An Index
to Book Reviews
in the Humanities

Volume 30
1989

Phillip Thomson
Williamston, Michigan

This volume of the Index contains data collected up to 31 December 1989.

This is an index to book reviews in humanities periodicals. Beginning with volume 12 of the Index (dated 1971), the former policy of selectively indexing reviews of books in certain subject categories only was dropped in favor of a policy of indexing all reviews in the periodicals indexed, with the one exception of children's books – the reviews of which will not be indexed.

The form of the entries used is as follows:

Author. Title.
Reviewer. Identifying Legend.

The author's name used is the name that appears on the title–page of the book being reviewed, as well as we are able to determine, even though this name is known to be a pseudonym. The title only is shown; subtitles are included only where they are necessary to identify a book in a series. The identifying legend consists of the periodical, each of which has a code number, and the date and page number of the periodical where the review is to be found. PMLA abbreviations are also shown (when a periodical has such an abbreviation, but such abbreviations are limited to four letters) immediately following the code number of the periodical. To learn the name of the periodical in which the review appears, it is necessary to refer the code number to the numerically arranged list of periodicals beginning on page iii. This list also shows the volume and number of the periodical issues indexed in this volume.

Reviews are indexed as they appear and no attempt is made to hold the title until all the reviews are published. For this reason it is necessary to refer to previous and subsequent volumes of this Index to be sure that the complete roster of reviews of any title is seen. As an aid to the user, an asterisk (*) has been added immediately following any title that was also indexed in Volume 29 (1988) of this Index.

Authors with hyphenated surnames are indexed under the name before the hyphen, and the name following the hyphen is not crossindexed. Authors with more than one surname, but where the names are not hyphenated, are indexed under the first of the names and the last name is cross-indexed. When alphabetizing surnames containing umlauts, the umlauts are ignored. Editors are always shown in the author–title entry, and they are cross–indexed (except where the editor's surname is the same as that of the author). Translators are shown only when they are necessary to identify the book being reviewed (as in the classics), and they are not cross–indexed unless the book being reviewed has no author or editor. Certain reference works and anonymous works that are known primarily by their title are indexed under that title and their editors are cross–indexed.

A list of abbreviations used is shown on page ii.

ABBREVIATIONS

Anon . . . . . Anonymous
Apr . . . . . . April
Aug . . . . . . August
Bk . . . . Book
Comp(s) . . . Compiler(s)
Cont . . . . . . Continued
Dec . . . . . . December
Ed(s) . . . . . Editor(s) [or] Edition(s)
Fasc . . . . . . Fascicule
Feb . . . . . . February
Jan . . . . . . January
Jul . . . . July
Jun . . . . . . June
Mar . . . . . . March
No . . . . Number
Nov . . . . . . November
Oct . . . . October
Prev . . . . . . Previous volume of this Index
Pt . . . . Part
Rev . . . . . . Revised
Sep . . . . September
Ser . . . . Series
Supp . . . . . . Supplement
Trans . . . . . Translator(s)
Vol . . . . Volume
* . . . . This title was also shown in
                    the volume of this Index
                    immediately preceding this
                    one

The periodicals in which the reviews appear are identified in this Index by a number. To supplement this number, and to promote ready identification, PMLA abbreviations are also given following this number. Every attempt will be made to index those issues shown here as "missing" in a later volume of this Index.

The following is a list of the periodicals indexed in volume 30:

90 – Burlington Magazine. London.
Jan88 thru Dec88 (Vol 130 complete)
91 – The Black Perspective in Music. Cambria Heights.
Spring88 & Fall88 (Vol 16 complete)
92(BH) – Bulletin Hispanique. Bordeaux.
Jan–Dec87 (Vol 89 complete)
95(CLAJ) – CLA Journal. Atlanta.
Sep88 thru Jun89 (Vol 32 complete)
97(CQ) – The Cambridge Quarterly. Cambridge.
Vol 17 complete
98 – Critique. Paris.
Jan/Feb88 thru Dec88 (Vol 44 complete)
99 – Canadian Forum. Toronto.
Feb/Mar88 (Vol 67 No 776/777)
102(CanL) – Canadian Literature. Vancouver.
Winter87 thru Autumn87 (No 115 thru No 118)
103 – Canadian Philosophical Reviews/Revue Canadienne de Comptes rendus en Philosophie. Edmonton.
Nov88 thru Dec89 (Vol 8 No 11 & 12 & Vol 9 complete)
104(CASS) – Canadian–American Slavic Studies/Revue canadienne-américaine d'études slaves. Irvine.
Fall–Winter87 (Vol 21 No 3/4) [no reviews indexed]
105 – Canadian Poetry. London, Ontario.
Spring/Summer88 & Fall/Winter88 (No 22 & 23)
106 – The Canadian Review of American Studies. London, Ontario.
Spring88 thru Fall88 (Vol 19 No 1–3)
107(CRCL) – Canadian Review of Comparative Literature/Revue Canadienne de Littérature Comparée. South Edmonton.
Sep/Dec87, Mar88 & Jun88 (Vol 14 No 3/4 & Vol 15 No 1 & 2)
108 – Canadian Theatre Review. Downsview.
Winter87 thru Winter88 (No 53–57)
110 – Carolina Quarterly. Chapel Hill.
Fall88 thru Spring89 (Vol 41 complete)
111 – Cauda Pavonis. Pullman.
Spring89 & Fall89 (Vol 8 complete)
112 – Celtica. Dublin.
Vol 20
115 – The Centennial Review. East Lansing.
Winter88 thru Fall88 (Vol 32 complete)
116 – Chinese Literature: Essays, Articles, Reviews. Madison.
Jul87 (Vol 9)
121(CJ) – Classical Journal. Greenville.
Oct–Nov88 thru Apr–May89 (Vol 84 complete)
122 – Classical Philology. Chicago.
Jan88 thru Oct88 (Vol 83 complete)
123 – Classical Review. Oxford.
Vol 38 complete
124 – Classical World. Pittsburgh.
Sep/Oct88 thru Jul/Aug89 (Vol 82 complete)
125 – Clio. Ft. Wayne.
Fall87 thru Summer88 (Vol 17 complete)
126(CCC) – College Composition and Communication. Urbana.
Feb88 thru Dec88 (Vol 39 complete)
127 – Art Journal. New York.
Spring88 thru Winter88 (Vol 47 complete)
128(CE) – College English. Urbana.
Jan88 thru Dec88 (Vol 50 complete)

130 – Comparative Drama. Kalamazoo.
Spring88 thru Winter88/89 (Vol 22 complete)
131(CL) – Comparative Literature. Eugene.
Winter88 thru Fall88 (Vol 40 complete)
133 – Colloquia Germanica. Bern.
Band 21 complete
136 – Conradiana. Lubbock.
Spring88 thru Autumn88 (Vol 20 complete)
137 – Contemporary Verse 2. Winnipeg.
Winter88 thru Fall88 (Vol 11 complete)
138 – Conjunctions. New York.
No 13 [no reviews indexed]
139 – American Craft. New York.
Feb/Mar88 thru Dec88/Jan89 (Vol 48 complete)
140(CH) – Crítica Hispánica. Pittsburgh.
Vol 10
141 – Criticism. Detroit.
Winter88 thru Fall88 (Vol 30 complete)
142 – Philosophy & Social Criticism. Chestnut Hill.
Vol 13 & 14 complete
143 – Current Musicology. New York.
No 43
144 – Critical Review. Chicago.
Winter89 thru Summer/Fall89 (Vol 3 complete)
148 – Critical Quarterly. Manchester.
Spring88 thru Autumn88 (Vol 30 No 1–3)
149(CLS) – Comparative Literature Studies. University Park.
Vol 25 complete
150(DR) – Dalhousie Review. Halifax.
Winter87/88 thru Fall88 (Vol 67 No 4, Vol 68 No 1/2 & 3)
151 – Dancemagazine. New York.
Jan88 thru Dec88 (Vol 62 complete)
152(UDQ) – The Denver Quarterly. Denver.
Summer88 thru Winter/Spring89 (Vol 23 complete) [some reviews from Spring88 issue, inadvertently deleted from prev vol, are indexed in this vol]
153 – Diacritics. Baltimore.
Summer86, Spring87, Spring88 thru Winter88 (Vol 16 No 2, Vol 17 No 1, Vol 18 complete)
154 – Dialogue. Waterloo.
Spring88 thru Winter88 (Vol 27 complete)
155 – The Dickensian. London.
Spring88 thru Autumn88 (Vol 84 complete)
156(ShJW) – Deutsche Shakespeare Gesellschaft West Jahrbuch. Bochum.
Jahrbuch 1988
157 – Drama/The Quarterly Theatre Review. London.
No 166 thru No 170
158 – Dickens Quarterly. Louisville.
Mar88 thru Dec88 (Vol 5 complete)
159 – Diachronica. Hildesheim.
Vol 5 complete
160 – Diálogos. Río Piedras.
Jan88 & Jul88 (Vol 23 complete)
161(DUJ) – Durham University Journal. Durham.
Dec87 (Vol 80 No 1) [issue of Jun87 missing]
162(TDR) – The Drama Review. Cambridge.
Spring88 thru Winter88 (Vol 32 complete)

165(EAL) – Early American Literature. Chapel Hill.
Vol 24 complete
166 – Eighteenth-Century Fiction. Hamilton.
Oct88 thru Jul89 (Vol 1 complete)
167 – Erkenntnis. Dordrecht.
Jan88 thru Nov88 (Vol 28 & 29 complete)
168(ECW) – Essays on Canadian Writing. Toronto.
Spring88 (No 36)
172(Edda) – Edda. Oslo.
1988/1 thru 1988/4 (Vol 88 complete)
173(ECS) – Eighteenth-Century Studies. Northfield.
Summer88 thru Spring89 (Vol 21 No 4, Vol 22 No 1 thru 3)
174(Éire) – Éire-Ireland. St. Paul.
Spring88, Summer88 & Winter88 (Vol 23 No 1, 2 & 4) [issue of Fall88 missing]
175 – English. Oxford.
Spring88 thru Autumn88 (Vol 37 complete)
177(ELT) – English Literature in Transition. Greensboro.
Vol 31 complete
178 – English Studies in Canada. Edmonton.
Mar88 thru Dec88 (Vol 14 complete)
179(ES) – English Studies. Lisse.
Feb88 thru Dec88 (Vol 69 complete)
181 – Epoch. Ithaca.
Vol 38 No 1 & 2
182 – Enclitic. Los Angeles.
Issue 21 thru 23 (Vol 11 No 1 thru 3)
183(ESQ) – ESQ: A Journal of the American Renaissance. Pullman.
Vol 33 No 2 thru 4
184(EIC) – Essays in Criticism. Oxford.
Jan88 thru Oct88 (Vol 38 complete)
185 – Ethics. Chicago.
Oct88 thru Jul89 (Vol 99 complete)
188(ECr) – L'Esprit Créateur. Baton Rouge.
Spring88 thru Winter88 (Vol 28 complete)
189(EA) – Etudes Anglaises. Paris.
Oct-Dec88 (Vol 41 No 4)
191(ELN) – English Language Notes. Boulder.
Jun88 & Sep88 thru Jun89 (Vol 25 No 4, Vol 26 complete)
192(EP) – Les Études Philosophiques. Paris.
Jan-Mar88 thru Oct-Dec88
193(ELit) – Etudes Littéraires. Québec.
Spring-Summer88 thru Winter88/89 (Vol 21 complete)
196 – Fabula. Berlin.
Band 29 complete
198 – The Fiddlehead. Fredericton.
Winter86 & Spring88 thru Winter88 (No 150 & 155 thru 158)
199 – Field. Oberlin.
Spring88 & Fall88 (Nos 38 & 39)
201 – Fifteenth-Century Studies. Detroit.
Vol 13 & 14
203 – Folklore. London.
Vol 99 complete
204(FdL) – Forum der Letteren. Leiden.
Mar88 thru Dec88 (Vol 29 complete)
206(FoLi) – Folia Linguistica. Berlin.
Vol 22 complete
207(FR) – French Review. Champaign.
Oct88 thru May89 (Vol 62 complete)
208(FS) – French Studies. London.
Jan88 thru Oct88 (Vol 42 complete)
209(FM) – Le Français Moderne. Paris.
Apr88 (Vol 56 No 1/2)

210(FrF) – French Forum. Lexington.
Jan88 thru Sep88 (Vol 13 complete)
215(GL) – General Linguistics. University Park.
Vol 28 complete
219(GaR) – Georgia Review. Athens.
Spring88 thru Winter88 (Vol 42 complete)
221(GQ) – German Quarterly. Cherry Hill.
Winter87 thru Fall88 & Winter88 thru Fall 88 (Vol 60 & 61 complete)
222(GR) – Germanic Review. Washington.
Winter88 thru Fall88 (Vol 63 complete)
223 – Genre. Norman.
Fall-Winter87 thru Winter88 (Vol 20 No 3/4, Vol 21 complete)
224(GRM) – Germanisch-Romanische Monatsschrift. Heidelberg.
Band 38 complete
228(GSLI) – Giornale storico della letteratura italiana. Torino.
Vol 165 complete
229 – Gnomon. München.
Band 60 complete
234 – The Hemingway Review. Ada.
Fall88 & Spring88 (Vol 8 complete)
235 – Hermathena. Dublin.
Summer88 (No 144)
236 – The Hiram Poetry Review. Hiram.
Spring-Winter88 (No 44 & 45)
238 – Hispania. University.
Mar88 thru Dec88 (Vol 71 complete)
240(HR) – Hispanic Review. Philadelphia.
Winter88 thru Autumn88 (Vol 56 complete)
241 – Hispanófila. Chapel Hill.
Jan88 thru Sep88 (No 92 thru 94)
244(HJAS) – Harvard Journal of Asiatic Studies. Cambridge.
Jun88 & Dec88 (Vol 48 complete)
249(HudR) – Hudson Review. New York.
Spring88 thru Winter89 (Vol 41 complete)
250(HLQ) – The Huntington Library Quarterly. San Marino.
Winter88 thru Autumn88 (Vol 51 complete)
257(IRAL) – IRAL: International Review of Applied Linguistics in Language Teaching. Heidelberg.
Feb88 thru Nov 88 (Vol 26 complete)
258 – International Philosophical Quarterly. New York and Namur.
Mar88 thru Dec88 (Vol 28 complete)
259(IIJ) – Indo-Iranian Journal. Dordrecht.
Jan88 thru Oct88 (Vol 31 complete)
260(IF) – Indogermanische Forschungen. Berlin.
Band 93
262 – Inquiry. Oslo.
Mar88 thru Dec88 (Vol 31 complete)
263(RIB) – Revista Interamericana de Bibliografía/Inter-American Review of Bibliography. Washington.
Vol38 complete
264(I&L) – Ideologies and Literature. Minneapolis/Valencia.
Spring88 & Fall 88 (Vol 3 No 1 & 2) [no reviews indexed]
268(IFR) – The International Fiction Review. Fredericton.
Winter89 (Vol 16 No 1)
269(IJAL) – International Journal of American Linguistics. Chicago.
Jan88 thru Oct88 (Vol 54 complete)

357 – Legacy. Amherst.
Fall88 thru Fall89 (Vol 5 No 2 & Vol 6 complete)
358 – Liber. Paris.
Oct89 & Dec89 (No 1 & No 2)
359 – Linguistics and Philosophy. Dordrecht.
Feb88 thru Aug88 (Vol 11 No 1-3)
361 – Lingua. Amsterdam.
Jan88 thru Dec88 (Vol 74, Vol 75 & Vol 76 complete)
363(LitR) – The Literary Review. Madison.
Fall88 thru Summer89 (Vol 32 complete)
364 – London Magazine. London.
Feb87, Mar87 & Apr–May87, Nov87 thru Feb/Mar89 (Vol 26 No 11 & 12; Vol 27 No 1/2, Vol 27 No 8-12; Vol 28 complete)
365 – Literary Research. College Park.
Winter87 thru Winter88 (Vol 12 complete, Vol 13 No 1)
366 – Literature and History. London.
Spring88 & Autumn88 (Vol 14 complete)
367(L&P) – Literature and Psychology. Providence.
Vol 34 complete
376 – Malahat Review. Victoria.
Mar88 thru Dec88 (No 82-85)
377 – Manuscripts St. Louis.
Mar88 thru Nov88 (Vol 32 complete)
379(MedR) – Medioevo romanzo. Bologna.
Aug86 & Apr88 thru Dec88 (Vol 11 No 2 & Vol 13 Complete)
380 – Master Drawings. New York.
Winter87 thru Winter88 (Vol 25 No 4 & Vol 26 complete)
381 – Meanjin Quarterly. Parkville.
Autumn88 thru Summer88 (Vol 47 complete)
382(MAE) – Medium Aevum. Oxford.
1988/1 & 1988/2 (Vol 57 complete)
385(MQR) – Michigan Quarterly Review. Ann Arbor.
Winter89 thru Fall89 (Vol 28 complete)
389(MQ) – The Midwest Quarterly. Pittsburg.
Autumn88 thru Summer89 (Vol 30 complete)
390 – Midstream. New York.
Jan88 thru Dec88 (Vol 34 complete)
391 – Milton Quarterly. Athens.
Dec87 thru Dec88 (Vol 21 No 4 & Vol 22 complete)
392 – The Mississippi Quarterly. Mississippi State.
Winter87/88 thru Fall88 (Vol 41 complete)
393(Mind) – Mind. Oxford.
Jan88, Apr88 & Oct88 (Vol 97 No 385, 386 & 388) [issue of Jul88 missing]
394 – Mnemosyne. Leiden.
Vol 41 complete
395(MFS) – Modern Fiction Studies. West Lafayette.
Spring88 thru Winter88 (Vol 34 complete)
396(ModA) – Modern Age. Bryn Mawr.
Winter88 thru Fall89 (Vol 32 complete)
397(MD) – Modern Drama. Toronto.
Mar88 thru Dec88 (Vol 31 complete)
399(MLJ) – Modern Language Journal. Madison.
Spring88 thru Winter88 (Vol 72 complete)
400(MLN) – MLN [Modern Language Notes]. Baltimore.
Jan88 thru Dec88 (Vol 103 complete)

401(MLQ) – Modern Language Quarterly. Seattle.
Dec86 thru Sep87 (Vol 47 No 4 & Vol 48 No 1-3)
402(MLR) – Modern Language Review. London.
Jan89 thru Oct89 (Vol 84 complete)
403(MLS) – Modern Language Studies. Middlebury.
Winter88 thru Fall88 (Vol 18 complete)
405(MP) – Modern Philology. Chicago.
Aug88 thru May89 (Vol 86 complete)
406 – Monatshefte. Madison.
Spring88 thru Winter88 (Vol 80 complete)
407(MN) – Monumenta Nipponica. Tokyo.
Spring88 thru Winter88 (Vol 43 complete)
410(M&L) – Music & Letters. Oxford.
Jan88 thru Oct88 (Vol 69 complete)
411 – Music Analysis. Oxford.
Mar88 thru Oct88 (Vol 7 complete)
412 – Music Review. Cambridge.
Feb88 thru Aug88 (Vol 48 No 1-3)
413 – Music Perception. Berkeley.
Fall88 thru Summer89 (Vol 6 complete)
414(MusQ) – Musical Quarterly. New York.
Vol 73 complete
415 – The Musical Times. London.
Jan88 thru Dec88 (Vol 129 complete)
416 – Musiktheorie. Laaber.
Band 3 complete
424 – Names. New York.
Mar–Jun88 & Sep–Dec88 (Vol 36 complete)
432(NEQ) – New England Quarterly. Boston.
Mar88 thru Dec88 (Vol 61 complete)
434 – New England Review and Bread Loaf Quarterly. Middlebury.
Autumn88 thru Summer89 (Vol 11 complete)
438 – The New Scholasticism. Washington.
Winter88 thru Autumn88 (Vol 62 complete)
439(NM) – Neuphilologische Mitteilungen. Helsinki.
1988/1 thru 1988/4 (Vol 89 complete)
440 – New York Folklore. Newfield.
Winter–Spring88 & Summer–Fall88 (Vol 14 complete)
441 – New York Times Book Review. New York.
1Jan89 thru 31Dec89 (Vol 94 complete)
442(NY) – New Yorker. New York.
2Jan89 thru 25Dec89 (Vol 64 No 46-52, Vol 65 No 1-45) [Vol65 begins with issue dated 20Feb89]
445(NCF) – Nineteenth-Century Literature. Berkeley.
Jun88 thru Mar89 (Vol 43 complete)
446(NCFS) – Nineteenth-Century French Studies. Fredonia.
Fall–Winter88/89 & Spring–Summer89 (Vol 17 complete)
447(N&Q) – Notes & Queries. Oxford.
Mar88 thru Dec88 (Vol 35 complete)
448 – Northwest Review. Eugene.
Vol 26 complete
449 – Noûs. Bloomington.
Jun87 & Mar88 thru Dec88 (Vol 21 No 2 & Vol 22 complete)
450(NRF) – La Nouvelle Revue Française. Paris.
Jan88 thru Dec88 (Vol 71 & Vol 72 complete)

451 – 19th Century Music. Berkeley.
Spring88 thru Spring89 (Vol 11 No 3 & Vol 12 complete)
452(NJL) – Nordic Journal of Linguistics. Oslo.
Vol 11 complete
453(NYRB) – The New York Review of Books. New York.
19Jan89 thru 21Dec89 (Vol 35 No 21/22, Vol 36 No 1–20)
454 – Novel. Providence.
Fall 88 thru Spring89 (Vol 22 complete)
455 – The North American Review. Cedar Falls.
Mar88 thru Dec88 (Vol 273 complete)
459 – Obsidian II. Raleigh.
Spring88 thru Winter88 (Vol 3 complete)
460(OhR) – The Ohio Review. Athens.
No 42 & No 43
462(OL) – Orbis Litterarum. Copenhagen.
Vol 43 complete
463 – Oriental Art. Richmond.
Summer87 & Spring88 thru Winter88/89 (Vol 33 No 2, Vol 34 complete)
465 – The Opera Quarterly. Chapel Hill.
Autumn88 thru Summer89 (Vol 6 complete)
466 – Oxford Studies in Ancient Philosophy. Oxford.
Vol 6
468 – Paideuma. Orono.
Spring88 & Fall&Winter88 (Vol 17 complete)
470 – Papers of the Bibliographical Society of Canada/Cahiers de la Société bibliographique du Canada. Toronto.
Vol 26
472 – Parnassus: Poetry in Review. New York.
Vol 15 complete
473(PR) – Partisan Review. Boston.
Vol 55 complete
475 – Papers on French Seventeenth Century Literature. Seattle & Tübingen.
Vol 15 complete
476 – Journal of Arts Management and Law. Washington.
Spring88 thru Fall88 (Vol 18 No 1–3)
477(PLL) – Papers on Language and Literature. Edwardsville.
Winter88 & Spring88 (Vol 24 No 1 & 2)
478(P&L) – Philosophy and Literature. Baltimore.
Apr88 & Oct88 (Vol 12 complete)
479(PhQ) – The Philosophical Quarterly. Oxford.
Jan88 thru Oct88 (Vol 38 complete)
480(P&R) – Philosophy & Rhetoric. University Park.
Vol 21 complete
481(PQ) – Philological Quarterly. Iowa City.
Winter88 thru Fall88 (Vol 67 complete)
482(PhR) – Philosophical Review. Ithaca.
Jan88 thru Oct88 (Vol 97 complete)
483 – Philosophy. Cambridge.
Jan88 thru Oct88 (Vol 63 complete)
484(PPR) – Philosophy & Phenomenological Research. Providence.
Sep88 thru Jun89 (Vol 49 complete)
485(PE&W) – Philosophy East & West. Honolulu.
Jan88 thru Oct88 (Vol 38 complete)

486 – Philosophy of Science. East Lansing.
Mar88 thru Dec88 (Vol 55 complete)
487 – Phoenix. Toronto.
Spring88 thru Winter88 (Vol 42 complete)
488 – Philosophy of the Social Sciences. Waterloo.
Mar88 thru Dec88 (Vol 18 complete)
489(PJGG) – Philosophisches Jahrbuch. Freiburg.
Band 95 complete
490 – Poetica. Amsterdam.
Band 20 complete
491 – Poetry. Chicago.
Apr88 thru Mar89 (Vol 152 & 153 complete)
493 – Poetry Review. London.
Spring88 thru Winter88/89 (Vol 78 complete)
494 – Poetics Today. Durham.
Vols 8 & 9 complete
495(PoeS) – Poe Studies. Pullman.
Jun88 (Vol 21 No 1)
496 – Poet Lore. Bethesda.
Spring88 thru Winter88/89 (Vol 83 complete)
497(PolR) – Polish Review. New York.
Vol 33 complete
498 – Popular Music and Society. Bowling Green.
Spring88 thru Winter88 (Vol 12 complete)
500 – Post Script. Jacksonville.
Fall88 & Winter89 (Vol 8 No 1 & 2)
502(PrS) – Prairie Schooner. Lincoln.
Spring88 thru Winter88/89 (Vol 62 complete)
505 – Progressive Architecture. Cleveland.
Jan88 thru Dec88 (Vol 69 complete)
506(PSt) – Prose Studies. London.
May88 thru Dec88 (Vol 11 complete)
507 – Print. New York.
Jan/Feb88 thru Nov/Dec88 (Vol 42 complete)
508 – Prooftexts. Baltimore.
Jan88 thru Sep88 (Vol 8 complete)
510 – The Piano Quarterly. Wilmington.
Winter87/88 thru Fall88 (Vol 36 complete)
511 – Plays and Players. London.
Feb88 thru Oct88 (No 413–421) [issue of Jan88 missing]
513 – Perspectives of New Music. Seattle.
Winter88 & Summer88 (Vol 26 complete)
517(PBSA) – Papers of the Bibliographical Society of America. Brooklyn.
Vol 82 complete
518 – Philosophical Books. Oxford.
Jan88 thru Oct88 (Vol 29 complete)
519(PhS) – Philosophical Studies. Dordrecht.
Jan88 thru Nov88 (Vol 53 & 54 complete)
520 – Phronesis. Assen.
Vol 33 complete
521 – Philosophical Investigations. Oxford.
Jan88 thru Oct88 (Vol 11 complete)
526 – Quarry. Kingston.
Winter88 thru Autumn88 (Vol 37 complete)
529(QQ) – Queen's Quarterly. Kingston.
Spring88 thru Winter88 (Vol 95 complete)
530 – Recherches sur Diderot et sur l'"Encyclopédie." Paris.
Apr88 & Oct88 (No 4 & 5)

532(RCF) – The Review of Contemporary Fiction. Elmwood Park.
Spring88 thru Fall88 (Vol 8 complete)
533 – Raritan. New Brunswick.
Summer88 thru Spring89 (Vol 8 complete)
534(RALS) – Resources for American Literary Study. College Park.
Vol 16 complete
535(RHL) – Revue d'Histoire Littéraire de la France. Vineuil.
Jan–Feb88 thru Nov–Dec88 (Vol 88 complete)
536(Rev) – Review. Charlottesville.
Vol 10
537 – Revue de Musicologie. Paris.
Vol 74 complete
538(RAL) – Research in African Literatures. Austin.
Spring88 thru Winter88 (Vol 19 complete)
539 – Renaissance & Reformation/Renaissance et Réforme. Toronto.
Summer88 thru Summer89 (Vol 12 No 3&4, Vol 13 No 1&2)
540(RIPh) – Revue Internationale de Philosophie. Wetteren.
Vol 42 fasc 1–3
541(RES) – Review of English Studies. Oxford.
Feb88 thru Nov88 (Vol 39 complete)
542 – Revue Philosophique de la France et de l'Étranger. Paris.
Jan–Mar88 thru Oct–Dec88 (Vol 178 complete)
543 – Review of Metaphysics. Washington.
Sep88 thru Jun89 (Vol 42 complete)
544 – Rhetorica. Berkeley.
Winter88 thru Autumn88 (Vol 6 complete)
545(RPh) – Romance Philology. Berkeley.
Aug88 thru May 89 (Vol 42 complete)
546(RR) – Romanic Review. New York.
Jan88 thru Nov88 (Vol 79 complete)
547(RF) – Romanische Forschungen. Frankfurt am Main.
Band 99 Heft 4 & Band 100 complete
548 – Revista Española de Lingüística. Madrid.
Jan–Jun88 & Jul–Dec88 (Vol 18 complete)
549(RLC) – Revue de Littérature Comparée. Paris.
Jan–Mar88 thru Oct–Dec88 (Vol 62 complete)
550(RusR) – Russian Review. Cambridge.
Jan88 thru Oct88 (Vol 47 complete)
551(RenQ) – Renaissance Quarterly. New York.
Spring88 thru Winter88 (Vol 41 complete)
552(REH) – Revista de estudios hispánicos. Poughkeepsie.
Jan88 thru Oct88 (Vol 22 complete)
553(RLiR) – Revue de Linguistique Romane. Strasbourg.
Jan–Jun88 & Jul–Dec88 (Vol 52 complete)
554 – Romania. Paris.
Vol 107 No 4 & Vol 108 No 1
555 – Revue de Philologie. Paris.
Vol 61 fasc 1&2
556 – Russell. Hamilton.
Summer/Winter88 (Vol 8 No 1&2) [no reviews indexed]

558(RLJ) – Russian Language Journal. East Lansing.
Winter–Spring–Fall88 (Vol 42 complete)
559 – Russian Linguistics. Dordrecht.
Vol 12 complete
560 – Salmagundi. Saratoga Springs.
Spring–Summer88 & Fall88 (No 78/79 & 80)
561(SFS) – Science Fiction Studies. Montréal.
Nov87 thru Nov88 (Vol 14 No 3, Vol 15 complete)
562(Scan) – Scandinavica. Norwich.
May88 & Nov88 (Vol 27 complete)
563(SS) – Scandinavian Studies. Eugene.
Winter88 thru Autumn88 (Vol 60 complete)
564 – Seminar. Downsview.
Feb88 thru Nov88 (Vol 24 complete)
565 – Stand Magazine. Newcastle upon Tyne.
Winter87/88 thru Autumn88 (Vol 29 complete)
566 – The Scriblerian. Philadelphia.
Autumn88 (Vol 21 No 1)
567 – Semiotica. Berlin.
Vol 68 thru Vol 72 complete
568(SCN) – Seventeenth–Century News. University Park.
Spring–Summer88 thru Winter88 (Vol 46 complete)
569(SR) – Sewanee Review. Sewanee.
Winter88 thru Fall88 (Vol 96 complete)
570(SQ) – Shakespeare Quarterly. Washington.
Spring88 thru Winter88 (Vol 39 complete)
571(ScLJ) – Scottish Literary Journal. Aberdeen.
May88 thru Winter88 (Vol 15 complete & supps 28 & 29)
572 – Shaw: The Annual of Bernard Shaw Studies. University Park.
Vol 8
573(SSF) – Studies in Short Fiction. Newberry.
Winter88 & Spring88 (Vol 25 No 1 & 2)
574(SEEJ) – Slavic & East European Journal. Tucson.
Spring88 thru Winter88 (Vol 32 complete)
575(SEER) – Slavonic and East European Review. London.
Jan88 thru Oct88 (Vol 66 complete)
576 – Journal of the Society of Architectural Historians. Philadelphia.
Mar88 thru Dec88 (Vol 47 complete)
577(SHR) – Southern Humanities Review. Auburn.
Winter88 thru Fall88 (Vol 22 complete)
578 – Southern Literary Journal. Chapel Hill.
Fall88 thru Fall89 (Vol 21 complete, Vol 22 No 1)
579(SAQ) – South Atlantic Quarterly. Durham.
Winter88 thru Fall88 (Vol 87 complete)
580(SCR) – The South Carolina Review. Clemson.
Fall88 & Spring89 (Vol 21 complete)
581 – Southerly. Sydney.
Mar88 thru Dec88 (Vol 48 complete)
585(SoQ) – The Southern Quarterly. Hattiesburg.
Fall88 thru Spring89 (Vol 27 No 1–3)
587(SAF) – Studies in American Fiction. Boston.
Spring88 & Autumn88 (Vol 16 complete)

588(SSL) – Studies in Scottish Literature.
Columbia.
   Vol 23
589 – Speculum. Cambridge.
   Jan88 thru Oct88 (Vol 63 complete)
590 – Studies in the Humanities. Indiana.
   Dec88 & Jun89 (Vol 15 No 2 & Vol 16 No
   1)
591(SIR) – Studies in Romanticism. Boston.
   Spring88 thru Winter88 (Vol 27 complete)
592 – Studio International. London.
   Vol 201 No 1019 & 1020
593 – Symposium. Washington.
   Spring88 thru Winter89 (Vol 42 complete)
594 – Studies in the Novel. Denton.
   Spring88 thru Winter88 (Vol 20 complete)
597(SN) – Studia Neophilologica. Stockholm.
   Vol 60 complete
598(SoR) – The Southern Review. Baton
Rouge.
   Winter89 thru Autumn89 (Vol 25 complete)
599 – Style. De Kalb.
   Winter88 thru Fall89 (Vol 22 No 4 & Vol
   23 No 1–3)
600 – Simiolus. Utrecht.
   Vol 18 complete
601(SuF) – Sinn und Form. Berlin.
   Jan–Feb88 thru Nov–Dec88 (Vol 40 complete)
602 – Sprachkunst. Vienna.
   Band 19 complete
603 – Studies in Language. Amsterdam.
   Vol 12 complete
604 – Spenser Newsletter. Chapel Hill.
   Winter88 thru Fall88 (Vol 19 complete)
   [issue of Fall87 missing]
605(SC) – Stendhal Club. Grenoble.
   15Oct88 thru 15Jul89 (Vol 31 complete)
606 – Synthese. Dordrecht.
   Jan88 thru Dec88 (Vol 74–77 complete)
607 – Tempo. London.
   Mar88 thru Dec88 (No 164–167)
608 – TESOL Quarterly. Washington.
   Mar87 & Mar89 thru Dec89 (Vol 21 No 1 &
   Vol 23 complete)
609 – Theater. New Haven.
   Summer/Fall88 thru Spring89 (Vol 19 No
   3 & Vol 20 No 1–2) [no reviews indexed]
610 – Theatre Research International.
Oxford.
   Spring88 thru Autumn88 (Vol 13 complete)
611(TN) – Theatre Notebook. London.
   Vol 42 complete
612(ThS) – Theatre Survey. Bloomington.
   May88 (Vol 29 No 1) [no reviews indexed]
615(TJ) – Theatre Journal. Baltimore.
   Dec87 thru Dec88 (Vol 39 No 4 & Vol 40
   complete)
616 – Thalia. Ottawa.
   Vol 10 No 1
617(TLS) – Times Literary Supplement. London.
   6–12Jan89 thru 29Dec89/4Jan90 (No
   4475–4526)
618 – Trivia. North Amherst.
   Spring88 & Fall88 (No 12 & No 13)
619 – Transactions of the Charles S. Peirce
Society. Buffalo.
   Winter88 thru Fall88 (Vol 24 complete)

627(UTQ) – University of Toronto Quarterly.
Toronto.
   Fall87 thru Summer89 (Vol 57 & Vol 58
   complete) [in Fall87 & Fall88 issues only
   the "Humanities" section is indexed]
628(UWR) – University of Windsor Review.
Windsor.
   Vol 21 complete
635(VPR) – Victorian Periodicals Review.
Edwardsville.
   Spring88 thru Winter88 (Vol 21 complete)
636(VP) – Victorian Poetry. Morgantown.
   Spring–Summer88 thru Winter88 (Vol 26
   complete)
637(VS) – Victorian Studies. Bloomington.
   Autumn88 thru Summer89 (Vol 32 com-
   plete)
639(VQR) – Virginia Quarterly Review.
Charlottesville.
   Winter88 thru Autumn88 (Vol 64 complete)
640 – Vivarum. Leiden.
   May88 & Nov88 (Vol 26 complete)
646(WWR) – Walt Whitman Quarterly Review.
Iowa City.
   Summer88 thru Spring89 (Vol 6 complete)
647 – Wascana Review. Regina.
   Spring88 & Fall88 (Vol 23 complete)
648(WCR) – West Coast Review. Burnaby.
   Vol 22 No 4 & Vol 23 No 1
649(WAL) – Western American Literature.
Logan.
   May88 thru Feb89 (Vol 23 complete)
650(WF) – Western Folklore. Glendale.
   Jan88 thru Oct88 (Vol 47 complete)
651(WHR) – Western Humanities Review. Salt
Lake City.
   Spring88 thru Winter88 (Vol 42 complete)
654(WB) – Weimarer Beiträge. Berlin.
   1/1988 thru 12/1988 (Vol 34 complete)
656(WMQ) – William & Mary Quarterly.
Williamsburg.
   Jan88 thru Oct88 (Vol 45 complete)
658 – Winterthur Portfolio. Chicago.
   Spring88 thru Winter88 (Vol 23 complete)
659(ConL) – Contemporary Literature. Madison.
   Spring89 thru Winter89 (Vol 30 complete)
660(Word) – Word. New York.
   Apr88 thru Dec88 (Vol 39 complete)
661(WC) – The Wordsworth Circle. Philadelphia.
   Winter88 thru Autumn88 (Vol 19 complete)
662 – Woman's Art Journal. Knoxville.
   Spring/Summer88 & Fall88/Winter89 (Vol
   9 complete)
676(YR) – Yale Review. New Haven.
   Summer88 thru Winter89 (Vol 77 No 4,
   Vol 78 No 1 & 2)
677(YES) – The Yearbook of English Studies.
London.
   Vol 19
679 – Zeitschrift für allgemeine Wissenschaftstheorie. Stuttgart.
   Band 19 complete
680(ZDP) – Zeitschrift für deutsche Philologie. Berlin.
   Band 106 Heft 4 & Band 107 complete
682(ZPSK) – Zeitschrift für Phonetik,
Sprachwissenschaft und Kommunikations-
forschung. Berlin.
   Band 41 complete

683 – Zeitschrift für Kunstgeschichte.
München.
Band 51 complete
684(ZDA) – Zeitschrift für deutsches Altertum und deutsche Literatur [Anzeiger sec-
tion]. Stuttgart.
Band 117 complete
685(ZDL) – Zeitschrift für Dialektologie und
Linguistik. Stuttgart.
2/1987 thru 3/1988 (Band 54 Heft 2&3 &
Band 55 complete)
687 – Zeitschrift für Philosophische Forschung. Meisenheim/Glan.
Jan–Mar88 thru Oct–Dec88 (Vol 42 complete)
688(ZSP) – Zeitschrift für slavische Philologie. Heidelberg.
Band 48 complete
702 – Shakespeare Studies. New York.
Vol 20
703 – Sulfur. Ypsilanti.
Fall88 (No 23) [issue No 22 missing]
704(SFR) – Stanford French Review. Saratoga.
Spring88 & Fall–Winter88 (Vol 12 complete)
705 – The Wallace Stevens Journal. Potsdam.
Spring88 & Fall88 (Vol 12 complete)
706 – Studia Leibnitiana. Stuttgart.
Band 20 complete
707 – Sight and Sound. London.
Winter87/88 thru Autumn88 (Vol 57 complete)
708 – Studi Linguistici Italiani. Rome.
Vol 14 fasc 1
709 – Studies in Art Education. Reston.
Fall88 thru Summer89 (Vol 30 complete)
711(RHM) – Revista Hispánica Moderna. New
York.
Jun88 & Dec88 (Vol 41 complete)

275(IQ) – Italian Quarterly. New Brunswick.
278(IS) – Italian Studies. London.
279 – International Journal of Slavic Linguistics and Poetics. Columbus.
283 – Jabberwocky – The Journal of the
Lewis Carroll Society. Burton-on-Trent.
296(JCF) – Journal of Canadian Fiction.
Montreal.
300 – Journal of English Linguistics.
Whitewater.
326 – Journal of the William Morris Society.
London.
343 – Komparatistische Hefte. Bayreuth.
346(KJ) – The Kipling Journal. London.
417 – Die Musikforschung. Kassel.
456(NDQ) – North Dakota Quarterly. Grand
Forks.
457(NRFH) – Nueva Revista de Filología Hispánica. Mexico City.
464 – Orbis. Louvain.
509 – Philosophy & Public Affairs. Princeton.
531 – Revue de Synthèse. Paris.
557 – Renaissance Studies. Oxford
582(SFQ) – Southern Folklore. Lexington.
595(ScS) – Scottish Studies. Edinburgh.
596(SL) – Studia Linguistica. Stockholm.
620(TSWL) – Tulsa Studies in Women's Literature. Tulsa.
675(YER) – Yeats Eliot Review. Little Rock.
678(YCGL) – Yearbook of Comparative &
General Literature. Bloomington.
710 – Studies in Second Language Acquisition. New York.

Each year we are unable (for one reason or
another) to index the reviews appearing in
all of the periodicals scanned. The following
is a list of the periodicals whose reviews
were not included in this volume of the
Index. Every attempt will be made to index
these reviews in the next volume of the
Index.

29(APR) – The American Poetry Review.
Philadelphia.
34 – American Theatre. New York.
67 – AUMLA (Journal of the Australasian
Universities Language and Literature
Assn.). Nedlands.
134(CP) – Concerning Poetry. Bellingham.
146 – Crazyhorse. Little Rock.
147 – Critical Texts. New York.
187 – Ethnomusicology. Bloomington.
202(FMod) – Filología Moderna. Madrid.
205(ForL) – Forum Linguisticum. Lake Bluff.
214 – Gambit. London.
239 – Hispanic Linguistics. Pittsburgh.
242 – History of European Ideas. Oxford.
254 – Hypatia. Bloomington.

Achinstein, P. & O. Hannaway, eds. Observation, Experiment, and Hypothesis in Modern Physical Science.
G. Hon, 486:Sep88-482
Acke, D., ed. Europese moralisten.
F. Gevrey, 535(RHL):Mar-Apr88-345
Acker, K. Literal Madness.*
I. Malin, 532(RCF):Fall88-153
Acker, K. Young Lust.
R. Kaveney, 617(TLS):19-25May89-536
Acker, R. & M. Burkhard, eds. Blick auf die Schweiz.
M. Pender, 402(MLR):Oct89-1048
Ackerman, G.M. The Life and Work of Jean-Léon Gérôme.*
J. House, 90:Mar88-238
Ackerman, R. J.G. Frazer.*
J.B. Vickery, 637(VS):Summer89-607
Ackerman, T.F. & others, eds. Clinical Medical Ethics.
B.H., 185:Apr89-688
Ackermann, I. & H. Weinrich, eds. Eine nicht nur deutschen Literatur.
H. Suhr, 221(GQ):Spring88-332
Ackland, V. For Sylvia.
P.N. Furbank, 617(TLS):28Jul-3Aug89-815
Ackrill, J.L. - see Aristotle
Ackroyd, P. Chatterton.*
P. Saari, 42(AR):Spring88-267
P. Vansittart, 364:Nov87-105
Ackroyd, P. T.S. Eliot.
G. Wolfe, 396(ModA):Spring89-172
Ackroyd, P. First Light.
J. Crowley, 441:17Sep89-15
C. Rawson, 617(TLS):28Apr-4May89-453
Ackroyd, P. Hawksmoor.
I. Malin, 532(RCF):Spring88-189
Acorn, M. The Uncollected Acorn. (J. Deahl, ed) Whiskey Jack.
M.T. Lane, 198:Spring88-99
Acorn, M., with J. Deahl. A Stand of Jack-pine.
M.T. Lane, 198:Spring88-99
"Acta Classica Universitatis Scientiarum Debrecenensis." (Vols 20 & 21)
J-M. André, 555:Vol61fasc2-351
"Acta Universitatis Szegediensis de Atilla József Nominatae, Dissertationes Slavicae, (Sectio Historiae Litterarum, 18.)."
C.J.G. Turner, 575(SEER):Jul88-474
"Actas do Congreso Internacional de Estudios sobre Rosalía de Castro e o seu tempo."
R. Landeira, 238:Dec88-826
"Actes du Colloque 'Marceline Desbordes-Valmore et son temps.'"
J. Voisine, 549(RLC):Jan-Mar88-105
"Actes du Xe Congrès de l'Association Internationale de Littérature Comparée, New York 1982."
J. Hervier, 549(RLC):Jul-Sep88-403
"Actes du XVIIe Congrès international de linguistique et philologie romanes (Aix-en-Provence, 29 août-3 septembre 1983)." (Vols 1, 3, 4, 6, 8 & 9)
G. Price, 208(FS):Jan88-117
Acton, E. Russia.
M. Perrie, 575(SEER):Apr88-286
Lord Acton. Selected Writings of Lord Acton. (J.R. Fears, ed)
J.V. Schall, 396(ModA):Fall89-360

Adam, J., ed. Employment Policies in the Soviet Union and Eastern Europe. (2nd ed)
J.L. Porket, 575(SEER):Jan88-148
Adam, P. Eileen Gray.
F. Anderton, 46:Apr88-10
I. Anscombe, 90:Oct88-782
J.V. Iovine, 45:Feb88-79
de Adam, S. - see under Salimbene de Adam
Adam de la Halle. The Lyrics and Melodies of Adam de la Halle. (D.H. Nelson & H. van der Werf, eds & trans)
S.N. Rosenberg, 589:Apr88-351
Adamo Muscettola, S., A. Balasco & D. Gianpaola, eds. Benevento: l'arco e la città.
M. Pfanner, 229:Band60Heft6-567
Adams, A. After You've Gone.
R. Carlson, 441:8Oct89-27
Adams, A. Manzanar. (J. Armor & P. Wright, eds)
L.E. Nesbitt, 441:12Feb89-19
Adams, A. & others, eds. The Changing Face of Arthurian Romance.
C. Houswitschka, 72:Band225Heft2-382
M. Lambert, 402(MLR):Jul89-704
"Ansel Adams: Letters and Images 1916-1984." (M.S. Alinder & A.G. Stillman, eds)
R.M. Adams, 453(NYRB):16Feb89-33
442(NY):6Feb89-108
Adams, D. The Long Dark Tea-Time of the Soul.
P-L. Adams, 61:Apr89-99
C. Schine, 441:12Mar89-11
Adams, D.J. Diderot: Dialogue and Debate.*
H.D. Rothschild, 403(MLS):Summer88-88
J. Undank, 210(FrF):Jan88-119
Adams, G. Dancing on Coral.
G. Oldham, 42(AR):Summer88-395
Adams, G. The Hottest Night of the Century. Games of the Strong.
C. Lansbury, 441:30Jul89-9
Adams, H., ed. John La Farge.
E. Johns, 127:Fall88-241
Adams, H. & L. Searle, eds. Critical Theory since 1965.
A.S., 295(JML):Fall87/Winter88-236
S. Scobie, 376:Mar88-101
478(P&L):Oct88-325
Adams, J. AIDS.
J. Weber, 617(TLS):2-8Jun89-601
Adams, J.R. The Big Fix.
K.W. Arenson, 441:17Dec89-19
Adams, L. & Y. Meissen Porcelain Figures.
J.E. Poole, 39:Dec88-448
Adams, M.M. William Ockham.
W.A. Frank, 543:Jun89-817
Adams, R.J. The Eastern Portal of the North Transept at Chartres.
M.F. Hearn, 589:Jan88-114
Adams, R.M. Shakespeare: The Four Romances.
E.A.J. Honigmann, 453(NYRB):28Sep89-44
Adams, R.M. The Virtue of Faith and Other Essays in Philosophical Theology.*
T.V. Morris, 543:Mar89-607
K. Seeskin, 185:Oct88-184
Adams, W. & J.W. Brock. Dangerous Pursuits.
M.A. Reichek, 441:17Dec89-28
Adamson, J. "Troilus and Cressida."*
M. Baron, 175:Spring88-94
Adamson, M.J. May's Newfangled Mirth.
M. Stasio, 441:27Aug89-22
Adas, M. Machines as the Measure of Men.
A.C. Kors, 441:10Sep89-20

Adatte, E. "Les Fleurs du Mal" et "Le Spleen de Paris."*
   R. Lloyd, 208(FS):Apr88-219
   G. Robb, 535(RHL):Nov-Dec88-1152
Adcock, F., ed. The Faber Book of 20th Century Women's Poetry.*
   L. Sail, 565:Spring88-73
Adcock, F. The Incident Book.*
   S. Rae, 364:Mar87-87
Adcock, F. Meeting the Comet.
   L. Mackinnon, 617(TLS):26May-1Jun89-593
Addiss, S. The Art of Zen.
   K. Butler, 441:9Jul89-18
Addiss, S., ed. Japanese Quest for a New Vision.
   P. Berry, 293(JASt):Aug88-631
Addiss, S. Tall Mountains and Flowing Waters.*
   P. Berry, 407(MN):Winter88-505
Adelman, K.L. The Great Universal Embrace.
   L.D. Freedman, 441:19Nov89-28
Adelson, A. & R. Lapides, with M. Web. Lódź Ghetto.
   I. Deak, 453(NYRB):28Sep89-63
Adelson, L.A. Crisis of Subjectivity.
   R.A. Berman, 221(GQ):Fall87-687
Adelugba, D., ed. Before Our Very Eyes.*
   J. Gibbs, 538(RAL):Fall88-408
Adeney, M. The Motor Makers.*
   G. Howard, 324:Apr89-314
Adey, L. Class and Idol in the English Hymn.
   G. Irvine, 617(TLS):4-10Aug89-852
Adey, L. Hymns and the Christian "Myth."
   R. Arnold, 178:Sep88-350
Adhyatman, S. Kendi.
   N.V. Robinson, 60:Sep-Oct88-155
Adkins, A.W.H. & P. White, eds. The Greek Polis.*
   K.O. O'Keeffe, 568(SCN):Winter88-82
Adler, D. Philip Massinger.
   N.A. Brittin, 570(SQ):Summer88-260
   C. Milsum, 481(PQ):Summer88-385
Adler, E. The Power of Ideology.
   P.J. McDonough, 263(RIB):Vol38No2-212
Adler, H.G. Die unsichtbare Wand. Hausordnung.
   J.J. White, 617(TLS):13-19Oct89-1129
Adler, K. & T. Garb - see Morrisot, B.
Adler, T.P. Mirror on the Stage.
   M.D. Whitlatch, 615(TJ):May88-287
Adorno, R. Guaman Poma.
   L.H. Dowling, 238:Mar88-86
   K. Ross, 240(HR):Winter88-125
Adorno, T. The Jargon of Authenticity.
   D.H., 355(LSoc):Sep88-461
Adorno, T.W. Against Epistemology.
   C.W. Harvey, 606:Dec88-415
Adorno, T.W. Gesammelte Schriften. (Vol 20, Pts 1 & 2) (R. Tiedemann, ed)
   W. Goetschel, 221(GQ):Fall88-556
Adorno, T.W. Kierkegaard: Construction of the Aesthetic.
   R. Martinez, 103:Oct89-391
Adrados, F.R., ed. Diccionario griego-español (D.G.E.). (Vol 2)
   P. Monteil, 555:Vol61fasc2-295
Adrados, F.R. Nuevos estudios de Lingüística General y de Teoría Literaria.
   E. Martinell, 548:Jan-Jun88-255
Adravanti, F. Gengis-Khan.
   C-P. Pérez, 450(NRF):May88-102

Aebi, M. Kants Begründung der "Deutschen Philosophie."
   R.M., 342:Band79Heft2-254
Aelfric. Fifty-Six Aelfric Fragments. (E. Fausbøll, ed)
   N.F. Blake, 402(MLR):Apr89-431
   M. Clayton, 382(MAE):1988/2-297
   M.R. Godden, 541(RES):Nov88-529
   D. Yerkes, 589:Oct88-890
Aélion, R. Euripide héritier d'Eschyle.
   D. van Ness, 394:Vol41fasc1/2-153
Aelius Aristides - see under Aristides
Aellen, R. Redeye.*
   T.J. Binyon, 617(TLS):17-23Nov89-1288
Aers, D. Chaucer.*
   D. Pearsall, 402(MLR):Jan89-112
   J. Simons, 366:Spring88-116
Aers, D., ed. Medieval Literature.*
   A. Samson, 402(MLR):Oct89-917
   P. Strohm, 589:Apr88-352
Aerts, W.J., E.R. Smits & J.B. Voorbij. Vincent of Beauvais and Alexander the Great.
   G.G. Guzman, 589:Apr88-354
Aertsen, H. Play in Middle English.
   J. Holland, 447(N&Q):Dec88-516
Aeschbach, M. - see Lefèvre, R.
Aeschylus. Choephori. (A. Bowen, ed)
   P.G. Mason, 123:Vol38No2-394
Aeschylus. Choephori. (A.F. Garvie, ed)
   W.G. Thalmann, 124:Nov-Dec88-129
Aeschylus. Septem contra Thebas.* (G.O. Hutchinson, ed)
   P. Demont, 555:Vol61fasc2-306
Aǵa, 'O. - see under 'Osmān Aǵa
Agacinski, S. Aparté.
   K. Newmark, 153:Spring87-70
Aganbegyan, A., ed. Perestroika 1989.
   A.B. Ulam, 441:2Apr89-24
Agar, E. A Look at My Life
   R. Cardinal, 617(TLS):31Mar-6Apr89-336
   G. Ewart, 364:Oct/Nov88-138
Agard, F.B. A Course in Romance Linguistics.
   J.R. Craddock, 545(RPh):Feb89-314
Agazzi, E., ed. Epistemologia.
   A. Mercier, 84:Sep88-415
Agazzi, E. Philosophie, science, métaphysique.
   A. Reix, 542:Oct-Dec88-493
"The Age of Correggio and the Carracci."
   F. Russell, 39:Jan88-70
Agee, J. James Agee: Selected Journalism. (P. Ashdown, ed)
   V.A. Kramer, 534(RALS):Vol16No1&2-242
   T.O., 295(JML):Fall87/Winter88-287
Agee, J. Bend This Heart.
   A. Hempel, 441:16Jul89-22
Aggeler, G. Confessions of Johnny Ringo.
   R.E. Morsberger, 649(WAL):Nov88-246
Agnew, J-C. Worlds Apart.
   P. Borsay, 83:Spring88-86
   R.D. Hume, 402(MLR):Oct89-921
   J. Pick, 610:Summer88-160
   I.K. Steele, 106:Fall88-385
Agnon, S.Y. Shira.
   G. Schulman, 441:24Dec89-6
Agoncillo, T.A. The Burden of Proof.
   A.W. McCoy, 293(JASt):Feb88-189
Agoos, J. Above the Land.*
   L. Sail, 565:Spring88-73
   639(VQR):Winter88-26
Agosin, M. Scraps of Life.
   662:Fall88/Winter89-53

Agosín, M. Women of Smoke.
  G. Martin, 617(TLS):14-20Jul89-782
El-Agraa, A.M. Japan's Trade Frictions?
  M. Bronfenbrenner, 293(JASt):Nov88-881
Agricola, C., ed. Volkssagen aus Schottland.
  W.F.H. Nicolaisen, 196:Band29Heft1/2-
  168
Agricola, E., J. Schildt & D. Viehweger, eds.
  Wortschatzforschung heute.
  G. Kleiber, 553(RLiR):Jul-Dec88-482
Agricola, S. White Mercedes.
  G. Conoley, 152(UDQ):Winter/Spring89-
  129
  D. Revell, 460(OhR):No43-116
"Agronyms: Mélanges de toponymie et de dia-
  lectologie en hommage à Pierrette Dubuis-
  son."
  F.R. Hamlin, 424:Mar-Jun88-118
Aguilar, R. & others, eds. Palabra Nueva.
  S. Rodríguez del Pino, 36:Summer88-98
Aguirre y Ortiz, J. & F. Lázaro Carreter. Dis-
  curso.
  J. Dowling, 240(HR):Winter88-89
Agulhon, M. Histoire Vagabonde.
  H. Cronel, 450(NRF):Sep88-118
Agurskii, M. & M. Shklovskaia, eds. Maksim
  Gor'kii.
  I. Weil, 550(RusR):Jul88-353
Agursky, M. The Third Rome.
  A. Kustarev, 550(RusR):Oct88-461
Agustoni, L. & J.B. Göschl. Einführung in die
  Interpretation des Gregorianischen Chorals.
  (Vol 1)
  A. Traub, 416:Band3Heft3-284
Ahearn, B. - see Pound, E. & L. Zukofsky
Ahenakew, F., ed & trans. Kiskinahamawak-
  an-Ackimowinisa/Student Stories.
  R. Darnell, 355(LSoc):Sep88-462
Ahenakew, F. Stories of the House People.
  B.L. Pearson, 350:Sep89-652
Ahituv, S. Canaanite Toponyms in Ancient
  Egyptian Documents.
  A.F. Rainey, 318(JAOS):Jul-Sep87-534
Ahl, F. Metaformations.*
  W.S. Anderson, 24:Fall88-457
  G. Davis, 122:Jul88-260
  E. Doblhofer, 229:Band60Heft2-155
Ahlheid, F. Quintilian.*
  K. Schöpsdau, 394:Vol41fasc1/2-210
Ahlin, J. Sigurd Lewerentz, Architect.
  M.A. Branch, 505:Apr88-173
  B. Linn, 46:Feb88-84
  W.C. Miller, 576:Jun88-205
Ahlstedt, E. La Pudeur en Crise.*
  R. Gibson, 402(MLR):Apr89-481
Ahmad, Z.H., ed. Government and Politics of
  Malaysia.
  W.R. Roff, 293(JASt):Nov88-927
Ahmed, M. The British Labour Party and the
  Indian Independence Movement, 1917-1939.
  W.W. Reinhardt, 293(JASt):May88-392
Ahnlund, H. Johan Eberhard Carlberg, Stock-
  holms stads arkitekt 1727-1773.
  D.K. Underwood, 576:Jun88-203
Ahooja-Patel, K., A.G. Drabek & M. Nerfin,
  eds. World Economy in Transition.
  S.J. Burki, 293(JASt):May88-319
"Ahornblätter."
  E. Schafroth, 547(RF):Band100Heft4-371
Ahston, T.H. & C.H.E. Philpin, eds. The Bren-
  ner Debate.
  A.J. Slavin, 551(RenQ):Autumn88-483

Ainsa, F. Identidad cultural de Iberoamérica
  en su narrativa.*
  J.S. Brushwood, 238:Sep88-559
Aitchison, J. The Golden Harvester.
  A. Noble, 617(TLS):3-9Mar89-218
Aitchison, J. Linguistics.
  A. Pousada, 350:Mar89-174
Aitchison, J. Words in the Mind.
  R. Shillcock, 297(JL):Sep88-569
Aitchison, S. Utah Wildlands.
  R. Burrows, 649(WAL):Nov88-275
Aitken, J.L. Masques of Morality.
  C.B. Atkinson, 628(UWR):Vol21No1-96
Aitken, W.R. - see Soutar, W.
Aitmatov, C. The Place of the Skull.
  M. Scammell, 441:30Apr89-22
Aizenshtat, I. Isk docheri Shaliapina i drugie
  ocherki moskovskogo advokata.
  E. Huskey, 550(RusR):Jan88-98
Akbar, M.J. Nehru.
  D. Arnold, 617(TLS):31Mar-6Apr89-334
Akenson, D. The Orangeman.
  C. Gaffield, 529(QQ):Spring88-179
  C. Wilton-Siegel, 298:Winter88/89-135
Åkerstrom, A. Berbati. (Vol 2)
  R.L.N. Barber, 123:Vol38No2-446
Akhamlich, M-L. - see Guérin de Bouscal, D.
Akhand, D.G. Grammar Practice.
  M.A. Maxwell-Paegle, 399(MLJ):
  Summer88-224
Akins, E. Home Movie.*
  D. Jersild, 441:15Jan89-22
Akio, M. & Ishihara Shintaro - see under
  Morita Akio & Ishihara Shintaro
Aksyonov, V. In Search of Melancholy Baby.
  42(AR):Winter88-124
Aksyonov, V. Our Golden Ironburg.
  A. Mobilio, 441:23Jul89-18
Aksyonov, V. Say Cheese!
  A. Donald, 441:30Jul89-13
"Akten zur deutschen auswärtigen Politik
  1918-1945." (Ser A, Vols 3-5)
  F.L. Carsten, 575(SEER):Jul88-496
Akurgal, E. Alt-Smyrna. (Vol 1)
  W. Schiering, 229:Band60Heft3-249
Akutagawa, R. Hell Screen; Cogwheels; A
  Fool's Life.*
  L. Allen, 617(TLS):28Apr-4May89-466
Alain. The Gods.
  W. Schwarz, 617(TLS):24Feb-2Mar89-203
Aland, K. - see Mühlenberg, H.M.
Alas, L. Relatos breves. (R. Rodríguez Marín,
  ed)
  J. Rutherford, 402(MLR):Oct89-1012
  N.M. Valis, 86(BHS):Jul88-309
Alazraki, J., ed. Critical Essays on Jorge
  Luis Borges.
  P. Beardsell, 402(MLR):Apr89-511
  H.D. Oberhelman, 238:Mar88-91
Albanese, V. Slow Mist.
  D. Manganiello, 102(CanL):Spring88-220
Albert, M. Unausgesprochene Botschaften.
  C.W. Thompson, 208(FS):Jul88-351
Alberti, L.B. Dinner Pieces. (D. Marsh, trans)
  L.V.R., 568(SCN):Spring-Summer88-35
Alberti, L.B. On the Art of Building in Ten
  Books.
  A. Hughes, 617(TLS):26May-1Jun89-590
Albertini, P. L'Enseignement classique à
  travers les exercices manuscrits des élèves
  (1600-1940).
  P. Gerbod, 535(RHL):Nov-Dec88-1175

4

Albertinus, A. Verachtung dess Hoflebens/
Vnd Lob dess Landtlebens (1598). (C.E.
Schweitzer, ed)
J. Hardin, 133:Band21Heft2/3-204
Albi, J. La defensa de las Indias (1764-
1799).
M.A. De Marco, 263(RIB):Vol38No3-396
Albinus, R. Lexikon der Stadt Königsberg.
R.M., 342:Band79Heft2-250
Albrecht, U. Von der Burg zum Schloss.
P. Crossley, 90:May88-375
Alciati, A. Andreas Alciatus: "Index Emblem-
aticus."* (Vol 1 ed by P.M. Daly & V. Cal-
lahan, with S. Cuttler; Vol 2 ed by P.M.
Daly, with S. Cuttler)
M. Bath, 541(RES):Aug88-426
Alcott, L.M. Alternate Alcott. (E. Showalter,
ed)
K.B. Meyers, 357:Fall88-68
Alcott, L.M. A Double Life. (M.B. Stern, ed)
S. Mackay, 617(TLS):31Mar-6Apr89-332
Aldercroft, D.H. - see Landau, Z. & J. Tomas-
zewski, J.
Alderman, G. London Jewry and London Poli-
tics 1889-1986.
R.S. Wistrich, 617(TLS):20-26Oct89-1157
Alderson, W.T. & S.P. Low. Interpretation of
Historic Sites. (2nd ed)
M. Leone, 292(JAF):Jan-Mar88-86
Aldiss, B. Forgotten Life.*
S. Hynes, 441:30Apr89-10
Aldiss, B. Last Orders.
G. Jonas, 441:21May89-26
Aldiss, B.W., with D. Wingrove. Trillion Year
Spree.
V. Hollinger, 561(SFS):Mar88-102
Aldouri-Lauber, M. Zwischen Defaitismus
und Revolte.
S. Heiler, 72:Band225Heft2-447
Aldridge, A. The Scientific World View in
Dystopia.*
K-K.T. Ho, 149(CLS):Vol25No1-93
Aldridge, A.O. The Reemergence of World
Literature.*
M. Détrie, 549(RLC):Jan-Mar88-67
Aldrin, B. & M. McConnell. Men from Earth.
F. Howard, 441:2Jul89-8
Alegría, C. & D.J. Flakoll. Ashes of Izalco.
F. Handman, 441:5Nov89-25
Alegría, F. Nueva historia de la novela his-
panoamericana.
M.A. Salgado, 238:Mar88-88
Aleixandre, V. A Longing for the Light. (L.
Hyde, ed)
K. Warren, 577(SHR):Winter88-89
Aleixandre, V. Shadow of Paradise.*
A.M. Gullón, 240(HR):Summer88-384
Alekperov, A.K. Leksičeskaja semantika
prostyx glagolov v sovremennom azerbajd-
žanskom jazyke.
G.F. Meier, 682(ZPSK):Band41Heft5-657
Aleksandrov, V.A. Rossiia na dal'nevostoch-
nikh rubezhakh (vtoraia polovina-XVII v.).
A. Allison, 550(RusR):Jul88-330
Aler, J. & J. Enklaar, eds. Hermann Broch
1886-1986.
R.H. Watt, 402(MLR):Jan89-257
Aleu Benítez, J. Filosofia y libertad en Kant.
A. Reix, 542:Apr-Jun88-260
Alexander, A. Thomas Hardy.
W.E. Davis, 395(MFS):Winter88-675
Alexander, A. - see O'Dea, A.C.

Alexander, C. A New Theory of Urban Design.
G. Rand, 47:Feb88-35
Alexander, C. - see Brontë, C.
Alexander, E.P. Fighting for the Confed-
eracy. (G.W. Gallagher, ed)
J.M. McPherson, 453(NYRB):12Oct89-43
Alexander, J. & P. Binski, eds. Age of Chiv-
alry.
78(BC):Autumn88-313
Alexander, J.H. Reading Wordsworth.
Z. Leader, 175:Autumn88-229
Alexander, J.J.G., T.J. Brown & J. Gibbs - see
Wormald, F.
Alexander, J.T. Catherine the Great.
A.G. Cross, 617(TLS):23-29Jun89-682
C.S. Leonard, 441:22Jan89-9
Alexander, M. "The Miller's Tale" by Geoffrey
Chaucer.
D. Pearsall, 402(MLR):Jan89-112
Alexander, P. Ideas, Qualities and Corpus-
cles.*
G.A.J. Rogers, 483:Oct88-548
Alexander, P.F. William Plomer.
P.N. Furbank, 617(TLS):3-9Mar89-219
Alexander, R. The Structure of Vasko Popa's
Poetry.*
E.C. Hawkesworth, 575(SEER):Jan88-129
V.D. Mihailovich, 574(SEEJ):Spring88-
154
Alexander, R.D. The Biology of Moral Sys-
tems.*
M. Ruse, 185:Oct88-182
Alexander, R.M. Dynamics of Dinosaurs and
Other Extinct Giants.
G.S. Paul, 441:13Aug89-8
Alexander, S. The Pizza Connection.*
M. Massing, 453(NYRB):30Mar89-22
Alexander, T.M. John Dewey's Theory of Art,
Experience, and Nature.*
A. Berleant, 619:Spring88-293
M.H. Mitias, 290(JAAC):Summer88-526
K. Price, 89(BJA):Autumn88-385
S.B. Rosenthal, 543:Sep88-129
Alexander, W. The Laird of Drammochdyle
and His Contemporaries. (W. Donaldson, ed)
I.R. Carter, 571(ScLJ):Winter88-8
W. Crome, 635(VPR):Summer88-72
Alexandrescu, S., F. Drijkoningen & W. Noo-
men - see van den Boogaard, N.
Alexiou, M. & V. Lambropoulos, eds. The Text
and its Margins.*
L.D. Tsitsipis, 567:Vol70No1/2-175
Alfau, F. Locos, A Comedy of Gestures.
A. Shapiro, 442(NY):5Jun89-105
Alfieri, V.E. - see Fichte, J.G.
Alföldi, A. Caesar in 44 v. Chr. (Vol 1) (H.
Wolff, E. Alföldi-Rosenbaum & G. Stumpf,
eds) Caesariana. (E. Alföldi-Rosenbaum,
ed)
E. Rawson, 123:Vol38No2-324
Alföldy, G. Die römische Gesellschaft. Rö-
mische Heeresgeschichte: Beiträge 1962-
1985.
T. Wiedemann, 123:Vol38No2-335
Alfonso X el Sabio. La historia novelada de
Alejandro Magno. (T. González Rolán & P.
Saquero Suárez-Somonte, eds)
O.T. Impey, 545(RPh):May89-503
Alford, C.F. Narcissism.
A.W. Price, 617(TLS):3-9Feb89-115
J. Wallulis, 103:May89-175

Allsen, T.T. Mongol Imperialism.
D. Sinor, 293(JASt):Aug88-580
Allworth, E., ed. Tartars of the Crimea.
(British title: Tatars of the Crimea.)
J. Keep, 617(TLS):21-27Apr89-415
639(VQR):Autumn88-118
Almond, B. Moral Concerns.
R. Keshen, 185:Oct88-159
H. Meynell, 483:Jul88-405
Almond, B. Philosophy or Sophia.
R. Crisp, 291:Vol5No2-233
Alon, G. The Jews in Their Land in the Tal-
mudic Age. (G. Levi, ed & trans)
D. Berger, 441:30Jul89-21
Alpers, S. Rembrandt's Enterprise.*
D. Carrier, 290(JAAC):Summer88-521
M. Edmundson, 385(MQR):Summer89-437
D. Freedberg, 453(NYRB):19Jan89-29
M. Russell, 324:Dec88-60
E. White, 62:Dec88-111
639(VQR):Summer88-103
van Alphen, E. Bang voor schennis?
J. van Luxemburg, 204(FdL):Jun88-139
van Alphen, E. & I. de Jong, eds. Door het
oog van de tekst.
J.J.M. Westenbroek, 204(FdL):Dec88-309
Alshawi, H. Memory and Context for Lan-
guage Interpretation.
R. Chen, 350:Sep89-652
Altabé, D. Temas y diálogos. (5th ed)
D.L. Heyck, 399(MLJ):Winter88-491
Altena, J.Q.V. - see under van Regteren
Altena, J.Q.
Altenberg, B. Prosodic Patterns in Spoken
English.
D.L. Bolinger, 361:Dec88-348
J. Pierrehumbert, 452(NJL):Vol11No1/2-
209
Altenburg, D. & R. Kleinertz - see Liszt, F.
Alter, P. The Reluctant Patron.*
R. Yeo, 637(VS):Summer89-581
Alter, R. The Pleasures of Reading.
R. Boyers, 441:25Jun89-22
442(NY):21Aug89-94
Alter, R., with C. Cosman. A Lion for Love.*
W. Fowlie, 569(SR):Winter88-xv
L.W. Marvick, 599:Spring89-174
Alter, R. & F. Kermode, eds. The Literary
Guide to the Bible.*
W.S. Anderson, 124:Mar-Apr89-317
M. Bal, 204(FdL):Dec88-314
H. Goldgar, 249(HudR):Spring88-203
V. Nemoianu, 400(MLN):Dec88-1139
S. Pinsker, 219(GaR):Spring88-194
B.V. Qualls, 533:Spring89-134
Alter, S. The Godchild.
E. Hower, 441:14May89-22
Alter, S. Renuka.
S. Curtis, 617(TLS):10-16Mar89-256
Altes, W.L.K. - see under Korthals Altes, W.L.
Altet, X.B. - see under Barral y Altet, X.
Althusser, L. Schriften. (Vols 1 & 2)
G.L., 185:Oct88-197
Altick, R.D. Paintings from Books.*
K. Garlick, 447(N&Q):Mar88-134
Altick, R.D. Writers, Readers and Occasions.
D. Grylls, 617(TLS):29Sep-5Oct89-1066
Altieri, J. The Theatre of Praise.
M.H. Wikander, 570(SQ):Autumn88-384
Altman, R. The American Film Musical.*
S. Snyder, 106:Spring88-89

Alvar, C. & A. Gómez Moreno. La poesía lírica
medieval.
I.A. Corfis, 240(HR):Summer88-365
Alvar, M. El mundo novelesco de Miguel
Delibes.
L. González-del-Valle, 238:Dec88-834
J. Rodríguez, 240(HR):Autumn88-516
Alvar Ezquerra, M. & others - see "The
Oxford-Duden Pictorial Spanish-English
Dictionary"
Alvarez, N.E. Análisis arquetípico, mítico y
simbólico de "Pedro Páramo."
Z. Gutiérrez-Vega, 345(KRQ):Feb88-125
Amado, J. Showdown.*
J. Gledson, 617(TLS):20-26Jan89-58
G. Kidder, 37:Sep/Oct88-61
Amado, J. Tocaia Grande.
E. Engler, 654(WB):9/1988-1528
Amado Lévy-Valensi, E. A la gauche du
seigneur ou l'illusion idéologique.
B.D. Hercenberg, 542:Jan-Mar88-114
Amann, K. & A. Berger, eds. Österreichische
Literatur der dreissiger Jahre.*
J. Koppensteiner, 221(GQ):Summer87-499
Ambrazas, V., ed-in-chief. Grammatika lit-
ovskogo jazyka.
W.R. Schmalstieg, 260(IF):Band93-381
Ambrière, F. Le Siècle des Valmore.
M. Brix, 356(LR):Aug88-244
J. Gaulmier, 535(RHL):Jan-Feb88-136
"Saint Ambroise, 'Les devoirs.'" (Bk 1) (M.
Testard, ed & trans)
M. Reydellet, 555:Vol61fasc1-150
Ambrose, J. Syntaxe comparative du français
et de l'anglais.
J.T. Chamberlain, 207(FR):May89-1080
Ambrose, S.E. Nixon. (Vol 1)
G.S. Smith, 529(QQ):Winter88-797
R.A. Strong, 639(VQR):Summer88-525
Ambrose, S.E. Nixon. (Vol 2)
R.W. Apple, Jr., 441:12Nov89-1
442(NY):4Dec89-187
Ambrosini, R. Tendenze della linguistica
teorica attuale.
L. Zgusta, 350:Jun89-418
Ambrosoli, L. - see Cattaneo, C.
Amburger, E. Deutsche in Staat, Wirtschaft
und Gesellschaft Russlands.
R.P. Bartlett, 575(SEER):Jan88-141
Amelang, J.S. Honored Citizens of Barcelona.
J-L. Marfany, 86(BHS):Jul88-315
Amell, S. La narrativa de Juan Marsé, conta-
dor de aventis.
C.C. Soufas, Jr., 345(KRQ):Nov88-499
"The American Heritage Larousse Spanish
Dictionary."
W.W. Moseley, 399(MLJ):Spring88-103
"American Paradise."
D.M. Sokol, 658:Summer/Autumn88-187
A. Wilton, 90:May88-378
Amery, C. Wren's London.
A. Paine, 46:Dec88-10
Ames, J. I Pass Like Night.
M. Stimpson, 617(TLS):3-9Nov89-1217
Ames, R.T. The Art of Rulership.
J.S. Major, 485(PE&W):Apr88-197
Amichai, Y. Selected Poetry of Yehuda Ami-
chai.* (C. Bloch & S. Mitchell, eds & trans)
L. Bar-Yaacov, 577(SHR):Fall88-402
Amis, J. & M. Rose, eds. Words about Music.
J. Rosselli, 617(TLS):27Oct-2Nov89-1190
Amis, K. The Crime of the Century.
E. Lotozo, 441:12Nov89-54

Amis, K. Difficulties with Girls.*
G. Annan, 453(NYRB):15Jun89-12
J. Grossman, 441:2Apr89-11
C. McGrath, 442(NY):12Jun89-121
J. Mellors, 364:Dec88/Jan89-132
Amis, M. London Fields.
M. Imlah, 617(TLS):29Sep-5Oct89-1051
Ammianus. Ammianus Marcellinus, "Histoire."
(Vol 5, Bks 26-28) (M-A. Marié, ed & trans)
M. Reydellet, 555:Vol61fasc1-151
Ammianus. Ammianus Marcellinus: The Later
Roman Empire (A.D. 354-378). (W. Hamil-
ton, ed & trans)
R.B. Hitchner, 124:Jan-Feb89-206
Ammons, A.R. Sumerian Vistas.*
J.F. Cotter, 249(HudR):Spring88-225
D. McDuff, 565:Autumn88-61
W. Scammell, 493:Spring88-48
639(VQR):Spring88-65
Ammons, E. - see Cooke, R.T.
Amore, A.P. - see Behn, A.
Amorelli, M.T.F. - see under Falconi Amorelli,
M.T.
Amprimoz, A.L. A l'ombre de Rimbaud.*
G. De Wulf, 356(LR):Feb-May88-144
F.R. Smith, 108(FS):Apr88-222
Amrouche, J. & J. Roy. D'une amitié.
D. Brahimi, 535(RHL):Mar-Apr88-337
Amselek, P., ed. Théorie des actes de lan-
gage.
M. Adam, 542:Jan-Mar88-97
Anaya, R., ed. Voces.
L. Torres, 649(WAL):Nov88-251
Ancono, F.A. Writing the Absence of the Fa-
ther.
S.P., 295(JML):Fall87/Winter88-261
van Andel, T.H. & C. Runnels. Beyond the
Acropolis.*
L.T. Pearcy, 124:Nov-Dec88-131
Anderberg, T., T. Nilstun & I. Persson, eds.
Aesthetic Distinction.
S. Davies, 103:Sep89-360
Anderegg, J. Sprache und Verwandlung.
D. Barnouw, 221(GQ):Summer87-458
R.C. Holub, 406:Fall88-364
G. Michel, 682(ZPSK):Band41Heft1-140
Anderle, M. Die Landschaft in den Gedichten
Hölderlins.
D. Constantine, 83:Spring88-118
H. Gaskill, 133:Band21Heft2/3-220
A.A. Kuzniar, 221(GQ):Fall87-670
C. Ullmann, 564:Sep88-281
Anderman, J. The Edge of the World.
M. Mestrovic, 441:19Mar89-22
Anders, S.B. The Bus Home.
455:Mar88-72
Andersen, F.G. Commonplace and Creativity.*
W.E. Richmond, 64(Arv):Vol42-197
Andersen, H., ed. Sandhi Phenomena in the
Languages of Europe.*
J. Klausenburger, 320(CJL):Jun88-191
K.H. Schmidt, 685(ZDL):2/1988-256
Andersen, L. Studies in Oracular Verses.
R. Parker, 123:Vol38No2-401
G. Rougemont, 555:Vol61fasc2-300
Andersen, W.K. & S.D. Damle. The Brother-
hood in Saffron.
K.W. Jones, 293(JASt):Feb88-162
Anderson, A. & D.L. Bark, eds. Thinking
About America.
P. Kennedy, 453(NYRB):16Mar89-36

Anderson, A.B. & G.W. Pickering. Confronting
the Color Line.
J.M.O., 185:Jul89-981
Anderson, B.S. & J.P. Zinsser. A History of
Their Own.* (Vol unknown)
639(VQR):Autumn88-117
Anderson, C. Style as Argument.*
E.S. Fussell, 27(AL):Mar88-154
D. Hesse, 126(CCC):May88-243
Anderson, D. The Toe-Rags.
C. Hope, 617(TLS):17-23Mar89-275
Anderson, D.A. Management Education in De-
veloping Countries.
S. Keith, 263(RIB):Vol38No1-69
Anderson, D.L. Imperialism and Idealism.
H. Schmidt, 302:Vol24No1-79
Anderson, F. At Glasgow Cross.
E. Morgan, 493:Spring88-42
Anderson, F. Espacio urbano y novela.
J. Whiston, 86(BHS):Apr88-190
Anderson, G. Philostratus.*
J.R. Morgan, 123:Vol38No2-235
Anderson, G. The White-Blouse Revolution.
D. Atkinson, 617(TLS):15-21Sep89-1014
Anderson, J. Billarooby.*
T. Wilhelmus, 249(HudR):Autumn88-554
Anderson, J. In Extremis.
L. Graeber, 441:13Aug89-16
Anderson, J. & J. Durand, eds. Explorations
in Dependency Phonology.
E.V. Hume, 350:Sep89-653
Anderson, J.A. A Taste of Kentucky.
N. Groce, 292(JAF):Jan-Mar88-93
Anderson, J.E., ed & trans. Two Literary
Riddles in the Exeter Book.*
M. Nelson, 589:Jul88-614
J. Stevenson, 382(MAE):1988/2-298
Anderson, K. Sympathy for the Devil.*
R. Warde, 152(UDQ):Summer88-119
Anderson, L. Dear Dad.
L. Stone, 441:24Dec89-17
Anderson, M. - see Bachmann, I.
Anderson, N.F. Woman Against Women in Vic-
torian England.*
V. Colby, 445(NCF):Dec88-407
S. Mitchell, 637(VS):Autumn88-138
Anderson, O. Rotten Borough.
J. Melmoth, 617(TLS):7-13Apr89-364
Anderson, O. Suicide in Victorian and
Edwardian England.*
B.T. Gates, 637(VS):Autumn88-117
Anderson, P. The Boat of a Million Years.
G. Jonas, 441:19Nov89-32
Anderson, P. Busybodies.
M. Orth, 441:26Nov89-37
Anderson, P.B. No East or West.
P. Walters, 575(SEER):Jan88-149
Anderson, P.V. Technical Writing.
P.J. Lindholdt, 126(CCC):Dec88-484
Anderson, R.B. Dostoevsky.*
P. Debreczeny, 574(SEEJ):Spring88-135
Anderson, R.R., U. Goebel & O. Reichmann,
eds. Frühneuhochdeutsches Wörterbuch.
(Vol 1, Pt 1 comp by O. Reichmann)
N.R. Wolf, 684(ZDA):Band117Heft3-111
Anderson, S. The Sherwood Anderson Diaries,
1936-1941. (H.H. Campbell, ed)
Y. Butts, 219(GaR):Spring88-208
P.A. Greasley, 395(MFS):Summer88-237
J. Schevill, 536(Rev):Vol10-285
42(AR):Spring88-278
Anderson, S. An English Consul in Turkey.
R. Irwin, 617(TLS):29Sep-5Oct89-1073

8

Anderson, S. Letters to Bab.* (W.A. Sutton, ed)
G.A. Love, 534(RALS):Vol16No1&2–161
Anderson, S. & E. Erb, eds. Berührung ist nur eine Randerscheinung.
A. Hartmann, 133:Band21Heft1–94
Anderson, S.C. Grass and Grimmelshausen.
D. Aren, 133:Band21Heft2/3–265
I.E. Hunt, 221(GQ):Spring88–325
Anderson, W. Cecil Collins.
M. James, 364:Oct/Nov88–103
F. Spalding, 90:Sep88–709
Andersson, A.Ö. – see under Östling Andersson, A.
Andersson, B. Studien zu Jacob Böhmes "Aurora oder Morgen Röte im auffgang."
R.E. Schade, 221(GQ):Summer87–470
Andersson, H.O. & F. Bedoire. Swedish Architecture, Drawings 1640–1970.
M.A. Branch, 505:Apr88–173
D.K. Underwood, 576:Jun88–203
Andersson, T.M. A Preface to the "Nibelungenlied."*
A. Classen, 221(GQ):Fall88–568
J.L. Flood, 562(Scan):Nov88–181
M.E. Gibbs, 406:Winter88–502
P.W. Tax, 400(MLN):Apr88–674
de Andrade, C.D. – see under Drummond de Andrade, C.
de Andrade, M.P. – see under Pardo de Andrade, M.
André, J. Etre médecin à Rome.
P. Flobert, 555:Vol61fasc2–344
André, J. – see Isidore of Seville
André, J. & J. Filliozat. L'Inde vue de Rome.
P. Flobert, 555:Vol61fasc2–339
W. Schmitthenner, 229:Band60Heft6–551
André, R. La Belle Saison.
J. Blot, 450(NRF):Mar88–88
André, R. – see Stendhal
Andreae, B. Die Symbolik der Löwenjagd.
R.R.R. Smith, 123:Vol38No2–362
Andreassen, T. Det litteraere system i Norge.
L. Furuland, 172(Edda):1988/2–176
Andres, G., J.M. Hunisak & A.R. Turner. The Art of Florence.
J. Russell, 441:3Dec89–9
Andrés de Uztarroz, J.F. Certamen poético que la Universidad de Zaragoza consagró al arzobispo d. Pedro de Apaolaza en 1642. (A. San Vicente, ed)
T. Dadson, 86(BHS):Jul88–303
C. Maurer, 240(HR):Summer88–373
Andrés-Suárez, I. Los cuentos de Ignacio Aldecoa.
R. Fiddian, 86(BHS):Jul88–311
D. Lytra, 238:Mar88–84
G. Pérez Firmat, 240(HR):Spring88–275
Andrew, D., ed. Breathless.
J.J. Michalczyk, 207(FR):May89–1083
Andrew, D.S. Louis Sullivan and the Polemics of Modern Architecture.*
M. Donougho, 289:Fall88–114
Andrewes, G. Behind the Waterfall.
R. Gibson, 617(TLS):16–22Jun89–670
Andrews, E. The Poetry of Seamus Heaney.
D. Johnston, 617(TLS):8–14Sep89–983
Andrews, J.F., ed. William Shakespeare.
J.L. Halio, 570(SQ):Spring88–108
Andrews, K. Catalogue of Netherlandish Drawings in the National Gallery of Scotland.
G. Gordon, 380:Spring88–49

Andrews, M. The Search for the Picturesque.
A. Broyard, 441:1Oct89–28
Andrews, N., Jr. The Case Against Camões.
K.S. Larsen, 238:Dec88–822
Andrews, P.B. An Introduction to Mathematical Logic and Type Theory.
M. Yasuhara, 316:Mar88–312
Andrews, W.L., ed. Sisters of the Spirit.*
D.C. Dance, 534(RALS):Vol16No1&2–59
A.S. Newson, 115:Spring88–203
Andrews, W.L. To Tell a Free Story.*
D.C. Dance, 534(RALS):Vol16No1&2–59
P. Edwards, 538(RAL):Winter88–559
F. Hobson, 115:Winter88–79
B.A. McCaskill, 392:Winter87/88–89
Andreyev, C. Vlasov and the Russian Liberation Movement.*
J.A. Armstrong, 550(RusR):Apr88–200
P.J.S. Duncan, 575(SEER):Oct88–659
Andreyev, L. Visions. (O.A. Carlisle, ed)
639(VQR):Summer88–94
Andrian, G.W., ed. Modern Spanish Prose, with a Selection of Poetry. (4th ed)
D.N. Flemming, 399(MLJ):Spring88–102
Andrzejewski, B.W., S. Piłaszewicz & W. Tyloch, eds. Literatures in African Languages.
W.F. Feuser, 538(RAL):Fall88–380
Aneirin. Y Gododdin. (A.O.H. Jarman, ed & trans)
P.P. Sims-Williams, 617(TLS):21–27Apr89–434
Anesko, M. "Friction with the Market."*
N. Baym, 301(JEGP):Jan88–136
N. Bradbury, 541(RES):Nov88–582
C.B. Cox, 569(SR):Summer88–497
J. Gooder, 97(CQ):Vol17No2–177
S.M. Griffin, 405(MP):Feb89–321
H. Parker, 536(Rev):Vol10–211
Ang, L. – see under Li Ang
Angehrn, E. Geschichte und Identität.
K. Röttgers, 687:Oct–Dec88–701
P. Trotignon, 542:Jan–Mar88–99
Angehrn, E. & G. Lohmann, eds. Ethik und Marx.*
A. Künzli, 687:Jul–Sep88–486
Angels Santa i Banyeres, M., ed. Stendhal.
V.D.L., 605(SC):15Jan89–159
Angermüller, R. Mozart's Operas.
P. Constantine, 441:23Apr89–20
des Anges, J. Jeanne des Anges, Autobiografia. (M. Bergamo, ed)
G. Malquori Fondi, 475:Vol15No28–259
Angier, C. Jean Rhys.
C.J.B., 295(JML):Fall87/Winter88–375
Anglès, A. André Gide et le premier groupe de la "Nouvelle Revue Française." (Vol 2)
P. McCarthy, 546(RR):May88–529
M. Tilby, 208(FS):Apr88–225
Anglès, A. André Gide et le premier groupe de la "Nouvelle Revue Française." (Vol 3)
P. McCarthy, 546(RR):May88–529
"The Anglo-Saxon Chronicle."* (Vol 3) (J.M. Bately, ed)
N.F. Blake, 677(YES):Vol19–298
E.G. Stanley, 541(RES):Feb88–96
"The Anglo-Saxon Chronicle."* (Vol 4)(S. Taylor, ed)
D.B. Schneider, 72:Band224Heft2–389
"The Anglo-Saxon Chronicle."* (Vol 17)(D. Dumville & M. Lapidge, eds)
M. Griffith, 382(MAE):1988/1–98
H. Vollrath, 38:Band106Heft1/2–211

9

Angulo, D. & A.E. Pérez Sánchez. A Corpus of Spanish Drawings. (Vol 4)
T. Mullaly, 324:Jul89-519
P. Troutman, 617(TLS):22-28Sep89-1033
Angus, I. & S. Jhally, eds. Cultural Politics in Contemporary America.*
L. Menand, 617(TLS):21-27Jul89-796
Angus, I.H. George Grant's Platonic Rejoinder to Heidegger.
R. Burch, 103:Sep89-345
Ankori, Z. Yahaduth ve-Yavanuth noṣrith, miphgash ve-imut bi-meruṣath-hadoroth.
S. Bowman, 589:Jan88-114
"Annales Benjamin Constant, 5."
P. Delbouille, 535(RHL):Mar-Apr88-287
"Annales Universitatis Scientiarum Budapestinensis de Rolando Eötvös Nominatae." (Vols 13 & 14)
J-P. Chambon, 209(FM):Apr88-153
"Annali d'Italianistica." (Vol 3)
S.L. Bermann, 276:Summer88-154
Annan, N. Leslie Stephen.*
B. Lightman, 637(VS):Spring89-442
Annas, G.J. Judging Medicine.
B.A. Brody, 185:Jul89-956
Annas, J. & J. Barnes. The Modes of Scepticism.*
J.F. Finamore, 124:Jan-Feb89-218
N.P. White, 482(PhR):Apr88-256
"Annual Bibliography of Victorian Studies 1984." (B. Chaudhuri, ed)
R. Morton, 178:Mar88-94
Ansa, T.M. Baby of the Family.
V. Sayers, 441:26Nov89-6
Saint Anselm. L'oeuvre de saint Anselme de Cantorbery. (Vol 1 ed & trans by M. Corbin; Vol 2 ed & trans by A. Galonnier, M. Corbin & R. de Ravinel)
H. Merle, 192(EP):Jul-Sep88-436
Ansen, A. The Vigilantes.
S. Moore, 532(RCF):Fall88-170
Ansermet, E. Les fondements de la musique dans la conscience humaine. (rev by J-C. Piguet)
A. Reix, 542:Jan-Mar88-88
Anson, R.S. War News.
H.E. Salisbury, 441:27Aug89-9
442(NY):25Sep89-122
Antal, F. Florentine Painting and its Social Background.
C. Juler, 592:Vol201No1019-67
Anthonioz, M. L'album "Verve."
J. Piel, 98:Mar88-254
Anthony, C., ed. Family Portraits.
J.K. Conway, 441:19Nov89-11
Antkowiak, B., ed. Elegie.
D. Witschew, 654(WB):11/1988-1890
Antle, M. Théâtre et poésie surréalistes.
S. Tokatlian, 207(FR):May89-1077
Antler, J. Lucy Sprague Mitchell.
E. Haller, 77:Fall88-331
Antón, A.M.G. - see under Galilea Antón, A.M.
Antonelli, R. Repertorio metrico della scuola poetica siciliana.
W.T. Elwert, 72:Band225Heft1-227
Antoni, K. Miwa, der Heilige Trank.
F.G. Bock, 407(MN):Winter88-510
Antonini, R., L. del Tutto Palma & S. Renzetti Marra. Bibliografia dell'Italia Antica: Epigrafia, linguistica e scienze ausiliarie (1950-1984).
P. Flobert, 555:Vol61fasc2-357

Antonius, S. Where the Jinn Consult.
R. Kabbani, 364:Feb88-103
Antosh, R.B. Reality and Illusion in the Novels of J-K. Huysmans.*
P. Cogny, 535(RHL):Mar-Apr88-311
Anyi, W. - see under Wang Anyi
Anzieu, D. The Skin Ego.
S. Gardner, 617(TLS):7-13Jul89-751
Apeltauer, E., ed. Gesteuerter Zweitspracherwerb.
M.P. Alter, 399(MLJ):Autumn88-340
Apfel, E. Sämtliche herausgegebenen musikalischen Satzlehren vom 12. Jahrhundert bis gegen Ende des 15. Jahrhunderts in deutschen Übersetzungen.
A. Traub, 416:Band3Heft1-91
Apicius. The Roman Cookery of Apicius. (J. Edwards, trans)
C.R. Freis, 124:Jul-Aug89-451
Apollonius. Apollonio Rodio: "Le Argonautiche."* (G. Paduano & M. Fusillo, eds)
R.L. Hunter, 303(JoHS):Vol108-230
Apostolou, J.L. & M.H. Greenberg, eds. The Best Japanese Science Fiction Stories.
G. Jonas, 441:9Apr89-38
Appadurai, A., ed. The Social Life of Things.
C.S. Smith, 39:Mar88-217
Appel, R. & P. Muyksen. Language Contact and Bilingualism.
R.C. Troike, 399(MLJ):Autumn88-342
Appelfeld, A. For Every Sin.
D. Donoghue, 453(NYRB):28Sep89-39
G. Josipovici, 617(TLS):1-7Sep89-952
F. Prose, 441:21May89-9
442(NY):4Sep89-106
Appelfeld, A. The Immortal Bartfuss.*
D. Donoghue, 453(NYRB):28Sep89-39
T. Wilhelmus, 249(HudR):Autumn88-556
Appelfeld, A. To the Land of the Cattails.* (British title: To the Land of the Reeds.)
L. Elkin, 287:Jul/Aug87-33
Appiah, A. Assertion and Conditionals.*
K. Arnold, 320(CJL):Mar88-92
Appiah, A. For Truth in Semantics.*
M.J. Cresswell, 353:Vol26No1-162
Apple, R.W., Jr. Apple's Europe.*
42(AR):Winter88-123
Appleby, D.P. Heitor Villa-Lobos.
L.M. Peppercorn, 607:Sep88-65
Appleman, P. Apes and Angels.
A. Mobilio, 441:23Apr89-20
Appleman-Jurman, A. Alicia.
S. Taitz, 441:1Jan89-15
Applewhite, J. Ode to the Chinaberry Tree and Other Poems.*
J. Mazzaro, 569(SR):Winter88-149
Applewhite, J. River Writing.
A. Corn, 491:Jan89-229
639(VQR):Summer88-99
Applewhite, J. Seas and Inland Journeys.
I.M. Findlay, 447(N&Q):Mar88-133
Appleyard, B. The Pleasures of Peace.
M. Bull, 617(TLS):25-31Aug89-922
April, J-P. Nord électrique.
T. Vuong-Riddick, 102(CanL):Spring88-133
Apter, E.S. André Gide and the Codes of Homotextuality.
P.A. Genova, 446(NCFS):Spring-Summer89-422
Aptheker, H. - see Du Bois, W.E.B.

Aquinas, T. St. Thomas Aquinas on Politics and Ethics. (P.E. Sigmund, ed & trans)
  P.J. Weithman, 543:Mar89-638
Arac, J. Critical Genealogies.
  D.H. Bialostosky, 661(WC):Autumn88-194
  V.B. Leitch, 395(MFS):Summer88-319
Arac, J., ed. Postmodernism and Politics.*
  S. Connor, 402(MLR):Oct89-904
  B. Foley, 149(CLS):Vol25No2-197
  T. Pinkney, 366:Spring88-110
  L.V., 295(JML):Fall87/Winter88-237
Arad, Y. Belzec, Sobibor, Treblinka.
  M.I. Teicher, 390:Apr88-56
Aragón, L.G. - see under García Aragón, L.
Aragonés, J.E. Veinte años de teatro español (1960-1980).
  P. Zatlin, 240(HR):Autumn88-520
Araluce-Cuenca, J.R. Sintaxis de la paremia en el Arcipreste de Talavera.
  E.M. Gerli, 86(BHS):Apr88-181
Arancón, M.R.G. - see under García Arancón, M.R.
de Aranda, G.M. - see under Martínez de Aranda, G.
Arapi, F. Këngë të moçme shqiptare.
  S-B. Jansson, 64(Arv):Vol42-199
Arasanayagam, J. Trial by Terror.
  N. Simms, 314:Winter-Spring88-234
Aravena, F.R. & L.G. Solis Rivera - see under Rojas Aravena, F. & L.G. Solis Rivera
Arazi, A., ed. Al-Aḥādīth al-Ḥisān fī Faḍl al-Ṭaylasān li-Djalāl al-Dīn al-Suyūṭī.
  Y.K. Stillman, 318(JAOS):Jul-Sep87-528
Arbena, J.L., ed. Sport and Society in Latin America.
  D.G. La France, 263(RIB):Vol38No4-531
Arblaster, A. Democracy.
  T.D.C., 185:Apr89-664
"Arcana Mundi." (G. Luck, trans)
  R.M. Berchman, 41:Spring88-145
  J.R. Bram, 24:Spring88-148
  A. Le Boeuffle, 555:Vol61fasc2-340
  D. Martinez, 121(CJ):Dec88-Jan89-168
Arce, J. Estudios sobre el emperador Fl. Cl. Juliano (Fuentes literarias, epigrafía, numismática).
  R.B.E. Smith, 313:Vol78-270
Archambault, G. Standing Flight.*
  A.J. Harding, 102(CanL):Spring88-163
Archer, J. A Twist in the Tale.
  M. Stasio, 441:19Feb89-23
Archer, L., ed. Slavery and Other Forms of Unfree Labour.
  P. Morgan, 617(TLS):3-9Feb89-104
Archer, M., S. Crewe & P. Cormack. English Heritage in Stained Glass.
  S. Grover, 617(TLS):10-16Feb89-149
Archer, M. & T. Falk. India Revealed.
  A. Motion, 617(TLS):26May-1Jun89-586
Archer, M., C. Rowell & R. Skelton. Treasures from India.
  J.P. Losty, 39:Sep88-211
Archer, R. The Pervasive Image.*
  K. McNerney, 238:Mar88-75
  J.R. Webster, 589:Jan88-115
"Architettura etrusca nel Viterbese."
  D. Ridgway, 123:Vol38No1-180
dell' Arco, M.F. - see under Fagiolo dell' Arco, M.
Ardagh, J. Germany and the Germans.*
  J. Steffen, 364:Apr-May87-151
  639(VQR):Spring88-59

Arden, H.M. The Romance of the Rose.
  H.R. Runte, 207(FR):Mar89-678
  D.A. Trotter, 402(MLR):Jul89-737
Ardoin, J. Callas at Juilliard.
  L. Green, 465:Autumn88-102
Arduini, M.L. Neue Studien über Rupert von Deutz.
  J. Van Engen, 589:Apr89-355
Arenas, R. Singing from the Well.
  639(VQR):Winter88-22
Arends, S.F. The Central Dakota Germans.
  G. Bevington, 350:Dec89-873
Arens, A., ed. Text-Etymologie.
  J.M. Jeep, 350:Dec89-874
de Arguijo, J. Obra completa de Don Juan de Arguijo.* (S.B. Vranich, ed)
  D.G. Walters, 86(BHS):Apr88-183
Arhammar, N. & others, eds. Aspects of Language. (Vols 1 & 2)
  K. Heger, 685(ZDL):3/1988-343
"Ariadne's Thread." (S. Bassnett & P. Kuhiwczak, trans)
  L. Chamberlain, 617(TLS):24Feb-2Mar89-200
Aridjis, H. Persephone.
  I. Malin, 532(RCF):Spring88-194
Ariff, M. & H. Hill. Export-Oriented Industrialisation.
  C.W. Lindsey, 293(JASt):May88-410
Aris, M. Bhutan.
  S.B. Goodman, 318(JAOS):Oct-Dec87-840
Aris, M. Hidden Treasures and Secret Lives.
  J.H. Crook, 617(TLS):18-24Aug89-899
Aristides. Aelius Aristide, "Discours sacrés."* (A.J. Festugière, ed & trans) [shown in prev under Aelius Aristides]
  L. Pernot, 555:Vol61fasc2-311
Aristides. P. Aelius Aristides, The Complete Works Translated into English. (Vol 1) (C.A. Behr, ed & trans)
  A.R.R. Sheppard, 123:Vol38No2-233
Aristides. Elio Aristides, "Discursos I." (F. Gascó & A. Ramírez de Verger, eds & trans)
  N.G. Wilson, 123:Vol38No2-406
Aristophanes. Birds. (A.H. Sommerstein, ed & trans)
  W.G. Arnott, 123:Vol38No2-211
  S.D. Olson, 124:May-Jun89-386
Aristophanes. Lysistrata. (J. Henderson, ed)
  D.M. Macdowell, 123:Vol38No2-213
  J.H. Turner, 124:Jan-Feb89-210
Aristophanes. Peace. (A.H. Sommerstein, ed & trans)
  S.D. Olson, 124:Nov-Dec88-118
Aristophanes of Byzantium. Aristophanis Byzantii Fragmenta. (W.J. Slater, ed)
  B. Baldwin, 589:Oct88-891
  J.J. Keaney, 24:Fall88-450
  D.M. Schenkeveld, 394:Vol41fasc1/2-178
Aristotle. Aristote, "Politique." (Vol 3, Pt 1, Bk 7) (J. Aubonnet, ed & trans)
  P. Louis, 555:Vol61fasc2-309
  R.W., 555:Vol61fasc1-119
Aristotle. A New Aristotle Reader. (J.L. Ackrill, ed)
  D.J. De Moss, 518:Jul88-130
Aristotle. Nicomachean Ethics. (T. Irwin, trans)
  C.C.W. Taylor, 482(PhR):Apr88-247
Aristotle. The Politics. (S. Everson, ed; B. Jowett, trans)
  M. Cranston, 617(TLS):21-27Apr89-433

Arjomand, S.A. The Shadow of God and the Hidden Imam.
R.W. Bulliet, 318(JAOS):Jan–Mar87–185
Arkin, M. & B. Shollar, eds. Longman Anthology of World Literature by Women 1875–1975.
A. Leighton, 617(TLS):22–28Sep89–1024
Arksey, L., N. Pries & M. Reed, eds. American Diaries.* (Vol 2) [entry in prev is of Vols 1 & 2]
D.J. Winslow, 40(AEB):Vol2No4–184
Arkush, R.D. & L.O. Lee. Land Without Ghosts.
A. Broyard, 441:3Dec89–22
Arlen, M.J. The Camera Age.
R. Berman, 289:Summer88–101
Armani, G. Notizie su Carlo Cattaneo.
A. Cavaglion, 228(GSLI):Vol165fasc530–313
de Armas, F.A. The Return of Astraea.*
R. ter Horst, 240(HR):Spring88–265
R.P. Kinkade, 111:Fall89–10
Armen, M. La Fontaine d'Heghnar.
L. Kovacs, 450(NRF):Mar88–96
Armenini, G.B. De' veri precetti della pittura. (M. Gorreri, ed)
D. Ekserdjian, 617(TLS):5–11May89–488
Armistead, S.G. & J.H. Silverman, with I.J. Katz. Folk Literature of the Sephardic Jews. (Vol 2, Pt 1)
H. Goldberg, 238:Mar88–77
Armitage, C.M., comp. Sir Walter Ralegh.
W.J. Scheick, 568(SCN):Fall88–50
Armitage, S. John Held, Jr.
42(AR):Summer88–400
Armor, J. & P. Wright – see Adams, A.
Armour, D.A. The Merchants of Albany, New York, 1686–1760.
O.A. Rink, 656(WMQ):Oct88–799
Armour, P. The Door of Purgatory.
Z.G. Barański, 545(RPh):Aug88–51
Armstrong, A.H., ed. Classical Mediterranean Spirituality.
G.P. Corrington, 124:Nov–Dec88–143
Armstrong, J.C.W. Champlain.
J. Pritchard, 529(QQ):Winter88–905
Armstrong, K. Holy War.
N. Housley, 617(TLS):20–26Jan89–64
Armstrong, N. Desire and Domestic Fiction.*
N. Auerbach, 301(JEGP):Jul88–429
C. Gallagher, 637(VS):Spring89–412
R. Markley, 223:Summer88–236
J. Prostko, 191(ELN):Jun88–87
Armstrong, N. & L. Tennenhouse, eds. The Ideology of Conduct.*
E. Jordan, 366:Autumn88–222
Arnaldus de Villanova. Commentum supra tractatum Galieni de malicia complexionis diverse. (L. García Ballester & E. Sánchez Salor, eds) Doctrina Galieni de interioribus. (R.J. Durling, ed) Translatio libri Galieni de rigore et tremore et iectigacione et spasmo. (M.R. McVaugh, ed)
L. Demaitre, 589:Jan88–117
Arnason, M., S. Sigmundsson & Ö. Thorsson. Orðabók um slangur, slettur, bannorð og annað utangarðsmál.
A. Liberman, 563(SS):Winter88–87
Arnaud, C. Chamfort.
A. Clerval, 450(NRF):Sep88–116
Arnaud, J. Recherches sur la littérature maghrebine de langue française.
M. Mortimer, 538(RAL):Fall88–393

Arnaud, P. Robert Bresson.
J.J. Michalczyk, 207(FR):Dec88–356
Arndt, H.W. Economic Development.
J.P.P., 185:Oct88–210
Arnheim, R. New Essays on the Psychology of Art.*
M.J. Rosen, 560:Spring–Summer88–113
Arnold, B. German Knighthood, 1050–1300.
S. Jenks, 589:Jul88–617
Arnold, D. Famine.
M. Douglas, 617(TLS):7–13Apr89–355
Arnold, D. Police Power and Colonial Rule.
D. Ludden, 293(JASt):Aug88–669
Arnold, D. Situations.
G. Gessert, 448:Vol26No2–118
Arnold, K. Niklashausen 1476.
N.F. Palmer, 382(MAE):1988/2–331
Arnold, M. Willa Cather's Short Fiction.
L. Wagner-Martin, 659(ConL):Fall89–444
Arnold, M. The Oxford Authors: Matthew Arnold. (M. Allott & R.H. Super, eds)
639(VQR):Spring88–52
Arnold, P. & P. Wynne-Thomas, eds. An Ashes Anthology.
A.L. Le Quesne, 617(TLS):23–29Jun89–696
Arnott, P.D. Public and Performance in the Greek Theatre.
O. Taplin, 617(TLS):27Oct–2Nov89–1187
Arnson, C.J. Crossroads.
R. Caplan, 441:12Nov89–21
Arntzen, S. – see Ikkyū Sōjun
Aron, P. Le Écrivains belges et le socialisme (1880–1913).*
H-J. Lope, 547(RF):Band100Heft4–443
M. Voisin, 193:Autumn88–144
Aron, P., ed. Entre l'évangile et la révolution, Charles Plisnier.
M. Voisin, 193:Autumn88–133
Aron, R. History, Truth, Liberty.* (F. Draus, ed)
I.L. Horowitz, 473(PR):Vol55No2–338
Aronoff, M. & R.T. Oehrle, with others, eds. Language Sound Structure.
W. Zonneveld, 603:Vol12No1–243
Aronowitz, S. Science as Power.
D. Kevles, 617(TLS):14–20Jul89–785
Aronson, N. Mademoiselle de Scudéry ou le voyage au pays de Tendre.*
M. Gérard, 535(RHL):Mar–Apr88–264
J. Trethewey, 208(FS):Jan88–79
Aronson, R. Sartre's Second Critique.*
S.K., 185:Oct88–197
G.J. Stack, 319:Oct89–634
Arrighetti, G. Poeti, eruditi e biografi.
G.M. Kirkwood, 24:Winter88–602
Arrillaga, M. Los silencios de María Bibiana Benítez.
E.J. Ordóñez, 238:Sep88–554
Arrivé, M., F. Gadet & M. Galmiche. La Grammaire d'aujourd'hui.
F. Martin-Berthet, 209(FM):Apr88–93
Arroyo, C.M. – see under Morón Arroyo, C.
Arroyuelo, F.F. – see under Flores Arroyuelo, F.
"The Art of Paul Gauguin."
R.D. Reck, 207(FR):May89–1105
Arter, D. & others. Western Europe 1989.
D. Leonard, 617(TLS):21–27Apr89–428
Arthur, R.G. Medieval Sign Theory and "Sir Gawain and the Green Knight."
J.M.P. Donatelli, 627(UTQ):Fall88–104
D. Wurtele, 178:Jun88–221

"Arthurian Literature." (Vol 6) (R. Barber, ed)
  J.M. Cowen, 447(N&Q):Sep88-359
  P.J.C. Field, 541(RES):Feb88-152
"Le arti in Sicilia nel Settecento."
  M. Estella, 48:Jan-Mar88-87
"Arts of Africa, Oceania and the Americas."
  2(AfrA):Nov87-83
Artsruni, T. History of the House of the Artsrunik'.
  N.G. Garsoïan, 589:Apr88-355
Arveiller, R. & G. Gouiran — see Falquet de Romans
Arvidsson, C. & L.E. Blomqvist. Symbols of Power.
  S. Welch, 575(SEER):Oct88-662
Asche, S. Die Liebe, der Tod und das Ich im Spiegel der Kunst.
  K. Arens, 221(GQ):Winter87-124
Ascher, A. The Revolution of 1905.
  639(VQR):Autumn88-117
Ascherson, N. The Struggles for Poland.
  S. Baranczak, 473(PR):Vol55No4-682
  P. Kuhivchak, 97(CQ):Vol17No3-247
Aschkenasy, N. Eve's Journey.*
  A. Balaban, 403(MLS):Summer88-89
  E.M. Makowski, 219(GaR):Spring88-206
  N.B. Sokoloff, 508:Jan88-143
Ascoli, A.R. Ariosto's Bitter Harmony.
  C.P. Brand, 131(CL):Fall88-399
  A. Reynolds, 551(RenQ):Summer88-300
Asenjo Barbieri, F., ed. Cancionero musical de los siglos xv y xvi.
  G. Carnero, 240(HR):Autumn88-496
Ash, J. Disbelief.*
  R. Garfitt, 364:Jun88-86
Ashbee, A., ed. Records of English Court Music. (Vol 2)
  P. Holman, 415:Jan88-25
Ashbee, A., ed. Records of English Court Music. (Vol 3)
  P. Holman, 617(TLS):29Sep-5Oct89-1068
Ashbery, J. April Galleons.*
  R. Jackson, 219(GaR):Winter88-856
  D. Revell, 152(UDQ):Summer88-104
  W. Scammell, 493:Spring88-48
  V. Shetley, 491:May88-109
  D. Young, 199:Spring88-76
  639(VQR):Spring88-63
Ashbery, J., ed. The Best American Poetry, 1988.
  R.T. Smith, 496:Winter88/89-52
Ashbery, J. Selected Poems.*
  D. McDuff, 565:Autumn88-61
  F. Worsham, 577(SHR):Winter88-94
Ashbery, J. & J. Schuyler. A Nest of Ninnies.
  G. Ward, 97(CQ):Vol17No1-99
Ashcraft, R. Locke's Two Treatises of Government.
  A. Reeve, 402(MLR):Oct89-928
Ashcraft, R. Revolutionary Politics and Locke's "Two Treatises of Government."*
  J.D. Rabb, 529(QQ):Summer88-487
Ashcroft, J., D. Huschenbett & W.H. Jackson, eds. Liebe in der deutschen Literatur des Mittelalters.
  A. Classen, 406:Spring88-123
Ashdown, P. — see Agee, J.
Ashe, G. The Discovery of King Arthur.
  M. Whitaker, 102(CanL):Autumn88-180
Ashihara, Y. The Hidden Order.
  J. Shulevitz, 441:17Dec89-19

Ashliman, D.L. A Guide to Folktales in the English Language.
  U. Marzolph, 196:Band29Heft1/2-169
Ashmore, H.S. Unseasonable Truths.
  R.A. McCaughey, 441:3Sep89-10
  G. Steiner, 442(NY):23Oct89-142
Ashton, D. Fragonard in the Universe of Painting.
  M. Levey, 90:Oct88-779
Ashton, R. Little Germany.*
  T.H. Pickett, 133:Band21Heft2/3-229
  A. Varty, 541(RES):Feb88-129
Ashworth, M. Beyond Methodology.*
  S.K. Gill, 355(LSoc):Jun88-308
"Asian Art in the Arthur M. Sackler Gallery: The Inaugural Gift."
  J. Sweetman, 463:Spring88-55
Asimov, I. Nemesis.
  G. Jonas, 441:19Nov89-32
Asimov, I. The Relativity of Wrong.
  J.D. Barrow, 617(TLS):29Sep-5Oct89-1072
Askew, R.R. The Dragonflies of Europe.
  M. Ridley, 617(TLS):3-9Feb89-118
Aslanoff, S. Manuel typographique du russiste.
  R. Scrivens, 575(SEER):Oct88-637
Åslund, A. Gorbachev's Struggle for Economic Reform.
  O. Figes, 617(TLS):4-10Aug89-841
  P. Taubman, 441:13Aug89-25
Asmis, E. Epicurus' Scientific Method.
  J. Boulogne, 555:Vol61fasc1-120
  D. Furley, 53(AGP):Band70Heft1-108
  A.A. Long, 482(PhR):Apr88-249
Asor Rosa, A., ed. Letteratura italiana. (Pt 7; Vol 1 & Vol 2, Pt 1) Scrittori e popolo.
  D. Robey, 617(TLS):17-23Feb89-172
"Aspects du théâtre dans le théâtre au XVIIe siècle."
  C. Mazouer, 535(RHL):Mar-Apr88-263
Assad, M.L. La Fiction et la mort dans l'oeuvre de Stéphane Mallarmé.
  K.C. Kurk, 446(NCFS):Fall-Winter88/89-242
Asscher-Pinkhof, C. Star Children.
  M.I. Teicher, 390:Apr88-56
Assion, P., ed. Transformationen der Arbeiterkultur.
  H. Groschopp, 654(WB):4/1988-701
de Assis, J.M.M. — see under Machado de Assis, J.M.
Assollant, A. Lettres inédites à Ernest Havet et à quelques autres. (A. Carriat, ed)
  R. Mathé, 535(RHL):Mar-Apr88-325
Assoun, P-L. L'Ecole de Francfort.
  A. Reix, 542:Jul-Sep88-356
Astafiev, V. Triste polar.
  J. Blot, 450(NRF):Feb88-105
Astås, R. Et bibelverk fra middelalderen.
  M. Rindal, 172(Edda):1988/4-367
Astbury, R. — see Varro
Asthana, S. Pre-Harappan Cultures of India and the Borderlands.
  G.L. Possehl, 318(JAOS):Oct-Dec87-839
Astiazarain Achabal, M.I. La Iglesia Parroquial de Elgoibar.
  A. Rodríguez G. de Ceballos, 48:Apr-Jun88-186
Astill, G. & A. Grant, eds. The Countryside of Medieval England.
  R.B. Dobson, 617(TLS):6-12Jan89-20

13

Astley, N. Darwin Survivor.
  M. Wormald, 617(TLS):9–15Jun89–641
Astley, N., ed. Poetry with an Edge.
  M. Wormald, 617(TLS):9–15Jun89–641
Astley, T. An Item from the Late News.
  R.D. Haynes, 581:Jun88–138
Aston, M. England's Iconoclasts. (Vol 1)
  P. Collinson, 617(TLS):17–23Feb89–155
Åström, P. & others. Corpus Vasorum Anti-
  quorum. (Sweden, Vol 3)
  B.A. Sparkes, 303(JoHS):Vol108–268
Aswell, E.C. & E. Nowell. In the Shadow of
  the Giant: Thomas Wolfe. (M.A. Doll & C.
  Stites, eds)
  J. Halberstadt, 441:30Jul89–14
Asztalos, M., ed. The Editing of Theological
  and Philosophical Texts from the Middle
  Ages.
  A. Classen, 597(SN):Vol60No2–263
Atherton, S.A. & S.P. Nandan, eds. Creative
  Writing from Fiji.
  D. Brydon, 49:Apr88–96
Atkins, B.T. & others – see "Collins-Robert
  French-English English-French Dictionary"
Atkins, G.D. Quests of Difference.*
  J.D. Canfield, 405(MP):Feb89–309
  E. Pollak, 301(JEGP):Jan88–116
Atkins, J. The British Spy Novel.*
  J.R. Cohn, 594:Fall88–323
Atkins, S. – see von Goethe, J.W.
Atkinson, P. Language, Structure, and Re-
  production.
  P. McLaren, 355(LSoc):Jun88–263
Atkinson, R. The Long Gray Line.
  T. Buckley, 441:22Oct89–18
Atlan, L. Les Passants.
  B.L. Knapp, 207(FR):May89–1088
Attfield, R. A Theory of Value and Obliga-
  tion.
  B. Mayo, 518:Jan88–53
  C. Megone, 291:Vol5No2–237
  S. Mendus, 483:Jul88–406
  H. Oberdiek, 185:Apr89–638
"Atti del Convegno Virgiliano di Brindisi nel
  Bimillenario della Morte."
  J. den Boeft, 394:Vol41fasc1/2–198
Attoe, D. Lion at the Door.
  E. Stumpf, 441:30Jul89–16
Attridge, D. Peculiar Language.
  P. McGee, 329(JJQ):Fall88–129
Attridge, D., G. Bennington & R. Young, eds.
  Post-Structuralism and the Question of
  History.
  R.D. Ackerman, 478(P&L):Oct88–307
  A. Montefiore, 447(N&Q):Sep88–414
  A. Pagden, 322(JHI):Jul–Sep88–519
  J. Thompson, 141:Spring88–269
Attridge, D. & D. Ferrer, eds. Post-Structur-
  alist Joyce.
  R.A. Cave, 541(RES):May88–321
  P. Parrinder, 402(MLR):Jan89–141
Attwood, W. The Twilight Struggle.
  639(VQR):Winter88–16
Atwell, J.E. Ends and Principles in Kant's
  Moral Thought.*
  S.E., 185:Apr89–678
Atwood, M., ed. The CanLit Foodbook.
  M. Matthews, 376:Mar88–106
Atwood, M. Cat's Eye.
  A. McDermott, 441:5Feb89–1
  S. Mackay, 617(TLS):3–9Feb89–113
  C. Rooke, 376:Dec88–131
    [continued]

[continuing]
  J. Thurman, 442(NY):29May89–108
  R. Towers, 453(NYRB):27Apr89–50
Atwood, M. Interlunar.
  L.W. Norfolk, 617(TLS):18–24Aug89–903
Atwood, M. Selected Poems II.*
  L. York, 102(CanL):Spring88–185
Atwood, W.G. Fryderyk Chopin.*
  T. Higgins, 309:Vol8No3/4–395
Aubailly, J–C. La Fée et le chevalier.
  K. Busby, 382(MAE):1988/1–130
Auberger, G. L'unanimité cistercienne primi-
  tive.
  C.H. Berman, 589:Apr88–357
Aubert, J., ed. Joyce avec Lacan.*
  E. Ragland-Sullivan & R.B. Kershner,
  329(JJQ):Fall88–115
Aubonnet, J. – see Aristotle
Auburger, L. Funktionale Sprachvarianten.
  G. Van der Elst, 685(ZDL):2/1987–262
Auchard, J. Silence in Henry James.*
  C.B. Cox, 569(SR):Summer88–497
  R. Gard, 447(N&Q):Mar88–137
  J.W. Gargano, 587(SAF):Spring88–124
Auchincloss, L. Fellow Passengers.
  I. Colegate, 441:26Mar89–8
Auchincloss, L. The Golden Calves.*
  I. Fonseca, 617(TLS):24Feb–2Mar89–191
Auchincloss, L. The Vanderbilt Era.
  P–L. Adams, 61:Sep89–112
  A.E. Johnson, 441:28May89–19
Auden, W.H. Paul Bunyan.
  J. Fuller, 493:Autumn88–42
Auden, W.H. & C. Isherwood. Plays and Other
  Dramatic Writings by W.H. Auden 1928–
  1938. (E. Mendelson, ed)
  M. Wood, 617(TLS):4–10Aug89–849
von Aue, H. – see under Hartmann von Aue
Auerbach, E.R. & N. Wallerstein. ESL for
  Action.
  S–K. Lai, 608:Jun89–321
Auerbach, N. Romantic Imprisonment.*
  K. Swann, 591(SIR):Winter88–605
Auerbach, N. Ellen Terry.*
  J. Fisher, 610:Autumn88–287
  G. Rowell, 611(TN):Vol42No3–126
  639(VQR):Summer88–90
Auerbacher, I. I Am a Star.
  M.I. Teicher, 390:Apr88–57
Augros, R. & G. Stanciu. The New Biology.
  P.W. Colgan, 529(QQ):Winter88–945
Augst, G., ed. Graphematik und Orthogra-
  phie.
  B.J. Koekkoek, 221(GQ):Fall88–566
Augst, G., ed. New Trends in Graphemics and
  Orthography.
  B.J. Koekkoek, 221(GQ):Fall88–566
  J. Scharnhorst, 682(ZPSK):Band41Heft5–
  676
Augst, G. Regeln zur deutschen Rechtschrei-
  bung vom 1. Januar 2001.
  G. Feudel, 682(ZPSK):Band41Heft5–658
Saint Augustine. Oeuvres de Saint Augustin:
  "La Vie heureuse." (J. Doignon, ed & trans)
  P.G. Walsh, 123:Vol38No1–157
Saint Augustine. Sant'Agostino, "La Vera
  Religione." (A. Lamacchia, ed)
  A. Bastiaensen, 640:Nov88–156
Auhuber, F. In einem fernen dunklen Spiegel.
  J.M. McGlathery, 406:Summer88–231
Aujoulat, N. Le Néoplatonisme alexandrin:
  Hiéroclès d'Alexandrie.
  J. Dillon, 319:Jul89–466

Bagwell, J.T. American Formalism and the Problem of Interpretation.*
M.P.L., 295(JML):Fall87/Winter88-237

Bahl, R., C.K. Kim & C.K. Park, eds. Public Finances During the Korean Modernization Process.
K. Moskowitz, 293(JASt):Nov88-902

Bahn, P.G. & J. Vertut. Images of the Ice Age.
C. Chippindale, 617(TLS):15-21Sep89-1011

Bahner, W. & W. Neumann, eds. Sprachwissenschaftliche Germanistik.*
E-M. Heinle, 685(ZDL):3/1987-353

Bai, L. - see under Li Bai

Bailey, A. Major André.
A. Rosenheim, 617(TLS):21-27Apr89-436

Bailey, A. The Outer Banks.
P. Kopper, 441:23Jul89-22

Bailey, A. Spring Jaunts.*
S. Pickering, 569(SR):Fall88-673

Bailey, B.L. From Front Porch to Back Seat.*
639(VQR):Autumn88-136

Bailey, C.J. Catalogue of the Collection of Drawings in the Ashmolean Museum.* (Vol 5)
G. Scheffler, 90:Aug88-639

Bailey, C-J.N. English Phonetic Transcription.*
G. Bailey, 350:Mar89-174
J. Kelly, 353:Vol26No5-879

Bailey, D. Bring Me Your Passion.
A. Brennan, 198:Autumn88-108

Bailey, D.R.S. - see under Shackleton Bailey, D.R.

Bailey, F.A. Class and Tennessee's Confederate Generation.
J.T. O'Brien, 106:Fall88-339
639(VQR):Winter88-12

Bailey, G. The Making of Andrei Sakharov.
R. Penrose, 617(TLS):29Sep-5Oct89-1058

Bailey, H. A Stranger to Herself.
P. Raine, 617(TLS):3-9Nov89-1218

Bailey, J. Conflicts in Cricket.
A.L. Le Quesne, 617(TLS):23-29Jun89-696

Bailey, L. Soup Meals.
R. Flaste, 441:11Jun89-18

Bailey, P. Gabriel's Lament.*
639(VQR):Winter88-21

Bailey, P., ed. Music Hall.
K. Barker, 611(TN):Vol42No2-87
G. Speaight, 610:Summer88-169
J.W. Stedman, 637(VS):Autumn88-121

Bailey, S.D. War and Conscience in the Nuclear Age.*
C.A.J.C., 185:Jul89-980

Baillargeon, J-P., ed. Les Pratiques culturelles des Québécois.
B-Z. Shek, 627(UTQ):Fall87-192

Bailyn, B. The Peopling of British North America.*
J.C.A. Stagg, 639(VQR):Spring88-361

Bailyn, B., with B. De Wolfe. Voyagers to the West.*
J.C.A. Stagg, 639(VQR):Spring88-361

Bain, R. & J.M. Flora, eds. Fifty Southern Writers Before 1900.
27(AL):Oct88-522

Bainbridge, B. An Awfully Big Adventure.
L. Duguid, 617(TLS):15-21Dec89-1385

Baine, R.M., with M.R. Baine. The Scattered Portions.*
A. Lincoln, 541(RES):Feb88-117
M. Storch, 402(MLR):Oct89-936

Baird-Lange, L.Y. & H. Schnuttgen. A Bibliography of Chaucer, 1974-1985.
R. Beadle, 617(TLS):16-22Jun89-676
S. Ferris, 365:Fall87-215

Baird-Smith, R., ed. Winter's Tales: New Series, 5.
M. Illis, 617(TLS):1-7Dec89-1337

Bak, K. P.D.A. Atterboms sagospel Lycksalighetens ö som initiatorisk drama.
J.W. Dietrichson, 172(Edda):1988/2-179

Bakalar, J.B. & L. Grinspoon. Drug Control in a Free Society.
D.A.J.R., 185:Apr89-686

Bakalla, M.H. & B. Ingham - see Ali, A.S.M.

Baker, D.C. - see Chaucer, G.

Baker, D.L. Narcissus and the Lover.*
J.C. Nash, 210(FrF):May88-243

Baker, D.Z. Mythic Masks in Self-Reflexive Poetry.
C. Dumoulié, 549(RLC):Jan-Mar88-83
P. Merivale, 107(CRCL):Jun88-306

Baker, G. Wittgenstein, Frege and the Vienna Circle.
G. Currie, 617(TLS):17-23Feb89-163

Baker, G.P. & P.M.S. Hacker. Scepticism, Rules and Language.
P. Leonardi, 449:Dec88-618
L. Reinhardt, 63:Mar88-113

Baker, G.P. & P.M.S. Hacker. Wittgenstein.*
P. Carruthers, 479(PhQ):Jan88-131
P. Engel, 542:Jul-Sep88-357
A. Lugg, 486:Sep88-486

Baker, H.A., Jr. Modernism and the Harlem Renaissance.*
W.L. Howard, 219(GaR):Fall88-638
N.I. Huggins, 538(RAL):Winter88-580
C.A. Wall, 27(AL):Dec88-680

Baker, J.H. Mary Todd Lincoln.
639(VQR):Spring88-50

Baker, J.M. The Music of Alexander Scriabin.
R.J. Guenther, 317:Spring88-194
A. Pople, 411:Jul88-215
T.J. Samson, 308:Fall88-353

Baker, K., ed. The Faber Book of English History in Verse.*
C. Rumens, 493:Autumn88-8

Baker, M. The Winnipeg School of Art.
M. Waddington, 102(CanL):Winter87-205

Baker, N. The Mezzanine.*
B. Leithauser, 453(NYRB):17Aug89-15
R. Plunket, 441:5Feb89-9
N. Smith, 617(TLS):15-21Sep89-998

Baker, P. Modern Poetic Practice.
V.S., 295(JML):Fall87/Winter88-269

Baker, R. The Good Times.
P-L. Adams, 61:Jul89-96
W. Just, 441:28May89-1
442(NY):3Jul89-95

Baker, R.L. Jokelore.
R.O. Ribnick, 650(WF):Jan88-60

Baker, S.S. Radical Beginnings.
F. Matthews, 106:Spring88-69

Baker, W. Mountain Blood.*
L. Domina, 502(PrS):Summer88-136

Bakhtin, M.M./P.N. Medvedev. Problems of Dostoevsky's Poetics.* (C. Emerson, ed)
J. Goodlife, 478(P&L):Apr88-152

Bakhtin, M.M. Speech Genres and Other Late Essays.* (C. Emerson & M. Holquist, eds)
  D.K. Danow, 567:Vol72No1/2-179
  W. van Peer, 204(FdL):Jun88-143
  N. Perlina, 574(SEEJ):Fall88-461
  W.G. Regier, 223:Fall88-369
  A. Shukman, 575(SEER):Jan88-125
Bakina, M.A. & E.A. Nekrasova. Èvoljucija poztičeskoj reču XIX-XX vv.
  D. Sloane, 574(SEEJ):Summer88-314
Bakker, B.H., with C. Becker - see Zola, É.
Bakker, D.M. De macht van het woord. (T.A.J.M. Janssen, J. Noordegraaf & A. Verhagen, eds)
  R.S. Kirsner, 204(FdL):Dec88-306
Bakker, H. Ayodhyā.
  J.W. de Jong, 259(IIJ):Apr88-147
Bakker, J. Ernest Hemingway in Holland, 1925-1981.*
  H. Beaver, 402(MLR):Oct89-969
  T.D., 295(JML):Fall87/Winter88-329
  E. Margolies, 179(ES):Jun88-267
Bakker, J., J.A. Verleun, & J.V.D. Vriesenaerde, eds. Essays on English and American Literature and a Sheaf of Poems.
  R. Asselineau, 189(EA):Oct-Dec88-500
Bal, M. Narratology.*
  W. Martin, 188(ECr):Spring88-112
  H.F. Mosher, Jr., 494:Vol8No3/4-694
  G. Prince, 567:Vol68No3/4-355
Balaguer, J.R. - see under Rubió i Balaguer, J.
Balanza, F. & others. Guerrilles al Baix Llobregat.
  J-L. Marfany, 86(BHS):Jul88-316
Balard, M., ed. Fortunes de Jacques Amyot.
  S. Bamforth, 402(MLR):Jan89-159
Balavoine, C., J. Lafond & P. Laurens, eds. Le Modèle à la Renaissance.*
  F. Lestringant, 535(RHL):Mar-Apr88-253
Balavoine, C. & P. Laurens, eds. La Statue et l'empreinte.
  P. Ford, 208(FS):Jan88-74
  J-F. Maillard, 535(RHL):Sep-Oct88-1019
Balayé, S. La Bibliothèque Nationale des origines à 1800.
  W.H. Barber, 617(TLS):24-30Nov89-1305
Balayé, S. & L. Omacini - see Madame de Staël
Balbert, P. & P.L. Marcus, eds. D.H. Lawrence.*
  M. Bell, 402(MLR):Jan89-146
Balcer, J.M. Herodotus and Bisitun.
  T.S. Kawami, 124:Jul-Aug89-455
  R. Stevenson, 123:Vol38No2-434
Balcer, J.M. Sparda by the Bitter Sea.
  J. Wiesehöfer, 229:Band60Heft6-544
Balcou, J., ed. La mer au siècle des encyclopédies.
  A.M. Chouillet, 530:Apr88-172
Bald, R.C. John Donne.
  D.F. Bratchell, 447(N&Q):Mar88-86
Baldassarri, M. La logica stoica. (Vols 5b, 7b & 8)
  J. Barnes, 123:Vol38No2-426
Balderston, D. El precursor velado.*
  A. Hayes, 345(KRQ):Feb88-123
Baldi, P. An Introduction to the Indo-European Languages.
  P. Swiggers, 553(RLiR):Jan-Jun88-245
Baldi, S. Studi Miltoniani.
  R. Flannagan, 391:Mar88-26

Baldick, C. In Frankenstein's Shadow.*
  W.P. Day, 637(VS):Summer89-577
Baldick, C. The Social Mission of English Criticism, 1848-1932.
  R. Crawford, 447(N&Q):Dec88-560
Baldick, J. Mytstical Islam.
  R. Irwin, 617(TLS):8-14Dec89-1371
Baldinger, K. Dictionnaire étymologique de l'ancien français. (fasc G5)
  G. Roques, 553(RLiR):Jul-Dec88-510
Baldinger, K. Dictionnaire onomasiologique de l'ancien occitan. (fasc 3 & 4) Dictionnaire onomasiologique de l'ancien occitan Supplément. (fasc 2 & 3) Dictionnaire onomasiologique de l'ancien gascon. (fasc 5 & 6) (I. Popelar, ed of all)
  G. Roques, 553(RLiR):Jul-Dec88-509
Baldini, A. Ricerche sulla storia di Eunapio di Sardi.*
  T.M. Banchich, 229:Band60Heft1-73
Baldissone, G. Filippo Tommaso Marinetti.
  S.W. Vinall, 402(MLR):Oct89-1006
Baldon, C. & I. Melchior. Steps & Stairways.
  P. Goldberger, 441:3Dec89-21
Baldwin, D.R. H.E. Bates.*
  R. Wasson, 395(MFS):Summer88-282
Baldwin, J.W. The Government of Philip Augustus.*
  J.B. Henneman, Jr., 589:Apr88-360
Baldwin, N. Man Ray.
  R. Lippincott, 441:8Jan89-22
  L.E. Nesbitt, 55:Oct88-93
Baldwin, W. Beware the Cat. (W.A. Ringler, Jr. & M. Flachmann, eds)
  K. Duncan-Jones, 617(TLS):7-13Apr89-369
Bale, J. The Complete Plays of John Bale. (P. Happé, ed)
  C. Gauvin, 189(EA):Oct-Dec88-476
Balfour, M. Withstanding Hitler in Germany: 1933-1945.*
  G. Craig, 453(NYRB):2Feb89-10
Balibar, R. L'Institution du français.*
  P. Pupier, 320(CJL):Mar88-114
Balis, A. Corpus Rubenianum Ludwig Burchard. (Pt 18, Vol 1)
  M. Jaffé, 90:Oct88-775
Balis, A. Corpus Rubenianum Ludwig Burchard.* (Pt 18, Vol 2)
  C. Brown, 39:Mar88-216
  M. Jaffé, 90:Oct88-775
  C. White, 380:Summer88-138
Balk, H.W. Performing Power.
  C. Kitka, 610:Summer88-183
Ball, M., F. Gray & L. McDowell. The Transformation of Britain.
  F. Cairncross, 617(TLS):1-7Dec89-1326
Ball, M.J., ed. The Use of Welsh.
  J. Fife, 350:Jun89-418
Ball, R.J. Reading Classical Latin.
  B. Thurman & W. Spencer, 399(MLJ):Autumn88-344
Ball, T. & J. Farr, eds. After Marx.
  J. Dunn, 488:Jun88-270
Ball, T., J. Farr & R.L. Hanson, eds. Political Innovation and Conceptual Change.
  D. Miller, 617(TLS):8-14Sep89-980
Ball, T. & J.G.A. Pocock, eds. Conceptual Change and the Constitution.
  W. Brock, 617(TLS):8-14Sep89-979
Ballabriga, A. Le Soleil et le Tartare.
  R.G.A. Buxton, 123:Vol38No2-291

Ballard, J.G. The Day of Creation.*
  H. Mantel, 364:Nov87-98
Ballard, J.G. Memories of the Space Age.
  P. Kincaid, 617(TLS):13-19Jan89-42
Ballard, J.G. Running Wild.
  P. Kincaid, 617(TLS):13-19Jan89-42
  J. Marcus, 441:17Dec89-19
Ballard, M.B. A Long Shadow.*
  R.G. Haycock, 106:Spring88-105
Ballester, L.G. & E. Sánchez Salor - see under
  García Ballester, L. & E. Sánchez Salor
Balliett, W. American Musicians.*
  P. Baker, 498:Spring88-86
  R. Middleton, 415:Jul88-347
Ballmer, T.T. & W. Brennenstuhl. Deutsche
  Verben.
  T.F. Shannon, 350:Mar89-175
Ballmer, T.T. & R. Posner, eds. Nach-
  Chomskysche Linguistik.
  S. Freytag, 682(ZPSK):Band41Heft3-389
Balmas, E. & M. Dassonville, eds. Théâtre
  français de la Renaissance.* (1st Ser, Vol
  1)
  R.A. Carr, 207(FR):Oct88-162
  G. Schrenck, 535(RHL):Sep-Oct88-1020
Balme, M. & J. Morwood. Oxford Latin Course.
  (Pt 1)
  W.A. Williams, 123:Vol38No2-433
Balmer, R. Mine Eyes Have Seen the Glory.
  G. Wills, 453(NYRB):21Dec89-20
Bammesberger, A. Der Aufbau des german-
  ischen Verbalsystems.
  U. Hempen, 680(ZDP):Band107Heft3-465
Bammesberger, A. English Etymology.*
  P. Bierbaumer, 260(IF):Band93-333
  F. Wenisch, 38:Band106Heft1/2-146
Bammesberger, A. Linguistic Notes on Old
  English Poetic Texts.
  N. Jacobs, 382(MAE):1988/1-92
Bammesberger, A., ed. Problems of Old En-
  glish Lexicography.*
  K.R. Grinda, 260(IF):Band93-344
  D.G. Scragg, 38:Band106Heft1/2-150
Bammesberger, A. A Sketch of Diachronic
  English Morphology.
  P. Bierbaumer, 38:Band106Heft1/2-147
  J. Insley, 72:Band225Heft2-365
  K. Toth, 260(IF):Band93-331
Banac, I. With Stalin against Tito.
  M. Wheeler, 617(TLS):16-22Jun89-659
Bancheri, S. & others. Lettura e Conversa-
  zione.
  J.L. Laurenti, 399(MLJ):Winter88-480
Bancquart, M-C. Anatole France.
  J. Beecher, 446(NCFS):Spring-Summer89-
  414
Bandle, O., W. Baumgartner & J. Glauser, eds.
  Strindbergs Dramen im Lichte neuerer
  Methodendiskussionen.
  H. Uecker, 52:Band23Heft2-198
Banerjee, N.V. Towards Perpetual Peace.
  W. Eastman, 103:Nov89-433
Banerjee, S.P. & S. Moitra, eds. Communica-
  tion, Identity and Self-Expression.
  D. Krishna, 485(PE&W):Oct88-431
Banerji, S. The Wedding of Jayanthi Mandel.
  J. Mellors, 364:Nov87-102
Banes, S. Terpsichore in Sneakers. (2nd ed)
  S. Manning, 162(TDR):Winter88-32
Banister, J. China's Changing Population.
  L.A. Orleans, 293(JASt):May88-333
Bankei. Bankei Zen. (P. Haskel, trans)
  T.P. Kasulis, 485(PE&W):Jan88-82

Banker, J.R. Death in the Community.
  L. Martines, 617(TLS):1-7Sep89-956
Banks, M. & A. Swift. The Joke's On Us.
  S. Carlson, 615(TJ):Dec88-574
Banks, O. Becoming a Feminist.
  639(VQR):Winter88-32
Banks, R. Affliction.
  E. Tallent, 441:17Sep89-7
  R. Towers, 453(NYRB):7Dec89-46
Banks, R. Success Stories.
  42(AR):Spring88-274
Banney, H.F. Return to Sender.
  B.L. Cooper, 498:Fall88-109
  R.S. Denisoff, 498:Summer88-84
Banta, M. Imaging American Women.*
  S. Albertine, 405(MP):May89-448
  T.A. Carbone, 658:Spring88-98
Banta, M. & O.A. Silverman - see Joyce, J.
Banton, M. Racial Consciousness.
  N.D. Deakin, 617(TLS):3-9Mar89-216
Banville, J. The Book of Evidence.
  P. Craig, 617(TLS):31Mar-6Apr89-344
Banyeres, M.A.S. - see under Angels Santa i
  Banyeres, M.
Bar-On, A.Z., ed. On Shmuel Hugo Berman's
  Philosophy.
  M. Adam, 542:Jul-Sep88-357
Bara, B.G. & G. Guida, eds. Computational
  Models of Natural Language Processing.
  L.A. Connolly, 603:Vol12No1-165
Barale, M.A. Daughters and Lovers.*
  E.C.R., 295(JML):Fall87/Winter88-395
Barańczak, S. A Fugitive from Utopia.*
  M.G. Levine, 574(SEEJ):Winter88-675
  N. Taylor, 402(MLR):Jul89-815
Barasch, M. Giotto and the Language of Ges-
  ture.
  H.B.J. Maginnis, 90:Sep88-702
  639(VQR):Summer88-102
Barash, C. - see Schreiner, O.
Baratto, M. La letteratura teatrale del set-
  tecento in Italia. (G. Da Pozzo, F. Fido &
  M. Santagata, eds)
  J.I. Cope, 173(ECS):Fall88-70
Barayón, R.S. - see under Sender Barayón, R.
Barba, E. Beyond the Floating Islands.
  K.Q.Z., 295(JML):Fall87/Winter88-274
Barba, V. - see Diderot, D.
Barber, B. The Conquest of Politics.*
  M. Walzer, 453(NYRB):2Feb89-42
Barber, C.L. Creating Elizabethan Tragedy.
  M. Charney, 551(RenQ):Winter88-746
Barber, C.L. & R.P. Wheeler. The Whole Jour-
  ney.*
  T. Cartelli, 702:Vol20-283
  K. Muir, 402(MLR):Oct89-924
  L. Salingar, 131(CL):Summer88-259
  M.A. Skura, 570(SQ):Spring88-90
Barber, N. The Weeping and the Laughter.
  J. Cohen, 441:5Feb89-24
Barber, R. King Arthur.
  N.J. Lacy, 589:Oct88-896
Barber, R. - see "Arthurian Literature"
Barber, R.L.N. The Cyclades in the Bronze
  Age.
  J.C. Overbeck, 124:Jul-Aug89-464
Barbera, J., W. McBrien & H. Bajan. Stevie
  Smith.
  C.K. Doreski, 87(BB):Mar88-70
  S. Hills, 78(BC):Spring88-136
Bàrberi Squarotti, G., ed. I bersagli della
  satira.
  D. Gorret, 228(GSLI):Vol165fasc530-305

19

Barner, W., E. Lämmert & N. Oellers, eds. Unser Commercium.
  A. Aurnhammer, 52:Band23Heft2-187
Barner, W. & A.M. Reh, eds. Nation und Gelehrtenrepublik.*
  H. Madland, 221(GQ):Spring87-281
  J.W. Van Cleve, 406:Summer88-222
Barnes, B. The Nature of Power.
  H. Laycock, 103:Oct89-394
Barnes, D. Djuna Barnes: Interviews. (A. Barry, ed)
  S.E. Grace, 534(RALS):Vol16No1&2-164
Barnes, D. New York. (A. Barry, ed)
  L. Tillman, 441:1Oct89-27
Barnes, J. A History of the World in 10 1/2 Chapters.
  R. Adams, 453(NYRB):26Oct89-7
  J.C. Oates, 441:1Oct89-12
  M. Wood, 617(TLS):30Jun-6Jul89-713
Barnes, J. Staring at the Sun.*
  I. Malin, 532(RCF):Summer88-327
Barnes, L. A Hero Travels Light.*
  E. MacNiven, 526:Summer88-86
  G. Noonan, 102(CanL):Summer88-135
Barnes, L. The Snake Tattoo.
  M. Stasio, 441:16Apr89-31
Barnes, L. A Trouble of Fools.*
  T.J. Binyon, 617(TLS):10-16Mar89-262
Barnes, P. A Companion to Post-War British Theatre.*
  W.B. Worthen, 615(TJ):Mar88-131
Barnes, T.D. Constantine and Eusebius. The New Empire of Diocletian and Constantine.
  F. Kolb, 229:Band60Heft1-45
Barnett, A.D. The Making of Foreign Policy in China.
  A.H.Y. Lin, 302:Vol24No1-91
Barnett, C., ed. Hitler's Generals.
  R.J. Overy, 617(TLS):1-7Sep89-937
Barnett, F. & S. Working Together.
  P.S. Estess, 441:29Oct89-41
Barnett, G.A. Lanford Wilson.
  M. Wolf, 511:May88-44
Barnett, J. The Elusive City.*
  F. Gutheim, 47:Jan88-42
Barnett, M.A. Lire avec plaisir.
  H.J. Siskin, 207(FR):Dec88-377
Barnett, R.D. Ancient Ivories in the Middle East and Neighboring Lands.*
  H. Leibowitz, 318(JAOS):Jan-Mar87-138
Barnett, R.L. Dynamics of Detour.
  M.J. Muratore, 345(KRQ):May88-233
Barnett, R.L., ed. Re-lectures raciniennes.*
  B. Chédozeau, 535(RHL):Nov-Dec88-1139
Barnett, S. Dossiers Secrets.
  H. Buckingham, 566:Winter87/88-71
Barnett, S.W. & J.K. Fairbank, eds. Christianity in China.
  M.S. Gewurtz, 293(JASt):Feb88-105
Barnette, D. & L.J., eds. Studies in Eighteenth-Century Spanish Literature and Romanticism in Honor of John Clarkson Dowling.
  R.L. Irvin, 552(REH):Oct88-138
Barnhardt, W. Emma Who Saved My Life.
  J. Olshan, 441:16Jul89-24
Barnhart, D.K. The Barnhart Dictionary Companion Index (1982-1985).
  G. Cannon, 660(Word):Aug88-140
Barnhart, M.A. Japan Prepares for Total War.
  A.D. Coox, 407(MN):Spring88-112
  M.R. Peattie, 293(JASt):May88-370

Barnhart, R.K. & S. Steinmetz, eds. The Barnhart Dictionary of Etymology.
  J. Algeo, 350:Dec89-848
Barnie, J. Lightning Country.
  J. May, 493:Summer88-54
Barnouw, D. & G. van der Stroom - see Frank, A.
Barny, R. Rousseau dans la Révolution.
  J.H. Bloch, 402(MLR):Apr89-475
  N. Hampson, 208(FS):Jul88-347
Baro, J. Glosario completo de "Los Milagros de Nuestra Señora" de Gonzalo de Berceo.
  J.T. Snow, 238:Dec88-820
Baroja, P. La nave de los locos. (F. Flores Arroyuelo, ed)
  B.J. Dendle, 240(HR):Autumn88-508
Barolini, T. Dante's Poets.*
  D. Parker, 276:Summer88-156
Barolsky, P. Walter Pater's Renaissance.*
  F.E. Court, 177(ELT):Vol31No2-197
Baron, D.E. Grammar and Gender.*
  W.N. Francis, 350:Mar89-176
  P.L. Lundberg, 35(AS):Summer88-169
Baron, H. In Search of Florentine Civic Humanism.
  G. Holmes, 617(TLS):17-23Mar89-287
Baron, J.H. Chamber Music.
  J. Dack, 410(M&L):Oct88-524
Baron, S.H. & C. Pletsch, eds. Introspection in Biography.
  L.A. Renza, 77:Winter88-79
Baroncelli, G. - see Cavalieri, B.
Barone, P. The Wind.
  G.L. Morris, 455:Sep88-68
Baroni, M. & M.G. Tavoni, eds. Giuseppe Sarti.
  M. Hunter, 410(M&L):Jan88-83
"Du Baroque aux Lumières."*
  J. Hennequin, 475:Vol15No28-271
Barr, A.H., Jr. Defining Modern Art.* (I. Sandler & A. Newman, eds)
  G. van Hensbergen, 90:Apr88-301
Barr, M.S. Alien to Femininity.
  P.D. Murphy, 590:Dec88-163
  E.B. Thompson, 395(MFS):Summer88-257
Barr, M.S., R. Salvaggio & R. Law. Suzy McKee Charnas/Octavia Butler/Joan D. Vinge.
  K.L. Spencer, 561(SFS):Nov87-407
Barr, R. Roseanne.
  M.L. Polak, 441:5Nov89-25
Barr, W. - see Persius
Barra Bagnasco, M. Protomi in terracotta da Locri Epizefiri.
  G. Olbrich, 229:Band60Heft2-176
Barral, C. Catalogue raisonné du Musée des Beaux-Arts, Dijon: Faiences Italiennes.
  T.H.W., 90:Jun88-476
Barral y Altet, X., ed. Artistes, Artisans et production artistique au Moyen Age. (Vol 1)
  M. Camille, 90:Feb88-143
Barral i Altet, X., ed. Le paysage monumental de la France autour de l'an Mil.
  T.W. Lyman, 576:Sep88-299
Barratt, A. Between Two Worlds.
  J. Curtis, 575(SEER):Oct88-647
  P. Doyle, 402(MLR):Jul89-813
  P.R. Hart, 395(MFS):Summer88-307
Barreca, R., ed. Last Laughs.
  M.R. Higonnet, 617(TLS):29Dec89/4Jan90-1437

Barrelet, M–T., ed. Problèmes concernant les Hurrites 2.
  O.W. Muscarella, 318(JAOS):Jan–Mar87–135
Barrell, J. Poetry, Language and Politics.*
  M. Baron, 175:Summer88–175
Barrell, J. The Political Theory of Painting from Reynolds to Hazlitt.*
  M. Eaves, 591(SIR):Fall88–429
  W. Pressly, 324:Jul89–517
Barrero Pérez, O. La novela existencial española de la posguerra.
  G. Sobejano, 711(RHM):Jun88–81
Barresi, D. The Judas Clock.
  F. Muratori, 448:Vol26No1–113
Barrett, A. Lucid Stars.
  M. Brandham, 617(TLS):12–18May89–518
  J. Marcus, 441:29Jan89–30
Barrett, B. Eva Hesse Sculpture.
  J. Russell, 441:11Jun89–56
Barrett, H. & J. Phillips. Suburban Style.
  S. Meacham, 637(VS):Winter89–281
Barrett, W. Death-Bed Visions.
  G. Bennett, 203:Vol99No1–132
Barrett, W. Death of the Soul.*
  A. O'Hear, 483:Jan88–124
Barricelli, G.P. Giacomo Leopardi.
  M. Caesar, 402(MLR):Jan89–192
Barricelli, J–P. & J. Gibaldi, eds. Interrelations of Literature.
  H.A. Pausch, 107(CRCL):Mar88–110
Barrick, M.E. German-American Folklore.
  W.F.H. Nicolaisen, 650(WF):Oct88–316
Barrick, W.B. & J.R. Spencer, eds. In the Shelter of Elyon.
  P.E. Dion, 318(JAOS):Jan–Mar87–132
Barrie, D. – see Ruskin, J.
Barrington, R. Health, Medicine and Politics in Ireland 1900–1970.
  M.E. Daly, 272(IUR):Spring88–149
Barroll, J.L. 3d, ed. Medieval and Renaissance Drama in England. (Vol 2)
  L. Manley, 677(YES):Vol19–318
Barron, R. A Guide to Minnesota Writers.
  T. Pribek, 649(WAL):Nov88–272
Barron, W.R.J. English Medieval Romance.
  N. Jacobs, 447(N&Q):Dec88–507
Barrow, J. The Mutiny of the Bounty.
  G. Milner, 617(TLS):19–25May89–538
Barrow, J.D. The World Within the World.
  T. Ferris, 617(TLS):18–24Aug89–892
Barry, A. – see Barnes, D.
Barry, B. A Treatise on Social Justice. (Vol 1)
  J. Dunn, 617(TLS):6–12Oct89–1079
Barry, D. Dave Barry Slept Here.
  R. Lingeman, 441:18Jun89–11
Barry, J.M. The Ambition and the Power.
  R. Dugger, 441:19Nov89–12
Barry, K. Susan B. Anthony.
  M. Saxton, 441:12Feb89–19
Barry, K. Language, Music, and the Sign.
  P.H. Fry, 173(ECS):Winter88/89–238
  M. Storey, 410(M&L):Oct88–532
Barry, L. The Good Times Are Killing Me.*
  442(NY):6Mar89–111
Barry, N.P. The New Right.
  M.B., 185:Jul89–973
Barry, N.P. On Classical Liberalism and Libertarianism.
  D. Miller, 518:Jul88–169
  T.P., 185:Apr89–677

Barsam, R. The Vision of Robert Flaherty.
  B. Winston, 707:Autumn88–277
Barsby, J. – see Plautus
Barshay, A.E. State and Intellectual in Imperial Japan.
  I. Nish, 617(TLS):28Apr–4May89–460
Barson, J. La Grammaire à l'oeuvre.* (4th ed)
  E. McKee, 399(MLJ):Spring88–86
Barstow, A.L. Joan of Arc.
  M. Hunt, 589:Jul88–620
Barstow, A.L. Married Priests and the Reforming Papacy.
  Z.P. Thundy, 201:Vol14–203
Barstow, S. Give Us This Day.
  V. Cunningham, 617(TLS):1–7Sep89–953
Bartel, P. The Complete "Gone With the Wind" Trivia Book.
  D. Finkle, 441:10Dec89–7
Barth, E.M. & R.T.P. Wiche. Problems, Functions and Semantic Roles.
  B. Abbott, 316:Mar88–317
Barth, R.L. A Soldier's Time.
  G. Powell, 150(DR):Fall88–373
Barthel, J. Love or Honor.
  M. Gallagher, 441:18Jun89–21
Barthelemy, A.G. Black Face Maligned Race.
  E.D. Jones, 538(RAL):Winter88–554
  B. Nakhjavani, 570(SQ):Summer88–242
Barthelme, D. Forty Stories.*
  T. Wilhelmus, 249(HudR):Autumn88–549
Barthelme, D. Paradise.*
  L. Lemon, 502(PrS):Fall88–132
Barthelme, D. Sixty Stories.
  W. Steiner, 617(TLS):14–20Apr89–403
Barthelme, F. Two against One.*
  R. Kaveney, 617(TLS):15–21Sep89–998
Barthelme, S. And He Tells the Little Horse the Whole Story.
  M. Gorra, 249(HudR):Summer88–406
  G. Locklin, 573(SSF):Spring88–160
  639(VQR):Summer88–82
Bartholomae, D. & A. Petrosky. Ways of Reading.
  D. George, 126(CCC):May88–239
Bartholomew, J. The Richest Man in the World.
  R. Flamini, 617(TLS):22–28Sep89–1040
Bartley, W.W. 3d. Wittgenstein.* (rev)
  478(P&L):Oct88–329
Bartley, W.W. 3d – see Hayek, F.A.
Bartley, W.W. 3d – see Popper, K.R.
Barton, G.E., R.C. Berwick & E.S. Ristad. Computational Complexity and Natural Language.
  S. Pulman, 297(JL):Sep88–573
Barton, J. People of the Book?
  J.L. Houlden, 617(TLS):5–11May89–496
Bartoš, F.M. The Hussite Revolution, 1424–1437. (J.M. Klassen, ed & trans)
  H. Kaminsky, 589:Jul88–622
Bartsch, R. Norms of Language.*
  J.R. Hagland, 452(NJL):Vol11No1/2–201
Bartsch, R. Sprachnormen.
  K–H. Jäger, 406:Spring88–118
  C. Gnutzmann, 38:Band106Heft3/4–427
  M. Görlach, 260(IF):Band93–255
Bartsch, W. Übungen im Joch.
  J. Engler, 654(WB):12/1988–2018
Baruch, E.H. & L.J. Serrano. Women Analyze Women.
  L.E. Nesbitt, 441:23Apr89–21

Barwise, J. & J. Perry. Situations and Attitudes.
P. Werth, 307:Apr88-54
de Bary, W.T. East Asian Civilizations.
R.J. Smith, 293(JASt):Nov88-835
Barzun, J. The Culture We Deserve. (A. Krystal, ed)
B.F. Williamson, 441:17Sep89-25
Barzun, J. A Word or Two Before You Go...*
J.M.M., 295(JML):Fall87/Winter88-238
E.L. Steeves, 403(MLS):Fall88-91
Basalla, G. The Evolution of Technology.
D. Joravsky, 453(NYRB):7Dec89-11
E. Regis, 441:9Apr89-28
Basavaṇṇa. The Lord of the Meeting Rivers.*
(K.V. Zvelebil, trans) [shown in prev under trans]
I.V. Peterson, 318(JAOS):Apr-Jun87-350
Basbøll, H. & J. Wagner. Kontrastive Phonologie des Deutschen und Dänischen.*
R. Bannert, 685(ZDL):3/1987-362
Basch, L. Le musée imaginaire de la marine antique.
A. Göttlicher, 229:Band60Heft8-759
Basdekis, D. The Evolution of Ortega y Gasset as Literary Critic.*
M. Austin, 89(BJA):Winter88-85
S. Miller, 238:May88-298
H. Raley, 240(HR):Winter88-121
D.L. Shaw, 86(BHS):Oct88-414
Base, R. Foreign Object.
R.W. Ingram, 102(CanL):Autumn88-145
Baselt, B. Händel-Handbuch. (Vol 3)
T. Best, 410(M&L):Jan88-66
Bashford, H.H. Augustus Carp Esq. by Himself.*
42(AR):Spring88-276
Basile, B. L'invenzione del vero.
F. Arato, 228(GSLI):Vol165fasc532-613
Basker, J.G. Tobias Smollett.
R. Cohen, 166:Jan89-158
Basker, M. & S.D. Graham - see Gumilev, N.
Baskerville, P. The Bank of Upper Canada.
C. Wilton-Siegel, 298:Winter88/89-195
Baskerville, S. & R. Willett, eds. Nothing Else to Fear.
H.W. Emerson, 366:Autumn88-264
Bass, R. Oil Notes.
R. Wright, 617(TLS):24-30Nov89-1297
Bass, R. The Watch.
S. Lowell, 441:5Mar89-11
Bassani, E. Nobili o selvaggi?
2(AfrA):Feb88-93
Bassein, B.A. Women and Death.
J. Perreault, 107(CRCL):Mar88-106
Bassett, S. Sylvia Plath.
J. Banerjee, 179(ES):Jun88-280
Bassnett, S. & P. Kuhiwczak - see "Ariadne's Thread"
Bastein, F.H., ed. Kanada heute.
529(QQ):Winter88-971
Bastert, U. Modalpartikel und Lexikographie.
U. Brausse, 682(ZPSK):Band41Heft3-383
A. Lötscher, 685(ZDL):2/1988-263
Bastian, H.G. Musik im Fernsehen.
W. Rathert, 416:Band3Heft3-267
Bastin, B. Red River Blues.
F.J. Hay, 292(JAF):Jan-Mar88-100
Bastos, A.R. - see under Roa Bastos, A.
Bataille, G. The Accursed Share. (Vol 1)
Guilty. Oeuvres complètes. (Vols 11 & 12)
D. Coward, 617(TLS):4-10Aug89-857

Bataille, G.M. & K.M. Sands. American Indian Women, Telling Their Lives.
P. Reedy, 649(WAL):May88-93
Bataille, L. L'ombilic du rêve.
E.S. Apter, 98:Apr88-336
Bate, A.K. - see Joseph of Exeter
Bate, J. Shakespeare and the English Romantic Imagination.*
Z. Leader, 591(SIR):Fall88-463
C.M. Mazer, 340(KSJ):Vol37-206
N. Roe, 447(N&Q):Mar88-128
Bate, M. & G. Hare, eds. Communicative Approaches to French in Higher Education.
R. McLure, 208(FS):Apr88-246
Bately, J.M. - see "The Anglo-Saxon Chronicle"
Bates, H.E. Elephant's Nest in a Rhubarb Tree & Other Stories.
B. Baker, 441:11Jun89-43
Bates, H.E. A Month By the Lake and Other Stories.
D. Baldwin, 573(SSF):Winter88-79
639(VQR):Summer88-93
Bates, M.J. Wallace Stevens.*
J. Applewhite, 569(SR):Winter88-121
F.J. Lepkowski, 77:Fall88-326
Bateson, M.C. Composing a Life.
J. O'Reilly, 441:26Nov89-7
Baticle, J., with others. Zurbarán.
N.A. Mallory, 127:Fall88-233
Batinski, M.C. The New Jersey Assembly, 1738-1775.
R.J. Dinkin, 656(WMQ):Jan88-184
Batkin, J. Pottery of the Pueblos of New Mexico.
H.K. Crotty, 2(AfrA):May88-84*
Batman, R. James Pattie's West.*
I.H.W. Engstrand, 77:Fall88-349
Batra, R. Regular Economic Cycles.
W.N. Parker, 441:29Oct89-31
Batsleer, J. & others. Rewriting English.*
D. Longhurst, 49:Jul88-110
C.H. Smith, 128(CE):Mar88-318
Battail, J-F. & M. Le Suédois sans Peine/ Svenska på lätt sätt.
C. Bord, 563(SS):Summer88-422
Battat, J.Y. Management in Post-Mao China.
D.F. Simon, 293(JASt):Feb88-106
Battestin, M.C., with R.R. Battestin. Henry Fielding.
W.B. Carnochan, 617(TLS):20-26Oct89-1145
Baud-Bovy, S. Essai sur la chanson populaire grecque.
W.J. Aerts, 394:Vol41fasc1/2-190
Baudin, F. How Typography Works.
B. Crutchley, 324:Nov89-824
Baudot, G. - see de Motolinía, T.
Baudouin de Courtenay, J. Ausgewählte Werke in deutscher Sprache.* (J. Mugdan, ed)
G. Rössler, 685(ZDL):2/1987-236
Baudrillard, J. America.*
R. Hughes, 453(NYRB):1Jun89-29
J. Marcus, 441:12Feb89-19
Bauer, D. Dexterity.
J. Clute, 617(TLS):29Dec89/4Jan90-1447
B. De Mott, 61:May89-97
M. Pellecchia, 441:7May89-24
Bauer, H-J. & J. Forner - see Wagner, R.
Bauer, L. & others. American English Pronunciation.
A. Wollmann, 38:Band106Heft1/2-191

Beales, D. Joseph II. (Vol 1)
   F.A.J. Szabo, 150(DR):Fall88–336
Bean, J.M.W. From Lord to Patron.
   N. Saul, 617(TLS):1–7Dec89–1343
Bean, P. & J. Melville. Lost Children of the
   Empire.
   P. Willmott, 617(TLS):19–25May89–539
Beard, G. The Work of Grinling Gibbons.
   D. Esterly, 617(TLS):24–30Nov89–1299
Beard, G. & J. Goodison. English Furniture
   1500–1840.
   90:Jun88–477
Beard, M. The Good Working Mother's Guide.
   M. Lefkowitz, 617(TLS):14–20Jul89–768
Beard, R. & B. Szymanek, comps. Bibliography
   of Morphology 1960–1985.
   E.A. Ebbinghaus, 215(GL):Vol28No3–240
   R. Raffelsiefen, 350:Dec89–875
Beards, V. – see Somerville, E.O. & M. Ross
Beardsell, P.R. Quiroga.
   D.L. Shaw, 402(MLR):Jan89–218
Beardsmore, H.B. Bilingualism. (2nd ed)
   M. Mack, 399(MLJ):Spring88–79
Bearth, T. L'articulation du temps et de l'as-
   pect dans le discours toura.
   S. Brauner, 682(ZPSK):Band41Heft6–810
Beasley, B. Spirituals.
   M. Jarman, 249(HudR):Winter89–734
   639(VQR):Summer88–99
Beasley, J.C. – see Smollett, T.
Beasley, W.G. Japanese Imperialism, 1894–
   1945.
   R.H. Myers, 293(JASt):Aug88–633
Beaton, C. The Glass of Fashion.
   D. Atkinson, 617(TLS):30Jun–6Jul89–722
Beaton, M.C. Death of a Perfect Wife.
   M. Stasio, 441:10Dec89–41
Beattie, A., ed. The Best American Short
   Stories 1987.
   P. La Salle, 573(SSF):Spring88–159
Beattie, A. Alex Katz.
   M.I. James, 90:Apr88–304
Beattie, J.M. Crime and the Courts in En-
   gland, 1660–1800.*
   H.T. Dickinson, 566:Autumn88–82
   S. Staves, 173(ECS):Summer88–535
Beatty, B. Byron's "Don Juan."*
   F.L. Beaty, 661(WC):Autumn88–186
   A. Nicholson, 402(MLR):Jan89–131
   A. Rutherford, 447(N&Q):Jun88–252
   M. Storey, 339:Autumn88–101
Beatty, D.M. Putting the Charter to Work.
   G.A. Leigh, 529(QQ):Summer88–490
Beaty, F.L. Byron the Satirist.*
   B.A. Hirsch, 401(MLQ):Dec86–443
de Beaugrande, R–A. & W.U. Dressler. Ein-
   führung in die Textlinguistik.
   G. Tschauder, 685(ZDL):2/1987–253
Beaulieu, V–L. Chroniques polissonnes d'un
   téléphage enragé.
   I. Oore, 102(CanL):Spring88–113
Beaumont, A. Busoni the Composer.
   J.C.G. Waterhouse, 410(M&L):Jan88–99
Beaumont, A. – see Busoni, F.
de Beaumont, J. Au hasard de la chance,
   l'amour de vivre.
   J. Labat, 207(FR):Mar89–712
Beausoleil, C. Il y a des nuits que nous hab-
   itons tous.
   K.W. Meadwell, 102(CanL):Spring88–111
"Beauties, Beasts and Enchantment." (J.
   Zipes, trans)
   R. McKinley, 441:24Dec89–25

Beauvois, D., ed. Les Confins de l'ancienne
   Pologne.
   J. Dingley, 402(MLR):Oct89–1054
Beaver, H. "Huckleberry Finn."*
   L. Budd, 402(MLR):Oct89–964
   G.C. Carrington, Jr., 26(ALR):Fall88–76
   C. Gerrard, 541(RES):Nov88–594
Beavis, I.C. Insects and Other Invertebrates
   in Classical Antiquity.
   J. Scarborough, 617(TLS):3–9Feb89–118
Bebbington, D.W. Evangelicalism in Modern
   Britain.
   B. Godlee, 617(TLS):27Oct–2Nov89–1188
Bec, C. La memoria di un pittore fiorentino
   del XVII secolo.
   A. Di Benedetto, 228(GSLI):Vol165
   fasc529–124
Bec, P. Burlesque et obscenité ches les trou-
   badours.
   G. Lachin, 379(MedR):Aug86–302
Beccaria, C. Dei delitti e delle pene. (G.
   Francioni, ed) [together with] Firpo, L. Le
   edizioni italiane del "Dei delitti e del
   pene."
   S. Romagnoli, 228(GSLI):Vol165fasc531–
   444
Beccaria, C. Scritti filosofici e letterari. (L.
   Firpo, G. Francioni & G. Gaspari, eds)
   S. Romagnoli, 228(GSLI):Vol165fasc531–
   444
Beccaria, G.L. Italiano antico e nuovo.
   E. Radtke, 72:Band225Heft2–462
Béchade, H–D. Syntaxe du français moderne
   et contemporain.*
   J–M. Léard, 320(CJL):Sep88–280
Becher, J.R. & H.F.S. Bachmair. Johannes R.
   Becher – Heinrich F.S. Bachmair: Brief-
   wechsel 1914–1920. (M. Kühn–Ludewig,
   ed)
   A. Obermayer, 564:Nov88–394
Bechert, H., ed. Zur Schulzugehörigkeit von
   Werken der Hīnayāna–Literatur. (Pt 1)
   S. Lienhard, 318(JAOS):Jul–Sep87–509
Bechert, H. – see Geiger, W.
Bechtel, R., R. Marans & W. Michelson, eds.
   Methods in Environmental and Behavioral
   Research.
   C.C. Marcus, 47:Aug88–39
Beck, B. Stella Corfou.
   S. Puttit, 207(FR):Apr89–900
Beck, B.E.F., P.J. Claus & others, eds. Folk-
   tales of India.
   U. Parameswaran, 268(IFR):Winter89–71
Beck, F.A.G. Bibliography of Greek Education
   and Related Topics.
   L. Ascher, 24:Jul–Aug89–464
Beck, H., ed. Parliament House Canberra.
   R. Spence, 46:Oct88–12
Beck, H. & J. Turnbull – see "Critiques"
Beck, H.H.H. The Elusive "I" in the Novel.
   J. Kohnen, 680(ZDP):Band107Heft2–295
Beck, J., ed. Raphael before Rome.*
   D.G. Wilkins, 589:Oct88–898
Beck, J. Théâtre et propagande aux débuts
   de la Réforme.*
   G. Jondorf, 539:Summer89–243
Beck, L.W., with others – see Kant, I.
Becker, C., ed. Emile Zola: La Fabrique de
   "Germinal."*
   D. Baguley, 535(RHL):Mar–Apr88–321
Becker, F., ed. Afrikanische Fabeln und
   Mythen.
   R. Schott, 196:Band29Heft1/2–173

Becker, J. Eugenio Montale.
  E. Tandello, 402(MLR):Jul89-754
Becker, J. Pattern and Loom.
  M. Straub, 324:Mar89-259
Becker, J., with A.H. Feinstein, eds. Karawi-
  tan. (Vol 2)
  M. Kartomi, 293(JASt):Aug88-692
  N. Sorrell, 410(M&L):Oct88-502
Becker, J-J. Histoire politique de la France
  depuis 1945.
  H.B. Sutton, 207(FR):May89-1104
Becker, L.C. Reciprocity.*
  M. Davis, 482(PhR):Jul88-432
Becker, L.F. Françoise Mallet-Joris.
  M. Mercier, 535(RHL):Mar-Apr88-340
Becker, S. Nobility and Privilege in Late Im-
  perial Russia.*
  T. Fallows, 550(RusR):Jul88-339
Becker-Bertau, F., ed. Die Inschriften von
  Klaudiu Polis.
  C.P. Jones, 229:Band60Heft3-272
  D.M. Lewis, 123:Vol38No1-124
Becker-Cantarino, B., ed. Satire der frühen
  Neuzeit.
  W.A. Coupe, 402(MLR):Jul89-777
Becker-Cantarino, B. - see Handke, P.
Beckers, H., ed. Bauernpratik und Bauern-
  klage.*
  F.B. Brévart, 684(ZDA):Band117Heft1-33
Beckett, O. Horses and Movement.
  A. Stewart, 324:Apr89-318
Beckett, S. A Samuel Beckett Reader. (J.
  Calder, ed)
  D. McMillan, 299:No11&12-166
Beckett, S. Nohow On.
  A. Jenkins, 617(TLS):10-16Mar89-255
Beckett, S. Stirrings Still.
  A. Jenkins, 617(TLS):10-16Mar89-255
  442(NY):26Jun89-91
Beckmann, K. & H-J. Schulze - see Walther,
  J.G.
Beckson, K. Arthur Symons.
  R. Crawford, 447(N&Q):Sep88-394
  I. Fletcher, 636(VP):Winter88-484
  A. Johnson, 177(ELT):Vol31No4-451
  I. Murray, 161(DUJ):Dec87-152
  J. Stokes, 402(MLR):Apr89-450
Beckson, K. & J.M. Munro - see Symons, A.
Beckwith, C.I. The Tibetan Empire in Central
  Asia.
  M. Rossabi, 293(JASt):Aug88-583
Beckwith, J., ed. Sing Out the Glad News.*
  W.J. Gatens, 410(M&L):Oct88-534
  A.M. Gillmor, 627(UTQ):Fall88-211
  A. Luff, 415:Mar88-157
Becq, A. Genèse de l'esthétique française
  moderne.
  H.M. Block, 188(ECr):Fall88-94
Bécquer, G.A. Desde mi celda.* (D. Vil-
  lanueva, ed)
  M.A. Rees, 86(BHS):Apr88-189
Bécquer, G.A. The "Rimas" of Gustavo Adolfo
  Bécquer.
  M.A. Rees, 86(BHS):Jul88-307
Bedau, H.A. Death Is Different.
  J.H. Bogart, 185:Oct88-167
Beddard, R. A Kingdom Without a King.
  J.P. Kenyon, 617(TLS):28Jul-3Aug89-828
Beddow, M. Goethe: "Faust" I.
  O. Durrani, 402(MLR):Jul89-780
Mrs. Bedford. A Visit to Don Otavio.
  A. Broyard, 441:3Dec89-22

Bedford, S. Jigsaw.
  G. Annan, 453(NYRB):27Apr89-22
  L. Duguid, 617(TLS):12-18May89-519
  D. Plante, 441:28May89-13
Bedient, C. He Do the Police in Different
  Voices.*
  M. Dickie, 301(JEGP):Jan88-151
  W. Harmon, 569(SR):Winter88-105
  M. Moran, 27(AL):Mar88-128
  M. O'Connor, 529(QQ):Winter88-927
  V.S., 295(JML):Fall87/Winter88-312
Bedient, C. In the Heart's Last Kingdom.
  R. Gray, 677(YES):Vol19-357
Beecher, J. Charles Fourier.
  R. Carlisle, 446(NCFS):Spring-Summer89-
  441
Beegel, S.F. Hemingway's Craft of Omission.
  C.S. Burhans, Jr., 27(AL):Dec88-682
  P. Hays, 234:Spring89-52
  W.J. Stuckey, 395(MFS):Winter88-621
Beehler, M. T.S. Eliot, Wallace Stevens, and
  the Discourses of Difference.*
  W. Harmon, 569(SR):Winter88-105
  M. Moran, 27(AL):Mar88-128
Beekes, R.S.P. The Origins of the Indo-Euro-
  pean Nominal Inflection.
  F.R. Adrados, 260(IF):Band93-292
Beeman, R., S. Botein & E.C. Carter 2d, eds.
  Beyond Confederation.
  J.M. Banner, Jr., 656(WMQ):Apr88-355
  P.J. King, 106:Summer88-279
Beeman, W.O. Language, Status, and Power in
  Iran.*
  N. Haeri, 355(LSoc):Sep88-431
de Beer, E.S. - see Locke, J.
Beer, J. Sämtliche Werke.* (Vol 3)(F. van
  Ingen & H-G. Roloff, eds)
  H. Pörnbacher, 196:Band29Heft1/2-174
Beer, J.M.A. Narrative Conventions of Truth
  in the Middle Ages.
  J. Blacker, 545(RPh):Aug88-121
Beer, M. Romanzi di cavalleria.
  N. Harris, 354:Dec88-349
de Beer, M. Who Did What in South Africa.
  S. Uys, 617(TLS):25-31Aug89-915
Beer, P. Collected Poems.
  P. Reading, 617(TLS):20-26Jan89-59
Beerbohm, M. Letters of Max Beerbohm,
  1892-1956.* (R. Hart-Davis, ed)
  J. Gross, 453(NYRB):23Nov89-42
Beers, J.M., ed. A Commentary on the Cister-
  cian Hymnal.
  A. Hughes, 447(N&Q):Sep88-347
Beetham, D. Bureaucracy.
  G.P., 185:Oct88-195
Beevers, R. The Garden City Utopia.
  S. Meacham, 637(VS):Winter89-281
Beevor, A. The Enchantment of Christina von
  Retzen.
  T. Glyde, 617(TLS):18-24Aug89-901
Begemann, C. Furcht und Angst im Prozess
  der Aufklärung.
  J.M. Tudor, 402(MLR):Oct89-1026
  C. Zelle, 72:Band225Heft2-358
Begnal, M.H. Dreamscheme.
  H.B. Staples, 329(JJQ):Spring89-453
Behan, B. An Giall [and] The Hostage.
  R.H., 305(JIL):Jan88-60
Behar, R. Santa María del Monte.
  J.R. Llobera, 86(BHS):Jul88-313

Behn, A. Love-Letters Between a Nobleman and his Sister. (M. Duffy, ed)
  B. Dhuicq, 189(EA):Oct-Dec88-486
  J.G. Turner, 536(Rev):Vol10-1
  566:Autumn88-85
Behn, A. Oroonoko and Other Stories. (M. Duffy, ed)
  B. Dhuicq, 189(EA):Oct-Dec88-485
Behn, A. Oroonoko, or, The Royal Slave. (A.P. Amore, ed)
  M.A. O'Donnell, 166:Apr89-248
  566:Autumn88-84
Behn, R. Paper Bird.
  M. Jarman, 249(HudR):Winter89-733
Behne, K-E., G. Kleinen & H. de la Motte-Haber, eds. Musik Psychologie.
  S. Helms, 416:Band3Heft1-85
Behnen, M. Rüstung – Bündnis – Sicherheit.
  F.L. Carsten, 575(SEER):Jan88-142
Behr, C.A. – see Aristides
Behr, E. Hirohito.
  I. Buruma, 453(NYRB):26Oct89-31
  J.W. Dower, 441:8Oct89-8
Behrends, R., E. Hollmann & T. Webli. The Lorraine Apocalypse.
  78(BC):Autumn88-313
Behrens, P. Night Driving.
  M.A. Jarman, 376:Mar88-91
Behrman, J.N. Essays on Ethics in Business and the Professions.
  R.J., 185:Apr89-685
Bei Dao. The August Sleepwalker.
  D.J. Enright, 617(TLS):17-23Mar89-269
Bei Dao. Waves.*
  N. Tisdall, 364:Nov87-111
Beierwaltes, W. Denken des Einen.
  F.M. Schroeder, 489(PJGG):Band95Heft1-195
Beilharz, P. Trotsky, Trotskyism and the Transition to Socialism.
  D. Filtzer, 575(SEER):Apr88-313
Beilin, E.V. Redeeming Eve.
  M.P. Hannay, 604:Spring/Summer88-31
  L. Woodbridge, 551(RenQ):Summer88-347
  639(VQR):Spring88-54
Beils, K.B. Transzendenz und Zeitbewusst-sein.
  P. Trotignon, 542:Jul-Sep88-358
Beinfeld, S. & S.J. Stang – see Ford, F.M.
Beinhart, L. You Get What You Pay For.
  M. Stasio, 441:22Jan89-30
Beiser, F.C. The Fate of Reason.*
  G. di Giovanni, 319:Apr89-314
Beit-Hallahmi, B. The Israeli Connection.
  R. Jean & E. Isaac, 390:May88-58
Beizer, J.L. Family Plots.*
  G.R. Besser, 207(FR):Dec88-331
  W. Paulson, 210(FrF):May88-250
  C. Robinson, 447(N&Q):Sep88-419
Beja, M. & others, eds. James Joyce.*
  V.J. Cheng, 405(MP):Feb89-328
  V. Mahaffey, 177(ELT):Vol31No2-249
  J.C.C. Mays, 541(RES):Nov88-588
  J. Voelker, 295(JML):Fall87/Winter88-336
Béjin, A. & J. Freund, eds. Racismes, antiracismes.
  L. Marcil-Lacoste, 154:Summer88-374
Belardi, W. Filosofia, grammatica e retorica nel pensiero antico.
  G. Holtus, 72:Band225Heft1-236

Belben, R. Is Beauty Good. Dreaming of Dead People.
  R. Moss, 617(TLS):22-28Sep89-1022
Belcher, M. Bird Imagery in the Lyric Poetry of Tristan L'Hermite.
  C. Abraham, 475:Vol15No28-257
  P.J. Wolfe, 568(SCN):Spring-Summer88-20
Belcher, M. A.W.N. Pugin.
  M. Bright, 576:Dec88-418
Beld, S.G., W.W. Hallo & P. Michalowski. The Tablets of Ebla.
  V. Davidović, 318(JAOS):Apr-Jun87-330
Belfrage, B. – see Berkeley, G.
Belfrage, S. Living with History.
  639(VQR):Winter88-25
Belich, J. "I Shall Not Die."
  G. Palmer, 617(TLS):15-21Dec89-1396
Belin, D.W. Final Disclosure.
  R. Dugger, 441:29Jan89-11
Bélis, A. Aristoxène de Tarente et Aristote.
  P. Louis, 555:Vol61fasc2-310
  P. Pellegrin, 542:Apr-Jun88-239
  M.L. West, 303(JoHS):Vol108-235
Belitt, B. Possessions.*
  J. Mazzaro, 569(SR):Winter88-149
  W. Spiegelman, 472:Vol15No1-185
Bell, B.W. The Afro-American Novel and Its Tradition.
  J.L. Gray, 590:Dec88-157
  N. Harris, 219(GaR):Winter88-870
Bell, D.F. Models of Power.
  L. Kamm, 207(FR):May89-1076
  P. Livingston, 400(MLN):Sep88-908
  P. Walker, 446(NCFS):Spring-Summer89-415
Bell, I.A. Defoe's Fiction.*
  P.R. Backscheider, 403(MLS):Winter88-201
Bell, I.F.A. & D.K. Adams, eds. American Literary Landscapes.
  B. Wolf, 617(TLS):16-22Jun89-672
Bell, J.L. – see Ivanov, L.L.
Bell, M. New and Selected Poems.*
  S. McCartney, 376:Mar88-95
  R.B. Shaw, 491:Apr88-35
  639(VQR):Winter88-27
  639(VQR):Spring88-62
Bell, M.S. Soldier's Joy.
  D. Bradley, 441:2Jul89-3
Bell, M.S. Waiting for the End of the World.
  G. Davenport, 569(SR):Fall88-695
Bell, N., with D. Bessai, eds. Five from the Fringe.
  J. Noonan, 102(CanL):Winter87-235
Bell, R., ed. The Grammar of the Heart.
  W.R., 185:Jul89-990
Bell, S.H. Across the Narrow Sea.
  J. Hendry, 571(ScLJ):Winter88-58
Bell, V. & L. Lerner, eds. On Modern Poetry.
  C. Wilmer, 617(TLS):26May-1Jun89-578
Bell, W.G. Will James.
  P.K. Kett, 649(WAL):Nov88-241
Bellamy, J. Robin Hood.*
  J. Scattergood, 677(YES):Vol19-301
Bellamy, R. Game, Set and Deadline.
  K.B. Sayeed, 529(QQ):Winter88-964
Bellamy, R. Modern Italian Social Theory.*
  H.S. Harris, 185:Oct88-176
Belleau, A. Surprendre les voix.
  P-Y. Mocquais, 102(CanL):Spring88-221
  B-Z. Shek, 627(UTQ):Fall88-173

Belleau, I. & G. Dorion, eds. Les oeuvres de
creation et le français au québec. (Vol 3)
P.G. Socken, 102(CanL):Winter87-164
Belleau, R. Commentaire au Second Livre des
"Amours" de Ronsard.* (M-M. Fontaine & F.
Lecercle, eds)
Y. Bellenger, 535(RHL):Sep-Oct88-1016
de Bellefeuille, N. Catégoriques un deux et
trois.
A.L. Amprimoz, 102(CanL):Autumn88-140
de Bellefonds, P.L. - see under Linant de
Bellefonds, P.
Bellemare, P. - see Dray, W.H.
Bellenger, Y. Montaigne.
R.D. Cottrell, 207(FR):Feb89-519
Beller, S. Vienna and the Jews, 1867-1938.
M. Ignatieff, 453(NYRB):29Jun89-21
Bellier, P. & others. Paysages de Macédoine.
G.P. Henderson, 303(JoHS):Vol108-276
Bellingham, S. Isabel Ecclestone Mackay Bib-
liography.
T. Craig, 470:Vol26-170
Bellmann, G., ed. Beiträge zur Dialektologie
am Mittelrhein.
A. Mihm, 685(ZDL):3/1988-351
Bellos, D. Honoré de Balzac: "Old Goriot."
K.M. Hewitt, 447(N&Q):Dec88-552
Bellosi, L. La pecora di Giotto.*
J. Cannon, 90:Sep88-701
Bellow, S. The Bellarosa Connection.
G. Josipovici, 617(TLS):27Oct-2Nov89-
1181
W.H. Pritchard, 441:1Oct89-11
G. Wills, 453(NYRB):12Oct89-34
442(NY):23Oct89-146
Bellow, S. More Die of Heartbreak.*
G. Davenport, 569(SR):Fall88-695
Bellow, S. A Theft.
R. Boyers, 617(TLS):24-30Mar89-299
J.C. Oates, 441:5Mar89-3
R. Towers, 453(NYRB):27Apr89-50
J. Updike, 442(NY):1May89-111
Belnap, N.D., Jr. & T.B. Steel, Jr. Logik von
Frage und Antwort.
J. Dölling, 682(ZPSK):Band41Heft1-141
Beloff, M. Imperial Sunset. (Vol 2)
A. Porter, 617(TLS):15-21Dec89-1396
Belov, S. Žena pisatelja.
T. Pachmuss, 574(SEEJ):Fall88-469
Belsey, C. John Milton.
M. Stocker, 617(TLS):27Jan-2Feb89-90
Belsey, C. The Subject of Tragedy.*
R. Wilson, 366:Autumn88-210
Belting, H. The End of the History of Art?
J. Brodsky, 290(JAAC):Winter87-309
Beltrán, M.J.S. - see under Sánchez Beltrán,
M.J.
Beltrán Fernández de los Ríos, L. La arqui-
tectura del humo.*
A.A. Anderson, 86(BHS):Jul88-310
Beltrán Pepió, V. - see de Berceo, G.
Belyj, A. Gibel' senatora (Peterburg).* (J.
Malmstad, ed)
M. Carlson, 550(RusR):Apr88-226
G. Donchin, 575(SEER):Jan88-124
Belyj, A. Stixotvorenija.* (J.E. Malmstad, ed)
V.E. Alexandrov, 550(RusR):Apr88-225
R.J. Keys, 574(SEEJ):Summer88-324
van der Ben, N. The Charmides of Plato.*
P. Louis, 555:Vol61fasc1-118
S.R. Slings, 394:Vol41fasc3/4-409

van der Ben, N. & J.M. Bremer. Aristoteles
"Poetica."
O.J. Schrier, 204(FdL):Mar88-69
"BEN: La Vérité de A à Z."
C. Phillpot, 62:Dec88-110
Benabu, I. & J. Sermoneta, eds. Judeo-
Romance Languages.
L.P. Harvey, 86(BHS):Apr88-178
Benardete, J.A. Metaphysics.
A.W. Moore, 617(TLS):30Jun-6Jul89-724
Benardete, S., ed & trans. The Being of the
Beautiful.
M. Davis, 41:Vol7-191
Bence-Jones, M. A Guide to Irish Country
Houses.
D. Cruickshank, 617(TLS):24-30Mar89-
317
Ben Chaim, D. Distance in the Theatre.
I. Smith, 223:Summer88-245
Benchley, P. Rummies.
A.T. Wallach, 441:17Dec89-21
Bencivenga, E. Kant's Copernican Revolution.
R. Hahn, 543:Dec88-375
Benda, W., G. Hemmerich & U. Schödlbauer -
see Cooper, A.A. (Lord Shaftesbury)
Bender, E.T. Joyce Carol Oates.
J.V. Creighton, 395(MFS):Summer88-254
R. Donahoo, 27(AL):Mar88-150
Bender, J. Imagining the Penitentiary.*
D. Blewett, 627(UTQ):Spring89-415
P. Brückmann, 166:Oct88-75
A.M. Duckworth, 191(ELN):Jun89-80
L.B. Faller, 405(MP):May89-430
S. Varey, 141:Fall88-522
Bender, P. Deutsche Parallelen.
R. Morgan, 617(TLS):13-19Oct89-1115
Bender, S. Plain and Simple.
P. Finn, 441:31Dec89-13
Bender, T. New York Intellect.*
639(VQR):Winter88-10
Bender, T., ed. The University and the City.
J. Catto, 617(TLS):26May-1Jun89-584
Bender, T.K. A Concordance to Henry James's
"Daisy Miller."
S.B. Daugherty, 26(ALR):Fall88-81
Bendixen, A. - see James, H. & others
Bendixen, A. - see Spofford, H.P.
Bendixson, T. The Peterborough Effect.
R. Cowan, 324:Oct89-748
Benedetti, C. La soggettività nel racconto.
S. Knaller, 547(RF):Band99Heft4-470
Benedetti, J. Stanislavski.
E. Proffer, 441:5Mar89-27
Benedikt, M. The Prose Poem.
S. Birkerts, 472:Vol15No1-163
Benestad, F. & D. Schjelderup-Ebbe. Edvard
Grieg. (new ed)
L. Kuhn, 441:19Mar89-22
Benet, D. Something to Love.*
C.J.B., 295(JML):Fall87/Winter88-373
Benet, G. A Short Dance in the Sun.
J. Kaye, 441:30Apr89-38
Benewick, R. & P. Wingrove, eds. Reforming
the Revolution.
J. Mirsky, 617(TLS):28Apr-4May89-463
Benford, G. Tides of Light.
G. Jonas, 441:9Apr89-38
Benhabib, S. Critique, Norm, and Utopia.*
A.W. Wood, 482(PhR):Jan88-107
Benhabib, S. & D. Cornell, eds. Feminism as
Critique.
A.F., 185:Jan89-463
P.D. Murphy, 590:Dec88-163

van Bentham, J.F.A.K. Essays in Logical
Semantics.*
   K. Arnold, 320(CJL):Mar88-89
   J. Hawthorn, 316:Sep88-990
Bentini, J. & L. Spezzaferro, eds. L'impresa di
Alfonso II.
   K. Lippincott, 39:Jul88-70
Bentley, D.M.R. - see Crawford, I.V.
Bentley, D.M.R., with C.R. Steele - see Kidd,
A.
Bentley, E. The Brecht Memoir.
   P. Brady, 617(TLS):1-7Dec89-1335
   V.K., 295(JML):Fall87/Winter88-300
Bentley, G.E., Jr. Blake Records Supplement.
   J. Warner, 627(UTQ):Spring89-421
Bentley, M. The Climax of Liberal Politics.*
   B.L. Kinzer, 637(VS):Spring89-445
Bentley, N., M. Slater & N. Burgis. The Dick-
ens Index.
   G. Storey, 617(TLS):17-23Feb89-173
Bentman, R. Robert Burns.
   D. Daiches, 661(WC):Autumn88-190
   A.T. McKenzie, 173(ECS):Winter88/89-253
Bentsen, C. Maasai Days.
   L. Dawkins, 441:8Oct89-13
   442(NY):20Nov89-155
Benvenisti, M. Conflicts and Contradictions.
   J. Riemer, 287:May/Jun88-30
   D.V. Segre, 473(PR):Vol55No2-341
Benvenuti, A.T. - see under Tissoni Benven-
uti, A.
Benware, W.A. Phonetics and Phonology of
Modern German.*
   C. Hoequist, 353:Vol26No1-173
Benya, R., comp. Children and Languages.
(K.E. Müller, ed)
   J.S. Wilson, 399(MLJ):Winter88-459
Benyuch, O.P. & G.V. Chernov. Russian-
English English-Russian.
   S. Lubensky, 399(MLJ):Spring88-101
"Beowulf."* (G. Roberts, trans)
   C-D. Wetzel, 38:Band106Heft1/2-200
Beran, H. The Consent Theory of Political
Obligation.
   D.J.C. Carmichael, 185:Jul89-949
   N.E. Snow, 518:Oct88-239
Bérard, F. & others. Guide de l'épigraphiste.
   P-L. Gatier, 555:Vol61fasc2-317
Berberova, N. Liudi i lozhi.
   L. Hecht, 574(SEEJ):Fall88-474
   B.T. Norton, 550(RusR):Jul88-341
Berberova, N. The Revolt.
   S. Roe, 617(TLS):13-19Oct89-1132
Bercaw, M.K. Melville's Sources.*
   W. Kelley, 534(RALS):Vol16No1&2-19
de Berceo, G. El libro de los "Milagros de
Nuestra Señora." (J. Montoya Martínez, ed)
   I.A. Corfis, 240(HR):Winter88-94
   J. Lang, 547(RF):Band99Heft4-480
de Berceo, G. Milagros de Nuestra Señora. (V.
Beltrán Pepió, ed)
   J. Lang, 547(RF):Band99Heft4-480
Bercovitch, S., ed. Reconstructing American
Literary History.*
   F. Alam, 580(SCR):Fall88-65
   D.H. Hirsch, 432(NEQ):Mar88-149
   J.A.L. Lemay, 402(MLR):Oct89-960
Bercovitch, S. & M. Jehlen, eds. Ideology and
Classic American Literature.*
   E. Carton, 533:Winter89-99
Bercuson, D.J., R. Bothwell & J.L. Granatstein.
The Great Brain Robbery.*
   J. Agassi, 488:Jun88-251

Berend, I.T. The Crisis Zone of Europe.
   R. Pearson, 575(SEER):Apr88-302
Bérenger, J. Finances et absolutisme aut-
richien dans la seconde moitié du XVIIe
siècle.
   F.A.J. Szabo, 150(DR):Fall88-336
Berenson, B. & I.S. Gardner, with M. Berenson.
The Letters of Bernard Berenson and Isa-
belle Stewart Gardner, with Correspondence
by Mary Berenson.* (R.V. Hadley, ed)
   J. Davies, 55:Nov88-106
   D. Sutton, 90:Sep88-710
   W.L. Vance, 432(NEQ):Dec88-575
Berent, M. Rolling Thunder.
   N. Callendar, 441:17Sep89-30
Beresford, D. Ten Men Dead.
   J. Thomas, 441:2Apr89-20
Berg, A. & A. Schoenberg. The Berg-
Schoenberg Correspondence: Selected Let-
ters. (J. Brand, C. Hailey & D. Harris, eds)
   C. Hatch, 465:Autumn88-90
   A. Whittall, 410(M&L):Oct88-547
Berg, A.S. Goldwyn.
   L. Anderson, 617(TLS):15-21Dec89-1387
   J.G. Dunne, 453(NYRB):18May89-28
   M. Richler, 441:26Mar89-1
   442(NY):19Jun89-100
Berg, M. Jane Eyre.
   J. Maynard, 637(VS):Spring89-419
Berg, S. In It.*
   D. Revell, 460(OhR):No43-116
van den Berg, S.J. The Action of Ben Jon-
son's Poetry.
   J. Brady, 627(UTQ):Summer88-565
   L.S. Young, 391:Dec88-136
Bergale, A., ed. Jean-Luc Godard par Jean-
Luc Godard.
   F. Worth, 207(FR):Oct88-191
Bergamo, M. - see des Anges, J.
Bergan, R. The Great Theatres of London.
   F. Barker, 511:Feb88-44
Bergenholtz, H. & J. Mugdan, eds. Lexi-
kographie und Grammatik.
   H-G. Maak, 685(ZDL):3/1987-358
Berger, C. Forms of Farewell.
   J. Applewhite, 569(SR):Winter88-121
Berger, E. Der Parthenon in Basel.
   G.B. Waywell, 229:Band60Heft1-57
Berger, E., ed. Parthenon-Kongress Basel.
   B. Fehr, 229:Band60Heft7-624
Berger, G., ed. Zur Geschichte von Buch und
Leser in Frankreich des Ancien Régime.
   M. Delon, 535(RHL):Mar-Apr88-284
Berger, P. Blood Season.
   C. Salzberg, 441:20Aug89-21
Berger, P. The Goddess Obscured.
   J.S. Neaman, 589:Jan88-119
Berger, R. Malerinnen auf dem Weg ins 20.
Jahrhundert Kunstgeschichte als Sozial-
geschichte.
   M.L. Wagener, 662:Spring/Summer88-45
Berger, R. & others. Computergestützter
Fremdsprachenunterricht.
   B.A. Beatie, 399(MLJ):Spring88-70
   H. Bobek, 682(ZPSK):Band41Heft5-662
Berger, S.M. Forever Young.
   J. Viorst, 441:9Apr89-30
Berger, T. Being Invisible.*
   L. Lemon, 502(PrS):Fall88-132
   J. Saari, 42(AR):Spring88-266
Berger, T. Changing the Past.
   D. Glover, 441:27Aug89-12

Berger, T. The Houseguest.*
J. Clute, 617(TLS):4-10Aug89-851
J. Saari, 42(AR):Summer88-390
Bergeron, D.M. Shakespeare's Romances and the Royal Family.*
N. Council, 570(SQ):Autumn88-371
J.L. Levenson, 627(UTQ):Winter87/88-321
K. Sharpe, 250(HLQ):Spring88-96
Bergh, G. The Neuropsychological Status of Swedish-English Subsidiary Bilinguals.
M. Paradis, 353:Vol26No5-886
Berghahn, K.L. Schiller.*
A. Bohm, 564:May88-195
Bergier, J-F. Guillaume Tell.
M. Vale, 617(TLS):3-9Mar89-213
Bergin, T.G. & J. Speake, eds. The Encyclopaedia of the Renaissance.
T. Tuohy, 39:Dec88-448
Bergland, M. A Farm Under a Lake.
D. O'Brien, 441:9Jul89-7
Bergman, E.F. Woodlawn Remembers.
R.F. Shepard, 441:22Jan89-22
Bergman, I. The Magic Lantern.* (French title: Laterna Magica.)
A. Suied, 450(NRF):Mar88-97
Bergman, M. Karin.
M. Wolf, 441:31Dec89-12
Bergmann, G. Kleines sächsisches Wörterbuch.
R. Hinderling, 685(ZDL):2/1988-240
Bergmann, P. Nietzsche, "the Last Antipolitical German."*
M.C., 186:Oct88-201
R.F. Krummel, 133:Band21Heft4-354
G.J. Stack, 543:Sep88-131
Bergmann Loizeaux, E. Yeats and the Visual Arts.
S. Gurney, 396(ModA):Winter88-81
D.T.O., 295(JML):Fall87/Winter88-406
Bergon, F. Shoshone Mike.*
A. Ronald, 649(WAL):Nov88-250
Bergonzi, B. The Myth of Modernism and Twentieth Century Literature.*
P. Brooker, 366:Spring88-136
Bergougnioux, P. L'Arbre sur la rivière.
R. Jacquelin, 450(NRF):Oct88-96
Bergougnioux, P. La Maison rose.*
K. O'Neill, 207(FR):Feb89-545
Bergstein, E. Ex-Lover.
R. Sassone, 441:10Sep89-26
Bergström, I. Grammatical Correctness and Communicative Ability.
R.C. Major, 257(IRAL):May88-168
Bering, D. Der Name als Stigma.
D.C.G. Lorenz, 221(GQ):Fall88-606
Beringer, R.E. & others. Why the South Lost the Civil War.
R.G. Haycock, 106:Spring88-105
Berkeley, G. George Berkeley's Manuscript Introduction. (B. Belfrage, ed)
G. Brykman, 542:Apr-Jun88-261
Berkeley, G. Oeuvres I: Épiméthée. (G. Brykman, ed)
B. Belfrage, 235:Summer88-125
Berkley, G.E. Vienna and its Jews.
M. Ignatieff, 453(NYRB):29Jun89-21
C. Landauer, 390:Oct88-58
Berkoff, S. I Am Hamlet.
D. Nokes, 617(TLS):20-26Oct89-1151
Berkove, L.I. - see De Quille, D.
Berkow, I. Pitchers Do Get Lonely.
639(VQR):Autumn88-137

Berkow, I. - see Greenberg, H.
Berkowitz, D.S. John Selden's Formative Years.
A. Hamilton, 617(TLS):13-19Oct89-1120
Berkowitz, L. & K.A. Squitier, with W.A. Johnson. Thesaurus Linguae Graecae.* (2nd ed)
A.C. Bowen, 41:Spring88-136
Berkson, C. The Caves of Aurangabad.
G.M. Tartakov, 293(JASt):May88-395
Berkson, D. - see Stowe, H.B.
Berlanga, J.L.V. - see under Villacañas Berlanga, J.L.
Berlau, R. Brechts Lai-Tu. (H. Bunge, ed)
G.E. Bahr, 615(TJ):Dec87-524
R.J. Rundell, 221(GQ):Summer88-480
Berlin, A. Poetics and Interpretation of Biblical Narrative.
G.A. Rendsburg, 318(JAOS):Jul-Sep87-554
Berlin, E.A. Reflections and Research on Ragtime.*
P. Dickinson, 410(M&L):Oct88-545
P. Oliver, 415:Aug88-407
Berlin, I. - see Gutman, H.G.
Berlin, J.A. Rhetoric and Reality.
S. Crowley, 126(CCC):May88-245
Berlin, J.A. Writing Instruction in Nineteenth-Century Colleges.
D.R. Russell, 128(CE):Apr88-437
Berlowitz, L., D. Donoghue & L. Menand, eds. America in Theory.
W. Brock, 617(TLS):8-14Sep89-979
Berman, A. From the New Criticism to Deconstruction.
27(AL):Dec88-706
639(VQR):Autumn88-122
Berman, A. & others. Les Tours de Babel.
S. Simon, 107(CRCL):Jun88-275
Berman, C.H. Medieval Agriculture, the Southern French Countryside, and the Early Cistercians.
F.L. Cheyette, 589:Apr88-362
Berman, D., ed. George Berkeley.*
E.J. Lowe, 161(DUJ):Dec87-164
H.M. Robinson, 447(N&Q):Dec88-541
Berman, I.V. - see "The Talmud"
Berman, L. Lyndon Johnson's War.
R. Caplan, 441:13Aug89-17
R. Smith, 617(TLS):15-21Dec89-1381
Berman, R.A. The Rise of the Modern German Novel.*
S. Dowden, 221(GQ):Winter88-150
T. Ziolkowski, 569(SR):Spring88-319
Berman, W.C. William Fulbright and the Vietnam War.
639(VQR):Autumn88-130
Bermeo, N.G. The Revolution within the Revolution.*
T.C. Bruneau, 529(QQ):Summer88-492
Bermingham, A. Landscape and Ideology.*
T. Erwin, 141:Summer88-408
W. Vaughan, 59:Jun88-293
Bermond Montanari, G., ed. La formazione della città in Emilia Romagna.
F.R. Serra Ridgway, 90:Sep88-700
Bernabò Brea, L. Menandro e il teatro greco nelle terracotte liparesi.
E. Simon, 229:Band60Heft7-637
Bernad, M.A. The February Revolution and Other Reflections.
V.L. Rafael, 293(JASt):May88-411

Bernal, M. Black Athena.
J. Griffin, 453(NYRB):15Jun89-25
D. Konstan, 538(RAL):Winter88-551
M. Savvas, 124:Jul-Aug89-469
Bernanos, G. Le Chemin de la Croix-des-
Ames. (new ed) (B. & J-L. Bernanos, eds)
J-C. Polet, 356(LR):Nov88-531
Bernanos, G. Monsieur Ouine. (J-L. Ber-
nanos, ed)
P.P. Delvaux, 356(LR):Nov88-527
Bernanos, J-L., ed. Album Bernanos.
G. Gaucher, 356(LR):Nov88-529
Bernanos, J-L. Georges Bernanos à la merci
des passants.*
G. Gaucher, 356(LR):Nov88-529
Bernanos, J-L. & L. Balbont. Bernanos au-
jourd'hui.
J-C. Polet, 356(LR):Nov88-533
Bernard, A. Blackbird Bye Bye.
H. Vendler, 453(NYRB):17Aug89-26
Bernard, J.D., ed. Vergil at 2000.*
R.W. Condee, 149(CLS):Vol25No3-263
K.W. Gransden, 402(MLR):Jul89-689
M.C.J. Putnam, 24:Summer88-267
J. Romeuf, 549(RLC):Jul-Sep88-429
Bernard, P. Fouilles d'Aï Khanoum.* (Vol 4)
T. Fischer, 229:Band60Heft3-261
Bernard of Clairvaux. San Bernardo, Lettere.
(Vol 1) (E. Paratore, ed & trans)
C. Waddell, 589:Oct88-900
Bernasconi, R. - see Gadamer, H-G.
Bernasconi, R. & D. Wood, eds. The Provoca-
tion of Levinas.
S. Richmond, 617(TLS):23-29Jun89-698
Bernays, A. Professor Romeo.
M. Bradbury, 441:23Jul89-1
Bernd, C.A., ed. Grillparzer's "Der arme
Spielmann."
W.E. Yates, 402(MLR):Apr89-527
Bernet, C. Le vocabulaire des tragédies de
Jean Racine.
W. Henning, 72:Band224Heft2-449
de Berneville, G. Les poésies. (K. Fresco, ed)
G. Roques, 553(RLiR):Jul-Dec88-551
Bernhard, T. Des arbres à abattre.
L. Kovacs, 450(NRF):Jan88-113
Bernhard, T. Holzfällen.*
P. Görlich, 654(WB):8/1988-1327
Bernhard, T. Wittgenstein's Nephew.
L. Hafrey, 441:19Feb89-16
J. Updike, 442(NY):9Oct89-132
Bernhard, T. Woodcutters.*
T. Wilhelmus, 249(HudR):Autumn88-554
Bernhardt, P. Wily Violets & Underground
Orchids.
S.B. Stein, 441:9Jul89-10
Bernhardt, R. Polis und römische Herrschaft
in der späten Republik (149-31 v. Chr.).
D. Braund, 313:Vol78-219
Bernhardt, U. Die Funktion der Kataloge in
Ovids Exilpoesie.
M.J. McGann, 123:Vol38No2-413
Bernheim, E. Un couple.
M. Alhau, 450(NRF):Apr88-95
Bernier, O. Words of Fire, Deeds of Blood.
D. Walton, 441:9Jul89-13
Bernlef, J. Out of Mind.*
A. Desai, 441:17Sep89-13
Berns, G.N. Greek Antiquity in Schiller's
"Wallenstein."*
J. Simons, 221(GQ):Winter87-119
Bernstein, C. Loyalties.
E. Langer, 441:5Mar89-9

Bernstein, G.L. & H. Fukui, eds. Japan and
the World.
J. Parry, 617(TLS):13-19Jan89-31
Bernstein, J. In the Himalayas.
A. Broyard, 441:3Dec89-22
Bernstein, J.A. Nietzsche's Moral Philosophy.
D. Conway, 543:Jun89-819
A.H., 185:Oct88-200
M. Tanner, 617(TLS):12-18May89-509
Bernstein, J.M. The Philosophy of the Novel.*
494:Vol8No2-451
Bernstein, L.S. Getting Published.
G. Garrett, 569(SR):Summer88-516
Bernstein, M. The Great Depression.
639(VQR):Autumn88-115
Bernstein, R.B., with K.S. Rice. Are We to be
a Nation?
C.E. Prince, 656(WMQ):Apr88-379
Berofsky, B. Freedom from Necessity.
R.W. Binkley, 103:Apr89-129
M. Curd, 543:Mar89-608
Berra, Y., with T. Horton. Yogi: It Ain't
Over...
M. Lichtenstein, 441:23Apr89-37
Berres, T. Die Entstehung der "Aeneis."*
W. Suerbaum, 229:Band60Heft5-401
Berrian, B.F. Bibliography of African Women
Writers and Journalists.
E.S. Fido, 538(RAL):Summer88-272
Berrong, R.M. Every Man for Himself.*
M. Brunyate, 208(FS):Jan88-76
Berrong, R.M. Rabelais and Bakhtin.*
B.C. Bowen, 535(RHL):Mar-Apr88-243
S. Farquhar, 400(MLN):Sep88-951
F.M. Weinberg, 207(FR):Dec88-325
Berry, H. The Boar's Head Playhouse.*
A. Gurr, 611(TN):Vol42No3-138
Berry, H. Shakespeare's Playhouses.*
K.S. Rothwell, 130:Winter88/89-378
Berry, J., J. Foose & T. Jones. Up from the
Cradle of Jazz.*
G.L. Starks, Jr., 91:Fall88-254
Berry, W. The Collected Poems of Wendell
Berry, 1957-1982.*
J. Askins, 472:Vol15No1-317
R.B. Shaw, 491:Apr88-37
Berry, W. Home Economics.
D. Allen, 249(HudR):Summer88-409
J. Askins, 472:Vol15No1-317
Berry, W. Remembering.
G. Johnson, 441:1Jan89-14
Berry, W. Sabbaths.
J. Askins, 472:Vol15No1-317
J.F. Cotter, 249(HudR):Spring88-229
R.B. Shaw, 491:Apr88-37
639(VQR):Winter88-26
Berry, W. Standing by Words. Recollected
Essays 1965-1980. The Gift of Good Land.
J. Askins, 472:Vol15No1-317
Berryman, J. Collected Poems, 1937-1971.
(C. Thornbury, ed)
E. Hirsch, 441:8Oct89-32
Bersani, L. The Freudian Body.*
S. Kimball, 367(L&P):Vol34No3-64
Bersani, L. & U. Dutoit. The Forms of Vio-
lence.*
W. Davis, 59:Sep88-445
Berschin, W. Biographie und Epochenstil im
lateinischen Mittelalter. (Vol 1)
D. Norberg, 229:Band60Heft3-213
Bertaud, J-P. The Army of the French Revo-
lution.
W. Scott, 617(TLS):19-25May89-554

Bertaud, M. "L'Astrée" et "Polexandre."*
    H.T. Barnwell, 208(FS):Jan88−78
    M. Lathuillère, 535(RHL):Mar−Apr88−261
Bertelli, S. The Courts of the Italian Renaissance.
    W. Gundersheimer, 551(RenQ):Spring88−114
Bertelsen, E., ed. Doris Lessing.
    R. Rubinstein, 538(RAL):Summer88−258
Bertelsen, L. The Nonsense Club.*
    F. Doherty, 83:Spring88−95
    B.S. Hammond, 541(RES):Feb88−116
    R.D. Hume, 301(JEGP):Apr88−260
    J.M. Kuist, 125:Fall87−83
    A.J. Van Sant, 402(MLR):Oct89−931
    D. Womersley, 447(N&Q):Sep88−378
Berthier, P. 60 Ans de travail.
    P.J. Siegel, 446(NCFS):Spring−Summer89−434
Berthier, P. Stendhal et Chateaubriand.
    G. De Wulf, 356(LR):Aug88−243
    J.P. Gilroy, 446(NCFS):Fall−Winter88/89−218
    V.D.L., 605(SC):15Apr89−246
Berthier, P., ed. Stendhal et la presse.*
    G. Strickland, 208(FS):Jan88−94
Berthier, P. − see "Barbey d'Aurevilly"
Berthier, P. & others. L'Ensorcelée.
    A. Toumayan, 446(NCFS):Spring−Summer89−409
Berthoff, W. Literature and the Continuances of Virtue.*
    D. Jasper, 161(DUJ):Dec87−155
    S.P., 295(JML):Fall87/Winter88−238
Berthoud, R. The Life of Henry Moore.*
    L. Cooke, 90:Apr88−302
Bertil, E. Le Tour du Québec par deux enfants.
    A. Raspa, 102(CanL):Winter87−172
Bertin, M., ed. The Play and Its Critic.
    G.S. Argetsinger, 563(SS):Summer88−425
    V.K., 295(JML):Fall87/Winter88−274
Bertolucci, A. La camera da letto. (Bks 1 & 2)
    P. Hainsworth, 617(TLS):24 30Nov89−1292
Berton, P. Starting Out.
    W.C. James, 529(QQ):Autumn88−718
Bertran de Born. L'Amour et la Guerre.* (G. Gouiran, ed & trans)
    L.M. Paterson, 382(MAE):1988/1−138
Bertran de Born. The Poems of the Troubadour Bertran de Born.* (W.D. Paden, Jr., T. Sankovitch & P.H. Stäblein, eds)
    M.R. Blakeslee, 589:Jan88−121
    L.M. Paterson, 382(MAE):1988/1−138
Bertrand−Jennings, C. Espaces romanesques: Zola.*
    C. Alcorn, 207(FR):Feb89−529
    D. Baguley, 627(UTQ):Fall88−132
    G. Woollen, 402(MLR):Jan89−180
de Berval, R., ed. Présence du bouddhisme.
    B. Faure, 293(JASt):Nov88−834
Besch, W., ed. Sprachverhalten in ländlichen Gemeinden. (Vol 1)
    H. Tatzreiter, 685(ZDL):1/1988−98
Besch, W., ed. Sprachverhalten in ländlichen Gemeinden. (Vol 2)
    H. Tatzreiter, 685(ZDL):1/1988−104
Besch, W., O. Reichmann & S. Sonderegger, eds. Sprachgeschichte.* (Vols 1 & 2)
    H. Penzl, 350:Sep89−638
    E. Seebold, 260(IF):Band93−274

Beschloss, M.R. Mayday.
    J. Snyder, 550(RusR):Apr88−219
Besler, B. The Besler Florilegium.
    L. Yang, 441:3Dec89−74
Besner, N.K. The Light of Imagination.
    K. Dwyer, 395(MFS):Winter88−654
Besnier, P. − see Darien, G.
Besomi, O. & M. Regoliosi − see Tavoni, M.
Bessai, D. & D. Kerr, eds. NeWest Plays by Women.
    T.C. Davis, 108:Summer88−95
    B. Powell, 647:Spring88−116
Besset, M. Who Was Le Corbusier?
    M. Spens, 592:Vol201No1019−62
Bessière, J., ed. Absurde et renouveaux romanesques (1960−1980).
    J. Guérin, 535(RHL):Nov−Dec88−1173
Best, G., ed. The Permanent Revolution.
    W. Scott, 617(TLS):19−25May89−554
Best, J. Expérimentation et adaptation.*
    C. Bertrand−Jennings, 207(FR):Apr89−895
    C. Thomson, 446(NCFS):Fall−Winter 88/89−247
Best, M.R. − see Markham, G.
Besterman, T. − see de Voltaire, F.M.A.
Betancourt, P.P. The History of Minoan Pottery.*
    K. Branigan, 303(JoHS):Vol108−256
    S. Hood, 123:Vol38No1−110
Betken, W.T. − see Shakespeare, W.
Betsko, K. & R. Koenig. Interviews with Contemporary Women Playwrights.
    P.F. Behrendt, 502(PrS):Summer88−129
    J.R., 615(TJ):May88−282
Bettagno, A., with M. Cazort & C. Giudici, eds. I Gandolfi, Ubaldo, Gaetano, Mauro.
    J.B. Shaw, 90:Nov88−862
Betten, A. Sprachrealismus im deutschen Drama der siebziger Jahre.*
    L.C. De Meritt, 221(GQ):Spring87−311
    C.J. Wickham, 301(JEGP):Jan88−94
Bettencourt, P. Fables fraîches pour lire à jeun.
    J. Taylor, 207(FR):Dec88−359
Bettini, M. Antropologia e cultura romana.
    T. Barton, 313:Vol78−206
    A. Douglas, 123:Vol38No2−432
    V. Pöschl, 229:Band60Heft2−148
Bettini, M. & C. Questa, eds. Materiali e discussioni per l'analisi dei testi classici, 14.
    J. Soubiran, 555:Vol61fasc2−326
Bettsworth, M. Marking Time.
    T. Parker, 617(TLS):24−30Mar89−318
Betz, A. Exil und Engagement.
    A. Graczyk, 72:Band224Heft2−376
    A. Stephan, 406:Winter88−528
Beugnot, B., ed. Voyages.
    C.N. Smith, 208(FS):Apr88−207
Beumann, H. & W. Schröder, eds. Frühmittelalterliche Ethnogenese im Alpenraum.
    D. Messner, 547(RF):Band99Heft4−422
Beurdeley, M. & G. Raindre. Qing Porcelain.*
    "Skipjack," 463:Summer88−144
Bevan, D. André Malraux.*
    E. Fallaize, 402(MLR):Jan89−187
    G.W. Ireland, 529(QQ):Spring88−206
Bevan, D.G. Michel Tournier.*
    A. Purdy, 535(RHL):Nov−Dec88−1172
    B. Scheiner, 72:Band225Heft1−217
    A. Smith, 295(JML):Fall87/Winter88−391
    M.J. Worton, 208(FS):Apr88−237

Bever, T.G., J.M. Carroll & L.A. Miller, eds. Talking Minds.
  C. Futter, 320(CJL):Mar88-97
Beveridge, C. & R. Turnbull. The Eclipse of Scottish Culture.
  P. Drew, 617(TLS):18-24Aug89-891
Beverly, A., M. Kittel & K.J. Jewell, eds. The Defiant Muse.
  M.R. Vitti-Alexander, 399(MLJ):Summer88-243
Bevington, D. - see Shakespeare, W.
Bevis, R.W. English Drama: Restoration and Eighteenth Century, 1660-1789.
  M. Baron, 175:Summer88-178
  R. Folkenflik, 617(TLS):10-16Mar89-253
Bew, P. Conflict and Conciliation in Ireland, 1890-1910.
  M.E. Daly, 272(IUR):Spring88-147
Bewell, A. Wordsworth and the Enlightenment.
  K. Blank, 617(TLS):15-21Dec89-1380
Beyen, R. Bibliographie de Michel de Ghelderode.
  M. Voisin, 193:Autumn88-136
Beyer, V., C. Wild-Block & F. Zschokke. Les Vitraux de la cathédrale Notre-Dame de Strasbourg.*
  G. Laipple, 683:Band51Heft3-450
de Beynac, J.C. & M. Magnien - see under Cubelier de Beynac, J. & M. Magnien
Bezold, C., R.J. Carlson & J.C. Peck. The Future of Work and Health.
  J.V. Milligan, 529(QQ):Spring88-217
de Bhaldraithe, T. Foirisiún Focal as Gaillimh.
  B. Ó Cuív, 112:Vol20-212
Bhalla, A., ed. García Márquez and Latin America.
  P. Finnegan, 395(MFS):Summer88-263
  G.R. McMurray, 238:Sep88-558
Bhatia, T.K. A History of the Hindi Grammatical Tradition.
  R. Singh, 320(CJL):Sep88-298
Bhatt, S. Brunizem.
  J. Welch, 493:Spring88-31
Bhattacharya, B. So Many Hungers!
  K.V. Reddy, 314:Summer-Fall87-43
Bhattacharya, L. Pages sur la chambre; les Marches du vide.
  G. Macé, 450(NRF):May88-109
Bhattacharya, S. Landschenkungen und Staatliche Entwicklung in Frühmittelalterlichen Bengalen (6 bis 13. Jh. n. Chr.).
  W.L. Smith, 318(JAOS):Jul-Sep87-523
Bhattacharya, S. & R. Thapar, eds. Situating Indian History.
  N.B. Dirks, 293(JASt):Nov88-910
Bhutto, B. Daughter of Destiny.* (British title: Daughter of the East.)
  I. Buruma, 453(NYRB):2Mar89-8
  B. Palling, 441:19Mar89-6
Biale, D. Power and Powerlessness in Jewish History.
  R. Kronish, 390:Nov88-52
Bialer, S., ed. Politics, Society and Nationality.
  A.G. Meyer, 385(MQR):Fall89-771
Bialer, S. The Soviet Paradox.*
  A. Brown, 575(SEER):Apr88-325
Bialostocki, J. Dürer and his Critics.
  K. Andrews, 90:Jun88-470
Bialostosky, D.H. Making Tales.*
  J. Sturrock, 677(YES):Vol19-337

Bianchi, L. Le stele funerarie della Dacia.*
  I. Skupinska-Løvset, 229:Band60Heft4-378
Bianchi, U., ed. Transition Rites.
  S. Siporin, 292(JAF):Apr-Jun88-244
de Biasi, P-M. - see Flaubert, G.
von Biberach, R. De septem itineribus aeternitatis. Die siben strassen zu got. (M. Schmidt, ed & trans of both)
  W. Breuer, 680(ZDP):Band107Heft1-143
de Bibiena, J.G. La Poupée.
  S. Davies, 83:Autumn88-236
"Biblia Pauperum." (A. Henry, ed)
  P. Needham, 617(TLS):31Mar-6Apr89-346
  78(BC):Autumn88-313
"Biblia Sacra iuxta Latinam Vulgatam versionem ad codicum fidem."
  W. Thiele, 229:Band60Heft8-716
"Bibliografia degli scritti di Cesare Segre."
  A.V., 379(MedR):Dec88-472
Bibolet, J-C., ed. Le "Mystère de la Passion" de Troyes.*
  G.A. Runnalls, 208(FS):Jul88-337
Bickel, G.A.C. Jean Genet.
  P. Thody, 617(TLS):21-27Apr89-419
  R. Zaiser, 547(RF):Band100Heft4-448
Bickerman, E.J. The Jews in the Greek Age.
  J. Griffin, 453(NYRB):16Mar89-6
Bickerton, L.M. Eighteenth-Century English Drinking Glasses. (2nd ed)
  R.J.C., 90:Jun88-477
Bickley, R.B., Jr. Joel Chandler Harris.
  W. Mixon, 578:Fall88-86
Bickmann, C. Der Gattungsbegriff im Spannungsfeld zwischen historischer Betrachtung und Systementwurf.
  R.C. Holub, 406:Fall88-364
Biddle, A.W. & D.L. Bean. Writer's Guide: Life Sciences.
  T. Haring-Smith, 126(CCC):Dec88-485
Biddle, A.W. & K.M. Holland. Writer's Guide: Political Science.
  T. Haring-Smith, 126(CCC):Dec88-485
Bideault, M. & C. Lautier. Ile de France Gothique, I.
  N. Coldstream, 90:Aug88-633
Bideaux, M., ed. Jacques Cartier: Relations.
  J.S. Moir, 627(UTQ):Fall87-173
Biebuyck, D. The Arts of Zaire.* (Vols 1 & 2)
  A.P. Bourgeois, 54:Jun88-362
Bieder, R.E. Science Encounters the Indian, 1820-1880.*
  D.R. Mandell, 292(JAF):Jan-Mar88-84
Biehl, C.D. Mit ubetydelige Levnets Løb.
  A. Heitmann, 562(Scan):May88-77
Biehl, W. Euripides, "Kyklops."
  H. Hillgruber, 229:Band60Heft6-490
Bien, J. History, Revolution and Human Nature.
  W.H. Shaw, 488:Sep88-407
Bienek, H. Earth and Fire.
  A. Huyssen, 441:15Jan89-26
Bienek, H. September Light.*
  42(AR):Fall88-532
Bienne, G. Premières alliances.
  F. Mary, 450(NRF):Jun88-82
Bier, C., ed. Woven from the Soul, Spun from the Heart.
  R. Chenciner, 39:Jul88-67
  J. Wearden, 463:Autumn88-221
Bierds, L. Off the Aleutian Chain.
  F. Muratori, 448:Vol26No1-113

Bierman, J. Napoleon III and his Carnival Empire.
    J. Ridley, 617(TLS):12-18May89-522
Biermans, J.T. The Odyssey of New Religious Movements.
    J.K. Ohles, 87(BB):Dec88-277
Biers, J.C. The Great Bath on the Lechaion Road.
    A. Farrington, 123:Vol38No2-446
Bietenholz, P.G. - see Erasmus
Bietenholz, P.G. & T.B. Deutscher, eds. Contemporaries of Erasmus.* (Vol 1)
    J. Kraye, 447(N&Q):Mar88-72
Bietenholz, P.G. & T.B. Deutscher, eds. Contemporaries of Erasmus. (Vol 3)
    A. Hamilton, 617(TLS):8-14Sep89-981
Bigazzi, V.L. - see under Lippi Bigazzi, V.
Bill, E.G.W. Education at Christ Church, Oxford, 1660-1800.
    V.H.H. Green, 617(TLS):14-20Apr89-400
Bill, J.A. The Eagle and the Lion.*
    639(VQR):Autumn88-130
Bill, V.T. Chekhov.
    J.L. Conrad, 574(SEEJ):Summer88-321
    M.J. Hanak, 403(MLS):Fall88-94
    R.A. Peace, 575(SEER):Oct88-644
Billcliffe, R. The Scottish Colourists.
    F. Spalding, 617(TLS):13-19Oct89-1118
Billi, M., ed. Il gotico inglese.
    R. Ceserani, 494:Vol8No1-202
Billick, D.J. & S.N. Dworkin. A Bibliography of Concordances, Glossaries, Vocabularies and Selected Word Studies.
    F M Waltman 240(HR):Spring88-249
Billick, D.J. & S.N. Dworkin. Lexical Studies of Medieval Spanish Texts.
    A.V., 379(MedR):Dec88-463
Billings, R. The Revels.
    R. Berry, 102(CanL):Autumn88-147
Billings, W. The Complete Works of William Billings. (Vol 3) (K. Kroeger, ed)
    N. Temperley, 317:Spring88-179
Billingsley, P. Bandits in Republican China.
    R.V. Des Forges, 617(TLS):31Mar-6Apr89-334
Billington, M. Peggy Ashcroft.*
    T. Foster, 324:Nov89-822
Billington, M. Stoppard.*
    J. Morris, 397(MD):Dec88-591
Billot, M., G. de Diesbach & J. d'Hendecourt - see Mugnier, A.
Billy, T., ed. Critical Essays on Joseph Conrad.
    S. Pinsker, 177(ELT):Vol31No2-200
Bilton, P. & others, eds. Essays in Honour of Kristian Smidt.
    J. Lothe, 172(Edda):1988/1-87
    C. Schaar, 179(ES):Apr88-187
Binchy, M. Silver Wedding.
    R. Plunket, 441:10Sep89-18
Binder, G., ed. Saeculum Augustum, I.
    R. Seager, 123:Vol38No2-326
Binder, M., ed. Contemporary Chicano Poetry.
    F.A. Lomeli, 36:Summer88-96
Binder, W. & others - see Naumann, B.
Binding, P. Lorca.
    D. Eisenberg, 86(BHS):Oct88-415
Bindman, D., ed. Colour Versions of William Blake's Book of Job Designs from the Circle of John Linnell.*
    M. Butlin, 88:Winter88/89-105

Bindman, D., G. Keynes & R. Essick. William Blake's Illustrations to the Book of Job.*
    M. Butlin, 88:Winter88/89-105
Bingham, A.M. Portrait of an Explorer.
    W.F. Buckley, Jr., 441:8Oct89-35
    C. Miller, 617(TLS):26May-1Jun89-586
Bingham, C. The History of Royal Holloway College 1886-1986.*
    J.S. Pedersen, 637(VS):Spring89-457
Bingham, S. Passion and Prejudice.
    P.L. Adams, 61:Feb89-83
    H. Dudar, 441:5Feb89-13
    L. Harris, 442(NY):11Sep89-118
Binion, R. After Christianity.*
    G.A. Wells, 402(MLR):Jul89-698
Binni, W. Incontri con Dante.
    Z.G. Barański, 545(RPh):Aug88-51
Binns, R. Malcolm Lowry.*
    P. Tiessen, 102(CanL):Winter87-157
Binski, P. The Painted Chamber at Westminster.
    J.A. Holladay, 589:Oct88-900
    A. Stones, 90:Feb88-142
Binswanger, L. Mélancolie et manie.
    P. Trotignon, 542:Oct-Dec88-511
Binur, Y. My Enemy, My Self.
    A. Edgar, 441:26Mar89-17
    B. Wasserstein, 617(TLS):18-24Aug89-887
Binyon, T.J. "Murder Will Out."
    J. Symons, 617(TLS):7-13Jul89-740
Bioy Casares, A. The Adventures of a Photographer in La Plata.
    I. Stavans 441:19Nov89-24
de Biran, M. - see under Maine de Biran
Birbrajer, J. Friends and False Friends.*
    R. & L. Sobel, 399(MLJ):Winter88-488
Bircher, M. & F. Kemp - see von Greiffenberg, C.R.
Bird, A. A History of Russian Painting.
    J.E. Bowlt, 39:Nov88-373
Bird, C. Woodpecker Point & Other Stories.
    E. Gillooly, 441:28May89-18
Bird, G. William James.*
    M. Migotti, 518:Apr88-65
    E.K. Suckiel, 619:Fall88-563
Bird, L., with B. Ryan. Drive.
    C. Paikert, 441:10Dec89-33
Birgegård, U. Johan Gabriel Sparwenfeld and the Lexicon Slavonicum.*
    H. Keipert, 559:Vol12No2-234
Birke, V. Italian Masters of the Sixteenth and Seventeenth Centuries.
    B. Bohn, 380:Winter88-369
Birkeland, B. & B.N. Kvalsvik. Folkemål og danning.
    T. Steinfeld, 172(Edda):1988/2-173
Birkerts, S. The Electric Life.
    H. Benedict, 441:16Apr89-21
Birkett, D. Spinsters Abroad.
    G. Tindall, 617(TLS):5-11May89-493
Birkett, J. The Sins of the Fathers.*
    P.W.M. Cogman, 402(MLR):Jan89-182
    I. Collins, 366:Autumn88-257
Birkinshaw, P. Freedom of Information.
    J. Waldron, 617(TLS):27Jan-2Feb89-79
Birkmann, T. Präteritopräsentia.
    J.E. Cathey, 452(NJL):Vol11No1/2-197
Birks, T. Lucie Rie.*
    R. Hildyard, 39:Dec88-448
    A. Stewart, 592:Vol201No1020-63
Birley, A. Marcus Aurelius.* (rev)
    J.B. Gould, 319:Apr89-325

Birley, A. – see Syme, R.
Birmingham, S. Shades of Fortune.
   F. Stanfill, 441:23Jul89-18
Birnbacher, D. & A. Burkhardt, eds. Sprach-
spiel und Methode.
   W. Franzen, 687:Apr-Jun88-327
   R. Wimmer, 489(PJGG):Band95Heft2-439
Birnbaum, H. – see Issatschenko, A.
Birnbaum, L.C. Liberazione della donna.
   R. Holub, 276:Winter88-346
Birrell, T.A. English Monarchs and Their
Books from Henry VII to Charles II.
   K.Z. Derounian, 568(SCN):Fall88-51
   D. McKitterick, 354:Dec88-350
Birt, P.W. Lé Jèrriais pour tous.
   J-P.Y. Montreuil, 207(FR):Apr89-920
Birtel, W. & C-H. Mahling, eds. Aufklärungen.
(Vol 2)
   S. Wollenberg, 410(M&L):Jul88-382
Birus, H. Vergleichung.
   W. Koepke, 221(GQ):Summer88-449
Bishop, A. Gentleman Rider.
   D.A.N. Jones, 617(TLS):21-27Jul89-805
Bishop, D.H., ed. Chinese Thought.*
   R.E. Allinson, 302:Vol24No1-81
Bishop, J. Joyce's Book of the Dark.*
   B.B., 295(JML):Fall87/Winter88-337
   M.H. Begnal, 149(CLS):Vol25No3-272
   C. Herr, 481(PQ):Summer88-399
   J. Hurt, 301(JEGP):Oct88-587
   J.C.C. Mays, 541(RES):Nov88-588
Bishop, J.D. Seneca's Daggered Stylus.*
   H. Zehnacker, 555:Vol61fasc1-143
Bissett, B. Canada Gees Mate for Life.
   B. Whiteman, 102(CanL):Winter87-148
Bisson, T.N. The Medieval Crown of Aragon.*
   D.W. Lomax, 382(MAE):1988/2-330
Bissoondath, N. A Casual Brutality.
   M.A. Jarman, 376:Dec88-132
   T. Keneally, 441:26Feb89-14
   J. Mellors, 364:Oct/Nov88-114
Bisztray, G. Hungarian-Canadian Literature.
   R. Sullivan, 627(UTQ):Fall88-138
Bitov, A. Pushkin House.*
   639(VQR):Summer88-92
Bitterli, U. Cultures in Conflict.
   A. Pagden, 617(TLS):4-10Aug89-844
Bix, H.P. Peasant Protest in Japan, 1590-
1884.*
   R. Bowen, 293(JASt):Nov88-821
Biyidi, O. XVIIe siècle, 1600-1699.
   B. Cap, 207(FR):Dec88-327
Bizzarro, S. Historical Dictionary of Chile.
(2nd ed)
   E. Echevarria, 263(RIB):Vol38No2-213
Bjarkman, P.C. & V. Raskin, eds. The Real-
World Linguist.*
   E.P. Hamp, 269(IJAL):Jan88-112
   A.S. Kaye, 361:May88-96
Bjørhovde, G. Rebellious Structures.
   B.L. Harman, 637(VS):Summer89-601
Björk, L.A. – see Hardy, T.
Bjork, R.E. The Old English Verse Saints'
Lives.
   N.F. Blake, 402(MLR):Apr89-431
   M.M. Gatch, 301(JEGP):Oct88-576
   J. Harris, 589:Jan88-123
Bjorklund, B., ed & trans. Contemporary Aus-
trian Poetry.
   J. Koppensteiner, 221(GQ):Winter88-160
   K. Weissenberger, 133:Band21Heft2/3-
262

Björkman, S. "L'incroyable, romanesque, pic-
aresque épisode barbaresque."
   T.J. Walsh, 545(RPh):Aug88-82
Björkvall, G. Corpus troporum V.
   J. Caldwell, 410(M&L):Jul88-365
Bjørnson, B. Bjørnstjerne Bjørnsons Brief-
wechsel mit Duetschen. (Pts 1 & 2) (A.
Keel, ed)
   S.C. Brantly, 563(SS):Summer88-405
Bjornson, R., ed. Approaches to Teaching
Cervantes' "Don Quixote."*
   G.W. Frey, 72:Band225Heft1-221
Bjurstrom, C.G., ed. French Folktales.
   R. McKinley, 441:24Dec89-25
Bjurström, P. French Drawings in the Nation-
almuseum, Stockholm. (Vol 3)
   P. ten-Doesschate Chu, 380:Winter87-
420
   P. Rosenberg, 90:May88-379
Blaché, A.G. The Memoirs of Alice Guy
Blaché. (A. Slide, ed)
   W.W. Dixon, 502(PrS):Spring88-127
Black, C.E. Understanding Soviet Politics.
   A. Yanov, 550(RusR):Apr88-207
Black, C.F. Italian Confraternities in the
Sixteenth Century.
   L. Martines, 617(TLS):17-23Nov89-1284
Black, E.C. The Social Politics of Anglo-
Jewry 1880-1920.
   R.S. Wistrich, 617(TLS):20-26Oct89-1157
Black, G. The Good Neighbor.
   M. Davidson, 441:30Apr89-35
Black, J. British Foreign Policy in the Age of
Walpole.*
   M. Harris, 161(DUJ):Dec87-138
Black, J. The Collapse of the Anglo-French
Alliance 1727-1731.
   S. Soupel, 189(EA):Oct-Dec88-488
Black, J. The English Press in the Eighteenth
Century.*
   J. Derry, 83:Autumn88-211
   H.L. Snyder, 354:Jun88-170
Black, J. Natural and Necessary Enemies.*
   S. Soupel, 189(EA):Oct-Dec88-487
Black, J. You Can't Win.
   L. Sante, 453(NYRB):27Apr89-15
Black, J.L. G-F. Müller and the Imperial Rus-
sian Academy.*
   A. Gleason, 550(RusR):Apr88-185
Black, L.C. Mikhail Chekhov as Actor, Direc-
tor and Teacher.
   L. Senelick, 610:Autumn88-295
Black, R. Benedetto Accolti and the Floren-
tine Renaissance.*
   P.F. Grendler, 276:Summer88-157
   R.G. Witt, 589:Apr88-364
Black, S.T. Child Star.*
   P. French, 617(TLS):11-17Aug89-871
Blackburn, A., with C. Lesley & J. Landem,
eds. The Interior Country.
   R.A. Roripaugh, 649(WAL):Aug88-165
Blackburn, J. Charles Waterton, 1782-1865.
   D. King-Hele, 617(TLS):26May-1Jun89-
586
Blackburn, R. The Overthrow of Colonial
Slavery, 1776-1848.*
   D.B. Davis, 453(NYRB):30Mar89-29
Blackburn, S.H. & A.K. Ramanujan, eds. An-
other Harmony.
   F.W. Clothey, 293(JASt):Feb88-164
Blackburn, T. The Adjacent Kingdom. (J.
MacVean, ed)
   K. Raine, 4:Autumn88-27

Bloch, A.A. Studies in Arabic Syntax and Semantics.
    M.G. Carter, 318(JAOS):Oct-Dec87-812
Bloch, C. & S. Mitchell - see Amichai, Y.
Bloch, E. Briefe 1903-1975. (K. Bloch & others, eds)
    F.W. Graf, 489(PJGG):Band95Heft1-214
Bloch, E. The Utopian Function of Art and Literature.
    C.F. Breslin, 103:Nov88-423
Bloch, J. Recueil d'articles de Jules Bloch, 1906-1955. (C. Caillat, comp)
    M.C. Shapiro, 350:Jun89-421
Bloch, M. Les Caractères originaux de l'histoire rurale française.
    R.B. Dobson, 617(TLS):23-29Jun89-684
Bloch, R. & C. Guittard - see Livy
Bloch, R.H. The Scandal of the Fabliaux.*
    G.S. Burgess, 382(MAE):1988/2-325
    C. Lee, 379(MedR):Aug88-301
    P. Nykrog, 545(RPh):Feb89-285
    S. White, 589:Jan88-126
Bloch, R.H. Visionary Republic.*
    M. Fitzpatrick, 83:Spring88-87
    P.F. Gura, 432(NEQ):Sep88-439
    M. Heale, 617(TLS):10-16Mar89-261
Block, F. Revising State Theory.
    J.A.G., 185:Jul89-972
Block, J. Les XX and Belgian Avant-Gardism 1868-1894.
    A. van den Hoven, 107(CRCL):Mar88-146
Block, L. Out on the Cutting Edge.
    G.A. Haywood, 441:15Oct89-46
Blockley, R.C., ed. The Fragmentary Classicising Historians of the Later Roman Empire. (Vol 2)
    R. Scott, 303(JoHS):Vol108-238
Blockley, R.C. - see Menander Protector
Blodgett, E.D. & others. Driving Home.
    A. Sirois, 107(CRCL):Jun88-269
Blodgett, H. Centuries of Female Days.
    R. Dinnage, 617(TLS):18-24Aug89-890
    K. Weber, 441:22Jan89-23
Bloom, A. The Closing of the American Mind.*
    C.T. Asplund, 529(QQ):Summer88-432
    R. Nelson, 628(UWR):Vol21No2-92
    S. Rudikoff, 249(HudR):Autumn88-531
    R. Scholes, 128(CE):Mar88-323
    D. Steiner, 560:Fall88-204
    A. Wolfe, 473(PR):Vol55No1-156
Bloom, A. Prodigal Sons.
    M. Greenstein, 106:Fall88-333
    I. Saposnik, 659(ConL):Spring89-160
Bloom, C. Reading Poe Reading Freud.
    P. Brooks, 617(TLS):13-19Jan89-40
Bloom, H., ed. British Modernist Fiction, 1920 to 1945.
    E.J. Higgins, 95(CLAJ):Jun89-513
Bloom, H., ed. Joseph Conrad.
    J.H. Stape, 177(ELT):Vol31No2-237
Bloom, H., ed. E.M. Forster. E.M. Forster's "A Passage to India."
    F.P.W. McDowell, 177(ELT):Vol31No4-487
Bloom, H., ed. Genesis.
    R.T. Anderson, 115:Winter88-87
Bloom, H., ed. Thomas Hardy. Thomas Hardy's "Jude the Obscure." Thomas Hardy's "Tess of the d'Urbervilles."
    H. Orel, 177(ELT):Vol31No2-205
Bloom, H., ed. Henry James.
    J.W. Tuttleton, 177(ELT):Vol31No1-111
Bloom, H., ed. Rudyard Kipling.
    W.W. Robson, 177(ELT):Vol31No2-230

Bloom, H., ed. Rudyard Kipling's "Kim."
    L.A.F. Lewis, 177(ELT):Vol31No3-334
Bloom, H., ed. D.H. Lawrence's "Women in Love."
    J. Meyers, 177(ELT):Vol31No4-489
Bloom, H., ed. Ursula K. Le Guin.
    E. Cummins, 561(SFS):Mar88-99
Bloom, H., ed. Arthur Miller. James Baldwin.
    E.J. Higgins, 95(CLAJ):Dec88-256
Bloom, H., ed. Cynthia Ozick.
    E.M. Kauvar, 659(ConL):Fall89-452
Bloom, H., ed. Walter Pater.
    I. Small, 177(ELT):Vol31No2-195
Bloom, H. Poetics of Influence. (J. Hollander, ed)
    L. Sage, 617(TLS):14-20Apr89-389
Bloom, H., ed. Thomas Pynchon.
    S. Moore, 532(RCF):Summer88-321
Bloom, H. Ruin the Sacred Truths.
    H. Beaver, 617(TLS):18-24Aug89-900
    D. Donoghue, 453(NYRB):2Mar89-22
    C.H. Sisson, 441:26Feb89-18
Bloom, H., ed. The Tales of Poe.
    M. Fisher, 573(SSF):Spring88-171
Bloom, H., ed. Edith Wharton.
    P.L. Yongue, 26(ALR):Fall88-82
Bloom, H., ed. Oscar Wilde.
    K. Powell, 177(ELT):Vol31No1-79
Bloom, H., ed. Virginia Woolf.
    E.K. Ginsberg, 177(ELT):Vol31No1-107
Bloom, H., ed. William Butler Yeats.
    R.J. Finneran, 177(ELT):Vol31No3-320
Bloom, I. - see Lo Ch'in-shun
Bloom, P., ed. Music in Paris in the Eighteen-Thirties.
    D. Charlton, 415:Mar88-134
Bloomfield, B.P., ed. The Question of Artificial Intelligence.
    P.A. Facione, 103:Apr89-131
Bloomfield, L. A Leonard Bloomfield Anthology. (abridged) (C.F. Hockett, ed)
    W. Cowan, 320(CJL):Jun88-176
Blotkamp, C. Mondriaan in Detail.
    A. Doig, 90:Dec88-936
Blotkamp, C. & others. De Stijl: The Formative Years 1917-22.*
    R. Alley, 39:Sep88-211
    P. Overy, 592:Vol201No1020-61
Blotner, J. & others - see Faulkner, W.
Blount, R., Jr. Now, Where Were We?
    D. Mason, 441:2Apr89-9
Blowers, G.H. & A.M. Turtle, eds. Psychology Moving East.
    R.W. Brislin, 293(JASt):May88-320
Bluche, F. & S. Rials, eds. Les Révolutions françaises.
    A. Forrest, 617(TLS):6-12Oct89-1097
Bluche, F., & J-F. Solnon. La Véritable Hiérarchie sociale de l'ancienne France.
    C.G.S. Williams, 207(FR):Feb89-574
Blüher, K.A., ed. Paul Valéry, Perspectives de la réception.
    P. Jourdan, 535(RHL):Jan-Feb88-144
Blum, A. & P. McHugh. Self-reflection in the Arts and Sciences.
    A.W. McHoul, 488:Mar88-125
Blum, C. Rousseau and the Republic of Virtue.*
    N. Le Coat, 173(ECS):Winter88/89-235
    J. Lough, 83:Autumn88-218
    J.F. McMillan, 617(TLS):21-27Jul89-792
    R.C. Rosbottom, 405(MP):May89-438
    J. Still, 208(FS):Jul88-347

38

Blum, P.Z. - see Crosby, S.M.
Blum, R. The Book of Runes.
  W.C. Watt, 567:Vol68No3/4-367
Blum, S. Wortschatz und Übersetzungs-
  leistung in den althochdeutschen Canones-
  glossen.
  B. Meineke, 685(ZDL):1/1988-86
Blumenberg, H. The Genesis of the Coperni-
  can World.
  M. Donougho, 103:Apr89-134
Blumenberg, H. Höhlenausgänge.
  P. Winch, 617(TLS):13-19Oct89-1127
Blumenberg, H. Lebenszeit und Weltzeit.
  K. Harries, 311(JP):Sep87-516
Blumenberg, H. Die Sorge geht über den
  Fluss.
  P. Trotignon, 542:Oct-Dec88-494
Blumenthal, M. Against Romance.
  P. Stitt, 491:Jun88-171
Blumenthal, P. Vergangenheitstempora,
  Textstrukturerung und Zeitverständnis in
  der französischen Sprachgeschichte.
  H. Bonnard, 553(RLiR):Jul-Dec88-530
  M. Harris, 208(FS):Oct88-498
Blundell, M.W. Helping Friends and Harming
  Enemies.
  O. Taplin, 617(TLS):27Oct-2Nov89-1187
Blundell, S. The Origins of Civilization in
  Greek and Roman Thought.*
  J.M. Alonso-Núñez, 123:Vol38No1-163
Bly, P.A. Vision and the Visual Arts in
  Galdós.*
  B.J. Dendle, 86(BHS):Oct88-413
  M.A. Schnepf, 552(REH):Jan88-139
  P.L. Ullman, 238:May88-294
  D.F. Urey, 345(KRQ):Aug88-375
Bly, R. A Love of Minute Particulars.
  R. Pybus, 565:Summer88-72
Bly, R. Selected Poems.*
  A. Melnyczuk, 473(PR):Vol55No1-167
  R. Mitchell, 460(OhR):No42-86
Bly, R. The Winged Life.
  H. Nelson, 460(OhR):No42-93
Boa, E. The Sexual Circus.*
  W.G. Sebald, 89(BJA):Autumn88-399
Boardman, J. Greek Sculpture: The Classical
  Period.*
  M. Robertson, 303(JoHS):Vol108-266
Boardman, J. & others, eds. The Cambridge
  Ancient History. (Vol 4)
  S. Hornblower, 617(TLS):24Feb-2Mar89-
  204
Boardman, J. & others - see "The Oxford His-
  tory of the Classical World"
Boardman, J. & C.E. Vaphopoulou-Richardson,
  eds. Chios.
  F.M. Combellack, 124:May-Jun89-395
  C. Emlyn-Jones, 123:Vol38No2-305
Boatwright, M.T. Hadrian and the City of
  Rome.*
  J. vander Leest, 487:Autumn88-276
  T.P. Wiseman, 123:Vol38No2-357
Bobbio, N. Which Socialism?
  A.V., 185:Apr89-668
Bober, P.P. & R.O. Rubenstein, with S. Wood-
  ford. Renaissance Artists and Antique
  Sculpture.*
  A.A. Donohue, 124:Jan-Feb89-216
  M. Greenhalgh, 380:Autumn88-272
  R. Harprath, 229:Band60Heft1-78
  W.S. Sheard, 683:Band51Heft2-281
  I.M. Veldman, 600:Vol18No3-164

Boberg, J., T. Fichter & E. Gillen, eds. Exer-
  zierfeld der Moderne. Die Metropole.
  H. Groschopp, 654(WB):3/1988-524
Bobes Naves, M.D. Semiología de la obra dra-
  mática.
  E. Giordano, 711(RHM):Dec88-181
Bobrowski, J. Ce qui vit encore.
  J-P. Cometti, 98:May88-445
  J. Stéfan, 450(NRF):Apr88-100
Bobrowski, J. Gesammelte Werke in sechs
  Bänden.* (Vols 1-4) (E. Haufe, ed)
  B. Leistner, 601(SuF):Nov-Dec88-1308
Boccaccio, G. Amorosa visione.
  T. Boli, 589:Jul88-625
Boccassini, D. La Parola riscritta.
  J. Pineaux, 535(RHL):Jan-Feb88-124
Bock, C.V. Untergetaucht unter Freunden.
  U.K. Goldsmith, 222(GR):Summer88-154
Bock, H. & W. Heise, eds. Unzeit des Bieder-
  meiers.
  H-G. Werner, 654(WB):7/1988-1220
Bockarie, S. & H. Hinzen, comps. Limba Stor-
  ies and Songs.
  R. Finnegan, 538(RAL):Fall88-424
Böckle, F. & E-W. Böckenförde, eds. Natur-
  recht in der Kritik.
  C. Schefold, 489(PJGG):Band95Heft2-376
Bockris, V. The Life and Death of Andy War-
  hol.
  P. Schjeldahl, 441:12Nov89-3
Bodden, M-C., ed & trans. The Old English
  Finding of the True Cross.
  A.S.G. Edwards, 402(MLR):Apr89-429
Bode, B. No Bells to Toll.
  R. Wright, 441:13Aug89-6
Bodea, C. & H. Seton-Watson. R.W. Seton-
  Watson and the Romanians, 1906-1920.
  C.M. Woodhouse, 617(TLS):3-9Nov89-
  1208
Boden, A. F.W. Harvey.
  D. Hibberd, 617(TLS):10-16Feb89-134
Boden, M.A. Computer Models of Mind.
  A. Smith, 617(TLS):17-23Feb89-163
Bodenheimer, R. The Politics of Story in Vic-
  torian Social Fiction.
  J. Kucich, 445(NCF):Mar89-531
  F.S. Schwarzbach, 617(TLS):6-12Jan89-
  15
Bodi, L. & S. Jeffries, eds. The German Con-
  nection.
  A. Scott-Prelorentzos, 564:Feb88-80
Bodman, J.W. & J.B. McKoy. Spaghetti For-
  ever.
  J. Kaplan, 608:Jun89-325
Body, J. Jean Giraudoux.
  M. Autrand, 535(RHL):Mar-Apr88-333
  A.J. Singerman, 207(FR):Feb89-533
"Boek, bibliotheek en geesteswetenschappen."
  S. Roach, 354:Mar88-78
Boër, S.E. & W.G. Lycan. Knowing Who.*
  D.H., 355(LSoc):Sep88-463
  S. Soames, 316:Jun88-657
  K. Sterelny, 486:Dec88-654
Boesche, R. The Strange Liberalism of Alexis
  de Tocqueville.
  D.C. Large, 207(FR):Apr89-928
Boese, H. - see Proclus
Boethius. De Consolatione Philosophiae.
  (Notker der Deutsche, trans; P.W. Tax, ed)
  J.C. Frakes, 684(ZDA):Band117Heft3-123

Boethius of Dacia. On the Supreme Good, On the Eternity of the World, On Dreams.* (J.F. Wippel, trans)
    F.E. Kelley, 589:Oct88-904
Boetsch, L. José Díaz Fernández y la otra Generación del 27.*
    S. Miller, 345(KRQ):May88-247
Boffey, J. Manuscripts of English Courtly Love Lyrics in the Later Middle Ages.*
    M.J. Franklin, 382(MAE):1988/1-114
Bogard, T. - see O'Neill, E.
Bogdan, R. Freak Show.*
    V. Crapanzano, 617(TLS):17-23Feb89-158
Bogen, D. After the Splendid Display.
    R. Pybus, 565:Summer88-72
Bogen, J. & J.E. McGuire, eds. How Things Are.
    R. Smith, 41:Vol7-248
Bogue, M., with G.B. Reilly. Ish Kabibble.
    G.T. Simon, 441:11Jun89-28
van Boheemen, C. The Novel as Family Romance.
    R. Battaglia, 329(JJQ):Winter89-299
    K.V. Lindberg, 454:Winter89-234
    M. Power, 395(MFS):Winter88-691
van Boheemen-Saaf, C. Between Sacred and Profane.
    M. Buning, 204(FdL):Jun88-145
Bohlke, L.B. - see Cather, W.
Böhme, R. Die verkannte Muse.
    E. Heitsch, 229:Band60Heft2-97
    M.R. Wright, 303(JoHS):Vol108-226
Bohn, W. The Aesthetics of Visual Poetry, 1914-1928.*
    M. Cranston, 207(FR):Dec88-322
    G.J. Janecek, 345(KRQ):May88-239
    A. Robinson, 402(MLR):Apr89-454
    E.S., 295(JML):Fall87/Winter88-270
Bohnen, K., U. Hansen & F. Schmöe, eds. Fin de Siècle.
    J. Hardin, 406:Summer88-242
Böhr, E. Corpus Vasorum Antiquorum. (Deutschland, Vol 52, fasc 4)
    D. von Bothmer, 229:Band60Heft2-180
    B.A. Sparkes, 303(JoHS):Vol108-268
Böhr, E. & W. Martini, eds. Studien zur Mythologie und Vasenmalerei.
    E. Moignard, 123:Vol38No1-178
Boime, A. A Social History of Modern Art. (Vol 1)
    C.S. Smith, 59:Dec88-574
Boisvert, L., C. Poirier & C. Verreault. La lexicographie québécoise.
    C.A. Demharter, 207(FR):Dec88-380
    A. Lapierre, 320(CJL):Sep88-277
    T.R. Wooldridge, 627(UTQ):Fall87-203
Boitani, P. Chaucer and the Imaginary World of Fame.*
    G. Schmitz, 38:Band106Heft1/2-221
Boitani, P. & J. Mann, eds. The Cambridge Chaucer Companion.
    W. Erzgräber, 72:Band225Heft2-386
    C. Gauvin, 189(EA):Oct-Dec88-472
    P. Hardman, 541(RES):Nov88-534
    J. Simons, 366:Spring88-116
Bojtár, E. Slavic Structuralism.
    M. Burri, 494:Vol8No3/4-732
Bok, D. Higher Learning.
    N. McMillan, 577(SHR):Spring88-173
Bok, S. A Strategy for Peace.
    D. Schorr, 441:19Mar89-8

Böker, U. Loyale Illoyalität.
    K. Otten, 72:Band224Heft2-415
Bokobza, S. Contribution à la titrologie romanesque.*
    G. Strickland, 208(FS):Jan88-94
Boland, E. Selected Poems.
    M. O'Neill, 617(TLS):7-13Jul89-737
Bold, A. MacDiarmid.*
    W.N. Herbert, 493:Winter88/89-23
    W. Scammell, 364:Feb/Mar89-116
Bold, A. Summoned by Knox.
    R. Watson, 588(SSL):Vol23-254
Bold, C. Selling the Wild West.*
    M.W. Fishwick, 627(UTQ):Fall88-196
    J.D. Nesbitt, 649(WAL):May88-56
Bold, J., with J. Reeves. Wilton House and English Palladianism.
    A. Gomme, 617(TLS):8-14Sep89-982
Bölhoff, R. - see Pyritz, H. & I.
Bolinger, D.L. Intonation and its Parts.
    G. Brown, 297(JL):Mar88-248
Bolkestein, A.M. Problems in the Description of Modal Verbs.
    P.H. Matthews, 394:Vol41fasc3/4-424
Böll, H. Und sagte kein einziges Wort. (W. Hanson, ed)
    J.H. Reid, 402(MLR):Jul89-806
Böll, H. Women in a River Landscape.*
    M. Hulse, 617(TLS):17-23Nov89-1272
Bollas, C. Forces of Destiny.
    S. Sutherland, 617(TLS):27Oct-2Nov89-1178
Bollenbeck, G. Till Eulenspiegel.*
    W. Wunderlich, 684(ZDA):Band117Heft1-36
Bolon, C.R., R.S. Nelson & L. Seidel, eds. The Nature of Frank Lloyd Wright.
    W.J.R. Curtis, 617(TLS):24-30Mar89-315
Bolter, J.D. Turing's Man.
    E. Halper, 121(CJ):Oct-Nov88-64
Bolton, H.P. Dickens Dramatized.
    B. Bell, 610:Spring88-60
    J.S. Bratton, 155:Spring88-50
    G.J. Worth, 637(VS):Winter89-255
Bolton, M. The Testing.
    N. Callendar, 441:15Jan89-39
Bolton, S. Evaluation de la compétence communicative en langue étrangère.
    R.A. Schulz, 399(MLJ):Autumn88-331
Boltz, I. - see Shakespeare, W.
Bombeck, E. I Want to Grow Hair, I Want to Grow Up, I Want to Go to Boise.
    A. Banks, 441:26Nov89-26
Bomchil, S. & V. Carreño. El mueble colonial de las Américas.
    O. Etorena, 37:Jul/Aug88-59
Bömer, F. P. Ovidius Naso, "Metamorphosen."
    E.J. Kenney, 123:Vol38No2-247
Bomhard, A.R. Toward Proto-Nostratic.
    E. Helimski, 318(JAOS):Jan-Mar87-97
Bonaccorso, G. & others. Flaubert e il pensiero del suo secolo.
    B.F. Bart, 593:Summer88-167
Bonaccorso, R. Sean O'Faolain's Irish Vision.
    P. O'Leary, 395(MFS):Summer88-286
Bonafin, M., ed. Il viaggio di Carlomagno in Oriente.
    S. Luongo, 379(MedR):Apr88-135
Bonafoux, P. The Impressionists.
    90:Mar88-241

Booth–Clibborn, E., ed. The Best of British Packaging.
  B. Robinson, 324:Jan89–123
Borbein, V., J. Laubépin & M–L. Parizet. Le Français actif.
  N.A. Poulin, 207(FR):Feb89–562
Borch–Jacobsen, M. The Freudian Subject.
  M.N–S., 185:Jul89–975
Borchardt, E. Mythische Strukturen im Werk Heinrich von Kleists.
  L.C. De Meritt, 133:Band21Heft4–345
Borchardt, R. "Das Gespräch über Formen und Platons Lysis deutsch," mit einem Essay von Botho Strauss.
  H. Hummel, 224(GRM):Band38Heft3–356
Borchers, H. Freud und die amerikanische Literatur (1920–1940).
  A. Guttmann, 27(AL):Oct88–488
Bord, A. Pascal et Jean de la Croix.
  M. Adam, 542:Apr–Jun88–252
Bordillon, H. Gestes et Opinions d'Alfred Jarry, Ecrivain.
  J.A. Cutshall, 402(MLR):Jan89–181
Bordwell, D. Ozu & the Poetics of Cinema.
  M. Le Fanu, 707:Autumn88–288
Borg, A. Cypriot Arabic.
  A.S. Kaye, 318(JAOS):Oct–Dec87–810
Borgeaud, P. The Cult of Pan in Ancient Greece.
  S. Goldhill, 617(TLS):30Jun–6Jul89–723
Borgen, R. Sugawara no Michizane and the Early Heian Court.*
  R.L. Backus, 318(JAOS):Oct–Dec87–818
  M. Ury, 244(HJAS):Jun88–276
Borger, R. & others. Texte aus der Umwelt des Alten Testaments. (Vol 1, Pt 2) (O. Kaiser, ed)
  M. Weinfeld, 318(JAOS):Apr–Jun87–335
Borges, J.L. Atlas.
  F. de Mèredieu, 450(NRF):Jun88–86
Borges, J.L. Les Conjurés, [together with] Le Chiffre.
  S. Brussell, 450(NRF):Nov88–119
Borges, J.L. Le Livre des Etres imaginaires.
  H. Cronel, 450(NRF):Oct88–92
Borges, J.L. Textos cautivos. (E. Sacerio Carí & E. Rodríguez Monegal, eds)
  M. Breton, 37:May/Jun88–60
Borges, J.L., S. Ocampo & A. Bioy Casares, eds. The Book of Fantasy.
  P–L. Adams, 61:Mar89–98
Borgeson, P.W., Jr. Hacia el nombre nuevo.*
  J. Walker, 345(KRQ):Feb88–126
Borghese, L., ed. Karl Hillebrand Eretico d'Europa.
  M. Jakob, 549(RLC):Jul–Sep88–430
Borghi Cedrini, L. Via de lo Paraiso.
  G. Holtus, 72:Band225Heft1–228
Borgolte, M. Die Grafen Alemanniens in merowingischer und karolingischer Zeit.
  R.W. Mathisen, 589:Apr88–371
Borgolte, M., D. Geuenich & K. Schmid, eds. Subsidia Sangallensia. (Vol 1)
  J.H. Lynch, 589:Oct88–905
Borgomano, M. L'appel des arènes d'Aminata Sow Fall.
  A. Adebayo, 538(RAL):Summer88–250
Borie, B. 4th. Farming and Folk Society. (G. Sharrow, ed)
  M.J. Chiarappa, 292(JAF):Jan–Mar88–113
Borisova, E. & G. Sternin. Russian Art Nouveau.
  L. Hughes, 617(TLS):28Apr–4May89–449

Bork, R.H. The Tempting of America.
  J.P. Diggins, 441:19Nov89–15
Borman, F., with R.J. Serling. Countdown.
  A. Salpukas, 441:8Jan89–37
Borman, W. Gandhi and Non–Violence.*
  M.D., 185:Oct88–199
de Born, B. – see under Bertran de Born
Bornäs, G. Ordre alphabétique et classement méthodique du lexique.*
  K.E.M. George, 208(FS):Oct88–495
  F.J. Hausmann, 547(RF):Band100Heft4–363
Borne, D. Histoire de la société française depuis 1945.
  H.B. Sutton, 207(FR):May89–1104
Bornstein, D. – see Compagni, D.
Borowski, L.E., R.B. Jachmann & E.A. Wasianski. Kant intime. (J. Mistler, ed & trans)
  R.M., 342:Band79Heft1–112
Borrás, A.A., ed. The Theatre and Hispanic Life.
  R.A. Young, 107(CRCL):Mar88–114
Borsay, P. The English Urban Renaissance.
  P. Clark, 617(TLS):29Sep–5Oct89–1067
Borsi, F. & E. Godoli. Vienna 1900.*
  P.D., 46:May88–14
Borsò–Borgarello, V. Metapher: Erfahrungs- und Erkenntnismittel.
  S. Kupsch–Losereit, 72:Band225Heft1–210
Borson, R. & K. Maltman. The Transparence of November/Snow.*
  529(QQ):Spring88–224
Borsook, E. & F. Superbi Gioffredi, eds. Tecnica e Stile.*
  A. Conti, 551(RenQ):Summer88–308
  M. Kemp, 90:Sep88–698
Boruah, B.H. Fiction and Emotion.
  B. Falk, 617(TLS):30Jun–6Jul89–724
Borzsák, S. – see Horace
Böschenstein, H. Selected Essays on German Literature. Zur deutschen Literatur und Philosophie. (R. Symington, ed of both)
  H. Spencer, 564:Sep88–269
Bosco, G. Il "Meraviglioso" barocco come segno della transgressione.
  V. De Gregorio Cirillo, 475:Vol15No28–266
Bosco, U. Altre pagine dantesche.
  M. Marti, 228(GSLI):Vol165fasc532–602
Bose, M. & C. Gunn. Fraud.
  J.H.C. Leach, 617(TLS):9–15Jun89–632
Bose, S. Agrarian Bengal.
  P. Chatterjee, 293(JASt):Aug88–670
Bose, T. – see Colbeck, N.
Bosher, J.F. The Canada Merchants, 1713–1763.
  C. Nish, 656(WMQ):Jul88–602
Bosinelli, R.M., P. Pugliatti & R. Zacchi, eds. Myriad–Minded Man.
  R. Rutelli, 494:Vol8No1–208
Boskovits, M. Gemäldegalerie Berlin Katalog der Gemälde. (E. Schleier, ed & trans)
  C.B. Strehlke, 90:Nov88–859
Bosse, M. Stranger at the Gate.
  C. Salzberg, 441:20Aug89–20
Bosshardt, H–G., ed. Perspektiven auf Sprache.
  W. Viereck, 685(ZDL):3/1988–396
Bossi, F. Studi sul "Margite."
  M. Davies, 303(JoHS):Vol108–222
  J. Smart, 123:Vol38No2–202

Bostock, D. Plato's "Theaetetus."
C. Rowe, 617(TLS):31Mar–6Apr89–341
Bostock, W.W. Francophonie.
F.J. Hausmann, 257(IRAL):Feb88–72
Boston, R. Osbert.
H. Carpenter, 617(TLS):4–10Aug89–846
Boswell, J. Boswell: The English Experiment
1785–1789.* (I.S. Lustig & F.A. Pottle,
eds)
T. Crawford, 571(ScLJ):Winter88–1
A.F.T. Lurcock, 541(RES):Nov88–562
N. Page, 506(PSt):May88–108
Boswell, J. Robinson Jeffers and the Critics,
1912–1983.
C.S. Abbott, 40(AEB):Vol2No4–186
R.J. Brophy, 649(WAL):Feb89–367
Boswell, J. The Kindness of Strangers.
B. Knox, 453(NYRB):29Jun89–9
M.M. McLaughlin, 441:19Mar89–16
G. Steiner, 442(NY):6Feb89–103
K. Thomas, 617(TLS):25–31Aug89–913
Boswell, J. Edwin Arlington Robinson and the
Critics.
C.S. Abbott, 40(AEB):Vol2No4–186
Boswell, R. The Geography of Desire.
R.P. Brickner, 441:1Oct89–25
442(NY):30Oct89–118
Boswinkel, E. & P.W. Pestman, eds. Les
archives privées de Dionysios, fils de
Kephalas.
H. Heinen, 229:Band60Heft2–128
Botha, R.P. Morphological Mechanisms.
H. Sauer, 38:Band106Heft3/4–421
von Bothmer, D. The Amasis Painter and his
World.*
T.H. Carpenter, 303(JoHS):Vol108–269
Bothorel, A. & others. Cinémarradiographie
des voyelles et consonnes du français.*
V. Marrero, 548:Jul–Dec88–438
Bothwell, R., I. Drummond & J. English. Can-
ada, 1900–1945.
G.W., 102(CanL):Summer88–180
Botta, C. Per questi dilettosi monti. (L. Ba-
dini Confalonieri, ed)
C. Sensi, 228(GSLI):Vol165fasc529–129
Böttcher, K. & J. Mittenzwei. Zwiegespräch.
D.C. Riechel, 221(GQ):Spring87–319
Bottigheimer, R.B., ed. Fairy Tales and Soci-
ety.*
G. Avery, 447(N&Q):Jun88–270
D.P. Haase, 221(GQ):Summer88–488
J.M. McGlathery, 301(JEGP):Jul88–423
Bottigheimer, R.B. Grimms' Bad Girls and Bold
Boys.*
L. Bluhm, 196:Band29Heft1/2–175
A.C. Ulmer, 406:Winter88–511
Bottineau, Y. El arte cortesano en la España
de Felipe V (1700–1746). (rev) (M.C.
Martín Montero, ed & trans) L'Art de cour
dans l'Espagne des Lumières 1746–1808.
C. Whistler, 90:Oct88–778
Botting, G. Lady of My House and Other
Poems.
529(QQ):Autumn88–752
Bottoms, D. Any Cold Jordan.*
D. Kirby, 569(SR):Spring88–xxxvi
Bottoms, D. Under the Vulture-Tree.*
D. Kirby, 569(SR):Spring88–xxxvi
V. Shetley, 491:May88–100
Boucé, P.G. & S. Halimi, eds. Le Corps et
l'âme en Grande Bretagne au XVIIIe siècle.*
M. Bignami, 677(YES):Vol19–327
S. Davies, 83:Spring88–85

Bouchardeau, H. Choses dites de profil.
R. O'Callaghan, 207(FR):Feb89–546
Boucher, A–M., M. Duplantie & R. Le Blanc,
eds. Propos sur la pédagogie de la commu-
nication en langues secondes.
E.K. Horwitz, 399(MLJ):Spring88–71
M–C.W. Koop, 207(FR):Feb89–556
Boucher, D. The Fairies Are Thirsty.
J.J. O'Connor, 102(CanL):Summer88–126
Boucicault, D. Selected Plays. (A. Parkin,
ed)
A. Roche, 272(IUR):Spring88–139
Boucourechliev, A. Stravinsky.*
P. Driver, 607:Dec88–45
S. Walsh, 415:Jul88–345
Boudon, R. L'idéologie ou l'origine des idées
reçues.
A. Reix, 542:Jan–Mar88–99
Bouelet, R.S. Espaces et dialectique du héros
césairien.
A.J. Arnold, 538(RAL):Winter88–586
Bougard, R.G. Erotisme et amour physique
dans la littérature française du XVIIe
siècle.
J–C. Vuillemin, 207(FR):Feb89–520
Bouissac, P., M. Herzfeld & R. Posner, eds.
Iconicity.
J. Davies, 567:Vol71No1/2–153
S.E. Larsen, 462(OL):Vol43No1–73
Boulad-Ayoub, J., ed. L'efficacité du sym-
bolique.
R. Miguelez, 154:Autumn88–541
Boulanger, M. Promenade avec Gustave Roud.
F. Mary, 450(NRF):Apr88–89
Bouloumié, A. Michel Tournier.
C. Davis, 208(FS):Oct88–492
Boulter, C.G. & K.T. Luckner. Corpus Vasorum
Antiquorum. (U.S.A., Vol 20, fasc 2)
B.A. Sparkes, 303(JoHS):Vol108–268
Boulton, D.J.D. The Knights of the Crown.
639(VQR):Winter88–31
Boulton, J.T. & L. Vasey – see Lawrence, D.H.
Boulton, M., ed. Les Enfaunces de Jesu
Crist.*
J. Beer, 589:Oct88–906
T.D. Hemming, 208(FS):Apr88–198
G. Hesketh, 382(MAE):1988/1–127
Bouraoui, H. Echosmos.
C. Tapping, 102(CanL):Summer88–145
Bourdieu, P. Distinction.
T.J. Diffey, 89(BJA):Summer88–291
E. Wilson, 153:Summer88–47
Bourdieu, P. L'ontologie politique de Martin
Heidegger.*
R.R., 98:May88–437
Bourdieu, P. La Noblesse d'état.
T. Judt, 617(TLS):18–24Aug89–889
Bourdon, D. Warhol.
P. Schjeldahl, 441:12Nov89–3
Bourdouxhe, M. A Nail, A Rose, and Other
Stories.
A. Duchêne, 617(TLS):13–19Oct89–1129
Bourg, T. & F. Wilhelm, eds. Le Grand-Duché
de Luxembourg dans les Carnets de Victor
Hugo.
S. Gaudon, 535(RHL):Mar–Apr88–305
Bourgin, F. The Great Challenge.
P. Maier, 441:30Jul89–11
Bourne, J.M. Patronage and Society in Nine-
teenth–Century England.*
L. James, 635(VPR):Winter88–166
de Bouscal, D.G. – see under Guérin de Bous-
cal, D.

Boutwell, J.D., P. Doty & G.F. Treverton, eds. The Nuclear Confrontation in Europe.
 P. Rogers, 575(SEER):Apr88-333
Bouveresse, J. La Force de la Règle.
 J-M. Monnoyer, 98:Nov88-914
 R. Schmit, 540(RIPh):Vol42fasc1-105
Bouysse, P. Essai sur la jeunesse d'un moraliste.
 Q.M. Hope, 475:Vol15No29-735
 P.J. Wolfe, 568(SCN):Spring-Summer88-20
Bové, P.A. Intellectuals in Power.*
 A. Stoekl, 577(SHR):Winter88-49
Bow, D. Mojave.
 455:Mar88-72
Bowden, J. Jesus.
 A. Webster, 617(TLS):17-23Feb89-176
Bowen, A. - see Aeschylus
Bowen, E. The Mulberry Tree. (H. Lee, ed)
 639(VQR):Winter88-7
Bowen, R. Innocence Is Not Enough.
 E.P. Tsurumi, 293(JASt):Nov88-880
Bowen, R.W., ed. E.H. Norman.
 H.D. Harootunian, 293(JASt):Nov88-878
Bower, T. The Red Web.
 R. Cecil, 617(TLS):10-16Nov89-1232
Bowering, A. Figures Cut in Sacred Ground.
 S. Scobie, 376:Dec88-141
Bowering, G. Caprice.*
 S. Dragland, 648(WCR):Vol23No1-74
Bowering, G., ed. The Contemporary Canadian Poem Anthology. (2nd ed)
 D. Precosky, 168(ECW):Spring88-123
Bowering, G. Delayed Mercy and Other Poems.
 G. Harding-Russell, 526:Winter88-99
Bowering, G., ed. Sheila Watson and "The Double Hook."
 M. Peterman, 102(CanL):Winter87-144
Bowers, F. The Work.
 D. Martin, 617(TLS):22-28Sep89-1035
Bowers, F. - see "Dictionary of Literary Biography"
Bowers, J. Stonewall Jackson.
 J.M. McPherson, 453(NYRB):12Oct89-43
 R. Snow, 441:10Sep89-34
Bowers, J. & J. Tick, eds. Women Making Music.*
 T. Carter, 410(M&L):Jan88-61
Bowers, J.E. A Sense of Place.
 P. Wild, 649(WAL):Feb89-382
Bowers, J.M. The Crisis of Will in "Piers Plowman."
 P. Martin, 250(HLQ):Summer88-227
Bowie, M. Freud, Proust and Lacan.*
 B. Stoltzfus, 395(MFS):Summer88-298
Bowie, M., A. Fairlie & A. Finch, eds. Baudelaire, Mallarmé, Valéry.
 G. Cesbron, 356(LR):Feb-May88-145
Bowie, N.E., ed. Equal Opportunity.
 D.W.H., 185:Jan89-450
Bowlby, R. Just Looking.*
 Y. Chevrel, 107(CRCL):Mar88-145
 D. Knight, 494:Vol8No1-196
 L. Logue, 223:Summer88-243
Bowlby, R. Virginia Woolf.
 J.E. Fisher, 395(MFS):Winter88-692
 S. Roe, 617(TLS):3-9Feb89-100
Bowler, P.J. The Mendelian Revolution.
 R. Olby, 617(TLS):15-21Dec89-1384
Bowler, P.J. Theories of Human Evolution.
 R. Barton, 637(VS):Winter89-276
Bowles, B. & R. Tyson. They Love a Man in the Country.
 D. McWhorter, 441:30Jul89-16

Bowles, G. Louise Bogan's Aesthetic of Limitation.
 S. Schendler, 27(AL):May88-314
Bowles, P. Their Heads Are Green and Their Hands Are Blue. A Distant Episode.
 R. Craft, 453(NYRB):23Nov89-6
Bowles, P. Unwelcome Words.
 J. Ryle, 617(TLS):15-21Sep89-995
Bowlt, J.E. - see Lavrentiev, A.
Bowman, A.K. Egypt After the Pharaohs: 332 B.C.-A.D. 642.*
 H. Goedicke, 124:Mar-Apr89-310
Bowman, R. - see Bligh, W.
Bown, M.C. Contemporary Russian Art.
 L. Hughes, 617(TLS):6-12Oct89-1100
Boxill, R. Tennessee Williams.*
 R.B. Parker, 397(MD):Mar88-119
Boyd, B. Nabokov's "Ada."*
 J. Grayson, 575(SEER):Apr88-280
Boyd, B. - see Chaucer, G.
Boyd, G. Balzac's Dolls and Other Essays, Studies, and Literary Sketches.
 C.M. Wright, 649(WAL):May88-90
Boyd, W. The New Confessions.*
 J. Mellors, 364:Dec87/Jan88-136
 T. Wilhelmus, 249(HudR):Autumn88-552
Boyde, P. Dante Philomythes and Philosopher.
 T. Barolini, 545(RPh):Nov88-234
Boydston, J.A. - see Dewey, J.
Boyer, J. Richard Brautigan.
 R. Burrows, 649(WAL):Aug88-156
Boyer, J.W. & J. Kirshner, eds. Readings in Western Civilization.
 C.C. Rostankowski, 258:Jun88-230
Boyer, M.C. Manhattan Manners.*
 F. Gutheim, 47:Nov88-58
Boyer, R. Eléments de grammaire de l'islandais ancien.
 C. Bord, 563(SS):Spring88-311
Boyer, R. Le Mythe viking dans les lettres françaises.
 P. Michel, 535(RHL):Nov-Dec88-1185
Boylan, C. Black Baby.*
 A. Gelb, 441:10Dec89-33
Boylan, E. Working Murder.
 M. Stasio, 441:30Jul89-18
Boyle, A.J. The Chaonian Dove.*
 S.J. Harrison, 313:Vol78-234
 A.M. Shaw, 124:Nov-Dec88-127
Boyle, A.J. - see Seneca
Boyle, C. Sleeping Rough.*
 H. Lomas, 364:Jul88-92
 S. O'Brien, 493:Autumn88-56
Boyle, D. Building Futures.
 A. Saint, 617(TLS):8-14Dec89-1351
Boyle, N. & M. Swales, eds. Realism in European Literature.*
 T.G. Sauer, 221(GQ):Spring88-314
 T. Wright, 402(MLR):Apr89-426
Boyle, T.C. If the River Was Whiskey.
 E. Benedict, 441:14May89-1
Boyle, T.C. World's End.*
 639(VQR):Spring88-57
Boyne, W.J. Trophy for Eagles.
 T. Ferrell, 441:27Aug89-16
Boyt, R. Sexual Intercourse.
 A. Vaux, 617(TLS):26May-1Jun89-592
Bozell, L.B. Mustard Seeds.
 E.T. Miles, 396(ModA):Summer89-259
Bozeman, T.D. To Live Ancient Lives.
 G.S. Wood, 453(NYRB):9Nov89-26

Braccesi, L. L'Ultimo Alessandro (dagli antichi ai moderni).
J.R. Hamilton, 229:Band60Heft2-165
Bracewell, M. Divine Concepts of Physical Beauty.
J. O'Grady, 617(TLS):27Oct-2Nov89-1180
Brack, O.M., Jr., ed. Twilight of Dawn.
R. Gagnier, 177(ELT):Vol31No1-84
Brack, O.M., Jr. — see under "Studies in Eighteenth-Century Culture"
Brackenbury, A. Christmas Roses and Other Poems.
C. Wills, 617(TLS):23-29Jun89-694
Brackman, A.C. The Other Nuremberg.
I. Buruma, 453(NYRB):26Oct89-31
C. Thorne, 617(TLS):28Apr-4May89-460
Bradbrook, M. Shakespeare in His Context.
R. Hapgood, 617(TLS):25-31Aug89-927
Bradbrook, M.C. The Collected Papers of Muriel Bradbrook.
T.W. Craik, 161(DUJ):Dec87-145
Bradbury, M. Cuts.
J. Saari, 42(AR):Winter88-115
639(VQR):Spring88-56
Bradbury, M. No, Not Bloomsbury.
42(AR):Summer88-400
Bradbury, M., ed. The Penguin Book of Modern British Short Stories.*
42(AR):Summer88-401
Bradbury, M. Unsent Letters.*
P. Lewis, 364:Aug/Sep88-131
639(VQR):Autumn88-124
Bradbury, M. & S. Ro, eds. Contemporary American Fiction.
B.K. Horvath, 395(MFS):Winter88-649
Bradbury, N. An Annotated Critical Bibliography of Henry James.
R.A. Hocks, 26(ALR):Fall88-83
Braden, G. Renaissance Tragedy and the Senecan Tradition.*
U. Baumann, 229:Band60Heft2-161
G.W. Pigman 3d, 131(CL):Winter88-81
Braden, J. Just Enough Rope.
M. Dowd, 441:31Dec89-13
Bradfield, S. The History of Luminous Motion.
F.L. Block, 441:24Sep89-11
R. Kaveney, 617(TLS):8-14Dec89-1368
Bradford, C.I., Jr. & W.H. Branson, eds. Trade and Structural Change in Pacific Asia.
P. Eng-Fong, 293(JASt):Nov88-930
Bradford, M.E. Remembering Who We Are.* Generations of the Faithful Heart.
J.J. Thompson, Jr., 569(SR):Spring88-xxvi
Bradford, S. George VI.
F. Donaldson, 617(TLS):24-30Nov89-1298
Bradlee, B., Jr. Guts and Glory.*
T. Draper, 453(NYRB):19Jan89-38
R.S. Leiken, 617(TLS):10-16Feb89-127
Bradley, A.C. Shakespearean Tragedy.*
J. McLauchlan, 447(N&Q):Mar88-80
Bradley, C.H. & B.E. Hollenbach, eds. Studies in the Syntax of Mixtecan Languages.
T. Kaufman, 350:Mar89-177
Bradley, G. Terms to be Met.*
L. Sail, 565:Spring88-73
Bradley, G.V. Church-State Relationships in America.
T.J. Curry, 656(WMQ):Jul88-618
Bradley, I., ed. The Penguin Book of Hymns.
G. Irvine, 617(TLS):4-10Aug89-852

Bradley, J. Power Lines.
M. Childress, 441:24Sep89-38
Bradley, J.E. Popular Politics and the American Revolution in England.
J.L. Bullion, 656(WMQ):Jul88-608
Bradley, J.L. & I. Ousby — see Ruskin, J. & C.E. Norton
Bradley, K.R. Slaves and Masters in the Roman Empire.*
J-C. Dumont, 555:Vol61fasc2-337
Bradshaw, B. & E. Duffy, eds. Humanism, Reform and the Reformation.
A. Hamilton, 617(TLS):21-27Jul89-812
Bradshaw, G. The Colour of Power.
C. Mango, 617(TLS):22-28Dec89-1421
Bradshaw, G. Imperial Purple.
D.L. Patrick, 441:29Jan89-30
Bradshaw, G. Shakespeare's Scepticism.
A.D. Nuttall, 184(EIC):Apr88-149
P.L. Rudnytsky, 551(RenQ):Winter88-754
Bradshaw, L. Acting and Thinking.
P. Fuss, 103:Dec89-477
Bradshaw, T., with B. Martin. Looking Deep.
A. Barra, 441:19Nov89-45
Brady, F. Citizen Welles.
J.R. Baker, 441:23Apr89-16
G. Vidal, 453(NYRB):1Jun89-12
Brady, J.P. A Voyage to Inishneefa.
J. Cronin, 174(Éire):Summer88-155
Brady, P. Rococo Style versus Enlightenment Novel.
G. Poe, 478(P&L):Apr88-129
Braet, A. De klassieke statusleer in modern perspectief.
J.A.E. Bons, 394:Vol41fasc3/4-390
Braet, H., J. Nowé & G. Tournoy, eds. The Theatre in the Middle Ages.*
J.A. Dane, 545(RPh):Aug88-113
A.E. Knight, 345(KRQ):Nov88-479
Bragg, B., with E. Bergman. Lessons in Laughter.
L.J. Davis, 441:24Sep89-42
Bragg, M. Richard Burton.
D. Kaufman, 441:12Mar89-15
J. Osborne, 453(NYRB):27Apr89-24
Bragger, J.D. & D.B. Rice. Allons-y! (2nd ed)
D. Stamato, 207(FR):Apr89-915
Bragger, J.D. & D.B. Rice. Du Tac au tac.*
A. Caprio, 399(MLJ):Spring88-87
J.P. Kaplan, 207(FR):Feb89-563
Braham, R.L., ed. The Treatment of the Holocaust in Textbooks.
M.I. Teicher, 390:Apr88-57
Brahm, O. & G. Hauptmann. Otto Brahm-Gerhart Hauptmann Briefwechsel, 1889-1912.* (P. Sprengel, ed)
F. Amrine, 133:Band21Heft2/3-239
K.W. Jonas, 221(GQ):Spring87-292
E.A. McCormick, 301(JEGP):Apr88-304
Brailey, N.J. Thailand and the Fall of Singapore.
D.K. Wyatt, 293(JASt):May88-413
Brain, P. Galen on Bloodletting.
P. De Lacy, 124:Nov-Dec88-135
J. Longrigg, 123:Vol38No1-19
Braine, D. The Reality of Time and the Existence of God.*
P.L. Quinn, 543:Dec88-378
A. Reix, 542:Oct-Dec88-495
Braithwaite, M. All The Way Home.*
L. Irvine, 102(CanL):Winter87-264

45

Brakhage, P.S. The Theology of "La Lozana andaluza."
 T. O'Reilly, 402(MLR):Jan89-204
 A. Soons, 86(BHS):Oct88-406
Brakkee, R. - see Machiavelli, N.
Bramlett, J. Ride for the High Points.
 P.K. Kett, 649(WAL):Nov88-241
Bramwell, A. Ecology in the Twentieth Century.
 D. King-Hele, 617(TLS):20-26Oct89-1160
 R. Willson, 324:Nov89-818
Branagh, K. Beginning.
 D. Nokes, 617(TLS):20-26Oct89-1151
Brancacci, A. Rhetorike philosophousa.*
 É. des Places, 555:Vol61fasc1-130
 D.A. Russell, 303(JoHS):Vol108-237
 E. Spinelli, 319:Oct89-610
 M.B. Trapp, 123:Vol38No1-147
Branch, E.M., M.B. Frank & K.M. Sanderson - see Twain, M.
Branch, T. Parting the Waters.*
 W.S. McFeely, 617(TLS):3-9Nov89-1209
 442(NY):13Feb89-93
Brand, J., C. Hailey & D. Harris - see Berg, A. & A. Schoenberg
Branden, B. The Passion of Ayn Rand.
 M.R. Gladstein, 534(RALS):Vol16No1&2-236
Branden, N. Judgment Day.
 S. Brownmiller, 441:25Jun89-15
Brandon, H. Special Relationships.
 R. MacNeil, 441:12Feb89-7
Brandon, R.M. Country Textiles of Japan.
 M. Lyman, 407(MN):Spring88-130
 T. Mertel, 60:Nov-Dec87-148
Brandstetter, G. Erotik und Religiostät.*
 M. Winkler, 221(GQ):Fall87-675
 M. Winkler, 221(GQ):Summer88-466
Brandt, B.E. Christopher Marlowe and the Metaphysical Problem Play.
 D. Feldmann, 156(ShJW):Jahrbuch1988-287
Brandt, R. & W. Stark, eds. Kant-Forschungen. (Vol 1)
 W. Ritzel, 342:Band79Heft4-493
Brandys, K. Letters to Mrs. Z. (M. Edelson, ed & trans)
 J.R. Clark, 497(PolR):Vol33No4-479
Brandys, K. Rondo.
 P. Lopate, 441:19Nov89-30
Branick, V.P. Wonder in a Technical World.
 D.E. Cody, 438:Autumn88-486
Branson, C. Howard Hawks.
 M. Busby, 649(WAL):Aug88-147
Brantlinger, P. Rule of Darkness.*
 V.G. Kiernan, 366:Autumn88-260
 J. Kucich, 454:Winter89-216
 42(AR):Summer88-397
Brater, E., ed. Becket at 80/Beckett in Context.*
 M.B., 295(JML):Fall87/Winter88-292
 J. Hansford, 541(RES):Feb88-145
Brater, E. Beyond Minimalism.*
 D.I. Grossvogel, 130:Summer88-185
Brathwaite, E.K. X/Self.
 J. Figueroa, 364:Aug/Sep88-116
 L. Sail, 565:Spring88-73
Bratman, M.E. Intention, - Plans, - and - Practical - Reason.
 A.R. Mele, 393(Mind):Oct88-632
Bratton, J.S., ed. Music Hall.
 K. Barker, 611(TN):Vol42No2-87
 [continued]

[continuing]
 G. Speaight, 610:Summer88-169
 J.W. Stedman, 637(VS):Autumn88-122
Bratton, J.S., ed. Plays in Performance: "King Lear."
 C.C. Rutter, 611(TN):Vol42No3-140
Bratton, J.S. - see Shakespeare, W.
Braude, S.E., ed. The Limits of Influence.
 A. Flew, 484(PPR):Dec88-353
Braudel, F. The Identity of France. (Vol 1)
 442(NY):10Apr89-123
Braudel, F. L'identité de la France.
 P. Carrard, 153:Fall88-2
Braudy, L. The Frenzy of Renown.
 S.A.S., 295(JML):Fall87/Winter88-239
 S.L. Schein, 141:Spring88-253
Brault, G.J. The French-Canadian Heritage in New England.*
 J. Pritchard, 529(QQ):Spring88-199
Brault, J. Death-Watch.
 R. Dole, 198:Summer88-103
Braun, F. Terms of Address.
 J.E. Joseph, 350:Dec89-852
Braun, L.J. The Cat Who Went Underground.
 M. Stasio, 441:2Apr89-33
Braun, P. Tendenzen in der deutschen Gegenwartssprache. (2nd ed)
 D. Herberg, 682(ZPSK):Band41Heft2-237
Braune, W. Gotische Grammatik. (19th ed) (E.A. Ebbinghaus, ed)
 J. Udolph, 260(IF):Band93-371
Brauner, S. & I. Herms. Lehrbuch des modernen Swahili.
 A. Almeida, 685(ZDL):2/1987-281
Braunfels, W. Urban Design in Western Europe.*
 J.S. Curl, 324:Oct89-749
Braunmüller, K. Deutsch-Skandinavisch im Vergleich.
 S-G. Andersson, 452(NJL):Vol11No1/2-193
 T. Milosch, 682(ZPSK):Band41Heft5-660
Brautigan, R. Forellenfischen in Amerika.
 K-H. Schönfelder, 654(WB):3/1988-461
Bray, F. Science and Civilization in China. (Vol 6, Pt 2)
 P-T. Ho, 318(JAOS):Apr-Jun87-347
 E-T.Z. Sun, 302:Vol24No1-96
Bray, L. César-Pierre Richelet (1626-1698).*
 R. Arveiller, 209(FM):Apr88-145
 R. Zuber, 535(RHL):Jul-Aug88-765
Bray, M. Are Small Schools the Answer?
 E. Edmonds, 324:Sep89-679
Braybrooke, D. Meeting Needs.*
 G. Graham, 479(PhQ):Jul88-381
 A.C. Michalos, 154:Autumn88-507
 R. Young, 63:Dec88-563
Braybrooke, D. Philosophy of Social Science.
 B. Warren, 63:Sep88-428
Braybrooke, N., ed. Seeds in the Wind.
 P.N. Furbank, 617(TLS):17-23Nov89-1261
Brazeau, P. Parts of a World.*
 J. Applewhite, 569(SR):Winter88-121
 F.J. Lepkowski, 77:Fall88-326
 E.P. Nassar, 396(ModA):Spring89-166
Brazier, R. Constitutional Practice.
 G. Marshall, 617(TLS):30Jun-6Jul89-707
Brea, L.B. - see under Bernabò Brea, L.
Breazeale, D. - see Fichte, J.G.
Brecher, R. Anselm's Argument.
 P.J.W. Miller, 319:Oct89-612

"The Brecht Yearbook." (Vol 12) (G. Breuer, ed)
J. Bailey, 221(GQ):Fall87-685
Bredero, A.H. Cluny et Cîteaux au douzième siècle.
D.S. Buczek, 589:Apr88-372
Bredin, J-D. The Affair.* (French title: L'Absence.)
V. Caron, 287:Jul/Aug87-30
van Bree, C. Historische Grammatica van het Nederlands.
W. Zonneveld, 204(FdL):Jun88-148
Breen, T.H. Imagining the Past.
P-L. Adams, 61:Aug89-92
D. Walton, 441:13Aug89-17
Breeskin, A. Romaine Brooks.
662:Spring/Summer88-52
Bregenhoj, C. Ṛg Veda as the Key to Folklore.
B. Hansen, 292(JAF):Jul-Sep88-373
Breinig, H. Satire und Roman.
H. Isernhagen, 494:Vol8No3/4-722
Breit, M.E. & R.E. Daggy, eds. Thomas Merton. (new ed)
V.A. Kramer, 534(RALS):Vol16No1&2-229
Breitinger, E. & R. Sander, eds. Drama and Theatre in Africa.
W.F. Feuser, 538(RAL):Fall88-434
Brejon de Lavergnée, B. Musée du Louvre, Cabinet des Dessins, Inventaire général des dessins, École française, Dessins de Simon Vouet 1590-1649.
P. Rosenberg, 380:Winter87-414
Breland, H.M. & others. Assessing Writing Skill.
K.L. Greenberg, 126(CCC):Dec88-478
Brelich, M. The Work of Betrayal.
E. Gillooly, 441:27Aug89-18
Breman, J. Of Peasants, Migrants, and Paupers.
S. Bose, 293(JASt):Nov88-912
Bremer, J. On Plato's Polity.
J.M. Alonso-Núñez, 303(JoHS):Vol108-242
Bremmer, J., ed. Interpretations of Greek Mythology.
N. Marinatos, 121(CJ):Oct-Nov88-67
D. Sider, 124:Nov-Dec88-127
Brenkman, J. Culture and Domination.*
E.S. Clemens, 185:Apr89-658
Brennan, J.F. Enlightened Despotism in Russia.
R.P. Bartlett, 575(SEER):Apr88-290
Brent, R. Liberal Anglican Politics.
J. von Arx, 637(VS):Winter89-278
Brentano, F. Philosophical Investigations on Space, Time and the Continuum. (S. Körner & R. Chisholm, eds)
G. Koehn, 103:Mar89-87
Brentano, F. Über Aristoteles. (R. George, ed)
J. Barnes, 484(PPR):Sep88-162
M. Husain, 41:Vol7-239
Brenton, H. Diving for Pearls.
L. Taylor, 617(TLS):23-29Jun89-695
Brereton, J., ed. Traditions of Inquiry.
D.R. Russell, 128(CE):Apr88-437
Breslauer, B.H. The Uses of Bookbinding Literature.
P.S. Koda, 87(BB):Mar88-66
Breslin, J. Table Money.
G. Davenport, 569(SR):Fall88-695

Breslin, J.B., ed. The Substance of Things Hoped For.
P. La Salle, 573(SSF):Winter88-86
Breslin, J.E.B. — see Williams, W.C.
Breslin, P. The Psycho-Political Muse.
H. Fromm, 491:Jul88-229
639(VQR):Autumn88-120
Bresnan, J., ed. Crisis in the Philippines.
R.E. Welch, Jr., 529(QQ):Spring88-211
Bresson, D. & others. Zur gesprochenen deutschen Umgangssprache I.
M. Durrell, 685(ZDL):2/1988-204
Breton, A. Mad Love (L'amour fou).*
P. Powrie, 402(MLR):Jan89-183
Breton, S. Poétique du sensible.
P. Somville, 542:Oct-Dec88-514
Breton, S. Rien ou quelque chose.*
M. Adam, 542:Jan-Mar88-117
Bretonneau, G. L'exigence des valeurs chez Louis Lavelle.
A. Reix, 542:Jul-Sep88-359
Brett, S. Mrs. Presumed Dead.
M. Stasio, 441:16Apr89-31
Brett, S. A Series of Murders.
T.J. Binyon, 617(TLS):28Apr-4May89-470
M. Stasio, 441:8Oct89-20
Bretz, M.L., T. Dvorak & C. Kirschner. Pasajes: Lengua. Pasajes: Literatura. Pasajes: Actividades. Pasajes: Cultura. (each is 2nd ed)
M.J. Treacy, 399(MLJ):Spring88-103
Bretzigheimer, G. Johann Elias Schlegels poetische Theorie im Rahmen der Tradition.
K.F. Hilliard, 83:Autumn88-243
J.A. Kowalik, 221(GQ):Spring88-304
Breuer, G. — see "The Brecht Yearbook."
Breuer, R. Literatur.
J.H. Petersen, 52:Band23Heft1-91
M. Pfister, 38:Band106Heft1/2-272
Brewer, D. An Introduction to Chaucer.*
G.H.V. Bunt, 179(ES):Spring88-103
Brewer, J. The Common People and Politics 1750-1790s.* (M. Duffy, ed)
J.E. Hill, 173(ECS):Summer88-530
Brewer, J. The Sinews of Power.
J. Cannon, 617(TLS):25-31Aug89-926
D. Simpson, 441:6Aug89-19
Brewer, J. After Soweto.
T. Couzens, 538(RAL):Winter88-576
Brewer, J.D., ed. Can South Africa Survive?
G.M. Fredrickson, 453(NYRB):26Oct89-48
S. Uys, 617(TLS):25-31Aug89-915
Brewer, R.J. Corpus of Sculpture of the Roman World: Great Britain; Wales.
M.A.R. Colledge, 123:Vol38No1-182
Brewster, E. Selected Poems of Elizabeth Brewster.
P. Keeney, 102(CanL):Autumn88-150
Brewster, E. Visitations.*
B. Pell, 102(CanL):Autumn88-169
K. Tudor, 198:Winter88-103
Breymayer, R. — see Hölderlin, F.
Breytenbach, B. Memory of Snow and of Dust.
W. Kendrick, 441:22Oct89-9
Brian, D., ed. The True Gen.*
W.J. Stuckey, 395(MFS):Winter88-621
42(AR):Winter88-122
Brians, P. Nuclear Holocausts.
J. Dewey, 395(MFS):Summer88-322
Briant, P. Rois, tributs et paysans.
J. Wiesehöfer, 229:Band60Heft1-33

Briceland, A.V. Westward from Virginia.
W.M. Billings, 656(WMQ):Apr88–372
Brick, H. Daniel Bell and the Decline of In-
tellectual Radicalism.*
F. Matthews, 106:Spring88–69
Brickell, C., ed-in-chief. The American Hor-
ticultural Society Encyclopedia of Garden
Plants.
L. Yang, 441:3Dec89–74
Brickhouse, T.C. & N.D. Smith. Socrates on
Trial.
G. Vlastos, 617(TLS):15–21Dec89–1393
Bridge, C. Holding India to the Empire.
W.W. Reinhardt, 293(JASt):May88–392
Bridges, B. Korea and the West.
Y.W. Kihl, 293(JASt):Aug88–668
Bridges, H. & T.C. Boodman. Gone With the
Wind.
D. Finkle, 441:10Dec89–7
Bridges, H. & T.C. Boodman – see Howard, S.
Bridges, M.E. Generic Contrast in Old English
Hagiographical Poetry.*
R.D. Fulk, 481(PQ):Spring88–270
D.G. Scragg, 38:Band106Heft3/4–484
Bridgman, R. Traveling in Mark Twain.*
L.J. Budd, 26(ALR):Fall88–72
J.D. Wilson, 27(AL):May88–298
Bridgwater, P. The German Poets of the First
World War.*
R.E. Lorbe, 301(JEGP):Jan88–90
Bridgwater, P. George Moore and German
Pessimism.
D.B. Eakin, 177(ELT):Vol31No4–471
Bridgwater, P. Arthur Schopenhauer's En-
glish Schooling.
H. Reiss, 402(MLR):Oct89–1032
Bridson, G. & G. Wakeman. Printmaking &
Picture Printing.
P.S. Koda, 87(BB):Mar88–67
Briegleb, K. Opfer Heine?
G.F. Peters, 221(GQ):Fall87–679
Briels, J. Vlaamse schilders in de Noordelijke
Nederlanden in het begin van de gouden
eeuw, 1585–1630.
B. Haak, 600:Vol18No4–262
Brien, K.M. Marx, Reason, and the Art of
Freedom.*
M. Nissim-Sabat, 185:Apr89–647
Brienza, S.D. Samuel Beckett's New Worlds.
M.P. Gillespie, 594:Spring88–100
J.R. Moore, 573(SSF):Spring88–168
J. Reinelt, 223:Summer88–231
F.N. Smith, 395(MFS):Winter88–719
Briers, R. Coward & Company.
S. Morley, 157:No168–47
Brigantini, I. & M. de Vos, eds. Le decora-
zioni della villa romana della Farnesina.
P.H. von Blanckenhagen, 229:Band60
Heft4–356
Briggs, C.L. Learning How to Ask.
P. Nusbaum, 292(JAF):Jan–Mar88–75
A.E. Shuman, 650(WF):Jan88–68
Briggs, R. Communities of Belief.
J.K. Powis, 617(TLS):5–11May89–491
Briggs, W.W., Jr. – see Gildersleeve, B.L.
Brijder, H.A.G., A.A. Drukker & C.W. Neeft,
eds. Enthusiasmos.
E. Moignard, 123:Vol38No1–178
Brill, L. The Hitchcock Romance.
D. Coward, 617(TLS):15–21Dec89–1387
Brimelow, P. The Patriot Game.*
R. Collins, 488:Jun88–239
Brindle, R.S. – see under Smith Brindle, R.

Bringhurst, R. Pieces of Map, Pieces of
Music.*
S. Pugmire, 649(WAL):May88–88
Brink, A. States of Emergency.
J. Mellors, 364:Jul88–105
Brink, C.O. English Classical Scholarship.*
J-P. Levet, 555:Vol61fasc2–321
Brinker-Gabler, G., K. Ludwig & A. Wöffen.
Lexikon deutschsprachiger Schriftsteller-
innen: 1800–1945.
R. Tenberg, 439(NM):1988/1–110
Brinkley, D. Washington Goes to War.*
C. Thorne, 617(TLS):7–13Apr89–371
Brinkley, J. The Circus Master's Mission.
D. Traxel, 441:2Jul89–10
Brinkley, R. Richard Brinkley's Theory of
Sentential Reference. (M.J. Fitzgerald, ed
& trans)
G. Nuchelmans, 640:Nov88–153
Brinkmann, K. Aristoteles' allgemeine und
spezielle Metaphysik.
T. Bole, 303(JoHS):Vol108–241
Brinkmann to Broxten, E. Stadtsprache –
Stadtmundart.
J. Herrgen, 685(ZDL):2/1988–225
G. Lerchner, 682(ZPSK):Band41Heft4–545
Brinkmeyer, R.H., Jr. Three Catholic Writers
of the Modern South.*
E. Gregory, 396(ModA):Fall89–375
Brint, S. & J. Karabel. The Diverted Dream.
G. Mantsios, 441:24Dec89–17
Briscoe, J. – see Livy
Briskin, J. The Naked Heart.
S. Paulos, 441:20Aug89–2Q
Brisson, L. – see Plato
Bristol, M.D. Carnival and Theater.*
D. Freake, 627(UTQ):Fall87–108
N.C. Liebler, 702:Vol20–288
M. Pfister, 156(ShJW):Jahrbuch1988–235
Britnell, J. Jean Bouchet.*
E. Armstrong, 535(RHL):Nov–Dec88–1134
C.J. Brown, 207(FR):Dec88–324
I.D. McFarlane, 551(RenQ):Autumn88–491
M. Simonin, 210(FrF):May88–243
de Brito, M.C. Opera in Portugal in the Eigh-
teenth Century.
M. Robinson, 617(TLS):8–14Sep89–985
Britt, S. Long Tall Dexter.
F. Davis, 617(TLS):22–28Sep89–1032
Brittan, G. Kant's Theory of Science.
J.M. Young, 342:Band79Heft1–92
Britton, C. Claude Simon.
J.T. Booker, 207(FR):Feb89–536
J.H. Duffy, 402(MLR):Jul89–745
D.Y. Kadish, 268(IFR):Winter89–79
42(AR):Summer88–398
Britton, F. London Delftware.
I.L., 90:Jun88–476
A. Ray, 39:May88–372
Brivic, S. Joyce the Creator.*
R.A. Cave, 541(RES):May88–321
P. Parrinder, 402(MLR):Jan89–141
Briz, A. & M. Prunyonosa. Sintaxi i semàntica
de l'article.
C. Fuentes Rodríguez, 548:Jul–Dec88–442
Broadie, A. Introduction to Medieval Logic.*
E.J. Ashworth, 640:Nov88–141
S. Read, 518:Jan88–22
J.A. Trentman, 103:Apr89–138
Brock, W.R. Welfare, Democracy, and the New
Deal.
D. Montgomery, 617(TLS):21–27Jul89–
795

Brock-Broido, L. A Hunger.
 H. Vendler, 442(NY):7Aug89-93
Brockett, C.D. Land, Power, and Poverty.
 J. Saunders, 263(RIB):Vol38No4-533
Brockington, J.L. Righteous Rāma.
 B. von Nooten, 318(JAOS):Jan-Mar87-197
 S.J.M. Sutherland, 293(JASt):May88-396
Brockington, J.L. Vier Pole expression-
istischer Prosa.
 R. Furness, 402(MLR):Jul89-803
Brodbeck-Jucker, S. Mykenische Funde von
Kephallenia im archäologischen Museum
Neuchâtel.
 H. Gallet de Santerre, 555:Vol61fasc1-111
Brodeur, H. Chroniques du Nouvel-Ontario.
 M. Benson, 102(CanL):Winter87-251
Brodey, V., ed. Las Coplas de Mingo Revulgo.*
 J.R. Rank, 240(HR):Winter88-98
Brodhead, R.H. The School of Hawthorne.*
 N. Bradbury, 541(RES):Nov88-567
 M. Lopez, 115:Spring88-197
 T. Martin, 27(AL):Dec88-666
Brodkey, H. The Abundant Dreamer.
 W. Steiner, 617(TLS):3-9Nov89-1217
Brodman, J.W. Ransoming Captives in Cru-
sader Spain.
 J.C. Shideler, 589:Jan88-128
Brodsky, C.J. The Imposition of Form.
 M.P. Ginsburg, 446(NCFS):Fall-Winter
88/89-249
 S.G. Kellman, 395(MFS):Winter88-743
Brodsky, J. Less Than One.*
 G.S. Smith, 575(SEER):Apr88-282
 L. Toker, 577(SHR):Winter88-65
Brodsky, J. Poèmes 1961-1987.
 J. Blot, 450(NRF):Jul-Aug88-222
Brodsky, J. To Urania.*
 B. Howard, 491:Nov88-106
 S. O'Brien, 364:Feb/Mar89-107
 G. Szirtes, 493:Winter88/89-40
Brodsky, L.D. & R.W. Hamblin, eds. Faulkner.*
(Vol 4)
 C S Brown, 569(SR):Spring00-271
Brodsky, M. Dyad.
 P. West, 441:24Dec89-8
Brodsky, M. X in Paris.
 A. Gelb, 441:12Feb89-18
Brodsky, P.P. Rainer Maria Rilke.
 M. Jacobs, 402(MLR):Jul89-800
Brody, J. "Fate" in Oedipus Tyrannus.*
 A. Giorgi-Chevrel, 549(RLC):Jul-Sep88-418
 D.H. Roberts, 124:Sep-Oct88-68
de Broer, W. & D. Kopp, eds. Grabbe im Drit-
ten Reich.
 R.C. Cowen, 406:Fall88-398
 G.R. Cuomo, 221(GQ):Fall88-599
Broerman, B.M. The German Historical Novel
in Exile after 1933.*
 G. Brude-Firnau, 564:Feb88-91
 M. Goth, 221(GQ):Winter88-109
 R. Kieser, 406:Winter88-527
 W. Paulsen, 133:Band21Heft2/3-253
Brogan, J.V. Stevens and Simile.*
 J. Applewhite, 569(SR):Winter88-121
 R.W.B., 295(JML):Fall87/Winter88-386
 M. Dickie, 677(YES):Vol19-365
 P. McDonald, 541(RES):Aug88-461
 M. Perloff, 405(MP):Nov88-217
 R.I. Scott, 106:Summer88-266

de Broglie, G. Le Français, pour qu'il vive.*
 D. Nott, 402(MLR):Jan89-150
Brogyanyi, B. & T. Krömmelbein, eds. Ger-
manic Dialects.*
 F. van Coetsem, 133:Band21Heft4-382
Broido, V. Lenin and the Mensheviks.
 S.F. Jones, 575(SEER):Jul88-498
Brokoph-Mauch, G. Robert Musils "Nachlass
zu Lebzeiten."
 E. Geyer, 680(ZDP):Band107Heft4-632
Brombert, V. The Hidden Reader.*
 C. Smethurst, 617(TLS):17-23Feb89-173
Brombert, V. Victor Hugo and the Visionary
Novel.* (French title: Victor Hugo et le
roman visionnaire.)
 S. Noakes, 591(SIR):Winter88-617
Bromiley, G.N. Thomas's Tristan and the
Folie Tristan d'Oxford.
 R. Pensom, 402(MLR):Apr89-462
Brommer, F. Der Parthenonfries.
 M. Gisler, 229:Band60Heft2-178
Brommer, P., ed. Capitula episcoporum. (Vol
1) "Capitula episcoporum."
 U-R. Blumenthal, 589:Apr88-374
Bromwich, R. Aspects of the Poetry of Dafydd
ap Gwilym.
 A.H. Diverres, 545(RPh):Nov88-246
 N. Jacobs, 382(MAE):1988/1-124
Bronner, E. Battle for Justice.
 G. Wills, 441:10Sep89-7
Bronner, E.B. & D. Fraser. William Penn's
Published Writings 1660-1726.
 D.J. Hall, 354:Mar88-71
Bronner, S.E. & D. Kellner, eds. Passion and
Rebellion.
 J. Joll, 453(NYRB):27Apr89-53
 L. Krukowski, 103:Sep89-349
Bronner, S.J. American Folklore Studies.
 C.H. Carpenter, 292(JAF):Jan-Mar88-76
 B. Vorpagel, 650(WF):Jan88-66
Bronner, S.J. Grasping Things.*
 J.D. Dorst, 658:Spring88-97
 B. Mergen, 292(JAF):Jan-Mar88-95
Bronner, S.J. Old-Time Music Makers of New
York State.
 M. Collins, 440:Winter-Spring88-150
Brönnimann-Egger, W. – see Shakespeare, W.
Bronson, B.H. & J.M. O'Meara – see Johnson,
S.
Brontë, C. An Edition of the Early Writings of
Charlotte Brontë.* (Vol 1) (C. Alexander,
ed)
 G.B. Tennyson, 445(NCF):Sep88-274
Brontë, C. The Poems of Charlotte Brontë.*
(V.A. Neufeldt, ed)
 G.B. Tennyson, 445(NCF):Sep88-274
Brontë, C. The Professor. (M. Smith & H.
Rosengarten, eds)
 D. Mehl, 72:Band225Heft2-404
 M. Slater, 175:Summer88-169
Brook, M., ed. Bibliography of British News-
papers: Nottinghamshire.
 P. Hoare, 635(VPR):Fall88-121
Brook, P. The Shifting Point.*
 G. Martin, 465:Spring89-112
Brook, S. The Club.
 R. Klein, 617(TLS):21-27Apr89-421
Brooke, C. The Medieval Idea of Marriage.
 R.M. Smith, 617(TLS):22-28Sep89-1037
Brooke, C. & R. Highfield. Oxford and Cam-
bridge.*
 G. Cavaliero, 324:Dec88-59

Brooke, C.N.L. A History of Gonville and Caius College.
  N. Orme, 551(RenQ):Summer88-335
Brookeman, C. American Culture and Society Since the 1930s.
  B. Michelson, 677(YES):Vol19-358
Brooker, P. Bertolt Brecht.
  A.D. White, 402(MLR):Jan89-258
Brookfield, A. Alice Alone.
  J. Grant, 617(TLS):24Feb-2Mar89-190
Brookner, A. A Friend from England.*
  A. Bloom, 249(HudR):Autumn88-544
Brookner, A. Latecomers.*
  R. Dinnage, 453(NYRB):1Jun89-34
  D. Leavitt, 441:2Apr89-3
  J. Updike, 442(NY):1May89-111
Brookner, A. The Misalliance.* (British title: A Misalliance.)
  P. Iyer, 473(PR):Vol55No4-692
Brookner, A. Lewis Percy.
  J. Symons, 617(TLS):25-31Aug89-917
Brooks, A.A. Children of Fast-Track Parents.
  R. Atkins, 441:26Nov89-26
Brooks, C. The Language of the American South.*
  J.L. Dillard, 35(AS):Winter88-376
Brooks, C. On the Prejudices, Predilections, and Firm Beliefs of William Faulkner.
  A.F. Kinney, 587(SAF):Autumn88-251
Brooks, E. Riding High.
  J. Cohen, 441:17Dec89-19
Brooks, H.F. T.S. Eliot as Literary Critic.
  K. Smidt, 179(ES):Dec88-534
Brooks, H.F., with R. Selden - see Oldham, J.
Brooks, M.W. John Ruskin and Victorian Architecture.
  M. Bright, 445(NCF):Sep88-259
  K.O. Garrigan, 637(VS):Autumn88-142
  N. Jackson, 576:Dec88-419
  P.F. Morgan, 635(VPR):Winter88-162
Brooks, P. Two Park Street.*
  G. Garrett, 569(SR):Summer88-516
Brooks, P., S. Felman & J.H. Miller, eds. The Lesson of Paul de Man.
  C. Norris, 506(PSt):May88-89
Brooks, W. - see Poinsinet de Sivry, L.
Brooks-Davies, D. Pope's "Dunciad" and the Queen of the Night.*
  V. Carretta, 536(Rev):Vol10-267
Brookshaw, D. Race and Color in Brazilian Literature.
  D. Treece, 86(BHS):Jan88-110
Broonzy, W.L.C. & Y. Bruynoghe. Big Bill Blues.
  G. Goffette, 450(NRF):Feb88-107
Brophy, E.B. Samuel Richardson.
  J.I. Schwarz, 166:Apr89-252
Brossard, C. Postcards.
  S. Moore, 532(RCF):Fall88-170
Brossard, N. The Aerial Letter.
  A. Parker, 618:Fall88-104
Brossard, N. French Kiss; or, A Pang's Progress.
  J. Williamson, 168(ECW):Spring88-75
Brossard, N. Sous La Langue/Under Tongue. Lovhers.
  S. Scobie, 376:Mar88-95
Broude, N. The Macchiaioli.*
  D. Stewart, 324:Feb89-185
Broudy, H.S. The Role of Imagery in Learning.
  R. Arnheim, 289:Summer88-113
Broué, P. Trotsky.
  A. Nove, 617(TLS):10-16Mar89-246

Broughton, T.A. Preparing to Be Happy.
  P. Filkins, 363(LitR):Winter89-241
Broughton, T.R.S. The Magistrates of the Roman Republic.* (Vol 3)
  J. Briscoe, 313:Vol78-268
  T.J. Cadoux, 123:Vol38No2-314
  R.E.A. Palmer, 24:Winter88-609
Brouwers, J. Sunken Red.
  M. Wolf, 441:26Feb89-34
Brovkin, V.N. The Mensheviks after October.
  639(VQR):Summer88-84
Browder, C. The Wickedest Woman in New York.*
  R. Porter, 617(TLS):13-19Jan89-39
Brower, K. A Song for Satawal.
  S. Pickering, 569(SR):Fall88-673
Brown, A. - see Sophocles
Brown, A.C. - see Cave Brown, A.
Brown, A.L. The Governance of Late Medieval England 1272-1461.
  N. Saul, 617(TLS):1-7Dec89-1343
Brown, A.P. Joseph Haydn's Keyboard Music.* Performing Haydn's "The Creation."*
  S.C. Fisher, 173(ECS):Fall88-120
Brown, C. A Year Inside.
  M. Trend, 617(TLS):30Jun-6Jul89-727
Brown, C. - see Mandelstam, O.
Brown, C. & J.A. Pechman, eds. Gender in the Workplace.
  M.C.B., 185:Oct88-207
Brown, C.B. Clara Howard; in a Series of Letters [and] Jane Talbot, a Novel. (S.J. Krause, general ed)
  D. Berthold, 534(RALS):Vol16No1&2-76
Brown, C.J. The Shaping of History and Poetry in Late Medieval France.*
  A. Moss, 208(FS):Apr88-200
Brown, C.S. Music & Literature.
  F. Claudon, 549(RLC):Jan-Mar88-87
  R. Miles, 569(SR):Summer88-lxi
Brown, C.S. The Tall Tale in American Folklore and Literature.
  D.R. Sewell, 27(AL):May88-297
Brown, C.S. - see Clark, S.
Brown, D. Continental Philosophy and Modern Theology.
  F.J.C., 185:Jul89-992
Brown, D. Day of the Cheetah.
  N. Callendar, 441:17Sep89-30
Brown, E.G., with D. Adler. Public Justice, Private Mercy.
  A. Lewis, 441:20Aug89-7
Brown, G.M. The Golden Bird.
  B. Dickson, 571(ScLJ):Spring88-63
  P. Lewis, 565:Spring88-35
Brown, G.M. The Masked Fisherman and Other Stories.
  D. Profumo, 617(TLS):30Jun-6Jul89-714
Brown, G.M. - see Muir, E.
Brown, H.D. Principles of Language Learning and Teaching. (2nd ed)
  M.E. Call, 399(MLJ):Spring88-69
Brown, H.I. Observation and Objectivity.
  N. Everitt, 518:Jul88-148
  P.K. Moser, 84:Dec88-551
Brown, H.I. Rationality.
  G. Gutting, 103:Dec88-467
Brown, H.P. Egalitarianism and the Generation of Inequality.
  B. Barry, 617(TLS):20-26Jan89-51
Brown, I.G., ed. Scott's Interleaved Waverley Novels.*
  J. Rubenstein, 571(ScLJ):Winter88-7

Bruce, D. Sudden Hunger.
G. Kuzma, 496:Winter88/89–49
Bruce, G. Perspectives.
R. Crawford, 571(ScLJ):Spring88–39
Bruce, R.V. The Launching of Modern Amer-
ican Science, 1846–1876.
A.H. Dupree, 432(NEQ):Jun88–269
Bruce, S. The Rise and Fall of the New Chris-
tian Right.
M. Ruthven, 617(TLS):9–15Jun89–629
Bruckberger, R-L. Bernanos vivant.
J-C. Polet, 356(LR):Nov88–534
Brucker, C. Sage et sagesse au moyen âge
(XIIe et XIIIe siècles).
P. Rickard, 208(FS):Apr88–244
Brucker, G. Giovanni and Lusanna.*
P.A. McCoy, 568(SCN):Spring–Summer88–
21
E.B. Welles, 276:Autumn88–264
Brückner, T. Die erste französische Aeneis.
A. Vermeylen, 356(LR):Feb–May88–119
Brückner, W., P. Blickle & D. Breuer, eds.
Literatur und Volk im 17. Jahrhundert.
H. Langer, 654(WB):5/1988–865
Brügmann, M. Amazonen der Literatur.*
K.L. Komar, 221(GQ):Spring88–330
Bruijn, J.R. & others. Dutch-Asiatic Shipping
in the Seventeenth and Eighteenth Centu-
ries. (Vol 1)
J.E. Wills, Jr., 293(JASt):Aug88–567
Brulé, G. – see under Gace Brulé
Brulez, W. Cultuur en getal.
M.J. Bok, 600:Vol18No1/2–63
Brülisauer, B. Moral und Konvention.
P. Trotignon, 542:Oct–Dec88–496
Brulotte, G. Ce qui nous tient.
C.D. Fisher, 207(FR):May89–1089
Brumberg, J.J. Fasting Girls.*
M. Warner, 617(TLS):21–27Apr89–420
Brun, V. & T. Schumacher. Traditional Herbal
Medicine in Northern Thailand.
L. Golomb, 293(JASt):Aug88–693
Brundage, J.A. Law, Sex and Christian Socie-
ty in Medieval Europe.*
J. Shatzmiller, 627(UTQ):Summer89–546
Brundell, B. Pierre Gassendi.
S. Gaukroger, 63:Jun88–275
L.S. Joy, 319:Jul89–476
R.H. Popkin, 103:Oct89–396
Bruneau, M-F. Racine le jansénisme et la
modernité.*
B. Chedozeau, 535(RHL):Jul–Aug88–764
Brunel, G. Boucher.*
P. Conisbee, 39:Apr88–296
A. Laing, 90:Jul88–541
Brunelin, A. Gabin.
D. Coward, 617(TLS):20–26Jan89–68
Bruner, J. Actual Minds, Possible Worlds.
C. Kneupper, 126(CCC):Feb88–93
B.M., 494:Vol8No2–452
B. Sutton-Smith, 355(LSoc):Jun88–298
Bruni, L. Leonardo Bruni, traduttore di De-
mostene: la "Pro Ctesiphonte." (M. Accame
Lanzillotta, ed)
M.C. Davies, 123:Vol38No1–131
Bruni, L. The Humanism of Leonardo Bruni.
L.V.R., 568(SCN):Spring–Summer88–34
Bruni, S. I lastroni a scala.
S. Weber & S. Steingräber, 229:Band60
Heft8–742
Brüning, E., ed. 1935 New York 1937.*
D. Pike, 400(MLN):Apr88–704
Brunner, F. & others – see Meister Eckhart

Brunner, L. Tragic Victory.*
M.H. Thuente, 177(ELT):Vol31No2–220
"Brünner Beiträge zur Germanistik und Nord-
istik." (Vol 3)
N.R. Wolf, 685(ZDL):3/1987–370
Bruns-Özgan, C. Lykische Grabreliefs des 5.
und 4. Jahrhunderts v. Chr.
J. Borchhardt, 229:Band60Heft6–556
Brunvand, J.H. The Mexican Pet.*
R. McGillivray, 650(WF):Jan88–69
Brusatin, M. Histoire des couleurs.*
F. de Mèredieu, 450(NRF):Mar88–93
Bruscagli, R., ed. Trionfi e canti carnascia-
leschi del Rinascimento.
M. Pozzi, 228(GSLI):Vol165fasc532–605
Brusselback, H. Los Clavos.
G. Gessert, 448:Vol26No3–85
Bruter, C.P. De l'intuition à la controverse.
M. Espinoza, 542:Jul–Sep88–375
Bruter, C-P. Topologie et perception.*
M. Espinoza, 192(EP):Apr–Jun88–266
de Bruyne, P. & others. La justice sociale en
question?
F. Giroux, 103:Mar89–92
Bruyninx, E. L'art du Laiton chez les Dan et
Guere-Wobe.
2(AfrA):Feb88–93
Bruzelius, C.A. The Thirteenth-Century
Church at St.–Denis.*
C.F. Barnes, Jr., 576:Mar88–80
Bryan, S. Objects of Affection.
P. Breslin, 491:Oct88–30
Bryant, J., ed. A Companion to Melville
Studies.*
R. Milder, 534(RALS):Vol16No1&2–99
Bryant, J.A., Jr. Shakespeare and the Uses of
Comedy.*
W.M. Jones, 130:Fall88–276
N. Sanders, 570(SQ):Spring88–98
Bryant, J.A., Jr. Understanding Randall Jar-
rell.
M.K. Spears, 569(SR):Winter88–95
Bryce, T.R. The Lycians in Literary and Epi-
graphic Sources.
P. Frei, 229:Band60Heft8–720
Bryden, R. & B. Neil – see Whittaker, H.
Bryer, A. & D. Winfield. The Byzantine Monu-
ments and Topography of the Pontos.
C. Foss, 589:Apr88–377
Bryer, J.R., ed. Conversations with Lillian
Hellman.*
J.F. Desmond, 392:Fall88–553
V.A. Kramer, 392:Spring88–197
Brykman, G. – see Berkeley, G.
Brynner, R. Yul.
B. Shulgasser, 441:12Nov89–59
Bryson, B. The Lost Continent.
M. Slung, 441:17Sep89–26
Bryson, K. Flowers and Death.
M. Brannigan, 103:Dec88–469
Bryson, N., ed. Calligram.
M. Berger, 62:Dec88–109
R. Snell, 617(TLS):6–12Jan89–17
Brzezinski, Z. The Grand Failure.
G.W. Lapidus, 441:26Mar89–10
A.G. Meyer, 385(MQR):Fall89–771
Buache, F. Le Cinéma français des années
soixante.
J. Anzalone, 207(FR):May89–1086
Buber-Neumann, M. Milena.*
J. Adler, 617(TLS):16–22Jun89–661

Bullivant, K., ed. The Modern German Novel.
  K.S. Parkes, 402(MLR):Jan89-263
Bullivant, K. Realism Today.
  K.S. Parkes, 402(MLR):Jan89-263
Bulloch, A.W., ed. Callimachus, "The Fifth
  Hymn."*
  A. Griffiths, 303(JoHS):Vol108-230
  W.H. Mineur, 394:Vol41fasc1/2-175
Bullock, A., ed. Domenico Tordi e il carteggio
  colonnese della Biblioteca Nazionale di
  Firenze.
  G. Rabitti, 402(MLR):Apr89-490
Bulman, J.C. The Heroic Idiom of Shake-
  spearean Tragedy.*
  A.F. Kinney, 250(HLQ):Autumn88-325
Bultot, R. & G. Hasenohr – see Crapillet, P.
Bulygin, E., J-L. Gardies & I. Niiniluoto, eds.
  Man, Law and Modern Forms of Life.
  L. Green, 488:Mar88-107
Bumke, J. Höfische Kultur.
  H. Heinen, 301(JEGP):Apr88-291
  W.H. Jackson, 589:Oct88-907
Bumsted, J.M. Land, Settlement, and Politics
  on Eighteenth-Century Prince Edward Is-
  land.* The People's Clearance.
  N.E.S. Griffiths, 656(WMQ):Jul88-603
Bundy, E.L. Studia Pindarica.
  D.E. Gerber, 24:Summer88-252
Bundy, M. Danger and Survival.*
  S. Hoffmann, 453(NYRB):2Feb89-28
Bungay, S. Beauty and Truth.*
  R. Wicks, 482(PhR):Apr88-281
Bunge, H. – see Berlau, R.
Bunge, M. Das Leib-Seele-Problem.
  R. Blutner, 682(ZPSK):Band41Heft3-393
Bunge, N. Finding the Words.
  P. Stitt, 534(RALS):Vol16No1&2-271
Bunim, A. A Fire in His Soul.
  S. Steinmetz, 441:31Dec89-13
Bunn, T. Worse Than Death.
  M. Stasio, 441:8Oct89-20
Bunt, H.C. Mass Terms and Model-Theoretic
  Semantics.*
  P. Bricker, 316:Jun88-653
Bunting, B. & M.H. Floyd. Harvard.
  D.P. Myers, 576:Sep88-310
Bunyan, J. The Miscellaneous Works of John
  Bunyan.* (Vol 3) (J.S. McGee, ed)
  N.H. Keeble, 447(N&Q):Sep88-374
  N. Smith, 541(RES):Nov88-553
Bunyan, J. The Miscellaneous Works of John
  Bunyan.* (Vol 5) (G. Midgley, ed)
  M. Hardman, 677(YES):Vol19-323
  N.H. Keeble, 447(N&Q):Jun88-233
  T.H. Luxon, 405(MP):Nov88-205
  N. Smith, 541(RES):Nov88-553
Bunyan, J. The Miscellaneous Works of John
  Bunyan.* (Vol 11) (R.L. Greaves, ed)
  [shown in prev under subtitle: Good News
  for the Vilest of Men; The Advocateship of
  Jesus Christ.]
  U.M. Kaufmann, 301(JEGP):Oct88-583
  N.H. Keeble, 447(N&Q):Jun88-233
Bunyard, P. & E. Goldsmith, eds. Gaia.
  S.R.L. Clark, 617(TLS):20-26Oct89-1143
Buonocore, M. Bibliografia dei fondi mano-
  scritti della Biblioteca Vaticana (1968-
  1980).
  H. Walter, 229:Band60Heft6-540
Buora, A.S.B. – see under Scarpa Bonazza
  Buora, A.
Burac, R. – see Péguy, C.

Burbick, J. Thoreau's Alternative History.
  L.N. Neufeldt, 432(NEQ):Jun88-308
  S. Paul, 301(JEGP):Oct88-594
Burchfield, R., ed. The New Zealand Pocket
  Oxford Dictionary.
  C. Balme, 38:Band106Heft3/4-460
Burchfield, R., ed. Studies in Lexicography.
  A. Bammesberger, 447(N&Q):Jun88-199
Burchfield, R.W. – see "The Compact Edition
  of the Oxford English Dictionary"
Burckhardt, J. The Altarpiece in Renaissance
  Italy. (P. Humfrey, ed)
  M. Jaffé, 617(TLS):30Jun-6Jul89-725
Burdick, N.B. Legacy.
  I. Poliski, 441:27Aug89-17
Burford, B. The Threshing Floor.
  G. Wilentz, 459:Spring88-105
Bürgel, J.C., ed & trans. Steppe im Staub-
  korn.
  H. Moayyad, 318(JAOS):Oct-Dec87-805
Burgelin, C., ed. Lectures de Sartre.*
  J. Pacaly, 535(RHL):Jul-Aug88-792
Burger, E.K. – see Joachim of Fiore
Burger, H. Brenner. (Vol 1)
  J. Neves, 617(TLS):13-19Oct89-1129
Burgess, A. Any Old Iron.
  P-L. Adams, 61:Mar89-97
  D. Donoghue, 453(NYRB):30Mar89-35
  S.F. Schaeffer, 441:26Feb89-12
  J. Symons, 617(TLS):7-13Apr89-363
Burgess, A. The Devil's Mode.
  H. Benedict, 441:10Dec89-38
  J. Melmoth, 617(TLS):15-21Dec89-1385
Burgess, A. Flame into Being.*
  M. Bell, 402(MLR):Jan89-146
Burgess, A. Little Wilson and Big God.*
  P. Boytinck, 529(QQ):Summer88-448
  J. Lewis, 364:Mar87-96
Burgess, G.S. The Lais of Marie de France.
  N.J. Lacy, 207(FR):Feb89-515
  R. Pensom, 402(MLR):Apr89-463
Burgess, G.S. Marie de France. (Supp 1)
  H.R. Runte, 207(FR):Apr89-885
Burgess, G.S. & R.A. Taylor, eds. The Spirit
  of the Court.*
  R. Morse, 382(MAE):1988/1-85
Burggraeve, R. & E. Levinas. Une bibliog-
  raphie primaire et secondaire (1929-1985).
  C. Chalier, 192(EP):Oct-Dec88-559
Burgin, R. Man Without Memory.
  S.S. Wells, 441:5Nov89-24
Burgin, V. Between. The End of Art Theory.
  M. Iversen, 59:Mar88-133
  A. Robinson, 402(MLR):Apr89-416
Burgin, V., J. Donald & C. Kaplan, eds. For-
  mations of Fantasy.
  M. Del Sapio, 677(YES):Vol19-362
Burgos, F. La novela moderna hispanoameri-
  cana.*
  P. Swanson, 86(BHS):Oct88-423
Burgos, F., ed. Los ochenta mundos de Cortá-
  zar.
  J. Roy, 263(RIB):Vol38No4-532
Burgos, F., ed. Prosa hispánica de vanguar-
  dia.
  W.H. Corral, 552(REH):Oct88-134
Burgoyne, M.H. Mamluk Jerusalem.*
  J. Folda, 576:Sep88-319
Burguière, P. & P. Évieux – see Saint Cyril of
  Alexandria
Burian, P., ed. Directions in Euripidean Crit-
  icism.
  P. Demont, 555:Vol61fasc2-308

Burian, P. – see Else, G.F.
Buridant, C., ed. La Lexicographie au Moyen
Age.
  R. Blumenfeld-Kosinski, 589.Oct88–909
  P. Rickard, 208(FS):Jul88–372
Buridant, C., ed. La traduction de l'"Historia
Orientalis" de Jacques de Vitry.*
  P.S. Noble, 382(MAE):1988/1–131
  J.G. Rowe, 589:Jan88–130
Burk, K. Britain, America and the Sinews of
War, 1914–1918.
  F.M. Carroll, 106:Summer88–211
Burkard, M. Fictions from the Self.
  R. McDowell, 249(HudR):Autumn88–568
Burke, B. I Want to Take Picture.
  G. Gessert, 448:Vol26No1–74
Burke, D. Street French.
  Y. de la Quérière, 207(FR):Oct88–205
  T. Scanlan, 399(MLJ):Autumn88–352
Burke, J.L. Black Cherry Blues.
  M. Stasio, 441:8Oct89–20
Burke, J.L. Heaven's Prisoners.*
  639(VQR):Summer88–93
Burke, K. & M. Cowley. The Selected Corres-
pondence of Kenneth Burke and Malcolm
Cowley, 1915–1981. (P. Jay, ed)
  442(NY):27Mar89–116
Burke, P. & R. Porter, eds. The Social History
of Language.
  H. Kahane, 350:Jun89–419
  V.K. Kiernan, 366:Autumn88–222
Burkert, W. Ancient Mystery Cults.
  R. Beck, 487:Autumn88–266
  M. Colakis, 124:Jul–Aug89–447
  S. Goldhill, 617(TLS):30Jun–6Jul89–723
  H.A. Pohlsander, 121(CJ):Dec88–Jan89–
167
Burkhardt, M. & E. Waldstein – see "Women in
German Yearbook"
Burkhardt, A. & K-H. Körner, eds. Pragman-
tax.
  B.J. Koekkoek, 221(GQ):Fall87–653
Burkhardt, F. & S. Smith – see Darwin, C.
Burkhardt, F.H. & F. Bowers – see James, W.
Burkhardt, F.H., F. Bowers & I.K. Skrupskelis
– see James, W.
Burkhart, K. From Under the 8-Ball.
  G. Gessert, 448:Vol26No2–124
Burkholder, R.E. & J. Myerson. Emerson.^
  L. Buell, 534(RALS):Vol16No1&2–84
Burkholtz, H. Strange Bedfellows.
  639(VQR):Autumn88–128
Burkman, K.H. The Arrival of Godot.*
  J.W. Flannery, 615(TJ):Dec87–542
Burkman, K.H., ed. Myth and Ritual in the
Plays of Samuel Beckett.
  J. Schlueter, 130:Winter88/89–376
Burlingham, M.J. The Last Tiffany.
  N. Bliven, 442(NY):31Jul89–82
  R. Scheier, 441:27Aug89–17
Burman, P. St. Paul's Cathedral.
  N.C., 90:Oct88–784
Burn, M. Mary and Richard.*
  A. Ross, 364:Jun88–106
Burnard, B., ed. The Old Dance.
  M. Junyk, 529(QQ):Summer88–450
Burnett, D. Harold Town.
  L. Dompierre, 627(UTQ):Fall88–207
Burnett, J., D. Vincent & D. Mayall. The
Autobiography of the Working Class. (Vol
2)
  P.S. Bagwell, 366:Spring88–129

Burnett, V. Farewell Tour.
  K. Wilson, 102(CanL):Autumn88–182
Burney, C. Memoirs of Dr. Charles Burney:
1726–1769.* (S. Klima, G. Bowers & K.S.
Grant, eds)
  M.S. Cole, 465:Summer89–90
Burney, F. Cecilia, or Memoirs of an Heiress.*
  P. Sabor, 402(MLR):Oct89–933
  H. Wilcox, 83:Autumn88–227
Burney, F. Selected Letters and Journals. (J.
Hemlow, ed)
  I. Grundy, 447(N&Q):Mar88–101
  H. Wilcox, 83:Autumn88–227
Burnheim, J. Is Democracy Possible?
  P. Pettit, 63:Mar88–105
Burns, C. About the Body.
  D. Durrant, 364:Dec88/Jan89–136
Burns, C. The Flint Bed.
  L. Doughty, 617(TLS):21–27Jul89–804
Burns, E. Restoration Comedy.*
  R.A. Zimbardo, 566:Autumn88–71
Burns, E. – see Stein, G. & C. Van Vechten
Burns, E.J. Arthurian Fictions.*
  A. Leupin, 131(CL):Spring88–177
Burns, G. The Sports Pages.
  J. Gindin, 385(MQR):Spring89–283
Burns, G., with D. Fisher. All My Best
Friends.
  D. Nasaw, 441:5Nov89–13
Burns, J. Beyond the Silver River.
  R. Wright, 617(TLS):14–20Jul89–776
Burns, J. Out of the Past.
  G. Mort, 493:Winter88/89–57
Burns, J.H., ed. The Cambridge History of
Medieval Political Thought.
  A.G., 185:Jul89–977
  G. Leff, 617(TLS):7–13Jul89–756
Burns, J.H. & H.L.A. Hart – see Bentham, J.
Burns, J.M. The Crosswinds of Freedom.
  J.A. Garraty, 441:14May89–14
Burns, J.P. & S. Rosen, eds. Policy Conflicts
in Post-Mao China.
  D.L. Shambaugh, 293(JASt).Feb88–107
Burns, M. Suburbs of the Arctic Circle.*
  B. Leckie, 102(CanL):Winter87–278
  E. Thompson, 198:Winter86–104
Burns, R. The Complete Letters of Robert
Burns. (J.A. Mackay, ed)
  D.A. Low, 588(SSL):Vol23–289
Burns, R. Two Glossaries by Robert Burns.
  G.R.R., 588(SSL):Vol23–313
Burnshaw, S. Robert Frost Himself.*
  P.R.J., 295(JML):Fall87/Winter88–320
  R. Zaller, 4:Autumn88–65
Burnside, J. The Hoop.
  M. Wormald, 617(TLS):17–23Feb89–169
Burnyeat, M., ed. The Skeptical Tradition.
  T. Scaltsas, 479(PhQ):Jan88–130
Burow, J., comp. Corpus Vasorum Antiquorum.
(Deutschland, 54)
  H.A. Shapiro, 229:Band60Heft2–182
Burrell, D.B. Knowing the Unknowable God.*
  T.M. Rudavsky, 319:Jul89–468
Burros, M. 20-Minute Menus.
  P. Simon, 441:11Jun89–20
Burroughs, S. Memoirs of Stephen Burroughs.
  L. Buell, 165(EAL):Vol24No1–82
Burroughs, W. Interzone.
  P. Baker, 617(TLS):27Oct–2Nov89–1181
Burroughs, W.S. The Western Lands.*
  S.E. Olson, 42(AR):Winter88–110

Burrow, J.A. The Ages of Man.*
  H.A. Kelly, 589:Jul88-630
  D. Pearsall, 402(MLR):Jan89-111
  H. White, 382(MAE):1988/1-81
Burrowes, J. Incomers.
  I. Rankin, 571(ScLJ):Spring88-65
Burrowes, R. The Yemen Arab Republic.
  F. Halliday, 617(TLS):20-26Jan89-54
Burrows, J.F. Computation into Criticism.
  H. Bonheim, 677(YES):Vol19-332
  W.A. Craik, 447(N&Q):Dec88-542
  P. Honan, 83:Spring88-100
Burrus, V. Chastity as Autonomy.
  R.L.S., 185:Apr89-692
Burst, A. The Three Families of H.L. Hunt.
  D. Cole, 441:5Feb89-25
Burstein, S.M. Translated Documents of
    Greece and Rome. (Vol 3)
  A.J.L. van Hooff, 394:Vol41fasc3/4-452
Burt, J. Robert Penn Warren and American
    Idealism.
  W.B. Clark, 598(SoR):Spring89-514
  J.N. Hathcock, 30:Spring89-87
  J.R. Millichap, 395(MFS):Winter88-638
  H. Ruppersburg, 27(AL):Dec88-694
Burt, J. The Way Down.
  639(VQR):Autumn88-133
Burt, R. Rock and Roll, the Movies.
  R.S. Denisoff, 498:Summer88-82
Burt, R.A. Two Jewish Justices.
  639(VQR):Summer88-96
Burton, J., ed. Cinema and Social Change in
    Latin America.*
  J.M., 295(JML):Fall87/Winter88-279
Burton, S. Impossible Dream.
  J.M. Hamilton, 441:21May89-13
Burton-Roberts, N. Analysing Sentences.
  N.J. Robat, 179(ES):Feb88-93
Buruma, I. God's Dust.
  D.J. Enright, 617(TLS):6-12Oct89-1101
  J. Fallows, 441:9Jul89-10
  J. Sterba, 453(NYRB):28Sep89-52
  442(NY):21Aug89-94
Burunat, S., J. Burunat & E.D. Starčević. El
    español y su sintaxis.
  T.A. Morgan, 399(MLJ):Autumn88-368
Burwick, F. The Haunted Eye.
  T. Ziolkowski, 445(NCF):Jun88-125
Bury, J.P.T. & R.P. Tombs. Thiers 1797-1877.
  D.H. Barry, 161(DUJ):Dec87-140
  W.H.C. Smith, 208(FS):Jul88-371
Burzio, L. Italian Syntax.*
  A. Belletti, 603:Vol12No1-255
  G. Lepschy, 545(RPh):May89-422
Busard, H.L.L. — see Euclid
Busby, M. Lanford Wilson.
  R. Burrows, 649(WAL):Aug88-156
Busch, F. Absent Friends.
  S. Hearon, 441:7May89-7
Busch, F. War Babies.
  G. Johnson, 441:5Nov89-24
Busch, F. When People Publish.*
  G. Garrett, 569(SR):Summer88-516
Busch, G. Paula Modersohn-Becker.
  E.C. Oppler, 54:Dec88-709
Busch, G. & L. von Reinken — see Modersohn-
    Becker, P.
Busch, H. — see Verdi, G.
Busch, N. The Titan Game.
  N. Callendar, 441:26Nov89-33

Busch, R.L. Humor in the Major Novels of F.M.
    Dostoevsky.
  W.J. Leatherbarrow, 402(MLR):Oct89-
    1051
Busch, U. Die klitischen Pronomina des Ital-
    ienischen.*
  W. Schweickard, 72:Band225Heft2-464
Busch, W. Wilhelm Busch: "Max and Moritz" in
    English Dialects and Creoles.* (M. Görlach,
    ed)
  D. Nehls, 257(IRAL):May88-172
  A.M. Stewart, 571(ScLJ):Spring88-23
"Wilhelm Busch, Max und Moritz: In deutschen
    Dialekten, Mittelhochdeutsch und Jid-
    disch." (M. Görlach, ed)
  D. Nehls, 257(IRAL):May88-172
Bush, A. Bonnettstown.
  J. Malcolm, 442(NY):26Jun89-89
Bush, S., Jr. & C.J. Rasmussen. The Library
    of Emmanuel College, Cambridge, 1584-
    1637.
  F.J. Bremer, 165(EAL):Vol24No1-77
  P. Collinson, 78(BC):Autumn88-426
Bushman, J.H. Teaching the English Lan-
    guage.
  S.D. Spangehl, 350:Dec89-878
Busi, A. Seminar on Youth.
  A. Cancogni, 441:13Aug89-13
  P. Parker, 364:Oct/Nov88-142
Busi, A. The Standard Life of a Temporary
    Pantyhose Salesman.*
  P. Bailey, 617(TLS):11-17Aug89-878
Buskirk, W. The Western Apache.
  C.S. Fowler, 649(WAL):Aug88-187
Busoni, F. Ferruccio Busoni: Selected Let-
    ters.* (A. Beaumont, ed & trans)
  J.C.G. Waterhouse, 410(M&L):Jan88-99
Buss, A.E., ed. Max Weber in Asian Studies.
  M. Juergensmeyer, 293(JASt):Feb88-93
Buss, R. Cocteau: "Les Enfants terribles."
  M. Autrand, 535(RHL):Nov-Dec88-1166
  E. Freeman, 208(FS):Apr88-231
  P. Read, 402(MLR):Jan89-186
Busse, W. & J. Trabant, eds. Les Idéologues.
  J. Andresen, 567:Vol72No3/4-271
  B. Herting, 682(ZPSK):Band41Heft2-238
Busselle, M. Landscape in Spain.
  L. Gross, 441:2Apr89-28
Busselle, R. An Exposure of the Heart.
  S. Jacoby, 441:12Mar89-11
Büssing, S. Aliens in the Home.
  D.A. Ringe, 395(MFS):Summer88-317
Bussmann, H. Lexikon der Sprachwissen-
    schaft.
  H-D. Kreuder, 685(ZDL):3/1988-370
de Bustos Tovar, J.J. & J.H. Silverman, eds.
    Homenaje a Américo Castro.
  S.G. Armistead, 240(HR):Spring88-243
Buszynski, L. Soviet Foreign Policy and
    Southeast Asia.*
  D. Pike, 293(JASt):May88-414
Butchvarov, P. Skepticism in Ethics.
  J.C. Morrison, 103:Jun89-220
Butler, A.M. Daughters of Joy, Sisters of
    Misery.
  M. Honey, 115:Summer88-313
Butler, C. Statistics in Linguistics.*
  L. Hamp-Lyons, 608:Mar89-127
Butler, F., M.R. Higonnet & B. Rosen — see
    "Children's Literature"
Butler, J. Nightshade.
  G. Benford, 441:3Sep89-7
  442(NY):13Nov89-147

Butler, J., R. Elphick & D. Welch, eds. Demo-
cratic Liberalism in South Africa.*
G.M. Fredrickson, 453(NYRB):26Oct89-48
Butler, L.S. Samuel Beckett and the Meaning
of Being.
P. Müller, 72:Band225Heft2-411
Butler, M. Jane Austen and the War of Ideas.
M. De Forest, 166:Jul89-345
Butler, M. Theatre and Crisis, 1632-1642.*
F.J. Levy, 702:Vol20-294
Butler, R.O. The Deuce.
S. Spencer, 441:3Sep89-10
Butlin, R. Ragtime in Unfamiliar Bars.*
R. Watson, 588(SSL):Vol23-254
Butlin, R. The Sound of My Voice.*
T. Nolan, 441:31Dec89-12
"Michel Butor: regards critiques sur son
oeuvre."
L.S. Roudiez, 535(RHL):Jan-Feb88-157
Butrica, J.L. The Manuscript Tradition of
Propertius.
G.P. Goold, 487:Spring88-87
Butscher, E. Conrad Aiken.* (Vol 1)
D. Davis, 617(TLS):19-25May89-537
Butt, G. To Toslow We'll Go and Other Plays.
an ear and a fear.
D. Lynde, 108:Spring88-93
Butt, J. & C. Benjamin. A New Reference
Grammar of Modern Spanish.
R.M. De Keyser, 350:Jun89-420
Butt, R. A History of Parliament: The Middle
Ages.
G.L. Harriss, 617(TLS):28Apr-4May89-
468
Butter, P.H. - see Muir, E.
Butterfield, J., ed. Language, Mind and
Logic.*
A. George, 479(PhQ):Jan88-117
Butterick, G.F. - see Olson, C.
Butterworth, C.E. - see Averroes
Buttigieg, J.A., ed. Criticism without Bound-
aries.
V.B. Leitch, 395(MFS):Summer88-319
Buttigieg, J.A. "A Portrait of the Artist" in
Different Perspective.*
M. Fludernik, 395(MFS):Winter88-687
R. Mason, 447(N&Q):Dec88-550
Button, G. & J.R.E. Lee, eds. Talk and Social
Organisation.
S. Colville-Hall, 399(MLJ):Winter88-484
Butts, R.E., ed. Kant's Philosophy of Physical
Science.
P.A.R., 185:Oct88-203
van Buuren, M. "Les Rougon-Macquart"
d'Émile Zola: de la métaphore au mythe.*
A. Dezalay, 535(RHL):Nov-Dec88-1159
R. Lethbridge, 208(FS):Oct88-483
Buxbaum, M.H., ed. Critical Essays on Benja-
min Franklin.
C. Looby, 165(EAL):Vol24No1-79
Buxton, W. Talcott Parsons and the Capital-
ist Nation-State.
D. Sciulli, 488:Dec88-566
de Buzon, F. - see Descartes, R.
Buzzoni, A., ed. Torquato Tasso tra lettera-
tura, musica, teatro e arti figurative.
M. Bongiovanni Bertini, 549(RLC):Oct-
Dec88-569
Byam Shaw, C. - see Mackenzie, J.
Byatt, A. Sugar and Other Stories.
K. Cushman, 573(SSF):Winter88-80
Byatt, A.S. Unruly Times.
617(TLS):22-28Dec89-1426

Byerman, K.E. Fingering the Jagged Grain.*
C.A. Ridley, 459:Spring88-90
Byers, E. The Nation of Nantucket.
P.R. Virgadamo, 432(NEQ):Jun88-274
Bynon, T. & F.R. Palmer, eds. Studies in the
History of Western Linguistics In Honour of
R.H. Robins.
R. Posner, 353:Vol26No2-312
Bynum, C.W. Holy Feast and Holy Fast.
H.G. Gelber, 401(MLQ):Sep87-281
Byrne, F. Grammatical Relations in a Radical
Creole.
D. Winford, 361:Nov88-258
Byrnes, H. & S. Fink. Wendepunkt.
I.H.R. McCoy, 399(MLJ):Summer88-237
Byron, H.J. Plays by H.J. Byron. (J. Davis,
ed)
K. Tetzeli von Rosador, 72:Band224
Heft2-409
Lord Byron. Byron I: Poems 1807-1818. (A.
Levine & J.J. McGann, eds)
F.L. Beaty, 340(KSJ):Vol37-185
Lord Byron. The Complete Poetical Works.*
(Vol 4) (J.J. McGann, ed)
J. Clubbe, 340(KSJ):Vol37-181
D.H. Reiman, 339:Autumn88-89
A. Rutherford, 447(N&Q):Jun88-252
Lord Byron. The Complete Poetical Works.*
(Vol 5) (J.J. McGann, ed)
J. Clubbe, 340(KSJ):Vol37-181
P. Morgan, 179(ES):Apr88-180
D.H. Reiman, 339:Autumn88-89
A. Rutherford, 447(N&Q):Jun88-252
M. Storey, 541(RES):May88-309
Lord Byron. The Manuscripts of the Younger
Romantics: Lord Byron. (Vol 2) (A. Levine
& J.J. McGann, eds)
J. Clubbe, 340(KSJ):Vol37-181
Lord Byron. The Oxford Authors: Byron. (J.J.
McGann, ed)
J. Clubbe, 340(KSJ):Vol37-181
M. Storey, 339:Autumn88-101

Cabada Castro, M. Feuerbach y Kant.
M.P.M. Caimi, 342:Band79Heft1-105
Cabanne, P. Dialogues with Marcel Duchamp.
E. Heartney, 55:Summer88-89
Cable, J. The Geneva Conference of 1954 on
Indochina.
W.J. Duiker, 293(JAST):May88-416
Cabrera Infante, G. Holy Smoke.
J. Byrne, 532(RCF):Fall88-152
Cabrera Infante, G. View of Dawn in the
Tropics.
N. Rankin, 617(TLS):20-26Jan89-58
Cadogan, M. Richmal Crompton.
P. Parker, 364:Feb87-107
Caduff, G.A. Antike Sintflutsagen.
W. Fauth, 229:Band60Heft6-531
Cady, E.H. & L.J. Budd, eds. On Whitman.
D.D. Kummings, 646(WWR):Summer88-33
Caesar. C. Iulius Caesar, "Commentarii rerum
gestarum." (Vol 1: Bellum Gallicum.) (W.
Hering, ed)
E. Mensching, 229:Band60Heft8-696
Caesar, M. & P. Hainsworth, eds. Writers and
Society in Contemporary Italy.*
L.V., 295(JML):Fall87/Winter88-203
"Caesar Augustus: Seven Aspects." (F. Millar
& E. Segal, eds)
A. Chastagnol, 555:Vol61fasc1-161

Caetano, J.A.P. & others – see under Palma
   Caetano, J.A. & others
Cafagna, L. Dualismo e sviluppo nella storia
   d'Italia.
      G. Reid, 617(TLS):6–12Oct89–1083
Caffee, G.L., comp & trans. The Breton and
   His World.
      O. Lerch, 292(JAF):Jul–Sep88–381
Caffrey, M.M. Ruth Benedict.
      M. Beard, 617(TLS):29Sep–5Oct89–1050
      M.B. Norton, 441:7May89–20
Cagnon, M. The French Novel of Quebec.
      M. Naudin, 403(MLS):Winter88–203
Cahalan, J.M. The Irish Novel.
      P. Craig, 617(TLS):26May–1Jun89–577
      D. O'Brien, 329(JJQ):Summer89–629
Cahan, A. Grandma Never Lived in America.*
   (M. Rischin, ed)
      A. Waldinger, 26(ALR):Spring89–74
"Les Cahiers Colette, No. 8."
      P. D'Hollander, 535(RHL):Nov–Dec88–
         1168
"Cahiers de l'Université, No. 7: Yves Bon-
   nefoy; Poésie, Art et Pensée."
      C. Jordens, 356(LR):Aug88–262
"Cahiers Jean Giraudoux, No. 15."
      A. Duneau, 535(RHL):Nov–Dec88–1167
"Cahiers pour la littérature populaire."
      R. Mathé, 535(RHL):Nov–Dec88–1181
Cahill, T. A Wolverine is Eating My Leg.
      C. Sommers, 441:14May89–23
Cahn, S. Industry of Devotion.
      639(VQR):Spring88–44
Cahoone, L.E. The Dilemma of Modernity.
      G.J. Galgan, 543:Sep88–132
Caiger–Smith, A. Lustre Pottery.
      90:Jun88–476
Caillat, C. – see Bloch, J.
Caine, B. Destined to be Wives.
      D. Rubinstein, 637(VS):Autumn88–115
Cairncross, A., ed. The Robert Hall Diaries,
   1947–1953.
      M. Stewart, 617(TLS):3–9Nov89–1206
Cairncross, A. & N. Watts. The Economic Sec-
   tion, 1939–1961.
      M. Stewart, 617(TLS):3–9Nov89–1206
Cairns, C. Pietro Aretino and the Republic of
   Venice.*
      P.H. Labalme, 551(RenQ):Summer88–302
Cairns, D. Berlioz. (Vol 1)
      J. Warrack, 617(TLS):24Feb–2Mar89–187
Cairns, E. Caught in Crossfire.
      J.B. Davenport, 174(Éire):Summer88–150
Cairns, F., ed. Papers of the Liverpool Latin
   Seminar. (Vol 5)
      N. Horsfall, 123:Vol38No2–270
Cairns, F. Virgil's Augustan Epic.
      S. Harrison, 617(TLS):8–14Sep89–984
Cairns, P. Depression.
      G. Gessert, 448:Vol26No1–79
Cairns, P. Synthetic Fabric.
      G. Gessert, 448:Vol26No1–78
Caistor, N., ed. The Faber Book of Contempo-
   rary Latin American Short Stories.
      G. Martin, 617(TLS):14–20Jul89–782
Caizergues, P. – see Cocteau, J.
Calaferte, L. Promenade dans un parc.
      R.E. Anderson, 207(FR):Dec88–359
Calame–Griaule, G. Words and the Dogon
   World.
      C. Bird, 292(JAF):Apr–Jun88–241
      M.H. Krieger, 650(WF):Jul88–232

Calame–Griaule, G., V. Görög–Karady & M.
   Chiche, eds. Le Conte, Pourquoi? Com-
   ment?/Folktales, Why and How?
      A. Schmetzke, 203:Vol99No1–135
Calasso, R. Le Nozze di Cadmo e Armonia.
      D. Davis, 617(TLS):3–9Feb89–112
Calboli Montefusco, L. La dottrina degli
   "status" nella retorica greca e romana.
      I.C. Rutherford, 123:Vol38No2–264
Calbris, G. & J. Montredon. Des gestes et des
   mots pour le dire.
      P. Léon, 207(FR):Mar89–695
      T.A. Sebeok, 567:Vol69No1/2–185
Calciati, R. Corpus Nummorum Siculorum: La
   monetazione de bronzo/The Bronze Coinage.
   (Vols 1–3)
      G. Manganaro, 229:Band60Heft5–455
Caldenby, C. & O. Hultin. Asplund.
      W.C. Miller, 576:Jun88–205
Calder, D.G. & T.C. Christy, eds. Germania.
      A.M. Mellini Rizzi, 350:Dec89–879
Calder, J., ed. As No Other Dare Fail.
      J. Pilling, 402(MLR):Oct89–957
Calder, J. – see Beckett, S.
Calder, J. – see Stevenson, R.L.
Calder, N. & J. Newell, eds. Future Earth.
      F.W. Taylor, 617(TLS):16–22Jun89–662
Calder, R. Willie.
      F. Raphael, 617(TLS):31Mar–6Apr89–329
Calder, W.M. 3d & R.L. Fowler – see von Wil-
   amowitz–Moellendorff, U.
Calder, W.M. 3d & D.A. Traill, eds. Myth,
   Scandal, and History.*
      J.T. Hooker, 303(JoHS):Vol108–258
Caldera, E. – see de Saavedra, A., Duque de
   Rivas
Calderini, I.G.G. – see Galen
Calderón de la Barca, P. El castillo de Linda-
   brides. (V.B. Torres, ed)
      W.R. Blue, 304(JHP):Spring88–271
Calderón de la Barca, P. Love Is No Laughing
   Matter ('No hay burlas con el amor'). (D.
   Cruickshank & S. Page, eds & trans)
      F.A. De Armas, 86(BHS):Oct88–411
      A.L. Mackenzie, 402(MLR):Jul89–762
"Calderón 1600–1681."
      E. Oostendorp, 547(RF):Band99Heft4–484
Calderwood, J.L. If It Were Done.*
      R.A. Foakes, 541(RES):May88–292
      D.R.C. Marsh, 447(N&Q):Jun88–224
Calderwood, J.L. Shakespeare and the Denial
   of Death.
      639(VQR):Autumn88–118
Calderwood, J.L. To Be and Not to Be.
      V. Bourgy, 189(EA):Oct–Dec88–481
Caldwell, E. With All My Might.
      M.J. Bolsterli, 395(MFS):Winter88–642
      J.S. Leonard, 27(AL):Mar88–140
      D.R. Noble, 392:Winter87/88–110
"The Caledonian Phalanx."
      L. Hughes, 575(SEER):Oct88–656
Calhoun, R.M. Evangelicals and Conserva-
   tives in the Early South, 1740–1861.
      W.H. Daniel, 392:Fall88–567
Calin, W. In Defense of French Poetry.
      P. Broome, 208(FS):Jul88–375
      J.L. Pallister, 568(SCN):Winter88–78
      R. Pensom, 402(MLR):Oct89–972
Calin, W. A Muse for Heroes.
      L.S. Crist, 545(RPh):Feb89–375
Calinescu, M. – see Eliade, M.
Calkins, R.G. Monuments of Medieval Art.
      90:Feb88–148

Call, M.J. Back to the Garden.
P.H. Dubé, 166:Jul89-352
Callahan, D. What Kind of Life.
C.E. Rosenberg, 441:24Dec89-1
Callahan, N. Carl Sandburg.*
D.A. Carpenter, 27(AL):Oct88-508
Callamand, M. Grammaire vivante du fran-
çais.
A. Duménil, 207(FR):May89-1080
D.A. Kibbee, 399(MLJ):Winter88-471
Callard, D.A. "Pretty Good for a Woman."
L.P. Rudnick, 534(RALS):Vol16No1&2-232
Callebat, L., with P. Fleury – see Vitruvius
Callebaut, W. & R. Pinxten, eds. Evolutionary
Epistemology.
J. Collier, 103:Feb89-43
Calleo, D.P. Beyond American Hegemony.
639(VQR):Summer88-97
Callewaert, W.M., ed. Early Hindī Devotional
Literature in Current Research.
M.C. Shapiro, 318(JAOS):Jan-Mar87-200
Callicott, J.B., ed. Companion to "A Sand
County Almanac."*
S. Paul, 271:Fall88-163
"Callimachus: Hymns, Epigrams, Select Frag-
ments." (S. Lombardo & D. Rayor, eds &
trans)
N. Hopkinson, 123:Vol38No2-400
639(VQR):Summer88-100
Callot, E. Les étapes de la biologie.
A. Reix, 542:Jul-Sep88-377
Calloway, C.G. Crown and Calumet.
C.A. Sims, 106:Summer88-243
Calloway, S. Twentieth-Century Decoration.*
P. Garner, 617(TLS):3-9Mar89-233
B. Scott, 324:Aug89-594
Callwood, J. Twelve Weeks in Spring.
J. McSherry, 529(QQ):Spring88-220
Calvetti, P. The Ashio Copper Mine Revolt
(1907).
F.G. Notehelfer, 407(MN):Winter88-488
Calvié, L. – see Furet, F.
Calvino, I. Six Memos for the Next Millen-
nium.*
A.J. Tamburri, 395(MFS):Winter88-723
P. Valesio, 599:Summer89-325
Calvino, I. The Uses of Literature.*
E.P. Nassar, 396(ModA):Summer89-269
A.J. Tamburri, 577(SHR):Fall88-390
Calvo, A.G. – see under García Calvo, A.
Calvocoressi, P., G. Wint & J. Pritchard. Total
War. (rev)
M. Carver, 617(TLS):1-7Sep89-935
Camaiora, L.C. Gray – Keats – Hopkins.
M. Bignami, 402(MLR):Apr89-444
Camartin, I. Nichts als Worte?
G. Holtus, 72:Band225Heft2-473
W. Marxgut, 547(RF):Band100Heft4-345
W. Müller, 685(ZDL):1/1988-122
Cambiano, G., ed. Storiografia e dossografia
nella filosofia antica.
P.M. Huby, 123:Vol38No1-67
A. Laks, 229:Band60Heft8-675
Cambitoglou, A., C. Aellen & J. Chamay. Le
peintre de Darius et son milieu.
P.E. Arias, 229:Band60Heft7-631
"Cambridge/Signorelli Italian/English, En-
glish/Italian Dictionary."* (M.P. Fontanelli
& B. Reynolds, eds)
J.R. Woodhouse, 447(N&Q):Jun88-198

Cameron, A. Procopius and the Sixth Cen-
tury.*
J. Herrin, 313:Vol78-263
S. Krautschick, 229:Band60Heft3-277
Cameron, A. & others – see "The Dictionary of
Old English"
Cameron, A.D. The New North. (D. Richeson,
ed)
M. Peterman, 649(WAL):Nov88-280
Cameron, C. Daddy Boy.
W.J. Harding, 441:18Jun89-20
Cameron, D.K. A Kist of Sorrows.
G. Telfer, 571(ScLJ):Winter88-23
Cameron, E. Irving Layton.
B. Jones, 102(CanL):Winter87-160
Cameron, J. & P.J. Christman. The Art of
"Gone With the Wind."
D. Finkle, 441:10Dec89-7
Cameron, K. – see Palissy, B.
Cameron, K.C., W.S. Dodd & S.P.Q. Rahtz, eds.
Computers and Modern Language Studies.*
P. Meara, 402(MLR):Oct89-895
R. Middleton, 208(FS):Oct88-498
R. Sinyor, 276:Spring88-34
Cameron, S. Thinking in Henry James.
J. Bayley, 453(NYRB):7Dec89-21
Cameron, S. Writing Nature.*
D.S. Gross, 223:Spring88-93
Cammann, A. Aus der Welt der Erzähler.
K. Horn, 196:Band29Heft1/2-177
Camoin, F. Deadly Virtues.*
S.E. Gunter, 649(WAL):Feb89-378
Camon, F. La Femme aux liens.
H. Cronel, 450(NRF):May88-107
Camp, D. – see Lindsay, V.
Camp, J. The Fool's Run.
F. Siegel, 441:15Oct89-52
Camp, J.M. The Athenian Agora.
A.W. Johnston, 303(JoHS):Vol108-261
S.I. Rotroff, 124:Nov-Dec88-128
Campailla, S. Mal di luna e d'altro.
J. Smith, 402(MLR):Oct89-1008
Campana, A. & P.M. Masotti, eds. Bartolomeo
Sacchi, Il Platina.
C.H. Clough, 402(MLR):Jul89-750
Campbell, A. Death is an Anxious Mother.
L. Hutchman, 102(CanL):Winter87-263
Campbell, B.M. Sweet Summer.
B. Mukherjee, 441:11Jun89-47
Campbell, C. The French Procuress.*
E.J. Campion, 475:Vol15No28-269
Campbell, C. & others. Ramsay Traquair and
His Successors: A Guide to the Archive/
Ramsay Traquair et ses successeurs: guide
du fonds.
J.F. Tener, 470:Vol26-189
Campbell, H.H. – see Anderson, S.
Campbell, J. The Improbable Machine.
G. Johnson, 441:24Dec89-12
Campbell, J. Joy in Work, German Work.
R.J. Evans, 617(TLS):1-7Dec89-1342
Campbell, J. Mythic Black Fiction.*
P.A. Muckley, 295(JML):Fall87/Winter88-
204
Campbell, K. A Stoic Philosophy of Life.
D. Browne, 63:Sep88-420
Campbell, L. The Linguistics of Southeast
Chiapas, Mexico.
W. Bright, 350:Dec89-880
Campbell, L. & F. Steer. A Catalogue of Man-
uscripts in the College of Arms, Collec-
tions. (Vol 1)
A. Payne, 617(TLS):14-20Apr89-400

Campbell, M. The Great Cellists.
R. Anderson, 415:Aug88-403
Campbell, M. & C. Greated. The Musician's
Guide to Acoustics.
D. Vaughan, 415:Oct88-536
Campbell, R. Juice.
M. Stasio, 441:28May89-27
Campbell, R. Nibbled to Death by Ducks.
M. Stasio, 441:10Dec89-41
Campbell, R. & D. Collinson. Ending Lives.
M.J. Coughlan, 518:Oct88-234
Campbell, T. Justice.
P. Pettit, 617(TLS):28Jul-3Aug89-818
Campbell, T. The Left and Rights.
D.F.B. Tucker, 144:Summer/Fall89-554
Campbell, T.P. & C. Davidson, eds. The Fleu-
ry Playbook.
T.J. McGee, 589:Jan88-131
Campbell, W.A.B. & R. Melchin. Western Se-
curity and the Strategic Defence Initiative.
529(QQ):Spring88-222
Campbell-Kelly, M. & others - see Babbage,
C.
Camporesi, P. Bread of Dreams. I balsami di
Venere.
V. Nutton, 617(TLS):7-13Jul89-743
de Campos, A.L.V. A República do Picipau
Amarelo.
D. Brookshaw, 86(BHS):Jan88-107
Campschreur, W. & J. Divendal, eds. Culture
in Another South Africa.
D. Papineau, 617(TLS):25-31Aug89-915
Camus, A. American Journals.
P.B. Koppisch, 115:Summer88-329
P. McCarthy, 617(TLS):1-7Sep89-954
Camus, A. Carnets. (Vol 3)
P. McCarthy, 617(TLS):1-7Sep89-954
Can Xue. Dialogues in Paradise.
C. Innes, 441:24Sep89-48
Canals Vidal, F. Sobre la esencia del conoci-
miento.
A. Reix, 542:Oct-Dec88-496
Canardo, M.R. - see under Rigau Canardo, M.
Cañas, D. Poesía y percepción.
S. Daydí-Tolson, 240(HR):Summer88-387
Canavaggio, J. Cervantès.
M. Chevalier, 92(BH):Jan-Dec87-378
E.L. Rivers, 400(MLN):Mar88-457
Canby, J.V. & others, eds. Ancient Anatolia.
D. Small, 124:Mar-Apr89-328
Cancogni, A. The Mirage in the Mirror.
P.R.J., 295(JML):Fall87/Winter88-359
Canerot, M-F. Mauriac après 1930.
B. Chochon, 535(RHL):Jan-Feb88-150
Canet Vallés, J.L. Teatro y prácticas escéni-
cas. (Vol 2)
M.M. Ruano de la Haza, 402(MLR):Apr89-
501
Canetti, E. Jeux de regards.
J. Blot, 450(NRF):Jun88-90
Canetti, E. The Play of the Eyes.
N. Ritter, 577(SHR):Spring88-185
Canetti, E. The Torch in My Ear.
J. Campbell, 617(TLS):25-31Aug89-929
Canfield, D.L. - see Castillo, C., O.F. Bond &
B.M. Garcia
Canfield, J.V., ed. The Philosophy of Witt-
genstein.
C. Cordura, 160:Jul88-164
Canin, E. Emperor of the Air.*
G. Johnson, 219(GaR):Summer88-423
E. McGraw, 455:Sep88-64
42(AR):Spring88-272

Cannadine, D. The Pleasures of the Past.
R. Davenport-Hines, 617(TLS):21-
27Apr89-432
E. Hower, 441:19Nov89-11
Canning, J. The Political Thought of Baldus
de Ubaldis.
T. Kuehn, 551(RenQ):Autumn88-470
P. Riesenberg, 589:Oct88-910
Cannon, G. Historical Change and English
Word-Formation.
R. Raffelsiefen, 350:Dec89-880
Cannon, J. & others, eds. Blackwell Diction-
ary of Historians.
J.P. Kenyon, 617(TLS):21-27Apr89-428
Canny, N. & A. Pagden, eds. Colonial Identity
in the Atlantic World, 1500-1800.*
D. Alden, 656(WMQ):Oct88-784
I.K. Steele, 106:Fall88-353
Cano González, A.M. El habla de Somiedo.
A. Monjour, 553(RLiR):Jan-Jun88-275
Canseco, L.G. - see under Gómez Canseco, L.
Cantacuzino, S. Re/Architecture.
J.M. Richards, 617(TLS):8-14Dec89-1359
Cantalapiedra Erostarbe, F. Lectura semió-
tico-formal de "La Celestina."*
D. Hook, 402(MLR):Jan89-202
Cantarella, E. Pandora's Daughters.
B.K. Gold, 124:Jul-Aug89-454
L.A. Jones, 41:Spring88-138
H. King, 303(JoHS):Vol108-248
W. Schuller, 229:Band60Heft5-445
Cantarella, M., ed. Bibliografia salveminiana,
1892-1984.
D. Forgacs, 402(MLR):Jan89-195
Canter, D., M. Comber & D.L. Uzzell. Football
in its Place.
B. Glanville, 617(TLS):30Jun-6Jul89-710
Canth, S.M. Sanoi Minna Canth, Pioneer Re-
former. (R. Heikkilä, ed)
K.O. Dana, 563(SS):Autumn88-514
Cantin, R. J'ai besoin de personne.
N.J. Lamoureux, 207(FR):May89-1090
Canto, M. L'Intrigue philosophique.
R.S.W. Hawtrey, 123:Vol38No2-221
Canto, M. - see Plato
Cantril, H. The Invasion from Mars.
I.F. Clarke, 561(SFS):Jul88-240
Cao, A.F. Federico García Lorca y las van-
guardias.*
H. Rogmann, 547(RF):Band99Heft4-485
Cao Yu. Peking Man.
M.K. Spring, 318(JAOS):Jul-Sep87-503
Capasso, M. & T. Dorandi - see Cavallo, G.
Capel Margarito, M. La platería de la cate-
dral de Jaén.
A. López-Yarto Elizalde, 48:Apr-Jun88-
192
Caplan, D. Neurolinguistics and Linguistic
Aphasiology.
J. Niemi, 452(NJL):Vol11No1/2-205
Caplan, J. Framed Narratives.*
V. Mylne, 530:Apr88-163
494:Vol8No2-453
Caplan, P., ed. The Culture Construction of
Sexuality.
C.O., 185:Apr89-670
Caplan, U. & M.W. Steinberg - see Klein, A.M.
Capote, T. Answered Prayers.
P. Saari, 42(AR):Winter88-112
Capp, B. Cromwell's Navy.
N.A.M. Rodger, 617(TLS):29Dec89/
4Jan90-1434

Cappelletti, A.J. La Filosofía de Anaxágoras.
M. Schofield, 41:Fall88-297
Cappelletti, S. Luigi Riccoboni e la riforma del teatro.
T.A. Emery, 276:Autumn88-265
Capurro, R. Hermeneutik der Fachinformation.
K. Leidlmair, 489(PJGG):Band95Heft1-216
Caputi, A. Pirandello and the Crisis of Modern Consciousness.
J. Mazzaro, 130:Winter88/89-371
Caputo, J. Radical Hermeneutics.
G.D. Atkins, 478(P&L):Oct88-313
J.L. Marsh, 258:Dec88-459
Caputo, J.D. Heidegger and Aquinas.*
M.E. Zimmerman, 438:Summer88-365
Caputo-Mayr, M.L. & J.M. Herz. Franz Kafka.
E.M. Rajec, 221(GQ):Spring88-320
J.J. White, 402(MLR):Apr89-529
Caramel, L. & A. Longatti. Antonio Sant'Elia.
J. Rykwert, 617(TLS):12-18May89-523
Carandini, A. & A. Ricci. Settefinestre.
N. Purcell, 313:Vol78-194
Caras, R.A. A Cat is Watching.
E. Janeway, 441:1Oct89-13
Caratini, R. Histoire critique de la pensée sociale. (Vol 1)
A. Reix, 542:Jan-Mar88-100
Caravaggi, G. & others. Poeti cancioneriles del sec. XV.
L. Mendia Vozzo, 379(MedR):Apr88-157
Caray, H., with B. Verdi. Holy Cow!
J. Weinberg, 441:23Apr89-36
Carby, H.V. Reconstructing Womanhood.*
A. Costanzo, 27(AL):Oct88-481
Card, O.S. Treason. (rev)
G. Jonas, 441:26Feb89-32
Carden, J. A Piano Teacher's Guide to Electronic Keyboards.
510:Fall88-10
Cardenal, E. Flights of Victory/Vuelos de Victoria. (M. Zimmerman, ed & trans)
M.A. Rygiel, 577(SHR):Winter88-63
Cardenal, E. Nicaraguan New Time.
E. Williamson, 617(TLS):14-20Jul89-779
Cardinal, R. Breton: "Nadja."
P. Powrie, 208(FS):Apr88-232
Cardona, C. Metafísica del bien y del mal.
A. Reix, 542:Oct-Dec88-498
Cardus, N. Cardus on the Ashes. (M. Hughes, ed)
A.L. Le Quesne, 617(TLS):23-29Jun89-696
Cardwell, D.S.L. James Joule.
W.H. Brock, 617(TLS):29Sep-5Oct89-1070
Cardwell, R.A., ed. Essays in Honour of Robert Brian Tate from his Colleagues and Pupils.*
R.K. Britton, 402(MLR):Jul89-756
Cardwell, R.A. & J. Hamilton, eds. Virgil in a Cultural Tradition.*
K.W. Gransden, 402(MLR):Jul89-689
Care, N.S. On Sharing Fate.
L.E.L., 185:Jan89-465
Careri, E. Catalogo dei manoscritti musicali dell'Archivio delle Scuole Pie a San Pantaleo.
G. Dixon, 410(M&L):Oct88-510
Carette, M. & D. Deroeux. Carreaux de pavement médiévaux de Flandre et d'Artois (XIIIe-XIVe siècles).
S. Bonde & C. Maines, 589:Jul88-634

Carettoni, G. Das Haus des Augustus auf dem Palatin.
W. Ehrhardt, 229:Band60Heft7-640
Carew, A. Labour under the Marshall Plan.
C. Maier, 358:Dec89-16
Carey, B. Undressing the Dark.
K. McGuirk, 137:Fall88-50
Carey, C. & R.A. Reid — see Demosthenes
Carey, P. Oscar & Lucinda.*
T. Wilhelmus, 249(HudR):Autumn88-552
639(VQR):Autumn88-128
Carí, E.S. & E. Rodríguez Monegal — see under Sacerio Carí, E. & E. Rodríguez Monegal
Carley, J.P. — see John of Glastonbury
Carley, L. — see Delius, F.
Carlier, A. Guide de la documentation bibliographique en linguistique générale et française.
P. Swiggers, 553(RLiR):Jan-Jun88-252
Carlier, B. Deux lettres à un ami.
M. Alhau, 450(NRF):Jan88-107
Carlier, P. La royauté en Grèce avant Alexandre.*
A.J. Podlecki, 487:Summer88-181
J. Seibert, 229:Band60Heft5-413
Carlisle, O.A. — see Andreyev, L.
Carlisle, R.B. The Proffered Crown.
J. Beecher, 446(NCFS):Spring-Summer89-442
Carlitz, K. The Rhetoric of "Chin p'ing mei."
P. Rushton, 293(JASt):Feb88-109
Carlson, E.W., ed. Critical Essays on Edgar Allan Poe.
K. Ljungquist, 392:Winter87/88-99
Carlson, M. The Italian Shakespearians.*
D. Barrett, 610:Summer88-166
Carlson, M. Theories of the Theatre.*
P. Hernadi, 494:Vol8No2-439
Carlson, R. The News of the World.*
J.L. Jacobsen, 649(WAL):May88-58
Carlson, S. Women of Grace.
J. Auchard, 177(ELT):Vol31No2-242
M. Little, 481(PQ):Winter88-124
Carlut, C. & W. Meiden. French for Oral and Written Review. (4th ed)
T. Carr, 399(MLJ):Winter88-473
T. Scanlan, 207(FR):Oct88-209
Carlyle, T. A Carlyle Reader. (G.B. Tennyson, ed)
W. Myers, 402(MLR):Jan89-132
Carlyle, T. & J.W. The Collected Letters of Thomas and Jane Welsh Carlyle.* (Vols 10-12) (C.R. Sanders, ed)
B. Küster, 72:Band224Heft2-405
W. Myers, 402(MLR):Jan89-132
Carlyle, T. & J.W. The Collected Letters of Thomas and Jane Welsh Carlyle.* (Vols 13-15) (C.D. Ryals & K.J. Fielding, eds)
C. Moore, 588(SSL):Vol23-274
Carman, B. Windflower.
R. Hatch, 102(CanL):Winter87-223
Carman, J.B. & F.A. Marglin, eds. Purity and Auspiciousness in Indian Society.
S. Oleksiw, 318(JAOS):Jul-Sep87-506
Carmassi, C. La letteratura tedesca nei periodici italiani del primo Ottocento (1800-1847).
M. Beller, 52:Band23Heft2-182
Carney, R. American Vision.
L.J. Leff, 219(GaR):Spring88-211

Carswell, J. The Porcupine.
    J. Miller, 617(TLS):4-10Aug89-853
Carswell, J., with E.A. Maser & J.M. Mudge.
Blue and White.
    J. Sweetman, 463:Summer87-191
Carter, A.H. 3d. Italo Calvino.*
    S. Donatelli, 454:Fall88-113
Carter, B. Dartmoor. (B. Skilton, ed)
    J.W. Blench, 161(DUJ):Dec87-163
Carter, H.L. The Life and Times of Little
Turtle.
    B.W. Sheehan, 77:Fall88-345
    C.A. Sims, 106:Summer88-243
Carter, J.C. The Sculpture of the Sanctuary
of Athena Polias at Priene.
    C.E. Vafopoulou-Richardson, 123:
      Vol38No2-347
Carter, J.C.D. & D.L. Schmidt, eds. José
Agustín: "Onda" and Beyond.
    J.A. Duncan, 402(MLR):Jan89-222
    M.I. Lichtblau, 552(REH):May88-135
    H.R.M., 295(JML):Fall87/Winter88-288
    G. Woodyard, 238:Sep88-560
Carter, L.B. The Quiet Athenian.*
    J.M. Hurwit, 124:Sep-Oct88-59
    D. Whitehead, 303(JoHS):Vol108-253
Carter, M.L. Specter or Delusion?
    J. Wilt, 637(VS):Autumn88-137
Carter, P. The Road to Botany Bay.
    M. Aveling, 381:Summer88-745
Carter, R. Prints in the Valley.
    F. Baveystock, 617(TLS):1-7Dec89-1338
Carter, R.B. Descartes' Medical Philosophy.
    J.J. Furlong, 679:Band19Heft1-148
Carter, S. Twentieth Century Type Designers.
    K.F. Schmidt, 507:Mar/Apr88-152
Carter, S.D. The Road to Komatsubara.
    T.B. Hare, 407(NM):Autumn88-363
Carter, T. Mozart: "Le nozze di Figaro."*
    R. Parker, 465:Spring89-110
    S. Sadie, 415:Dec88-667
"Henri Cartier-Bresson: Photoportraits."
    R.L. Bray, 441:10Sep89-27
Cartledge, P. Agesilaos and the Crisis of
Sparta.
    M. Clauss, 229:Band60Heft5-417
    C.D. Hamilton, 24:Winter88-605
    R. Rousselle, 124:Nov-Dec88-119
Carton, E. The Rhetoric of American Ro-
mance.*
    R.C. De Prospo, 153:Fall88-43
Cartwright, J. Interior.*
    R. Fuller, 441:13Aug89-16
Carvalho, J. & S. Moore, eds. Connections
Project/Conexus.
    G. Gessert, 448:Vol26No2-122
Carvalho dos Santos, M.H., ed. Diderot.
    R. Rey, 530:Oct88-169
Carver, M. Out of Step.
    J. Erickson, 617(TLS):20-26Oct89-1158
Carver, R. Elephant and Other Stories.*
    D. Durrant, 364:Jul88-111
Carver, R. In a Marine Light.
    W. Scammell, 493:Spring88-48
Carver, R. A New Path to the Waterfall.
    L. Norfolk, 617(TLS):15-21Sep89-1000
Carver, R. Ultramarine.*
    C. Smart, 529(QQ):Spring88-185
Carver, R. Where I'm Calling From.*
    P. Skenazy, 182:Issue21-77
Carver, T.K. & S.D. Fotinos. A Conversation
Book.
    J. Giannotti, 399(MLJ):Spring88-82

Casa, F.P. & M.D. McGaha, eds. Editing the
"Comedia."*
    J.A. Parr, 552(REH):Jan88-135
    M.G. Profeti, 86(BHS):Apr88-184
Casagrande, P.J. Hardy's Influence on the
Modern Novel.
    W.E. Davis, 395(MFS):Winter88-675
    A. Sisson, 637(VS):Winter89-242
    J.D. Woolf, 177(ELT):Vol31No2-211
Casanave, C.P. & D. Williams. The Active
Reader.
    M.R. Gitterman, 399(MLJ):Autumn88-347
Casares, A.B. - see under Bioy Casares, A.
Casarico, L. Il controllo della popolazione
nell'Egitto romano. (Vol 1)
    C. Wehrli, 229:Band60Heft4-370
Cascardi, A.J. The Bounds of Reason.*
    D. Schier, 569(SR):Spring88-316
    G. Wihl, 478(P&L):Apr88-114
Cascardi, A.J., ed. Literature and the Ques-
tion of Philosophy.*
    C. Rapp, 125:Summer88-400
Casciato, A.D. & J.L.W. West 3d - see Kromer,
T.
Case, F.I. The Crisis of Identity.
    C.H. Bruner, 107(CRCL):Mar88-173
Casey, E.S. Remembering.
    E.F. Kaelin, 103:Nov88-428
    S.H. Watson, 543:Dec88-379
Casey, J. Spartina.
    S. Kenney, 441:25Jun89-7
Casey, P.F. Paul Rebhun.*
    J.P. Aikin, 221(GQ):Winter88-124
    R. Ambacher, 406:Winter88-508
Cash, A.H. Lawrence Sterne: The Later
Years.*
    E.A. Bloom, 301(JEGP):Oct88-686
    P.J. Casagrande, 594:Summer88-206
    W.G. Day, 536(Rev):Vol10-193
    O.W. Ferguson, 569(SR):Summer88-lxiv
    J. Smitten, 541(RES):Feb88-114
Casillo, R. The Genealogy of Demons.*
    J. Kronick, 598(SoR):Autumn89-859
    H. Levin, 453(NYRB):9Nov89-45
Caso González, J.M., ed. Historia y crítica de
la literatura española. (Vol 4)
    P. Deacon, 86(BHS):Jul88-305
van Caspel, P. Bloomers on the Liffey.*
    P. Parrinder, 402(MLR):Jan89-141
Cassell, E.J. Talking With Patients.
    A. Chacoff & E. Ness, 355(LSoc):Mar88-
      148
Cassell, R.A., ed. Critical Essays on Ford
Madox Ford.
    R.C. Schweik, 177(ELT):Vol31No1-89
Cassian, N. Call Yourself Alive?
    L. Chamberlain, 617(TLS):24Feb-2Mar89-
      200
Cassidy, F.G. - see "Dictionary of American
Regional English"
Cassill, R.V. Collected Stories.
    F. Wilson, 441:31Dec89-12
Cassin, B., ed. Le plaisir de parler.*
    F. Wolff, 192(EP):Apr-Jun88-249
Cassin, B. & M. Canto, eds. Positions de la
sophistique.*
    F. Wolff, 192(EP):Apr-Jun88-249
Casson, H., ed. The V & A Album, Gold Edi-
tion.
    C. Blair, 39:Mar88-219
Castagnola, R. - see de' Medici, L.
Castellana, M. Epistemologia debole.
    P. Engel, 542:Jul-Sep88-377

63

Castelvecchi, A. – see Trissino, G.G.
Casteras, S.P. Images of Victorian Womanhood in English Art.
   B.C. Rezelman, 637(VS):Spring89-429
Castiglioni, A., A. Castiglioni & G. Negro. Fiumi di pietra.
   M.B. Visonà, 2(AfrA):Aug88-85
de Castilla y León, J., ed. Literatura contemporánea en Castilla y León.
   I-J. López, 240(HR):Summer88-391
del Castillo, A., ed. Ejército y Sociedad.
   N. Mackie, 123:Vol38No2-443
Castillo, A. The Mixquiahuala Letters.
   B.D. May, 238:May88-313
Castillo, C., O.F. Bond & B.M. Garcia, comps. The University of Chicago Spanish Dictionary. (4th ed) (rev by D.L. Canfield)
   W.W. Moseley, 399(MLJ):Summer88-248
Castillo, G. Augusto Torres.
   90:Jan88-45
Castillo, J.R. – see under Romera Castillo, J.
Castle, T. Masquerade and Civilization.*
   I.A. Bell, 566:Autumn88-63
   L. Bertelsen, 401(MLQ):Jun87-195
   J.P. Carson, 481(PQ):Fall88-528
   R. Howells, 83:Spring88-93
   S.K. Marks, 594:Spring88-102
   M. Seidel, 166:Oct88-79
   W.B. Warner, 400(MLN):Dec88-1144
Castleman, R. Jasper Johns.
   P.B. Arnold, 127:Spring88-53
Castro, J.G. The Art and Life of Georgia O'Keeffe.
   M. Lennon, 106:Spring88-113
Castro, M.C. – see under Cabada Castro, M.
Castro, I. – see Pessoa, F.
Castro-Amaya, R.A. & J. Kattan-Zablah. Dos amigos.*
   S.E. Torres, 238:Mar88-99
Castronovo, D. The English Gentleman.*
   S. Pickering, 569(SR):Spring88-259
   42(AR):Winter88-124
   639(VQR):Spring88-54
Castronovo, D. Thornton Wilder.*
   R.C., 295(JML):Fall87/Winter88-398
Catalano, J.S. A Commentary on Jean-Paul Sartre's "Critique of Dialectical Reason." (Vol 1)
   A. Leak, 208(FS):Apr88-233
   W.L. McBride, 103:Nov88-430
   G.J. Stack, 319:Jan89-167
   H. Wardman, 402(MLR):Apr89-484
"Catalogue of Seventeenth-Century Italian Books in the British Library."
   L. Baldacchini, 354:Mar88-61
"A Catalogue of the Libraries of Sir Thomas Browne and Dr. Edward Browne, His Son." (J.S. Finch, ed)
   G. Mandelbrote, 78(BC):Summer88-279
   J.F.S. Post, 250(HLQ):Summer88-232
Catan, J.R. – see Reale, G.
Catanach, J.N. Brideprice.
   M. Stasio, 441:18Jun89-28
Catanzaro, R. Il delitto come impresa.
   A. Lyttelton, 617(TLS):3-9Mar89-211
Cate, P.D., ed. The Graphic Arts and French Society, 1871-1914.
   R.D. Reck, 207(FR):Apr89-930
Cather, W. Willa Cather in Person. (L.B. Bohlke, ed)
   B. Bair, 594:Fall88-340
   P.A. Greasley, 395(MFS):Summer88-237
         [continued]

[continuing]
   D.D. Quantic, 649(WAL):Aug88-151
   L. Wagner-Martin, 659(ConL):Fall89-444
Cather, W. The Short Stories of Willa Cather.
   C. Bold, 617(TLS):17-23Nov89-1259
Cato the Censor. Caton, "Les Origines (Fragments)." (M. Chassignet, ed & trans)
   J. Briscoe, 123:Vol38No1-153
   T.J. Cornell, 313:Vol78-211
Cattaneo, C. Il Politecnico 1839-1844. (L. Ambrosoli, ed)
   N. Bobbio, 358:Oct89-11
Catteau, J. Dostoyevsky and the Process of Literary Creation.
   L. Knapp, 617(TLS):17-23Nov89-1261
Catullus. Catullus: Love and Hate. (L.M. Kaiser, ed)
   J. Sarkissian, 124:Sep-Oct88-51
Caudill, H.M. Slender is the Thread.
   639(VQR):Summer88-91
Caudle, N. Voices from Home.
   A. McDermott, 441:13Aug89-8
Caudwell, C. Collected Poems.*
   T. Eagleton, 565:Winter87/88-65
Caudwell, S. The Sirens Sang of Murder.
   T.J. Binyon, 617(TLS):1-7Sep89-953
   M. Stasio, 441:5Nov89-28
Caufield, C. Multiple Exposures.
   E. Marshall, 441:16Jul89-20
Caunitz, W.J. Black Sand.
   M. Stasio, 441:2Apr89-33
Caute, D. Veronica, or The Two Nations.
   M. Wormald, 617(TLS):25-31Aug89-918
Cauthen, K. The Passion for Equality.
   J.P.S., 185:Oct88-187
Cauville, S. & D. De Vauchelle. Le Temple D'Edfou.
   R.S. Bianchi, 318(JAOS):Jul-Sep87-550
Cauvin, J. & O. Aurenche, eds. Cahiers de l'Euphrate no 4.
   J. Yakar, 318(JAOS):Oct-Dec87-793
Cavalcanti, G. The Poetry of Guido Cavalcanti. (L. Nelson, Jr., ed & trans)
   D. Anderson, 402(MLR):Jul89-748
   S. Pearce, 382(MAE):1988/1-141
Cavalieri, B. Carteggio. (G. Baroncelli, ed)
   F. Arato, 228(GSLI):Vol165fasc532-612
Cavallo, G. Libri, scritture, scribi a Ercolano. (M. Capasso & T. Dorandi, eds)
   H. Maehler, 229:Band60Heft5-398
Cavallo, G. & H. Maehler. Greek Bookhands of the Early Byzantine Period, AD 300-800.
   R. Browning, 617(TLS):13-19Jan89-46
Cavallo, S. La poética de José Hierro.
   E.E. De Torre Gracia, 711(RHM):Dec88-187
Cavanagh, C. Love and Forgiveness in Yeats's Poetry.
   M.H. Begnal, 174(Éire):Spring88-147
Cavarocchi, M. La certezza che toglie la speranza.
   R. Robertson, 402(MLR):Oct89-1037
Cavazza, F. – see Gellius
Cave, R.A., ed. The Romantic Theatre.
   C.M. Mazer, 340(KSJ):Vol37-206
Cave, T. Recognitions.*
   639(VQR):Autumn88-120
Cave Brown, A. "C."
   639(VQR):Summer88-90
Cavell, S. Disowning Knowledge in Six Plays of Shakespeare.*
   M. Elliott, 175:Autumn88-224
   J. Marenbon, 483:Oct88-546

Cavell, S. In Quest of the Ordinary.
  G. Steiner, 442(NY):19Jun89-97
  W. Steiner, 617(TLS):28Jul-3Aug89-817
Cavillac, C. L'Espagne dans la trilogie "pic-
aresque" de Lesage.
  D-H. Pageaux, 535(RHL):Jul-Aug88-771
Caviness, M.H. & others. Stained Glass before
1700 in American Collections.
  H. Wayment, 90:Jun88-470
Cawelti, J.G. & B. Rosenberg. The Spy Story.
  J.S. Dean, 125:Spring88-310
  L.D. Harred, 395(MFS):Summer88-331
Caws, M.A. Reading Frames in Modern Fic-
tion.*
  E.D. Ermarth, 301(JEGP):Jan88-141
Caws, M.A., ed. Textual Analysis.
  J.R. Bennett, 128(CE):Sep88-566
Cayton, A.R.L. The Frontier Republic.
  M.J. Rohrbough, 656(WMQ):Apr88-384
de Cazanove, O. & others. L'Association dio-
nysiaque dans les sociétés anciennes:
Actes de la table ronde organisée par
l'Ecole Française de Rome (Rome 24-25 mai
1984).
  J. Linderski, 313:Vol78-207
Cazelles, B. Le Corps de sainteté, d'après
Jehan Bouche d'Or, Jehan Paulus, et quel-
ques vies des XIIe et XIIIe siècles.
  D. Robertson, 545(RPh):May89-435
Cazelles, B. & P. Johnson. Le Vain siècle
guerpir.
  D. Robertson, 545(RPh):May89-435
Cazzullo, A. La verità della parola.
  J. Protevi, 543:Mar89-612
Cèbe, J-P. - see Varro
Cébeillac-Gervasoni, M., ed. Les "bour-
geoisies" municipales italiennes aux IIe et
Ier siècles av. J-C.
  H. Wolff, 229:Band60Heft3-239
Ceccarelli, L. L'allitterazione a vocale inter-
posta variabile in Virgilio.
  S.J. Harrison, 123:Vol38No2-411
Cecchetti, D. L'evoluzione del latino umanis-
tico in Francia.
  R.M. Rosado Fernandes, 547(RF):Band
  100Heft4-373
Cecil, H. Independent Witness.
  M. Stasio, 441:30Apr89-45
Cecil, R. A Divided Life.*
  R.W. Winks, 441:16Apr89-1
Cedeño, R.N. & I. Páez Urdaneta & J.M. Gui-
tart - see under Núñez Cedeño, R., I. Páez
Urdaneta & J.M. Guitart
Cederberg, F. The Last Hunter.
  R.W. Ingram, 102(CanL):Autumn88-145
Cedrini, L.B. - see under Borghi Cedrini, L.
Čejka, J., M. Černík & K. Sýs. The New Czech
Poetry.
  S. O'Brien, 364:Feb/Mar89-107
  M. Parker, 617(TLS):24Feb-2Mar89-200
Celan, P. Poems of Paul Celan.
  G. Steiner, 442(NY):28Aug89-93
Celant, G. Unexpressionism.
  J. Hall, 617(TLS):31Mar-6Apr89-336
Celati, G. Voices from the Plains. Quattro
novelle sulle apparenze. Verso la foce.
  A. Tahourdin, 617(TLS):13-19Oct89-
  1131
Celce-Murcia, M. & D. Larsen-Freeman. The
Grammar Book.
  G.P. Delahunty, 351(LL):Mar88-141
Celeyrette-Pietri, N. & J. Robinson-Valéry -
see Valéry, P.

Çelik, Z. The Remaking of Istanbul.
  H. Crane, 576:Sep88-305
Cellini, B. La vie de Benvenuto Cellini écrite
par lui-même (1500-1571).
  N. Heinich, 98:Mar88-183
Cendrars, B. Hollywood, La Mecque du cinéma
[suivi de] l'ABC du cinéma.
  G. Colvile, 207(FR):Feb89-543
Cenkner, W. A Tradition of Teachers.
  R.W. Lariviere, 318(JAOS):Oct-Dec87-778
Cense, A.A. Makassaars-Nederlands Wooden-
boek, met Nederlands-Makassaars register.
  J.U. Wolff, 318(JAOS):Jan-Mar87-194
Censer, J.R. & J.D. Popkin, eds. Press and
Politics in Pre-Revolutionary France.
  D. Stephens, 207(FR):Dec88-347
"Cent ans de littérature française (1850-
1950)."
  L. Le Guillou, 535(RHL):Nov-Dec88-1180
Cerasuolo, S., M. Capasso & A. D'Ambrosio.
Carlo Maria Rosini (1748-1836).
  I.C. McIlwaine, 123:Vol38No1-190
Cerf, M. Street Girl.
  S. Rance, 617(TLS):13-19Oct89-1130
Čermák, F. & others, eds. A Course of Czech
Language. (Vols 1-3)
  J. McGinley, 575(SEER):Apr88-261
Černá, J. Kafka's Milena.
  J. Adler, 617(TLS):16-22Jun89-661
Cerny, L. "Beautie and the use thereof."
  G. Schmitz, 72:Band225Heft1-155
Černyx, V.A. - see Axmatova, A.
de Cervantes Saavedra, M. Don Quixote de la
Mancha. (T. Smollett, trans)
  N.M. Valis, 396(ModA):Fall89-368
Červenka, M. Z večerní školy versologie.*
  H. Eagle, 494:Vol8No1-142
"Aimé Césaire ou l'athanor d'un alchimiste."
  A.J. Arnold, 538(RAL):Winter88-586
"Césaire d'Arles, Sermons au peuple." (Vol
3)(M-J. Delage, ed & trans)
  O. Hiltbrunner, 229:Band60Heft6-537
César de Nostredame. Les Perles, ou les
larmes de la saincte Magdeleine.* (R.T.
Corum, Jr., ed)
  O. Millet, 535(RHL):Sep-Oct88-1025
Cessi, V. Erkennen und Handeln in der Theo-
rie des Tragischen bei Aristoteles.
  M. Heath, 123:Vol38No2-404
Chabon, M. The Mysteries of Pittsburgh.*
  639(VQR):Autumn88-128
Chabot, J-L. Histoire de la pensée politique
(XIXe et XXe siècles).
  D. Damamme, 542:Oct-Dec88-517
Chace, J. & C. Carr. America Invulnerable.*
  639(VQR):Autumn88-129
Chace, S. Intimacy.
  C. Gaiser, 441:12Feb89-15
Chacel, J.M., P.S. Falk & D.V. Fleischer, eds.
Brazil's Economic and Political Future.
  S.M. Cunningham, 263(RIB):Vol38No3-398
Chadwick, H. Augustine.*
  P. Habermehl, 229:Band60Heft3-209
Chadwick, J. Linear B and Related Scripts.
  B. Vine, 124:Mar-Apr89-321
Chadwick, R.F., ed. Ethics, Reproduction and
Genetic Control.
  H.K., 185:Apr89-688
Chadwick, W. Women Artists and the Surreal-
ist Movement.
  J. Kaplan, 662:Fall88/Winter89-47

Chafe, W. & J. Nichols, eds. Evidentiality.
Co Vet, 320(CJL):Mar88-65
T. Willett, 353:Vol26No3-498
Chafets, Z. Heroes and Hustlers, Hard Hats
and Holy Men.
J. Riemer, 287:Jul/Aug88-33
Chafets, Z. Members of the Tribe.
A.L. Goldman, 441:22Jan89-23
Chaffee, J.W. The Thorny Gates of Learning
in Sung China.*
P. Ebrey, 244(HJAS):Dec88-493
Chafuen, A.A. Christians for Freedom.
M.N. Rothbard, 258:Mar88-112
"Marc Chagall Arabian Nights."
P-L. Adams, 61:Jan89-120
Chai, L. The Romantic Foundations of the
American Renaissance.*
M. Anesko, 432(NEQ):Sep88-456
R. Asselineau, 189(EA):Oct-Dec88-494
E.S. Fussell, 27(AL):Oct88-469
J. McWilliams, 445(NCF):Dec88-399
Chaillou, M. La Croyance des voleurs.
R. Buss, 617(TLS):21-27Jul89-802
Chaim, D.B. Distance in the Theatre.
M. Carlson, 610:Autumn88-297
de Chaisemartin, N. & E. Örgen. Les docu-
ments sculptés de Silahtarağa.
R. Fleischer, 229:Band60Heft1-61
Chalfant, W.Y. Cheyennes and Horse Soldiers.
I. Frazier, 441:24Sep89-35
Chalfen, R. Snapshot Versions of Life.
D.H., 355(LSoc):Sep88-463
Lord Chalfont. By God's Will.
R. Flamini, 617(TLS):22-28Sep89-1040
Chalier, C. La persévérance du mal.
P. Trotignon, 542:Jan-Mar88-117
Chamberlain, L. The Food and Cooking of
Eastern Europe.
S. Beller, 617(TLS):22-28Dec89-1410
Chambers, C. The Story of Unity Theatre.
B. Nightingale, 617(TLS):3-9Nov89-1214
Chambers, C. & M. Prior. Playwrights' Prog-
ress.
V. Lustig, 157:No170-49
Chambers, F.M. An Introduction to Old Pro-
vençal Versification.*
W.D. Paden, 589:Jan88-132
Chambers, H., ed. An Enormous Yes.
W. Scammell, 493:Winter88/89-20
Chambers, H., ed. Peterloo Preview I.
S. O'Brien, 617(TLS):25-31Aug89-916
Chambers, H. & C. Faram, eds. Neighbours.
S. O'Brien, 617(TLS):25-31Aug89-916
Chambers, J. Milestones I. Milestones II.
R. Witmer, 627(UTQ):Fall87-229
Chambers, R. A Course of Lectures on the
English Law, Delivered at the University of
Oxford 1767-1773 by Sir Robert Chambers,
Second Vinerian Professor of English Law,
and Composed in Association with Samuel
Johnson. (T.M. Curley, ed)
J. Hackney, 541(RES):Nov88-561
D. Ibbetson, 447(N&Q):Dec88-540
Chambers, R. Mélancolie et opposition.
D.F. Bell, 400(MLN):Sep88-939
B. Howells, 402(MLR):Oct89-988
Chambers, R. Story and Situation.*
C. Warner, 107(CRCL):Mar88-92
Chambon, J-P., ed. Französisches Etymolo-
gisches Wörterbuch. (Vol 25, fasc 146)
R. Arveiller, 209(FM):Apr88-136

Chambon, J-P., ed. Französisches Etymolo-
gisches Wörterbuch. (Vol 25, fasc 148)
R. Arveiller, 209(FM):Apr88-141
Chametzky, J. Our Decentralized Literature.
S.P., 295(JML):Fall87/Winter88-204
von Chamisso, A. A Voyage Around the World
with the Romanzov Exploring Expedition in
the Years 1815-1818 in the Brig "Rurik,"
Captain Otto von Kotzebue. (H. Kratz, ed &
trans)
H.M. Kastinger Riley, 133:Band21Heft4-
347
Chamoiseau, P. Solibo magnifique.
R. Linkhorn, 207(FR):Apr89-901
Chamot, A.U. America: The Early Years.
America: After Independence.
J. Dungey, 608:Mar89-133
Champagne-Muzar, C.M., J.S. Bourdage & E.I.
Schneiderman. Accent on Accent.
J. Walz, 207(FR):Apr89-922
Champfleury. Le Violon de faïence, Les En-
fants du professeur Turck, La Sonnette de
M. Berloquin. (M. Weatherilt, ed)
K.G. McWatters, 208(FS):Jan88-99
Champigny, R. Sense, Antisense, Nonsense.
J. Baetens, 535(RHL):Mar-Apr88-348
C. Shorley, 208(FS):Jan88-115
Champlin, C. Back There Where the Past Was.
E. Hanson, 441:17Sep89-25
Chan Heng Chee. A Sensation of Indepen-
dence.
T.J. Bellows, 293(JASt):Aug88-695
Chan, M. & H. Kwok. A Study of Lexical Bor-
rowing from Chinese into English with Spe-
cial Reference to Hong Kong.
Yan Shunchiu, 302:Vol24No1-104
Chan, S. Songs of the Maori King.
G. Boire, 102(CanL):Spring88-194
Chan, W-T., ed. Chu Hsi and Neo-Confucian-
ism.
H.C. Tillman, 485(PE&W):Jan88-77
Chan, W-T. - see Ch'en Ch'un
Chanady, A. Magical Realism and the Fan-
tastic.
L. Olsen, 70:Apr88-76
Chanan, M. The Cuban Image.
P. Bacarisse, 86(BHS):Apr88-207
Chance, J. Woman as Hero in Old English
Literature.*
C. Brewer, 541(RES):May88-280
J.W. Nicholls, 402(MLR):Jan89-114
H. O'Donoghue, 382(MAE):1988/2-299
H. Weissman, 589:Jan88-134
Chand, M. House of the Sun.
J. Banerjee, 617(TLS):21-27Jul89-804
Chander, N.J., ed. Dynamics of State Politics,
Kerala.
T.J. Nossiter, 293(JASt):Aug88-672
Chandès, G. Le Serpent, la femme et l'épée.
T. Hunt, 402(MLR):Jan89-157
E. Kennedy, 447(N&Q):Dec88-520
P.S. Noble, 208(FS):Oct88-458
Chandler, B.J. King of the Mountain.
C. Duggan, 617(TLS):26May-1Jun89-572
Chandler, D.P. & M.C. Ricklefs, eds. Nine-
teenth and Twentieth Century Indonesia.
R.S. Kipp, 293(JASt):May88-417
Chandler, H., with V.H. Trimble. Heroes, Plain
Folks, and Skunks.
M.E. Ross, 441:23Apr89-37

Chandler, J.H., ed. Wiltshire Dissenters'
Meeting House Certificates and Registra-
tions 1689–1852.
  M.H. Port, 447(N&Q):Jun88–236
Chandler, R. Selected Letters of Raymond
Chandler. (F. MacShane, ed)
  E. Fontana, 649(WAL):May88–60
Chandler, R. & R.B. Parker. Poodle Springs.
  E. McBain, 441:15Oct89–35
  L. Rose, 61:Oct89–113
Chaney, E. The Grand Tour and the Great
Rebellion.
  J. Bury, 90:Jul88–542
Chang, D.W–W. China under Deng Xiaoping.
  J. Mirsky, 617(TLS):28Apr–4May89–463
Chang, H. Chinese Intellectuals in Crisis.
  J.B. Grieder, 293(JASt):Aug88–584
  G. Mathews, 31(ASch):Autumn88–624
Chang, K.C., ed. Studies of Shang Archaeol-
ogy.
  E.L. Shaughnessy, 318(JAOS):Jul–Sep87–
  500
Chang, K–I.S. Six Dynasties Poetry.*
  D. Holzman, 244(HJAS):Jun88–244
Chang-Rodríguez, E. Poética e ideología en
José Carlos Mariátegui.
  D.R. Reedy, 86(BHS):Jul88–322
"Chanson de Guillaume."* (B. Schmolke-
Hasselmann, trans)
  G. Pinkernell, 72:Band224Heft2–446
Chao, K. Man and Land in Chinese History.
  R.M. Hartwell, 293(JASt):May88–335
Chao, S.R. & T.D. Abramson, eds. Kohn Pe-
dersen Fox.
  S. Gutterman, 45:Mar88–77
Chapallaz, M. The Pronunciation of Italian.
  R.A. Hall, Jr., 276:Spring88–36
Chapelot, J. & R. Fossier. The Village and
House in the Middle Ages.
  S. Bonde, 589:Jul88–637
Chapman, G. The Plays of George Chapman:
The Tragedies with "Sir Gyles Goose-
cappe."* (A. Holaday, G.B. Evans & T.L.
Berger, eds)
  M. Baron, 175:Spring88–87
  G. Monsarrat, 189(EA):Oct–Dec88–484
Chapman, M. South African English Poetry.
  J. Alvarez-Péreyre, 538(RAL):Spring88–
  111
Chapman, R. The Sense of the Past in Victo-
rian Literature.*
  M. Hardman, 402(MLR):Oct89–944
Chapman, R.A. Ethics in the British Civil
Service.
  A. Cairncross, 617(TLS):6–12Jan89–5
Chapman, R.W. – see Johnson, S.
Chapman, W. Inside the Philippine Revolu-
tion.
  M. Leifer, 617(TLS):28Apr–4May89–465
Chappaz, M. Un homme qui vivait couché sur
un banc. Verdures de la Nuit. Les Grandes
Journées de Printemps.
  F. Mary, 450(NRF):Sep88–104
Chappell, F. Brighten the Corner Where You
Are.
  S.O. Warner, 441:1Oct89–26
Chappell, F. The Fred Chappell Reader.
  S. Wright, 569(SR):Spring88–xxxiv
Chapple, C. Karma and Creativity.
  J.W. de Jong, 259(IIJ):Apr88–146
  A. Malhotra, 485(PE&W):Jan88–88

Chapple, J.A.V. Science and Literature in the
Nineteenth Century.*
  E. Block, Jr., 637(VS):Winter89–285
  C. Jones, 506(PSt):May88–111
  N. Vance, 402(MLR):Jul89–723
Chapsal, M. Adieu l'amour.
  R.J. Hartwig, 207(FR):Dec88–360
Chapuis, N. – see Qian Zhongshu
Char, R. Éloge d'une soupçonnée.
  M. Hutchinson, 617(TLS):29Dec89/
  4Jan90–1443
  J. Roudaut, 450(NRF):Sep88–103
Charlebois, J. Tâche de naissance.
  K.W. Meadwell, 102(CanL):Spring88–111
Charles, D. Aristotle's Philosophy of Action.*
  S. Sauvé, 482(PhR):Jul88–411
Charles-Edwards, T.M., M.E. Owen & D.B.
Walters, eds. Lawyers and Laymen.
  F. Kelly, 112:Vol20–227
Charles-Roux, E. Chanel.
  617(TLS):29Sep–5Oct89–1072
Charlesworth, B. & C. Hagen. Private Enemy
– Public Eye. (T.W. Stack & C. Stainback,
eds)
  A. Grundberg, 441:3Dec89–73
Charlton, D.G., ed. The French Romantics.
  M. Philip, 345(KRQ):Feb88–89
Charlton, G. Nightshift Workers.
  M. Wormald, 617(TLS):9–15Jun89–641
Charlton, W. Philosophy and Christian Belief.
  S. Grover, 617(TLS):19–25May89–534
Charney, M., ed. "Bad" Shakespeare.
  R. Hapgood, 617(TLS):25–31Aug89–927
Charnon-Deutsch, L. The Nineteenth-Cen-
tury Spanish Story.*
  A.H. Clarke, 345(KRQ):Aug88–370
  T.A. Sackett, 552(REH):Jan88–138
Charpin, D. Le clergé d'Ur au siècle d'Ham-
murabi (XIXe–XVIIIe siècles av. J.–C.).
  M. Stol, 318(JAOS):Oct–Dec87–792
Charters, A. Beats & Company.*
  R. Ardinger, 649(WAL):May88–64
  A.J. Sabatini, 296(JML):Fall87/Winter88–
  191
Chartier, R. Cultural History.
  P. Curry, 617(TLS):17–23Feb89–156
Chartier, R., ed. A History of Private Life.
(Vol 3)
  M. Quilligan, 441:16Apr89–24
  K. Thomas, 453(NYRB):9Nov89–15
Charyn, J. Movieland.
  R. Sklar, 441:16Jul89–17
Chase, C. Decomposing Figures.*
  J. Baldo, 141:Winter88–141
  L.R. Furst, 107(CRCL):Jun88–298
  P. Kamuf, 131(CL):Fall88–404
  A.K. Mellor, 445(NCF):Jun88–128
  S. Simpkins, 128(CE):Nov88–812
Chase, G. America's Music.
  D. Nicholls, 410(M&L):Oct88–542
Chase, J. The Evening Wolves.
  J. Conarroe, 441:28May89–11
  442(NY):14Aug89–90
Chase, J. Exterior Decoration.
  A. Dannatt, 46:Dec87–10
Chase, W.J. Workers, Society, and the Soviet
State.
  W.G. Rosenberg, 550(RusR):Jul88–342
Chase-Riboud, B. Echo of Lions.
  M. Southgate, 441:14May89–22
Chassignet, M. – see Cato the Censor
Chastain, K. & G. Guntermann. ¡Imagínate!
  M.E. Beeson, 399(MLJ):Spring88–106

Chastel, A. & J. Guillaume, eds. La maison de
ville à la Renaissance. L'escalier dans
l'architecture de la Renaissance.
N. Miller, 576:Jun88-197
de Chateaubriand, F.R. Correspondance gén-
érale.* (Vol 5) (P. Riberette, ed)
J-C. Berchet, 535(RHL):Mar-Apr88-288
Châtenet, M. Le château de Madrid au bois de
Boulogne.
D. Thomson, 90:May88-375
Chatham, R. Dark Waters.
C. Verderese, 441:20Aug89-21
Châtillon, J. - see de Saint-Victor, R.
Chatterjee, U. English, August.*
J. Mellors, 364:Jul88-105
Chatterjee, V., ed. The Romantic Tradition.
N. Roe, 447(N&Q):Mar88-128
Chatto, B. The Green Tapestry.
A. Lacy, 441:11Jun89-30
Chattopadhyay, M. Petition to Agitation.
J.R. McLane, 293(JASt):Aug88-673
Chattopadhyaya, D. Knowledge and Inter-
vention.
D. Allen, 485(PE&W):Jan88-79
Chatwin, B. The Songlines.
C. Matthews, 376:Dec88-142
Chatwin, B. Utz.*
P.L. Adams, 61:Feb89-83
G. Annan, 453(NYRB):2Feb89-6
R. Stone, 441:15Jan89-3
Chatwin, B. What Am I Doing Here.
D. Ackerman, 441:10Sep89-9
P-L. Adams, 61:Nov89-136
H.M. Enzensberger, 617(TLS):16-
22Jun89-657
Chaucer, G. The Canterbury Tales.* (D.
Wright, ed & trans)
E.H.C., 382(MAE):1988/1-152
Chaucer, G. The Miller's Tale. (T.W. Ross,
ed) The Manciple's Tale. (D.C. Baker, ed)
M. Gretsch, 38:Band106Heft3/4-498
E.G. Stanley, 447(N&Q):Dec88-512
Chaucer, G. The Nun's Priest's Tale.* (D.A.
Pearsall, ed)
E.G. Stanley, 447(N&Q):Dec88-512
Chaucer, G. The Physician's Tale. (H.S.
Corsa, ed)
N.F. Blake, 179(ES):Dec88-571
E.G. Stanley, 447(N&Q):Dec88-512
Chaucer, G. The Prioress's Tale. (B. Boyd,
ed) Geoffrey Chaucer: The Minor Poems.
(Pt 1) (G.B. Pace & A. David, eds)
E.G. Stanley, 447(N&Q):Dec88-512
Chaucer, G. The Riverside Chaucer. (3rd ed)
(L. Benson, ed)
M. Baron, 175:Summer88-177
B. Bowden, 184(EIC):Jan88-75
L. Brosnahan, 589:Jul88-641
Chaudhuri, B. - see "Annual Bibliography of
Victorian Studies 1984"
Chaudhuri, N.C. Thy Hand, Great Anarch.*
P-L. Adams, 61:Jun89-98
A. Ross, 364:Feb88-109
Chaudhuri, S. Index Internationalis Indicus.
(Vols 2-4) Index to the Transactions of
the International Congress of Orientalists
1873-1973. (Pt 1)
R. Rocher, 318(JAOS):Oct-Dec87-846
Chaudhuri, S, ed. Proceedings of the Asiatic
Society. (Vol 1)
R. Rocher, 318(JAOS):Oct-Dec87-780
Chaudron, C. Second Language Classrooms.
D. Barnwell, 399(MLJ):Winter88-458

Chaumartin, F-R. Le "De beneficiis" de Sén-
èque, sa signification philosophique, poli-
tique et sociale.
A. Novara, 555:Vol61fasc1-143
Chauveau, J-P., ed. Anthologie de la poésie
française du XVIIe siècle.
C. Abraham, 475:Vol15No28-279
Chavée, A. Petit Traité d'agnosticisme.
M. Voisin, 193:Autumn88-145
Chaves, J., ed & trans. The Columbia Book of
Later Chinese Poetry.
S. Owen, 244(HJAS):Jun88-260
R.E. Strassberg, 293(JASt):May88-337
Chavez, A. The Short Stories of Fray Angeli-
co Chavez. (G. Padilla, ed)
R. Gish, 649(WAL):Aug88-158
Chávez, H.A.H. - see under Helberg Chávez,
H.A.
Checa, J. Gracián y la imaginación arquitec-
tónica.
D.J. Hildner, 238:Mar88-82
Checkland, S. The Elgins, 1766-1917.*
J. Griffin, 453(NYRB):20Jul89-14
Chedid, A. Mondes miroirs magies.
B.L. Knapp, 207(FR):May89-1091
Chee, C.H. - see under Chan Heng Chee
Cheek, M. Pause Between Acts.
E. Pall, 441:5Mar89-22
Cheever, J. The Letters of John Cheever.*
(B. Cheever, ed)
J. Campbell, 617(TLS):15-21Sep89-996
Cheever, S. Elizabeth Cole.
C. See, 441:19Nov89-13
Chefdor, M., R. Quinones & A. Wachtel, eds.
Modernism: Challenges and Perspectives.*
S. Connor, 402(MLR):Jul89-699
Chehak, S.T. The Story of Annie D.
M. Stasio, 441:9Jul89-24
Cheles, L. The Studiolo of Urbino.*
E. Verheyen, 539:Summer89-236
P.F. Watson, 276:Autumn88-267
C.W. Westfall, 589:Apr88-379
Chelkowski, P.J. & R.J. Pranger, eds. Ideology
and Power in the Middle East.*
639(VQR):Autumn88-132
Chemain, R. L'imaginaire dans le roman afri-
cain d'expression française.
D. Whitman, 538(RAL):Fall88-398
Chemparathy, G. L'autorité du Veda selon les
Nyāya-Vaiśeṣikas.
P. Olivelle, 318(JAOS):Apr-Jun87-364
Ch'en Ch'un. Neo-Confucian Terms Explained
(The "Pei-hsi tzu-i"). (W-T. Chan, ed &
trans)
J. Berthrong, 293(JASt):Feb88-110
Chen, K.C. China's War with Vietnam, 1979.
C-T. Hsüeh, 293(JASt):Nov88-847
Chen, L.F. The Confucian Way.
R. Ptak, 318(JAOS):Oct-Dec87-823
Chen, Y-S. Realism and Allegory in the Early
Fiction of Mao Tun.
D.D.W. Wang, 293(JASt):Feb88-111
L.Y-X., 295(JML):Fall87/Winter88-352
Ch'en Ying-chen. Exiles at Home.
C. Yu, 293(JASt):Feb88-113
Chen Yung-fa & G. Benton. Moral Economy
and the Chinese Revolution.
S.C. Averill, 293(JASt):Aug88-615
Chênerie, M-L. Le Chevalier errant dans les
romans arthuriens en vers des XIIe et XIIIe
siècles.*
J. Chaurand, 549(RLC):Jan-Mar88-90
[continued]

Ching-hwang, Y. – see under Yen Ching-hwang

Chinul. The Korean Approach to Zen.
Young Bong Oh, 293(JASt):Aug88–660

Chinweizu, ed. Voices from Twentieth-Century Africa.*
A. Maja-Pearce, 364:Feb/Mar89–142

de Chirico, G. Hebdomeros.
L.E. Nesbitt, 55:Summer88–89

Chisholm, D. The Civil War Notebook of Daniel Chisholm. (W.S. Menge and J.A. Shimrak, eds)
442(NY):4Sep89–108

Chisholm, R.M. Brentano and Intrinsic Value.*
D. Jacquette, 321:Oct88–331

Chistov, K.V. Narodnye traditsii i fol'klor.
M. Perrie, 550(RusR):Apr88–179

Chitham, E. A Life of Emily Brontë.*
C. Lemon, 82:Vol19No6–275
J. Maynard, 637(VS):Spring89–419

Chitty, S. That Singular Person Called Lear.*
K. Weber, 441:5Mar89–14

Chiu, H., Y.C. Jao & Y-L. Wu, eds. The Future of Hong Kong.
A.Y. So, 293(JASt):Aug88–588

Cho, D-S. The General Trading Company.
A.K. Young, 293(JASt):May88–322

Chocheyras, J. & G.A. Runnalls, eds. La Vie de Marie Magdaleine par personnages, Bibliothèque Nationale de Paris, Réserve Yf 2914.*
R. Horville, 535(RHL):Sep–Oct88–1024
L.R. Muir, 382(MAE):1988/1–135

Chock, P.P. & J.R. Wyman, eds. Discourse and the Social Life of Meaning.
D.H., 355(LSoc):Sep88–464

Choe-Wall, Y-H. – see Lady Hong

Chomarat, J., M-M. Fragonard & G. Mathieu-Castellani – see de Muret, M-A.

Chomsky, N. Barriers.*
M.R. Manzini, 297(JL):Mar88–252

Chomsky, N. Knowledge of Language.*
N. Hornstein, 482(PhR):Oct88–567
N.V. Smith, 297(JL):Mar88–189

Chomsky, N. La nouvelle syntaxe.
R. Martin, 209(FM):Apr88–112

Chomsky, N. On Power and Ideology.
M.A. Rygiel, 577(SHR):Winter88–63

Chŏngju, S. – see under Sŏ Chŏngju

Choquette, R. La Foi, Gardienne de la langue en Ontario 1900-1950.
J.S. Moir, 627(UTQ):Fall88–192

Chou Hsun & Kao Ch'un-ming. 5000 Years of Chinese Costumes.
J.E. Vollmer, 60:Sep–Oct88–153

Chou, J-H. & C. Brown. The Elegant Brush.
H. Butz, 293(JASt):Aug88–589

Chouillet, A-M., ed. Colloque International Diderot (1713-1784).*
G. Bremner, 83:Spring88–110

Chouillet, J. Denis Diderot-Sophie Volland.
S. Davies, 83:Spring88–110

Choyce, L. Conventional Emotions.
P. Klovan, 102(CanL):Spring88–211

Chrétien, G. – see Nonnos

Chrétien, J-L. L'effroi du beau.
M-A. Lescourret, 98:Mar88–252
P. Somville, 542:Oct–Dec88–515

Chrétien de Troyes. Arthurian Romances.
(D.D.R. Owen, ed & trans)
G.S Burgess, 208(FS):Oct88–458
E. Kennedy, 447(N&Q):Dec88–519

Chrétien de Troyes. Guillaume d'Angleterre.
(A.J. Holden, ed)
G. Roques, 553(RLiR):Jul–Dec88–548

Chrétien de Troyes. The Knight with the Lion, or Yvain (Le Chevalier au Lion).
(W.W. Kibler, ed & trans)
G.S. Burgess, 589:Jan88–136
382(MAE):1988/1–154

Christensen, D.E. Hegelian/Whiteheadian Perspectives.
G.R. Lucas, Jr., 103:Aug89–305

Christensen, D.E. The Search for Concreteness.
J.M. Zycinski, 543:Jun89–821

Christensen, J. Practicing Enlightenment.*
W.B. Carnochan, 402(MLR):Apr89–442
D. Womersley, 541(RES):Aug88–449

Christensen, J. & J. From Arnold Schoenberg's Literary Legacy.
O. Neighbour, 415:Oct88–532

Christensen, M. Mortal Belladaywic.
M.D. Wood, 448:Vol26No3–103

Christensen, T. Reel Politics.*
D. Jeffcock, 707:Summer88–216

Christian, W.A., Sr. Doctrines of Religious Communities.
R. Attfield, 518:Oct88–252

Christiansen, R., ed. The Grand Obsession.*
E. Forbes, 415:Sep88–462

Christiansen, R. Romantic Affinities.*
H. Bevington, 441:15Jan89–14

Christianson, C.P. Memorials of the Book Trade in Medieval London.*
78(BC):Autumn88–313

Christison, M.A. & S. Bassano. Look Who's Talking. (2nd ed)
E. Fischer-Kohn, 399(MLJ):Autumn88–348

Christmann, H.H. Filología idealista y lingüística moderna.
P. Swiggers, 553(RLiR):Jul–Dec88–496

Christoff, D. & others. La philosophie de la Haute Ecole de Lausanne 1542-1955.
A. Reix, 542:Jan–Mar88–118

Christopher, N. The Soloist.
G. Davenport, 569(SR):Fall88–695

Christopher, R.C. Crashing the Gates.
M.M. Thomas, 441:4Jun89–10

Christopher, T. In Search of Lost Roses.
B. Lowry, 441:3Dec89–75

Christy, T.C. Uniformitarianism in Linguistics.
F. Lebsanft, 685(ZDL):3/1987–355

Chrysaphes, M. The Treatise of Manuel Chrysaphes, the Lampadarios. (D.E. Conomos, ed & trans)
D. Stefanović, 410(M&L):Jul88–366

Chūhei Sugiyama & Hiroshi Mizuta, eds. Enlightenment and Beyond.
B.K. Marshall, 407(MN):Winter88–486

Ch'un, C. – see under Ch'en Ch'un

Chung Sei-wha, ed. Challenges for Women.
L.S. Lewis, 293(JASt):Nov88–905

Churchill, L.R. Rationing Health Care in America.
N. Daniels, 185:Jan89–444

Churchill, S. The Education of Linguistic and Cultural Minorities in the OECD Countries.
J.A. Fishman, 399(MLJ):Summer88–227
O. García, 355(LSoc):Dec88–597

Churchland, P.M. & C.A. Hooker, eds. Images of Science.*
R. Fellows, 518:Apr88–120

Churchland, P.S. Neurophilosophy.*
  M. Donald, 529(QQ):Winter88-947
  C.S. Hill, 482(PhR):Oct88-573
  C.A. Hooker, 63:Jun88-340
Chute, C. Letourneau's Used Auto Parts.*
  A. Bloom, 249(HudR):Autumn88-546
  J. Parini, 617(TLS):24-30Nov89-1313
Cicero. M. Tulli Ciceronis orationes: Divin-
  atio in Q. Caecilium, In C. Verrem actio I, In
  C. Verrem actio II.
  W.D. Lebek, 229:Band60Heft3-193
Cicero. Fragmenta ex libris philosophicis, ex
  aliis libris deperditis, ex scriptis incertis.
  (G. Garbarino, ed)
  M. Plezia, 229:Band60Heft2-152
  J.G.F. Powell, 313:Vol78-216
Cicero. Philippics.* (D.R. Shackleton Bailey,
  ed & trans)
  P. Fedeli, 229:Band60Heft4-296
  H.M. Hine, 123:Vol38No1-40
  J.J. Hughes, 24:Fall88-452
  J.G.F. Powell, 313:Vol78-216
Cicero. Pro Roscio Amerino. (E.H. Donkin, ed)
  P. Harvey, 124:Jul-Aug89-448
Cicero. Second Philippic Oration. (W.K.
  Lacey, ed & trans)
  A.T. Edwards, 124:Jul-Aug89-454
Cicero. Tusculan Disputations I.* (A.E.
  Douglas, ed & trans)
  J.P. Adams, 124:Sep-Oct88-53
Cicero. Verrines. (Vol 2, Pt 1) (T.N. Mitchell,
  ed & trans)
  H.C. Gotoff, 123:Vol38No1-37
  R. Hock, 124:Jul-Aug89-481
  J.G.F. Powell, 313:Vol78-216
Cielens, I. Trois fonctions de l'exil dans les
  oeuvres de fiction d'Albert Camus.*
  G. Jacobs, 345(KRQ):Feb88-104
  J. Sarrochi, 535(RHL):Jan-Feb88-154
de la Cierva, R. La Derecha sin remedio
  (1801-1987).
  V. Nemoianu, 396(ModA):Summer89-276
Cifuentes, L.F. - see under Fernández Cifu-
  entes, L.
Ciliberto, M. La ruota del tempo.
  M. Pozzi, 228(GSLI):Vol165fasc529-125
da Cingoli, G. - see under Gentile da Cingoli
Cipolla, G. - see Meli, G.
Cipriani, G. Cesare e la retorica dell'
  assedio.
  J.G.F. Powell, 123:Vol38No2-415
Cipriani, G. - see Postel, G.
Cirni, J. The Come On.
  M. Stasio, 441:30Jul89-18
Cisneros, S. The House on Mango Street.
  A. Nash, 608:Jun89-326
Citron, M.J. - see Hensel, F.
Cixous, H. & C. Clement. The Newly Born
  Woman (La Jeune Née).
  E. Jordan, 366:Autumn88-218
  H. Michie, 494:Vol8No3/4-661
  E. Wright & D. Chisholm, 402(MLR):
  Apr89-418
Clabburn, P. The National Trust Book of Fur-
  nishing Textiles.
  B. Scott, 324:Dec88-63
Claiborne, S. A Craving for Women.
  R. Short, 441:1Jan89-14
Clair, J. Paradoxe sur le conservateur.
  R. Jacquelin, 450(NRF):Oct88-102
de Claireville, O.S. Le Gascon extravagant.
  (F. Robello, ed)
  G. Malquori Fondi, 475:Vol15No28-332

Clampitt, A. Archaic Figure.*
  D.M. Halperin, 473(PR):Vol55No3-508
  M. O'Neill, 493:Summer88-60
  W. Scammell, 364:Aug/Sep88-108
Clampitt, A. What The Life Was Like.
  R. Pybus, 565:Summer88-72
Clancy, T. Clear and Present Danger.
  D. Wise, 441:13Aug89-9
Clarà, J.B.C. - see under Culla i Clarà, J.B.
de Claramonte, A. El Burlador de Sevilla. (A.
  Rodríguez López-Vázquez, ed)
  J.A. Parr, 238:May88-288
  B. Wittmann, 547(RF):Band100Heft4-473
de Claramonte, A. Púsoseme el sol, salióme la
  luna.* (A. Rodríguez López-Vázquez, ed)
  S.N. McCrary, 345(KRQ):Feb88-111
Clare, J. John Clare and the Bounds of Cir-
  cumstance.
  W. Howard, 627(UTQ):Fall88-110
Clare, J. The Early Poems of John Clare,
  1804-1822. (E. Robinson & D. Powell, eds)
  G. Lindop, 617(TLS):8-14Dec89-1366
Clare, J. Selected Poetry and Prose. (M. & R.
  Williams, eds)
  M. Grainger, 541(RES):Nov88-565
  D. Groves, 447(N&Q):Jun88-250
Clareson, T. Frederik Pohl.
  D.N. Samuelson, 561(SFS):Nov88-361
Clark, A. Rock and Roll Memories.
  B.L. Cooper, 498:Summer88-85
Clark, A. Women's Silence, Men's Violence.*
  A.G. Jones, 83:Autumn88-211
Clark, A. - see Neff, W., Jr.
Clark, A.R. La France dans l'Histoire selon
  Bernanos.
  M. Watthee-Delmotte, 356(LR):Nov88-526
Clark, B.L. Talking About Writing.*
  M.S. Rugger, 608:Sep89-535
Clark, C. Three Augustan Women Play-
  wrights.*
  J.W. Lafler, 610:Autumn88-282
  L. Woods, 615(TJ):Mar88-127
Clark, C.E., Jr. The American Family Home,
  1800-1960.
  B.L. Herman, 658:Summer/Autumn88-185
  D. Schuyler, 576:Jun88-208
  M.A. Williams, 650(WF):Apr88-157
Clark, D.N. Christianity in Modern Korea.
  D.H. Bays, 293(JASt):Aug88-661
Clark, D.N., ed. The Kwangju Uprising.
  D.I. Steinberg, 293(JASt):Aug88-662
Clark, E. The Want Makers.
  J. Williamson, 441:2Jul89-14
Clark, G. American Ceramics: 1876 to the
  Present. (rev)
  J. Perreault, 139:Dec88/Jan89-18
Clark, J., with J. Picard. Laying Down the
  Law.
  E.L. Sturz, 441:9Jul89-14
Clark, J.C.D. Revolution and Rebellion.
  J. Childs, 83:Autumn88-207
Clark, K. & M. Holquist. Mikhail Bakhtin.*
  G. Woodcock, 569(SR):Spring88-306
Clark, M. Dos Passos's Early Fiction, 1912-
  1938.*
  J. Rohrkemper, 395(MFS):Summer88-242
Clark, M.H. The Anastasia Syndrome.
  B. Kent, 441:3Dec89-82
Clark, M.H. While My Pretty One Sleeps.
  J. Curtin, 441:18Jun89-20
Clark, P., ed. The European Crisis of the
  1590s.
  R. Major, 551(RenQ):Autumn88-486

Clark, P.P. Literary France.*
    A. Sonnenfeld, 207(FR):Apr89-925
    R.W. Tobin, 478(P&L):Oct88-308
    C.D.E. Tolton, 627(UTQ):Spring89-411
Clark, R.W. Lenin.*
    A. Stent, 441:5Feb89-14
Clark, S. Ready from Within. (C.S. Brown, ed)
    J. Carson, 77:Fall88-340
Clark, T. The Exile of Céline.
    S. Day, 529(QQ):Autumn88-732
Clark, T.L. The Dictionary of Gambling and
    Gaming.
    L.R.N. Ashley, 424:Sep-Dec88-235
    G. Cannon, 660(Word):Dec88-239
    A.S. Kaye, 350:Mar89-178
Clark, V.M. Aldous Huxley and Film.
    J. Meckier, 395(MFS):Winter88-705
Clark, W.B., ed. Naval Documents of the
    American Revolution. (Vols 3 & 4)
    D. Syrett, 656(WMQ):Jan88-196
Clark, W.W. & R. King. Laon Cathedral.
    E. Fernie, 59:Jun88-289
Clarke, A.C. & G. Lee. Rama II.
    G. Jonas, 441:31Dec89-4
Clarke, D., ed. The Penguin Encyclopedia of
    Popular Music.
    P. Oldfield, 617(TLS):18-24Aug89-904
Clarke, D.M. Occult Powers and Hypotheses.
    S. James, 617(TLS):29Sep-5Oct89-1069
Clarke, E.G., with others. Targum Pseudo-
    Jonathan of the Pentateuch.
    J.C. Greenfield, 318(JAOS):Apr-Jun87-
    333
Clarke, G. Letting in the Rumour.
    M. Wormald, 617(TLS):29Sep-5Oct89-
    1065
Clarke, G.S. Fortification.
    S. Pepper, 617(TLS):22-28Dec89-1424
Clarke, G.W. - see Saint Cyprian
Clarke, J. From Feathers to Iron.
    G. Lansing, 703:Fall88-223
Clarke, J.S., comp. Margaret Oliphant (1828-
    1897).
    R.A. Colby, 635(VPR):Spring88-38
    P. Scott, 588(SSL):Vol23-298
Clarke, L. The Chymical Wedding.
    L.B. Osborne, 441:12Nov89-54
    A. Thwaite, 617(TLS):14-20Apr89-403
Clarke, L. Sunday Whiteman.
    J. Mellors, 364:Dec87/Jan88-136
Clarke, P. The Keynesian Revolution in the
    Making, 1924-1936.
    R. Middleton, 617(TLS):10-16Mar89-243
Clarke, R.W. & R.P. Lawry, eds. The Power of
    the Professional Person.
    M.R., 185:Jul89-983
Clarke, S. Keynesianism, Monetarism and the
    Crisis of the State.
    P. Clarke, 617(TLS):13-19Jan89-32
Clarke, T. Equator.*
    J. Hone, 617(TLS):7-13Jul89-758
    442(NY):23Jan89-120
Classe, O. - see Pradon, J.
Classen, A. Zur Rezeption norditalienischer
    Kultur des Trecento im Werk Oswalds von
    Wolkenstein (1376/77-1445).
    A. Robertshaw, 402(MLR):Oct89-1020
Classen, C.J. Die Stadt im Spiegel der Des-
    criptiones und Laudes urbium.
    P. Flobert, 555:Vol61fasc1-166
Clastres, P. Society Against the State.
    D. Schweickart, 103:Apr89-139

"Paul Claudel No. 14."
    J-N. Segrestaa, 535(RHL):Mar-Apr88-330
Clausen, C. The Moral Imagination.
    S.P., 295(JML):Fall87/Winter88-240
    W. Poznar, 577(SHR):Fall88-395
Clausen, R.R. & N.H. Ekstrom. Perennials for
    American Gardens.
    A. Lacy, 441:11Jun89-30
Clausen, W. Virgil's "Aeneid" and the Tradi-
    tion of Hellenistic Poetry.
    N. Gross, 124:Mar-Apr89-325
Clausing, S. English Influence on American
    German and American Icelandic.*
    P. Schach, 133:Band21Heft4-378
    J. Wilson, 685(ZDL):2/1988-266
Clayton, B., with N.M. Elliott. Buck Clayton's
    Jazz World.
    P. Baker, 498:Spring88-87
Clayton, J. Romantic Vision and the Novel.
    T. Doody, 454:Spring89-354
    J. Hill, 115:Spring88-212
    A.K. Mellor, 445(NCF):Jun88-128
    D. Schwarz, 661(WC):Autumn88-203
    M. Steig, 637(VS):Winter89-263
    G. Stewart, 191(ELN):Jun89-85
Clayton, P. Explanation from Physics to The-
    ology.
    J. King-Farlow, 103:Nov89-434
Cleary, J.J., ed. Proceedings of the Boston
    Area Colloquium in Ancient Philosophy.
    (Vol 1)
    J. Bogen, 41:Vol7-256
Cleary, J.J., ed. Proceedings of the Boston
    Area Colloquium in Ancient Philosophy.*
    (Vol 2)
    J. Creed, 123:Vol38No2-277
Cleary, J.J., ed. Proceedings of the Boston
    Area Colloquium in Ancient Philosophy.
    (Vol 3)
    L. Spellman, 103:Jan89-1
Cleaver, E. The Enchanted Caribou.
    A. Kertzer, 102(CanL):Winter87-165
Cleaves, F. Rock of Chickamauga.
    R.M. Magnaghi, 77:Fall88-343
Cleaves, P.S. Professions and the State.
    D.J. Mabry, 263(RIB):Vol38No1-71
Clément, C. Opera, or the Undoing of Women.
    P. Robinson, 441:1Jan89-3
    J. Rosselli, 617(TLS):2-8Jun89-614
Clement, X.C. - see under Company i Clement,
    X.
Clemente, V., ed. John Ciardi.
    B. Raffel, 363(LitR):Winter89-272
Clements, M. Rock Me.
    M. Mifflin, 441:26Feb89-34
Clements, P. Baudelaire and the English Tra-
    dition.*
    W.T. Bandy, 107(CRCL):Mar88-137
    P.P. Ferguson, 405(MP):Aug88-103
    C. Robinson, 447(N&Q):Jun88-283
Clements, W.M. Native American Folklore in
    Nineteenth-Century Periodicals.
    D.R. Mandell, 292(JAF):Jan-Mar88-84
Clemo, J. A Different Drummer.
    J. May, 493:Summer88-54
Clemoes, P. & others, eds. Anglo-Saxon En-
    gland.* (Vol 14)
    N.F. Blake, 677(YES):Vol19-298
Cleveland, H. & L.P. Bloomfield, eds. Pros-
    pects for Peace Making.
    T. Martin, 42(AR):Winter88-117

Clewlow, C. A Woman's Guide to Adultery.
    M. Beard, 617(TLS):12–18May89–504
    M. Seymour, 441:26Mar89–11
Cliff, W. En orient.
    A. Moorhead, 207(FR):Apr89–902
Clifford, J. The Predicament of Culture.*
    H. Foster, 62:Feb89–16
Clifford, P. "La Chastelaine de Vergi" and
    Jean Renart.
    J. Fox, 402(MLR):Jan89–157
Clifton, L. Good Woman.
    H. Lazer, 598(SoR):Summer89–760
    L. Rosenberg, 441:19Feb89–24
Clifton, L. New Poems.*
    H. Lazer, 598(SoR):Summer89–760
Clifton, L. Next.*
    G. Kuzma, 219(GaR):Fall88–624
    L. Rosenberg, 441:19Feb89–24
Clingman, S. – see Gordimer, N.
Clingman, S.R. The Novels of Nadine Gor-
    dimer.
    N. Ascherson, 453(NYRB):30Mar89–12
    T.B., 395(MFS):Winter88–756
    B. Harlow, 538(RAL):Summer88–255
    M.P.L., 295(JML):Fall87/Winter88–324
    R.G. Martin, 49:Jul88–104
Clodfelter, M. The Limits of Air Power.
    R. Halloran, 441:16Jul89–18
Clough, A.H. The Poems of Arthur Hugh
    Clough. (A.L.P. Norrington, ed)
    A. St. George, 447(N&Q):Jun88–263
Cloutier–Wojciechowska, C. & R. Robidoux,
    eds. Solitude rompue.
    A.L. Amprimoz, 345(KRQ):May88–223
    A. Purdy, 107(CRCL):Jun88–301
Clover, C.J. & J. Lindow, eds. Old Norse–
    Icelandic Literature.*
    S.A. Mitchell, 589:Jan88–137
    P. Schach, 301(JEGP):Jul88–416
Clowes, E.W. Maksim Gorky.
    A. Barratt, 402(MLR):Apr89–537
Clulee, N.H. John Dee's Natural Philosophy.
    P. Curry, 617(TLS):14–20Jul89–785
Clutton–Brock, J., ed. The Walking Larder.
    P.G. Bahn, 617(TLS):11–17Aug89–881
Coale, S.C. In Hawthorne's Shadow.
    M. Kobre, 219(GaR):Summer88–437
Coales, J., ed. The Earliest English Brasses.
    J.A. Goodall, 90:Jun88–468
Coan, R.W. Human Consciousness and Its
    Evolution.
    G. Hélal, 154:Spring88–181
Coarelli, F., ed. Fregellae. (Vol 2)
    B. Bouloumié, 229:Band60Heft5–472
    T.W. Potter, 313:Vol78–209
Coates, E. Suite in Four Movements.
    S. Banfield, 415:Jul88–348
Coates, P. Words After Speech.
    S. Sandler, 497(PolR):Vol33No1–35
Coates, P.D. China Consuls.
    A. Iriye, 617(TLS):10–16Mar89–242
Coats, G.W., ed. Saga, Legend, Tale, Novella,
    Fable.
    W.F.H. Nicolaisen, 203:Vol99No2–267
Cobb, R. The People's Armies.*
    J.F. McMillan, 617(TLS):21–27Jul89–792
Cobb, R. Something to Hold Onto.*
    J. Lewis, 364:Dec88/Jan89–143
Cobb, R., general ed. Voices of the French
    Revolution.
    A. Barnet, 441:9Jul89–13

Cobb, S.R. Optomotrist on a Scottish Hebri-
    dean Island.
    N.M. Curme, 571(ScLJ):Spring88–22
Cobban, A.B. The Medieval English Universi-
    ties.
    J. Catto, 617(TLS):26May–1Jun89–584
Cobbett, W. & R. Cohen, eds. Popular Strug-
    gles in South Africa.
    S. Uys, 617(TLS):25–31Aug89–915
Coburn, A. Godilocks.
    C. Salzberg, 441:7May89–24
Coburn, T.B. Devī-Māhātmya.
    P. Olivelle, 318(JAOS):Oct–Dec87–773
Cocalis, S.L., ed. The Defiant Muse.*
    S.L. Clark, 221(GQ):Spring88–298
    K.L. Komar, 221(GQ):Fall87–651
Cocchiarella, N.B. Logical Investigations of
    Predication Theory and the Problem of Uni-
    versals.
    J. Corcoran & Woosuk Park, 316:Sep88–
    991
Cocco de Filippis, D. & E.J. Robinett. Poems
    of Exiles and Other Concerns.
    J.J. Davis, 95(CLAJ):Mar89–382
Cochetti, S. Mythos und "Dialektik der Auf-
    klärung."*
    J. Früchtl, 489(PJGG):Band95Heft2–418
Cochrane, E. Italy 1530–1630. (J. Kirshner,
    ed)
    A. Brown, 617(TLS):29Sep–5Oct89–1067
Cochrane, E. & J. Kirshner, eds. The Renais-
    sance.
    K.O. O'Keeffe, 568(SCN):Winter88–82
Cocker, M. Richard Meinertzhagen.
    D. Pryce–Jones, 617(TLS):11–17Aug89–
    870
Cocking, R.R. & J.P. Mestre, eds. Linguistic
    and Cultural Influences on Learning
    Mathematics.
    C. Kessler, 608:Jun89–317
Cocks, R.C.J. Sir Henry Maine.
    S. Collini, 617(TLS):12–18May89–520
Cockshut, A.O.J. – see Kipling, R.
Cockton, P. Subject Catalogue of the House of
    Commons Parliamentary Papers 1801–1900.
    N. Gash, 617(TLS):14–20Apr89–408
Cocteau, J. Journal: 1942–1945. (J. Touzot,
    ed) Lettres à sa mère. (Vol 1) (P. Caizer-
    gues, ed)
    P. Pollard, 617(TLS):6–12Oct89–1090
Cocteau, J. & A. de Noailles. Correspondance
    1911–1931. (C. Mignot–Ogliastri, ed)
    P. Pollard, 617(TLS):6–12Oct89–1090
Code, L. Epistemic Responsibility.
    J. Heil, 484(PPR):Jun89–742
    B. Hunter, 103:Nov88–433
    P.K. Moser, 518:Jul88–154
    H. Redner, 543:Sep88–134
Code, L., S. Mullett & C. Overall, eds. Femi-
    nist Perspectives.
    C. Bray, 103:Apr89–142
Code, M. Order and Organism.*
    S. Malin, 606:Jun88–423
Codoñer Merino, C. Evolución del concepto de
    historiografía en Roma.
    J.W. Rich, 123:Vol38No1–159
Coe, J. A Touch of Love.
    M. Illis, 617(TLS):2–8Jun89–619
Coe, R.M. Toward a Grammar of Passages.
    J.M. Williams, 126(CCC):Dec88–474
Coe, R.N. When the Grass Was Taller.*
    L.K. Penrod, 107(CRCL):Mar88–101

Coedès, G. The Making of South-East Asia.
  M. Nihom, 318(JAOS):Oct-Dec87-844
Coelho, A., F. Lhomeau & J-L. Poitevin.
  Julien Gracq.
  J. Taylor, 617(TLS):2-8Jun89-618
Coelho, E., L. Winer & J.W-B. Olsen. All Sides
  of the Issue.
  C. Matthews, 608:Sep89-533
van Coetsem, F. Loan Phonology and the Two
  Transfer Types in Language Contact.
  J. Heath, 350:Jun89-384
Coetzee, J.M. White Writing.*
  S. Irlam, 400(MLN):Dec88-1147
Cofer, J.O. The Line of the Sun.
  R. Márquez, 441:24Sep89-46
Coffler, G.H. Melville's Classical Allusions.
  D. Yannella, 534(RALS):Vol16No1&2-96
Cogan, F.B. All-American Girl.
  A.S. Grossman, 617(TLS):15-21Dec89-
  1395
Cogan, T.J., ed & trans. The Tale of the Soga
  Brothers.
  S. Matisoff, 407(MN):Spring88-101
Coggan, D. Cuthbert Bardsley.
  G. Irvine, 617(TLS):3-9Nov89-1222
Coghill, N. The Collected Papers of Nevill
  Coghill, Shakespearian and Medievalist.*
  (D. Gray, ed)
  P.R. Cross, 366:Autumn88-230
Coghlan, B. - see Storm, T. & W. Petersen
Cogswell, T. English Politics and the Coming
  of War, 1621-1624.
  R. Lockyer, 617(TLS):29Dec89/4Jan90-
  1434
Cohan, S. Violation and Repair in the English
  Novel.*
  G. Campbell, 529(QQ):Autumn88-735
Cohen, A.A. Artists & Enemies.
  I. Gold, 473(PR):Vol55No1-159
Cohen, D., D. Menuez & R.G. Tussy. Fifteen
  Seconds.
  R. Lippincott, 441:24Dec89-16
Cohen, F.G. The Poetry of Christian Hofmann
  von Hofmannswaldau.*
  E. Spence, 564:Sep88-272
Cohen, G., ed. Etymology and Linguistic
  Principles. (Vol 1)
  E.P. Hamp, 424:Sep-Dec88-243
Cohen, G.A. History, Labour, and Freedom.
  D. McLellan, 617(TLS):21-27Jul89-809
Cohen, H.R., ed. Répertoire International de
  la Presse Musicale.
  R.L. Smith, 617(TLS):31Mar-6Apr89-342
Cohen, J. Disappearance.
  M. Stasio, 441:10Sep89-28
Cohen, M. Engaging English Art.*
  J.A. Dando, 637(VS):Winter89-250
Cohen, M. Living on Water.
  P. Gunn, 617(TLS):1-7Dec89-1338
Cohen, M. Nadine.*
  L. Boone, 102(CanL):Spring88-151
Cohen, M. Zion & State.
  J.V. Mallow, 287:Sep/Oct88-29
Cohen, M.A. Poet and Painter.
  G. MacLeod, 27(AL):May88-311
Cohen, M.N., ed. Lewis Carroll.
  A. Bell, 617(TLS):22-28Sep89-1025
Cohen, M.N. & A. Gandolfo, eds. Lewis Carroll
  and the House of Macmillan.
  B. Menikoff, 536(Rev):Vol10-273
Cohen, R.I. The Burden of Conscience.
  R.A. Kingcaid, 207(FR):Mar89-731

Cohen, S.F. & K. vanden Heuvel. Voices of
  Glasnost.
  H. Goodman, 441:26Nov89-25
Cohen, S.P. Island of Steel.
  M. Stasio, 441:1Jan89-23
Cohen, T. Remaking Japan.* (H. Passin, ed)
  T.W. Burkman, 407(MN):Summer88-250
Cohen, W.S. & G.J. Mitchell. Men of Zeal.*
  T. Draper, 453(NYRB):19Jan89-38
Cohen-Solal, A. Sartre.
  J. Parini, 249(HudR):Summer88-363
Cohen-Stratyner, B. - see Fabris, J. & C.
  Boullet
Cohler, A.M. Montesquieu's Comparative Pol-
  itics and the Spirit of American Constitu-
  tionalism.
  W. Brock, 617(TLS):8-14Sep89-979
Cohn, J. Creating America.
  M. Nichols, 441:8Oct89-21
Cohn, J. Romance and the Erotics of Proper-
  ty.
  K. Ellis, 395(MFS):Winter88-749
Cohn, R. From "Desire" to "Godot."
  D. Bradby, 615(TJ):Oct88-427
Cohn, R.G. A Critical Work. (Vol 2)
  B. Norman, 475:Vol15No28-281
  A. Thiher, 207(FR):Dec88-321
Cohn, R.G. Mallarmé's Prose Poems.
  U. Franklin, 546(RR):May88-525
  42(AR):Summer88-398
Cohn, S.K., Jr. Death and Property in Siena,
  1205-1800.
  L. Martines, 617(TLS):1-7Sep89-956
Cohn-Bendit, D. Nous l'avons tant aimée la
  révolution.
  A. Prévos, 207(FR):Feb89-578
Colacurcio, M.J., ed. New Essays on "The
  Scarlet Letter."*
  R. Belflower, 541(RES):May88-333
Colafrancesco, P. & M. Massaro, with M.L.
  Ricci, eds. Concordanze dei Carmina Latina
  epigraphica.
  H. Solin, 229:Band60Heft7-619
Colajanni, N. La resistibile ascesa di Achille
  Occhetto.
  P. McCarthy, 617(TLS):10-16Nov89-1234
Colbeck, N. A Bookman's Catalogue. (T. Bose,
  ed)
  R. Alston, 354:Mar88-77
  M. O'Connor, 470:Vol26-161
Colby, W., with J. McCargar. Lost Victory.
  R. Manning, 441:12Nov89-18
Colchester, L.S. Wells Cathedral.
  N.C., 90:Oct88-784
Colchie, T. & M. Strand - see Drummond de
  Andrade, C.
Coldrey, B.M. Faith and Fatherland.
  J. Rogers, 174(Eire):Winter88-158
Cole, D.B. & J.J. McDonough - see French, B.B.
Cole, J.H. Shaohsing.*
  M. Zelin, 318(JAOS):Oct-Dec87-827
Cole, R. The Glass Children.*
  455:Mar88-72
Cole, R.C. Irish Booksellers and English Writ-
  ers 1740-1800.*
  N. Barker, 173(ECS):Winter88/89-269
  N. Jameson, 354:Mar88-70
  D. Patterson, 470:Vol26-199
Cole, R.W. An Innocent in Britain.
  R. Oliver, 617(TLS):3-9Feb89-104
Cole, S.G. Theoi megaloi.*
  R.A. Tomlinson, 303(JoHS):Vol108-246

"Collins–Robert French–English English–French Dictionary." (2nd ed) (B.T. Atkins & others, comps.)
    T. Piotrowski, 257(IRAL):Aug88–253
Collinson, D. Fifty Major Philosophers.
    G.A.J. Rogers, 518:Apr88–80
Collinson, P. The Birthpangs of Protestant England.
    J.J. Scarisbrick, 617(TLS):28Jul–3Aug89–828
Collomb, M. La Littérature art déco.
    B. Thibault, 207(FR):Feb89–531
"Colloque Louis Hémon."
    B–Z. Shek, 627(UTQ):Fall87–179
Collot, M., ed. Autour d'André Du Bouchet.
    C. Jordens, 356(LR):Aug88–259
Colls, R. The Pitmen of the Northern Coalfield.
    D. Harker, 637(VS):Autumn88–136
Colls, R. & P. Dodd, eds. Englishness.*
    R. Howell, Jr., 366:Spring88–133
de Colombí–Monguió, A. Petrarquismo peruano.*
    D.R. Reedy, 345(KRQ):Feb88–120
Colter, C. The Amoralists & Other Tales.
    B. Atkinson, 441:12Feb89–16
Colton, E.O. The Jackson Phenomenon.
    E. Cose, 441:16Jul89–11
Colton, R.E. Juvenal and Boileau.
    L.T. Pearcy, 124:Jan–Feb89–199
Coluccia, R. – see Ferraiolo
Columbus, C.K. Mythological Consciousness and the Future.
    J. Labanyi, 402(MLR):Oct89–1014
Columella. Columelle: "De l'agriculture: les arbres."* (R. Goujard, ed & trans)
    K.D. White, 123:Vol38No1–154
Colussi, G., ed. Glossario degli antichi volgari italiani. (Vols 1–3)
    M. Fanfani, 545(RPh):Nov88–203
    A. Scolari, 379(MedR):Aug86–309
de Combarieu du Gres, M. & J. Subrenat. Le Roman de Renart, index des thèmes et des personnages.
    R. Bellon, 553(RLiR):Jul–Dec88–544
Combe, C. Hérault de Séchelles héros stendhalien.
    V.D.L., 605(SC):15Jan89–160
de Combray, R. Lost in the City of Light.
    442(NY):20Nov89–155
Combs, D.W. Early Gravestone Art in Georgia and South Carolina.*
    G. Stone, 658:Spring88–82
Comella, A. I materiali votivi di Falerii.
    T.W. Potter, 313:Vol78–209
Comito, T. In Defense of Winters.
    H. Davidson, 301(JEGP):Jul88–425
    F. Murphy, 569(SR):Summer88–lvii
Commins, D. – see O'Neill, E. & S. Commins
Comotti, G. Music in Greek and Roman Culture.
    A. Barker, 617(TLS):25–31Aug89–923
"The Compact Edition of the Oxford English Dictionary." (Vol 3) (R.W. Burchfield, ed)
    K. Sørensen, 179(ES):Dec88–573
Compagni, D. Dino Compagni's Chronicle of Florence. (D. Bornstein, ed & trans)
    G. Dameron, 539:Summer89–240
Compagnon, A. Proust entre deux siècles.
    E. Hughes, 617(TLS):13–19Oct89–1112
Compagnon, A. – see Proust, M.

Company i Clement, X. La Pintura del Renaixement.
    I. Mateo Gómez, 48:Jul–Sep88–328
"The Complete Book of Covers from the New Yorker, 1925–1989."
    A. Hirschfeld, 441:3Dec89–44
"Santiago de Compostela."
    90:Mar88–242
Comrie, B. Tense.*
    K. Schubert, 603:Vol12No1–194
Comrie, B., ed. The World's Major Languages.*
    E.P. Hamp, 269(IJAL):Jan88–110
    42(AR):Fall88–530
Comstock, C. Disruption and Delight in the Nineteenth–Century Novel.
    W.P. Day, 637(VS):Summer89–577
Comte-Sponville, A. Le mythe d'Icare. Vivre.
    F. George, 98:May88–393
Comyns, B. The House of Dolls.
    P. Craig, 617(TLS):24Feb–2Mar89–190
Conacher, D.J. Aeschylus' "Oresteia."
    M. Davies, 123:Vol38No2–393
    A.N. Michelini, 124:May–Jun89–386
    M.E. Reesor, 529(QQ):Summer88–443
Conacher, J.B. Britain and the Crimea, 1855–56.
    D. Read, 617(TLS):13–19Jan89–43
Conche, M. Montaigne et la philosophie.*
    J. Bernhardt, 319:Oct89–616
    A. Reix, 542:Apr–Jun88–253
    J.J. Supple, 208(FS):Jul88–340
Conche, M. – see Heraclitus
Conchess, B.J., comp. Bibliography of Old Catalan Texts.*
    A.M. Perrone Capano Compagna, 379(MedR):Apr88–155
Condé, M. The Children of Segu.
    D. Goodwin, 441:31Dec89–13
de Condillac, E.B. Traité des animaux.
    J. Ecole, 192(EP):Jul–Sep88–423
Condon, J. & K. Kurata. In Search of What's Japanese about Japan.
    Y–H. Tohsaku, 399(MLJ):Autumn88–364
Marquis de Condorcet & A. Suard. Correspondance inédite de Condorcet et Madame Suard, 1771–1791. (E. Badinter, ed)
    W.H. Barber, 617(TLS):6–12Jan89–3
Condren, C. The Status and Appraisal of Classic Texts.
    T.W. Simon, 518:Jul88–141
Conermann, K., ed. Fruchtbringende Gesellschaft.
    G. van den Heuvel, 706:Band20Heft1–117
Confalonieri, L.B. – see under Badini Confalonieri, L.
"Il Confronto Letterario."
    M. Berthomieu, 535(RHL):Jul–Aug88–794
Confucius. Les Entretiens de Confucius. (P. Ryckmans, ed & trans)
    A. Comte-Sponville, 98:Apr88–350
    J–L. Gautier, 450(NRF):Mar88–83
Conger, J.A. The Charismatic Leader.
    C.L. Harris, 441:29Oct89–40
Conio, G. Le constructivisme russe: Les arts plastiques. (Vol 1)
    R. Micha, 98:May88–403
Conisbee, P. Chardin.
    G. Inkster, 83:Autumn88–246
Conkin, P.K. The Southern Agrarians.
    T.D. Clark, 392:Fall88–564
Conlon, D., ed. Simon de Puille.
    G. Roques, 553(RLiR):Jul–Dec88–550

Conlon, D.J., ed. G.K. Chesterton.*
  R. Mason, 447(N&Q):Mar88–118
  W.J. Scheick, 177(ELT):Vol31No3–330
Conlon, P.M. Le Siècle des Lumières. (Vol 4)
  P. Jansen, 535(RHL):Nov–Dec88–1141
Conlon, R.M. Distance and Duties.
  C. Armstrong, 298:Spring/Summer88–240
Conn, J. The Fabulous Disguise of Our-
  selves.*
  L. York, 102(CanL):Summer88–142
Conn, P. Literature in America.
  S. Gubar, 441:8Oct89–28
Conn, S. In the Kibble Palace.
  E. Morgan, 493:Spring88–42
  C. Whyte, 571(ScLJ):Spring88–48
Connaughton, S. A Border Station.
  M. Stimpson, 617(TLS):27Jan–2Feb89–89
Connell, R.J. The Empirical Intelligence.
  T.A. Russman, 103:May89–177
Connell, R.J. Substance and Modern Science.
  J.F.X. Knasas, 543:Mar89–614
Connelly, J. Man's Work.
  P. Glasser, 455:Jun88–61
  G. Johnson, 219(GaR):Summer88–423
Conner, K.P. Blood Moon.
  G. Haslam, 649(WAL):May88–86
Connolly, J.E. Translation and Poetization in
  the "Quaderna Vía."
  N.S. Miguel, 240(HR):Autumn88–494
Connolly, J.M. & T. Keutner, eds. Hermeneu-
  tics Versus Science?
  P.A. Heelan, 543:Mar89–615
Connolly, J.W. & S.I. Ketchian, eds. Studies
  in Russian Literature in Honor of Vsevolod
  Setchkarev.
  G. McVay, 402(MLR):Jul89–810
Connor, L., P. Asch & T. Asch. Jero Tapakan.
  T.A. Volkman, 293(JASt):Nov88–932
Connor, S. Charles Dickens.*
  M. Moseley, 569(SR):Spring88–243
  P. Preston, 447(N&Q):Dec88–545
Connor, S. & S. Kingman. The Search for the
  Virus.*
  S. Sutherland, 617(TLS):1–7Dec89–1344
Connor, W.R. Thucydides.
  C.W. Kalkavage, 24:Summer88–259
Connors, J. The Robie House of Frank Lloyd
  Wright.*
  W.J.R. Curtis, 617(TLS):24–30Mar89–315
Connors, L. The Emperor's Adviser.
  Itō Takashi & G. Akita, 285(JapQ):Apr–
  Jun88–208
  D.A. Titus, 293(JASt):May88–372
Connors, R.J., L.S. Ede & A.A. Lunsford, eds.
  Essays on Classical Rhetoric and Modern
  Discourse.
  J. Poulakos, 480(P&R):Vol21No2–165
Conoley, G. Some Gangster Pain.
  L. Upton, 152(UDQ):Spring88–106
Conolly, L.W., ed. Canadian Drama and the
  Critics.
  A. Leggatt, 108:Winter88–93
Conomos, D.E. – see Chrysaphes, M.
Conoway, J. The Kingdom in the Country.
  P. Wild, 649(WAL):Nov88–264
Conquest, R. The Harvest of Sorrow.*
  K. Neilson, 529(QQ):Spring88–193
  D.W. Treadgold, 396(ModA):Winter88–66
Conquest, R. Stalin and the Kirov Murder.
  E. Mawdsley, 617(TLS):8–14Sep89–977
  P.H. Solomon, Jr., 441:15Jan89–13
Conrad, B. 3d. Absinthe.
  L. Tillman, 441:12Mar89–23

Conrad, B. Two Essays on Reference Without
  Meaning.
  L. Zgusta, 350:Mar89–178
Conrad, J. The Collected Letters of Joseph
  Conrad.* (Vol 2) (F.R. Karl & L. Davies,
  eds)
  J. Batchelor, 541(RES):Nov88–583
  E.K. Hay, 136:Summer88–167
  O. Knowles, 447(N&Q):Mar88–117
  Z. Najder, 575(SEER):Apr88–271
  G.B. Tennyson, 445(NCF):Sep88–275
  I.V., 295(JML):Fall87/Winter88–306
Conrad, J. Oeuvres III. (S. Monod, general
  ed)
  J.H. Stape, 136:Summer88–176
Conrad, P. Behind the Mountain.
  C. Kizer, 441:9Apr89–14
Conrad, P. The Everyman History of English
  Literature.*
  S. Monod, 189(EA):Oct–Dec88–499
Conrad, P. A Song of Love and Death.*
  W. Dean, 410(M&L):Oct88–536
Conradi, P.J. Iris Murdoch.*
  E. Schiller, 295(JML):Fall87/Winter88–
  357
Conran, T., ed & trans. Welsh Verse.
  D. McDuff, 565:Spring88–64
Conroy, J. Belfast Diary.*
  T.D. Redshaw, 174(Éire):Summer88–153
"La Conscience européenne au XVe et au XVIe
  siècle."
  J–M. Hannick, 356(LR):Aug88–239
Constant, B. Political Writings. (B. Fontana,
  ed & trans)
  M. Cranston, 617(TLS):21–27Apr89–433
Constantin–Weyer, M. Avec plus ou moins de
  rire.
  P. Hebert, 102(CanL):Summer88–136
Constantine, D. Madder.*
  M. Grucefin, 400(Spring88–67
  R. Garfitt, 364:Jun88–86
Constantinescu, N. Lectura textului folcloric.
  M.H. Beissinger, 292(JAF):Jul–Sep88–362
Conta, G. Asculum II. (Bk 1, Vol 1)
  H. Galsterer, 229:Band60Heft3–266
Contardi, B. & S. Romana – see Titi, F.
Conte, G.B. The Rhetoric of Imitation.* (C.
  Segal, ed & trans)
  E. Block, 122:Oct88–373
  N. Gross, 124:Sep–Oct88–50
"Contemporary Inuit Drawings."
  M. Bell, 529(QQ):Spring88–228
Content, D.J., ed. Islamic Rings and Gems,
  The Zucker Collection.
  R. Ward, 90:Nov88–858
Conti, A. Storia del restauro e della conser-
  vazione delle opere d'arte.
  J. Anderson, 59:Dec88–565
Contini, G. Breviario di ecdotica.
  R. Coluccia, 228(GSLI):Vol165fasc532–
  591
Contini, G. Ultimi esercizî ed elzeviri.
  Z. Barański, 617(TLS):3–9Feb89–112
Conway, J.K. The Road From Coorain.
  V. Klinkenborg, 441:7May89–3
  442(NY):26Jun89–92
Cooey, P., S.A. Farmer & M.E. Ross, eds. Em-
  bodied Love.
  S.E.H., 185:Apr89–669
Cook, A. Changing the Signs.
  K. Moxey, 201:Vol14–207
Cook, A. Figural Choice in Poetry and Art.
  J.E. Stoll, 569(SR):Winter88–xi

Cook, A. History/Writing.
   B.A. Haddock, 617(TLS):25-31Aug89-926
Cook, A. Thresholds.*
   J.F. Fetzer, 222(GR):Summer88-152
   A.C. Goodson, 591(SIR):Spring88-167
   S. Simpkins, 128(CE):Nov88-812
Cook, B.F. Greek Inscriptions.
   M.M. Austin, 123:Vol38No2-451
Cook, D. Crying Out Loud.*
   J. Mellors, 364:Dec88/Jan89-132
Cook, D. Forging the Alliance.
   D. Middleton, 441:21May89-9
Cook, E. Poetry, Word-Play, and Word-War in
   Wallace Stevens.
   M. Beehler, 705:Fall88-188
Cook, E. Seeing Through Words.*
   G.E. Rowe, 131(CL):Winter88-84
   H. Smith, 570(SQ):Summer88-262
Cook, G.M. My Diary of Earth.
   M. Estok, 198:Winter88-106
Cook, M. - see Chénier, M-J.
Cook, N. A Guide to Musical Analysis.*
   M.G. Brown & D.J. Dempster,
   308:Spring88-148
   W. Drabkin, 415:Feb88-81
Cook, R. Mutation.
   J. Kaufman, 441:19Feb89-20
Cook, R. The Regenerators.
   L. Armour, 102(CanL):Winter87-246
Cook, S.C. Opera for a New Republic.
   J.K. Law, 465:Winter88/89-97
Cook, T.H. Flesh and Blood.
   M. Stasio, 441:19Feb89-23
Cook, T.H. Streets of Fire.
   M. Stasio, 441:24Sep89-29
Cook-Gumperz, J., ed. The Social Construc-
   tion of Literacy.
   W. Grabe, 361:Jul88-262
   J. John, 257(IRAL):May88-169
   K. Walters, 355(LSoc):Dec88-593
Cooke, E.S., Jr., ed. Upholstery in America
   and Europe from the Seventeenth Century
   to World War I.
   S. Jervis, 39:May88-372
   K.M. Walton, 658:Spring88-84
Cooke, J. The Novels of Nadine Gordimer.*
   M. Wade, 538(RAL):Summer88-252
Cooke, J.B. South of the Border.
   H. Mittelmark, 441:7May89-24
Cooke, M.G. Afro-American Literature in the
   Twentieth Century.
   W.E. Cain, 128(CE):Feb88-190
   E. Kreutzer, 72:Band225Heft2-420
Cooke, P. The Fiddle Tradition in the Shet-
   land Isles.
   R. Anderson, 415:Jan88-22
Cooke, R. Velimir Khlebnikov.
   R.R. Milner-Gulland, 402(MLR):Jan89-270
Cooke, R.T. "How Celia Changed Her Mind"
   and Selected Stories.* (E. Ammons, ed)
   W.H. Shurr, 534(RALS):Vol16No1&2-79
Cooley, D. The Vernacular Muse.
   B. Almon, 649(WAL):Nov88-243
Coolidge, C. Solution Passage. Space. The
   Maintains. Mine. The Crystal Text.
   A. Mack & J. Rome, 472:Vol15No1-257
Coolidge, J. Patrons and Architects.
   M. Kemp, 617(TLS):29Dec89/4Jan90-1435
van Coolput, C-A. Aventures querant et le
   sens du monde.
   E. Kennedy, 208(FS):Jul88-334
Coombs, D. Spreading the Word.
   B.C. Bloomfield, 617(TLS):3-9Feb89-121

Cooney, T.A. The Rise of the New York Intel-
   lectuals.*
   F. Matthews, 106:Spring88-69
   A. Wald, 385(MQR):Winter89-130
Coonts, S. The Minotaur.
   N. Callendar, 441:22Oct89-37
Coontz, S. The Social Origins of Private Life.
   N.F. Cott, 617(TLS):22-28Sep89-1037
Cooper, A. Cairo in the War, 1939-1945.
   P.L. Fermor, 617(TLS):1-7Sep89-938
Cooper, A.A. (Lord Shaftesbury). Complete
   Works, Selected Letters and Posthumous
   Writings in English with a Parallel German
   Translation. (Vol 2, Pt 1) (W. Benda, G.
   Hemmerich & U. Schödlbauer, eds & trans)
   P. Carrive, 542:Jul-Sep88-335
   E. Vollrath, 489(PJGG):Band95Heft2-428
Cooper, B. Modern African Writing.
   R. Aitken, 538(RAL):Spring88-126
Cooper, C.R., ed. Researching Response to
   Literature and the Teaching of Literature.
   R.R. Hellenga, 223:Fall88-359
Cooper, D. Closer.
   T.R. Edwards, 453(NYRB):17Aug89-52
   W. Ferguson, 441:14May89-23
Cooper, D. The Horn Fellow.
   P. Williams, 571(ScLJ):Spring88-60
Cooper, D.E. Metaphor.*
   M. Lewis, 483:Jan88-129
   P. Mühlhäusler, 353:Vol26No3-495
Cooper, J. Players.
   J. Jarvis, 441:30Apr89-26
Cooper, J. Scaffolding.*
   R. Hadas, 472:Vol15No1-217
Cooper, J. Victorian and Edwardian Furniture
   and Interiors.
   P. Davey, 46:Apr88-10
Cooper, J.F. Gleanings in Europe: The Rhine.
   (T. Philbrick & M. Geracht, eds) The Pilot;
   A Tale of the Sea. (K.S. House, ed)
   R. Lawson-Peebles, 541(RES):Nov88-563
Cooper, M. Judgements of Value. (D. Cooper,
   ed)
   W. Dean, 617(TLS):17-23Mar89-274
Cooper, R.K. The American Shakespeare The-
   atre, Stratford, 1955-1985.
   D. Richman, 570(SQ):Autumn88-378
Cooper, R.R. The Last to Go.*
   L. Duguid, 617(TLS):18-24Aug89-901
   442(NY):27Mar89-114
Cooper, W. The Country of Here Below.
   W.H. Green, 649(WAL):Nov88-266
Cooper, W.F. Claude McKay.*
   A. Rampersad, 115:Winter88-81
Coote, J., ed. The Faber Book of the Sea.
   T.J. Binyon, 617(TLS):19-25May89-538
Coover, R. Spanking the Maid.
   J. Mellors, 364:Feb87-103
Cope, E.S. Politics Without Parliaments
   1629-1640.
   C. Herrup, 250(HLQ):Autumn88-337
   E. Skerpan, 568(SCN):Fall88-48
Cope, J.I. Robert Coover's Fictions.*
   P.J. Bailey, 659(ConL):Fall89-448
   K. Hume, 454:Fall88-122
   S. Moore, 532(RCF):Spring88-199
   A.W., 295(JML):Fall87/Winter88-308
Cope, J.I. Dramaturgy of the Daemonic.
   D. Radcliff-Umstead, 276:Summer88-159
Copeland, A. The Golden Thread.
   P. Hampl, 441:22Oct89-24

Copeland, J.G., & others. Puertas a la Lengua
Española. Puertas al Mundo Hispánico.
Puertas a la Comunicación. (each is 2nd
ed)
  M.P. Mellgren, 399(MLJ):Spring88-107
Copernicus, N. Nicholas Copernicus Minor
Works. (P. Czartoryski, ed)
  P.W. Knoll, 497(PolR):Vol33No4-468
Coplan, D. In Township Tonight!
  B. King, 538(RAL):Spring88-103
Copley, A. Sexual Moralities in France,
1780-1980.
  M. Mason, 617(TLS):19-25May89-542
Copley, S. Literature and the Social Order in
Eighteenth-Century England.*
  N.C. Jaffe, 677(YES):Vol19-325
Copp, D., ed. Nuclear Weapons, Deterrence,
and Disarmament.*
  W.E. Seager, 103:Nov88-436
  J. Thompson, 63:Jun88-280
Copp, D. & D. Zimmerman, eds. Morality, Rea-
son, and Truth.
  D. Odegard, 154:Spring88-135
Coppa, F.J., ed-in-chief. Dictionary of
Modern Italian History.
  W.S. Linsenmeyer, 276:Summer88-163
Coppens, P. Enfants d'Hermès.
  J.P. Gilroy, 102(CanL):Winter87-260
Coquin, F-X. & C. Gervais-Francelle, eds.
1905.
  M. Perrie, 575(SEER):Jan88-143
Corbea, A. & O. Nicolae, eds. Interferenţe
culturale româno-germane/Rumänisch-
deutsche Kultur-Interferenzen.
  A. von Brunn, 224(GRM):Band38Heft1/2-
228
Corbeil, J-C. & A. Archambault. The Facts on
File English/French Visual Dictionary.
  J.E. Joseph, 399(MLJ):Autumn88-353
Corbet, P. Les saints ottoniens.
  C.B. Bouchard, 589:Jul88-645
Corbin, A. The Foul and the Fragrant.
  B.G. Mittman, 125:Fall87-97
Corbin, D. Morphologie dérivationnelle et
structuration du lexique.
  G. Gorcy, 553(RLiR):Jul-Dec88-521
  F. Rainer, 547(RF):Band100Heft4-355
Corbin, H. Histoire de la philosophie islam-
ique.* L'alchimie comme art hiératique.
(P. Lory, ed)
  A. Reix, 542:Jan-Mar88-119
Corbin, H. - see Shîrâzî, M.S.
Corbin, H. - see Sohravardî, S.Y.
Corbin, M. - see Saint Anselm
Corbin, P. & D. Sedge, eds. Three Jacobean
Witchcraft Plays.
  S.J. Steen, 568(SCN):Spring-Summer88-
16
Corbin, S. No Easy Place to Be.
  J. Johnson, 441:2Jul89-12
Corbluth, E. St. Patrick's Night.
  G. Mort, 493:Winter88/89-57
  S. O'Brien, 617(TLS):25-31Aug89-916
Corcoran, N. Seamus Heaney.
  R.W.B., 295(JML):Fall87/Winter88-328
  R.J.C. Watt, 541(RES):Nov88-592
Cordasco, F. Junius.
  J. Black, 447(N&Q):Jun88-241
Cordasco, F. & G. Simonson. Junius and his
Works.
  J. Black, 447(N&Q):Jun88-241
Corder, J.W. Lost in West Texas.
  D. Heaberlin, 649(WAL):Nov88-246

Cordero, N.L. & others, eds & trans. Los filó-
sofos presocráticos. (Vol 2)
  R. Torretti, 160:Jan88-221
Cordié, A. Un enfant devient psychotique.
  E. Jalley, 542:Oct-Dec88-511
Cordroc'h, M., R. Pierrot & L. Chotard - see de
Musset, A.
Coren, M. Gilbert.
  P. Dickinson, 364:Feb/Mar89-143
  M. Seymour-Smith, 617(TLS):31Mar-
6Apr89-330
Corey, P.L., ed. Faces, Voices and Dreams.
  A. Wardwell, 2(AfrA):Aug88-88
Corfis, I.A., ed. Historia de la linda Melosina.
  M.J. Kelley, 238:May88-291
Corfis, I.A. - see de San Pedro, D.
Corino, K. Robert Musil.
  P. Payne, 617(TLS):7-13Jul89-736
Corley, C.F.V. The Second Continuation of
the Old French "Perceval."
  E. Kennedy, 402(MLR):Apr89-467
  P. Sullivan, 382(MAE):1988/2-324
Cormack, M. Bonington.
  G. Reynolds, 617(TLS):30Jun-6Jul89-725
Cormack, R. Writing in Gold.
  A.W. Carr, 54:Mar88-145
  E. Fernie, 59:Mar88-147
Corman, C. And the Word.
  D. Sampson, 249(HudR):Summer88-391
Cormier, R. Fade.
  B.L. Clark, 441:12Feb89-18
Cormier, R., ed & trans. Three Ovidian Tales
of Love.
  B. Guthmüller, 72:Band225Heft2-437
Corn, A. The West Door.*
  R. McDowell, 249(HudR):Autumn88-572
  V. Shetley, 491:May88-102
  639(VQR):Summer88-97
Corn, J.J., ed. Imagining Tomorrow.*
  639(VQR):Autumn88-137
Corneille, P. Le Cid. (V.J. Cheng, trans)
  D.A. Watt, 402(MLR):Jul89-739
Corneille, P. Théâtre Complet. (Vol 1) (A.
Niderst, ed)
  H.A. Garrity, 403(MLS):Winter88-197
Corneille, P. Théâtre complet.* (Vol 3) (A.
Niderst, ed)
  A. Couprie, 535(RHL):Mar-Apr88-267
Cornelissen, R. Drama und Sprachakttheorie.
  G.J. Mallinson, 208(FS):Jan88-80
Cornell, L.L. - see Kipling, R.
Cornfield, R. & W. Mackay - see Denby, E.
Cornford, J. Collected Writings.* (A. Young,
ed)
  T. Eagleton, 565:Winter87/88-65
Corngold, S. Frank Kafka.
  L. Hafrey, 617(TLS):16-22Jun89-661
de Cornière, F. J'ai beau marcher.
  R. Jacquelin, 450(NRF):Oct88-96
Cornish, F. Anaphoric Relations in English
and French.*
  L.G. Kelly, 320(CJL):Sep88-275
  D.J. Napoli, 350:Dec89-881
  M-P. Woodley, 402(MLR):Jul89-682
Cornwell, J. A Thief in the Night.
  E. Kennedy, 441:5Nov89-15
  M. Walsh, 617(TLS):1-7Sep89-940
Cornwell, N. Pasternak's Novel.*
  J.W. Connolly, 402(MLR):Apr89-539
  M. Sendich, 558(RLJ):Winter-Spring-
Fall88-362
  J.S. Toomre, 574(SEEJ):Summer88-332

Cottom, D. Social Figures.*
    C. Crosby, 637(VS):Autumn88-119
    639(VQR):Spring88-53
Cotton, E.G. & J.M. Sharp. Spanish in the
    Americas.
    T. Kaufman, 350:Mar89-179
Cotton, M.A. & G.P.R. Métraux. The San Rocco
    Villa at Francolise.*
    P. Arthur, 229:Band60Heft2-187
Cottrell, R.D. The Grammar of Silence.*
    M. Dassonville, 188(ECr):Summer88-100
    O. Millet, 535(RHL):Jul-Aug88-760
Couliano, I.P. Eros and Magic in the Renais-
    sance.
    W. Schwarz, 617(TLS):24Feb-2Mar89-203
Coulmas, F., ed. With Forked Tongues.
    C.B. Paulston, 350:Sep89-656
Coulmas, F. The Writing Systems of the
    World.
    J.T. Hooker, 617(TLS):17-23Nov89-1264
Coulon, M. - see de la Cruz, R.
Coulonges, H. Farwell, Dresden.
    A. Barnet, 441:12Mar89-19
Couloubaritsis, L. Mythe et philosophique
    chez Parménide.
    J. Dillon, 319:Jul89-461
    D. Sider, 124:May-Jun89-393
    P. Trotignon, 542:Apr-Jun88-240
    M.R. Wright, 123:Vol38No2-274
Coulson, W.D.E. The Dark Age Pottery of
    Messenia.
    M. Popham, 303(JoHS):Vol108-267
Coulter, J. Rethinking Cognitive Theory.
    A.W. McHoul, 488:Mar88-129
Couper-Kuhlen, E. An Introduction to En-
    glish Prosody.*
    C.A. Brewster, 350:Jun89-422
    E. Standop, 38:Band106Heft1/2-154
Coupland, N., ed. Styles of Discourse.
    C. Myers-Scotton, 350:Dec89-882
Coupry, F. Avec David Bloom dans le rôle de
    David Bloom.
    M. Fougères, 207(FR):Oct88-197
Courbin, P. What is Archaeology?
    A. Sherratt, 617(TLS):3-9Mar89-228
de Courcy, A. 1939.
    I. Colegate, 617(TLS):26May-1Jun89-571
Courier, P-L. Correspondance générale. (Vol
    0) (G. Viollet-le-Duc, ed)
    R. Bourgeois, 535(RHL):Nov-Dec88-1146
Courtenay, B. The Power of One.
    E. Stumpf, 441:2Jul89-12
de Courtenay, J.B. - see under Baudouin de
    Courtenay, J.
Courtney, C.P. A Guide to the Published
    Works of Benjamin Constant.*
    P. Jansen, 535(RHL):Mar-Apr88-287
Courtney-Clarke, M. Ndebele.
    J. Wilson, 662:Spring/Summer88-47
Cousins, J. & others. Les Demoiselles d'Avig-
    non.
    Y-A. Bois, 98:Oct88-834
Cousins, M. & A. Hussain. Michel Foucault.
    K. Minogue, 144:Winter89-138
Coutau-Bégarie, H. & C. Huan. Darlan.
    M.R.D. Foot, 617(TLS):1-7Sep89-937
Couzens, T. The New African.
    S. Roberts, 538(RAL):Spring88-99
Cova, P.V. & others. Studi sulla lingua di
    Plinio il Vecchio.
    J.B. Hall, 313:Vol78-247
    M. Winterbottom, 123:Vol38No1-155

Coval, S.C. & J.C. Smith. Law and its Presup-
    positions.*
    R.A. Duff, 479(PhQ):Jul88-378
Covarrubias, J.I. Convergencias.
    M. de Semprún Donahue, 37:Mar/Apr88-
    59
Coveri, L. & D. Moreno, eds. Studi di etno-
    grafia e dialettologia ligure in memoria di
    Hugo Plomteux.
    M.M. Parry, 545(RPh):Feb89-342
Covington, V. Gathering Home.
    A. Whitehouse, 441:1Jan89-14
Cowan, W. & J. Rakušan. Source Book for Lin-
    guists. (2nd ed)
    P. Stevens, 399(MLJ):Winter88-486
Coward, R. The Whole Truth.
    D. Gould, 617(TLS):7-13Jul89-748
Cowart, J., J. Hamilton & S. Greenough.
    Georgia O'Keeffe Art and Letters.
    M. Lennon, 106:Spring88-113
Cowdery, L.T. The Nouvelle of Henry James
    in Theory and Practice.*
    J. Auchard, 177(ELT):Vol31No2-242
Cowler, R. - see Pope, A.
Cowley, M. Conversations with Malcolm Cow-
    ley. (T.D. Young, ed)
    J.M. Kempf, 534(RALS):Vol16No1&2-169
Cowling, M. The Artist as Anthropologist.
    R.D. Altick, 617(TLS):15-21Dec89-1397
Cowling, M. Religion and Public Doctrine in
    Modern England.
    M. Le Fanu, 97(CQ):Vol17No1-84
Cowper, W. The Letters and Prose Writings of
    William Cowper.* (Vol 5) (J. King & C. Rys-
    kamp, eds)
    K. Williamson, 541(RES):May88-301
Cox, A. & N. O'Sullivan, eds. The Corporate
    State.
    C. Townshend, 617(TLS):10-16Feb89-144
Cox, C. & J. Marks. The Insolence of Office.
    S.J. Prais, 617(TLS):17-23Feb89-175
Cox, C.B. Two-Headed Monster.*
    J. Forth, 364:Apr-May87-128
Cox, H. Many Mansions.
    J.M. Washington, 441:29Jan89-26
Cox, J.D. Shakespeare and the Dramaturgy of
    Power.
    R. Hapgood, 617(TLS):25-31Aug89-927
Cox, J.N. In the Shadows of Romance.*
    J. Ehrstine, 130:Summer88-187
Cox, M. - see James, M.R.
Cox, M. & R.A. Gilbert, eds. The Oxford Book
    of English Ghost Stories.*
    R. Beecham, 447(N&Q):Jun88-268
    S. Pickering, 569(SR):Winter88-xiii
Coxon, A.H. The Fragments of Parmenides.*
    R. Bodéüs, 154:Autumn88-563
    M.R. Wright, 123:Vol38No2-274
Coyle, B. & A. Filreis - see Stevens, W. & J.
    Rodríguez Feo
Cozzens, J.G. James Gould Cozzens: Selected
    Notebooks 1960-1967. James Gould Coz-
    zens: A Time of War - Air Force Diaries.
    (M.J. Bruccoli, ed of both)
    J.A. Parrish, Jr., 534(RALS):Vol16No1&2-
    222
Crabb, C.V., Jr. & K.V. Mulcahy. Presidents
    and Foreign Policy Making.
    639(VQR):Winter88-24
Crabbe, G. George Crabbe: Selected Poetry.
    (J. Poster, ed)
    M. Storey, 447(N&Q):Mar88-103

Crabbe, G. Selected Letters and Journals of
George Crabbe.* (T.C. Faulkner, with R.L.
Blair, eds)
   D. Feldmann, 38:Band106Heft1/2-252
Crabbe, K.W. Evelyn Waugh.
   639(VQR):Autumn88-124
Crace, J. The Gift of Stones.*
   R. Fainlight, 364:Oct/Nov88-117
   J. Smiley, 441:16Jul89-12
Cracraft, J. The Petrine Revolution in Rus-
sian Architecture.
   A.G. Cross, 617(TLS):12-18May89-523
Craddock, P.B. Edward Gibbon: Luminous
Historian, 1772-1794.
   J. Kenyon, 617(TLS):15-21Dec89-1379
Craig, C., ed. The History of Scottish Litera-
ture.* (Vol 4)
   T. Crawford, 571(ScLJ):Winter88-19
Craig, C., ed. Noun Classes and Categoriza-
tion.
   A. Carstairs, 320(CJL):Jun88-173
Craig, D. Against Looting.
   J. May, 493:Summer88-54
Craig, E. The Mind of God and the Works of
Man.*
   M. Beaney, 521:Jul88-270
Craig, F. & P. Britain's Poisoned Water.
   D. Hammerton, 324:Nov89-817
Craig, G.A. The Triumph of Liberalism.
   L. Gossman, 453(NYRB):26Oct89-56
   R. Grew, 441:18Jun89-15
Craig, P.R. A Beautiful Place to Die.
   M. Stasio, 441:24Dec89-23
Craig, R.C., ed. The Humor of H.E. Taliaferro.
   C. Ficken, 536(Rev):Vol10-137
Craig, T., ed & trans. Musui's Story.
   A. Walthall, 407(MN):Autumn88-374
Craig, W.L. The Only Wise God.
   B.R. Reichenbach, 258:Sep88-340
Craik, T.W. & R.J. - see Donne, J.
Crais, R. The Monkey's Raincoat.
   T.J. Binyon, 617(TLS):28Apr-4May89-
470
Cramer, K. Nicht-reine synthetische Urteile
a priori.
   T. Pinder, 687:Jan-Mar88-154
Cramer, T. Die kleineren Liederdichter des
14. und 15. Jahrhunderts. (Vol 4)
   C. Petzsch, 72:Band224Heft2-370
Cramp, R. The British Academy Corpus of
Anglo-Saxon Stone Sculpture in England.
(Vol 1, Pts 1 & 2)
   L. Nees, 589:Apr88-383
Crandall, J.A., ed. ESL Through Content-
Area Instruction.
   N. Evans, 399(MLJ):Summer88-228
Crane, D.M. & T.A. Breslin. An Ordinary Re-
lationship.
   J. Grasso, 293(JASt):Feb88-114
Crane, E.F. A Dependent People.
   I.H. Polishook, 656(WMQ):Apr88-376
Crane, H. Playbill.
   K. Barker, 611(TN):Vol42No2-88
Crane, S. The Correspondence of Stephen
Crane. (S. Wertheim & P. Sorrentino, eds)
   H. Beaver, 617(TLS):20-26Jan89-55
   C. Benfey, 453(NYRB):16Mar89-31
Crane, S. Stephen Crane: Prose and Poetry.
(J.C. Levenson, ed)
   C. Benfey, 453(NYRB):16Mar89-31

Crane, S.D. Insular Romance.*
   J.A. Dane, 545(RPh):Feb89-381
   R.W. Hanning, 589:Jul88-647
   A.T. Harrison, 207(FR):Oct88-160
   T. Hunt, 541(RES):May88-283
   C. Lee, 379(MedR):Apr88-144
   R.A. Shoaf, 301(JEGP):Jul88-437
Cranston, M. Philosophers and Pamphle-
teers.*
   M. Adereth, 402(MLR):Jan89-169
Crapillet, P. Le "Cur Deus homo" d'Anselme
de Canterbury et le "De arrha animae"
d'Hugues de Saint-Victor, traduits pour
Philippe le Bon.* (R. Bultot & G. Hasenohr,
eds)
   W. Rothwell, 208(FS):Jan88-71
Craven, W. Colonial American Portraiture.*
   D. Irwin, 83:Spring88-120
Crawford, B.E., ed. St. Magnus Cathedral and
Orkney's Twelfth Century Renaissance.
   H.G. Slade, 617(TLS):10-16Mar89-259
Crawford, I.V. Malcolm's Katie. (D.M.R. Bent-
ley, ed)
   G. Warkentin, 627(UTQ):Fall88-159
Crawford, M. The Anglo-American Crisis of
the Mid-Nineteenth Century.
   K. Brauer, 637(VS):Winter89-241
Crawford, R. The Savage and the City in the
Work of T.S. Eliot.*
   B. Jackson, 175:Autumn88-241
Crawford, S. Mayordomo.
   L.M. Vause, 649(WAL):Nov88-279
Crawford, T. Angels in the Rain.*
   M. Estok, 198:Winter86-101
Crawford, T., D. Hewitt & A. Law, eds. Longer
Scottish Poems.* (Vol 2)
   F. Stafford, 447(N&Q):Dec88-523
   K. Sutherland, 571(ScLJ):Spring88-3
Crean, S. Newsworthy.
   M. Lang, 102(CanL):Winter87-277
Creech, J. Diderot.*
   G. Bremner, 208(FS):Jan88-89
   R. Waldinger, 188(ECr):Winter88-124
Creed, J.L. - see Lactantius
Creese, W.L. The Crowning of the American
Landscape.*
   R.G. Wilson, 639(VQR):Winter88-164
Cremades, E.R. - see under Rubio Cremades,
E.
Cremin, L.A. American Education.*
   639(VQR):Autumn88-116
Cremonesi, C. Studi romanzi di filologia e
letteratura.
   M.E. Winters, 545(RPh):May89-455
de Crenne, H. - see under Helisenne de
Crenne
de Crescenzo, L. The History of Greek Phil-
osophy. (Vol 1)
   W. Jordan, 617(TLS):30Jun-6Jul89-724
de Crespigny, R. Northern Frontier.
   W.G. Boltz, 318(JAOS):Oct-Dec87-819
Cresswell, M.J. Adverbial Modification.*
   B. Taylor, 63:Sep88-435
Cressy, D. Coming Over.*
   D.G. Allen, 656(WMQ):Oct88-787
   R. Howell, Jr., 366:Autumn88-235
   N. Pettit, 432(NEQ):Dec88-604
Le comte de Creutz. Lettres inédites de Paris
(1766-1770). (M. Molander, ed) Un Am-
bassadeur à la Cour de France. (G. Mary,
ed)
   C. Jones, 402(MLR):Jul89-741

Crevel, R. Difficult Death.*
  P. Hallam, 364:Dec88/Jan89-128
van Creveld, M. Technology and War.
  G.A. Craig, 453(NYRB):17Aug89-31
Crew, S.R. Field to Factory.
  M.L.S. Heininger, 658:Summer/Autumn88-
  169
Crewe, J. Hidden Designs.
  M.G. Brennan, 541(RES):May88-287
  A.B. Dawson, 570(SQ):Spring88-94
  J. Gouws, 447(N&Q):Jun88-217
  P. Hyland, 568(SCN):Fall88-42
Crewe, Q. In the Realms of Gold.
  J. Ure, 617(TLS):14-20Jul89-776
Crews, F. Skeptical Engagements.*
  F. McCombie, 447(N&Q):Dec88-558
  M.D.O., 295(JML):Fall87/Winter88-241
  K. Shabetai, 144:Winter89-105
Crews, H. All We Need of Hell.*
  E.C. Lynskey, 502(PrS):Summer88-141
Crichton, R. - see Smyth, E.
Crick, B. & J. Ferns - see Whalley, G.
Crick, F. What Mad Pursuit.*
  A.R. Hall, 324:Oct89-750
  R. Olby, 617(TLS):26May-1Jun89-568
Crisler, J.S. - see Norris, F.
Crisp, O. & L. Edmondson, eds. Civil Rights in
  Imperial Russia.
  J. Keep, 617(TLS):22-28Sep89-1039
Crispell, K.R. & C.F. Gomez. Hidden Illness in
  the White House.
  H.L. Abrams, 441:1Jan89-17
"Critique et édition de textes."
  F. Lebsanft, 547(RF):Band99Heft4-441
"Critiques 1." "Critiques 2." (H. Beck & J.
  Turnbull, eds of both)
  N. Quarry, 46:Oct88-12
Croce, A. Sight Lines.*
  O. Stuart, 151:Dec88-64
Crombie, W. Free Verse and Prose Style.
  Seiichi Suzuki, 361:Dec88-337
Crome, L. Unbroken.
  I. Deak, 453(NYRB):28Sep89-63
Crompton, L. Byron and Greek Love.*
  M. Lynch, 637(VS):Autumn88-129
Crompton, R. Just William [& others].
  P. Parker, 364:Feb87-107
Cromwell, A.M. An African Victorian Femi-
  nist.
  J.A. Berkman, 637(VS):Autumn88-126
Crone, A.L. & C.V. Chvany, eds. New Studies
  in Russian Language and Literature.*
  M.G. Basker, 575(SEER):Oct88-642
  D. Rancour-Laferrière, 558(RLJ):Winter-
  Spring-Fall88-359
Cronin, A. No Laughing Matter.
  D. Donoghue, 617(TLS):27Oct-2Nov89-
  1171
Cronin, G.L. & B.H. Hall. Saul Bellow. (2nd
  ed)
  S.E. Marovitz, 87(BB):Mar88-67
Cronin, R. Colour and Experience in Nine-
  teenth-Century Poetry.
  A. St. George, 617(TLS):21-27Jul89-807
Cronjé, J.V. Dionysius of Halicarnassus, "De
  Demosthene."
  S. Usher, 123:Vol38No1-146
Crook, J.M. The Dilemma of Style.*
  A. Saint, 46:Apr88-10
Crook, N. and D. Guiton. Shelley's Venomed
  Melody.*
  M.A. Quinn, 340(KSJ):Vol37-191
  R. Rooksby, 447(N&Q):Jun88-250

Crookall, D. & others, eds. Simulation-Gam-
  ing in the Late 1980s.
  P.A. Dunkel, 608:Mar89-136
Cropp, M., E. Fantham & S.E. Scully, eds.
  Greek Tragedy and its Legacy.
  J. Gregory, 487:Spring88-74
  A.N. Michelini, 24:Winter88-594
Cropp, M. & G. Fick. Resolutions and Chrono-
  logy in Euripides.
  D.J. Mastronarde, 487:Winter88-366
Cropper, E. The Ideal of Painting.
  D.S. Pepper, 380:Winter88
Cropper, E., with others. Pietro Testa, 1612-
  1650: Prints and Drawings.
  F. Haskell, 453(NYRB):20Jul89-36
Cros, E. Literatura, ideología y sociedad.
  M.I. Millington, 86(BHS):Jul88-285
Crosby, B. A Catalogue of Durham Cathedral
  Music Manuscripts.*
  J. Morehen, 410(M&L):Jul88-371
Crosby, D.A. The Specter of the Absurd.
  J. McBride, 103:Dec88-473
Crosby, J. One Touch of Shakespeare. (J.W.
  Velz & F.N. Teague, eds)
  I.G. Dash, 570(SQ):Summer88-253
  M. Eccles, 405(MP):Aug88-106
  J.P. Hammersmith, 577(SHR):Spring88-
  187
Crosby, S.M. The Royal Abbey of St-Denis.
  (P.Z. Blum, ed)
  E. Fernie, 59:Jun88-289
  H.R. Loyn, 39:Feb88-142
Crosley, M.L. The Architect's Guide to Com-
  puter-Aided Design.
  R.L. King, 47:Nov88-58
Cross, A. A Trap for Fools.
  M. Stasio, 441:14May89-30
Cross, A.G. The Russian Theme in English
  Literature from the Sixteenth Century to
  1980.*
  G. Lewinson, 575(SEER):Jan88-119
Cross, N. The Common Writer.*
  A. Easson, 366:Spring88-125
Cross, T., ed. The Lost Voices of World War
  One.
  J. Joll, 453(NYRB):27Apr89-53
  P. McCarthy, 617(TLS):10-16Feb89-133
"Cross Currents." (Vol 5) (L. Matejka, ed)
  R.L. Aczel, 575(SEER):Jan88-131
Crossley, P. Gothic Architecture in the Reign
  of Kasimir the Great.*
  P.W. Knoll, 497(PolR):Vol33No4-469
  W. Leedy, 576:Dec88-416
Crossley, R. H.G. Wells.
  D.Y. Hughes, 561(SFS):Mar88-95
Crossley, R. - see Stapledon, O. & A. Miller
Crossley-Holland, K., ed. The Oxford Book of
  Travel Verse.*
  R. Cockcroft, 447(N&Q):Sep88-401
Crossley-Holland, K. The Painting Room.*
  S. Knight, 364:Dec88/Jan89-118
"El Crotalón." (Vol 1)
  K. Kohut, 547(RF):Band100Heft4-466
Crouch, D. The Beaumont Twins.
  J.W. Alexander, 589:Jul88-650
Crouch, D.P. History of Architecture.
  J.W. Stamper, 576:Mar88-74
Crouch, T. The Bishop's Boys.
  442(NY):4Sep89-107
Crouse, J. & D. Trusheim. The Case Against
  the SAT.
  A. Hacker, 453(NYRB):12Oct89-63

Crouthamel, J.L. Bennett's New York Herald and the Rise of the Popular Press.
    J. Ziomek, 441:8Oct89-42
Croutier, A.L. Harem.
    P-L. Adams, 61:Aug89-91
    B. Small, 441:11Jun89-22
Crouzet, M. Essai sur la genèse du romantisme.
    J.T. Booker, 207(FR):Oct88-175
Crouzet, M. Le Héros fourbe chez Stendhal.
    G. May, 207(FR):Feb89-523
Crouzet, M. Nature et société chez Stendhal.*
    K. Ringger, 535(RHL):Mar-Apr88-294
Crouzet, M. Le Naturel, la grâce et le réel dans la poétique de Stendhal.
    R.T. Denommé, 210(FrF):Sep88-375
Crouzet, M. La Poétique de Stendhal.* Le Naturel, la grâce et le réel dans la poétique de Stendhal.
    A. Michel, 535(RHL):Jul-Aug88-779
Crowe, C. The Night-Side of Nature.
    G. Bennett, 203:Vol99No1-131
Crowe, M.J. The Extraterrestrial Life Debate 1750-1900.*
    D. Knight, 83:Autumn88-222
Crowley, B.L. The Self, the Individual, and the Community.
    W. Kymlicka, 518:Oct88-242
    D.J. Levy, 144:Spring89-336
Crowley, J. Novelty.
    G. Jonas, 441:21May89-26
Crown, A.D. A Bibliography of the Samaritans.
    J.C. Greenfield, 318(JAOS):Jul-Sep87-545
Crowther, P. – see Perelman, S.J.
Croxton, P.C.L. & L.H. Martin. Solving Problems in Structures.
    D.E. Gordon, 47:Mar88-61
Crozier, A. & T. Longville, eds. A Various Art.
    K. Edwards, 703:Fall88-228
    D. Houston, 493:Autumn88-51
Crozier, L. Angels of Flesh, Angels of Silence.
    B. Rendall, 647:Fall88-82
Crozier, L. The Garden Going on Without Us.
    F.W. Kaye, 102(CanL):Winter87-138
Cruden, R.M., ed. Traffic of Ideas Between India and America.
    S.R. Glazer, 293(JASt):Aug88-674
Cruden, S. Scottish Medieval Churches.
    R.N. Bailey, 447(N&Q):Jun88-206
Cruickshank, D. & S. Page – see Calderón de la Barca, P.
Cruikshank, J.L. A Delicate Experiment.
    R. Cuff, 106:Spring88-128
Cruise, E.J. English Grammar for Students of Russian.
    K.L. Nalibow, 574(SEEJ):Summer88-347
Crummey, R.O. The Formation of Muscovy 1304-1613.
    L. Hughes, 575(SEER):Apr88-285
Crump, G.M., ed. Approaches to Teaching Milton's "Paradise Lost."*
    G. Campbell, 447(N&Q):Dec88-536
    L. Potter, 402(MLR):Jan89-128
Crupi, C.W. Robert Greene.
    E. Heale, 677(YES):Vol19-309
"La Crusca nella tradizione letteraria e linguistica italiana."
    D. Hay, 551(RenQ):Autumn88-497

Cruse, D.A. Lexical Semantics.*
    A. Lehrer, 297(JL):Mar88-203
    B. Peeters, 320(CJL):Jun88-197
Crusius, C.A. Die philosophischen Hauptwerke. (Vol 4, Pt 1)
    J. Ecole, 192(EP):Oct-Dec88-549
Crusz, R. A Time for Loving.
    C. Tapping, 102(CanL):Summer88-145
Cruttenden, A. Intonation.*
    B. Williams, 353:Vol26No2-330
Cruz, A., Jr. Memoirs of a Counterrevolutionary.
    A.J. Glass, 441:15Oct89-11
Cruz, A.J. Imitación y transformación.
    D.H. Darst, 304(JHP):Spring88-257
de la Cruz, R. Sainetes.* (M. Coulon, ed)
    P. Deacon, 86(BHS):Apr88-188
de Cruz-Sáenz, M.S., ed. Romancero tradicional de Costa Rica.
    M. Da Costa Fontes, 292(JAF):Jan-Mar88-115
    E. Gargurevich, 552(REH):May88-132
    R.D. Woods, 238:Sep88-554
    R. Wright, 86(BHS):Jul88-320
Crystal, D. The Cambridge Encyclopedia of Language.*
    E.A. Ebbinghaus, 215(GL):Vol28No1-77
    M.H. Sable, 263(RIB):Vol38No1-72
Crystal, D., ed. Linguistic Controversies.
    P.H. Salus, 567:Vol70No1/2-169
Cua, A.S. Ethical Argumentation.*
    A.H. Black, 293(JASt):Aug88-590
Cuadra, P.A. The Birth of the Sun.
    G. Simon, 448:Vol26No3-58
Cuadros, E.R. – see under Rodríguez Cuadros, E.
Cubelier de Beynac, J. & M. Magnien, eds. Acta Scaligeriana.*
    P. Ford, 208(FS):Jan88-74
Cudahy, S. Nectar at Noon.
    N. Sonenberg, 441:8Oct89-12
Cude, W. The Ph.D. Trap.
    M. Fee, 376:Sep88-165
Cuevas, C. – see de Herrera, F.
Cugusi, P. Aspetti letterari dei "Carmina Latina Epigraphica."*
    A. Bastiaensen, 394:Vol41fasc3/4-444
Cui Wenhua, comp. He shang lun.
    F. Wakeman, Jr., 453(NYRB):2Mar89-19
Culla i Clarà, J.B. El republicanisme lerrouxista a Catalunya (1901-1923).
    J-L. Marfany, 86(BHS):Oct88-421
Cullamar, E.T. Babaylanism in Negros: 1896-1907.
    M. Cullinane, 293(JASt):Aug88-696
Cullen, B., ed. Hegel Today.
    J.B., 185:Jul89-976
Cullen, C.T. & L. Tobias – see Marshall, J.
Culler, A.D. The Victorian Mirror of History.*
    R. Keefe, 158:Mar88-36
    K. Sutherland, 541(RES):Aug88-455
Culler, J., ed. On Puns.
    639(VQR):Autumn88-140
Culler, J. Ferdinand de Saussure.* (rev)
    G. Sampson, 144:Winter89-93
Culley, M., ed. A Day at a Time.
    E. Hampsten, 534(RALS):Vol16No1&2-64
Culme, J. The Directory of Gold and Silversmiths, Jewellers and Allied Traders 1838-1914.
    R. Edgcumbe, 39:Sep88-216
    M. Snodin, 90:Oct88-782

Cummings, D.W. American English Spelling.
  M. Aronoff, 350:Sep89-591
Cummings, J. Once a Legend.
  B.J. Frye, 649(WAL):Feb89-372
Cummings, S. Mark Twain and Science.
  F. Crews, 453(NYRB):20Jul89-39
Cummins, J. The Hound and the Hawk.
  S. Anglo, 617(TLS):12-18May89-522
Cummins, J.G. - see López de Ayala, P.
Cummins, M. The Lamplighter. (N. Baym, ed)
  B.A. White, 357:Fall89-70
Cummins, R. Meaning and Mental Representa-
tion.
  A. Clark, 617(TLS):27Oct-2Nov89-1189
Cunliffe, B. The City of Bath.*
  D. Leatherbarrow, 173(ECS):Winter88/89-
  274
  T.H. Watkins, 124:Jan-Feb89-200
Cunliffe, B. Greeks, Romans and Barbarians.*
  J. Griffin, 453(NYRB):16Mar89-6
Cunningham, E. Masterpieces of the American
West.
  S. Armitage, 649(WAL):Nov88-263
Cunningham, L. Sleeping Arrangements.
  C.L. Glickfeld, 441:31Dec89-19
Cunningham, N.E., Jr. In Pursuit of Reason.*
  R.J. Brugger, 639(VQR):Spring88-349
  W.S. Price, Jr., 27(AL):Mar88-114
  J.N. Rakove, 656(WMQ):Apr88-377
Cunningham, R. Apples on the Flood.
  C.S. Brown, 131(CL):Spring88-172
Cunningham, V. British Writers of the Thir-
ties.*
  M. Baron, 175:Spring88-84
  T. Pinkney, 175:Autumn88-246
  W. Scammell, 364:Jun88-95
  L.M. Schwerdt, 395(MFS):Winter88-700
Cuno, J., ed. French Caricature and the
French Revolution, 1789-1799.
  W. Scott, 617(TLS):19-25May89-554
Cupitt, D. The New Christian Ethics.
  483:Oct88-555
Cupitt, D. Radicals and the Future of the
Church.
  A. Webster, 617(TLS):27Oct-2Nov89-
  1188
Curley, E. Behind the Geometrical Method.
  L.M., 185:Apr89-680
  G.H.R. Parkinson, 617(TLS):3-9Feb89-
  115
Curley, T.M. - see Chambers, R.
Curnonsky. Larousse Traditional French
Cooking.
  R. Flaste, 441:3Dec89-18
Curnow, A. Continuum.
  L. Mackinnon, 617(TLS):26May-1Jun89-
  593
Curnow, A. The Loop in Lone Kauri Road.*
  J. Forth, 364:Apr-May87-128
  B. O'Donoghue, 493:Spring88-34
Curran, C.E. Tensions in Moral Theology.
  J. Garvey, 441:19Mar89-11
Curran, J. K2, Triumph and Tragedy.
  M. Cart, 441:30Apr89-39
Curran, S. Poetic Form and British Romanti-
cism.*
  R.L. Brett, 541(RES):Feb88-120
  M. Brown, 340(KSJ):Vol37-166
  P.H. Fry, 141:Winter88-131
  K.R. Johnston, 405(MP):Feb89-316
  M.G.H. Pittock, 447(N&Q):Mar88-127
Current, R.N. Arguing with Historians.
  639(VQR):Spring88-43

Currey, C.B. Edward Lansdale.
  R. Manning, 441:26Feb89-9
Currie, G. & A. Musgrave, eds. Popper and
the Human Sciences.*
  C.B. McCullagh, 63:Jun88-266
  B.T. Wilkins, 488:Sep88-418
Currie, H.M. Silver Latin Epic.
  R.C. Lounsbury, 124:May-Jun89-396
Currie, R. Learning on the Job.*
  S.R. Dorscht, 102(CanL):Winter87-257
Currie-McDaniel, R. Carpetbagger of Con-
science.
  R.P. Fuke, 106:Summer88-270
Curry, J. Woodstock.
  J. Wiener, 441:21May89-19
Curry, P. Prophecy and Power.
  J. Henry, 617(TLS):1-7Dec89-1345
Curry, R.K. En torno a la poesía de Luis Cer-
nuda.*
  G. Barrow, 86(BHS):Apr88-195
Curtin, M. Propriety and Position.
  M. Burgan, 637(VS):Spring89-428
Curtis, G.L. The Japanese Way of Politics.
  Shiratori Rei, 285(JapQ):Oct-Dec88-439
Curtis, J.A.E. Bulgakov's Last Decade.
  A. Barratt, 575(SEER):Oct88-648
  B.A. Beatie & P.W. Powell, 395(MFS):
  Winter88-712
  P. Doyle, 402(MLR):Jul89-813
  D.M. Fiene, 574(SEEJ):Winter88-666
  E.C. Haber, 550(RusR):Jul88-354
Curtis, R.L., ed. Le roman de Tristan en
prose.* (Vol 3)
  L.A.M. Sumberg, 589:Jan88-141
Curtis, W.J.R. Le Corbusier.*
  R. Becherer, 505:Mar88-121
  K. Kimball, 45:May88-91
  M. Spens, 592:Vol201No1019-62
Cusamano, C. The New Foods.
  R. Flaste, 441:11Jun89-18
Cushman, K. - see Lawrence, D.H.
Cushman, S. William Carlos Williams and the
Meanings of Measure.*
  G.S. Lensing, 569(SR):Winter88-113
Cutler, A.H. & H.E. The Jew as Ally of the
Muslim.
  S. Bowman, 589:Apr88-386
Cutler, B. Dark Fire.
  A. Cooper, 389(MQ):Winter89-254
Cutrer, E.F. The Art of the Woman.
  E. Johns, 617(TLS):17-23Feb89-160
Cutting, P. Children of the Siege.*
  S. MacNeille, 441:2Apr89-29
Cuvigny, H. L'arpentage par espèces dans
l'Égypte ptolémaïque d'après les papyrus
grecs.
  A. Bülow-Jacobsen, 229:Band60Heft3-
  236
  D.J. Thompson, 303(JoHS):Vol108-255
Cuvigny, M. - see Plutarch
Cuzzani, A. Teatro completo.
  O. Pellettieri, 352(LATR):Spring89-139
Cymbalista, D. Danger.
  G. Glickman, 441:25Jun89-11
Saint Cyprian. The Letters of St. Cyprian of
Carthage.* (Vols 2 & 3) (G.W. Clarke, ed &
trans)
  R.P.C. Hanson, 123:Vol38No1-156
Saint Cyril of Alexandria. Cyrille d'Alexan-
drie, "Contre Julien." (Vol 1, Bks 1 & 2) (P.
Burguière & P. Évieux, eds & trans)
  É. des Places, 555:Vol61fasc2-316

Czarnecka, E. & A. Fiut. Conversations with Czeslaw Milosz.
B. Wormser, 472:Vol15No2-67
Czarnecki, J.P. Last Traces.
A. Knopf, 441:20Aug89-20
Czartoryski, P. - see Copernicus, N.
Czerniawski, A., ed & trans. The Burning Forest.*
D. O'Driscoll, 493:Spring88-18
Czerwinski, E.J., ed. Chekhov Reconstructed.
M. Ehre, 574(SEEJ):Fall88-471

Dabit, E. Journal intime 1928-1936. (P-E. Robert, ed)
P. McCarthy, 617(TLS):29Dec89/4Jan90-1444
Dabydeen, C., ed. A Shapely Fire.
R. Sullivan, 627(UTQ):Fall88-138
Dabydeen, D., ed. The Black Presence in English Literature.
Z.T. Sullivan, 677(YES):Vol19-361
Dabydeen, D. Coolie Odyssey.
F. D'Aguiar, 493:Summer88-64
Dabydeen, D. Hogarth, Walpole and Commercial Britain.
R. Paulson, 173(ECS):Fall88-90
Dabydeen, D. Hogarth's Blacks.*
M.G. Cooke, 173(ECS):Winter88/89-225
Dacey, P. & D. Jauss, eds. Strong Measures.
W. Harmon, 472:Vol15No1-99
Dacy, D.C. Foreign Aid, War, and Economic Development.
W.J. Duiker, 293(JASt):May88-416
Daemmrich, H.S. & I. Themen und Motive in der Literatur.
H. Foltinek, 602:Band19Heft1-202
Dagan, A. The Court Jesters.
A. Rome, 441:12Nov89-55
Dagan, E.A. Man and his Vision.
C.D. Roy, 2(AfrA):Aug88-87
Daggy, R.E. - see Merton, T.
d'Agostino, F. Chomsky's System of Ideas.*
D.H., 355(LSoc):Jun88-311
D'Aguiar, F. Airy Hall.
S. O'Brien, 617(TLS):7-13Jul89-737
D'Aguiar, F. & others, eds. The New British Poetry.
M. Horovitz, 493:Winter88/89-64
Dahl, C.C. Louis Auchincloss.*
K. King, 27(AL):May88-308
R.P. Moses, 295(JML):Fall87/Winter88-290
Dahl, M.K. Political Violence in Drama.
E.C. Ramírez, 615(TJ):Dec88-572
Dahl, Ö. Tense and Aspect Systems.*
S. Fleischman, 545(RPh):Nov88-186
K. Schubert, 603:Vol12No1-194
Dahl, R.A. Democracy and Its Critics.
R.N. Bellah, 441:12Nov89-22
Dahl, T. Working for Love.
D. Jacobs, 441:12Mar89-22
Dahlhaus, C. Ludwig van Beethoven und seine Zeit.
K. von Fischer, 416:Band3Heft3-254
Dahlhaus, C. Die Musiktheorie im 18. und 19. Jahrhundert. (Pt 1)
L.A. Rothfarb, 308:Spring88-133
Dahlhaus, C. Nineteenth-Century Music.
J. Drummond, 617(TLS):1-7Dec89-1329
P. Gossett, 453(NYRB):26Oct89-21

Dahlhaus, C. Schoenberg and the New Music.
M. Miller, 607:Jun88-49
O. Neighbour, 410(M&L):Jul88-410
Dahlhaus, C. & H.H. Eggebrecht. Was ist Musik?
B. Sponheuer, 416:Band3Heft3-249
Dahlie, H. Varieties of Exile.*
D. Dowling, 102(CanL):Winter87-216
S.E. Grace, 295(JML):Fall87/Winter88-205
D.B. Jewison, 627(UTQ):Fall87-151
Dahlsten, D.L. & R. Garcia, eds. Eradication of Exotic Pests.
M. Ridley, 617(TLS):24-30Nov89-1297
Dahrendorf, E. - see Schapiro, L.
Dahrendorf, R. The Modern Social Conflict.
S. Hoffmann, 441:5Feb89-18
J. Waldron, 617(TLS):10-16Feb89-144
Daiches, D., P. Jones & J. Jones, eds. A Hotbed of Genius.*
S.H., 185:Apr89-679
A.T. McKenzie, 173(ECS):Winter88/89-253
Daichman, G.S. Wayward Nuns in Medieval Literature.
P.D. Johnson, 589:Apr88-388
K. Varty, 382(MAE):1988/2-295
Daigle, J. Au septième ciel.
C.F. Coates, 102(CanL):Winter87-255
Daikichi, I. - see under Irokawa Daikichi
Dailey, J. Rivals.
R. Short, 441:5Mar89-22
Daiser, W. Künstliche-Intelligenz-Forschung und ihre epistemologischen Grundlagen.
J. Schopman, 679:Band19Heft1-153
Daitch, S. L.C.
S. Moore, 532(RCF):Fall88-166
Dakubu, M.E.K. - see under Kropp Dakubu, M.E.
Dalby, D. Africa and the Written Word.
L. Arvanites, 2(AfrA):Nov87-78
Dal Co, F., ed. Kevin Roche.
S. Gutterman, 45:Mar88-77
Daldry, G. Charles Dickens and the Form of the Novel.*
S. Monod, 402(MLR):Jan89-137
Dale, P., with others. Dangerous Families.
D.L., 185:Jan89-468
Dale, P.N. The Myth of Japanese Uniqueness.*
G. Sampson, 307:Nov88-236
J.M. Unger, 293(JASt):Nov88-891
Dale, R.C. The Films of René Clair.
H.A. Garrity, 207(FR):Oct88-192
Dales, R.C. & E.B. King - see Grosseteste, R.
Daley, J. Honourable Friends.
J-A. Goodwin, 617(TLS):3-9Nov89-1218
D'Alfonso, A. The Other Shore.
L. McKinney, 102(CanL):Winter87-232
Lord Dalhousie. The Dalhousie Journals. (Vol 3) (M. Whitelaw, ed)
G.W., 102(CanL):Spring88-259
Dallapiccola, A., with S. Zingel-Ave Lallemant, eds. Vijayanagara City and Empire New Currents of Research.
J.F. Mosteller, 318(JAOS):Oct-Dec87-846
Dallapiccola, L. Dallapiccola on Opera. (Vol 1) (R. Shackelford, ed)
D. Osmond-Smith, 415:Aug88-405
K. Pendle, 465:Spring89-104
C. Shaw, 607:Jun88-48
Dalla Valle, D., ed. Manierismo e letteratura.
M. Bastiaensen, 549(RLC):Oct-Dec88-572

Dallin, A. & C. Rice. The Gorbachev Era.
　A.G. Meyer, 385(MQR):Fall89-771
Dallmayr, F.R. Critical Encounters.
　F.A. Olafson, 484(PPR):Sep88-180
Dalrymple, W. In Xanadu.
　M. Alexander, 617(TLS):29Sep-5Oct89-
　1073
Dalton, H.L. & others, eds. AIDS and the Law.
　J.B., 185:Oct88-213
Daly, B.M., ed. Moral Conduct and Authority.
　J.C. Bürgel, 318(JAOS):Jan-Mar87-186
Daly, G. Pre-Raphaelites in Love.
　K. Flint, 617(TLS):14-20Apr89-393
Daly, P.M., ed. The English Emblem and the
　Continental Tradition.
　J.M. Massing, 617(TLS):21-27Jul89-806
Daly, P.M., ed. The European Emblem.
　F.D. Hoeniger, 107(CRCL):Jun88-281
Daly, P.M. & V. Callahan, with S. Cuttler –
　see Alciati, A.
Daly, P.M., with S. Cuttler – see Alciati, A.
Daly, P.M., with L.T. Duer & A. Raspa, eds.
　The English Emblem Tradition. (Vol 1)
　J.M. Massing, 617(TLS):21-27Jul89-806
Dalyell, T. Dick Crossman.
　M. Pugh, 617(TLS):3-9Nov89-1207
van Dam, H-J. P. Papinius Statius, "Silvae,"
　Book II.*
　J.A. Willis, 394:Vol41fasc1/2-207
Damascius. Traité des premiers principes.
　(Vol 1) (L.G. Westerink, ed; J. Combès,
　trans)
　É. des Places, 555:Vol61fasc2-314
Damblemont, A. Le Français pour la profes-
　sion.
　J.T. Day, 207(FR):Mar89-707
Damen, F. Crisis and Religious Renewal in
　the Drahmo Samaj (1860-1884).
　R.J. Young, 318(JAOS):Oct-Dec87-842
Dameron, J.L. & J.W. Mathews, eds. No Fairer
　Land.*
　C.S. Watson, 392:Fall88-575
Damisch, H. L'origine de la perspective.*
　B. Vouilloux, 98:Apr88-301
von Damm, H. At Reagan's Side.
　J. Didion, 453(NYRB):21Dec89-3
　M. Dowd, 441:15Jan89-8
Damm, S. Vögel, die verkünden Land.*
　K.A. Wurst, 221(GQ):Winter87-115
Damm, S. – see Lenz, J.M.R.
Dammann, E. Was Herero erzählten und
　sangen.
　R. Schott, 196:Band29Heft1/2-179
Damrosch, D. The Narrative Covenant.
　E.L. Greenstein, 508:Sep88-347
Damrosch, L., Jr. God's Plot and Man's
　Stories.*
　J.D. Canfield, 125:Fall87-85
　L. Lerner, 128(CE):Sep88-572
Damrosch, L., Jr. The Imaginative World of
　Alexander Pope.
　M.R. Brownell, 401(MLQ):Sep87-290
　P. Rogers, 191(ELN):Mar89-88
　K. Williamson, 184(EIC):Jul88-254
Damrosch, L., Jr., ed. Modern Essays on
　Eighteenth-Century Literature.
　B. Hammond, 166:Apr89-241
Dan, J. Jewish Mysticism and Jewish Ethics.
　I.G. Marcus, 589:Jan88-143
Dana, Mrs. W.S. How to Know the Wild
　Flowers.
　L. Yang, 441:3Dec89-74

Dance, D.C., ed. Fifty Caribbean Writers.*
　E. Skinner, 395(MFS):Summer88-262
　H. Tiffin, 538(RAL):Fall88-441
Dance, D.C. Folklore from Contemporary Ja-
　maicans.*
　C.B. Davies, 538(RAL):Fall88-438
　J.P. Homiak, 292(JAF):Jan-Mar88-125
Dance, H.O. Stormy Monday.*
　A.F. Kinney, 585(SoQ):Winter89-101
Danchin, L. Jean Dubuffet, peintre-philos-
　ophe.
　R. Cardinal, 617(TLS):13-19Oct89-1118
Danchin, P., ed. The Prologues and Epilogues
　of the Restoration 1660-1700.* (Pts 1-3)
　A.H. Scouten, 173(ECS):Fall88-82
Dancocks, D.G. Legacy of Valour.*
　M. Milner, 529(QQ):Spring88-183
Dancourt, F.C. La Maison de campagne
　(1688), La Foire Saint-Germain (1696), Les
　Eaux de Bourbon (1696), comédies.* (A.
　Blanc, ed)
　H.G. Hall, 208(FS):Jan88-81
Dancy, J. Berkeley.*
　P.J. Bagley, 518:Apr88-85
　G.P., 185:Oct88-204
Dancz, V.H. Women and Party Politics in Pen-
　insular Malaysia.
　W.R. Roff, 293(JASt):Nov88-927
Dandamaev, M.A. & V.G. Lukonin. The Cul-
　ture and Social Institutions of Ancient
　Iran. (P.L. Kohl, with D.J. Dadson, eds)
　A.D.H. Bivar, 617(TLS):6-12Oct89-1096
Dandekar, H.C. Men to Bombay, Women at
　Home.
　A. Thorner, 293(JASt):Feb88-166
Dandridge, R.B. Ann Allen Shockley.
　H.R. Houston, 459:Spring88-96
Dano, J.A. "Res/Verba."*
　G.R. Muller, 589:Jul88-651
Daneloň, F. "Note" di Giovita Scalvini su i
　Promessi Sposi.
　P. De Marchi, 228(GSLI):Vol165fasc529-
　131
Danica, E. Don't: A Woman's Word.
　S. Hartwell, 618:Fall88-48
　H. Meunch, 137:Fall88-48
Daniel, E.V. Fluid Signs.*
　R.C. Lester, 318(JAOS):Apr-Jun87-353
Daniel, G. Le Style de Diderot.
　D.J. Adams, 83:Spring88-112
　J. Chouillet, 535(RHL):Mar-Apr88-277
　D. Fourny, 207(FR):Dec88-329
　A. Judge, 402(MLR):Jan89-173
　H. Mason, 208(FS):Jul88-346
Daniel, K.W. Francis Poulenc.
　R.L. Smith, 617(TLS):16-22Jun89-667
Daniel, L. Falling Together.
　A. Brooks, 102(CanL):Summer88-160
Daniel, W.C. "De Lawd."
　C.G. Holloway, 95(CLAJ):Mar89-385
　J. Mason, 459:Winter88-137
Daniele, A. – see de' Dottori, C.
Daniell, D., ed. Tyndale's New Testament.
　(W. Tyndale, trans)
　G. Hill, 617(TLS):17-23Nov89-1273
Daniels, A. Zanzibar to Timbuktu.*
　J. Lewis, 364:Jul88-104
Daniels, B.C., ed. Power and Status.
　J.K. Martin, 656(WMQ):Jan88-182
Daniels, L.J. Tales of an Old Horse Trader.*
　(H.S. Herrick, ed)
　R. Wright, 617(TLS):25-31Aug89-929

Daniels, N. Am I My Parents' Keeper?
R. George, 103:Nov88-439
Daniels, N. Just Health Care.
J. Taylor, 185:Oct88-171
Daniels, R. Asian America.
L. Pan, 617(TLS):22-28Sep89-1026
Daniloff, N. Two Lives, One Russia.*
G. Webb, 617(TLS):9-15Jun89-631
Danly, S. & L. Marx, eds. The Railroad in
American Art.*
658:Winter88-296
Dann, J.C. - see Nagle, J.
Dann, O. & J. Dinwiddy, eds. Nationalism in
the Age of the French Revolution.
W. Scott, 617(TLS):19-25May89-554
Danner, R. Patterns of Irony in the "Fables"
of La Fontaine.*
H. Mydlarski, 345(KRQ):May88-234
Danon, R. Work in the English Novel.*
G. Channon, 366:Spring88-131
G. Channon, 366:Autumn88-250
Danson, L. Max Beerbohm and the Act of
Writing.
K. Beckson, 617(TLS):24-30Nov89-1308
Dantanus, U. Brian Friel.*
G. O'Connor, 511:Jun88-44
Danto, A.C. Connections to the World.
J. Annas, 441:14May89-18
Danto, A.C. Mysticism and Morality.
E. Grimbergen, 543:Sep88-135
Danto, A.C. The Philosophical Disenfran-
chisement of Art.*
S. Davies, 63:Jun88-277
D.A. Hoekema, 127:Winter88-379
A. Nehamas, 311(JP):Apr88-214
D. Novitz, 290(JAAC):Winter87-307
R. Shusterman, 494:Vol8No3/4-651
Danto, A.C. The State of the Art.*
J. Brodsky, 290(JAAC):Summer88-517
P. Crowther, 89(BJA):Summer88-284
E. Fox, 364:Dec87/Jan88-130
G. van Hensbergen, 90:Nov88-866
D.A. Hoekema, 127:Winter88-379
A. Nehamas, 311(JP):Apr88-214
d'Antonio, M. Fall From Grace.
G. Wills, 453(NYRB):21Dec89-20
Danylewycz, M. Taking the Veil.
J. Sangster, 298:Spring/Summer88-234
Dao, B. - see under Bei Dao
Da Pozzo, G., F. Fido & M. Santagata - see
Baratto, M.
Darbellay, E. - see Frescobaldi, G.
Darby, P. Three Faces of Imperialism.
N. Etherington, 637(VS):Summer89-573
Darby, W. Necessary American Fictions.
M. Light, 395(MFS):Summer88-246
Dardis, T. The Thirsty Muse.
P. Rose, 61:Jun89-93
Dargan, J. Balzac and the Drama of Perspec-
tive.*
J. Frölich, 535(RHL):Mar-Apr88-297
Darien, G. Le Voleur. (P. Besnier, ed)
W. Redfern, 208(FS):Apr88-223
Darlington, D. In Condor Country.
G. Haslam, 649(WAL):May88-82
Darnton, R. The Business of Enlightenment.
C. Michael, 599:Spring89-170
Darnton, R. & D. Roche, eds. Revolution in
Print.
R. Bernstein, 441:9Jul89-12
A. Forrest, 617(TLS):6-12Oct89-1097

Darras, J. Arpentage de la poésie contempo-
raine.
O. Merzoug, 98:Dec88-1021
Daruwalla, K.N. The Keeper of the Dead.
S.C. Narula, 314:Summer-Fall87-161
D'Arvor, O.P. - see under Poivre D'Arvor, O.
Darwall, S.L. Impartial Reason.
M.G. Singer, 484(PPR):Mar89-507
Darwin, C. The Correspondence of Charles
Darwin.* (Vols 1-3) (F. Burkhardt & S.
Smith, eds)
J.R. Durant, 447(N&Q):Sep88-386
Darwin, C. The Correspondence of Charles
Darwin. (Vol 4) (F. Burkhardt & S. Smith,
eds)
D.L. Hull, 617(TLS):18-24Aug89-892
Darwish, M., S. al-Qasim & Adonis. Victims
of a Map. (A. al-Udhari, ed & trans)
S.M. Toorawa, 294:Sep88-193
Dary, D. Entrepreneurs of the Old West.*
C.S. Peterson, 649(WAL):Aug88-181
Das, V. Structure and Cognition.
R.W. Lariviere, 318(JAOS):Oct-Dec87-837
Das, V., ed. The Word and the World.
F.J. Korom, 292(JAF):Jul-Sep88-369
Dascal, M. Leibniz: Language, Signs and
Thought.*
L. Zgusta, 350:Jun89-423
Dasenbrock, R.W. - see Lewis, W.
Dash, L. When Children Want Children.
D. Wycliff, 441:12Feb89-19
Da Silva, G. Le texte et le lecteur comme
interaction objective.
P. Somville, 542:Jan-Mar88-94
Da Silva, Z.S. Beginning Spanish. (6th ed)
D. McAlpine, 399(MLJ):Autumn88-369
Dassonville, M., ed. Ronsard et l'imaginaire.
F. Cornilliat, 535(RHL):Mar-Apr88-247
Daston, L. Classical Probability in the En-
lightenment.
L.J. Cohen, 617(TLS):2-8Jun89-616
d'Aubigné, A. Sa vie à ses enfants.* (G.
Schrenck, ed)
O. Millet, 535(RHL):Sep-Oct88-1023
Daudet, A. Oeuvres. (Vol 1) (R. Ripoll, ed)
F. Garavini, 535(RHL):Jul-Aug88-786
Dauenhauer, B.P. The Politics of Hope.*
D. Pellauer, 543:Dec88-381
Dauenhauer, N.M. & R., eds. Haa Shuká.
J. Miller, 650(WF):Apr88-154
S. Scollon, 649(WAL):Nov88-271
Dauenhauer, R. Frames of Reference.
S. Preston, 649(WAL):Nov88-258
d'Aurevilly, J.B. - see under Barbey d'Aure-
villy, J.
Daurio, B. If Summer Had a Knife.
S. Scobie, 376:Sep88-162
Dauses, A. Grundbegriffe der Grammatik.
K-H. Körner, 72:Band225Heft1-146
Dauster, F. The Double Strand.
R. Bravo, 238:Dec88-842
A.P. Debicki, 240(HR):Autumn88-529
Dauxois, J. Charlotte Corday.
M. & P. Higonnet, 617(TLS):19-25May89-
541
Davenport, G. The Jules Verne Steam Bal-
loon.
S. Moore, 532(RCF):Fall88-158
Davenport-Hines, R.P.T., ed. Markets and
Bagmen.
A.J. Marrison, 637(VS):Winter89-267

Daviau, D.G., ed. Major Figures of Contemporary Austrian Literature.
   M, McInnes, 133:Band21Heft2/3-260
David, A., ed. The Charts and Coastal Views of Captain Cook's Voyages: The Voyage of the "Endeavour" 1768-1771.
   B.A.L. Cranstone, 617(TLS):7-13Apr89-375
David, D. Intellectual Women and Victorian Patriarchy.*
   B.C. Gelpi, 445(NCF):Dec88-396
   J.B. Taylor, 637(VS):Winter89-272
David, H. The Fitzrovians (1900-1955).*
   G. Ewart, 364:Oct/Nov88-138
David, M. & L. Stubenberg, eds. Philosophische Aufsätze zu Ehren von Roderick M. Chisholm.
   P. Trotignon, 542:Jul-Sep88-359
David-Ménard, M. L'hystérique entre Freud et Lacan.
   G. Vachon, 154:Autumn88-556
David-Ménard, M. & others. Les identifications.
   A. Reix, 542:Jan-Mar88-75
Davidoff, L. & C. Hall. Family Fortunes.
   E. Jordan, 366:Autumn88-218
   E. Yeo, 637(VS):Winter89-254
Davidow, W.H. & B. Uttal. Total Customer Service.
   D. Graulich, 441:29Oct89-40
Davidsen, L. The Sardine Deception.
   P. Vinten-Johansen, 563(SS):Summer88-426
Davidson, A. Seafood.
   R. Flaste, 441:3Dec89-40
Davidson, C., ed. The Saint Play in Medieval Europe.*
   H. Phillips, 382(MAE):1988/1-87
Davidson, C., C.J. Gianakaris & J.H. Stroupe, eds. Drama in the Renaissance.
   L. Manley, 677(YES):Vol19-318
Davidson, C.N. Revolution and the Word.*
   L. Buell, 27(AL):May88-286
   E. Carton, 533:Winter89-99
   J. Franchot, 534(RALS):Vol16No1&2-9
   C.S. Jordan, 165(EAL):Vol24No1-73
   B. Rosenthal, 594:Winter88-426
Davidson, D. Wahrheit und Interpretation.
   S. Majetschak, 489(PJGG):Band95Heft2-434
Davidson, H.M. Blaise Pascal.
   L.A. MacKenzie, Jr., 546(RR):May88-520
Davidson, R. Ancestors.
   R. Brain, 617(TLS):25-31Aug89-918
   R. Hansen, 441:12Nov89-15
Davie, D. Czeslaw Milosz and the Insufficiency of Lyric.*
   A. Czerniawski, 447(N&Q):Mar88-140
   R. Gorczynski, 497(PolR):Vol33No2-207
Davie, D. To Scorch or Freeze.
   M. Walters, 617(TLS):7-13Apr89-365
Davie, D. Under Briggflatts.
   T. Eagleton, 617(TLS):24-30Nov89-1291
Davie, E. Coming to Light.
   S. Mackay, 617(TLS):18-24Aug89-902
Davie, G.E. The Crisis of the Democratic Intellect.*
   R.L.H., 185:Oct88-199
Davie, M. & S., eds. The Faber Book of Cricket.
   D. Durrant, 364:Dec87/Jan88-143
Davies, A. Getting Hurt.
   G. Craig, 617(TLS):16-22Jun89-669

Davies, A. Literary London.
   D. Piper, 617(TLS):21-27Apr89-426
Davies, A. Other Theatres.
   C. Barker, 610:Autumn88-299
   R. Cornish, 615(TJ):Dec88-576
   M. Etherton, 366:Autumn88-268
Davies, A.M. & Y. Duhoux - see under Morpurgo Davies, A. & Y. Duhoux
Davies, C.B. & A.A. Graves, eds. Ngambika.
   R. Cobham, 538(RAL):Summer88-232
Davies, G.I. Megiddo.
   A.M. Berlin, 124:Jul-Aug89-467
Davies, H. Like Angels from a Cloud.*
   G.R. Evans, 541(RES):Feb88-160
   P.G. Stanwood, 301(JEGP):Apr88-254
Davies, H. Sartre and "Les Temps Modernes."*
   C. Howells, 323:May88-212
   M. Kelly, 402(MLR):Apr89-483
Davies, H.S. Wordsworth and the Worth of Words. (J. Kerrigan & J. Wordsworth, eds)
   M. Baron, 175:Spring88-54
   P.F. Morgan, 179(ES):Oct88-455
   G. Jackson, 661(WC):Autumn88-168
   N. Roe, 541(RES):May88-305
Davies, M. & J. Kathirithamby. Greek Insects.
   M.A.T. Natunewicz, 124:May-Jun89-403
Davies, P. The Cosmic Blueprint.
   J.D. Barrow, 617(TLS):29Sep-5Oct89-1072
Davies, P. Dollarville.
   B. Levine, 441:19Nov89-24
Davies, R., ed. Leonid Andreyev.
   M.J. Rosen, 441:25Jun89-24
Davies, R. The Lyre of Orpheus.*
   D. Lodge, 453(NYRB):13Apr89-35
   J. Mellors, 364:Oct/Nov88-115
   P. Rose, 441:8Jan89-7
   442(NY):20Mar89-115
Davies, R.W. Soviet History in the Gorbachev Revolution.
   A. Nove, 617(TLS):17-23Nov89-1258
Davies, S. The Feminine Reclaimed.*
   J.A. Roberts, 570(SQ):Autumn88-370
   J. Di Salvo, 301(JEGP):Jan88-109
Davies, S. The Idea of Woman in Renaissance Literature.
   W. Schleiner, 111:Fall89-12
Davies, W. Small Worlds.
   J.L. Nelson, 617(TLS):28Apr-4May89-468
Davies, W.V. Egyptian Hieroglyphs.
   R.S. Bianchi, 124:Jul-Aug89-461
Davignon, R. Le mal chez Gabriel Marcel.
   C. Chalier, 192(EP):Apr-Jun88-265
   T. Langan, 627(UTQ):Fall87-219
Dávila Flores, O. - see under Monreal, D.
Davis, A.Y. Women, Culture & Politics.
   L. Wenzel, 441:26Mar89-17
Davis, B.H. Thomas Percy.
   R. Foster, 617(TLS):14-20Jul89-770
Davis, C. Michel Tournier.
   M. Sheringham, 617(TLS):11-17Aug89-879
Davis, C.T. & H.L. Gates, Jr., eds. The Slave's Narrative.
   W.E. Cain, 128(CE):Feb88-190
Davis, D. Devices and Desires.
   L. Mackinnon, 617(TLS):30Jun-6Jul89-715
Davis, G. & M. Murch. Grounds For Divorce.
   N. Wikeley, 617(TLS):24-30Mar89-318
Davis, H., ed. Ethics and Defence.
   C.W.M., 185:Jul89-979

Davis, J. Dangerous Amusement.
P. Breslin, 491:Oct88-30
Davis, J. - see Byron, H.J.
Davis, J.A. Conflict and Control.
P. Ginsborg, 617(TLS):17-23Nov89-1284
Davis, J.C. Fear, Myth and History.
R. Smolinski, 568(SCN):Fall88-46
Davis, J.E. The Spanish of Argentina and Uruguay.
D. Woll, 685(ZDL):1/1988-124
Davis, J.H. Mafia Kingfish.
R. Dugger, 441:29Jan89-11
Davis, K. Fugue and Fresco.
W. Harmon, 468:Fall&Winter88-261
Davis, K. Labrador.
M. Brandham, 617(TLS):12-18May89-518
Davis, L. The Philippines.
M. Leifer, 617(TLS):28Apr-4May89-465
Davis, L. The Silver Pigs.
P. Howell, 617(TLS):17-23Nov89-1271
Davis, L.E. & R.A. Huttenback, with S.G. Davis. Mammon and the Pursuit of Empire.
N. Etherington, 637(VS):Summer89-573
Davis, L.H. Onward and Upward.
E. Prioleau, 27(AL):May88-315
Davis, L.J. Resisting Novels.*
T. Docherty, 541(RES):Nov88-602
Davis, M., with Q. Troupe. Miles.
G. Giddins, 441:15Oct89-7
Davis, N.Z. Fiction in the Archives.
R.M. Adams, 453(NYRB):16Mar89-35
E. Benson, 207(FR):Feb89-573
J. Bossy, 617(TLS):7-13Apr89-359
639(VQR):Summer88-79
Davis, P. Deadfall.
K. Reed, 441:22Oct89-22
Davis, P. English Structure in Focus. (Bk 1) (rev)
N.R. Wason, 399(MLJ):Spring88-82
Davis, P. English Structure in Focus. (Bk 2) (2nd ed)
H. Kim, 608:Dec89-691
Davis, P.J. & R. Hersh. Descartes' Dream.
J.D. Barrow, 617(TLS):29Sep-5Oct89-1072
Davis, R. Muang Metaphysics.
M.R. Rhum, 293(JAst):Feb88-191
Davis, R.C., ed. Contemporary Literary Criticism.*
J.R. Bennett, 128(CE):Sep88-566
J-M. Rabaté, 189(EA):Oct-Dec88-492
Davis, R.C. & R. Schleifer, eds. Rhetoric and Form.
C. Reeves, 494:Vol9No4-843
Davis, R.L. Court and Family in Sung China, 960-1279.*
P. Ebrey, 244(HJAS):Dec88-493
Davis, R.M. - see Waugh, E.
Davis, R.M. - see Wister, O.
Davis, S. Bob Marley.
D.E.M., 91:Fall88-252
Davis, S. A Miner's Christmas Carol.
C.S. McClure, 649(WAL):Aug88-189
Davis, S., Jr., J. Boyar & B. Boyar. Why Me?
M. Jefferson, 441:7May89-13
Davis, S.D. & P.D. Beidler, eds. The Mythologizing of Mark Twain.
E.L. Galligan, 569(SR):Spring88-265
Davis, W.R. Thomas Campion.
E.S. Ryding, 551(RenQ):Autumn88-517
R.H. Wells, 410(M&L):Oct88-509

Davis-Goff, A. Walled Gardens.
M. Pakenham, 441:24Sep89-20
442(NY):30Oct89-118
Davison, A. & G.M. Green, eds. Linguistic Complexity and Text Comprehension.
C.A. Perfetti, 350:Sep89-643
Davoli, S., ed. Civiltà teatrale e Settecento emiliano.
E. Cross, 410(M&L):Jan88-76
d'Avray, D. The Preaching of the Friars.
A.J. Fletcher, 382(MAE):1988/1-134
Dawani, T. Jemen.
F. Halliday, 617(TLS):20-26Jan89-54
Dawe, R.D. - see Sophocles
Dawidowicz, L.S. From That Place and Time.
I. Deak, 453(NYRB):28Sep89-63
T. Venclova, 441:23Jul89-31
Dawkins, R. The Blind Watchmaker.*
M. Levin, 31(ASch):Winter88-137
K. Sterelny, 63:Sep88-421
Dawley, A. & P. Buhle, eds. Working for Democracy.
E.G. Nellis, 106:Summer88-195
Dawson, C. Christianity and the New Age.
R. Hittinger, 396(ModA):Fall89-372
Dawson, C. Prophets of Past Time.
J.H. Buckley, 637(VS):Summer89-584
G.B. Tennyson, 445(NCF):Mar89-551
Dawson, J. Judasland.
T. Glyde, 617(TLS):2-8Jun89-620
Day, A. Jokerman.
N. Corcoran, 617(TLS):7-13Apr89-376
Day, G. From Fiction to the Novel.*
M.E. Novak, 536(Rev):Vol10-59
Day, H.T. & H. Sturges, with others, eds. Art of the Fantastic.
E.J. Sullivan, 127:Winter88-376
Day, J.P. Liberty and Justice.
B. Hooker, 518:Oct88-244
W. Wasserman, 103:Nov88-441
Day, J.T. Stendhal's Paper Mirror.*
J. Rosenthal, 207(FR):Feb89-524
Day, R. Larkin.
J. Banerjee, 179(ES):Jun88-280
Day, R.B., R. Beiner & J. Masciulli, eds. Democratic Theory and Technological Society.
R.H.B., 185:Jul89-972
Day, W.G., ed. The Pepys Ballads.*
D. McKitterick, 78(BC):Winter88-461
Day, W.P. In the Circles of Fear and Desire.*
D. Gates, 627(UTQ):Winter87/88-346
Dāya - see under Rāzī, N.A.
Dayan, J. Fables of Mind.*
S. Hutchinson, 447(N&Q):Dec88-552
J.G. Kennedy, 495(PoeS):Jun88-21
K. Ljungquist, 27(AL):May88-295
Dayan, P. Mallarmé's "Divine Transposition."*
F.S. Heck, 207(FR):Feb89-528
Daydí-Tolson, S. Voces y ecos en la poesía de José Angel Valente.
A. Hoyle, 86(BHS):Oct88-417
Dayley, J.P. Tzutujil Grammar.
J. Brody, 269(IJAL):Oct88-473
Deacon, R. The Greatest Treason.
N. Clive, 617(TLS):24-30Nov89-1298
Deahl, J. - see Acorn, M.
Deák, G.G. Picturing America, 1497-1899.
H. Brogan, 441:19Mar89-10
De Albuquerque, L. & I. Guerreiro, eds. II Seminário internacional de história Indoportuguesa.
G. Parker, 318(JAOS):Jul-Sep87-524

Dean, C. Arthur of England.
J.P. Carley, 178:Sep88-347
P. Rogers, 529(QQ):Winter88-920
Dean, M. In Search of the Perfect Lawn.
J.R. Wytenbroek, 102(CanL):Spring88-140
Dean, T. Land and Power in Late Medieval Ferrara.*
W. Gundersheimer, 551(RenQ):Winter88-708
Dean, W. & J.M. Knapp. Handel's Operas: 1704-1726.*
R. Strohm, 410(M&L):Oct88-516
Deane, S. Celtic Revivals.
G. Verstraete, 272(IUR):Spring88-157
Deane, S. A Short History of Irish Literature.*
R.A. Cave, 541(RES):May88-321
J.J.M., 295(JML):Fall87/Winter88-205
B. Tippett, 366:Autumn88-262
Dear, W.C. & C. Stowers. "Please...Don't Kill Me."
O. Levy, 441:15Oct89-51
Dearborn, M.V. Love in the Promised Land.
B.P. Taylor, 432(NEQ):Dec88-638
Dearden, S. A Nest of Corsairs.
S. Soucek, 318(JAOS):Jul-Sep87-532
Dearstyne, H. Inside the Bauhaus.* (D. Spaeth, ed)
J.R. Mellow, 139:Feb/Mar88-14
Deathridge, J., M. Geck & E. Voss. Wagner Werk-Verzeichnis.
B. Millington, 410(M&L):Jul88-396
Deaver, M.K., with M. Herskowitz. Behind the Scenes.
J. Didion, 453(NYRB):21Dec89-3
Deaver, P.F. Silent Retreats.*
639(VQR):Autumn88-127
Debenedetti, S. Studi filologici.
L. De Vendittis, 228(GSLI):Vol165 fasc531-469
A. Scolari, 379(MedR):Apr88-147
Debray-Genette, R. & J. Neefs, eds. Romans d'Archives.
M. Lukacher, 446(NCFS):Spring-Summer-89-397
Debreuille, J-Y. L'École de Rochefort.
I. Higgins, 208(FS):Jul88-367
De Brosse, J. The Serpentine Wall.
M. Stasio, 441:22Jan89-30
Debus, F. & E. Dittmer, eds. Sandbjerg 85.
G. Kolde, 685(ZDL):1/1988-73
Debussy, C. Letters.* (F. Lesure & R. Nichols, eds)
R. Orledge, 410(M&L):Apr88-285
Debussy, C. Piano Trio in G Major. (E. Derr, ed)
L. Berman, 451:Spring88-291
Debyser, F. L'Immeuble.*
M-C.W. Koop, 207(FR):Oct88-210
Decaudin, M. & D. Leuwers, eds. Littérature française: de Zola à Guillaume Apollinaire, 1869-1920.
M.A. Caws, 207(FR):Apr89-884
Decroux, E. Words on Mime.
A. Lust, 615(TJ):Dec87-534
Décsy, G. A Select Catalogue of Language Universals.
J. Aitchison, 215(GL):Vol28No3-227
S. De Lancey, 350:Jun89-423
Dédéyan, C. Montesquieu ou l'alibi persan.
M-H. Chabut, 166:Jul89-340

Dee, P.S. Financial Markets and Economic Development.
K. Moskowitz, 293(JASt):Nov88-902
Deely, J. Introducing Semiotic.
R.S. Corrington, 438:Winter88-118
Deely, J.N., with R.A. Powell – see Poinsot, J.
Dees, A., ed. Actes du IVe colloque international sur le moyen français.
M. Offord, 208(FS):Apr88-245
Dees, A. Atlas des formes linguistiques des textes littéraires de l'ancien français.
H. Geisler, 547(RF):Band100Heft4-366
L. Wolf, 685(ZDL):3/1988-349
Defaux, G. Marot, Rabelais, Montaigne.
D.G. Coleman, 402(MLR):Apr89-470
F. Gray, 210(FrF):Sep88-369
I.S. Majer, 400(MLN):Sep88-954
De Felice, E. I nomi degli italiani.
G. Holtus, 72:Band224Heft2-470
Deford, F. Casey on the Loose.
M-A.T. Smith, 441:18Jun89-20
Deforge, B. Eschyle, poète cosmique.
M. Comber, 123:Vol38No2-395
De Francis, J. Visible Speech.
J.T. Hooker, 617(TLS):17-23Nov89-1264
De Graff, A. The Tower and the Well.
R.C. Capasso, 403(MLS):Winter88-205
De Grand, A. The Italian Left in the Twentieth Century.
M. Clark, 617(TLS):28Jul-3Aug89-821
Deguy, M. La poésie n'est pas seule.
D.P. Kinloch, 208(FS):Oct88-493
Dehejia, V. – see Lear, E.
Deibe, C.F. – see under Feal Deibe, C.
Deighton, L. Spy Hook.*
T.J. Binyon, 617(TLS):20-26Jan89-70
Deighton, L. Spy Line.
N. Callendar, 441:17Dec89-17
Dekker, G. The American Historical Romance.*
C. Mulvey, 366:Autumn88-263
G. Scharnhorst, 395(MFS):Winter88-611
J. Woodress, 27(AL):Oct88-466
Dekker, R.M. & L.C. van de Pol. The Tradition of Female Transvestism in Early Modern Europe.
E.S. Turner, 617(TLS):17-23Mar89-281
De Kok, D. Unseen Danger.
S.P. Schneider, 106:Fall88-373
De Koninck, R. & J. Nadeau, eds. Ressources, problèmes et défis de l'Asie du Sud-Est.
J. Bowen, 293(JASt):May88-434
Dekovic, G. Looking at a Spanish Village. Looking at Spanish Food. Looking at Spanish Signs.
R.W. Fairchild, 399(MLJ):Spring88-110
Delacorta. Alba.
442(NY):18Sep89-139
Delage, M-J. – see "Césaire d'Arles, Sermons au peuple"
De-la-Noy, M. – see Welch, D.
Delany, P. The Neo-Pagans.*
M.L. Ross, 627(UTQ):Spring88-442
P. Stansky, 177(ELT):Vol31No4-467
42(AR):Winter88-125
639(VQR):Winter88-16
Delatour, Y. & others. 350 Exercices de grammaire.
R. Reynolds-Cornell, 207(FR):Apr89-916
Delbanco, A. The Puritan Ordeal.
G.S. Wood, 453(NYRB):9Nov89-26
442(NY):10Apr89-124

De Mille, J. A Strange Manuscript Found in a Copper Cylinder. (M. Parks, ed)
    R.G. Moyles, 470:Vol26-167
Demoriane, H. The Tightrope Walker.
    J. Rees, 617(TLS):17-23Nov89-1285
Demosthenes. Selected Private Speeches.* (C. Carey & R.A. Reid, eds)
    A.H.M. Kessels, 394:Vol41fasc3/4-414
De Mott, R. - see Steinbeck, J.
Dempsey, H.A. The Gentle Persuader.
    O.P. Dickason, 298:Fall88-170
Dempster, N. Heiress.
    M. Grover, 441:24Dec89-17
Demus, O. The Mosaic Decoration of San Marco, Venice. (H.L. Kessler, ed)
    C. Mango, 617(TLS):13-19Oct89-1117
Denby, E. Dance Writings. (R. Cornfield & W. Mackay, eds)
    O. Stuart, 151:Dec88-64
d'Encausse, H.C. - see under Carrère d'Encausse, H.
Dendle, B.J. Galdós: The Early Historical Novels.*
    S. Miller, 238:Sep88-548
    G.M. Scanlon, 402(MLR):Apr89-503
Dendy, W. & W. Kilbourn. Toronto Observed.
    D. Gebhard, 576:Mar88-94
    A. Payne, 627(UTQ):Fall88-204
Denecke, L., ed. Brüder Grimm Gedenken. (Vol 7)
    J. Rissmann, 196:Band29Heft1/2-180
Denham, R.D. Northrop Frye.
    M. Fee, 376:Sep88-166
    J.M. Mellard, 40(AEB):Vol2No3-113
Denina, C. Storia delle lingue e polemiche linguistiche (dai saggi berlinesi 1783-1804). (C. Marazzini, ed)
    P. Swiggers, 553(RLiR):Jul-Dec88-494
Denis, J. Treatise on Harpsichord Tuning by Jean Denis. (V.J. Panetta, Jr., ed)
    H. Schott, 410(M&L):Jul88-374
"Edison Denisov: A Complete Catalogue."
    A.F.L.T., 412:May88-158
Denkler, H. Neues über Wilhelm Raabe.
    W. Hanson, 402(MLR):Oct89-1034
Dennerline, J. Qian Mu and the World of Seven Mansions.
    D. Wilson, 617(TLS):23-29Jun89-681
Dennett, D.C. Elbow Room.* (German title: Ellenbogenfreiheit.)
    R. Hesse, 687:Oct-Dec88-716
    P. van Inwagen, 449:Dec88-609
Dennett, D.C. The Intentional Stance.*
    D. Jacquette, 393(Mind):Oct88-619
Denning, M. Cover Stories.
    J.R. Cohn, 594:Fall88-323
    D. Monaghan, 395(MFS):Summer88-293
Denning, M. Mechanic Accents.
    J.G. Cawelti, 27(AL):Oct88-485
Dennis, B. & D. Skilton, eds. Reform and Intellectual Debate in Victorian England.
    C. Jones, 506(PSt):May88-111
Dennis, C. The Outskirts of Troy.*
    D. Revell, 152(UDQ):Summer88-104
Dennis, G.T., ed & trans. Three Byzantine Military Treatises.
    W.E. Kaegi, 589:Jan88-145
Dennis, I. Bagdad.*
    L. Irvine, 102(CanL):Winter87-264
Dennis, N. José Bergamín.*
    D. Harris, 86(BHS):Oct88-415
    A. Hoyle, 402(MLR):Jul89-765
    [continued]

[continuing]
    G. Pérez Firmat, 345(KRQ):May88-248
    S.G. Polansky, 552(REH):Jan88-145
Dennis, N. & A.H. Halsey, eds. English Ethical Socialism.
    R. Pinker, 617(TLS):24-30Mar89-320
Denselow, R. When the Music's Over.
    T.W. Ryback, 617(TLS):21-27Jul89-794
Dent, N.J.H. The Moral Psychology of the Virtues.*
    E. Simpson, 449:Mar88-155
Dentinger, J. Death Mask.*
    T.J.B., 617(TLS):31Mar-6Apr89-343
Denvir, B., ed. The Impressionists at First Hand.
    90:Mar88-241
Deo, S.B. & K. Paddayya. Recent Advances in Indian Archaeology.
    H.S. Converse, 318(JAOS):Apr-Jun87-368
Déon, M. Where Are You Dying Tonight?
    G.S. Bourdain, 441:8Oct89-24
De Porte, A.W. France.
    T. Scanlan, 207(FR):May89-1110
Deprun, J., J. Ehrard & A. Lourenceau - see Diderot, D.
De Puma, R.D. Corpus Speculorum Etruscorum, USA 1.
    F.R. Serra Ridgway, 123:Vol38No2-354
De Puma, R.D. Etruscan Tomb-Groups.
    G. Davies, 123:Vol38No1-116
De Quille, D. Dan De Quille: Dives and Lazarus. (L.I. Berkove, ed)
    R. Dwyer, 649(WAL):Feb89-377
De Quille, D./W. Wright. Little Lucy's Papa.
    C.M. Wright, 649(WAL):May88-89
Derbyshire, D.C. & G.K. Pullum, eds. Handbook of Amazonian Languages.* (Vol 1)
    M.R. Key, 297(JL):Sep88-542
Deroeux, D., ed. Terres cuites architecturales au moyen âge.
    S. Bonde & C. Maines, 589:Jul88-634
Derouet, C. - see Léger, F.
Derounian, K.Z. - see Wister, S.
Derr, E. - see Debussy, C.
Derré, J-R. Littérature et Politique dans l'Europe du XIXe siècle.
    S. Jeune, 549(RLC):Jan-Mar88-99
Derrida, J. Glas.*
    C. Howells, 447(N&Q):Dec88-556
    H. Rapaport, 223:Spring88-108
    C. Sartiliot, 153:Winter88-68
    S. Scobie, 376:Mar88-101
Derrida, J. De l'esprit.* Psyché.*
    M-A. Lescourret, 98:Apr88-259
    A. Reix, 542:Jul-Sep88-360
Derrida, J. Parages.
    J-R. Mantion, 98:Mar88-224
Derrida, J. The Post Card.*
    I.E. Harvey, 103:May89-180
    S. Scobie, 376:Mar88-101
    F. Sparshott, 529(QQ):Winter88-939
Derrida, J. The Truth in Painting.*
    D. Carrier, 311(JP):Apr88-219
    R.A. Cavell, 627(UTQ):Summer89-521
    J.C. Gilmour, 290(JAAC):Summer88-519
    I.E. Harvey, 103:Dec88-475
    M. Podro, 59:Sep88-433
    S. Scobie, 376:Mar88-101
    F. Sparshott, 529(QQ):Winter88-939
Derron, P. - see Pseudo-Phocylides
Derry, A. Stages of Twilight.
    S. Corey, 219(GaR):Spring88-161

    [continued]

Dertouzos, M.L., R.K. Lester and R.M. Solow.
Made in America.
  A. Kessler-Harris, 441:23Jul89-13
Derval, B. & M.H. Lenoble, eds. La critique
littéraire et l'ordinateur/Literary Criticism
and the Computer.
  G. Pauls, 356(LR):Feb-May88-115
Desai, A. Baumgartner's Bombay.*
  R. Dinnage, 453(NYRB):1Jun89-34
  R. Fainlight, 364:Oct/Nov88-116
  P. West, 441:9Apr89-3
Desai, A.R., ed. Agrarian Struggles in India
After Independence.
  R.J. Herring, 293(JASt):Feb88-168
Desai, P. Perestroika in Perspective.
  O. Figes, 617(TLS):4-10Aug89-841
  P. Taubman, 441:13Aug89-25
Desai, P. The Soviet Economy.
  W. Brus, 575(SEER):Apr88-323
De Salvo, L. Virginia Woolf.
  L.E. Beattie, 441:23Jul89-19
  K. Fraser, 442(NY):6Nov89-154
  A. Motion, 617(TLS):10-16Nov89-1230
Desan, W. The Planetary Man. (Vol 3)
  L. Dupré, 543:Jun89-822
"Marceline Desbordes-Valmore et son temps."
  A. Michel, 535(RHL):Jul-Aug88-782
Descartes, R. Abrégé de musique. (F. de
Buzon, ed & trans)
  G. Durosoir, 537:Vol74No1-105
"René Descartes: Meditations on First Philos-
ophy with Selections from the Objections
and Replies." (J. Cottingham, trans)
  R. Burch, 568(SCN):Spring-Summer88-13
  S. Gaukroger, 63:Sep88-414
Descombes, V. Proust.*
  M. Jarrety, 450(NRF):Feb88-100
  C. Lang, 400(MLN):Sep88-902
Descotes, M. Victor Hugo et Waterloo.
  S. Gaudon, 535(RHL):Mar-Apr88-305
Descrains, J. Jean-Pierre Camus (1584-
1652) et ses "Diversités" (1609-1618) ou la
culture d'un évêque humaniste.*
  B. Chedozeau, 535(RHL):Mar-Apr88-260
Desgraves, L. Répertoire des programmes des
pièces de théâtre jouées dans les collèges
en France (1601-1700).*
  J. Hennequin, 535(RHL):Mar-Apr88-265
  C. Smith, 354:Sep88-267
Deshpande, M.M. Ellipsis and Syntactic
Overlapping.*
  R. Rocher, 318(JAOS):Oct-Dec87-780
De Silva, R.K. & W.G.M. Beumer. Illustrations
and Views of Dutch Ceylon, 1602-1796.
  J.M. Richards, 617(TLS):26May-1Jun89-
591
Desmond, J.F. Risen Sons.*
  R.H. Brinkmeyer, Jr., 573(SSF):Spring88-
169
  E. Brown-Guillory, 27(AL):Oct88-497
  W. Burke, 395(MFS):Summer88-247
Desmond, R. Wonders of Creation.
  90:Mar88-242
Desmond, W. Art and the Absolute.*
  C.L. Carter, 319:Jan89-163
  M.W. Roche, 221(GQ):Fall88-554
  G. Shapiro, 290(JAAC):Fall87-86
Desnoyers, F. Derrière le silence.
  J.P. Gilroy, 102(CanL):Winter87-260
Desportes, Y. Das System der räumlichen
Präpositionen im Deutschen.
  A. Greule, 685(ZDL):3/1988-388

Des Pres, T. Praises & Dispraises.*
  S.C., 219(GaR):Winter88-881
  A. Libby, 344:Spring89-140
Desréaux, C. Lettre impossible hélas à sig-
ner, destinée à un seul lecteur à qui elle
ne peut être envoyée.
  C. Bobin, 450(NRF):Jan88-109
Dessau, A. & others, comps. Politisch-
ideologische Strömungen in Lateinamerika.
  O.C. Stoetzer, 263(RIB):Vol38No3-399
Dessaulles, H. Hopes and Dreams.
  V. Raoul, 102(CanL):Spring88-173
Dessen, A.C. Shakespeare and the Late Moral
Plays.*
  D.S. Kastan, 128(CE):Oct88-694
  R.W.F. Martin, 541(RES):Feb88-104
De Swaan, A. In Care of the State.
  R. Klein, 617(TLS):3-9Mar89-215
Detienne, M. The Creation of Mythology.*
(French title: L'invention de la mytholo-
gie.)
  T. di Piero, 153:Summer86-21
  J. Romm, 124:Jul-Aug89-459
Detienne, M. L'Écriture d'Orphée. Dionysos
at Large.
  S. Goldhill, 617(TLS):30Jun-6Jul89-723
Detienne, M. Les Maîtres de vérité dans la
Grèce archaïque.
  R.P. Harrison, 153:Summer86-14
Detienne, M. & J-P. Vernant. Les Ruses de
l'intelligence.
  R. Klein, 153:Summer86-2
Detlefsen, M. Hilbert's Program.
  A.D. Irvine, 103:Apr89-145
Deuchar, S. Sporting Art in Eighteenth-Cen-
tury England.
  A. Bermingham, 617(TLS):4-10Aug89-840
  A. Stewart, 324:Apr89-318
Deussen, C. Erinnerung und Rechtfertigung.
  W. Paulsen, 221(GQ):Fall88-601
Deutsch, K.L. & W. Soffer, eds. The Crisis of
Liberal Democracy.
  F. Canavan, 258:Mar88-110
"Devant l'histoire."
  C. Bouchindhomme, 98:May88-384
Develin, R. Athenian Officials, 684-321 B.C.
  P. Millett, 617(TLS):29Dec89/4Jan90-
1449
Develin, R. The Practice of Politics at Rome
366-167 B.C.*
  M. Ducos, 555:Vol61fasc1-160
  H. Kloft, 229:Band60Heft5-422
Devitt, M. & K. Sterelny. Language and Real-
ity.
  S. Guttenplan, 479(PhQ):Jan88-127
  G. Hunter, 518:Apr88-88
  G. Stahl, 542:Jul-Sep88-377
Devlin, A.J., ed. Conversations with Ten-
nessee Williams.*
  R.C., 295(JML):Fall87/Winter88-399
  J.F. Desmond, 392:Fall88-553
  O.C. Walker, 615(TJ):Oct88-442
Devlin, A.J., ed. Welty.
  V.A. Kramer, 395(MFS):Winter88-631
Devlin, D.D. The Novels and Journals of
Fanny Burney.*
  R.L. Brett, 541(RES):May88-338
Devlin, H. Portraits of American Architec-
ture.
  P. Goldberger, 441:3Dec89-21
Devlin, K. Mathematics.*
  M. Gardner, 453(NYRB):16Mar89-26

De Vos, G.A. & T. Sofue, eds. Religion and the Family in East Asia.
  D.L. Overmyer, 293(JASt):Feb88-95
De Vos, J. Lebendig begraben.
  W. Paulsen, 221(GQ):Spring87-295
Dewar, J., comp. True Canadian War Stories.
  E. Thompson, 102(CanL):Spring88-127
Dewdney, C. The Immaculate Perception.
  J. Thurston, 529(QQ):Spring88-188
Dewey, F.L. Thomas Jefferson, Lawyer.
  A. Hast, 656(WMQ):Jan88-200
Dewey, J. John Dewey, The Later Works, 1925-1953. (Vol 4) (J.A. Boydston, ed)
  G.S. Pappas, 619:Winter88-147
Dewey, J. John Dewey: The Later Works, 1925-1953. (Vol 12) (J.A. Boydston, ed)
  H.S. Thayer, 619:Fall88-521
Dewhurst, C.K. Grand Ledge Folk Pottery.
  J.A. Chinn, 650(WF):Jul88-230
Dews, P. Logics of Disintegration.*
  M. Sprinker, 400(MLN):Dec88-1151
Dexter, P. Paris Trout.*
  R. Towers, 453(NYRB):16Feb89-18
Deyermond, A. El "Cantar de Mio Cid" y la épica medieval española.
  M. de la Concepción Piñero Valverde, 547(RF):Band100Heft4-467
Dharmasiri, G. Fundamentals of Buddhist Ethics.
  B. Gujer, 485(PE&W):Oct88-439
d'Holbach, P.H.D. Die gesamte erhaltene Korrespondenz. (H. Sauter & E. Loos, eds)
  S. Mason, 208(FS):Apr88-209
D'Hondt, J. Hegel in His Time.
  T. Pinkard, 103:Apr89-148
Diakonoff, I.M. Afrasian Languages.
  J.A.C. Greppin, 617(TLS):17-23Nov89-1264
Diamond, M.C. Enriching Heredity.
  S. Rose, 617(TLS):7-13Jul89-748
Díaz Migoyo, G. Guía de "Tirano Banderas."*
  F. López-Criado, 552(REH):Jan88-143
Dibba, E. Fafa.
  R. Brain, 617(TLS):15-21Sep89-1006
Di Benedetto, A. Vittorio Alfieri.*
  J. Lindon, 402(MLR):Jul89-752
Dichy, A. & P. Fouché. Jean Genet.
  P. Thody, 617(TLS):21-27Apr89-419
Di Cicco, P.G. Post-Sixties Nocturne.
  E. Tihanyi, 102(CanL):Winter87-200
Di Cicco, P.G. Virgin Science.
  E. Folsom, 529(QQ):Autumn88-726
  D. Manganiello, 102(CanL):Spring88-220
Dick, B.F. William Golding.
  S. Vice, 447(N&Q):Jun88-264
Dick, P.K. The Broken Bubble.*
  J. Clute, 617(TLS):8-14Dec89-1368
Dick, S. & others, eds. Omnium Gatherum.
  P. Craig, 617(TLS):27Oct-2Nov89-1192
Dickel, G. & H. Speer, comps. Deutsches Rechtswörterbuch. (Vol 7)
  H.H. Munske, 684(ZDA):Band117Heft1-5
Dickens, C. The Annotated Dickens. (E. Guiliano & P. Collins, eds)
  M. McGowan, 155:Spring88-52
Dickens, C. Esquisses de Boz; Martin Chuzzlewit.* (S. Monod, with H. Bordenave & F. du Sorbier, eds)
  M. Cardwell, 677(YES):Vol19-338
Dickens, C. George Silverman's Explanation. (H. Stone, ed)
  R. Glancy, 158:Jun88-95

Dickens, C. The Letters of Charles Dickens.* (Vol 6) (G. Storey, K. Tillotson & N. Burgis, eds)
  M. Reynolds, 155:Autumn88-180
Dickens, C. Master Humphrey's Clock.
  A. Easson, 158:Mar88-39
Dickens, C. The Pickwick Papers.* (J. Kinsley, ed)
  P. Preston, 447(N&Q):Sep88-389
  M. Reynolds, 155:Summer88-114
  J. Sutherland, 541(RES):May88-311
  K. Tetzeli von Rosador, 72:Band225 Heft2-403
  W.P. Williams, 40(AEB):Vol2No4-182
Dickens, C. The Speeches of Charles Dickens. (K.J. Fielding, ed)
  G. Storey, 617(TLS):17-23Feb89-173
"Dickens' London."
  A. Sanders, 155:Summer88-110
  G.J. Worth, 637(VS):Winter89-255
"Dickens Studies Annual." (Vol 14) (M. Timko, F. Kaplan & E. Guiliano, eds)
  W.J. Palmer, 158:Dec88-198
  K. Sutherland, 541(RES):Aug88-455
"Dickens Studies Annual."* (Vol 15) (M. Timko, F. Kaplan & E. Guiliano, eds)
  M.T. Chialant, 677(YES):Vol19-340
Dickenson, D. George Sand.*
  R. Lloyd, 364:Jun88-111
Dickey, J. & W.A. Bake. Wayfarer.
  P-L. Adams, 61:Jan89-120
Dickie, M. On the Modernist Long Poem.*
  R. Franciosi, 481(PQ):Winter88-126
  S. Fredman, 27(AL):Oct88-506
Dickinson, C. The Widows' Adventures.
  H. Wolitzer, 441:24Sep89-14
Dickinson, D. Fighting the Upstream.
  C. Bond, 526:Autumn88-100
Dickinson, H.T. Caricatures and the Constitution 1760-1832.
  J.E. Hill, 173(ECS):Summer88-530
Dickinson, J. & B. Russell. Family, Economy and State.
  L.D. Harman, 298:Fall88-160
Dickinson, P. The Music of Lennox Berkeley.
  R. Crichton, 617(TLS):22-28Dec89-1409
Dickinson, P. Skeleton-in-Waiting.
  C. Lansbury, 441:31Dec89-5
Dickson, P.G.M. Finance and Government under Maria Theresia, 1740-1780.
  F.A.J. Szabo, 150(DR):Fall88-336
Dickson, W.J. - see Scarron, P.
"Dictionary of American Regional English."* (Vol 1) (F.G. Cassidy, chief ed)
  W.N. Francis, 355(LSoc):Jun88-287
"Dictionary of Canadian Biography." (Vol 6) (F.G. Halpenny, general ed)
  R. Cook, 470:Vol26-159
  M. Prang, 529(QQ):Winter88-912
"Dictionary of Literary Biography." (Vol 55) (W.B. Thesing, ed)
  G.H. Brookes, 635(VPR):Winter88-163
  W.A. Madden, 637(VS):Autumn88-147
"Dictionary of Literary Biography." (Vol 57) (W.B. Thesing, ed)
  W.A. Madden, 637(VS):Autumn88-147
"Dictionary of Literary Biography." (Vol 58) (F. Bowers, ed)
  R. Vince, 610:Autumn88-276
"Dictionary of Old English: Preface and List of Texts and Index of Editions." (A. Cameron & others, eds)
  H. Sauer, 72:Band225Heft2-370

Dilman, I. Mind, Brain, and Behaviour.
  D.J. Howard, 103:Jul89-259
Dilworth, S. The Long White.
  C. Goodrich, 441:5Feb89-24
Dilworth, T. The Shape of Meaning in the
  Poetry of David Jones.
  W. Cookson, 4:Winter88-81
  W.J. Keith, 627(UTQ):Summer89-532
Di Maggio, P.J., ed. Nonprofit Enterprise in
  the Arts.
  A.S. Keller, 476:Fall88-78
Dimand, R.W. The Origins of the Keynesian
  Revolution.
  P. Clarke, 617(TLS):13-19Jan89-32
Dimer, E. Ogljadyeajas' nazad.
  V. Terras, 574(SEEJ):Winter88-658
Dimock, G.E. The Unity of "The Odyssey."
  G. Steiner, 617(TLS):8-14Sep89-984
Dimond, F. & R. Taylor. Crown & Camera.
  R. Tobias, 637(VS):Winter89-292
Dinesen, R. & others, eds. Deutschsprachiges
  Exil in Dänemark nach 1933.
  R. Kieser, 406:Winter88-527
Ding Ling. I Myself Am a Woman. (T.E. Bar-
  low, with G.J. Bjorge, eds)
  S. Brownmiller, 441:3Sep89-7
  J. Mirsky, 453(NYRB):26Oct89-27
Dingbo, W. & P.D. Murphy, eds. Science Fic-
  tion From China.
  G. Jonas, 441:31Dec89-4
Dinnage, R. Annie Besant.
  S. Mitchell, 637(VS):Autumn88-138
Dinnage, R. One to One.
  P. Fuller, 617(TLS):27Jan-2Feb89-78
Dinnerstein, L. Uneasy at Home.
  L. Grossman, 390:Apr88-51
Dinzelbacher, P. & H-D. Mück, eds. Volkskul-
  tur des europäischen Spätmittelalters.
  A. Hartmann, 196:Band29Heft1/2-182
Di Pietro, R.J., ed. Linguistics and the Pro-
  fessions.
  E.W. McMullen, 660(Word):Aug88-129
Di Pietro, R.J. Strategic Interaction.*
  C.K. Knop, 207(FR):Dec88-374
  A.G. Lo Ré, 238:Sep88-563
Di Pino, G. Pause e intercanti nella "Divina
  Commedia" e altri studi.
  Z.G. Barański, 545(RPh):Aug88-51
D'Ippolito, F. Giuristi e Sapienti in Roma
  Arcaica.
  B.W. Frier, 229:Band60Heft3-268
Dirlik, A. The Origins of Chinese Communism.
  M.B. Yahuda, 617(TLS):11-17Aug89-869
Dirscherl, K. Der Roman der Philosophen.*
  H. Coulet, 535(RHL):Mar-Apr88-280
Dirven, R. & V. Fried, eds. Functionalism in
  Linguistics.
  A. Liberman, 215(GL):Vol28No4-302
  D.C. Walker, 350:Sep89-658
Di Scala, S.M. Renewing Italian Socialism.
  M. Clark, 617(TLS):28Jul-3Aug89-821
Disch, T. Yes, Let's.
  L. Norfolk, 617(TLS):15-21Sep89-1000
Disraeli, B. Benjamin Disraeli: Letters. (Vol
  3) (M.G. Wiebe & others, eds)
  A. Robson, 529(QQ):Winter88-914
  D. Sultana, 447(N&Q):Sep88-385
Disraeli, B. Benjamin Disraeli: Letters. (Vol
  4) (M.G. Wiebe, J.B. Conacher & J. Mat-
  thews, eds)
  N. Gash, 617(TLS):22-28Sep89-1025
Disselbeck, K. Geschmack und Kunst.
  L. Sharpe, 402(MLR):Oct89-1030

Dittmar, N., P. Schlobinski & I. Wachs. Ber-
  linisch.
  D. Stellmacher, 685(ZDL):3/1987-373
Dittmer, L. China's Continuous Revolution.
  R. Kraus, 293(JASt):May88-341
Ditz, T.L. Property and Kinship.
  M.A. Bellesiles, 106:Summer88-233
  C.H. Dayton, 656(WMQ):Jan88-189
"Le Dix-huitième siècle." (Vol 19)
  C. Jones, 402(MLR):Oct89-978
Dixit, K.K. Ślokavārtika.
  J.A. Taber, 318(JAOS):Jan-Mar87-203
Dixon, G. The Gilbert and Sullivan Concor-
  dance.*
  A. Lamb, 410(M&L):Oct88-541
Dixon, M. Ride Out the Wilderness.*
  C.A. Wall, 27(AL):Dec88-680
Dixon, M. Trouble the Water.
  C.D. Kennedy, 441:24Sep89-48
Dixon, P. – see Farquhar, G.
Dixon, P.B. Reversible Readings.*
  J. Gledson, 86(BHS):Jan88-108
Dixon, S. Garbage.
  639(VQR):Autumn88-129
Dixon, S. Love and Will.
  J.R. Kornblatt, 441:17Dec89-23
Dixon, S. The Play and Other Stories.
  J. Levin, 441:4Jun89-19
Dixsaut, M. Le naturel philosophe.
  A. Preus, 41:Vol7-227
D'jačkov, M.V. Kreol'skie Jazyki.
  M. Perl, 682(ZPSK):Band41Heft3-395
Djelantik, A.A.M. Balinese Paintings.
  A.P. McCauley, 293(JASt):Nov88-934
Djelassi, M.S. – see Rosidor
Djerassi, C. Cantor's Dilemma.
  L. Shainberg, 441:5Nov89-14
Djerassi, C. The Futurist and Other Stories.
  C. Greenland, 617(TLS):21-27Apr89-436
Djian, P. Betty Blue.*
  42(AR):Fall88-531
Djwa, S. The Politics of the Imagination.*
  M. Fee, 376:Mar88-106
  P. Morley, 298:Winter88/89-159
  P. Stevens, 627(UTQ):Fall88-168
Dmitrenko, A. & others, eds. Fifty Russian
  Artists.
  C. Lodder, 575(SEER):Jul88-469
Doane, J. & D. Hodges. Nostalgia and Sexual
  Difference.*
  E. Jordan, 366:Autumn88-222
  J.D. Kalb, 115:Summer88-333
  P.D. Murphy, 590:Dec88-163
  S. Shuttleworth, 141:Winter88-115
Doane, M. The Surprise of Burning.*
  B. Morton, 617(TLS):13-19Jan89-42
Doane, M.A. The Desire to Desire.
  S. Snyder, 106:Spring88-89
Dobbin, C. Islamic Revivalism in a Changing
  Peasant Economy.
  J.R. Bowen, 293(JASt):Aug88-697
Döblin, A. A People Betrayed. Karl and Rosa.
  M. Hulse, 364:Feb87-99
Dobozy, M. Full Circle.*
  E.R. Haymes, 406:Summer88-219
Dobrez, L.A.C. The Existential and Its Exits.
  D.B., 295(JML):Fall87/Winter88-207
Dobson, A. An Introduction to the Politics
  and Philosophy of José Ortega y Gasset.
  R. Carr, 617(TLS):13-19Oct89-1113
Dobson, J. – see Southworth, E.D.E.N.
Dobson, R., G. Brangham & R.A. Gilbert – see
  Machen, A.

Dobyns, S. A Boat off the Coast.*
  639(VQR):Spring88-58
Dobyns, S. Cemetery Nights.*
  T. Lux, 651(WHR):Summer88-174
Dobyns, S. Saratoga Bestiary.
  E. Weiner, 441:16Apr89-20
  442(NY):10Apr89-124
Docherty, T. John Donne, Undone.*
  M. Elsky, 551(RenQ):Autumn88-520
  N.H. Keeble, 447(N&Q):Dec88-529
  N. Rhodes, 541(RES):Aug88-439
Docherty, T. On Modern Authority.
  T. Pinkney, 366:Spring88-110
Dock, A. Flurnamen der Börde Lamstedt. (D.
  Stellmacher, ed)
  E. Neuss, 685(ZDL):3/1987-418
Dockstader, F. The Song of the Loom.
  N. Luomala, 662:Spring/Summer88-42
Doctorow, E.L. Billy Bathgate.
  T. Rafferty, 442(NY):27Mar89-112
  A. Tyler, 441:26Feb89-1
  G. Wills, 453(NYRB):2Mar89-3
  M. Wood, 617(TLS):15-21Sep89-997
Dod, E. Die Vernünftigkeit der Imagination in
  Aufklärung und Romantik.
  J. Barnouw, 301(JEGP):Apr88-303
  B. Bjorklund, 406:Summer88-225
  J. Simons, 133:Band21Heft2/3-212
Dodd, P., ed. Modern Selves.*
  I.B.N., 295(JML):Fall87/Winter88-242
Dode, R-E. Ästhetik als Vernunftkritik.
  J-E. Pleines, 342:Band79Heft1-114
von Doderer, H. Commentarii 1957 bis 1966.
  (Vol 2) (W. Schmidt-Dengler, ed)
  A.C. Ulmer, 400(MLN):Apr88-701
Dodsley, R. The Correspondence of Robert
  Dodsley 1733-1764. (J.E. Tierney, ed)
  J.L. Abbott, 324:Oct89-748
  P. Rogers, 617(TLS):14-20Jul89-770
Dodwell, B., ed. The Charters of Norwich
  Cathedral Priory. (Vol 2)
  D.R. Carr, 589:Jan88-146
Doe, J. Speak into the Mirror.
  Z. Salzmann, 350:Sep89-659
D'Oench, E.G. & J.E. Feinberg. Jim Dine
  Prints, 1977-1985.
  P.B. Arnold, 127:Spring88-53
Doerflinger, T.M. A Vigorous Spirit of Enter-
  prise.*
  M. Egnal, 656(WMQ):Jan88-193
Dogaer, G. Flemish Miniature Painting in the
  Fifteenth and Sixteenth Centuries.
  C. Reynolds, 90:Oct88-775
  78(BC):Autumn88-313
Dohnal, J. Basic Course in Czech.
  D. Short, 575(SEER):Oct88-631
Doig, A. Theo van Doesburg.*
  P. Overy, 592:Vol201No1020-61
Doig, I. Dancing at the Rascal Fair.
  A.C. Bredahl, 649(WAL):Aug88-169
Doignon, J. - see Saint Augustine
Dokulil, M. & others, eds. Mluvnice češtiny I.
  D. Short, 575(SEER):Oct88-631
Dolamore, C.E.J. Ionesco: "Rhinocéros."
  J. Knowlson, 208(FS):Jan88-111
Dolbeau, F. & others. Indices librorum.
  B.C. Barker-Benfield, 123:Vol38No2-368
Dolezal, F. Forgotten But Important Lexicog-
  raphers: John Wilkins and William Lloyd.*
  E. Standop, 260(IF):Band93-352
d'Olivet, F. - see under Fabre d'Olivet
Doll, M.A. & C. Stites - see Aswell, E.C. & E.
  Nowell

Dolmetsch, C.L. The German Press of the
  Shenandoah Valley.*
  T.G. Gish, 221(GQ):Fall87-689
Dolto, F. Inconscient et destins.
  F. Dupuy-Sullivan, 207(FR):May89-1092
Dombroski, R.S. L'apologia del vero.
  M. Puppo, 547(RF):Band99Heft4-474
Dombrowa, R. Strukturen in Shakespeares
  "King Henry the Sixth."
  H. Keiper, 224(GRM):Band38Heft1/2-229
  W. Weiss, 72:Band225Heft1-171
Domenichini, D. Analecta montaniana.
  J.A. Jones, 86(BHS):Oct88-406
Domes, J. Untersuchungen zur Sprache der
  Kölner "Willehalm"-Handschrift K.
  H. Beckers, 680(ZDP):Band107Heft1-141
Domingo, E.G. Sandhi en Indoeuropeo.
  D. Weber, 260(IF):Band93-294
Domínguez, J.I. To Make a World Safe for
  Revolution.
  W.S. Smith, 441:21May89-23
Domini, S. & others. Vocabolario fraseologico
  del dialetto "bisiàc."
  E.F. Tuttle, 545(RPh):Aug88-107
Dominicis, M. & J.J. Reynolds. Repase y
  escriba.
  A. Roca, 399(MLJ):Autumn88-371
Dominik, M. William Shakespeare and "The
  Birth of Merlin."*
  D.W. Foster, 570(SQ):Spring88-118
Donagan, A. Choice.*
  K. Rankin, 103:Jan89-4
Donagan, A. Spinoza.
  G.H.R. Parkinson, 617(TLS):28Jul-
    3Aug89-818
Donaghy, M. Shibboleth.
  S. O'Brien, 364:Feb/Mar89-107
  B. O'Donoghue, 617(TLS):1-7Dec89-1336
Donahue, J.D. The Privatization Decision.
  R. Heilbroner, 441:17Dec89-13
Donald, A. Poor Dear Charlotte.*
  42(AR):Fall88-531
Donald, A. Smile, Honey.*
  S. McCauley, 441:8Oct89-13
Donald, C.M. The Fat Woman Measures Up.
  M. Harry, 198:Autumn88-97
  C. Tapping, 102(CanL):Summer88-168
Donald, D.H. Look Homeward.*
  T.D. Adams, 219(GaR):Fall88-651
  J. Groth, 31(ASch):Winter88-134
  M.M. Harper, 578:Fall88-88
  J. Howland, Jr., 569(SR):Spring88-280
  R.S. Kennedy, 536(Rev):Vol10-203
  R.A. Martin, 115:Summer88-322
Donaldson, D.J. Cajun Nights.
  A. Brumer, 441:22Jan89-22
Donaldson, F. The Royal Opera House in the
  Twentieth Century.
  E. Forbes, 415:Apr88-191
Donaldson, I. - see Jonson, B.
Donaldson, I.M. The Life and Work of Samuel
  Rutherford Crockett.
  J. Calder, 617(TLS):20-26Oct89-1163
Donaldson, S. John Cheever.*
  M. Pinker, 152(UDQ):Fall88-100
Donaldson, S., ed. Conversations with John
  Cheever.
  L.M. Waldeland, 395(MFS):Winter88-648
Donaldson, T.E. Hindu Temple Art of Orissa.
  (Vols 2 & 3)
  W. Smith, 293(JASt):Nov88-916
Donaldson, W. - see Alexander, W.

Donaldson-Evans, M. A Woman's Revenge.*
  U. Dethloff, 547(RF):Band100Heft4-441
  R. Lethbridge, 208(FS):Jul88-358
Donatelli Noble, C. Pronuncia e fonetica
  dell'italiano.
  R.J. Di Pietro, 276:Spring88-42
Donderer, M. Die Chronologie der römischen
  Mosaiken in Venetien und Istrien bis zur
  Zeit der Antonine.
  K.M.D. Dunbabin, 123:Vol38No2-360
Donkin, E.H. – see Cicero
Donne, J. Devotions Upon Emergent
  Occasions. (A. Raspa, ed)
  T. R. Langley, 97(CQ):Vol17No2-166
Donne, J. Selected Poetry and Prose. (T.W. &
  R.J. Craik, eds)
  M.G. Brennan, 447(N&Q):Sep88-363
Donnelly, F. Shake Down the Stars.
  L.B. Osborne, 441:28May89-18
Donnelly, G. Faulty Ground.
  S. Ferguson, 441:17Dec89-18
Donno, E.S. – see Shakespeare, W.
D'Onofrio, G. Fons Scientiae.
  M. Mugnai, 319:Apr89-302
Donoghue, D. Reading America.*
  639(VQR):Summer88-80
Donoghue, D. We Irish.*
  M. O'Brien, 184(EIC):Jan88-84
Donoso, A. & H.C. Raley. José Ortega y Gas-
  set.
  N.R. Orringer, 238:Sep88-549
Donoso, J. Curfew.*
  R. Garis, 249(HudR):Winter89-753
Donovan, H. Right Places, Right Times.
  T. Goldstein, 441:12Nov89-13
Doob, L.W. Slightly beyond Skepticism.
  A.J. Damico, 185:Oct88-175
Doody, M.A. Frances Burney.
  D. Nokes, 617(TLS):25-31Aug89-911
Doody, M.A. The Daring Muse.*
  P. Hughes, 173(ECS):Fall88-78
  R.P. Lessenich, 72:Band224Heft2-401
  R.J. Merrett, 178:Jun88-225
Dooley, M. Turbulence.
  S. Pugh, 493:Winter88/89-49
  M. Wormald, 617(TLS):9-15Jun89-641
Dor, J. Structure et perversions.
  A. Reix, 542:Jan-Mar88-77
Dore, R.P. & R. Sinha, eds. Japan and World
  Depression.
  E.M. Hadley, 293(JASt):Nov88-885
Dorfman, A. Last Waltz in Santiago.
  639(VQR):Autumn88-134
Dorfman, A. My House is on Fire.
  B. Mukherjee, 441:31Dec89-8
Dorian, N. The Tyranny of Tide.
  D.H., 355(LSoc):Dec88-622
Dörig, J. La frise est de l'Héphaisteion.*
  F. Felten, 229:Band60Heft3-253
Dorion, G. & M. Voisin, eds. Littérature qué-
  bécoise, voix d'un peuple, voies d'une
  autonomie.
  I. Oore, 102(CanL):Autumn88-168
Dorion, H. Hors champ.
  T. Vuong-Riddick, 102(CanL):Spring88-
  132
Dorment, R. British Painting in the Philadel-
  phia Museum of Art: From the Seventeenth
  through the Nineteenth Century.*
  R. Paulson, 173(ECS):Summer88-527
Dorn, J.A. & H.G. Manne, eds. Economic Lib-
  erties and the Judiciary.
  A.A.S., 185:Apr89-681

Dorney, L., G. Noonan & P. Tiessen, eds. A
  Public and Private Voice.*
  A. Archer, 49:Jan88-97
  L. Early, 178:Mar88-112
  J. Hart, 298:Winter88/89-145
  S. Hutchison, 102(CanL):Spring88-205
Dörrie, D. Love, Pain, and the Whole Damn
  Thing.
  L. Chamberlain, 617(TLS):22-28Dec89-
  1422
  H. Coale, 441:10Sep89-26
Dörrie, H. Der Platonismus in der Antike.
  (Vol 1) (A. Dörrie, ed)
  M. Schofield, 123:Vol38No1-69
Dorris, M. The Broken Cord.
  P. Guthrie, 441:30Jul89-1
Dorris, M. A Yellow Raft in Blue Water.*
  L. Dawson-Evans, 565:Summer88-54
  J. Mellors, 364:Feb88-105
Dorsett, T. & H. Frommer. Running Tough.
  R. Strauss, 441:19Nov89-44
Dorsi, M.L. I libretti d'opera da 1800 al 1825
  nella biblioteca del conservatorio "G.
  Verdi" di Milano.
  P. Gossett, 410(M&L):Apr88-262
  S. Mamy, 537:Vol74No1-101
Dorsinville, M. Le Pays natal.*
  C. Bouygues, 102(CanL):Winter87-211
Dorwick, T. & others. ¿Qué tal? (2nd ed)
  A.L. Prince, 399(MLJ):Spring88-108
Dostoevsky, F. Fyodor Dostoevsky: Complete
  Letters.* (Vol 1) (D. Lowe & R. Meyer, eds
  & trans)
  V. Terras, 574(SEEJ):Fall88-468
Dostoevsky, F. Fyodor Dostoevsky: Complete
  Letters. (Vol 2) (D.A. Lowe, ed & trans)
  S.J. Parker, 441:4Jun89-13
Dotoli, G. & F. Fiorino. Viaggiatori francesi
  in Puglia nell' Ottocento.*
  L. Le Guillou, 535(RHL):Mar-Apr88-327
Dotson, J. The Enduring Voice.
  R.J. Brophy, 649(WAL):Feb89-367
  E. Lueders, 651(WHR):Summer88-172
de' Dottori, C. L'asino. (A. Daniele, ed)
  L. Serianni, 708:Vol14fasc1-124
Doty, W.G. Mythography.
  R.B., 295(JML):Fall87/Winter88-242
  D. Kelly, 124:Nov-Dec88-142
Doubrovsky, S. Writing and Fantasy in
  Proust.*
  A. Smith, 295(JML):Fall87/Winter88-372
Dougherty, D. Valle-Inclán y la Segunda
  República.
  J.J. Gilabert, 238:May88-296
  L.J. Herrera, 552(REH):May88-130
  J. Lyon, 402(MLR):Jan89-213
  A. Risco, 240(HR):Autumn88-507
Doughtie, E. English Renaissance Song.*
  E.B. Jorgens, 551(RenQ):Summer88-342
Doughtie, E., ed. Liber Lilliati.*
  P. Thomson, 677(YES):Vol19-311
Doughty, R.W. At Home in Texas.
  L. Rodenberger, 649(WAL):Aug88-188
Douglas, A. & P. Greenfield, eds. Records of
  Early English Drama: Cumberland, West-
  morland and Gloucestershire.
  C.C. Rutter, 611(TN):Vol42No2-83
  W.P. Williams, 447(N&Q):Mar88-74
Douglas, A.E. – see Cicero
Douglas, C. – see Khlebnikov, V.
Douglas, G. Kodachromes at Midday.
  L. Hutchman, 102(CanL):Winter87-263

Douglas, I.H. Abdul Kalam Azad. (G. Minault & C.W. Troll, eds)
D. Arnold, 617(TLS):31Mar–6Apr89–334
Douglas, J. & F.C. Atwell. Love, Intimacy and Sex.
A.S., 185:Jul89–985
Douglas, J.L. The Free Yemeni Movement 1935–1962.
F. Halliday, 617(TLS):20–26Jan89–54
Douglas, K. Keith Douglas: The Complete Poems. (D. Graham, ed)
P. Parker, 364:Jul88–101
Douglas, N. Isole d'estate/Summer Islands. (C. Knight, ed)
D. Ridgway, 617(TLS):9–15Jun89–633
Douglas, S.J. Inventing American Broadcasting, 1899–1922.
M. Banta, 432(NEQ):Sep88–458
Douglass, P. Bergson, Eliot, and American Literature.*
S.S. Baskett, 115:Winter88–92
K.E. Csengeri, 131(CL):Fall88–409
M.A. Gillies, 49:Apr88–101
W. Harmon, 569(SR):Winter88–105
P. Lamarque, 677(YES):Vol19–355
A. Robinson, 541(RES):Aug88–463
I.V., 295(JML):Fall87/Winter88–242
Doumato, L. Architecture and Women.
47:Nov88–58
Dourado, A. The Bells of Agony.
J. Gledson, 617(TLS):20–26Jan89–58
Dove, M. The Perfect Age of Man's Life.*
G. Schmitz, 72:Band225Heft2–375
T. Turville-Petre, 541(RES):Aug88–424
Dove, R. Fifth Sunday.*
K. Warren, 577(SHR):Winter88–87
Dove, R. Thomas and Beulah.*
P. Harris, 639(VQR):Spring88–270
Dover, K.J. Greek and the Greeks.
P.E. Easterling, 617(TLS):11–17Aug89–876
H. Lloyd-Jones, 123:Vol38No2–377
Dover, K.J. The Greeks and Their Legacy.
P.E. Easterling, 617(TLS):11–17Aug89–876
Dovlatov, S. Čemodan.
T. Pogacar, 574(SEEJ):Summer88–337
Dovlatov, S. Ours.
P-L. Adams, 61:Jul89–94
S. Ruta, 441:30Apr89–1
Dow, J.R. & R.W. Brednich, eds. Internationale Volkskundliche Bibliographie/International Folklore Bibliography/Bibliographie Internationale d'Ethnologie für die Jahre 1981 und 1982 mit Nachträgen für die vorausgehenden Jahre.
M. Taft, 292(JAF):Jul–Sep88–373
Dow, J.R. & H. Lixfeld, eds & trans. German Volkskunde.*
P. Dinzelbacher, 133:Band21Heft4–373
C. Fees, 203:Vol99No2–263
Dowden, S.D. Sympathy for the Abyss.
P.M. Lützeler, 221(GQ):Winter88–149
Dowley, T., ed. Discovering the Bible.
J. Russell, 124:Sep–Oct88–65
Dowling, L. Language and Decadence in the Victorian Fin de Siècle.*
G.A.O., 295(JML):Fall87/Winter88–195
R.O. Preyer, 301(JEGP):Apr88–276
J. Stokes, 402(MLR):Oct89–949
Downar, J. The Old Noise of Truth.
M. Wormald, 617(TLS):22–28Dec89–1417

Downer, L. On the Narrow Road. (British title: On the Narrow Road to the Deep North.)
P-L. Adams, 61:Aug89–91
B. Moeran, 617(TLS):9–15Jun89–633
J.D. Morley, 441:30Jul89–13
Downes, K. Sir John Vanbrugh.*
J. Vernon, 90:Aug88–635
Downes, K. Sir Christopher Wren. The Architecture of Wren.
D. Watkin, 617(TLS):26May–1Jun89–590
Downie, G. An X-ray of Longing.
M. Cookshaw, 376:Jun88–193
K. McGuirk, 137:Fall88–50
Downs, R.B. Images of America.
W.R. Kime, 649(WAL):May88–77
639(VQR):Winter88–30
Downton, E. Pacific Challenge.
D.M. Schurman, 529(QQ):Summer88–485
Dowty, D.R., L. Karttunen & A.M. Zwicky, eds. Natural Language Parsing.*
L.A. Connolly, 603:Vol12No1–165
Dowty, D.R., L. Karttunen & A.M. Zwicky. Natural Language Understanding.
H. Goodluck, 320(CJL):Jun88–182
Doyal, L. & R. Harris. Empiricism, Explanation and Rationality.
G. Brown, 518:Apr88–124
Doyle, A.C. The Unknown Conan Doyle.* (J.M. Gibson & R.L. Green, eds)
L.O. Manning, 635(VPR):Winter88–161
Doyle, A.I., ed. The Vernon Manuscript.
R. Beadle, 617(TLS):13–19Jan89–46
E.G. Stanley, 447(N&Q):Jun88–209
Doyle, R. The Commitments.
K. Friedman, 441:23Jul89–11
Doyle, R.E. Atē.
J. Gruber, 229:Band60Heft5–385
Doyle, W. Origins of the French Revolution. (2nd ed)
C. Lucas, 617(TLS):19–25May89–554
Doyle, W. The Oxford History of the French Revolution.
L. Groopman, 441:9Jul89–13
C. Jones, 617(TLS):21–27Jul89–791
Drabble, M. A Natural Curiosity.
J. Grossman, 441:3Sep89–3
H. Mantel, 453(NYRB):23Nov89–18
P. Reading, 617(TLS):29Sep–5Oct89–1052
442(NY):18Sep89–139
Drabble, M. The Radiant Way.*
A. Bloom, 249(HudR):Autumn88–541
Drabble, M. & J. Stringer, eds. The Concise Oxford Companion to English Literature.
R. Crawford, 447(N&Q):Sep88–400
Drabeck, B.A. & H.E. Ellis – see MacLeish, A.
Drachenberg, E. Die mittelalterliche Glasmalerei in Erfurt.
E. Frodl-Kraft, 683:Band51Heft3–442
G. Schmidt, 683:Band51Heft3–445
Drage, C.L. Russian and Church Slavonic Books 1701–1800 in United Kingdom Libraries.
H. Rothe, 688(ZSP):Band48Heft2–398
Drakakis, J., ed. Alternative Shakespeares.*
M. Pfister, 156(ShJW):Jahrbuch1988–235
R. Wilson, 366:Autumn88–211
Drake, B. What We Say to Strangers.
G. Kuzma, 219(GaR):Fall88–624
Drake, R. Survivors and Others.
J.H. Justus, 396(ModA):Winter88–88
Drake, W. The First Wave.
B.M. Perkins, 27(AL):May88–313

Dransfield, M. Michael Dransfield Collected Poems. (R. Hall, ed)
　M. Roberts, 581:Dec88-481
Drapeau, R-B. Féminins singuliers.
　Λ-M. Picard, 627(UTQ).Fall87-200
Draper, H. The Marx-Engels Cyclopedia.
　B. Frohmann, 470:Vol26-208
Draper, R.P., ed. D.H. Lawrence: The Critical Heritage.
　K. Cushman, 177(ELT):Vol31No3-353
Draper, R.P., ed. The Literature of Region and Nation.
　T. Paulin, 617(TLS):8-14Sep89-983
Draus, F. - see Aron, R.
Dray, W.H. Perspectives sur l'histoire. (rev by P. Bellemare)
　A. Reix, 542:Oct-Dec88-518
Dreher, D.E. Domination and Defiance.*
　M. Novy, 551(RenQ):Spring88-167
　A. Thompson, 677(YES):Vol19-316
Dreiser, T. Theodore Dreiser's "Heard in the Corridors" Articles and Related Writings. (T.D. Nostwich, ed)
　R.W. Dowell, 26(ALR):Spring89-93
Dreiser, T. Sister Carrie; Jennie Gerhardt; Twelve Men. (R. Lehan, ed)
　J.K. Davis, 569(SR):Summer88-507
　A. Delbanco, 453(NYRB):23Nov89-32
Dreiser, T. & H.L. Mencken. Dreiser-Mencken Letters.* (T.P. Riggio, ed)
　P.L. Gerber, 536(Rev):Vol10-85
　M.D.O., 295(JML):Fall87/Winter88-229
　D. Pizer, 395(MFS):Summer88-235
Dresler-Brumme, C. Nietzsches Philosophie in Musils Roman "Der Mann ohne Eigenschaften."
　K. Marko, 602:Band19Heft2-169
Dressler, W.U. Morphonology.*
　W. Haas, 685(ZDL):3/1988-380
　A.S. Kaye, 603:Vol12No2-527
Dressler, W.U. & others, eds. Phonologica 1984.
　S.L. Fulmer, 350:Dec89-883
Dretske, F. Explaining Behavior.
　J. Hornsby, 617(TLS):3-9Mar89-227
　A.J. Jacobson, 103:Aug89-306
　R.G. Meyers, 543:Jun89-824
Dreuilhe, E. Mortal Embrace.*
　J. Weber, 617(TLS):2-8Jun89-601
Drevet, P. Une Chambre dans les bois.
　J. Kirkup, 617(TLS):13-19Oct89-1130
Drevet, P. Le Visiteur de hasard.*
　G.E. Reed, 207(FR):Mar89-713
Drew, B. Nelson Algren.
　J. Atlas, 441:26Nov89-18
Drew, D. Kurt Weill.*
　M. Bowen, 415:Sep88-462
　T. Levitz & b.d. mcclung, 465:Autumn88-95
Drew, E. Election Journal.
　C. Dean, 441:2Apr89-29
Drew, J. India and the Romantic Imagination.
　N. Mirsky, 447(N&Q):Dec88-555
Drew, J. The Lesser Vehicle.*
　L. Sail, 565:Spring88-73
Drewry, G. & T. Butcher. The Civil Service Today.
　A. Cairncross, 617(TLS):6-12Jan89-5
Drews, R. Basileus.
　H.W. Singor, 394:Vol41fasc1/2-218
Dreyfus, L. Bach's Continuo Group.*
　C.M.B., 412:Aug88-227
　P. Williams, 317:Summer88-349

Drifte, R. Arms Production in Japan.
　J.H. Buck, 293(JASt):Feb88-140
Drigo, P. Maria Zef.
　A. Johnson, 441:26Nov89-30
Drinkard, M. Green Bananas.
　A. Solomon, 441:17Sep89-24
Drinkwater, J.F. The Gallic Empire.
　R. Bland, 313:Vol78-258
Driscoll, P. Spearhead.
　N. Callendar, 441:25Jun89-31
Driver, E. A Bibliography of Cookery Books Published in Britain 1875-1914.
　J. Grigson, 617(TLS):22-28Dec89-1410
"Droits." (No. 6)
　S. Goyard-Fabre, 154:Summer88-372
Droixhe, D. De l'origine du langage aux langues du monde.
　P. Swiggers, 553(RLiR):Jul-Dec88-490
Dronke, P. Dante and Medieval Latin Traditions.*
　T. Barolini, 551(RenQ):Summer88-293
　J.H. Whitfield, 382(MAE):1988/1-145
Dronke, P., ed. A History of Twelfth-Century Western Philosophy.
　G. Leff, 617(TLS):7-13Jul89-756
Dronke, P. Poetic Individuality in the Middle Ages. (2nd ed)
　F.P. Knapp, 72:Band225Heft1-152
　C.J. McDonough, 447(N&Q):Sep88-346
Drost, W., ed. Fortschrittsglaube und Dekadenzbewusstsein im Europa des 19. Jahrhunderts.*
　R. Lloyd, 208(FS):Jan88-103
Droste, F.G. & Y. d'Hulst, eds. Nuove prospettive nella linguistica contemporanea.
　P. Swiggers, 553(RLiR):Jul-Dec88-479
von Droste-Hülshoff, A. Historisch-kritische Ausgabe. (Vol 8, Pt 1 ed by W. Gödden; Vol 13, Pt 1 ed by A. Kansteiner)
　J. Guthrie, 400(MLR):Jan89-200
Drotner, K. English Children and their Magazines 1751-1945.
　G. Avery, 617(TLS):3-9Feb89-120
Drucker, P.F. The New Realities.
　B.R. Barber, 441:18Jun89-15
"Drug Abuse Prevention."
　M. Massing, 453(NYRB):30Mar89-22
Drummond de Andrade, C. Travelling in the Family. (T. Colchie & M. Strand, eds)
　C. de Oliveira, 577(SHR):Spring88-199
Drüppel, C.J. Altfranzösische Urkunden und Lexikologie.
　W. Müller, 685(ZDL):3/1987-360
　A.M. Muth, 545(RPh):May89-459
Druse, K. The Natural Garden.
　A. Lacy, 441:11Jun89-30
Drux, R. Marionette Mensch.
　J.M. McGlathery, 406:Winter88-513
Dryden, J. The Oxford Authors: John Dryden.* (K. Walker, ed)
　T. Mason, 541(RES):Aug88-443
Dryden, J. The Works of John Dryden.* (Vol 13) (M.E. Novak, G.R. Guffey & A. Roper, eds)
　D. Hughes, 677(YES):Vol19-322
Duarte i Montserrat, C. El vocabulari jurídic del "Llibre de les costums de Tortosa."
　A.M. Perrone Capano Compagna, 379(MedR):Aug88-313
Duberman, M.B. Paul Robeson.
　E. Bentley, 617(TLS):12-18May89-507
　J.P. Diggins, 441:12Feb89-1
　M. Kempton, 453(NYRB):27Apr89-3

Dubie, N. The Springhouse Poems.*
  C. Bedient, 569(SR):Winter88-137
Dubin, L.S. The History of Beads.
  J. Bamberger, 139:Apr/May88-16
Dubin, S.C. Bureaucratizing the Muse.
  J. Hutchens, Jr., 289:Summer88-120
  G.C. Koch & J. Jeffri, 476:Spring88-83
Dubinsky, R. Stormy Applause.
  J. Skvorecky, 441:25Jun89-12
  442(NY):11Sep89-123
Dubois, E. - see Quinault, P.
Dubois, L. Recherches sur le dialecte
arcadien.
  R. Schmitt, 229:Band60Heft1-1
Du Bois, W.E.B. Against Racism. (H. Aptheker, ed)
  E. Peters, 534(RALS):Vol16No1&2-148
Duboy, P. Lequeu.
  B. Bergdoll, 576:Jun88-200
"Jacques Du Broeucq."
  B. Boucher, 90:Mar88-233
Dubrow, H. Captive Victors.
  W. Keach, 551(RenQ):Winter88-752
Dubuffet, J. Asphyxiating Culture and Other
Writings.
  R. Cardinal, 617(TLS):13-19Oct89-1118
Dubuffet, J. Bonpiet beau neuille. Bâtons
rompus. Asphyxiante culture.
  M. Thévoz, 98:Jan/Feb88-77
Dubus, A. 3d. The Cage Keeper and Other
Stories.
  D. Solomon, 441:5Feb89-24
Duby, G., ed. A History of Private Life.* (Vol
2)
  M.E. Hussey, 42(AR):Fall88-524
Duby, G. Mâle Moyen Age.
  M. Vale, 617(TLS):31Mar-6Apr89-347
Duchen, C. Feminism in France from May '68
to Mitterand.*
  M. Sarde, 207(FR):Mar89-724
Duchêne, R. Madame de La Fayette, la romancière aux cent bras.
  M-O. Sweetser, 207(FR):Feb89-576
Duchesneau, L. The Voice of the Muse.
  D. Huron, 411:Mar88-110
Duckworth, C. The d'Antraigues Phenomenon.*
  R. Niklaus, 83:Spring88-82
Duclos, C. Mémoires pour servir à l'histoire
des moeurs du XVIIIe siècle.
  J. Brengues, 535(RHL):Jul-Aug88-772
Duclos-Faure, D. & others. Manuel de catalogage automatisé des livres anciens en
format Intermarc.
  S. Rawles, 402(MLR):Jul89-733
Ducornet, R. Entering Fire.
  S. Slemon, 102(CanL):Spring88-122
Ducos, M. Les Romains et la loi.*
  W.M. Gordon, 123:Vol38No1-76
Ducrey, P. Guerre et guerriers dans la Grèce
antique.
  H-J. Gehrke, 229:Band60Heft3-219
  G. Schepens, 394:Vol41fasc3/4-454
Dudek, L. Zembla's Rocks.*
  A.R. Kizuk, 102(CanL):Autumn88-152
  P.J.M. Robertson, 529(QQ):Summer88-483
"Duden." (Vol 1) (19th ed)
  G. Kempcke, 682(ZPSK):Band41Heft2-240
Duemer, J. Customs.
  L. Upton, 152(UDQ):Spring88-106
Duerr, H.P. Nacktheit und Scham.
  G. Baumann, 617(TLS):6-12Jan89-18

Duff, R.A. Trials and Punishments.*
  T.S. Champlin, 518:Apr88-107
Duffey, B. A Poetry of Presence.*
  G.S. Lensing, 569(SR):Winter88-113
Duffy, B. The World as I Found It.*
  639(VQR):Spring88-55
Duffy, C.A. Selling Manhattan.*
  S. O'Brien, 364:Apr/May88-118
Duffy, C.A. Thrown Voices.
  J. Saunders, 565:Autumn88-72
Duffy, D. Sounding the Iceberg.*
  C. Thomas, 627(UTQ):Fall87-158
Duffy, M. Change.
  J. Mellors, 364:Mar87-98
Duffy, M. The Englishman and the Foreigner.
  J.E. Hill, 173(ECS):Summer88-530
Duffy, M. The Passionate Shepherdess.
  A. Leighton, 617(TLS):1-7Sep89-950
Duffy, M. A Thousand Capricious Chances.
  J. Sutherland, 617(TLS):11-17Aug89-864
Duffy, M. - see Behn, A.
Duffy, M. - see Brewer, J.
Dufilho, A. Le Temps des joies secrètes.
  J. Abrate, 207(FR):May89-1093
Dufour, R.P. Modernization in Colonial Massachusetts, 1630-1763.
  J.A. Schutz, 656(WMQ):Oct88-797
Dufournet, J. & M. Rousse. Sur la "Farce de
Maître Pierre Pathelin."
  J. Crow, 382(MAE):1988/1-136
  A. Hindley, 208(FS):Jul88-336
  E. Suomela-Härmä, 439(NM):1988/3-431
Dufrenne, M. In the Presence of the Sensuous. (M.S. Roberts & D. Gallagher, eds &
trans)
  S. Bann, 617(TLS):20-26Jan89-66
Dugas, J-Y. Répertoire des gentilés du
Québec.
  W. Schweickard, 553(RLiR):Jan-Jun88-
315
Dugas, K. - see Wordsworth, W.
Duggan, C. Fascism and the Mafia.
  A. Lyttelton, 617(TLS):3-9Mar89-211
Duggan, J.J., ed. A Fragment of "Les Enfances Vivien."*
  C. Di Girolamo, 379(MedR):Aug88-298
Duggan, W. Lovers of the African Night.*
  42(AR):Fall88-531
Dugrand, A. Une Certaine Sympathie.
  L.A. Di Benedetto, 207(FR):Oct88-199
Duiker, W.J. China and Vietnam.
  S.W. Simon, 293(JASt):Feb88-193
Dujardin, P., ed. Le secret.
  B. Beugnot, 154:Winter88-734
Duke, B. The Japanese School.*
  J.L. Huffman, 399(MLJ):Autumn88-364
Dull, J.R. A Diplomatic History of the American Revolution.
  P.E. Russell, 106:Spring88-124
Dulles, A. The Reshaping of Catholicism.
  J. Garvey, 441:19Mar89-11
Dumas, A. Dumas on Food. (A. & J. Davidson,
trans)
  F.W.J. Hemmings, 208(FS):Oct88-481
Dumas, D. Nos façons de parler.
  L.B. Mignault, 627(UTQ):Fall88-182
Dumm, T.L. Democracy and Punishment.
  D.M.F., 185:Oct88-193
Dumont, J-P. Introduction à la méthode
d'Aristote.
  B. Dumoulin, 192(EP):Jul-Sep88-426
Dumville, D. & M. Lapidge - see "The Anglo-
Saxon Chronicle"

Dumville, D.N., ed. The "Historia Brittonum."*
(Vol 3)
  L.M. Matheson, 589:Jan88-147
  B.K. Vollmann, 38:Band106Heft1/2-213
Dunae, P.A., ed. Ranchers' Legacy.
  B. Ferguson, 298:Spring/Summer88-219
Dunant, S. Snowstorms in a Hot Climate.
  M. Freitag, 441:1Jan89-14
Dunaway, D.K. Huxley in Hollywood.
  K. Quinn, 441:22Oct89-25
Dunayevskaya, R. Marxism and Freedom. The
Philosophic Moment of Marxist-Humanism.
  N. Gibson, 150(DR):Fall88-357
Dunbabin, J. France in the Making, 843-
1180.*
  M.T. Clanchy, 382(MAE):1988/1-127
Duncan, A. American Art Deco.*
  139:Apr/May88-68
Duncan, A.B., ed. Claude Simon.*
  S. Petit, 345(KRQ):May88-237
  E. Smyth, 535(RHL):Jan-Feb88-158
Duncan, E. Breaking the Curfew.
  M. Ispahani, 441:24Sep89-28
Duncan, E. Those Giants Let Them Rise!
  J. Hendin, 532(RCF):Spring88-207
Duncan, J., ed. Walter Burley Griffin.
  P. Drew, 46:Oct88-12
Duncan, J.A. Voices, Visions, and a New
Reality.*
  S. Bacarisse, 86(BHS):Oct88-424
  R.W. Fiddian, 402(MLR):Jan89-221
Duncan, R. Ground Work II.*
  639(VQR):Summer88-99
Dundes, A., ed. Little Red Riding Hood. Cin-
derella.
  M. Warner, 617(TLS):24-30Nov89-1309
Dunkley, J. Gambling.*
  A-M. Anthonioz, 535(RHL):Jul-Aug88-
766
Dunkley, J. - see Regnard, J-F.
Dunkling, L. & G. Wright. A Dictionary of Pub
Names.
  A. Room, 424:Sep-Dec88-247
Dunkling, L.A. You Name It!
  A. Room, 424:Sep-Dec88-241
Dunlap, S. Pious Deception.
  M. Stasio, 441:10Sep89-28
Dunlop, J.B., R.S. Haugh & M. Nicholson, eds.
Solzhenitsyn in Exile.*
  J. Curtis, 574(SEEJ):Spring88-142
Dunlop, M. Body Defences.
  D.R. Forsdyke, 529(QQ):Winter88-949
Dunlop, P. Short Latin Stories.
  H.E. Moritz, 399(MLJ):Autumn88-344
Dunmore, H. The Raw Garden.
  M. Wormald, 617(TLS):9-15Jun89-641
Dunmore, H. The Sea Skater.
  D. McDuff, 565:Spring88-64
Dunn, D. Northlight.*
  S. O'Brien, 493:Winter88/89-45
Dunn, D. Selected Poems 1964-1983.*
Elegies.
  R. Watson, 588(SSL):Vol23-254
Dunn, J. The Politics of Socialism.
  R. Riemer, 488:Sep88-403
Dunn, K. Geek Love.
  S. Dobyns, 441:2Apr89-11
  R. Kaveney, 617(TLS):8-14Sep89-968
Dunn, R. The Possibility of Weakness of
Will.*
  N.O. Dahl, 185:Oct88-160
  G. Marshall, 63:Sep88-425

Dunn, R.E. The Adventures of Ibn Battūta.
  I.R. Netton, 294:Sep88-192
Dunn-Lardeau, B., ed. "Legenda Aurea."*
  R. Blumenfeld-Kosinski, 545(RPh):Feb89-
370
Dunne, J.G. Harp.
  H. Kenner, 441:10Sep89-3
Dunphy, J. The Murderous McLaughlins.*
  42(AR):Fall88-532
Dunsby, J. & A. Whittall. Music Analysis in
Theory and Practice.
  W. Drabkin, 415:May88-247
Dunwoodie, P. Camus, "L'Envers et l'Endroit"
and "L'Exil et le Royaume."
  J. Levi-Valensi, 535(RHL):Mar-Apr88-
335
Du Plessis, R.B. H.D.*
  M.P.L., 295(JML):Fall87/Winter88-310
Dupont, B., K. Sørensen & J. Vaeth, eds. At-
lanteren har så mange mil.
  R. Birn, 563(SS):Autumn88-518
Dupont, P. - see Ferenczi, S.
Dupont, P. & F. Renevier. On n'attrape pas
les filles avec du vinaigre.
  A.J.M. Prévos, 207(FR):Dec88-351
Dupré, S. Porsuk 1.
  M.J. Mellink, 318(JAOS):Jul-Sep87-553
Duque, A.M., J.M. Blázquez Martínez & J.M.
Solana Sáinz - see under Montenegro
Duque, A., J.M. Blázquez Martínez & J.M.
Solana Sáinz
Durand, J., ed. Dependency and Non-Linear
Phonology.*
  H. Basbøll, 603:Vol12No2-485
Durand, J-L. Sacrifice et labour en Grèce
ancienne.
  D. Arnould, 555:Vol61fasc1-107
Durand, L. Daddy.
  B. Hochberg, 441:2Apr89-28
Durand-Sandrail, B. - see Diderot, D.
Durant, S. Ornament.*
  T. Reese, 507:Sep/Oct88-162
Duranton, H., ed. Correspondance littéraire
du Président Bouhier. (Vols 4 & 5)
  P. Rétat, 535(RHL):Jan-Feb88-126
Duras, M. Emily L.
  A. Solomon, 441:28May89-18
Duras, M. La Vie matérielle.
  D.D. Fisher, 207(FR):Dec88-361
Duras, M. Les Yeux verts.
  M. Cottenet-Hage, 207(FR):Mar89-703
Duras, M. & X. Gauthier. Woman to Woman.
  639(VQR):Summer88-81
Durham, L.L. Heart of a Western Woman.
  S. Preston, 649(WAL):Aug88-160
Durham, W.B., ed. American Theatre Com-
panies, 1749-1887.*
  D.J. Watermeier, 610:Summer88-163
Durham, W.B., ed. American Theatre Com-
panies, 1888-1930.*
  R. Moody, 610:Summer88-164
Durliat, M. Die Kunst des frühen Mittelalters.
  V.H. Elbern, 683:Band51Heft3-454
Durling, R.J. - see Arnaldus de Villanova
Durova, N. The Cavalry Maiden.* (M.F. Zirin,
ed & trans)
  A. Fitzlyon, 364:Aug/Sep88-142
Dürr, V., R. Grimm & K. Harms, eds.
Nietzsche.
  A. Del Caro, 133:Band21Heft4-352
  M. Tanner, 617(TLS):12-18May89-509

103

East, J.P. The American Conservative Movement.
  E.B. McLean, 396(ModA):Winter88-62
Easterling, P.E. - see Sophocles
Easterling, P.E. & B.M.W. Knox, eds. The Cambridge History of Classical Literature.* (Vol 1)
  J. Herington, 487:Spring88-79
Easthope, A. British Post-Structuralism.
  M. Ellmann, 617(TLS):17-23Feb89-172
Easthope, A. Poetry and Phantasy.
  M. Walters, 617(TLS):22-28Dec89-1419
Easthope, A. What a Man's Gotta Do.
  E. Jordan, 366:Autumn88-222
Eastlake, W. Prettyfields [together with] Haslam, G. The Man Who Cultivated Fire & Other Stories.
  G.I. Locklin, 649(WAL):Aug88-161
Eastman, L.E. Family, Fields, and Ancestors.
  W.T. Rowe, 293(JASt):Nov88-848
Easton, C. The Search for Sam Goldwyn.
  J.G. Dunne, 453(NYRB):18May89-28
Eaton, C.E. New and Selected Poems, 1942-1987.
  W. Shear, 389(MQ):Summer89-529
  T. Swiss, 569(SR):Winter88-x
Eaton, C.E. New and Selected Stories, 1959-1989.
  P. Kaganoff, 441:17Dec89-18
Eaton, C.L.G. Islam and the Destiny of Man.
  M.A. Adeel, 485(PE&W):Jan88-92
  M.S. Stern, 589:Jan88-149
Eaton, M.M. Basic Issues in Aesthetics.
  S.L. Feagin, 103:Nov88-444
  P.H. Werhane, 290(JAAC):Spring88-424
Eaton, R. & others, eds. Papers from the 4th International Conference on English Historical Linguistics, Amsterdam, 10-13 April, 1985.*
  W. Elmer, 38:Band106Heft3/4-462
Eaves, M. & M. Fischer, eds. Romanticism and Contemporary Criticism.*
  J.E. Grant, 88:Spring89-124
  K. Kroeber, 591(SIR):Summer88-339
Ebbesen, S. - see Simon of Faversham
Ebbinghaus, E.A. - see Braune, W.
Ebeling, H. & L. Lütkehaus, eds. Schopenhauer und Marx.
  P. Trotignon, 542:Jul-Sep88-342
Eberhard, W. A Dictionary of Chinese Symbols.*
  L.G. Thompson, 318(JAOS):Jul-Sep87-493
  J.L. Watson, 293(JASt):Feb88-116
Eberhardt, I. The Oblivion Seekers and Other Writings.*
  D. Flower, 364:Jun88-93
Eberhardt, I. The Passionate Nomads.*
  H. Mantel, 364:Feb88-99
Eberhart, R. Collected Poems: 1930-1986. Maine Poems.
  J. Parini, 617(TLS):23-29Jun89-694
Eberle, M. World War I and the Weimar Artists.
  C.V. Poling, 54:Mar88-156
  529(QQ):Winter88-970
Ebermann, E. Die Sprache der Mauka.
  M. Dietrich-Friedländer, 682(ZPSK):Band41Heft2-242
Eble, K.E. Old Clemens and W.D.H.*
  E.L. Galligan, 569(SR):Spring88-265

Ebobisse, C. Les verbaux du dangaléat de l'est (Guera, Tchad).
  Z. Frajzyngier, 350:Dec89-885
Eby, C.D. The Road to Armageddon.
  J. Sutherland, 617(TLS):6-12Jan89-15
  G.B. Tennyson, 445(NCF):Jun88-134
  F. Warner, 637(VS):Spring89-464
Eccles, W.J. Essays on New France.*
  G.W., 102(CanL):Summer88-178
Echenoz, J. Lac.
  P. Burton-Page, 617(TLS):8-14Dec89-1369
Echevarría C., E. La novela social de Bolivia.
  C.S. Mathieu, 238:May88-307
Echevarría, R.G. - see under González Echevarría, R.
Echeverria, R. Furacão Elis.
  M. Holston, 37:Jan/Feb88-61
Echols, P.C. & N. Zahler - see Ives, C.
Eck, J-F. Histoire de l'economie française depuis 1945.
  H.B. Sutton, 207(FR):May89-1104
Eckelaar, J. & J. Bell, eds. Oxford Essays in Jurisprudence. (3rd Ser)
  S. Guest, 518:Oct88-199
Ecker, G., ed. Feminist Aesthetics.
  N.B. Kampen, 662:Fall88/Winter89-45
  M. Keller, 290(JAAC):Summer88-531
  S. Lennox, 221(GQ):Winter88-115
Eckert, G. Sprachtypus und Geschichte.*
  L. Löfstedt, 439(NM):1988/2-223
Eckert, R., E. Crome & C. Fleckenstein. Geschichte der russischen Sprache.
  A. Sjöberg, 559:Vol12No1-82
Eckhardt, F. Music from Within.
  H. Kallmann, 102(CanL):Winter87-267
Meister Eckhart. L'Oeuvre Latine de Maître Eckhart. (Vol 1) (F. Brunner & others, eds) Oeuvres (Sermons, Traités).
  F.F. Nef, 98:Oct88-811
Eckstein, A.M. Senate and General.*
  H.C. Boren, 124:Jan-Feb89-201
  S.P. Oakley, 24:Winter88-611
  J.W. Rich, 123:Vol38No2-315
Eckstut, S. & T. Miller. Interlink 1. Interlink 2.
  E. Fischer-Kohn, 399(MLJ):Autumn88-348
Eco, U. Art and Beauty in the Middle Ages.*
  M. Mothersill, 290(JAAC):Winter87-311
  A.V.C.S., 382(MAE):1988/2-291
Eco, U. Foucault's Pendulum. (Italian title: Il pendolo di Foucault.)
  R. Adams, 453(NYRB):9Nov89-3
  A. Burgess, 441:15Oct89-1
  A. Stille, 61:Nov89-125
  C. Vita-Finzi, 617(TLS):3-9Mar89-225
  C. Vita-Finzi, 617(TLS):17-23Nov89-1272
Eco, U. The Open Work.
  C. Vita-Finzi, 617(TLS):17-23Nov89-1272
Eco, U. Travels in Hyperreality.* (W. Weaver, ed & trans)
  S. Slemon, 102(CanL):Spring88-122
Eco, U. & T.A. Sebeok, eds. The Sign of Three.
  M. Shepherd, 567:Vol68No1/2-155
Eddy, P., with H. Sabogal & S. Walden. The Cocaine Wars.*
  M. Massing, 453(NYRB):30Mar89-22
Edel, D. Helden auf Freiersfüssen.
  T. Ó Cathasaigh, 112:Vol20-169

105

Edel, L. Henry James.
  W.W. Stowe, 534(RALS):Vol16No1&2-131
Edel, L. - see James, H.
Edel, L. & L.H. Powers - see James, H.
Edel, L. & A.R. Tintner, eds. The Library of
Henry James.*
  J. Auchard, 177(ELT):Vol31No3-349
  P. Buitenhuis, 106:Fall88-325
  R.L. Gale, 26(ALR):Fall88-80
Edel, L., with M. Wilson - see James, H.
Edelberg, C.D. Jonathan Odell.*
  R.D. Arner, 27(AL):May88-293
Edelman, B. The House that Kant Built.*
(French title: La maison de Kant, conte
moral.)
  R. George, 627(UTQ):Fall88-219
  L.A. Mulholland, 154:Summer88-375
Edelman, G.M. Topobiology.
  R.C. Lewontin, 453(NYRB):27Apr89-18
  N.C. Spitzer, 441:22Jan89-12
Edelman, L. Transmemberment of Song.
  M. Dickie, 27(AL):Oct88-507
Edelsky, C. Writing in a Bilingual Program.
  M. Brisk, 608:Sep89-536
Edelson, M. Psychoanalysis.
  B. Farrell, 617(TLS):15-21Sep89-1009
  R.S. Wallerstein, 441:26Feb89-36
Edelson, M. - see Brandys, K.
Edelstein, L. & I.G. Kidd - see "Posidonius"
Eden, K. Poetic and Legal Fiction in the Ar-
istotelian Tradition.*
  D.G. Marshall, 481(PQ):Spring88-262
  P. Mitsis, 124:Sep-Oct88-74
Eder, J.F. On the Road to Tribal Extinction.
  M.D. Zamora, 293(JASt):Nov88-935
Edey, M.A. & D.C. Johanson. Blueprints.
  R. Dawkins, 441:9Apr89-34
Edgerton, H. Stopping Time.
  J. Sturman, 55:Feb88-52
Edgeworth, M. Patronage.
  J. Wheare, 447(N&Q):Jun88-248
Edie, J.M. William James and Phenomenol-
ogy.*
  R. Cobb-Stevens, 619:Summer88-436
  G.E. Myers, 484(PPR):Mar89-538
Edison, T.A. The Papers of Thomas A. Edison.
(Vol 1) (R.V. Jenkins & others, eds)
  D. Joravsky, 453(NYRB):7Dec89-11
  R. McCormmach, 441:16Jul89-13
  S. Schaffer, 617(TLS):29Sep-5Oct89-
  1047
"Les Éditeurs belges de Victor Hugo et le
Banquet des "Misérables.""*
  S. Gaudon, 535(RHL):Mar-Apr88-305
Edmiston, W.F. Diderot and the Family.*
  R. Buisine & J-M. Dolle, 535(RHL):Mar-
  Apr88-276
  L. Perol, 530:Apr88-167
Edmond, L. Seasons and Creatures.
  D. McDuff, 565:Spring88-64
  B. O'Donoghue, 493:Spring88-34
Edmond, L. Selected Poems.
  R. Pybus, 565:Summer88-72
Edmond, L. Summer Near the Arctic Circle.
  L. Mackinnon, 617(TLS):26May-1Jun89-
  593
Edmonson, M.S., ed & trans. Heaven Born
Mérida and Its Destiny.*
  W.F. Hanks, 269(IJAL):Jul88-331
Edmunds, J.B., Jr. Francis W. Pickens and the
Politics of Destruction.
  J.T. O'Brien, 106:Fall88-339

Edmunds, L. Cleon, "Knights," and Aristoph-
anes' Politics.
  D.M. Macdowell, 123:Vol38No2-215
  S.D. Olson, 124:Jul-Aug89-453
Edmunds, L. Oedipus.
  V. Bers, 124:Sep-Oct88-49
  S. Hobbs, 203:Vol99No2-258
Edmunds, L. & A. Dundes, eds. Oedipus.*
  S. Hobbs, 203:Vol99No2-258
Edmundson, B. Two Voices.
  M.A. Jarman, 376:Mar88-91
Edson, L. Henri Michaux and the Poetics of
Movement.*
  H. Merkl, 72:Band225Heft1-214
  C. Rigolot, 207(FR):Dec88-344
  S. Winspur, 546(RR):Nov88-688
Edson, R. The Wounded Breakfast.
  S. Birkerts, 472:Vol15No1-163
Edwards, A.S.G., ed. Middle English Prose.*
  G.C. Britton, 447(N&Q):Sep88-350
Edwards, A.T. Achilles in the "Odyssey."*
  D. Arnould, 555:Vol61fasc1-113
  D. Sinos, 24:Spring88-133
Edwards, D. Neale Pottery and Porcelain.
  G. Blake-Roberts, 39:Sep88-218
Edwards, E.W. British Diplomacy and Finance
in China, 1895-1914.
  J.A. Thompson, 637(VS):Winter89-271
Edwards, G. - see Tirso de Molina
Edwards, J. Language, Society and Identity.
  M.G. Clyne, 355(LSoc):Mar88-103
Edwards, J. Positive Discrimination, Social
Justice, and Social Policy.*
  B. Shaw, 291:Vol5No2-235
Edwards, L.M., with J.S. Ramirez & T.A. Bur-
gard. Domestic Bliss.*
  662:Spring/Summer88-50
Edwards, M. Poetry and Possibility.
  J. Bayley, 617(TLS):24Feb-2Mar89-201
Edwards, M.W. Homer, Poet of the "Iliad."*
  M.E. Reesor, 529(QQ):Summer88-443
  J.E. Rexine, 124:Sep-Oct88-56
  M.M. Willcock, 123:Vol38No2-201
Edwards, P. Heidegger und der Tod.
  N. Hoerster, 167:Jan88-135
Edwards, P. The Horse Trade of Tudor and
Stuart England.
  P. Clark, 617(TLS):20-26Jan89-63
Edwards, P. Shakespeare.*
  G.K. Hunter, 402(MLR):Jan89-121
Edwards, R. Life before Birth.
  J. Godfrey, 617(TLS):3-9Nov89-1202
van Eeden, W. Invățături preste toate zilele
(1642).
  K-H. Schroeder, 72:Band224Heft2-445
Eekelaar, J.M. & D. Pearl, eds. An Aging
World.
  P. Willmott, 617(TLS):29Dec89/4Jan90-
  1431
Effe, B., ed. Theokrit und die griechische
Bukolik.
  M. Jakob, 52:Band23Heft2-176
van Effen, J. Le Misanthrope. (J.L. Schorr,
ed)
  D.J. Culpin, 402(MLR):Jan89-171
Egan, M.D. Architectural Acoustics.
  F. Wilson, 47:Oct88-46
Egan, P. - see Hulten, P., N. Dumitresco & A.
Istrati
Eggebrecht, H.E. & others. Die mittelalter-
liche Lehre von der Mehrstimmigkeit.
  M. Everist, 410(M&L):Jan88-57
  L.A. Rothfarb, 308:Spring88-133

Eggers, D. & J.N. Hardin – see Gryphius, C.
Eggers Lan, C. & V.E. Juliá, eds & trans. Los filósofos presocráticos. (Vol 1)
R. Torrotti, 160:Jan88–221
Eggleston, W. The Democratic Forest.
A. Grundberg, 441:3Dec89–20
Egnal, M. A Mighty Empire.
639(VQR):Autumn88–115
Egorov, S.F. & others, eds. Antologiia pedagogicheskoi mysli Drevnei Rusi i Russkogo gosudarstva XIV–XVII vv.
M.J. Okenfuss, 550(RusR):Oct88–445
Egremont, M. Painted Lives.
T. Glyde, 617(TLS):18–24Aug89–901
Egri, P. Chekhov and O'Neill.*
V.K., 295(JML):Fall87/Winter88–364
Ehle, J. The Widow's Trial.
R. Fuller, 441:15Oct89–50
Ehlers, W–W. G. Valerius Flaccus Setinus Balbus, Argonautica.
A.J. Kleywegt, 394:Vol41fasc1/2–202
Ehlich, K. Interjektionen.
J. Paternost, 215(GL):Vol28No3–228
Ehre, M. Isaac Babel.*
T.W. Clyman, 574(SEEJ):Summer88–327
J. Grayson, 575(SEER):Apr88–277
C. Rougle, 550(RusR):Apr88–228
Ehrenberg, M. Women in Prehistory.
J. Clutton–Brock, 617(TLS):13–19Oct89–1126
Ehrenreich, B. Fear of Falling.
J. Morley, 441:6Aug89–12
442(NY):4Sep89–107
Ehrhardt, S. & others. New Chatto Poets: Number 2.
B. O'Donoghue, 617(TLS):1–7Dec89–1336
Ehrich, V. & H. Vater, eds. Temporalsemantik.
B. Comrie, 350:Dec89–885
Ehrismann, O. "Nibelungenlied."
A. Classen, 221(GQ):Fall88–568
M.E. Gibbs, 406:Winter88–502
Ehrlich, C. Harmonious Alliance.
R. Davenport–Hines, 617(TLS):10–16Feb89–130
Ehrlich, J.R. & B.J. Rehfeld. The New Crowd.
R. Rosenbaum, 441:29Oct89–34
Ehrman, E. Mme du Châtelet.*
C.J. Betts, 208(FS):Jul88–345
G. May, 77:Winter88–85
Eichholz, B. Kommentar zur Sigune– und Ither–Szene im 3. Buch von Wolframs "Parzival" (138,9–161,8).
D.H. Green, 402(MLR):Apr89–516
Eichler, E. & H. Walther. Städtnamenbuch der DDR.
W.F.H. Nicolaisen, 424:Sep–Dec88–239
Eichmann, R. & J. Du Val, eds & trans. The French Fabliau, B.N. MS 837.* (Vol 2)
B.J. Levy, 382(MAE):1988/1–131
J. Tattersall, 208(FS):Jan88–70
Eickel, N., ed. Russia, The Land, The People.
C. Lodder, 575(SEER):Jul88–469
Eidlin, F., ed. Constitutional Democracy.
W.T. Bluhm, 488:Sep88–409
Eigeldinger, F.S., ed. Table de concordances rythmique et syntaxique des "Illuminations" d'Arthur Rimbaud.
C.A. Hackett, 208(FS):Jan88–101
Eigeldinger, J–J. Chopin. (R. Howat, ed)
W. Hughes, 510:Spring88–60
Eigeldinger, M. Mythologie et intertextualité.
I. Piette, 356(LR):Feb–May88–114

"Eighteenth–Century Ireland/Iris an dá chultúr."* (Vol 1)(A. Carpenter, ed)
S. Gilley, 83:Spring88–75
Eigner, E.M. The Dickens Pantomime.
F.S. Schwarzbach, 617(TLS):3–9Nov89–1214
Einbein, E. & R. Jones. Manners and Morals.
T. Murdoch, 59:Dec88–581
Eisenberg, D. A Study of "Don Quixote."*
E.H. Friedman, 238:Dec88–822
Eisenberg, P. Grundriss der deutschen Grammatik.
P. Suchsland, 682(ZPSK):Band41Heft2–245
Eisenbichler, K. & O.Z. Pugliese, eds. Ficino and Renaissance Neoplatonism.
L.V.R., 568(SCN):Spring–Summer88–33
Eisenhower, J.S.D. So Far From God.
S.W. Sears, 441:2Apr89–13
Eisenman, P. Houses of Cards.
T. Fisher, 505:Feb88–149
H. Muschamp, 139:Jun/Jul88–21
Eisenstadt, J. From Rockaway.
J. Saari, 42(AR):Winter88–116
Eisenstadt, S.N., ed. Patterns of Modernity.* (Vol 2) [entry in prev is of Vols 1 & 2]
C.E. Black, 293(JASt):Aug88–568
Eisenstein, S. Nonindifferent Nature.* Immoral Memories.
L. Anderson, 617(TLS):31Mar–6Apr89–337
Eisenstein, S.M. Selected Works. (Vol 1) (R. Taylor, ed & trans)
D. Robinson, 707:Spring88–140
Eismann, W. – see Ivanov, V.V.
Eismann, W. & P. Grzybek. Semiotische Studien zum Rätsel.
A. Schwarz, 196:Band29Heft1/2–185
Eisner, M. Zur Typologie der Grabbauten im Suburbium Roms.
G. Davies, 123:Vol38No2–359
Eisner, R. The Road to Daulis.
S. Goldhill, 123:Vol38No1–75
L.J. Parker, 124:Jan–Feb89–215
Ekeland, I. Mathematics and the Unexpected.*
42(AR):Fall88–529
Eklof, B. Russian Peasant Schools.
M.J. Okenfuss, 550(RusR):Jul88–334
Ekman, P., with M.A.M. & T. Ekman. Why Kids Lie.
C. Samuels, 441:26Nov89–27
Ekstein, N.C. Dramatic Narrative.
P. Desan, 207(FR):Mar89–682
L.A. Gregorio, 494:Vol8No3/4–726
R. Howells, 402(MLR):Jan89–167
R.W. Tobin, 475:Vol15No28–286
Eksteins, M. Rites of Spring.
P. Fussell, 61:Mar89–94
J. Joll, 453(NYRB):27Apr89–53
L. McDiarmid, 441:23Jul89–24
Elam, K., ed. La grande festa del linguaggio.
R. Ceserani, 494:Vol8No1–202
Elam, K. Shakespeare's Universe of Discourse.*
K. Bartenschlager, 38:Band106Heft3/4–534
Elbaz, R. The Changing Nature of Self.
P. Grosskurth, 627(UTQ):Spring89–422
von Elbe, J. Witness to History.
K.E. Meyer, 441:10Dec89–33
Elbert, S. A Hunger for Home.
K.B. Meyers, 357:Fall88–68

Elbert, S.H. Echo of a Culture.
  M. Kana, 350:Dec89-886
Elbow, P. Embracing Contraries.
  B. Hilbert, 126(CCC):Dec88-480
Elder, J. Imagining the Earth.*
  E.D. Mackerness, 447(N&Q):Jun88-274
Elderfield, J. Frankenthaler.
  J. Russell, 441:11Jun89-56
Elders, L. Autour de Saint Thomas d'Aquin.
  E. de Jong, 543:Sep88-137
El Din, M.S. & J. Rodenbeck - see Mahfouz, N.
Elejabeitia, A. - see de Zabaleta, J.
Elgar, E. Elgar and His Publishers. (J.N.
  Moore, ed)
  R. Anderson, 415:Feb88-79
  M. Kennedy, 410(M&L):Oct88-551
  D. Mitchell, 617(TLS):26May-1Jun89-587
  M. Smith, 607:Sep88-61
Elgar, E. Edward Elgar, The Windflower Let-
  ters. (J.N. Moore, ed)
  D. Mitchell, 617(TLS):26May-1Jun89-587
Elgin, C.Z. With Reference to Reference.
  O.R. Scholz, 687:Apr-Jun88-336
Eliade, M. Autobiography. (Vol 2)
  R. Irwin, 441:5Mar89-24
  N. Malcolm, 617(TLS):10-16Feb89-137
Eliade, M. Youth Without Youth and Other
  Novellas. (M. Calinescu, ed)
  R. Irwin, 441:5Mar89-24
Elías-Olivares, L. & others, eds. Spanish
  Language Use and Public Life in the USA.*
  S. Sotillo, 355(LSoc):Jun88-272
Eliav, A.L. New Heart, New Spirit.
  A. Knopf, 441:7May89-25
Elie, M. - see Schopenhauer, A.
Eliot, G. Daniel Deronda.* (G. Handley, ed)
  Scenes of Clerical Life.* (T.A. Noble, ed)
  Felix Holt the Radical. (F.C. Thomson, ed)
  P. Shillingsburg, 301(JEGP):Jul88-456
Eliot, G. Middlemarch.* (D. Carroll, ed)
  R. Ashton, 541(RES):Feb88-138
  A.W. Bellringer, 179(ES):Feb88-89
  K.M. Hewitt, 447(N&Q):Mar88-111
  A. Jumeau, 189(EA):Oct-Dec88-489
  S. Shatto, 445(NCF):Sep88-255
  P. Shillingsburg, 301(JEGP):Jul88-456
Eliot, T.S. The Letters of T.S. Eliot.* (Vol 1)
  (V. Eliot, ed)
  S. Helmling, 344:Summer89-153
  P. Levi, 493:Winter88/89-4
  H. Lomas, 364:Feb/Mar89-118
  J. Olney, 598(SoR):Spring89-503
Elisseeff, D. Moi Arcade interprète chinois
  du Roi-Soleil.
  M. Détrie, 549(RLC):Jan-Mar88-68
Elkana, Y. Anthropologie der Erkenntnis.
  W. Kutschmann, 687:Jul-Sep88-489
Elkin, S. The Rabbi of Lud.
  L. Lemon, 502(PrS):Fall88-132
  N. Teitel, 390:Jan88-61
Elkin, S.L. City and Regime in the American
  Republic.
  I.K., 185:Jul89-982
Elkins, A. Curses!
  M. Stasio, 441:2Apr89-33
Elling, B., ed. Kafka-Studien.
  P.F. Dvorak, 221(GQ):Summer87-492
Elliot, V. - see Shaw, G.B.
Elliott, B.S. Irish Migrants in the Canadas.
  P. Brode, 174(Éire):Summer88-157
Elliott, D. New Worlds.*
  C. Lodder, 575(SEER):Jul88-469

Elliott, E. & others, eds. Columbia Literary
  History of the United States.*
  J.D. Bloom, 534(RALS):Vol16No1&2-1
  G. Gunn, 676(YR):Autumn88-119
  P.F. Gura, 27(AL):Oct88-461
  S. Pinsker, 219(GaR):Summer88-402
  T. Wortham, 445(NCF):Dec88-417
Elliott, G. Althusser.*
  M. Sprinker, 400(MLN):Dec88-1151
Elliott, J. Life On The Nile.
  L. Duguid, 617(TLS):31Mar-6Apr89-344
Elliott, J.H. The Count-Duke of Olivares.
  F.A. de Armas, 238:Sep88-547
  H. Nader, 551(RenQ):Autumn88-494
  R.A. Stradling, 86(BHS):Oct88-409
Elliott, J.H. Richelieu and Olivares.
  R.A. Stradling, 86(BHS):Oct88-408
Elliott, J.H. Spain and Its World 1500-1700.
  J. Lynch, 617(TLS):7-13Apr89-359
Elliott, M. Partners in Revolution.
  J.F. McMillan, 617(TLS):21-27Jul89-792
Elliott, M. Wolfe Tone.
  A. Macintyre, 617(TLS):27Oct-2Nov89-
  1174
Elliott, R.W.V. Runes.
  J.T. Hooker, 617(TLS):17-23Nov89-1264
Ellis, A., ed. Ethics and International Rela-
  tions.*
  B. Almond, 483:Jan88-130
Ellis, A.T. The Fly in the Ointment.
  P. Craig, 617(TLS):10-16Nov89-1243
Ellis, B.E. The Rules of Attraction.*
  639(VQR):Winter88-22
Ellis, C.G. Oriental Carpets in the Philadel-
  phia Museum of Art.
  M. Straub, 324:Apr89-317
Ellis, D. Wordsworth, Freud, and the Spots of
  Time.*
  T.R. Frosch, 591(SIR):Spring88-134
Ellis, F.H., ed. Swift vs. Mainwaring.*
  J. Black, 447(N&Q):Mar88-95
  H-J. Müllenbrock, 38:Band106Heft1/2-
  246
Ellis, J. The Russian Orthodox Church.
  P. Valliere, 550(RusR):Jan88-94
Ellis, J.M. Against Deconstruction.
  M. Walters, 617(TLS):22-28Dec89-1419
Ellis, R. India by Rail.
  D. Murphy, 617(TLS):8-14Dec89-1370
Ellis, R. Patterns of Religious Narrative in
  the "Canterbury Tales."*
  H. Cooper, 541(RES):Feb88-102
  T. Lawler, 402(MLR):Jul89-708
  H.L. Spencer, 382(MAE):1988/1-106
Ellis, S. The Baby Project.
  M. Steig, 102(CanL):Spring88-236
Ellis, S. Home And Away.*
  J. Forth, 364:Nov87-85
Ellis, T. Platitudes.
  D.J. Austin, 441:19Feb89-20
  442(NY):13Feb89-93
Ellis, W.M. Alcibiades.
  P. Millett, 617(TLS):10-16Nov89-1237
Ellison, H. Angry Candy.
  G. Jonas, 441:8Jan89-31
Ellison, H. Harlan Ellison's Watching.
  R.F. Moss, 441:17Sep89-12
Ellison, H.J., ed. Japan and the Pacific Qua-
  drille.
  E.A. Olsen, 293(JASt):Nov88-886
Ellison, K. Imelda.
  C.R. Herron, 441:8Jan89-23

Ellmann, L. Sweet Desserts.*
    D. Finkle, 441:2Jul89-12
Ellmann, M. The Poetics of Impersonality.*
    J. Kronick, 598(SoR):Autumn89-859
    W. Pratt, 27(AL):Dec88-690
    42(AR):Spring88-273
    639(VQR):Summer88-82
Ellmann, R. Samuel Beckett.*
    M.B., 295(JML):Fall87/Winter88-293
Ellmann, R. Four Dubliners.*
    R.M. Kain, 329(JJQ):Winter89-303
    R.B. Kershner, Jr., 219(GaR):Fall88-617
Ellmann, R. a long the riverrun.*
    A. Goreau, 441:19Mar89-21
    W. Scammell, 364:Oct/Nov88-122
Ellmann, R. Oscar Wilde.*
    M. Baron, 175:Spring88-85
    S. Bick, 42(AR):Fall88-527
    J.H. Buckley, 536(Rev):Vol10-51
    T. Eldeman, 305(JIL):Jan88-57
    I. Fletcher, 177(ELT):Vol31No3-309
    M.P. Gillespie, 594:Fall88-343
    R.B. Kershner, Jr., 219(GaR):Fall88-617
    D. Mills, 157:No167-49
    A. Rogers, 324:Dec88-65
    A. Shelley, 184(EIC):Apr88-156
    P.E. Smith 2d, 637(VS):Spring89-459
Ellowitch, A. Tell Me About It.
    E. Auerbach, 608:Jun89-327
Ellsberg, M.R. Created to Praise.*
    P.E. Mitchell, 177(ELT):Vol31No3-361
Ellsworth, R.H. Later Chinese Painting and
    Calligraphy 1800-1950.*
    P.C. Swann, 463:Summer88-140
Ellul, J. The Humiliation of the Word.
    D. Lovekin, 480(P&R):Vol21No1-65
Elman, B.A. From Philosophy to Philology.*
    S.W. Durrant, 318(JAOS):Apr-Jun87-346
Elmer, W. Diachronic Grammar.
    A. Lutz, 38:Band106Heft3/4-466
Elon, A. Jerusalem.
    P. Grose, 441:1Oct89-9
    442(NY):20Nov89-156
El Saadawi, N. The Circling Song.
    S. Roe, 617(TLS):22-28Dec89-1421
El Saadawi, N. The Fall of the Imam.*
    J. Mellors, 364:Aug/Sep88-135
El Saadawi, N. Memoirs of a Woman Doctor.
    J. Mellors, 364:Aug/Sep88-135
El Saffar, R., ed. Critical Essays on Cervan-
    tes.*
    F. Domínguez, 241:May88-85
    F. Pierce, 402(MLR):Jan89-206
Else, G.F. Plato and Aristotle on Poetry. (P.
    Burian, ed)
    A. Ford, 124:Jul-Aug89-460
    F. Sparshott, 478(P&L):Oct88-298
Elshtain, J.B. Women and War.*
    S. Kress, 560:Fall88-227
Elster, J. An Introduction to Karl Marx.*
    S. James, 483:Oct88-545
Elster, J., ed. The Multiple Self.*
    P. Brockelman, 125:Spring88-294
Elster, J. & G. Hernes - see Coleman, J.S.
Elster, J. & A. Hylland, eds. Foundations of
    Social Choice Theory.*
    P. Shaw, 518:Apr88-126
Eltis, W. & P. Sinclair, eds. Keynes and Eco-
    nomic Policy.
    D.E. Moggridge, 617(TLS):9-15Jun89-632
Elton, B. Stark.
    R. Kaveney, 617(TLS):14-20Apr89-404

Elton, G.R. F.W. Maitland.
    R. Brentano, 589:Jan88-151
Elvers, R. - see Mendelssohn, F.
Elwood, D.J. Philippine Revolution 1986.
    V.L. Rafael, 293(JASt):May88-411
Elytis, O. The Little Mariner.
    639(VQR):Autumn88-134
Embree, A.T. - see "Encyclopedia of Asian
    History"
Embree, B. No Wild Dog Howled.
    S. Preston, 649(WAL):Aug88-183
van Emden, J. The Metaphysical Poets.
    G. Hammond, 402(MLR):Jan89-124
Emeljanow, V. Victorian Popular Dramatists.*
    M.R. Booth, 677(YES):Vol19-344
Emenyonu, E., ed. Essential Ekwensi.
    Ezenwa-Ohaeto, 538(RAL):Fall88-411
Emenyonu, E.N., ed. English and the Nigerian
    Situation.
    I. Hancock, 538(RAL):Fall88-420
Emerson, C. Boris Godunov.
    E. Garden, 410(M&L):Jan88-90
    S. Golub, 615(TJ):Dec88-578
    H. McLean, 131(CL):Summer88-299
    G. McVay, 575(SEER):Jan88-121
Emerson, C. - see Bakhtin, M.M./P.N. Med-
    vedev
Emerson, C. & M. Holquist - see Bakhtin, M.M.
Emerson, L.J. The Selected Letters of Lidian
    Jackson Emerson. (D.B. Carpenter, ed)
    R.D. Habich, 432(NEQ):Jun88-290
    L.C. Johnson, 27(AL):Mar88-119
Emerson, R.W. The Poetry Notebooks of Ralph
    Waldo Emerson.* (R.H. Orth & others, eds)
    R.M. Aderman, 534(RALS):Vol16No1&2-81
Emery, K., Jr. Renaissance Dialectic and
    Renaissance Poetry.
    R. Bocnig, 668(SCN):Winter88-75
Émile-Zola, F. - see Zola, E.
Emin, G. For You on New Year's Day.
    D. McDuff, 565:Spring88-64
Emlen, R.P. Shaker Village Views.
    R.L. Emerson, 106:Fall88-369
Emmerson, S., ed. The Language of Electro-
    acoustic Music.
    J. Harrison, 410(M&L):Apr88-296
    A. MacDonald, 415:Jun88-303
Emmons, T. - see Got'e, I.V.
Emmott, R. The Sun Also Sets.
    J. Dreyfuss, 441:29Oct89-35
Empson, W. Argufying.* The Royal Beasts
    and Other Works. (J. Haffenden, ed of
    both)
    T. Miller, 400(MLN):Dec88-1155
Empson, W. Essays on Shakespeare.* (D.B.
    Pirie, ed)
    R. Gill, 447(N&Q):Dec88-528
    M. Grivelet, 189(EA):Oct-Dec88-482
    M. Lomax, 366:Spring88-117
    H.F. Plett, 156(ShJW):Jahrbuch1988-294
del Encina, J. Teatro y poesía. (S. Zimic, ed)
    A.M. Rambaldo, 240(HR):Winter88-101
    R. Surtz, 86(BHS):Jul88-297
Enckell, P. - see Quemada, B.
"Encyclopedia of Asian History." (A.T.
    Embree & others, eds)
    H. Conroy & S.C. Ushioda, 293(JASt):
    Nov88-837
Endicott, S. Red Earth.
    J. Mirsky, 617(TLS):13-19Jan89-31
Endō, S. Foreign Studies.
    L. Allen, 617(TLS):28Apr-4May89-466

Endō, S. Scandal.*
  B. Leithauser, 442(NY):6Mar89-107
  J. Mellors, 364:Apr/May88-133
Endres, R. Am Anfang war die Stimme.
  K. Schoell, 72:Band224Heft2-454
Engberg-Pedersen, T. Aristotle's Theory of
  Moral Insight.
  R. Hursthouse, 466:Vol6-201
Engdahl, E. Constituent Questions.
  F. Kiefer, 297(JL):Sep88-566
Engdahl, H. Den romantiska texten.
  A. Melberg, 172(Edda):1988/2-180
Engel, A. Variant.
  N. Callendar, 441:19Mar89-29
Engel, D. In the Shadow of Auschwitz.
  N. Pease, 497(PolR):Vol33No3-347
Engel, D.H. Creating a Chinese Garden.
  S. Markbreiter, 60:Jan-Feb88-129
Engel, H. A City Called July.
  R.W. Harvey, 102(CanL):Winter87-214
Engel, H. A Victim Must Be Found.*
  T.J. Binyon, 617(TLS):20-26Jan89-70
Engel, J. Addicted.
  L.B. Schorr, 441:27Aug89-7
Engel, M. Rilkes "Duineser Elegien" und die
  moderne Lyrik.
  B. Maché, 406:Winter88-520
Engel, P. Identité et référence.*
  F. Clementz, 540(RIPh):Vol42fasc1-101
Engel, P. La Norme du Vrai.
  L.J. Cohen, 617(TLS):15-21Sep89-1010
Engel, U. Deutsche Grammatik.
  D. Nehls, 257(IRAL):Aug88-249
Engel, U. & P. Mrazović, eds. Kontrastive
  Grammatik Deutsch-Serbokroatisch.
  W. & H. Fleischer, 682(ZPSK):Band41
  Heft2-253
Engel-Braunschmidt, A. & C. Heithus. Biblio-
  graphie der sowjetdeutschen Literatur
  1960-1985.
  P. Bruhn, 688(ZSP):Band48Heft2-415
Engelhard, J. Indecent Proposal.
  B. Raskin, 441:19Mar89-17
Engelhardt, H.T., Jr. The Foundations of
  Bioethics.*
  J. Harris, 482(PhR):Jul88-440
  H. Upton, 518:Apr88-99
Engelkamp, J., ed. Psychologische Aspekte
  des Verstehens.
  U. Nitsche, 682(ZPSK):Band41Heft1-119
Engelmann, B. In Hitler's Germany.*
  E. Kurzweil, 473(PR):Vol55No1-143
  A.J. Nicholls, 364:Mar88-88
Engels, J. Cardinals in the Ice Age.
  455:Mar88-72
Engfors, C., ed. Lectures and Briefings from
  the International Symposium on the Archi-
  tecture of Erik Gunnar Asplund.
  W.C. Miller, 576:Jun88-206
Engh, M.J. Wheel of the Winds.
  G. Jonas, 441:8Jan89-31
Engineer, A.A., ed. The Shah Bano Contro-
  versy.
  G. Minault, 293(JASt):Nov88-814
Englebretsen, G., ed. The New Syllogistic.
  V. Balowitz, 103:Dec88-481
Engler, E. Lehrbuch des brasilianischen Por-
  tugiesisch.
  D. Woll, 72:Band225Heft2-461
Engler, R. Bibliographie saussurienne, 4.
  P. Swiggers, 553(RLiR):Jul-Dec88-488

Englert, W.G. Epicurus on the Swerve and
  Voluntary Action.
  T.J. Saunders, 123:Vol38No2-284
"English Poets: British Academy Chatterton
  Lectures."
  M. Ford, 617(TLS):21-27Jul89-807
Enklaar, J. & P. Küpper, eds. Kafka-Kollo-
  quium: Utrecht, Mai 1984.*
  M. Harman, 133:Band21Heft2/3-246
Enninger, W., ed. Studies on the Languages
  and the Verbal Behavior of the Pennsyl-
  vania Germans I.
  P.T. Roberge, 685(ZDL):3/1988-356
Ennius. The "Annals" of Quintus Ennius.*
  (O. Skutsch, ed)
  S.M. Goldberg, 121(CJ):Oct-Nov88-59
  J.K. Newman, 24:Fall88-431
  D.O. Ross, Jr., 122:Jul88-251
Enos, J.L. & W.H. Park. The Adoption and
  Diffusion of Imported Technology.
  L.E. Westphal, 293(JASt):Nov88-906
Enrico, H. Rip Current.
  B. Pell, 102(CanL):Autumn88-171
Enright, A. & others. First Fictions: Intro-
  duction 10.
  P. Magrath, 617(TLS):17-23Feb89-170
Enright, D.J. The Alluring Problem.
  F. McCombie, 447(N&Q):Jun88-271
  P. Rogers, 31(ASch):Summer88-466
Enright, D.J., ed. The Faber Book of Fevers
  and Frets.
  R. Porter, 617(TLS):8-14Dec89-1367
Enros, P.C., comp. Biobibliography of Pub-
  lishing Scientists in Ontario between 1914
  and 1939.
  B.H. MacDonald, 470:Vol26-173
Ensslen, K. Einführung in die schwarz-
  amerikanische Literatur.
  E. Kreutzer, 72:Band225Heft2-420
Enzensberger, H.M. Europe, Europe.*
  (German title: Ach Europa!)
  N. Ascherson, 453(NYRB):28Sep89-13
  H.S. Hughes, 441:4Jun89-13
Eph'al, I. The Ancient Arabs.
  G. Frame, 318(JAOS):Jan-Mar87-130
Epp, R.H., ed. Spindel Conference 1984: Re-
  covering the Stoics.
  G.B. Kerferd, 41:Spring88-134
Eprile, T. Temporary Sojourner.
  H. Rochman, 441:20Aug89-19
Epstein, D. Beyond Orpheus.
  V.K. Agawu, 410(M&L):Jul88-407
Epstein, D.F. Personal Enmity in Roman Poli-
  tics, 218-43 B.C.*
  D. Nightingale, 123:Vol38No2-319
Epstein, E.J. Deception.
  J. Bamford, 441:7May89-30
  T. Powers, 453(NYRB):17Aug89-40
Epstein, J. Once More around the Block.
  S. Pinsker, 639(VQR):Spring88-342
Epstein, J. Partial Payments.
  T.J. Binyon, 617(TLS):13-19Oct89-1134
  J. Bloom, 441:12Mar89-23
Epstein, J. Remembering Charlie.
  R. Lippincott, 441:28May89-19
Epstein, S. Light.
  M. Giles, 441:8Oct89-19
Epstein, W.H. Recognizing Biography.
  J.W. Crowley, 177(ELT):Vol31No4-461
  M. Seymour-Smith, 617(TLS):27Jan-
  2Feb89-92

Esteva Fabregat, C. El mestizaje en Ibero-
américa.
  L.M. Díaz Soler, 263(RIB):Vol38No3-400
Estève, M., ed. Études bernanosiennes 16.
  M. Watthee-Delmotte, 356(LR):Nov88-517
Estève, M., ed. Études bernanosiennes 17.
  M. Watthee-Delmotte, 356(LR):Nov88-518
Estève, M., ed. Études bernanosiennes 18.
  M. Watthee-Delmotte, 356(LR):Nov88-523
Estévez, M.V. - see under Vázquez Estévez,
  M.
Esthus, R.A. Double Eagle and Rising Sun.
  I. Nish, 293(JASt):Nov88-887
  R.B. Valliant, 407(MN):Autumn88-377
Estleman, L.D. General Murders.
  E. Stumpf, 441:29Jan89-34
Estleman, L.D. Peeper.
  G.A. Effinger, 441:15Oct89-45
Estleman, L.D. Silent Thunder.
  T.J.B., 617(TLS):8-14Sep89-969
  M. Stasio, 441:16Apr89-31
Estrada, E.M. - see under Martínez Estrada,
  E.
Estrich, S. Real Rape.
  M.E. Becker, 185:Jan89-443
Etherington-Smith, M. & J. Pilcher. The "It"
  Girls.
  639(VQR):Spring88-51
Etiemble, ed. Romanciers du XVIIIe siècle.
  (Vol 1)
  D. Coward, 617(TLS):6-12Jan89-14
Étienne, M. La Face et le lointain.
  M-N. Little, 207(FR):Feb89-547
Etienne, M-F. Gérard de Nerval.
  S. Carpenter, 207(FR):Dec88-335
  N. Rinsler, 402(MLR):Jan89-179
Étienvre, J-P. Figures de jeu.
  E. Martinell, 548:Jul-Dec88-435
Etter, A. Die Fragesätze im Ṛgveda.
  S. Migron, 259(IIJ):Jul88-220
  D. Weber, 260(IF):Band93-295
Ettin, A.V. Literature and the Pastoral.
  S. Chaudhuri, 447(N&Q):Mar88-76
  M. Jakob, 52:Band23Heft1-99
Ettinger, E. Kindergarten.
  M. Halahmy, 617(TLS):10-16Feb89-148
Ettinghausen, R. & O. Grabar. The Art and
  Architecture of Islam: 650-1250.
  B. Gray, 90:Mar88-231
Ettinghausen, R. & E. Yarshater, eds. High-
  lights of Persian Art.
  L. Komaroff, 318(JAOS):Jan-Mar87-193
"Études Historiques Hongroises 1985."
  L. Péter, 575(SEER):Jan88-144
"Études littéraires sur le XVe siècle." (Vol 3)
  J. Britnell, 208(FS):Apr88-201
Euclid. The First Latin Translation of
  Euclid's "Elements" Commonly Ascribed to
  Adelard of Bath. (H.L.L. Busard, ed)
  D. Edwards, 41:Vol7-261
Euripides. Euripides' "Kresphontes" and
  "Archelaos." (A. Harder, ed)
  J. Wilkins, 123:Vol38No2-209
Euripides. Euripidis Fabulae. (Vol 1) (J.
  Diggle, ed)
  D.J. Mastronarde, 122:Apr88-151
Euripides. Hippolytus. (J. Ferguson, ed)
  G.T. Cockburn, 123:Vol38No2-398
Euripides. Orestes. (M.L. West, ed & trans)
  G.T. Cockburn, 123:Vol38No2-398
Euripides. Orestes. (C.W. Willink, ed)
  D. Arnould, 555:Vol61fasc2-309
  J.D. Pheifer, 235:Summer88-101

Euripides. Trojan Women.* (S.A. Barlow, ed &
  trans)
  J.M. Dillon, 235:Summer88-103
  S.F. Wiltshire, 124:Nov-Dec88-133
Evans, C. & M. Thornton. Woman and Fash-
  ion.
  D. Atkinson, 617(TLS):30Jun-6Jul89-722
Evans, D.S. Medieval Religious Literature.
  J. Scattergood, 677(YES):Vol19-301
Evans, E.N. Judah P. Benjamin.*
  S. Horowitz, 390:Jun/Jul88-61
Evans, F. - see West, R.
Evans, G. Collected Papers.*
  C. McGinn, 482(PhR):Apr88-278
Evans, G. The Varieties of Reference.* (J.
  McDowell, ed)
  S. Schiffer, 311(JP):Jan88-33
Evans, G.R. Anselm.
  P. Hebblethwaite, 617(TLS):29Dec89/
  4Jan90-1450
Evans, G.R. The Language and Logic of the
  Bible: The Road to Reformation.
  T. Reist, 589:Apr88-391
Evans, G.R. The Thought of Gregory the
  Great.
  C. Straw, 589:Jul88-654
Evans, H.B. Publica Carmina.*
  V. Schmidt, 394:Vol41fasc1/2-200
Evans, J., P. Reed & P. Wilson, comps. A
  Britten Source Book.*
  P. Driver, 607:Mar88-43
Evans, J.D.G. Aristotle.
  A.D.M. Walker, 518:Jan88-20
  R. Wardy, 123:Vol38No1-161
Evans, M. Signifying Nothing.*
  D.S. Kastan, 128(CE):Oct88-694
  M. Pfister, 156(ShJW):Jahrbuch1988-235
Evans, R.J. In Hitler's Shadow.
  I. Buruma, 453(NYRB):26Oct89-31
Evans, R.J. & D. Geary, eds. The German Un-
  employed.
  H. James, 161(DUJ):Dec87-143
Evans, R.J.W. The Making of the Habsburg
  Monarchy, 1550-1700.
  F.A.J. Szabo, 150(DR):Fall88-336
Evans, S. The Penetration of "Exiles."
  R.B., 295(JML):Fall87/Winter88-337
Evans, S.M. Born for Liberty.
  M. Lee, 441:20Aug89-14
Evans, S.M. & B.J. Nelson. Wage Justice.
  W. Kaminer, 441:30Jul89-29
Evel'son, E. Sudebnye protsessy po ekonomi-
  cheskim delam v SSSR.
  J.N. Hazard, 550(RusR):Apr88-210
Evelyn, J. - see under Mackenzie, G.
Everett, B. Poets in Their Time.*
  P. Hammond, 541(RES):May88-330
Evers, K. Studien zu den Vorlagen des
  schwedischen Neuen Testaments vom Jahre
  1526.
  U. Bichel, 685(ZDL):2/1987-265
Evers, L. & F.S. Molina. Yaqui Deer Songs,
  Maso Bwikam.
  A. Robinson, 650(WF):Jan88-62
Everson, S. - see Aristotle
Evin, A.Ö. Origins and Development of the
  Turkish Novel.
  E.W. Ervin, 318(JAOS):Oct-Dec87-809
Ewals, L. Ary Scheffer.
  M.S. Kinsey, 446(NCFS):Spring-Sum-
  mer89-432
Ewart, G. Penultimate Poems.
  G. Maxwell, 617(TLS):3-9Nov89-1216

Ewart-Biggs, J. Pay, Pack and Follow.
    S. Pickering, 569(SR):Fall88-673
Ewers, J.C. Plains Indian Sculpture.
    C. Kaut, 292(JAF):Jan-Mar88-79
    C. Taylor, 2(AfrA):Nov87-77
Ewin, R.E. Liberty, Community and Justice.
    A. Mason, 518:Oct88-247
"Exhibition Road."
    P. Overy, 592:Vol201No1020-60
Exley, F. Last Notes from Home.* A Fan's
Notes. Pages from a Cold Island.
    T.R. Edwards, 453(NYRB):19Jan89-36
"Exotisme et création."*
    N. Dodille, 535(RHL):Jul-Aug88-797
Exum, F., ed. Essays on Comedy and the
"Gracioso" in Plays by Agustín Moreto.
    J.A. Castañeda, 238:Sep88-544
    A.A. Heathcote, 402(MLR):Jan89-210
    C. Stern, 240(HR):Summer88-375
Eyer, P. Perlokutionen.
    H. Harnisch, 682(ZPSK):Band41Heft4-522
Eyles, A. Sherlock Holmes.
    E. Lauterbach, 177(ELT):Vol31No4-481
Ezawa, K. Sprachsystem und Sprechnorm.
    A. Loprieno, 260(IF):Band93-257
Ezell, E.C. The AK47 Story.
    C.D. Bellamy, 575(SEER):Apr88-328
Ezergailis, I.M., ed. Critical Essays on
Thomas Mann.
    A.D. Latta, 268(IFR):Winter89-73
    H. Siefken, 402(MLR):Oct89-1041
Ezorsky, G., ed. Moral Rights in the Work-
place.
    J.K., 185:Jan89-452
Ezquerra, M.A. & others - see under Alvar
Ezquerra, M. & others
Ezra, K. Art of the Dogon.
    R. Hoffman, 2(AfrA):Aug88-14

Faarlund, J.T., ed. Germanic Linguistics.
    T.F. Shannon, 350:Mar89-181
Faas, E. Tragedy and After.*
    J. Kleinstück, 38:Band106Heft1/2-241
Fabb, N. & others, eds. The Linguistics of
Writing.
    R. Fowler, 402(MLR):Oct89-897
    S. Scobie, 376:Dec88-144
Faber, R. Young England.
    D. Roberts, 637(VS):Autumn88-143
Fabian, A.C., ed. Origins.
    F.W. Taylor, 617(TLS):16-22Jun89-662
Fabian, B. - see Jefcoate, G. & K. Kloth
Fabian, J. Time and the Other.
    M. Roche, 488:Mar88-119
Fabre, G., ed. European Perspectives on His-
panic Literature of the United States.
    U. Krauter, 649(WAL):Nov88-270
Fabre, G., M. Mayer & I. Rodà. Inscriptions
Romaines de Catalogne.
    J. d'Encarnação, 229:Band60Heft8-757
Fabre, M. The World of Richard Wright.*
    C. Werner, 395(MFS):Spring88-125
Fabre d'Olivet. La Langue d'oc rétablie:
Grammaire. (G. Kremnitz, ed)
    J-P. Chambon, 553(RLiR):Jul-Dec88-541
Fabregat, C.E. - see under Esteva Fabregat,
C.
Fabris, J. & C. Boullet. Scenes and Machines
from the 18th Century. (B. Cohen-Straty-
ner, ed)
    D. Bradby, 402(MLR):Jul89-705
Faci, C.R. - see under Rábanos Faci, C.

Faden, G. Der Schein der Kunst.
    C. Jamme, 489(PJGG):Band95Heft1-187
Faerber, T. & M. Luchsinger. Joyce in Zürich.
    P. Herring, 329(JJQ):Summer89-621
Faerch, C. & G. Kasper, eds. Introspection in
Second Language Research.
    W.D. Davies, 350:Jun89-424
Fagan, B.M. The Great Journey.*
    J.D. Jennings, 656(WMQ):Oct88-782
    639(VQR):Spring88-68
Faggin, G. Vocabolario della lingua friulana.
    W. Belardi, 545(RPh):Aug88-96
Fagiolo dell' Arco, M. Balla, the Futurist.
    N.V. Halliday, 39:Apr88-299
Fähnrich, H. Kurze Grammatik der georgis-
chen Sprache.
    R. Smeets, 682(ZPSK):Band41Heft2-247
Fain, H. Normative Politics and the Commun-
ity of Nations.
    A. Edel, 103:Mar89-96
    K. Kipnis, 185:Jan89-433
Fainlight, R. Selected Poems.*
    S. Knight, 364:Dec88/Jan89-118
    J. Mole, 493:Summer88-44
Fairbairn, S. & G., eds. Psychology, Ethics
and Change.
    M.N-S., 185:Jul89-985
Fairbank, J.K. China Watch.*
    639(VQR):Winter88-25
Fairbank, J.K. & A. Feuerwerker, eds. The
Cambridge History of China.* (Vol 13, Pt 2)
    J.A. Fogel, 293(JASt):May88-342
Fairbanks, C. Prairie Women.*
    A.L. Anderson, 102(CanL):Winter87-249
    M.L. Briscoe, 128(CE):Nov88-802
    L. Ricou, 627(UTQ):Fall87-154
    L.H. Rodenberger, 357:Spring89-73
Fairchild, J. Chic Savages
    S. Menkes, 441:3Dec89-31
Faiz, F.A. The True Subject.
    639(VQR):Spring88-65
Falck, C. Myth, Truth and Literature.
    M. Walters, 617(TLS):22-28Dec89-1419
Falck, C. - see Jeffers, R.
Falconi Amorelli, M.T. Vulci.
    D. Ridgway, 123:Vol38No2-352
Faldbakken, K. Adam's Diary.* The Sleeping
Prince.
    M. Casserley, 617(TLS):3-9Feb89-114
Falkner, J.M. The Nebuly Coat.
    P. Dickinson, 364:Oct/Nov88-142
Fallaize, E. Étienne Carjat and "Le Boule-
vard" (1861-1863).*
    D.R. Gamble, 446(NCFS):Fall-Winter
    88/89-253
    F.W.J. Hemmings, 208(FS):Jul88-354
Faller, L. Turned to Account.
    K.L. Cope, 594:Winter88-428
Fallon, R.T. Captain or Colonel.*
    E. Jones, 391:Mar88-28
Fallowell, D. To Noto, or London to Sicily in
a Ford.
    M. Alexander, 617(TLS):29Sep-5Oct89-
    1073
Fallows, J. More Like Us.
    A. Hacker, 453(NYRB):30Mar89-6
    D.H. Wrong, 441:26Mar89-7
Falquet de Romans. L'oeuvre poétique de
Falquet de Romans, troubadour. (R.
Arveiller & G. Gouiran, eds)
    G. Roques, 553(RLiR):Jul-Dec88-539

Fawkner, H.W. The Ecstatic World of John Cowper Powys.
  D. Lane, 395(MFS):Summer88-284
Fay, B., E.O. Golob & R.T. Vann - see Mink, L.O.
Feal, R.G. - see under Geisdorfer Feal, R.
Feal Deibe, C. En Nombre de Don Juan (Estructura de un mito literario).*
  J. Mandrell, 400(MLN):Mar88-463
  S. Miller, 345(KRQ):Feb88-118
Fears, J.R. - see Lord Acton
Feather, J. The Provincial Book Trade in Eighteenth-Century England.*
  N. Barker, 173(ECS):Winter88/89-269
  J. Black, 366:Spring88-122
  B. Fabian, 38:Band106Heft3/4-541
Féau, E., ed. L'art africain.
  2(AfrA):Feb88-92
Feaver, W. Pitmen Painters.
  F. Spalding, 617(TLS):9-15Jun89-640
Fecher, C.A. - see Mencken, H.L.
Fechner, G.T. Le petit livre de la vie après la mort.
  A. Reix, 542:Jul-Sep88-343
Fedeli, P. Properzio, Il libro terzo delle elegie.*
  M. Citroni, 229:Band60Heft4-318
Fedeli, P. - see Propertius
Feder, G., H. Hüschen & U. Tank, eds. Joseph Haydn - Tradition und Rezeption.
  T. Emmerig, 416:Band3Heft1-88
Federhofer, H. Heinrich Schenker.*
  W. Rothstein, 411:Jul88-233
Federici, F. Quegli anni con Joyce/Those Years with Joyce.
  C. del Greco Lobner, 329(JJQ):Fall88-156
Federighi, L. Cantare il jazz.
  A.J.M.P., 91:Spring88-114
Feffer, M. Radical Constructionism.
  D. Levy, 103:Jul89-261
Fegert, H. Die Formenbildung des Verbs im Russischen.*
  M. Kirkwood, 575(SEER):Apr88-253
Fehér, Z. Az ördögnek eladott lányok.
  A. Dömötör, 196:Band29Heft1/2-186
Fehling, D. Herodotus and His "Sources."
  S. Hornblower, 617(TLS):10-16Nov89-1237
Fehr, K. Jeremias Gotthelf.
  E. Gallati, 133:Band21Heft2/3-231
  G.H. Hart, 221(GQ):Winter88-142
Feibleman, P. Lilly.*
  D. Rifkind, 617(TLS):17-23Mar89-275
Feijoo, B.J. Obras. (I.L. McClelland, ed)
  P. Deacon, 86(BHS):Apr88-187
Feijoo, G. Lo fantástico en los relatos de Carlos Fuentes.*
  S. Boldy, 86(BHS):Apr88-207
Feil, E. Religio. Antithetik neuzeitlicher Vernunft "Autonomie-Heteronomie" und "rational-irrational."
  J. Stallmach, 489(PJGG):Band95Heft2-426
Fein, J.M. Toward Octavio Paz.*
  C. Cosgrove, 86(BHS):Jul88-323
Fein, R. Medical Care, Medical Costs.
  S. Sutherland, 617(TLS):1-7Dec89-1344
Feinberg, D.B. Eighty-Sixed.
  C. Texier, 441:26Feb89-9
Feinberg, J. Harm to Self.*
  S.S. Kleinberg, 521:Apr88-177

Feinberg, J. The Moral Limits of the Criminal Law.
  J-C. Wolf, 687:Jul-Sep88-454
Feinstein, E. All You Need.
  T. Glyde, 617(TLS):8-14Sep89-969
Feinstein, E. A Captive Lion.*
  A. Smith, 575(SEER):Apr88-274
Feinstein, E. Mother's Girl.*
  P. Erens, 441:12Feb89-18
Feinstein, J. A Season Inside.
  A. Heisch, 441:22Jan89-14
Feist, P.H. Geschichte der deutschen Kunst 1760-1848. Geschichte der deutschen Kunst 1848-1890.
  W. Hütt, 654(WB):8/1988-1397
Feistner, E. Ottes "Eraclius" vor dem Hintergrund der französischen Quelle.
  A. Classen, 597(SN):Vol60No2-280
  D.H. Green, 402(MLR):Jan89-230
Fekete, J., ed. Life After Postmodernism.
  D. Cook, 627(UTQ):Fall88-216
  M.A. Weinstein, 103:Oct89-404
Fekete, J., ed. The Structural Allegory.
  E. Morot-Sir, 535(RHL):Nov-Dec88-1182
Feldbusch, E. Geschriebene Sprache.*
  M. Faust, 685(ZDL):1/1988-83
  J. Knobloch, 680(ZDP):Band107Heft3-476
Feldhaus, A., ed & trans. The Deeds of God in Ṛddhipur.
  J.D. Redington, 318(JAOS):Jul-Sep87-518
Feldman, F. & S. Weil, with S.D. Biederman. Art Law.*
  B. Hoffman, 55:Mar88-93
  H.E. Nass, 662:Spring/Summer88-54
Feldman, I. All of Us Here.*
  C. Bedient, 569(SR):Winter88-137
Feldman, P.R. & B. Norman. The Wordworthy Computer.
  H.J. Schwartz, 126(CCC):Oct88-362
Feldman, P.R. & D. Scott-Kilvert - see Shelley, M.
Feldman, Y.S. Modernism and Cultural Transfer.
  J. Berman, 390:Dec88-54
Feldmann, H. Wenceslau de Moraes (1854-1929) und Japan.*
  P.E.H. Hair, 86(BHS):Jan88-104
Felice, D. Montesquieu in Italia (1800-1985).
  G. Bremner, 208(FS):Apr88-208
  J-M. Le Lannou, 542:Apr-Jun88-264
  V. Santi, 549(RLC):Jan-Mar88-92
Felipe, C. Teatro. (J.A. Escarpanter & J.A. Madrigal, eds)
  M. Montes-Huidobro, 352(LATR):Spring89-134
Fell, C., C. Clark & E. Williams. Women in Anglo-Saxon England and the Impact of 1066.
  A. Fischer, 38:Band106Heft3/4-488
Fellinger, R., ed. Peter Handke.
  T.F. Barry, 221(GQ):Winter87-88
Fellman, M. Inside War.
  442(NY):19Jun89-100
Fellner, H. Hemingway as Playwright.
  R.S. Kennedy, 295(JML):Fall87/Winter88-330
Fellows, O. & D.G. Carr - see "Diderot Studies"
Felman, S. Jacques Lacan and the Adventure of Insight.*
  R.C. Davis, 400(MLN):Dec88-1159
  [continued]

Felman, S. Jacques Lacan and the Adventure of Insight. [continuing]
    S. Scobie, 376:Mar88-101
    T.H. Thompson, 455:Mar88-57
    E. Wright, 494:Vol8No3/4-700
Felmingham, M. The Illustrated Gift Book 1880-1930.*
    T. Russell-Cobb, 324:Mar89-261
Felmy, S., comp & trans. Märchen und Sagen aus Hunza.
    E. Ettlinger, 203:Vol99No1-133
Felperin, H. Beyond Deconstruction.*
    R. Champion, 144:Winter89-77
    M. Folch-Serra, 529(QQ):Autumn88-618
    N. Jacobs, 447(N&Q):Jun88-273
Fel'shtinskii, I. - see Trotsky, L.
Felsing, R.H. - see Price, E.J.
Feltes, N.N. Modes of Production of Victorian Novels.*
    R. Clark-Beattie, 627(UTQ):Fall87-120
    J. Pilditch, 478(P&L):Apr88-144
    W. Ruddick, 366:Autumn88-255
    P.L. Shillingsburg, 301(JEGP):Apr88-262
    P.T. Srebrnik, 177(ELT):Vol31No3-379
    J. Sutherland, 541(RES):May88-311
Femling, J. Hush, Money.
    M. Stasio, 441:10Sep89-28
Fénelon, F.D.D. Correspondance. (Vols 6-9) (J. Orcibal, with J. Le Brun & I. Noye, eds)
    A. Vermeylen, 356(LR):Aug88-241
Fenik, B. Homer and the "Nibelungenlied."*
    S.L. Clark, 221(GQ):Fall87-659
Fenlon, I., ed. Early Music History. (Vol 5)
    J. Glixon, 410(M&L):Jul88-367
Fenno, R.F., Jr. The Making of a Senator.
    N. Lemann, 453(NYRB):30Mar89-27
    L. Wertheimer, 441:5Feb89-19
Fenton, C.L. & M.A. The Fossil Book. (rev by P.V. Rich, T.H. Rich & M.A. Fenton)
    J. Gorman, 441:8Oct89-11
Fenton, J. All the Wrong Places.*
    M. Leifer, 617(TLS):28Apr-4May89-465
    442(NY):6Mar89-112
Fenton, J. Manila Envelope.
    B. Morrison, 617(TLS):30Jun-6Jul89-715
Fenton, W.N. The False Faces of the Iriquois.
    Z. Pearlstone, 2(AfrA):Feb88-17
Féral, J., J.L. Savona & E.A. Walker, eds. Théâtralité, Ecriture et Mise en Scène.*
    I. Yaron, 494:Vol8No2-453
Ferber, M. The Social Vision of William Blake.*
    N. Hilton, 403(MLS):Winter88-195
Ferber, R. Platos Idee des Guten.*
    P. Louis, 555:Vol61fasc1-118
Ferdinand, J. Gionisme et panthéisme.
    S. Mittler, 627(UTQ):Fall88-133
de Ferdinandy, M. Die hispanischen Königs-gesta.
    H. Pietschmann, 547(RF):Band99Heft4-482
Ferenczi, S. The Clinical Diary of Sandor Ferenczi.* (J. Dupont, ed)
    P. Lomas, 617(TLS):5-11May89-480
    S. Schneiderman, 441:15Jan89-24
Ferguson, H. Manual for Multicultural Education. (2nd ed)
    L.M. Crawford-Lange, 399(MLJ):Winter88-459
Ferguson, J. A Prosopography to the Poems of Juvenal.
    F. Jones, 123:Vol38No2-255
Ferguson, J. - see Euripides

Ferguson, M.A., ed. Images of Women in Literature. (4th ed)
    M.L. Briscoe, 128(CE):Nov88-802
Ferguson, M.W., M. Quilligan & N.J. Vickers, eds. Rewriting the Renaissance.*
    V.A. Conley, 188(ECr):Summer88-99
    E.H. Hageman, 570(SQ):Summer88-247
Ferguson, P.M., J.E. Breen & J.O. Jirsa. Reinforced Concrete Fundamentals. (5th ed)
    M.S. Stubbs, 47:Mar88-61
Ferguson, R. Enigma.*
    H.S. Naess, 563(SS):Autumn88-514
Ferguson, R. The Unbalanced Mind.*
    D. Fairer, 83:Spring88-105
    D. Griffin, 405(MP):Nov88-210
Ferguson, T. Sentimental Journey.
    E. Waterston, 102(CanL):Winter87-155
Ferguson, T. & J. Rogers. Right Turn.*
    W.B. Hixson, Jr., 115:Summer88-315
Fernandes, S.L.D. Foundations of Objective Knowledge.
    W. Sauer, 342:Band79Heft2-246
Fernandez, J.W. Persuasions and Performances.
    L. Brodkey, 128(CE):Jan88-89
    D.J. Crowley, 2(AfrA):Nov87-78
Fernández, P.H. La paradoja en Ortega y Gasset.*
    H.C. Raley, 552(REH):May88-126
Fernández-Armesto, F. The Spanish Armada.*
    J.R. Hale, 453(NYRB):16Feb89-30
Fernández Cifuentes, L. García Lorca en el teatro.
    D. Harris, 86(BHS):Jul88-309
    M. Thompson, 402(MLR):Apr89-504
Fernández-Galiano, M. & A. Heubeck. Omero, "Odissea, VI": libri XXI-XXIV.
    R. Janko, 303(JoHS):Vol108-218
    M.M. Willcock, 123:Vol38No1-1
Fernández Jiménez, J., ed. Textos y concordancias de Biblioteca Nacional MS. 22019 y Biblioteca Colombina MS. 5-3-20.
    J.J. Gwara, 304(JHP):Spring88-263
Fernández-Morera, D. & G. Bleiberg - see de León, L.
Fernández Ramírez, S. La nueva gramática académica.
    M. Angeles Alvarez Martínez, 548:Jul-Dec88-447
Fernández Turienzo, F. - see de Unamuno, M.
Fernández-Vázquez, A.A. - see Keller, J.E.
Ferraiolo. Cronaca. (R. Coluccia, ed)
    M. Marti, 228(GSLI):Vol165fasc531-458
Ferrán, J. J.V. Foix.
    P.J. Boehme, 238:Dec88-830
    P.J. Boehne, 240(HR):Autumn88-522
Ferrari, G.R.F. Listening to the Cicadas.
    C.J. Rowe, 123:Vol38No2-223
    R.B. Rutherford, 520:Vol33No2-216
Ferré, F. Philosophy of Technology.
    R. Burch, 103:Oct89-407
Ferreira, M.E.V. - see under Vaz Ferreira, M.E.
Ferreira, M.J. Scepticism and Reasonable Doubt.
    P. Dear, 637(VS):Summer89-583
    H.G. Van Leeuwen, 319:Apr89-312
    R.S. Woolhouse, 521:Jul88-249
Ferreira, M.P. O som de Martin Codax/The Sound of Martin Codax.
    D. Fallows, 415:Feb88-82
    S. Parkinson, 402(MLR):Jul89-759

Ferrer, E.B. – see under Blasco Ferrer, E.
Ferrero, P., E. Hedges & J. Silber. Hearts and Hands.*
    S. James, 662:Spring/Summer88–51
Ferrier, J–L., with Y. le Pichon, eds. Art of Our Century.
    J. Russell, 441:3Dec89–77
Ferrill, A. The Origins of War: from the Stone Age to Alexander the Great.*
    M. Cooper, 318(JAOS):Apr–Jun87–337
Ferris, T. Coming of Age in the Milky Way.*
    J.D. North, 617(TLS):3–9Nov89–1221
Ferro-Luzzi, G.E. Cool Fire.
    M.A. Selby, 293(JASt):May88–399
Ferry, J–M. Habermas.
    P. Trotignon, 542:Jul–Sep88–361
Ferry, L. & A. Renaut. La Pensée 68.
    A.M. Hjort, 154:Summer88–367
    M. Lilla, 617(TLS):17–23Nov89–1255
Ferry, L. & A. Renaut. 68–86.
    F. Giroux, 154:Spring88–171
Ferster, J. Chaucer on Interpretation.*
    K.A. Bleeth, 589:Jul88–656
    G.C. Britton, 447(N&Q):Sep88–357
Fertig, M. 4722 Rue Berri.
    R. Attridge, 102(CanL):Autumn88–143
Festugière, A.J. – see Aristides
Fet, J. Allmugens diktar.
    I. Nymoen, 172(Edda):1988/2–186
Fetherling, D. & D. – see Sandburg, C.
"Fétis on Clarinettists and Clarinet Repertoire." (J. Rees–Davies, trans)
    M. O'Loughlin, 415:Oct88–535
Fetting, H., ed. Von der "Freien Bühne" zum "Politischen Theater."
    H. Pollow, 654(WB):10/1988–1754
Fetzer, J.H., ed. Principles of Philosophical Reasoning.
    M.A. Finocchiaro, 480(P&R):Vol21No4–304
Fetzer, J.H., ed. Sociobiology and Epistemology.*
    R.R. Sullivan, 488:Dec88–565
Feuer, L. Imperialism and the Anti-Imperialist Mind.
    L.H. Gann, 31(ASch):Winter88–145
Feyerabend, P. Farewell to Reason.
    483:Jan88–133
Ffinch, M. G.K. Chesterton.
    J. Lucas, 637(VS):Autumn88–134
Fiacc, P. Missa Terribilis.
    H. Buckingham, 565:Winter87/88–71
Fichner-Rathus, L. Understanding Art.
    P. Smith, 709:Fall88–63
Fichte, J.G. Early Philosophical Writings. (D. Breazeale, ed & trans)
    F. Beiser, 617(TLS):7–13Apr89–373
Fichte, J.G. La missione del dotto. (V.E. Alfieri, ed & trans)
    J–M. Gabaude, 542:Jul–Sep88–343
Fichte, J.O., ed. Chaucer's Frame Tales.
    L. Carruthers, 189(EA):Oct–Dec88–474
Fichte, J.O., K.H. Göller & B. Schimmelpfennig, eds. Zusammenhänge, Einflüsse, Wirkungen.
    E.E. Du Bruck, 201:Vol14–209
    D. Kartschoke, 684(ZDA):Band117 Heft4–157
Ficino, M. Commentary on Plato's Symposium on Love. (S. Jayne, ed & trans)
    J.C. Nelson, 276:Summer88–164

von Ficker, L. Ludwig von Ficker: Briefwechsel 1909–1914. (I. Zangerle & others, eds)
    R. Detsch, 564:Feb88–88
Fickett, H. & D.R. Gilbert. Flannery O'Connor.*
    M.D.O., 295(JML):Fall87/Winter88–362
Ficowski, J. – see Schulz, B.
Fidjestøl, B. & others. Festskrift til Ludvig Holm-Olsen på hans 70-årsdag den 9. juni 1984.*
    R. McTurk, 562(Scan):Nov88–175
Fiebach, J. Die Toten als die Macht der Lebenden.
    B. Forstreuter, 654(WB):9/1988–1574
    M. Schipper, 538(RAL):Fall88–433
Field, A. VN.*
    J.M. Kopper, 574(SEEJ):Summer88–333
    D. Rampton, 627(UTQ):Winter88/89–332
Field, C., with R. Kauffman. The Hill Towns of Italy.
    P–L. Adams, 61:Aug89–92
Field, E. New and Selected Poems.
    L. Goldstein, 472:Vol15No1–240
Field, F. Losing Out.
    F. Cairncross, 617(TLS):1–7Dec89–1326
Field, J.V. Kepler's Geometrical Cosmology.
    P. Barker & R. Ariew, 543:Jun89–826
Field, L. Thomas Wolfe and His Editors.
    J. Halberstadt, 31(ASch):Autumn88–616
    C. Johnston, 580(SCR):Spring89–84
    J.S. Phillipson, 40(AEB):Vol2No4–189
    J.S. Phillipson, 395(MFS):Winter88–628
    J.S. Phillipson, 587(SAF):Autumn88–252 42(AR):Summer88–399
Field, R.S. Richard Hamilton.
    P.B. Arnold, 127:Spring88–53
Field, R.S. & R.E. Fine. A Graphic Muse.
    662:Spring/Summer88–53
Field, S., ed & trans. Tian Wen.
    Y.F. Blanford, 318(JAOS):Oct–Dec87–829
    V.H. Mair, 116:Jul87–127
Fielding, H. Dzieje Przygód Józefa Andrewsa i Jego Przyjaciela Pana Abrahama Adamsa.
    G. Bystydzieńska, 566:Autumn88–75
Fielding, H. "An Enquiry into the Causes of the Late Increase of Robbers" and Related Writings. (M.R. Zirker, ed) "The Covent-Garden Journal" and "A Plan of the Universal Register-Office." (B.A. Goldgar, ed)
    D. Nokes, 617(TLS):7–13Apr89–361
Fielding, H. An Institute of the Pleas of the Crown.
    566:Autumn88–74
Fielding, H. The "True Patriot" and Related Writings.* (W.B. Coley, ed)
    J. Black, 447(N&Q):Sep88–377
Fielding, J. The Deep End.
    M. Jensen, 102(CanL):Winter87–176
Fielding, K.J. – see Dickens, C.
Fiero, G.K., W. Pfeffer & M. Allain, eds & trans. Three Medieval Views of Women.
    M. Keen, 453(NYRB):7Dec89–32
Fifield, C. Max Bruch.*
    R. Anderson, 415:Jun88–304
"The Fifteen Joys of Marriage (Les XV. Joies de Mariage)." (B.A. Pitts, trans)
    S.M. Taylor, 201:Vol14–229
Figes, E. Sex and Subterfuge.
    L.E. Nesbitt, 441:8Jan89–23
Figueiredo Martins, I.D., comp. Bibliografia do Humanismo em Portugal no Século xvi.
    T.F. Earle, 123:Vol38No1–189

Fikentscher, W. Methoden des Rechts.
   C. Schefold, 489(PJGG):Band95Heft2-376
Fildes, V. Wet Nursing.
   L. Pollock, 617(TLS):17-23Mar89-281
Filedt Kok, J.P., comp. The Master of the
   Amsterdam Cabinet, or The Housebook Mas-
   ter, ca. 1470-1500.*
   R.G. Calkins, 589:Jan88-184
Filewod, A. Collective Encounters.
   T. Goldie, 108:Winter88-92
   R. Nunn, 627(UTQ):Fall88-153
Filgis, M.N. & W. Radt. Altertümer von Per-
   gamon, XV. (Pt 1)
   P. Gros, 229:Band60Heft2-142
Filipović, R. Teorija jezika u kontaktu.
   J.L. Conrad, 574(SEEJ):Spring88-166
   R. Katičić, 206(FoLi):Vol22No1/2-203
de Filippis, D.C. & E.J. Robinett - see under
   Cocco de Filippis, D. & E.J. Robinett
Fillitz, H. Die Schatzkammer in Wien.
   G.B. Ladner, 589:Oct88-916
Filtzer, D. Soviet Workers and Stalinist In-
   dustrialization.*
   H. Kuromiya, 550(RusR):Apr88-198
Finamore, J.F. Iamblichus and the Theory of
   the Vehicle of the Soul.*
   J. Dillon, 303(JoHS):Vol108-243
   R. Ferwerda, 394:Vol41fasc1/2-181
Finch, A. Selected Poems. (D. Thompson, ed)
   M.G. Brennan, 447(N&Q):Sep88-363
   D. Crane, 83:Autumn88-227
Finch, J.S. - see "A Catalogue of the Li-
   braries of Sir Thomas Browne and Dr.
   Edward Browne, His Son"
Finch, R. For the Back of a Likeness.
   L-A. Hales, 102(CanL):Spring88-161
Findley, C.V. Ottoman Civil Officialdom.
   J.M. Rogers, 617(TLS):11-17Aug89-868
Findley, S.E. Rural Development and Migra-
   tion.
   F. Arnold, 293(JASt):May88-420
Findley, T. The Telling of Lies.*
   L. Hutcheon, 102(CanL):Winter87-225
Fine, A. The Shaky Game.*
   J. Butterfield, 393(Mind):Apr88-291
   P. Teller, 486:Mar88-155
Fine, J., ed. Second Language Discourse.
   C. van Kerckvoorde, 350:Jun89-443
Fine, K. Reasoning with Arbitrary Objects.*
   J. Macnamara, 316:Mar88-305
   M. Santambrogio, 449:Dec88-630
Fine, R. Hollywood and the Profession of
   Authorship, 1928-1940.
   F. Walgren, 295(JML):Fall87/Winter88-
   280
Fine, R.E. Gemini G.E.L.
   P.B. Arnold, 127:Spring88-53
Fine, S. Molly Dear.
   G. Jonas, 441:8Jan89-31
Fineman, J. Shakespeare's Perjured Eye.*
   R.P. Wheeler, 405(MP):Aug88-87
Fingarette, H. Heavy Drinking.*
   M. Moore, 185:Apr89-660
Fink, C. Marc Bloch.
   M.R. Marrus, 441:1Oct89-24
Fink, G-L., ed. Cosmopolitisme, Patriotisme
   et Xénophobie en Europe au Siècle des
   Lumières.
   F. Baasner, 547(RF):Band100Heft4-413
Fink, H. & J. Jackson, eds. All the Bright
   Company.
   J.T. Goodwin, 108:Summer88-94

Fink, I. A Scrap of Time and Other Stories.*
   (Polish title: Skrawek czasu.)
   E. Kurzweil, 473(PR):Vol55No1-143
   E. Sartori, 502(PrS):Summer88-132
Fink, L. & B. Greenberg. Upheaval in the
   Quiet Zone.
   J. Klein, 441:24Sep89-40
Fink, M. - see Smith, J.
Finkel, D. Selected Shorter Poems.
   R.B. Shaw, 491:Apr88-38
Finkel, D. The Wake of the Electron.
   639(VQR):Summer88-98
Finkel, N.J. Insanity on Trial.
   K.F.T. Cust, 103:Sep89-351
Finkelstein, J. Dining Out.
   L. Taylor, 617(TLS):17-23Nov89-1286
Finkelstein, N. Andy Warhol: The Factory
   Years 1964-1967.
   M. Nixon, 441:12Nov89-3
Finkielkraut, A. La Défaite de la pensée.
   L. Lazar, 207(FR):Feb89-571
Finkielkraut, A. La Mémoire vaine.
   I. Buruma, 453(NYRB):26Oct89-31
Finkler, K. Spiritualist Healers in Mexico.
   L. Camino, 292(JAF):Jan-Mar88-121
Finlay, J. The Salt of Exposure.
   R.L. Barth, 598(SoR):Winter89-255
Finlayson, I. The Sixth Continent.*
   M.P.L., 295(JML):Fall87/Winter88-191
Finley, M.I. Ancient History.
   J.T. Roberts, 124:Sep-Oct88-63
Finley, M.I. Politics in the Ancient World.
   N.F. Jones, 41:Vol7-232
Finnegan, R. Literacy and Orality.
   O. Murray, 617(TLS):16-22Jun89-655
Finneran, R.J., ed. Critical Essays on W.B.
   Yeats.
   D.T.O., 295(JML):Fall87/Winter88-406
Finneran, R.J. - see "Yeats: An Annual of
   Critical and Textual Studies"
Finnis, J., J.M. Boyle, Jr. & G. Grisez. Nuclear
   Deterrence, Morality and Realism.*
   A. Hockaday, 483:Apr88-277
   J. McMahan, 185:Jan89-407
Finnissy, M. & R. Wright, eds. New Music 87.
   R. Samuel, 410(M&L):Apr88-298
Finscher, L., ed. Claudio Monteverdi.
   T. Carter, 410(M&L):Jan88-65
Finson, J.W. Robert Schumann and the Study
   of Orchestral Composition.
   E. Sams, 617(TLS):3-9Nov89-1215
Fiore, R. & others, eds. Studies in Honour of
   William C. McCrary.*
   P. Evans, 86(BHS):Jul88-304
Fiorenza, A., ed. Comporre arcano.
   D. Kämper, 416:Band3Heft3-285
Fiori, G. Vita di Enrico Berlinguer.
   P. McCarthy, 617(TLS):10-16Nov89-1234
Firchow, P.E. The Death of the German
   Cousin.*
   P. Brantlinger, 177(ELT):Vol31No1-77
   E. Schlant, 221(GQ):Spring88-335
Firmat, G.P. - see under Pérez Firmat, G.
Firpo, L. - see under Beccaria, C.
Firpo, L., G. Francioni & G. Gaspari - see
   Beccaria, C.
Firpo, M. & D. Marcatto, eds. Il processo in-
   quisitoriale del Cardinal Giovanni Morone.
   (Vol 4)
   P.F. Grendler, 551(RenQ):Winter88-713
"Elena Firsova: A Complete Catalogue."
   A.F.L.T., 412:May88-158

118

"First Fictions: Introduction 10."
D. Durrant, 364:Feb/Mar89-133
"The First Printed Catalogue of the Bodleian Library, 1605."
D. McKitterick, 354:Mar88-58
E.G. Stanley, 447(N&Q):Sep88-348
Fisch, H. A Remembered Future.
J.B. Vickery, 301(JEGP):Apr88-251
Fisch, M.H. Peirce, Semeiotic, and Pragmatism.* (K.L. Ketner & C.J.W. Kloesel, eds)
M. Migotti, 518:Apr88-65
Fischer, A. Engagement, Wedding and Marriage in Old English.*
K.R. Grinda, 38:Band106Heft3/4-476
Fischer, B. "Gehen" von Thomas Bernhard.
R. Leventhal, 222(GR):Summer88-148
P.C. Pfeiffer, 221(GQ):Winter87-147
Fischer, E.P. & C. Lipson. Thinking about Science.
S. Rose, 617(TLS):31Mar-6Apr89-333
Fischer, F. & J. Forester, eds. Confronting Values in Policy Analysis.
S. Hetcher, 185:Apr89-659
Fischer, H. Georg Büchner und Alexis Muston.
R. Grimm, 406:Summer88-233
Fischer, H.R. Sprache und Lebensform.
P. Trotignon, 542:Jul-Sep88-361
Fischer, I. Latina Dunăreană.
J. André, 555:Vol61fasc2-348
Fischer, L., ed. Literatur der Bundesrepublik Deutschland bis 1967.
F. Futterknecht, 222(GR):Fall88-212
Fischer, W., R.M. McInnis & J. Schneider, eds. The Emergence of a World Economy, 1500-1914.
F. Perlin, 293(JASt):May88-324
Fischer-Dieskau, D. Reverberations.
W I Taitte 441:24Sep89-25
Fish, S. Doing What Comes Naturally.
P. Meisel, 441:21May89-22
Fishburn, K. The Unexpected Universe of Doris Lessing.*
R. Rubenstein, 538(RAL):Summer88-264
Fisher, A. Let Us Now Praise Famous Women.
662:Spring/Summer88-52
Fisher, B. The House as a Symbol.
C. Cook, 447(N&Q):Sep88-398
A.S.L., 295(JML):Fall87/Winter88-303
B. Murray, 395(MFS):Summer88-285
Fisher, D.E. & R. Albertazzie. Hostage One.
N. Callendar, 441:17Sep89-30
Fisher, J. Commercial Relations between Spain and Spanish America in the Era of Free Trade 1778-1796.
P.T. Bradley, 86(BHS):Apr88-205
Fisher, J., ed. Perceiving Artworks.
D.E. Cody, 438:Spring88-229
Fisher, L. Constitutional Dialogues.
G. Marshall, 617(TLS):30Jun-6Jul89-707
Fisher, M.F.K. Here Let Us Feast. Among Friends. The Art of Eating. Serve It Forth. Consider the Oyster. How to Cook a Wolf. The Gastronomical Me. Sister Age.
P. Storace, 453(NYRB):7Dec89-42
Fisher, P. Hard Facts.*
R. Gray, 402(MLR):Apr89-451
M. Lopez, 115:Spring88-200
Fisher, P. Poems 1955-1987.
R. Sheppard, 617(TLS):10-16Mar89-257
Fisher, R.K. Aristophanes "Clouds."
D.M. MacDowell, 123:Vol38No1-141

Fisher, S. In the Patient's Best Interests.
R.T., 185:Apr89-687
Fisher, S. Revelatory Positivism?
D. Jenkins, 617(TLS):17-23Feb89-176
Fisher, S.T. The Merchant-Millers of the Humber Valley.
C. Armstrong, 298:Spring/Summer88-240
Fishkin, S.F. From Fact to Fiction.
G. Scharnhorst, 395(MFS):Winter88-611
Fishman, A. Amish Literacy.
J. Livingston-Webber, 350:Dec89-887
Fishman, J.A. Ideology, Society and Language.
A.S. Kaye, 350:Jun89-425
Fishman, J.A. & others, eds. The Fergusonian Impact.
L.G. Kelly, 320(CJL):Jun88-188
S. Romaine, 353:Vol26No1-176
Fishman, J.A. & others. The Rise and Fall of the Ethnic Revival.*
A. Thomas, 320(CJL):Sep88-306
Fishman, R. Bourgeois Utopias.
S. Meacham, 637(VS):Winter89-281
639(VQR):Spring88-62
Fishwick, D. The Imperial Cult in the Latin West. (Vol 1)
S.R.F. Price, 487:Winter88-371
Fishwick, N. English Football and Society, 1910-1950.
J. Walvin, 617(TLS):10-16Nov89-1248
Fiske, J. Understanding Popular Culture.
D. Papineau, 617(TLS):8-14Dec89-1364
Fitch, B.T. & A. Oliver - see "Texte"
Fitch, G.W. Naming and Believing.
J.E. Tomberlin, 484(PPR):Mar89-521
Fitch, J.G. - see Seneca
Fitchen, J. Building Construction Before Mechanization.*
T.F. Peters, 505:Jul88-111
Fitting, M. Computability Theory, Semantics, and Logic Programming.
J.C. Shepherdson, 316:Dec88-1257
Fitzgerald, A.E. The Pentagonists.
R.I. Bell, 441:26Feb89-35
N. Lemann, 453(NYRB):26Oct89-3
Fitzgerald, M.J. - see Brinkley, R.
Fitzgerald, P. The Beginning of Spring.*
J. Mellors, 364:Feb/Mar89-136
R. Plunket, 441:7May89-15
Fitzgerald, P. Charlotte Mew and Her Friends.*
H. Fromm, 31(ASch):Autumn88-632
Fitzgerald, R. All About Anthrax. Pushed from the Wings.
R. Brain, 617(TLS):3-9Nov89-1218
Fitzgerald, R. British Labour Management and Industrial Welfare 1846-1939.
P. Stead, 637(VS):Spring89-448
Fitzpatrick, F. The Open Door.
A. Pousada, 350:Jun89-426
Fiva, T. Possessor Chains in Norwegian.
T.A. Afarli, 452(NJL):Vol11No1/2-215
Fix, H., ed. Jenseits von Index und Konkordanz.
L.E. Janus, 563(SS):Spring88-318
Fix, H. Wortschatz der Jónsbók.
L.E. Janus, 563(SS):Spring88-323
Flacelière, R. & others - see Plutarch
Flachmann, K. & M. The Prose Reader.
D. George, 126(CCC):May88-239
Flacks, R. Making History.*
T. Martin, 42(AR):Fall88-525

Flage, D.E. Berkeley's Doctrine of Notions.*
  A. Flew, 319:Oct89-622
  D.R. Raynor, 518:Jul88-131
  T.L.S. Sprigge, 479(PhQ):Jan88-134
Flam, J. Matisse.*
  J.D. Herbert, 59:Jun88-298
Flanagan, B. Written in My Soul.
  G.M. Plasketes, 498:Fall88-103
Flanagan, M. Trust.*
  42(AR):Fall88-532
Flanagan, S. Hildegard of Bingen, 1098-1179.
  M. Keen, 453(NYRB):7Dec89-32
Flanders, J. Timepiece.
  A. Hudgins, 249(HudR):Winter89-740
Flanner, J. Darlinghissima. (N.D. Murray, ed)
  P. Craig, 617(TLS):7-13Apr89-362
Flannery, S. The Zebra Network.
  N. Callendar, 441:23Apr89-33
Flaphan, S. The Birth of Israel.*
  R. Jean & E. Isaac, 390:May88-58
Flathman, R.E. The Philosophy and Politics
  of Freedom.*
  P. Cole, 518:Jul88-175
Flaubert, G. Carnets de travail.* (P-M. de
  Biasi, ed)
  M. Jarrety, 450(NRF):Jul-Aug88-214
Flavell, M.K. George Grosz.*
  D.F. Anstis, 324:Apr89-322
  T. Benson, 90:Dec88-936
  639(VQR):Autumn88-123
de Flavilis, G. Kant e Spinoza.
  A. Stanguennec, 542:Apr-Jun88-263
Fleckenstein, J., ed. Das ritterliche Turnier
  im Mittelalter.
  K-H. Borck, 684(ZDA):Band117Heft4-176
  D.H. Green, 402(MLR):Oct89-901
Fleetwood, H. The Past.
  J. Mellors, 364:Mar87-98
Fleischhauer, C. & B.W. Brannan, eds. Docu-
  menting America, 1935-1943.
  S. MacNeille, 441:30Apr89-39
Fleischmann, U. Das Französisch-Kreolische
  in der Karibik.
  M. Perl, 682(ZPSK):Band41Heft6-813
Fleishman, L. & others - see "Stanford Slavic
  Studies"
Fleissner, R.F. The Prince and the Professor.
  D. Daphinoff, 156(ShJW):Jahrbuch1988-
  281
Fleming, B. Captain Bennett's Folly.
  A. Solomon, 441:6Aug89-12
Fleming, J. Blacks in College.
  A. Hacker, 453(NYRB):12Oct89-63
Fleming, R.E. James Weldon Johnson.
  C. Werner, 395(MFS):Spring88-125
Fleming, T. The Politics of Human Nature.
  P. Gottfried, 543:Jun89-828
Fletcher, A. Reform in the Provinces.
  K. Sharpe, 250(HLQ):Spring88-120
Fletcher, A. & J. Stevenson, eds. Order and
  Disorder in Early Modern England.
  K. Sharpe, 250(HLQ):Spring88-117
Fletcher, G.A. The Keynesian Revolution and
  Its Critics.
  G. Selgin, 144:Summer/Fall89-435
Fletcher, G.P. A Crime of Self-Defense.*
  R.A. Shiner, 103:Sep89-353
Fletcher, H.G. 3d. New Aldine Studies.
  M. Lowry, 617(TLS):28Jul-3Aug89-833
Fletcher, I., ed. British Poetry and Prose
  1870-1905.*
  P.M.S. Dawson, 541(RES):Aug88-458

Fletcher, I. W.B. Yeats and His Contempo-
  raries.
  M.S. Helfand, 637(VS):Summer89-604
  R. Hogan, 177(ELT):Vol31No2-218
Fletcher, I. - see Gray, J.
Fletcher, J.G. Selected Poems. (L. Carpenter
  & L. Rudolph, eds)
  D. Davis, 617(TLS):5-11May89-478
Fletcher, K.K. The Paris Conservatoire and
  the Contest Solos for Bassoon.
  N. O'Loughlin, 415:Dec88-669
Fletcher, L. Modernismo.
  R.D. Woods, 238:May88-302
Fletcher, M.D. Contemporary Political Satire.
  E.A. Kaplan, 395(MFS):Winter88-733
  J. Seaton, 115:Summer88-326
Fletcher, P. A Child's Learning of English.
  B. Glauser, 38:Band106Heft1/2-180
Fletcher, P. Education and Music.*
  J. Paynter, 410(M&L):Jan88-116
Fletcher, P. & M. Garman, eds. Language Ac-
  quisition.* (2nd ed)
  S.W. Felix, 603:Vol12No2-518
Fletcher, R. The Quest for El Cid.
  P. Linehan, 617(TLS):6-12Oct89-1098
Fletcher, W.C. Soviet Charismatics.
  P. Valliere, 550(RusR):Jan88-94
Flew, A. David Hume.*
  J. Harrison, 483:Oct88-539
  A.J. Jacobson, 393(Mind):Apr88-295
  P. Russell, 518:Jan88-27
Flew, A. Thinking About Social Thinking.*
  W.W. Miller, 488:Sep88-411
Flew, A. & others. Hume's Philosophy of Re-
  ligion.*
  G. Scarre, 518:Apr88-86
Flew, A. & G. Vesey. Agency and Necessity.
  M. Adam, 542:Oct-Dec88-500
  S. Botros, 518:Apr88-94
Flexner, S.B. - see "The Random House Dic-
  tionary of the English Language, Un-
  abridged"
Flick, J.F. Handbuch der Buchdruckerkunst.
  Beschreibung der elastischen Auftrage-
  Walzen.
  J.L. Flood, 354:Dec88-359
Fliedl, K. Zeitroman und Heilsgeschichte.
  M.K. Kremer, 406:Fall88-402
  K. Weissenberger, 133:Band21Heft2/3-
  255
Flier, M. & R.D. Brecht, eds. Issues in Rus-
  sian Morphosyntax.*
  M. Kirkwood, 575(SEER):Apr88-256
Flier, M.S. & A. Timberlake, eds. The Scope of
  Slavic Aspect.*
  J. Lindstedt, 559:Vol12No3-303
  O.T. Yokoyama, 574(SEEJ):Spring88-157
Flinn, D.M. What They Did For Love.
  B. Gelb, 441:13Aug89-2
Flint, K. Dickens.*
  K. Sutherland, 541(RES):Aug88-455
Flobert, P. - see Varro
Flood, C. The Animals in Their Elements.
  M.A. Jarman, 376:Mar88-92
Flood, C.B. Hitler.
  G.A. Craig, 441:16Apr89-15
  442(NY):3Jul89-96
Flood, J.L., ed. Ein Moment des erfahrenen
  Lebens.
  F. König, 133:Band21Heft1-96

Flood, R. & M. Lockwood, eds. The Nature of
Time.
  P.M. Huby, 518:Apr88-122
  A. Reix, 542:Jan-Mar88-120
Flora, J.M. & R. Bain, eds. Fifty Southern
Writers After 1900.*
  S. Felton, 395(MFS):Summer88-259
Florence, P. Mallarmé, Manet and Redon.*
  N. Bryson, 208(FS):Jul88-357
Flores, A. & K., eds. The Defiant Muse.*
  P. Bacarisse, 86(BHS):Jul88-286
Flores, A.B. - see under Baeza Flores, A.
Flores, O.D. - see under Dávila Flores, O.
Flores Arroyuelo, F. - see Baroja, P.
Floros, C. Gustav Mahler.* (Vol 3)
  S. Cut, 537:Vol74No2-244
Flory, S. The Archaic Smile of Herodotus.
  T.J. Luce, 124:Mar-Apr89-318
Flory, W.S. The American Ezra Pound.
  H. Levin, 453(NYRB):9Nov89-45
Flot, Y. Les Producteurs.
  M-N. Little, 207(FR):Oct88-193
Flotzinger, R. - see von Hausegger, F.
Flower, J.E., ed. France Today. (6th ed)
  D.J. Daniels, 207(FR):Oct88-187
Flowers, B.S. - see Moyers, B.
Floyd, S.A. Jr. & M.J. Reisser. Black Music
Biography.
  D.E. McGinty, 91:Spring88-106
Flukinger, R. The Formative Decades.
  J.L., 90:Jun88-479
Flusser, V. Die Schrift.
  A. Assmann, 490:Band20Heft3/4-284
Flynn, D. A Suitcase in Berlin.
  N. Callendar, 441:17Dec89-17
Flynn, E.A. & P.P. Schweickart, eds. Gender
and Reading.*
  C.V.B., 295(JML):Fall87/Winter88-244
Flynn, R. Wanderer Springs.
  J. Stull, 649(WAL):Aug88-172
Flynn, S. A Parameter-Setting Model of L2
Acquisition.
  G. de Haan, 603:Vol12No2-538
Foakes, R.A. - see Coleridge, S.T.
Fodor, J.A. Psychosemantics.*
  A. Clark, 393(Mind):Oct88-605
  D.C. Dennett, 311(JP):Jul88-384
  W.S. Robinson, 543:Mar89-619
  K. Sterelny, 63:Mar88-107
Fogarasi, M. Nuovo manuale di storia della
lingua italiana.
  P. Tekavčić, 553(RLiR):Jan-Jun88-268
Fogel, A. Coercion to Speak.*
  J. Batchelor, 541(RES):Nov88-585
Fogel, J.A. Ai Ssu-ch'i's Contribution to the
Development of Chinese Marxism.
  J. Israel, 293(JASt):Aug88-586
Fogel, R.W. Without Consent or Contract.
  M.P. Johnson, 453(NYRB):21Dec89-51
  C.V. Woodward, 441:5Nov89-15
  442(NY):30Oct89-118
Fogelin, R.J. Figuratively Speaking.
  A. Margalit, 617(TLS):14-20Apr89-399
Fogelin, R.J. Hume's Skepticism in the "Trea-
tise of Human Nature."*
  M. Williams, 482(PhR):Apr88-263
Fogelklou, E. Reality and Radiance.* (H.T.
Lutz, ed & trans)
  E.A. Andersen, 562(Scan):Nov88-193
Föhl, H. & A. Benger, eds. Katalog der Stifts-
bibliothek Xanten.
  P.R. Quarrie, 354:Dec88-362

Fokkema, D. & H. Bertens, eds. Approaching
Postmodernism.*
  S. Connor, 402(MLR):Jul89-699
Fokkema, D. & E. Ibsch. Theories of Litera-
ture in the Twentieth Century.
  R.L., 295(JML):Fall87/Winter88-244
Folda, J. The Nazareth Capitals and the Cru-
sader Shrine of the Annunciation.
  A. Borg, 589:Oct88-922
  P. Williamson, 90:Dec88-934
Foley, B. Telling the Truth.*
  J. Hollowell, 395(MFS):Summer88-243
  B.M., 494:Vol8No2-455
  P.J. Rabinowitz, 405(MP):May89-450
Foley, J.M., ed. Comparative Research on
Oral Traditions.
  N.K. Moyle, 574(SEEJ):Winter88-679
Foley, R. The Theory of Epistemic Rational-
ity.
  L. Code, 543:Jun89-829
  J. Somerville, 518:Oct88-220
Foley, W.A. The Papuan Languages of New
Guinea.
  B. Comrie, 297(JL):Mar88-224
Folgarait, L. So Far from Heaven.
  D.G. La France, 263(RIB):Vol38No1-73
Folkenflik, V. - see Madame de Staël
Follett, K. The Pillars of the Earth.
  C. Holland, 441:10Sep89-41
Folse, H.J. The Philosophy of Niels Bohr.
  H.D. Sanchez, 160:Jan88-153
  R.H. Schlagel, 543:Sep88-140
Fonagy, I. La vive voix.
  R. Jolivet, 209(FM):Apr88-121
Foner, N., ed. New Immigrants in New York.*
  M.C. McKenna, 106:Fall88-359
Fong, G.S. Wu Wenying and the Art of South-
ern Song Ci Poetry.
  R.C. Miao, 293(JASt):Aug88-593
  S.H. Sargent, 116:Jul87-153
Fonquerne, Y-R. & A. Egido, eds. Formas
breves del relato.
  B.M. Damiani, 240(HR):Summer88-363
Fontaine, J. Culture et spiritualité en
Espagne du IVe au VIIe siècle.
  J.N. Hillgarth, 589:Jul88-657
Fontaine, J., C. Prato & A. Marcone, eds.
Giuliano Imperatore.
  R.B.E. Smith, 313:Vol78-262
Fontaine, M-M. & F. Lecercle - see Belleau,
R.
Fontaine, P.F.M. The Light and the Dark.
(Vol 1)
  R.W. Jordan, 123:Vol38No2-424
Fontana, B. - see Constant, B.
Fontana, B.L. & J.P. Schaefer. Tarahumara.
  J.T. Groulx, 649(WAL):Aug88-185
Fontane, T. Der Schleswig-Holsteinsche
Krieg im Jahre 1864. Der deutsche Krieg
von 1866. (H. Nürnberger, ed of both)
  W. Paulsen, 406:Summer88-238
Fontanella, L. - see Marguerite de Navarre
Fontanelli, M.P. & B. Reynolds - see "Cam-
bridge/Signorelli Italian/English, En-
glish/Italian Dictionary"
Fontbona, F. & F. Miralles. Història de l'art
català. (Vol 7)
  J-L. Marfany, 86(BHS):Apr88-202
Fontes, M.D. - see under da Costa Fontes, M.
Foon, C.S. - see under Chew Sock Foon
Foon, K.H. - see under Kwong Hing Foon
Foot, P. Who Framed Colin Wallace?
  T. Hadden, 617(TLS):1-7Sep89-940

Fowler, R.L. The Nature of Early Greek Lyric.
 A. Burnett, 24:Fall88-442
 D.A. Campbell, 627(UTQ):Fall88-99
 C. Carey, 487:Summer88-177
 A. Carson, 121(CJ):Apr-May89-362
 M. Davies, 229:Band60Heft6-486
 J.T. Hooker, 303(JoHS):Vol108-222
 M.E. Reesor, 529(QQ):Summer88-443
Fox, A. History and Heritage.
 R. Glen, 637(VS):Winter89-237
Fox, A. & J. Guy. Reassessing the Henrician
 Age.
 A.J. Slavin, 551(RenQ):Winter88-727
 R. Tittler, 539:Summer88-231
Fox, C. Londoners.
 G. Pollock, 59:Jun88-275
Fox, C., ed. Psychology and Literature in the
 Eighteenth Century.
 G.S. Gross, 173(ECS):Winter88/89-248
Fox, D. - see Henryson, R.
Fox, G. The Deepening of the Colours.*
 K. Dawes, 198:Summer88-110
 E. Folsom, 529(QQ):Autumn88-727
Fox, M. The Coming of the Cosmic Christ.
 C. Zaleski, 441:15Jan89-12
Fox, M.V. The Song of Songs and the Ancient
 Egyptian Love Songs.*
 J.M. Sasson, 318(JAOS):Oct-Dec87-733
Fox, M.W. & L.D. Mickley, eds. Advances in
 Animal Welfare Science, 1986/87.
 B.R., 185:Oct88-214
Fox, R.E. Conscientious Sorcerers.
 C. Werner, 395(MFS):Spring88-125
Fox, R.L. Pagans and Christians.*
 G. Fowden, 313:Vol78-173
Fox, R.W. Reinhold Niebuhr.*
 V. Guroian, 396(ModA):Spring89-175
Fox, S. Blood and Power.
 S. Raab, 441:2Jul89-9
Fox, S., ed. The Medieval Woman.
 M-M. Dubois, 189(EA):Oct-Dec88-470
Fox-Genovese, E. Within the Plantation
 Household.*
 G.M. Fredrickson, 617(TLS):5-11May89-
 477
 M. Sobel, 441:8Jan89-1
 442(NY):23Jan89-119
Foxe, C. Locke and the Scriblerians.
 J. Mullan, 617(TLS):4-10Aug89-853
Foxley, A. Chile y su futuro.
 J.S. Valenzuela, 263(RIB):Vol38No4-528
Fradejas Rueda, J.M. - see Moamin
Fradkin, P.L. Fallout.
 K. Schneider, 441:9Apr89-32
Fraga Iribarne, M. El pensamiento conser-
 vador español.
 V. Nemoianu, 396(ModA):Summer89-276
Fraisat, N., ed. Poems in Their Place.
 K.R. Johnston, 340(KSJ):Vol37-172
Fraisse, J-C. L'Intériorité sans retrait.*
 A. Sheppard, 123:Vol38No2-428
Fraisse, S., ed. Péguy, un romantique malgré
 lui.
 F. Gerbod, 535(RHL):Jan-Feb88-147
Frame, J. The Carpathians.*
 N. Wartik, 441:22Jan89-22
Frame, R. Penelope's Hat.
 P. Craig, 617(TLS):11-17Aug89-878
França, J-A., ed. L'Humanisme Portugais et
 l'Europe.
 R.C. Willis, 86(BHS):Apr88-197
Francioni, G. - see Beccaria, C.

Francis, D. Controlling Interest.
 J. Niosi, 529(QQ):Autumn88-714
Francis, D. The Edge.*
 P-L. Adams, 61:Mar89-97
 S. Grafton, 441:12Feb89-9
Francis, D. Hot Money.*
 A. Ross, 364:Dec87/Jan88-141
Francis, D. Portugal 1715-1808.*
 P.E.H. Hair, 86(BHS):Jan88-103
Francis, D. Straight.
 P-L. Adams, 61:Dec89-127
 M. Stasio, 441:3Dec89-32
Francis, M. WHOM.
 A. Rosenheim, 617(TLS):10-16Nov89-
 1243
Francis, R.D. & H. Palmer, eds. The Prairie
 West.
 B. Ferguson, 298:Spring/Summer88-219
Francisco, P.W. Cold Feet.
 D. Ackerman, 441:19Feb89-22
Franck, K.A. & S. Ahrentzen, eds. New
 Households, New Housing.
 P. Goldberger, 441:3Dec89-21
Franco, E. Perception, Knowledge, and Dis-
 belief.
 S. Pollock, 293(JASt):Nov88-917
Franco, J. Plotting Women.
 M. Wood, 617(TLS):14-20Jul89-778
Franey, P. & B. Miller. Cuisine Rapide.
 P. Simon, 441:11Jun89-20
Frank, A. The Diary of Anne Frank. (D. Bar-
 nouw & G. van der Stroom, eds)
 J. Thurman, 442(NY):18Dec89-116
 R. Wisse, 441:2Jul89-2
Frank, F.S. The First Gothics.
 W.H. Hildebrand, 87(BB):Dec88-274
 D.P. Varma, 166:Jan89-165
Frank, H., Y. Frank-Böhringer & B. Frank-
 Böhringer, eds. Lingvokibernetiko-Sprach-
 kybernetik.
 G.F. Meier, 682(ZPSK):Band41Heft5-668
Frank, J. Dostoevsky: The Stir of Liberation,
 1860-1865.*
 R.L. Belknap, 574(SEEJ):Summer88-317
 P.J. Casagrande, 594:Summer88-206
 C.V. Ponomareff, 627(UTQ):Winter88/89-
 330
 E. Wasiolek, 131(CL):Summer88-297
 G. Woodcock, 569(SR):Spring88-306
Frank, M. Das Bild des Juden in der deut-
 schen Literatur im Wandel der Zeit-
 geschichte.*
 R. Robertson, 402(MLR):Jan89-261
Frank, M. - see Tieck, L.
Frank, R. The Lines of My Hand.
 A. Grundberg, 441:3Dec89-04
Frank, R.H. Passions within Reason.
 A. Ryan, 453(NYRB):18May89-25
Frank, S.L. The Spiritual Foundations of
 Society.
 K.B., 185:Jan89-470
Franke, P., W. Leschhorn & A.U. Stylow,
 comps. Sylloge Nummorum Graecorum,
 Deutschland: Sammlung v. Aulock; Index.
 W. Szaivert, 229:Band60Heft6-548
Franke-Benn, C. Die Wayangwelt.
 J.U. Wolff, 318(JAOS):Jan-Mar87-195
Frankfurt, H.G. The Importance of What We
 Care About.
 M. Klein, 617(TLS):11-17Aug89-882
Frankl, R. Televangelism.
 A. Woolfolk, 585(SoQ):Winter89-105

Franklin, A. The Neglect of Experiment.
J. Forge, 63:Mar88-116
I. Hacking, 486:Jun88-306
Franklin, B. The Papers of Benjamin Franklin. (Vol 25)(W.B. Willcox, ed)
W.R. Ward, 83:Autumn88-205
Franklin, B. Writings.* (J.A.L. Lemay, ed)
D. Seed, 83:Autumn88-205
Franklin, C. Printing and the Mind of Morris.
D. McKitterick, 78(BC):Spring88-134
Franklin, D.O., ed. Bach Studies.
M. Boyd, 617(TLS):27Oct-2Nov89-1190
Franklin, H.B. War Stars.
P. Conrad, 617(TLS):1-7Sep89-939
Franko, M. The Dancing Body in Renaissance Choreography.
S.L. Foster, 615(TJ):Oct88-429
Frankovits, A., ed. Seduced and Abandoned.
G.P. Bennington, 208(FS):Jul88-369
Fransman, M., ed. Machinery and Economic Development.
B.M. Koppel, 293(JASt):Feb88-97
Frantzen, A.J. King Alfred.
H. Sauer, 38:Band106Heft3/4-487
E.G. Stanley, 447(N&Q):Jun88-203
Frantzen, A.J. The Literature of Penance in Anglo-Saxon England.
B. Lindström, 597(SN):Vol60No1-139
P.E. Szarmach, 589:Apr88-392
Franz, U. Deng Xiaoping.
J. Mirsky, 617(TLS):17-23Mar89-270
Franzen, B. Hearing from Wayne, and Other Stories.*
639(VQR):Autumn88-128
Fraser, A. The Warrior Queens.
P-L. Adams, 61:May89-100
N. Bliven, 442(NY):24Apr89-108
G.A. Craig, 453(NYRB):17Aug89-31
G. Garrett, 441:2Apr89-18
Fraser, H. Beauty and Belief.*
A.D. Culler, 131(CL):Winter88-91
J.C. Livingston, 506(PSt):Sep88-103
Fraser, J. Telling Tales.
G.W., 102(CanL):Winter87-294
Fraser, K. Foreign Affairs.
N. Besner, 168(ECW):Spring88-64
Fraser, K. Scenes from the Fashionable World.
A.F. Collins, 662:Fall88/Winter89-52
Fraser, R. The Brontës.
V. Tiger, 441:5Feb89-16
Fraser, R. The Three Romes.
S. Pickering, 569(SR):Fall88-673
Fraser, R. West African Poetry.
A. Maja-Pearce, 364:Apr/May88-142
G. Moore, 538(RAL):Winter88-574
H.A. Waters, 403(MLS):Summer88-86
Fraser, R. Young Shakespeare.*
S. Schoenbaum, 617(TLS):20-26Jan89-63
Fraser, R. - see Barker, G.
Fraser, R. - see Shakespeare, W.
Fraser, S. My Father's House.*
C. Matthews, 376:Mar88-92
Fraser, T.P. The French Essay.*
H. Sonneville, 356(LR):Feb-May88-117
Fraser-Lu, S. Indonesian Batik.
G.N. Gartenberg, 293(JASt):Feb88-194
Frastein, S., ed. När kvinder skriver, en antologi.
B. Baldwin, 563(SS):Summer88-414
Frauenfelder, U.H. & L.K. Tyler, eds. Spoken Word Recognition.
B.H. Repp, 348(L&S):Apr-Jun88-207

Frayling, C. The Royal College of Art.
C.S. Smith, 90:Jun88-474
Frayn, J.M. Sheep-rearing and the Wool Trade in Italy during the Roman Period.
N. Purcell, 123:Vol38No1-96
Frayn, M. The Trick of It.
G. Craig, 617(TLS):22-28Sep89-1021
Frazer, T.C. Midland Illinois Dialect Patterns.
M.I. Miller, 35(AS):Winter88-353
R.K. Seymour, 215(GL):Vol28No2-154
Frazier, I. Great Plains.
S. Hubbell, 441:18Jun89-9
Frazier, W., with N. Offen. Walt Frazier.
M. Caruso, 441:29Jan89-31
Freadman, R. Eliot, James, and the Fictional Self.
R. Hull, 594:Fall88-345
W. Veeder, 395(MFS):Summer88-231
Freberg, S. It Only Hurts When I Laugh.
S. Elliott, 441:8Jan89-23
Frécaut, J-M. & D. Porte, eds. Journées Ovidiennes de Parménie.
B. Liou-Gille, 555:Vol61fasc1-142
Freccero, J. Dante.* (R. Jacoff, ed)
M. Marcus, 589:Jan88-152
L. Pertile, 382(MAE):1988/1-143
T. Wlassics, 551(RenQ):Winter88-707
Frechette, J-M. Le Corps de l'infini.
M. Andersen, 102(CanL):Spring88-142
Fredborg, K.M. The Latin Rhetorical Commentaries by Thierry of Chartres.
O. Weyers, 640:Nov88-152
Frede, M. Essays in Ancient Philosophy.*
G.B. Kerferd, 123:Vol38No2-290
Frederick the Great. Friedrich der Grosse, "Das Palladion." (J. Ziechmann & others, eds)
P. Wagner, 83:Spring88-117
Fredrickson, G.M. The Arrogance of Race.*
D.B. Davis, 453(NYRB):30Mar89-29
Fredriksen, P. From Jesus to Christ.
G. Vermes, 617(TLS):24-30Mar89-321
Freeborn, P. The Stark Truth.
S. Lee, 441:5Nov89-26
Freedberg, D. The Power of Images.
R. Arnheim, 617(TLS):22-28Sep89-1033
Freedland, M. Leonard Bernstein.*
A. Jacobs, 415:Jan88-21
Freedman, E.B. & J. D'Emilio. Intimate Matters.
C. Stevens, 42(AR):Fall88-525
Freedman, F.B. William Douglas O'Connor.
M.J. Killingsworth, 534(RALS):Vol16 No1&2-118
Freeling, N. Not as Far as Velma.
M. Stasio, 441:9Jul89-24
Freeman, B. Danger on the Tracks.
M. Steig, 102(CanL):Spring88-236
Freeman, C. The Bride of Ambrose and Other Stories.
J. Clute, 617(TLS):21-27Jul89-803
Freeman, C. Technology Policy and Economic Performance.
Funaba Masatomi, 285(JapQ):Jul-Sep88-326
Freeman, G. Termination Rock.
J. O'Grady, 617(TLS):25-31Aug89-918
Freeman, J. The Chinchilla Farm.
T. Sandlin, 441:17Dec89-13
442(NY):13Nov89-147

125

Freeman, J. Family Attractions.*
  J.L. Jacobsen, 649(WAL):Feb89-375
  G.L. Morris, 455:Sep88-68
Freeman, M.J. - see Jodelle, E.
Freeman, P. & D. Kennedy, eds. The Defence
  of the Roman and Byzantine East.
  B. Isaac, 313:Vol78-240
Freeman, S. Fair Weather Foul.
  R.G. Topp, 569(SR):Summer88-lxvii
Freeman, S. Mutton and Oysters.
  J. Burnett, 617(TLS):22-28Dec89-1410
Freeman, T. Hans Henny Jahnn.
  R. Furness, 402(MLR):Jul89-803
"The 'Freeman's Journal' of Bloomsday."
  M. O'Toole, 329(JJQ):Summer89-632
Freemantle, B. The Run Around.
  N. Callendar, 441:25Jun89-31
Freese, P., ed. The American Short Story.
  P. Bischoff, 72:Band225Heft2-475
Frege, G. Die Grundlagen der Arithmetik. (C.
  Thiel, ed)
  M. Schirn, 316:Sep88-993
Freidin, G. A Coat of Many Colors.
  P. France, 617(TLS):10-16Mar89-245
Freimark, P., F. Kopitzsch & H. Slessarev, eds.
  Lessing und die Toleranz.*
  F. Genton, 549(RLC):Jan-Mar88-93
  K.A. Wurst, 221(GQ):Summer88-463
Freitag, M. Dialectique et société. (Vol 1)
  A. Stanguennec, 542:Jan-Mar88-101
Fremlin, D.H. Consequences of Martin's
  Axiom.
  W. Weiss, 316:Jun88-650
French, A. All Cretans Are Liars and Other
  Poems.
  L. Mackinnon, 617(TLS):26May-1Jun89-
  593
French, B.B. Witness to the Young Republic.
  (D.B. Cole & J.J. McDonough, eds)
  P-L. Adams, 61:Nov89-136
French, D. Jitters.
  V. Comensoli, 102(CanL):Autumn88-136
French, P.A., T.E. Uehling & H.K. Wettstein,
  eds. Midwest Studies in Philosophy. (Vol
  11)
  C.M., 185:Oct88-192
Frend, W.H.C. The Rise of Christianity.
  Saints and Sinners in the Early Church.
  P. Habermehl, 229:Band60Heft8-725
Frenk, M., ed. Corpus de la antigua lírica
  popular hispánica (siglos xv a xvii).
  J. Gornall, 304(JHP):Winter88-162
  A. Vermeylen, 356(LR):Feb-May88-121
Frenz, T. Die Kanzlei der Papste der Hoch-
  renaissance (1471-1527).
  C.L. Stinger, 551(RenQ):Summer88-291
Frere, S. Britannia. (3rd ed)
  T.W. Potter, 123:Vol38No2-438
Frere, S.S., A.L.F. Rivet & N.H.H. Sitwell.
  Tabula Imperii Romani: Britannia Septen-
  trionalis.
  L. Keppie, 123:Vol38No2-439
Fresco, K. - see de Berneville, G.
Frescobaldi, G. Il primo libro di Capricci fatti
  sopra diversi soggetti et arie. (E. Darbel-
  lay, ed)
  F. Hammond, 317:Fall88-527
"Freshman Admissions at Berkeley."
  A. Hacker, 453(NYRB):12Oct89-63
Fretwell, B. Clematis.
  L. Yang, 441:3Dec89-74

Freud, S. Briefe an Wilhelm Fliess 1887-
  1904. (J.M. Masson, ed)
  W. Goetschel, 221(GQ):Summer88-484
Freud, S. The Interpretation of Dreams.
  C. Sartiliot, 153:Winter88-68
Freudenstein, R. & C.V. James, eds. Confi-
  dence through Competence in Modern Lan-
  guage Learning.
  P.B. Nimmons, 399(MLJ):Spring88-72
Freudenthal, G. Atom and Individual in the
  Age of Newton.
  M.A. Finocchiaro, 262:Mar88-103
  D. Kubrin, 319:Jan89-154
Freud, E. The Return of the Reader.
  W.E. Cain, 395(MFS):Winter88-729
  A.C. Pugh, 494:Vol8No3/4-689
Freund, J. Politique et impolitique.
  A. Reix, 542:Oct-Dec88-519
Freund, W. & H. Schumacher, eds. Spiegel im
  dunklen Wort.
  W. Paulsen, 221(GQ):Spring87-296
Freundlich, R. Verbalsubstantive als Namen
  für Satzinhalte in der Sprache des Thuky-
  dides.
  M.H.B. Marshall, 123:Vol38No2-403
Frewin, L. The Late Mrs. Dorothy Parker.*
  H.L. Hill, 27(AL):Mar88-149
Frey, C. The Nefertiti Look.
  M. Kenyon, 376:Sep88-160
Frey, J.A. Les Contemplations of Victor Hugo.
  J.D. Erickson, 446(NCFS):Fall-Winter
  88/89-228
Freyburger, G. Fides.
  J.H.W.G. Liebeschuetz, 123:Vol38No2-296
  J. Ramminger, 229:Band60Heft1-18
Freyburger-Galland, M.L., G. Freyburger &
  J.C. Tautil. Sectes religieuses en Grèce et
  à Rome dans l'antiquité païenne.
  J.H.W.G. Liebeschuetz, 123:Vol38No2-296
  J. Linderski, 313:Vol78-207
Freydank, H. Hethitische Rituale und Fest-
  beschreibungen.
  C. Carter, 318(JAOS):Oct-Dec87-790
Freyer, B. Royal Benin Art.
  B.W. Blackmun, 2(AfrA):May88-14
Freyre, G. The Masters and the Slaves. The
  Mansions and the Shanties. Order and Pro-
  gress.
  A. Hennessy, 617(TLS):14-20Jul89-763
Frick, N.A. Image in the Mind.
  J.T. Goodwin, 108:Summer88-94
Fridén, A. "Macbeth" in the Swedish Theatre
  1838-1986.
  K-P. Steiger, 156(ShJW):Jahrbuch1988-
  299
Friebert, S. & D. Young, eds. The Longman
  Anthology of Contemporary American
  Poetry 1950-1980.
  C. Clausen, 569(SR):Winter88-131
Fried, E. 100 Poems without a Country.
  L. Sail, 565:Spring88-73
Fried, M. Realism, Writing, Disfiguration.*
  R. Carney, 473(PR):Vol55No3-464
  R.A. Cavell, 627(UTQ):Summer89-521
  L. Jordanova, 59:Mar88-115
  C. Landauer, 89(BJA):Spring88-187
  J.H. Levi, 55:Feb88-51
  J. Nagel, 27(AL):Oct88-479
  S. Wertheim, 26(ALR):Fall88-85
Friedberg, A.L. The Weary Titan.
  P. Kennedy, 453(NYRB):16Mar89-36

Friedberg, R.C. American Art Song and American Poetry. (Vol 3)
P. Dickinson, 410(M&L):Apr88-293
von Friedeburg, L. & J. Habermas, eds. Adorno-Konferenz 1983.
W. van Reijen, 687:Jan-Mar88-162
Frieden, K. Genius and Monologue.
M. Gullick, 89(BJA):Summer88-298
Frieden, S. Autobiography.*
R. Delphendahl, 221(GQ):Spring87-310
Friedenberg, J. & C. Bradley. Finding a Job in the United States.
R.M. Ramsey, 399(MLJ):Summer88-226
Friedl, E. Women of Deh Koh.
P. Glazebrook, 441:14May89-13
Friedländer, S. Reflections of Nazism.
H.A. Schmitt, 569(SR):Winter88-158
Friedman, A. Agnelli and the Network of Italian Power.
G.G. Migone, 617(TLS):2-8Jun89-617
Friedman, A. & T. Schwarz. Power and Greed.
G. Tyler, 441:9Jul89-9
Friedman, A.J. & C.C. Donley. Einstein: Myth and Muse.*
J.D. Barrow, 617(TLS):29Sep-5Oct89-1072
Friedman, A.T. House and Household in Elizabethan England.
H. Colvin, 617(TLS):1-7Sep89-948
Friedman, A.W., ed. Critical Essays on Lawrence Durrell.
H.M. Kay, 115:Summer88-320
Friedman, A.W. William Faulkner.
R.D. Parker, 402(MLR):Jan89-148
Friedman, A.W., C. Rossman & D. Sherzer, eds. Beckett Translating/Translating Beckett.
S.E. Gontarski, 395(MFS):Winter88-722
J.C.C. Mays, 272(IUR):Spring88-141
A. Otten, 42(AR):Winter88-113
L. Powlick, 615(TJ):Dec88-588
Friedman, B.J. The Current Climate.
C. Bloom, 441:1Oct89-26
Friedman, E.G. & M. Fuchs, eds. Breaking the Sequence.
E. Hirsh, 659(ConL):Winter89-578
Friedman, E.H. The Antiheroine's Voice.*
B.M. Damiani, 238:Dec88-821
R.L. Fiore, 115:Fall88-433
M.J. Lemaître, 599:Spring89-147
Friedman, J. Blasphemy, Immorality, and Anarchy.
D. Underdown, 551(RenQ):Summer88-327
Friedman, J. & P. Aprahamian. Inside London.
A. Youngman, 441:27Aug89-17
Friedman, K. Frequent Flyer.
D. Murray, 441:15Oct89-50
Friedman, L.D. Hollywood's Image of the Jew.
R.L. Macmillan, 488:Sep88-427
Friedman, M. Deadly Reflections.
T.J.B., 617(TLS):3-9Nov89-1218
Friedman, M. Foundations of Space-Time Theories.*
L. Sklar, 311(JP):Mar88-158
Friedman, M. The Utopian Dilemma.*
D. Stone, 287:May/Jun87-29
Friedman, M.L. The Emperor's Kites.
P. Finnegan, 395(MFS):Summer88-263
G.R. Shivers, 552(REH):Oct88-131
Friedman, P. Serious Trouble.*
B.K. Horvath, 532(RCF):Spring88-208
Friedman, R. An Eligible Man.
J. Grant, 617(TLS):24Feb-2Mar89-190

Friedman, T. James Gibbs.*
D. Cast, 54:Jun88-352
Friedman, T.L. From Beirut to Jerusalem.
R. Rosenblatt, 441:9Jul89-1
442(NY):14Aug89-91
Friedman, Y. - see Peter the Venerable
Friedrich, O. City of Nets.
J.G. Dunne, 453(NYRB):18May89-28
Friedrich, O. Glenn Gould.
E. Zukerman, 441:23Apr89-22
Friedrich, P. The Language Parallax.*
J.T. Andresen, 355(LSoc):Dec88-600
D. Tannen, 350:Mar89-169
Friel, J. Taking the Veil.
G. Gardiner, 617(TLS):1-7Dec89-1337
Friend, J.W. Seven Years in France.
P. McCarthy, 617(TLS):22-28Dec89-1406
Frier, B.W. The Rise of the Roman Jurists.*
D. Cohen, 122:Apr88-163
W.M. Gordon, 123:Vol38No1-38
Fries, J. Der Zweikampf.*
F. Ahlheid, 394:Vol41fasc3/4-430
E. Burck, 229:Band60Heft4-323
Fries, U. Einführung in die Sprache Chaucers.*
H. Peters, 72:Band224Heft2-393
"Elizabeth Frink, Sculpture."
R. Berthoud, 90:Jun88-473
Frisbie, C.J., ed. Explorations in Ethnomusicology.
R. Provine, 415:Jan88-22
Frisch, M. Schweiz ohne Armee?
M. Butler, 617(TLS):8-14Dec89-1356
Frisch, P. Zehn agonistische Papyri.
R.S. Bagnall, 229:Band60Heft1-42
J.D. Thomas, 123:Vol38No2-453
Frisch, W. Brahms and the Principle of Developing Variation.*
V. Kofi Agawu, 411:Mar88-99
Frisch, W., ed. Schubert.*
N. Rast, 411:Mar88-105
Frith, S. Music for Pleasure.
T.W. Ryback, 617(TLS):21-27Jul89-794
Fritz, A.D. Thought and Vision.
W.H. Green, 580(SCR):Spring89-80
Frizell, B.S. Asine II, Results of the Excavations East of the Acropolis, 1970-1974. (Fasc 3)
E. French, 123:Vol38No2-444
Frobose, M. Récits divertissants.
A.J. Salvas, 207(FR):Feb89-565
Frodon, J-M. & J-C. Loiseau. Jean de Florette.
H. Charney, 207(FR):Mar89-704
Froeschle, H., ed. Beiträge zur schwäbischen Literatur- und Geistesgeschichte. (Vol 3)
M. Hałub, 680(ZDP):Band106Heft4-626
Froissart, J. Le Paradis d'amour; L'Orloge amoureus.* (P.F. Dembowski, ed)
L.S. Crist, 589:Apr88-394
N. Wilkins, 208(FS):Apr88-197
Frome, F. Some Dare to Dream.
I. Deak, 453(NYRB):28Sep89-63
Froment-Meurice, M. La Disparue.
J.T. Letts, 207(FR):Apr89-903
Fromkin, D. A Peace to End All Peace.
N. Bliven, 442(NY):11Dec89-154
W.R. Louis, 441:27Aug89-9
Fromm, G.G., ed. Essaying Biography.
I.B. Nadel, 177(ELT):Vol31No4-465
Fromm, H., ed. Der deutsche Minnesang.* (Vol 2)
H. Heinen, 406:Summer88-215

Frontinus, S.J. Frontino, "Los Acueductos de Roma." (T. González Rolán, ed & trans)
  L. Callebat, 555:Vol61fasc1-140
Frost, E.L. For Richer, For Poorer.
  Suzuki Sunao, 285(JapQ):Jul-Sep88-322
Frow, J. Marxism and Literary History.*
  R. McNutt, 577(SHR):Summer88-277
  M. Sinfield, 506(PSt):May88-113
  R. Strickland, 454:Fall88-111
  D. Watson, 366:Spring88-113
Frucht, A. Fruit of the Month.*
  42(AR):Fall88-532
  639(VQR):Autumn88-129
Frühwald, W. & others - see "Aurora"
Frum, L. Linda Frum's Guide to Canadian Universities.
  G.S. Smith, 529(QQ):Autumn88-751
Frutkin, M. The Alchemy of Clouds.
  R. Maggs, 102(CanL):Winter87-280
Fry, J. Visual Variations.
  R.B. Phillips, 529(QQ):Spring88-230
Fryckstedt, M.C. Geraldine Jewsbury's "Athenaeum" Reviews.*
  E.M. Casey, 635(VPR):Summer88-80
Frye, N. Northrop Frye on Shakespeare.* (R. Sandler, ed)
  T.W. Craik, 161(DUJ):Dec87-145
  M. Grivelet, 189(EA):Oct-Dec88-482
  E.A.J. Honigmann, 677(YES):Vol19-314
  A.W. Lyle, 541(RES):Aug88-434
  J. Rees, 447(N&Q):Jun88-220
Fryer, J. Felicitous Space.*
  B. Bair, 594:Fall88-340
Frykman, J. & O. Löfgren. Culture Builders.
  B. Klein, 292(JAF):Apr-Jun88-239
Fu, C.W-H. & G.E. Spiegler, eds. Movements and Issues in World Religions.
  J.W. Laine, 293(JASt):May88-326
Fu, S., G.D. Lowry & A. Yonemura - see under Shen Fu, G.D. Lowry & A. Yonemura
Fubini, E. Musica e cultura nel Settecento europeo.
  R. Monelle, 410(M&L):Jul88-381
Fuchs, D. Saul Bellow.
  E. Hollahan, 594:Spring88-104
Fuchs, E. Israeli Mythogynies.*
  B. Lyons, 395(MFS):Winter88-750
  N.B. Sokoloff, 508:Jan88-143
Fuchs, E., ed. Plays of the Holocaust.
  M.I. Teicher, 390:Apr88-57
Fuchs-Sumiyoshi, A. Orientalismus in der deutschen Literatur.*
  A.A. Teraoka, 221(GQ):Spring87-304
Fuegi, J. Bertolt Brecht.*
  M. Esslin, 615(TJ):Dec87-523
  D. Fogg, 610:Spring88-63
  R.C. Lamont, 397(MD):Sep88-459
  R.J. Rundell, 221(GQ):Summer88-480
Fuentes, C. Aura. (P. Standish, ed)
  R.W. Fiddian, 402(MLR):Jan89-221
Fuentes, C. Christopher Unborn.
  J. King, 617(TLS):15-21Dec89-1386
  S. Ruta, 441:20Aug89-1
Fuentes, N. Ernest Hemingway Rediscovered.
  S.F. Beegel, 234:Spring89-51
Fuerst, N. Das Dramenwerk Max Zweigs.
  R. Kieser, 406:Winter88-527
Fuerst, N. Paul Ernst.
  R.E. Lorbe, 406:Summer88-249
Fugard, S. A Revolutionary Woman.
  J. Byrne, 532(RCF):Spring88-204

Fügedi, E. Castle and Society in Medieval Hungary (1000-1437).*
  J. Klassen, 589:Jul88-661
Fühmann, F. & D. Riemann. Was für eine Insel in was für einem Meer.
  G. Klatt, 654(WB):4/1988-641
Fujimura, O., ed. Vocal Physiology.
  W.S-Y. Wang, 350:Sep89-660
Fuks, A. Social Conflict in Ancient Greece.
  A.J.L. van Hooff, 394:Vol41fasc1/2-226
Fukuzawa Yukichi. Fukuzawa Yukichi on Japanese Women.
  J.C. Lebra, 407(MN):Autumn88-376
Fulbeck, W. Fulbeck's Direction, or Preparative to the Study of the Law.
  D. Ibbetson, 447(N&Q):Dec88-540
Fulbright, J.W., with S.P. Tillman. The Price of Empire.
  W.F. Kimball, 617(TLS):7-13Jul89-742
  G. Smith, 441:19Feb89-7
  R. Steel, 453(NYRB):29Jun89-47
Fulcher, J.F. The Nation's Image.*
  P. Gumplowicz, 537:Vol74No2-240
  R. Macdonald, 415:Aug88-405
Fulghum, R. All I Really Need to Know I Learned in Kindergarten.
  R.B. Smith, 441:19Mar89-23
Fulghum, R. It Was on Fire When I Lay Down on It.
  G. Kolata, 441:17Sep89-25
Fülleborn, U. & M. Engel, eds. Das neuzeitliche Ich in der Literatur des 18. und 20. Jahrhunderts.
  A. Fiddler, 402(MLR):Jul89-805
Fuller, B. A Butterfly Net and a Kingdom.
  L. Graeber, 441:19Mar89-22
Fuller, G.E. How to Learn a Foreign Language.
  C.L. McKay, 399(MLJ):Autumn88-332
Fuller, J. The Burning Boys.
  J.K.L. Walker, 617(TLS):30Jun-6Jul89-714
Fuller, J. Tell It Me Again.* The Grey among the Green.*
  J. Lucas, 493:Autumn88-59
Fuller, J. - see Gay, J.
Fuller, M. The Letters of Margaret Fuller. (R.N. Hudspeth, ed)
  D. Berkson, 357:Fall88-64
Fuller, P. Theoria.*
  M. Yorke, 324:Jun89-442
Fuller, P. Towards an Antipodean Aesthetic.
  R. Carmichael, 592:Vol201No1019-68
Fuller, R. Available for Dreams.
  M. O'Neill, 617(TLS):23-29Jun89-694
Fuller, R. Consolations.*
  J. Forth, 364:Nov87-85
Fuller, R. Image of a Society.
  J. Lewis, 364:Mar87-62
Fuller, R. The Ruined Boys.
  J. Lewis, 364:Mar87-67
Fuller, R. The Strange and the Good.
  617(TLS):1-7Dec89-1344
Fuller, T. - see Oakeshott, M.
Fulton, A. Palladium.*
  C. Bedient, 569(SR):Winter88-137
Fulton, R., ed. A Garioch Miscellany.
  J. Saunders, 565:Autumn88-72
Fulton, R.D. & C.M. Colee, eds. Union List of Victorian Serials.*
  J.D. Vann, 40(AEB):Vol2No2-68
Fulwiler, T., ed. The Journal Book.
  A. Johnstone, 126(CCC):Oct88-363

Fumerton, R.A. Metaphysical and Epistemological Problems of Perception.*
G. Dicker, 449:Sep88-483
Fung, S.S.K. & S.T. Lai. T'ang Poets.
Chow Tse-Tsung, 302:Vol24No1-73
Funkenstein, A. Theology and the Scientific Imagination from the Middle Ages to the Seventeenth Century.*
R. Palter, 319:Apr89-305
Furbank, P.N. E.M. Forster.
P. Craig, 617(TLS):7-13Apr89-362
Furbank, P.N. & W.R. Owens. The Canonisation of Daniel Defoe.*
A.J. McGeoch, 364:Jul88-98
M.E. Novak, 166:Jan89-147
Furet, F. Marx and the French Revolution.* (French title: Marx et la Révolution française.) (L. Calvié, ed)
W. Scott, 617(TLS):19-25May89-554
Furet, F., ed. Unanswered Questions.
I. Deak, 453(NYRB):28Sep89-63
Furet, F. & M. Ozouf, eds. A Critical Dictionary of the French Revolution.
L. Hunt, 441:10Sep89-12
Furler, B. Augen-Schein.
H. Kaulen, 680(ZDP):Band107Heft4-630
Furley, D. Cosmic Problems.
D. Sedley, 617(TLS):13-19Oct89-1128
Furley, D.J. The Greek Cosmologists.* (Vol 1)
N. Austin, 124:Mar-Apr89-315
M. Schofield, 520:Vol33No1-113
Furnas, J.C. My Life in Writing.
S.G. Lanes, 441:10Sep89-27
Furrow, M.M., ed. Ten Fifteenth-Century Comic Poems.*
J.M.P. Donatelli, 627(UTQ):Fall87-104
S. Mapstone, 382(MAE):1988/2-318
S.M. Taylor, 201:Vol14-213
A. Wawn, 402(MLR):Apr89-435
Furtwangler, A. American Silhouettes.*
M. Breitwieser, 173(ECS):Summer88-547
J. Matthews, 529(QQ):Winter88-911
Furtwängler, W. Notebooks 1924-1954. (M. Tanner, ed)
B. Goldschmidt, 617(TLS):28Jul-3Aug89-826
Furukawa, N. L'article et le problème de la référence en français.*
R. Martin, 209(FM):Apr88-110
Fusco, A.C. Inigo Jones Vitruvius Britannicus.
E. Chaney, 90:Aug88-633
Füssel, S. Riccardus Bartholinus Perusinus: Humanistische Panegyrik am Hofe Kaiser Maximilians I.
L.V.R., 568(SCN):Fall88-68
Fussell, P., ed. The Norton Book of Travel.
639(VQR):Summer88-103
Fussell, P. Wartime.
N. Annan, 453(NYRB):28Sep89-3
N. Bliven, 442(NY):16Oct89-127
S. Schama, 441:3Sep89-1
J. Treglown, 617(TLS):22-28Sep89-1027
Füst, M. The Story of My Wife.*
P. Sherwood, 617(TLS):10-16Mar89-255
Fyfield, F. A Question of Guilt.
M. Stasio, 441:27Aug89-22
Fynsk, C. Heidegger.
R. Gasché, 543:Mar89-616
D.F. Krell, 323:Jan88-96
B. Radloff, 627(UTQ):Summer88-561
A. Schwarz, 400(MLN):Apr88-698

Fyrth, J. The Signal was Spain.*
M. Alpert, 86(BHS):Oct88-416

Gabbard, K. & G.O. Psychiatry and the Cinema.
D. Polan, 500:Winter89-64
S. Snyder, 106:Spring88-89
Gabbay, D. & F. Guenthner, eds. Handbook of Philosophical Logic. (Vol 3)
L. Humberstone, 63:Mar88-120
Gabelmann, H. Antike Audienz- und Tribunalszenen.
M. Ducos, 555:Vol61fasc1-167
Gable, R. - see Williams, R.
Gabler, H.W., with C. Melchior & W. Steppe - see Joyce, J.
Gabler, N. An Empire of Their Own.*
L. Anderson, 617(TLS):15-21Dec89-1387
J.G. Dunne, 453(NYRB):18May89-28
Gaboriau, F. Philosophie issue des sciences.
M. Adam, 542:Jan-Mar88-121
Gaborieau, M., ed. Islam et société en Asie du Sud/Islam and Society in South Asia.
B.D. Metcalf, 293(JASt):Feb88-176
Gabriel, E. Einführung in den Vorarlberg Sprachatlas mit Einschluss des Fürstentums Liechtenstein, Westtirols und des Allgäus (VALTS).
H. Löffler, 685(ZDL):3/1988-346
Gabriel, E., ed. Vorarlberger Sprachatlas mis Schluss des Fürstentums Liechtenstein, Westtirols und des Allgäus (VALTS). (Vol 1)
H. Löffler, 685(ZDL):3/1988-346
Gace Brulé. The Lyrics and Melodies of Gace Brulé. (S.N. Rosenberg & S. Danon, eds & trans)
S. Haynes, 208(FS):Apr88-196
Gachnang, J., ed. Sigmar Polke.
M. Wechsler, 62:Sep88-19
Gadamer, H-G. The Idea of the Good in Platonic-Aristotelian Philosophy.* (P.C. Smith, ed & trans)
R.B. Louden, 41:Fall88-298
L.P. Schrenk, 124:Sep-Oct88-51
Gadamer, H-G. The Relevance of the Beautiful and Other Essays.* (R. Bernasconi, ed)
S. Bann, 617(TLS):20-26Jan89-66
R.J. Bernstein, 290(JAAC):Spring88-421
S. Stern-Gillet, 89(BJA):Summer88-289
Gadda, C.E. Lettere a Gianfranco Contini.
U. Varnai, 617(TLS):3-9Feb89-112
Gadenne, P. Le Jour que voici.
F. Mary, 450(NRF):Apr88-91
Gadenne, P. Scènes dans le château.*
J. Taylor, 532(RCF):Spring88-193
Gadet, F. Saussure and Contemporary Culture.
M. Sprinker, 617(TLS):18-24Aug89-898
Gadney, R. Nightshade.
N. Callendar, 441:15Jan89-39
Gado, F. The Passion of Ingmar Bergman.
H.T.B., 295(JML):Fall87/Winter88-281
Gadourek, C. William Faulkner and the American Dilemma.
J.L. Sensibar, 27(AL):Dec88-684
Gaefke, P. & D.A. Utz, eds. Science and Technology in South Asia.
K.G. Zysk, 318(JAOS):Oct-Dec87-838
Gaehtgens, T.W., ed. Johann Joachim Winckelman 1717-1768.*
N. Gabriel, 52:Band23Heft1-107

Gaskell, P. A Bibliography of the Foulis
Press.* (2nd ed)
   B. Gerrard, 40(AEB):Vol2No4–175
   G.R.R., 588(SSL):Vol23–309
Gaskell, P. From Writer to Reader.
   B. Fabian, 38:Band106Heft3/4–524
Gaskill, W. A Sense of Direction.*
   T. Dunn, 511:Oct88–46
Gaskin, J.C.A. Hume's Philosophy of Religion.
(2nd ed)
   M.A. Stewart, 319:Jul89–481
Gasnault, F. Guinguettes et lorettes.
   J-C. Lebensztejn, 98:Mar88–236
Gass, S.M. & C.G. Madden, eds. Input in Sec-
ond Language Acquisition.
   B.F. Freed, 355(LSoc):Mar88–137
Gasset, J.O. – see under Ortega y Gasset, J.
Gateau, J-C. Abécédaire critique.
   D. Knight, 402(MLR):Oct89–973
Gates, H. Chinese Working-Class Lives.
   J.W. Salaff, 293(JASt):Nov88–849
Gates, H.L., Jr., ed. Black Literature and
Literary Theory.*
   H.K. Bhabha, 494:Vol8No1–181
   W.E. Cain, 128(CE):Feb88–190
   G. Lang, 107(CRCL):Jun88–259
Gates, H.L., Jr. Figures in Black.*
   R.D. Abrahams, 538(RAL):Fall88–448
   K. Kinnamon, 27(AL):Oct88–483
   C. Werner, 395(MFS):Spring88–125
Gates, H.L., Jr. The Signifying Monkey.*
   H.V. Carby, 617(TLS):29Dec89/4Jan90–
   1446
Gatrell, P. The Tsarist Economy 1850–1917.
   C.S. Leonard, 550(RusR):Jul88–338
Gatrell, S. Hardy the Creator.
   K. Millard, 617(TLS):29Dec89/4Jan90–
   1445
Gatrell, S. – see Hardy, T.
Gatwood, L.E. Devi and the Spouse Goddess.
   E.B. Findly, 318(JAOS):Oct–Dec87–781
Gauchet, M. Le désenchantement du monde.
   A. Reix, 542:Oct–Dec88–499
Gauchet, M. La Révolution des droits de
l'homme.
   W. Scott, 617(TLS):19–25May89–554
Gaudriault, R. Répertoire de la gravure de
mode française des origines à 1815.*
   A. Kleinert, 683:Band51Heft3–458
Gauger, H-M., W. Oesterreicher & R. Windisch.
Einführung in die romanische Sprachwis-
senschaft.
   N.R. Wolf, 685(ZDL):2/1987–244
Gaulmier, J., J. Boissel & M-L. Concasty – see
de Gobineau, J.A.
Gaulmier, J., with P. Lésétieux & V. Monteil –
see de Gobineau, A.
Gault, C. Some of Eve's Daughters.
   J.K. Keefer, 102(CanL):Spring88–218
   C. Mavrow, 376:Jun88–185
Gaume, M. Ruth Crawford Seeger.*
   P. Dickinson, 410(M&L):Jan88–112
Gaur, A., ed. South Asian Studies.
   M.L.P. Patterson, 293(JASt):Feb88–177
Gauthier, D.P. Morals by Agreement.*
   D.W. Brock, 484(PPR):Sep88–157
   R. Campbell, 479(PhQ):Jul88–343
Gauthier, R.A., ed. Lectura in Librum de
anima a quodam discipulo reportata (Ms.
Roma Naz. V.E. 828).
   S.P. Marrone, 589:Oct88–924

Gautier, T. Correspondance générale de
Théophile Gautier.* (Vol 1) (C. Lacoste-
Veysseyre, ed)
   H. Cockerham, 208(FS):Apr88–217
Gautier, T. Correspondance générale de
Théophile Gautier.* (Vol 2) (C. Lacoste-
Veysseyre & P. Laubriet, eds)
   H. Cockerham, 208(FS):Apr88–217
   J. Gaulmier, 535(RHL):Mar–Apr88–293
   P. Whyte, 402(MLR):Apr89–478
Gautier, T. Correspondance générale de
Théophile Gautier.* (Vol 3) (C. Lacoste-
Veysseyre & P. Laubriet, eds)
   P. Whyte, 402(MLR):Apr89–478
Gautier, T. Les Grotesques.* (C. Rizza, ed)
   G. Bosco, 475:Vol15No28–329
Gauvin, L. & J-M. Klinkenberg, eds. Trajec-
toires.*
   E-M. Kroller, 345(KRQ):May88–240
Gavin, W.J., ed. Context Over Foundation.
   J.L. Safford, 103:Oct89–411
Gavison, R., ed. Issues in Contemporary Legal
Philosophy.*
   J.H.B., 185:Oct88–188
   S. Guest, 518:Oct88–197
   M.A. Menlowe, 518:Apr88–105
Gawlick, G. – see Reimarus, H.S.
Gawlick, G. & L. Kreimendahl. Hume in der
deutschen Aufklärung.*
   H.B. Nisbet, 402(MLR):Jan89–231
   R. Palaia, 706:Band20Heft2–214
Gay, J. Dramatic Works. (J. Fuller, ed)
   C. Price, 541(RES):Nov88–558
Gay, P. The Bourgeois Experience. (Vol 1)
   V. Raoul, 102(CanL):Spring88–173
Gay, P. Freud.*
   S.B. Girgus, 30:Winter89–93
   A. Storr, 249(HudR):Winter89–723
   S. Tapscott, 219(GaR):Winter88–850
   S. Weiland, 385(MQR):Spring89–270
Gay, P. A Godless Jew.*
   G. Weiler, 390:Jun/Jul88–60
Gay, P. La Vitalité littéraire de l'Ontario
français.
   L.E. Doucette, 627(UTQ):Fall87–206
Gaycken, H-J. Christoph Martin Wieland.
   J. Curran, 83:Spring88–115
Gazdar, G. & others. Generalized Phrase
Structure Grammar.*
   W. O'Grady, 320(CJL):Sep88–284
   T. Torris, 603:Vol12No2–425
Gaze, J. Figures in a Landscape.
   T. O'Riordan, 617(TLS):31Mar–6Apr89–
   348
Geahchan, D.J. Temps et désir du psychan-
alyste.
   A. Reix, 542:Jan–Mar88–78
Gearey, J. – see von Goethe, J.W.
Gearhart, S. The Open Boundary of History
and Fiction.*
   T.M. Kavanagh, 125:Spring88–297
   H. Mason, 83:Autumn88–233
Geary, J.S., ed. Historia del Conde Fernán
González.
   S.D. Kirby, 304(JHP):Autumn88–69
Geckeler, H. & D. Kattenbusch. Einführung in
die italienische Sprachwissenschaft.
   J. Jernej, 547(RF):Band100Heft4–374
Geddes, G. Changes of State.
   T. Marshall, 168(ECW):Spring88–133
   L. Ricou, 102(CanL):Summer88–171

Geddes, G. Hong Kong Poems.*
  M. Estok, 198:Winter88-106
  L. Ricou, 102(CanL):Summer88-171
  E.D. Rutland, 529(QQ):Winter88-940
Geddes, G. The Unsettling of the West.
  L. Ricou, 102(CanL):Summer88-171
  P. Stevens, 529(QQ):Autumn88-568
Geddes, G., ed. Vancouver.
  M. Doyle, 102(CanL):Winter87-188
Geduld, H.M. – see Wells, H.G.
Gee, M. Grace.*
  J. Mellors, 364:Oct/Nov88-116
Gee, S. Spring Will Be Ours.
  M. Kott, 441:3Sep89-15
Geeraerts, D. Paradigm and Paradox.
  G. Proni, 567:Vol68No1/2-145
Geertz, C. Works and Lives.*
  N. Bromell, 219(GaR):Winter88-873
Geffray, G. – see Mozart, W.A.
Gehlen, A. Man.
  K. Peter, 103:Mar89-99
Gehring, W.D., ed. Handbook of American Film
    Genres.
  P.D. Murphy, 590:Jun89-47
Gehring, W.D. The Marx Brothers.
  S. Snyder, 106:Spring88-89
  C. Ward, 500:Winter89-66
Gehrke, H.J. Jenseits von Athen und Sparta.
  G.J.D. Aalders H. Wzn., 394:Vol41
    fasc3/4-458
  S. Hornblower, 123:Vol38No1-87
  J.B. Salmon, 229:Band60Heft4-366
Geier, M. Die Schrift und die Tradition.
  T.C. Fox, 221(GQ):Winter88-117
  W. Moser, 107(CRCL):Jun88-261
Geiger, R.L. To Advance Knowledge.*
  B. McArthur, 577(SHR):Summer88-280
Geiger, W. Culture of Ceylon in Medieval
    Times. (H. Bechert, ed)
  E. Bender, 318(JAOS):Oct-Dec87-847
Geisdorfer Feal, R. Novel Lives.
  J. Chrzanowski, 345(KRQ):Nov88-503
  H.R.M., 295(JML):Fall87/Winter88-228
Geisen, H. – see Shakespeare, W.
Geisler, H. Studien zur typologischen Ent-
    wicklung, Lateinisch – Altfranzösisch –
    Neufranzösisch.
  G. Holtus, 72:Band224Heft2-433
Geismann, G. & H. Oberer, eds. Kant und das
    Recht der Lüge.
  S. Nachtsheim, 342:Band79Heft3-374
Geist, S. Interpreting Cézanne.
  R. Wollheim, 617(TLS):4-10Aug89-839
Gelb, N. Dunkirk.
  A. Boyer, 441:8Oct89-25
Gelderman, C. Mary McCarthy.*
  A. Chisholm, 617(TLS):16-22Jun89-672
  P.M. Spacks, 534(RALS):Vol16No1&2-37
Gelfant, B.H. Woman Writing in America.*
  M. Peterman, 102(CanL):Winter87-144
Gella, A., ed. Sprawy polskie w perspektywie
    światowej.
  S. Dąbrowski, 497(PolR):Vol33No2-247
Gelley, A. Narrative Crossings.*
  L. Hafrey, 617(TLS):13-19Jan89-41
  G. Handwerk, 52:Band23Heft1-92
  M.G. Sokolyansky, 402(MLR):Jul89-686
Gellhorn, M. The View from the Ground.
  A. Wilentz, 617(TLS):8-14Dec89-1370
Gellius. Aulo Gellio: Le "Notti attiche," Libri
    I–III.* (F. Cavazza, ed & trans)
  P.K. Marshall, 122:Jan88-87

Gellner, E. Relativism and the Social Sci-
    ences.
  H.V. McLachlan, 488:Mar88-113
Gellrich, J.M. The Idea of the Book in the
    Middle Ages.*
  R. Copeland, 545(RPh):Feb89-366
  L. Patterson, 589:Jul88-664
Gelly, D. & D. Smith. Giants of Jazz.
  J.K. Skipper, Jr., 498:Spring88-91
Gelpi, A. A Coherent Splendor.
  L. Keller, 27(AL):Dec88-688
Gelpi, A., ed. Wallace Stevens.*
  R. Berry, 102(CanL):Autumn88-147
Gelsomino, R. Ferentinum del sistema viario
    Romano (primo secolo a.C. – quarto secolo
    d.C.).
  H.E. Herzig, 229:Band60Heft5-460
  N. Purcell, 123:Vol38No1-181
Gély, C. – see de Guérin, M.
Gendre, A., ed. Ronsard.
  J. O'Brien, 402(MLR):Jan89-161
Genesee, F. Learning Through Two Lan-
    guages.
  M.A. Snow, 608:Mar89-137
Genet, J. Lettres à Olga et Marc Barbezat.
  P. Bougon, 450(NRF):Oct88-94
  P. Thody, 617(TLS):21-27Apr89-419
Genet, J. Prisoner of Love.* (French title:
    Un Captif amoureux.)
  P. Thody, 617(TLS):21-27Apr89-419
Genette, G. Seuils.*
  J. Baetens, 494:Vol8No3/4-713
  G. Cesbron, 535(RHL):Nov-Dec88-1177
  J-M. Klinkenberg, 209(FM):Apr88-125
  W. Nelles, 599:Spring89-141
  C. Robyns, 494:Vol8No2-466
Genette, R.D. Métamorphoses du récit.
  B.L. Knapp, 207(FR):Mar89-677
Genevois, D.B., ed. Typologie de la presse
    hispanique.
  P-J. Guinard, 92(BH):Jan-Dec87-386
Geniušienė, E. The Typology of Reflexives.
  W.R. Schmalstieg, 215(GL):Vol28No2-134
Geno, M.G. A la française.
  D. Aynesworth, 207(FR):Dec88-376
Genova, J., ed. Power, Gender, Values.
  A. Minas, 103:May89-182
  M.S., 185:Jul89-969
Gensini, S. Elementi di storia linguistica
    italiana.
  H.W. Haller, 545(RPh):May89-466
Gent, P. North Dallas After Forty.
  M. Chambers, 441:19Nov89-45
Gentile da Cingoli. Quaestiones supra Pris-
    ciano minori. (R.M. Vico, ed)
  G.L. Bursill-Hall, 589:Jul88-667
Gentili, A. & C. O'Brien, eds. The Green
    Flame.
  P. Hainsworth, 402(MLR):Apr89-493
Gentili, B., ed. Giuliano Imperatore.
  R. Browning, 123:Vol38No1-172
Gentili, B. Poetry and Its Public in Ancient
    Greece.
  O. Murray, 617(TLS):16-22Jun89-655
Gentili, B. & G. Paioni, eds. Oralità.
  S. Siporin, 292(JAF):Apr-Jun88-244
Gentili, B. & R. Pretagostini, eds. Edipo: il
    teatro greco e la cultura europea.
  A.L. Brown, 123:Vol38No2-421
Gentle, M. Ancient Light.
  G. Jonas, 441:2Jul89-15
"David Gentleman's Coastline."
  G. Heptonstall, 324:Feb89-184

Giancotti, F. Poesia e Filosofia in Seneca Tragico.
  R. Mayer, 123:Vol38No1-152
Giannantoni, G., ed. Socraticorum Reliquae.
  G. Vlastos, 319:Oct89-605
Giannaris, G. Greek Immigrants and the Greek-American Novel.
  J. Taylor, 268(IFR):Winter89-70
Giannetti, G. & M. Bruno. Un Kaléidoscope de Mots.
  P. Siegel, 207(FR):Feb89-561
Gianotti, G.F. "Romanzo" e Ideologia.
  G. Anderson, 123:Vol38No1-155
  H.E. Elsom, 313:Vol78-248
  B.L. Hijmans, 229:Band60Heft6-535
Giantvalley, S. Edward Albee.
  T.P. Adler, 365:Winter88-51
Giardina, A., ed. Società romana e impero tardoantico. (Vol 3)
  C. Wickham, 313:Vol78-183
Giardina, A., ed. Tradizione dei classici, trasformazioni della cultura.
  H.D. Jocelyn, 123:Vol38No2-365
Gibbal, J-M. Les Génie du Fleuve.
  H. Carn, 450(NRF):Dec88-90
Gibbins, P. Particles and Paradoxes.
  J.L. Bell, 479(PhQ):Oct88-536
  H. Krips, 518:Oct88-253
Gibbons, J. Code-Mixing and Code Choice.
  M.K.M. Chan, 399(MLJ):Summer88-223
Gibbons, K. A Virtuous Woman.
  R. Kaveney, 617(TLS):15-21Sep89-998
  P. Powell, 441:30Apr89-12
Gibbs, J. Wole Soyinka.
  G. Moore, 447(N&Q):Mar89-122
Gibbs, J., K.H. Katrak & H.L. Gates, Jr., comps. Wole Soyinka.*
  M. Banham, 295(JML):Fall87/Winter88-383
  S.L. Richards, 615(TJ):Mar88-137
Gibian, G. - see Seifert, J.
Gibson, I. Federico García Lorca.
  P-L. Adams, 61:Nov89-135
  A. Josephs, 441:8Oct89-1
  P. Preston, 617(TLS):7-13Jul89-735
Gibson, J.M. & R.L. Green - see Doyle, A.C.
Gibson, J.W. The Perfect War.
  A. Panaritis, 293(JASt):Aug88-698
Gibson, M. Revolutionary Rexroth.*
  S. Pugmire, 649(WAL):Aug88-148
  V.S., 295(JML):Fall87/Winter88-375
Gibson, M.E. History and the Prism of Art.
  T.J. Collins, 445(NCF):Dec88-411
  H.F. Tucker, 637(VS):Autumn88-151
  D.M. Weed, 85(SBHC):Vol15-85
  639(VQR):Winter88-9
Gibson, R. Alain-Fournier, "Le Grand Meaulnes."*
  M. Autrand, 535(RHL):Nov-Dec88-1166
Gibson, R.F., Jr. Enlightened Empiricism.
  C.H., 185:Jul89-974
Gidal, P. Understanding Beckett.*
  M.B., 295(JML):Fall87/Winter88-293
  N.K. Langford, 397(MD):Mar88-132
  J. Reinelt, 223:Summer88-231
Giddings, R., ed. Matthew Arnold.*
  M. Allott, 447(N&Q):Mar89-109
  M. Hardman, 402(MLR):Oct89-944
  J.C. Livingston, 506(PSt):May88-109
Giddins, G. Satchmo.
  C. Fox, 617(TLS):7-13Apr89-376
  T. Piazza, 441:26Feb89-35

Gide, A. Les Cahiers et les Poésies d'André Walter.* (C. Martin, ed)
  A. Goulet, 535(RHL):Mar-Apr88-332
Gide, A. Correspondance avec Francis Vielé-Griffin 1891-1931. (H. de Paysac, ed)
  A. Goulet, 535(RHL):Mar-Apr88-333
  M. Tilby, 208(FS):Jan88-105
Gide, A. Correspondance avec sa mère 1880-1895. (C. Martin, ed)
  P. Pollard, 617(TLS):27Jan-2Feb89-76
Gide, A. & T. Sternheim. Correspondance, 1927-1950. (C. Foucart, ed)
  A. Goulet, 535(RHL):Nov-Dec88-1168
Gies, D.T. - see de Grimaldi, J.
Gies, F. & J. Marriage and the Family in the Middle Ages.
  639(VQR):Summer88-86
Giff, P.R. Laura Ingalls Wilder.
  S.N. Maher, 649(WAL):Nov88-244
Gifford, H. Poetry in a Divided World.
  D. Davie, 402(MLR):Jul89-695
  P. Martin, 366:Autumn88-207
Gifford, J. William Adam 1689-1748.
  H.G. Slade, 617(TLS):1-7Sep89-948
Gifford, J. Fife.
  I. Gow, 617(TLS):10-16Mar89-259
Gigante, M., ed. Contributi alla storia della Officina dei Papiri Ercolanesi, 2.
  I.C. McIlwaine, 123:Vol38No1-186
Gigante, M., ed. La fortuna di Virgilio.
  N. Horsfall, 123:Vol38No1-151
Giguère, R. La Main au feu.
  A.L. Amprimoz, 102(CanL):Autumn88-140
Gikandi, S. Reading the African Novel.
  C.P. Sarvan, 395(MFS):Winter88-755
Gil-Albert, J. & M.J. Kahn, eds & trans. Yehudá Haleví.
  M.R. Menocal, 240(HR):Autumn88-493
Gilbert, B. God Gave Us This Country.
  R. Sanders, 441:6Aug89-10
Gilbert, B.B. David Lloyd George. (Vol 1)
  J.M. Lipkis, 31(ASch):Summer88-472
  D.R. Woodward, 637(VS):Spring89-465
Gilbert, D. Sandinistas.
  A. Husarska, 441:15Jan89-23
Gilbert, G.G., ed. Pidgin and Creole Languages.
  M. Perl, 682(ZPSK):Band41Heft3-397
  E.C. Polomé, 215(GL):Vol28No4-291
  W. Washabaugh, 350:Mar89-127
Gilbert, K., ed. Inside Black Australia.
  A. Burke, 581:Dec88-470
Gilbert, M. Winston S. Churchill.* (Vol 8: "Never Despair," 1945-1965.)
  D. Cannadine, 453(NYRB):15Jun89-36
Gilbert, M. "Fraudsters."
  J. Symons, 364:Apr/May88-141
Gilbert, M. Paint, Gold and Blood.
  T.J. Binyon, 617(TLS):17-23Nov89-1288
Gilbert, M. The Second World War.
  M. Carver, 617(TLS):1-7Sep89-935
  G.A. Craig, 441:26Nov89-16
Gilbert, R.A. A.E. Waite.
  T. Willard, 111:Spring89-15
Gilbert, S.M. Blood Pressure.
  B. Bennett, 441:12Mar89-38
Gilbert, S.M. & S. Gubar. The Madwoman in the Attic.
  L.E. Donaldson, 153:Fall88-65
  K. Hamilton, 391:Dec88-132

Gilbert, S.M. & S. Gubar. No Man's Land.*
(Vol 1)
   M. Banta, 27(AL):Oct88-463
   W.H. Pritchard, 249(HudR):Summer88-370
   E.B. Thompson, 395(MFS):Winter88-747
Gilbert, S.M. & S. Gubar. No Man's Land. (Vol
2)
   T. Castle, 617(TLS):2-8Jun89-607
   W. Kendrick, 441:19Feb89-9
Gilbert, S.M. & S. Gubar, eds. The Norton
Anthology of Literature by Women.*
   M.L. Briscoe, 128(CE):Nov88-802
Gilborn, C. Adirondack Furniture and the
Rustic Tradition.
   B. Hansson, 139:Aug/Sep88-18
   G.W.R. Ward, 658:Spring88-100
Gilcher, E. Supplement to a Bibliography of
George Moore.
   D.B. Eakin, 177(ELT):Vol31No4-471
   E. Grubgeld, 365:Fall87-218
Gilchrist, E. The Anna Papers.
   M. Paley, 441:15Jan89-16
   W. Steiner, 617(TLS):27Oct-2Nov89-1181
Gilchrist, E. Falling through Space.*
   G. Garrett, 569(SR):Summer88-516
   W. Steiner, 617(TLS):27Oct-2Nov89-1181
Gilchrist, E. Light Can Be Both Wave and
Particle.
   R. Hoffman, 441:22Oct89-13
Gilchrist, J.B., comp. Inventory of Ontario
Newspapers, 1793-1986.
   E. Hulse, 470:Vol26-163
Gilder, G. Microcosm.
   L. Winner, 441:15Oct89-15
Gildersleeve, B.L. The Letters of Basil Lan-
neau Gildersleeve. (W.W. Briggs, Jr., ed)
   N. Horsfall, 123:Vol38No2-389
Gildner, G. A Week in South Dakota.* The
Second Bridge.*
   J. Waldmeir, 115:Winter88-83
Giles, P. Hart Crane: The Contexts of "The
Bridge."
   M. Dickie, 301(JEGP):Jan88-148
   P.R.J., 295(JML):Fall87/Winter88-308
   M. Perloff, 402(MLR):Oct89-965
Gilfillan, M. Magpie Rising.*
   P. Wild, 649(WAL):Nov88-275
Gilfoy, P.S. Patterns of Life.
   R. Hoffman, 2(AfrA):Feb88-15
Giliomee, H. & L. Schlemmer, eds. Negotiating
South Africa's Future.
   S. Uys, 617(TLS):25-31Aug89-915
Gilje, P.A. The Road to Mobocracy.
   H.B. Rock, 656(WMQ):Jul88-589
   639(VQR):Spring88-43
Gill, A. The Early Mallarmé.* (Vol 2)
   B. Marchal, 535(RHL):Nov-Dec88-1161
   F.S. Heck, 207(FR):Dec88-337
Gill, B. The Death of a Joyce Scholar.
   M. Stasio, 441:18Jun89-28
Gill, B. Many Masks.
   R. Campbell, 47:Jan88-39
   W.J.R. Curtis, 617(TLS):24-30Mar89-315
   P.L. Donhauser, 55:Apr88-53
   H. Muschamp, 139:Jun/Jul88-20
   A. Saint, 576:Dec88-426
   F. Schulze, 45:Jun88-79
   E. Weiss, 505:Sep88-133
Gill, E. An Essay on Typography.
   P. Rand, 441:10Sep89-22
Gill, L. Peasants, Entrepreneurs, and Social
Change.
   T.E. Millington, 263(RIB):Vol38No3-401

Gill, R., ed. Theology and Sociology.
   S.E.H., 185:Apr89-692
Gill, R. - see Marlowe, C.
Gill, S. William Wordsworth.
   M.H. Abrams, 453(NYRB):21Dec89-45
   N. Fruman, 617(TLS):5-11May89-475
   P.D. Sheats, 441:11Jun89-49
Gill, S.D. Mother Earth.*
   T. McElwain, 650(WF):Oct88-314
Gilles, P. The Antiquities of Constantinople.
(2nd ed) (R.G. Musto, ed)
   L.V.R., 568(SCN):Fall88-67
Gillespie, A.K. & M.A. Rockland. Looking for
America on the New Jersey Turnpike.
   E. Allen, 441:19Nov89-14
Gillespie, C.K. Justifiable Homicide.
   T. Lewin, 441:31Dec89-17
Gillespie, D.C. Valentin Rasputin and Soviet
Russian Village Prose.*
   R. Freeborn, 575(SEER):Jan88-164
   M. Winchell, 574(SEEJ):Summer88-336
Gillespie, M.A. & T.B. Strong, eds. Nietzsche's
New Seas.
   A.D. Schrift, 103:Nov89-437
Gillespie, M.P., with E.B. Stocker. James
Joyce's Trieste Library.*
   M.H. Begnal, 174(Éire):Spring88-149
   A. Hammond, 354:Mar88-75
   J.C.C. Mays, 541(RES):Nov88-588
Gillespie, R. The Spanish Socialist Party.
   P. Preston, 617(TLS):8-14Sep89-977
Gillette, J.M. Theatrical Design and Produc-
tion.
   J.E. Travis, 615(TJ):May88-292
Gilliatt, P. A Woman of Singular Occupation.*
   E. Munro, 441:14May89-24
   442(NY):19Jun89-100
Gillies, M. Bartók in Britain.
   P. Griffiths, 617(TLS):24Feb-2Mar89-188
Gilligan, C. & others, eds. Mapping the Moral
Domain.
   M. Csikszentmihalyi, 441:28May89-6
Gillilan, P. That Winter.*
   D. McDuff, 565:Spring88-64
Gillis, C. A Question of Final Belief.
   S. Grover, 617(TLS):22-28Dec89-1404
Gillispie, C.C. & M. Dewachter, eds. Monu-
ments of Egypt.
   L. Golub, 62:Dec88-110
Gillman, S. Dark Twins.
   F. Crews, 453(NYRB):20Jul89-39
Gillmor, A.M. Erik Satie.
   N. Wilkins, 415:Oct88-533
Gillon, R. Philosophical Medical Ethics.*
   S.E. Marshall, 483:Oct88-552
Gilly, C. Spanien und der Basler Buchdruck
bis 1600.*
   T.S. Beardsley, Jr., 240(HR):Winter88-92
Gilman, C. & M.J. Schneider. The Way to In-
dependence.
   R.L. Welsch, 658:Winter88-288
Gilman, E.B. Iconoclasm and Poetry in the
English Reformation.*
   T.H. Luxon, 250(HLQ):Summer88-235
   C.H. Miller, 477(PLL):Winter88-94
   D.H. Parker, 539:Summer88-229
Gilman, S.L., ed. Conversations with
Nietzsche.* (German title: Begegnungen mit
Nietzsche.)
   A. Del Caro, 221(GQ):Summer87-510
   M. Tanner, 617(TLS):12-18May89-509
Gilman, S.L. Disease and Representation.
   A. Scull, 617(TLS):10-16Mar89-239

Gilman, S.L. Jewish Self-Hatred.*
 S. Bauschinger, 406:Summer88-211
 P. Milbouer, 221(GQ):Spring88-337
Gilmour, D. Back on Tuesday.
 D. Brydon, 102(CanL):Winter87-194
Gilmour, J.C. Picturing the World.
 T.J. Flynn, 543:Mar89-620
 P.N. Humble, 89(BJA):Winter88-89
Gilmour, P. Ken Tyler.
 P.B. Arnold, 127:Spring88-53
Gilmour, R. The Novel in the Victorian Age.*
 N. Bradbury, 541(RES):Feb88-133
 C.A. Howells, 447(N&Q):Mar88-104
Gilomen-Schenkel, E., ed. Frühe Klöster, die
 Benediktiner und Benediktinerinnen in der
 Schweiz.
 R.H. Schmandt, 589:Apr88-399
Gilroy, D. Sight Unseen.
 N. Callendar, 441:16Jul89-23
Giltaj, J. The Drawings by Rembrandt and His
 School in the Museum Boymans-Van Beu-
 ningen.
 M. Russell, 617(TLS):10-16Nov89-1247
Gindin, J. John Galsworthy's Life and Art.*
 L. Strahan, 177(ELT):Vol31No4-455
Gingold, H. How To Grow Old Disgracefully.
 J. Wilders, 617(TLS):24-30Mar89-301
Ginouvès, R. & R. Martin. Dictionnaire
 méthodique de l'architecture grecque et
 romaine.* (Vol 1)
 R.L. Gordon, Jr., 124:Nov-Dec88-118
Ginsberg, A. White Shroud.*
 L. Sail, 565:Spring88-73
 D. Sampson, 249(HudR):Summer88-389
Ginsberg, J. Ángel Ganivet.*
 J. Belmonte Serrano, 345(KRQ):Aug88-
 381
Ginsberg, R., ed. The Philosopher as Writer.*
 P. Walmsley, 173(ECS):Winter88/89-250
Ginsburg, F.D. Contested Lives.
 M. Phillips, 441:23Jul89-19
Ginsburg, M.P. Flaubert Writing.*
 P. Force, 546(RR):Mar88-398
 D.Y. Kadish, 207(FR):Dec88-333
 T. Unwin, 208(FS):Jan88-98
Ginsburg, N. – see under Penna, S.
Ginzburg, C. The Enigma of Piero della Fran-
 cesca: The Baptism, The Arezzo Cycle, The
 Flagellation.*
 T. Martone, 54:Sep88-523
Ginzburg, C. Storia notturna.
 I.P. Couliano, 358:Dec89-14
Ginzburg, N. Family.
 J. Marcus, 441:1Jan89-14
Ginzburg, N. Valentino and Sagittarius.* All
 Our Yesterdays.
 R. Signorelli-Pappas, 532(RCF):Fall88-
 151
Ginzburg, N. Voices in the Evening.
 442(NY):23Oct89-146
Gioia, D. Daily Horoscope.*
 S. Kuzma, 448:Vol26No3-111
 J. Mazzaro, 569(SR):Winter88-149
 R. Squires, 577(SHR):Winter88-92
Giono, J. Colline. (B. Nelson, ed)
 P. Citron, 535(RHL):Mar-Apr88-335
 W. Redfern, 208(FS):Jan88-107
Giorgis, D.W. Red Tears.
 H. Kebede, 441:18Jun89-21
Gioscio, J. Il dialetto lucano di Calvello.
 M. Maiden, 545(RPh):May89-469
Giovangli, O.C. & G. Petrocchi – see under
 Costa Giovangli, O. & G. Petrocchi

di Giovanni, G. & H.S. Harris, eds & trans.
 Between Kant and Hegel.*
 J. Burbidge, 154:Summer88-378
Giovanni, N. Sacred Cows...And Other Edi-
 bles.
 42(AR):Summer88-397
di Giovanni, N.T., ed. Celeste Goes Dancing
 and Other Stories.
 G. Martin, 617(TLS):14-20Jul89-782
di Giovine, P. Il gruppo "ct" latino in
 albanese.
 H.M. Ölberg, 260(IF):Band93-312
Giralt, E.F. – see under Forment Giralt, E.
Girard, R. The Scapegoat.*
 A. Demaitre, 577(SHR):Fall88-394
 A.S., 295(JML):Fall87/Winter88-246
Girard, R. Things Hidden Since the Founda-
 tion of the World.
 639(VQR):Spring88-68
Girardet, J., J. Schelle-Mervelay & S. Toux.
 Il était une petite grenouille, 2.
 J.J. Smith, 207(FR):Feb89-564
de Girardin, D. Chroniques parisiennes:
 1836-1848. (J-L. Vissière, ed)
 P. Park, 446(NCFS):Fall-Winter88/89-226
Giraud, M. The Métis in the Canadian West.
 N.J. Christie, 656(WMQ):Jan88-186
Giraud, Y., ed. Le premier livre d'"Amadis de
 Gaule."*
 M. Cuénin, 535(RHL):Mar-Apr88-251
Giraudeau, M. Les notions juridiques et soci-
 ales chez Hérodote.
 C. Coulet-Caquot, 555:Vol61fasc1-116
Giraudon, L. Quel jour sommes-nous.
 C. Tarting, 98:Mar88-253
Girke, W., H. Jachnow & J. Schrenk. Handbib-
 liographie zur slavistischen und allgemein-
 en Linguistik in Osteuropa. (Vol 2)
 P. Ivić, 685(ZDL):2/1987-246
Girouard, M. Cities and People.*
 J.S. Ackerman, 576:Mar88-90
Girouard, M. A Country House Companion.
 639(VQR):Spring88-67
Giroud, F. – see Michelet, J.
Giroux, R. – see Lowell, R.
Giroux, R. – see Malamud, B.
Giry-Schneider, J. Les Prédicats nominaux
 en français.
 W.A. Bennett, 402(MLR):Jan89-152
 D.J. Napoli, 350:Jun89-428
Gish, T.G. & R. Spuler, eds. Eagle in the New
 World.
 C.L. Dolmetsch, 221(GQ):Summer88-486
 R. Kondert, 406:Winter88-499
Gisolfi, A.M. Caudine Country.
 G. Volpe, 276:Summer88-165
Gitler, I. Swing to Bop.
 G.L. Starks, Jr., 91:Spring88-109
Gittings, J. China Changes Face.
 M.B. Yahuda, 617(TLS):11-17Aug89-869
Giuliani, L. Bildnis und Botschaft.
 R.R.R. Smith, 229:Band60Heft8-761
Giusti, P. & P.L. de Castris. "Forastieri e
 regnicoli."
 N. Dacos, 90:Jul88-538
Giusti, P.P. Berichte der diplomatischen Ver-
 treter des Wiener Hofes aus Spanien in der
 Regierungszeit Karls III. (1759-1788).
 (Vols 12 & 13) (H-O. Kleinmann, ed)
 J.H.R. Polt, 240(HR):Autumn88-502
Giusto, J-P. Le Champ clos de l'Écriture.
 H. Levillain, 535(RHL):Mar-Apr88-330

Giustolisi, V. Nakone et Entelle alla luce degli antichi decreti recentemente apparsi e di un nuovo decreto inedito.
P.A. Lomas, 303(JoHS):Vol108-262
Given-Wilson, C. The Royal Household and the King's Affinity.*
F.A. Cazel, Jr., 589:Jan88-155
J. Sherborne, 382(MAE):1988/2-307
Givner, J., ed. Conversations with Katherine Anne Porter.
M.J. Bolsterli, 395(MFS):Winter88-642
J.F. Desmond, 392:Fall88-553
Givner, J. Mazo de la Roche.
A. Pringle, 617(TLS):10-16Nov89-1230
Glaeser, B., ed. Learning from China?
V. Smil, 293(JASt):Aug88-594
von Glahn, R. The Country of Streams and Grottoes.
W.W. Lo, 293(JASt):Aug88-628
Glancey, J. New British Architecture.
A. Saint, 617(TLS):8-14Dec89-1351
Glanville, B. The Catacomb.
J. Mellors, 364:Mar88-102
Glaser, E. Graphische Studien zum Schreibsprachwandel vom 13. bis 16. Jahrhundert.
H. Singer, 685(ZDL):3/1987-369
Gläser, E. Tropical Depressions.
639(VQR):Autumn88-134
Gläser, R. Phraseologie der englischen Sprache.
G. Bourcier, 189(EA):Oct-Dec88-468
Glasgow, E. Ellen Glasgow's Reasonable Doubts. (J.R. Raper, ed)
B. Harrison, 392:Fall88-569
F. Pullin, 617(TLS):16-22Jun89-668
Glasrud, C.A., ed. L'Héritage Tranquille.
J.H. Bourque, 207(FR):Dec88-346
Glass, B. Lotte Lehmann.
C. Hatch, 465:Winter88/89-103
Glass, J.M. Private Terror/Public Life.
F. Klagsbrun, 441:8Oct89-15
Glass, J.W. The Pennsylvania Culture Region.
M.J. Chiarappa, 292(JAF):Jan-Mar88-113
Glass, P. Opera on the Beach.* (R.T. Jones, ed)
P. Dickinson, 324:Dec88-60
K. Potter, 415:Nov88-602
Glass, R. Clichés of Urban Doom and Other Essays.
D. Harvey, 617(TLS):7-13Apr89-356
Glasscoe, M., ed. The Medieval Mystical Tradition in England.
L. Carruthers, 189(EA):Oct-Dec88-471
Glasser, P. Singing on the Titanic.
C. Hardesty, 455:Mar88-67
Glasser, R. Gorbals Boy at Oxford.*
P. Vansittart, 364:Jun88-97
Glassgold, P. Hwaet, A Little Old English Anthology of American Modernist Poetry.
A. Lefevere, 107(CRCL):Mar88-109
Glatzer, N.N. The Loves of Franz Kafka.*
M.H. Gelber, 395(MFS):Summer88-303
Glaysher, F. - see Hayden, R.
Glazer, I.R. Philadelphia Theatres, A-Z.*
M.K. Fielder, 615(TJ):Dec87-536
Glazer, M.P. & P.M. The Whistleblowers.
H. Goodman, 441:13Aug89-17
Glazer, N. & M. Lilla, eds. The Public Face of Architecture.
R. Campbell, 47:Dec88-61
A.W. Levi, 289:Fall88-113
Glazer, P.M. & M. Slater. Unequal Colleagues.
V. Strong-Boag, 106:Fall88-384

Gleckner, R.F. Blake and Spenser.*
J.M.Q. Davies, 541(RES):Feb88-118
Gledson, J. Machado de Assis.
M. Peixoto, 240(HR):Summer88-400
M. Silverman, 238:May88-303
Gleeck, L.E., Jr. President Marcos and the Philippine Political Culture.
M.P. Onorato, 293(JASt):Nov88-936
Glenday, J. The Apple Ghost.
M. Wormald, 617(TLS):1-7Dec89-1336
Glendinning, V. The Grown-Ups.
D. Dunn, 617(TLS):31Mar-6Apr89-344
Glendinning, V. Rebecca West.*
H. Orel, 177(ELT):Vol31No4-447
42(AR):Spring88-274
639(VQR):Summer88-86
Glendon, M.A. Abortion and Divorce in Western Law.*
N.D., 185:Jul89-987
Glenn, E.M. The "Metamorphoses."*
E. Fantham, 124:May-Jun89-387
Glenny, R.E. The Manipulation of Reality in Works by Heinrich von Kleist.
H.M. Brown, 402(MLR):Jul89-788
Glezer, A. Russkie xudožniki na zapade.
M. Tupitsyn, 574(SEEJ):Winter88-674
Glezer, A. & S. Petrunis, comps. Russkie poèty na zapade.
G.J. Janecek, 574(SEEJ):Fall88-479
Glickfeld, C.L. Useful Gifts.
M. Childress, 441:21May89-21
Glickman, N.J. & D.P. Woodward. The New Competitors.
J. Dreyfuss, 441:21May89-51
Glienke, B. Fatale Präzedenz.
L. Hernø, 172(Edda):1988/1-83
Glier, I., ed. Die deutschsprachige Literatur im späten Mittelalter (1250-1370). (Pt 2)
U. Liebertz-Grün, 406:Spring88-122
Glier, I., ed. Geschichte der Deutschen Literatur von den Anfängen bis zur Gegenwart (De Boor/Newald). (Vol 3, Pt 2)
J.E. Tailby, 402(MLR):Jul89-771
Gliksohn, J-M. Iphigénie, de la Grèce antique à l'Europe des Lumières.*
A. Giorgi-Chevrel, 549(RLC):Jul-Sep88-420
The Knight of Glin, N. Robinson & D. Griffin. Vanishing Country Houses of Ireland.
D. Cruickshank, 617(TLS):24-30Mar89-317
Glissant, E. Mahagony.
J. Silenieks, 207(FR):Dec88-362
"The Glory of the Page."
78(BC):Autumn88-313
Glouberman, M. Descartes.
S. Gaukroger, 63:Sep88-414
R.A. Watson, 319:Oct89-618
Glover, D. The South Will Rise at Noon.
M. Pellecchia, 441:19Mar89-22
Glover, J. I: The Philosophy and Psychology of Personal Identity.
A. Morton, 617(TLS):27Jan-2Feb89-77
S. Sutherland, 617(TLS):1-7Dec89-1344
Glover, J. Our Photographs.*
H. Buckingham, 565:Winter87/88-71
Glover, J.G. The Cubist Theatre.
E.S., 295(JML):Fall87/Winter88-275
Gluck, C. Japan's Modern Myths.*
B.K. Marshall, 318(JAOS):Jan-Mar87-168
Glück, L. The Triumph of Achilles.*
D. McDuff, 565:Autumn88-61
W. Scammell, 493:Spring88-48

Glynn, J. Prince of Publishers.*
P.T. Srebrnik, 637(VS):Winter89-253
Glynn, S., ed. European Philosophy and the
Human and Social Sciences.
N. Parker, 323:May88-210
Glynn, S., ed. Sartre.
J. Howarth, 518:Jul88-135
Glynn, T. Watching the Body Burn.
U. Hegi, 441:5Mar89-16
Gnüg, H. Kult der Kälte.
H. Denman, 617(TLS):4-10Aug89-849
Gnutzmann, R. Roberto Arlt o el arte del cal-
idoscopio.*
E.A. Giordano, 238:Dec88-842
de Gobineau, A. Oeuvres. (Vol 2) (J. Gaul-
mier, with P. Lésétieux & V. Monteil, eds)
A. Smith, 446(NCFS):Fall-Winter88/89-
256
de Gobineau, J.A. Oeuvres. (Vol 3) (J. Gaul-
mier, J. Boissel & M-L. Concasty, eds)
R. Béziau, 446(NCFS):Spring-Summer89-
437
M.D. Biddiss, 208(FS):Apr88-218
Gochet, P. Ascent to Truth.*
J-L. Gardies, 542:Jul-Sep88-380
Gocke, R. Shakespeare's Tragedies.
H. Antor, 156(ShJW):Jahrbuch1988-303
Goddard, D. Undercover.
C. Salzberg, 441:1Jan89-15
Godden, R. A House with Four Rooms.
S. Rudikoff, 441:24Dec89-24
Gödden, W. - see von Droste-Hülshoff, A.
Godding, P. Le droit privé dans les Pays-Bas
méridionaux du 12e au 18e siècle.
D. Nicholas, 589:Oct88-927
Godfrey, J.J. A Philosophy of Human Hope.
B.P. Dauenhauer, 543:Jun89-831
Godfrey, M. Plan B is Total Panic.
R.E. Jones, 102(CanL):Spring88-167
Godfrey, T.J. & W.M. Collins. Una encuesta
dialectal en el area mam de Guatemala.
T. Kaufman, 350:Mar89-182
Godin, D. Translating Genesis.
C. Tapping, 102(CanL):Summer88-168
Godin, G. Soirs sans Atout.
M. Benson, 102(CanL):Summer88-169
Godineau, D. Citoyennes tricoteuses.
M. & P. Higonnet, 617(TLS):19-25May89-
541
Godman, P. Poetry of the Carolingian Renais-
sance.
T.A-P. Klein, 229:Band60Heft7-591
Godman, P. Poets and Emperors.
T. Hunt, 541(RES):Aug88-422
C.J. McDonough, 447(N&Q):Sep88-345
Godwin, G. A Southern Family.
639(VQR):Winter88-21
Godwin, J. Harmonies of Heaven and Earth.
F. Sparshott, 415:Jul88-345
Godwin, J. - see Lucretius
Godwin, W. Damon and Delia. (P. Marshall,
ed)
R. Lansdown, 617(TLS):25-31Aug89-912
Godwin-Jones, R. Narrative Strategies in the
Novels of Jeremias Gotthelf.
E. Gallati, 133:Band21Heft2/3-233
L. Tatlock, 221(GQ):Fall87-681
Godzich, W. & N. Spadaccini, eds. Literature
Among Discourses.*
T.E. Case, 552(REH):Oct88-141
P.J. Smith, 86(BHS):Jul88-294
Goebel, R.J. Kritik und Revision.*
M. Harman, 133:Band21Heft2/3-245

Goertz, R.O.W., ed. Iberia.
N.J. Lamb, 86(BHS):Oct88-403
Goesch, K. Hervé Bazin I.
G. Cesbron, 535(RHL):Mar-Apr88-341
Goesch, K. - see Mauriac, F.
von Goethe, J.W. La Chasse.
J-P. Naugrette, 98:May88-444
von Goethe, J.W. Essays on Art and Litera-
ture. (J. Gearey, ed)
T. Ziolkowski, 249(HudR):Autumn88-506
von Goethe, J.W. Faust I & II. (S. Atkins, ed
& trans)
R.B. Bottigheimer, 221(GQ):Winter88-132
T. Ziolkowski, 249(HudR):Autumn88-504
von Goethe, J.W. Goethe's Collected Works.
(Vols 4 & 5) (T.P. Saine & J.L. Sammons,
eds)
R.B. Bottigheimer, 221(GQ):Fall88-578
T. Ziolkowski, 249(HudR):Autumn88-509
von Goethe, J.W. Recension einer Anzahl
französischer satyrischer Kupferstiche.
(K.H. Kiefer, ed)
N. Boyle, 402(MLR):Apr89-526
von Goethe, J.W. Selected Poems. (C. Middle-
ton, ed)
T. Ziolkowski, 249(HudR):Autumn88-501
von Goethe, J.W. Verse Plays and Epic. (C.
Hamlin & F. Ryder, eds)
T. Ziolkowski, 249(HudR):Autumn88-510
"Goethe Yearbook."* (Vol 2) (T.P. Saine, ed)
H. Froeschle, 221(GQ):Summer88-444
Goetinck, J.F. Essai sur le rôle des
Allemands dans le "Dictionnaire Historique
et Critique" (1697) de Pierre Bayle.
G. Sauder, 52:Band23Heft1-105
Goetz, H-W. Leben im Mittelalter.
R.C. Hoffmann, 589:Apr88-401
Goetz, W.R. Henry James and the Darkest
Abyss of Romance.*
C.B. Cox, 569(SR):Summer88-497
R. Gard, 447(N&Q):Mar88-137
Goffart, W. The Narrators of Barbarian His-
tory.
R. Collins, 617(TLS):5-11May89-492
Goffen, R. Piety and Patronage in Renais-
sance Venice.*
J. Anderson, 59:Dec88-565
C.M. Rosenberg, 276:Autumn88-270
Goffen, R. Spirituality in Conflict.
J. Czarnecki, 617(TLS):5-11May89-488
Goffi, J-Y. La philosophie de la technique.
C. Mitcham, 103:Jan89-10
Goga, O. Poezii - Poésies. (O. Galatanu, ed
& trans)
J. Amsler, 549(RLC):Jan-Mar88-114
Gohdes, C. & S.E. Marovitz, eds. Bibliograph-
ical Guide to the Study of the Literature of
the U.S.A. (5th ed)
D. Van Leer, 534(RALS):Vol16No1&2-49
Golby, J.M., ed. Culture and Society in Brit-
ain 1850-1890.*
J. Thompson, 447(N&Q):Mar88-105
M. Woodfield, 402(MLR):Jan89-136
Gold, B.K. Literary Patronage in Greece and
Rome.
N. Horsfall, 123:Vol38No2-268
Gold, D. The Lord as Guru.
P. van der Veer, 293(JASt):Aug88-678
Gold, P.S. The Lady and the Virgin.
R. Blumenfeld-Kosinski, 545(RPh):
May89-493
Gold, V. & L. Cheney. The Body Politic.
J. Johnson, 441:5Feb89-24

Goldberg, B. Bertha Broadfoot and Pepin the Short.
  W.H. Green, 363(LitR):Winter89-235
Goldberg, J. La culpabilité, axiome de la psychanalyse.
  G. Charron, 154:Summer88-321
Goldberg, J. Voice Terminal Echo.*
  D. Norbrook, 447(N&Q):Mar88-78
  M. Pfister, 156(ShJW):Jahrbuch1988-235
  H. Rapaport, 301(JEGP):Jan88-107
  G.E. Rowe, 131(CL):Winter88-84
  M. Stocker, 402(MLR):Jan89-126
Goldberg, N. Writing Down the Bones.
  G. Garrett, 569(SR):Summer88-516
Goldberg, V. Margaret Bourke-White.
  639(VQR):Summer88-90
Goldberger, A.H., ed. Woman as Mediatrix.
  K.L. Komar, 221(GQ):Summer88-453
Golden, J.L. & J.J. Pilotta, eds. Practical Reasoning in Human Affairs.
  B. Warnick, 480(P&R):Vol21No2-158
Goldfinger, C. La géo-finance.
  M.A. Sinaceur, 98:Apr88-290
Goldgar, B.A. - see Fielding, H.
Goldhill, S. Reading Greek Tragedy.*
  D. Bain, 303(JoHS):Vol108-239
  C. Segal, 122:Jul88-234
Goldie, S.M. - see Nightingale, F.
Golding, W. Fire Down Below.
  D. Bair, 441:2Apr89-37
  S. Medcalf, 617(TLS):17-23Mar89-267
Goldman, A.H. Empirical Knowledge.
  E.L. Holman, 543:Jun89-832
Goldman, A.H. Moral Knowledge.
  R.C.S. Walker, 617(TLS):28Jul-3Aug89-818
Goldman, A.I. Epistemology and Cognition.*
  R. Audi, 484(PPR):Jun89-733
  A. Clark, 479(PhQ):Oct88-526
  F. Dretske, 311(JP):May88-265
  B. Freed, 486:Sep88-479
  D.H. Sanford, 262:Dec88-519
Goldman, A.J. The Rabbi is a Lady.
  J. Riemer, 287:Mar/Apr88-31
Goldman, E. The Social Significance of Modern Drama.
  M. Kearns, 42(AR):Winter88-118
Goldman, M. Acting and Action in Shakespearean Tragedy.*
  A.W. Bellringer, 447(N&Q):Mar88-82
  J.L. Levenson, 627(UTQ):Winter87/88-321
Goldman, M., with T. Cheek & C.L. Hamrin, eds. China's Intellectuals and the State.
  J. Israel, 293(JASt):Aug88-586
Goldman, M.I. Gorbachev's Challenge.*
  L. Gruliow, 42(AR):Summer88-383
  A.G. Meyer, 385(MQR):Fall89-771
  639(VQR):Winter88-24
Goldman, P., T. Mathews & others. The Quest for the Presidency 1988.
  S.V. Roberts, 441:10Dec89-38
Goldman, R.P., ed & trans. The Rāmāyana of Vālmīki.
  R.W. Lariviere, 318(JAOS):Apr-Jun87-356
Goldman, R.P. & S.J. Sutherland. Devavāṇīpraveśikā. (2d ed)
  R. Salomon, 293(JASt):Nov88-919
Goldman, S.R. & H.T. Trueba, eds. Becoming Literate in English as a Second Language.
  J. Battenburg, 350:Sep89-660

Goldman, W. & M. Lupica. Wait Till Next Year.
  C. Sommers, 441:5Feb89-25
Goldsborough, R. Death on Deadline.
  T.J. Binyon, 617(TLS):10-16Mar89-262
Goldschmidt, H.L. Xanthippe - keine Xanthippe.
  W. Goetschel, 221(GQ):Winter88-161
Goldsmith, E.C., ed. Writing the Female Voice.
  T. Castle, 617(TLS):2-8Jun89-607
  A. Clampitt, 344:Fall89-178
Goldsmith, J. - see Spender, S.
Goldstein, C. Visual Fact over Verbal Fiction.
  C. Dempsey, 617(TLS):5-11May89-488
Goldstein, J. Console and Classify.
  E. & R.E. Peschel, 446(NCFS):Fall-Winter88/89-260
Goldstein, L. The Flying Machine and Modern Literature.*
  S. James, 569(SR):Summer88-lxvi
  S.P., 295(JML):Fall87/Winter88-246
Goldstein, L. Tourists.
  442(NY):11Sep89-123
Goldstein, R. The Late-Summer Passion of a Woman of Mind.
  R. Cohen, 441:7May89-28
Goldstein, R.D. Mother-Love and Abortion.
  N."A." Davis, 185:Jul89-957
Golenbock, P. Personal Fouls.
  T. Whitaker, 441:27Aug89-12
Göller, K.H., ed. Spätmittelalterliche Artusliteratur.
  K. Gamerschlag, 72:Band224Heft2-399
Gollin, J. Broken Consort.
  M. Stasio, 441:24Dec89-23
Golomb, D.M. A Grammar of Targum Neofiti.
  S.A. Kaufman, 318(JAOS):Jan-Mar87-142
Golovskoy, V.S., with J. Rimberg. Behind the Soviet Screen.
  V. Kepley, Jr., 574(SEEJ):Spring88-148
  A. Lawton, 550(RusR):Apr88-203
Gom, L. Housebroken.
  A.J. Harding, 102(CanL):Spring88-163
  L. Irvine, 168(ECW):Spring88-81
  P. Stevens, 529(QQ):Autumn88-568
Gom, L. Private Properties.*
  B. Almon, 102(CanL):Winter87-206
Gombrich, R. & G. Obeyesekere. Buddhism Transformed.
  M. Southwold, 617(TLS):28Jul-3Aug89-819
Gombrowicz, W. Diary.* (Vol 1) (J. Kott, ed) Dziennik.
  J. Bloinski, 617(TLS):3-9Feb89-102
Gombrowicz, W. Diary. (Vol 2) (J. Kott, ed)
  S. Gavronsky, 441:5Nov89-34
Gómez Canseco, L. Rodrigo Caro.
  J.A. Jones, 86(BHS):Oct88-411
  S.B. Vranich, 240(HR):Winter89-106
Gomez de Silva, G. Elsevier's Concise Spanish Etymological Dictionary.*
  S.N. Dworkin, 545(RPh):Feb89-353
  D. Nehls, 257(IRAL):Feb88-75
Gómez-Moriana, A. La subversion du discours rituel.*
  G. Díaz-Migoyo, 240(HR):Summer88-370
Gonda, J. Prajāpati and the Year.
  R.W. Lariviere, 318(JAOS):Oct-Dec87-837
Gonda, J. Prajāpati's Rise to Higher Rank.
  K. Mylius, 259(IIJ):Apr88-139
Gonda, J. Pūṣan and Sarasvatī.*
  L. Rocher, 318(JAOS):Oct-Dec87-778

Gonelli, L.M., ed. Carteggio D'Ancona. (Vol 7)
    A.V., 379(MedR):Aug88-318
de Góngora, L. Antología poética. (A. Carreira, ed)
    P.J. Smith, 402(MLR):Jul89-761
de Góngora, L. Romances. (2nd ed) (A. Carreño, ed)
    E.T. Aylward, 238:Mar88-83
Gonnaud, M. An Uneasy Solitude.
    L.C. Johnson, 27(AL):Dec88-665
    639(VQR):Summer88-88
Gontarski, S.E. The Intent of Undoing in Samuel Beckett's Dramatic Texts.*
    M. Esslin, 299:No11&12-178
    E.A. Falsey, 517(PBSA):Vol82No3-381
Gontarski, S.E., ed. On Beckett.*
    V.K., 295(JML):Fall87/Winter88-295
    J. Schlueter, 130:Winter88/89-376
Gonzales, R. Twilights and Chants.
    S. Hamill, 649(WAL):Nov88-261
González, A. Antonio Machado.
    M.P. Predmore, 240(HR):Winter88-117
Gonzalez, A. & M.A. Español para el Hispanohablante en los Estados Unidos.
    S. Cavazos Pena, 399(MLJ):Spring88-110
González, A.M.C. – see under Cano González, A.M.
González, G. Rainbow's End.
    C.R. Shirley, 649(WAL):Feb89-388
González, J.J.M. & others – see under Martín González, J.J. & others
González, J.M.C. – see under Caso González, J.M.
Gonzalez, R., ed. City Kite on a Wire.
    R.D. Harper, 649(WAL):Aug88-178
Gonzalez-Crussi, F. The Five Senses.
    A. Fels, 441:9Apr89-35
González Echevarría, R. La ruta de Severo Sarduy.
    R.S. Minc, 238:Dec88-840
    A. Moreiras, 400(MLN):Mar88-466
González Echevarría, R. The Voice of the Masters.*
    S. Boldy, 86(BHS):Apr88-204
González Faus, J.I. Where the Spirit Breathes.
    P. Hebblethwaite, 617(TLS):22-28Sep89-1035
González-Palacios, A. Il Tempio del Gusto.
    S. Jervis, 39:May88-370
González Rolán, T. – see Frontinus, S.J.
González Rolán, T. & P. Saquero Suárez-Somonte – see Alfonso X el Sabio
Gonzalo, I.O. – see under Oceja Gonzalo, I.
Gooch, J. Army, State and Society in Italy, 1870-1915.
    P. Ginsborg, 617(TLS):17-23Nov89-1284
Good, R.M. The Sheep of His Pasture.
    G.A. Rendsburg, 318(JAOS):Jul-Sep87-558
Goodall, G. Parallel Structures in Syntax.
    L. Haegeman, 361:Jul88-275
Goodden, A. "Actio" and Persuasion.*
    D.F. Connon, 83:Spring88-112
    M. de Rougemont, 535(RHL):Nov-Dec88-1142
    M. de Rougemont, 610:Summer88-162
Goodden, A. The Complete Lover.
    D. Coward, 617(TLS):17-23Mar89-284
Gooddy, W. Time and the Nervous System.
    D. King-Hele, 617(TLS):21-27Jul89-793

Goodheart, E. Pieces of Resistance.
    R. Newsom, 395(MFS):Winter88-740
Goodin, R. Protecting the Vulnerable.
    T. Mautner, 291:Vol5No1-114
Goodin, R.E. & J. Le Grand, with others. Not Only the Poor.
    T.R. Marmor, 185:Jan89-442
Gooding, D., T. Pinch & S. Schaffer, eds. The Uses of Experiment.
    B. Pippard, 617(TLS):29Sep-5Oct89-1057
Goodman, A. Total Immersion.
    R. Hacker, 441:10Sep89-26
Goodman, N. Of Mind and Other Matters.*
    R. Shusterman, 494:Vol8No3/4-651
Goodman, N. & C.Z. Elgin. Reconceptions in Philosophy and Other Arts and Sciences.
    S. Gardner, 617(TLS):6-12Jan89-17
Goodrich, N.L. King Arthur. Merlin.
    A. Chesterman, 439(NM):1988/3-433
Goodrich, P. Legal Discourse.
    E. Battistella, 350:Jun89-387
Goodsell, C.T. The Social Meaning of Civic Space.
    T. Fisher, 505:Aug88-109
Goodwin, D.K. The Fitzgeralds and the Kennedys.
    S.M. Gillon, 432(NEQ):Mar88-134
Goodwin, G. A History of Ottoman Architecture.
    J. Sweetman, 463:Summer87-191
Goodwin, M. & N. Wise. On the Edge.
    A. Cooper, 441:10Dec89-33
Goody, J. The Interface between the Written and the Oral.
    B. King, 350:Sep89-661
    O. Murray, 617(TLS):16-22Jun89-655
Goody, J. The Logic of Writing and the Organization of Society.
    O. Murray, 617(TLS):16-22Jun89-655
Goold, G.P. – see Manilius
Goonetilleke, D.C.R.A. Images of the Raj.*
    V.G. Kiernan, 366:Autumn88-260
Goorney, H. & E. MacColl, eds. Agit-Prop to Theatre Workshop.
    R.N.C., 295(JML):Fall87/Winter88-276
Goosse, A. – see Grevisse, M.
Gorak, J. Critic of Crisis.
    G. Henderson, 627(UTQ):Summer89-543
Gorak, J. God the Artist.*
    B.M., 494:Vol8No2-467
    D. Seed, 402(MLR):Jul89-731
Gorbachev, M. Perestroika.*
    L. Gruliow, 42(AR):Summer88-383
Gorbman, C. Unheard Melodies.
    B. Covey, 599:Winter88-676
Gordenker, L. Refugees in International Politics.
    A.R.Z., 185:Jan89-460
Gordimer, N. The Essential Gesture.* (S. Clingman, ed)
    N. Ascherson, 453(NYRB):30Mar89-12
    A. Maja-Pearce, 364:Oct/Nov88-141
Gordimer, N. A Sport of Nature.*
    J. Mellors, 364:Apr-May87-153
Gordis, R. Judaic Ethics for a Lawless World.
    E.N.D., 185:Apr89-663
Gordon, A. The Dead Pull Hitter.
    D. Cole, 441:22Oct89-22
Gordon, D. The Low Road Hame.
    C. Gow, 571(ScLJ):Spring88-36

Gordon, D.E. Expressionism.
  C. Rhodes, 59:Dec88-590
  M. Yorke, 324:Apr89-323
  639(VQR):Spring88-67
Gordon, E.A. Mark the Music.
  D. Shewey, 441:16Jul89-16
Gordon, G. & R.E. Cohen. Down to the Wire.
  J.D. Atwater, 441:24Dec89-10
Gordon, G. & D. Hughes, eds. Best Short
  Stories 1987.
  L. Dawson-Evans, 565:Summer88-54
Gordon, G. & D. Hughes, eds. Best Short
  Stories 1988.
  M. Illis, 617(TLS):1-7Dec89-1337
Gordon, I. - see Lowry, B.
Gordon, J. "Finnegans Wake."*
  J.C.C. Mays, 272(IUR):Spring88-141
Gordon, J.S. The Golden Guru.
  42(AR):Spring88-273
Gordon, L. Eliot's New Life.*
  J.M.B., 179(ES):Dec88-539
  J. Haffenden, 493:Winter88/89-6
  S. Helmling, 344:Summer89-153
  H. Lomas, 364:Feb/Mar89-118
  J. Olney, 598(SoR):Spring89-503
  M. Pinker, 152(UDQ):Winter/Spring89-173
Gordon, L. Maricopa Morphology and Syntax.
  B. Comrie, 353:Vol26No1-159
Gordon, M. The Other Side.
  M.S. Bell, 441:15Oct89-9
Gordon, M.T. & S. Riger. The Female Fear.
  P. Dye, 441:7May89-25
Gordon, P.H., with S. Waller & P. Weinman.
  Diamonds Are Forever.
  C.R. Herron, 441:23Apr89-36
Gordon, R.L. & D.M. Stillman. En primera per-
  sona.
  J.B. McInnis, 399(MLJ):Autumn88-372
Gordon, R.M. The Structure of Emotions.
  K. Bach, 484(PPR):Dec88-362
  A.R. Mele, 518:Oct88-224
Gordon, V. Mrs. Rushworth.
  L. Duguid, 617(TLS):13-19Jan89-42
Gordon, W.T. Semantics.
  J.F. Kess, 320(CJL):Mar88-106
Gorgias, J. Veriphantors Betrogener Frontal-
  bo [1670?]. (H. Rölleke, ed)
  J. Hardin, 221(GQ):Winter87-111
Gori, L. & S. Lucarelli. Vocabolario Pistoiese.
  (G. Giacomelli, ed)
  R. Stefanini, 545(RPh):Aug88-102
Görlach, M. - see Busch, W.
Görlach, M. - see "Wilhelm Busch, Max und
  Moritz: In deutschen Dialekten, Mittelhoch-
  deutsch und Jiddisch"
Gorn, E.J. The Manly Art.*
  R. Roberts, 598(SoR):Summer89-771
  A.J. Young, 106:Spring89-122
Górnowicz, H. Gewässernamen im Flussgebiet
  der unteren Weichsel.
  W. Kaestner, 260(IF):Band93-372
van Gorp, H. & others. Lexicon van literaire
  Termen.*
  M. Angenot, 107(CRCL):Mar88-73
Gorreri, M. - see Armenini, G.B.
Gorz, A. Métamorphoses du travail. Quête du
  sens.
  S. Khilnani, 617(TLS):5-11May89-490
Gorzond, I. Die Linguistik der unpersönlichen
  Ausdrücke.
  E. Kaiser, 547(RF):Band100Heft4-359
Goscilo, H., ed. Balancing Acts.
  H. Gifford, 453(NYRB):1Jun89-3

Gose, E.B., Jr. The World of the Irish Wonder
  Tale.
  G. Thomas, 102(CanL):Winter87-242
Goshawke, W., I.D.K. Kelly & J.D. Wigg. Com-
  puter Translation of Natural Language.
  L. Proctor, 350:Dec89-888
Goss, M. The Evidence for Phantom Hitch-
  Hikers.
  A. Schmetzke, 203:Vol99No2-265
Gossett, P. "Anna Bolena" and the Artistic
  Maturity of Gaetano Donizetti.
  G. Duval-Wirth, 537:Vol74No1-117
  J.A. Hepokoski, 451:Summer88-74
  R. Parker, 317:Summer88-368
Gotchi, I. A Bit of Witchcraft.
  J.K.L. Walker, 617(TLS):30Jun-6Jul89-
  714
Got'e, I.V. Time of Troubles.* (T. Emmons, ed
  & trans)
  N. Davies, 453(NYRB):15Jun89-46
  J. Keep, 617(TLS):13-19Jan89-29
Göthel, F. Thematisch-bibliographisches
  Verzeichnis der Werke von Louis Spohr.
  C. Brown, 410(M&L):Jul88-389
Gottcent, J.H. The Bible.
  S.G. Nugent, 124:Jul-Aug89-480
Gottfried, P. & T. Flemming. The Conserva-
  tive Movement.
  E. Papa, 543:Dec88-382
Gotthelf, A., ed. Aristotle on Nature and
  Living Things.*
  G.E.R. Lloyd, 466:Vol6-221
Gotthelf, A. & J.G. Lennox, eds. Philosophical
  Issues in Aristotle's Biology.
  M. Schofield, 520:Vol33No1-114
Gottlieb, R.S. History and Subjectivity.
  V.G., 185:Jul89-976
Gottschall, E. Typographic Communications
  Today.
  D.P. Doordan, 441:26Nov89-31
Gottwald, N.K. The Tribes of Yahweh.
  A.F. Rainey, 318(JAOS):Jul-Sep87-541
Götze, H. Castel del Monte.
  F. Toker, 576:Dec88-415
Götze, K-H. Heinrich Böll: "Ansichten eines
  Clowns."
  E. Friedrichsmeyer, 221(GQ):Spring88-
  324
Goubert, J-P. The Conquest of Water.
  J. Burnett, 617(TLS):15-21Dec89-1383
Goubert, P. The Course of French History.
  639(VQR):Autumn88-115
Goudge, E. Garden of Lies.
  R. Weinreich, 441:9Jul89-18
van Goudoever, A.P. The Limits of Destalini-
  zation in the Soviet Union.
  W. Taubman, 550(RusR):Apr88-208
Goudriaan, T., ed & trans. The Viṇāśikha-
  tantra, a Śaiva Tantra of the Left Current.
  H. Brunner, 259(IIJ):Jul88-224
de Gouges, O. Oeuvres. (B. Groult, ed)
  M. & P. Higonnet, 617(TLS):19-25May89-
  541
Gough, H. The Newspaper Press in the French
  Revolution.
  W. Scott, 617(TLS):19-25May89-554
Gouhier, H. L'anti-humanisme au XVIIe
  siècle.^
  F. Lagarde, 475:Vol15No28-292
  J-M. Le Lannou, 98:Oct88-863
Gouhier, H. Blaise Pascal.*
  F. Lagarde, 704(SFR):Fall-Winter88-405
  P. Magnard, 192(EP):Oct-Dec88-554

Gouillart, C. – see Livy
Gouinlock, J. Excellence in Public Discourse.*
  A.J. Reck, 319:Jan89–166
  H. Wenkart, 619:Winter88–141
Gouiran, G. – see Bertran de Born
Goujard, R. – see Columella
Goujon, J–P. "Tes blessures sont plus douces que leurs caresses."
  J. Dupont, 535(RHL):Nov–Dec88–1163
Goujon, J–P. – see Vivien, R.
Gould, B. A Future for Socialism.
  J. Lively, 617(TLS):3–9Nov89–1199
Gould, C.C. Rethinking Democracy.
  M. Cranston, 617(TLS):20–26Jan89–52
  F. Cunningham, 103:Jan89–13
Gould, E., ed. The Sin of the Book.
  H. Shillony, 535(RHL):Mar–Apr88–344
Gould, G. The Glenn Gould Reader. (T. Page, ed)
  K. Bazzana, 414(MusQ):Vol73No2–284
Gould, H.A. The Hindu Caste System.
  R.I. Crane, 293(JASt):Nov88–920
Gould, I. The Gould Collection of Netsuke.
  L. Bandini, 60:Sep–Oct88–157
Gould, J. Herodotus.
  S. Hornblower, 617(TLS):10–16Nov89–1237
Gould, S.J. Time's Arrow, Time's Cycle.*
  A. Bewell, 173(ECS):Fall88–125
  S. Herbert, 637(VS):Winter89–239
Gould, S.J. An Urchin in the Storm.*
  A.B. Stewart, 42(AR):Spring88–270
Gould, S.J. Wonderful Life.
  P–L. Adams, 61:Nov89–136
  J. Gleick, 441:22Oct89–1
Gould, W. – see "Yeats Annual"
Goulet, A. Fiction et vie sociale dans l'oeuvre d'André Gide.
  C.L. Kaplan, 207(FR):Dec88–340
  P. Pollard, 208(FS):Jul88–361
Goulet–Cazé, M–O. L'ascèse cynique.*
  J. Mansfeld, 123:Vol38No1–162
  É. des Places, 555:Vol61fasc2–315
Goulyga, A. Emmanuel Kant, une vie.
  A. Stanguennec, 542:Apr–Jun88–264
Gounaropoulou, L. & M.B. Hatzopoulos. Les Milliaires de la Voie Egnatienne entre Héraclée des Lyncestes et Thessalonique.
  A. Aichinger, 229:Band60Heft3–241
  É. des Places, 555:Vol61fasc1–121
Gourlay, E. The Celluloid Barrette.
  K. Tudor, 198:Winter88–103
Gourvish, T.R. & A. O'Day, eds. Later Victorian Britain, 1867–1900.
  C.R. Perry, 637(VS):Summer89–606
  639(VQR):Autumn88–116
Gouws, J. – see Greville, F.
Goux, J–J. Économie et symbolique.
  P. Reynaud–Pactat, 153:Summer88–69
Goux, J–J. Les Monnayeurs du langage.
  T. Di Piero, 153:Summer88–2
  P. Reynaud–Pactat, 153:Summer88–69
Govier, T. Selected Issues in Logic and Communication.
  D. Romain, 103:Dec89–480
Gowans, A. The Comfortable House.*
  G. Dodds, 106:Summer88–261
  J.S. Hull, 576:Jun88–208
Gowers, R. Emily Carr.
  D. Farr, 529(QQ):Winter88–894
Gowing, L. Paintings in the Louvre.
  C. McCorquodale, 39:Oct88–294

Gowing, N. The Wire.
  A. Husarska, 441:26Mar89–16
Goy, R.J. Chioggia and the Villages of the Venetian Lagoon.*
  D.E. Queller, 276:Autumn88–274
"Goya: Nuevas visiones."
  Yasunari Kitaura, 48:Oct–Dec88–453
Goyard–Fabre, S. & R. Sève. Les grandes questions de la philosophie du droit.
  G. Fraysse, 542:Jan–Mar88–102
Goyet, F. – see Tabourot, É.
Goytisolo, J. Count Julian.
  A.L. Six, 617(TLS):17–23Nov89–1272
Goytisolo, J. Forbidden Territory.
  J. Butt, 617(TLS):19–25May89–537
  W. Gimbel, 441:12Feb89–12
Goytisolo, J. Landscapes after the Battle.*
  T. Whalen, 532(RCF):Summer88–318
Gözö, Y. – see under Yoshimasu Gözö
Grab, W. Georg Büchner und die Revolution von 1848.
  D. Sevin, 406:Summer88–236
Grabo, N.S. Edward Taylor. (rev)
  J.D. Patterson, 165(EAL):Vol24No3–264
Grabovac, J. Ethische und didaktisch–aufklärerische Tendenzen bei Filip Grabovac "Cvit razgovora."
  E.D. Goy, 575(SEER):Apr88–288
Graça Moura, V. Camões e a divina proporção.
  T.F. Earle, 86(BHS):Jan88–101
Grace, G. A Sacrifice of Fire.*
  B. Pell, 102(CanL):Autumn88–171
Gracia, J.J.E. Individuality.
  P. Weiss, 543:Sep88–143
Gracia, J.J.E. Introduction to the Problem of Individuation in the Early Middle Ages.*
  I. Boh, 438:Spring88–243
  P. King, 482(PhR):Oct88–564
Gracia, J.J.E. & I. Jaksic. Filosofía e identidad cultural en América Latina.
  263(RIB):Vol38No4–546
Gracq, J. Autour des sept collines.
  A. Derasse, 605(SC):15Jul89–336
  J. Taylor, 617(TLS):2–8Jun89–618
Gracq, J. Oeuvres complètes.
  J. Taylor, 617(TLS):2–8Jun89–618
Gradenwitz, P. Leonard Bernstein.*
  A. Jacobs, 415:Jan88–21
Graef, R. Talking Blues.
  R. Klein, 617(TLS):19–25May89–539
Graf, K. Gmünder Chroniken im 16. Jahrhundert.
  E. Moser–Rath, 196:Band29Heft1/2–190
Graf, M. The Kraków Ghetto and the Plaszów Camp Remembered.
  I. Deak, 453(NYRB):28Sep89–63
Graf, O.A. Die Kunst des Quadrats.
  A. Alofsin, 576:Dec88–428
Grafen, A., ed. Evolution and its Influence.
  P.J. Bowler, 617(TLS):1–7Dec89–1345
Graff, G. Professing Literature.*
  L.R. Furst, 149(CLS):Vol25No3–277
  A. Golding, 405(MP):May89–411
  L. Groening, 150(DR):Winter87/88–511
  P. Jay, 223:Spring88–118
  T.L. Jeffers, 125:Spring88–287
  G. Levine, 533:Spring89–121
  D. Novitz, 478(P&L):Apr88–118
  R. Ohmann, 125:Spring88–283
  J.M. Perl, 536(Rev):Vol10–171
  R. Scholes, 128(CE):Mar88–323
                  [continued]

[continuing]
K. Vanderbilt, 27(AL):Mar88-108
S.P. Zitner, 627(UTQ):Summer88-554
42(AR):Winter88-125
Grafström, Å. La langue du comte Robert
Joseph de la Cerda de Villelongue, corres-
pondant de Voltaire.
J-P. Chambon, 553(RLiR):Jan-Jun88-302
Grafton, A. & L. Jardine. From Humanism to
the Humanities.*
J. Kraye, 319:Jan89-150
I. Maclean, 131(CL):Winter88-78
W. Poznar, 577(SHR):Summer88-279
R.G. Witt, 551(RenQ):Autumn88-479
Grafton, A., G.W. Most & J.E.G. Zetzel - see
Wolf, F.A.
Grafton, S. "F" is for Fugitive.
E. Weiner, 441:21May89-17
Graham, A.C. Yin-Yang and the Nature of
Correlative Thinking.
J. Sellmann, 485(PE&W):Apr88-203
Graham, C. Death of a Hollow Man.
T.J.B., 617(TLS):30Jun-6Jul89-714
Graham, D. Magic Shows.*
E. Nelson, 219(GaR):Summer88-440
Graham, D. No Name on the Bullet.
G. Johnson, 441:10Sep89-27
Graham, D. - see Douglas, K.
Graham, G. Politics in its Place.*
J-M. Gabaude, 542:Jan-Mar88-103
Graham, J. The End of Beauty.*
D.M. Halperin, 473(PR):Vol55No3-508
W. Scammell, 493:Spring88-48
455:Mar88-72
Graham, J.F., ed. Difference in Translation.*
C. Norris, 131(CL):Winter88-52
Graham, K. Hokusai's Wave.*
J. Mellors, 364:Apr/May88-133
Graham, K. Indirections of the Novel.*
D.R. Schwarz, 445(NCF):Mar89-545
Graham, P. Iban Shamanism.
A.L. Tsing, 293(JASt):Aug88-699
Graham, S.L. House and Street.
A. Hennessy, 617(TLS):14-20Jul89-763
Graham, T. The Book of the Royal Year.
639(VQR):Spring88-66
Gram, M.S. The Transcendental Turn.*
G. Franzwa, 342:Band79Heft3-348
Gramley, S. & K.M. Pätzold. Das moderne En-
glisch.
F.W. Gester, 72:Band224Heft2-378
Grampp, W.D. Pricing the Priceless.
G. Glueck, 441:19Nov89-33
Grana, G. La "rivoluzione fascista."
S. de Pretis, 547(RF):Band100Heft4-460
Granatstein, J.L. Canada: 1957-1967.*
R. Graham, 529(QQ):Spring88-178
de Granda Gutiérrez, G. Estudios de lingüís-
tica afro-románica.
W.W. Megenney, 545(RPh):May89-475
Grande, F. Once artistas y un dios.
F. Dauster, 240(HR):Winter88-131
Grand'Henry, J. - see Ibn Riḍwān
Grandin, J.M. Kafka's Prussian Advocate.
M. Harman, 221(GQ):Fall88-593
C. Koelb, 395(MFS):Winter88-716
"Les Grands Rhétoriqueurs."* (Vol 1)
F. Cornilliat, 535(RHL):Mar-Apr88-250
"Grandville: Dessins originaux."
J. Cuno, 54:Sep88-530

Grandy, R.E. & R. Warner, eds. Philosophical
Grounds of Rationality.
G. Macdonald, 518:Jul88-137
M. Platts, 393(Mind):Jan88-138
Grangaud, M. Memento-fragments.
A. Chevrier, 98:May88-416
Granger, B. Henry McGee is Not Dead.
N. Callendar, 441:15Jan89-39
Granger, G-G. Essai d'une philosophie du
style. (rev)
A. Reix, 542:Oct-Dec88-501
Granier, J. L'intelligence métaphysique.
P. Trotignon, 542:Jan-Mar88-122
Granqvist, R., ed. Distorted Perspectives.
A.P.A. Busia, 538(RAL):Winter88-557
Granshaw, L. & R. Porter, eds. The Hospital
in History.
R. Pinker, 617(TLS):28Jul-3Aug89-820
Grant, B.K., ed. Film Genre Reader.*
P.D. Murphy, 590:Jun89-47
Grant, G. The World We Created at Hamilton
High.*
639(VQR):Autumn88-132
Grant, G.P. Technology and Justice.* En-
glish-Speaking Justice.
D. Gauthier, 154:Spring88-121
Grant, J.N. Studies in the Textual Tradition
of Terence.*
J. Barsby, 123:Vol38No1-21
S.M. Goldberg, 124:Nov-Dec88-126
S. Prete, 229:Band60Heft2-150
Grant, M. The Rise of the Greeks.*
W.G. Forrest, 441:22Jan89-16
Grant, M. & E. Frankl. Cambridge.
G. Cavallero, 324:Dec88-59
Grant, M. & R. Kitzinger, eds. Civilization of
the Ancient Mediterranean.
D.J.R. Bruckner, 441:22Jan89-16
Grant, P. Reading the New Testament.
J.L. Houlden, 617(TLS):15-21Dec89-1398
Grant, R.M. Gods and the One God.
W.C. Stephens, 124:May-Jun89-401
Granville-Barker, H. Granville Barker and
His Correspondents.* (E. Salmon, ed)
J. Fisher, 397(MD):Sep88-465
D. Kennedy, 615(TJ):Dec87-537
Granville-Barker, H. Plays by Harley Gran-
ville Barker. (D. Kennedy, ed)
J. Fisher, 397(MD):Sep88-465
Gras, M. Trafics tyrrhéniens archaïques.
D. Ridgway, 123:Vol38No1-113
Grasberger, R. Bruckner-Bibliographie (bis
1974).
P. Banks, 410(M&L):Jan88-95
Grass, G. On Writing and Politics, 1967-
1983.*
M.P.L., 295(JML):Fall87/Winter88-325
Grass, G. The Rat.* (German title: Die Rät-
tin.)
639(VQR):Winter88-20
Grass, G. Show Your Tongue.
P-L. Adams, 61:Jun89-96
C. Blaise, 441:21May89-12
442(NY):18Sep89-140
Grasselli, M.M. & P. Rosenberg, with others.
Watteau 1684-1721.
H. Opperman, 54:Jun88-354
Grasskamp, W. Trivialität und Geschichtlich-
keit.
S.E. Larsen, 462(OL):Vol43No2-193
Grasso, J.M. Truman's Two China Policy.
C.A. Buss, 293(JASt):May88-346
Grathoff, R. - see Schütz, A. & A. Gurwitsch

Gratwick, A.S. – see Terence
Gratz, R.B. The Living City.
  R. Campbell, 441:14May89-26
Graulich, M. – see Austin, M.
de Grauwe, L. De Wachtendonckse psalmen en
  glossen.
  H. von Gadow, 72:Band225Heft1-150
  E. Neuss, 685(ZDL):3/1987-412
Graves, A.B. Italo-Hispanic Ballad Relation-
  ships.
  J. Cummins, 402(MLR):Apr89-497
Graves, R. Poems About War.
  D. Hibberd, 617(TLS):10-16Feb89-134
Graves, R. Share of Honor.
  D. Murray, 441:5Mar89-22
Graves, R.P. Robert Graves.* (Vol 1)
  S. Helmling, 569(SR):Fall88-lxxxii
  J.M. Perl, 473(PR):Vol55No1-163
Graves, W. & others. Four New Comedies.
  M. Westley, 108:Winter88-91
Gravil, R., L. Newlyn & N. Roe, eds. Cole-
  ridge's Imagination.*
  P. Martin, 366:Autumn88-207
Grawe, C. Theodor Fontane: "Effi Briest."*
  D.C. Riechel, 221(GQ):Spring87-291
Gray, C.S. Klaus Rifbjerg.
  H.C. Andersen, 562(Scan):May88-73
Gray, D., ed. The Oxford Book of Late Medie-
  val Verse and Prose.*
  A.V.C.S., 382(MAE):1988/1-115
Gray, D. – see Bennett, J.A.W.
Gray, D. – see Coghill, N.
Gray, F. Noel Coward.
  J. Fisher, 397(MD):Dec88-596
Gray, F. La Bruyère amateur de caractères.*
  L.A. Gregorio, 475:Vol15No28-295
  M.S. Koppisch, 210(FrF):Jan88-114
Gray, J. Liberalisms.
  K.F.T. Cust, 103:Dec89-483
Gray, J. The Poems of John Gray. (I. Fletch-
  er, ed)
  G.B. Tennyson, 445(NCF):Sep88-275
  R. Wells, 617(TLS):6-12Jan89-16
Gray, J.A. & D.S. Lee, eds. The Federal Cyl-
  inder Project. (Vol 2)
  R. Keeling, 292(JAF):Jan-Mar88-82
Gray, J.C., ed. Mirror up to Shakespeare.*
  J.L. Levenson, 570(SQ):Spring88-106
Gray, N. The Paintings of David Jones.
  C. Reid, 617(TLS):25-31Aug89-922
Gray, P. Ring Doves and Snakes.
  E. Herring, 617(TLS):7-13Jul89-758
Gray, P., with C. Sargood. Honey From a
  Weed.
  639(VQR):Spring88-66
Gray, R. The Imperative of Modernity.
  R. Carr, 617(TLS):13-19Oct89-1113
Gray, R. Writing the South.*
  R.H. Brinkmeyer, Jr., 392:Spring88-187
Gray, R.G. The Treble V.
  J.D. Nesbitt, 649(WAL):May88-85
Gray, R.T. Constructive Destruction.
  S. Dowden, 221(GQ):Fall88-595
  R.V. Gross, 406:Winter88-488
  J.L. Hibberd, 133:Band21Heft4-364
Gray, S. How's That for Telling 'Em, Fat
  Lady?*
  G. Gordon, 511:Aug88-43
Gray, S., ed. The Penguin Book of Southern
  African Stories.
  C. Style, 364:Mar87-112
Gray, S. Time of Our Darkness.
  P. Parker, 364:Oct/Nov88-142

Grayling, A.C. Berkeley.*
  C.J. McCracken, 319:Jan89-159
Grayling, A.C. Wittgenstein.
  M. Budd, 617(TLS):3-9Feb89-115
  483:Oct88-556
Grayson, G.W. Oil and Mexican Foreign Pol-
  icy.
  G. Poitras, 263(RIB):Vol38No3-403
"The Graywolf Annual Four."* (S. Walker, ed)
  J.R. Dickey, 649(WAL):Feb89-372
de Grazia, S. Machiavelli in Hell.
  W.A. Rebhorn, 441:5Nov89-25
Greaves, R.L. – see Bunyan, J.
"Devis Grebu: Through an Artist's Eye."
  R. Siegel, 441:29Jan89-31
Greeley, A.M. Love Song.
  K. Olson, 441:22Jan89-23
Greeley, A.M. St. Valentine's Night.
  S. Paulos, 441:17Sep89-24
Green, C. Cubism and Its Enemies.*
  L. Malen, 55:Apr88-54
  D. Stephens, 207(FR):Mar89-730
  A. Summerfield, 324:Mar89-263
Green, D. Shaping Political Consciousness.*
  639(VQR):Autumn88-130
Green, H.G. The Devil is Innocent.
  R.J. Merrett, 102(CanL):Autumn88-158
Green, J. Against the Tide.
  J. Stanton, 529(QQ):Summer88-494
Green, J. The 1987 Green Book.
  B.L. Cooper, 498:Summer88-80
Green, J. Les Pays lointains.
  R. Stanley, 207(FR):Feb89-548
Green, K. Night Angel.
  M. Stasio, 441:19Feb89-23
Green, L. The Authority of the State.
  R.E. Flathman, 103:Oct89-412
Green, L.D. – see Rainold, J.
Green, M. Mountain of Truth.*
  P. Milbouer, 221(GQ):Fall88-608
Green, M. & J. Swan. The Triumph of Pierrot.*
  J. Fisher, 397(MD):Jun88-310
Green, M.J. Fiction in the Historical
  Present.*
  J. Cruickshank, 208(FS):Apr88-237
  S. Day, 529(QQ):Spring88-205
  M. LaVallée-Williams, 295(JML):Fall87/
  Winter88-209
  D.A. Orlando, 704(SFR):Fall-Winter88-
  417
Green, R.L., ed. The Sherlock Holmes Letters.
  E.S. Lauterbach, 395(MFS):Summer88-294
Green, T.M. The Woman Who Is The Midnight
  Wind.
  K. Wilson, 102(CanL):Autumn88-182
Green, V. Love in a Cool Climate.
  A.F. McGill, 635(VPR):Spring88-32
Green-Pedersen, N.J. The Tradition of the
  "Topics" in the Middle Ages.*
  M. Beuchot, 449:Jun87-282
Greenawalt, K. Conflicts of Law and Moral-
  ity.*
  B.R. Gross, 185:Oct88-168
Greenbaum, S. Good English and the Gram-
  marian.*
  E. Finegan, 350:Sep89-662
Greenberg, C. The Collected Essays and Crit-
  icism.* (J. O'Brian, ed)
  E. Frank, 560:Fall88-246
  S.P., 295(JML):Fall87/Winter88-326

Greenberg, D.F. The Construction of Homo-
sexuality.
J. Boswell, 61:Feb89-74
N.B. Dirks, 441:15Jan89-9
A. Scull, 617(TLS):28Jul-3Aug89-820
Greenberg, H. Hank Greenberg: The Story of
My Life. (I. Berkow, ed)
P. Constantine, 441:18Jun89-21
W. Sheed, 453(NYRB):12Oct89-49
Greenberg, M. Corneille, Classicism and the
Ruses of Symmetry.*
C. Carlin, 207(FR):Oct88-166
T. Cave, 208(FS):Oct88-468
Greenberg, M. The Hamlet Vocation of Cole-
ridge and Wordsworth.*
Z. Leader, 591(SIR):Fall88-463
L. Newlyn, 541(RES):Aug88-450
Greenblatt, S. Renaissance Self-Fashioning.
M. Waller, 153:Spring87-2
Greenblatt, S., ed. Representing the English
Renaissance.*
S.L. Wofford, 604:Fall88-53
Greenblatt, S. Shakespearean Negotiations.*
M. Edmundson, 385(MQR):Summer89-437
M. Elliott, 175:Autumn88-224
Greene, B. Homecoming.
D. Anderson, 441:22Jan89-24
Greene, D. - see Johnson, S.
Greene, G. The Captain and the Enemy.*
J. Bayley, 453(NYRB):16Mar89-3
Greene, G. Yours etc. (C. Hawtree, ed)
J. Symons, 617(TLS):10-16Nov89-1231
Greene, G. & C. Kahn, eds. Making A Differ-
ence.
S. Neuman, 49:Jul88-99
C.H. Smith, 128(CE):Mar88-318
Greene, J.P. Peripheries and Center.
H. Hartog, 656(WMQ):Oct88-773
Greene, J.P. Pursuits of Happiness.
R.C. Simmons, 617(TLS):19-25May89-532
Greene, K. The Archaeology of the Roman
Economy.
P. Culham, 124:Sep-Oct88-58
Greenfeld, H. The Devil and Dr. Barnes.
J. Sturman, 55:Oct88-93
Greenfield, S.B. & D.G. Calder. A New Critical
History of Old English Literature.*
H. Sauer, 447(N&Q):Dec88-506
E.G. Stanley, 131(CL):Summer88-286
Greenhalgh, P. Ephemeral Vistas.
D. Jenkins, 46:Jul88-64
T. Prasch, 637(VS):Spring89-427
"Elizabeth Greenhill Bookbinder."
C. Franklin, 78(BC):Spring88-138
Greenleaf, S. Impact.
442(NY):30Oct89-118
Greenough, S. & others. On the Art of Fixing
a Shadow.
A. Grundberg, 441:3Dec89-20
Greenslade, D. Welsh Fever.
J.A. Fishman, 355(LSoc):Dec88-621
Greenspahn, F.E. Hapax Legomena in Biblical
Hebrew.
E.L. Greenstein, 318(JAOS):Jul-Sep87-
538
Greenspan, P.S. Emotions and Reasons.
C. Armon-Jones, 617(TLS):22-28Dec89-
1425
Greenstein, F.I., ed. Leadership in the Mod-
ern Presidency.*
42(AR):Summer88-399

Greenwald, M.L. Directions by Indirections.*
C.H. Shattuck, 405(MP):Aug88-114
G.J. Williams, 570(SQ):Summer88-255
Greenwald, R. - see Jacobsen, R.
Greer, G. Daddy, We Hardly Knew You.
S. Sutherland, 617(TLS):17-23Mar89-275
Greer, G. Shakespeare.
M. Quilligan, 570(SQ):Spring88-105
R. Simard, 610:Autumn88-280
Gregersen, K. & H. Basbøll, eds. Nordic Pros-
ody IV.
I. Lehiste, 348(L&S):Apr-Jun88-211
Gregg, R.C., ed. Arianism.
D.W.H. Arnold, 161(DUJ):Dec87-169
Gregor, B. & M. Krifka, eds. Computerfibel für
die Geisteswissenschaften.*
W.H. Veith, 685(ZDL):2/1988-260
Gregor, F. Die alte ungarische und slowak-
ische Bergbauterminologie mit ihren deut-
schen Bezügen.*
W. Fiedler, 682(ZPSK):Band41Heft1-137
Gregory, B. Inventing Reality.
J. Polkinghorne, 617(TLS):17-23Mar89-
273
Gregory, G. Japanese Electronics Technology.
M.A. Cusumano, 293(JASt):May88-380
Gregory, P.N., ed. Traditions of Meditation in
Chinese Buddhism.
P.B. Watt, 293(JASt):Aug88-595
Gregory, R.L., with O.L. Zangwill, eds. The
Oxford Companion to the Mind.*
K. Baker, 62:Dec88-110
483:Apr88-289
Gregory, S. The Woodwitch.
B. Kent, 441:19Mar89-22
Gregory of Rimini. Lectura super primum et
secundum Sententiarum. (A.D. Trapp &
others, eds)
K.H. Tachau, 589:Oct88-929
Greider, W. Secrets of the Temple.*
R.E. Wagner, 144:Summer/Fall89-505
von Greiffenberg, C.R. Sämtliche Werke. (M.
Bircher & F. Kemp, eds)
R.E. Schade, 221(GQ):Fall87-663
Greiner, W. & G. Stilz, eds. Naturalismus in
England 1880-1920.
J.P. Becker, 52:Band23Heft1-110
S. Kohl, 177(ELT):Vol31No1-94
Grene, M. Descartes.*
L. Frankel, 482(PhR):Apr88-261
S. Gaukroger, 63:Sep88-414
J. Westphal, 393(Mind):Jan88-133
Grene, M. & D. Nails, eds. Spinoza and the
Sciences.
D. Garrett, 486:Sep88-480
E.G.E. van der Wall, 319:Jul89-479
Grenfell, J. Darling Ma. (J. Roose-Evans, ed)
A. Strachan, 511:Oct88-47
Grenier, R. Albert Camus.*
T. Keefe, 402(MLR):Apr89-482
Grenier, R. La Mare d'Auteuil.
R. Jacquelin, 450(NRF):Jul-Aug88-211
Grensemann, H. Knidische Medizin. (Pt 2)
V. Nutton, 123:Vol38No2-454
Grenville, K. Dream House.*
42(AR):Winter88-120
Grenville, K. Joan Makes History.*
442(NY):27Mar89-114
du Gres, M.D. & J. Subrenat - see under de
Combarieu du Gres, M. & J. Subrenat
Gresset, M. A Faulkner Chronology.*
C.S. Brown, 569(SR):Spring88-271

147

Gresset, M. & K. Ohashi, eds. Faulkner: After the Nobel Prize.
  D.G. Ford, 578:Spring89-118
"La grève des philosophes."
  M. Adam, 542:Jan-Mar88-121
Greville, F. The Prose Works of Fulke Greville, Lord Brooke.* (J. Gouws, ed)
  K. Duncan-Jones, 402(MLR):Jan89-122
  F.J. Levy, 250(HLQ):Summer88-228
Grevisse, M. Le bon usage.* (12th ed) (A. Goosse, ed)
  P. Osswald, 547(RF):Band99Heft4-419
  A. Rodríguez Somolinos, 548:Jan-Jun88-241
Grey, E. Jordan.
  J. Coles, 617(TLS):6-12Oct89-1104
Grice, P. Studies in the Way of Words.
  S. Blackburn, 617(TLS):17-23Nov89-1265
Grieder, J. Anglomanie in France (1740-1789).
  A. Grewe, 72:Band224Heft2-473
Griep, W. & H-W. Jäger, eds. Reisen im 18. Jahrhundert.
  M. Maurer, 224(GRM):Band38Heft3-353
Grier, K.C. Culture and Comfort.
  W. Rybczynski, 453(NYRB):9Nov89-35
Grier, P.T., ed. Dialectic and Contemporary Science.
  J. Burbidge, 103:Dec89-486
Grierson, P. & M. Blackburn. Medieval European Coinage, with a Catalogue of the Coins in the Fitzwilliam Museum, Cambridge. (Vol 1)
  A.M. Stahl, 589:Oct88-933
Griesbach, H. Deutsch mit Erfolg 1.
  G.A. Everett, 399(MLJ):Winter88-476
Griesbach, H. Neue deutsche Grammatik.
  H. Lederer, 399(MLJ):Summer88-239
  G. Starke, 682(ZPSK):Band41Heft4-523
Grieve, P. Desire and Death in the Spanish Sentimental Romance (1440-1550).
  B.F. Weissberger, 304(JHP):Spring88-255
Griffin, C. The Crombergers of Seville.
  J. Lynch, 617(TLS):7-13Apr89-359
Griffin, D. Regaining Paradise.*
  C. Hill, 366:Spring88-121
  P. Rogers, 173(ECS):Summer88-502
Griffin, J. Homer: The "Odyssey."
  C. Leach, 447(N&Q):Sep88-345
Griffin, J. Latin Poets and Roman Life.*
  R.F. Thomas, 122:Jan88-54
Griffin, J. Virgil.*
  E.S. de Angeli, 124:Jul-Aug89-473
  R. Astbury, 235:Summer88-120
Griffin, J. Well-Being.
  D. Braybrooke, 185:Apr89-625
  D.M. Taylor, 483:Jan88-127
Griffin, M.T. Nero.*
  G.J.D. Aalders H. Wzn., 394:Vol41 fasc3/4-465
Griffin, N. Spanish Incunabula in the John Rylands University Library of Manchester.
  J.J. Gwara, 304(JHP):Autumn88-71
Griffin, P. Along With Youth.*
  E. Margolies, 179(ES):Jun88-267
  E. Pifer, 677(YES):Vol19-351
Griffin, S. Unremembered Country.
  L. Runciman, 649(WAL):Nov88-256
Griffith, J. Universities and the State.
  J. Campbell, 617(TLS):29Dec89/4Jan90-1432
Griffith, J.S. Celebrating a Heritage.
  L. Fish, 440:Winter-Spring88-152

Griffith, J.S. & others. Respect and Community.
  L. Fish, 440:Winter-Spring88-152
Griffith, M. Aeschylus, "Prometheus Bound."
  W.J. Verdenius, 394:Vol41fasc3/4-398
Griffith, N.S. Edward Bellamy.
  K.M. Roemer, 26(ALR):Fall88-95
Griffith, S.F. Home Town News.
  D.B. Johnson, 441:5Feb89-25
  D.M. Kennedy, 61:Jan89-111
Griffith, T.G. - see Migliorini, B.
Griffiths, E. The Printed Voice of Victorian Poetry.
  A. St. George, 617(TLS):12-18May89-521
Griffiths, L. Personification in "Piers Plowman."*
  A. Henry, 382(MAE):1988/1-108
  G. Schmitz, 38:Band106Heft3/4-511
Griffiths, P. Myself and Marco Polo.
  R. Irwin, 617(TLS):15-21Dec89-1385
Griffiths, P.J. On Being Mindless.
  T. Abbott, 293(JASt):Feb88-178
  R.R. Jackson, 485(PE&W):Oct88-443
  J.W. de Jong, 259(IIJ):Apr88-160
Griffiths, R. Le Centre perdu.
  C. Lucas, 617(TLS):19-25May89-554
Grignani, M.A. Prologhi ed epiloghi.
  D. Zancani, 402(MLR):Apr89-492
Grignani, M.A., ed. La vita della foresta di W.H. Hudson nella traduzione di Eugenio Montale.
  D. Zancani, 402(MLR):Apr89-492
Grignon, C-H. Un homme et son péché. (A. Sirois & Y. Francoli, eds)
  B-Z. Shek, 627(UTQ):Fall88-185
Grigor'ev, V.P., ed. Problemy strukturnoj lingvistiki, 1983.
  B.P. Scherr, 574(SEEJ):Spring88-162
Grigson, G. Persephone's Flowers.
  J. Loveday, 4:Autumn88-71
Grimal, P. Cicéron.
  J.G.F. Powell, 313:Vol78-216
Grimal, P. Rome.
  P. Flobert, 555:Vol61fasc2-324
  M. Griffin, 123:Vol38No2-379
de Grimaldi, J. La pata de cabra. (D.T. Gies, ed)
  E.V. Coughlin, 238:Dec88-825
  I.L. McClelland, 86(BHS):Jul88-306
Grimes, M. The Old Silent.
  M. Stasio, 441:24Sep89-29
Grimes, M. Send Bygraves.
  M. Stasio, 441:24Dec89-23
Grimes, M.G., ed. The Knights in Fiction.
  S. de Paul, 106:Summer88-253
Grimm, G.E. & H-P. Bayerdörfer, eds. Im Zeichen Hiobs.
  M.H. Gelber, 462(OL):Vol43No2-184
  K. Weissenberger, 221(GQ):Spring87-303
Grimm, H-J. Untersuchungen zum Artikelgebrauch im Deutschen.
  E. Bauer, 685(ZDL):2/1988-265
  G. Kleiber, 553(RLiR):Jul-Dec88-488
Grimm, J. Molière.
  I. Maclean, 208(FS):Oct88-469
Grimm, J. Reden in der Akademie. (W. Neumann & H. Schmidt, eds)
  H-W. Eroms, 685(ZDL):2/1987-234
Grimm, J. - see de La Fontaine, J.
Grimm, J. & W. The Complete Fairy Tales of the Brothers Grimm.* (J. Zipes, trans)
  D.C. Riechel, 399(MLJ):Autumn88-363

Grimm, J. & W. Kinder- und Hausmärchen. (H. Rölleke, ed)
J.M. McGlathery, 301(JEGP):Jan88-85
E. Moser-Rath, 196:Band29Heft1/2-191
Grimm, J. & W. Unbekannte Märchen. (H. Rölleke, ed)
S. Ude-Koeller, 196:Band29Heft1/2-192
Grimm, R. Love, Lust, and Rebellion.*
D.G. Richards, 222(GR):Summer88-150
Grimm, R. & J. Hermand, eds. Our Faust?
G. Mahal, 133:Band21Heft4-337
von Grimmelshausen, J.J.C. An Unabridged Translation of "Simplicius Simplicissimus." (M. Adair, trans)
J. Hardin, 133:Band21Heft2/3-206
Grimminger, R. Die Ordnung, das Chaos, die Kunst.
M. Seel, 687:Oct-Dec88-712
Grimshaw, J. Philosophy and Feminist Thinking.*
H. Heise, 615(TJ):May88-283
Grimshaw, J.A., Jr., ed. Time's Glory.
E.T. Carroll, 395(MFS):Summer88-251
Grimwood, M. Heart in Conflict.*
L. Butts, 594:Winter88-430
M. Millgate, 27(AL):Mar88-142
Grinter, L.E. & P.M. Dunn, eds. The American War in Vietnam.
M. Young, 293(JASt):Nov88-937
Griolet, P. Cadjins et créoles en Louisiane.
M.M. Marshall, 207(FR):May89-1081
Grissom, K. Dropoff.
N. Callendar, 441:15Jan89-39
Griswold, C.J., Jr. Self-Knowledge in Plato's "Phaedrus."*
G.R.F. Ferrari, 482(PhR):Jul88-408
C. Hampton, 319:Oct89-606
J.A. Mason, 478(P&L):Apr88-141
G.J. de Vries, 394:Vol41fasc1/2-161
Griswold, W. Renaissance Revivals.*
A.W. Bloom, 130:Fall88-281
M. Scott, 611(TN):Vol42No2-93
Grivel, C. & F. Rutten, eds. Recherches sur le roman. (Vol 2)
R. Mahieu, 535(RHL):Jan-Feb88-155
Grivel, M. Le Commerce de l'estampe à Paris au XVIIe siècle.
A. Griffiths, 354:Sep88-269
H. Zerner, 90:Aug88-635
Grizzard, L. Chili Dawgs Always Bark at Night.
D. McWhorter, 441:19Nov89-25
Grizzard, L. Don't Bend Over in the Garden, Granny, You Know Them Taters Got Eyes.
B. Kent, 441:2Apr89-29
Grmek, M.D. Les maladies à l'aube de la civilisation occidentale.
A. Debru, 555:Vol61fasc2-345
Grobel, L. The Hustons.
P-L. Adams, 61:Dec89-128
N. Johnson, 441:19Nov89-20
Grobstein, C. Science and the Unborn.
A.H. Malcolm, 441:8Jan89-10
Groce, N.E. Everyone Here Spoke Sign Language.
42(AR):Summer88-399
Grocock, C.W., ed & trans. The Ruodlieb.
W.S. Anderson, 124:Sep-Oct88-70
Grodecki, L. & C. Brisac. Gothic Stained Glass, 1200-1300.*
M.H. Caviness, 589:Jul88-669
Gromyko, A. Memories.*
A. Nove, 617(TLS):9-15Jun89-631

Grondin, J. Le tournant dans la pensée de Martin Heidegger.
J-F. Mattéi, 154:Winter88-675
von Gronicka, A. The Russian Image of Goethe.* (Vol 2)
E. Kostka, 222(GR):Summer88-147
Grønvik, O. Runene på Eggjasteinen.
S. Kramarz, 680(ZDP):Band107Heft3-470
Groom, N. A Dictionary of Arabic Topography and Placenames.
M.C. Astour, 318(JAOS):Apr-Jun87-339
Groos, A. & R. Parker, eds. Reading Opera.
J.K. Law, 465:Summer89-85
J. Rosselli, 617(TLS):2-8Jun89-614
Grootings, P., ed. Technology and Work.
D. Lane, 575(SEER):Apr88-312
Gros, P. Byrsa III.*
S.R. Wolff, 124:Nov-Dec88-117
Grose, C. Milton and the Sense of Tradition.
N. Forsyth, 617(TLS):22-28Sep89-1036
Gross, F. Ideologies, Goals and Values.
A.J. Matejko, 497(PolR):Vol33No2-246
Gross, K. Spenserian Poetics.*
C. Martin, 405(MP):Aug88-85
Gross, L., J.S. Katz & J. Ruby, eds. Image Ethics.
P. Whitehead, 617(TLS):26-31Aug89-924
Gross, N.P. Amatory Persuasion in Antiquity.*
A.H.F. Griffin, 123:Vol38No1-56
J.P. Sullivan, 124:Nov-Dec88-141
Gross, P. Cat's Whisker.*
S. O'Brien, 364:Feb88-83
Gross, P. & S. Kantaris. The Air Mines of Mistila.*
G. Maxwell, 493:Winter88/89-48
Gross, S., ed. Maurice Maeterlinck und die deutschsprachige Literatur.
P. Gorceix, 72:Band225Heft1-213
Gross, S. & J. Thomas. Belgien-Literatur und Politik.
P. Gorceix, 356(LR):Feb-May88-136
Grosse, E.U. & H-H. Lüger. Frankreich verstehen.
G. Barthel, 547(RF):Band100Heft4-450
Grosse, G. Kołowokoło Budyšina.
G. Stone, 575(SEER):Jul88-499
Grosseteste, R. De cessatione legalium. (R.C. Dales & E.B. King, eds)
G.J. Etzkorn, 589:Jul88-671
Grosskurth, P. Melanie Klein.*
A. Brink, 627(UTQ):Fall87-216
R.S. Steele, 77:Fall88-329
Grossman, D. See Under: Love.
D. Donoghue, 453(NYRB):28Sep89-39
E. White, 441:16Apr89-7
442(NY):7Aug89-96
Grossman, D. The Yellow Wind.*
639(VQR):Autumn88-129
Grossman, J.R. Land of Hope.
G.M. Fredrickson, 617(TLS):15-21Dec89-1395
Grossman, K.M. The Early Novels of Victor Hugo.*
C. Bernard, 546(RR):May88-522
P.W.M. Cogman, 208(FS):Jan88-95
M. Sachs, 210(FrF):Sep88-373
Groult, B. - see de Gouges, O.
Groulx, L. The Iron Wedge.
G.W., 102(CanL):Winter87-290
Grove, J.M. The Little Ice Age.
B. Funnell, 617(TLS):17-23Mar89-272

149

Grover, K., ed. Dining in America 1850-1900.
639(VQR):Spring88-43

Groves, D. James Hogg and the St. Ronan's Border Club.
G.H. Hughes, 571(ScLJ):Winter88-10
J. Rubenstein, 588(SSL):Vol23-291

Groves, D. – see Hogg, J.

Groves, P. Academe.
L. Norfolk, 617(TLS):5-11May89-495

Grubb, K.B. Razzle Dazzle.
H. Dudar, 441:17Dec89-20

Gruber, J. Die Dialektik des "Trobar."
L. Rossi, 547(RF):Band99Heft4-457

Grubmüller, K. & G. Hess, eds. Kontroversen, alte und neue. (Vol 7)
J. Schmidt, 564:May88-184

Gruen, E.S. The Hellenistic World and the Coming of Rome.*
M.G. Morgan, 122:Jul88-245

Gruenais, M-P., ed. Etats de langue.
A. Hull, 207(FR):Apr89-919

Grujić, P.M. Čičerin, Plechanov und Lenin.
G.M. Hamburg, 550(RusR):Jan88-103

Grünbaum, A. & W.C. Salmon, eds. The Limitations of Deductivism.
L.J. Cohen, 617(TLS):7-13Apr89-373

Grundlehner, P. The Poetry of Friedrich Nietzsche.
A. Del Caro, 221(GQ):Spring88-318
J. Rolleston, 301(JEGP):Jul88-413

Grundy, I. Samuel Johnson & the Scale of Greatness.*
J.T. Boulton, 447(N&Q):Mar88-97

Grunebaum, J.O. Private Ownership.*
P. Day, 518:Jan88-58

Grunfeld, A.T. The Making of Modern Tibet.
J.T. Dreyer, 293(JASt):May88-347

Grunfeld, F.V. Rodin.*
V. Jirat-Wasiutyński, 90:Sep88-708
42(AR):Spring88-276

Grünfeld, J. Method and Language.
J-M. Salanskis, 192(EP):Jan-Mar88-117

Gruzinski, S. La Colonisation de l'Imaginaire.
H. Cronel, 450(NRF):Nov88-117

Gruzinski, S. Man-Gods in the Mexican Highlands.
D. Brading, 617(TLS):25-31Aug89-925

Grylls, D. The Paradox of Gissing.*
C. Burkhart, 177(ELT):Vol31No3-326
J. Halperin, 405(MP):Aug88-108
E. Mengel, 38:Band106Heft3/4-545
P.T. Srebrnik, 635(VPR):Fall88-133
A. Trodd, 366:Autumn88-256

Gryphius, C. Poetische Wälder.* (J.N. Hardin & D. Eggers, eds) Der Deutschen Sprache unterschiedene Alter und Wachsthum.* (D. Eggers & J.N. Hardin, eds)
J. Alexander, 406:Spring88-125
A.J. Harper, 83:Spring88-114

Grziwotz, H. Der moderne Verfassungsbegriff und die "Römische Verfassung" in der deutschen Forschung des 19. und 20. Jahrhunderts.
W. Nippel, 123:Vol38No2-442
T.E.J. Wiedemann, 313:Vol78-267

Gsell, O. & U. Wandruszka. Der romanische Konjunktiv.
G. Kleiber, 209(FM):Apr88-119
E. Schepper, 439(NM):1988/3-436

Guagnini, E., ed. Il punto su Saba.
E. Favretti, 228(GSLI):Vol165fasc532-580

Guagnini, E. & B. Maier, eds. Il punto su Saba.
E. Favretti, 228(GSLI):Vol165fasc532-580

Gualdani, E.N. – see under Norti Gualdani, E.

"Guanzi."* (Vol 1) (W.A. Rickett, trans)
R.T. Ames, 302:Vol24No1-68
R.D.S. Yates, 293(JASt):Feb88-128

Gudmundson, W. & M. Moos, comps. A Long Way to See.
P.D. Morrow, 649(WAL):Nov88-276

Guenette, D. Empiècements.
J.P. Gilroy, 102(CanL):Winter87-260

Guenette, D. L'Irrésolue.
M. Andersen, 102(CanL):Spring88-142

Guentherodt, I. Dudenrode Kr. Witzenhausen; Netra Kr. Eschwege.
H.J. Dingeldein, 685(ZDL):2/1987-264

de Guérin, M. Le Cahier vert. (C. Gély, ed)
J.A. Hiddleston, 208(FS):Jan88-97

Guérin, M. Qu'est-ce qu'une oeuvre?
G. Cesbron, 535(RHL):Nov-Dec88-1181

Guérin de Bouscal, D. Dom Quichot de la Manche, Seconde partie.* (M-L. Akhamlich, ed)
C. Mazouer, 535(RHL):Mar-Apr88-263

Gueroult, M. Histoire de l'histoire de la philosophie. (Vol 1)
L. Geldsetzer, 53(AGP):Band70Heft2-212

Guers-Villate, Y. Continuité/Discontinuité de l'oeuvre durassienne.*
A. Zielonka, 345(KRQ):Nov88-492

Guéry, R. La Nécropole orientale de Sitifis (Sétif, Algérie): Fouilles de 1966-1967.
E. Fentress, 313:Vol78-255

Guest, B. & J.M. Sellers, eds. Enterprise and Exploitation in a Victorian Colony.
J.M. MacKenzie, 637(VS):Spring89-432

Guest, R. & A.V. John. Lady Charlotte.
F. McLynn, 617(TLS):18-24Aug89-890

Guglielmi, G. Prosa italiana del novecento.
S. Sora, 72:Band225Heft2-471

Gugliotta, G. & J. Leen. Kings of Cocaine.
D.H. Bain, 441:30Apr89-13
M. Massing, 453(NYRB):30Mar89-22

Guibbory, A. The Map of Time.*
P. Hammond, 541(RES):Feb88-105
T. Hayes, 125:Spring88-292
W. Lamont, 366:Autumn88-264
J.M. Steadman, 405(MP):Feb89-304
E.W. Tayler, 551(RenQ):Summer88-360

Guicciardi, J-P. – see de Ligne, C.J.

Guicciardini, F. Le Lettere. (Vol 1) (P. Jodogne, ed)
M.M. Bullard, 551(RenQ):Autumn88-477

Guichemerre, R. – see Scarron, P.

"The Guide to Writers Conferences."
42(AR):Summer88-400

Guildford, D. & others. Four Books by Four Artists.
G. Gessert, 448:Vol26No3-83

Guilhamet, L. Satire and the Transformation of Genre.*
K. Combe, 447(N&Q):Dec88-537
R. Morton, 191(ELN):Jun88-84
529(QQ):Winter88-968

Guiliano, E. & P. Collins – see Dickens, C.

Guillaume, G. Leçons de linguistique de Gustave Guillaume, 1945-1946. (Série A, No. 7) Leçons de linguistique de Gustave Guillaume, 1947-1948. (Série C, No. 8) (R. Valin, W. Hirtle & A. Joly, eds of both)
A. Montaut, 529(QQ):Summer88-460

Guillaume, J. & C. Pichois, with others – see de Nerval G.

Guillaume, L. Agenda.
  Y. Leclair, 450(NRF):Dec88-80

Guillaume de Tyr. Chronique. (R.B.C. Huygens, ed)
  J.G. Rowe, 589:Jan88-157

Guillevic. Motifs, Creusement.
  J-M. Le Sidaner, 450(NRF):Feb88-92

Guillou-Varga, S. Mythes, mythographies et poésie lyrique au Siècle d'Or espagnol.
  E.L. Rivers & R.H. Chinchilla, 240(HR):Spring88-257

Guiraud-Weber, M. Les propositions sans nominatif en russe moderne.
  A.G.F. Van Holk, 559:Vol12No3-342

Gulden, A. Nur auf der Grenze bin ich zu Haus.
  K. Kehr, 685(ZDL):2/1987-275

Gullace, G. Il "Candide" nel pensiero di Voltaire.
  C.J. Betts, 208(FS):Jan88-86

Gullette, D. – see "Nicaraguan Peasant Poetry from Solentiname"

Gullette, M.M. Safe at Last in the Middle Years.
  F. Conroy, 441:1Jan89-9

Gullón, G., ed. "Fortunata y Jacinta" de Benito Pérez Galdós.
  D.F. Urey, 240(HR):Spring88-267

Gumbrecht, H.U. & K.L. Pfeiffer, eds. Stil.
  P. Monteath, 494:Vol8No1-192

Gumilev, N. Neizdannoe i nesobrannoe. (M. Basker & S.D. Graham, eds)
  S.I. Ketchian, 550(RusR):Apr88-224

Gummerman, J. We Find Ourselves in Moontown.
  J. Clute, 617(TLS):21-27Jul89-803
  J. Humphreys, 441:28May89-9

Gumplowicz, P., ed. Doctor Jazz?
  A.J.M. Prévos, 91:Spring88-112

Gunn, D. Psychoanalysis and Fiction.
  P. Brooks, 617(TLS):13-19Jan89-40

Gunn, G. The Culture of Criticism and the Criticism of Culture.*
  D. Dowling, 102(CanL):Summer88-149
  M. Folch-Serra, 529(QQ):Autumn88-618
  K.G., 185:Oct88-195
  J. Seaton, 115:Winter88-94

Gunn, J., ed. The New Encyclopedia of Science Fiction.
  J. Clute, 617(TLS):21-27Apr89-430

Gunn, N.M. Neil M. Gunn: Selected Letters.* (J.B. Pick, ed)
  J.B. Caird, 571(ScLJ):Winter88-11

Gunn, N.M. Landscape and Light.* (A. McCleery, ed)
  M. McCulloch, 571(ScLJ):Spring88-19

Gunn, T. Undesirables.*
  N. Powell, 493:Autumn88-66

Gunning, D. Good Stuff.
  J.K.L. Walker, 617(TLS):3-9Nov89-1218

Gunter, P.A.Y. Henri Bergson. (2nd ed)
  K. Gore, 402(MLR):Apr89-480
  J. Theau, 154:Autumn88-562

Güntert, G. & J.L. Varela, eds. Entre pueblo y corona.
  D.T. Gies, 240(HR):Winter88-112

Günther, W. Dichter der neueren Schweiz. (Vol 3)
  T.S. Evans, 133:Band21Heft4-371
  C.C. Zorach, 406:Fall88-382

Guppy, S. The Blindfold Horse.*
  A. McCarthy, 441:12Feb89-17

Gupta, R.K. The Great Encounter.
  S.S. Korom, 318(JAOS):Oct-Dec87-847

Gupta, S.K. The Scheduled Castes in Modern Indian Politics.
  O.M. Lynch, 293(JASt):Aug88-679

Guptara, P. Black British Literature.
  C.L. Innes, 538(RAL):Winter88-595

Guralnick, P. Searching for Robert Johnson.
  P. Romanowski, 441:5Nov89-25

Gurevič, A.J. Contadini e santi.
  L. Minervini, 379(MedR):Apr88-131

Gurganus, A. Oldest Living Confederate Widow Tells All.
  J. Wilcox, 441:13Aug89-1

Gurganus, A.E. The Art of Revolution.
  W. Koepke, 221(GQ):Fall88-596

Gurney, R. La poesía de Juan Larrea.
  G. Barrow, 86(BHS):Apr88-192

Gurney, S. Alain-Fournier.
  R. Gibson, 208(FS):Oct88-489
  R. Stanley, 207(FR):Dec88-338

Gurock, J. The Men and Women of Yeshiva.*
  E.S. Shapiro, 390:Dec88-56

Gurr, A. Playgoing in Shakespeare's London.
  J.F. Andrews, 570(SQ):Winter88-503
  M. Butler, 447(N&Q):Sep88-368
  C. Jansohn, 72:Band225Heft2-393
  P. Thomson, 610:Autumn88-275

Gurr, A., with J. Orrell. Rebuilding Shakespeare's Globe.
  K. Brown, 617(TLS):8-14Sep89-966
  J.R. Mulryne, 324:Nov89-822

Gussmann, E., ed. Rules and the Lexicon.
  D.C. Walker, 350:Sep89-663

Gustafson, R. Winter Prophecies.
  L.M. York, 628(UWR):Vol21No2-90

Gustafson, R.F. Leo Tolstoy.*
  J.M. Coetzee, 131(CL):Spring88-185
  C. Lock, 627(UTQ):Summer88-542
  G. Woodcock, 569(SR):Spring88-306

Gustafsson, L. Funeral Music for Freemasons.
  W.G. Jones, 562(Scan):May88-78

"Gutenberg-Jahrbuch 1988." (H-J. Koppitz, ed)
  J.L. Flood, 617(TLS):14-20Apr89-408

Guterman, H. & B. Llewellyn, comps. David Roberts.
  C. Newton, 39:Sep88-215

Guterson, D. The Country Ahead of Us, the Country Behind.
  L.E. Nesbitt, 441:3Sep89-14

Guthrie, A.B., Jr. Big Sky, Fair Land. (D. Petersen, ed)
  T.W. Ford, 649(WAL):Feb89-379

Guthrie, A.B., Jr. Murder in the Cotswolds.
  M. Stasio, 441:28May89-27

Guthrie, G.P. A School Divided.
  M. McCaskey, 399(MLJ):Winter88-463

Guthrie, J. – see Büchner, G.

Guthrie, S. A Japanese New Religion.
  D.L. Barnhill, 293(JASt):Nov88-890
  R.F. Young, 407(NM):Autumn88-370

de Gutiérrez, A. The Movement Against Teaching English in Schools of Puerto Rico.
  A. Pousada, 350:Sep89-657

Gutierrez, A.R. – see under Ropero Gutierrez, A.

Gutierrez, D. The Dark and Light Gods.
  M. Magalaner, 395(MFS):Winter88-738

Gutierrez, D. The Maze in the Mind and the World.
  R.I. Scott, 106:Summer88-264
Gutiérrez, G.D. - see under de Granda Gutiérrez, G.
Gutman, H.G. Power and Culture.* (I. Berlin, ed)
  639(VQR):Summer88-94
Gutman, H.G. & D.H. Bell, eds. The New England Working Class and the New Labor History.
  E.G. Nellis, 106:Summer88-195
Gutman, R. Architectural Practice.
  H. Muschamp, 62:Dec88-108
Gutman, R. Banana Diplomacy.*
  M. Falcoff, 617(TLS):12-18May89-524
Gutmann, A., ed. Democracy and the Welfare State.
  A.B.C., 185:Apr89-665
Gutmann, A. Democratic Education.*
  C.T. Asplund, 529(QQ):Summer88-432
  M. Rickard, 63:Sep88-438
  D. Steiner, 560:Fall89-204
  M.G. Yudof, 185:Jan89-439
Gutsche, G.J. Moral Apostasy in Russian Literature.*
  V. Belenkaya, 573(SSF):Spring88-166
Guttenplan, S. The Language of Logic.*
  A. Reix, 542:Jul-Sep88-381
Guttmann, A. Sports Spectators.
  S. Miller, 31(ASch):Summer88-468
Guttmann, A. A Whole New Ball Game.*
  J. Gindin, 385(MQR):Spring89-283
  639(VQR):Autumn88-136
Gutwirth, M. Un Merveilleux sans éclat.*
  M-F. Bruneau, 210(FrF):May88-247
  J-P. Collinet, 475:Vol15No28-353
  G.J. Mallinson, 208(FS):Oct88-469
Guy, J. Tudor England.
  P. Williams, 617(TLS):2-8Jun89-616
Guy, J.S. Oriental Trade Ceramics in South-East Asia, Ninth to Sixteenth Centuries.
  J. Ayers, 324:Jun89-447
  U. Roberts, 60:Mar-Apr88-130
Guy, R.K. The Emperor's Four Treasuries.
  J.A. Whitbeck, 293(JASt):Nov88-850
Guyaux, A. Poétique du fragment.*
  C. Jordens, 356(LR):Aug88-245
Guyaux, A. - see Rimbaud, A.
Guyer, P. Kant and the Claims of Knowledge.*
  R. Hanna, 543:Mar89-622
  F.P. Van De Pitte, 103:May89-184
de Guzman, R.P. & M.A. Reforma, eds. Government and Politics of the Philippines.
  M. Leifer, 617(TLS):28Apr-4May89-465
Gwin, M.C. Black and White Women of the Old South.*
  K. Kinnamon, 301(JEGP):Apr88-281
  H. Thomas, 295(JML):Fall87/Winter88-209
Gwynn, R.S. The Drive-In.
  N. German, 577(SHR):Winter88-98
Gwynne, H.A. The Rasp of War. (K. Wilson, ed)
  A.J.A. Morris, 617(TLS):7-13Jul89-742
Gyekye, K. An Essay on African Philosophical Thought.*
  D. Emmet, 483:Jul88-407

H.D. Nights.*
  L.M. Friebert, 50(ArQ):Summer88-108

H.D. Notes on Thought and Vision [and] The Wise Sappho.
  L. Mackinnon, 617(TLS):10-16Feb89-134
Ha, S-K., ed. Housing Policy and Practice in Asia.
  S. Tanphiphat, 293(JASt):Aug88-570
"Hans Haacke: Unfinished Business."
  W. Jeffett, 39:Jul88-69
de Haan, H. & I. Haagsma. Architects in Competition.*
  P. Davey, 46:Jun88-8
de Haan, T. The Child of Good Fortune.
  T. Shippey, 617(TLS):14-20Apr89-404
Haaparanta, L. & J. Hintikka, eds. Frege Synthesized.*
  E. Martin, 316:Mar88-318
Haar, J. Essays on Italian Poetry and Music in the Renaissance, 1350-1600.
  B.N.S. Gooch, 568(SCN):Winter88-80
Haar, M. Le Chant de la terre.*
  E. Escoubas, 192(EP):Jul-Sep88-431
  P. Trotignon, 542:Jul-Sep88-363
Haarman, L., P. Leech & J. Murray. Reading Skills for the Social Sciences.
  W. Schoener, 608:Dec89-686
Haarmann, H. Language in Ethnicity.
  J.M. Fayer, 399(MLJ):Spring88-72
Haarscher, G. Philosophie des droits de l'homme.
  R. Gervais, 103:Nov88-448
Haas, B. When California Was an Island.
  G.L. Morris, 455:Sep88-68
Haas, R. - see Salamun, T.
Haas, R. & C. Klein-Braley, eds. Literatur im Kontext.
  R. von Ledebur, 72:Band225Heft1-187
Haas, W. & G.B. Mathieu. Deutsch für alle. (3rd ed)
  R.A. Korb, 399(MLJ):Spring88-93
Haass, S. Gedichtanthologien der viktorianischen Zeit.
  G. Hönnighausen, 72:Band225Heft2-401
Haasse, H.S. In a Dark Wood Wandering. (rev) (A. Miller, ed)
  S. Paulos, 441:17Dec89-18
Habegger, A. Henry James and the "Woman Business."
  W.C. Booth, 441:24Sep89-54
Haberland, J. - see von Saar, F.
Haberley, D.T. Three Sad Races.
  A. Hennessy, 617(TLS):14-20Jul89-763
Haberman, D.C., ed. Bernard Shaw. (Vol 3)
  A. Silver, 365:Winter87-48
  S. Weintraub, 572:Vol8-147
Habermas, G.R. & A.G.N. Flew. Did Jesus Rise From the Dead?* (T.L. Miethe, ed)
  D.W. Viney, 389(MQ):Spring89-392
Habermas, J. Logique des sciences sociales et autres essais.
  P. Trotignon, 542:Jul-Sep88-363
Habermas, J. Die Neue Unübersichtlichkeit.*
  H-P. Krüger, 654(WB):3/1988-518
Habermas, J. The Philosophical Discourse of Modernity.* (German title: Der philosophische Diskurs der Moderne.)
  J.M. Bernstein, 59:Dec88-586
  A.M. Hjort, 154:Summer88-367
  H-P. Krüger, 654(WB):3/1988-518
  G. Zoeller, 271:Fall88-151
Habermas, J. The Theory of Communicative Action.* (Vols 1 & 2) (French title: Théorie de l'agir communicationnel. German title: [continued]

[continuing]
Theorie des kommunikativen Handelns.)
A. Reix, 542:Jan–Mar88–103
Habersetzer, K H. Politische Typologie und
dramatisches Exemplum.*
R.E. Schade, 221(GQ):Fall87–661
Habicht, C. Pausanias' Guide to Ancient
Greece.
D. Fehling, 123:Vol38No1–18
S.V. Tracy, 24:Summer88–278
Habicht, W., W–D. Lange & others, eds. Der
Literatur–Brockhaus.
H. Denman, 617(TLS):13–19Oct89–1136
von Habsburg, G. Fabergé.
B. Beaumont–Nesbitt, 324:Jun89–445
Hacke, C. Weltmacht wider Willen.
R. Morgan, 617(TLS):13–19Oct89–1115
Hacker, H–J. Zur Poetologie des mittelalter-
lichen Dramas in England.
M. Markus, 72:Band225Heft2–379
Hacker, P. Grundlagen indischer Dichtung
und indischen Denkens. (K. Rüping, ed)
H. Brinkhaus, 259(IIJ):Oct88–322
Hackett, C.A. – see Rimbaud, A.
Hackett, P. – see Warhol, A.
Hacking, I. Representing and Intervening.
D. Baird, 449:Jun88–299
Hacking, R.D. Such a Long Journey.
G. Irvine, 617(TLS):27Jan–2Feb89–82
Hackl, W. Kein Bollwerk der alten Garde –
keine Experimentierbude.
A. Reiter, 402(MLR):Oct89–1046
Hackworth, D.H. & J. Sherman. About Face.
B.E. Trainor, 441:30Apr89–7
Hadas, R. A Son from Sleep.
L. Upton, 152(UDQ):Fall88–119
Haddad, Y.Y. Contemporary Islam and the
Challenge of History.
S.I. Gellens, 318(JAOS):Jul–Sep87–526
Hadley, R.V. – see Berenson, B. & I.S. Gard-
ner, with M. Berenson
Hadot, I. Arts libéraux et philosophie dans la
pensée antique.*
R.L.S. Evans, 124:Sep–Oct88–71
Hadot, I. Simplicius.
A.H. Armstrong, 123:Vol38No2–428
Hadot, P. Exercices spirituels et philosophie
antique. (2nd ed)
A. Reix, 542:Apr–Jun88–242
Haertling, P. A Woman.
42(AR):Summer88–398
Haffner, S. Der Teufelspakt.
G.A. Craig, 453(NYRB):30Mar89–15
Hagan, C. Grand Ole Opry.
S. Liveten, 441:16Jul89–25
Hagan, D.V. Félicien David (1810–1876).
B. Friedland, 451:Spring88–282
Hagan, E.A. "High Nonsensical Words."
R.H., 305(JIL):Jan88–60
Hagedorn, J., with P. Macon. People and
Folks.
A. Campbell, 441:5Feb89–36
Hagège, C. Le Français et le siècles.*
J–C. Vuillemin, 207(FR):Feb89–570
Hagelin, O., comp. The Art of Writing and
Drawing.
N. Barker, 78(BC):Autumn88–427
Hagerfors, L. The Whales in Lake Tangan-
yika.
W. Ferguson, 441:30Jul89–16
Hagerman, E. The American Civil War and the
Origins of Modern Warfare.
D.H. Bain, 441:16Apr89–21

Hagland, J.R. Riksstyring og spraknorm.
S. Zempel, 563(SS):Spring88–321
Hagstrum, J.H. Eros and Vision.
D. Nokes, 617(TLS):11–17Aug89–880
Hagstrum, J.H. The Romantic Body.*
N. Brown, 591(SIR):Fall88–451
M. Eaves, 405(MP):Aug88–94
S. Simpkins, 128(CE):Nov88–812
Hahn, E. China to Me.
N. Tisdall, 364:Apr/May88–139
Hahn, H.G. & C. Behm 3d. The Eighteenth-
Century British Novel and Its Background.*
566:Autumn88–78
Hahn, J. & D. Lehmann – see Sochor, A.
Hahn, J.W. Soviet Grassroots.
O. Figes, 617(TLS):4–10Aug89–841
Hahn, L.E. & P.A. Schilpp, eds. The Philoso-
phy of W.V.O. Quine.
P. Hylton, 311(JP):Mar88–164
Hahn, M., ed. Der grosse Legendenkranz.
J.W. de Jong, 259(IIJ):Oct88–322
S. Lienhard, 318(JAOS):Jul–Sep87–510
Hahn, M. & K. Klaus. Das Mṛgajātaka (Harib-
haṭṭajātakamālā XL).
J.P. McDermott, 318(JAOS):Jul–Sep87–
511
Hahn, R. Kant's Newtonian Revolution in
Philosophy.
J.N. Catudal, 103:Jul89–267
Hahn, R.H. None of the Roads Were Paved.
E. Waterston, 102(CanL):Winter87–155
Hahn, S. & J. Prude, eds. The Countryside in
the Age of Capitalist Transformation.
R.D. Brown, 432(NEQ):Jun88–260
Haid, H. & J. Huber. Nachruf.
K. Kehr, 685(ZDL):2/1987–274
Haider, H. & M. Prinzhorn, eds. Verb Second
Phenomena in Germanic Languages.*
T.F. Shannon, 350:Sep89–663
Haig, B. Paul Kane Artist.
M. Waddington, 102(CanL):Winter87–205
Haig, S. Flaubert and the Gift of Speech.
L.K. Martin, 210(FrF):May88–251
A.W. Raitt, 402(MLR):Oct89–992
A. Tooke, 208(FS):Jan88–97
J.R. Williams, 207(FR):Feb89–525
Haig, S. The "Madame Bovary" Blues.
D. Aynesworth, 446(NCFS):Spring–Sum-
mer89–411
R.R. Brock, 594:Fall88–347
C.M. Crow, 208(FS):Oct88–485
M. Donaldson–Evans, 207(FR):May89–
1075
Haigh, C., ed. The English Reformation Re-
visited.*
A.J. Slavin, 551(RenQ):Winter88–727
Haigh, R.H., D.S. Morris & A.R. Peters. The
Years of Triumph?
F.L. Carsten, 575(SEER):Jan88–163
Hail, B.A. Patterns of Life, Patterns of Art.
A. Trevelyan, 2(AfrA):Feb88–91
Hailperin, T. Boole's Logic and Probability.
(2nd ed)
N.T. Gridgeman, 316:Dec88–1253
Haimo, E. & P. Johnson, eds. Stravinsky
Retrospectives.*
E. Antokoletz, 317:Fall88–547
Haine, M. Les Facteurs d'instruments de
musique à Paris ou 19e siècle.*
T. Zeldin, 410(M&L):Apr88–279
Haines, J. The Stars, the Snow, the Fire.
R.M. Pyle, 441:10Dec89–14
442(NY):11Sep89–124

Haines, J. Stories We Listened To.
  R. Hedin, 649(WAL):May88-74
Haines, R.M. Archbishop John Stratford.
  J. Dahmus, 589:Jan88-158
Hainsworth, P. Petrarch the Poet.
  R. Jacoff, 617(TLS):18-24Aug89-900
Hajime, T. - see under Tanabe Hajime
Hak, T., J. Haafkens & G. Nuhof, eds. Working
  Papers on Discourse and Conversational
  Analysis.
  D.H., 355(LSoc):Jun88-311
Haksar, N. Demystification of Law for Women.
  G. Minault, 293(JASt):Nov88-814
Haksar, V. Civil Disobedience, Threats and
  Offers.
  N.E.S., 185:Oct88-198
Hakuta, K. Mirror of Language.
  Y.N. Padron, 399(MLJ):Summer88-222
Halac, R. Teatro I.
  J.A. Dubatti, 352(LATR):Spring89-136
Halász, L., ed. Literary Discourse.
  G. Prince, 599:Spring89-150
Halbach, U. Der russische Fürstenhof vor
  dem 16. Jahrhundert.
  L. Hughes, 575(SEER):Jan88-136
  E. Myles, 550(RusR):Jan88-99
Halbach, U., H. Hecker & A. Kappeler, eds.
  Geschichte Altrusslands in der Begriffswelt
  ihrer Quellen.
  L. Hughes, 575(SEER):Apr88-287
Halberstam, D. Summer of '49.
  J. Kaplan, 441:7May89-9
  W. Sheed, 453(NYRB):12Oct89-49
Haldas, G. La Légende des repas.
  A.J.M. Prévos, 207(FR):Dec88-350
Haldeman, J. Buying Time.
  G. Jonas, 441:2Jul89-15
Hale, B. Abstract Objects.
  J.R. Brown, 154:Winter88-729
  D. Freedman, 518:Oct88-214
Hale, F., ed. Danes in North America.*
  P. Houe, 562(Scan):May88-45
Hale, J.A. The Broken Window.
  A. Moorjani, 207(FR):Mar89-694
  L. Papin, 210(FrF):Jan88-124
Hale, J.R. War and Society in Renaissance
  Europe, 1450-1620.
  C.C. Bayley, 589:Apr88-406
Haley, J.H. Charles N. Hunter and Race Rela-
  tions in North Carolina.
  R.P. Fuke, 106:Summer88-271
Haley, K.H.D. The British and the Dutch.
  J. Israel, 617(TLS):3-9Feb89-116
Halfmann, H. Itinera principum.
  W. Williams, 123:Vol38No2-333
  A. Winterling, 229:Band60Heft2-131
Halfmann, U. - see O'Neill, E.
Haliczer, S., ed & trans. Inquisition & Society
  in Early Modern Europe.
  J.K. Cameron, 161(DUJ):Dec87-136
Hall, A.R. & M.B. - see Oldenburg, H.
Hall, B. The Dreamers.
  L. Forestier, 441:23Apr89-23
Hall, D. The Happy Man.*
  T. Haddin, 577(SHR):Spring88-202
  R. Pybus, 565:Summer88-72
  V. Sherry, 569(SR):Winter88-viii
Hall, D.D. Worlds of Wonder, Days of Judg-
  ment.
  G.S. Wood, 453(NYRB):9Nov89-26
Hall, D.J. Robert Frost.*
  P.R.J., 295(JML):Fall87/Winter88-320

Hall, D.K. In Prison.
  R. Lippincott, 441:26Mar89-17
Hall, D.L. & R.T. Ames. Thinking Through
  Confucius.
  C. Hansen, 293(JASt):Nov88-852
Hall, H.W., ed. Science Fiction and Fantasy
  Reference Index, 1878-1985.
  R.M.P., 561(SFS):Nov88-383
Hall, J.B. Lope de Vega: "Fuenteovejuna."*
  S.N. McCrary, 238:Mar88-79
Hall, J.B. Prolegomena to Claudian.
  R.P.H. Green, 123:Vol38No1-32
Hall, J.D. & others. Like a Family.*
  L.M. Fine, 115:Summer88-334
  639(VQR):Summer88-89
Hall, J.W. Tropical Freeze.
  S. Paretsky, 441:15Oct89-38
Hall, J.W. Under Cover of Daylight.
  S.C., 219(GaR):Summer88-441
Hall, M.G. The Last American Puritan.*
  R.S. Bosco, 165(EAL):Vol24No3-257
Hall, P. London 2001.
  D. Harvey, 617(TLS):7-13Apr89-356
Hall, R. Captivity Captive.*
  J. Mellors, 364:Apr/May88-133
Hall, R. - see Dransfield, M.
Hall, R.A., Jr., ed. Leonard Bloomfield.*
  W. Cowan, 320(CJL):Jun88-176
  G.J. Metcalf, 215(GL):Vol28No4-295
Hall, R.A., Jr. Proto-Romance Morphology.
  C. Schmitt, 553(RLiR):Jan-Jun88-254
Hall, S. & J. Ramsey, eds. Approaches to
  Teaching Wordsworth's Poetry.
  S. Simpkins, 128(CE):Nov88-812
  J. Sturrock, 677(YES):Vol19-337
Hall, T. Planung europäischer Hauptstädte.
  J.S. Ackerman, 576:Mar88-90
Hallager, E. The Master Impression.
  N. Marinatos, 303(JoHS):Vol108-258
Hallahan, W.H. Tripletrap.
  N. Callendar, 441:16Jul89-23
Hallam, H.E., ed. The Agrarian History of
  England and Wales. (Vol 2)
  R.B. Dobson, 617(TLS):23-29Jun89-684
Hallberg, G., S. Isaksen & B. Pamp, eds.
  Nionde nordiska namnforskarkongressen.
  L.R.N. Ashley, 424:Mar-Jun88-115
von Hallberg, R. American Poetry and Culture
  1945-1980.*
  N. Corcoran, 402(MLR):Jan89-149
von Hallberg, R., ed. Politics and Poetic
  Value.
  J.N. Hathcock, 568(SCN):Fall88-43
Halldórsson, B. & others, eds. Islendinga
  sögur og þaettir. (Vol 2)
  M. Cormack, 563(SS):Spring88-311
Halldórsson, B. & others, eds. Sígildar sögur.
  (Vol 1)
  M. Cormack, 563(SS):Spring88-312
de la Halle, A. - see under Adam de la Halle
Haller, H.W. The Hidden Italy.*
  J. Ahern, 472:Vol15No2-91
Haller, R. Fragen zu Wittgenstein und Auf-
  sätze zur österreichischen Philosophie.*
  A. Janik, 319:Apr89-321
Haller, R. Non-existence and Predication.
  G. Stahl, 542:Jul-Sep88-382
Hallett, G.L. Language and Truth.
  E.L. Holman, 543:Dec88-383
Hallett, M. Cantorian Set Theory and Limita-
  tion of Size.*
  R. Bunn, 486:Sep88-461
  J.W. Dauben, 84:Dec88-541

Hamilton, I. In Search of J.D. Salinger.*
    J. Lewis, 364:Dec88/Jan89-123
    S. Pinsker, 219(GaR):Fall88-609
Hamilton, I. - see "Soho Square II"
Hamilton, J. The Book of Ruth.
    K. Burkett, 441:12Mar89-22
Hamilton, J. The Frogs Are Still Singing.
    J. Parini, 617(TLS):24-30Nov89-1313
Hamilton, J.M. Edgar Snow.
    J. Mirsky, 453(NYRB):16Feb89-15
    S. Topping, 441:8Jan89-13
Hamilton, J.R. & J.C. Batchelor. Thunder in
the Dust.
    L. Clayton, 649(WAL):Nov88-282
Hamilton, P. Wordsworth.
    W.J.B. Owen, 541(RES):Feb88-123
Hamilton, R. & M. Barrett, eds. The Politics
of Diversity.
    C. Strange, 529(QQ):Autumn88-744
Hamilton, W. - see Ammianus
Hamilton-Paterson, J. Gerontius.
    P. Reading, 617(TLS):24-30Mar89-300
Hamlin, C. & F. Ryder - see von Goethe, J.W.
Hamlyn, D.W. A History of Western Philos-
ophy.
    J. Cottingham, 479(PhQ):Jul88-376
Hamm, J-J. Le Texte stendhalien.*
    C. Bertrand-Jennings, 627(UTQ):Fall88-
    130
    A. Jefferson, 208(FS):Oct88-479
Hammel, E. Khe Sanh.
    P. Dye, 441:23Jul89-19
Hammer, A. Hammer.
    D.W. Treadgold, 396(ModA):Winter88-66
Hammerschmidt, V.W. Anspruch und Ausdruck
in der Architektur des späten Historismus
in Deutschland (1860-1914).
    D. Dolgner, 43:Band18Heft2-199
Hammerstein, R. Macht und Klang.
    B.S. Hall, 589:Oct88-939
    E.V. Williams, 317:Spring88-166
Hammet, M. - see Reade, C.
Hammick, G. People for Lunch.
    P. Lewis, 565:Spring88-35
Hammond, B. & P. O'Connor. Josephine Baker.
    A. Lively, 617(TLS):13-19Jan89-30
Hammond, F. Girolamo Frescobaldi.
    J. Harper, 410(M&L):Apr88-250
Hammond, G. A Brace of Skeet.
    T.J. Binyon, 617(TLS):29Dec89/4Jan90-
    1448
Hammond, J.H. Secret and Sacred. (C. Bleser,
ed)
    R. Brown, 441:29Jan89-22
    J.M. McPherson, 453(NYRB):19Jan89-16
    P. Morgan, 617(TLS):11-17Aug89-866
Hammond, N. Twentieth Century Wildlife
Artists.
    C. Ashwin, 592:Vol201No1019-67
Hammond, N.G.L. A History of Greece to 322
B.C. (3rd ed)
    P. Carlier, 555:Vol61fasc1-108
Hammond, P. John Oldham and the Renewal of
Classical Culture.*
    M. Stocker, 83:Spring88-91
Hammond, P. - see Pope, A.
Hammond, W.M. Public Affairs.
    N. Lemann, 441:2Jul89-5
Hamon, H. & P. Rotman. Génération.
    A.P. Colombat, 207(FR):Mar89-714
Hamon, P. Texte et idéologie.
    P. Starr, 400(MLN):Sep88-957

Hamp-Lyons, L. & B. Heasley. Study Writing.
    A. Bollati, 399(MLJ):Autumn88-349
Hampl, P. Spillville.
    S. Birkerts, 472:Vol15No1-163
    639(VQR):Winter88-30
Hampsch, G.H. Preventing Nuclear Genocide.
    C. Fowler, 103:Jun89-229
Hampson, N. Prelude to Terror.
    W. Doyle, 617(TLS):20-26Jan89-65
Hampton, J. Hobbes and the Social Contract
Tradition.*
    J.T. Edelman, 521:Jul88-257
    P. Russell, 319:Oct89-620
Hampton, L., with J. Haskins. Hamp.
    M. Miles, 441:3Dec89-24
Hamre, J.S. Georg Sverdrup.
    T. Hall, 563(SS):Winter88-103
Hamrick, W.S. An Existential Phenomenology
of Law.
    B.P. Dauenhauer, 323:May88-201
Hamrick, W.S., ed. Phenomenology in Practice
and Theory.*
    M.J. Burke, 438:Spring88-241
Han, S-B., ed. Asian Peoples and Their Cul-
tures.
    F. Moos, 293(JASt):Aug88-571
Han, S-J., ed. After One Hundred Years.
    B.C. Koh, 293(JASt):Feb88-158
Han Suyin, M. Langford & G. Mason. Han
Suyin's China.
    J. Sweetman, 463:Spring88-55
Hanák, P. Ungarn in der Donaumonarchie,
Probleme der bürgerlichen Umgestaltung
eines Vielvölkerstaates.
    L. Péter, 575(SEER):Apr88-296
Hanawalt, B.A. The Ties that Bound.*
    R.A. Houlbrooke, 382(MAE):1988/2-308
Hancher, M. The Tenniel Illustrations to the
"Alice" Books.*
    M.N. Cohen, 635(VPR):Spring88-35
Hancock, G. Lords of Poverty.
    T. Clarke, 441:12Nov89-12
Hand, J.O. & M. Wolff. Early Netherlandish
Painting: National Gallery of Art, Washing-
ton.
    M. Russell, 39:Sep88-219
Handa, O.C. Buddhist Monasteries in Himach-
al Pradesh.
    J.H. Crook, 617(TLS):3-9Feb89-119
Handel, M.I., ed. Leaders and Intelligence.
    N. Clive, 617(TLS):11-17Aug89-870
Handelman, S.A. The Slayers of Moses.
    S.P., 295(JML):Fall87/Winter88-211
Handelsman, M. Incursiones en el mundo lit-
erario del Ecuador.
    J. Hancock, 238:Dec88-835
Handjaras, L. & A. Marinotti - see Vasa, A.
Handke, P. The Afternoon of a Writer.
    L. Simon, 441:3Sep89-17
    J. Updike, 442(NY):25Dec89-104
Handke, P. Die Wiederholung.
    K. Pankow, 601(SuF):Jul-Aug88-876
Handke, P. Wunschloses Unglück. (B.
Becker-Cantarino, ed)
    P.F. Dvorak, 399(MLJ):Summer88-241
Handley, G. - see Eliot, G.
Handlin, O. & L. Liberty in Expansion 1760-
1850.
    R. Caplan, 441:1Oct89-27
Handurukande, R., ed & trans. Five Buddhist
Legends in the Campū Style.
    B.C. Hall, 318(JAOS):Jul-Sep87-512

Handwerk, G.J. Irony and Ethics in Narrative.*
    M. Bullock, 131(CL):Summer88-279
    J. Clayton, 591(SIR)·Fall88-446
    R.J. Dingley, 447(N&Q):Jun88-275
    T. Docherty, 541(RES):May88-336
Handy, C. The Age of Unreason.
    D. Howell, 324:Jul89-518
Hane, M., ed & trans. Reflections on the Way to the Gallows.
    E. Hanson, 441:1Jan89-15
Hanen, M. & K. Nielsen, eds. Science, Morality and Feminist Theory.
    J. Genova, 103:Feb89-45
    L.T., 185:Apr89-669
Hanfling, O., ed. Life and Meaning.
    E. Telfer, 518:Oct88-235
Hanham, A. The Celys and Their World.*
    M. Mate, 589:Apr88-407
Hankey, J., ed. Plays in Performance: "Othello."
    C.C. Rutter, 611(TN):Vol42No3-140
Hanna, R. 3d, comp. The Index of Middle English Prose, Handlist I.
    V. Gillespie, 382(MAE):1988/1-109
Hanna, W.L. The Life and Times of James Willard Schultz (Apikuni).*
    J.A. Stout, Jr., 77:Fall88-348
Hannah, B. Boomerang.
    T.R. Edwards, 453(NYRB):17Aug89-52
    J. Kennedy, 441:14May89-19
Hannestad, N. Roman Art and Imperial Policy.
    J. Linderski, 124:Nov-Dec88-140
    R.M. Schneider, 229:Band60Heft5-438
Hanrieder, W.F. Germany, America, Europe.
    D. Gress, 441:17Sep89-13
Hans, L-M. Karthago und Sizilien.
    S.P. Ellis, 123:Vol38No1-89
    R.J.A. Talbert, 303(JoHS):Vol108-263
Hanscombe, G. & V.L. Smyers. Writing for Their Lives.*
    R.M. Brownstein, 441:12Mar89-25
Hanse, J. Nouveau Dictionnaire des difficultés du français moderne. (2nd ed)
    F. Abel, 547(RF):Band100Heft4-364
    J.E. Joseph, 399(MLJ):Summer88-233
    A. Rodríguez Somolinos, 548:Jul-Dec88-450
Hansell, P. & J. Doves and Dovecotes.
    M. Girouard, 617(TLS):24-30Mar89-317
Hansen, B.B. La peur, le rire et la sagesse.*
    F.R. Atance, 539:Summer88-223
    M-C. Gomez-Geraud, 535(RHL):Jan-Feb88-123
Hansen, C. Language and Logic in Ancient China.*
    P.J. Ivanhoe, 116:Jul87-115
Hansen, E.C. Ludovic Halévy.
    F.W.J. Hemmings, 208(FS):Oct88-483
Hansen, J. Landsbyprosaen i den russiske sovjetliteratur i 1960rne og 1970rne.
    E. Egeberg, 172(Edda):1988/4-376
Hansen, M.H. The Athenian Assembly in the Age of Demosthenes.
    P.J. Rhodes, 123:Vol38No2-310
Hansen, M.H. Demography and Democracy.*
    L. de Blois & W. van Loon, 394:Vol41 fasc3/4-461
Hansen, M.H. & others, eds. Brev fra Amerika.
    P. Houe, 562(Scan):May88-45

Hansen, P.A. Carmina Epigraphica Graeca saeculorum VIII-V a. Chr. n.
    O. Masson, 555:Vol61fasc1-114
Hansen, P.A. A List of Greek Verse Inscriptions c. 400-300 B.C.
    C. Dobias-Lalou, 555:Vol61fasc2-309
Hansen, R. Nebraska.
    M. La Chapelle, 441:19Feb89-31
Hansen, S.G. & others. Bellman - en boheme i en brydningstid.
    A. Swanson, 563(SS):Summer88-401
Hansen, U. Conrad Ferdinand Meyer: "Angela Borgia."*
    A.T. Alt, 221(GQ):Winter88-143
    E.M.V. Plater, 564:Sep88-282
    G.W. Reinhardt, 133:Band21Heft2/3-237
Hanslick, E. Eduard Hanslick on the Musically Beautiful.* (G. Payzant, ed & trans)
    G. Epperson, 290(JAAC):Fall87-85
    J. Zwicky, 154:Spring88-167
Hanson, C. - see Mansfield, K.
Hanson, K. The Self Imagined.
    D. Carr, 484(PPR):Mar89-536
    E. Frazer, 393(Mind):Jan88-134
Hanson, R.L. The Democratic Imagination in America.
    F. Cunningham, 529(QQ):Spring88-209
Hanson, W. - see Böll, H.
Hanson, W.S. Agricola and the Conquest of the North.
    C. Martin, 123:Vol38No2-330
Häntzschel, G., ed. Bildung und Kultur bürgerlicher Frauen 1850-1918.
    K. Fliedl, 224(GRM):Band38Heft1/2-200
Hao, Y-P. The Commercial Revolution in Nineteenth-Century China.
    J.Y. Wong, 244(HJAS):Dec88-521
Happé, P., ed. Medieval English Drama.*
    G.H.V. Bunt, 179(ES):Jun88-273
Happé, P. - see Bale, J.
Haque, A. Trends in Pakistan's External Policy, 1947-1971, with Particular Reference to People's China.
    A. Jalal, 293(JASt):Aug88-680
Harap, L. Dramatic Encounters.
    J. Jacoby, 459:Winter88-141
Harap, L. In the Mainstream.
    L. Field, 395(MFS):Summer88-260
Harari, J.V. Scenarios of the Imaginary.
    T.M. Kavanagh, 400(MLN):Dec88-1166
    L. Kerslake, 627(UTQ):Spring89-413
    R.C. Rosbottom, 210(FrF):Sep88-371
Haraszti, M. The Velvet Prison.*
    S. Baranczak, 560:Spring-Summer88-29
Harbron, J.D. Trafalgar and the Spanish Navy.
    P. Whitlock, 324:Oct89-753
Harcourt, G. - see Tsushima, Y.
Hardacre, H. Kurozumikyō and the New Religions of Japan.
    J.C. Dobbins, 293(JASt):Feb88-141
Harden, E.F. Thackeray's "English Humourists" and "Four Georges."*
    I.B. Nadel, 637(VS):Winter89-248
Harden, T. Untersuchungen zur R-Realisation im Ruhrgebiet.
    H.H. Menge, 685(ZDL):1/1988-112
Harder, A. - see Euripides
Hardie, A. Statius and the Silvae.
    H-J. van Dam, 229:Band60Heft8-704
Hardie, P.R. Virgil's "Aeneid."*
    K.W. Gransden, 123:Vol38No1-24
    J. Griffin, 313:Vol78-229

Hardin, C.L. Color for Philosophers.
  D.L. Sepper, 543:Jun89-834
Hardin, J. Johann Beer.*
  L. Tatlock, 221(GQ):Winter87-113
Hardin, J. Christian Gryphius Bibliographie.
  J. Alexander, 406:Spring88-125
  G.R. Hoyt, 221(GQ):Spring87-280
Hardin, J.N. & D. Eggers - see Gryphius, C.
Harding, A.J. Coleridge and the Inspired
  Word.*
  E.S. Shaffer, 627(UTQ):Fall87-117
  J. Sturrock, 402(MLR):Oct89-934
Harding, A.J. Public Duties and Public Law.
  J. Griffith, 617(TLS):10-16Nov89-1236
Harding, C. & others. Imprisonment in En-
  gland and Wales.
  T.H. Ford, 161(DUJ):Dec87-134
Harding, E. & P. Riley. The Bilingual Family.*
  R. Muñoz, 238:Mar88-100
Harding, G. Opiate Addiction, Morality and
  Medicine.
  H.F., 185:Jan89-466
Harding, J. Gerald du Maurier.
  P. O'Connor, 617(TLS):20-26Oct89-1151
Harding, P. Translated Documents of Greece
  and Rome. (Vol 2)
  A.J.L. van Hooff, 394:Vol41fasc3/4-452
Harding, S. The Science Question in Femin-
  ism.*
  K. Shrader-Frechette, 606:Sep88-441
Hardison, O.B., Jr. Disappearing Through the
  Skylight.
  M. Bradbury, 441:31Dec89-3
Hardman, M. Ruskin and Bradford.*
  T. Steele, 366:Spring88-128
Hardy, B. Collected Essays. (Vol 1)
  M. Baron, 175:Autumn88-265
Hardy, E. Emma Hardy's Diaries.* (R.H. Tay-
  lor, ed)
  D. Taylor, 569(SR):Spring88-250
Hardy, J. Jane Austen's Heroines.*
  W.A. Craik, 447(N&Q):Dec88-542
Hardy, J.E. The Fiction of Walker Percy.
  J.N. Gretlund, 627(UTQ):Spring89-423
  L.A. Lawson, 578:Spring89-113
  J.R. Millichap, 395(MFS):Winter88-638
  639(VQR):Spring88-52
Hardy, R.E. & J.G. Cull. Hemingway.
  C.D. Cheney, 649(WAL):Nov88-269
  234:Spring89-51
Hardy, T. The Collected Letters of Thomas
  Hardy.* (Vol 5) (R.L. Purdy & M. Millgate,
  eds)
  D. Taylor, 569(SR):Spring88-250
Hardy, T. The Collected Letters of Thomas
  Hardy. (Vol 6) (R.L. Purdy & M. Millgate,
  eds)
  J. Halperin, 395(MFS):Winter88-672
  D. Taylor, 569(SR):Spring88-250
  G.B. Tennyson, 445(NCF):Sep88-275
  M. Williams, 447(N&Q):Jun88-259
  K. Wilson, 177(ELT):Vol31No4-469
Hardy, T. The Complete Poetical Works of
  Thomas Hardy.* (Vols 2 & 3) (S. Hynes, ed)
  D. Taylor, 569(SR):Spring88-250
Hardy, T. Far from the Madding Crowd.*
  (R.C. Schweik, ed)
  S. Gatrell, 177(ELT):Vol31No2-174
  K.M. Hewitt, 447(N&Q):Jun88-258
Hardy, T. Jude the Obscure. (P. Ingham, ed)
  A Pair of Blue Eyes. (A. Manford, ed)
    [continued]

[continuing]
  Under the Greenwood Tree. (S. Gatrell, ed)
  K. Brady, 301(JEGP):Apr88-271
  S. Gatrell, 177(ELT):Vol31No2-174
Hardy, T. The Life and Work of Thomas Hardy
  by Thomas Hardy.* (M. Millgate, ed)
  617(TLS):29Sep-5Oct89-1072
Hardy, T. The Literary Notebooks of Thomas
  Hardy.* (Vols 1 & 2) (L.A. Björk, ed)
  D. Taylor, 569(SR):Spring88-250
  R.H. Taylor, 301(JEGP):Apr88-267
Hardy, T. The Mayor of Casterbridge.* (D.
  Kramer, ed)
  K.M. Hewitt, 447(N&Q):Jun88-258
Hardy, T. Tess of the d'Urbervilles.* The
  Return of the Native.* (S. Gatrell, ed of
  both)
  A.L. Manford, 301(JEGP):Apr88-275
Hardy, T. The Well-Beloved.* (T. Hethering-
  ton, ed) The Woodlanders. (D. Kramer, ed)
  S. Gatrell, 177(ELT):Vol31No2-174
"Thomas Hardy Annual." (No. 5) (N. Page, ed)
  T. Pettersson, 179(ES):Oct88-459
  L. Siemens, 177(ELT):Vol31No1-87
  A. Sisson, 637(VS):Winter89-242
Hareven, S. The Miracle Hater.*
  A. Kaufman, 287:Sep/Oct88-23
Harf-Lancner, L., comp. Métamorphose et
  bestiaire fantastique au moyen âge.*
  K. Varty, 382(MAE):1988/1-84
Hargrave, S. London London.
  C. Hawtree, 617(TLS):23-29Jun89-695
Hargreaves, J.D. Decolonization in Africa.
  W.R. Louis, 617(TLS):10-16Feb89-146
Harington, D. The Cockroaches of Stay More.
  H. Middleton, 441:23Apr89-17
Harker, M.F. Henry Peach Robinson.
  S. Stevenson, 90:Aug88-640
Harland, C.R. Mark Rutherford.
  J. Lucas, 637(VS):Spring89-424
Harland, R. Superstructuralism.
  P. Caws, 103:Jun89-231
  S. Giles, 89(BJA):Spring88-195
  P. Kitson, 447(N&Q):Sep88-413
  T. Pinkney, 366:Spring88-110
Härle, G. Die Gestalt des Schönen.
  W.G. Cunliffe, 564:Sep88-286
Harlow, B. Resistance Literature.
  B. Flanagan, 141:Spring88-265
  J. Walker, 529(QQ):Winter88-923
Harman, C. Sylvia Townsend Warner.
  P.N. Furbank, 617(TLS):28Jul-3Aug89-
  815
Harman, G. Change in View.*
  H. Margolis, 185:Jul89-966
  H. Price, 518:Jan88-38
Harman, L.D. The Modern Stranger.
  N.C. Dorian, 350:Dec89-889
Harman, M., ed. Robert Walser Rediscovered.*
  R.B. Bottigheimer, 221(GQ):Spring87-306
Harmer, M. The Forgotten Hospital.
  J.E.O. Screen, 575(SEER):Apr88-332
Harms, W. & C. Kemp, eds. Deutsche Illus-
  trierte Flugblätter des 16. und 17. Jahr-
  hunderts. (Vol 4)
  W.A. Coupe, 402(MLR):Oct89-1022
Harms, W. & M. Schilling, with others, eds.
  Die Sammlung der Herzog August Bibliothek
  in Wolfenbüttel.* (Vol 1, Pt 1)
  J.R. Paas, 221(GQ):Winter87-109
Harness, C.L. Krono.
  G. Jonas, 441:26Feb89-32

Harnisch, F. Die Erforschung der nordbair-
ischen Mundart von den Anfängen bis 1980.
  P. Wiesinger, 685(ZDL):2/1988-217
Harnoncourt, N. The Musical Dialogue.
  J. Keates, 617(TLS):4-10Aug89-854
de Haro, P.A. - see under Aullón de Haro, P.
Harp, R.L. - see Johnson, S.
Harper, G.M. The Making of Yeats's "A
Vision."* W.B. Yeats and W.T. Horton.
  W.K. Chapman, 111:Spring89-11
Harper, M. Emigration from North-East Scot-
land.
  G. Shepperson, 617(TLS):24Feb-2Mar89-
  186
Harpham, G.G. The Ascetic Imperative in
Culture and Criticism.*
  639(VQR):Summer88-80
Harrán, D. Word-Tone Relations in Musical
Thought from Antiquity to the Seventeenth
Century.
  J. Haar, 551(RenQ):Summer88-316
  M.R. Maniates, 308:Fall88-357
Harran, M.J., ed. Luther and Learning.
  D.C. Steinmetz, 551(RenQ):Spring88-123
Harré, R., ed. The Physical Sciences Since
Antiquity.
  M.A. Sutton, 161(DUJ):Dec87-133
Harré, R. Varieties of Realism.*
  J.E. Malpas, 63:Jun88-253
Harrell, J.G. - see Ingarden, R.
Harries, M. & S. A Pilgrim Soul.
  R. Saxton, 617(TLS):1-7Dec89-1331
Harrington, K. Changing Ideas on Architec-
ture in the "Encyclopédie," 1750-1776.
  J. Carré, 530:Oct88-170
Harrington, M. The Long-Distance Runner.*
  M. Kazin, 453(NYRB):16Mar89-29
Harrington, M. Socialism Past and Future.
  P. Berman, 441:16Jul89-15
  J. Lively, 617(TLS):3-9Nov89-1199
Harris, A., ed. A World Unsuspected.
  P.C. Hoy 2d, 569(SR):Fall88-688
Harris, C. Travelling to Find a Remedy.
  529(QQ):Summer88-506
Harris, D.A. Tennyson and Personification.*
  D. Birch, 541(RES):Feb88-135
  C.W. Hassett, 85(SBHC):Vol15-81
  J. Kolb, 481(PQ):Fall88-532
Harris, E.E. Formal, Transcendental and Dia-
lectical Thinking.
  L. Byrne, 543:Mar89-624
Harris, E.T. Henry Purcell's "Dido and
Aeneas."*
  M. Laurie, 410(M&L):Oct88-511
  K.T. Rohrer, 465:Winter88/89-89
Harris, H. Angel Cake.
  J. Mellors, 364:Nov87-110
Harris, J. Phonological Variation and Change.
  J. Cheshire, 361:Apr88-346
  C. Feagin, 35(AS):Spring88-76
  M. Görlach, 260(IF):Band93-354
Harris, J. Samuel Richardson.*
  S.K. Marks, 594:Winter88-432
  H.D. Weinbrot, 166:Oct88-69
Harris, J. The Value of Life.
  R.E. Goodin, 291:Vol5No1-123
Harris, J. & G. Higgott. Inigo Jones.
  K. Downes, 617(TLS):7-13Jul89-755
Harris, J.H. The Short Fiction of D.H. Law-
rence.*
  H. Laird, 477(PLL):Winter88-103

Harris, L.L. & C.D. Abbey, eds. Nineteenth-
Century Literature Criticism. (Vol 2)
  S.M. Chase, 635(VPR):Spring88-39
Harris, L.L. & C.D. Abbey, eds. Nineteenth-
Century Literature Criticism. (Vol 12)
  L. Austin, 365:Winter87-52
  W.E. Smith, 470:Vol26-203
Harris, M. Do It Again.
  C. Hawtree, 617(TLS):27Oct-2Nov89-
  1180
Harris, M. & A. Lee, eds. The Press in English
Society from the Seventeenth to Nineteenth
Centuries.*
  R.A. Colby, 635(VPR):Summer88-85
  H.L. Snyder, 354:Jun88-170
Harris, M.E. The Arts at Black Mountain Col-
lege.*
  E. Hahn, 106:Fall88-381
  J.R. Mellow, 139:Feb/Mar88-14
  42(AR):Winter88-122
Harris, M.J. The Zanucks of Hollywood.
  D. Jacobs, 441:23Jul89-11
Harris, M.R. The Occitan Translations of
John XII and XIII-XVII from a Fourteenth-
Century Franciscan Codex (Assisi, Chiesa
Nuova Ms. 9).*
  T.T. Field, 589:Jan88-161
Harris, N. Connecting Times.
  E. Margolies, 27(AL):Dec88-686
Harris, R. The Language Machine.
  S. Levin, 215(GL):Vol28No3-220
Harris, R. The Language Myth.
  P.H. Salus, 567:Vol70No1/2-169
Harris, R. Language, Saussure and Wittgen-
stein.
  P. Lamarque, 617(TLS):24Feb-2Mar89-
  202
Harris, R., ed. Linguistic Thought in England,
1914-1945.
  P. Lamarque, 617(TLS):24Feb-2Mar89-
  202
Harris, R. Murders and Madness.
  E. Weber, 617(TLS):8-14Dec89-1367
Harris, R. Reading Saussure.
  A. Carstairs, 478(P&L):Oct88-314
Harris, R.C., ed. Historical Atlas of Canada.
(Vol 1)
  B.B. Petchenik, 529(QQ):Autumn88-720
Harris, R.S. English Studies at Toronto.
  L. Groening, 150(DR):Winter87/88-511
  R.D. McMaster, 178:Sep88-247
Harris, T. Black Women in the Fiction of
James Baldwin.
  A. Barthelemy, 295(JML):Fall87/
  Winter88-291
Harris, T. & T.M. Davis, eds. Afro-American
Poets since 1955.
  A. Rampersad, 534(RALS):Vol16No1&2-
  244
Harris, W.V. Interpretive Acts.
  P. Lamarque, 617(TLS):24Feb-2Mar89-
  202
Harrison, A.H. Christina Rossetti in Context.
  A. & C. Belsey, 637(VS):Summer89-591
  A. St. George, 617(TLS):21-27Jul89-807
  639(VQR):Autumn88-118
Harrison, A.H. Swinburne's Medievalism.
  M.K. Louis, 637(VS):Spring89-447
Harrison, B.G. Italian Days.
  C. Kummer, 61:Aug89-89
  A. Lee, 441:10Sep89-15
  442(NY):2Oct89-120

Harrison, C. Somebody's Baby.
  E. Feldman, 441:9Jul89-25
Harrison, D.D. Black Pearls.*
  D.E. McGinty, 91:Fall88-250
Harrison, E. Darkness at Night.*
  J.D. Barrow, 617(TLS):29Sep-5Oct89-
    1072
Harrison, J. Dalva.*
  J. Clute, 617(TLS):24-30Mar89-299
  S. McCartney, 376:Jun88-185
Harrison, J. A Philosopher's Nightmare.
  T. Metzinger, 167:Jul88-143
Harrison, J. The Singing Underneath.*
  M. Jarman, 249(HudR):Winter89-735
Harrison, N.R. Jean Rhys and the Novel as
  Women's Text.
  S. Roe, 617(TLS):2-8Jun89-608
Harrison, P. Storming Intrepid.
  N. Callendar, 441:23Apr89-33
Harrison, R. Aviation Lore in Faulkner.
  R.D. Parker, 402(MLR):Jan89-148
Harrison, R. Bentham.
  D. Lyons, 311(JP):Mar88-154
Harrison, R. Fathers Never Leave You.
  C. Levenson, 529(QQ):Winter88-943
Harrison, R.J. Spain at the Dawn of History.
  D. Ridgway, 617(TLS):3-9Mar89-228
Harrison, T. Selected Poems.*
  S. Birkerts, 473(PR):Vol55No3-484
Harrison, V.V. Changing Habits.
  B.B. Sigmund, 441:7May89-39
Harriss, G.L. Cardinal Beaufort.
  C.T. Allmand, 617(TLS):31Mar-6Apr89-
    347
Harrisson, B. Pusaka.
  J. Ayers, 324:Jun89-447
  K.L. Hutterer, 293(JASt):Aug88-700
Harrisson, T. Living Through the Blitz.
  N. Annan, 453(NYRB):28Sep89-3
Harsent, D. Selected Poems.
  L. Mackinnon, 617(TLS):30Jun-6Jul89-
    715
Harshav, B. & B., eds. American Yiddish Po-
  etry.*
  J. Lewis, 703:Fall88-173
  M.J. Mirsky, 390:Aug/Sep88-63
  A. Novershtern, 508:Sep88-355
  S.P., 295(JML):Fall87/Winter88-211
Harss, L. Sor Juana's Dream.
  G. Sabat-Rivers, 238:Sep88-567
Hart, C.G. A Little Class on Murder.
  M. Stasio, 441:24Dec89-23
Hart, L. Sam Shepard's Metaphorical Stages.
  W.M. Demastes, 130:Summer88-190
  J. Jain, 649(WAL):Aug88-146
  M.C. Roudané, 397(MD):Mar88-125
  C. Schuler, 615(TJ):Mar88-139
Hart, P. The Spanish Sleuth.
  G.J. Pérez, 238:Sep88-553
Hart, R. Remains To Be Seen.
  T.J. Binyon, 617(TLS):30Jun-6Jul89-713
Hart, T.G. Sino-Soviet Relations.
  R. Allison, 575(SEER):Oct88-664
Hart-Davis, R. - see Beerbohm, M.
Hart-Davis, R. - see Sassoon, S.
Härtel, G. & E. Pólay. Römisches Recht und
  römische Rechtsgeschichte.
  L. Capogrossi Colognesi, 229:Band60
    Heft5-459
Harter, C.C. & J.R. Thompson. John Irving.
  E.C.R., 295(JML):Fall87/Winter88-334
Harter, P. Arts anciens du Cameroun.
  C.M. Geary, 2(AfrA):Nov87-24

Harth, D. & M. Raether, eds. Diderot oder die
  Ambivalenz der Aufklärung.
  P.H. Meyer, 530:Apr88-164
Hartig, M., ed. Angewandte Soziolinguistik.
  L. Zehetner, 685(ZDL):1/1988-118
Hartill, R. Writers Revealed.
  M. L'Engle, 441:5Nov89-41
Hartle, A. Death and the Disinterested Spec-
  tator.
  R.A. Watson, 319:Jan89-156
Hartley, G., ed. Philip Larkin, 1922-1985.*
  W. Scammell, 493:Winter88/89-20
Hartley, J. Philip Larkin, the Marvell Press
  and Me.
  B. Morrison, 617(TLS):7-13Jul89-740
Hartley, J.M. Guide to Documents and Manu-
  scripts in the United Kingdom Relating to
  Russia and the Soviet Union.
  R.P. Bartlett, 575(SEER):Apr88-284
Hartlyn, J. The Politics of Coalition Rule in
  Colombia.
  D. Lehmann, 617(TLS):10-16Mar89-244
Hartman, C. Han Yü and the T'ang Search for
  Unity.*
  M.K. Spring, 318(JAOS):Jan-Mar87-155
Hartman, G. Criticism in the Wilderness.
  Deconstruction and the Question of Text.
  Psychoanalysis and the Question of Text.
  Saving the Text.
  A. Argyros & J.A. Flieger, 153:Spring87-
    52
Hartman, G.H. The Unremarkable Words-
  worth.*
  H.R. Elam, 661(WC):Autumn88-164
Hartman, G.H. & S. Budick, eds. Midrash and
  Literature.*
  A. Berlin, 318(JAOS):Jul-Sep87-548
  E.P., 555:Vol61fasc1-128
Hartmann, W., ed. Die Konzilien der karolin-
  gischen Teilreiche, 843-859.
  H.J. Ryan, 589:Jul88-677
Hartmann von Aue. Erec. (T.L. Keller, trans)
  J.W. Thomas, 133:Band21Heft4-330
Hartnett, D. House of Moon.
  L. Mackinnon, 617(TLS):7-13Apr89-365
Hartnett, M. Collected Poems. (Vol 2)
  T. Eagleton, 565:Summer88-67
den Hartog, D. Dickens and Romantic Psy-
  chology.
  D.F. Sadoff, 158:Dec88-192
  M. Steig, 637(VS):Winter89-263
de Hartog, J. The Centurion.
  P-L. Adams, 61:Jul89-96
  C. Dragonwagon, 441:30Jul89-16
de Hartog, L. Genghis Khan.
  D. Morgan, 617(TLS):24-30Nov89-1293
Hartshorne, C. Insights and Oversights of
  Great Thinkers.
  A.J. Reck, 449:Jun87-283
Hartshorne, C. Wisdom as Moderation.*
  R.N.B., 185:Apr89-676
Hartt, F. History of Italian Renaissance Art.*
  (new ed)
  T. Tuohy, 39:Dec88-448
Hartung, A.E., general ed. A Manual of the
  Writings in Middle English, 1050-1500.
  (Vol7)
  V. Di Marco, 365:Winter87-35
Hartung, W. & H. Schönfeld & others, eds.
  Kommunikation und Sprachvariation.
  H-W. Eroms, 685(ZDL):2/1988-195

160

Hayes, L.D. Politics in Pakistan.
A.H. Syed, 293(JASt):Nov88-921
Hayes, R. Dignaga on the Interpretation of Signs.
D. Sinha, 103:Aug89-310
Hayford, H. & others - see Melville, H.
Hayhoe, R. & M. Bastid. China's Education and the Industrialized World.
J. Kwong, 293(JASt):May88-348
Hayley, B. & E. McKay, eds. 300 Years of Irish Periodicals.
J.B. Davenport, 174(Éire):Spring88-144
Hayman, D. Re-forming the Narrative.
L. Hafrey, 617(TLS):13-19Jan89-41
L. Orr, 329(JJQ):Summer89-623
639(VQR):Summer88-80
Hayman, R. Sartre.*
J. Parini, 249(HudR):Summer88-363
Hayman, R. Writing Against.
P. Thody, 402(MLR):Oct89-999
Haymes, B. The Concept of the Knowledge of God.
F.J.C., 185:Apr89-691
Haymes, E.R. The "Nibelungenlied."*
E.S. Dick, 133:Band21Heft2/3-198
M.E. Gibbs, 406:Winter88-503
W. Hempel, 589:Oct88-940
Haymon, S.T. A Very Particular Murder.
M. Stasio, 441:27Aug89-22
Haynes, J. African Poetry and the English Language.
K. Goodwin, 49:Oct88-99
Hays, D. The Hangman's Children.
D. Mason, 441:13Aug89-10
Hays, J. & P. Haines, eds. Wingbone.
R.D. Harper, 649(WAL):Aug88-178
Hays, M. - see Szondi, P.
Hayslip, L.L., with J. Wurts. When Heaven and Earth Changed Places.
D.K. Shipler, 441:25Jun89-1
Hayter, C. Gilbert and Sullivan.
J.W. Stedman, 637(VS):Autumn88-121
S. Wyatt, 610:Autumn88-289
Haywood, E. Bath-Intrigues.
566:Autumn88-77
Haywood, E., ed. Dante Readings.
L. Santoro, 272(IUR):Spring88-164
P. Williams, 402(MLR):Jul89-747
Haywood, E. The History of Miss Betsy Thoughtless.
J. Wheare, 447(N&Q):Jun88-248
Haywood, E. & B. Jones, eds. Dante Comparisons.*
D. Cecchetti, 549(RLC):Oct-Dec88-571
Haywood, I. Faking It.
M. Brown, 173(ECS):Fall88-108
P. Lewis, 89(BJA):Spring88-189
Haywood, I. The Making of History.*
M. Brown, 173(ECS):Fall88-108
Haywood, J.I. The Musical Language of Hugo Wolf.
E.F.K., 412:Feb88-78
"Hē archaia sophiotichē."
B. Cassin, 229:Band60Heft2-145
Head, R. The Indian Style.*
C.D. Collins, 318(JAOS):Oct-Dec87-783
Headington, C., R. Westbrook & T. Barfoot. Opera.*
G. Martin, 465:Winter88/89-80
Headley, J.M. & J.B. Tomaro, eds. San Carlo Borromeo.
A. Hamilton, 617(TLS):11-17Aug89-867

Headrick, D.R. The Tentacles of Progress.
F. Lehmann, 293(JASt):Nov88-838
Heald, T. Business as Usual.
T.J. Binyon, 617(TLS):1-7Dec89-1337
Heald, T., ed. The Rigby File.
T.J. Binyon, 617(TLS):10-16Nov89-1244
Healey, D. The Time of My Life.
M. Pugh, 617(TLS):3-9Nov89-1207
Healy, J. Yesterday's News.
M. Stasio, 441:13Aug89-14
Healy, S. Lone Stars.
442(NY):3Jul89-95
Heaney, S. The Government of the Tongue.
M. Baron, 175:Summer88-176
J. Bayley, 493:Autumn88-46
L. McDiarmid, 441:5Mar89-25
H. Vendler, 442(NY):13Mar89-102
Heaney, S. The Haw Lantern.*
J. Drexel, 473(PR):Vol55No3-500
P. Filkins, 271:Spring-Summer88-184
V. Luftig & S. Reese, 219(GaR):Fall88-645
Heap of Birds, E. Sharp Rocks.
G. Gessert, 448:Vol26No3-82
Hearn, J. The Gender of Oppression.
M.D.W., 185:Jan89-462
Hearne, B. Beauty and the Beast.
M. Warner, 617(TLS):24-30Nov89-1309
Hearnshaw, L.S. The Shaping of Modern Psychology.
S. Sutherland, 617(TLS):1-7Dec89-1344
Hearon, S. Owning Jolene.
T. Sandlin, 441:22Jan89-10
442(NY):27Mar89-115
Heath, C., ed. The Land Called Morning.
J.T. Goodwin, 102(CanL):Spring88-157
Heath, J. Ablaut and Ambiguity.
G. Gragg, 350:Dec89-820
Heath, M. Political Comedy in Aristophanes.
D.M. Macdowell, 123:Vol38No2-215
Heath, M.J. Crusading Commonplaces.
M. Magnien, 535(RHL):Sep-Oct88-1023
J.J. Supple, 208(FS):Jan88-77
Heath, R. The Shadow Bride.
J. Mellors, 364:Oct/Nov88-115
Heath-Stubbs, J. Collected Poems 1943-1987.*
J. Greening, 493:Autumn88-54
P. Levi, 4:Autumn88-20
Hebditch, D. & N. Anning. Porn Gold.
H. Lomas, 364:Oct/Nov88-130
Hébert, A. Héloïse.
J.J. O'Connor, 102(CanL):Summer88-126
Hébert, A. Le Premier Jardin.
U. Doerr, 268(IFR):Winter89-87
E. Hamblet, 207(FR):Dec88-363
Hecht, A. Obbligati.*
S.A.S., 295(JML):Fall87/Winter88-328
Hecht, S. & A. Cockburn. The Fate of the Forest.
E. Gaspari, 441:24Dec89-10
Heck, E. "Mē theomachein" oder.
R.P.C. Hanson, 123:Vol38No1-164
I. Opelt, 229:Band60Heft7-651
Heckel, E. & others. Zur Geschichte der Kulturpolitik in der BRD.
E. Hexelschneider, 654(WB):7/1988-1227
Hecker, A. Geschichte als Fiktion.
W. Stauffacher, 406:Fall88-396
Heckmann, R., H. Krings & R.W. Meyer, eds. Natur und Subjektivität.*
P. Müller, 489(PJGG):Band95Heft2-431

Hedgepeth, C., Jr. Theories of Social Action in Black Literature.
    M. Awkward, 538(RAL):Fall88-450
    P.A. Muckley, 295(JML):Fall87/Winter88-212
Hedlund, S. Crisis in Soviet Agriculture.
    K. Brooks, 550(RusR):Jul88-347
Heepe, M., ed. Lautzeichen und ihre Anwendung in verschiedenen Sprachgebieten.
    G.F. Meier, 682(ZPSK):Band41Heft5-664
de Heer, P. The Care-taker Emperor.
    R. Taylor, 318(JAOS):Oct-Dec87-822
Heesterman, J.C. The Inner Conflict of Tradition.*
    T.R. Trautmann, 293(JASt):Aug88-681
Heffernan, T.J., ed. The Popular Literature of Medieval England.*
    J.M. Ziolkowski, 301(JEGP):Jan88-99
Heft, C. Crash and Burn.
    G. Gessert, 448:Vol26No1-73
Hegel, G.W.F. The Philosophy of Right.
    C. Sartiliot, 153:Winter88-68
Hegel, R.E. & R.C. Hessney, eds. Expression of Self in Chinese Literature.*
    A.A. Rickett, 116:Jul87-139
Heger, H. & J. Matillon, eds. Les Croates et la civilisation du livre.
    C.A. Simpson, 575(SEER):Oct88-638
    J. Voisine, 549(RLC):Jan-Mar88-106
Hegselmann, R. Formale Dialektik.
    A.F. Koch, 687:Jan-Mar88-159
Heidbreder, R. Don't Eat Spiders.
    A. Kertzer, 102(CanL):Winter87-165
Heidegger, M. Die Frage nach dem Ding.
    R.M., 342:Band79Heft1-113
Heidegger, M. Gesamtausgabe. (Pt 2; Vol 43 ed by B. Heimbüchl, Vol 44 ed by M. Heinz, Vol 48 ed by P. Jaeger)
    W. Patt, 489(PJGG):Band95Heft1-175
Heidegger, M. Hegel's Phenomenology of Spirit.
    F. Schalow, 543:Jun89-837
Heider, G.C. The Cult of Molek.
    D. Edelman, 318(JAOS):Oct-Dec87-727
Heifetz, H. - see Kālidāsa
Heikkilä, R. - see Canth, S.M.
Heilbroner, R. & P. Bernstein. The Debt and the Deficit.
    G. Daugherty, 441:16Jul89-25
Heilbrun, C.G. Writing a Woman's Life.
    W. Martin, 441:8Jan89-19
Heim, M. Electric Language.*
    D. Dutton, 478(P&L):Apr88-156
    P.B. Thompson, 103:Dec88-483
Heimbüchl, B. - see Heidegger, M.
Heimonet, J-M. Politiques de l'écriture, Bataille/Derrida.
    F. Chevillot, 207(FR):Mar89-688
Hein, C. The Distant Lover.
    K. Washburn, 441:7May89-33
Hein, C. Der Tangospieler.
    P. Graves, 617(TLS):21-27Jul89-802
Heine, H. Historisch-kritische Gesamtausgabe der Werke. (Vol 4 ed by W. Woesler; Vol 7 ed by M. Opitz)
    F. Mende, 680(ZDP):Band107Heft2-297
Heine, S. Existential and Ontological Dimensions of Time in Heidegger and Dōgen.*
    M.E. Zimmerman, 323:Jan88-103
Heinemann, M.E. Gender and Destiny.
    S. Bauschinger, 221(GQ):Winter88-154
    E.C.R., 295(JML):Fall87/Winter88-197
    M.I. Teicher, 390:Apr88-56

Heinen, H. & I. Henderson, eds. Genres in Medieval German Literature.
    S. Jefferis, 221(GQ):Spring88-299
Heinle, E. & F. Leonhardt. Towers.
    P. Goldberger, 441:3Dec89-21
Heinrich, B. Ravens in Winter.
    P-L. Adams, 61:Oct89-115
    M.J. West, 441:24Sep89-12
    442(NY):16Oct89-132
Heinrichs, W. Threshold of War.*
    W.F. Kimball, 617(TLS):12-18May89-505
Heintz, G. Stefan George.
    A.R. Wedel, 221(GQ):Summer88-476
Heinz, M. - see Heidegger, M.
Heinzle, J., ed. Heldenbuch. (Vol 2)
    J.L. Flood, 402(MLR):Jul89-774
Heinzle, J. Das "Nibelungenlied."
    M.E. Gibbs, 406:Winter88-503
Heise, E.T. & R.F. Muller. A Conversational Introduction to French. (2nd ed)
    L.R. Polly, 399(MLJ):Autumn88-354
Heisenberg, W. Physics and Philosophy.
    J.D. Barrow, 617(TLS):29Sep-5Oct89-1072
Heisserer, A.J., ed. Classical Antiquities.
    G.D. Weinberg, 124:Jul-Aug89-476
Heissig, W., ed. Fragen der mongolischen Heldendichtung. (Pt 4)
    C.R. Bawden, 196:Band29Heft1/2-195
Heitmann, K. Das Rumänenbild im deutschen Sprachraum 1775-1918.
    W. Engel, 72:Band225Heft1-233
    H. Fassel, 547(RF):Band99Heft4-490
Heitmann, K., ed. Rumänisch-deutsche Interferenzen.
    A. Marino, 107(CRCL):Jun88-291
Heitsch, E. Platon über die rechte Art zu reden und zu schreiben.
    T.A. Szlezák, 229:Band60Heft5-390
Helberg Chávez, H.A. Skizze einer Grammatik des Amarakaeri.
    K.H. Schmidt, 685(ZDL):2/1987-278
Helbig, A.K. & A.R. Perkins. Dictionary of American Children's Fiction, 1960-1984.
    A.M. Hildebrand, 87(BB):Jun88-159
Helbig, G. Entwicklung der Sprachwissenschaft seit 1970.
    J. Herrgen, 685(ZDL):2/1988-193
Held, V. Rights and Goods.
    D. Copp, 482(PhR):Jul88-430
Heldt, B. Terrible Perfection.
    M.V. Jones, 402(MLR):Apr89-541
Helgadóttir, G., ed. Hrafns saga Sveinbjarnarsonar.
    M.C. Seymour, 179(ES):Dec88-570
Helgesen, M., S. Brown & T. Mandeville. English Firsthand.
    E.L. Judd, 608:Mar89-134
Helisenne de Crenne. A Renaissance Woman. (M.M. Mustacchi & P.J. Archambault, eds & trans)
    B.L. Knapp, 188(ECr):Summer88-96
Helkkula, M., R. Nordström & O. Välikangas. Eléments de syntaxe contrastive du verbe.
    P. Swiggers, 553(RLiR):Jul-Dec88-534
Hellan, L. & K.K. Christensen, eds. Topics in Scandinavian Syntax.*
    H.Á. Sigurdsson, 603:Vol12No1-209
Hellenkemper, H. & F. Hild. Neue Forschungen in Kilikien.
    M. Waelkens, 229:Band60Heft2-185

Heller, A. & F. Feher, eds. Reconstructing
Aesthetics.
R. Shusterman, 494:Vol8No3/4-651
Heller, E. The Importance of Nietzsche.
A. Nehamas, 441:30Apr89-28
M. Tanner, 617(TLS):12-18May89-509
J.R. Watson, 103:Sep89-358
Heller, F., ed. The Use and Abuse of Social
Science.
P.D., 185:Apr89-682
Heller, H. The Conquest of Poverty.
D. Bitton, 551(RenQ):Autumn88-493
Heller, H-B. Literarische Intelligenz und
Film.*
J. Blackwell, 221(GQ):Spring87-324
Heller, M., ed. Codeswitching.
D. Hymes, 350:Sep89-588
Heller, M. & A. Nekrich. Utopia in Power.*
A.G. Meyer, 550(RusR):Jul88-344
Heller, P. Bad Intentions.
C. Sommers, 441:8Oct89-25
Heller, P. Tyson.
V. Scannell, 617(TLS):22-28Sep89-1041
Heller, R. The Decision Makers.
T.C. Hayes, 441:29Oct89-41
Heller, R. The State of Industry.
C. Carter, 324:Mar89-261
Heller, S. & S. Chwast. Graphic Style.
D.P. Doordan, 441:5Mar89-22
Heller, T.C., M. Sosna & D.E. Wellbery, eds.
Reconstructing Individualism.*
J.J. Baker, 141:Winter88-127
Hellinga, L. & J. Goldfinch, eds. Bibliography
& the Study of 15th-Century Civilisation.
T.A.B., 179(ES):Oct88-468
M.K. Duggan, 78(BC):Winter88-578
Hellinger, B. - see Collier, J.
Hellman, B., ed. Dikt i krig.
G.C. Schoolfield, 563(SS):Winter88-97
Hellman, S. Italian Communism in Transition.
M. Clark, 617(TLS):28Jul-3Aug89-821
Hellmann-Rajanayagam, D. Tamil als polit-
isches Symbol.
S.B. Steever, 318(JAOS):Apr-Jun87-355
Hellmuth, L. Gastfreundschaft und Gastrecht
bei den Germanen.*
A.C. Murray, 589:Jan88-163
Helly, D.O. Livingstone's Legacy.*
J.M. MacKenzie, 637(VS):Autumn88-140
Helm, A. Staffordshire Folk Drama.
S. Roud, 203:Vol99No1-132
Helman, D.H., ed. Analogical Reasoning.
A. Margalit, 617(TLS):14-20Apr89-399
Helms, C.N., ed. Diego Rivera.
O. Baddeley, 59:Jun88-271
Helsinger, E.K., R.L. Sheets & W. Veeder. The
Woman Question.*
R.D. Altick, 617(TLS):11-17Aug89-866
Helttula, A. Studies on the Latin Accusative
Absolute.
J.N. Adams, 123:Vol38No2-300
Helwig, D. Old Wars.
N. Callendar, 441:22Oct89-37
Helwig, D. & S. Martin, eds. Coming Attrac-
tions 4.
P. Morley, 102(CanL):Autumn88-164
Helwig, D. & S. Martin, eds. 86: Best Canadi-
an Stories.*
P. Morley, 102(CanL):Autumn88-164
P. Stevens, 529(QQ):Autumn88-568
Helwig, M. Eden.
M. Cookshaw, 376:Mar88-96

Helwig, M. Tongues of Men and Angels.
R. Maggs, 102(CanL):Winter87-280
Hemingway, E. The Complete Short Stories of
Ernest Hemingway.
234:Fall88-65
Hemingway, E. The Dangerous Summer.*
(French title: L'Été dangereux.)
J. Blot, 450(NRF):Dec88-81
Hemley, R. All You Can Eat.
J. Clute, 617(TLS):21-27Jul89-803
Hemlow, J. - see Burney, F.
Hemming, C. British Landscape Painters.
C. Newall, 617(TLS):10-16Nov89-1247
Hemming, J. Amazon Frontier.*
E.F. Moran, 263(RIB):Vol38No1-75
Hemmings, F.W.J. Culture and Society in
France 1789-1848.
J-M. Bailbé, 535(RHL):Nov-Dec88-1145
B. Rigby, 208(FS):Jul88-350
Hémon, L. Itinéraire de Liverpool à Québec.
B-Z. Shek, 627(UTQ):Fall87-179
Hempfer, K.W. & G. Regn, eds. Interpretation.
B. Marx, 547(RF):Band100Heft4-401
Hemphill, P. Me and the Boy.
S. Pickering, 569(SR):Fall88-673
Henderson, B. - see Sturges, P.
Henderson, B., P. Booth & J. Meek, eds. The
Pushcart Prize XIII.
C. Major, 441:21May89-18
Henderson, J. - see Aristophanes
Henderson, J.B. The Development and Decline
of Chinese Cosmology.
J.M. Kitagawa, 302:Vol24No1-99
J.S. Major, 293(JASt):May88-349
Henderson, K.U. & B.F. McManus, eds. Half
Humankind.
L. Woodbridge, 301(JEGP):Jan88-104
Henderson, M.C. Broadway Ballyhoo.
J. Papp, 441:3Dec89-44
Henderson, W.O. Manufactories in Germany.
T. Kemp, 83:Spring88-82
Hendrick, G. - see Jones, J.
Hendrick, G. - see Van Doren, M.
Hendrickson, D.C. The Future of American
Strategy.
P. Kennedy, 453(NYRB):16Mar89-36
Hendrie, D., Jr. A Survey of the Atlantic
Beaches.*
42(AR):Spring88-276
Hendrix, G. Nature of Language.
H. Huckabay, 350:Dec89-889
Hendry, J. Becoming Japanese.
D.K. Kondo, 293(JASt):Feb88-142
A.E. Murase, 407(MN):Autumn88-381
Hendry, J. Understanding Japanese Society.
D.W. Plath, 293(JASt):Aug88-636
Hendy, M.F. Studies in the Byzantine Mone-
tary Economy, c. 300-1450.
F. Millar, 313:Vol78-198
Henig, M. & A. King, eds. Pagan Gods and
Shrines of the Roman Empire.
J.H.W.G. Liebeschuetz, 123:Vol38No2-296
Henken, E.R. Traditions of the Welsh Saints.
T.A. Watkins, 112:Vol20-201
Henkin, L., J.D. Monk & A. Tarski. Cylindric
Algebras. (Pt 2)
R.D. Maddux, 316:Jun88-651
Henn-Memmesheimer, B. Nonstandardmuster.
B.J. Koekkoek, 221(GQ):Winter88-120
Henne, H., H. Sitta & H.E. Wiegand - see
Mode, D.

Hennei, I.N. "Ämnar kanske fröken publicera något?"
   P. Bjørby, 563(SS):Summer88-408
Hennessey, M. An Arch for the King & Other Stories.
   R.J. Merrett, 102(CanL):Autumn88-158
Hennessy, P. Whitehall.
   A. Cairncross, 617(TLS):6-12Jan89-5
Hennig, U., ed. Das Wiener Passionsspiel.
   E.E. Du Bruck, 201:Vol14-215
Henning, G. A Guide to Language Testing.
   L. Hamp-Lyons, 608:Mar89-127
Henny, S. & J-P. Lehmann, eds. Themes and Theories in Modern Japanese History.
   J.S. Brownlee, 407(MN):Winter88-494
Henrich, D., ed. All-Einheit.
   R. Margreiter, 489(PJGG):Band95Heft2-410
   G. Parkes, 485(PE&W):Jan88-85
Henriksen, L.L., with J.A. Boydston. Anzia Yezierska.*
   S.B. Purdy, 395(MFS):Winter88-742
Henry, A., ed. The Mirour of Mans Saluacioune.*
   R.P. McGerr, 447(N&Q):Sep88-360
   S.J. Ogilvie-Thomson, 541(RES):Nov88-537
   D. Pearsall, 589:Jul88-681
   O.S. Pickering, 382(MAE):1988/2-315
   78(BC):Autumn88-313
Henry, A., ed. The Pilgrimage of the Lyfe of the Manhode.* (Vol 1)
   R.P. McGerr, 179(ES):Feb88-85
   B. Millett, 382(MAE):1988/2-313
Henry, A. - see "Biblia Pauperum"
Henry, D. & E. The Mask of Power.*
   H. Hofmann, 394:Vol41fasc3/4-441
Henry, F.E.E. Saint-Leger Leger traducteur de Pindare.*
   R. Little, 208(FS):Apr88-229
Henry, L. Restoring the Chateau of the Marquis de Sade.
   F. Muratori, 448:Vol26No1-113
Henry, M. La Barbarie.*
   R. Kühn, 687:Jan-Mar88-124
Henry, M. An Ocean in my Ear.
   G. Mort, 493:Winter88/89-57
Henry, O. O. Henry's Texas Short Stories. (M. McClintock & M. Simms, eds)
   D. Heaberlin, 649(WAL):Aug88-164
Henry-Hermann, G. Ethik und praktische Erfahrung.
   D. Jakowljewitsch, 53(AGP):Band70Heft3-343
Henryson, R. The Poems.* (D. Fox, ed)
   A.A. MacDonald, 179(ES):Aug88-359
   S. Mapstone, 447(N&Q):Jun88-214
Hensel, F. The Letters of Fanny Hensel to Felix Mendelssohn. (M.J. Citron, ed & trans)
   C. Brown, 415:Apr88-187
Henshaw, M. Out of the Line of Fire.
   F. Baveystock, 617(TLS):10-16Mar89-256
Henson, M.A. A Black Explorer at the North Pole.
   K. Bouton, 441:13Aug89-11
Hentschel, E. Funktion und Geschichte deutscher Partikeln.*
   U. Bichel, 685(ZDL):1/1988-116
   U. Brausse, 682(ZPSK):Band41Heft3-383
   B.J. Koekkoek, 221(GQ):Fall87-653

Hepburn, F. Portraits of the Later Plantagenets.
   J.C. Smith, 589:Apr88-408
Hepburn, J. - see Bennett, A.
Hepokoski, J.A. Giuseppe Verdi: "Otello."
   F.W. Sternfeld, 410(M&L):Apr88-280
Heppenheimer, T.A. The Coming Quake.
   K.C. Cole, 441:1Jan89-11
Heraclitus. Héraclite, Fragments.* (M. Conche, ed & trans)
   J. Brunschwig, 319:Jan89-145
   M. Fattal, 192(EP):Apr-Jun88-267
Hérail, R.J. & E.A. Lovatt. Dictionary of Modern Colloquial French.
   J.E. Joseph, 399(MLJ):Spring88-89
"Le héraut du dix-septième siècle."
   M. Roethlisberger, 380:Spring88-52
Herbert, C. Trollope and Comic Pleasure.*
   R.C. Burke, 301(JEGP):Jul88-454
   J. Freedman, 402(MLR):Jul89-724
   S.M. Smith, 541(RES):Nov88-569
Herbert, M. - see Lawrence, D.H.
Herbert, R.L. Impressionism.*
   K. Cieszkowski, 324:Jun89-444
   J. Flam, 453(NYRB):28Sep89-20
   T. Hilton, 617(TLS):24-30Mar89-305
Herbert, W. The Noose of Laurels.
   K. Bouton, 441:13Aug89-11
Herbert, Z. Report from the Beseiged City and Other Poems.*
   D. McDuff, 565:Spring88-64
Herdman, J. Three Novellas.*
   C. McCullough, 571(ScLJ):Winter88-62
Heredia, J.L. - see under López Heredia, J.
Heres, G., comp. Corpus Speculorum Etruscorum. (Deutsche Demokratische Republik, fasc 1)
   U. Höckmann, 229:Band60Heft6-558
Hereth, M. Alexis de Tocqueville.
   S.H., 185:Jan89-459
Herf, J. Reactionary Modernism.*
   M.T. Jones, 221(GQ):Winter87-158
Herfort-Koch, M. Archaische Bronzeplastik Lakoniens.
   P. Cartledge, 123:Vol38No2-342
Herget, W., K.P. Jochum & I. Weber, eds. Theorie und Praxis im Erzählen des 19. und 20. Jahrhunderts.
   H. Foltinek, 224(GRM):Band38Heft3-359
   D. Mehl, 72:Band225Heft2-397
Hering, W. - see Caesar
Herlihy, D. Medieval Households.*
   R.S. Gottfried, 589:Jan88-165
Herlihy, P. Odessa.
   D.R. Brower, 550(RusR):Apr88-186
Herlinger, J.W. - see Marchetto of Padua
Herman, B.L. Architecture and Rural Life in Central Delaware, 1700-1900.
   M.A. Williams, 658:Spring88-87
Herman, J., ed. Latin vulgaire - latin tardif.
   B.I. Knott-Sharpe, 123:Vol38No1-167
Herman, J. Notes from a Welsh Diary, 1944-1955.
   F. Spalding, 617(TLS):9-15Jun89-640
Herman, N. Too Long a Child.
   M. Lefkowitz, 617(TLS):14-20Jul89-768
Herman, W. Understanding Contemporary American Drama.
   A. Woods, 610:Autumn88-303
Hermand, J. Kultur im Wiederaufbau.*
   A. Stephan, 222(GR):Fall88-208
Hermann, I. Probleme der heutigen Kultur.
   D. Ulle, 654(WB):4/1988-690

Hermans, T., ed. The Manipulation of Literature.
  J. Labanyi, 402(MLR):Apr89-420
  L.H. Malmberg, 161(DUJ):Dec87-162
Hermary, A. La sculpture archïque et classique. (Vol 1: Catalogue des sculptures classiques de Délos.)
  R.A. Tomlinson, 303(JoHS):Vol108-267
Hermenegildo, A. - see Lasso de la Vega, G.L.
Hermerén, G. The Nature of Aesthetic Qualities.
  S. Davies, 103:Sep89-360
Hermogenes. On Types of Style. (C.W. Wooten, ed & trans)
  S.M. Oberhelman, 568(SCN):Fall88-40
  S. Usher, 123:Vol38No2-406
Herms, I. Wörterbuch Hausa-Deutsch.
  S. Brauner, 682(ZPSK):Band41Heft2-251
Hernández, M. Epistolario. El torero más valiente. (A. Sánchez Vidal, ed of both)
  R. Berroa, 240(HR):Summer88-382
Hernández-Araico, S. Ironía y tragedia en Calderón.
  A.E. Wiltrout, 238:Mar88-80
Hernández Sacristán, C. Oraciones reflejas y estructuras actanciales en español.
  C. Company, 545(RPh):Feb89-348
  J.N. Green, 86(BHS):Apr88-177
Hernon, P. Earthly Remains.
  C. Salzberg, 441:26Nov89-30
Herodotus. The History of Herodotus. (D. Grene, trans)
  J. Dillon, 235:Summer88-99
  J. Hart, 123:Vol38No2-402
  H. Lloyd-Jones, 31(ASch):Winter88-130
  M. Simpson, 569(SR):Spring88-292
"Herodotus, Book I." (R.A. McNeal, ed)
  S. West, 123:Vol98No1-16
Herr, C. Joyce's Anatomy of Culture.*
  R.A. Battaglia, 454:Fall88-117
  M.P. Gillespie, 125:Spring88-290
  R.B. Kershner, Jr., 219(GaR):Summer88-431
  A. Martin, 272(IUR):Spring88-144
  J.C.C. Mays, 541(RES):Nov88-588
  J. Voelker, 295(JML):Fall87/Winter88-338
Herraiz, J.J.L. & J. Fernández Jiménez - see under Labrador Herraiz, J.J. & J. Fernández Jiménez
de Herrera, F. Poesía castellana original completa.* (C. Cuevas, ed)
  D.G. Walters, 86(BHS):Apr88-182
Herrera, M.T. - see de Ketham, J.
Herrera-Sobek, M. & H.M. Viramontes, eds. Chicana Creativity and Criticism.
  U. Krauter, 649(WAL):Nov88-270
Herrick, H.S. - see Daniels, L.J.
Herrin, J. The Formation of Christendom.*
  D. Obolensky, 575(SEER):Oct88-650
Herring, P.F. Joyce's Uncertainty Principle.
  C. Herr, 395(MFS):Winter88-684
  L. Knuth, 329(JJQ):Fall88-145
  J.L. McDonald, 268(IFR):Winter89-67
Hersak, D. Songye Masks and Figure Sculpture.
  M. Adams, 2(AfrA):Aug88-17
Hersey, G. The Lost Meaning of Classical Architecture.
  M.A. Branch, 505:May88-107
  D. Clarke, 47:Aug88-41
Hersey, J. Blues.
  639(VQR):Winter88-31

Hersey, J. Life Sketches.
  H. Benedict, 441:7May89-25
Hershey, O. Truck Dance.
  V. Weissman, 441:23Apr89-21
Hershiser, O., with J.B. Jenkins. Out of the Blue.
  C. Salzberg, 441:4Jun89-23
  W. Sheed, 453(NYRB):12Oct89-49
Hershman, D.J. & J. Lieb. The Key to Genius.
  S. Sutherland, 617(TLS):27Jan-2Feb89-78
Herszlikowicz, M. Philosophie de l'antisémitisme.
  F. Giroux, 103:Mar89-102
Hertz, D.M. The Tuning of the Word.
  L.B. Brown, 290(JAAC):Spring88-439
  P. Citron, 535(RHL):Mar-Apr88-315
  L. Kramer, 149(CLS):Vol25No2-193
Hertz, N. The End of the Line.*
  T.R. Frosch, 591(SIR):Spring88-134
Hertzberg, A. The Jews in America.
  J.A. Garraty, 441:26Nov89-5
Hervey, A. A Soldier of the Company. (C. Allen, ed)
  P-L. Adams, 61:Oct89-116
Herviant, C. Le Soleil des taupes.
  L.A. Olivier, 207(FR):Mar89-715
Herz, J.S. The Short Narratives of E.M. Forster.
  R.J. Voorhees, 395(MFS):Winter88-702
Herzfeld, M. Anthropology Through the Looking-Glass.
  C. Stewart, 617(TLS):6-12Jan89-18
Herzog, A. The Woodchipper Murder.
  R. Grant, 441:15Oct89-52
Herzog, I. The Royal Purple and the Biblical Blue. (E. Spanier, ed)
  R. Hoffmann, 358:Dec89-17
von Hesberg-Tonn, B. Coniunx carissima.
  P. Guyot, 229:Band60Heft2-170
Heschel, A.J. Maimonides.
  M. Skakun, 390:Jan88-62
Heseltine, M. The Challenge of Europe.
  A. Howard, 617(TLS):2-8Jun89-602
Hesiod. Theogony [and] Works and Days. (M.L. West, ed & trans)
  C. Martindale, 617(TLS):31Mar-6Apr89-341
Hesketh, P. Netting the Sun.
  M. Wormald, 617(TLS):22-28Dec89-1417
Hess, D. & M. Muller. Dorfsman & CBS.*
  T. Reese, 507:Mar/Apr88-151
Hess, H-J. - see Leibniz, G.W.
Hesse, M.G. Gabrielle Roy.
  P. Socken, 102(CanL):Winter87-193
Hetherington, T. - see Hardy, H.
Hettrich, H. Untersuchungen zur Hypotaxe im Vedischen.
  W.P. Lehmann, 159:Vol5-207
Heubeck, A. & A. Hoekstra. A Commentary on Homer's "Odyssey." (Vol 2)
  G. Steiner, 617(TLS):8-14Sep89-984
Heubeck, A., S. West & J.B. Hainsworth. A Commentary on Homer's "Odyssey." (Vol 1)
  G. Steiner, 617(TLS):8-14Sep89-984
Heubner, H. Kommentar zum "Agricola" des Tacitus.*
  P. Flobert, 555:Vol61fasc1-146
Heuermann, H. & B-P. Lange, eds. Die Utopie in der angloamerikanischen Literatur.
  R. Beck, 72:Band224Heft2-420

Heurgon, J. Scripta Varia.
    P. Flobert, 555:Vol61fasc2-334
    J-C. Richard, 229:Band60Heft5-449
Heuser, A. - see MacNeice, L.
von Heusinger, C., ed. Das Gestochene Bild,
von der Zeichnung Zum Kupferstich.
    C. Hartley, 90:Jul88-539
van den Heuvel, P. Parole, mot, silence.
    J. Baetens, 204(FdL):Mar88-73
Heuzé, P. L'Image du corps dans l'oeuvre de
Virgile.
    F. della Corte, 229:Band60Heft2-154
    P.R. Hardie, 313:Vol78-269
    A. Novara, 555:Vol61fasc2-328
Hewison, R. The Heritage Industry.*
    D. Lowenthal, 59:Sep88-467
Hewitt, D. English Fiction of the Early Mod-
ern Period, 1890-1940.
    D. Trotter, 617(TLS):29Sep-5Oct89-1066
Hewitt, J. Freehold and Other Poems.
    H. Buckingham, 565:Winter87/88-71
Hewitt, N., ed. The Culture of Reconstruc-
tion.
    B. Appleyard, 617(TLS):14-20Jul89-765
Hewitt, R.L. Structure, Meaning and Ritual in
the Narratives of the Southern San.
    T. Geider, 196:Band29Heft1/2-198
Hexter, R.J. Ovid and Medieval Schooling.
    F.T. Coulson, 377:Mar88-52
Hey, G. Die slavischen Siedlungen im König-
reich Sachsen mit Erklärung ihrer Namen.
    J. Udolph, 260(IF):Band93-376
Heydenreich, L.H. Leonardo-Studien.
    M. Kemp, 617(TLS):5-11May89-488
Heyen, W. The Chestnut Rain.
    D. Revell, 460(OhR):No43-116
Heyerdahl, T. Easter Island.
    P-L. Adams, 61:Dec89-127
Heyert, E. Metropolitan Places.
    P. Goldberger, 441:3Dec89-21
Heym, S. Nachruf.
    P. Graves, 617(TLS):24Feb-2Mar89-197
Heymann, C.D. A Woman Called Jackie.
    M. Filler, 617(TLS):30Jun-6Jul89-722
    K. Olson, 441:28May89-19
Heyndels, I. Le Conflit racinien.*
    N. Ekstein, 494:Vol8No2-449
Heyndels, R. La pensée fragmentée.
    W. Moser, 107(CRCL):Mar88-128
    P. Saint-Amand, 704(SFR):Fall-
    Winter88-409
Heynen, J., V. Krahn & J. Lessmann. Italien-
ische Renaissancekunst im Kaiser Wilhelm
Museum Krefeld.
    C.B. Strehlke, 90:Nov88-860
Heytesbury, W. On Maxima and Minima.* (J.
Longeway, ed & trans)
    R. Wood, 589:Jul88-682
Heywood, C. Childhood in 19th-Century
France.
    J.F. McMillan, 617(TLS):3-9Feb89-117
Heywood, C., ed. D.H. Lawrence.*
    D.R. Schwarz, 395(MFS):Summer88-279
Heyworth, P.L. - see Wanley, H.
Hiaasen, C. Skin Tight.
    K. Dunn, 441:15Oct89-42
Hiatt, H.H. America's Health in the Balance.
    L.B. McGuire, 639(VQR):Winter88-148
Hibbard, G.R. - see Shakespeare, W.
Hibberd, D. Owen the Poet.*
    W. Blazek, 295(JML):Fall87/Winter88-366
    R. Hoffpauir, 177(ELT):Vol31No1-96

Hibbert, C. Cities and Civilizations.*
    J.S. Ackerman, 576:Mar88-90
Hibbert, C. The Grand Tour.
    B. Ford, 39:Mar88-218
Hibbert, C. Venice.
    C. Pittel, 441:23Jul89-19
Hibbert, C. & M. Black. London's Churches.
    H. Thorold, 324:Feb89-183
Hick, J. An Interpretation of Religion.
    S. Grover, 617(TLS):22-28Dec89-1404
Hickey, D.J. & J.E. Doherty. A Dictionary of
Irish History, 1800-1980.
    F. D'Arcy, 272(IUR):Autumn88-351
Hickmann, M., ed. Social and Functional
Approaches to Language and Thought.
    N. Besnier, 350:Jun89-413
Hicks, J.V. Rootless Tree.
    B. Whiteman, 102(CanL):Winter87-148
Hicks, M.A. Richard III as Duke of Gloucester.
    J.R. Lander, 161(DUJ):Dec87-135
Hicks, S. The Oxtail Cocktail.
    J.L. Jacobsen, 649(WAL):Nov88-250
Hidalgo-Serna, E. Das ingeniöse Denken bei
Baltasar Gracián.*
    C. Strosetzki, 72:Band224Heft2-457
Hiddleston, J., ed. Laforgue aujourd'hui.*
    B.L. Knapp, 446(NCFS):Spring-Summer89-
    418
Hiddleston, J.A. Baudelaire and "Le Spleen
de Paris."*
    J. Dargan, 446(NCFS):Fall-Winter88/89-
    237
Hieatt, C.B. & S. Butler, eds. Curye on In-
glysch.
    G.R. Keiser, 589:Apr88-410
Hiebel, H.H. Die Zeichen des Gesetzes. Franz
Kafka "Ein Landarzt."
    P. Horn, 680(ZDP):Band107Heft4-623
Hielscher, K. Tschechow.
    W. Busch, 688(ZSP):Band48Heft2-400
Hieronymi, S. Presbyteri Opera. (Pt 3) (P.
Lardet, ed)
    P. Flobert, 555:Vol61fasc2-331
Hiersche, R. Deutsches etymologisches Wör-
terbuch. (Buchstabe A, Pts 1 & 2)
    E. Seebold, 260(IF):Band93-360
Hiestand, R. Papsturkunden für Kirchen im
Heiligen Lande.
    G.T. Dennis, 589:Oct88-943
Hiestand, R. Papsturkunden für Templer und
Johanniter, Neue Folge.
    M. Gervers, 589:Jan88-167
Higgins, A. Helsingor Station and Other
Departures.
    J. Melmoth, 617(TLS):24-30Nov89-1312
Higgins, A. Ronda Gorge and Other Preci-
pices.
    J. Hone, 617(TLS):18-24Aug89-894
Higgins, D. Pattern Poetry.*
    L.V.R., 568(SCN):Fall88-65
Higgins, G.V. The Progress of the Seasons.
    P-L. Adams, 61:May89-99
    L.S. Ritter, 441:23Apr89-11
    W. Sheed, 453(NYRB):12Oct89-49
Higgins, G.V. Trust.
    J. Symons, 617(TLS):29Dec89/4Jan90-
    1447
Higgins, I., ed. The Second World War in Lit-
erature.
    D. Blackbourn, 402(MLR):Oct89-908
    S.B. John, 208(FS):Oct88-494
Higgins, J. A History of Peruvian Literature.
    S. Boldy, 402(MLR):Jul89-766

Higgins, J. A Season in Hell.
N. Callendar, 441:19Mar89-29
Higgins, J. & J. Ross. Southeast Asians.
C. Cook, 608:Jun89-028
Higgins, K. Nietzsche's "Zarathustra."
D.W. Conway, 543:Dec88-385
Higgins, M.B. & C.M. Raphael - see Reich, W.
Higgins, R. Tanagra and the Figurines.*
C.E. Vafopoulou-Richardson, 123:
Vol38No2-448
Higginson, F.H. A Bibliography of the Writings of Robert Graves.* (2nd ed rev by W.P. Williams)
J. Meyers, 87(BB):Jun88-162
Higgs, R.J. Laurel & Thorn.
J. Gindin, 385(MQR):Spring89-283
Higham, C. & R. Moseley. Cary Grant.
B. Shulgasser, 441:30Apr89-19
Highsmith, P. Mermaids on the Golf Course.
E. Stumpf, 441:29Jan89-34
Higonnet, M.R. & J. Jenson, eds. Behind the Lines.*
M.E. Rose, 366:Autumn88-266
Higonnet, P. Sister Republics.
N. Hampson, 617(TLS):19-25May89-556
Hijirida, K. & M. Yoshikawa. Japanese Language and Culture for Business and Travel.
P.J. Wetzel, 399(MLJ):Summer88-244
Hijuelos, O. The Mambo Kings Play Songs of Love.
M. Jefferson, 441:27Aug89-1
442(NY):16Oct89-132
Hilbert, D.R. Color and Color Perception.
C.L. Hardin, 103:Feb89-47
D.L. Sepper, 543:Jun89-834
Hilbert, R. - see under Brown, S.E.
Hilbig, W. La Lettre.
L. Kovacs, 450(NRF):Dec88-83
Hildy, F.J. Shakespeare at the Maddermarket.
C. Smith, 610:Summer88-171
Hill, A.G. - see Wordsworth, W. & D.
Hill, B., ed. The First English Feminist.
F.A. Nussbaum, 173(ECS):Summer88-499
Hill, B.W. Sir Robert Walpole.
J. Cannon, 617(TLS):25-31Aug89-926
Hill, C. The Collected Essays of Christopher Hill.* (Vol 3)
R. Howell, Jr., 366:Autumn88-242
Hill, C. A Tinker and a Poor Man.
R.M. Adams, 453(NYRB):2Mar89-27
M. Ferguson, 441:12Mar89-31
442(NY):27Mar89-116
Hill, D. "Out of His Skin."
M. Phillips, 617(TLS):22-28Sep89-1041
Hill, D. Prince.
T. Hibbert, 617(TLS):7-13Apr89-376
Hill, D.E. - see Ovid
Hill, F. A Fatal Delusion.
L. Duguid, 617(TLS):18-24Aug89-901
Hill, G. Heartwood.
R. Maggs, 102(CanL):Winter87-280
Hill, P. & R. Keynes - see Lopokova, L. & J.M. Keynes
Hill, S. The Accumulation of Small Acts of Kindness.
M. O'Neill, 617(TLS):4-10Aug89-850
Hill, S. My Darling Camel.*
R. Hill, 493:Autumn88-64
Hill, W.E. The Oregon Trail.
P.A. Owens, 649(WAL):Nov88-234
Hill, W.H. - see Soloviev, S.M.
Hillel, S. Operation Babylon.*
N. Rejwan, 390:May88-63

Hillerman, T. Talking God.
P-L. Adams, 61:Oct89-116
T. Foote, 441:18Jun89-9
442(NY):14Aug89-92
Hillerman, T. A Thief of Time.
B. Waters, 649(WAL):Feb89-376
Hillerman, T. & B. Kalman. Indian Country.
J.T. Groulx, 649(WAL):Aug88-185
Hilliard, S.S. The Singularity of Thomas Nashe.*
N. Rhodes, 447(N&Q):Mar88-79
Hillier, B. Young Betjeman.*
J. Bayley, 364:Aug/Sep88-119
S. Gaisford, 324:Jan89-125
J. Whitworth, 493:Winter88/89-10
Hillier, J. The Art of the Japanese Book.
O. Impey, 39:Sep88-207
L. Smith, 617(TLS):28Jul-3Aug89-833
Hillier, J., ed. Cahiers du Cinéma.* (Vol 1)
H.T.B., 295(JML):Fall87/Winter88-281
Hillis, D., ed. Voices & Visions.*
W. Dodge, 168(ECW):Spring88-161
Hillocks, G., Jr. Research on Written Composition.*
R.A. Schwegler, 128(CE):Apr88-444
Hills, P. The Light of Early Italian Painting.
E.S. Barelli, 89(BJA):Winter88-92
M. Kemp, 90:Sep88-698
A. Martindale, 59:Dec88-568
Hills, P., ed. John Singer Sargent.*
W.A. Coles, 432(NEQ):Mar88-122
Hilmy, S.S. The Later Wittgenstein.
D. Freedman, 518:Jul88-133
Hilscher, E. Gerhart Hauptmann.
R. Bernhardt, 654(WB):12/1988-2101
Hilton, B. The Age of Atonement.
J.W. Burrow, 617(TLS):7-13Apr89-358
Hilton, I. Peter Huchel.
S. Parker, 402(MLR):Jul89-808
Hilton, N., ed. Essential Articles for the Study of William Blake, 1970-1984.*
K.E. Smith, 83:Spring88-97
Hilton, R.H. & T.H. Aston, eds. The English Rising of 1381.
B.A. Hanawalt, 589:Apr88-412
Hilzinger, S. "Als ganzer Mensch zu leben..."
I.M. Goessl, 221(GQ):Summer87-505
Hilzinger, S. Christa Wolf.*
A. Stephan, 406:Fall88-407
Himka, J-P. Galician Villagers and the Ukrainian National Movement in the Nineteenth Century.
J. Keep, 617(TLS):21-27Apr89-415
Himmelfarb, G. The New History and the Old.*
P. Divinsky, 529(QQ):Winter88-826
H. Fromm, 249(HudR):Summer88-377
639(VQR):Winter88-15
Himmelfarb, M. Tours of Hell.
C. McDannell, 124:Jan-Feb89-204
Himmelheber, G. Biedermeier: 1815-1835.
J. Russell, 441:3Dec89-77
Himmelheber, G. Biedermeiermöbel.* (rev)
S.J., 90:Jun88-477
Hinago, M. Japanese Castles.
B.A. Coats, 407(MN):Spring88-123
Hinchcliffe, P. & E. Jewinski, eds. Magic Realism and Canadian Literature.*
P. Stevens, 529(QQ):Autumn88-568
Hinderer, W. & H.J. Schmidt - see Büchner, G.
Hinderling, R. - see under Wickham, C.J.
Hindle, P. Maps for Local History.
S. Bendall, 617(TLS):21-27Apr89-426

Hindley, J.R. & J.P. Seldin. Introduction to Combinators and [lambda]-Calculus.
J.L. Krivine, 316:Sep88-985
Hindman, S.L. Christine de Pizan's "Epistre Othéa."
A.T. Harrison, 201:Vol14-217
Hinds, J. Japanese.*
S.E. Martin, 293(JASt):Feb88-144
Hinds, J., S.K. Maynard & S. Iwasaki, eds. Perspectives on Topicalization.
K. Takahara, 350:Dec89-890
Hinds, S. The Metamorphosis of Persephone.
M. von Albrecht, 24:Fall88-461
B.R. Nagle, 124:Jul-Aug89-449
W.S.M. Nicoll, 123:Vol38No2-245
Hindus, M. The Crippled Giant.*
N. Hewitt, 208(FS):Jan88-106
Hindus, M. Essays.
M. Syrkin, 390:Oct88-34
Hine, D. Academic Festival Overtures.
L. Ricou, 102(CanL):Summer88-173
Hine, D.C., ed. The State of Afro-American History.
W.E. Cain, 128(CE):Feb88-190
Hine, T. Populuxe.*
R.G. Liebman, 505:Feb88-149
Hinojosa, R. Claros varones de Belken/Fair Gentlemen of Belken County.
O.U. Somoza, 36:Fall-Winter88-234
Hinojosa, R. Klail City.
A. Ramírez, 238:Mar88-97
L. Torres, 649(WAL):Nov88-251
Hinrichs, B. Utopische Prosa als Längeres Gedankenspiel.
T. Menke, 221(GQ):Summer88-483
W. Paulsen, 301(JEGP):Apr88-313
M.M. Schardt, 680(ZDP):Band107Heft4-634
Hinsch, W. Erfahrung und Selbstbewusstsein.
W. Becker, 342:Band79Heft3-356
Hinske, N. Lebenserfahrung und Philosophie.
W. Farr, 489(PJGG):Band95Heft1-198
Hinson, M. Guide to the Pianist's Repertoire. (2nd ed)
J. Banowetz, 510:Winter87/88-63
C. Ehrlich, 415:Feb88-87
Hintikka, M.B. & J. Investigating Wittgenstein.*
P. Carruthers, 479(PhQ):Apr88-244
R.M. Gomm, 521:Apr88-162
J-M. Monnoyer, 98:Nov88-914
E.M. Zemach, 484(PPR):Sep88-171
Hinton, M., with D.G. Berger. Bass Line.*
E.S., 91:Fall88-259
Hinton, S. Cindy and Myself.
G. Gessert, 448:Vol26No1-73
von Hinüber, O. Das ältere Mittelindisch im Überblick.
J.W. de Jong, 259(IIJ):Apr88-152
Hinz, E.J., ed. "For Better or Worse."*
H. Hoy, 627(UTQ):Fall87-138
Hinz, M. Die Zukunft der Katastrophe.*
E. Leube, 72:Band225Heft1-230
Hinze, C., ed. Das alte Köln in Sagen und Bräuchen.
G. Petschel, 196:Band29Heft1/2-200
Hinzler, H.I.R. Catalogue of Balinese Manuscripts in the Library of the University of Leiden and Other Collections in the Netherlands.
H. Geertz, 293(JASt):Nov88-938

Hippolytus. Refutatio omnium haeresium. (M. Marcovich, ed)
J.N. Birdsall, 123:Vol38No1-149
R.W. Sharples, 303(JoHS):Vol108-243
Hirai, A. Individualism and Socialism.*
A.E. Barshay, 293(JASt):May88-373
B-A. Shillony, 407(MN):Summer88-245
Hirdt, W., ed. Der Bauer im Wandel der Zeit.*
F.H. Bäuml, 133:Band21Heft2/3-202
P. Zimmermann, 52:Band23Heft3-321
Hiro, D. The Longest War.
M. Yapp, 617(TLS):4-10Aug89-842
"Hiroshige: One Hundred Famous Views of Edo."* (French title: Hiroshige: Cent vues célèbres d'Edo.)
P.W. Kroll, 318(JAOS):Oct-Dec87-831
A. Suied, 450(NRF):Feb88-108
M. Takeuchi, 293(JASt):May88-367
Hirsch, E. The Night Parade.
H. Vendler, 453(NYRB):17Aug89-26
Hirsch, E.D., Jr. Cultural Literacy.*
C.T. Asplund, 529(QQ):Summer88-432
R. Scholes, 128(CE):Mar88-323
P. Scott, 128(CE):Mar88-333
639(VQR):Winter88-23
Hirsch, E.D., Jr., with W.G. Rowland, Jr. and M. Stanford, eds. A First Dictionary of Cultural Literacy.
J. Shenker, 441:17Dec89-22
Hirsch, H. Schallplatten zwischen Kunst und Kommerz.
W. Rathert, 416:Band3Heft3-267
Hirsch, K. Songs from the Alley.
D.C. Anderson, 441:16Jul89-25
Hirsch, S.W. The Friendship of the Barbarians.*
S. Hornblower, 123:Vol38No1-144
P.W. Sage, 24:Spring88-139
Hirschhorn, L. The Workplace Within.
H. Rahmanian, 42(AR):Summer88-396
Hirschon, R. Heirs of the Greek Catastrophe.
N. Clive, 617(TLS):4-10Aug89-843
Hirsh, J.C., ed. Barlam and Iosaphat.*
M. Glasscoe, 382(MAE):1988/2-316
R. Hanna 3d, 589:Apr88-414
V.M. O'Mara, 38:Band106Heft3/4-514
M. Rigby, 541(RES):Nov88-553
Hirson, D. The House Next Door to Africa.*
S.E. Olson, 42(AR):Fall88-527
Hirst, D. Authority and Conflict.*
K. Sharpe, 250(HLQ):Spring88-127
Hirst, D.L. Edward Bond.*
M. Göring, 402(MLR):Apr89-428
Hirst, E. & others. Energy Efficiency in Buildings.
D. Watson, 47:Mar88-56
Hirst, M. Michelangelo and His Drawings.*
C. Hope, 453(NYRB):17Aug89-16
D. Summers, 617(TLS):26May-1Jun89-591
Hirst, M. Michelangelo Draftsman.
C. Hope, 453(NYRB):17Aug89-16
Hirst, P.Q. Law, Socialism, and Democracy.
S.L.E., 185:Apr89-667
Hisatoyo Ishida. Esoteric Buddhist Painting. (E.D. Saunders, ed & trans)
M. Saso, 407(MN):Winter88-500
Hiskes, A.L. & R.P. Science, Technology, and Policy Decisions.
C.A.S., 185:Jan89-465
Hitchens, C. Imperial Spoils.* (British title: The Elgin Marbles.)
S. Coates, 441:1Oct89-26
J. Griffin, 453(NYRB):20Jul89-14

Hitchens, C. Prepared for the Worst.
  C.C. O'Brien, 617(TLS):28Apr-4May89-
  447
Hittinger, R. A Critique of the New Natural
Law Theory.
  E.L. Fortin, 543:Jun89-838
  G. Grisez, 438:Autumn88-438
  H.B. Veatch, 438:Summer88-353
Hixson, R.F. Privacy in a Public Society.
  N.E. Bowie, 185:Oct88-161
Hjartarson, P., ed. A Stranger to My Time.
  P. Morley, 298:Winter88/89-159
  J.J. O'Connor, 627(UTQ):Fall88-165
  M. Rubio, 529(QQ):Winter88-934
"Hmong Art, Tradition and Change."
  M.G. Forsythe, 60:Jul-Aug88-125
Hoad, L., ed. Literary Manuscripts at the
National Library of Canada.
  H. Hoy, 102(CanL):Spring88-203
Hoagland, E. Heart's Desire.
  J. Dunford, 441:30Apr89-39
Hobbs, D. Doing the Business.
  P. Smith, 617(TLS):8-14Sep89-971
Hobbs, R. Edward Hopper.
  R. Bass, 55:Apr88-53
  G. Levin, 432(NEQ):Sep88-475
Hobday, C. Edgell Rickword.
  J. Lucas, 617(TLS):3-9Nov89-1204
Hoberg, U. Die Wortstellung in der geschrie-
benen deutschen Gegenwartssprache.
  D. Stellmacher, 685(ZDL):3/1987-364
Hoberman, R. Modernizing Lives.*
  T.S.W. Lewis, 77:Summer88-256
Hobhouse, H. Forces of Change.
  D. Arnold, 617(TLS):25-31Aug89-914
Hobhouse, J. The Bride Stripped Bare.
  A. Graham-Dixon, 617(TLS):24-30Mar89-
  306
Hobhouse, J. November.
  J. Mellors, 364:Feb87-103
Hobsbaum, P. A Reader's Guide to Robert
Lowell.
  M. Hofmann, 617(TLS):26May-1Jun89-
  578
Hobsbawm, E. Politics for a Rational Left.
  R.W. Johnson, 617(TLS):26May-1Jun89-
  569
Hobsbawm, E.J. The Age of Empire 1875-
  1914.*
  H.G. Pitt, 364:Feb88-93
  A. Silvera, 637(VS):Spring89-460
Hobson, C. & others - see Marshall, J.
Hobson, J.A. The Dreaming Brain.*
  B. Farrell, 453(NYRB):15Jun89-28
Hoch, S.L. Serfdom and Social Control in Rus-
sia.
  R.P. Bartlett, 575(SEER):Apr88-292
  B. Eklof, 550(RusR):Jul88-336
Hochberg, H. Logic, Ontology, and Language.
  E. & J. Dölling, 682(ZPSK):Band41Heft4-
  524
Hoche, H-U. & W. Strube. Analytische Phil-
osophie. (E. Ströcker & W. Wieland, eds)
  J. Dölling, 682(ZPSK):Band41Heft4-526
Hochheim, R. & others. Nikolaus Lenau.
  C. Gibbon, 602:Band19Heft1-173
Hochman, E.S. Architects of Fortune.
  W. Marlin, 441:18Jun89-26
Hochschild, A., with A. Machung. The Second
Shift.
  R. Kuttner, 441:25Jun89-3

Hock, H.H. Principles of Historical Linguis-
tics.
  B.D. Joseph, 350:Mar89-162
  A.S. Kaye & A. della Volpe, 603:
  Vol12No2-457
Hockett, C.F. Refurbishing Our Foundations.
  D. Bolinger, 350:Sep89-602
Hockett, C.F. - see Bloomfield, L.
Hockings, P., with C. Pilot-Raichoor. Counsel
from the Ancients.
  W. Bright, 350:Dec89-891
Hodges, D.L. Renaissance Fictions of Anat-
omy.*
  S.K. Heninger, Jr., 131(CL):Fall88-401
Hodges, G.R. New York City Cartmen, 1667-
1850.
  S. Rosswurm, 656(WMQ):Jul88-621
Hodgman, H. Broken Words.
  L. Taylor, 617(TLS):17-23Feb89-170
Hodgman, H. Ducks.
  J. Gummerman, 441:10Dec89-18
Hodgson, A. The Romances of William Morris.
  P. Faulkner, 402(MLR):Apr89-448
Hodin, J.P. Friedrich Karl Gotsch.
  90:Jun88-478
Hodson, L., ed. Marcel Proust: The Critical
Heritage.
  E. Hughes, 617(TLS):13-19Oct89-1112
Hoefert, S. Internationale Bibliographie zum
Werk Gerhart Hauptmanns. (Vol 1)
  I. M. Goessl, 406:Winter88-517
  K.W. Jonas, 301(JEGP):Oct88-607
  G. Oberembt, 680(ZDP):Band107Heft2-304
  P. Skrine, 402(MLR):Jul89-796
van den Hoek, T. & others. Grammaticaal
woordenboek.
  H. Hulshof, 204(FdL):Dec88-318
Hoerder, D., ed. "Struggle a Hard Battle."
  J.H. Silverman, 106:Spring88-99
Hoerr, J.P. And the Wolf Finally Came.
  C.F. Sabel, 441:5Feb89-3
Hoey, A. A Fire in the Cold House of Being.
  R. McDowell, 249(HudR):Autumn88-571
Hofer, E. & E. Barish. Emerson in Italy.
  O. Conant, 441:17Sep89-24
Höffe, O. Introduction à la philosophie pra-
tique de Kant.
  A-M. Roviello, 540(RIPh):Vol42fasc3-383
  A. Stanguennec, 542:Jul-Sep88-333
  R. Theis, 342:Band79Heft3-367
Höffe, O. Sittlich-politische Diskurse.
  E. Fulda, 687:Oct-Dec88-709
Hoffman, D. Hang-Gliding from Helicon.
  A. Hudgins, 249(HudR):Winter89-742
Hoffman, E. Lost in Translation.
  P. Conrad, 441:15Jan89-1
  C. Rumens, 617(TLS):17-23Nov89-1263
Hoffman, E. The Right to Be Human.
  42(AR):Fall88-530
Hoffman, F. Jazz Advertised in the Negro
Press. (Vol 1)
  E. Southern, 91:Fall88-257
Hoffman, L. & M. Culley, eds. Women's Per-
sonal Narratives.
  C.P. Havely, 447(N&Q):Sep88-416
  J. Perreault, 107(CRCL):Jun88-257
von Hoffman, N. Citizen Cohn.*
  A. Katz, 287:Jul/Aug88-29
Hoffmann, D. Frank Lloyd Wright's Robie
House.*
  W.J.R. Curtis, 617(TLS):24-30Mar89-315

Hoffmann, E.T.A. Klein Zaches genannt Zinnober. (G.R. Kaiser, ed) Klein Zaches genannt Zinnober: Ein Märchen.
  H. Steinecke, 680(ZDP):Band106Heft4-625
Hoffmann, F. & G. Albert, comps. The Cashbox Album Charts 1955-1974. The Cashbox Album Charts 1975-1985.
  R.S. Denisoff, 498:Summer88-85
Hoffmann, J. Die Welt der Begriffe.
  R. Blutner, 682(ZPSK):Band41Heft6-815
Hoffmann, L-F. Essays on Haitian Literature.
  J-L. Joubert, 535(RHL):Jan-Feb88-163
Hoffmann, M.E. Negatio contrarii.
  I. Kajanto, 229:Band60Heft4-362
Hoffmann, P. German Resistance to Hitler.
  639(VQR):Autumn88-117
Hoffmann, P. Symbolismus.
  H.R. Klieneberger, 402(MLR):Jul89-797
  M. Winkler, 221(GQ):Fall88-589
Hoffmann, W. Das "Nibelungenlied."
  M.E. Gibbs, 406(Winter88-506
Hoffmeister, G. Deutsche und europäische Barockliteratur.
  P. Skrine, 402(MLR):Jul89-778
Hoffmeister, G., ed. Der moderne deutsche Schelmenroman.
  G.R. Hoyt, 133:Band21Heft2/3-256
  I.E. Hunt, 221(GQ):Fall88-602
Höffner, J.C. Economic Systems and Economic Ethics.
  P.H., 185:Oct88-208
Hoffpauir, R. Romantic Fallacies.
  L. Mathews, 178:Mar88-104
Hofland, K., K. Natvig & H. Noreng. Henrik Ibsens ordskatt.
  A. Aarseth, 172(Edda):1988/3-282
Höfler, J. Die Tafelmalerei der Gotik in Kärnten, 1420-1500.
  C. Grössinger, 90:May88-374
Hofman, M. & J. Morehen, comps. Latin Music in British Sources c. 1485 - c. 1610.
  I. Rumbold, 415:Dec88-691
Hofmann, D. & M.J. Greenberg. Sport$biz.
  A. Barra, 441:11Jun89-44
Hofmann, L. Exempelkatalog zu Martin Pruggers Beispielkatechismus von 1824.
  H. Schade, 196:Band29Heft1/2-200
Hofmann, M. Acrimony.*
  J. Saunders, 565:Autumn88-72
  H. Vendler, 453(NYRB):17Aug89-26
Hofmann, P. The Viennese.*
  M. Ignatieff, 453(NYRB):29Jun89-21
"Hofmannsthal-Forschungen 8." (W. Mauser, ed)
  M.K.E. Hoppe, 221(GQ):Summer87-489
Hofstein, F. Au Miroir du jazz.
  A.J.M.P., 91:Spring88-114
Hofstetter, W. Winchester und der spätaltenglische Sprachgebrauch.
  C. van Kerckvoorde, 350:Mar89-183
Hogan, D. A Link With the River.
  D. Donoghue, 441:16Jul89-3
Hogan, J.C. A Commentary on the Complete Greek Tragedies: Aeschylus.
  S. Fineberg, 124:May-Jun89-389
Hogan, L. Seeing Through the Sun.
  R. Pybus, 565:Summer88-72
Hogan, P. The Lawn.
  D.P. Myers, 576:Sep88-310
Hogate, A. The Art in Structural Design.
  M.S. Stubbs, 47:Mar88-49

Hoge, J.O., ed. Literary Reviewing.*
  P. Harkin, 40(AEB):Vol2No3-129
  P.J. Klemp, 365:Spring/Summer87-151
  G.B. Tennyson, 445(NCF):Jun88-137
Högemann, P. Alexander der Grosse und Arabien.*
  S. Hornblower, 123:Vol38No2-435
Hogg, J. Selected Poems and Songs.* (D. Groves, ed)
  I. Campbell, 447(N&Q):Jun88-246
  J. Rubenstein, 588(SSL):Vol23-291
Hogg, J. - see Keller, H.
Hogg, R. Heat Lightning.
  R. Berry, 102(CanL):Autumn88-147
Hogg, R. & C.B. McCully. Metrical Phonology.*
  M. Jessen, 361:Sep88-99
Hoggart, R. A Local Habitation.* (Vol 1)
  R. Fuller, 364:Dec88/Jan89-139
Hogsett, C. The Literary Existence of Germaine de Staël.*
  G.R. Besser, 207(FR):Apr89-891
  N. Le Coat, 400(MLN):Sep88-960
Hohendahl, P.U., ed. Geschichte der deutschen Literaturkritik (1730-1980).
  M.T. Jones, 221(GQ):Fall87-644
Hohendahl, P.U. Literarische Kultur im Zeitalter des Liberalismus 1830-1870.*
  J.M. Ellis, 131(CL):Winter88-90
  W. Paulsen, 406:Summer88-229
  J.M. Peck, 221(GQ):Winter87-129
Hohmann, C. Thomas Pynchon's "Gravity's Rainbow."
  S. Moore, 532(RCF):Summer88-321
Hoile, D. Mozambique.
  J. Harding, 617(TLS):20-26Oct89-1161
Hokenson, J. & H. Pearce, eds. Forms of the Fantastic.
  R. Steele, 188(ECr):Fall88-90
"Hokusai: One Hundred Views of Mount Fuji."
  A. Stewart, 324:Oct89-754
Holaday, A., G.B. Evans & T.L. Berger - see Chapman, G.
Holbek, B. Interpretation of Fairy Tales.
  S.S. Jones, 650(WF):Oct88-310
  W. Scherf, 196:Band29Heft1/2-202
Holbrook, C.A. Jonathan Edwards: The Valley and Nature: An Interpretative Essay.*
  S.G.P., 185:Oct88-204
Holbrook, D. Evolution and the Humanities.*
  R. Barton, 637(VS):Winter89-276
  M. Stuart-Fox, 115:Summer88-318
  M. Stuart-Fox, 381:Summer88-762
Holbrook, D. The Novel and Authenticity.
  P. Swinden, 447(N&Q):Sep88-410
Holbrook, D. Qualitative Utilitarianism.
  J.R., 185:Jul89-967
Holden, A. Laurence Olivier.*
  M. Hoyle, 511:Aug88-42
Holden, A.J., ed. Le Roman de Waldef (Cod. Bodmer 168).*
  I. Short, 208(FS):Oct88-460
Holden, A.J. - see Chrétien de Troyes
Holden, H. After the Fact.*
  S. Whaley, 102(CanL):Spring88-136
Holden, J. Style and Authenticity in Postmodern Poetry.
  T.O., 295(JML):Fall87/Winter88-270
Holden, M. Selected Poems.*
  D. Sutton, 493:Summer88-51
Holden, U. A Bubble Garden.
  P. Craig, 617(TLS):3-9Feb89-113
  D. Durrant, 364:Dec88/Jan89-136

Hölderlin, F. Friedrich Hölderlin: Essays and Letters on Theory. (T. Pfau, ed & trans)
    H. Gaskill, 402(MLR):Jul89−783
Hölderlin, F. Hymne an die Heiterkeit.* (R. Breymayer, ed)
    P. Hayden-Roy, 221(GQ):Summer87−477
Holderness, G. D.H. Lawrence.
    J.E. Michaels, 268(IFR):Winter89−89
Holderness, G., ed. The Shakespearean Myth.
    R. Hapgood, 617(TLS):25−31Aug89−927
Holderness, G., N. Potter & J. Turner. Shakespeare.
    R. Hapgood, 617(TLS):25−31Aug89−927
Holdstock, P. The Blackbird's Song.
    M. Kenyon, 376:Mar88−93
Holdsworth, C. & T.P. Wiseman, eds. The Inheritance of Historiography, 350−900.
    J.M. Alonso-Núñez, 123:Vol38No1−160
    H−W. Goetz, 229:Band60Heft1−51
Holgate, D. New Hall.*
    R. Hildyard, 39:Oct88−296
Holl, H.P. Gotthelf im Zeitgeflecht.
    E. Gallati, 133:Band21Heft2/3−233
    G.K. Hart, 221(GQ):Winter87−124
Holland, H. The Iceland Journal of Henry Holland 1810. (A. Wawn, ed)
    P.M. Mitchell, 562(Scan):Nov88−183
Holland, V. Son of Oscar Wilde.
    P. Craig, 617(TLS):7−13Apr89−362
Hollander, A. Moving Pictures.
    M. Vaizey, 441:17Sep89−22
Hollander, J. Harp Lake.
    J. Parini, 441:22Oct89−16
Hollander, J. In Time and Place.*
    S. Cushman, 473(PR):Vol55No3−493
Hollander, J. Melodious Guile.
    L. Mackinnon, 617(TLS):11−17Aug89−880
Hollander, J. − see Bloom, H.
Hollander, L.M. − see "The Poetic Edda"
Hollander, R. Il Virgilo dantesco.
    Z.G. Barański, 545(RPh):Aug88−51
Holley, M. The Poetry of Marianne Moore.
    L. Leavell, 365:Winter88−48
    639(VQR):Summer88−100
Hollier, D., ed. The College of Sociology, 1937−1939.
    D. Coward, 617(TLS):4−10Aug89−857
Hollier, D. The Politics of Prose.
    C.S. Brosman, 478(P&L):Oct88−321
    P. Carrard, 210(FrF):May88−254
    D. Polan, 494:Vol8No3/4−706
Hollingdale, R.J. − see Nietzsche, F.
Hollinghurst, A. The Swimming-Pool Library.*
    J. Mellors, 364:Jun88−100
Hollingsworth, M. Willful Acts.
    D. Rubin, 168(ECW):Spring88−135
Hollis, M. The Cunning of Reason.*
    A.C. Birch, 543:Dec88−389
Hollis, M. Invitation to Philosophy.
    R. Crisp, 291:Vol5No2−233
Holloway, J., ed. The Oxford Book of Local Verses.*
    J. Simpson, 203:Vol99No1−130
Holloway, K.F.C. The Character of the Word.
    K. Byerman, 395(MFS):Winter88−634
    C.N. Pondrom, 27(AL):May88−306
Holloway, K.F.C. & S. Demetrakopoulos. New Dimensions of Spirituality.
    K. Byerman, 395(MFS):Winter88−634
Hollyman, S. We the Homeless.
    R. Lippincott, 441:16Apr89−21
Holman, M. − see Hwang Sun-won

Holmes, G. Florence, Rome and the Origin of the Renaissance.
    M. McLaughlin, 382(MAE):1988/1−142
    G. Mazzotta, 551(RenQ):Spring88−112
Holmes, J.C. Passionate Opinions.
    C. Cagle, 389(MQ):Summer89−531
Holmes, J.C. Representative Men.*
    C. Cagle, 389(MQ):Winter89−258
Holmes, R. Coleridge.
    S. Gill, 617(TLS):3−9Nov89−1203
Holoman, D.K. Catalogue of the Works of Hector Berlioz.
    J. Warrack, 617(TLS):24Feb−2Mar89−187
Holroyd, M. Bernard Shaw.* (Vol 1)
    J. Symons, 364:Dec88/Jan89−121
    J. Updike, 442(NY):2Jan89−62
Holroyd, M. Bernard Shaw. (Vol 2)
    J. Gross, 453(NYRB):21Dec89−27
    M. Peters, 441:17Sep89−9
    J. Sutherland, 617(TLS):8−14Sep89−965
Hölscher, L. The Reality of the Mind.*
    B. Bubacz, 319:Jan89−148
Holst, I. The Music of Gustav Holst. (3rd ed)
    A. Frogley, 410(M&L):Jan88−110
Holstun, J. A Rational Millennium.*
    J.A.L. Lemay, 27(AL):May88−290
Holt, E.G., ed. The Expanding World of Art, 1874-1902.* (Vol 1)
    M.L. Clausen, 576:Dec88−423
Holt, M.P. & G.W. Woodyard, eds. Drama Contemporary: Latin America.*
    R.A. Kerr, 238:Mar88−103
    E.C. Ramirez, 615(TJ):Dec88−572
Holt, R. Sport and the British.
    J. Walvin, 617(TLS):10−16Nov89−1248
Höltgen, K.J. Aspects of the Emblem.*
    T.A.B., 179(ES):Oct88−464
    H. Kelliher, 38:Band106Heft3/4−527
    J. Manning, 541(RES):May88−327
Höltgen, K.J. & others, eds. Tradition und Innovation in der englischen und amerikanischen Lyrik des 20. Jahrhunderts.
    N. Kohl, 72:Band225Heft1−183
Holthoer, R. & T. Linders, eds. Sundries − in Honour of Torgny Säve-Söderbergh.
    P. Lacovara, 318(JAOS):Jul−Sep87−549
Holthusen, H.E. Gottfried Benn.
    M. Winkler, 221(GQ):Fall87−684
Holtmeier, K. Religiöse Elemente in der sowjetrussischen Gegenwartsliteratur.
    H. Röhling, 688(ZSP):Band48Heft2−410
Holton, M. & H. Kuhner, eds & trans. Austrian Poetry Today/Österreichische Lyrik heute.
    B. Bjorklund, 222(GR):Spring88−108
Holtus, G., ed. La versione franco-italiana della "Bataille d'Aliscans."*
    E. Blasco Ferrer, 379(MedR):Aug86−299
    R.F. Cook, 589:Jul88−683
Holtus, G. & J. Kramer, eds. Romania et Slavia Adriatica.
    J.E. Joseph, 350:Jun89−373
Holtus, G. & E. Radtke, eds. Gesprochenes Italienisch in Geschichte und Gegenwart.
    J. Kramer, 72:Band224Heft2−441
Holtus, G. & E. Radtke, eds. Sprachlicher Substandard.
    T. Stehl, 547(RF):Band100Heft4−351
Holtus, G. & K. Ringger, eds. Raetia antiqua et moderna.
    D. Messner, 547(RF):Band100Heft4−381
Holtz, L., with J. Heisler. The Fighting Spirit.
    M.E. O'Connell, 441:19Nov89−44

Hopkinson, L.P. Nothing to Forgive.*
  H. Mantel, 364:Dec88/Jan89-130
Hopkinson, N., ed. Callimachus: "Hymn to Demeter."*
  A. Griffiths, 303(JoHS):Vol108-230
Hoppe, H. Sintassi e stile di Tertulliano. (G. Allegri, ed)
  R. Braun, 555:Vol61fasc2-333
Höppe, W. Karl Marx - Friedrich Engels.
  D. Stellmacher, 685(ZDL):1/1988-81
Hoppen, K.T. Elections, Politics, and Society in Ireland 1832-1885.
  R.E. Ward, 174(Éire):Spring88-145
Hoppen, K.T. Ireland since 1800.
  G. Ó Tuathaigh, 617(TLS):15-21Dec89-1394
Horace. The Epistles. (C. Macleod, trans)
  R. Mayer, 123:Vol38No1-26
Horace. Q. Horati Flacci Opera. (D.R. Shackleton Bailey, ed)
  J. Delz, 229:Band60Heft6-495
  D. Mankin, 24:Summer88-270
  R. Renehan, 122:Oct88-311
Horace. Horatius Opera. (S. Borzsák, ed)
  D. Mankin, 24:Summer88-270
Horak, S.M. Russia, the USSR, and Eastern Europe.
  W. Zalewski, 497(PolR):Vol33No3-363
Höricht, L.A.S. - see under Scatozza Höricht, L.A.
Hörisch, J. Gott, Geld und Glück.
  E. Wright, 494:Vol8No2-454
Horn, M. Der holsteinische Niederelberaum.
  H. Menke, 685(ZDL):2/1988-232
Hornblower, S. Thucydides.
  A.L. Boegehold, 124:Jan-Feb89-202
Hornby, R. Drama, Metadrama, and Perception.*
  G.G. Cima, 615(TJ):Dec87-545
  S. Stone-Blackburn, 49:Apr88-93
Horne, A. Harold Macmillan.* (Vol 1: 1894-1956)
  D. Cannadine, 453(NYRB):27Apr89-36
  P. Jenkins, 441:5Mar89-1
Horne, A. Harold Macmillan. (Vol 2: 1957-1986.)
  P. Brendon, 441:26Nov89-11
  P. Clarke, 617(TLS):23-29Jun89-679
  H. Young, 453(NYRB):23Nov89-47
Horne, D. The Great Museum.
  D.B. Driscoll, 658:Summer/Autumn88-197
Horner, J. Recent Mistakes.
  S. Scobie, 376:Sep88-162
Horner, J.R. & J. Gorman. Digging Dinosaurs.*
  P-L. Adams, 61:Jun89-98
Horner, P.J., ed. The Index of Middle English Prose: Handlist III.*
  V. Gillespie, 382(MAE):1988/1-112
  S.J. Ogilvie-Thomson, 541(RES):May88-284
  O.S. Pickering, 72:Band224Heft2-390
Horner, W.B., ed. The Present State of Scholarship in Historical and Contemporary Rhetoric.
  B. Vickers, 402(MLR):Apr89-455
Hornig, C. Giorgiones Spätwerk.
  P. Holberton, 90:Jul88-537
Horning, A.S. Teaching Writing as a Second Language.
  A. Raimes, 126(CCC):May88-249
Hornsby, D. & D. Sukarna, with J-A. Parry. Read On.
  J. Coady, 350:Dec89-892

Hornschuch, H. Orthotypographia, lateinisch/deutsch.
  J.L. Flood, 354:Dec88-358
Hornung, E., with A. Brodbeck & E. Staehelin. Das Buch von den Pforten des Jenseits. (Pt 2)
  E.S. Meltzer, 318(JAOS):Jul-Sep87-544
Hornung, M. - see Kranzmayer, E.
Horobin, G., ed. Sex, Gender and Care Work.
  E.P.S., 185:Jan89-462
Horosz, W. Search without Idols.
  C.L. Mui, 103:Jan89-16
  M.N-S., 185:Oct88-191
Horowitz, A. Rousseau, Nature and History.
  A. Rosenberg, 627(UTQ):Fall88-127
Horowitz, D.L. Ethnic Groups in Conflict.*
  R. Provencher, 293(JASt):Nov88-839
Horowitz, I.L. Communicating Ideas.*
  G. Garrett, 569(SR):Summer88-516
Horowitz, J. Understanding Toscanini.*
  D. Matthews, 410(M&L):Apr88-291
Horowitz, M. Karl Kraus.
  L.A. Lensing, 221(GQ):Spring88-287
Horrall, S.M. - see Thomas of Hales
Horrocks, G. Generative Grammar.
  G.S. Nathan, 350:Sep89-664
Horrox, R. Richard III.
  D. Starkey, 617(TLS):8-14Sep89-981
Horsford, H.C., with L. Horth - see Melville, H.
Horton, H.M. - see Nishi, K. & K. Hozumi
Horvath, B.M. Variation in Australian English.*
  L. Milroy, 355(LSoc):Dec88-577
Horvath, J. Focus in the Theory of Grammar and the Syntax of Hungarian.*
  L.K. Marácz, 603:Vol12No1-199
  M.S. Rochemont, 353:Vol26No2-319
Horwitt, S.D. Let Them Call Me Rebel.
  N. Lichtenstein, 441:12Nov89-23
Horwood, H. Dancing on the Shore.
  W.M. Bogaards, 627(UTQ):Fall88-148
Horwood, H. Remembering Summer.
  S.G. Mullins, 102(CanL):Autumn88-166
Hoskins, W.G. The Making of the English Landscape.
  T. O'Riordan, 617(TLS):31Mar-6Apr89-348
Hösle, J. Das italienische Theater von der Renaissance bis zur Gegenreformation.
  W.T. Elwert, 72:Band225Heft1-229
Hösle, V. Hegels System.
  M.W. Roche, 319:Oct89-630
  R. Schürmann, 543:Dec88-387
Hospital, J.T. Charades.
  R. Loewinsohn, 441:12Mar89-14
Hospital, J.T. Dislocations.*
  P.A. Taylor, 102(CanL):Spring88-238
Hoston, G.A. Marxism and the Crisis of Development in Prewar Japan.*
  A.H. Ion, 529(QQ):Summer88-498
Hotman, F. La Vie de Messire Gaspar de Colligny Admiral de France. (E-V. Telle, ed)
  K. Cameron, 402(MLR):Jan89-163
  J. Przybylak, 539:Summer89-247
Hottois, G., ed. Philosophies et sciences.
  A. Reix, 542:Jul-Sep88-383
Hough, J. Russia and the West.*
  A.G. Meyer, 385(MQR):Fall89-771
Hough, R. & D. Richards. The Battle of Britain.
  N. Annan, 453(NYRB):28Sep89-3
  D. Henahan, 441:31Dec89-11

Houghton, S.G. A Trace of Desert Waters.
N.J. Warner, 649(WAL):Nov88–238
Houghton, W.E., E.R. Houghton & J.H. Slinger-
land, eds. The Wellesley Index to Victorian
Periodicals, 1824–1900.* (Vol 4)
P.L. Shillingsburg, 40(AEB):Vol2No3–126
G.B. Tennyson, 445(NCF):Sep88–276
Houle, G. Meter in Music, 1600–1800.
E.T. Boal, 415:Jun88–300
Houle, G. & G. – see Paras, J.
Houlgate, L.D. Family and State.
F. Schoeman, 185:Apr89–651
Houlgate, S. Hegel, Nietzsche and the Criti-
cism of Metaphysics.
D.W. Conway, 543:Sep88–145
Hourani, G.F. Reason and Tradition in Islamic
Ethics.*
L.V. Berman, 589:Apr88–416
House, K.S. – see Cooper, J.F.
Housley, N. The Avignon Papacy and the
Crusaders, 1305–1378.
J.G. Rowe, 589:Jul88–685
Houston, J.D. The Men in My Life.
D.A. Carpenter, 649(WAL):May88–75
Houston, J.P. Patterns of Thought in Rimbaud
and Mallarmé.*
C.A. Hackett, 208(FS):Jan88–101
J. Lawler, 210(FrF):Jan88–121
Houston, R.A. & I.D. Whyte, eds. Scottish
Society 1500–1800.
G. Donaldson, 617(TLS):18–24Aug89–891
Houts, P.S., P.C. Cleary & T–W. Hu. The Three
Mile Island Crisis.
T. O'Riordan, 617(TLS):17–23Mar89–272
Hovannisian, R.G. The Republic of Armenia.
(Vol 2)
J.R. Russell, 318(JAOS):Apr–Jun87–381
Howard, A. RAB.
H.G. Pitt, 364:Apr–May87–144
Howard, B. Northern Interior.
W.J. Smith, 502(PrS):Summer88–138
Howard, D., comp. Directory of Theatre Re-
sources.
A. Cameron, 610:Spring88–70
Howard, D. From Marx to Kant.*
P. Livet, 192(EP):Jul–Sep88–441
Howard, D., ed. Philip Massinger.*
C. Milsum, 481(PQ):Summer88–385
Howard, D.R. Chaucer.*
42(AR):Winter88–122
Howard, J. & J. Watters. Jean Howard's
Hollywood.
J. Didion, 453(NYRB):21Dec89–3
D. Dunne, 441:3Dec89–12
Howard, J.E. Shakespeare's Art of Orchestra-
tion.*
J.L. Levenson, 627(UTQ):Winter87/88–
321
Howard, L. Essays on Puritans and Puritan-
ism. (J. Barbour & T. Quirk, eds)
M.A. Bellesiles, 106:Jun88–233
P. Lindholdt, 569(SR):Summer88–464
F. Shuffelton, 165(EAL):Vol24No1–75
Howard, M. The Early Tudor Country House.
G. Roberts, 59:Sep88–463
Howard, P. Breaking the Iron Rice Bowl.
G. Bennett, 293(JASt):Nov88–853
Howard, S. Gone With the Wind. (H. Bridges &
T.C. Boodman, eds)
D. Finkle, 441:10Dec89–7
Howard, V., with M. Reynolds. The Macken-
zie–Papineau Battalion.
G.W., 102(CanL):Winter87–290

Howarth, D. Lord Arundel and His Circle.*
J.M. Muller, 600:Vol18No3–172
K. Sharpe, 250(HLQ):Spring88–106
Howarth, D. & S. Lord Nelson.
D.A. Hofmann, 441:26Mar89–17
Howarth, J. & G. Ross, eds. Contemporary
France. (Vol 1)
K.A. Reader, 208(FS):Jul88–370
Howarth, W.D., C. Duckworth & J. Balcou – see
de Voltaire, F.M.A.
Howat, R. – see Eigeldinger, J–J.
Howatch, S. Glamorous Powers.
L.B. Osborne, 441:29Jan89–30
Howatch, S. Ultimate Prizes.
E. Pall, 441:19Nov89–24
Howatson, M.C., ed. The Oxford Companion to
Classical Literature. (2nd ed)
C.H. Sisson, 617(TLS):11–17Aug89–876
Howe, A. & R. Waller, eds. En Marge du Clas-
sicisme.
N.A. Peacock, 610:Summer88–157
Howe, E. The London Bookbinders, 1780–
1806.
W. Gardner, 324:Oct89–751
Howe, E.T. Mystical Imagery.
C. Swietlicki, 304(JHP):Autumn88–79
Howe, F. The Lives of a Spirit.
D. Kolokithas, 703:Fall88–181
Howe, I. The American Newness.*
D.W. Levy, 223:Fall88–374
Howe, I., R.R. Wisse & K. Shmeruk, eds. The
Penguin Book of Modern Yiddish Verse.*
M.J. Mirsky, 390:Aug/Sep88–63
A. Novershtern, 508:Sep88–355
S.S. Prawer, 617(TLS):10–16Mar89–257
Howe, M.J. The Mother Shadow.
M. Stasio, 441:27Aug89–22
Howe, N. The Old English Catalogue Poems.*
J.F. Kiteley, 382(MAE):1988/1–97
R.A. Shoaf, 223:Spring88–117
Howell, A. Why I May Never See the Walls of
China.*
S. Rae, 364:Mar87–87
Howell, B. Joy Ride.
J. Krauss, 441:25Jun89–24
Howell, B. Wuthering Depths.
T. Fitton, 617(TLS):14–20Apr89–404
Howell, C. Sea Change.
J. McDougall, 389(MQ):Spring89–388
Howell, D.W. Patriarchs and Parasites.
P.D.G. Thomas, 83:Autumn88–209
Howell, J. Smoke Signals.
S. O'Brien, 617(TLS):25–31Aug89–916
B. Turner, 493:Winter88/89–61
Howell, M.C. Women, Production, and Patri-
archy in Late Medieval Cities.*
D. Nicholas, 589:Jan88–170
Howell, P., M. Lock & S. Cobb, eds. The Jong-
lei Canal.
A. De Waal, 617(TLS):20–26Oct89–1161
Howell, R.C. The Royal Navy and the Slave
Trade.
D. Eltis, 637(VS):Summer89–587
Howells, C.A. Private and Fictional Words.*
H. Lutz, 49:Oct88–94
S. Neuman, 627(UTQ):Fall88–143
Howells, E.M. If Not Literature. (G.D. Merrill
& G. Arms, eds)
E.H. Cady, 27(AL):Dec88–673
Howells, R.J. Rousseau: "Julie, ou La Nou-
velle Héloïse."
A–M. Ashworth, 402(MLR):Apr89–475

Howells, R.J. & others, eds. Voltaire and his World.*
    C. Mervaud, 535(RHL):Jan–Feb88–127
Hower, A. & R.A. Preto-Rodas. Empire in Transition.
    M.L. Smolen, 238:Mar88–77
Howie, J., ed. Ethical Principles and Practice.
    J.V., 185:Apr89–662
    P. Vallentyne, 103:Oct89–416
Hoy, A. Fabrications.
    R.B. Woodward, 55:Sep88–101
Hoy, C.M. A Philosophy of Individual Freedom.
    J.W. Grove, 488:Sep88–422
Hoy, D., ed. Michel Foucault.
    J. Frow, 381:Autumn88–144
    J. Frow, 381:Winter88–353
Hoy, D.C., ed. Foucault.
    K. Minogue, 144:Winter89–138
Hoy, J. & T. Isern. Plain Folk.
    G.F. Day, 649(WAL):Aug88–175
Hoy, P. Les Carnets bibliographiques de la revue des lettres modernes.
    T. Mathews, 208(FS):Apr88–226
Høystad, O.M. Odin i Juvikfolke.
    E. Vannebo, 172(Edda):1988/3–274
Hoyt, E.P. The Death of the U-Boats.
    639(VQR):Summer88–85
Hrabal, B. I Served the King of England.* (French title: Moi qui ai servi le Roi d'Angleterre.)
    D.J. Enright, 453(NYRB):18May89–37
    R. Lourie, 441:19Mar89–13
    J. Naughton, 617(TLS):12–18May89–519
Hrotswitha of Gandersheim. The Plays of Hrotswitha of Gandersheim. (L. Bonfante & A. Bonfante-Warren, eds & trans)
    R.P. Sonkowsky, 124:May–Jun89–390
Hryciw-Wing, C.A. John Hawkes.
    D.J. Greiner, 534(RALS):Vol16No1&2–267
    P.F. Murphy, 87(BB):Sep88–213
Hsia, R.P-C., ed. The German People and the Reformation.
    A. Hamilton, 617(TLS):23–29Jun89–683
Hsia, R.P-C. The Myth of Ritual Murder.
    G.R. Elton, 453(NYRB):19Jan89–48
Hsu Tao-ching. The Chinese Conception of the Theatre.*
    P. Lovrick, 397(MD):Dec88–598
Hsun, C. & Kao Ch'un-ming – see under Chou Hsun & Kao Ch'un-ming
Huang Tsung-hsi. The Records of Ming Scholars. (J. Ching, with C. Fang & others, eds & trans)
    B.A. Elman, 293(JASt):May88–351
Hubala, E. Balthasar Neumann – seine Kunst zu bauen.
    H. Lorenz, 90:Jul88–540
Hubbard, T.K. The Pindaric Mind.
    W.J. Verdenius, 394:Vol41fasc1/2–136
Hubbell, S. A Book of Bees.*
    T.C. Holyoke, 42(AR):Fall88–523
    E. Perényi, 453(NYRB):16Feb89–8
Hubbell, S. A Country Year.
    E. Perényi, 453(NYRB):16Feb89–8
Hubbs, J. Mother Russia.
    M. Warner, 441:5Mar89–28
Huber, K., ed. Rätisches Namenbuch III.*
    W. Dahmen, 547(RF):Band99Heft4–438
Huberman, J.H. Late Victorian Farce.*
    J.W. Stedman, 637(VS):Autumn88–121
    R.W. Strang, 610:Spring88–61

Hubert, R.R. Surrealism and the Book.
    R. Cardinal, 617(TLS):29Sep–5Oct89–1064
    R. Hattendorf, 207(FR):Mar89–674
Hubka, T.C. Big House, Little House, Back House, Barn.*
    H.W. Marshall, 576:Jun88–209
Hübler, A. Einander verstehen.
    K-D. Barnickel, 38:Band106Heft3/4–442
Hübner, J. Zweymahl zwey und funffzig Auserlesene Biblische Historien Aus dem Alten und Neuen Testamente, Der Jugend zum Besten abgefasset. (R. Lachmann & C. Reents, eds)
    R. Schenda, 196:Band29Heft1/2–206
Hübner, K. Die Wahrheit des Mythos.*
    P. Marcou, 167:Jan88–139
Huchel, R., general ed. Sinn und Form.
    P. Brady, 617(TLS):30Jun–6Jul89–721
Huddle, D. The High Spirits.
    S. Lowell, 441:24Sep89–9
Huddleston, R. English Grammar.
    H.S. Kim, 608:Dec89–693
Hudgins, A. After the Lost War.
    P. Breslin, 491:Oct88–30
    P. Filkins, 363(LitR):Winter89–241
    L. Rector, 249(HudR):Summer88–396
Hudson, A. Lollards and their Books.*
    J. Frankis, 541(RES):Feb88–100
Hudson, B. Justice through Punishment.
    H.A.B., 185:Oct88–206
Hudson, C. Playing in the Sand.
    R. Brain, 617(TLS):20–26Oct89–1150
Hudson, D.W. & M.J. Mancini, eds. Understanding Maritain.
    F.J. Crosson, 103:Jul89–270
    J.P. Hittinger, 543:Dec88–390
Hudson, H.D., Jr. The Rise of the Demidov Family and the Russian Iron Industry in the Eighteenth Century.
    T. Esper, 550(RusR):Apr88–184
Hudson, K. Museums of Influence.
    B.F. Tolles, Jr., 658:Winter88–292
Hudson, M. Our Grandmothers' Drums.
    E. Gillies, 617(TLS):4–10Aug89–844
Hudson, N. Mobile Homes.
    L. Irvine, 102(CanL):Winter87–264
    P. Stevens, 529(QQ):Autumn88–568
    E. Thompson, 198:Winter86–104
Hudson, P. The Genesis of Industrial Capital.
    R. Glen, 637(VS):Winter89–237
    B.F. Duckham, 83:Autumn88–208
Hudspeth, R.N. – see Fuller, M.
Huebert, R. – see Shirley, J.
Huebner, W. Michel Butor auf der Harburg.
    D. Shepheard, 402(MLR):Oct89–1000
Hueckstedt, R.A. The Style of Bāṇa.*
    E. Gerow, 318(JAOS):Apr–Jun87–361
    D.L. Gitomer, 293(JASt):May88–400
Hueppauf, B., ed. Expressionismus und Kulturkrise.
    A. Arnold, 107(CRCL):Mar88–153
Huer, J. Art, Beauty, and Pornography.
    T.A. Gracyk, 289:Summer88–121
Hufeland, C.W. Makrobiotik oder die Kunst, das menschliche Leben zu verlängern.
    R.M., 342:Band79Heft2–251
Huffington, A.S. Picasso.*
    A. Berman, 55:Sep88–101
    D. Rees, 324:Dec88–66
Huggan, I. The Elizabeth Stories.
    L. Dawson-Evans, 565:Summer88–54

Huggett, R. Binkie Beaumont.
J. Wilders, 617(TLS):24-30Mar89-301
Hughes, G.J., ed. The Philosophical Assess-
ment of Theology.
L. Moonan, 518:Jul88-190
Hughes, H.S. Sophisticated Rebels.
P. Schneider, 441:8Jan89-8
Hughes, J. Pastors and Visionaries.
R.B. Dobson, 617(TLS):15-21Sep89-1008
Hughes, J.M. Reshaping the Psychoanalytic
Domain.
P.L. Rudnytsky, 617(TLS):7-13Jul89-750
Hughes, L. The Big Sea.
R.D.B., 295(JML):Fall87/Winter88-332
Hughes, L.K. The Manyfacèd Glass.*
S. Shatto, 447(N&Q):Dec88-549
Hughes, M. Blaine's Way.
D.W. Atkinson, 102(CanL):Spring88-143
Hughes, M. – see Cardus, N.
Hughes, R. The Fatal Shore.*
J. Neville, 364:Feb87-91
Hughes, R.S. Beyond the Red Pony.
S. Pinsker, 573(SSF):Spring88-164
Hughes, T. Moon-Whales. Tales of the Early
World.
W. Magee, 493:Autumn88-13
Hughes, T. Gabrielle Roy et Margaret Laur-
ence. (2nd ed)
R. Benson, 627(UTQ):Fall88-189
Hughes, T. Wolfwatching. Moortown Diary.
J. Lucas, 617(TLS):20-26Oct89-1148
Hughes, T.P. American Genesis.
D. Joravsky, 453(NYRB):7Dec89-11
R. Minkoff, 441:25Jun89-25
Hugo, V. Ruy Blas. (G. Rosa, ed)
S.L. Fairchild, 446(NCFS):Spring-Sum-
mer89-439
Huidobro, M.M. – see under Montes Huidobro,
M.
Huld, M.E. Basic Albanian Etymologies.
N. Boretzky, 260(IF):Band93-309
Hull, D.L. Business and Technical Com-
munication.
T. Dukes, 40(AEB):Vol2No2-78
Hull, D.L. Science as a Process.*
M. Ridley, 617(TLS):12-18May89-503
Hull, G.T. Color, Sex and Poetry.
W.L. Howard, 219(GaR):Fall88-638
Hull, N.E.H. Female Felons.
T.L. Ditz, 656(WMQ):Jul88-594
N.H. Rafter, 432(NEQ):Jun88-277
Hulme, P. Colonial Encounters.*
R.J.P. Williams, 366:Autumn88-233
K. Williamson, 541(RES):Feb88-153
Hülser, K. Die Fragmente zur Dialektik der
Stoiker.* (Vol 1)
J. Barnes, 123:Vol38No1-65
Hult, D.F. Self-fulfilling Prophecies.*
J. Brumlik, 345(KRQ):May88-231
J. Hill, 208(FS):Jul88-335
N.J. Lacy, 207(FR):Oct88-161
A. Leupin, 494:Vol8No3/4-727
K.D. Uitti, 210(FrF):Sep88-365
Hulten, P., ed. Futurism and Futurisms.
N.V. Halliday, 39:Apr88-299
139:Apr/May88-18
Hulten, P., N. Dumitresco & A. Istrati. Con-
stantin Brancusi.* (P. Egan, ed & trans)
E. Shanes, 39:Sep88-217
"Human Embryo Research: Yes or No?"
H.K., 185:Oct88-214
"The Human Experience."
H. Gifford, 453(NYRB):1Jun89-3

Humber, J.M. & R.F. Almeder, eds. Biomedical
Ethics Reviews 1987.
L.M.F., 185:Apr89-690
Hume, D. Dialogues sur la religion naturelle.
(M. Malherbe, ed & trans)
M.A. Stewart, 319:Jul89-481
Hume, D. Essays: Moral, Political, and Liter-
ary. (E.F. Miller, ed)
M. Bordelon, 396(ModA):Winter88-92
Hume, K. Pynchon's Mythography.*
C. Clerc, 268(IFR):Winter89-66
D. Eddins, 536(Rev):Vol10-155
B.M., 494:Vol8No2-456
S. Moore, 532(RCF):Summer88-321
J.W. Slade, 395(MFS):Winter88-665
Hume, R.D. Henry Fielding and the London
Theatre, 1728-1737.
R. Folkenflik, 617(TLS):10-16Mar89-253
Humesky, A. & V. Bolen. Elementary Ukrain-
ian. (Vols 1 & 2) Intermediate Ukrainian.
(Vol 1)
N.K. Moyle, 574(SEEJ):Spring88-175
Humesky, A., G. Perfecky & K. Dowbenko.
Intermediate Ukrainian. (Vol 2)
N.K. Moyle, 574(SEEJ):Spring88-175
Humfrey, P. – see Burckhardt, J.
Humm, M. Feminist Criticism.
M. Del Sapio, 402(MLR):Oct89-959
Humm, P., P. Stigant & P. Widdowson, eds.
Popular Fictions.*
P. Beilharz, 637(VS):Winter89-269
Hummer, T.R. Lower-Class Heresy.
J.F. Cotter, 249(HudR):Spring88-227
R. Jones, 496:Summer88-55
S. Pinsker, 363(LitR):Winter89-256
Humphrey, J.H. Roman Circuses.*
H.B. Evans, 121(CJ):Apr-May89-370
Humphrey, R. The Historical Novel as Philos-
ophy of History.
G. Brude-Firnau, 564:Feb88-91
Humphrey, T. – see Kant, I.
Humphrey, W. Farther Off from Heaven. The
Ordways. Home from the Hill. Hostages to
Fortune. Proud Flesh. The Collected Sto-
ries.
M.R. Winchell, 569(SR):Spring88-287
Humphrey, W. No Resting Place.
J. Clute, 617(TLS):1-7Dec89-1338
J. Ehle, 441:25Jun89-19
Humphrey, W. Open Season.
R. Benson, 569(SR):Spring88-xxx
Humphreys, H. Gods and Other Mortals.
A. & S. Munton, 102(CanL):Spring88-231
Humphreys, J. Rich in Love.*
D. Flower, 249(HudR):Spring88-213
Humphreys, J.R. Timeless Towns and Haunted
Places.
P-L. Adams, 61:Sep89-112
Humphries, J. Losing the Text.
A. Greenfield, 546(RR):Mar88-392
S. Hand, 208(FS):Oct88-501
W.F. Motte, Jr., 207(FR):Oct88-156
Humphries, J. Metamorphoses of the Raven.*
R.C. De Prospo, 153:Fall88-43
J.A. Hiddleston, 208(FS):Jan88-112
Humphries, J. The Puritan and the Cynic.
J.C. Austin, 149(CLS):Vol25No4-370
Humphries, R. Fritz Lang.
D. Coward, 617(TLS):15-21Dec89-1387
Hunczak, T. Symon Petliura and the Jews.
D. Saunders, 575(SEER):Jan88-161

Hundsnurscher, F. & J. Splett. Semantik der Adjektive im Deutschen.*
 G. Koller, 685(ZDL):2/1988-258
Huneker, J.G. Americans in the Arts, 1890-1920.* (A.T. Schwab, ed)
 P.J. Egan, 130:Fall88-277
Hungry Wolf, A. Off on a Wild Caboose Chase.
 E. Zotti, 441:26Feb89-35
Hunnicutt, B.K. Work Without End.
 N. Lichtenstein, 441:29Jan89-15
Hunnicutt, E. In the Music Library.
 P. Glasser, 455:Jun88-61
 G. Johnson, 219(GaR):Summer88-423
 639(VQR):Spring88-57
Hunnicutt, E. Suite for Calliope.
 L. Lemon, 502(PrS):Fall88-132
Hunt, H.T. Multiplicity of Dreams.
 R. Dinnage, 617(TLS):22-28Dec89-1403
Hunt, I.E. Krieg und Frieden in der deutschen Literatur.
 H.D. Osterle, 406:Summer88-212
Hunt, I.E. Mütter und Muttermythos in Günter Grass' Roman "Der Butt."
 I.T. Hasselbach, 221(GQ):Winter87-143
Hunt, J.D. Garden and Grove.*
 K. Downes, 90:Aug88-634
Hunt, J.D. William Kent.*
 J. Harris, 39:Sep88-212
 C.M. Sicca, 90:Aug88-638
Hunt, L. Politics, Culture and Class in the French Revolution.*
 C. Jones, 161(DUJ):Dec87-139
 G. Lewis, 83:Spring88-84
Hunt, T. Chrétien de Troyes: "Yvain" (Le Chevalier au Lion).*
 E. Kennedy, 447(N&Q):Dec88-519
Hunt, T., ed. Les Gius partiz des eschez.*
 G. Hesketh, 382(MAE):1988/1-126
 A.J. Holden, 208(FS):Jan88-69
Hunt, T. - see Jeffers, R.
Hunt, T. - see de Linham, R.
Hunt, W.R. Stef.
 P. Grosskurth, 102(CanL):Winter87-190
Hunter, I. Culture and Government.
 B. Cox, 617(TLS):11-17Aug89-865
Hunter, I. Nothing to Repent.
 C.A. Berst, 77:Fall88-350
Hunter, J.F.M. Understanding Wittgenstein.*
 C. McMullen, 482(PhR):Oct88-579
 L. Resnick, 154:Spring88-147
Hunter, R.L. The New Comedy of Greece and Rome.*
 D. Konstan, 24:Spring88-142
Hunter, S. The Day Before Midnight.
 N. Callendar, 441:23Apr89-33
Hunting, C. Collected Poems: 1969-1982.
 S. Mitchell, 472:Vol15No1-281
"The Huntington Art Collections."
 G. Ashton, 39:Jan88-68
Huot, S. From Song to Book.
 D.F. Hult, 599:Summer89-316
 H. Solterer, 546(RR):May88-517
Hupper, W.G. An Index to English Periodical Literature on the Old Testament and Ancient Near Eastern Studies. (Vol 1)
 J.K. Ohles, 87(BB):Dec88-277
Huppert, G. After the Black Death.
 A.J. Slavin, 551(RenQ):Autumn88-484
Hurford, P. Making Music on the Organ.
 A. Bond, 415:Dec88-693
Hurlbutt, R.H. 3d. Hume, Newton and the Design Argument. (rev)
 M.A. Stewart, 319:Jul89-481

Hurst, H.R. Gloucester, the Roman and Later Defences.
 D.P. Davison, 123:Vol38No1-122
Hursthouse, R. Beginning Lives.*
 I. Tipton, 518:Oct88-231
Husak, D. Philosophy of Criminal Law.
 L. Katz, 185:Jul89-953
Huse, N. & W. Wolters. Venedig.*
 J. Anderson, 59:Dec88-565
Huseman, W.H. La Personnalité littéraire de François de La Noue, 1531-1591.*
 N. Cazauran, 535(RHL):Sep-Oct88-1021
 J.J. Supple, 208(FS):Jan88-77
Huskey, E. Russian Lawyers and the Soviet State.*
 A.L. Tait, 575(SEER):Apr88-308
Husserl, E. Aufsätze und Vorträge (1911-1921). (T. Nenon & H.R. Sepp, eds)
 J.J. Drummond, 543:Jun89-841
Husserl, E. Phenomenology and the Foundations of the Sciences. (Bk 3)
 P. Trotignon, 542:Jul-Sep88-364
Hussey, J.M. The Orthodox Church in the Byzantine Empire.
 M. Philippides, 589:Jan88-172
Hussey, M. The Singing of the Real World.*
 E.K. Ginsberg, 177(ELT):Vol31No1-107
 C.G. Heilbrun, 301(JEGP):Jul88-460
 E. Jay, 447(N&Q):Jun88-261
 M.P.L., 295(JML):Fall87/Winter88-402
 H. Richter, 594:Winter88-417
Hutcheon, L. Formalism and the Freudian Aesthetic.
 P. Collier, 107(CRCL):Mar88-98
Hutcheon, L. A Poetics of Postmodernism.
 W. Steiner, 617(TLS):10-16Feb89-132
Hutcheon, L. A Theory of Parody.*
 L. Irvine, 102(CanL):Winter87-264
Hutcheson, F. Eine Untersuchung über den Ursprung unserer Ideen von Schönheit und Tugend.
 K. Haakonssen, 319:Oct89-626
Hutchinson, D.S. The Virtues of Aristotle.*
 A.W.H. Adkins, 185:Jan89-428
 P.M. Huby, 123:Vol38No1-64
Hutchinson, G.B. The Ecstatic Whitman.*
 N.S. Grabo, 27(AL):Dec88-668
Hutchinson, G.O. Hellenistic Poetry.
 F. Cairns, 617(TLS):27Jan-2Feb89-93
Hutchinson, G.O. - see Aeschylus
Hutchinson, M. The Prince of Wales: Right or Wrong?
 A. Saint, 617(TLS):8-14Dec89-1351
Hutchinson, T. & A. Waters. English for Specific Purposes.
 B.W. Robinett, 399(MLJ):Spring88-73
Hutchman, L. Blue Riders.*
 529(QQ):Spring88-226
"Hüter der Verwandlung."
 D. Barnouw, 221(GQ):Winter87-145
Huth, A. Such Visitors.
 R. Cobb, 617(TLS):7-13Jul89-738
Hutt, J. Understanding Far Eastern Art.
 J. Sweetman, 463:Spring88-55
Huxley, H.H. What Proper Person?
 J.V. Luce, 235:Summer88-138
Huxtable, A.L. Architecture, Anyone?*
 H. Muschamp, 139:Jun/Jul88-96
Huygens, C. Le Cycle Harmonique (Rotterdam, 1691). (R. Rasch, ed & trans)
 T. Christensen, 308:Fall88-379
 A. Cohen, 410(M&L):Jan88-68
Huygens, R.B.C. - see Guillaume de Tyr

Huyssen, A. After the Great Divide.
  M. Folch-Serra, 529(QQ):Autumn88-618
  R.C. Holub, 406:Fall88-364
  E.C.R., 295(JML):Fall87/Winter88-248
Hvidt, K. Edvard Brandes.
  L. Longum, 172(Edda):1988/3-285
Hwang Sun-won. The Book of Masks. (M.
  Holman, ed)
  E. Gillooly, 441:31Dec89-12
Hyams, N.M. Language Acquisition and the
  Theory of Parameters.
  J. Aitchison, 297(JL):Sep88-527
  K.F. Drozd, 350:Jun89-406
  J. Hildebrand, 320(CJL):Mar88-102
Hyde, E. Monoosook Valley.
  A. Boaz, 441:30Apr89-38
Hyde, L. The Gift.
  B. Leland, 153:Summer88-38
Hyde, L. - see Aleixandre, V.
Hyde, M. - see Shaw, G.B. & A. Douglas
Hyde, N. Four Faces of British Music.
  H.B.R., 412:Aug88-229
Hyde, T. The Poetic Theology of Love.*
  J.V. Mirollo, 276:Autumn88-277
Hyder, Q. A Woman's Life.
  F.W. Pritchett, 314:Winter-Spring88-247
Hyett, B.H. In Evidence.
  A. Balaban, 385(MQR):Winter89-149
Hyland, A. & K. Milne, eds. Irish Educational
  Documents. (Vol 1)
  P.B. Gallagher, 272(IUR):Spring88-150
Hyland, P. The Black Heart.*
  S. MacNeille, 441:5Mar89-23
Hyland, W.G. Mortal Rivals.
  639(VQR):Summer88-97
Hylson-Smith, K. Evangelicals in the Church
  of England: 1734-1984.
  B. Godlee, 617(TLS):27Oct-2Nov89-1188
Hyman, A. - see Averroes
Hyman, A. - see Babbage, C.
Hymes, D. "In Vain I Tried to Tell You."
  E. Désveaux, 98:Dec88-989
Hymes, R.P. Statesmen and Gentlemen.
  P. Ebrey, 244(HJAS):Dec88-493
Hynes, S. Flights of Passage.*
  C. Thorne, 617(TLS):7-13Apr89-371
Hynes, S. - see Hardy, T.
Hyun, P. Man Sei!
  A.C. Nahm, 293(JASt):May88-385

Iannace, G.A. Interferenza linguistica ai
  confini fra Stato e Regno.
  G. Holtus, 72:Band224Heft2-472
Iannone, A.P., ed. Contemporary Moral Con-
  troversies in Technology.
  D.R.F., 185:Oct88-215
Ibarz, J.M.O. - see under Ortiz Ibarz, J.M.
Ibbotson, E. Madensky Square.
  K. Blickle, 441:15Jan89-22
Ibn Abi 'l-Dunyā. Kitāb al-Mawt (The Book
  of Death) and Kitāb al-Qubūr (The Book of
  Graves). (L. Kinberg, ed)
  R. Weipert, 318(JAOS):Jan-Mar87-180
Ibn Aṭ-Ṭayyib. Proclus' Commentary on the
  Pythagorean Golden Verses. (N. Linley, ed
  & trans)
  C.E. Butterworth, 589:Jan88-174
Ibn Buṭlān. Das Ärziebankett. (F. Klein-
  Franke, trans)
  I. Lichtenstädter, 318(JAOS):Apr-Jun87-
  377

Ibn Riḍwān. Le livre de la méthode du mede-
  cin de 'Alī b. Riḍwān (998-1067). (J.
  Grand'Henry, ed & trans)
  G. Saliba, 318(JAOS):Jan-Mar87-189
Ibn Riḍwān. Medieval Islamic Medicine. (A.S.
  Gamal, ed)
  G. Saliba, 318(JAOS):Jan-Mar87-174
Ida, M., S. Wechsler & D. Zec, eds. Working
  Papers in Grammatical Theory and Dis-
  course Structure.
  D.H., 355(LSoc):Jun88-312
"Idaho+, Contemporary Poetry From the
  American West."
  J. Harris, 649(WAL):Nov88-255
Idol, J.L., Jr. A Thomas Wolfe Companion.
  J.M. Flora, 573(SSF):Spring88-165
  R.S. Kennedy, 365:Fall87-224
  J.S. Phillipson, 395(MFS):Winter88-628
Idone, C. Salad Days.
  R. Flaste, 441:11Jun89-18
Idris, Y. A Leader of Men.
  I.J. Boullata, 268(IFR):Winter89-82
Idzerda, S.J., A.C. Loveland & M.H. Miller.
  Lafayette, Hero of Two Worlds.
  M. Kammen, 441:2Jul89-7
Ife, B.W. Reading and Fiction in Golden-Age
  Spain.*
  F.A. de Armas, 238:May88-292
  M.R. Greer, 345(KRQ):May88-246
Iga, M. The Thorn in the Chrysanthemum.
  M.I. White, 293(JASt):Feb88-145
Ige, S. Comparative Literature as a Distinct
  Discipline.
  W.F. Feuser, 538(RAL):Fall88-377
de la Iglesia, M.R.S. - see under Saurín de la
  Iglesia, M.R.
Ignar, S. Rodzina chłopska i gospodarstwo
  rolne.
  T.N. Cieplak, 497(PolR):Vol33No2-215
Ignashev, D.N. - see Ratušinskaja, I.
Ignatow, D. New and Collected Poems, 1970-
  1985.*
  J. Mazzaro, 569(SR):Winter88-149
  L. Van Brunt, 496:Fall88-51
Ihwe, J.F. Konversationen über Literatur.
  D. Posdzech, 654(WB):9/1988-1570
Iijima, T. & J.M. Vardaman, Jr., eds. The
  World of Natsume Soseki.
  S.J. Napier, 293(JASt):Aug88-636
Ijsseling, S., ed. Jacques Derrida.
  J. Colette, 192(EP):Jul-Sep88-424
Ikeda, D. & B. Wilson. L'avenir de l'humanité
  et le rôle de la religion.
  A. Reix, 542:Jan-Mar88-124
Ikkyū Sōjun. Ikkyū and the Crazy Cloud An-
  thology.* (S. Arntzen, ed & trans)
  D. Pollak, 293(JASt):May88-369
Iliescu, M. & H. Siller-Runggaldier. Rätoro-
  manische Bibliographie.
  W. Müller, 685(ZDL):1/1988-123
  C. Schmitt, 72:Band224Heft2-473
Iljic, R. L'exploitation aspectuelle de la
  notion de franchissement en chinois con-
  temporain.
  B. King, 350:Sep89-665
Iljic, R. Le marque de détermination nominale
  "de" en chinois contemporain.
  B. King, 350:Sep89-666
Illis, M. A Chinese Summer.
  R. Kaveney, 617(TLS):13-19Jan89-42
  N. Sonenberg, 441:1Oct89-27

Ives, C. The Unanswered Question. (P.C. Echols & N. Zahler, eds) Trio for Violin, Violoncello, and Piano. (J. Kirkpatrick, ed)
  W. Rathert, 414(MusQ):Vol73No4-575
Ives, R., ed. From Timberline to Tidepool.
  D. Whipple, 649(WAL):Feb89-371
Ivo, L. Snakes' Nest or A Tale Badly Told.
  J. Gledson, 617(TLS):15-21Dec89-1386
Ivry, B. Regatta.
  N. Hildes-Heim, 441:22Jan89-23
Iyer, R. - see Gandhi, M.
Izzi, E. The Booster.
  M. Stasio, 441:2Apr89-33

Jabès, E. Un Étranger avec, sous le bras, un livre de petit format. Le Livre des questions, 2.
  M. Edwards, 617(TLS):29Dec89/4Jan90-1443
Jablonski, E. Gershwin.*
  M. Bowen, 415:Nov88-599
Jack, D. Me So Far.
  E. Stumpf, 441:24Dec89-16
Jack, R.D.S. Alexander Montgomerie.*
  D. Norbrook, 447(N&Q):Jun88-227
Jack, R.D.S. Scottish Literature's Debt to Italy.
  C. Whyte, 588(SSL):Vol23-305
Jackall, R. Moral Mazes.
  J.N.B., 185:Jan89-469
Jäckel, E. Hitler in History.
  H.A. Schmitt, 569(SR):Winter88-158
Jackendoff, R. Consciousness and the Computational Mind.
  D.S. Clarke, Jr., 543:Sep88-147
  A. Flores, 103:Feb89-53
Jackson, A. The Ulster Party.
  G. Ó Tuathaigh, 617(TLS):15-21Dec89-1394
Jackson, B. Fieldwork.*
  T.A. Green, 650(WF):Jan88-71
Jackson, B. Honest Graft.*
  T.B. Edsall, 453(NYRB):20Jul89-20
Jackson, C. Hattie.
  A. Young, 441:15Oct89-13
Jackson, F. Conditionals.
  P. Mott, 518:Jul88-156
  D.E. Over, 393(Mind):Oct88-626
  G. Stahl, 542:Jul-Sep88-384
Jackson, G. & others. Octubre 1934.
  H. Graham, 86(BHS):Apr88-193
Jackson, H.J. - see Coleridge, S.T.
Jackson, K.D., ed. Cambodia 1975-1978.
  R. Smith, 617(TLS):15-21Dec89-1381
Jackson, K.D. & W. Mungkandi, eds. United States-Thailand Relations.
  C.D. Neher, 293(JASt):Feb88-195
Jackson, M.P. & M. Neill - see Marston, J.
Jackson, M.W. Matters of Justice.
  R. Elliot, 63:Jun88-281
Jackson, P. George Scharf's London Sketches and Watercolours of a Changing City 1820-1850.
  D.E. Nord, 637(VS):Autumn88-149
  G. Pollock, 59:Jan88-275
Jackson, R. Acts of Mind.
  S.P., 295(JML):Fall87/Winter88-270
Jackson, R. Doctors and Diseases in the Roman Empire.
  J. Scarborough, 617(TLS):21-27Apr89-420

Jackson, R. & R. Smallwood, eds. Players of Shakespeare, 2.
  R. Hapgood, 617(TLS):25-31Aug89-927
Jackson, R.L. Black Literature and Humanism in Latin America.
  M. De Costa-Willis, 459:Winter88-132
  I.I. Smart, 263(RIB):Vol38No3-404
Jackson, R.L. & L. Nelson, Jr., eds. Vyacheslav Ivanov.
  J.D. Elsworth, 575(SEER):Jan88-122
  R.F. Gustafson, 550(RusR):Jan88-91
Jackson, T.R. The Legends of Konrad von Würzburg.*
  N.F. Palmer, 402(MLR):Jul89-773
Jackson, W.A., F.S. Ferguson & K.F. Pantzer - see "A Short-Title Catalogue of Books Printed in England, Scotland, and Ireland and of English Books Printed Abroad 1475-1640"
Jackson, W.T.H. The Challenge of the Medieval Text.*
  J.F. Poag, 221(GQ):Spring87-275
Jacob, G. & C. de Givray - see Truffaut, F.
Jacob, J-L., ed. Louis Guilloux.
  Y. Chevrel, 535(RHL):Nov-Dec88-1170
Jacob, P., ed & trans. Vacances du pouvoir.
  M. Détrie, 549(RLC):Jan-Mar88-67
Jacob, P. - see Li Bai
Jacob, S. La Passion Selon Galatée.
  E. Potvin, 102(CanL):Summer88-156
Jacobo de Junta. Oeuvres, I. (J. Roudil, ed)
  P. Linehan, 86(BHS):Jul88-290
Jacobs, A. The Pan Book of Orchestral Music.
  W. Mann, 415:Aug88-402
Jacobs, D. Haarlem Road.
  G. Mort, 493:Winter88/89-57
  S. O'Brien, 617(TLS):25-31Aug89-916
Jacobs, D. Terminus.
  H. Buckingham, 565:Winter87/88-71
Jacobs, H.A. Incidents in the Life of a Slave Girl, Written by Herself.* (L.M. Child, ed; new ed rev by J.F. Yellin)
  B.A. St. Andrews, 219(GaR):Spring88-203
  42(AR):Winter88-124
  639(VQR):Winter88-18
Jacobs, M. What Feathers Are For.
  A. Adamson, 102(CanL):Winter87-230
Jacobs, M., ed. With Other Words.
  A. & S. Munton, 102(CanL):Spring88-231
Jacobsen, B. Modern Transformational Grammar.
  A. Radford, 297(JL):Mar88-207
Jacobsen, J. On the Island.
  S.G. Kellman, 441:27Aug89-20
Jacobsen, J. The Sisters.*
  R.B. Shaw, 491:Apr88-40
Jacobsen, R. The Silence Afterwards.* (R. Greenwald, ed & trans)
  C. Leland, 627(UTQ):Fall87-170
Jacobson, D. Adult Pleasures.*
  M. Baron, 175:Autumn88-265
  P. Lewis, 364:Aug/Sep88-131
Jacobson, W.S. The Companion to "The Mystery of Edwin Drood."*
  T.J. Cribb, 541(RES):Feb88-136
  P. Preston, 447(N&Q):Sep88-389
Jacobsson, R., ed. Pax et Sapientia.
  J. Caldwell, 410(M&L):Jan88-60
Jacobus, M. Reading Woman.*
  T. Cosslett, 447(N&Q):Jun88-282
  E. Jordan, 366:Autumn88-218
  E.C.R., 295(JML):Fall87/Winter88-249

Jacoby, M. Germanisches Recht und Rechts-
sprache zwischen Mittelalter und Neuzeit
unter besonderer Berücksichtigung des
skandinavischen Rechts.
　　P-A. Wiktorsson, 684(ZDA):Band117
　　Heft2-51
Jacoby, R. The Last Intellectuals.
　　T.H. Adamowski, 627(UTQ):Summer89-526
　　S. Pinsker, 390:Apr88-49
　　S. Rudikoff, 249(HudR):Autumn88-534
　　639(VQR):Spring88-58
Jacoff, R. - see Freccero, J.
Jacquemin, J-P. & Monkasa-Bitumba, eds.
Forces littéraires d'Afrique.
　　G. De Wulf, 356(LR):Feb-May88-118
Jacques, F. Le privilège de liberté.*
　　M. Kleijwegt & H.W. Pleket, 394:Vol41
　　fasc1/2-233
Jaeger, C.S. The Origins of Courtliness.*
　　G.A. Bond, 545(RPh):May89-479
Jaeger, P. - see Heidegger, M.
Jaeggli, O. & C. Silva-Corvalán, eds. Studies
in Romance Linguistics.*
　　F. Drijkoningen, 603:Vol12No2-533
　　S.N. Dworkin, 320(CJL):Jun88-179
Jaeschke, W. & others, eds. Buchstabe und
Geist.
　　R. Imbach, 687:Oct-Dec88-720
Jaffé, H.L.C. De Stijl, 1917-1931.
　　P. Overy, 592:Vol201No1020-61
Jaffe, J.A. Arthur Conan Doyle.
　　E.S. Lauterbach, 395(MFS):Summer88-294
Jaffé, M. Old Master Drawings from Chats-
worth.
　　J.B. Shaw, 90:Nov88-862
"Madhur Jaffrey's Cookbook."
　　R. Flaste, 441:11Jun89-16
Jäger, A. John McGrath und die 7:84 Com-
pany Scotland.
　　P. Zenzinger, 588(SSL):Vol23-294
Jägerskiöld, S. Oskuld och arsenik.
　　A. Melberg, 172(Edda):1988/2-180
Jahn, R.G. & B.J. Dunne. Margins of Reality.
　　42(AR):Fall88-529
Jahn, W. The Art of Gilbert & George.
　　D. Kaufman, 441:3Sep89-14
"Jahrbuch des Vereins für niederdeutsche
Sprachforschung." (Jahrgang 1986)
　　A. Classen, 221(GQ):Summer87-466
Jai, J.R., ed. Shah Bano.
　　G. Minault, 293(JASt):Nov88-814
Jain, D. & N. Banerjee, eds. Tyranny of the
Household.
　　G. Minault, 293(JASt):Nov88-814
Jakes, J. California Gold.
　　M. Pellecchia, 441:8Oct89-24
Jaki, S.L. Lord Gifford and his Lectures.
　　P. Trotignon, 542:Jul-Sep88-344
Jaki, S.L. Uneasy Genius.*
　　J.C. Caiazza, 396(ModA):Spring89-154
Jakob-Rost, L. & J. Marzahn. Assyrische
Königsinschriften auf Ziegeln aus Assur.
　　A.K. Grayson, 318(JAOS):Apr-Jun87-331
Jakober, M. Sandinista.*
　　C. Kanaganayakam, 102(CanL):Winter87-
　　270
Jakobson, R. Language in Literature. (K.
Pomorska & S. Rudy, ed)
　　F.W. Galan, 617(TLS):13-19Jan89-41
　　M.C. Haley, 580(SCR):Spring89-83
　　D. Shepherd, 402(MLR):Oct89-1049
　　M. Tarlinskaja, 599:Spring89-152

Jakobson, R. & L.R. Waugh. Die Lautgestalt
der Sprache.
　　E. Lang, 682(ZPSK):Band41Heft4-527
Jalard, M-C. Le Jazz est-il encore possible?*
　　A.J.M. Prévos, 91:Spring88-112
Jalland, P. Women, Marriage and Politics
1860-1914.
　　D. Rubinstein, 637(VS):Autumn88-115
Jalland, P. - see Wilberforce, O.
James, A. John Morris-Jones.
　　B. Ó. Cuív, 112:Vol20-203
James, A.R.W., ed. Victor Hugo et la Grande-
Bretagne.*
　　P.W.M. Cogman, 208(FS):Jan88-95
　　A. Laster, 535(RHL):Jul-Aug88-783
　　A.C. Ritchie, 546(RR):Nov88-685
　　J. Van Eerde, 446(NCFS):Fall-Winter
　　88/89-230
James, B. Historical Baseball Abstract.
　　J. Gindin, 385(MQR):Spring89-283
James, C. Snakecharmers in Texas.*
　　P. Lewis, 364:Aug/Sep88-131
James, D. Qur'ans of the Mamluks.
　　B. Gray, 617(TLS):12-18May89-525
James, D.E. Allegories of Cinema.
　　J. Bowen, 617(TLS):17-23Nov89-1286
James, E. Judge Not.
　　J.L. Houlden, 617(TLS):1-7Sep89-958
James, E.N. George Farquhar.*
　　S.S. Kenny, 40(AEB):Vol2No2-80
James, F. Semantics of the English Subjunc-
tive.*
　　D.F. Stermole, 627(UTQ):Fall87-142
James, H. The Complete Notebooks of Henry
James.* (L. Edel & L.H. Powers, eds)
　　M. Anesko, 27(AL):Mar88-120
　　T. Follini, 97(CQ):Vol17No3-263
　　R. Gard, 447(N&Q):Sep88-422
　　R.S. Lyons, 569(SR):Summer88-492
　　N. Page, 177(ELT):Vol31No1-110
　　B. Richards, 541(RES):Nov88-578
　　W. Veeder, 395(MFS):Summer88-231
James, H. A German Identity.
　　R.J. Evans, 617(TLS):23-29Jun89-683
James, H. Henry James Selected Letters.* (L.
Edel, ed)
　　C.B. Cox, 569(SR):Summer88-497
　　R.L. Gale, 26(ALR):Fall88-78
　　R. Hewitt, 395(MFS):Winter88-617
　　N. Page, 177(ELT):Vol31No3-346
　　B. Redford, 27(AL):Oct88-478
James, H. Literary Criticism.* (Vols 1 & 2)
(L. Edel, with M. Wilson, eds)
　　S. Gurney, 396(ModA):Fall89-351
　　G. Watson, 569(SR):Summer88-485
James, H. & others. The Whole Family. (A.
Bendixen, ed)
　　N. Baym, 534(RALS):Vol16No1&2-135
James, J.D. & R.B. Bottoms - see Kaplan, F.,
M. Goldberg & F.J. Fielding
James, M. Society, Politics and Culture.
　　J. Scattergood, 589(YES):Vol19-301
James, M.R. The Ghost Stories of M.R. James.
(M. Cox, ed)
　　S. Pickering, 569(SR):Winter88-xiii
James, P. Unity in Diversity.
　　H.E. Elsom, 313:Vol78-248
　　B. Hijmans, 229:Band60Heft5-409
James, P.D. Devices and Desires.
　　T.J. Binyon, 617(TLS):10-16Nov89-1244
James, R.R. Anthony Eden.
　　M. Curtis, 390:Jun/Jul88-56

184

James, S. The Content of Social Explana-
tion.*
   R. Keat, 482(PhR):Apr88-283
James, W. Manuscript Lectures. (F.H. Burk-
hardt, F. Bowers & I.K. Skrupskelis, eds)
   E. Taylor, 441:16Apr89-30
James, W. Selected Unpublished Correspon-
dence, 1885-1910.* (F.J.D. Scott, ed)
   R.N. Hudspeth, 432(NEQ):Jun88-292
James, W. The Works of William James.* (Vol
16: Essays in Psychical Research.) (F.H.
Burkhardt & F. Bowers, eds)
   A. Flew, 484(PPR):Dec88-353
James, W. The Works of William James. (Vol
17: Essays, Comments, and Reviews.) (F.H.
Burkhardt, F. Bowers & I.K. Skrupskelis,
eds)
   G. Cotkin, 26(ALR):Spring89-79
   M. Mendell, 619:Fall88-572
James, W.A. Ricardo Bofill 1960-1985.
(Spanish title: Ricardo Bofill, Taller de
Arquitectura.)
   M. Filler, 617(TLS):24-30Mar89-295
   D. Waterman, 55:Nov88-105
Jamie, K. The Way We Live.*
   E. Morgan, 493:Spring88-42
   T. Nairn, 571(ScLJ):Spring88-44
Jamie, K. & A. Greig. A Flame in Your Heart.*
   E. Morgan, 493:Spring88-42
   R. Watson, 588(SSL):Vol23-254
Jamieson, R.A. Shoormal.
   T. Eagleton, 565:Summer88-67
Jamison, S.W. Function and Form in the
"áya-"Formations of the Rig Veda and
Atharva Veda.
   Toshifumi Gotō, 259(IIJ):Oct88-303
Jamme, F.A. Pour les simples.
   V. Wackenhelm, 450(NRF):Sep88-106
Janáček, L. Janáček's Uncollected Essays on
Music. (M. Zemanová, ed & trans)
   C. Mackerras, 617(TLS):1-7Dec89-1331
   J. Peyser, 441:17Sep89-38
Janaway, C. Self and World in Schopen-
hauer's Philosophy.
   P. Gardiner, 617(TLS):22-28Sep89-1034
Janda, L.A. A Semantic Analysis of the Rus-
sian Verbal Prefixes za-, pere-, do-, and
ot-.
   J.A. Dunn, 575(SEER):Jan88-119
Janeway, E. The Economics of Chaos.
   J.E. Garten, 441:12Feb89-12
Janicaud, D. & others. Les pouvoirs de la
science.
   A. Reix, 542:Jul-Sep88-384
Janik, D. Literatursemiotik als Methode.
   H.T. Siepe, 72:Band224Heft2-360
Janko, R. Aristotle on Comedy.*
   E. Belfiore, 41:Vol7-236
   J.M. Bremer, 394:Vol4fasc1/2-166
Jankowski, P. Communism and Collaboration.
   J. Hayward, 617(TLS):28Jul-3Aug89-821
   R.O. Paxton, 453(NYRB):27Apr89-42
Jannetta, A.B. Epidemics and Mortality in
Early Modern Japan.*
   W. Johnston, 293(JASt):May88-376
Janovic, V. The House of the Tragic Poet.
   S. O'Brien, 364:Feb/Mar89-107
   M. Parker, 617(TLS):24Feb-2Mar89-200
Janowitz, G.J. Leonardo da Vinci, Brunelles-
chi, Durer.
   J. White, 551(RenQ):Winter88-733

Janowitz, P. Temporary Dwellings.
   H. Hart, 385(MQR):Summer89-417
   R. McDowell, 249(HudR):Autumn88-567
Janowitz, T. American Dad.
   M. Brandham, 617(TLS):12-18May89-518
Jansen, E.G. Rural Bangladesh.
   J. Bhattacharyya, 293(JASt):May88-401
Jansen, M. Die Indus Zivilisation.
   G.L. Possehl, 318(JAOS):Oct-Dec87-845
Jansen, M.B., ed. Japanese Studies in the
United States. (Pt 1)
   C. Totman, 407(MN):Winter88-519
Jansen, S.C. Censorship.
   C. Gearty, 617(TLS):21-27Jul89-796
Janssen, T.A.J.M., J. Noordegraaf & A. Ver-
hagen – see Bakker, D.M.
Jansson, H. Per Olov Enquist och det in-
ställda upproret.
   L.E. Hansen & I. Laerkesen, 172(Edda):
1988/4-373
Janvier, L. Monstre, Va.
   D. Di Bernardi, 532(RCF):Fall88-159
   J. Réda, 450(NRF):Mar88-87
Janvier, Y. La géographie d'Orose.
   M. Reydellet, 555:Vol61fasc1-155
Janz, M. Marmorbilder.
   J.F. Fetzer, 564:Nov88-388
   M.A. Weiner, 406:Winter88-518
   M. Winkler, 221(GQ):Fall87-675
   M. Winkler, 221(GQ):Summer88-466
Jaquier, C. Gustave Roud et la tentation du
romantisme.
   P. Blanc, 546(RR):May88-533
Jarczyk, G. & P-J. Labarrière. Les premiers
combats de la reconnaissance.
   A. Reix, 542:Jul-Sep88-344
Jardí, E. Quatre escriptors marginats.
   J-L. Marfany, 86(BHS):Apr88-201
Jardin, A. Tocqueville.*
   H. Brogan, 617(TLS):6-12Jan89-4
   R.O. Paxton, 453(NYRB):2Mar89-16
   J.W. Scott, 441:19Feb89-12
Jardine, A. & P. Smith, eds. Men in Femi-
nism.*
   N. Segal, 402(MLR):Jul89-685
Jardine, A.A. Gynesis.*
   S. Willis, 153:Spring88-29
Jardine, N. The Birth of History and Philos-
ophy of Science.
   J.C. Pitt, 53(AGP):Band70Heft1-116
Jardine, N. The Fortunes of Inquiry.
   J. Heil, 393(Mind):Apr88-303
   J.E. & M. Tiles, 518:Jan88-41
Jarman, A.O.H. – see Aneirin
Jarman, D. Alban Berg: "Wozzeck."
   A. Whittall, 617(TLS):28Jul-3Aug89-826
Jaro, B.K. The Key.*
   F. Mench, 124:May-Jun89-399
Jaron, N., R. Möhrmann & H. Müller. Berlin –
Theater der Jahrhundertwende.
   G.J. Carr, 402(MLR):Jan89-248
   R.C. Cowen, 301(JEGP):Jul88-415
   P. Sprengel, 680(ZDP):Band107Heft2-308
Jaroslawski, J. Die marxistische Bewegung
und die Polenfrage.
   Z. Bauman, 617(TLS):22-28Dec89-1406
Jarrett, D. The Sleep of Reason.
   S. Collini, 617(TLS):6-12Jan89-15
Jarvie, I. Philosophy of the Film.
   C.B. Daniels, 154:Autumn88-554
   B. Salt, 89(BJA):Summer88-293
de Jasay, A. The State.
   D. Shapiro, 258:Sep88-342

185

Jasienica, P. The Commonwealth of Both Nations.
N. Pease, 497(PolR):Vol33No4-471
Jasińska-Kania, A., ed. Osobowość, Orientacje Moralne i Postawy Polityczne.
Z. Bauman, 617(TLS):24-30Nov89-1295
Jasinski, R. Autour de l'"Esther" racinienne.*
J. Moravcevich, 475:Vol15No28-297
Jasmin, C. Alice vous fait dire bonsoir.
P-Y. Mocquais, 102(CanL):Spring88-221
Jasmin-Bélisle, H. Le Père Emile Legault et ses Compagnons de saint Laurent.
L.E. Doucette, 627(UTQ):Fall87-189
E.F Nardocchio, 102(CanL):Autumn88-167
Jasper, D., ed. The Interpretation of Belief.*
P. Hamilton, 541(RES):Feb88-127
Jasper, D. Das Papstwahldekret von 1059.
R.C. Figueira, 589:Jul88-686
Jasper, P. Recycling.
R. Maggs, 102(CanL):Winter87-280
Jasper, P. & K. Turner, eds. Art Among Us/Arte Entre Nosotros.
J.S. Griffith, 292(JAF):Jan-Mar88-126
Jaspers, K. Philosophie.*
J. Chevalier, 540(RIPh):Vol42fasc2-254
Jastrow, R. Journey to the Stars.
W.G. Kolata, 441:19Nov89-25
Jaume, L. Le Discours jacobin et la démocratie.
W. Scott, 617(TLS):19-25May89-554
Jauss, H.R. Aesthetic Experience and Literary Hermeneutics.
R.R. Hellenga, 223:Fall88-359
Jauss, H.R. Die Epochenschwelle von 1912.
E. Leube, 547(RF):Band100Heft4-447
T. Mathews, 208(FS):Apr88-226
Javadi, H. Satire in Persian Literature.
D. Davis, 617(TLS):28Apr-4May89-450
Javeau, C. Le Petit Murmure et le bruit du monde.
M. Voisin, 193:Autumn88-143
Jay, B. & M. Moore, eds. Bernard Shaw on Photography.
A. Hollinghurst, 617(TLS):20-26Oct89-1155
Jay, E. Faith and Doubt in Victorian Britain.*
E. Block, Jr., 506(PSt):Sep88-105
A. Kiff, 447(N&Q):Sep88-408
T. Pettersson, 179(ES):Oct88-458
B. Richards, 541(RES):Aug88-454
N. Vance, 402(MLR):Jul89-723
Jay, E. - see Wesley, J.
Jay, M. Fin-de-Siècle Socialism and Other Essays.
J. Gray, 617(TLS):24Feb-2Mar89-183
Jay, P. - see Burke, K. & M. Cowley
Jay, R. The Trade Card in Nineteenth-Century America.*
E.R. McKinstry, 658:Summer/Autumn88-196
Jayal, N.G. - see Webb, S. & B.
Jayne, S. - see Ficino, M.
Jaynes, G.D. & R.M. Williams, Jr., eds. A Common Destiny.
A. Hacker, 453(NYRB):12Oct89-63
Jeal, T. Baden-Powell.
P. Fussell, 617(TLS):13-19Oct89-1119
Jeanne des Anges. Autobiographie d'une hystérique possédée. (G. Legué & G. de la Tourette, eds)
S.E. Miller, 153:Spring88-2

Jeanneret, M. Des mets et des mots.*
P. Burke, 208(FS):Oct88-467
L.W. Johnson, 207(FR):Mar89-679
D.N. Losse, 400(MLN):Sep88-948
M. Tetel, 210(FrF):Sep88-367
Jeannet, A.M., ed. Parliamo dell'Italia.
U. Skubikowski, 276:Spring88-38
Jeansonne, G. Gerald L.K. Smith.*
M. Ruthven, 617(TLS):9-15Jun89-629
Jeay, M., ed. Les Évangiles des quenouilles.*
M. Angenot, 107(CRCL):Jun88-278
N. Corbett, 545(RPh):Nov88-225
R.L. Krueger, 589:Oct88-943
Jeay, M. Savoir faire.*
M. Angenot, 107(CRCL):Jun88-278
N. Corbett, 545(RPh):Nov88-225
M.W. Morris, 589:Jan88-178
Jefcoate, G. & K. Kloth. A Catalogue of English Books Printed Before 1801 Held By the University Library at Göttingen.* (Pt 1) (B. Fabian, ed) [entry in prev was of Pts 1 & 2]
R. Alston, 354:Mar88-64
Jeffares, A.N. W.B. Yeats.
B. O'Donoghue, 617(TLS):10-16Mar89-252
Jeffares, A.N. & M. Alexander, general eds. Macmilan Anthology of English Literature. (Vols 1-5)
D. Hibberd, 617(TLS):29Dec89/4Jan90-1445
Jeffers, R. The Collected Poetry of Robinson Jeffers. (Vol 1) (T. Hunt, ed)
42(AR):Fall88-530
Jeffers, R. Rock and Hawk.* (R. Hass, ed)
R.J. Brophy, 649(WAL):Feb89-367
P.W. Rea, 152(UDQ):Spring88-113
R. Zaller, 4:Autumn88-53
639(VQR):Summer88-98
Jeffers, R. Selected Poems. (C. Falck, ed)
D. McDuff, 565:Autumn88-61
W. Scammell, 493:Spring88-48
R. Zaller, 4:Autumn88-53
Jeffers, R. The Women at Point Sur and Other Poems. Dear Judas and Other Poems. The Double Axe and Other Poems.
D. McDuff, 565:Autumn88-61
Jefferson, A. Reading Realism in Stendhal.*
R. Dénier, 605(SC):15Apr89-249
Jefferson, A. & D. Robey, eds. Modern Literary Theory. (2nd ed)
S. Vice, 447(N&Q):Jun88-280
Jeffrey, D.L., ed. Chaucer and Scriptural Tradition.*
G.H.V. Bunt, 179(ES):Jun88-275
Jeffreys, S. The Spinster and Her Enemies.
P. Summerfield, 637(VS):Summer89-595
Jeffreys-Jones, R. The CIA and American Democracy.
D.P. Calleo, 441:5Mar89-14
R. Cecil, 617(TLS):10-16Nov89-1232
Jeffries, R. Dead Clever.
T.J.B., 617(TLS):19-25May89-536
Jehlen, M. American Incarnation.*
E. Carton, 533:Winter89-99
S.B. Girgus, 26(ALR):Spring89-72
R.J. Maiman, 366:Spring88-114
Jehne, M. Der Staat des Dictators Caesar.
H. Botermann, 229:Band60Heft7-613
Jelavich, P. Munich und Theatrical Modernism.
L.C. De Meritt, 221(GQ):Summer87-487

Jelinek, E. Lust.
  M. Hulse, 617(TLS):21-27Jul89-802
Jelinek, E.C. The Tradition of Women's Auto-
  biography.
  J.M. Mueller, 77:Fall88-338
  S.A.S., 295(JML):Fall87/Winter88-250
Jencks, C. Le Corbusier and the Tragic View
  of Architecture.
  M. Spens, 592:Vol201No1019-62
Jencks, C. Post-Modernism.*
  M. Filler, 617(TLS):24-30Mar89-295
  H. Muschamp, 139:Jun/Jul88-21
Jencks, C. The Prince, the Architects and
  New Wave Monarchy.
  D. Jenkins, 46:Aug88-10
  D. Lewis, 47:Dec88-55
Jencks, C. What is Post-Modernism? Archi-
  tecture Today.
  M. Filler, 617(TLS):24-30Mar89-295
Jenista, F.L. The White Apos.
  S.D. Russell, 293(JASt):Aug88-702
Jenkins, A. In the Hot-House.*
  S. O'Brien, 364:Oct/Nov88-99
  D. O'Driscoll, 493:Autumn88-60
Jenkins, A. The Theatre of Tom Stoppard.*
  J. Morris, 397(MD):Dec88-591
  R.W. Strang, 447(N&Q):Dec88-551
  A. Thomas, 627(UTQ):Fall88-123
Jenkins, D.E. God, Politics and the Future.
  D. Jenkins, 617(TLS):6-12Jan89-6
Jenkins, L. An Almost Human Gesture.
  S. Birkerts, 472:Vol15No1-163
Jenkins, P. Across China.
  S. Pickering, 569(SR):Fall88-673
Jenkins, P. Mrs. Thatcher's Revolution.*
  442(NY):23Jan89-118
Jenkins, R. European Diary 1977-81.
  D. Leonard, 617(TLS):17-23Mar89-271
Jenkins, R. Just Duffy.*
  C. Milton, 571(ScLJ):Winter88-27
Jenkins, R.V. & others - see Edison, T.A.
Jennings, C. The Confidence Trick.
  C. Johnson, 617(TLS):10-16Mar89-243
Jennings, E. Tributes.
  G. Maxwell, 617(TLS):5-11May89-495
Jennings, H.D. Os dois exílios.
  J. Parker, 86(BHS):Oct88-419
Jennings, J. & H. Gottfried. American Ver-
  nacular Interior Architecture, 1870-1940.
  658:Winter88-296
Jens, W., ed. Kindlers Neues Literatur Lexi-
  kon.
  H. Denman, 617(TLS):13-19Oct89-1136
Jensen, E.M. Emancipation som lidenskab.*
  K.A. Seaver, 562(Scan):May88-90
Jensen, F., ed & trans. The Poetry of the
  Sicilian School.*
  H.W. Storey, 545(RPh):Nov88-236
Jensen, J.M. Loosening the Bonds.
  M.L. Briscoe, 128(CE):Nov88-802
Jensen, L. Giuseppe Verdi and Giovanni
  Ricordi.
  J. Rosselli, 617(TLS):1-7Dec89-1329
Jensen, P.A. & others, eds. Text and Context.
  C. Kelly, 575(SEER):Oct88-641
  G. McVay, 402(MLR):Jul89-810
Jentleson, B.W. Pipeline Politics.
  R. Campbell, 550(RusR):Apr88-219
Jentsch-Grooms, L. Exile and the Process of
  Individuation.
  S.K. Ugalde, 238:Mar88-95
  F.B. Vecchio, 552(REH):May88-133
  R. Warner, 86(BHS):Jul88-311

Jeppesen, K. & A. Luttrell. The Maussolleion
  at Halikarnassos. (Vol 2)
  S. Hornblower, 123:Vol38No1-175
Jeremy, D., ed. Business and Religion in
  Britain.
  M. Coulter, 637(VS):Spring89-436
Jernudd, B.H. & M.H. Ibrahim, eds. Aspects of
  Arabic Sociolinguistics.*
  A.S. Kaye, 361:Jan88-74
Jerome, J., ed. 1988 Poet's Market.
  639(VQR):Spring88-65
Jerome, J. Stone Work.
  M.E. Guthrie, 441:20Aug89-21
  442(NY):14Aug89-92
Saint Jérôme. Apologie contre Rufin. (P.
  Lardet, ed)
  P. Flobert, 555:Vol61fasc2-331
Jersild, P.C. Children's Island.
  L.G. Warme, 563(SS):Summer88-419
Jervis, R. The Meaning of the Nuclear Revo-
  lution.
  G.A. Craig, 453(NYRB):17Aug89-31
  M. Krepon, 441:1Oct89-30
Jeter, K.W. Death Arms.
  G. Jonas, 441:19Nov89-32
Jeter, K.W. Farewell Horizontal.
  G. Jonas, 441:9Apr89-38
Jettmar, K. The Religions of the Hindukush.
  (Vol 1)
  J. Frembgen, 259(IIJ):Oct88-329
  S. Lavan, 293(JASt):Feb88-181
Jeune, S., ed. Stendhal à Bordeaux (1838).
  R.M. Pauly, 446(NCFS):Fall-Winter88/89-
  222
  J.G. Shields, 208(FS):Apr88-216
Jewitt, J.R., with R. Alsop. The Adventures
  and Sufferings of John R. Jewitt, Captive of
  Maquinna.*
  E. Willis, 649(WAL):Nov88-253
Jhabvala, R.P. Three Continents.
  D. Flower, 249(HudR):Spring88-214
  J. Mellors, 364:Nov87-102
  639(VQR):Winter88-22
Ji Cheng. The Craft of Gardens.
  P-L. Adams, 61:Apr89-100
  M. Sullivan, 617(TLS):19-25May89-558
Jie, Z. - see under Zhang Jie
Jiles, P. The Jesse James Poems.
  S. Scobie, 376:Jun88-194
Jiles, P. The Late Great Human Road Show.*
  P. Jacob, 102(CanL):Spring88-209
  P. Stevens, 529(QQ):Autumn88-568
Jiménez, J.F. - see under Fernández Jiménez,
  J.
Jiménez, J.R. Selección de poemas. (G. Azam,
  ed)
  J.P. Devlin, 402(MLR):Oct89-1013
Jimenez, M.A. Changing Faces of Madness.
  L. Handlin, 432(NEQ):Jun88-301
  J.D. Pressman, 656(WMQ):Jul88-606
Jiménez, S.G. - see under García Jiménez, S.
Jiménez-Fajardo, S. Multiple Spaces.*
  C.G. Bellver, 345(KRQ):Aug88-383
Jin, Z. & Q. Zhou - see "June Four"
Joachim di Fiore. Enchiridion super Apoca-
  lypsim. (E.K. Burger, ed)
  R.E. Lerner, 589:Oct88-945
Joas, H. G.H. Mead.
  O. Flanagan, 185:Oct88-180
Jobse-van Putten, J. "'n Brood is ginnen
  stoeten."
  A. Berteloot, 685(ZDL):2/1987-268

Jochim, C. Chinese Religions.*
   J. Lagerwey, 318(JAOS):Jan-Mar87-162
Jodelle, E. L'Eugène. (M.J. Freeman, ed)
   R.W. Tobin, 207(FR):Dec88-327
Jodogne, P. - see Guicciardini, F.
Joeres, R-E.B. & M.J. Maynes, eds. German
Women in the Eighteenth and Nineteenth
Centuries.*
   L.K. Worley, 221(GQ):Fall87-692
Jofen, J. - see Ule, L.
Joffe, E. The Chinese Army After Mao.
   P.H.B. Godwin, 293(JASt):Aug88-596
Johanson, D. & J. Shreeve. Lucy's Child.
   J.N. Wilford, 441:12Nov89-14
Johanson, S. & P. Lysvåg. Understanding
English Grammar. (Pt 2)
   W.S. Chisholm, 350:Dec89-893
Johansson, G.V. Kristen demokrati på sven-
ska.
   M. Micheletti, 563(SS):Winter88-101
Johansson, S. Plural Attributive Nouns in
Present-Day English.
   R. Emons, 38:Band106Heft3/4-424
John, E.E. Creative Responses of Mongo Beti
and Ferdinand Oyono to Historical Realities
in Cameroun. The Rise of the Camerounian
Novel in French.
   R. Bjornson, 538(RAL):Winter88-569
John, E.E. Literature and Development.
   C. Wood, 538(RAL):Winter88-571
"The Elton John Collection."
   A. Solomon, 62:Dec88-111
John, N., ed. Pyotr Tchaikovsky: "Eugene
Onegin."
   D. Brown, 415:Sep88-464
John of Glastonbury. The Chronicle of Glas-
tonbury Abbey.* (J.P. Carley, ed)
   B.K. Vollmann, 38:Band106Heft1/2-212
John-Steiner, V. Notebooks of the Mind.*
   B. Sutton-Smith, 355(LSoc):Jun88-298
Johns, B. & D. Strecker, eds. The Hmong
World.
   J.F. Hartmann, 293(JASt):Feb88-197
Johns, J. & others. Foirades/Fizzles.
   W. Gass, 453(NYRB):2Feb89-22
Johns-Lewis, C., ed. Intonation in Dis-
course.*
   D.A. Zwierzynski, 320(CJL):Sep88-313
Johnsgard, P.A., with L. Agassiz Fuertes.
North American Owls.
   R.O. Paxton, 453(NYRB):21Dec89-39
Johnson, A.F. Children of Disobedience.
   D. Profumo, 617(TLS):30Jun-6Jul89-714
Johnson, B. Lady of the Beasts.
   K.A. Rabuzzi, 441:5Feb89-22
Johnson, B., ed. The Oxford Companion to
Australian Jazz.
   A. Shipton, 415:Nov88-598
Johnson, B. A World of Difference.
   B. Marie, 400(MLN):Dec88-1170
   P.D. Murphy, 590:Dec88-163
   S. Rava, 207(FR):Mar89-676
   R. Wolfs, 204(FdL):Dec88-307
Johnson, C. Jane Austen.
   K. Ellis, 166:Apr89-260
Johnson, C., Jr. Henry James and the Evolu-
tion of Consciousness.
   R. Hewitt, 395(MFS):Winter88-617
   R.B. Salomon, 27(AL):Dec88-676
Johnson, D. Irish Murdoch.
   S. Felton, 395(MFS):Summer88-291
Johnson, D. Persian Nights.*
   P. Iyer, 473(PR):Vol55No4-692

Johnson, D. The Veil.
   P. Breslin, 491:Oct88-30
   L. Upton, 152(UDQ):Spring88-106
Johnson, D. & M. The Age of Illusion.*
   P. Lewis, 565:Spring88-34
Johnson, D.B. Worlds in Regression.*
   J. Grayson, 575(SEER):Apr88-279
Johnson, D.H. & D.M. Anderson, eds. The
Ecology of Survival.
   A. De Waal, 617(TLS):20-26Oct89-1161
Johnson, E.P. The Moccasin Maker.*
   C. Lillard, 102(CanL):Autumn88-154
Johnson, G. Emily Dickinson.*
   L.Y. Gossett, 569(SR):Summer88-469
Johnson, G. Understanding Joyce Carol
Oates.
   W.R. Allen, 27(AL):Oct88-495
Johnson, J. In the Night Cafe.
   P. Lopate, 441:30Apr89-11
Johnson, J. Princely Chandos.
   A. McInnes, 83:Spring88-73
Johnson, L. True Confessions of the Last
Cannibal.
   J. Forth, 364:Apr-May87-128
Johnson, L. & J. - see Manley, W.L. & others
Johnson, L.A. The Experience of Time in
"Crime and Punishment."*
   G. Rosenshield, 574(SEEJ):Winter88-650
Johnson, L.C. Thoreau's Complex Weave.*
   R.H. Du Pree, 577(SHR):Fall88-398
   S. Fink, 534(RALS):Vol16No1&2-113
Johnson, L.S. The Voice of the "Gawain"-
Poet.*
   G.C. Britton, 447(N&Q):Sep88-356
Johnson, M. The Body in the Mind.*
   R.J. Wallace, 518:Oct88-225
Johnson, M. Les mots anglais dans un maga-
zine pour jeunes (Hit-magazine 1972-
1979).
   G. Holtus, 72:Band225Heft2-476
   J-M. Klinkenberg, 209(FM):Apr88-135
Johnson, M.A. Robert Duncan.
   P. Varner, 649(WAL):Nov88-273
Johnson, P. Intellectuals.*
   W.D. O'Flaherty, 441:12Mar89-3
   B. Williams, 453(NYRB):20Jul89-11
"Philip Johnson/John Burgee: Architecture
1979-1985."*
   S. Gutterman, 45:Mar88-77
Johnson, P.A. Duke Richard of York 1411-
1460.
   C.T. Allmand, 617(TLS):28Apr-4May89-
468
Johnson, P.O. The Critique of Thought.
   J. Burbridge, 103:Nov89-440
Johnson, R. The Film Industry in Brazil.*
   L.S. Chang, 399(MLJ):Spring88-100
Johnson, R. Simple Fare.
   R. Flaste, 441:11Jun89-18
Johnson, R.G. Good Grief.
   M. Cart, 441:8Oct89-25
Johnson, R.L. El ser y la palabra en Gabriel
Miró.*
   I.R. MacDonald, 86(BHS):Apr88-191
   F. Márquez Villanueva, 240(HR):
Autumn88-514
Johnson, S. Dr. Johnson's Critical Vocabu-
lary.* (R.L. Harp, ed)
   W.J. Ong, 536(Rev):Vol10-97
Johnson, S. The Letters of Samuel Johnson.
(Vols 1-3)(R.W. Chapman, ed)
   C. Rawson, 83:Spring88-98

Johnson, S. The Oxford Authors: Samuel Johnson.* (D. Greene, ed)
  J. Mezciems, 541(RES):May88-297
Johnson, S. Selections from Johnson on Shakespeare. (B.H. Bronson & J.M. O'Meara, eds)
  J.D. Fleeman, 447(N&Q):Mar88-98
Johnson, S., ed. Shout Africa.
  G.M. Fredrickson, 453(NYRB):26Oct89-48
Johnson, S.K. The Japanese Through American Eyes.
  T.S. Lebra, 407(MN):Winter88-517
Johnson, U. Anniversaries II.
  T. McGonigle, 532(RCF):Summer88-317
Johnson, W.R. Momentary Monsters.*
  J.F. Makowski, 124:Jul-Aug89-447
Johnson-Laird, P.N. The Computer and the Mind.
  S.R. Anderson, 350:Dec89-800
Johnston, A.F., ed. Editing Early English Drama.
  C. Davidson, 130:Spring88-82
Johnston, B. It's Been a Piece of Cake.
  A.L. Le Quesne, 617(TLS):23-29Jun89-696
Johnston, B.F. & others, eds. U.S.-Mexico Relations: Agriculture and Rural Development.
  O. Bedini, 263(RIB):Vol38No2-214
Johnston, C. Jack London – an American Radical?
  E. Labor, 534(RALS):Vol16No1&2-151
Johnston, C. Thomas Wolfe.
  R.S. Kennedy, 365:Fall87-223
  J.S. Phillipson, 40(AEB):Vol2No2-94
  J.S. Phillipson, 87(BB):Mar88-69
Johnston, C., G.V. Shepherd & M. Worsdale. Vatican Splendour.
  G. Scavizzi, 627(UTQ):Fall87-223
Johnston, D. The Rhetoric of "Leviathan."*
  A.J. Arscott, 529(QQ):Spring88-213
  D.M.F., 185:Oct88-205
  C. Hill, 366:Autumn88-240
  A.P. Martinich, 319:Jul89-474
Johnston, G. – see Whalley, G.
Johnston, J. Fool's Sanctuary.*
  J. Mellors, 364:Mar87-98
Johnston, K.G. The Tip of the Iceberg.*
  W.J. Stuckey, 395(MFS):Summer88-240
Johnston, K.R. Wordsworth and "The Recluse."
  J.A. Hodgson, 591(SIR):Spring88-129
Johnston, M.D. The Spiritual Logic of Ramon Llull.
  E.J. Ashworth, 103:Jan89-22
Johnston, R.H. "New Mecca, New Babylon."
  H. Shukman, 617(TLS):31Mar-6Apr89-335
Johnston, W. The Time of their Lives.
  H. Barratt, 198:Autumn88-112
Johnston, W.M. In Search of Italy.
  639(VQR):Summer88-101
Johnston, W.M. L'esprit viennois.
  M. Pollak, 542:Jan-Mar88-67
Johnstone, M., ed. Illuminating Dance.
  J. Amstutz, 154:Autumn88-543
Johnstone, R. Eden to Edenderry.
  W. Scammell, 617(TLS):3-9Nov89-1216
Jolivet, V. Corpus Vasorum Antiquorum. (France, Vol 33, fasc 22)
  B.A. Sparkes, 303(JoHS):Vol108-268

Jolley, E. My Father's Moon.
  V. Gornick, 441:30Apr89-9
  P. Raine, 617(TLS):28Jul-3Aug89-831
  442(NY):24Apr89-111
Jolley, E. The Newspaper of Claremont Street.*
  A. Bloom, 249(HudR):Autumn88-545
Jolley, E. Stories.*
  P. Saari, 42(AR):Summer88-393
Jolley, E. The Sugar Mother.*
  P. Craig, 617(TLS):3-9Mar89-226
Jolly, C., ed. Histoire des bibliothèques françaises.
  W.H. Barber, 617(TLS):24-30Nov89-1305
Jonaitis, A. Art of the Northern Tlingit.*
  M.M. Halpin, 54:Sep88-534
Jonas, G. The Circuit Riders.
  N. Angier, 441:2Apr89-30
Jonassaint, J. Le Pouvoir des mots, les maux du pouvoir.
  S. Crosta, 627(UTQ):Fall87-212
  J. Samuel, 102(CanL):Spring88-235
Jones, A.H. Ideas and Innovations.*
  P.M. Spacks, 677(YES):Vol19-335
  R. Stamper, 594:Summer88-224
  B. Stovel, 166:Jan89-162
Jones, A.R. – see Wordsworth, W.
Jones, B.T., ed. Dance as Cultural Heritage.* (Vol 2)
  A. Miner, 318(JAOS):Oct-Dec87-842
Jones, C. Chuck Amuck.
  M. Goodman, 441:3Dec89-11
Jones, C. The Longman Companion to the French Revolution.
  A. Forrest, 617(TLS):6-12Oct89-1097
Jones, D.C. Come Winter.
  S.S. Wells, 441:10Dec89-32
Jones, D.C. & I. MacPherson, eds. Building Beyond the Homestead.
  B. Ferguson, 298:Spring/Summer88-219
Jones, D.K. Stewart Mason.
  E.F. Candlin, 324:Nov89-823
Jones, D.R. Peter Brook and "Marat/Sade."
  R. Gordon, 611(TN):Vol42No2-91
Jones, E. Gentlemen and Jesuits.*
  C.J. Jaenen, 298:Spring/Summer88-243
Jones, F.J. The Modern Italian Lyric.
  S. Pearce, 402(MLR):Jan89-193
  L.V., 295(JML):Fall87/Winter88-212
Jones, G. Kairos.
  J. Clute, 617(TLS):6-12Jan89-21
Jones, G. The Norse Atlantic Saga. (2nd ed)
  E. Haugen, 589:Apr88-418
Jones, G.R. Red Revolution.
  J. Fallows, 61:Sep89-107
  L. Lopez Torregrosa, 441:10Sep89-36
Jones, H. "A New Kind of War."
  N. Clive, 617(TLS):15-21Dec89-1382
Jones, J. To Reach Eternity. (G. Hendrick, ed)
  B. De Mott, 441:30Jul89-10
Jones, J.B. – see Fauré, G.
Jones, J.T. Wayward Skeptic.*
  D.T.O., 295(JML):Fall87/Winter88-297
Jones, K. Quite the Other Way.
  D. Finkle, 441:27Aug89-16
Jones, L.E. German Liberalism and the Dissolution of the Weimar Party System, 1918-1933.
  J. Joll, 453(NYRB):27Apr89-53
Jones, M. The Daily Express Guide to Names.
  E. Callary, 424:Mar-Jun88-122

Jones, M., ed. Gentry and Lesser Nobility in Late Medieval Europe.*
N. Saul, 382(MAE):1988/1-89
Jones, M. Last Things.
D. Finkle, 441:24Sep89-48
Jones, M. Talking Jazz.*
G.L. Starks, Jr., 91:Fall88-254
Jones, M.O. Exploring Folk Art.
C.K. Dewhurst, 115:Fall88-428
Jones, N. Mischief Makers.
V.J. Mercer, 441:16Jul89-24
Jones, P.M. The Peasantry in the French Revolution.
W. Scott, 617(TLS):19-25May89-554
Jones, R.A. Arthur Ponsonby.
M. Pugh, 617(TLS):3-9Nov89-1207
Jones, R.B. & M.T. Latimer - see Toomer, J.
Jones, R.C. Engagement with Knavery.*
L. Potter, 447(N&Q):Mar88-85
Jones, R.T. - see Glass, P.
Jones, S.G. Sport, Politics and the Working Class.
J. Walvin, 617(TLS):10-16Nov89-1248
Jones, T. Outward Leg.
S. Pickering, 569(SR):Fall88-673
Jones-Davies, M-T., ed. La Satire au temps de la Renaissance.
I.D. McFarlane, 402(MLR):Apr89-469
de Jonge, A. Stalin and the Shaping of the Soviet Union.
D.W. Treadgold, 396(ModA):Winter88-66
Jongeneel, E. Michel Butor et le pacte romanesque.
C. Sherak, 704(SFR):Fall-Winter88-415
de Jongh, E. Portretten van echt en trouw.
D.R. Smith, 54:Dec88-705
de Jongh-Rossel, E.M. El krausismo y la generación de 1898.*
L.V. Braun, 552(REH):May88-128
J.M. Ruano de la Haza, 345(KRQ):Aug88-382
Jonsen, A.R. & S. Toulmin. The Abuse of Casuistry.
K.W. Kemp, 185:Jul89-945
Jonson, B. The Oxford Authors: Ben Jonson.* (I. Donaldson, ed)
G. Parfitt, 447(N&Q):Jun88-229
Jonsson, B.R., S-B. Jansson & M. Jersild, eds. Sveriges medeltida ballader. (Vol 2)
L. Isaacson, 563(SS):Spring88-323
Jonsson, M. La cura dei monumenti alle origini.
C. Gasparri, 229:Band60Heft6-527
D. Ridgway, 123:Vol38No1-184
Jönsson, R. Ma vie de chien.
D. Pobel, 450(NRF):Dec88-86
Jönsson, R. My Life as a Dog.
M. Stimpson, 617(TLS):13-19Oct89-1132
Joós, E. Poetic Truth and Transvaluation in Nietzsche's "Zarathustra."*
P. Preuss, 154:Winter88-732
Joppien, R. & B. Smith. The Art of Captain Cook's Voyages.* (Vol 3)
J. Egerton, 90:Oct88-780
Jordan, B. Rethinking Welfare.
B.B., 185:Jan89-454
Jordan, C. Babies of Illinois.
G. Gessert, 448:Vol26No1-70
Jordan, C. Pulci's "Morgante."
A.R. Ascoli, 551(RenQ):Spring88-148
Jordan, C. A Terrible Beauty.
639(VQR):Summer88-82

Jordan, D.K. & D.L. Overmyer. The Flying Phoenix.
S. Harrell, 293(JASt):Feb88-119
Jordan, F., with others, eds. The English Romantic Poets.* (4th ed)
S.J. Wolfson, 340(KSJ):Vol37-209
Jordan, J.E. - see Wordsworth, W.
Jordan, J.N. Western Philosophy.
C.C. Rostankowski, 258:Jun88-230
Jordan, K. Henry the Lion.
P.W. Strait, 589:Oct88-946
Jordan, L. The Toy Cupboard.
T.J. Binyon, 617(TLS):22-28Sep89-1022
Jordan, R. & H. Love - see Southerne, T.
Jordan, R.M. Chaucer's Poetics and the Modern Reader.
J. Craig, 178:Dec88-467
Jordan, R.W. Plato's Arguments for Forms.
G.J. Boter, 394:Vol41fasc1/2-157
Jordan, T.E. Victorian Childhood.
H. Cunningham, 637(VS):Winter89-252
Jordan, W.C. From Servitude to Freedom.
F.J. Pegues, 589:Oct88-948
Jordanova, L. Sexual Visions.
E. Showalter, 617(TLS):27Oct-2Nov89-1177
Jordanova, L.J., ed. Languages of Nature.*
E. Block, Jr., 637(VS):Winter89-285
D.G. Charlton, 83:Spring88-107
A.B. Shteir, 173(ECS):Winter88/89-242
Jorden, E.H., with M. Noda. Japanese: The Spoken Language. (Pt 1)
Y. Nakano, 350:Dec89-894
Jørgensen, A. Dansk litteraturhistorisk bibliografi 1967. Danske forfattere pa plade. Litteratur om Johannes V. Jensen.
S.H. Rossel, 563(SS):Winter88-108
Jørgensen, A., ed. Grundtvig-litteratur 1963-1985.
N.L. Jensen, 563(SS):Winter88-95
Jørgensen, J.C. Hamskiftet.
F. Ingwersen, 562(Scan):May88-89
Jørgensen, J.C. Leif Panduro.
S.H. Rossel, 562(Scan):Nov88-198
Jørgensen, K.S.R. La Théorie du roman.
C. Toloudis, 207(FR):Feb89-514
Jorgensen, P.A. William Shakespeare: The Tragedies.*
J. McLauchlan, 447(N&Q):Mar88-81
Jorgenson, D.A. Moritz Hauptmann of Leipzig.
W.J. Gatens, 410(M&L):Jul88-390
M.P. McCune, 308:Fall88-381
Jorro, F.A. - see under Aura Jorro, F.
Jorstad, H.L. & J.N. Davis. The Magazine.
J.A.M. Recker, 399(MLJ):Winter88-472
J.A. Reiter, 207(FR):Oct88-213
José, F.S. Ermita.
I. Buruma, 453(NYRB):1Jun89-7
Joseph, B.D. & I. Philippaki-Warburton. Modern Greek.
G. Horrocks, 297(JL):Mar88-243
Joseph, J.E. Eloquence and Power.
A. Scaglione, 350:Mar89-125
Joseph, L. Curriculum Vitae.
P. Breslin, 491:Oct88-30
H. Hart, 385(MQR):Summer89-417
Joseph, W.A. The Critique of Ultra-leftism in China, 1958-1981.
C-C. Lau, 302:Vol24No1-89
Joseph of Exeter. Trojan War I-III. (A.K. Bate, ed & trans)
A.E. Samuel, 124:Mar-Apr89-328

Josephson, H., ed. Biographical Dictionary of Modern Peace Leaders.
    T.J.K., 185:Oct88–196
Josipovici, G. The Book of God.*
    D. Donoghue, 617(TLS):31Mar–6Apr89–331
Josipovici, G. In the Fertile Land.*
    J. Mellors, 364:Feb88–105
Josselyn, J. John Josselyn, Colonial Traveler. (P.J. Lindholdt, ed)
    R.F. Dolle, 568(SCN):Fall88–54
    A.T. Vaughan, 165(EAL):Vol24No3–266
Jost, J.E. Ten Middle English Arthurian Romances.*
    S. Crane, 589:Jul88–689
Jotischky, A. Marco Polo's Tears.
    P. Reading, 617(TLS):30Jun–6Jul89–713
Jouanny, R. Les voies du lyrisme dans les "Poèmes" de Léopold Sédar Senghor (Chants d'ombre, Hosties noires, Ethiopiques, Nocturnes).
    J. Spleth, 538(RAL):Fall88–406
Joubert, A.J. "La Chronique des Pasquier" et "Cécile parmi nous" de Duhamel. (Vol 1)
    J. Cruickshank, 208(FS):Apr88–229
"Joufroi de Poitiers." (R. Noel, trans)
    N.J. Lacy, 207(FR):Apr89–885
Jourdan, P-A. Les Sandales de paille. (Y. Leclair, ed)
    F-R. Daillie, 450(NRF):Feb88–93
Joussaume, R. Dolmens for the Dead.
    639(VQR):Summer88–103
Jouve, M-A. & J. Demornex. Balenciaga.
    J. Simon, 441:3Dec89–44
Jouve, N.W. Colette.
    S. Freeman, 402(MLR):Oct89–998
Jouve, P-J. Oeuvre.* (J. Starobinski, ed)
    R. Vernier, 207(FR):Oct88–170
    A. Wyss, 98:Mar88–163
Jovino, M.B. – see under Bonghi Jovino, M.
Jowett, B. Dear Miss Nightingale. (V. Quinn & J. Prest, eds)
    A. Summers, 637(VS):Spring89–454
Joy, L.S. Gassendi the Atomist.
    R.H. Popkin, 103:Oct89–396
Joyce, J. James Joyce's Letters to Sylvia Beach, 1921–1940. (M. Banta & O.A. Silverman, eds)
    S. Pinsker, 177(ELT):Vol31No4–499
    B.K. Scott, 329(JJQ):Fall88–141
Joyce, J. Ulysses.* (H.W. Gabler, with C. Melchior & W. Steppe, eds)
    J. Kidd, 517(PBSA):Vol82No4–411
Joyce, J.A. Richard Wright's Art of Tragedy.*
    W.J. Hug, 577(SHR):Summer88–301
    J.B. Moore, 392:Winter87/88–94
    P. Muckley, 295(JML):Fall87/Winter88–405
    C. Werner, 395(MFS):Spring88–125
Joyce, W., H. Ticktin & S. White, eds. Gorbachev and Gorbachevism.
    O. Figes, 617(TLS):4–10Aug89–841
Joye, J-C. Amour, pouvoir et transcendance chez Pierre Corneille.
    C.B. Kerr, 475:Vol15No28–299
Joynson, R.B. The Burt Affair.
    L. Hudson, 617(TLS):3–9Nov89–1201
Juarroz, R. Poésie et Réalité.
    P. Dubrunquez, 450(NRF):Dec88–78
Juchem, J.G. Der notwendig konfliktäre Charakter der Kommunikation.
    F. Unger, 682(ZPSK):Band41Heft3–399

Judd, A. The Noonday Devil.
    J. Lewis, 364:Nov87–100
"Judentum in Wien: Sammlung Max Berger."
    M. Ignatieff, 453(NYRB):29Jun89–21
Judovitz, D. Subjectivity and Representation in Descartes.*
    J.I. Porter, 400(MLN):Sep88–915
Judycka, J., ed. Aristoteles Latinus IX, 1.
    P. Hossfeld, 53(AGP):Band70Heft2–227
Juilland, A. Les Verbes de Céline.* (Pt 1)
    G. Holtus, 72:Band225Heft1–192
    J-P. Saint-Gérand, 535(RHL):Nov-Dec88–1166
Juler, C. Les Orientalistes de l'École Italienne.
    C. Newton, 39:Sep88–215
Juliet, C. Accords.
    F. Mary, 450(NRF):Mar88–86
Jullien, F. La valeur allusive.
    M. Détrie, 549(RLC):Jan–Mar88–68
    G. Siary, 549(RLC):Jan–Mar88–111
Jumsai, S.. Naga.
    N. Barley, 617(TLS):6–12Jan89–18
al-Jundi, A. Al-Sahyuniyya wa'l Islam.
    N. Rejwan, 390:Jan88–51
"June Four." (Z. Jin & Q. Zhou, trans)
    M. Gottschalk, 441:10Dec89–13
Jung, C.G. Psychology and Western Religion.
    W. Schwarz, 617(TLS):24Feb–2Mar89–203
Jung, K.D. – see under Kim Dae Jung
Junghyo, A. White Badge.
    B. Kent, 441:2Jul89–12
Jungraithmayr, H. & W.J.G. Möhlig, eds. Lexikon der Afrikanistik.
    R.M. Voigt, 685(ZDL):2/1987–279
Junius, M. Die Tälas der Nordindischen Musik.
    J. Katz, 410(M&L):Oct88–500
de Junta, J. – see under Jacobo de Junta
Jupp, U., ed. Home Port: Victoria. Deep Sea Stories from the Thermopylae Club.
    E. Thompson, 102(CanL):Spring88–127
Jussawalla, F.F. Family Quarrels.
    R. Ross, 49:Jul88–97
Just, W. Jack Gance.
    J. Martin, 441:1Jan89–1
Justice, D. The Sunset Maker.*
    M. Collier, 473(PR):Vol55No3–490
    D. St. John, 42(AR):Winter88–102
    W. Scammell, 493:Spring88–48
Justinian. Justinian's "Institutes." (P. Birks & G. McLeod, trans)
    Z.M. Packman, 124:May–Jun89–389
Jusufu, A. Love, Women, and Men in Stories from Mendeland.
    R. Finnegan, 538(RAL):Fall88–424
Juszezak, J. L'apologie de la passion.
    A. Reix, 542:Jan–Mar88–124
Juszezak, J. Les sources du symbolisme.
    P. Somville, 542:Jan–Mar88–90
Juvenal. Satires, I, III, X. (2nd ed) (N. Rudd & E. Courtney, eds)
    R.A. La Fleur, 124:Nov–Dec88–122

Kabbani, R. Europe's Myths of Orient.
    F.N. Bohrer, 127:Spring88–49
    J.R. Goodman, 568(SCN):Spring-Summer88–11
    G. Levin, 364:Feb/Mar89–128
Kablitz, A. Lamartines "Méditations poétiques."
    F. Claudon, 535(RHL):Jan–Feb88–131

Kadare, I. Doruntine.*
S. Salisbury, 441:27Aug89-16
Kadir, D. Questing Fictions.*
D. Gerdes, 238:Sep88-560
M. Giammarco, 295(JML):Fall87/Winter88-213
Kadish, A. Historians, Economists and Economic History.
R. Davenport-Hines, 617(TLS):10-16Nov89-1246
Kadish, D.Y. The Literature of Images.*
D.F. Bell, 210(FrF):May88-253
Kadohata, C. The Floating World.
D. O'Hehir, 441:23Jul89-16
C. Ong, 617(TLS):29Dec89/4Jan90-1447
Kaegi, W.E., Jr. & P. White, eds. Rome: Late Republic and Principate.*
K.O. O'Keeffe, 568(SCN):Winter88-82
J.W. Rich, 123:Vol38No1-171
Kael, P. Hooked.
R. Sklar, 441:19Mar89-7
von Kaenel, H-M. Münzprägung und Münzbildnis des Claudius.
J-B. Giard, 229:Band60Heft2-174
Kaes, A. From Hitler to Heimat.
I. Buruma, 453(NYRB):26Oct89-31
Kagan, D. The Fall of the Athenian Empire.*
639(VQR):Spring88-44
Kagan, J. Unstable Ideas.
R.M. Restak, 441:28May89-16
Kagan, J. & S. Lamb, eds. The Emergence of Morality in Young Children.
O. Flanagan, 185:Apr89-644
J. Youniss, 543:Dec88-393
Kagan, S. The Limits of Morality.
S. Scheffler, 617(TLS):1-7Sep89-941
Kagarlitsky, B. The Thinking Reed.
R. Pipes, 617(TLS):3-9Feb89-103
Kahan, S. The Wolf of the Kremlin.
R. Brackman, 390:Feb/Mar88-60
Kahane, H. & R. Graeca et romanica. (Vol 3)
G.M. Messing, 350:Mar89-184
Kahin, A.R., ed. Regional Dynamics of the Indonesian Revolution.
W.H. Frederick, 293(JASt):May88-426
Kähler, H. Berlin - Asphalt und Licht.
A. Drescher, 654(WB):2/1988-337
Kahn, A. J-K. Huysmans.
R. Griffiths, 208(FS):Oct88-484
Kahn, G. & R. Kühn - see Weil, S.
Kahn, J.E., ed. Reader's Digest Reverse Dictionary.
L. Mackinnon, 617(TLS):21-27Apr89-431
Kahn, V. Rhetoric, Prudence, and Skepticism in the Renaissance.*
E. Garver, 125:Fall87-102
S. Rendall, 131(CL):Winter88-59
Kahrs, E., ed. Kalyāṇamitrārāgaṇam.
D.Q. Adams, 318(JAOS):Oct-Dec87-784
Kaikō, T. Darkness in Summer.
L. Allen, 617(TLS):28Apr-4May89-466
Kain, P.J. Marx and Ethics.
D. McLellan, 617(TLS):21-27Jul89-809
Kaiser, G. & J-D. Müller, eds. Höfische Literatur, Hofgesellschaft, Höfische Lebensformen um 1200.*
H. Kratz, 133:Band21Heft2/3-188
Kaiser, G.R. - see Hoffmann, E.T.A.
Kaiser, L.M. - see Catullus
Kaiser, N.A. Social Integration and Narrative Structure.
K. Hasselbach, 406:Fall88-395
Kaiser, O. - see Borger, R. & others

Kakonis, T. Michigan Roll.*
T.J. Binyon, 617(TLS):11-17Aug89-878
Kal, V. On Intuition and Discursive Reasoning in Aristotle.
L.P. Schrenk, 543:Jun89-842
Kalakuckaja, L.P. Sklonenie familij i ličnyx imen v russkom literaturnom jazyke.
A. Mustajoki, 559:Vol12No1-100
Kalechofsky, R. The Persistence of Error.
R.L. Greenwood, 103:Oct89-418
Kalia, N.N. From Sexism to Equality.
G. Minault, 293(JASt):Nov88-814
Kālidāsa. The Origin of the Young God. (H. Heifetz, ed & trans)
R.A. Hueckstedt, 318(JAOS):Apr-Jun87-363
B.S. Miller, 293(JASt):Feb88-179
Kalikoff, B. Murder and Moral Decay in Victorian Popular Literature.*
L. Fletcher, 177(ELT):Vol31No3-383
N.J. Tyson, 635(VPR):Summer88-86
Kalinowski, G. Sémiotique et philosophie.*
M. Seymour, 154:Spring88-165
Kalinowski, G. - see Regneri, C.
Kalish, J. Josef Škvorecký.
S. Latham, 470:Vol26-171
R.B. Pynsent, 575(SEER):Jul88-500
Kallet, M. Honest Simplicity in William Carlos Williams' "Asphodel, That Greeny Flower."*
G.S. Lensing, 569(SR):Winter88-113
Kallgren, J.K. & D.F. Simon, eds. Educational Exchanges.
S.P. Ogden, 293(JASt):Aug88-601
Kálmán, B., ed. Wogulisches Wörterbuch.
P. Hauel, 682(ZPSK):Band41Heft1-134
Kalnins, M., ed. D.H. Lawrence.*
C. Jansohn, 72:Band224Heft2-466
D.T.O., 295(JML):Fall87/Winter88-345
Kalpakian, L. The Swallow Inheritance.
L. Dawson-Evans, 565:Summer88-54
Kalpaxis, T.E. Hemiteles.
R.A. Tomlinson, 303(JoHS):Vol108-265
Kalsi, M-L.S. - see under Schubert Kalsi, M-L.
Kalupahana, D.J. Nāgārjuna.
C. Hallisey, 293(JASt):May88-402
Kalupahana, D.J. The Principle of Buddhist Psychology.
A. Sponberg, 293(JASt):Aug88-573
Kalven, H., Jr. A Worthy Tradition.* (J. Kalven, ed)
D.M., 185:Jul89-978
639(VQR):Summer88-95
Kalwies, H.H. - see Salel, H.
Kamensky, A. Chagall: The Russian Years 1907-1922.
J. Russell, 441:3Dec89-9
Kaminski, A. Kith and Kin.*
R. Di Antonio, 390:Nov88-57
Kaminski, T. The Early Career of Samuel Johnson.
C.E. Pierce, Jr., 173(ECS):Fall88-102
Kaminsky, H. & S. Talent.
W. Smith, 441:6Aug89-18
"Madeleine Kamman's Savoie."
R. Flaste, 441:3Dec89-18
Kammen, R. Big Horn Gunfighter. Long Henry. Wind River Kill. Wyoming Gunsmoke.
J.D. Nesbitt, 649(WAL):Feb89-373
Kampers-Manhe, B. & C. Vet, eds. Études de linguistique française offertes à Robert de
[continued]

[continuing]
Dardel par ses amis et collègues.
   M.A. Jones, 402(MLR):Jul89-734
   Y. Roberge, 350:Sep89-667
Kampits, P. Ludwig Wittgenstein.
   R. Wimmer, 489(PJGG):Band95Heft2-439
Kanatchikov, S.I. A Radical Worker in Tsarist
   Russia.* (R.E. Zelnik, ed & trans)
   H. Hogan, 550(RusR):Jan88-102
Kanda, C.G. Shinzō.*
   C. Wheelwright, 318(JAOS):Apr-Jun87-
   344
Kändler, K., H. Karolewski & I. Siebert, eds.
   Berliner Begegnungen.
   J. Schebera, 654(WB):6/1988-1042
Kandzia, C., ed. Behnisch & Partners: Designs
   1952-1987.
   P.B. Jones, 46:Jun88-8
Kane, C.J. Blood and Sable.
   639(VQR):Summer88-93
Kane, E.J. The S & L Insurance Mess.
   A.M. Solomon, 441:29Oct89-27
Kane, J. Running the Amazon.
   J. Paine, 441:30Jul89-17
Kane, R. Free Will and Values.
   R. Double, 518:Apr88-96
Kaneko Mitsuharu. Shijin. (A.D. Syrokomla-
   Stefanowska, ed)
   S.M. Strong, 407(MN):Winter88-476
Kanellos, N. Mexican American Theater.
   C. Morton, 352(LATR):Fall88-141
   O.U. Somoza, 238:Dec88-843
Kanfer, S. A Summer World.
   J. Cohen, 441:24Dec89-24
Kang, W.J. Religion and Politics Under the
   Japanese Rule.
   D.N. Clark, 293(JASt):Aug88-663
Kang, Y.A. Schema and Symbol.
   S. Feldman, 342:Band79Heft2-239
Kaniuk, Y. His Daughter.
   B. Cheyette, 617(TLS):3-9Feb89-114
   D. Donoghue, 453(NYRB):28Sep89-39
   J. Henkin, 441:4Jun89-11
Kansteiner, A. - see von Droste-Hülshoff, A.
Kant, I. Grundlegung zur Metaphysik der
   Sitten. (T. Valentiner, ed)
   W. Steinbeck, 342:Band79Heft1-111
Kant, I. Kant's Latin Writings.* (L.W. Beck,
   with others, eds)
   D.E. Walford, 482(PhR):Jul88-427
Kant, I. Observations in the Feeling of the
   Beautiful and Sublime. (J.T. Goldthwait,
   trans)
   R.M., 342:Band79Heft2-251
Kant, I. Perpetual Peace and Other Essays on
   Politics, History and Morals. (T. Humphrey,
   ed & trans)
   T. Mautner, 342:Band79Heft4-481
Kant, I. Der Streit der Fakultäten. (S.
   Dietzsch, ed)
   R.M., 342:Band79Heft1-112
Kant, I. Zum ewigen Frieden.
   R.M., 342:Band79Heft1-111
Kanter, R.M. When Giants Learn to Dance.
   M.G. Butler, 441:29Oct89-40
   C. Handy, 324:Nov89-821
"Kantian Ethical Thought."
   R.M., 342:Band79Heft2-253
Kantorowicz, E. L'Empereur Frédéric II.
   H. Cronel, 450(NRF):Jun88-83
Kany, R. Mnemosyne als Programm.
   H. Lloyd-Jones, 123:Vol38No1-136

Kao, M., ed. Twentieth-Century Chinese
   Painting.
   J. Rawson, 617(TLS):6-12Oct89-1099
Kao, S. Lire Valéry.*
   H. Laurenti, 535(RHL):Jan-Feb88-145
   S. Nash, 188(ECr):Spring88-108
Kaoru, U. - see under Umehara Kaoru
Kaplan, A.R., M.A. Hoover & W.B. Moore. The
   Minnesota Ethnic Food Book.*
   N. Groce, 292(JAF):Jan-Mar88-93
Kaplan, A.Y. Reproductions of Banality.
   R. Wagner-Pacifici, 295(JML):Fall87/
   Winter88-198
Kaplan, C. & E.C. Rose, ed. Doris Lessing.
   B. Draine, 395(MFS):Winter88-709
Kaplan, E. - see Michelet, J.
Kaplan, E.A., ed. Postmodernism and its Dis-
   contents.
   M. Walters, 617(TLS):22-28Dec89-1419
Kaplan, E.A. Rocking Around the Clock.*
   R.S. Denisoff, 498:Summer88-63
Kaplan, F. Dickens.*
   J. Bayley, 453(NYRB):19Jan89-11
   P. Rogers, 617(TLS):7-13Apr89-360
   442(NY):6Feb89-107
Kaplan, F. Sacred Tears.*
   R. Beum, 569(SR):Spring88-xxiv
Kaplan, F., M. Goldberg & F.J. Fielding. Lec-
   tures on Carlyle & his Era. (J.D. James &
   R.B. Bottoms, eds)
   W. Myers, 402(MLR):Jan89-132
Kaplan, J. Pearl's Progress.
   J. Marcus, 441:23Apr89-20
Kaplan, J.A. Unexpected Journeys.
   R. Cardinal, 617(TLS):31Mar-6Apr89-336
   G.A. Cevasco, 324:Aug89-596
Kaplan, M. Science, Language and the Human
   Condition.
   J.P. Dougherty, 543:Jun89-843
Kaplan, P.H.D. The Rise of the Black Magus in
   Western Art.*
   J.C. Smith, 589:Jan88-181
Kaplan, S.H. L.A. Lost & Found.
   D. Gantenbein, 45:Jan88-53
   R. Herron, 46:Dec87-10
Kaplan, W. Everything that Floats.
   J. Stanton, 529(QQ):Summer88-494
Kaplowitt, S.J. The Ennobling Power of Love
   in the Medieval German Lyric.
   H. Bekker, 133:Band21Heft2/3-196
   S.L. Clark, 221(GQ):Summer88-459
   H. Heinen, 406:Summer88-215
   W.E. Jackson, 589:Apr88-419
   W.C. McDonald, 301(JEGP):Jul88-406
Kapp, R. Studien zum Spätwerk Robert Schu-
   manns.
   L.C. Roesner, 410(M&L):Jul88-392
Kappeler, S. The Pornography of Representa-
   tion.
   E. Bronfen, 59:Mar88-123
   J. Jiambalvo, 532(RCF):Spring88-195
   E. Rooney, 454:Fall88-106
Kapur, B.K. Singapore Studies.
   Chew Sock Foon, 293(JASt):Feb88-198
Kapur, H., ed. As China Sees the World.
   W-C. Lee, 293(JASt):Aug88-597
Karadžić, V.S. Les Contes populaires serbes.
   L. Kovacs, 450(NRF):Feb88-105
Karasch, M.C. Slave Life in Rio de Janeiro,
   1808-1850.
   A. Hennessy, 617(TLS):14-20Jul89-763

Karayannis, G.S. L'amour pédagogique dans la Grèce antique.
  A. Reix, 542:Apr-Jun88-243
Karbo, K. Trespassers Welcome Here.
  E.S. Brockman, 441:21May89-11
Karch, D. Dahn Kr. Pirmasens. Wilgartwiesen Kr. Pirmasens. Iggelbach Kr. Bad Dürkheim.
  H. Tatzreiter, 685(ZDL):3/1987-376
Karcher, C.L. - see Child, L.M.
Karius, I. Die Ableitung der denominalen Verben mit Nullsuffigierung im Englischen.*
  E. Leitzke, 38:Band106Heft1/2-169
Karl, F.R. William Faulkner.
  J.W. Aldridge, 441:14May89-3
Karl, F.R. & L. Davies - see Conrad, J.
Karlin, D. The Courtship of Robert Browning and Elizabeth Barrett.*
  C.D. Ryals, 677(YES):Vol18-346 [inadvertently deleted from prev]
  K. Tetzeli von Rosador, 38:Band106 Heft1/2-256
Karlin, D. - see Browning, R. & E.B.
Karlinger, F. Zauberschlaf und Entrückung.
  N.F. Palmer, 196:Band29Heft1/2-209
Karlinger, F. & J. Pögl, eds & trans. Märchen aus der Karibik.
  E. Ettlinger, 203:Vol99No1-134
Karlinsky, S. Marina Tsvetaeva.*
  H.B., 295(JML):Fall87/Winter88-391
Karlsen, C.F. The Devil in the Shape of a Woman.
  B. Rosenthal, 432(NEQ):Sep88-468
Karman, J. Robinson Jeffers.*
  R.J. Brophy, 649(WAL):Feb89-367
Karmay, S.G. Secret Visions of the Fifth Dalai Lama.
  J. Snelling, 617(TLS):3-9Feb89-119
Karnein, A. "De Amore" in volksprachlicher Literatur.*
  P. Cherchi, 379(MedR):Aug86-292
Karnow, S. In Our Image.
  R. Bonner, 442(NY):30Oct89-112
  I. Buruma, 453(NYRB):1Jun89-7
  P. Kreisberg, 441:2Apr89-1
Karodia, F. Coming Home and Other Stories.
  J.R. Moehringer, 441:19Feb89-20
Karpeles, M. - see Sharp, C.
Karr, M. Abacus.
  R. Katrovas, 434:Spring89-340
Karsh, E., ed. The Iran-Iraq War.
  M. Yapp, 617(TLS):4-10Aug89-842
Karumanchiri Polesini, L. & J. Vizmuller-Zocco. L'uso delle preposizioni in italiano.
  D. Maceri, 399(MLJ):Spring88-98
Kasack, W. Lexikon der russischen Literatur ab 1917.
  F. Scholz, 688(ZSP):Band48Heft2-402
Kasatkin, L.L. Russkij dialektnyj konsonantizm kak istočnik istorii russkogo jazyka.
  W. Lehfeldt, 559:Vol12No1-77
Kaser, M. Römische Rechtsquellen und angewandte Juristenmethode.
  J.A. Crook, 313:Vol78-250
Kashap, S.P. Spinoza and Moral Freedom.
  D.G., 185:Jan89-458
Kasinec, E. Slavic Books and Bookmen.
  W.F. Ryan, 575(SEER):Jan88-129
Kasper, G., ed. Learning, Teaching and Communication in the Foreign Language Classroom.
  J. John, 257(IRAL):Nov88-329

Kasper, W. Semantik des Konjunktivs II in Deklarativsätzen des Deutschen.
  M.R. Barnes, 133:Band21Heft4-380
  B.J. Koekkoek, 221(GQ):Summer88-456
Kassel, R. & C. Austin, eds. Poetae comici Graeci. (Vol 3, Pt 2)
  W.G. Arnott, 303(JoHS):Vol108-226
Kassel, R. & C. Austin, eds. Poetae Comici Graeci. (Vol 5)
  R.L. Hunter, 123:Vol38No1-14
Kasten, I. Frauendienst bei Trobadors und Minnesängern im 12. Jahrhundert.
  H. Bekker, 301(JEGP):Apr88-286
  M. Eikelmann, 684(ZDA):Band117Heft2-77
  D.H. Green, 402(MLR):Jul89-701
Kaster, R.A. Guardians of Language.
  A. Cameron, 617(TLS):14-20Apr89-399
Kastner, M.S. - see under Santiago Kastner, M.
Kastner, R. Geistlicher Rauffhandel.
  J. Schwitalla, 680(ZDP):Band107Heft1-149
Kastovsky, D. & A. Szwedek, eds. Linguistics across Historical and Geographical Boundaries.*
  W. Elmer, 38:Band106Heft1/2-145
Kasulis, T.P. - see Yuasa, Y.
Kasun, J. The War against Population.
  T. Martin, 42(AR):Fall88-526
Kasza, G.J. The State and the Mass Media in Japan 1918-1945.
  Haruhara Akihiko, 285(JapQ):Oct-Dec88-437
  R.H. Mitchell, 407(MN):Winter88-495
Katai, T. Literary Life in Tōkyō 1885-1915.
  W.E. Naff, 407(MN):Summer88-236
Kates, J. The Taste of Things.
  M. Matthews, 376:Jun88-196
Katič, I. Dansk-russiske veterinaere forbindelser 1796-1976.
  M.F. Metcalf, 550(RusR):Jul88-332
Katičić, R. Sintaksa hrvatskoga književnog jezika.
  V. Žegarac, 575(SEER):Apr88-265
Katō Shuichi. Histoire de la littérature japonaise.
  M. Détrie, 549(RLC):Jan-Mar88-67
Kato, W. Escape from Idi Amin's Slaughterhouse.
  A. Maja-Pearce, 617(TLS):15-21Sep89-992
Katrak, K.H. Wole Soyinka and Modern Tragedy.
  M. Banham, 295(JML):Fall87/Winter88-383
  S.L. Richards, 615(TJ):Mar88-137
  M.B. Wilkerson, 610:Summer88-179
Katre, S.M. "Aṣṭādhyāyi" of Pānini in Roman Transliteration.
  E.A. Ebbinghaus, 215(GL):Vol28No1-77
Katsh, M.E. The Electronic Media and the Transformation of Law.
  P.J. Williams, 441:20Aug89-23
Kattan, N. Le Repos et L'oubli.
  S. Drache, 526:Autumn88-87
Katz, D.S. Sabbath and Sectarianism in Seventeenth-Century England.
  P. Collinson, 617(TLS):17-23Feb89-155
Katz, G.S. Dialogues for Practice in Idiomatic Italian.
  J.L. Laurenti, 399(MLJ):Winter88-480

Kearney, R. Modern Movements in European Philosophy.
  J.M. Carvalho, 103:Aug89-312
  J. Dunphy, 63:Jun88-272
Kearney, R. Poétique du possible.
  A. Reix, 542:Jan-Mar88-90
Kearney, R. Transitions. The Wake of Imagination.
  T. Eagleton, 617(TLS):10-16Feb89-132
Kearns, C.M. T.S. Eliot and Indic Traditions.
  W. Harmon, 569(SR):Winter88-105
Kearns, M.S. Metaphors of Mind in Fiction and Psychology.
  W. Hughes, 637(VS):Spring89-416
Keating, M. The City That Refused to Die: Glasgow.
  D. Harvey, 617(TLS):7-13Apr89-356
Keating, M. To the Last Drop.
  A. Crowder, 529(QQ):Autumn88-747
Keating, M. & P. Hainsworth. Decentralisation and Change in Contemporary France.
  R. Kuhn, 208(FS):Apr88-250
Keating, P. The Haunted Study.
  D. Trotter, 617(TLS):29Sep-5Oct89-1066
Keaveney, A. Rome and the Unification of Italy.*
  T.J. Cornell, 313:Vol78-202
Keay, S.J. Roman Spain.
  J.J. Wilkes, 617(TLS):7-13Apr89-374
Kebric, R.B. The Paintings in the Cnidian Lesche at Delphi and their Historical Context.
  T. Hölscher, 229:Band60Heft5-465
  G. Roux, 555:Vol61fasc1-103
Kecskési, M. African Masterpieces from Munich.
  S.P. Blier, 2(AfrA):Nov87-75
Kedourie, E. Perestroika in the Universities.
  J. Campbell, 617(TLS):29Dec89/4Jan90-1432
Kedrov, B.M. 1986.
  N. Zitzelsberger, 574(SEEJ):Summer88-341
Kee, H.C. Medicine, Miracle and Magic in New Testament Times.
  H. King, 303(JoHS):Vol108-248
Kee, R. Munich.*
  A.J. Nicholls, 364:Oct/Nov88-119
Keeble, N.H. The Literary Culture of Nonconformity in Later Seventeenth-Century England.*
  P.R. Backscheider, 173(ECS):Winter88/89-261
  R. Sharrock, 166:Oct88-67
Keefe, R. & J.A. Walter Pater and the Gods of Disorder.
  L. Dowling, 637(VS):Spring89-455
  B.A. Inman, 445(NCF):Mar89-539
  639(VQR):Autumn88-138
Keefe, T. French Existentialist Fiction.*
  D.B., 295(JML):Fall87/Winter88-213
Keefer, J.K. The Paris-Napoli Express.*
  P. Klovan, 102(CanL):Spring88-211
Keefer, J.K. Transgressions.
  S.H. Elderkin, 526:Autumn88-97
Keefer, J.K. Under Eastern Eyes.
  W.M. Bogaards, 627(UTQ):Fall88-148
Keefer, J.K. White of the Lesser Angels.*
  S.H. Elderkin, 526:Autumn88-97
  D. Precosky, 102(CanL):Spring88-172

Keegan, J. The Price of Admiralty.
  P-L. Adams, 61:Apr89-99
  G.A. Craig, 453(NYRB):17Aug89-31
  K.J. Hagan, 441:16Apr89-12
  442(NY):26Jun89-92
Keegan, J. The Second World War.
  M. Carver, 617(TLS):1-7Sep89-935
  P. Kennedy, 441:31Dec89-10
Keegan, J. - see "The Times Atlas of the Second World War"
Keegan, W. Mr. Lawson's Gamble.
  F. Cairncross, 617(TLS):1-7Dec89-1326
Keel, A. - see Bjørnson, B.
Keele, A.F. Understanding Günter Grass.
  A.D. White, 402(MLR):Oct89-1047
Keeler, W. Javanese Shadow Plays, Javanese Selves.
  J. Peacock, 293(JASt):May88-428
Keeley, E. The Salonika Bay Murder.
  S. Salisbury, 441:25Jun89-25
  C.M. Woodhouse, 453(NYRB):12Oct89-58
Keenan, E.L. & L.M. Faltz. Boolean Semantics for Natural Language.*
  A. Cormack, 297(JL):Sep88-532
Keenan, J. Blue Heaven.
  A. Hornaday, 441:29Jan89-30
  42(AR):Fall88-532
Keene, D. The Pleasures of Japanese Literature.
  E. Hanson, 441:12Mar89-23
  J. McMullen, 617(TLS):7-13Apr89-370
Keene, D. Survey of Medieval Winchester.
  J. Blair, 382(MAE):1988/1-99
Keene, D. Travelers of a Hundred Ages.
  442(NY):25Sep89-121
Keene, R. & N. Divinsky. Warriors of the Mind.
  J. Speelman, 617(TLS):22-28Sep89-1041
Keepnews, O. The View From Within.*
  A. Lively, 617(TLS):29Dec89/4Jan90-1438
Kees, W. Weldon Kees and the Midcentury Generation.* (R.E. Knoll, ed)
  R. McPhillips, 502(PrS):Summer88-123
  P.T.S., 295(JML):Fall87/Winter88-343
Keesey, D., ed. Contexts for Criticism.
  J.R. Bennett, 128(CE):Sep88-566
Keeshan, B. Growing Up Happy.
  K. Lynch, 441:17Sep89-20
Keesing, N. Riding the Elephant.
  S.E. Lee, 581:Sep88-336
Keillor, G. We Are Still Married.
  B. Henderson, 441:9Apr89-13
  E. Korn, 617(TLS):3-9Nov89-1217
Keith, W.J. Regions of the Imagination.
  R. Inboden, 395(MFS):Winter88-682
  F.S. Schwarzbach, 617(TLS):6-12Jan89-15
  K.E. Welsh, 637(VS):Spring89-422
Keith-Smith, B. & K. Mills, eds. Büchner in Britain.
  T.M. Holmes, 402(MLR):Jan89-240
Kekes, J. The Examined Life.
  N.J.H. Dent, 103:Sep89-369
Kell, R. In Praise of Warmth.
  L. Sail, 565:Spring88-73
Keller, E. & M. Gopnik, eds. Motor and Sensory Processes of Language.
  J.F. Kess, 320(CJL):Mar88-107
Keller, E.F. Reflections on Gender and Science.*
  L. Ratcliffe, 529(QQ):Spring88-215

Keller, H. Criticism. (J. Hogg, ed)
P. Stadlen, 410(M&L):Jul88-402
S. Walsh, 607:Mar88-41
Keller, H. The Great Haydn Quartets.
J. Dack, 410(M&L):Jan88-80
W.D. Sutcliffe, 411:Oct88-349
Keller, H-E., with others, eds. Studia Occitanica in memoriam Paul Remy.* (Vol 1)
E. Poe, 589:Apr88-420
Keller, H-E. & others, eds. Studia Occitanica. (Vol 2)
M.B. Booth, 402(MLR):Jan89-154
Keller, J.E. Las narraciones breves piadosas versificadas en el castellano y gallego del medievo de Berceo a Alfonso X. (A.A. Fernández-Vázquez, ed & trans)
G.D. Grennia, 140(CH):Vol10-135
Keller, M. Rude Awakening.
A.B. Fisher, 441:29Oct89-38
Kellerman, F. The Ritual Bath.
J. Riemer, 287:Mar/Apr88-31
Kellerman, J. Silent Partner.
R. Herbert, 441:22Oct89-20
Kellermann, H. Die Weltanschauung im Romanwerk von Doris Lessing.
E. Auberlen, 72:Band224Heft2-416
Kelley, A.V. To the Lighthouse.
J.E. Fisher, 395(MFS):Winter88-692
Kelley, D. The Evidence of the Senses.
D. Gordon, 258:Sep88-337
Kelley, K.L. Models for the Multitudes.
B. Bair, 594:Spring88-108
Kelley, P. & R. Hudson - see Browning, R. & E.B.
Kellner, B., ed. The Harlem Renaissance.*
D.E. McGinty, 91:Spring88-106
Kellner, B. - see Van Vechten, C.
Kelly, A.A. Mary Lavin.
M. Koenig, 272(IUR):Spring88-146
Kelly, B. & M. London. The Four Little Dragons.
F. Gibney, 441:29Oct89-37
Kelly, B.P. To the Place of Trumpets.
A. Corn, 491:Jan89-234
J. Kitchen, 219(GaR):Summer88-407
A. Klauke, 448:Vol26No1-121
639(VQR):Autumn88-133
Kelly, C. Rousseau's Exemplary Life.^
A. Hartle, 103:Nov88-452
A. Rosenberg, 627(UTQ):Spring89-417
639(VQR):Summer88-89
Kelly, D., ed. The Romances of Chrétien de Troyes.
N.J. Lacy, 589:Jul88-690
Kelly, F. & G.L. Carr. The Early Landscapes of Frederic Edwin Church 1845-1854.
A. Wilton, 90:May88-378
Kelly, H.A. Canon Law and the Archpriest of Hita.*
F. Domínguez, 241:Jan88-87
Kelly, H.A. The Devil at Baptism.
C.W. Marx, 382(MAE):1988/1-82
Kelly, I. Hong Kong.
E. Cooper, 293(JASt):May88-353
Kelly, J., with E. Domville - see Yeats, W.B.
Kelly, J.P. Look into the Sun.
G. Jonas, 441:21May89-26
Kelly, L., ed. Tobias Smollett: The Critical Heritage.*
G.S. Rousseau, 173(ECS):Winter88/89-256
Kelly, L. Women of the French Revolution.
J.F. McMillan, 617(TLS):21-27Jul89-792

Kelly, M. Florrie's Girls.
P. Craig, 617(TLS):1-7Dec89-1337
Kelly, M.T. A Dream Like Mine.
A.B. Nicholas, 198:Summer88-98
Kelly, R. Doctor of Silence.
S. Moore, 532(RCF):Fall88-158
Kelly, W.W. Deference and Defiance in Nineteenth-Century Japan.*
W.B. Hauser, 318(JAOS):Jan-Mar87-167
Kelman, J. A Disaffection.
M. Kirby, 441:18Jun89-14
G. Mangan, 617(TLS):24Feb-2Mar89-191
Kelman, J. Greyhound for Breakfast.* A Chancer.
P. Lewis, 565:Spring88-35
Kelman, S. Making Public Policy.
S. Elkin, 185:Jan89-438
Kelsall, M. Byron's Politics.
M. Storey, 541(RES):May88-309
Kelsen, H. Théorie pure du droit. (2nd ed)
M. Hartney, 103:Nov89-442
Kelton, E. The Man Who Rode Midnight.
L. Clayton, 649(WAL):May88-86
Kelvin, N. - see Morris, W.
Kemal, S. Kant and Fine Art.*
E. Schaper, 479(PhQ):Oct88-537
Kemme, T. Political Fiction, the Spirit of the Age, and Allen Drury.
J.G. Cawelti, 27(AL):Oct88-485
Kemmelman, H. One Fine Day the Rabbi Bought a Cross.
J. Riemer, 287:Mar/Apr88-31
Kemp, B.J. Ancient Egypt.
T.G.H. James, 617(TLS):6-12Oct89-1096
Kemp, I. Hector Berlioz: "Les Troyens."
J. Warrack, 617(TLS):24Feb-2Mar89-187
Kemp, J. Architectural Ornamentalism.
H. Muschamp, 139:Jun/Jul88-96
Kemp, M. - see da Vinci, L.
Kemp, M. & J. Roberts, with P. Steadman. Leonardo da Vinci.
C. Hope, 453(NYRB):17Aug89-16
Kemp, S. Kipling's Hidden Narratives.
J.M. Lyon, 617(TLS):26May-1Jun89-576
Kemp, S. - see Kipling, R.
Kemper, H-G. Deutsche Lyrik der frühen Neuzeit. (Vols 1 & 2)
P. Macardle, 402(MLR):Jul89-775
Kempers, B. Kunst, macht en mecenaat.
J.L. de Jong, 600:Vol18No3-160
Kendall, F. & L. Louw. After Apartheid.
G.M. Fredrickson, 453(NYRB):26Oct89-48
Kendall, L. The Life and Hard Times of a Korean Shaman.
L.S. Lewis, 293(JASt):Nov88-907
Kendall, L. & G. Dix, eds. Religion and Ritual in Korean Society.
G.F. Kennedy, 293(JASt):May88-387
Kendall, R.D. The Drama of Dissent.
L.H. Carlson, 551(RenQ):Spring88-162
I. Clark, 301(JEGP):Oct88-577
P. Happé, 401(MLQ):Mar87-96
J. Mueller, 604:Winter88-1
Kendon, A. Sign Languages of Aboriginal Australia.
W.C. Stokoe, 617(TLS):25-31Aug89-925
Kendrick, C. Milton.*
G. Campbell, 402(MLR):Jan89-127
D. Chambers, 541(RES):Feb88-108
M. Grossman, 551(RenQ):Spring88-175
R. Helgerson, 301(JEGP):Oct88-582
G. Teskey, 153:Spring88-42

Kerman, C.E. & R. Eldridge. The Lives of Jean Toomer.*
 R.P. Bryd, 459:Spring88-83
 C. Werner, 395(MFS):Spring88-125
Kerman, J. Contemplating Music.
 R. Cox, 577(SHR):Winter88-86
Kermode, F. An Appetite for Poetry.
 N. Auerbach, 441:1Oct89-12
Kermode, F. Forms of Attention.*
 R. Lundin, 290(JAAC):Winter87-316
Kermode, F. History and Value.*
 A. Leighton, 617(TLS):1-7Sep89-950
Kernan, A. Printing Technology, Letters and Samuel Johnson.*
 P. Alkon, 191(ELN):Sep88-73
 S. Fix, 173(ECS):Summer88-521
 P.J. Korshin, 470:Vol26-194
 W.J. Ong, 536(Rev):Vol10-97
 M. Rose, 494:Vol8No3/4-714
 D. Womersley, 541(RES):Nov88-559
Kernfeld, B., ed. The New Grove Dictionary of Jazz.
 W. Balliett, 442(NY):14Aug89-88
 E.J. Hobsbawm, 617(TLS):3-9Feb89-105
Kerr, C.B., ed. Une Fenêtre ouverte sur la création.
 J. Cruickshank, 208(FS):Apr88-239
Kerr, F. Theology after Wittgenstein.*
 J. Haldane, 479(PhQ):Apr88-259
Kerr, L. Suspended Fictions.*
 C.S. Mathieu, 238:Sep88-557
Kerrigan, J. & J. Wordsworth - see Davies, H.S.
Kerrigan, W. The Sacred Complex.
 G. Teskey, 153:Spring88-42
Kerth, T., ed. Hermann von Sachsenheim: "Des Spiegels Abenteuer."
 A. Classen, 201:Vol14-218
Kesey, K. Demon Box.*
 C.J. Fox, 364:Mar87-109
Kessler, E. Flannery O'Connor and the Language of the Apocalypse.*
 M.D.O., 295(JML):Fall87/Winter88-363
Kessler, H.L. - see Demus, O.
Kessler, R. Moscow Station.
 D. Wise, 441:19Mar89-12
Kessler, R. Spy vs. Spy.*
 639(VQR):Autumn88-130
Kessner, T. Fiorello H. La Guardia and the Making of Modern New York.
 K. Auletta, 441:15Oct89-3
Kestner, J. Protest and Reform.*
 H.G. Klaus, 224(GRM):Band38Heft1/2-232
 T. Ørum, 462(OL):Vol43No1-88
Ketcham, M.G. Transparent Designs.*
 R.W.F. Kroll, 83:Autumn88-226
 A.F.T. Lurcock, 447(N&Q):Mar88-94
Ketcham, R. Individualism and Public Life.*
 N.S.C., 185:Oct88-188
Ketchian, S. The Poetry of Anna Akhmatova.
 W. Rosslyn, 575(SEER):Jan88-127
Keteyian, A. Big Red Confidential.
 A. Barra, 441:22Oct89-29
de Ketham, J. The Text and Concordance of the "Compendio de la humana salud," I-51, Biblioteca Nacional, Madrid. (M.T. Herrera, ed)
 T.M. Capuano, 304(JHP):Winter88-155
Ketner, K.L. & C.J.W. Kloesel - see Fisch, M.H.
Ketterer, D. Imprisoned in a Tesseract.
 D.M. Hassler, 395(MFS):Summer88-325
 H. Molitor, 178:Jun88-235

Kettering, E. Nähe.
 H. Mörchen, 489(PJGG):Band95Heft1-183
Kettle, M. Russia and the Allies. (Vol 2)
 E. Mawdsley, 617(TLS):31Mar-6Apr89-335
Keun, I. Ich lebe in einem wilden Wirbel. (G. Kreis & M.S. Strauss, eds)
 S. Parkes, 402(MLR):Jul89-804
Kevles, D.J. The Physicists.
 J. Polkinghorne, 617(TLS):17-23Mar89-273
Keyes, C. The Aesthetics of Power.*
 R.B.D., 295(JML):Fall87/Winter88-376
 W.H. Green, 580(SCR):Spring89-80
Keyes, C.F. Thailand.
 C.J. Reynolds, 293(JASt):Nov88-940
Keyserlingk, R.H. Austria in World War II.
 R. Knight, 617(TLS):21-27Jul89-797
Keyssar, A. Out of Work.
 R.D. Brown, 432(NEQ):Jun88-260
Khačikjan, M.L. Khurritskii i urartskii jazyki.
 P. Michalowski, 318(JAOS):Apr-Jun87-332
Khalid, F. Black Mirrors.
 J. Mellors, 364:Feb87-103
Khalidi, T., ed. Land Tenure and Social Transformation in the Middle East.
 M.L. Venzke, 318(JAOS):Apr-Jun87-382
Khan, H-U., with S. Cantacuzino & C. Correa. Charles Correa.
 S. Gutterman, 45:Jul88-65
Khan, M.M.R. The Long Wait.
 J. Malcolm, 441:9Apr89-25
Khan, N. Women's Poetry of the First World War.
 T. Castle, 617(TLS):2-8Jun89-607
Khan-Magomedov, S.O. Pioneers of Soviet Architecture.*
 E.K. Beaulour, 574(SEEJ):Fall88-491
 Y-A. Bois, 55:Mar88-93
Khan-Magomedov, S.O. Alexandr Vesnin and Russian Constructivism.*
 J.E. Bowlt, 90:Aug88-640
 P. Lizon, 47:Oct88-43
 C. Lodder, 575(SEER):Jul88-469
 V. Margolin, 574(SEEJ):Fall88-489
al-Kharrat, E. City of Saffron.
 R. Irwin, 617(TLS):15-21Sep89-1006
Khlebnikov, V. The Collected Works. (Vol 1) (C. Douglas, ed)
 M. Perloff, 703:Fall88-184
Khong Cho Oon. The Politics of Oil in Indonesia.
 D.Y. King, 293(JASt):May88-429
Khoury, P.S. Urban Notables and Arab Nationalism.
 M. Muslih, 318(JAOS):Jan-Mar87-179
Kibbey, A. The Interpretation of Material Shapes in Puritanism.*
 M.A. Bellesiles, 106:Summer88-233
 G. Breese, 27(AL):Oct88-467
 S. Bush, Jr., 402(MLR):Oct89-962
 P. Lindholdt, 569(SR):Summer88-464
 M. Lowance, Jr., 551(RenQ):Autumn88-535
 S.E. Marovitz, 506(PSt):May88-101
 N. Smith, 541(RES):Feb88-107
Kibler, W.W. - see Chrétien de Troyes
Kidd, A. The Huron Chief. (D.M.R. Bentley, with C.R. Steele, eds)
 G. Warkentin, 627(UTQ):Fall88-159
Kidd, D. Peking Story.*
 J.K. Fairbank, 453(NYRB):16Mar89-17

Kidd, I.G. Posidonius. (Vol 2)
 R.W. Sharples, 617(TLS):25-31Aug89-923
Kidd, R. The Popular Performing Arts, Non-
 Formal Education and Social Change in the
 Third World.
 A. Wilson, 108:Winter87-80
Kidder, T. Among Schoolchildren.
 P. Theroux, 441:17Sep89-1
Kiddle, M.E. & B. Wegmann. Perspectivas.
 (4th ed)
 V. Babb, 399(MLJ):Autumn88-372
Kidwell, C. Marullus.
 A. Grafton, 617(TLS):22-28Dec89-1405
Kidwell, C.B. & V. Steele. Men and Women.
 P-L. Adams, 61:Jul89-94
Kiefer, A. A Book by Anselm Kiefer/Erotik im
 Fernen Osten, oder.
 M. Rudman, 55:Sep88-101
 F. Tuten, 62:Dec88-111
Kiefer, A. Erotik im Fernen Osten.
 A. Ross, 364:Oct/Nov88-140
Kiefer, K.H. - see von Goethe, J.W.
Kiefer, W. Outlaw.
 R. Singleton, 441:12Nov89-54
Kieffer, B. The Storm and Stress of Language.
 A.C. Leidner, 221(GQ):Spring88-305
 H. Madland, 301(JEGP):Oct88-601
 W. Paulsen, 406:Summer88-224
 L. Weissberg, 400(MLN):Apr88-683
Kiely, B. Nothing Happens in Carmincross.
 J. Byrne, 532(RCF):Spring88-191
Kiernan, K.S. The Thorkelin Transcripts of
 "Beowulf."
 R.P. Creed, 191(ELN):Sep88-75
 M. Griffith, 382(MAE):1988/2-296
 B. Lindström, 597(SN):Vol60No2-264
 J. Wilcox, 481(PQ):Spring88-267
Kiernan, R.F. Noel Coward.
 J. Fisher, 397(MD):Dec88-596
Kiesel, H. Literarische Trauerarbeit.*
 U-K. Ketelsen, 224(GRM):Band38Heft4-
 463
 H.T. Tewarson, 221(GQ):Summer88-478
Kightly, C. Country Voices.
 G. Boyes, 203:Vol99No2-258
Kijewski, K.J. Katwalk.
 T.J. Binyon, 617(TLS):24-30Nov89-1312
 M. Stasio, 441:27Aug89-22
Kilani-Schoch, M. Introduction à la morphol-
 ogie naturelle.
 K.G. Ottósson, 350:Dec89-894
Kilgo, J. Deep Enough for Ivorybills.*
 D. Miller, 569(SR):Fall88-684
Killingley, S-Y. A New Look at Cantonese
 Tones, Five or Six?*
 H. Kwok, 302:Vol24No1-102
Kilmister, C.W. Russell.
 P. Hager, 63:Sep88-417
Kilodney, C., ed. Worst Canadian Stories.
 T. Whalen, 532(RCF):Summer88-325
Kilvert, F. Kilvert's Cornish Diary. (Journal
 No 4) (R. Maber & A. Tregoning, eds)
 A. Powell, 617(TLS):30Jun-6Jul89-716
Kim Dae Jung. Prison Writings.
 G. Henderson, 293(JASt):Feb88-161
Kimball, B.A. Orators and Philosophers.
 R. Hariman, 544:Spring88-199
Kimitada, M. - see under Miwa Kimitada
Kimmel, A. Vous avez dit France?
 T. Scanlan, 207(FR):Oct88-185
Kimpel, D., ed. Mehrsprachigkeit in der deut-
 schen Aufklärung.
 H. Penzl, 301(JEGP):Apr88-295

Kimpel, D. & R. Suckale. Die gotische Archi-
 tektur in Frankreich 1130-1270.
 C. Bruzelius, 576:Jun88-190
Kinberg, L. - see Ibn Abi 'l-Dunyā
Kincaid, J. A Small Place.*
 I. Fonseca, 617(TLS):13-19Jan89-30
Kinchin, P. & J., with N. Baxter. Glasgow's
 Great Exhibitions.
 D. Jenkins, 46:Jul88-64
Kinderman, W. Beethoven's Diabelli Varia-
 tions.*
 B. Cooper, 410(M&L):Jul88-387
 N. Marston, 451:Summer88-80
Kindleberger, C.P. Manias, Panics, and
 Crashes. (rev)
 F. Norris, 441:29Oct89-39
King, B. Modern Indian Poetry in English.
 J. Welch, 493:Spring88-31
King, C. & I.C. Smith, eds. Twelve More Mod-
 ern Scottish Poets.
 J. Saunders, 565:Autumn88-72
King, D. Lyndon La Rouche and the New
 American Fascism.
 G. Johnson, 441:18Jun89-7
King, D.B. The Crisis of Our Time.
 639(VQR):Autumn88-132
King, F. Frozen Music.
 639(VQR):Autumn88-128
King, F. Reflections in a Jaundiced Eye.
 F. Gannon, 441:9Apr89-11
King, F. The Woman Who Was God.*
 C. See, 441:15Jan89-11
King, G.H. Existenz, Denken, Stil.
 J. Disse, 687:Jul-Sep88-483
King, J. William Cowper.*
 D. Groves, 447(N&Q):Jun88-241
 D.L. MacDonald, 627(UTQ):Fall87-115
 B. Redford, 405(MP):Aug88-92
King, J. Interior Landscapes.
 R. Cork, 90:Apr88-303
King, J., ed. Modern Latin American Fiction.
 D.L. Shaw, 402(MLR):Apr89-510
King, J. "Sur."
 M.L. Bastos, 240(HR):Autumn88-531
 D.L. Shaw, 402(MLR):Jan89-220
King, J. & C. Ryskamp - see Cowper, W.
King, J.C. - see Notker der Deutsche
King, J.N. English Reformation Literature.*
 D.H. Parker, 539:Fall88-328
King, L., with B.D. Colen. "Mr. King, You're
 Having a Heart Attack."
 G. Kolata, 441:9Apr89-33
King, L.D. & C.A. Maley, eds. Selected Papers
 from the XIIIth Linguistic Symposium on
 Romance Languages.
 K. Klingebiel, 545(RPh):Nov88-179
King, M. Freedom Song.
 639(VQR):Spring88-46
King, M.C. The Drama of J.M. Synge.*
 J. Coakley, 130:Spring88-84
 A. Parkin, 397(MD):Jun88-309
King, M.L. Venetian Humanism in an Age of
 Patrician Dominance.*
 D.E. Queller, 589:Jul88-692
King, S. The Dark Half.
 G. Stade, 441:29Oct89-12
King, S. The Dark Tower.
 R. Fuller, 441:8Jan89-22
King, S.R. Passionate Journey.
 W. Davis, 293(JASt):Aug88-638
Kingdon, M. & G. Stobart. GCSE Examined.
 S.J. Prais, 617(TLS):17-23Feb89-175

Kingdon, R.M. Myths about the St. Barth-
olomew's Day Massacres, 1572–1576.
M.E. Hussey, 42(AR):Fall88–523
639(VQR):Autumn88–116
Kingsolver, B. Homeland and Other Stories.
R. Banks, 441:11Jun89–16
Kingston, M.H. Tripmaster Monkey.
C. Ong, 617(TLS):15–21Sep89–998
L.A. Schreiber, 441:23Apr89–9
P. Skenazy, 182:Issue23–36
Kinkley, J.C. The Odyssey of Shen Congwen.*
Y–T.M. Feuerwerker, 293(JASt):Aug88–
598
P. Link, 395(MFS):Winter88–753
E. Widmer, 244(HJAS):Dec88–553
Kinneavy, J.L. Greek Rhetorical Origins of
Christian Faith.
C. Kallendorf, 544:Spring88–195
Kinnell, G. The Past.*
R. Pybus, 565:Summer88–72
Kinney, A.F. Humanist Poetics.
M.G. Brennan, 541(RES):Nov88–540
J. Crewe, 551(RenQ):Summer88–339
C. Ross, 405(MP):May89–421
S. Sim, 179(ES):Aug88–361
Kinney, A.F. John Skelton.
J.L. Mills, 604:Spring/Summer88–32
J. Scattergood, 191(ELN):Jun88–89
Kinney, D. – see More, T.
Kinnier Wilson, J.V. The Legend of Etana.
J. Williams, 124:Nov–Dec88–120
Kinsella, T. Blood and Family.
W. Logan, 441:28May89–24
Kinsella, T. The New Oxford Book of Irish
Verse.*
Z.B., 295(JML):Fall87/Winter88–213
Kinsella, W.P. The Iowa Baseball Confed-
eracy.
A.E. Hye, 102(CanL):Winter87–162
Kinsella, W.P. The Moccasin Telegraph and
Other Tales.
E. Cook-Lynn, 649(WAL):Aug88–141
Kinsley, J. – see Dickens, C.
Kinstler, C. The Moon Under Her Feet.
R. Irwin, 441:9Jul89–14
Kintzler, C. Condorcet.
N. Hampson, 208(FS):Oct88–476
Kipling, R. The Day's Work. (T. Pinney, ed)
The Jungle Book. (W.W. Robson, ed) The
Second Jungle Book. (W.W. Robson, ed)
Kim. (A. Sandison, ed) Life's Handicap.
(A.O.J. Cockshut, ed) "The Man Who Would
be King" and Other Stories. (L.L. Cornell,
ed) Plain Tales From the Hills. (A. Ruth-
erford, ed) Stalky & Co. (I. Quigly, ed)
Rudyard Kipling: Selected Stories. (S.
Kemp, ed)
Z.T. Sullivan, 402(MLR):Oct89–951
Kipling, R. Kipling's India.* (T. Pinney, ed)
B. Gasser, 447(N&Q):Sep88–395
Kipnis, K. & D.T. Meyers, eds. Political Real-
ism and International Morality.
H. Fain, 103:Jan89–25
T.N., 185:Jan89–451
Kipp, R.S. & S. Rodgers, eds. Indonesian Reli-
gions in Transition.
M.R. Woodward, 293(JASt):May88–431
Kippenberg, H.G., editor-in-chief. Visible
Religion. (Vol 2)
J.J. Buckley, 318(JAOS):Jan–Mar87–207
Kipperman, M. Beyond Enchantment.*
F. Garber, 661(WC):Autumn88–210
[continued]

[continuing]
S. Prickett, 541(RES):Feb88–122
F.W. Shilstone, 577(SHR):Fall88–396
Király, B.K., B. Lotze & N.F. Dreisziger, eds.
The First War between Socialist States.*
G.F. Cushing, 575(SEER):Apr88–305
Kirby, D. Saving the Young Men of Vienna.
S. Corey, 219(GaR):Spring89–161
455:Mar88–72
Kirby, D. War, Peace and Revolution.*
G. Eley, 550(RusR):Jan88–104
Kirby, D.G. & P. Herring – see Polvinen, T.
Kirby, I.J. Bible Translation in Old Norse.*
K. Wolf, 563(SS):Spring88–313
Kirchberger, L. Franz Kafka's Use of Law in
Fiction.
R.V. Gross, 406:Winter88–488
Kircher, E.W.G. Anweisung in der Buchdruck-
erkunst so viel davon das Drucken betrifft.
J.J. Flood, 354:Dec88–359
Kirchner, E.J. Liberal Parties in Western
Europe.
C. Townshend, 617(TLS):10–16Feb89–144
Kirk, E.K. Music at the White House.
P. Dickinson, 415:Feb88–89
R.A. Schellhous, 115:Spring88–208
Kirk, G.S. "The Iliad": A Commentary.* (Vol
1, Bks 1–4)
R.D. Dawe, 121(CJ):Oct–Nov88–69
Kirk, G.S., J.E. Raven & M. Schofield. The
Presocratic Philosophers. (2nd ed)
R. Torretti, 160:Jan88–230
Kirk, J.M., S. Sanderson & J.D.A. Widdowson,
eds. Studies in Linguistic Geography.*
W.N. Francis, 355(LSoc):Mar88–124
M. Görlach, 685(ZDL):1/1988–63
Kirk, R. Translation Determined.*
B.M. Humphries, 482(PhR):Jul88–447
Kirkham, M. Jane Austen, Feminism and Fic-
tion.*
S. Tave, 454:Winter89–231
Kirkham, M. The Imagination of Edward
Thomas.
H.B., 295(JML):Fall87/Winter88–389
A. Hertz, 627(UTQ):Fall88–121
R. Hoffpauir, 49:Jul88–107
P. McDonald, 541(RES):May88–316
M.G.H. Pittock, 677(YES):Vol19–346
M. Scofield, 175:Spring88–65
Kirkpatrick, J. – see Ives, C.
Kirkpatrick, R. Dante: "The Divine Comedy."
G. Holmes, 382(MAE):1988/1–144
J. Took, 402(MLR):Jul89–746
Kirkup, J. I, of all people.*
W. Magee, 493:Winter88/89–24
Kirkwood, J. Diary of a Mad Playwright.
W. Wasserstein, 441:24Sep89–11
Kirp, D.L. Learning by Heart.
L. May, 441:4Jun89–23
Kirschbaum, E. The Eradication of German
Culture in the United States: 1917–1918.
C.A. Bernd, 406:Fall88–383
Kirshner, J. – see Cochrane, E.
Kirshner, J. & K.F. Morrison, eds. Medieval
Europe.
K.O. O'Keeffe, 568(SCN):Winter88–82
Kirwan, C. Augustine.
S. Clark, 617(TLS):18–24Aug89–899
T.A. Losoncy, 103:Aug89–315
Kiš, D. The Encyclopedia of the Dead.
A. Carter, 441:23Apr89–14
W. Gass, 453(NYRB):26Oct89–18
J. Hofmann, 617(TLS):30Jun–6Jul89–713

Kishel, J.F. – see Wordsworth, W.
al-Kishtainy, K. Takwin al-Sahyuniyya.
N. Rejwan, 390:Jan88-51
Kismaric, C., with W. Shawcross. Forced Out.
K.E. Meyer, 441:9Apr89-15
Kiss, E., ed. Hermann Broch.
H.D. Osterle, 133:Band21Heft2/3-249
E. Schlant, 221(GQ):Spring87-297
Kiss, J. Magyar madárnevek.
M. Katzschmann, 685(ZDL):2/1987-273
Kiss, J. Mihályi tájszótár (Rábaköz). Nyelvj-
árási tanulmányok. A rábaközi Mihályi
nyelvjárásának hang- és alaktana. Fejez-
etek a Mihályi nyelvjárás mondattanából.
T. Kesztyüs, 685(ZDL):1/1988-129
Kiss, K.É. Configurationality in Hungarian.
J. Horvath, 353:Vol26No6-1085
Kisseloff, J. You Must Remember This.
M. Tax, 441:9Jul89-17
Kitagawa, J.M. On Understanding Japanese
Religion.
T.M. Ludwig, 293(JASt):Aug88-639
Kitaj, R.B. First Diasporist Manifesto.
H. Kramer, 617(TLS):8-14Sep89-970
Kitarō, N. – see under Nishida Kitarō
Kitchen, J. Perennials.*
K. West, 502(PrS):Fall88-118
Kitcher, P. Vaulting Ambition.*
C. Murphy, 449:Sep88-479
K. Sterelny, 63:Dec88-538
Kitching, G. Karl Marx and the Philosophy of
Praxis.
S. Meikle, 103:Feb89-56
Kiteley, B. Still Life with Insects.
H. Mittelmark, 441:22Oct89-23
Kitman, M. The Making of the Prefident 1789.
P. Maier, 441:17Dec89-10
Kittay, E.F. Metaphor.
T.A. Deibler, 103:Nov88-456
G. McFee, 89(BJA):Autumn88-392
A. Margalit, 617(TLS):14-20Apr89-399
Kittay, E.F. & D.T. Meyers, eds. Women and
Moral Theory.
C. Card, 185:Oct88-125
Kittelson, J.M. Luther the Reformer.
J.M. Headley, 551(RenQ):Summer88-325
Kittler, F.A. Aufschreibesysteme 1800-1900.
F. Futterknecht, 494:Vol8No3/4-675
R.C. Holub, 221(GQ):Fall87-641
J. Kruse, 406:Fall88-378
Kittredge, W. Owning it All.
C.S. Long, 649(WAL):May88-80
G.A. Love, 448:Vol26No2-133
Kitzinger, C. The Social Construction of Les-
bianism.
S.E.H., 185:Apr89-671
Kivy, P. Osmin's Rage.
R. Osborne, 617(TLS):16-22Jun89-667
W.R. Wians, 465:Summer89-95
Kiyooka, R. Pear Tree Pomes.
S. Scobie, 376:Mar88-97
Kjetsaa, G. Fyodor Dostoyevsky.*
R.M. Davison, 402(MLR):Apr89-534
42(AR):Summer88-397
Kjørven, J. Robert Frost's Emergent Design.
Ø.T. Gulliksen, 172(Edda):1988/1-77
E.J. Ingebretsen, 27(AL):Mar88-127
Klancher, J.P. The Making of English Reading
Audiences, 1790-1832.*
S. Bennett, 445(NCF):Jun88-123
P.M. Spacks, 677(YES):Vol19-335
S.A. Zemka, 223:Summer88-234

Klare, J., ed. Wörterbuch Portugiesisch-
Deutsch.
H. Kröll, 72:Band224Heft2-438
Klassen, A.D., C.J. Williams & E.E. Levitt.
Sex and Morality in the U.S. (H.J. O'Gor-
man, ed)
D. Johnson, 453(NYRB):12Oct89-25
Klassen, J.M. – see Bartoš, F.M.
Klaus, G. Das etymologische Wörterbuch des
Französischen im 19. Jahrhundert.*
M. Pfister, 72:Band225Heft1-201
Klaus, H.G. The Literature of Labour.*
A.D.B., 506(PSt):Sep88-109
J. Goode, 677(YES):Vol19-328
D. Longhurst, 366:Spring88-130
Klaus, H.G., ed. The Rise of Socialist Fiction
1880-1914.
P. Beilharz, 637(VS):Winter89-269
S.B. Purdy, 395(MFS):Winter88-742
M.E. Rose, 366:Autumn88-259
Klausenburger, J. French Liaison and Lin-
guistic Theory.*
J. Durand, 208(FS):Oct88-496
Klausmann, H. Die Breisgauer Mundarten.
H. Singer, 685(ZDL):1/1988-97
Kleber, P. Exceptions and Rules.
R.C. Lamont, 397(MD):Sep88-459
Kleber, R.E. Build Your Case.
B.A. Encinas, 399(MLJ):Winter88-466
Klecko, J., J. Fields & G. Logan. Nose to
Nose.
M. Mehler, 441:19Nov89-44
Kleeblatt, N.L. The Dreyfuss Affair.
R. Kimball, 560:Fall88-198
Kleefeld, G. Das Gedicht als Sühne.*
R. Salter, 221(GQ):Summer87-491
R. Schier, 301(JEGP):Jan88-88
Kleege, G. Home for the Summer.
C. Goodrich, 441:27Aug89-16
Kleemann, I. Frühe Bewegung.* (Vol 1)
E. Guralnick, 229:Band60Heft5-463
Kleiber, G. Relatives restrictives et relatives
appositives.
K. Klingebiel, 215(GL):Vol28No3-222
Klein, A.M. Literary Essays and Reviews. (U.
Caplan & M.W. Steinberg, eds)
J. Kertzer, 49:Jan88-99
Klein, G. La politica linguistica del fascis-
mo.*
G. Lepschy, 545(RPh):Feb89-337
Klein, H.M. – see Shakespeare, W.
Klein, K.G. The Woman Detective.
P. Raine, 617(TLS):31Mar-6Apr89-332
Klein, K.K. & others – see Oswald von Wol-
kenstein
Klein, L. Exhibits.
E.K. Carpenter, 507:Mar/Apr88-151
Klein, T. & C. Minis. Zwei Studien zu Veldeke
und zum Strassburger Alexander.*
L. de Grauwe, 680(ZDP):Band107Heft1-
120
Klein, W. Second Language Acquisition.*
F.W. Gester, 38:Band106Heft3/4-434
Klein-Franke, F. Die klassische Antike in
der Tradition des Islam.
E.K. Rowson, 318(JAOS):Jan-Mar87-187
Kleinfield, S. The Hotel.
S. Rea, 441:27Aug89-20
Kleinhenz, C. The Early Italian Sonnet: The
First Century (1220-1321).*
S. Pearce, 382(MAE):1988/1-140
Kleinig, J. Ethical Issues in Psychosurgery.*
M.A. Warren, 63:Jun88-283

Kleinman, A. Social Origins of Distress and Disease.
　F.M. Cheung, 293(JASt):Nov88-854
Kleinman, S., ed. Mind and Body.
　S.K. Wertz, 485(PE&W):Apr88-207
Kleinmann, H-O. - see Giusti, P.P.
Kleinow, H.G. Die Überwindung der Polis im frühen 4. Jahrhundert v. Chr.
　G. Dobesch, 229:Band60Heft8-680
"Kleist-Jahrbuch 1985." (H.J. Kreutzer, ed)
　B. Fischer, 221(GQ):Summer87-483
"Kleist-Jahrbuch 1986." (H.J. Kreutzer, ed)
　K. Arens, 221(GQ):Winter88-138
Kleparski, G. Semantic Change and Componential Analysis.*
　P. Mühlhäusler, 447(N&Q):Jun88-200
Klier, J.D. Russia Gathers Her Jews.
　K. Neilson, 529(QQ):Winter88-918
　H.M. Scott, 83:Autumn88-219
Klíma, I. My First Loves.*
　D.J. Enright, 453(NYRB):18May89-37
Klíma, L. Némésis La Glorieuse.
　L. Arénilla, 98:Nov88-955
Klima, S., G. Bowers & K.S. Grant - see Burney, C.
Klimo, K. Labor Pains.
　A. Clyde, 441:15Jan89-22
Kline, M-J. A Guide to Documentary Editing.*
　T.H. Howard-Hill, 536(Rev):Vol10-149
　F.J. Teute, 656(WMQ):Apr88-386
Klingaman, W.K. 1929.
　M.B. Grover, 441:29Oct89-40
Klingebiel, K. Bibliographie linguistique de l'ancien occitan (1960-1982).*
　N.B. Smith, 589:Jan88-183
Klingler, B. Emma Bovary und ihre Schwestern - Die unverstandene Frau.
　S. Volckmann, 52:Band23Heft3-323
Klitzman, R. A Year-Long Night.
　K. Hughes, 441.10Jul89-23
Kloefkorn, W. Honeymoon.
　A. Ortolani, 389(MQ):Autumn88-120
Kloesel, C.J.W. - see Peirce, C.S.
Klooster, H.A.J. Indonesiers schrijven hun geschiedenis.
　T. Abdullah, 293(JASt):May88-432
Kloppenberg, J.T. Uncertain Victory.*
　G. Cotkin, 26(ALR):Spring89-79
Kloppenburg, J.R., Jr. First the Seed.
　G. Prance, 617(TLS):4-10Aug89-845
Klopstock, F.G. Werke und Briefe.* (Werke IV; Vol 5, Pts 1 & 2) (E. Höpker-Herberg, ed)
　P.M. Mitchell, 301(JEGP):Jul88-409
Klose, K. Russia and the Russians.
　M. McCauley, 575(SEER):Apr88-320
Klosko, G. The Development of Plato's Political Theory.*
　C. Osborne, 319:Jan89-146
Kloss, H., ed. Deutsch als Muttersprache in den Vereinigten Staaten. (Pt 2)
　G.G. Gilbert, 355(LSoc):Jun88-267
Klossowski, P. Roberte ce Soir [and] The Revocation of the Edict of Nantes. The Baphomet.
　D. Coward, 617(TLS):4-10Aug89-857
Klotz, H. The History of Postmodern Architecture.
　M. Filler, 617(TLS):24-30Mar89-295
　H. Muschamp, 139:Jun/Jul88-21
Klotz, H. 20th Century Architecture.
　P. Goldberger, 441:3Dec89-21

Klotz, H., with L. Sabau, eds. New York Architecture: 1970-1990.
　P. Goldberger, 441:3Dec89-21
Klotz, V. Das europäische Kunstmärchen.*
　A.C. Ulmer, 406:Spring88-117
Kluncker, K. Das Geheime Deutschland.
　K.L. Komar, 221(GQ):Spring87-299
Klussmann, P.G. & H. Mohr, eds. Literatur und bildende Kunst.*
　S.G. Leonhard, 133:Band21Heft1-91
Klüver, B. & J. Martin. Kiki's Paris.
　E. White, 441:11Jun89-42
Knapp, B.L. Archetype, Architecture, and the Writer.
　N. Lane, 345(KRQ):Nov88-494
　B.E. Savedoff, 290(JAAC):Fall87-98
Knapp, B.L. Stephen Crane.*
　D.E. Gribble, 649(WAL):May88-76
　S. Wertheim, 26(ALR):Fall88-87
Knapp, B.L. Music, Archetype, and the Writer.
　R. Donington, 617(TLS):17-23Mar89-274
Knapp, B.L. Women in Twentieth-Century Literature.
　B.K. Scott, 395(MFS):Summer88-329
Knapp, B.L. Word/Image/Psyche.*
　R. Koren, 549(RLC):Jan-Mar88-81
Knapp, F.P. "Chevalier errant" und "fin'-amor."
　K. Pratt, 589:Apr88-422
Knapp, F.P., ed. Nibelungenlied und Klage.
　D.H. Green, 402(MLR):Apr89-517
Knapp, G. Friedrich Dürrenmatt: Romulus der Grosse.
　D.H. Haenicke, 221(GQ):Spring87-307
Knapp, K., W. Enninger & A. Knapp-Potthoff, eds. Analyzing Intercultural Communication.
　K. Takahara, 350:Dec89-895
Knapp, L., ed & trans. Dostoevsky as Reformer.
　G. Rosenshield, 574(SEEJ):Summer88-318
Knapp, M. Doris Lessing.
　E. Bertelsen, 538(RAL):Summer88-261
Knapp, P.A., ed. Assays. (Vol 2)
　R.P. McGerr, 677(YES):Vol19-307
Knapp, S. Personification and the Sublime.
　P. Hamilton, 447(N&Q):Mar88-130
Knauss, J. Die Melioration des Kopaisbeckens durch die Minyer im 2. Jahrhundert v. Chr. (Kopais 2)
　G. Garbrecht, 229:Band60Heft8-754
Kneale, M. Inside Rose's Kingdom.
　C. Hawtree, 617(TLS):31Mar-6Apr89-344
Knechtes, D.R. - see Xiao Tong
Knetschke, E. & M. Sperlbaum, eds. Monumenta Germaniae acustica: Katalog 1978.
　L. Zehetner, 685(ZDL):3/1987-371
Knight, A., ed. Robert Louis Stevenson in the South Seas.
　R.A. Boyle, 637(VS):Spring89-450
Knight, A. & K., eds. The Beat Vision.*
　M. Green, 363(LitR):Fall88-123
　M.G. Porter, 649(WAL):May88-65
Knight, A. & K., eds. Kerouac and the Beats.
　M. Green, 363(LitR):Fall88-123
　S. Moore, 532(RCF):Fall88-170
Knight, C. - see Douglas, N.
Knight, D. The Age of Science.
　R. Barton, 637(VS):Winter89-276
Knight, K.L. The Widow of Oz.
　B. Probst, 441:19Nov89-24
Knight, R.C. - see Vinaver, E.

Knight, R.P. Expedition into Sicily. (C.
Stumpf, ed)
P.A. Lomas, 303(JoHS):Vol108-276
Knight, S. Geoffrey Chaucer.*
N.R. Havely, 382(MAE):1988/2-309
J. Simons, 366:Spring88-116
Knight, V., comp. The Works of Art of the
Corporation of London.*
C. Harrison, 89(BJA):Spring88-184
Knightley, P. The Master Spy.* (British title:
Philby.)
N. Annan, 453(NYRB):13Apr89-24
R.W. Winks, 441:16Apr89-1
Knightley, P. & C. Kennedy. An Affair of
State.*
639(VQR):Summer88-94
Knobel, L. International Interiors.
T. Crosby, 324:Feb89-182
Knoblock, J. - "Xunzi: A Translation and
Study of the Complete Works"
Knoche, M. Volksliteratur und Volksschrift-
envereine im Vormärz.
T. Salumets, 406:Summer88-232
Knodel, J., A. Chamratrithirong & N. Debaval-
ya. Thailand's Reproductive Revolution.
T.H. Hull, 293(JASt):Aug88-703
Knodt, R. Friedrich Nietzsche.
R.F. Krummel, 133:Band21Heft4-354
Knoespel, K.J. Narcissus and the Invention
of Personal History.*
R. Levine, 589:Apr88-423
Knoll, R.E. - see Kees, W.
de Knop, S. Metaphorische Komposita in Zeit-
ungsüberschriften.
C. Schäffner, 682(ZPSK):Band41Heft4-529
Knorr, W.R. The Ancient Tradition of Geo-
metric Problems.
D.H. Fowler, 41:Vol7-201
Knowles, G. Patterns of Spoken English.
A. Ward, 447(N&Q):Jun88-200
Knox, B. Essays Ancient and Modern.
J. Griffin, 453(NYRB):26Oct89-46
Knox, E. & H-L. Plus ça change.
D.J. Daniels, 207(FR):Oct88-187
Y. de la Quérière, 207(FR):Apr89-918
Knox, P.E. Ovid's "Metamorphoses" and the
Traditions of Augustan Poetry.
W.S. Anderson, 24:Fall88-457
A.A.R. Henderson, 123:Vol38No1-27
Knox-Shaw, P. The Explorer in English Fic-
tion.
H.M. Daleski, 136:Summer88-173
D. Hewitt, 541(RES):Nov88-601
C. Mulvey, 366:Autumn88-228
Knudsen, J.B. Justus Möser and the German
Enlightenment.
R. Stauf, 224(GRM):Band38Heft1/2-212
J.W. Van Cleve, 221(GQ):Winter88-127
H. Williams, 83:Autumn88-219
Knuuttila, S. & J. Hintikka, eds. The Logic of
Being.
A. Reix, 542:Jan-Mar88-126
Knystautas, A. The Natural History of the
USSR.
639(VQR):Winter88-31
"Knytlinga saga." (H. Pálsson & P. Edwards,
trans)
H. O'Donoghue, 447(N&Q):Sep88-350
Kobak, A. Isabelle.*
D. Flower, 364:Jun88-93
M-K. Wilmers, 441:23Apr89-24
Kobal, J., ed. Hollywood Glamor Portraits.
J.G. Dunne, 453(NYRB):18May89-28

Kobel, E. Alfred Döblin.
W. Koepke, 221(GQ):Spring87-301
W. Paulsen, 222(GR):Summer88-154
Kobler, J. Otto the Magnificent.
M.B. Grover, 441:25Jun89-25
Kobo, Y., R. Mori & G. Okuhara. Japanese for
Children.
P.J. Wetzel, 399(MLJ):Autumn88-365
Koch, C.J. Crossing the Gap.*
P. Lewis, 364:Apr-May87-148
Koch, E. Shah Jahan and Orpheus.
P. Mitter, 90:Nov88-865
Koch, G., ed. Indien.
D.S. Low, 402(MLR):Jan89-262
Kockelmans, J.J. Heidegger and Science.
D. Moran, 323:Jan88-97
J. Weinsheimer, 488:Sep88-413
Kočović, B. Žrtve Drugog svetskog rata u
Jugoslaviji.
S.K. Pavlowitch, 575(SEER):Jan88-151
Kodama, S. - see Pound, E.
Kodama de Larroche, C. Les Cercles d'un
Regard.
J. Pigeot, 549(RLC):Jul-Sep88-436
Kodish, D. Good Friends and Bad Enemies.
C.H. Carpenter, 292(JAF):Jan-Mar88-77
Koelb, C. & V. Lokke, eds. The Current in
Criticism.
J. Fekete, 395(MFS):Winter88-736
J.H. Petersen, 52:Band23Heft2-171
Koenen, M.J. & J.B. Drewes. Wolters' Woor-
denboek Eigentijds Nederlands.
A. Sassen, 204(FdL):Mar88-74
Koenig, J. Smugglers Notch.
M. Stasio, 441:5Feb89-26
Koepke, W. Johann Gottfried Herder.
H.B. Nisbet, 402(MLR):Apr89-525
Koeppen, W. Gesammelte Werke in sechs Bän-
den. (M. Reich-Ranicki, with D. von Briel &
H-U. Treichel, eds)
E. Oehlenschläger, 680(ZDP):
Band106Heft4-631
Koeppen, W. Pigeons on the Grass.*
A. Otten, 42(AR):Fall88-522
Koerner, E.F.K. & M. Tajima, with C.P. Otero,
comps. Noam Chomsky.
B.D. Joseph, 350:Dec89-896
Koerner, K. Saussurean Studies/Etudes saus-
suriennes.
J.E. Joseph, 350:Sep89-595
Kofman, S. The Childhood of Art.
N. Korda, 400(MLN):Dec88-1172
Kogan, B.S. Averroes and the Metaphysics of
Causation.*
A.L. Ivry, 318(JAOS):Jul-Sep87-527
Kogan, J. Nothing but the Best.
639(VQR):Winter88-31
Kogan, S. The Hieroglyphic King.*
C.F. Main, 551(RenQ):Summer88-356
Kogawa, J. Woman in the Woods.
L. Hutchman, 102(CanL):Winter87-263
Kohl, P.L., with D.J. Dadson - see Dandamaev,
M.A. & V.G. Lukonin
Kohl, S. Das englische Spätmittelalter.
A. Classen, 201:Vol14-222
S. Wenzel, 589:Apr88-425
Köhler, E. Sociologia della "fin'amor." (2nd
ed)
C. Di Girolamo, 379(MedR):Aug88-300
Kohler, S. The Perfect Place.
G. Pool, 441:3Sep89-14
Kohn, A. Fortune or Failure.
D. Brin, 617(TLS):29Sep-5Oct89-1071

Kohnen, J. Theodor Gottlieb von Hippel
1741-1796.
 H.H.H. Beck, 342:Band79Heft4-491
Kohrt, M. Phonetik, Phonologie und die "Rel-
ativität der Verhältnisse."
 E. Bauer, 685(ZDL):3/1988-379
Kohrt, M. Problemgeschichte des Graphembe-
griffs und des frühen Phonembegriffs.
 E. Bauer, 685(ZDL):3/1988-378
Kojima, R. Urbanization and Urban Problems
in China.
 C.W. Pannell, 293(JASt):Nov88-855
de Kok, A. La Place du pronom personnel
régime conjoint en français.*
 R. de Dardel, 603:Vol12No1-153
Kok, J.P.F. - see under Filedt Kok, J.P.
Kokotailo, P. John Glassco's Richer World.
 S. Scobie, 376:Dec88-141
Koktová, E. Sentence Adverbials in a Func-
tional Description.
 Y. Bader, 257(IRAL):Nov88-332
 M. Bílý, 361:Jul88-251
Kolakowski, L. Bergson.
 R.J. Fąfara, 497(PolR):Vol33No1-104
Kolakowski, L. Histoire du marxisme.
 J-M. Gabaude, 542:Jul-Sep88-345
Kolakowski, L. Metaphysical Horror.
 A.C. Danto, 617(TLS):28Apr-4May89-448
Kolakowski, L. The Presence of Myth.
 A. Kuper, 617(TLS):6-12Oct89-1086
Kolb, D. The Critique of Pure Modernity.*
 G.J. Galgan, 543:Mar89-628
 H.S. Harris, 484(PPR):Jun89-752
Kolb, F. Die Stadt im Altertum.
 M. Woloch, 487:Spring88-85
Kolb, P. - see Proust, M.
Kolchin, P. Unfree Labor.*
 P. Morgan, 656(WMQ):Jul88-592
 C.A. Ruud, 106:Summer88-273
Kolenda, K., ed. Organizations and Ethical
Individualism.
 D.F.T., 185:Jul89-983
 P.H. Werhane, 103:May89-186
Kolesov, V.V. Mir čeloveka v slove Drevnej
Rusi.
 H. Birnbaum, 574(SEEJ):Fall88-464
Kolin, P.C. David Rabe.
 M. Charney, 580(SCR):Spring89-86
Kolin, P.C. & J.M. Davis, eds. Critical Essays
on Edward Albee.*
 C. Johnson, 295(JML):Fall87/Winter88-
288
 R.A. Martin, 115:Winter88-97
 G. Mast, 405(MP):Feb89-331
 K.M. Sullivan, 577(SHR):Summer88-297
 L.H. Weaver, 397(MD):Mar88-124
Kolkenbrock-Netz, J., G. Plumpe & H.J.
Schrimpf, eds. Wege der Literaturwissen-
schaft.
 R.J. Rundell, 221(GQ):Winter87-102
Kolker, M.Z. - see under Zelaya Kolker, M.
Koller, G. Computative Graphematik.
 W. Hofrichter, 682(ZPSK):Band41Heft1-
141
 W. Lenders, 685(ZDL):2/1987-269
Kolleritsch, O., ed. Egon Wellesz.
 D. Symons, 410(M&L):Apr88-289
Kollmann, E. & M. Jarchow. Berliner Porzel-
lan.
 H. Morley-Fletcher, 39:Sep88-209
Kollmann, N.S. Kinship and Politics.*
 D.J. Dunn, 377:Mar88-51
 L. Hughes, 575(SEER):Oct88-652

Kølln, H. Der Bericht über den Dänenkönig in
den St. Wenzel-Biographien des 13. und 14.
Jahrhunderts.
 J.M. Jochens, 563(SS):Winter88-90
Kolve, V.A. Chaucer and the Imagery of Nar-
rative.*
 G.C. Britton, 447(N&Q):Jun88-211
Kölving, U. & J. Carriat. Inventaire de la
"Correspondance littéraire" de Grimm et de
Meister.*
 M. Moog-Grünewald, 52:Band23Heft3-317
no Komachi, O. & I. Shikibu. The Ink Dark
Moon. (J. Hirshfield, with M. Aratani,
trans)
 E.A. Cranston, 293(JASt):Aug88-646
 J. McMullen, 617(TLS):7-13Apr89-370
Komar, K.L. Transcending Angels.*
 M. Jacobs, 402(MLR):Jul89-800
Komárek, M. & others, eds. Mluvnice češtiny
II.
 D. Short, 575(SEER):Oct88-631
Kome, P. Women of Influence.
 J. Sangster, 298:Spring/Summer88-234
Kometani, F. Passover.
 S. Chira, 441:22Oct89-27
Kominis, A.D., ed. Patmos.
 G. Fowden, 617(TLS):22-28Dec89-1424
Komunyakaa, Y. Dien Cai Dau.
 A. Aubert, 181:Vol38No1-67
 W. Koestenbaum, 441:24Sep89-50
Kondrašov, N.A. Slavjanskie jazyki.
 J.A. Van Campen, 574(SEEJ):Spring88-
155
Konecky, E. A Place at the Table.
 B.F. Williamson, 441:4Jun89-22
Koner, P. Solitary Song.
 E. Resnikova, 441:24Sep89-56
König, D. Das Tor zur Unterwelt.
 J.W. de Jong, 259(IIJ):Apr88-144
König, W. & H. Stopp, eds. Historische, geo
graphische und soziale Übergänge im ale-
mannischen Sprachraum.
 H. Tatzreiter, 685(ZDL):3/1987-396
Konigsberg, I. Narrative Technique in the
English Novel: Defoe to Austen.*
 P. Honan, 83:Spring88-100
Konigson, E., ed. Figures théâtrales du
peuple.*
 J. Emelina, 535(RHL):Jan-Feb88-160
Konikoff, A. Sarcophagi from the Jewish Cat-
acombs of Ancient Rome.*
 L.H. Kant & L.V. Rutgers, 229:Band60
Heft4-376
Konishi, J. A History of Japanese Litera-
ture.* (Vol 2) (E. Miner, ed)
 M.S. Viswanathan, 293(JASt):May88-377
Konstan, D. Roman Comedy.
 D.E. Majewski, 615(TJ):Dec88-574
"Kontroversen, alte und neue: Akten des VII.
Internationalen Germanisten-Kongresses
Göttingen 1985." (Vol 4)
 E.G. Fichtner, 133:Band21Heft4-375
Konvitz, M.R., ed. The Legacy of Horace M.
Kallen.*
 A. Weston, 619:Summer88-427
Koontz, D.R. Midnight.
 D. Murray, 441:26Mar89-16
Koonz, C. Mothers in the Fatherland.*
 E. Kurzweil, 473(PR):Vol55No1-143
Koopmann, H. & T. Stammen, eds. Bertolt
Brecht.
 A. Tatlow, 133:Band21Heft1-87

Koopmans, J. & P. Verhuyck. Sermon joyeux et truanderie (Villon – Nemo – Ulespiègle).
  J. Fox, 208(FS):Oct88–462
Köpeczi, B., ed. Erdély története.
  M. Rady, 575(SEER):Jul88–482
Köpeczi, B. A Francia Felvilágosodás.
  T. Gorilovics, 535(RHL):Nov–Dec88–1143
Köpeczi, B. & P. Sárközy, eds. Venezia, Italia, Ungheria, fra Arcadia e Illuminismo.
  P. Mildonian, 107(CRCL):Jun88–286
Koppel, E.M. Die römischen Skulpturen von Tarraco.*
  S. Keay, 313:Vol78–253
Koppel, G. The Religious Dimension of Jane Austen's Novels.
  H.K. Girling, 166:Jul89–350
  S. Tave, 454:Winter89–231
Koppelman, S., ed. The Other Woman. Between Mothers & Daughters.
  E.K. Trimberger, 534(RALS):Vol16No1&2–125
Koppensteiner, J., ed. So loch doch.
  R. Minert, 399(MLJ):Winter88–476
Koppes, C.R. & G.D. Black. Hollywood Goes to War.
  S. Snyder, 106:Spring88–89
Koppitz, H–J. – see "Gutenberg–Jahrbuch"
Korbonski, S. The Jews and the Poles in World War II.
  I. Deak, 453(NYRB):28Sep89–63
Korczak, J. King Matt the First.*
  M.G. Levine, 497(PolR):Vol33No1–109
Korda, M. The Fortune.
  M. Ivins, 441:26Feb89–11
Korelitz, J.H. The Properties of Breath.
  T. Dooley, 617(TLS):4–10Aug89–850
Korff, W. Norm und Sittlichkeit. Wie kann der Mensch glücken?
  C. Schefold, 489(PJGG):Band95Heft2–376
Korhonen, J., ed. Beiträge zur allgemeinen und germanistischen Phraseologieforschung.
  F. Hundsnurscher, 685(ZDL):3/1988–382
  D. Steffens, 682(ZPSK):Band41Heft6–811
Korkmaz, J. Le Cinéma de Claude Sautet.
  T. Conley, 207(FR):Apr89–937
Kornberg, A. For the Love of Enzymes.
  J. Adams, 617(TLS):29Sep–5Oct89–1071
Kornblith, L., ed. Naturalizing Epistemology.
  M. Clarke, 486:Mar88–152
Körner, K–H. Korrelative Sprach–Typologie.
  G. Kleiber, 553(RLiR):Jul–Dec88–484
Körner, S. Metaphysics.
  B. Leftow, 258:Mar88–114
Körner, S. & R. Chisholm – see Brentano, F.
Korshin, P.J., ed. The American Revolution and Eighteenth–Century Culture.*
  J.E. Crowley, 656(WMQ):Jul88–616
Korshin, P.J., ed. Johnson after Two Hundred Years.*
  T.F. Bonnell, 405(MP):May89–427
  J.F. Woodruff, 627(UTQ):Spring89–419
Kortekaas, G.A.A., ed. Historia Apollonii regis Tyri.*
  R. Hexter, 589:Jan88–186
Korthals Altes, W.L. Changing Economy in Indonesia. (Vol 7)
  R. Van Niel, 293(JASt):Aug88–705
Kortländer, B. & F. Nies, eds. Französische Literatur in deutscher Sprache.
  C. Foucart, 72:Band225Heft2–450

Korzen, H. "Pourquoi" et l'inversion finale en français.
  M. Mahler, 207(FR):May89–1078
Kosai, Y. The Era of High–Speed Growth.
  L.E. Hein, 293(JASt):Feb88–147
Kosáry, D.G. The Press During the Hungarian Revolution of 1848–1849.
  R.L. Aczel, 575(SEER):Jul88–490
Koschmann, V.J. The Mito Ideology.
  Matsumoto Sannosuke, 285(JapQ):Jan–Mar88–93
  P. Nosco, 407(MN):Summer88–241
  B.T. Wakabayashi, 293(JASt):Aug88–640
Kosicka, J. & D. Gerould. A Life of Solitude.
  D. Jacobs, 441:8Oct89–39
  B. Shallcross, 497(PolR):Vol33No2–239
Kositsky, R. & others. Edward & W.S. Maxwell: Guide to the Archives/Edward & W.S. Maxwell: guide to fonds.
  J.F. Tener, 470:Vol26–189
Kosok, H. O'Casey the Dramatist.*
  P. Corbin, 72:Band224Heft2–410
Kossoff, A.D. & others, eds. Actas del VIII Congreso de la Asociación Internacional de Hispanistas.
  K. Kohut, 547(RF):Band100Heft4–465
Kostabi, M. Sadness Because the Video Rental Store Was Closed & Other Stories.
  E. Hill & S. Bloom, 62:Dec88–108
Kostelanetz, R. The Old Fictions and the New.
  J. Hollowell, 395(MFS):Summer88–243
Koster, C. Word Recognition in Foreign and Native Language.
  W. Grabe, 350:Dec89–897
Kostof, S. America by Design.
  C.H. Krinsky, 576:Sep88–314
  R. Moore, 46:Aug88–10
Kostof, S. A History of Architecture.
  L.K. Eaton, 576:Mar88–75
Kosztolányi, D. L'oeil–de–mer.
  P. Chardin, 549(RLC):Jan–Mar88–115
Kotelovoj, N.Z., ed. Novoe v russkoj leksike.
  S. Lubensky, 574(SEEJ):Spring88–160
Kotkin, S. – see Scott, J.
Kott, J. The Bottom Translation.
  R. Gross, 615(TJ):Mar88–142
  B.W. Kliman, 125:Spring88–309
Kott, J. Kamienny Potok.
  J.T. Baer, 497(PolR):Vol33No1–91
Kott, J. – see Gombrowicz, W.
von Kotzebue, A. & C.A. Böttiger. Der Briefwechsel zwischen August von Kotzebue und Carl August Böttiger. (B. Maurach, ed)
  G. Kurscheidt, 680(ZDP):Band107Heft4–606
Kotzwinkle, W. The Exile.
  J. Saari, 42(AR):Summer88–391
Kotzwinkle, W. The Midnight Examiner.
  G. Jacobs, 441:14May89–27
Kouassi, M. Untersuchungen zu den Akan–Erzählungen.
  R. Schott, 196:Band29Heft1/2–262
Kovacs, D. The Heroic Muse.
  S. Ireland, 123:Vol38No2–208
Kovács, I., ed. Début et fin de lumières en Hongrie, en Europe centrale et en Europe orientale.
  G.F. Cushing, 575(SEER):Oct88–640
Kovacs, K.S. Le Réve et la Vie.
  A.C. Ritchie, 546(RR):Nov88–684

Koval'chenko, I.D., N.B. Selunskaia & B.M. Litvakov. Sotsial'no-ekonomicheskii stroi pomeshchich'ego khoziaistva Evropeiskoi Rossii v epokhu kapitalizma.
C.S. Leonard, 550(RusR):Apr88-187
Kövecses, Z. Metaphors of Anger, Pride and Love.
B. King, 350:Mar89-185
Kovner, A. My Little Sister and Selected Poems of Abba Kovner.* (S. Kaufman, ed & trans)
L. Bar-Yaacov, 577(SHR):Fall88-402
Kowalke, K.H., ed. A New Orpheus.*
M. Gilbert, 615(TJ):Mar88-136
A.W., 412:Feb88-79
Kožin, A.N. Literaturnyj jazyk Moskovskoj Rusi: Učebnoe posobie.
A. Grannes, 559:Vol12No1-87
Kozol, J. Rachel and Her Children.*
S. Halpern, 453(NYRB):16Feb89-24
Kozulin, A. Psychology in Utopia.
E. Gellner, 575(SEER):Apr88-309
Kraatz, A. Lace.
P-L. Adams, 61:Jul89-96
Kraft, H. Mein Indien liegt in Rüschhaus.
R.E. Panny, 400(MLN):Apr88-687
Kraft, M.E. & N.J. Vig, eds. Technology and Politics.
L.A.H., 185:Jul89-982
Kraft, P.B. Das anfängliche Wesen der Kunst.
C. Jamme, 489(PJGG):Band95Heft1-187
Krag, H. & M. Warburg, eds. Der var engang ...amol iz geven.
S.L. Sampson, 575(SEER):Apr88-278
Kraggerud, E. Horaz und Actium.
L.C. Watson, 313:Vol78-227
Kragh, H. An Introduction to the Historiography of Science.
B. Gower, 518:Apr88-112
Kramer, B. & D. Hagedorn, eds. Griechische Papyri der Staats- und Universitätsbibliothek Hamburg (P. Hamb. III).
H. Maehler, 229:Band60Heft4-289
Kramer, B. & D. Hagedorn, eds. Griechische Texte der Heidelberger Papyrus-Sammlung (P. Heid. IV).*
R.A. Coles, 229:Band60Heft5-448
Kramer, C.E. Analytic Modality in Macedonian.
C.M. MacRobert, 575(SEER):Apr88-257
Kramer, D. Theorien zur historischen Arbeiterkultur.
K. Nicolai, 654(WB):5/1988-877
Kramer, D. - see Hardy, T.
Kramer, H., ed. The New Criterion Reader.*
639(VQR):Summer88-79
Kramer, L. Music and Poetry.*
P. Epstein, 295(JML):Fall87/Winter88-250
Kramer, L. Reports from the Holocaust.
G. Hochman, 441:2Apr89-29
Kramer, L. The Shoemaker's Wife and Other Poems.*
L. Sail, 565:Spring88-73
Kramer, Y. Primal Scene.
M. Stasio, 441:29Jan89-16
Krämling, G. Die systembildende Rolle von Ästhetik und Kulturphilosophie bei Kant.
R.A. Makkreel, 319:Oct89-628
Kranzler, D. Thy Brother's Blood.
M.I. Teicher, 390:Apr88-56

Kranzmayer, E. Glossar zur Laut- und Flexionslehre der deutschen zimbrischen Mundart. (M. Hornung, ed)
A. Rowley, 685(ZDL):3/1987-387
Krashen, S.D. The Input Hypothesis.*
P. Balboni, 351(LL):Mar88-149
Krasnov, V. Soviet Defectors.*
D.W. Treadgold, 396(ModA):Winter88-66
Krašovec, J. Antithetic Structure in Biblical Hebrew Poetry.
A. Berlin, 318(JAOS):Jan-Mar87-140
Kratochvil, L., ed. Rolling Stone: The Photographs.
T. Gitlin, 441:3Dec89-14
Kratz, H. - see von Chamisso, A.
Krätzer, A. Studien zum Amerikabild in der neueren deutschen Literatur.
U. Riese, 107(CRCL):Mar88-156
Kratzmann, G. & J. Simpson, eds. Medieval English Religious and Ethical Literature.
P. Gradon, 447(N&Q):Sep88-357
A. Hudson, 402(MLR):Apr89-432
M. Lang, 201:Vol14-224
Kraus, F.R. Briefe aus kleineren westeuropäischen Sammlungen.
W.L. Moran, 318(JAOS):Jan-Mar87-134
Kraus, K. Heine und die Folgen. Aphorismen. Die letzten Tage der Menschheit. (C. Wagenknecht, ed of all)
L.A. Lensing, 221(GQ):Spring88-287
Kraus, R.K. Pianos and Politics in China.
C. Ehrlich, 617(TLS):20-26Oct89-1156
Kraus, T., ed. Stefan Baumgartner.
A. Classen, 201:Vol14-227
Krause, S.J. - see Brown, C.B.
Krauss, B. Keneti.
G. Dening, 441:5Mar89-13
Krauss, F. Nordsiebenbürgisch-sächsisches Wörterbuch. (Vol 1 comp by G. Richter)
H-H. Smolka, 685(ZDL):3/1988-367
Krauss, R.E. The Originality of the Avant-Garde and other Modernist Myths.*
D.R. Karp, 290(JAAC):Spring88-426
M.D.O., 295(JML):Fall87/Winter88-251
Kreamer, C.M. Art of Sub-Saharan Africa.
F.T. Smith, 2(AfrA):Feb88-23
Krebs, B. Handbuch der Buchdruckerkunst.
J.L. Flood, 354:Dec88-359
Kreiner, J., ed. Japan und die Mittelmächte.
F.G. Notehelfer, 293(JASt):Feb88-148
Kreis, G. & M.S. Strauss - see Keun, I.
Kreiser, L. Deutung und Bedeutung.
R. Blutner, 682(ZPSK):Band41Heft1-124
Kreiter-Kurylo, C. Contrary Visions.
F. Allen, 496:Summer88-49
Kreitman, N. Touching Rock.
C. Gow, 571(ScLJ):Spring88-36
Krell, D.F. Intimations of Mortality.*
M. Haar, 192(EP):Jan-Mar88-128
T. Kisiel, 323:Jan88-93
Krell, D.F. Postponements.*
N. Davey, 323:May88-205
S.L. Gilman, 221(GQ):Winter88-118
M. Haar, 192(EP):Jan-Mar88-130
Krell, D.F. & D. Wood, eds. Exceedingly Nietzsche.
M. Tanner, 617(TLS):12-18May89-509
Kremer-Marietti, A. L'éthique.
M. Adam, 542:Oct-Dec88-503
Kremnitz, G. Das Okzitanische, Sprachgeschichte und Soziologie.
T.T. Field, 545(RPh):Nov88-213
Kremnitz, G. - see Fabre d'Olivet

Kreps, M. Texnika komičeskogo u Zoščenko.
  L.H. Scatton, 574(SEEJ):Winter88-658
Krettek, T., ed. Creativity and Common
  Sense.
  J.P. Surber, 543:Mar89-629
Kretzmann, N., A. Kenny & J. Pinborg, eds.
  The Cambridge History of Later Medieval
  Philosophy.
  M. Beuchot, 449:Dec88-635
Kreutel, R.F. - see 'Oṣmān Aġa
Kreutzer, E. New York in der Zeitgenös-
  sischen amerikanischen Erzählliteratur.
  U.S., 295(JML):Fall87/Winter88-262
Kreutzer, H.J. - see "Kleist-Jahrbuch"
Kreuzer, J. Erinnerung.
  R. Wiegmann, 406:Summer88-228
de Krey, G.S. A Fractured Society.
  A. McInnes, 83:Spring88-77
Kreyder, L. L'Enfance des saints et des
  autres.
  M. Bannister, 208(FS):Oct88-480
  R. Lloyd, 402(MLR):Jan89-178
Kreyenbroek, G. Sraoša in the Zoroastrian
  Tradition.*
  W.W. Malandra, 318(JAOS):Apr-Jun87-
  369
Kreyling, M. Figures of the Hero in Southern
  Narrative.*
  E.T. Carroll, 395(MFS):Summer88-251
  P. Castille, 594:Winter88-433
  R.D. Watson, Jr., 578:Fall88-99
Krich, J. El Beisbol.
  T. Miller, 441:4Jun89-7
Krieger, G. Der Begriff der praktischen Ver-
  nunft nach Johannes Buridanus.
  A. Goddu, 319:Oct89-613
Krieger, M. Words About Words About Words.*
  W.E. Cain, 395(MFS):Winter88-729
Krier, F. La Zone frontière du francoproven-
  çal et de l'alémanique dans le Valais.
  A. Schwegler, 545(RPh):Feb89-322
Krinsky, C.H. Gordon Bunshaft of Skidmore,
  Owings and Merrill.*
    D. Gebhard, 617(TLS):1-7Sep89-948
Krishnamurti, B. & J.P.L. Gwynn. A Grammar
  of Modern Telugu.*
  S.B. Steever, 318(JAOS):Jul-Sep87-515
Kristeva, J. The Kristeva Reader.* (T. Moi,
  ed)
  S.A.S., 295(JML):Fall87/Winter88-251
Kristeva, J. Soleil noir.
  A-M. Picard, 627(UTQ):Summer88-550
Kristof, A. The Notebook.
  A. Dorfman, 441:15Jan89-10
  S. Roe, 617(TLS):22-28Dec89-1421
Krizanc, J. Prague.
  V. Comensoli, 102(CanL):Autumn88-136
  V. Taborsky, 108:Fall88-85
Kroeber, K. British Romantic Art.*
  R.N. Essick, 340(KSJ):Vol37-204
  M.D. Paley, 591(SIR):Fall88-442
  S.M. Smith, 89(BJA):Spring88-186
  J.R. Watson, 402(MLR):Jul89-721
Kroeger, K. - see Billings, W.
Kroetsch, R. Advice to My Friends.
  P. Hjartarson, 102(CanL):Winter87-135
Kroetsch, R. & R.M. Nischik, eds. Gaining
  Ground.*
  S.S. Atherton, 102(CanL):Winter87-184
  K. Mezei, 677(YES):Vol19-359
Kröger, J. Sasanidischer Stuckdekor.
  C.A. Bromberg, 318(JAOS):Apr-Jun87-
  336

Krogseth, O. Den tyske historismen.
  L. Hermodsson, 597(SN):Vol60No2-270
Krohn, D. Die Verben der menschlichen Körp-
  erteilbewegung im heutigen Deutsch.
  F. Hundsnurscher, 685(ZDL):1/1988-96
Krois, J.M. Cassirer.
  W.H. Werkmeister, 319:Jul89-493
Kroker, A. & D. Cook. The Postmodern Scene.
  T. Carmichael, 627(UTQ):Fall87-144
Kroll, J. The Electrolux Man and Other
  Stories.
  D. Adelaide, 581:Sep88-339
"Lucien Kroll: Buildings and Projects."
  P.B. Jones, 46:Apr88-12
Kröller, E-M. Canadian Travellers in Europe,
  1851-1900.
  J. Doyle, 178:Dec88-472
  A. Ryall, 637(VS):Summer89-597
Krolop, K. Sprachsatire als Zeitsatire bei
  Karl Kraus.
  G.J. Carr, 402(MLR):Apr89-528
Kromer, T. Waiting for Nothing and Other
  Writings. (A.D. Casciato & J.L.W. West 3d,
  eds)
  D.C. Wixson, 534(RALS):Vol16No1&2-29
Kroos, R. Der Schrein des heiligen Servatius
  in Maastricht und die vier zugehörigen
  Reliquiare in Brussel.
  A. Legner, 683:Band51Heft1-148
Kropp Dakubu, M.E., ed. The Languages of
  Ghana.
  L.M. Hyman, 350:Sep89-668
Krueger, H.C. Navi e proprietà navale a Gen-
  ova, seconda metà del sec. XII.
  B.Z. Kedar, 589:Jul88-695
Krüger, J. S. Lorenzo Maggiore in Neapel,
  eine Franziskanerkirche zwischen Orden-
  sideal und Herrschaftsarchitektur.
  C. Bruzelius, 576:Sep88-301
Kruijsen, J., ed. Liber amicorum Weijnen.
  L.M. Eichinger, 685(ZDL):1/1988-65
Krukowski, L. Art and Concept.*
  P.N. Humble, 89(BJA):Autumn88-379
  D. Kuspit, 290(JAAC):Summer88-524
Krumlinde, L. Carl Jonas Love Almqvist i
  Amerika.
  A. Melberg, 172(Edda):1988/2-180
Krupat, A. For Those Who Come After.*
  J. Rice, 128(CE):Feb88-206
  A.R. Velie, 223:Spring88-107
Krupnick, M. Lionel Trilling and the Fate of
  Cultural Criticism.*
  E.L. Steeves, 403(MLS):Fall88-91
Kruse, B-A. Apollinisch-Dionysisch.
  P. Trotignon, 542:Jul-Sep88-346
Kruse, J. Der Tanz der Zeichen.
  D.C. Riechel, 221(GQ):Winter88-135
Kruse, J.A. & B. Kortländer, eds. Das junge
  Deutschland.
  J.L. Sammons, 680(ZDP):Band107Heft4-
  611
Krystal, A. - see Barzun, J.
Krysztofiak, M. Die Thematisierung der Okk-
  upationszeit im dänischen Gegenwarts-
  roman.
  L. Marx, 562(Scan):Nov88-195
Krzyżanowski, J.R. Advanced Polish.
  C.A. Wertz, 574(SEEJ):Spring88-181
Krzyżanowski, J.R., C.Y. Bethin & W.A. Wier-
  zewski. Reading Polish. (Vol 1)
  C.A. Wertz, 574(SEEJ):Spring88-181

Krzyżanowski, J.R., Z.K. Mirski & D.W. Roney. Ememenary Polish. Intermediate Polish.
  C.A. Wertz, 574(SEEJ):Spring88–181
Krzyżanowski, J.R. & D.W. Roney. Reading Polish. (Vol 2)
  C.A. Wertz, 574(SEEJ):Spring88–181
Ku, D–Y. Korea Under Colonialism.
  A.C. Nahm, 293(JASt):May88–385
Kubar, Z.S. Double Identity.
  I. Deak, 453(NYRB):28Sep89–63
Kubiński, W. Reflexivization in English and Polish.
  S. Wiertlewski, 215(GL):Vol28No3–236
Kübler–Ross, E. AIDS.*
  639(VQR):Summer88–95
Kubovy, M. The Psychology of Perspective and Renaissance Art.*
  A.D. Nuttall, 89(BJA):Spring88–183
Kučera, A. & others – see "Lexicographica"
Kučera, J.P. & J. Rak. Bohuslav Balbín a jeho místo v české kultuře.
  L. Udolph, 688(ZSP):Band48Heft2–420
Kuch, P. Yeats and AE.
  J.J.M., 295(JML):Fall87/Winter88–228
Kucich, J. Repression in Victorian Fiction.*
  S. Cohan, 454:Spring89–350
  D. David, 637(VS):Winter89–231
  639(VQR):Summer88–80
Kučukalić, Z. Die Struktur des Kunstwerks.
  V.K. Agawu, 410(M&L):Jul88–404
Küçükerman, Ö. Turkish House.
  G. Fowden, 617(TLS):22–28Dec89–1424
Kuczaj, S.A. 2d, ed. Discourse Development.
  K. Meng, 682(ZPSK):Band41Heft1–117
Kuczynski, J. Die Intelligenz.
  H. Hanke, 654(WB):8/1988–1394
Kudelin, A.B. Srednevekovaia arabskaia po-etika.
  M. Tolmacheva, 318(JAOS):Apr–Jun87–378
Kuehn, H.R. Mixed Blessings.
  B. Finkelstein, 441:12Mar89–23
Kuehn, M. Scottish Common Sense in Ger-many, 1768–1800.
  R.D.G., 185:Oct88–202
  R. Malter, 319:Jul89–486
Kuenzli, R.E., ed. Dada and Surrealist Film.*
  D. Fisher, 400(MLN):Sep88–943
Kugel, J.L. & R.A. Greer. Early Biblical In-terpretation.
  R.D. Sider, 124:Jul–Aug89–461
Kühl, K. Eigentumsordnung als Freiheitsord-nung.
  H. Oberer, 342:Band79Heft3–369
Kühl de Mones, U. Los inicios de la lexico-grafía del español del Uruguay.
  C. Schmitt, 553(RLiR):Jul–Dec88–507
Kuhlen, R., with others. Informationslinguis-tik.
  R. Hoffmann, 682(ZPSK):Band41Heft6–829
Kühlmann, W. & W.E. Schäfer, eds. Des Jesai-as Romplers von Löwenhalt erstes gebüsch seiner Reimgetichte 1647, mit einem Nach-wort, Kommentaren und bibliographischen Anhang.
  W.A. Coupe, 402(MLR):Jul89–779
Kuhn, A.K. Christa Wolf's Utopian Vision.
  P. Graves, 617(TLS):21–27Apr89–435
Kühn, J–H. & U. Fleischer, eds. Index Hip-pocraticus. (fasc 1)
  H. King, 123:Vol38No1–143
  J. Longrigg, 303(JoHS):Vol108–228

Kühn, J–H. & U. Fleischer, eds. Index Hip-pocraticus. (fasc 2)
  H. King, 123:Vol38No2–402
  J. Longrigg, 303(JoHS):Vol108–228
Kühn–Ludewig, M. – see Becher, J.R. & H.F.S. Bachmair
Kuhns, R. Psychoanalytic Theory of Art.* (German title: Psychoanalytische Theorie der Kunst.)
  J.T. Adams, 221(GQ):Fall88–540
Kuhrt, A. & H. Sancisi–Weerdenburg, eds. Achaemenid History. (Vol 3)
  M.C. Root, 617(TLS):13–19Oct89–1126
Kuhse, H. The Sanctity–of–Life Doctrine in Medicine.*
  R. Crisp, 518:Oct88–236
Kuic, V. – see Simon, Y.R.
Kula, W., N. Assorodobraj–Kula & M. Kula, eds. Writing Home.
  K.R. Sword, 575(SEER):Jul88–492
Kulkarni, V.B. Princely India and Lapse of British Paramountcy.
  M. Dembo, 318(JAOS):Oct–Dec87–788
Kulke, H. & D. Rothermund. A History of India.
  A. Vergati, 161(DUJ):Dec87–144
Kulke, H. & D. Rothermund, eds. Regionale Tradition in Südasien.
  W.L. Smith, 318(JAOS):Jul–Sep87–524
Kull, S. Minds at War.
  M. Bundy, 453(NYRB):20Jul89–3
Kullman, C.H. & W.C. Young, eds. Theatre Companies of the World.
  M.C. Roudané, 405(MP):Nov88–220
  D. Wheeler, 577(SHR):Summer88–299
Kullman, W., H. Flashar & F. Hampl. Mythos.
  A. Griffiths, 123:Vol38No2–421
Kumar, K. Utopia and Anti–Utopia in Modern Times.
  W. Stafford, 366:Autumn88–225
Kumar, K. & J. Stackhouse. Classical Music of South India.
  J. Katz, 410(M&L):Oct88–500
Kumin, M. In Deep.
  D. Miller, 569(SR):Fall88–684
  639(VQR):Summer88–102
Kumin, M. Nurture.
  C. Muske, 441:5Nov89–32
Kunc, K. Lore of Gold.
  G. Gessert, 448:Vol26No2–118
Kundera, M. The Art of the Novel.* (French title: L'art du roman.)
  R. Porter, 364:Aug/Sep88–140
  42(AR):Summer88–400
Kundera, M. The Joke.
  J. Byrne, 532(RCF):Summer88–332
Kundera, M. The Unbearable Lightness of Being.
  J. Byrne, 532(RCF):Fall88–160
Kunitz, S. Next–to–Last Things.*
  C. Bedient, 569(SR):Winter88–137
Kuno, S. Functional Syntax.*
  S. Wright, 297(JL):Sep88–553
Kuntz, P.G. Bertrand Russell.*
  P. Hager, 63:Sep88–417
Kunze, E. Deutsch–finnische Literaturbezie-hungen.
  P.M. Mitchell, 301(JEGP):Jul88–420
Kuo, T–C. & R.H. Myers. Understanding Com-munist China.
  A. Goldstein, 293(JASt):Feb88–120

Labrador Herraiz, J.J. & J. Fernández Jimé-
nez, eds. Cervantes and the Pastoral.*
  T.R. Hart, 86(BHS):Jul88-303
Laca, B. Die Wortbildung als Grammatik des
Wortschatzes.
  J. Garrido, 603:Vol12No1-223
"L'Académie de Peinture et de Sculpture à
Valenciennes au XVIIIe siècle."
  H. Weston, 90:Jan88-39
La Capra, D. History, Politics, and the
Novel.*
  M.S. Fries, 395(MFS):Winter88-732
La Capra, D. Rethinking Intellectual His-
tory.* History and Criticism.*
  A. Pagden, 322(JHI):Jul-Sep88-519
La Capra, D. & S.L. Kaplan, eds. Modern Eu-
ropean Intellectual History.
  A. Pagden, 322(JHI):Jul-Sep88-519
Lacey, N. State Punishment.
  T.D. Campbell, 617(TLS):14-20Apr89-401
  W. Cragg, 103:Nov89-443
Lacey, N.J., ed. The Arthurian Encyclopedia.
  M. Whitaker, 102(CanL):Autumn88-180
Lacey, W.K. - see Cicero
La Charité, R.C., ed. Rabelais's Incomparable
Book.
  M. Bideaux, 535(RHL):Nov-Dec88-1135
  C. Clark, 208(FS):Jul88-338
  L.K. Donaldson-Evans, 210(FrF):Jan88-
  111
La Charité, V.A. The Dynamics of Space.
  M. Antle, 446(NCFS):Fall-Winter88/89-
  239
  R.T. Denommé, 207(FR):Feb89-527
  M.C. Olds, 494:Vol8No3/4-735
Lacher, R-P. Die integumentale Methode in
mittelhochdeutscher Epik.
  D.A. Wells, 402(MLR):Oct89-1017
Lachet, C. La Prise d'Orange, ou La Parodie
courtoise d'une épopée.*
  P.S. Noble, 382(MAE):1988/1-128
Lachmann, R. & C. Reents - see Hübner, J.
Lachs, J. George Santayana.
  P.G. Kuntz, 543:Mar89-631
Lackner, W. - see Nicephorus Blemmydes
Laclau, E. & C. Mouffe. Hegemony and Social-
ist Strategy.
  F. Dallmayr, 142:Vol13No3-283
Laclavetine, J-M. Donnafugata.
  P. Nathaniel, 450(NRF):Feb88-97
Lacoste-Veysseyre, C. - see Gautier, T.
Lacoste-Veysseyre, C. & P. Laubriet - see
Gautier, T.
La Croix, W.L. War and International Ethics.
  K.K., 185:Jul89-979
Lactantius. De mortibus persecutorum.* (J.L.
Creed, ed & trans)
  J. den Boeft, 394:Vol41fasc1/2-215
Lacy, N.J., ed. The Arthurian Encyclopedia.
  S.C.B. Atkinson, 577(SHR):Spring88-189
  A.H. Diverres, 545(RPh):Feb89-358
Lacy, N.J. & others, eds. The Arthurian En-
cyclopedia.
  R. Field, 589:Apr88-426
Lacy, N.J. & G. Ashe. The Arthurian Hand-
book.
  M. Fries, 377:Nov88-215
Ladell, J. & M. Inheritance.
  C.G. Holland, 102(CanL):Winter87-261
Laden, M-P. Self-Imitation in the Eigh-
teenth-Century Novel.*
  A. Gelley, 188(ECr):Winter88-122
[continued]

[continuing]
  P.H. Meyer, 173(ECS):Fall88-113
  M.E. Mulvihill, 166:Jan89-168
  M. New, 566:Autumn88-65
  W.A. Speck, 366:Autumn88-244
  H. Weich, 547(RF):Band100Heft4-415
Lafarga, F., ed. Diderot.
  R. Rey, 530:Oct88-168
La Feber, W. The American Age.
  M. Cunliffe, 441:5Mar89-30
Laferrière, D. How to Make Love to a Negro.
  C. Rooke, 376:Jun88-186
Laffan, M., ed. The Burden of German His-
tory, 1939-45.
  A.J. Nicholls, 364:Mar88-88
Laffi, U. Asculum II. (Bk 1, Vol 2 & Bk 2)
  H. Galsterer, 229:Band60Heft3-266
Lafler, J. The Celebrated Mrs. Oldfield.
  F. Morgan, 617(TLS):15-21Dec89-1380
La Fleur, R.A., ed. The Teaching of Latin in
American Schools.
  S.M. Goldberg, 124:Mar-Apr89-313
  J.H. Hall, 399(MLJ):Autumn88-345
Lafont, B. La Fiancée du cinéma.
  J. Van Baelen, 207(FR):Mar89-699
Lafontaine, D. Le parti-pris des mots.
  N. Gueunier, 209(FM):Apr88-128
de La Fontaine, J. Fabeln. (J. Grimm, ed)
  H. Stenzel, 547(RF):Band100Heft4-431
Lafrance, G., ed. Gaston Bachelard, profils
épistémologiques.
  A. Reix, 542:Jul-Sep88-364
Lafrance, G., ed. Pouvoir et tyrannie.
  A. Reix, 542:Jan-Mar88-104
Lafrance, Y. Pour interpréter Platon. (Vol 1)
  L. Brisson, 154:Autumn88-548
  T-A. Druart, 543:Sep88-149
Lafrenière, L. Les dimensions fondamentales.
  M. Espinoza, 542:Jul-Sep88-385
Lagadec-Sadoulet, É. Temps et récit dans
l'oeuvre romanesque de Georges Bernanos.
  P. Vandevelde, 356(LR):Nov88-524
de Lage, G.R. - see under Raynaud de Lage, G.
Lagercrantz, O. Scrivere come Dio.
  Z.G. Barański, 545(RPh):Aug88-51
Lagerwey, J. Taoist Ritual in Chinese Society
and History.
  M. Saso, 293(JASt):Aug88-600
Lagny, M. & others. Générique des années 30.
  T. Conley, 207(FR):Mar89-700
de La Gorce, J. Bérain.
  B. Pons, 683:Band51Heft1-153
de Lagrave, J-P. Fleury Mesplet (1734-
1794).*
  L. Van der Bellen, 470:Vol26-179
La Guardia, D.M. Advance on Chaos.*
  J. Applewhite, 569(SR):Winter88-121
Laguerre, M.S. Voodoo and Politics in Haiti.
  A. Wilentz, 617(TLS):15-21Sep89-992
de Laguna, A.R. - see under Rodríguez de
Laguna, A.
Lahiri, T. Crime and Punishment in Ancient
India.
  R.W. Lariviere, 293(JASt):Feb88-182
Lahnstein, P. Eduard Mörike.
  R. Pohl, 680(ZDP):Band106Heft4-628
Lahr, J. - see Orton, J.
Laidlaw, B. Three Nights in the Heart of the
Earth.*
  42(AR):Fall88-532
Laine, E.J. Affective Factors in Foreign Lan-
guage Learning and Teaching.
  A.S. Kaye, 350:Mar89-186

Laing, A. & others. François Boucher 1703–
1770.
P. Conisbee, 39:Apr88–296
Laing, S. Representations of Working-Class
Life 1957–1964.
A. Louvre, 366:Spring88–126
Laird, R.F. France, the Soviet Union, and the
Nuclear Weapons Issue.
J.M. Newton, 575(SEER):Jan88–159
Laird, R.F. The Soviet Union, the West and
the Nuclear Arms Race.
M. Kramer, 550(RusR):Jan88–97
Laird, R.F. & E.P. Hoffmann, eds. Soviet For-
eign Policy in a Changing World.
P.J.S. Duncan, 575(SEER):Jan88–156
Lajolo, C. Poesia e filosofia in Georg Trakl.
P. Trotignon, 542:Jan–Mar88–91
Lake, A. Somoza Falling.
J. Chace, 453(NYRB):17Aug89–46
P.S. Falk, 441:2Apr89–12
Lake, C. Rosehill.
T. Glyde, 617(TLS):21–27Jul89–804
Lake, C., with L. Eichhorn & S. Leach, eds.
No Symbols Where None Intended.
E.A. Falsey, 517(PBSA):Vol82No3–381
B. Mitchell, 299:No11&12–183
Lake, P. Another Kind of Travel.
M. Jarman, 249(HudR):Winter89–732
Laker, R. To Dance with Kings.
B. Probst, 441:12Mar89–22
Lakoff, G. Women, Fire, and Dangerous
Things.*
G.D. Prideaux, 320(CJL):Sep88–288
Lal, D. The Hindu Equilibrium.
C.A. Bayly, 617(TLS):8–14Sep89–978
Lalande, D. Jean II Le Meingre, dit Boucicaut
(1366–1421), étude d'une biographie
héroïque.
G. Roques, 553(RLiR):Jul–Dec88–543
"L'Album Verve."
F. de Mèredieu, 450(NRF):Feb88–109
Lalonde, R. Sweet Madness.
J.J. O'Connor, 102(CanL):Summer88–126
Lalonde, R. Une Belle journée d'avance.
N.B. Bishop, 102(CanL):Winter87–169
Lam, W.M.C. Sunlighting as Formgiver for
Architecture.
H. Bryan, 505:Jan88–151
J.S. McBride, 47:Mar88–52
Lamacchia, A. – see Saint Augustine
de Lamartine, A. & A. de Virieu. Correspon-
dance. (Vols 1 & 2) (M–R. Morin, ed)
C. Crossley, 208(FS):Jul88–352
J. Gaulmier, 535(RHL):Nov–Dec88–1147
L. Le Guillou, 535(RHL):Mar–Apr88–289
Lamb, D. Down the Slippery Slope.
J. Rudinow, 103:Jan89–26
Lamb, D., ed. Hegel and Modern Philosophy.*
R.C. Solomon, 518:Oct88–208
Lamb, D., T. Davies & M. Roberts, eds. Explo-
rations in Medicine. (Vol 1)
T.S. Champlin, 291:Vol5No2–240
J. Howie, 103:Jan89–30
Lambersy, W. Noces Noires.
S. Basch, 450(NRF):Apr88–89
Lambert, A. Love Among the Single Classes.
L. Chamberlain, 617(TLS):12–18May89–
519
Lambert, A. 1939.
I. Colegate, 617(TLS):26May–1Jun89–571
Lambert, S. The Image Multiplied.
J. Gage, 324:May89–384
T. Harrod, 39:Sep88–208

Lamberti, J–C. Tocqueville and the Two
Democracies.
R.O. Paxton, 453(NYRB):2Mar89–16
Lamberton, R. Hesiod.
C. Martindale, 617(TLS):31Mar–6Apr89–
341
J. Rexine, 124:Jul–Aug89–475
Lamberton, R.L. Homer the Theologian.*
G.L. Bruns, 131(CL):Fall88–384
J. Dillon, 303(JoHS):Vol108–244
A. Sheppard, 123:Vol38No2–288
Lambrechts, R. Corpus Speculorum Etruscor-
um, Belgique 1.
F.R. Serra Ridgway, 123:Vol38No2–354
Lambropoulos, V. & D.N. Miller, eds. Twen-
tieth–Century Literary Theory.
S. Giles, 89(BJA):Spring88–196
R.S. Leventhal, 221(GQ):Fall88–559
478(P&L):Oct88–326
Lambton, A. The Mountbattens.
J. Grigg, 617(TLS):26May–1Jun89–571
Lambton, A.K.S. Continuity and Change in
Medieval Persia.
E. Bosworth, 617(TLS):28Apr–4May89–
450
Lamonde, Y. & E. Trépanier, eds. L'Avène-
ment de la modernité culturelle au Québec.
B–Z. Shek, 627(UTQ):Fall87–192
La Mothe Le Vayer. Dialogues faits à l'imita-
tion des anciens.
L.J. Elders, 543:Jun89–844
Lamott, A. All New People.
R. Bausch, 441:22Oct89–8
442(NY):4Dec89–187
L'Amour, L. Education of a Wandering Man.
A. Solomon, 441:19Nov89–25
L'Amour, L. Last of the Breed.
S. Jenkins, 649(WAL):May88–84
Lamoureux, D. Fragments et Collages.
S.A. Bergersen, 102(CanL):Spring88–189
Lampert, N. Whistleblowing in the Soviet
Union.
M. Mommsen, 550(RusR):Jul88–349
Lamping, D., ed. Ludwig Marcuse.
L. Kahn, 221(GQ):Fall88–609
Lamplugh, G.R. Politics on the Periphery.
M.L. Ready, 656(WMQ):Oct88–812
Lampton, D.M., with J.A. Madancy & K.M. Wil-
liams. A Relationship Restored.
S.P. Ogden, 293(JASt):Aug88–601
Lampton, D.M., with Yeung Sai-cheung. Paths
to Power.
P.H. Chang, 293(JASt):Aug88–602
Lan, C.E. & V.E. Juliá – see under Eggers
Lan, C. & V.E. Juliá
Lana, I. La condizione dei minatori nelle
miniere secondo Plinio il Vecchio e altri
autori antichi.
H. Zehnacker, 555:Vol61fasc1–165
Lanc, E., with I. Hammer & E–M. Höhle. Die
mittelalterlichen Wandmalereien in Wien
und Niederösterreich.
P. Diemer, 90:Feb88–147
Lancashire, A. – see Leech, C.
Lancashire, I. Dramatic Texts and Records of
Britain: A Chronological Topography to
1558.*
T. Pettitt, 539:Fall88–318
Lancaster, B. Radicalism, Cooperation and
Socialism.
P. Stead, 637(VS):Spring89–448

Lapesa, R. Garcilaso.
  A. Porqueras-Mayo, 240(HR):Winter88-102
Lapidge, M. & H. Gneuss, eds. Learning and Literature in Anglo-Saxon England.
  A. Bammesberger, 38:Band106Heft1/2-198
  J.B. Trahern, Jr., 301(JEGP):Jul88-433
Lapidus, I.M. A History of Islamic Societies.
  R. Irwin, 617(TLS):3-9Mar89-216
La Pierre, J. Children's Games.
  M. Stasio, 441:4Jun89-24
La Pierre, L., ed. If You Love This Country.
  C. Pullen, 529(QQ):Winter88-881
Lapington, S. Legend of True Labour.*
  S. O'Brien, 364:Feb88-83
Laplanche, J. Nouveaux fondements pour la psychanalyse.
  F. Roustang, 98:Oct88-771
Lapointe, R. & L. Tessier. Histoire des Franco-Canadiens de la Saskatchewan.
  A. Chartier, 207(FR):Mar89-727
Laponce, J.A. Languages and their Territories.
  D. Cartwright, 298:Winter88/89-130
Laporte, R. Une Vie.
  G. Jallet, 98:Dec88-1008
"L'Approche historique en critique littéraire."
  G. Jacques, 356(LR):Feb-May88-113
Laqueur, W. The Long Road to Freedom.
  M.D. Shulman, 441:28May89-5
Lardet, P. - see Saint Jérôme
Lardet, P. - see Hieronymi, S.
Lardner, J. Fast Forward.
  E.I. Scherick, 18:Nov87-63
Lardreau, G. Discours philosophique et discours spirituel.
  P. Magnard, 192(EP):Oct-Dec88-558
Lardy, N.R. China's Entry into the World Economy.
  T.R. Gottschang, 293(JASt):Nov88-857
Large, A. The Artificial Language Movement.*
  H. Tonkin, 355(LSoc):Jun88-282
de Lario, D. El Comte-Duc d'Olivares i el Regne de València.
  P. Williams, 86(BHS):Jul88-296
de Larivey, P. Le Laquais. (M. Lazard & L. Zilli, eds)
  M.J. Freeman, 208(FS):Oct88-464
Larkin, E. The Consolidation of the Roman Catholic Church in Ireland, 1860-1870.
  S.J. Connolly, 637(VS):Winter89-283
Larkin, P. Collected Poems.* (A. Thwaite, ed)
  M. Baron, 175:Autumn88-267
  P. Davison, 61:May89-95
  C. James, 442(NY):17Jul89-88
  J.D. McClatchy, 441:21May89-24
  W. Scammell, 493:Winter88/89-20
  D. Walcott, 453(NYRB):1Jun89-37
Larmore, C.E. Patterns of Moral Complexity.*
  L. Haworth, 154:Winter88-711
  B. Schultz, 185:Jan89-423
Larose, R. Théories contemporaines de la traduction.
  A.R. Curtis, 627(UTQ):Fall88-180
Larouche-Thibault, M. Amorosa.
  N.B. Bishop, 102(CanL):Winter87-169
Larrabee, F.S., ed. The Two German States and European Security.
  D. Gress, 441:17Sep89-13
  R. Morgan, 617(TLS):13-19Oct89-1115

Larrissy, E. William Blake.*
  P. Martin, 366:Autumn88-207
de Larroche, C.K. - see under Kodama de Larroche, C.
Larsen, J. Silk Road.
  P-L. Adams, 61:Sep89-111
  E. Stumpf, 441:10Sep89-26
Larsen, J. - see Xue Tao
Larsen, J.P. & K. Wedin, eds. Die Sinfonie KV 16a "del Sigr. Mozart."
  J. Arthur, 415:Aug88-406
Larsen, N. Quicksand [and] Passing.* (D.E. McDowell, ed)
  W.H. Shurr, 534(RALS):Vol16No1&2-79
Larsen-Freeman, D. Techniques and Principles in Language Teaching.
  T.L. Ballman, 399(MLJ):Summer88-216
  L.A.W. van Lier, 608:Mar87-146
Larson, G. The Prehistory of the Far Side.
  R. Scheier, 441:12Nov89-54
Larson, G.D. Prelude to Revolution.
  B. Anderson, 293(JASt):Aug88-707
Larson, J.L. Dickens and the Broken Scripture.*
  M.W. Carpenter, 158:Jun88-82
  M. Moseley, 569(SR):Spring88-243
  J.R. Reed, 637(VS):Autumn88-114
  G.J. Worth, 405(MP):Aug88-101
Larson, K.C. Whitman's Drama of Consensus.
  R.W. French, 646(WWR):Spring89-198
Larson, K.E. "King Lear" in German Translation.
  W.G. Müller, 156(ShJW):Jahrbuch1988-273
Larson, P.C., ed. The Spirit of H.H. Richardson on the Midland Prairies.
  M.A. Branch, 505:Jun88-125
La Rue, R., with G. Vincent & B. St.-Onge. Clavis Scriptorum Graecorum et Latinorum.
  R.S. Bagnall, 487:Summer88-186
Lary, N.M. Dostoevsky and Soviet Film.*
  A. Batchan, 574(SEEJ):Winter88-670
  M. Deppermann, 529(QQ):Winter88-903
  J.B. Dunlop, 550(RusR):Jul88-324
  M. Schonberg, 627(UTQ):Fall87-236
  R. Taylor, 575(SEER):Oct88-668
Lasdun, J. A Jump Start.*
  A. Hudgins, 249(HudR):Winter89-738
  H. Lomas, 364:Dec87/Jan88-122
Lash, J.P. Dealers and Dreamers.*
  A. Schlesinger, Jr., 453(NYRB):16Feb89-20
Laskin, M., Jr. & M. Pantazzi. Catalogue of the National Gallery of Canada: European and American Painting, Sculpture and Decorative Arts 1300-1800.
  H. Brigstocke, 90:Dec88-935
Laslett, P. A Fresh Map of Life.
  P. Willmott, 617(TLS):29Dec89/4Jan90-1431
Laslett, P. - see Locke, J.
Lasowski, P.W. L'Ardeur et la Galanterie.*
  R. Waller, 402(MLR):Oct89-977
Lass, A.H., D. Kiremidjian & R.M. Goldstein. The Facts on File: Dictionary of Classical, Biblical, and Literary Allusions.*
  639(VQR):Winter88-30
Lass, R. The Shape of English.*
  J. Algeo, 159:Vol5-219
  A-M. Simon-Vandenbergen, 179(ES):Oct88-461

Lasso de la Vega, G.L. Tragedia de la honra de Dido restaurada.* (A. Hermenegildo, ed)
T.E. Case, 238:Sep88-543
D. Fox, 400(MLN):Mar88-460
N. Griffin, 402(MLR):Apr89-500
Lastra de Suárez, Y. Las áreas dialectales del náhuatl moderno.
J.H. Hill, 350:Mar89-129
"Late Picasso."
N. Glendinning, 39:Dec88-446
Latham, B.K. & R.J. Pazdro, eds. Not Just Pin Money.
K. Tudor, 102(CanL):Winter87-199
Latham, C. & D. Agresta. Dodge Dynasty.
K. Konolige, 441:21May89-27
Lathrop, T.A. ¡De acuerdo!
M.E. Beeson, 399(MLJ):Autumn88-374
A. Garfinkel, 238:May88-316
Lathrop, T.A. The Evolution of Spanish. (rev)
S.L. Hartman, 545(RPh):Feb89-352
Lathrop, T.A. ¡Tanto mejor!
E. Cannon, 399(MLJ):Spring88-111
A. Garfinkel, 238:May88-316
Latimer, J. Solomon's Vineyard.
M. Stasio, 441:30Apr89-45
de La Torre, A.S. - see under Sanchez de La Torre, A.
Latour, B. The Pasteurization of France.
E. Weber, 617(TLS):24Feb-2Mar89-185
Latour, B. Science in Action.*
G. Myers, 126(CCC):Dec88-465
Latourelle, R. Miracles de Jésus et théologie du miracle.
M. Adam, 542:Apr-Jun88-212
Latraverse, F. La pragmatique.
S. Attardo, 350:Jun89-430
Latulippe, L.D. Developing Academic Reading Skills.
C.F. McCreary, 399(MLJ):Autumn88-351
Laubenheimer, F. La Production des amphores en Gaule Narbonnaise.
J.J. Paterson, 313:Vol78-241
Laubenthal, A. Paul Hindemiths Einakter-Triptychon.
S. Hinton, 410(M&L):Apr88-289
Laudan, L. Science and Values.*
J. Worrall, 84:Jun88-263
Laudan, R. From Mineralogy to Geology.*
S. Herbert, 637(VS):Winter89-239
Laufer, B. Kleinere Schriften von Berthold Laufer.* (Pt 3) (H. Walravens, ed)
P.W. Kröll, 318(JAOS):Jan-Mar87-162
Laufer, D. Seule ce soir?
A.J.M. Prévos, 207(FR):Dec88-351
Laugaa, M. La Pensée du pseudonyme.*
B. Beugnot, 535(RHL):Jul-Aug88-798
Laughlin, J. The Master of Those Who Know. Selected Poems, 1935-1985.
J. Longenbach, 468:Fall&Winter88-277
Laughlin, J. The Owl of Minerva.
V. Shetley, 491:May88-98
Laughlin, J. Pound as Wuz.*
M. Jennings, 649(WAL):Feb89-384
J. Longenbach, 468:Fall&Winter88-277
Laughton, B. The Euston Road School.*
A. Ross, 364:Feb87-110
Laugwitz, D. Zahlen und Kontinuum.
H. Osswald, 316:Jun88-649
Laurén, C. Normer för Findlandssvenskan.
E. Haugen, 355(LSoc):Mar88-149
Lauren, P.G., ed. The China Hands' Legacy.
J.C. Thomson, Jr., 293(JASt):Feb88-122

Laurence, D.H. Bernard Shaw.*
A.E.W. Maurer, 536(Rev):Vol10-219
E. Mendelson, 40(AEB):Vol2No2-86
Laurence, D.H. - see Shaw, G.B.
Laurence, D.H. & M. Quinn - see Shaw, G.B.
Laurence, D.H. & J. Rambeau - see Shaw, G.B.
Laurence, J. A Deepe Coffyn.
T.J. Binyon, 617(TLS):21-27Jul89-810
Laurent, F. L'Oeuvre Romanesque de Marie-Claire Blais.
A. Hayward, 627(UTQ):Fall87-183
R. Morency, 102(CanL):Autumn88-163
de Lauretis, T., ed. Feminist Studies/Critical Studies.
K. Cummings, 615(TJ):May88-277
de Lauretis, T. Technologies of Gender.
J. Kittredge, 367(L&P):Vol34No4-58
P.D. Murphy, 590:Dec88-163
S. Scobie, 376:Mar88-101
Laurich, C. Der französische Malerroman.
W. Drost, 547(RF):Band99Heft4-469
Lauro, C. "Foire" e utopia nel teatro di M-A. Legrand.
H.G. Hall, 208(FS):Jan88-81
Lauter, E. & C.S. Rupprecht, eds. Feminist Archetypal Theory.
E.C.R., 295(JML):Fall87/Winter88-198
Lauter, H. Die Architektur des Hellenismus.
A. Frazer, 576:Sep88-297
P. Gros, 229:Band60Heft3-279
Lauter, H. Lathuresa.*
R.A. Tomlinson, 303(JoHS):Vol108-264
Lauterbach, A. Before Recollection.*
S. Ferguson, 271:Fall88-157
Lauth, R. Dostojewski und sein Jahrhundert.*
A. Philonenko, 192(EP):Jan-Mar88-113
P. Somville, 542:Jan-Mar88-92
Lauvergnat-Gagnière, C. & B. Yon, eds. Le juste et l'injuste à la Renaissance et à l'âge classique.
Y. Bellenger, 549(RLC):Jul-Sep88-422
Lavaud, C. Le tiers rétrouve.
A. Reix, 542:Apr-Jun88-214
Lavender, D. The Way to the Western Sea.
D.A. Hofmann, 441:19Feb89-21
442(NY):13Feb89-93
Lavergne, P. André Breton et le mythe.
M. Antle, 207(FR):Feb89-532
R. Cardinal, 208(FS):Jan88-108
de Lavergnée, B.B. - see under Brejon de Lavergnée, B.
Lavers, N. Pop Culture into Art.
D.V. Sloan, 268(IFR):Winter89-84
Lavezzi, G. & R. Saccani - see Saba, U.
Lavin, M.A. Piero della Francesca's Baptism of Christ.
T. Martone, 54:Sep88-523
Lavrentiev, A. Varvara Stepanova. (J.E. Bowlt, ed & trans)
N. Lynton, 617(TLS):28Jul-3Aug89-827
M.J. Rosen, 441:26Mar89-10
Lavrin, N. D.H. Lawrence.
M. Storch, 402(MLR):Oct89-954
Lawless, C. Musée National d'Art Moderne.
Y-A. Bois, 98:May88-440
Lawlor, E. In Bolivia.
A. Broyard, 441:3Dec89-22
Lawner, L. Lives of the Courtesans.
R. Goffen, 551(RenQ):Autumn88-501
Lawner, L. - see Romano, G. & others

Lawrence, D.H. The Letters of D.H. Lawrence.
(Vol 4)(W. Roberts, J.T. Boulton & E. Mans-
field, eds)
C. Jansohn, 72:Band224Heft2-412
Lawrence, D.H. The Letters of D.H. Lawrence.
(Vol 5) (J.T. Boulton & L. Vasey, eds)
D. Bradshaw, 617(TLS):17-23Nov89-1260
Lawrence, D.H. Love Among the Haystacks
and Other Stories. (J. Worthen, ed)
K. Cushman, 177(ELT):Vol31No3-353
Lawrence, D.H. Memoir of Maurice Magnus.
(K. Cushman, ed)
J. Meyers, 395(MFS):Winter88-695
Lawrence, D.H. Reflections on the Death of a
Porcupine and Other Essays. (M. Herbert,
ed)
J. Meyers, 177(ELT):Vol31No4-489
Lawrence, D.H. "Study of Thomas Hardy" and
Other Essays.* (B. Steele, ed)
M. Bell, 402(MLR):Jan89-146
Lawrence, D.H. Women in Love.* (D. Farmer,
L. Vasey & J. Worthen, eds)
C. Jansohn, 72:Band225Heft2-408
N. Miller, 42(AR):Winter88-110
C.L. Ross, 184(EIC):Oct88-342
Lawrence, H. Tales of the North Atlantic.*
E. Thompson, 102(CanL):Spring88-127
Lawrence, K. The Life of Helen Alone.
S. Whaley, 102(CanL):Spring88-138
Lawrence, K.R. The Last Room in Manhattan.
S. Chace, 441:12Mar89-26
Lawrence, T.E. T.E. Lawrence: The Selected
Letters. (M. Brown, ed)
S.E. Tabachnick, 441:16Jul89-19
Lawrenson, T.E. The French Stage and Play-
house in the XVII Century. (2nd ed)
W. Brooks, 402(MLR):Apr89-472
N.A. Peacock, 208(FS):Apr88-206
S. Rosenfeld, 611(TN):Vol42No2-86
J. Scherer, 610:Summer88-156
Lawson, A. Adultery.
M. Beard, 617(TLS):12-18May89-504
M.V. Miller, 441:29Jan89-14
Lawson, E.D., comp. Personal Names and
Naming.
L.E. Seits, 424:Mar-Jun88-116
Lawson, H. & L. Appignanesi, eds. Disman-
tling Truth.
E. James, 617(TLS):22-28Sep89-1034
Lawson, L.A. & V.A. Kramer, eds. Conversa-
tions with Walker Percy.*
J.F. Desmond, 392:Fall88-553
Lawson, R.H. Günter Grass.*
I.T. Hasselbach, 221(GQ):Spring87-309
Lawson, R.H. Franz Kafka.*
S.P., 295(JML):Fall87/Winter88-341
W. Phillips, 473(PR):Vol55No4-675
E. Schlant, 221(GQ):Summer88-472
Lawson, T. & H. Pesaran, eds. Keynes' Eco-
nomics.
D. Gillies, 84:Mar88-117
Lawson-Peebles, R. Landscape and Written
Expression in Revolutionary America.
D. Flower, 249(HudR):Winter89-748
W. Franklin, 165(EAL):Vol24No3-259
Lawton, D. Chaucer's Narrators.*
V. Gillespie, 382(MAE):1988/2-312
D. Mehl, 38:Band106Heft3/4-507
Laxalt, R. The Basque Hotel.
B. Allen, 441:24Sep89-48
Laxalt, R. A Man in the Wheatfield.
D.C. Grover, 649(WAL):Aug88-171

Layton, I. Dance with Desire.
S. Noyes, 198:Spring88-106
Layton, I. Fortunate Exile.
C. Messenger, 529(QQ):Winter88-942
Layton, R., ed. Who Needs the Past? Conflict
in the Archaeology of Living Traditions.
P.G. Bahn, 617(TLS):11-17Aug89-881
Lazard, M. & L. Zilli - see de Larivey, P.
Lazitch, B., with M.M. Drachkovitch. Bio-
graphical Dictionary of the Comintern.
(rev)
I. Banac, 550(RusR):Apr88-198
Lazzarino, G. Prego! (2nd ed)
G. Marrone, 276:Spring88-39
Lea, H.A. Gustav Mahler.
G. Jordan, 221(GQ):Spring87-316
Lea, S. A Place in Mind.
K. Bereday, 441:1Oct89-26
Leach, D.E. Roots of Conflict.*
I.D. Gruber, 656(WMQ):Apr88-370
Leach, E. & D.A. Aycock. Structuralist Inter-
pretations of Biblical Myth.
R.T. Anderson, 115:Winter88-100
Leach, G. The Afrikaners.
S. Uys, 617(TLS):25-31Aug89-915
Leach, P. James Paine.*
J.S. Curl, 324:Mar89-262
Leacock, J. John Leacock's "The First Book of
the American Chronicles of the Times,
1774-1775."* (C. Mulford, ed)
S. Fender, 617(TLS):20-26Jan89-56
Leacock, S. Un Eté à Mariposa.
E-M.K., 102(CanL):Spring88-265
Leader, D.R. A History of the University of
Cambridge. (Vol 1)
J. Catto, 617(TLS):26May-1Jun89-584
Leamer, L. King of the Night.
T. Buckley, 441:23Jul89-9
Leaming, B. If This Was Happiness.
S. Braudy, 441:19Nov89-7
Leaney, A.R.C. The Jewish and Christian
World 200 B.C. to A.D. 200.
D. Satran, 318(JAOS):Oct-Dec87-836
Lear, E. Impossible Picturesqueness. (V.
Dehejia, ed)
K. Weber, 441:22Oct89-22
Lear, E. Selected Letters.* (V. Noakes, ed)
D. Cody, 365:Winter88-45
Lear, J. Aristotle.*
D.K.W. Modrak, 543:Dec88-395
Léard, J-M., ed. Les Parlers français.
A.L. Amprimoz, 345(KRQ):May88-223
Leary, L. The Book-Peddling Parson.
J.A.L. Lemay, 534(RALS):Vol16No1&2-58
Leaska, M.A. & J. Phillips - see Trefusis, V.
Leaton, A. Blackbird, Bye Bye.
J. Clute, 617(TLS):24Feb-2Mar89-191
Leavens, I. B. From "291" to Zurich.
E.S., 295(JML):Fall87/Winter88-199
Leavey, J.P., Jr. & G.L. Ulmer. Glassary.*
C. Howells, 447(N&Q):Dec88-556
H. Rapaport, 223:Spring88-108
S. Scobie, 376:Mar88-101
Leavis, F.R. Valuation in Criticism and Other
Essays.* (G. Singh, ed)
P. Faulkner, 447(N&Q):Jun88-266
S.P., 295(JML):Fall87/Winter88-347
Leavis, Q.D. Collected Essays.* (Vols 1 & 3)
(G. Singh, ed)
M. Dodsworth, 617(TLS):8-14Sep89-963

Leavis, Q.D. Collected Essays.* (Vol 2) (G. Singh, ed)
  D.R. Crane, 396(ModA):Summer89-266
  M. Dodsworth, 617(TLS):8-14Sep89-963
Leavitt, D. Equal Affections.
  J. Keates, 617(TLS):9-15Jun89-634
  B. Lowry, 441:12Feb89-7
Lèbano, E. Italian, A Self-Teaching Guide.
  J. Diiuglio, 399(MLJ):Winter88-482
Leblanc, B. Bonaventure des Périers.
  D. Plaisance, 535(RHL):Mar-Apr88-245
Le Boeuffle, A. Astronomie, Astrologie.
  W. Hübner, 229:Band60Heft6-509
Lebovics, H. The Alliance of Iron and Wheat in the French Third Republic, 1860-1914.
  S. Englund, 617(TLS):13-19Jan89-32
Lebow, E.F. Cal Rodgers and the Vin Fiz.
  T. Ferrell, 441:31Dec89-6
Lebowitz, A. A Matter of Days.
  W. Grimes, 441:12Mar89-22
Lebra, T.S. Japanese Women.*
  N.R. Rosenberger, 293(JASt):Feb88-149
Lebrecht, N., ed. Mahler Remembered.*
  R. Crichton, 415:Mar88-133
Le Breton, A. Argotez, argotez...il en restera toujours quelque chose.
  A.J.M. Prévos, 207(FR):Apr89-921
Le Breton, E., P. Ouston & L. Watson, eds. Victor Hugo and the Parnassians.
  R. Lloyd, 535(RHL):Mar-Apr88-307
Lebrun, D. Paris-Hollywood.
  A.J.M. Prévos, 207(FR):Feb89-542
Le Caron, L. Dialogues. (J.A. Buhlmann & D. Gildman, eds)
  J. Jehasse, 535(RHL):Mar-Apr88-249
Lecercle, J-L. - see Rousseau, J-J.
Lecker, R. Robert Kroetsch.
  R. Brown, 627(UTQ):Fall87-161
  A. Hicks, 102(CanL):Autumn88-141
Lecker, R., J. David & E. Quigley, eds. Canadian Writers and Their Works: Poetry Series. (Vol 3)
  S. Gingell, 627(UTQ):Fall88-155
Le Clair, T. In the Loop.
  S. Moore, 532(RCF):Summer88-326
  T. Schaub, 659(ConL):Spring89-128
  S. Weisenburger, 395(MFS):Winter88-660
Leclair, Y. - see Jourdan, P-A.
Leclant, J. & G. Clerc. Inventaire bibliographique des Isiaca, L-Q.
  J.G. Griffiths, 123:Vol38No2-430
Le Cléguer, T. Les Soeurs de la nuit.
  M-T. Noiset, 207(FR):Oct88-200
Leclerc, I. The Philosophy of Nature.
  A. Gabbey, 319:Oct89-624
Leclerc, J. Langue et société.*
  S. Whalen, 627(UTQ):Fall87-204
Leclerc, M. - see Isaye, G.
Le Compte, J. Moon Passage.
  E. Tennant, 441:25Jun89-14
Le Corbusier. Journey to the East. (I. Zaknic, with N. Pertuiset, eds & trans)
  M.A. Branch, 505:Mar88-121
"Le Corbusier: Architect of the Century."
  M. Spens, 592:Vol201No1019-62
Lécrivain, A. & others. Introduction à la lecture de la Science de la logique de Hegel. (Vol 3)
  A. Reix, 542:Jul-Sep88-347
"Lectures, systèmes de lectures."
  M. Borgomano, 535(RHL):Jan-Feb88-166

Ledbetter, D. Harpsichord and Lute Music in 17th-Century France.
  G.S.J., 412:Aug88-226
  C. Meyer, 537:Vol74No1-106
Ledbetter, K. Not Enough Women.
  A.J. Harding, 102(CanL):Spring88-163
Ledeen, M.A. Perilous Statecraft.*
  T. Draper, 453(NYRB):19Jan89-38
  M. Falcoff, 617(TLS):12-18May89-524
Leder, J., comp. Women in Jazz.*
  D.E. McGinty, 91:Fall88-250
Lederer, H. Phantastik und Wahnsinn.
  G. Lehnert-Rodiek, 52:Band23Heft2-189
Lederer, R.M., Jr. Colonial American English.
  B.S. Phillips, 35(AS):Spring88-72
Le Diberder, A. & S. Pflieger. Crise et mutation du monde musical.
  D. Grignon-Goasguen, 537:Vol74No2-247
Lee, A.R., ed. The Nineteenth-Century American Short Story.*
  L.K. Barnett, 402(MLR):Apr89-453
  R. Lawson-Peebles, 541(RES):May88-332
Lee, A.R., ed. Edgar Allan Poe.*
  R. Mason, 447(N&Q):Sep88-420
Lee, A.R., ed. Edgar Allan Poe and the Design of Order.
  C. Gerrard, 541(RES):Nov88-594
Lee, C.C. & C.C. Soufas, Jr., eds. En torno al hombre y a los monstruos.
  C. Alborg, 240(HR):Summer88-389
  L. Hickey, 402(MLR):Jul89-765
  M. Junquera, 552(REH):Oct88-128
Lee, C.H. The British Economy since 1700.
  A.J. Marrison, 637(VS):Winter89-267
Lee, D., ed. The New Canadian Poets: 1970-1985.
  K. Norris, 168(ECW):Spring88-110
Lee, L-O-F. From Exile to Redemption.*
  M.A. Bernheim, 573(SSF):Winter88-91
  E.M. Kauvar, 659(ConL):Fall89-452
Lee, H. Willa Cather.
  C. Bold, 617(TLS):17-23Nov89-1259
Lee, H. - see Bowen, E.
Lee, J.B. Hired Hands.
  A. Adamson, 102(CanL):Winter87-230
Lee, J.W. Classics of Texas Fiction.
  L. Clayton, 649(WAL):May88-72
Lee, L-O-F. Voices from the Iron House.
  M. Doleželová-Velingerová, 293(JASt): Aug88-604
  P. Link, 395(MFS):Winter88-753
  D. Pollard, 244(HJAS):Jun88-272
Lee, L-Y. Rose.
  J. Kitchen, 219(GaR):Summer88-407
  E. Nobles, 577(SHR):Spring88-200
  S. Pinsker, 363(LitR):Winter89-256
  L. Rector, 249(HudR):Summer88-399
Lee, M., Jr. The Road to Revolution.*
  K. Sharpe, 250(HLQ):Spring88-124
Lee, P. Miss Peggy Lee.
  B. Hochberg, 441:16Apr89-21
Lee, R. & D. Morgan, eds. Birthrights.
  C. Overall, 103:Sep89-371
Lee, S., with L. Jones. Do the Right Thing.
  M. Kempton, 453(NYRB):28Sep89-37
Lee, T.H.C. Government Education and Examinations in Sung China.*
  J. Chaffee, 318(JAOS):Jul-Sep87-497
  P. Ebrey, 244(HJAS):Dec88-493

Lee, V. Love and Strategy in the Eighteenth-Century French Novel.*
R. Niklaus, 83:Autumn88-235
Lee, W.T. & R.F. Staar. Soviet Military Policy Since World War II.
M. Kramer, 550(RusR):Jan88-97
Lee, Y-B. & W. Patterson, eds. One Hundred Years of Korean-American Relations, 1882-1982.
B.C. Koh, 293(JASt):Feb88-158
Leech, C. Christopher Marlowe.* (A. Lancashire, ed)
R. Dutton, 402(MLR):Oct89-922
D. Feldmann, 156(ShJW):Jahrbuch1988-287
M.H. Keefer, 627(UTQ):Fall88-108
Leed, R.L. & S. Paperno. 5000 Russian Words With All Their Inflected Forms and Other Grammatical Information.
H.H. Keller, 574(SEEJ):Fall88-497
M.I. Levin, 558(RLJ):Winter-Spring-Fall88-337
Leedham-Green, E.S. Books in Cambridge Inventories.
K. Humphreys, 354:Mar88-55
Leeker, J. Die Darstellung Cäsars in den romanischen Literaturen des Mittelalters.*
F-R. Hausmann, 72:Band225Heft1-208
K. Pratt, 382(MAE):1988/2-294
Leersen, J.T. Mere Irish and Fíor-Ghael.
A. Harrison, 272(IUR):Spring88-153
G. O'Brien, 677(YES):Vol19-348
Lees, A. Cities Perceived.*
C. Cosentino, 222(GR):Summer88-157
Lees, G. Meet Me at Jim & Andy's.
E.J. Hobsbawm, 453(NYRB):13Apr89-32
A. Lively, 617(TLS):29Dec89/4Jan90-1438
Lees, G. Oscar Peterson.
B. Morton, 617(TLS):22-28Sep89-1032
Lees, G. Singers and the Song.
498:Winter88-92
Le Fanu, M. The Cinema of Andrei Tarkovsky.
G. Millar, 707:Spring88-142
Lefebure, M. The Bondage of Love.
B.K. Mudge, 661(WC):Autumn88-184
639(VQR):Winter88-18
Lefebvre, J-P. Der gute Trommler.*
F. Mende, 654(WB):5/1988-858
J.L. Sammons, 406:Winter88-514
Lefèvre, R. Le recoeil des histoires de Troyes. (M. Aeschbach, ed)
G. Roques, 553(RLiR):Jul-Dec88-556
Leff, L.J. Hitchcock and Selznick.*
R. Combs, 707:Summer88-215
Lefkovitz, L.H. The Character of Beauty in the Victorian Novel.
D. David, 637(VS):Winter89-231
H. Michie, 223:Fall88-376
Lefort, C. Democracy and Political Theory.
M. Cranston, 617(TLS):20-26Jan89-52
Lefort, C. The Political Forms of Modern Society.* (J.B. Thompson, ed)
B. Flynn, 142:Vol13No1-85
Legarreta, D. The Guernica Generation.
D.W. Pike, 86(BHS):Apr88-194
Legat, M. The Illustrated Dictionary of Western Literature.
42(AR):Spring88-277

Legenhausen, L. & D. Wolff, eds. Computer Assisted Language Learning and Innovative EFL Methodology.
P.R. Lutzeier, 257(IRAL):Aug88-255
Léger, F. Lettres à Simone. (C. Derouet, ed)
C. Green, 90:Oct88-772
Leggatt, A. Shakespeare's Political Drama.
R. Hapgood, 617(TLS):25-31Aug89-927
Leggett, B.J. Wallace Stevens and Poetic Theory.*
A. Filreis, 27(AL):Mar88-134
Leggett, T. Śaṅkara on the Yoga-sūtra-s. (Vol 2)
Sengaku Mayeda, 485(PE&W):Oct88-440
Le Goff, J. Medieval Civilization. The Medieval Imagination.
M.T. Clanchy, 617(TLS):27Jan-2Feb89-83
M. Keen, 453(NYRB):18May89-47
Le Goff, J. Your Money or Your Life.* (French title: La Bourse et la vie.)
M. Keen, 453(NYRB):18May89-47
Legué, G. & G. de la Tourette - see Jeanne des Anges
Le Guern, M. - see Pascal, B.
Le Guin, U.K. Dancing at the Edge of the World.
N. Perrin, 441:12Mar89-18
W. Steiner, 617(TLS):8-14Dec89-1368
Lehan, R. - see Dreiser, T.
Lehiste, I. Lectures on Language Contact.
V.A. Friedman, 350:Jun89-431
Lehiste, I. & P. Ivić. Word and Sentence Prosody in Serbocroatian.
W. Browne, 574(SEEJ):Spring88-164
J. Gvozdanović, 361:Aug88-363
D.H., 355(LSoc):Jun88-312
Lehman, A.L. & B. Richardson, eds. Oskar Schlemmer.*
C.V. Poling, 54:Mar88-156
Lehman, D., ed. Ecstatic Occasions, Expedient Forms.
R.T. Smith, 496:Winter88/89-52
Lehman, J.F., Jr. Command of the Seas.
R. Halloran, 441:19Feb89-13
Lehmann, G.A. Die mykenisch-frühgriechische Welt und der östliche Mittelmeerraum in der Zeit der "Seevölker"-Invasionen um 1200 v. Chr.
D.F. Easton, 303(JoHS):Vol108-259
Lehmann, J. Christopher Isherwood.
42(AR):Summer88-400
Lehmann, J. New and Selected Poems.
S. Rae, 364:Mar87-87
Lehmann, W.P. A Gothic Etymological Dictionary.*
E.A. Ebbinghaus, 215(GL):Vol28No1-58
Lehmberg, S.E. The Reformation of Cathedrals.
F. Heal, 617(TLS):8-14Sep89-981
Lehne, I. & L. Johnson. Vienna.
J. Rieckmann, 221(GQ):Summer87-514
Lehrer, J. Crown Oklahoma.
K. Ray, 441:25Jun89-24
Lehrer, K. Thomas Reid.
D.W. Hamlyn, 617(TLS):29Dec89/4Jan90-1439
Leib, F.A. Fire Arrow.
N. Callendar, 441:15Jan89-39
Leibniz, G.W. Political Writings. (P. Riley, ed & trans)
M. Cranston, 617(TLS):21-27Apr89-433

Leibniz, G.W. Sämtliche Schriften und Briefe. (Section 1, Vol 3) (G. Utermöhlen & S. Sell-schopp, eds)
    G.H.R. Parkinson, 706:Band20Heft1-115
A. Robinet, 192(EP):Jul-Sep88-444
Leibniz, G.W. Sämtliche Schriften und Briefe. (Section 3, Vol 2) (H-J. Hess, ed)
    G.H.R. Parkinson, 706:Band20Heft2-212
Leibowitz, H. Fabricating Lives.
    E.A.J. Honigmann, 453(NYRB):7Dec89-16
    M. Seymour, 441:5Nov89-30
    442(NY):20Nov89-155
Leidhold, W. Ethik und Politik bei Francis Hutcheson.
    K. Haakonssen, 319:Oct89-626
Leigh, D. The Wilson Plot.
    N. Annan, 453(NYRB):13Apr89-24
    N. Clive, 617(TLS):27Jan-2Feb89-80
Leigh, R.A. - see Rousseau, J-J.
Leighten, P. Re-Ordering the Universe.
    J. Russell, 441:11Jun89-13
Leighton, A. American Gardens of the Nine-teenth Century.
    M.J. Darnall, 658:Spring88-92
Leighton, A. Elizabeth Barrett Browning.*
    S. Donaldson, 85(SBHC):Vol15-77
Leiner, W., ed. Onze Nouvelles Études sur l'image de la femme dans la littérature française du dix-septième siècle.*
    E. Guild, 208(FS):Jan88-84
Leinsle, U.G. Das Ding und die Methode.
    P.R. Blum, 53(AGP):Band70Heft3-327
Leinster-Mackay, D. The Educational World of Edward Thring.
    G. Hogg, 637(VS):Summer89-592
Leinwand, T.B. The City Staged.*
    A.J. Cook, 405(MP):May89-423
    C.R. Forker, 401(MLQ):Dec86-436
    M. Garrett, 541(RES):Aug88-429
    L. Manley, 677(YES):Vol19-318
    G.K. Paster, 570(SQ):Summer88-257
Leiren, T. Marcus Thrane.
    J.R. Hagland, 172(Edda):1988/1-91
Leiris, M. A cor et à cri.
    D. Hollier, 98:Dec88-982
Leiris, M. Nights as Day and Days as Night.*
    D. Coward, 617(TLS):4-10Aug89-857
Leisi, E. Das heutige Englisch.* (7th ed)
    F.W. Gester, 72:Band224Heft2-378
Leisi, E. Praxis der englischen Semantik. (2nd ed)
    F.W. Gester, 72:Band224Heft2-385
Leiss, W. C.B. Macpherson.
    B. Cooper, 103:Sep89-374
Leiss, W., S. Kline & S. Jhally. Social Commu-nication in Advertising.
    T. McCormack, 529(QQ):Summer88-504
Leitch, M. Burning Bridges.
    A-M. Conway, 617(TLS):14-20Apr89-403
Leitch, T.M. What Stories Are.*
    R.J. Dingley, 447(N&Q):Sep88-412
    U. Margolin, 599:Winter88-661
    P.T.S., 295(JML):Fall87/Winter88-263
    D.N. Salvino, 115:Fall88-429
Leitch, V.B. American Literary Criticism from the Thirties to the Eighties.*
    T.H. Adamowski, 627(UTQ):Summer89-526
    V. Nemoianu, 400(MLN):Dec88-1174
Leitch, V.B. Deconstructive Criticism.
    J.P. Leavey, Jr., 125:Fall87-89
Leiter, S.L., ed. Shakespeare Around the Globe.
    Y. Shafer, 610:Summer88-172

Leites, E. The Puritan Conscience and Mod-ern Sexuality.
    M.A. Bellesiles, 106:Summer88-233
Leites, N. Soviet Style in Management.
    A. Stewart-Hill, 550(RusR):Apr88-209
Leith, J.A., ed. Symbols in Life and Art.
    W. Blissett, 627(UTQ):Fall88-101
Leithauser, B. Between Leaps.*
    D. McDuff, 565:Autumn88-61
Leithauser, B. Cats of the Temple.*
    C. Bedient, 569(SR):Winter88-137
Leithauser, B. Hence.
    R.M. Adams, 453(NYRB):30Mar89-20
    A. Rosenheim, 617(TLS):28Jul-3Aug89-830
    L. Shapiro, 441:22Jan89-1
Leitner, G. Gesprächsanalyse und Rundfunk-kommunikation.*
    W. Bublitz, 38:Band106Heft3/4-440
Lejeune, C. Age poétique, âge politique.
    M. Voisin, 193:Autumn88-139
Lejeune, P. Le Cinéma des femmes.
    F. Worth, 207(FR):May89-1084
Lejeune, P. Moi aussi.
    N. Mandel, 494:Vol8No2-458
Leland, C.T. The Last Happy Men.*
    S. Bullrich, 295(JML):Fall87/Winter88-214
    A. Rosman-Askot, 711(RHM):Dec88-183
Lellenberg, J.L., ed. The Quest for Sir Arthur Conan Doyle.
    E. Lauterbach, 177(ELT):Vol31No4-481
    E.S. Lauterbach, 395(MFS):Summer88-294
Lem, S. Eden.
    G. Jonas, 441:1Oct89-40
Lem, S. Hospital of the Transfiguration.*
    J. Clute, 617(TLS):3-9Mar89-226
Le Mahieu, D.L. A Culture for Democracy.
    P. Smith, 617(TLS):20-26Jan89-68
Lemay, J.A.L. The Canon of Benjamin Frank-lin, 1722-1776.*
    B. Granger, 534(RALS):Vol16No1&2-72
Lemay, J.A.L., ed. Deism, Masonry, and the Enlightenment.
    B. Granger, 656(WMQ):Jul88-614
Lemay, J.A.L. "New England's Annoyances."
    N.S. Grabo, 534(RALS):Vol16No1&2-73
Lemay, J.A.L. - see Franklin, B.
Lemieux, G. Les Vieux m'ont conté.
    G. Thomas, 102(CanL):Winter87-242
Lemire, M., ed. L'Institution littéraire.
    B-Z. Shek, 627(UTQ):Fall87-192
Lemmens, M. & H. Wekker. Grammar in En-glish Learners' Dictionaries.*
    A.S. Kaye, 361:Jan88-69
    P. Lucko, 682(ZPSK):Band41Heft4-530
Lemonnier-Delpy, M-F. Nouvelle étude thé-matique sur "Le Mariage de Figaro" de Beaumarchais.
    R. Niklaus, 208(FS):Oct88-475
de Lemos, C.T.G. "Ser" and "estar" in Brazil-ian Portuguese.
    F. Rainer, 547(RF):Band99Heft4-431
Lemos, R. Metaphysical Investigations.
    W.G. O'Neill, 543:Dec88-396
Lemos, R.M. Rights, Goods, and Democracy.*
    D.N. Husak, 484(PPR):Mar89-541
Lempen-Ricci, S. Le sens de l'imagination.
    M. Espinoza, 542:Jan-Mar88-79
de Lempicka-Foxhall, K., with C. Phillips. Passion by Design.
    662:Fall88/Winter89-55

Leneman, L. Living in Atholl.
  M. Pittock, 83:Autumn88-214
"L'Enfer de la Bibliothèque Nationale, 5."
  H. Coulet, 535(RHL):Jul-Aug88-774
Lenoir, Y. Folklore et transcendance dans
  l'oeuvre américaine de Béla Bartók (1940-
  1945).*
  M. Gillies, 410(M&L):Oct88-549
Lens, S. Permanent War.
  P.M.H., 185:Jul89-980
Lensing, G.S. Wallace Stevens.*
  J. Applewhite, 569(SR):Winter88-121
  J. Bayley, 432(NEQ):Jun88-252
  D.H. Hesla, 27(AL):Mar88-132
  P. McDonald, 541(RES):Aug88-461
  K.Z. Moore, 295(JML):Fall87/Winter88-
  387
Lensink, J.N., ed. Old Southwest/New South-
  west.
  D.C. Grover, 649(WAL):Nov88-262
Lentin, A. Lloyd George, Woodrow Wilson and
  the Guilt of Germany.
  F.M. Carroll, 106:Summer88-211
Lentricchia, F. Ariel and the Police.*
  J. Adamson, 627(UTQ):Summer89-541
  W.E. Cain, 432(NEQ):Dec88-615
  S. Helmling, 344:Spring89-151
  H. Kellner, 599:Winter88-654
  L.M. Steinman, 705:Spring88-74
Lentricchia, F. Criticism and Social Change.*
  S. Bretzius, 153:Spring87-21
Lentzen, M. Der spanische Bürgerkrieg und
  die Dichter.*
  J. Rodríguez Richart, 72:Band224Heft2-
  460
Lenz, C., ed. Hans von Marées.
  C.J. Bailey, 90:Mar88-236
Lenz, G.H., ed. History and Tradition in
  Afro-American Culture.
  C. Werner, 395(MFS):Spring88-125
Lenz, J.M.R. Werke und Briefe in drei Bänden.
  (S. Damm, ed)
  K. Wurst, 221(GQ):Fall88-572
Lenz, S. The Selected Stories of Siegfried
  Lenz. (B. Mitchell, ed & trans)
  P. Demetz, 441:26Nov89-14
Leon, E. Who'd a Thought It.
  M. Adams, 2(AfrA):Aug88-88
León, J.D. - see under de Castilla y León, J.
de Léon, L. Fray Luis de León: Poesía. (D.
  Fernández-Morera & G. Bleiberg, eds)
  F.A. Domínguez, 238:May88-292
  W. Ferguson, 240(HR):Summer88-372
  T. O'Reilly, 402(MLR):Apr89-499
Leonard, E. Killshot.
  T.J. Binyon, 617(TLS):17-23Nov89-1288
  A. Rule, 441:23Apr89-12
  442(NY):24Apr89-112
Leonard, H. Madigan's Lock [and] Pizzazz.
  The Mask of Moriarty.
  C. Murray, 272(IUR):Spring88-136
Leonard, J.S. & C.E. Wharton. The Fluent
  Mundo.
  J. Carroll, 705:Spring88-71
Leonard, N. Jazz.*
  P. Baker, 498:Spring88-88
  S. De Veaux, 414(MusQ):Vol73No3-435
Leonard, T. Situations Theoretical and Con-
  temporary.
  R. Watson, 588(SSL):Vol23-254
Leonard, T.C. The Power of the Press.*
  M. Heale, 617(TLS):10-16Mar89-261

"Léonard de Vinci: ingénieur et architecte."
  R. Schofield, 90:Sep88-702
Leonardi, S.J. Dangerous by Degrees.
  L. Simon, 617(TLS):1-7Sep89-954
Le Page, R.B. & A. Tabouret-Keller. Acts of
  Identity.*
  P. Mühlhäusler, 603:Vol12No1-240
Le Page, R.G. - see Rotrou, J.
Le Pichon, Y. L'Érotisme des chers Maîtres.
  D.A. Michaud, 450(NRF):Jan88-117
Leplin, J., ed. Scientific Realism.
  J. Worrall, 479(PhQ):Jul88-370
Le Pore, E., ed. Truth and Interpretation.*
  J.O. Young, 63:Jun88-249
Leppard, R. Authenticity in Music.
  C. Page, 617(TLS):24Feb-2Mar89-188
Leppert, R. Music and Image.
  P. Rogers, 617(TLS):2-8Jun89-614
Leppert, R. & S. McClary, eds. Music and So-
  ciety.*
  C. Ford, 89(BJA):Autumn88-383
  C. Small, 410(M&L):Jul88-421
Leppmann, W. Gerhart Hauptmann.
  G. Oberembt, 680(ZDP):Band107Heft4-617
Leprohon, J.L. The Manor House of De Viller-
  ay. (R. Sorfleet, ed)
  A. Raspa, 102(CanL):Winter87-172
Lepschy, A.L., J. Took & D.E. Rhodes, eds.
  Book Production and Letters in the Western
  European Renaissance.*
  P.R. Quarrie, 354:Jun88-166
Lercangee, F. Joyce Carol Oates.
  S.P., 295(JML):Fall87/Winter88-361
Lerdahl, F. & R. Jackendoff. A Generative
  Theory of Tonal Music.
  R.B. Cantrick, 290(JAAC):Fall87-94
Lerer, S. Boethius and Dialogue.*
  G.M. Cropp, 478(P&L):Apr88-139
  J.B. Friedman, 589:Apr88-428
Lerman, R. God's Ear.
  B. Singer, 441:2Jul89-6
Lerner, J. Caught in a Still Place.
  C. Fraser, 617(TLS):28Jul-3Aug89-830
Lerner, L. Rembrandt's Mirror.*
  639(VQR):Winter88-26
Lerner, L.S. - see under Schwartz Lerner, L.
Lerner, R. The Thinking Revolutionary.*
  P.K. Conkin, 656(WMQ):Apr88-380
  639(VQR):Spring88-61
Lernoux, P. People of God.
  D.P. McCann, 441:23Jul89-33
Lerond, A. Patois, français régional, français
  central.
  J. Chaurand, 209(FM):Apr88-147
  R. Lepelley, 553(RLiR):Jul-Dec88-537
Lerot, J. Analyse grammaticale.
  P. Swiggers, 553(RLiR):Jan-Jun88-248
Leroy, B. The Jews of Navarre in the Late
  Middle Ages.
  D.W. Lomax, 345(KRQ):May88-255
Leroy, C., ed. Blaise Cendrars 1.
  M. Watthee-Delmotte, 356(LR):Aug88-251
Leroy, G. - see Weil, S.
de Lértora, P.R. & R.A. Young - see under
  Rubio de Lértora, P. & R.A. Young
Lervik, A.H. Evig din.*
  M.K. Norseng, 563(SS):Winter88-93
Leschak, P.M. Letters from Side Lake.
  639(VQR):Winter88-17
Leschhorn, W. "Gründer der Stadt."*
  M. Casevitz, 555:Vol61fasc2-299

Le Scouëzec, G. & J-R. Masson. Bretagne mégalithique.
  J. Réda, 450(NRF):Mar88-92
Lesko, D. James Ensor: The Creative Years.
  C. Zemel, 54:Mar88-154
Lesley, C. River Song.
  P-L. Adams, 61:Sep89-111
  M. Lichtenstein, 441:30Jul89-16
Leslie, P.M., ed. Canada: The State of the Federation 1986.
  D.C. Wallace, 298:Fall88-150
Leslie, P.M. Federal, State, National Economy.
  D.C. Wallace, 298:Fall88-150
Leśmian, B. Mythematics and Extropy.
  S. Barańczak, 497(PolR):Vol33No1-85
Lesourne, J. Education et société.
  L.A. Olivier, 207(FR):Mar89-732
Lesser, E. The Shoplifter's Apprentice.
  T. Nolan, 441:4Jun89-22
Lesser, M.X. Jonathan Edwards.
  W.J. Scheick, 165(EAL):Vol24No1-80
Lessing, D. The Fifth Child.
  R. Garis, 249(HudR):Winter89-756
  C. Rooke, 376:Jun88-186
  639(VQR):Autumn88-126
Lessing, D. The Prisons We Choose To Live In.
  G.H.L. Le May, 364:Nov87-95
Lessnoff, M. Social Contract.
  A. Seller, 518:Jan88-61
Lester, D.G., comp. Irish Research.
  B. Dolan, 305(JIL):Jan88-61
Lester, G.A. The Index of Middle English Prose (Handlist II).*
  V. Gillespie, 382(MAE):1988/1-111
Lester, J. Conrad and Religion.
  D.R. Schwarz, 445(NCF):Mar89-546
Lester, J. The Rhythms of Tonal Music.
  W.E. Caplin, 317:Summer88-382
Lestringant, F. - see Marot, C.
Lestringant, F. & D. Ménager, eds. Études sur "La Satyre Ménippée."
  I.D. McFarlane, 402(MLR):Apr89-469
Lesure, F. & R. Nichols - see Debussy, C.
"L'Etat baroque."
  M-H. Belin, 192(EP):Jul-Sep88-428
"L'Etat de l'opinion: clés pour 1987."
  A.J.M. Prévos, 207(FR):Oct88-188
Lette, K. Girls' Night Out.
  E. Listfield, 441:23Jul89-13
Lettenbauer, W. Tolstoj.
  W. Busch, 688(ZSP):Band48Heft2-400
"Lettres françaises de Belgique - Dictionnaire des oeuvres."
  M. Voisin, 193:Autumn88-146
Letwin, O. Ethics, Emotion and the Unity of the Self.*
  P. Gilbert, 518:Jul88-158
Letwin, S.R. The Gentleman in Trollope.
  S. Pickering, 569(SR):Spring88-259
Leuci, B. Captain Butterfly.
  R. Short, 441:12Nov89-55
Leuilliot, B. - see Paulhan, J.
Leutner, R.W. Shikitei Sanba and the Comic Tradition in Edo Fiction.*
  R.L. Danly, 318(JAOS):Jan-Mar87-165
Leuwers, D., ed. Pierre Jean Jouve poète de la rupture.
  J-M. Maulpoix, 535(RHL):Jan-Feb88-146
Lev, M. Yordim.
  R. Glaser, 390:Jan88-64

Levao, R. Renaissance Minds and Their Fictions.*
  P. Erickson, 570(SQ):Spring88-114
  B.M., 494:Vol8No2-459
Levarie, S. - see Levy, E.
Le Varlet, B. Le Crime de combe jadouille.
  J.M. Laroche, 207(FR):Mar89-717
Le Vayer, L. - see under La Mothe Le Vayer
Levchev, L. Stolen Fire.
  J. Saunders, 565:Autumn88-72
Levenson, C. Arriving at Night.*
  D.M.A. Relke, 102(CanL):Spring88-118
  C. Smart, 529(QQ):Spring88-185
Levenson, C.B. The Dalai Lama.
  J.H. Crook, 617(TLS):3-9Feb89-119
Levenson, J.C. - see Crane, S.
Levenson, T. Ice Time.
  T. Bay, 441:3Sep89-15
Levenstein, H.A. Revolution at the Table.*
  J.T. Patterson, 432(NEQ):Dec88-610
Lever, B. Sometimes the Distance.
  D.M.A. Relke, 102(CanL):Spring88-118
Leverenz, D. Manhood and the American Renaissance.
  D. Van Leer, 357:Fall89-61
Lévesque, R. Attendez que je me rappelle...
  P. Hébert, 627(UTQ):Fall87-190
Levett, J. Skedaddle.*
  H. Lomas, 364:Nov87-90
Levey, M. Men at Work.
  L. Duguid, 617(TLS):24Feb-2Mar89-190
Levey, M. Giambattista Tiepolo.
  D. Howard, 59:Mar88-144
Levi, A.H.T. - see Erasmus
Levi, D.E. The Prados of São Paulo, Brazil.
  A. Hennessy, 617(TLS):14-20Jul89-763
Levi, G. - see Alon, G.
Levi, I. Hard Choices.
  G.M., 185:Apr89-674
Levi, P. Collected Poems.
  P. Hainsworth, 617(TLS):14-20Apr89-402
Levi, P. Collected Poems 1955-1975.*
  E. Morgan, 493:Winter88/89-16
Levi, P. The Drowned and the Saved.* (Italian title: I sommersi e i salvati.)
  E. Kurzweil, 473(PR):Vol55No4-678
  C.G. Segrè, 390:Oct88-60
Levi, P. Shadow and Bone. Goodbye to the Art of Poetry.
  M. O'Neill, 617(TLS):29Sep-5Oct89-1065
Levi, P. The Life and Times of William Shakespeare.
  S. Schoenbaum, 617(TLS):20-26Jan89-63
Levi, P. The Mirror Maker.
  P-L. Adams, 61:Nov89-136
Levi, P. Other People's Trades.
  P-L. Adams, 61:Sep89-111
  P. Bailey, 617(TLS):1-7Dec89-1339
  L. Michaels, 441:7May89-14
  442(NY):4Sep89-107
Lévi-Strauss, C. The Jealous Potter.*
  E. Gonzalez, 400(MLN):Dec88-1177
Levillain, H. Sur deux versants.
  R. Little, 208(FS):Jul88-365
  S. Winspur, 546(RR):May88-527
Levin, D.M. The Opening of Vision.
  D.A. Crosby, 103:Mar89-107
Levin, D.P. Irreconcilable Differences.
  J. Nocera, 441:23Apr89-14
Levin, E. The History of American Ceramics.
  J. Perreault, 139:Dec88/Jan89-18

Levin, H. Playboys and Killjoys.*
    C. Koelb, 131(CL):Fall88-396
    G. Mazzotta, 570(SQ):Autumn88-376
    N.W. Slater, 124:Nov-Dec88-130
Levin, P.L. Abigail Adams.
    M.B. Norton, 432(NEQ):Dec88-620
Levin, R.A. Love and Society in Shakespear-
    ean Comedy.*
    J.L. Levenson, 627(UTQ):Winter87/88-
    321
    N. Sanders, 570(SQ):Spring88-98
Levin, S.R. Metaphoric Worlds.
    A. Margalit, 617(TLS):14-20Apr89-399
Levine, A. The End of the State.
    K.D., 185:Apr89-667
Levine, A. & J.J. McGann - see Lord Byron
Levine, D.O. The American College and the
    Culture of Aspiration, 1915-1940.*
    B. McArthur, 577(SHR):Summer88-280
Levine, D.R., J. Baxter & P. McNulty. The
    Culture Puzzle.*
    N.R. Tumposky, 399(MLJ):Spring88-83
Levine, J. Inside Apartheid.
    G.M. Fredrickson, 453(NYRB):26Oct89-48
    R. Larson, 441:26Feb89-41
Levine, J.M. Humanism and History.*
    C.S.L. Davies, 541(RES):Nov88-605
    B.E. Mansfield, 551(RenQ):Summer88-330
    N.S.S., 185:Jan89-458
Levine, L.I., ed. The Synagogue in Late An-
    tiquity.
    S.S. Weinberg, 124:May-Jun89-391
Levine, L.W. Highbrow/Lowbrow.
    T. Tanner, 617(TLS):14-20Jul89-767
Levine, M.P. Hume and the Problem of Mira-
    cles.
    T. Penelhum, 103:Dec89-487
    M. Williams, 617(TLS):14-20Jul89-784
Levine, P. The Amateur and the Profession-
    al.*
    R. Jann, 125:Fall87-81
    C. Keeble, 635(VPR):Fall88-128
Levine, P. A Walk with Tom Jefferson.*
    P. Mariani, 344:Fall89-170
Le Vine, R.A. & M.I. White. Human Conditions.
    V.N. Kobayashi, 293(JASt):Feb88-98
Levine, R.M., ed. Windows on Latin America.
    L.B. Casagrande, 263(RIB):Vol38No4-535
Levine, S.I. Anvil of Victory.
    R.F. Grow, 293(JASt):May88-354
    639(VQR):Winter88-14
Levinson, M. Keats's Life of Allegory.
    T. McFarland, 617(TLS):27Jan-2Feb89-
    90
Levinson, M. The Romantic Fragment Poem.*
    K.R. Johnston, 340(KSJ):Vol37-172
    C. Rzepka, 661(WC):Autumn88-209
Levinson, M. Wordsworth's Great Period
    Poems.*
    M. Baron, 175:Spring88-54
    A. Bewell, 661(WC):Autumn88-170
    P. Martin, 366:Autumn88-207
    W.J.B. Owen, 541(RES):Feb88-123
    J. Sturrock, 677(YES):Vol19-337
Levinson, O., ed. John Piper - The Complete
    Graphic Works.
    A. Summerfield, 39:Apr88-298
Levitt, M.P. Modernist Survivors.*
    M.J. Friedman, 454:Spring89-341
Levy, A., ed & trans. Fleur en Fiole d'Or (Jin
    Ping Mei cihua).
    M. Détrie, 549(RLC):Jan-Mar88-67

Levy, B.E. & P.C.V. Bastien. Roman Coins in
    the Princeton University Library. (Vol 1)
    M. Deissmann, 229:Band60Heft3-271
Lévy, B-H. Les Derniers Jours de Charles
    Baudelaire.
    L. Lazar, 207(FR):May89-1094
    J. Weightman, 617(TLS):5-11May89-482
Lévy, B.H. L'Eloge des intellectuels.
    L. Lazar, 207(FR):Feb89-571
Levy, D. Beautiful Mutants.
    A. Mobilio, 441:17Dec89-18
    S. Roe, 617(TLS):23-29Jun89-695
Levy, D. Ophelia and the Great Idea.
    J. Marcus, 441:27Aug89-16
    S. Roe, 617(TLS):23-29Jun89-695
Lévy, E., ed. Le Système palatial en Orient,
    en Grèce et à Rome.
    N. Marinatos, 123:Vol38No1-108
Levy, E. A Theory of Harmony.* (S. Levarie,
    ed)
    J. Kelleher, 143:No43-62
Levy, R.J. Whistle Maker.
    S. Corey, 219(GaR):Spring88-161
Levy, T. Figures de l'infini.
    A. Dibi, 192(EP):Oct-Dec88-565
    A. Reix, 542:Jul-Sep88-387
Levy, Y., I.M. Schlesinger & M.D.S. Braine,
    eds. Categories and Processes in Language
    Acquisition.
    B. MacWhinney, 348(L&S):Oct-Dec88-383
Levy-Konesky, N. & others. Fronteras.
    L.S. Glaze, 399(MLJ):Spring88-112
Lévy-Valensi, E.A. - see under Amado Lévy-
    Valensi, E.
Lewalski, B.K. "Paradise Lost" and the Rhet-
    oric of Literary Forms.*
    J.M. Steadman, 131(CL):Spring88-181
Lewalski, B.K., ed. Renaissance Genres.*
    M.G. Brennan, 541(RES):Nov88-540
Lewandowski, J. & J. Szomberg. Samorząd w
    dobie "Solidarności."
    A.J. Matejko, 497(PolR):Vol33No3-357
Lewin, A. A Cup of Tears. (A. Polonsky, ed)
    D. Pryce-Jones, 617(TLS):24Feb-
    2Mar89-197
Lewin, D. Generalized Musical Intervals and
    Transformations.*
    W. Slawson, 413:Winter88-203
    D.T. Vuza, 513:Winter88-258
Lewin, M. The Gorbachev Phenomenon.*
    A.G. Meyer, 385(MQR):Fall89-771
    639(VQR):Autumn88-131
Lewis, B. Jean Mitry and the Esthetics of the
    Cinema.
    J. Anzalone, 207(FR):Dec88-358
Lewis, B. Semites and Anti-Semites.
    D. Stone, 287:Jan/Feb88-30
Lewis, C. Gemini to Joburg.
    S. Pickering, 569(SR):Fall88-673
Lewis, C.S. L'abolition de l'homme.
    D. Leduc-Fayette, 542:Apr-Jun88-215
Lewis, C.S. Letters. (W. Hooper, ed)
    W. Schwarz, 617(TLS):24Feb-2Mar89-203
Lewis, C.S. & G. Calabria. C.S. Lewis and Don
    Giovanni Calabria Letters. (M. Moynihan,
    ed & trans)
    C. Rawson, 617(TLS):11-17Aug89-863
Lewis, D. On the Plurality of Worlds.*
    G. Forbes, 479(PhQ):Apr88-222
    J-L. Gardies, 542:Jul-Sep88-388
    W.G. Lycan, 311(JP):Jan88-42
    N. Salmon, 482(PhR):Apr88-237
    [continued]

Liebich, H.S. L'art islamique, Bassin mediter-
raneen.
  R. Hillenbrand, 463:Summer87-190
Liebs, E. Kindheit und Tod.
  H-J. Uther, 196:Band29Heft1/2-212
Lienesch, M. New Order of the Ages.
  W. Brock, 617(TLS):8-14Sep89-979
Lietz, R. The Lindbergh Half-Century.
  F. Allen, 496:Summer88-49
Lietzmann, H. Das Neugebäude in Wien.
  D.J. Jansen, 90:May88-376
Lieu, S.N.C., ed. The Emperor Julian.*
  M. Di Maio, 124:Jan-Feb89-205
Lieu, S.N.C. Manichaeism in the Later Roman
Empire and Medieval China.*
  G. Bonner, 589:Apr88-431
Lieven, D. Russia's Rulers under the Old
Regime.
  J. Keep, 617(TLS):11-17Aug89-868
Lifson, B. Samaras.
  E. Newhall, 55:Nov88-105
Light, M. The Soviet Theory of International
Relations.
  R. Langhorne, 617(TLS):13-19Jan89-38
Light, R.L. & Fan Lan-Ying. Contemporary
World Issues.
  N.R. Tumposky, 608:Dec89-682
Light, S. Shūzō Kuki and Jean-Paul Sartre.
  J.P. Fell, 319:Apr89-323
Lightbown, R. Mantegna.*
  P.F. Brown, 551(RenQ):Summer88-305
  M.A. Jacobsen, 54:Mar88-148
Lightfoot, S.L. Balm in Gilead.
  H.J. Geiger, 441:1Jan89-7
  442(NY):3Apr89-116
Lightfoot, S.L., ed. Visions of a Better Way.
  A. Hacker, 453(NYRB):12Oct89-63
Lightman, B. The Origins of Agnosticism.
  E. Block, 637(VS):Autumn88-127
  639(VQR):Spring88-46
de Ligne, C.J. Lettres à la Marquise de
Coigny. (J-P. Guicciardi, ed)
  S. Davies, 83:Spring88-109
  R. Mortier, 535(RHL):Jul-Aug88-776
Lilburn, T. Names of God.
  C. Tapping, 102(CanL):Summer88-168
"L'Illustration du livre et de la littérature au
XVIIIe siècle en France et en Pologne."
  J. Voisine, 549(RLC):Jul-Sep88-426
Lilly, W. Christian Astrology.
  E. Mackenzie, 447(N&Q):Jun88-231
Lima, R. Valle-Inclán.
  D. Gagen, 617(TLS):31Mar-6Apr89-328
Limaye, M. Prime Movers.
  L.A. Gordon, 293(JASt):Aug88-683
Limentani, A. & M. Infurna, eds. L'epica.
  M. Bonafin, 379(MedR):Apr88-127
Limentani, U. Dante's "Comedy."*
  T. Barolini, 589:Jan88-191
Limerick, P.N. The Legacy of Conquest.*
  C.S. Peterson, 649(WAL):Aug88-181
  639(VQR):Winter88-16
Limon, J. Dangerous Matter.*
  M. Butler, 447(N&Q):Mar88-89
  M. Charney, 130:Winter88/89-370
  M. Garrett, 541(RES):Aug88-429
  M. Heinemann, 551(RenQ):Summer88-352
  C. Hill, 366:Spring88-119
  T.H. Howard-Hill, 570(SQ):Spring88-128
  F.J. Levy, 702:Vol20-294
  A. Thompson, 402(MLR):Jul89-713

Limon, J. Gentlemen of a Company.*
  M. Kobialka, 574(SEEJ):Summer88-338
  H.B. Segel, 551(RenQ):Spring88-153
Limor, O., ed. The Disputation of Majorca,
1286.
  J. Cohen, 589:Jan88-212
Limouzy, P. & J. Bourgeacq. Vous avez la
parole.
  R. Noël, 207(FR):Dec88-371
Lin, S-F. & S. Owen, eds. The Vitality of the
Lyric Voice.
  J.M. Hargett, 116:Jul87-141
Linant de Bellefonds, P. Sarcophages
attiques de la nécropole de Tyr.*
  G. Davies, 303(JoHS):Vol108-269
Lincoln, A. Abraham Lincoln: Speeches and
Writings 1832-1858. Abraham Lincoln:
Speeches and Writings 1859-1865.
  A. Kazin, 441:10Dec89-3
Lincoln, B. Myth, Cosmos, and Society.
  P. Milbouer, 221(GQ):Fall87-695
Lincoln, H.B. The Italian Madrigal and Relat-
ed Repertories.
  N. Fortune, 617(TLS):4-10Aug89-854
Lincoln, K. Native American Renaissance.
  E. Désveaux, 98:Dec88-989
Lincoln, K., with A.L. Slagle. The Good Red
Road.
  J.L. Davis, 649(WAL):Aug88-186
Lindahl, C. Earnest Games.
  N.F. Blake, 179(ES):Apr88-176
  B. Bowden, 650(WF):Jul88-228
  J.D. Dorst, 292(JAF):Jul-Sep88-379
  J. Erickson, 196:Band29Heft1/2-214
  G. Olson, 589:Oct88-949
Lindberg, D.G. & R.L. Numbers, eds. God &
Nature.
  R.H. Popkin, 319:Apr89-316
Lindberg, K.V. Reading Pound Reading.
  J. Kronick, 598(SoR):Autumn89-859
  E.P. Nassar, 184(EIC):Oct88-351
  C.D.K. Yee, 27(AL):Oct88-501
  639(VQR):Winter88-8
Lindberg, S. & S. Corey, eds. Keener Sounds.
  P. Samway, 392:Winter87/88-105
Lindberg-Seyersted, B. Ford Madox Ford and
His Relationship to Stephen Crane and
Henry James.
  S. Wertheim, 26(ALR):Spring89-85
  R. Wiebe, 177(ELT):Vol31No4-492
Lindemann, E., ed. Longman Bibliography of
Composition and Rhetoric: 1984-1985.*
Longman Bibliography of Composition and
Rhetoric: 1986.
  M. Chan, 608:Mar89-138
Lindemann, K. & V. Arnold Wesker.
  M. Göring, 402(MLR):Apr89-428
  G. Klotz, 72:Band224Heft2-418
van der Linden, H. Kantian Ethics and So-
cialism.
  M. Gregor, 543:Jun89-856
  J. McMurtry, 103:Oct89-426
Lindenbaum, P. Changing Landscapes.*
  M.G. Brennan, 541(RES):Nov88-540
  S. Chaudhuri, 447(N&Q):Dec88-525
  T. Comito, 551(RenQ):Summer88-349
  M.N. Proser, 568(SCN):Spring-Summer88-
  1
Lindenberger, H. Opera.*
  P. Hernadi, 494:Vol8No2-439
  M. Mueller, 107(CRCL):Mar88-111

Linder, K.P. Grammatische Untersuchungen zu Charakteristik des Rätoromanischen in Graubünden.
M. Iliescu, 553(RLiR):Jul−Dec88−499
Linder, L. − see Potter, B.
Lindgren, T. Bathsheba. Merab's Beauty and Other Stories.
C. Sinclair, 617(TLS):14−20Jul89−783
Lindholdt, P.J. − see Josselyn, J.
Lindley, D. Thomas Campion.
C. Gullans, 568(SCN):Spring−Summer88−4
E.S. Ryding, 551(RenQ):Autumn88−517
P. Walls, 410(M&L):Oct88−507
Lindley, R. Autonomy.*
L. Haworth, 518:Jul88−167
Lindner, B., ed. Walter Benjamin im Kontext.
M.W. Jennings, 222(GR):Summer88−149
Lindop, G. Tourists.*
S. O'Brien, 364:Feb88−83
Lindow, J., L. Lönnroth & G.W. Weber, eds. Structure and Meaning in Old Norse Literature.
J.M. Jochens, 562(Scan):Nov88−179
W.E. Richmond, 292(JAF):Jul−Sep88−365
Lindsay, D. The Haunted Woman.
I. Rankin, 571(ScLJ):Winter88−29
Lindsay, F. A Charm against Drowning.*
T. Bacciarelli, 571(ScLJ):Winter88−31
Lindsay, V. The Poetry of Vachel Lindsay. (Vol 2) (D. Camp, ed)
J.T. Flanagan, 534(RALS):Vol16No1&2−141
Lindsey, R. A Gathering of Saints.*
M. Ruthven, 617(TLS):9−15Jun89−629
Lindskoog, K. The C.S. Lewis Hoax.
C. Rawson, 617(TLS):11−17Aug89−863
Lindstedt, J. On the Semantics of Tense and Aspect in Bulgarian.*
B. Comrie, 361:Jan88−72
Ling, D. − see under Ding Ling
Lingeman, R. Theodore Dreiser. (Vol 1)
N.W. Barrineau, 26(ALR):Fall88−91
A.D. Casciato, 639(VQR):Spring88−336
J.K. Davis, 569(SR):Summer88−507
P.L. Gerber, 536(Rev):Vol10−85
D. Pizer, 395(MFS):Summer88−235
T.P. Riggio, 31(ASch):Winter88−151
Lingis, A. Libido.*
M. Whitford, 208(FS):Jan88−115
Lingis, A. Phenomenological Explanations.
D. Ihde, 103:Jan89−33
de Linham, R. Kalendar.* (T. Hunt, ed)
G. Hesketh, 382(MAE):1988/1−126
A.J. Holden, 208(FS):Jan88−69
Liniger−Goumaz, M. Small Is Not Always Beautiful.
D. Birmingham, 617(TLS):1−7Sep89−955
Link, H.A. Waves and Plagues.
P−L. Adams, 61:Jun89−96
Linklater, J., ed. The Red Hog of Colima.
M. Illis, 617(TLS):20−26Oct89−1150
Linklater, M. & C. Hesketh. For King and Conscience.
D. Stevenson, 617(TLS):18−24Aug89−891
Linley, N. − see Ibn Aṭ−Tayyib
Linnér, S., ed. Från dagdrivare till feminister.
S.B. Grønstøl, 172(Edda):1988/1−75
Linthicum, J. Love Poems.
S. Pinsker, 363(LitR):Winter89−256
Linton, D. & R. Boston, eds. The Newspaper Press in Britain.*
J.H. Wiener, 635(VPR):Fall88−123

Lipner, J.J. The Face of Truth.
J.R. Timm, 485(PE&W):Oct88−445
Lipovetsky, G. L'Empire de l'éphémère.
H. Cronel, 450(NRF):Jul−Aug88−219
M. Lilla, 617(TLS):17−23Nov89−1255
Lipovetsky, G. L'Ere du vide.
M. Lilla, 617(TLS):17−23Nov89−1255
Lipp, S. Francisco Giner de los Rίos.*
G.J.G. Cheyne, 86(BHS):Apr88−191
C. Mellizo, 552(REH):Jan88−142
Lippi Bigazzi, V., ed. I volgarizzamenti trecenteschi dell' "Ars amandi" e dei "Remedia amoris."
M. Zaggia, 228(GSLI):Vol165fasc532−596
Lippit, V.D. The Economic Development of China.
B. Naughton, 293(JASt):Aug88−606
Lippman, E.A., ed. Musical Aesthetics.* (Vol 1)
B. Bujic, 410(M&L):Oct88−496
Lippman, T.W. Egypt After Nasser.
L. Anderson, 441:5Feb89−25
Lippmann, F., ed. Colloquium "Johann Adolf Hasse und die Musik seiner Zeit" (Siena 1983).
M. Boyd, 415:Feb88−83
C−H. Mahling, 416:Band3Heft3−281
R. Monelle, 410(M&L):Apr88−256
Lipski, J.M. The Spanish of Equatorial Guinea.*
W.W. Mcgenney, 545(RPh):Nov88−208
C. Schmitt, 72:Band225Heft2−456
Lipstadt, D.E. Beyond Belief.
D. Stone, 287:Jul/Aug88−34
Lipton, E. Looking into Degas.*
B. Collins, Jr., 662:Spring/Summer88−39
Liptzin, S. Biblical Themes in World Literature.
E. Bernstein, 221(GQ):Spring87−322
Lish, G. Extravaganza.
R.F. Moss, 441:4Jun89−15
Lish, G. Mourner at the Door.*
G. Johnson, 219(GaR):Winter88−840
E. McGraw, 455:Sep88−64
I. Malin, 532(RCF):Fall88−157
Liskin−Gasparro, J. & J.K. Phillips. Academic Preparation in Foreign Language.
E. André, 399(MLJ):Summer88−216
de l'Isle−Adam, P.A.M.D. − see under de Villiers de l'Isle−Adam, P.A.M.
Lispector, C. The Passion According to G.H.
S. Ruta, 441:8Jan89−12
Lister, R. Catalogue Raisonné of the Works of Samuel Palmer.
G. Reynolds, 617(TLS):10−16Feb89−149
Lister, R. The Paintings of William Blake.*
The Paintings of Samuel Palmer.
S.M. Bennett, 88:Summer88−20
Liszt, F. An Artist's Journey. (C. Suttoni, ed & trans)
L. Botstein, 441:20Aug89−9
P. Griffiths, 358:Dec89−8
Liszt, F. Franz Liszt: Tagebuch 1827. (D. Altenburg & R. Kleinertz, eds)
P. Merrick, 410(M&L):Apr88−275
Litchfield, R.B. Emergence of a Bureaucracy.
M.B. Becker, 173(ECS):Summer88−555
"A Literary History of the American West."
J. Milton, 649(WAL):May88−50
Litherland, S.J. The Long Interval.*
L. Sail, 565:Spring88−73
Little, J. Different Dragons.
R.E. Jones, 102(CanL):Spring88−167

225

Littlefield, B. Prospect.
 B. De Mott, 61:May89-97
 442(NY):19Jun89-99
Littlefield, D.F., Jr. & J.W. Parins, eds.
 American Indian and Alaska Native News-
 papers and Periodicals, 1971-1985.
 V.S. Salabiye, 635(VPR):Spring88-32
Littleford, M.S. & J.R. Whitt. Giambattista
 Vico, Post-Mechanical Thought, and Con-
 temporary Psychology.
 T.O. Buford, 103:Jul89-273
Littlejohns, R. Wackenroder-Studien.
 J. Trainer, 402(MLR):Jan89-235
Littleton, J. Target Nation.*
 P.H. Russell, 529(QQ):Summer88-496
Littlewood, I. Paris.
 K. Weil, 395(MFS):Winter88-718
 639(VQR):Summer88-103
Litvak, L. Geografías mágicas.
 D.L. Shaw, 345(KRQ):Aug88-379
Litvak, L. El sendero del tigre.
 L. Rivkin, 240(HR):Summer88-376
 D.L. Shaw, 345(KRQ):Aug88-379
 M.L. Welles, 711(RHM):Jun88-75
Litvin, V. The Soviet Agro-Industrial Com-
 plex.
 D. Van Atta, 550(RusR):Apr88-214
Litz, A.W. & C. MacGowan - see Williams, W.C.
Liu, A.P.L. Phoenix and the Lame Lion.
 S. Appleton, 293(JASt):Nov88-858
Liu Zongren. 6 Tanyin Alley.
 G. Feldman, 441:2Jul89-11
Lively, A. Blue Fruit.*
 J. Mellors, 364:Feb88-105
Lively, A. The Burnt House.
 T. Adams, 617(TLS):23-29Jun89-695
Lively, P. Moon Tiger.*
 J. Mellors, 364:Apr-May87-153
 G. Oldham, 42(AR):Summer88-395
Lively, P. Pack of Cards.
 J. Parini, 441:21May89-13
Lively, P. Passing On.
 J.K.L. Walker, 617(TLS):7-13Apr89-363
Livesay, D. Selected Poems.*
 S. Hutchison, 102(CanL):Spring88-205
Livingston, D.W. Hume's Philosophy of Com-
 mon Life.
 F. Wilson, 488:Mar88-139
Livingston, J. Lee Miller: Photographer.
 A. Winand, 441:30Jul89-17
Livingston, J.C. Matthew Arnold and Chris-
 tianity.*
 R. Ashton, 541(RES):Nov88-577
 M. Hardman, 402(MLR):Oct89-944
Livingston, P. Literary Knowledge.
 S. Bonnycastle, 103:Jun89-235
 P. Miers, 400(MLN):Dec88-1180
Livingston, W. The Papers of William Living-
 ston. (Vols 1-4) (C.E. Prince & others,
 eds)
 M.C. Batinski, 656(WMQ):Oct88-807
Livingstone, D. Keeping Heart.
 J. O'Grady, 617(TLS):15-21Dec89-1392
Livingstone, K. Livingstone's Labour.
 M. Pugh, 617(TLS):3-9Nov89-1207
Livni, A. Le Retour d'Israël d'Abraham Livni.
 P-M. de Saint-Cheron, 192(EP):Oct-
 Dec88-551
"Le livre français en Russie au XVIIIe siècle."
 F. Petizon, 530:Apr88-173
Livrea, E. - see Musaeus
Livrea, E. - see Triphiodorus

Livy. T. Livius, "Ab urbe condita," libri
 XXVIII-XXX. (P.G. Walsh, ed)
 S.P. Oakley, 123:Vol38No1-42
Livy. Livius, "Ab Urbe Condita" libri XLI-
 XLV. (J. Briscoe, ed)
 E. Burck, 229:Band60Heft4-323
 T.J. Luce, 24:Fall88-455
Livy. Tite-Live, "Histoire Romaine." (Vol 8,
 Bk 8)(R. Bloch & C. Guittard, eds & trans)
 E. Burck, 229:Band60Heft4-323
 K. Gries, 124:Jul-Aug89-466
Livy. Tite-Live, "Histoire Romaine."* (Vol
 30, Bk 40)(C. Gouillart, ed & trans)
 E. Burck, 229:Band60Heft2-119
Lixačev, D.S. Issledovanija po drevnerusskoj
 literature. (O.V. Tvorogov, ed)
 N.W. Ingham, 574(SEEJ):Winter88-646
Lizoain Garrido, J.M., ed. Documentación del
 monasterio de Las Huelgas de Burgos
 (1116-1230; 1231-1262).*
 P. Freedman, 589:Apr88-452
Ljungquist, K. The Grand and the Fair.
 R.C. De Prospo, 153:Fall88-43
Llarena, F.J.P. - see under Pereda Llarena,
 F.J.
Lledó, E. La memoria del logos.
 A. Gómez-Lobo, 53(AGP):Band70Heft1-
 103
Llewellyn, C. Fragments from the Fire.*
 S. Corey, 219(GaR):Spring88-161
Llewellyn, J. Derrida on the Threshold of
 Sense.
 S. Cox, 144:Winter89-56
 M. Hobson, 208(FS):Jul88-368
Llewellyn, S. Death Roll.
 T.J. Binyon, 617(TLS):21-27Jul89-810
Llewelyn, J. Beyond Metaphysics?*
 T. O'Connor, 323:Jan88-100
Llompart, J. Die Geschichtlichkeit der
 Rechtsprinzipien.
 C. Schefold, 489(PJGG):Band95Heft2-376
Llosa, M.V. - see under Vargas Llosa, M.
Lloyd, C., with T. Bennett. Clematis. (rev)
 L. Yang, 441:3Dec89-74
Lloyd, P.M. From Latin to Spanish.* (Vol 1)
 R. de Gorog, 159:Vol5-227
Lloyd, R. - see Mallarmé, S.
Lloyd, S. English Society and the Crusade
 1216-1307.
 N. Housley, 617(TLS):20-26Jan89-64
Lloyd-Jones, R. & M.J. Lewis. Manchester
 and the Age of the Factory.
 W. Ashworth, 637(VS):Spring89-414
Llull, R. Selected Works of Ramon Llull
 (1232-1316).* (A. Bonner, ed & trans)
 E. Lorenz, 547(RF):Band100Heft4-488
Llywelyn, M. Red Branch.
 R.C. Skidmore, 441:16Jul89-24
Lo Ch'in-shun. Knowledge Painfully Acquir-
 ed. (I. Bloom, ed & trans)
 J. Ching, 293(JASt):May88-334
 R.E. Hegel, 116:Jul87-161
Lo, F. Morning Breeze.
 J.M. Hamilton, 441:10Sep89-27
Lo, I.Y. & W. Schultz, eds. Waiting for the
 Unicorn.*
 S. Owen, 244(HJAS):Jun88-260
 R.E. Strassberg, 293(JASt):May88-337
Lo, K.S. The Stonewares of Yixing from the
 Ming Period to the Present Day.
 M.C. Macfarlane, 463:Spring88-53
 U. Roberts, 60:May-Jun88-170

Lo, P.C. Treating Persons as Ends.*
  N.T.P., 185:Oct88-202
Lo, W.W. An Introduction to the Civil Service
  of Sung China.
  P.J. Smith, 293(JASt):Nov88-859
Loader, J. Wild America.
  J. Butler, 441:14May89-9
Loades, A.L. Kant and Job's Comforters.*
  S. Hauerwas & L.G. Jones, 83:Autumn88-
  221
Loades, D. The Tudor Court.
  A.J. Slavin, 551(RenQ):Spring88-128
"L'objet en psychanalyse."
  M. Bertrand, 542:Jan-Mar88-84
Locher, K.T. Gottfried Keller.*
  J.L. Sammons, 564:Feb88-82
Lochhead, D. Tiger in the Skull.*
  L. Boone, 102(CanL):Winter87-209
Lochhead, L. True Confessions and New
  Cliches.
  R. Watson, 588(SSL):Vol23-254
Lock, G. Forces in Motion.*
  E.S., 91:Fall88-259
Lockard, C.A. From Kampung to City.
  R.A. O'Connor, 293(JASt):Aug88-709
Locke, J. The Correspondence of John Locke.
  (Vols 1-7) (E.S. de Beer, ed)
  R.S. Woolhouse, 518:Apr88-74
Locke, J. The Correspondence of John Locke.
  (Vol 8) (E.S. de Beer, ed)
  K.H.D. Haley, 617(TLS):1-7Sep89-949
Locke, J. Two Treatises of Government. (P.
  Laslett, ed)
  M. Cranston, 617(TLS):21-27Apr89-433
Locke, R.P. Music, Musicians, and the Saint-
  Simonians.*
  B. Friedland, 451:Spring88-282
  D.K. Holoman, 317:Fall88-539
  J. Rushton, 415:Feb88-85
  C.G.S. Williams, 207(FR):Apr89-926
Lockemann, P.C. & J.W. Schmidt, eds. Daten-
  bank-Handbuch.
  U. Lindner, 682(ZPSK):Band41Heft5-669
Lockerd, B.G., Jr. The Sacred Marriage.
  C. Kahn, 551(RenQ):Winter88-749
  A.L. Prescott, 604:Winter88-4
Locklin, G. Gerald Haslam.
  R.L. Buckland, 573(SSF):Spring88-166
  R. Burrows, 649(WAL):Aug88-156
Lockridge, K.A. The Diary, and Life, of Wil-
  liam Byrd II of Virginia, 1674-1744.*
  R.S. Dunn, 656(WMQ):Oct88-779
  J.A.L. Lemay, 585(SoQ):Winter89-107
  P.D. Nelson, 392:Fall88-568
Lockwood, W.B. German Today.
  T.F. Barry, 399(MLJ):Winter88-477
  W.V. Davies, 402(MLR):Jan89-227
Lodge, D., ed. Modern Criticism and Theory.
  M. Baron, 175:Autumn88-262
  M. Ellmann, 617(TLS):17-23Feb89-172
Lodge, D. Nice Work.*
  G. Chandler, 324:Jan89-122
  J. Conarroe, 441:23Jul89-1
  H. Mantel, 453(NYRB):23Nov89-18
  J. Mellors, 364:Dec88/Jan89-132
  442(NY):4Sep89-106
Lodge, D. Out of the Shelter.
  442(NY):4Sep89-106
Loewald, H.W. Sublimation.
  J. Lear, 617(TLS):7-13Jul89-752
Loewald, U. Child of Vietnam.
  M. Simms, 581:Sep88-343

Lofgren, C.A. "Government from Reflection
  and Choice."
  P.J. King, 106:Summer88-278
Loftis, J. Renaissance Drama in England &
  Spain.
  F.J. Levy, 702:Vol20-294
  D.B.J. Randall, 551(RenQ):Winter88-744
Logan, G.M. The Meaning of More's "Utopia."*
  U. Baumann, 38:Band106Heft1/2-236
Logan, O.L., with K. Clark. Motherwit.
  P.C. McKissack, 441:10Sep89-14
Logan, R.K. The Alphabet Effect.
  V.L. Johnson, 608:Mar89-140
  J.E. Joseph, 350:Dec89-898
Logan, W. Sullen Weedy Lakes.
  B. Bennett, 441:12Mar89-38
Logsdon, L. & C.W. Mayer, eds. Since Flan-
  nery O'Connor.
  W. Burke, 395(MFS):Summer88-247
Logue, A.W. The Psychology of Eating and
  Drinking.
  A. Lehrer, 567:Vol69No3/4-363
Logue, C. War Music.*
  S. Birkerts, 473(PR):Vol55No3-484
  P. Parotti, 569(SR):Spring88-xli
Loi, M. Poètes chinois d'écoles françaises.
  M. Détrie, 549(RLC):Jan-Mar88-68
Loizeaux, E.B. - see under Bergmann Loi-
  zeaux, E.
Loizou, A. The Reality of Time.
  M. Redhead, 518:Apr88-118
Lokke, K. Gérard de Nerval.
  S. Dunn, 207(FR):Apr89-892
  S. Dunn, 207(FR):May89-1074
  S. Guers, 446(NCFS):Fall-Winter88/89-
  225
  N. Rinsler, 208(FS):Jul88-353
Lomasky, L.E. Persons, Rights, and the Moral
  Community.*
  L.W. Sumner, 185:Apr89-640
Lomax, M. The Peepshow Girl.
  B. O'Donoghue, 617(TLS):1-7Dec89-1336
Lomax, M. Stage Images and Traditions.
  M. Archer, 157:No166-50
  T.W. Craik, 447(N&Q):Dec88-531
  L. Potter, 610:Autumn88-279
  R. Wilcher, 611(TN):Vol42No3-139
Lombard, L.B. Events.*
  M. Brand, 484(PPR):Mar89-525
Lombardi, L.G. Moral Analysis.
  C.A.H.J., 185:Apr89-663
Lombardo, P. Edgar Poe et la Modernité.*
  A-M. Smith, 208(FS):Jan88-113
Lombardo, S. & D. Rayor - see "Callimachus:
  Hymns, Epigrams, Select Fragments"
Lomnitz, L.A. & M. Perez-Lizaur. A Mexican
  Elite Family, 1820-1980.
  639(VQR):Autumn88-125
Lomperis, T.J. "Reading the Wind."*
  N.B. Christie, 27(AL):Mar88-153
London, J. The Letters of Jack London.* (E.
  Labor, R.C. Leitz 3d & I.M. Shepard, eds)
  P. Kemp, 617(TLS):9-15Jun89-627
London, J. Jack London's California. With a
  Heart Full of Love. (S. Noto, ed of both)
  E. Labor, 649(WAL):May88-62
London, M. & J. Schwartz. The Mitchel Lon-
  don Gracie Mansion Cookbook.
  R. Flaste, 441:11Jun89-20
Long, A.A. & D.N. Sedley. The Hellenistic
  Philosophers.
  F.E. Romer, 124:Jul-Aug89-471
  L.P. Schrenk, 543:Sep88-150

Long, L.D. & J. Spiegel-Podnecky. In Print.
  A. Nash, 608:Jun89-329
  P.B. Nimmons, 399(MLJ):Winter88-467
Long, S.O. Family Change and the Life Course
  in Japan.
  A.E. Imamura, 407(MN):Spring88-125
Long, T. Barbarians in Greek Comedy.*
  P. Holt, 24:Fall88-444
  D. Konstan, 122:Apr88-160
  R.P. Martin, 124:Sep-Oct88-55
Long, T. Repetition and Variation in the
  Short Stories of Herodotus.
  S. West, 123:Vol38No1-16
Longenbach, J. Modernist Poetics of History.
  K.V. Lindberg, 27(AL):May88-310
Longenbach, J. Stone Cottage.*
  H. Haughton, 617(TLS):17-23Mar89-285
  D. Wyatt, 639(VQR):Autumn88-739
Longeway, J. - see Heytesbury, W.
Longford, E., ed. The Oxford Book of Royal
  Anecdotes.
  J. Grigg, 617(TLS):26May-1Jun89-571
Longley, E. Louis MacNeice.
  P. McDonald, 617(TLS):6-12Jan89-16
  J. Mole, 493:Autumn88-49
Longley, E. Poetry in the Wars.*
  D. Hibberd, 447(N&Q):Jun88-263
  J. Saunders, 565:Autumn88-72
Longley, M. - see MacNeice, L.
Longstreth, R. The Buildings of Main Street.
  B.F. Le Beau, 576:Sep88-316
Longuet-Higgins, C. Mental Processes.*
  J. Sloboda, 410(M&L):Jul88-406
Longum, L. Drømmen om det frie menneske.*
  J. Garton, 562(Scan):May88-75
Longus. Pastorales (Daphnis et Chloé). (J-R.
  Vieillefond, ed & trans)
  B.P. Reardon, 123:Vol38No2-237
Lönner, U.N. C.J.L. Almqvists Målaren.
  K. Petherick, 562(Scan):May88-84
Lonsbach, R.M. Friedrich Nietzsche und die
  Juden. (2nd ed) (H.R. Schlette, ed)
  S.L. Gilman, 221(GQ):Winter87-155
Lonsdale, R., ed. Eighteenth-Century Women
  Poets.
  T. Castle, 617(TLS):10-16Nov89-1227
Lonsdale, R., ed The New Oxford Book of
  Eighteenth Century Verse.
  J.P. Hunter, 173(ECS):Summer88-491
  J.H. Pittock, 83:Spring88-102
Looseley, D. The Theatre of Armand Sala-
  crou.
  M. Autrand, 535(RHL):Jul-Aug88-791
Lopate, P. Against Joie de Vivre.
  H. Gold, 441:14May89-13
Lope Blanch, J.M. El estudio del español
  hablado culto.
  S.N. Dworkin, 240(HR):Winter88-90
Lopes, F. Chronique du Roi D. Pedro I. (G.
  Macchi & J. Steunou, eds)
  M. Garcia, 86(BHS):Jan88-101
Lopez, B. Crossing Open Ground.*
  J. Aton, 649(WAL):Nov88-285
  S. Pickering, 569(SR):Fall88-673
Lopez, D.S., Jr. & S.C. Rockefeller, eds. The
  Christ and the Bodhisattva.
  D.W. Mitchell, 485(PE&W):Oct88-448
López, S.S. & A. Martín Caselles. El Coro de
  la Catedral de Orihuela.
  I. Mateo Gómez, 48:Jan-Mar88-89
López-Baralt, L. San Juan de la Cruz y el
  Islam.*
  C.P. Thompson, 86(BHS):Oct88-405

López de Ayala, P. Coronica del rey don
  Pedro.* (C.L. & H.M. Wilkins, eds)
  G. Orduna, 545(RPh):Aug88-124
López de Ayala, P. Libro de la caça de las
  aves. (J.G. Cummins, ed)
  M. Ciceri, 547(RF):Band100Heft4-469
López de Ayala, P. Rimado de palacio. (G.
  Orduna, ed)
  J. Joset, 304(JHP):Winter88-157
López Heredia, J. Milagro en el Bronx y otros
  relatos.
  R. Falcón, 238:Mar88-92
López Morales, H. - see de Torres Naharro, B.
López-Sanz, M. Naturalismo y espiritualismo
  en la novelística de Galdós y Pardo Bazán.*
  M-P. Aspe, 552(REH):May88-125
López Torrijos, R. La Mitología en la pintura
  española del Siglo de Oro.
  A. Rodríguez G. de Ceballos, 48:Apr-
  Jun88-185
López-Vázquez, A.R. - see under Rodríguez
  López-Vázquez, A.
Lopokova, L. & J.M. Keynes. Lydia and May-
  nard. (P. Hill & R. Keynes, eds)
  D. Pryce-Jones, 617(TLS):15-21Sep89-
  994
Lops, R.L.H., ed. La Bible de Macé de la
  Charité VII: Apocalypse.
  J.L. Grigsby, 545(RPh):Nov88-174
Loraux, N. Tragic Ways of Killing a Woman.*
  H.P. Foley, 24:Winter88-597
  M.B. Skinner, 599:Winter88-677
  W.G. Thalmann, 478(P&L):Oct88-316
  M. Waller, 580(SCR):Fall88-70
Loraux, P. Les sous-mains de Marx.
  P. Soulez, 542:Jul-Sep88-348
Lorca, F.G. Impressions and Landscapes.
  J.W. Zdenek, 399(MLJ):Autumn88-373
Lorca, F.G. In the Green Morning.*
  A.S.L., 295(JML):Fall87/Winter88-349
  P. Preston, 617(TLS):7-13Jul89-735
Lorca, F.G. Mariana Pineda. Yerma.
  C.W. Cobb, 238:May88-318
  D.J. Pasto, 615(TJ):May88-286
  R. Warner, 402(MLR):Jul89-764
Lorca, F.G. Poet in New York.* (C. Maurer,
  ed)
  G. Conoley, 152(UDQ):Fall88-108
  639(VQR):Autumn88-134
Lorch, M.D. A Defense of Life.
  O.Z. Pugliese, 276:Summer88-166
Lord, G.D. Classical Presences in Seven-
  teenth-Century English Poetry.
  F. Blessington, 566:Autumn88-86
  D. Hopkins, 447(N&Q):Dec88-530
  C.R. Phillips 3d, 124:Mar-Apr89-326
  J.M. Steadman, 551(RenQ):Summer88-358
  H. Toliver, 401(MLQ):Sep87-285
  R.B. Waddington, 191(ELN):Jun88-94
  639(VQR):Winter88-7
Lord, S. Faces.
  V. Weissman, 441:19Mar89-22
Lordan, B. August Heat.
  R. Hoffman, 441:13Aug89-16
Lorence-Kot, B. Child-Rearing and Reform.
  I. Nagurski, 497(PolR):Vol33No4-473
Lorentz, P. Lorentz on Film: Movies 1927-
  1941.
  M.D.O., 295(JML):Fall87/Winter88-282
Lorenz, D.C.G. Grillparzer.
  L. Tatlock, 221(GQ):Summer88-471
  K. Schaum, 133:Band21Heft2/3-225
  R.C. Cowen, 564:Nov88-391

Lorenz, H. Varianz und Invarianz.*
  M.T. Peischl, 221(GQ):Spring87-288
Lorenz, T. Serious Living.
  J. Howe, 441:19Feb89-20
Loretz, O. Habiru-Hebräer.
  A.F. Rainey, 318(JAOS):Jul-Sep87-539
Loretz, O. Der Prolog des Jesaja Buches (1,1-2,5).
  D. Pardee, 318(JAOS):Jan-Mar87-143
Loretz, O. Psalm 29 - Kanaanäische El- und Baaltraditionen in jüdischer Sicht.
  S.B. Parker, 318(JAOS):Jan-Mar87-144
Lorian, A. Souplesse et complexité de la proposition relative en français.
  O. Soutet, 553(RLiR):Jan-Jun88-297
Loroña, L.V. A Bibliography of Latin American Bibliographies, 1980-1984.
  H.C. Woodbridge, 238:May88-313
Lory, P. - see Corbin, H.
Lösch, W., comp. Umgangssprachen und Dialekte in der DDR.
  D. Stellmacher, 685(ZDL):1/1988-78
Losee, J. Philosophy of Science and Historical Enquiry. (2nd ed)
  A. Millar, 518:Apr88-113
  J.M. Smith, 103:Feb89-58
Loseff, L., ed. Poètika Brodskogo.
  I.K. Lilly, 574(SEEJ):Fall88-480
Loss, A.K. W. Somerset Maugham.
  R.H. Costa, 177(ELT):Vol31No3-385
Lötscher, A. Satzakzent und Funktionale Satzperspektive im Deutschen.
  L.M. Eichinger, 685(ZDL):3/1988-385
Lötscher, A. Text und Thema.
  T.F. Shannon, 350:Dec89-899
Lott, B. A Course in English Language and Literature.
  J. John, 257(IRAL):Feb88-70
Lott, B. A Dream of Old Leaves.
  E. Lotozo, 441:10Sep89-20
Lottman, H. Flaubert.
  P-L. Adams, 61:May89-99
  D. Bair, 441:5Mar89-15
  442(NY):20Mar89-116
Lotz, R.E. Hot Dance Bands in Germany. (Vol 1)
  E. Southern, 91:Fall88-257
de la Loubère, S. The Kingdom of Siam.
  M. Bannister, 208(FS):Jul88-342
"L'Ouest en nouvelles."
  P. Hebert, 102(CanL):Summer88-136
Lough, J. France Observed in the Seventeenth Century by British Travellers.*
  M. Merlini, 475:Vol15No28-304
Lough, J. France on the Eve of Revolution.
  J.H. Brumfitt, 208(FS):Jul88-349
Lough, J. & E. Merson. John Graham Lough 1798-1876.
  M. Stocker, 637(VS):Spring89-435
Loughrey, B., ed. The Pastoral Mode.
  S. Chaudhuri, 447(N&Q):Mar88-76
Louie, K. Inheriting Tradition.*
  W.A. Rickett, 293(JASt):Aug88-607
Louis, W.R. & H. Bull, eds. The Special Relationship.
  H.M. Mackenzie, 106:Spring88-125
Louis, W.R. & R. Owen, eds. Suez 1956.
  M. Yapp, 617(TLS):18-24Aug89-888
Lounsbury, R.C. The Arts of Suetonius.
  B. Baldwin, 121(CJ):Apr-May89-367
  E.S. Gruen, 124:Nov-Dec88-139

Louth, A. Denys the Areopagite.
  P. Hebblethwaite, 617(TLS):29Dec89/4Jan90-1450
Louw, J.P. & E.A. Nida, eds. Greek-English Lexicon of the New Testament Based on Semantic Domains.
  B.M. Sietsema, 350:Dec89-900
Lovejoy, C.D., Jr. & B.W. Watson, eds. China's Military Reforms.
  R.D.V. Sismanidis, 293(JASt):Feb88-123
Lovejoy, D.S. Religious Enthusiasm in the New World.
  R.M. Bliss, 83:Autumn88-244
Loveland, A.C. Lillian Smith.*
  E.C. Lynskey, 577(SHR):Summer88-290
Lovell, M.S. The Sound of Wings.
  D.M. Kennedy, 441:26Nov89-1
Lovell, T. Consuming Fiction.*
  C. Hoyser, 637(VS):Summer89-580
  J.E. Kennard, 395(MFS):Winter88-745
  S. Ledger, 366:Autumn88-246
Lovell, W.G. Conquest and Survival in Colonial Guatemala.
  S. Davis, 529(QQ):Spring88-196
Lovelock, J. The Ages of Gaia.*
  S.R.L. Clark, 617(TLS):20-26Oct89-1143
  F.W. Taylor, 617(TLS):16-22Jun89-662
Lovesey, P. On the Edge.
  T.J. Binyon, 617(TLS):28Apr-4May89-470
  M. Stasio, 441:12Mar89-24
Lovett, A.W. Early Habsburg Spain 1517-1598.
  P. Williams, 86(BHS):Jul88-295
Loving, J. Emily Dickinson.*
  C. Gerrard, 541(RES):Nov88-594
  L.Y. Gossett, 569(SR):Summer88-469
  L. Kelly, 402(MLR):Oct89-967
  D. Porter, 445(NCF):Sep88-244
Lovtrup, S. Darwinism.
  W. Montgomery, 637(VS):Spring89-444
Low, A.D. The Sino-Soviet Confrontation Since Mao Zedong.
  S.I. Levine, 293(JASt):Aug88-609
Low, B-B. & J. Hinsley. Sophie du Pont, a Young Lady in America.
  N.E. Davis, 658:Summer/Autumn88-192
Low, D. Starwater.
  J. McDougall, 389(MQ):Spring89-390
Low, D.A. Robert Burns.*
  D.S. Robb, 447(N&Q):Mar88-103
Lowe, D. Russian Writing since 1953.*
  G. Gibian, 574(SEEJ):Fall88-478
  A. McMillin, 402(MLR):Apr89-540
Lowe, D. & R. Meyer - see Dostoevsky, F.
Lowe, D.A. - see Dostoevsky, F.
Lowe, J.T. Our Colonial Heritage.
  639(VQR):Spring88-44
Lowe, M. Towards the Real Flaubert. (A.W. Raitt, ed)
  M. Wood, 208(FS):Apr88-220
Lowe, R. Education in the Post-War Years.
  S.J. Prais, 617(TLS):17-23Feb89-175
Lowe, V. Alfred North Whitehead.* (Vol 1)
  W.E. Schlaretzki, 396(ModA):Spring89-158
Lowell, R. Collected Prose.* (R. Giroux, ed)
  P. Lewis, 565:Spring88-35
  M.K. Spears, 569(SR):Winter88-95
Lowenberg, P.H., ed. Language Spread and Language Policy.
  C.M. Eastman, 350:Jun89-376

Lowenthal, A.F. Partners in Conflict.*
  M. Kryzanek, 263(RIB):Vol38No1-77
Lowenthal, A.W. Joachim Wtewael and Dutch
  Mannerism.
  T.D. Kaufmann, 90:Jan88-38
Łowmiański, H. Początki Polski.
  R. Radzik, 575(SEER):Jul88-487
Lowndes, N. Angel in the Sun.
  V. Rounding, 617(TLS):29Dec89/4Jan90-
  1448
Lowry, B. Building a National Image. (I. Gor-
  don, ed)
  S.W. Ksiajek, 505:Jun88-125
Lowry, E. The Filmology Movement and Film
  Study in France.
  H.T.B., 295(JML):Fall87/Winter88-283
  H. Charney, 207(FR):May89-1085
Lowry, M. & G. Noxon. The Letters of Malcolm
  Lowry and Gerald Noxon, 1940-1952. (P.
  Tiessen, with N. Strobel, eds)
  F.W. Kaye, 649(WAL):Feb89-386
  P. Morley, 298:Winter88/89-159
Lowry, S.T. The Archaeology of Economic
  Ideas.
  D.L., 185:Apr89-680
Lowsky, M. Karl May.
  H. Vollmer, 680(ZDP):Band107Heft4-615
Loyer, F. Paul Hankar.
  A. Willis, 576:Dec88-422
Loyer, F. Paris XIXe siècle.
  B. Bergdoll, 576:Dec88-420
  B. Comment, 98:Mar88-204
  C. Ellis, 46:May88-12
Loyrette, H. & others. Degas.
  E. Darragon, 98:May88-355
Lozano, J., C. Peña-Marín & G. Abril. Análi-
  sis del discurso.
  M. Rector, 567:Vol69No3/4-369
Lu Wenfu. The Gourmet and Other Stories of
  Modern China.*
  N. Tisdall, 364:Apr/May88-139
Luard, N. Gondar.
  D.L. Patrick, 441:19Mar89-22
de Lubac, H., M. Rougier & M. Sales - see
  Marcel, G. & G. Fessard
Lubbers, K. Geschichte der irischen Erzähl-
  prosa. (Vol 1)
  E. Lobsien, 38:Band106Heft1/2-259
von Lübeck, A. Gesta Gregorii Peccatoris. (J.
  Schilling, ed)
  F.J. Worstbrock, 684(ZDA):Band117Heft2-
  69
Lucas, A., ed. Local Opposition and Under-
  ground Resistance to the Japanese in Java,
  1942-1945.
  W.H. Frederick, 293(JASt):May88-426
Lucas, H-C. & O. Pöggeler, eds. Hegels
  Rechtsphilosophie im Zusammenhang der
  Europäischen Verfassungsgeschichte.
  J-F. Kervegan, 192(EP):Jan-Mar88-120
Lucas, J. Modern English Poetry from Hardy
  to Hughes.
  T. Gibbons, 447(N&Q):Mar88-125
  P. Levi, 541(RES):Feb88-139
  P.E. Mitchell, 177(ELT):Vol31No2-208
  A.D. Moody, 402(MLR):Jan89-139
Lucas, J. Studying Grosz on the Bus.
  M. Wormald, 617(TLS):1-7Dec89-1336
Lucas, M. The Southern Vision of Andrew
  Lytle.*
  M.J. Bolsterli, 395(MFS):Winter88-642
  E.C. Lynskey, 577(SHR):Summer88-288
  [continued]

[continuing]
  F. Walgren, 295(JML):Fall87/Winter88-
  350
  T.D. Young, 392:Winter87/88-117
Luce, L.F. & E.C. Smith, eds. Towards Under-
  standing. (2nd ed)
  T. Light, 399(MLJ):Summer88-217
Lucente, G.L. Beautiful Fables.*
  A.H. Carter 3d, 573(SSF):Winter88-94
  S. Donatelli, 454:Fall88-113
  F. Ricci, 593:Spring88-75
  L.V., 295(JML):Fall87/Winter88-215
Luchetti, C. Under God's Spell.
  A.A. Rhodes, 441:24Dec89-17
Lucian. Luciani opera: Tomus IV; Libelli 69-
  86. (M.D. MacLeod, ed)
  K. Sidwell, 235:Summer88-121
"Lucian." (K. Sidwell, ed)
  L.P. Wencis, 124:Nov-Dec88-137
Luck, C.D. The Field of Honour.
  E.R. Sicher, 402(MLR):Apr89-537
Luck, G. - see "Arcana Mundi"
von Luck, H. Panzer Commander.
  M.R.D. Foot, 617(TLS):10-16Nov89-1232
Lucretius. De Rerum Natura IV. (J. Godwin,
  ed & trans)
  P.M. Brown, 123:Vol38No2-409
  D.R. Edwards, 124:May-Jun89-401
Lüdi, G. & B. Py. Zweisprachig durch Migra-
  tion.
  C. Schmitt, 553(RLiR):Jul-Dec88-482
Ludwig, M. Besteuerung und Verpfändung
  königlicher Städte im spätmittelalterlichen
  Polen.
  P.W. Knoll, 575(SEER):Jul88-488
Ludwig, R.M. & C.A. Nault, Jr., eds. Annals of
  American Literature, 1602-1983.*
  T. Wortham, 445(NCF):Dec88-419
Ludwig, W. Römische Historie im deutschen
  Humanismus.
  W. Röll, 684(ZDA):Band117Heft3-150
Luelsdorff, P. Constraints on Error Variables
  in Grammar.
  E. Hajičová, 603:Vol12No1-249
Luelsdorff, P., ed. Orthography and Phonol-
  ogy.
  G.S. Nathan, 350:Jun89-432
Luelsdorff, P.A. - see Vachek, J.
Lugarini, L. Prospettive hegeliane.
  J-L. Vieillard-Baron, 192(EP):Apr-
  Jun88-269
Luhmann, N. Love as Passion.
  T. Nolden, 599:Winter88-694
Luhrmann, T.M. Persuasions of the Witch's
  Craft.
  R. Dinnage, 453(NYRB):12Oct89-3
  V. Ebin, 358:Dec89-14
  P. Zaleski, 441:25Jun89-13
Luijpen, W.A.M. Phänomenologie des Natur-
  rechts.
  C. Schefold, 489(PJGG):Band95Heft2-376
Luisi, F. Laudario Giustinianeo.
  J.E. Glixon, 317:Spring88-170
Lukacher, N. Primal Scenes.
  J.M. Todd, 131(CL):Summer88-274
Lukács, G. Dostojewski. (J.C. Nyiri, ed)
  M. Wegner, 654(WB):2/1988-326
Lukács, G. Selected Correspondence 1902-
  1920.* (J. Marcus & Z. Tar, eds & trans)
  L. Congdon, 473(PR):Vol55No1-152
  I.V., 295(JML):Fall87/Winter88-350

Lukacs, J. Budapest 1900.
    S. Beller, 617(TLS):16-22Jun89-660
    I. Deak, 453(NYRB):16Mar89-21
    I. Sanders, 441:22Jan89-13
Lukas, R.C. The Forgotten Holocaust.
    N. Pease, 497(PolR):Vol33No3-347
    K. Sword, 575(SEER):Apr88-316
Luker, N., ed. Fifty Years On.
    M. Pursglove, 402(MLR):Jul89-812
    A.L. Tait, 575(SEER):Oct88-646
Luks, L. Entstehung der kommunistischen
    Faschismustheorie.
    M. McCauley, 575(SEER):Jan88-162
Luling, V. Somali-English Dictionary.
    D. Biber, 350:Sep89-628
Lulli, R. Opera latina.
    A. Llinarès, 92(BH):Jan-Dec87-377
Lulofs, T.J. & H. Ostrom. Leigh Hunt.
    E.M. Gates, 340(KSJ):Vol37-202
Lumiansky, R.M. & D. Mills, eds. The Chester
    Mystery Cycle.* (Vol 2)
    S. Carpenter, 541(RES):May88-285
    L.M. Clopper, 589:Apr88-433
Lumière, C. Kalavrita.
    E. Thompson, 102(CanL):Spring88-127
"Des Lumières au Romantisme."*
    L. D'Hulst, 107(CRCL):Jun88-293
Lund, J. & N.B. Wamberg, eds. Djaevleriernes
    optog.
    W.G. Jones, 562(Scan):Nov88-203
Lund, M. Reading Thackeray.
    S.S. Prawer, 617(TLS):12-18May89-521
Lundquist, J. Jack London.*
    R.W. Etulain, 26(ALR):Fall88-89
    J.C. Reesman, 649(WAL):Aug88-149
Lundström, S. Zur Textkritik der "Tusculan-
    en."
    J.G.F. Powell, 123:Vol38No2-257
Lundström, S. Die Überlieferung der latein-
    ischen Irenaeusübersetzung.
    R. Braun, 555:Vol61fasc1-153
Lunenfeld, M. Keepers of the City.
    C.J. Fleener, 377:Nov88-209
Lunn, A.J.E. Développement économique de la
    Nouvelle France, 1712-1760.
    C. Armstrong, 298:Spring/Summer88-240
Luntley, M. Language, Logic and Experience.
    T. Baldwin, 617(TLS):3-9Mar89-227
    E. Fales, 103:Nov89-448
Lush, R. A Manual for Lying Down.
    A. Taylor, 102(CanL):Winter87-197
Lustbader, E.V. French Kiss.
    N. Callendar, 441:12Feb89-20
Lustig, I.S. & F.A. Pottle - see Boswell, J.
Lutz, A. Die Version G der angelsächsischen
    Chronik.*
    E.G. Stanley, 541(RES):May88-281
Lutz, B., ed. Metzler Autoren Lexikon.
    U. Rainer, 406:Spring88-115
Lutz, D.S. The Origins of American Constitu-
    tionalism.
    W. Brock, 617(TLS):8-14Sep89-979
Lutz, E.C. Rhetorica divina.*
    W. Freytag, 680(ZDP):Band107Heft1-124
Lutz, F. & D. Strehle. Rückläufiges Wörter-
    buch des Surselvischen/Dicziunari Invers
    dil Romontsch Sursilvan.
    P. Swiggers, 553(RLiR):Jul-Dec88-502
Lutz, H.T. - see Fogelklou, E.
Lutz, W. Doublespeak.
    B. Hochberg, 441:26Nov89-31
Lutzeier, P.R. Linguistische Semantik.
    C. Gansel, 682(ZPSK):Band41Heft5-672

Lutzeier, P.R. Wort und Feld.
    H. Franke, 685(ZDL):2/1987-255
Lützeler, P.M. Hermann Broch.*
    P. Hasubek, 301(JEGP):Apr88-307
    H.D. Osterle, 133:Band21Heft2/3-249
Lützeler, P.M. Geschichte in der Literatur.
    F.M. Fowler, 402(MLR):Apr89-515
van Luxemburg, J., M. Bal & W.G. Weststeijn.
    Over literatuur.
    W. Bronzwaer, 204(FdL):Jun88-149
Luxton, M. & H. Rosenberg. Through the Kit-
    chen Window.
    L.D. Harman, 298:Fall88-160
Luyster, R.W. Hamlet and Man's Being.
    D. Daphinoff, 156(ShJW):Jahrbuch1988-
    281
Lvov, A. The Courtyard.
    C. Innes, 441:19Nov89-25
Lvov, A. & A. Sumerkin - see Vysotskii, V.S.
Lycan, W.G. Consciousness.*
    P. Carruthers, 393(Mind):Oct88-640
    G. Graham, 103:Apr89-155
Lycan, W.G. Judgement and Justification.
    J.G., 185:Apr89-673
Lycan, W.G. Logical Form in Natural Lan-
    guage.*
    S.D. Guttenplan, 479(PhQ):Oct88-538
    J.E. Tomberlin, 449:Mar88-133
Lydall, H. Yugoslavia in Crisis.
    M. Wheeler, 617(TLS):16-22Jun89-659
Lydenberg, R. Word Cultures.
    T.L. Ebert, 27(AL):Oct88-498
    S. Moore, 532(RCF):Summer88-326
    L.D. Stewart, 395(MFS):Summer88-249
Lyman, T.A. A Grammar of Mong Njua (Green
    Miao).
    S. De Lancey, 350:Sep89-668
    D.B. Solnit, 318(JAOS):Oct-Dec87-844
Lynch, G. Stephen Leacock.
    B. Powell, 647:Fall88-76
Lynch, J.J. Henry Fielding and the Helio-
    doran Novel.*
    D. Nokes, 83:Autumn88-229
Lynch, M., ed. The Early Modern Town in
    Scotland.
    M. Prestwich, 161(DUJ):Dec87-138
Lynch, T. Skating with Heather Grace.*
    V. Shetley, 491:May88-104
Lyne, R.O.A.M. Further Voices in Vergil's
    "Aeneid."
    E. Block, 124:Mar-Apr89-320
    S.J. Harrison, 313:Vol78-234
    N. Horsfall, 123:Vol38No2-243
Lyngstad, S., ed. Norway.
    J. Sjåvik, 563(SS):Winter88-92
Lynn, K.S. Hemingway.*
    R. Asselineau, 189(EA):Oct-Dec88-496
    J.M. Cox, 569(SR):Summer88-511
    P. Craig, 617(TLS):7-13Apr89-362
    T.K. Meier, 191(ELN):Mar89-92
    W.H. Pritchard, 249(HudR):Spring88-218
    W.J. Stuckey, 395(MFS):Summer88-240
    234:Fall88-65
Lyons, A. Other People's Money.
    M. Stasio, 441:30Jul89-18
Lyons, C.R. Samuel Beckett.
    M. Kędzierski, 299:No11&12-185
Lyons, C.R., ed. Critical Essays on Henrik
    Ibsen.
    M. Hinden, 130:Fall88-279
    S. Mason, 615(TJ):Oct88-435

Lyons, J.B. Thrust Syphilis Down to Hell and Other Rejoyceana.
P. Hickock, Jr., 305(JIL):Jan88-59
Lyons, T.P. Economic Integration and Planning in Maoist China.
P.B. Prime, 293(JASt):Nov88-861
Lyons, W. The Disappearance of Introspection.*
D.C. Dennett, 486:Dec88-653
O. Flanagan, 484(PPR):Mar89-533
Lyotard, J-F. L'enthousiasme.
D. Carroll, 98:Apr88-263
M. Renault, 103:Mar89-110
Lyotard, J-F. Peregrinations.
G.A. Genosko, 103:Dec88-486
Lyotard, J-F. The Postmodern Condition.
F. Merrell, 567:Vol72No1/2-125
Lyotard, J-F. Le postmoderne expliqué aux enfants.
D. Carroll, 98:Apr88-263
Lyotard, J-F. & J-L. Thébaud. Just Gaming.*
G.P. Bennington, 208(FS):Oct88-500
Lysaght, P. The Banshee.*
G. Bennett, 203:Vol99No2-261
Lytle, A. Southerners and Europeans.
V.A. Kramer, 395(MFS):Winter88-631
L. Menand, 617(TLS):5-11May89-479
Lytle, A. & A. Tate. The Lytle-Tate Letters. (T.D. Young & E. Sarcone, eds)
W.B. Clark, 569(SR):Fall88-lxxvi
M.E. Cook, 27(AL):Oct88-505
V.A. Kramer, 395(MFS):Winter88-631
R.C. Petersen, 585(SoQ):Winter89-93
M.K. Spears, 453(NYRB):2Mar89-35

Maalouf, A. Leo Africanus.* (British title: Leo the African.)
A. Shammas, 441:12Mar89-13
Maas, M. & J.M. Snyder. Stringed Instruments of Ancient Greece.
A. Barker, 617(TLS):25-31Aug89-923
Maas, P. Father and Son.
J. Holland, 441:26Feb89-15
Maaskant-Kleibrink, M. The Engraved Gems.
G. Platz-Horster, 229:Band60Heft6-564
Mabala, R.S. Three Suitors...One Husband.
R. Bjornson, 538(RAL):Fall88-403
Maber, R. & A. Tregoning – see Kilvert, F.
MacAdam, A.J. Textual Confrontations.*
P. Finnegan, 395(MFS):Summer88-263
J.J. Hassett, 240(HR):Summer88-397
McAdam, D. Freedom Summer.
C. Senna, 441:23Apr89-21
MacAdam, H.I. Studies in the History of the Roman Province of Arabia: the Northern Sector.
G.W. Bowersock, 123:Vol38No1-101
McAdam, R. Hour of the Pearl.
R. Attridge, 102(CanL):Autumn88-143
McAlexander, H.H., ed. Conversations with Peter Taylor.
J.F. Desmond, 392:Fall88-553
J.R. Millichap, 395(MFS):Winter88-638
McAlindon, T. English Renaissance Tragedy.*
R. Dutton, 402(MLR):Jul89-711
R. Gill, 541(RES):Nov88-543
B.G. Lyons, 551(RenQ):Autumn88-533
G.K. Paster, 401(MLQ):Jun87-186
McAllister, L. The Blue House.
M. Kenyon, 376:Sep88-160

MacAndrews, C., ed. Central Government and Local Development in Indonesia.
D.R. Snodgrass, 293(JASt):May88-435
McArthur, M. Stolen Writings.
R. Spoo, 329(JJQ):Winter89-291
Macaulay, J. The Classical Country House in Scotland 1660-1800.
I. Gow, 90:Jul88-545
S. Houfe, 39:Sep88-210
A. Rowan, 324:Jun89-443
McAuley, M. & S. Wagg. Percy Erskine Nobbs and His Associates: A Guide to the Archive/Percy Erskine Nobbs et ses associés: guide du fonds.
J.F. Tener, 470:Vol26-189
McBain, E. Lullaby.
M. Stasio, 441:5Feb89-26
Macbain, W., ed. De Sainte Katerine.
A.J. Holden, 402(MLR):Jul89-736
MacBeth, G. Anatomy of a Divorce.*
S. O'Brien, 364:Oct/Nov88-99
J. Whitworth, 493:Autumn88-53
MacBeth, G. A Child of the War.*
I. Rankin, 571(ScLJ):Spring88-28
MacBeth, G. The Cleaver Garden.*
J. Saunders, 565:Autumn88-72
McBriar, A.M. An Edwardian Mixed Doubles.
J. Rose, 637(VS):Spring89-463
McBride, W.M., comp. Mark Twain.*
T.A. Tenney, 470:Vol26-197
McCabe, B. One Atom to Another.*
E. Morgan, 493:Spring88-42
L. Sail, 565:Spring88-73
MacCabe, C. Tracking the Signifier.
F. Leibowitz, 290(JAAC):Winter87-314
J. Rex, 494:Vol8No1-194
McCabe, P. Carn.
P. Craig, 617(TLS):19-25May89-536
McCaffery, L., ed. Postmodern Fiction.*
R. Kostelanetz, 115:Winter88-88
P.T.S., 295(JML):Fall87/Winter88-185
A. Wilde, 659(ConL):Spring89-133
McCaffery, L. & S. Gregory, eds. Alive and Writing.
B.K. Horvath, 395(MFS):Winter88-649
G. Krist, 249(HudR):Spring88-233
42(AR):Winter88-123
639(VQR):Winter88-7
McCaffery, S. Evoba.
S. Scobie, 376:Sep88-163
McCaffrey, A. Dragonsdawn.
G. Jonas, 441:8Jan89-31
McCagg, W.O., Jr. A History of Habsburg Jews, 1670-1918.
M. Ignatieff, 453(NYRB):29Jun89-21
McCaig, D. The Bamboo Cannon.
V. Weissman, 441:26Mar89-12
MacCaig, N. Collected Poems.*
R. Watson, 588(SSL):Vol23-254
MacCaig, N. Voice-Over.*
R. Crawford, 571(ScLJ):Winter88-38
E. Morgan, 493:Spring88-42
McCallion, J. Tough Roots.
M. Estok, 198:Winter88-106
MacCallum, H. Milton and the Sons of God.*
G.R. Evans, 541(RES):May88-294
B. Rajan, 627(UTQ):Fall87-113
J.J. Smith, 447(N&Q):Mar88-91
McCalman, I. Radical Underworld.
A. Humpherys, 637(VS):Spring89-411
S. Prickett, 445(NCF):Mar89-526
McCandless, R.G. Yukon Wildlife.
A. Senkpiel, 102(CanL):Spring88-120

McCann, A.M. & others. The Roman Port and Fishery of Cosa.
A.J. Parker, 123:Vol38No2-356
J. Rougé, 487:Spring88-91
D.L. Thompson, 124:Mar-Apr89-311
McCardle, A.W. Friedrich Schiller and Swabian Pietism.
J. Golz, 406:Fall88-391
J.D. Manton, 83:Autumn88-238
McCarey, P. Hugh MacDiarmid and the Russians.*
A. Pyman, 402(MLR):Oct89-1053
C. Whyte, 571(ScLJ):Winter88-40
McCarthy, C. Blood Meridian or, The Evening Redness in the West.
A. Hislop, 617(TLS):21-27Apr89-436
MacCarthy, D. Sailing with Mr. Belloc.
H. Lomas, 364:Feb87-101
MacCarthy, F. Eric Gill.
M. Bull, 617(TLS):17-23Feb89-160
B.G. Harrison, 441:7May89-11
M. Yorke, 324:May89-381
McCarthy, G. Edward Albee.*
P.C. Kolin, 397(MD):Mar88-121
McCarthy, G.E. Marx's Critique of Science and Positivism.
D. Baxter, 103:Apr89-158
McCarthy, M. The Origins of the Gothic Revival.*
M. Bright, 627(UTQ):Fall88-200
McCarthy, P.A., ed. Critical Essays on Samuel Beckett.
V.K., 295(JML):Fall87/Winter88-295
McCartney, G. Confused Roaring.
R. Wasson, 395(MFS):Summer88-282
McCaslin, D.E. Stone Anchors in Antiquity.
Y. Calvet, 555:Vol61fasc1-109
McCaughey, E.P. Government by Choice.
R.F. Jones, 656(WMQ):Jul88-620
McCaughrean, G. The Maypole.
E. Tristram, 617(TLS):24Feb-2Mar89-190
McCauley, M., ed. The Soviet Union under Gorbachev.
M. McAuley, 575(SEER):Apr88-322
A.G. Meyer, 385(MQR):Fall89-771
Macchi, G. & J. Steunou – see Lopes, F.
Macchi, V., ed. The Collins Sansoni Italian Dictionary. (3rd ed)
G. Lepschy, 617(TLS):21-27Apr89-430
Macchia, G. Paris en ruines.
J. Ducruet, 605(SC):15Apr89-245
McClatchy, J.D., ed. Poets on Painters.
J.H. Levi, 62:Dec88-110
C. Reid, 617(TLS):23-29Jun89-697
McClatchy, J.D. White Paper.
H. Beaver, 441:9Jul89-33
M. Ford, 617(TLS):15-21Sep89-1001
McCleery, A. – see Gunn, N.M.
McCleery, N. Staying the Winter.
R. Hedin, 649(WAL):Aug88-190
G. Kuzma, 496:Spring88-45
McClellan, G.B. The Civil War Papers of George B. McClellan. (S.W. Sears, ed)
J.M. McPherson, 453(NYRB):12Oct89-43
McClelland, B.W. & T.R. Donovan, eds. Perspectives on Research and Scholarship in Composition.*
R.A. Schwegler, 128(CE):Apr88-444
McClelland, I.L. – see Feijoo, B.J.
McClendon, C.B. The Imperial Abbey of Farfa.
S. Lewis, 589:Jul88-697
H.R. Loyn, 39:Sep88-216
McClintock, M. & M. Simms – see Henry, O.

McCloskey, D.N. The Rhetoric of Economics.*
R. Sassower, 488:Dec88-551
McCloskey, M.A. Kant's Aesthetic.
R.A. Sharpe, 483:Apr88-285
McCloy, K. Velocity.
R. Goodman, 441:8Jan89-22
McCombs, J., ed. Critical Essays on Margaret Atwood.
M. Fee, 376:Sep88-166
McConica, J., ed. The History of the University of Oxford. (Vol 3)
D. McKitterick, 354:Mar88-58
McConkey, J. To a Distant Island.
I. Malin, 532(RCF):Fall88-165
McConkey, K. British Impressionism.
F. Spalding, 617(TLS):13-19Oct89-1118
McConkey, K. Edwardian Portraits.
R.S., 90:Oct88-784
McConnel, P. Sing Soft, Sing Loud.
442(NY):14Aug89-90
McCorkle, J. Tending to Virginia.
639(VQR):Spring88-58
MacCormac, E.R. A Cognitive Theory of Metaphor.*
A. Margalit, 617(TLS):14-20Apr89-399
McCormack, E. Inspecting the Vaults.*
J.K. Keefer, 102(CanL):Spring88-218
McCormack, E. The Paradise Motel.
C. Greenland, 617(TLS):11-17Aug89-878
M. Stasio, 441:26Nov89-30
McCormack, G. & Y. Sugimoto, eds. Democracy in Contemporary Japan.
J. Lie, 293(JASt):Aug88-643
McCormack, G. & Y. Sugimoto, eds. Modernization and Beyond.
J.A.A. Stockwin, 617(TLS):28Apr-4May89-459
McCormack, M.H. What They Still Don't Teach You at Harvard Business School.
P. Baida, 441:29Oct89-41
McCormack, W.J. Ascendancy and Tradition in Anglo-Irish Literary History from 1789 to 1939.*
J. Klerkx, 179(ES):Feb88-92
B. Tippett, 366:Autumn88-262
McCormick, J. George Santayana.*
T.N. Munson, 432(NEQ):Mar88-154
I.K. Skrupskelis, 619:Winter88-155
McCormick, K., G. Waller & L. Flower. Reading Texts.
D. George, 126(CCC):May88-239
R.R. Hellenga, 223:Fall88-359
McCormick, M. Eternal Victory.
A. Cutler, 124:Jul-Aug89-473
McCormick, P.J., ed. The Reasons of Art/L'art a ses raisons.*
R.W. Beardsmore, 89(BJA):Winter88-81
E.A. Trott, 627(UTQ):Fall87-222
McCormick, P.J. – see Ingarden, R.
MacCoun, C. The Age of Miracles.
L. Belfer, 441:9Jul89-18
McCrary, S.N. "El último godo" and the Dynamics of Urdrama.
T.E. Case, 238:Dec88-825
McCraw, T.K., ed. America Versus Japan.
T.J. Pempel, 293(JASt):Feb88-150
McCrory, M. Bleeding Sinners.
D. Durrant, 364:Feb/Mar89-133
L. Taylor, 617(TLS):6-12Jan89-21
McCrum, M. Thomas Arnold, Headmaster.
C. Leach, 617(TLS):29Dec89/4Jan90-1433

Maccubbin, R.P., ed. Unauthorized Sexual Behavior during the Enlightenment.
C. Todd, 83:Spring88-81

McCullagh, C.B. Justifying Historical Descriptions.
W. Neely, 449:Dec88-639

McCulloch, M. The Novels of Neil M. Gunn.*
J.B. Caird, 571(ScI.J):Spring88-17

McCullough, H.C. Brocade by Night.*
E.A. Cranston, 407(MN):Autumn88-305
R.A. Miller, 318(JAOS):Oct-Dec87-745
R.H. Okada, 293(JASt):Feb88-29

McCullough, H.C., ed & trans. Kokin Wakashū.*
E.A. Cranston, 407(MN):Autumn88-305
R.A. Miller, 318(JAOS):Oct-Dec87-745
R.H. Okada, 293(JASt):Feb88-29

McCullough, H.C. - see "The Tale of the Heike"

MacCurdy, G.G. Federico García Lorca.*
C.C., 295(JML):Fall87/Winter88-349

McCutchan, P. Convoy South.
H. Knight, 441:26Feb89-34

McDermott, J.J. Streams of Experience.*
R. Asselineau, 189(EA):Oct-Dec88-493

McDermott, R.A. - see Steiner, R.

MacDonagh, O. The Emancipist.
P. Johnson, 617(TLS):27Oct-2Nov89-1173

MacDonagh, O. The Hereditary Bondsman.*
639(VQR):Autumn88-125

McDonald, A.P., ed. Shooting Stars.
J. Maddock, 649(WAL):Nov88-235

MacDonald, C.A. Korea.
G. Henderson, 293(JASt):May88-389

McDonald, C.V. The Dialogue of Writing.
M. Buffat, 530:Oct88-165
R. Runte, 107(CRCL):Mar88-127

MacDonald, E.E. & T.B. Inge. Ellen Glasgow.
J.R. Raper, 534(RALS):Vol16No1&2-193

McDonald, F. Novus Ordo Secolorum.*
R.L. Emerson, 106:Summer88-227

MacDonald, G. & C. Wright, eds. Fact, Science and Morality.*
D.B., 185:Apr89-676
P. Trotignon, 542:Jul-Sep88-390
N. Zangwill, 518:Jul88-145

McDonald, H. The Normative Basis of Culture.
J.R. Kelly, 396(ModA):Summer89-273

McDonald, I. Mercy Ward.
S. O'Brien, 617(TLS):25-31Aug89-916

MacDonald, J. The Bridge Out of Town.*
P. Klovan, 102(CanL):Spring88-211
E. Thompson, 198:Winter86-104

McDonald, J. The "New Drama" 1900-1914.
D. Kennedy, 615(TJ):Dec87-537
R.W. Strang, 447(N&Q):Mar88-114

McDonald, J. & G.D. Snooks. Domesday Economy.
S. Fenoaltea, 589:Oct88-954

Macdonald, L. 1914-1918.
R. McCarthy, 617(TLS):10-16Feb89-133

McDonald, O. Parliament at Work.
M. Trend, 617(TLS):30Jun-6Jul89-727

MacDonald, P.V. Court Jesters.
C. Batts, 616:Vol10No1-58

Macdonald, R. The Fifth Wind.
G. Palmer, 617(TLS):15-21Dec89-1396

MacDonald, R. & C. Travis. Libraries and Special Collections on Latin America and the Caribbean. (2nd ed)
L. Gutiérrez-Witt, 263(RIB):Vol38No3-408

MacDonald, R.K. Beatrix Potter.
G. Avery, 447(N&Q):Mar88-119

Macdonald, R.R. The Burial-Places of Memory.
R.W. Condee, 149(CLS):Vol25No3-263
T. Corse, 121(CJ):Apr-May89-369
J.V. Mirollo, 551(RenQ):Autumn88-512
J. Moore, 568(SCN):Winter88-71
D.M. Rosenberg, 115:Spring88-217
639(VQR):Winter88-7

McDonald, S. & P.A. McDonald, with E.J. Kahn 3d. The Steven McDonald Story.
B. Kent, 441:30Jul89-17

MacDonald, S.P. Anthony Trollope.*
R. apRoberts, 637(VS):Spring89-440

McDonald, W. After the Noise of Saigon.
A. Hudgins, 249(HudR):Winter89-739
P. Stitt, 491:Jun88-169

McDonald, W. The Flying Dutchman.
P. Stitt, 491:Jun88-169

MacDonald, W.L. The Architecture of the Roman Empire.* (Vol 2)
G.B. Waywell, 123:Vol38No1-121

Macdonell, D. Theories of Discourse.*
K. Hirschkop, 494:Vol8No1-189
M. Kelly, 402(MLR):Oct89-899

McDonnell, J. Waugh on Women.*
C.J.B., 295(JML):Fall87/Winter88-394

McDonough, R.M. The Argument of the "Tractatus."
M. Cohen, 518:Jan88-30

McDougal, S.Y., ed. Dante Among the Moderns.*
G. Gillespie, 107(CRCL):Mar88-161

MacDougall, C. Stone Over Water.
G. Mangan, 617(TLS):28Jul-3Aug89-831

MacDougall, E.B. Ancient Roman Villa Gardens.
D. Hemsoll, 90:Nov88-858
B.A. Sparkes, 39:Jul88-70

McDougall, J. & S. Lebovici. Dialogue with Sammy.
S. Sutherland, 617(TLS):1-7Dec89-1344

McDowall, D. Palestine and Israel.
B. Wasserstein, 617(TLS):18-24Aug89-887

McDowell, C. Shoes.
E. Jong, 441:3Dec89-45

McDowell, D.E. - see Larsen, N.

MacDowell, D.M. Spartan Law.*
H. Taeuber, 229:Band60Heft6-547
R.W., 555:Vol61fasc1-104

McDowell, J. - see Evans, G.

Macedo, S. The New Right v. the Constitution.
P.B., 185:Apr89-682

McElfresh, T. Yes, You Can Get More Publicity.
J.E. Gainor, 615(TJ):May88-291

McElroy, J. The Letter Left to Me.*
J. Tabbi, 532(RCF):Fall88-167

MacEwan, G. Charles Noble. Frederick Haultain.
B. Ferguson, 298:Spring/Summer88-219

McEwan, I. The Child in Time.*
H. Mantel, 364:Dec87/Jan88-134

McEwan, N. Graham Greene.
J. Bayley, 453(NYRB):16Mar89-3

MacEwen, G. Afterworlds.*
P. Keeney, 102(CanL):Autumn88-150
529(QQ):Autumn88-754

MacEwen, G. The Honey Drum.
R. Bevis, 102(CanL):Spring88-192

McGuirk, C. Robert Burns and the Sentimental Era.*
    H.W. Drescher, 38:Band106Heft1/2–250
Machado, A. Solitudes, Galleries, and other Poems.
    T.J. Rogers, 238:Dec88–850
Machado de Assis, J.M. The Devil's Church and Other Stories.
    J. Perkins, 86(BHS):Jan88–106
Machado de Assis, J.M. Helena.
    C.G. Janiga, 552(REH):Oct88–140
McHale, B. Postmodernist Fiction.
    E.A. Kaplan, 395(MFS):Winter88–733
    C.J. Laansma, 204(FdL):Sep88–231
Machan, T.W. Techniques of Translation.*
    D. Pearsall, 402(MLR):Jan89–112
Machann, C. & F.D. Burt, eds. Matthew Arnold in His Time and Ours.
    C. Baldick, 617(TLS):13–19Jan89–43
Machatzke, M. – see Hauptmann, G.
Machen, A. The Collected Arthur Machen. (C. Palmer, ed) Selected Letters. (R. Dobson, G. Brangham & R.A. Gilbert, eds)
    T.D. Smith, 617(TLS):10–16Mar89–253
McHenry, R.W., Jr., ed. Contexts 3: "Absalom and Achitophel."*
    J.E. Van Domelen, 568(SCN):Spring-Summer88–12
Machiavelli, N. The Prince. (Q. Skinner & R. Price, eds; R. Price, trans)
    M. Cranston, 617(TLS):21–27Apr89–433
Machiavelli, N. La vita di Castruccio Castracani. (R. Brakkee, ed)
    E. Bonora, 228(GSLI):Vol165fasc532–609
Machin, G.I.T. Politics and the Churches in Great Britain 1869–1921.
    J. von Arx, 637(VS):Winter89–278
Machin, R. & C. Norris, eds. Post–Structuralist Readings of English Poetry.*
    K.M. Newton, 89(BJA):Spring88–197
    T. Rajan, 661(WC):Autumn88–199
Machor, J.L. Pastoral Cities.
    P.K. Dooley, 27(AL):Mar88–111
McHugh, H. Shades.*
    G. Conoley, 152(UDQ):Winter/Spring89–129
    J. Kitchen, 219(GaR):Summer88–407
    639(VQR):Autumn88–135
McHugh, H. To the Quick.
    G. Conoley, 152(UDQ):Winter/Spring89–129
    P. Harris, 639(VQR):Spring88–273
    J. Kitchen, 219(GaR):Summer88–407
McIlvanney, W. Walking Wounded.
    G. Mangan, 617(TLS):20–26Jan89–57
McInerney, J. Story of My Life.*
    C. Rooke, 376:Dec88–134
McInnis, N. Shaking the Dreamland Tree.
    L–A. Hales, 102(CanL):Spring88–161
    C. Smart, 529(QQ):Spring88–185
McIntosh, A., M.L. Samuels & M. Benskin, with others. A Linguistic Atlas of Late Mediaeval English.*
    E. Wilson, 541(RES):Feb88–94
McIntosh, C. Common and Courtly Language.*
    J.C. McKusick, 191(ELN):Sep88–80
    L.T. Milic, 355(LSoc):Dec88–585
    S. Soupel, 189(EA):Oct–Dec88–488
    L.E. Warren, 301(JEGP):Jan88–118
McIntosh, J. – see Hawthorne, N.

MacIntyre, A. Whose Justice? Which Rationality?*
    G.M. Brodsky, 103:Jul89–276
    R.P. George, 543:Mar89–593
    M. Nussbaum, 453(NYRB):7Dec89–36
MacIntyre, A., A. Quinton & B. Williams. Education and Values. (G. Haydon, ed)
    P.A.R., 185:Jan89–467
    483:Jan88–134
McIntyre, R. & D.W. Smith. Husserl and Intentionality.
    G. Küng, 449:Mar88–158
    D. Willard, 323:May88–186
    D. Willard, 323:Oct88–311
MacIntyre, T. I Bailed Out at Ardee.
    N. MacMonagle, 272(IUR):Autumn88–343
McJimsey, G. Harry Hopkins.
    A. Schlesinger, Jr., 453(NYRB):16Feb89–20
    639(VQR):Winter88–17
Mack, M. Alexander Pope.*
    P. Bruckmann, 627(UTQ):Summer89–517
    J.E. Colquitt, 577(SHR):Winter88–73
McKale, D.M. Curt Prüfer.
    639(VQR):Summer88–89
Mackay, C. Red Ice.
    K. McCarra, 571(ScLJ):Winter88–45
MacKay, C. The Sound of the Sea.
    I. Bamforth, 617(TLS):20–26Oct89–1150
MacKay, C.H., ed. Dramatic Dickens.
    F.S. Schwarzbach, 617(TLS):3–9Nov89–1214
McKay, D. Sanding Down This Rocking Chair on a Windy Night.*
    L.K. MacKendrick, 628(UWR):Vol21No1–99
Mackay, J.A. – see Burns, R.
MacKay, J.C. A Guide to Germanic Reference Grammars.
    F. Hundsnurscher, 685(ZDL):1/1988–79
Mackay, L. & M. Thompson, eds. Something in the Wind.
    T. O'Riordan, 617(TLS):17–23Mar89–272
McKay, S.L. & S–L.C. Wong, eds. Language Diversity.
    M. Terdal, 608:Dec89–685
McKean, C. The Scottish Thirties.*
    90:Aug88–642
McKechnie, P. Outsiders in the Greek Cities in the Fourth Century BC.
    P. Millett, 617(TLS):29Dec89/4Jan90–1449
McKee, A. Uncle Henry's Last Stand.
    J. O'Grady, 617(TLS):10–16Nov89–1243
McKee, E. & M.M. Gruzs. A Votre Portée.
    F. Coulont–Henderson, 399(MLJ):Autumn88–354
    T. Scanlan, 207(FR):Dec88–373
McKee, P. Heroic Commitment in Richardson, Eliot, and James.*
    J. Clayton, 454:Fall88–119
    C.A. Howells, 301(JEGP):Apr88–265
    M. Price, 445(NCF):Jun88–118
McKeever, P. Adlai Stevenson.
    S.E. Ambrose, 441:16Jul89–14
Mackensen, M., with others. Resafa I.
    W. Djobadze, 318(JAOS):Jan–Mar87–129
McKenzie, D.F. Bibliography and the Sociology of Texts.
    T.H. Howard–Hill, 354:Jun88–151
    C. Hurst, 447(N&Q):Dec88–505
    G.W. Williams, 40(AEB):Vol2No3–122

MacLeod, R., ed. Government and Expertise.
A. Cairncross, 617(TLS):6-12Jan89-5
MacLeod, S. Lawrence's Men and Women.*
M. Bell, 402(MLR):Jan89-146
MacLow, J. Representative Works: 1938-
1985.
C.O. Hartman, 502(PrS):Spring88-115
J. Perreault, 472:Vol15No1-201
MacLow, J. The Virginia Woolf Poems.
C.O. Hartman, 502(PrS):Spring88-115
McLuhan, M. The Letters of Marshall McLu-
han.* (M. Molinaro, C. McLuhan & W. Toye,
eds)
F. Zingrone, 627(UTQ):Fall88-171
McLuhan, M. & E. Laws of Media.
B. Rotman, 617(TLS):25-31Aug89-924
J. Sturrock, 441:26Feb89-39
Maclure, S. Education Re-formed.
S.J. Prais, 617(TLS):17-23Feb89-175
McLynn, F. Stanley.
J. Spurling, 617(TLS):20-26Oct89-1161
McMahan, E., S. Day & R. Funk. Literature
and the Writing Process.
H. Brent, 126(CCC):Feb88-102
McMahon, L. Faith.
L. Upton, 152(UDQ):Fall88-119
McManamon, J.M. Funeral Oratory and the
Cultural Ideals of Italian Humanism.
L. Martines, 617(TLS):1-7Sep89-956
McManus, J. Ghost Waves.
J. Kaye, 441:4Jun89-22
McManus, P.F. The Night the Bear Ate
Goombaw.
M.E. Guthrie, 441:18Jun89-21
McMaster, J. Dickens the Designer.
P. Collins, 155:Summer89-109
M. Garson, 627(UTQ):Fall88-114
M. Stone, 178:Sep88-354
G.J. Worth, 637(VS):Winter89-255
McMaster, R.D. Trollope and the Law.*
M. Laine, 627(UTQ):Fall87-123
Mac Mathúna, S. Immram Brain.
L. Breatnach, 112:Vol20-177
P.D. Stempel, 260(IF):Band93-327
McMillan, C.H. Multinationals from the Sec-
ond World.
J. Garland, 550(RusR):Apr88-216
Macmillan, D. Painting in Scotland: The
Golden Age.
R. Gilmour, 571(ScLJ):Spring88-11
McMillan, D.J., ed. Approaches to Teaching
Goethe's "Faust."
O. Durrani, 402(MLR):Jul89-781
H.G. Haile, 133:Band21Heft4-335
McMillan, I. Selected Poems.*
H. Lomas, 364:Dec87/Jan88-122
McMillan, J. Game Theory in International
Economics.
A.R., 185:Apr89-675
McMillan, R.C., H.T. Engelhardt, Jr. & S.F.
Spicker, eds. Euthanasia and the Newborn.
F.M.F., 185:Apr89-689
McMillan, T. Disappearing Acts.
V. Sayers, 441:6Aug89-8
442(NY):13Nov89-147
McMillen, N.R. Dark Journey.
C.V. Woodward, 453(NYRB):29Jun89-15
McMillin, S. The Elizabethan Theatre & "The
Book of Sir Thomas More."
G.D. Johnson, 570(SQ):Winter88-519
R. Vince, 610:Autumn88-276

MacMullen, R. Corruption and the Decline of
Rome.
J. Griffin, 453(NYRB):16Mar89-6
McMullin, E., ed. Construction and Con-
straint.
G.E. Overvold, 103:Aug89-321
D.Z., 185:Jul89-973
McMurray, G.R., ed. Critical Essays on Gab-
riel García Márquez.
K. McNerney, 238:Dec88-839
McMurray, G.R. Spanish American Writing
since 1941.*
D.W. Foster, 238:Dec88-841
McMurry, R.M. Two Great Rebel Armies.
J.M. McPherson, 453(NYRB):12Oct89-43
McMurtry, J. Understanding War.
G.H. Hampsch, 103:Jul89-280
McMurtry, L. Anything for Billy.*
J. Loose, 617(TLS):3-9Nov89-1217
442(NY):23Jan89-118
McMurtry, L. Some Can Whistle.
B. Kingsolver, 441:22Oct89-8
442(NY):4Dec89-187
McNab, J.P. Raymond Radiguet.*
R. Griffiths, 208(FS):Apr88-233
McNally, P.F., ed. Readings in Canadian Lib-
rary History.
C. Spadoni, 470:Vol26-185
McNamara, B. & J. Dolan, eds. The Drama
Review.
J. Bull, 610:Summer88-178
McNamara, E. The Moving Light.*
A. Brooks, 102(CanL):Summer88-160
Macnamara, J. A Border Dispute.*
J.L. Garfield, 316:Mar88-314
MacNamara, M. Style and Vision in Maupas-
sant's "Nouvelles."*
R. Lethbridge, 402(MLR):Oct89-994
McNamara, R.S. Out of the Cold.
A.B. Ulam, 441:8Oct89-12
McNaugher, T.L. New Weapons, Old Politics.
N. Lemann, 453(NYRB):26Oct89-3
Macnaughton, W.R. Henry James: The Later
Novels.
P. Buitenhuis, 106:Fall88-325
S.B. Daugherty, 26(ALR):Spring89-82
MacNeacail, A. An Seachnadh agus Dain Eile/
The Avoiding and Other Poems.*
J. Saunders, 565:Autumn88-72
R. Watson, 588(SSL):Vol23-254
McNeal, R.A. - see "Herodotus, Book I"
McNeal, R.H. Tsar and Cossack, 1855-1914.*
J. Bushnell, 550(RusR):Apr88-188
W.G. Wagner, 575(SEER):Oct88-657
MacNeice, L. Louis MacNeice: Selected Poems.
(M. Longley, ed)
P. McDonald, 617(TLS):6-12Jan89-16
J. Mole, 493:Autumn88-49
MacNeice, L. Selected Literary Criticism of
Louis MacNeice.* (A. Heuser, ed)
J. Banerjee, 179(ES):Jun88-280
C.A. Buckley, 447(N&Q):Sep88-397
P. Scupham, 493:Summer88-14
639(VQR):Summer88-100
McNeil, F. War and Peace in Central America.
J. Chace, 453(NYRB):17Aug89-46
L. Robinson, 441:29Jan89-13
442(NY):27Mar89-116
MacNeil, J.N. Tales Until Dawn.
D. Waugh, 571(ScLJ):Winter88-14
McNeil, M. Under the Banner of Science.
A.B. Shteir, 173(ECS):Winter88/89-242

MacNeil, R. Wordstruck.
　H. Benedict, 441:26Mar89-6
MacNeill, S. & F. Richardson. Piobaireachd
　and its Interprotation.*
　R. Anderson, 415:Oct88-535
McNeill, W.H. Arnold J. Toynbee.
　M. Lefkowitz, 441:28May89-12
　H.R. Trevor-Roper, 453(NYRB):12Oct89-
　28
　C.M. Woodhouse, 617(TLS):18-24Aug89-
　893
McNeillie, A. - see Woolf, V.
McNerney, K., ed. On Our Own Behalf.
　K. Burkett, 441:12Feb89-18
　639(VQR):Autumn88-126
McNicoll, G. & M. Singarimbun. Fertility De-
　cline in Indonesia.
　T.H. Hull, 293(JASt):Aug88-703
Maconie, R. - see Stockhausen, K.
McPartland, M. All in Good Time.
　J.K. Skipper, Jr., 498:Summer88-77
MacPhail, L. My 9 Innings.
　D. Cole, 441:23Apr89-37
McPhee, J. The Control of Nature.
　S.J. Pyne, 441:6Aug89-1
McPheeters, D.W. Estudios humanísticos
　sobre "La Celestina."*
　J.R. Stamm, 238:May88-289
McPheron, W. Charles Olson.*
　W. Fox, 30:Spring89-88
McPherson, B.R., ed. Likely Stories.
　J. Byrne, 532(RCF):Spring88-196
Macpherson, C.B. The Rise and Fall of Eco-
　nomic Justice and Other Essays.*
　C.M. Coope, 291:Vol5No1-118
Macqueen, J.G. The Hittites and Their Con-
　temporaries in Asia Minor. (rev)
　A. Ramage, 124:Jan-Feb89 211
McRae, J.R. The Northern School and the
　Formation of Early Ch'an Buddhism.
　A. Sponberg, 293(JASt):May88-357
McRae, K.D. Conflict and Compromise in Mul-
　tilingual Societies: Belgium.
　G. Geerts, 355(LSoc):Dec88-582
Macrorie, K., ed. Twenty Teachers.
　D.R. Russell, 128(CE):Apr88-437
MacShane, F. Into Eternity.
　E.S. Uffen, 534(RALS):Vol16No1&2-247
MacShane, F. - see Chandler, R.
MacShane, F. - see O'Hara, J.
McSparran, F., ed. Octovian.*
　A.S.G. Edwards, 589:Apr88-436
McSweeney, K. Four Contemporary Novelists.
　P. Tiessen, 102(CanL):Winter87-157
McTaggart, J.M.E. The Nature of Existence.
　P. Geach, 617(TLS):2-8Jun89-599
Mactaggart, P. & A., eds. Musical Instruments
　in the 1851 Exhibition.*
　C. Ehrlich, 410(M&L):Jan88-90
McTear, M. The Articulate Computer.
　J.F. Kess, 350:Jun89-434
McTigue, B. - see under "The Medici Aesop"
Macuch, R. Grammatik des Samaritanischen
　Aramäisch.
　J.C. Greenfield, 318(JAOS):Apr-Jun87-
　332
McVaugh, M.R. - see Arnaldus de Villanova
MacVean, J. - see Blackburn, T.
McWatters, K.G. & C.W. Thompson, eds.
　Stendhal et l'Angleterre.
　V.D.L., 605(SC):15Jul89-335

MacWeeney, A., with A. Court, eds. Puck of
　the Droms.
　G. O'Brien, 402(MLR):Apr89-458
McWhirter, G. Cage.
　W. Connor, 198:Spring88-109
　R. Miles, 102(CanL):Summer88-155
McWilliam, C. A Little Stranger.
　T.M. Disch, 441:16Jul89-9
　J. Keates, 617(TLS):27Jan-2Feb89-89
Maddoli, G., ed. Strabone: contributi allo
　studio della personalità e dell'opera. (Vol
　2)
　J.M. Alonso-Núñez, 303(JoHS):Vol108-
　235
Maddox, B. Nora.*
　P. Carr, 395(MFS):Winter88-690
　M. O'Toole, 329(JJQ):Fall88-160
　M.T. Reynolds, 676(YR):Autumn88-127
Madelénat, D. L'Epopée.
　C. Crossley, 535(RHL):Nov-Dec88-1176
Madelung, W. Streitschrift des Zaiditenimams
　Aḥmad an-Nāṣir wider die ibaditische Prä-
　destinationslehre.
　E. Kohlberg, 318(JAOS):Oct-Dec87-806
Madgett, N.L. Octavia and Other Poems.
　L.A. Slade, Jr., 95(CLAJ):Sep88-105
Madison, G.B. The Logic of Liberty.*
　Y. Roy, 154:Summer88-365
Mádl, A. & A. Schwob, eds. Vergleichende
　Literaturforschung.
　W. Feudel, 654(WB):2/1988-341
Madrigal, L.I. - see under Iñigo Madrigal, L.
Maduakor, O. Wole Soyinka.
　M. Banham, 295(JML):Fall87/Winter88-
　383
Maeland, O.M., ed. Mellom tekst og tekst.
　T. Moi, 172(Edda):1988/4-363
Maeterlinck, M. Introduction à la psychologie
　des songes et autres écrits (1886-1896).
　M. Voisin, 193:Autumn88-147
Magee, B., ed. Modern British Philosophy.
　J.F. Donceel, 258:Sep88-344
Magee, B. The Philosophy of Schopenhauer.
　P. Trotignon, 542:Jul-Sep88-348
Magee, R.M., ed. Conversations with Flannery
　O'Connor.
　J.F. Desmond, 392:Fall88-553
Mager, K. Philosophie als Funktion.
　P. Trotignon, 542:Jul-Sep88-365
Magi, A.P. & R. Walser - see Wolfe, T.
Magnan, A. Dossier Voltaire en Prusse
　(1750-1753).
　E. Jacobs, 208(FS):Jan88-88
　D. Williams, 402(MLR):Apr89-473
Magnan, A. Voltaire: "Candide ou l'optim-
　isme."
　E. Showalter, Jr., 166:Oct88-73
Magno, C.T. & D.V. Erdman - see under Tra-
　montano Magno, C. & D.V. Erdman
"Magnus' Saga." (H. Pálsson & P. Edwards,
　trans)
　D. Whaley, 562(Scan):May88-86
Magnuson, P. Coleridge and Wordsworth.
　R. Haven, 661(WC):Autumn88-166
　R. Tetreault, 150(DR):Spring/Summer88-
　191
　639(VQR):Autumn88-121
Magnusson, U. & G. Person. Facets, Phases
　and Foci.
　C.W. Kreidler, 660(Word):Apr88-74
Magny, J. Claude Chabrol.
　R.J. Nelson, 207(FR):Apr89-936

Magocsi, P.R., with N.O. Diakun. Ucrainica at the University of Toronto Library.
  Y. Slavutych, 470:Vol26–169
Magowan, R. And Other Voyages.
  S. Pickering, 569(SR):Fall88–673
Magowan, R. Burning the Knife.
  R. Pybus, 565:Summer88–72
Magris, A. L'idea di destino nel pensiero antico.
  M. Adam, 542:Apr–Jun88–244
  R.W. Sharples, 303(JoHS):Vol108–246
Magris, C. Danube.
  G.M. Tamás, 617(TLS):18–24Aug89–894
  E. Weber, 441:1Oct89–14
Mahajan, A. Goan Vignettes and Other Poems.
  D. McDuff, 565:Spring88–64
Mahajan, J. The Raj Landscape.
  M. Archer, 60:Nov–Dec88–143
Mahapatra, J. Selected Poems.
  B. Howard, 491:Nov88–113
Mahapatra, L.N. The Night Without Moon and Other Poems.
  R.K. Singh, 314:Winter–Spring88–243
Mahdi, M., ed. The Thousand and One Nights.
  A. Hamori, 318(JAOS):Jan–Mar87–182
Mahé, J.P., ed. Hermès en Haute-Egypte.
  J.A.G. Ruijling, 111:Fall89–14
Maheux–Forcier, L. Amadou. Isle of Joy.
  R. Dole, 198:Summer88–72
Maheux–Forcier, L. A Forest for Zoe.
  M. Belcher, 102(CanL):Winter87–208
Mahfouz, N. Wedding Song.* (rev) (M.S. El Din & J. Rodenbeck, eds) The Beginning and the End.* (M.R. Smith, ed) The Thief and the Dogs.* (rev) (J. Rodenbeck, ed)
  C. Bardenstein, 441:10Dec89–9
Mähl, H–J. & E. Mannack, eds. Studien zur Goethezeit.
  F. Amrine, 221(GQ):Summer88–440
Mahlendorf, U.R. The Wellsprings of Literary Creation.*
  R.C. Holub, 406:Fall88–364
  F.M. Sharp, 222(GR):Winter88–49
Mahler, G. Mahler's Unknown Letters.* (H. Blaukopf, ed)
  B. Brisk, 465:Winter88/89–101
Mahler, M.S. The Memoirs of Margaret S. Mahler. (P.E. Stepansky, ed)
  L.E. Beattie, 441:12Feb89–19
Mahling, C–H. & S. Wiesmann, eds. Gesellschaft für Musikforschung.
  E. West, 410(M&L):Apr88–261
Mahmud, A.A. Mashari al-Istitan al-Yahudi munthu al–Thawra al–Faransiyya hatta Nihayat al–Harb al–Alamiyya al–Ula.
  N. Rejwan, 390:Feb/Mar88–52
Mahoney, T. We're Not Here.
  J.F. Clarity, 441:5Mar89–22
Mahony, P. Maurice Maeterlinck, Mystic and Dramatist.
  M. Autrand, 535(RHL):Jul–Aug88–789
Mahony, P.J. Freud and the Rat Man.*
  G. Moyal, 529(QQ):Summer88–502
Mahood, M.M. – see Shakespeare, W.
Mahrer, A.R. Experiental Psychotherapy.
  S. Sutherland, 617(TLS):1–7Dec89–1344
Mahulkar, D.D. The Prātiśakhya Tradition and Modern Linguistics.
  R. Rocher, 318(JAOS):Oct–Dec87–839
Maia, C.D. História do Galego–Português.
  S. Parkinson, 402(MLR):Oct89–1009

Maidment, B. The Poorhouse Fugitives.
  A. Humpherys, 637(VS):Winter89–235
  M. Vicinus, 636(VP):Winter88–493
Maier, C.S. The Unmasterable Past.
  G. Craig, 453(NYRB):2Feb89–10
  R.J. Evans, 441:29Jan89–28
Maika, P. Virginia Woolf's "Between the Acts" and Jane Harrison's Con/spiracy.
  M. Di Battista, 177(ELT):Vol31No4–494
Mailer, N. The Deer Park.
  J.G. Dunne, 453(NYRB):18May89–28
Maillet, A. The Devil is Loose!
  R. Buchanan, 102(CanL):Winter87–213
Maillet, A. Margot la folle.
  E. Hamblet, 207(FR):Mar89–718
Maillet, M. Histoire de la Littérature Acadienne.
  M. Lacombe, 102(CanL):Spring88–168
Mailloux, P. A Hesitation before Birth.
  L. Hafrey, 617(TLS):16–22Jun89–661
Mailloux, S. Interpretive Conventions.*
  T. Beers, 153:Winter88–82
  R.R. Hellenga, 223:Fall88–359
Mainardi, P. Art and Politics of the Second Empire.*
  R.D. Reck, 207(FR):Dec88–348
  P. Vergo, 59:Jun88–286
Maine de Biran. Oeuvres. (Vol 2)
  M. Henry, 542:Jul–Sep88–338
Maingueneau, D. Eléments de linguistique pour le texte littéraire.
  Y. Ozzello, 207(FR):Oct88–183
Mainstone, R.J. Hagia Sophia.*
  F.A., 46:Apr88–12
Maiorino, G. Adam, "New Born and Perfect."
  C. Trinkaus, 551(RenQ):Winter88–705
Mair, W.N. & H. Meter, eds. Italienisch in Schule und Hochschule.
  W. Schweickard, 72:Band224Heft2–440
Mairet, G. Le Dieu mortel.
  A. Reix, 542:Jan–Mar88–175
Mairs, N. Remembering the Bone House.
  N. Christopher, 441:6Aug89–23
Maitland, S. A Book of Spells.
  L. Dawson–Evans, 565:Summer88–54
Maitre, D. Literature and Possible Worlds.
  U. Margolin, 494:Vol9No4–863
Majaro, S. The Creative Gap.
  P. Graham, 324:Dec88–58
Majeska, G.P. Russian Travelers to Constantinople in the Fourteenth and Fifteenth Centuries.
  K.D. Seemann, 575(SEER):Jul88–485
Major, C. My Amputations.
  J.R. Saunders, 459:Spring88–100
Makeba, M., with J. Hall. Makeba.*
  D.E. McGinty, 91:Fall88–250
Maker, W., ed. Hegel on Economics and Freedom.
  P. Murray & J.A. Schuler, 543:Sep88–152
Makinda, S.H. Superpower Diplomacy in the Horn of Africa.
  D. Killingray, 575(SEER):Apr88–330
Makkreel, R.A. & J. Scanlon, eds. Dilthey and Phenomenology.
  F. Schreiner, 319:Apr89–318
Makoto, Ō. & T. Fitzsimmons – see under Ōoka Makoto & T. Fitzsimmons
Makower, J. Woodstock.
  R.R. Harris, 441:23Jul89–7
Makowsky, V.A. Caroline Gordon.
  A. Hulbert, 617(TLS):17–23Nov89–1260
Makowsky, V.A. – see Blackmur, R.P.

240

Mandel, E. The Family Romance.*
　A.E. Davidson, 102(CanL):Spring88-198
　D. Duffy, 627(UTQ):Fall88-137
Mandelbaum, J. - see Corsi, P.
Mandelbaum, K. A Chorus Line.
　B. Gelb, 441:13Aug89-2
Mandelbaum, M. The Fate of Nations.
　D. Holloway, 441:29Jan89-33
Mandelstam, O. Osip Mandelshtam: The Eye-
　sight of Wasps.
　P. France, 617(TLS):10-16Mar89-245
Mandelstam, O. The Noise of Time.* (C.
　Brown, ed & trans)
　P. France, 617(TLS):10-16Mar89-245
Mandel'štam, O. Slovo i kul'tura.
　J.G. Harris, 574(SEEJ):Winter88-660
Mandl, H., N.L. Stein & T. Trabasso, eds.
　Learning and Comprehension of Text.
　E.B. Bernhardt, 399(MLJ):Summer88-219
Mandle, W.F. The Gaelic Athletic Association
　and Irish Nationalist Politics, 1884-1924.*
　F. D'Arcy, 272(IUR):Autumn88-351
Månesköld-Öberg, I. Att spegla tiden - eller
　forma den.
　S.C. Brantly, 563(SS):Summer88-411
Manford, A. - see Hardy, T.
Manfred, F. Prime Fathers.
　G.F. Day, 649(WAL):Feb89-378
Manfred, F. Winter Count II.
　M. Westbrook, 649(WAL):Nov88-257
Mangan, J.A. & R.J. Park, eds. From "Fair
　Sex" to Feminism.
　B. Schrodt, 637(VS):Winter89-261
Mangelsdorf, T. A History of Steinbeck's
　Cannery Row.
　R.E. Morsberger, 649(WAL):May88-71
"The Mango Tree."
　M. Rhum, 608:Jun89-330
Mangold, M. Saarbrücker rückläufiges Wör-
　terbuch.
　E. Bauer, 685(ZDL):2/1988-238
Manguel, A. & G. Guadalupi, eds. The Dictio-
　nary of Imaginary Places.
　W.N., 102(CanL):Winter87-284
Manilius. M. Manilii, "Astronomica."* (G.P.
　Goold, ed)
　A. Le Boeuffle, 555:Vol61fasc1-139
Manley, F. Within the Ribbons.
　B. Levine, 441:20Aug89-20
Manley, W.L. & others. Escape from Death
　Valley. (L. & J. Johnson, eds)
　D. Wellenbrock, 649(WAL):May88-68
Manlove, C.N. C.S. Lewis.
　B. Murray, 395(MFS):Winter88-701
Manlove, C.N. Science Fiction.*
　S. Pell, 561(SFS):Jul88-246
Manly, L., ed. London in the Age of Shake-
　speare.
　S.P. Cerasano, 570(SQ):Summer88-251
Mann, B.H. Neighbors and Strangers.
　J.A. Henretta, 656(WMQ):Oct88-793
Mann, C. Rumors.
　S. Ferguson, 441:19Feb89-20
Mann, J. Beijing Jeep.
　G. Williams, 441:19Nov89-13
Mann, P. Hugo Ball.
　R. Robertson, 402(MLR):Oct89-1035
Mann, R.G. El Greco and His Patrons.*
　F. Marías, 48:Jan-Mar88-87
Mann, S. Local Merchants and the Chinese
　Bureaucracy, 1750-1950.
　P.C. Perdue, 293(JASt):Feb88-125
　M. Zelin, 244(HJAS):Jun88-281

Mann, T. & J. Ponten. Dichter oder Schrift-
　steller? (H. Wysling, with W. Pfister, eds)
　H. Siefken, 402(MLR):Oct89-1041
Manniche, L. City of the Dead.
　W.H. Peck, 124:Jan-Feb89-203
Manniche, L. Sexual Life in Ancient Egypt.
　A.R. Schulman, 124:May-Jun89-391
Manning, F. Her Privates We. The Middle
　Parts of Fortune.
　K. Haq, 364:Apr-May87-160
Manning, J. New Vocal Repertory.
　P. Dickinson, 410(M&L):Jan88-115
Manolidis, G. Die Rolle der Physiologie in der
　Philosophie Epikurs.
　R.W. Jordan, 123:Vol38No2-426
Manoliu-Manea, M. Tipología e historia.
　J.R. Craddock, 545(RPh):Aug88-84
Mansel, P. Sultans in Splendour.
　A. Mango, 617(TLS):10-16Feb89-137
Mansfeld, J., ed. Die Vorsokratiker.
　J. Barnes, 123:Vol38No1-161
Mansfield, K. The Collected Letters of Kath-
　erine Mansfield.* (Vol 2) (V. O'Sullivan &
　M. Scott, eds)
　S. Cassavant, 177(ELT):Vol31No1-103
　M. Flay, 179(ES):Apr88-185
　B. Hooper, 573(SSF):Winter88-92
　A.K. Weatherhead, 395(MFS):Summer88-
　323
Mansfield, K. The Critical Writings of Kath-
　erine Mansfield.* (C. Hanson, ed) [shown in
　prev under ed]
　A.K. Weatherhead, 395(MFS):Summer88-
　323
Mansilla, L.V. Una excursión a los indios
　Ranqueles.
　M. Deas, 617(TLS):14-20Jul89-777
Mansion, S. Études Aristoteliciennes.
　N.P. White, 41:Fall88-301
Manso, F.N. La narratividad de la Poesía
　lírica galaicoportuguesa.
　K.M. Ashley, 345(KRQ):May88-243
Manteiga, R.C., C. Galerstein & K. McNerney,
　eds. Feminine Concerns in Contemporary
　Spanish Fiction by Women.
　F. Colecchia, 140(CH):Vol10-138
Mantel, H. Eight Months on Ghazzah Street.*
　J. Mellors, 364:Jun88-100
Mantel, H. Fludd.
　L. Duguid, 617(TLS):8-14Sep89-968
Mantero, M. Poetas españoles de posguerra.
　L.F. Costa, 238:Sep88-551
Mantle, J. Fanfare.
　P. Holland, 617(TLS):8-14Dec89-1364
Manton, E.L. Roman North Africa.
　J.J. Wilkes, 617(TLS):7-13Apr89-374
Manuel, J. Libro del conde Lucanor.* (R.
　Ayerbe-Chaux, ed)
　I. MacPherson, 86(BHS):Jul88-293
Mao, I.P-I. Beginning Reader for Modern Chi-
　nese.
　M.E. Everson, 399(MLJ):Winter88-464
Mao Zedong. The Secret Speeches of Chair-
　man Mao. (R. MacFarquhar, T. Cheek, & E.
　Wu, with others, eds)
　J. Mirsky, 453(NYRB):29Jun89-18
　J.D. Spence, 441:10Dec89-12
Mao Zedong. The Writings of Mao Zedong,
　1949-1976.* (Vol 1) (M.Y.M. Kau & J.K.
　Leung, eds)
　A.J. Nathan, 293(JASt):May88-352
Ma'oz, M. Asad, the Sphinx of Damascus.*
　M.D. Charney, 441:1Jan89-15

Mapp, A.J., Jr. Thomas Jefferson.*
  J.E. Person, Jr., 396(ModA):Spring89-147
Mappin, J. & J. Archer. Bernard Amtmann,
  1907-1979.
  D.P. Ewens, 470:Vol26-175
Mapplethorpe, R. Some Women.
  A. Grundberg, 441:3Dec89-73
  A. Hollinghurst, 617(TLS):20-26Oct89-
    1155
Maraini, D. Devour Me Too.
  L. York, 102(CanL):Summer88-142
Marand-Fouquet, C. La Femme au temps de la
  Révolution.
  M. & P. Higonnet, 617(TLS):19-25May89-
    541
Maravall, J.A. The Culture of the Baroque.*
  J. Beverley, 81:Spring/Fall88-27
  A. Gérard, 549(RLC):Jul-Sep88-424
Maravall, J.A. La literatura picaresca desde
  la historia social.
  P.N. Dunn, 86(BHS):Jul88-279
Marazzini, C. - see Denina, C.
Marc, D. Comic Visions.
  M. Bayles, 441:30Apr89-30
  Z. Leader, 617(TLS):10-16Nov89-1242
Marceau, J. A Family Business?
  D. Leonard, 617(TLS):2-8Jun89-602
Marcel, A.J. & E. Bisiach, eds. Consciousness
  in Contemporary Science.
  C. McGinn, 617(TLS):14-20Apr89-391
Marcel, G. & G. Fessard. Correspondance
  1934-1971.* (H. de Lubac, M. Rougier & M.
  Sales, eds)
  G. Cesbron, 356(LR):Aug88-257
Marchais, P. Permanence et relativité du
  trouble mental.
  A. Reix, 542:Jan-Mar88-80
Marchalonis, S., ed. Patrons and Protégées.
  M.R. Chandler, 27(AL):Dec88-670
Marchand, J., R. Mortier & J. Renwick - see de
  Voltaire, F.M.A.
Marchello-Nizia, C. Dire la vrai.*
  N.L. Corbett, 545(RPh):Aug88-92
Marchello-Nizia, C. - see Tibaut
Marchenko, A. To Live Like Everyone.
  J. Shulevitz, 441:22Oct89-23
Marchesseau, D. Diego Giacometti.
  S. Jervis, 39:Sep88-219
Marchetta, C. Lovers and Friends.
  V. Weissman, 441:5Nov89-25
Marchetto of Padua. The "Lucidarium" of
  Marchetto of Padua.* (J.W. Herlinger, ed &
  trans)
  L.L. Perkins, 551(RenQ):Spring88-135
  L.L. Perkins, 551(RenQ):Autumn88-467
Marchi, C. Dante.
  Z.G. Barański, 545(RPh):Aug88-51
Marciales, M. - see de Rojas, F.
Marcil-Lacoste, L. La thématique contempo-
  raine de l'égalité.
  D. Merllié, 542:Jul-Sep88-366
Marcone, A. Commento storico al libro IV
  dell'Epistolario di Q. Aurelio Simmaco.
  R. Klein, 229:Band60Heft5-461
Marcovich, M. - see Hippolytus
Marcucci, S. Kant in Europa.
  A. Stanguennec, 542:Jul-Sep88-333
Marcus, C.C. & W. Sarkissian. Housing as if
  People Mattered.
  P. Langdon, 47:Jul88-45
Marcus, G. Lipstick Traces.
  J. Bowen, 617(TLS):17-23Nov89-1286
  T. Eagleton, 441:9Apr89-12

Marcus, J. Georg Lukács and Thomas Mann.
  K. Fickert, 395(MFS):Winter88-714
  H. Siefken, 402(MLR):Oct89-1041
  639(VQR):Autumn88-121
Marcus, J., ed. Virginia Woolf and Blooms-
  bury.
  M. De Koven, 395(MFS):Summer88-275
  H. Richter, 594:Winter88-417
  42(AR):Winter88-120
Marcus, J. Virginia Woolf and the Languages
  of Patriarchy.
  M. De Koven, 395(MFS):Summer88-275
  H. Richter, 594:Winter88-417
  639(VQR):Winter88-9
Marcus, J. & Z. Tar - see Lukács, G.
Marcus, L.S. The Politics of Mirth.*
  J.D. Cox, 405(MP):Feb89-298
  J. Goldberg, 301(JEGP):Apr88-257
  A. Guibbory, 529(QQ):Summer88-469
  J.E. Neufeld, 539:Summer88-234
  D. Underdown, 366:Autumn88-233
Marcus, L.S. Puzzling Shakespeare.
  R. Hapgood, 617(TLS):25-31Aug89-927
Marcus, P.L. Yeats and the Beginning of the
  Irish Renaissance. (2nd ed)
  A. Martin, 272(IUR):Spring88-144
Marek, R. Works of Genius.
  G. Garrett, 569(SR):Summer88-516
  639(VQR):Winter88-20
Marek, V. Roman Republican Coins in the
  Collection of the Charles University.
  M. Deissmann, 229:Band60Heft4-368
Marenbon, J. Later Medieval Philosophy
  (1150-1350).*
  O. Leaman, 483:Apr88-283
Margarito, M.C. - see under Capel Margarito,
  M.
Margetts, J., ed. Die mittelalterlichen Neid-
  hart-Spiele.
  A. Classen, 201:Vol14-228
Margolis, A.T. Henry James and the Problem
  of Audience.
  J. Auchard, 177(ELT):Vol31No2-242
Margolis, J., ed. Philosophy Looks at the
  Arts. (3rd ed)
  G. McFee, 89(BJA):Autumn88-377
Margolis, J. Pragmatism without Founda-
  tions.*
  R. Donovan, 258:Jun88-215
  M. Migotti, 518:Apr88-65
  F.G. Verges, 483:Jan88-125
Margolis, J. Science without Unity.*
  M. Espinoza, 542:Jul-Sep88-391
Margolis, J. & T. Rockmore - see Farías, V.
Margoshes, D. Small Regrets.*
  J. Doyle, 102(CanL):Spring88-183
Marguerite de Navarre. Miroir de Jhesus
  Christ crucifié.* (L. Fontanella, ed)
  O. Millet, 535(RHL):Jul-Aug88-762
Marguin, L. Poésie et liberté.
  P. Somville, 542:Jan-Mar88-92
Margulis, L. & D. Sagan. Microcosmos. Ori-
  gins of Sex.
  M. Anderson, 567:Vol72No3/4-361
Marié, M-A. - see Ammianus
Marie de France. Oeuvres complètes. (Y.
  Otaka, ed)
  G.S. Burgess, 208(FS):Oct88-459
"Marie de France: Fables." (H. Spiegel, ed &
  trans)
  P.E. Bennett, 447(N&Q):Dec88-518
  C. Evans, 627(UTQ):Fall88-125
                              [continued]

243

"Marie de France: Fables." (H. Spiegel, ed & trans) [continuing]
  C. Lee, 379(MedR):Dec88-460
  D.L. Schrader, 377:Mar88-53
  F. Vielliard, 554:Vol108No1-126
  M.J. Ward, 207(FR):May89-1070
Marienstras, R. New Perspectives on the Shakespearean World.
  C. Uhlig, 156(ShJW):Jahrbuch1988-297
  R. Wilson, 366:Autumn88-210
Marin, A.P., ed. Knižnaja torgovlja.
  N. Zitzelsberger, 574(SEEJ):Winter88-676
Marín, R.R. – see under Rodríguez Marín, R.
Marinari, A., ed. Francesco De Sanctis un secolo dopo.
  P. De Marchi, 228(GSLI):Vol165fasc529-135
Marinatos, N. Minoan Sacrificial Ritual.
  B.C. Dietrich, 123:Vol38No2-340
Marinelli, P.V. Ariosto and Boiardo.
  M. Dorigatti, 402(MLR):Oct89-1001
Marinus. Mario di Neapoli, vita di Proclo. (R. Masullo, ed & trans)
  R. Ferwerda, 394:Vol41fasc1/2-183
  A. Sheppard, 123:Vol38No2-408
Marion, R. The Intern Blues.
  R. Scheier, 441:9Apr89-32
Marius, R. Thomas More.*
  J. Patrick, 396(ModA):Spring89-144
Mark, C.B.D. Gaelic Verbs.
  B. Ó Cuív, 112:Vol20-224
Mark, J. A Stranger in Her Native Land.
  M.B. Norton, 441:7May89-20
Mark, J.P. The Empire Builders.
  639(VQR):Spring88-59
Markale, J. Le Mont-Saint-Michel et l'énigme du Dragon.
  J-L. Jacob, 450(NRF):Jan88-110
Marker, F.J. & L-L., eds. Ingmar Bergman.
  C. Leland, 397(MD):Dec88-590
Markham, E.A. Living in Disguise.*
  T. Eagleton, 565:Winter87/88-65
Markham, G. The English Housewife. (M.R. Best, ed)
  L. Woodbridge, 551(RenQ):Spring88-130
Markham, S. Workers, Women, and Afro-Americans.
  S. Bauschinger, 221(GQ):Fall87-691
Markie, P.J. Descartes's Gambit.*
  S. Gaukroger, 63:Sep88-414
Markman, S.D. Architecture and Urbanization in Colonial Chiapas, Mexico.
  W.T.D. Barbour, 576:Sep88-308
Markovits, F. L'Ordre des échanges.*
  P. Desan, 207(FR):Mar89-729
Marks, E., ed. Critical Essays on Simone de Beauvoir.
  M. De Julio, 546(RR):May88-532
Marks, J.H., ed. Advocacy in Health Care.
  J.L.N., 185:Apr89-687
Marks, S.K. "Sir Charles Grandison."
  L.V. Graves, 594:Spring88-109
Markson, D. Wittgenstein's Mistress.*
  S. Roe, 617(TLS):6-12Oct89-1104
Markus, G. Language and Production.
  M.A. Finocchiaro, 262:Mar88-103
Markus, M. Point of View im Erzähltext.
  R.M. Nischik, 72:Band225Heft2-417
Markwald, G. Die Homerischen Epigramme.
  M. Davies, 303(JoHS):Vol108-221
Marlatt, D. & B. Warland. Double Negative.
  S. Scobie, 376:Sep88-162
Marlin, W. – see Neutra, R.

Marling, K.A. Tom Benton and His Drawings.
  H. Adams, 658:Spring88-102
Marlowe, C. The Complete Works of Christopher Marlowe. (Vol 1) (R. Gill, ed)
  K. Duncan-Jones, 541(RES):Aug88-430
  R. Dutton, 402(MLR):Oct89-922
  D. Feldmann, 156(ShJW):Jahrbuch1988-287
  J. Jowett, 447(N&Q):Sep88-364
Marmo, V. Dalle fonti alle forme.
  A. Vermeylen, 356(LR):Aug88-237
Marody, M. & A. Sułek, eds. Rzeczywistość polska i sposoby radzenia sobie z nią.
  A.J. Matejko, 497(PolR):Vol33No4-482
Maron, M. & J. von Westphalen. Trotzdem herzliche Grüsse.
  P. Graves, 617(TLS):10-16Feb89-143
Marongiu, P. & G. Newman. Vengeance.
  J.L.S., 185:Oct88-188
Marot, C. L'Adolescence clémentine. (F. Lestringant, ed)
  A. Scholar, 208(FS):Apr88-202
Marotti, A.F. John Donne, Coterie Poet.*
  D.F. Bratchell, 447(N&Q):Mar88-86
  G. Hammond, 402(MLR):Jan89-124
Marowitz, C. Prospero's Staff.
  A.V. Bruegge, 615(TJ):Oct88-440
Marowski, D.G. Contemporary Literary Criticism. (Vol 40)
  L. Austin, 365:Winter87-52
Marowski, D.G. & R. Matuz. Contemporary Literary Criticism. (Vol 41)
  L. Austin, 365:Winter87-52
Marples, D.R. Chernobyl and Nuclear Power in the USSR.*
  639(VQR):Winter88-24
Marples, D.R. The Social Impact of the Chernobyl Disaster.
  T. O'Riordan, 617(TLS):17-23Mar89-272
Marquess, W.H. Lives of the Poet.*
  L. Waldoff, 77:Summer88-253
Márquez, G.G. – see under García Márquez, G.
Marqueze-Pouey, L. Le Mouvement décadent en France.
  P. Citti, 535(RHL):Jul-Aug88-787
Marquis, A.G. Alfred H. Barr, Jr.
  L. Auchincloss, 441:30Apr89-3
Marr, D. American Worlds Since Emerson.
  J. McWilliams, 445(NCF):Dec88-399
  D. Robinson, 432(NEQ):Dec88-631
Marrinan, M. Painting Politics for Louis-Philippe.*
  J.F. Codell, 207(FR):Apr89-927
Marriott, A. Letters from Some Islands.
  B. Almon, 102(CanL):Winter87-206
Marris, P. The Dreams of General Jerusalem.*
  J. Mellors, 364:Jun88-100
Marrone, S.P. Truth and Scientific Knowledge in the Thought of Henry of Ghent.*
  P.J.W. Miller, 319:Jan89-149
Marrus, M.R. The Holocaust in History.
  I. Deak, 453(NYRB):28Sep89-63
  J.R. Fischel, 390:Apr88-54
Marsh, A. & V. Ryan. The Seamen.
  R. Davenport-Hines, 617(TLS):1-7Dec89-1342
Marsh, D. The Heart of Rock & Soul.
  S. Liveten, 441:8Oct89-11
Marsh, J. Jane and May Morris.
  662:Fall88/Winter89-54
Marsh, J. Pre-Raphaelite Women.*
  L.M. Edwards, 637(VS):Spring89-431

Marsh, P. & P. Collett. Driving Passion.
D. Durrant, 364:Mar87-110
Marsh, R.J. Soviet Fiction since Stalin.*
N. Kolchevska, 574(SEEJ):Winter88-667
Marshall, B.A. A Historical Commentary on
Asconius.*
J.T. Ramsey, 122:Apr88-168
Marshall, D. The Surprising Effects of Sym-
pathy.
J. Lichtenstein, 400(MLN):Dec88-1182
R.L. Montgomery, 617(TLS):26May-
1Jun89-579
J. Quinlan, 207(FR):Feb89-522
Marshall, D.G., ed. Literature as Philosophy,
Philosophy as Literature.
B. Lang, 125:Summer88-404
Marshall, G. In a Distant Isle.*
H. Hewitt, 571(ScLJ):Spring88-15
Marshall, G., ed. Ministerial Responsibility.
M. Trend, 617(TLS):30Jun-6Jul89-727
Marshall, J. The Papers of John Marshall.
(Vols 3 & 4 ed by C.T. Cullen & L. Tobias;
Vol 5 ed by C. Hobson & others)
J.H. Broussard, 656(WMQ):Jan88-202
Marshall, J.M. Land Fever.*
P. Reedy, 649(WAL):May88-72
Marshall, M.H.B. Verbs, Nouns, and Postposi-
tives in Attic Prose.
A.C. Moorhouse, 123:Vol38No2-430
Marshall, M.M. The Dialect of Notre-Dame-
de-Sanilhac.
J-P.Y. Montreuil, 207(FR):Feb89-569
Marshall, P. The Chosen Place, the Timeless
People.
S. Talmor, 161(DUJ):Dec87-125
Marshall, P. - see Godwin, W.
Marshall, P.H. William Godwin.*
P.L. Thorslev, Jr., 591(SIR):Fall88-457
Marshall, P.K. - see Isidore of Seville
Marshall, T. Adele at the End of the Day.*
P. Stevens, 529(QQ):Autumn88-568
Marshall, W. The New York Detective.
M. Stasio, 441:10Dec89-41
Marston, J. The Selected Plays of John Mar-
ston.* (M.P. Jackson & M. Neill, eds)
T.W. Craik, 447(N&Q):Mar88-90
M. Garrett, 541(RES):May88-293
C.B. Kuriyama, 568(SCN):Spring-
Summer88-15
Marston, J.G. King and Congress.
J.A. Schutz, 432(NEQ):Dec88-617
Marteau, R. Venise en miroir.
D. Pierson, 207(FR):Feb89-550
Martens, E. & H. Schnädelbach, eds. Philoso-
phie.
G-W. Küsters, 687:Apr-Jun88-342
Martens, L. The Diary Novel.*
M. Eifler, 221(GQ):Spring87-274
V. Raoul, 107(CRCL):Jun88-272
Marti, W. Berndeutsch-Grammatik für die
heutige Mundart zwischen Thun und Jura.
A. Lötscher, 685(ZDL):3/1987-404
Martial. Epigrams of Martial Englished by
Divers Hands. (J.P. Sullivan & P. Whigham,
eds)
L. Ascher, 124:Mar-Apr89-322
Martin, A. The General Interruptor.
F. Pitt-Kethley, 617(TLS):2-8Jun89-620
Martin, A. The Knowledge of Ignorance.*
K. Berri, 188(ECr):Spring88-106
E.J. Mickel, Jr., 561(SFS):Nov87-400
S. Vierne, 535(RHL):Mar-Apr88-322

Martin, B.S. Juffie Kane.
K. Olson, 441:16Apr89-20
Martin, C., ed. American Indian and the
Problem of History.
B.W. Sheehan, 656(WMQ):Apr88-362
Martin, C. - see Gide, A.
Martin, C. & G. Parker. The Spanish Armada.*
J.R. Hale, 453(NYRB):16Feb89-30
Martin, D. One Out of Four.
R.R. Wilson, 102(CanL):Spring88-181
Martin, D.M. - see under Moyano Martin, D.
Martin, E. Federico García Lorca, heterodoxo
y mártir.*
D. Devoto, 92(BH):Jan-Dec87-331
C. Maurer, 240(HR):Spring88-271
Martin, E.W. Divided Counsel.
J. Grasso, 293(JASt):Feb88-114
Martin, G. Aspects of Verdi.
E. Downes, 465:Winter88/89-104
Martin, G.T. Corpus of Reliefs of the New
Kingdom from the Memphite Necropolis and
Lower Egypt. (Vol 1)
E.J. Dwyer, 124:Jul-Aug89-470
Martin, H.C. W.B. Yeats.
B. Henderson, 177(ELT):Vol31No2-226
D.T.O., 295(JML):Fall87/Winter88-407
Martin, H-J. Histoire et pouvoirs de l'écrit.
M.T. Clanchy, 617(TLS):8-14Dec89-1354
Martin, H-J. Le Livre français sous l'Ancien
Régime.
G. Barber, 354:Jun88-168
Martin, J. Treasure of the Land of Darkness.
P. Bushkovitch, 550(RusR):Jul88-329
R.E.F. Smith, 575(SEER):Jan88-135
Martin, J.N. Elements of Formal Semantics.
S.D. Spangehl, 350:Dec89-904
Martin, J-P., ed. Les États-Unis.
J-P. Brunet, 106:Fall88-393
Martin, J.R. Reclaiming a Conversation.
R. Riemer, 488:Dec88-561
Martin, L. Entre líneas.
A.L. Prince, 399(MLJ):Summer88-246
Martin, L.G., ed. The ASEAN Success Story.
D.E. Weatherbee, 293(JASt):May88-440
Martin, M. The Legal Philosophy of H.L.A.
Hart.
D. Dyzenhaus, 518:Oct88-250
Martin, M.W. Self-Deception and Morality.*
A. Gombay, 482(PhR):Jul88-442
Martin, P. Pursuing Innocent Pleasures.*
W.A. Brogden, 576:Jun88-201
G. Midgley, 541(RES):May88-299
Martin, P.M. L'idée de royauté à Rome I.
A.W.J. Holleman, 394:Vol41fasc1/2-230
Martin, P.W. Mad Women in Romantic Writing.
W. Hughes, 637(VS):Spring89-416
W. Ruddick, 366:Autumn88-248
Martin, R. Fashion and Surrealism.*
J.J. Spector, 127:Winter88-372
Martin, R. Langage et croyance.
Co Vet, 320(CJL):Mar88-65
J. Picoche, 209(FM):Apr88-95
Martin, R. Pour une logique du sens.
K. Mudersbach, 547(RF):Band100Heft4-
347
Martin, R. Rawls and Rights.*
P. Livet, 192(EP):Jul-Sep88-441
B. Schultz, 185:Oct88-155
Martin, R. Ishmael Reed and the New Black
Aesthetic Critics.*
K. Byerman, 395(MFS):Winter88-634
Martin, R. & H. Koda. Jocks and Nerds.
J. Weitz, 441:3Dec89-44

Martin, R.H. – see Traversagni, L.G.

Martin, R.K. Hero, Captain, and Stranger.*
    M. Lynch, 405(MP):Feb89–319

Martin, R.M. The Meaning of Language.
    J.F.M. Hunter, 154:Winter88–741

Martin, R.M. Mind, Modality, Meaning, &
Method.
    F. Recanati, 192(EP):Oct–Dec88–554

Martin, S. Orthodox Heresy.
    J. Symons, 617(TLS):28Apr–4May89–451

Martin, S.E. The Japanese Language Through
Time.*
    W.P. Lehmann, 215(GL):Vol28No4–289

Martin, T. Marianne Moore.*
    S. Burris, 536(Rev):Vol10–113
    D.T.O., 295(JML):Fall87/Winter88–356

Martin, T. Once Upon a Windowsill.
    A. Lacy, 441:11Jun89–30

Martin, T.R. Sovereignty and Coinage in
Classical Greece.*
    M. Ostwald, 122:Jul88–237

Martin, V. The Consolation of Nature and
Other Stories.*
    G.L. Morris, 455:Sep88–68

Martin, V. A Recent Martyr.*
    J. Mellors, 364:Aug/Sep88–135

Martin, W. Hinny Beata.
    R. Garfitt, 364:Jun88–86

Martin, W.R. Alice Munro.
    M. Holmgren, 376:Dec88–143
    L. McMullen, 627(UTQ):Fall88–172
    W.B. Stone, 573(SSF):Winter88–95
    S.J. Warwick, 178:Dec88–481

Martín Gaite, C. The Back Room.
    I. Malin, 532(RCF):Summer88–315

Martín Gaite, C. Usos amorosos de la post-
guerra española.
    J.L. Brown, 240(HR):Autumn88–518

Martín González, J.J. & others. Herrera y el
clasicismo.
    J.B.B., 90:Mar88–242

Martín Montero, M.C. – see Bottineau, Y.

Martín Morán, J.M. Ginevra y Finea.
    A. Soons, 86(BHS):Jul88–297

Martindale, A. Simone Martini.
    J. Pope-Hennessy, 617(TLS):24–
    30Mar89–311

Martindale, C. John Milton and the Transformation of Ancient Epic.*
    J.M. Evans, 541(RES):Nov88–552
    G.D. Lord, 402(MLR):Oct89–927
    C. Schaar, 597(SN):Vol60No2–268
    J.J. Smith, 447(N&Q):Mar88–91

Martine, J.J., ed. Contemporary Authors.
(Vol 1)
    J. Klinkowitz, 534(RALS):Vol16No1&2–
    240

Martines, L. Society and History in English
Renaissance Verse.*
    P. Stallybrass, 551(RenQ):Summer88–337

Martinet, A. Des steppes aux océans.*
    D.R. Seklaoui, 207(FR):Dec88–378
    R. Wallace, 159:Vol5–233

Martínez, J.A. & F. Lomelí, eds. Chicano Literature.
    R.A. Paredes, 534(RALS):Vol16No1&2–57

Martínez, J.M. – see under Montoya Martínez,
J.

Martínez, M. Schoolland.
    C.R. Shirley, 649(WAL):Feb89–388

Martínez-Alier, J. Ecological Economics.
    639(VQR):Autumn88–131

Martínez de Aranda, G. Cerramientos y trazas
de montea.
    F. Marías, 48:Jul–Sep88–329

Martínez Estrada, E. Panorama de los
Estados Unidos. (J. Roy, ed)
    J.M. Flint, 86(BHS):Jul88–322

Martínez García, F. – see Vallejo, C.

Martínez García, H. El suplemento en
español.
    M.A. Alvarez Martínez, 548:Jan–Jun88–
    251

Martínez García, L. El Hospital del Rey de
Burgos.
    T.F. Ruiz, 589:Oct88–952

Martinez Vasquez, E.P., with A.L. Sanarabia &
others. The Story of Ana; La Historia de
Ana.
    L. McGrail, 608:Jun89–332

Martini, F. Literarische Form und Geschichte.*
    E.S. Dick, 221(GQ):Winter87–100

Martino, P. Il nome Etrusco di Atlante.
    R. Wallace, 350:Mar89–187

Martins, I.D.F. – see under Figueiredo Martins, I.D.

Martinson, M. My Mother Gets Married.
    L. Belfer, 441:28May89–18

Martinson, M. Women and Appletrees.*
    L.M. Desertrain, 563(SS):Summer88–426

Marty, J-P. The Tempo Indications of Mozart.
    N. Kenyon, 617(TLS):4–10Aug89–854

Marty, M.E. Modern American Religion.* (Vol
1)
    A–J. Morey, 577(SHR):Summer88–284

Martz, L., with G. Carroll. Ministry of Greed.
    L. May, 441:29Jan89–31

Martz, L.L. Milton. (2nd ed)
    R. Lejosne, 189(EA):Oct–Dec88–500
    D. Loewenstein, 568(SCN):Spring–
    Summer88–7

Marubbi, M. Vincenzo Civerchio.
    D. Scrase, 90:Sep88–703

Maruya, S. Singular Rebellion.*
    B. Leithauser, 442(NY):6Mar89–105
    J. Mellors, 364:Jul88–105

Marvick, E.W. Louis XIII.
    D.M. Bessen, 539:Summer89–238
    P.A. McCoy, 568(SCN):Winter88–82
    N.L. Roelker, 551(RenQ):Autumn88–490

Marvick, L.W. Mallarmé and the Sublime.*
    S. Meitinger, 535(RHL):Nov–Dec88–1162
    K. Wais, 547(RF):Band100Heft4–445

Marwick, A., ed. Total War and Social
Change.
    A.J.A. Morris, 617(TLS):1–7Dec89–1342

Marwil, J. Frederic Manning.
    R. Spoo, 468:Fall&Winter88–283

Marx, G.T. Undercover.
    J.K., 185:Jul89–984

Marx, L. The Pilot and the Passenger.*
    R.M. Adams, 453(NYRB):16Feb89–33

Marx, W. Hegel's Phenomenology of Spirit.
    W. Desmond, 543:Jun89–845

Marx, W. & J.F. Drennan, eds. The Middle
English Prose Complaint of Our Lady and
Gospel of Nicodemus.
    N.F. Blake, 72:Band225Heft1–235

Mary, G. – see le comte de Creutz

Marzolph, U. Typologie des persischen
Volksmarchens.
    M. Omidsalar, 650(WF):Jan88–72

Masařík, Z. Die frühneuhochdeutsche Ge-
schäftssprache in Mähren.*
    E. Strassner, 685(ZDL):1/1988-95
Masefield, P. Divine Revelation in Pali Buddhism.
    I.W. Mabbett, 293(JASt):May88-403
Masereel, F. Passionate Journey.
    442(NY):10Apr89-124
al-Masiri, A.W.M. Al-Ideolojiyya al-Sahyuniyya.
    N. Rejwan, 390:Jan88-51
Maslov, S.Y. Theory of Deductive Systems
and its Applications.
    D.J. Dougherty, 316:Dec88-1260
Maslov, Y.S., ed. Contrastive Studies in Ver-
bal Aspect in Russian, English, French and
German.* (J. Forsyth, with J. Forsyth, eds
& trans)
    B. Comrie, 353:Vol26No1-160
Mason, B.A. Love Life.
    D. Jersild, 344:Summer89-163
    R. Kaveney, 617(TLS):24-30Nov89-1313
    L. Moore, 441:12Mar89-7
Mason, B.A. Spence + Lila.*
    D. Jersild, 344:Summer89-163
    R. Kaveney, 617(TLS):24-30Nov89-1313
    639(VQR):Autumn88-127
Mason, E. Stifter: "Bunte Steine."
    A. Stillmark, 402(MLR):Jul89-793
Mason, H.A. The Tragic Plane.*
    S.A. Black, 397(MD):Sep88-462
Mason, H.A. - see "Sir Thomas Wyatt, A Lit-
erary Portrait"
Mason, H.T. - see "Studies on Voltaire and
the Eighteenth Century"
Mason, J.K. Human Life and Medical Practice.
    C. Harrison, 103:Aug89-318
Mason, M. - see "William Blake"
Mason, P. The City of Men.
    W. Nippel, 229:Band60Heft8-756
Mason, P. The English Gentleman.
    S. Pickering, 569(SR):Spring88-259
Mason, R. Weapon.
    N. Callendar, 441:7May89-18
Masotti, P.M. - see under Medioli Masotti, P.
Mass, J.P. & W.B. Hauser, eds. The Bakufu in
Japanese History.
    W.R. Braisted, 318(JAOS):Jan-Mar87-169
Masser, A. & M. Siller, eds. Das Evangelium
Nicodemi in spätmittelalterlicher deutscher
Prosa.
    K. Kunze, 684(ZDA):Band117Heft4-194
Massey, A. The Fire Garden.*
    J. Saunders, 565:Autumn88-72
Massie, A. A Question of Loyalties.
    G. Mangan, 617(TLS):8-14Sep89-969
Masson, J.M. - see Freud, S.
Masson, M.C. Philosophy and Tradition.
    R. Eno, 318(JAOS):Jan-Mar87-159
Masson, O. & T.B. Mitford. Les inscriptions
syllabiques de Kouklia-Paphos.
    J.T. Hooker, 123:Vol38No1-185
    G. Neumann, 229:Band60Heft1-65
Mast, G. Howard Hawks, Storyteller.
    G.W. Linden, 289:Fall88-117
Masters, H. Cooper.
    G. Garrett, 569(SR):Summer88-516
Masullo, R. - see Marinus
Matas, C. The Fusion Factor.
    D.W. Atkinson, 102(CanL):Spring88-143
Matejka, L. - see "Cross Currents"
Materassi, M. - see Roth, H.

Mates, B. The Philosophy of Leibniz.*
    R.M. Adams, 393(Mind):Apr88-299
    G. Stock, 521:Jul88-245
Mateus, M.H.M. Aspectos da Fonologia Por-
tuguesa. (2nd ed)
    M.W. Wheeler, 545(RPh):Feb89-354
Mathabane, M. Kaffir Boy in America.
    L. Hahn, 441:13Aug89-19
Mather, B.B., with D.M. Karns. Dance Rhythms
of the French Baroque.
    M.I., 412:May88-145
Mather, J.Y. & H.H. Speitel, eds. The Linguis-
tic Atlas of Scotland. (Scots section, Vol
3)
    B. Glauser, 38:Band106Heft3/4-446
Matheson, D. Ninth Life.
    M. Stasio, 441:2Apr89-33
Matheus, M. Trier am Ende des Mittelalters.
    J.B. Freed, 589:Apr88-434
Mathews, H. Cigarettes.*
    I. Malin, 532(RCF):Fall88-150
Mathews, H. The Way Home.
    M. Freely, 617(TLS):15-21Sep89-997
Mathias, R. A Ride Through the Woods.
    K.Q.Z., 295(JML):Fall87/Winter88-215
Mathieu, J-C., ed. Territoires de l'imagin-
aire.
    G. Cesbron, 356(LR):Aug88-233
    G. Cesbron, 535(RHL):Nov-Dec88-1178
Mathis, G. Analyse stylistique du "Paradis
Perdu" de John Milton.
    T. Healy, 402(MLR):Jul89-717
Mathur, I. & Chen Jai-Sheng. Strategies for
Joint Ventures in the People's Republic of
China.
    R.J. Goossen, 293(JASt):Aug88-610
Matilal, B.K. Perception.*
    P. Trotignon, 542:Apr-Jun88-216
Matoré, G. Le vocabulaire et la société médi-
évale.*
    H-L. Krechel, 72:Band225Heft2-431
Matos, C.A.R. - see under Rodríguez Matos,
C.A.
Matos, J., ed. Guía a las reseñas de libros de
y sobre Hispanoamérica.
    M.A. Salgado, 238:Sep88-562
Matossian, N. Xenakis.*
    E.R. Flint, 513:Summer88-308
Matson, W.I. A New History of Philosophy.
    C.C. Rostankowski, 258:Jun88-230
Matsuhashi, A., ed. Writing in Real Time.
    R.K. Durst, 126(CCC):May88-247
Matsumoto, S. Inspector Imanishi Investi-
gates.
    J. van de Wetering, 441:15Oct89-40
Matsumoto, S. The Voice.
    M. Stasio, 441:14May89-30
Matteo, S. & L.H. Peer, eds. The Reasonable
Romantic.
    H. Blank, 72:Band225Heft2-469
Mattera, D. Sophiatown.
    S. Suzman, 441:14May89-29
Matterson, S. Berryman and Lowell.
    M. Hofmann, 617(TLS):26May-1Jun89-
578
Mattes, M.J. Platte River Road Narratives.
    W.R. Kime, 649(WAL):Feb89-387
Mattheier, K.J., ed. Aspekte der Dialekt-
theorie.
    N. Weinhold, 685(ZDL):2/1988-199
Matthew, H.C.G. Gladstone 1809-1874.
    A.J. Heesom, 161(DUJ):Dec87-142

Matthews, B. Louisa.
　D. Adelaide, 581:Jun88-229
　B. Kingston, 71(ALS):May88-383
　K. Stewart, 71(ALS):May88-386
Matthews, C. Business Interactions.
　R.M. Ramsey, 399(MLJ):Summer88-231
Matthews, C. Mabon and the Mysteries of
Britain.
　J. Wood, 203:Vol99No2-262
Matthews, E. The Structured World of Jorge
Guillén.
　G. Connell, 86(BHS):Apr88-196
　M.L. Miller, 345(KRQ):May88-249
Matthews, G. "Just a Housewife."
　J. Boydston, 432(NEQ):Sep88-465
Matthews, J. Ghostly Populations.*
　G. Johnson, 219(GaR):Winter88-840
　639(VQR):Winter88-21
Matthews, J.H. André Breton.
　M. Bishop, 210(FrF):Jan88-122
　R. Cardinal, 208(FS):Jul88-366
　B.L. Knapp, 207(FR):Apr89-898
Matthews, M. Poverty in the Soviet Union.*
　M. Swafford, 550(RusR):Jul88-348
Matthews, W. Foreseeable Futures.*
　S.C. Behrendt, 502(PrS):Fall88-121
　M. Collier, 473(PR):Vol55No3-490
Matthiesen, A. Die intonative Segmentierung
Französischer Aussagesätze.
　F. Carton, 553(RLiR):Jul-Dec88-528
Matthiessen, P. On the River Styx.
　T.R. Edwards, 441:14May89-11
　S. Medcalf, 617(TLS):22-28Sep89-1023
　442(NY):3Jul89-95
Mattick, P., Jr. Social Knowledge.
　W.J. Earle, 488:Dec88-580
　S. Turner, 488:Dec88-582
Mattina, A., comp. Colville-Okanagan Dic-
tionary.
　M. Noonan, 350:Jun89-433
Mattingly, G. The Armada.
　J.R. Hale, 453(NYRB):16Feb89-30
Mattisson, A-C. Medeltida nordiska borg-
och sätesgårdsnamn på "-holm."
　K. Haugseth, 563(SS):Winter88-85
Mattoso, J. Identificação de um país.
　C.A. Hanson, 589:Jan88-192
Matute, A.M. The Heliotrope Wall and Other
Stories.
　R. Burgin, 441:14May89-22
　A.E. Lee, 617(TLS):4-10Aug89-858
Mauch, H. O laborum dulce lenimen.
　H.P. Syndikus, 229:Band60Heft2-123
de Maulde, F. Passage des aveux.
　R. Kopp, 207(FR):Mar89-719
Maunoury, J-L. Le Saut de l'ange.
　M. Alhau, 450(NRF):Jul-Aug88-213
de Maupassant, G. Romans. (L. Forestier, ed)
　R. Bismat, 535(RHL):Nov-Dec88-1157
Maupin, A. Sure of You.
　D. Feinberg, 441:22Oct89-26
Maurach, B. - see von Kotzebue, A. & C.A
Böttiger
Maurer, C. - see Lorca, F.G.
Maurer, H. Strange Ground.
　J. Glenn, 441:14May89-23
Maurer, W.H. Pinnacles of India's Past.
　H. Falk, 259(IIJ):Jul88-219
Mauriac, F. Les Paroles restent. (K. Goesch,
ed)
　R. Griffiths, 208(FS):Jul88-365
"Mauriac et le théâtre."
　B. Chochon, 535(RHL):Jan-Feb88-151

Mauser, W. - see "Hofmannsthal-Forschungen
8"
Mawer, S. Chimera.
　M. Casserley, 617(TLS):10-16Nov89-1244
Maxwell, D.E.S. A Critical History of Modern
Irish Drama, 1891-1980.*
　R. Ayling, 107(CRCL):Mar88-148
　J. Coakley, 130:Spring88-84
Maxwell, W. The Outermost Dream.
　J. Baumel, 441:14May89-23
Maxwell, W. So Long, See You Tomorrow.
　A. Rosenheim, 617(TLS):17-23Feb89-170
May, E.R. & J.K. Fairbank, eds. America's
China Trade in Historical Perspective.
　S. Mazumdar, 293(JASt):Feb88-126
　W. Wei, 318(JAOS):Oct-Dec87-834
May, G. "Les Mille et Une Nuits" d'Antoine
Galland.*
　L. Gossman, 210(FrF):Jan88-117
May, H.F. Coming to Terms.
　639(VQR):Spring88-50
May, J.M. Trials of Character.
　P. MacKendrick, 124:Jul-Aug89-463
May, K.M. Nietzsche and Modern Literature.
　M. Tanner, 617(TLS):12-18May89-509
May, R. Law and Society East and West.
　L. Rocher, 318(JAOS):Jul-Sep87-520
Mayall, D. Gypsy-Travellers in Nineteenth-
Century Society.
　J.R. Reed, 637(VS):Winter89-284
Mayer, A.J. Why Did the Heavens Not Dark-
en?
　V.R. Berghahn, 441:19Feb89-1
　I. Deak, 453(NYRB):28Sep89-63
Mayer, B. Eduard Mörike.
　W.E. Yates, 402(MLR):Jan89-242
Mayer, G. A Heartache of Grass.
　G. Mort, 493:Winter88/89-57
　S. O'Brien, 617(TLS):25-31Aug89-916
Mayer, J. & D. McManus. Landslide.*
　T. Draper, 453(NYRB):19Jan89-38
　R.S. Leiken, 617(TLS):10-16Feb89-127
Mayer, M. Markets.*
　C. Johnson, 617(TLS):10-16Mar89-243
Mayer, M. Night Studio.*
　E. Heartney, 55:Oct88-93
Mayers, D. George Kennan and the Dilemmas
of U.S. Foreign Policy.*
　W.F. Kimball, 617(TLS):6-12Oct89-1081
　R. Steel, 453(NYRB):17Aug89-3
Mayers, D.A. Cracking the Monolith.*
　J.W. Garver, 293(JASt):Nov88-863
Mayinger, J. Hegels Rechtsphilosophie und
ihre Bedeutung in der Geschichte des
marxistischen Staats- und Gesellschafts-
lehre.
　P-P. Druet, 258:Dec88-470
　J-F. Kervegan, 192(EP):Jan-Mar88-131
Maylam, P. A History of the African People of
South Africa.
　J.M. MacKenzie, 637(VS):Spring89-432
Mayle, P. A Year in Provence.
　H. Winterbotham, 617(TLS):4-10Aug89-
844
Maynard, W. Elizabethan Lyric Poetry and its
Music.*
　L.P. Austern, 405(MP):Feb89-294
　E.B. Jorgens, 551(RenQ):Summer88-342
　J. Michon, 189(EA):Oct-Dec88-478
　C. Monson, 570(SQ):Autumn88-386
　P. Thomson, 402(MLR):Jan89-117
Mayne, S. Children of Abel.*
　D. Precosky, 102(CanL):Spring88-172

Mayoral, M. – see Pardo Bazán, E.

Mayr, E. Toward a New Philosophy of Biology.
M. Ridley, 617(TLS):17–23Mar89–273

Mayr, O. Authority, Liberty & Automatic Machinery in Early Modern Europe.
R. Burch, 529(QQ):Spring88–192

de la Maza, A.M.R. – see under Roteta de la Maza, A.M.

Mazur, O. – see Palau, B.

Mazza, C. Animal Acts.
W. Ferguson, 441:26Nov89–13

Mazzolani, L.S. – see under Storoni Mazzolani, L.

Mazzolini, R.G. & S.A. Roe – see Bonnet, C. & J.T. Needham

Mazzoni, J. Introduzione alla Difesa della "Commedia" di Dante. (E. Musacchio & G. Pellegrini, eds)
Z.G. Barański, 545(RPh):Aug88–51

Mazzotta, G. The World at Play in Boccaccio's "Decameron."*
J.H. Potter, 401(MLQ):Dec86–433
W.A. Rebhorn, 405(MP):Nov88–202
J. Usher, 402(MLR):Jan89–190
J.H. Whitfield, 382(MAE):1988/1–147

Mbaabu, I. New Horizons in Kiswahili.
C. Eastman, 538(RAL):Fall88–386

Meacham, S. Tonybee Hall and Social Reform, 1880–1914.*
M.J. Moore, 637(VS):Summer89–603

Meaney, C.S. Stability and the Industrial Elite in China and the Soviet Union.
J.L. Wilson, 293(JASt):Nov88–865

Meara, P., ed. Spoken Language.
M.E. Winters, 399(MLJ):Summer88–220

Mearns, B. & R. Biographies for Birdwatchers.
M. Ridley, 617(TLS):28Apr–4May89–469

Mearns, R., ed. The Vision of Tundale.
K. Bitterling, 38:Band106Heft1/2–217
N.F. Blake, 72:Band224Heft2–392
R. Easting, 382(MAE):1988/1–122
C.D. Eckhardt, 589:Jan88–193
K. Kerby-Fulton, 677(YES):Vol19–299

Mebane, J.S. Renaissance Magic and the Return of the Golden Age.
F. Kiefer, 111:Fall89–9

Mech, L.D. The Arctic Wolf.
B. Hall, 441:19Feb89–20

Meckier, J. Hidden Rivalries in Victorian Fiction.*
R.J. Dunn, 594:Summer88–225
P.K. Garrett, 445(NCF):Sep88–248
639(VQR):Spring88–52

Mecklenburg, N. Die grünen Inseln.
C.J. Wickham, 221(GQ):Fall88–557

Medaglia, S.M. Note di esegesi archilochea.
S.R. Slings, 394:Vol41fasc1/2–134

Medhurst, K.N. & G.H. Moyser. Church and Politics in a Secular Age.
D. Jenkins, 617(TLS):6–12Jan89–6

de' Medici, L. Stanze. (R. Castagnola, ed)
E. Bigi, 228(GSLI):Vol165fasc530–307
M. Bregoli-Russo, 276:Autumn88–279

"The Medici Aesop." (B. McTigue, trans)
D.J.R. Bruckner, 441:29Oct89–9

Medina, V. Teatro. (M. de Paco, ed)
B.J. Dendle, 240(HR):Summer88–381

Medine, P.E. Thomas Wilson.
E. Heale, 677(YES):Vol19–309

Medioli Masotti, P. – see Tavoni, M.

Mednikova, E.M., ed. anglo-russkij slovar' glagol'nyx slovosočetanij.
M. Benson, 574(SEEJ):Fall88–493
C.L. Drage, 575(SEER):Apr88–255

Medved, D. The Case Against Divorce.
N.B. Cardozo, 441:26Nov89–27

Medvedev, R. China and the Superpowers.*
D.M. Schurman, 529(QQ):Summer88–485

Medvedev, R. Let History Judge. (rev)
R. Hingley, 441:4Jun89–11
A. Nove, 617(TLS):17–23Nov89–1258

Medvedev, Z.A. Gorbachev.*
A.G. Meyer, 385(MQR):Fall89–771

Mee, M. In Search of Flowers of the Amazon Forests. (T. Morrison, ed)
A. Huxley, 617(TLS):3–9Feb89–118

Meech-Pekarik, J. The World of the Meiji Print.
H. Cortazzi, 60:Mar–Apr88–124
H.D. Smith 2d, 407(MN):Autumn88–383

Meehan, M. Liberty and Poetics in Eighteenth-Century England.*
J. Black, 366:Autumn88–243
N.C. Jaffe, 677(YES):Vol19–325

Meehan, P.J. – see Wright, F.L.

Meek, H.A. Guarino Guarini and His Architecture.*
E. Denby, 324:Nov89–825
K. Downes, 46:Sep88–12

Meek, J. McFarlane Boils the Sea.
A. Pulver, 617(TLS):2–8Jun89–620

Meek, M.R.D. A Loose Connection.
T.J.B., 617(TLS):7–13Jul89–739

Meek, M.R.D. A Worm of Doubt.
639(VQR):Autumn88–127

van der Meer, L.B. The Bronze Liver of Piacenza.
L. Bonfante, 313:Vol78–208
M. Cristofani, 229:Band60Heft6–561
D. Ridgway, 123:Vol138No2–450

Meerhoff, K. Rhétorique et poétique au XVIe siècle en France.*
D. Ménager, 535(RHL):Jul–Aug88–759

van Meeuwen, P. Elias Canetti und die bildende Kunst von Breugel bis Goya.
R. Robertson, 402(MLR):Oct89–1036

Megaw, J. How Safe?
T. O'Riordan, 617(TLS):17–23Mar89–272

Megenney, W.W. El palenquero.
J.R. Gutiérrez, 238:May88–314

Megill, A. Prophets of Extremity.*
M. McCanles, 494:Vol8No1–200

Mehew, E. – see Stevenson, R.L. & L. Osbourne

Mehl, D. Geoffrey Chaucer.
P. Hardman, 541(RES):Nov88–534
A.V.C. Schmidt, 447(N&Q):Dec88–511
E.G. Stanley, 72:Band225Heft2–389

Mehl, D. Shakespeare's Tragedies.* (German title: Die Tragödien Shakespeares.)
L.S. Champion, 179(ES):Feb88–86
R. Dutton, 402(MLR):Jul89–711
M. Lomax, 366:Autumn88–231
D.R.C. Marsh, 447(N&Q):Jun88–224
K. Otten, 72:Band225Heft1–172
C. Saunders, 541(RES):Nov88–546
M. Shapiro, 130:Fall88–268

Mehling, M., ed. London.
D. Piper, 617(TLS):21–27Apr89–426

Mehlinj, M., ed. Rome and Latium. Paris and the Ile de France.
M. Stirling, 39:Mar88–219

Mehta, A. The Coasts of India.
    V. Fitzpatrick, 364:Mar88-112
Mehta, G. Raj.
    R. Billington, 441:9Apr89-18
    I. Buruma, 453(NYRB):18May89-9
    S. Curtis, 617(TLS):7-13Jul89-739
Mehtā, N. Devotional Songs of Narsī Mehtā.
    (Swami Mahadevananda, trans)
    S.S. Korom, 318(JAOS):Oct-Dec87-847
Mehta, V. The Stolen Night.
    J. Clute, 617(TLS):12-18May89-508
    S.A. Toth, 441:12Mar89-17
Meibauer, J., ed. Satzmodus zwischen Grammatik und Pragmatik.
    R. Pasch, 682(ZPSK):Band41Heft4-511
Meid, V. Barocklyrik.
    K.F. Otto, Jr., 406:Winter88-509
Meid, V. - see von Zesen, P.
Meid, W. Der erste zimbrische Katechismus. Der zweite zimbrische Katechismus.
    E. Kühebacher, 685(ZDL):3/1987-395
Meier, A. & E. Rudwick. Black History and the Historical Profession, 1915-1980.
    W.E. Cain, 128(CE):Feb88-190
Meier, H. Aufsätze und Entwürfe zur romanischen Etymologie.
    J. Klare, 72:Band225Heft2-426
Meier, H. Prinzipien der etymologischen Forschung.
    S.N. Dworkin, 545(RPh):May89-447
    J. Klare, 72:Band225Heft2-426
Meier, T.K. Defoe and the Defence of Commerce.
    D. De Luna, 173(ECS):Fall88-87
Meiffert, T. Die enteignete Erfahrung.
    R.C. Holub, 406:Fall88-364
Meijer, B.W. I grandi disegni italiani del Teylers Museum di Haarlem.
    J. Bean, 380:Summer88-140
Meijer, F. A History of Seafaring in the Classical World.*
    L. Casson, 229:Band60Heft2-162
    J.F. Lazenby, 303(JoHS):Vol108-249
    P.F.D. Martin, 313:Vol78-268
Meikle, S. Essentialism in the Thought of Karl Marx.
    M. Fisk, 449:Sep88-477
    R. Nordahl, 488:Sep88-419
Meiland, J.W. & M. Krausz, eds. Relativism.
    J.G. Hanink, 438:Spring88-232
de Meilhan, G.S. - see under Sénac de Meilhan, G.
Meimaris, Y.E. Sacred Names, Saints, Martyrs and Church Officials in the Greek Inscriptions and Papyri Pertaining to the Christian Church of Palestine.
    E. des Places, 555:Vol61fasc1-131
    W. Wischmeyer, 229:Band60Heft7-664
Meindl, D. Der amerikanische Roman zwischen Naturalismus und Postmoderne 1930-1960.
    A. Hornung, 38:Band106Heft3/4-552
Meine, C. Aldo Leopold.*
    S. Paul, 271:Fall88-163
Meinig, D.W. The Shaping of America.* (Vol 1)
    J. Axtell, 656(WMQ):Jan88-173
Meinke, P. The Piano Tuner.*
    C. Barrow, 577(SHR):Spring88-194
Meisami, J.S. Medieval Persian Court Poetry.
    639(VQR):Winter88-29
Meisel, M. Realizations.*
    P. van der Merwe, 611(TN):Vol42No1-44

Meisel, P. The Myth of the Modern.
    W.E. Cain, 395(MFS):Winter88-729
    S. Coulling, 445(NCF):Dec88-414
    P.A. Dale, 637(VS):Winter89-289
Meisling, P. Agnetes latter.
    Å. Svensen, 172(Edda):1988/3-283
Meissner, K. Mālushāhī and Rājulā.
    T. Riccardi, Jr., 293(JASt):Nov88-923
Meister, M.W., ed. Discourses on Śiva.
    C.D. Collins, 318(JAOS):Apr-Jun87-365
Meister, M.W. & M.A. Dhaky, eds. Encyclopaedia of Indian Temple Architecture: South India - Upper Drāviḍadēśa, Early Phase, A.D. 550-1075.
    W.E. Begley, 293(JASt):Feb88-183
Mekki-Berrada, T., ed. Correspondance littéraire secrète, 7 janvier-24 juin 1775.
    J. Lough, 208(FS):Jan88-92
Mela, P. - see under Pomponius Mela
Melançon, R. Blind Painting.*
    P. Lanthier, 102(CanL):Winter87-140
"Mélanges pour Jacques Scherer."
    D.A. Watts, 475:Vol15No28-347
Melanson, R.A. & D. Mayers, eds. Reevaluating Eisenhower.
    R. Accinelli, 106:Spring88-129
    W.I. Cohen, 115:Winter88-85
Melazzo, L., ed. Calendario Siciliano.*
    G. Ineichen, 260(IF):Band93-327
Melbourne, L.L. Double Heart.
    M.H. Gelber, 395(MFS):Summer88-303
Mel'čuk, I.A. & A.K. Žolkovskij. Tolkovo-Kombintornyj Slovar' Sovremennogo Russkogo Literaturnogo Jazyka.*
    W.W. Derbyshire, 558(RLJ):Winter-Spring-Fall88-346
Meldrum, B.H., ed. Under the Sun.*
    D.P. Rask, 26(ALR):Spring89-75
Mele, A.R. Irrationality.*
    P. Boddington, 518:Jul88-157
    M. Cavell, 185:Jan89-429
Melhorn-Boe, L. Hairy Legs.
    G. Gessert, 448:Vol26No1-80
Melhorn-Boe, L. Powder Puff Pink. Colour Me Dutiful. Leaky Stories.
    G. Gessert, 448:Vol26No1-79
Meli, G. Don Chisciotti and Sanciu Panza. (G. Cipolla, ed & trans)
    G. Monorchio, 276:Autumn88-282
Melis, A.R. - see under Riera Melis, A.
Mellah, F. Le Conclave des pleureuses.
    W. Cloonan, 207(FR):Oct88-201
Mellanby, K., ed. Air Pollution, Acid Rain and the Environment.
    J.T. Farquhar, 324:Oct89-752
Mellard, J.M. Doing Tropology.*
    J.E. Bassett, 27(AL):Mar88-155
    J. McGowan, 115:Spring88-216
Mellers, W. François Couperin and the French Classical Tradition.
    J.R. Anthony, 410(M&L):Oct88-513
Mellers, W. Vaughan Williams and the Vision of Albion.
    R. Scruton, 617(TLS):1-7Dec89-1327
Melling, D.J. Understanding Plato.*
    S.S. Tigner, 103:Jun89-238
Mellinkoff, R. The Devil at Isenheim.
    J. Russell, 441:11Jun89-13
Mellon, J., ed. Bullwhip Days.
    D. Bradley, 441:8Jan89-1
    442(NY):20Mar89-115
Mellor, A.K. Mary Shelley.*
    L. Newlyn, 617(TLS):17-23Feb89-171

Mellors, A. & J. Radford, eds. Bibliography of British Newspapers: Derbyshire.
  P. Hoare, 635(VPR):Fall88-121
Meltzer, F. Salome and the Dance of Writing.*
  M. Brisson, 529(QQ):Winter88-937
  R.A. Cavell, 627(UTQ):Summer89-521
  C.J. Stivale, 207(FR):Oct88-154
Meltzer, F., ed. The Trial(s) of Psychoanalysis.
  S.B. Girgus, 30:Winter89-91
Meltzoff, S. Botticelli, Signorelli and Savonarola.
  M. Kemp, 617(TLS):24-30Mar89-312
Melville, H. Journals. (H.C. Horsford, with L. Horth, eds)
  J.D. Bloom, 441:12Nov89-58
Melville, H. The Piazza Tales and Other Prose Pieces, 1839-1860. (H. Hayford & others, eds)
  W. Kelley, 534(RALS):Vol16No1&2-19
Melville, J. Ellen and Edy.
  G. Rowell, 611(TN):Vol42No3-126
Melville, J. A Haiku for Hanae.
  T.J. Binyon, 617(TLS):17-23Nov89-1288
Melville, S.W. Philosophy Beside Itself.*
  S. Connor, 402(MLR):Oct89-904
  M. Conroy, 577(SHR):Summer88-274
  A. Montefiore, 447(N&Q):Sep88-414
  T. Pinkney, 366:Spring88-110
  D. Simpson, 149(CLS):Vol25No1-86
Melzer, G. & J. Tükel, eds. Die Arbeit am Glück.
  T.F. Barry, 221(GQ):Winter87-88
Melzer, S.E. Discourses of the Fall.*
  N. Ekstein, 345(KRQ):Nov88-482
  F. Lagarde, 704(SFR):Fall-Winter88-407
  E. Morot-Sir, 567:Vol70No1/2-105
Menand, L. Discovering Modernism.*
  W. Harmon, 569(SR):Winter88-105
  M. Moran, 27(AL):Mar88-128
  P.T.S., 295(JML):Fall87/Winter88-312
Menander Protector. The History of Menander the Guardsman.* (R.C. Blockley, ed & trans)
  A. Cameron, 487:Autumn88-281
Ménard, P., ed. Le Roman de Tristan en prose. (Vol 1)
  G. Roques, 553(RLiR):Jan-Jun88-320
Menashe, S. Collected Poems.*
  C. Bedient, 569(SR):Winter88-137
Menchi, S.S. - see under Seidel Menchi, S.
Mencken, H.L. The Diary of H.L. Mencken. (C.A. Fecher, ed)
  R. Ward, 441:24Dec89-3
Mencken, H.L. & S. Haardt. Mencken and Sara, a Life in Letters.* (M.E. Rodgers, ed)
  V. Fitzpatrick, 639(VQR):Spring88-355
  M.D.O., 295(JML):Fall87/Winter88-353
Mendelsohn, E. & H. Nowotny, eds. Nineteen Eighty-Four.
  B. Suits, 488:Jun88-265
Mendelson, E. - see Auden, W.H. & C. Isherwood
Mendelson, S.H. The Mental World of Stuart Women.
  M.J.M. Ezell, 568(SCN):Winter88-76
Mendelssohn, F. Felix Mendelssohn: A Life in Letters. (R. Elvers, ed)
  C. Brown, 410(M&L):Jan88-88
  J. Chissell, 617(TLS):28Jul-3Aug89-826
Méndez-Faith, T. Paraguay.
  J.M. Marcos, 238:Mar88-90

Mendilow, J. The Romantic Tradition in British Political Thought.*
  P. Marshall, 402(MLR):Oct89-940
Mendoza, E. City of Marvels.*
  A.E. Lee, 617(TLS):20-26Jan89-58
Mendus, S., ed. Justifying Toleration.*
  C.J.B., 185:Jul89-968
Mendus, S. & J. Rendall, eds. Sexuality and Subordination.
  A. Summers, 617(TLS):7-13Apr89-357
Meneghello, L. Bau-sète.
  P. Hainsworth, 617(TLS):21-27Apr89-418
Menéndez Pelayo, M. Epistolario. (Vols 6-9)(M. Revuelta Sañudo, ed)
  A. Baron, 92(BH):Jan-Dec87-380
  A.H. Clarke, 86(BHS):Oct88-412
Menéndez Pelayo, M. Epistolario. (Vols 10-12)
  A. Baron, 92(BH):Jan-Dec87-380
Menéndez Pidal, R. La lengua castellana en el siglo XVII.
  F. Abad, 548:Jan-Jun88-247
Meng, H. Mundartwörterbuch der Landschaft Baden nach Sachgruppen.
  A. Lötscher, 685(ZDL):2/1988-236
Menge, W.S. & J.A. Shimrak - see Chisholm, D.
Menges, C.C. Inside the National Security Council.
  F. Barnes, 441:29Jan89-12
  M. Falcoff, 617(TLS):12-18May89-524
Menikoff, B. Robert Louis Stevenson and "The Beach of Falesá."
  A. Stiebel, 250(HLQ):Spring88-145
Menke, T.R. Lenz-Erzählungen in der deutschen Literatur.
  H. Madland, 221(GQ):Spring87-273
Mennemeier, F.N. & C. Wiedemann, eds. Kontroversen, alte und neue. (Vol 9)
  G.W. Field, 664:May88-186
  A.A. Wallas, 602:Band19Heft1-207
Mennie-de Varennes, K. Annotated Bibliography of Genealogical Works in Canada. (Vol 1)
  E. Phelps, 470:Vol26-177
Menninger, K.A. The Selected Correspondence of Karl A. Menninger, 1919-1945. (H.J. Faulkner & V.D. Pruitt, eds)
  G.N. Grob, 441:19Mar89-25
Menocal, M.R. The Arabic Role in Medieval Literary History.
  J. Cummins, 304(JHP):Winter88-151
  D. Metlitzki, 589:Oct88-957
Mensching, S. Tuchfühlung.
  M. Gratz, 601(SuF):Sep-Oct88-1096
Mentré, M. Création et Apocalypse.
  L.J.V.D., 90:Feb88-148
de Meo, P., ed. Situations.
  R.W. Bjornson, 399(MLJ):Summer88-232
Mercer, D. & D. Puttnam. Rural England.
  E. Dennis, 324:Dec88-62
Mercer, P. Hamlet and the Acting of Revenge.*
  639(VQR):Summer88-81
Merchant, I. Hullabaloo in Old Jeypore.
  A. Aronson, 441:26Feb89-35
  G. Heptonstall, 324:Jun89-445
Merchant, M. Confrontation of Angels.
  J. MacVean, 4:Autumn88-35
Merchant, M. Jeshua.
  J. MacVean, 4:Autumn88-38
Mercier-Josa, S. Retour sur le jeune Marx.*
  R. Gervais, 154:Summer88-373

Meredeen, S. Managing Industrial Conflict.
S. Alderson, 324:May89–382
Meredith, C. Shifts.*
A. Whitehouse, 441:30Apr89–38
Meredith, D.R. Murder by Impulse.*
E.P. Sewell, 649(WAL):Nov88–247
Meredith, M. In the Name of Apartheid.*
G.M. Fredrickson, 453(NYRB):26Oct89–48
Meredith, M., ed. Meeting the Brownings.
M. Smith, 541(RES):May88–314
Meredith, P., ed. The Mary Play from the N-Town Manuscript.
S. Carpenter, 541(RES):Nov88–536
S. Spector, 130:Summer88–192
Mergenthaler, O. The Biography of Ottmar Mergenthaler, Inventor of the Linotype. (C. Schlesinger, ed)
R.B. Smith, 441:19Nov89–25
Merino, C.C. – see under Codoñer Merino, C.
Merkel, I. & A.G. Debus, eds. Hermeticism and the Renaissance.
S.J. Linden, 617(TLS):25–31Aug89–928
Merkelbach, R. Mani und seine Religions-system.
W.H.C. Frend, 123:Vol38No1–165
Merkl, H. Sor Juana Inés de la Cruz.
J.R. Jones, 86(BHS):Oct88–422
Merkley, P. The Greek and Hebrew Origins of Our Idea of History.
I. Robinson, 529(QQ):Winter88–895
Merle, R. The Idol.
S. Altinel, 617(TLS):29Dec89/4Jan90–1448
Merllié, F. Michel Tournier.
G. Hintzy, 542:Oct–Dec88–515
M. Sheringham, 617(TLS):11–17Aug89–879
Merlonghi, F.C., F. Merlonghi & J.A. Tursi. Oggi in Italia. (3rd ed)
A.P. Esposito, 399(MLJ):Winter88–482
Mermet, G. Francoscopie.
A.J.M. Prévos, 207(FR):Oct88–188
Merod, J. The Political Responsibility of the Critic.
H. Fromm, 219(GaR):Spring88–183
T.S., 185:Oct88–195
J. Seaton, 115:Summer88–327
Merquior, J.G. Foucault.*
Z. Elmarsafy, 400(MLN):Dec88–1185
M. Poster, 144:Winter89–155
42(AR):Fall88–529
Merquior, J.G. From Prague to Paris.*
R. Tallis, 144:Winter89–7
Merrel, F. Pararealities.* [shown in prev under Merrell]
U. Margolin, 494:Vol9No4–863
Merrell, F. A Semiotic Theory of Texts.
W.O. Hendricks, 567:Vol72No1/2–97
Merrick, P. Revolution and Religion in the Music of Liszt.
E.F. Jensen, 451:Fall88–184
D.P., 412:Feb88–75
J. Rosenblatt, 309:Vol8No1/2–169
A. Walker, 410(M&L):Apr88–272
Merrill, G.D. & G. Arms – see Howells, E.M.
Merrill, J. The Inner Room.
C. Kizer, 441:12Nov89–63
Merrill, R. Joseph Heller.
L.K. Barnett, 402(MLR):Jul89–732
Merrills, J.G. The Development of International Law by the European Court of Human Rights.
J. Waldron, 617(TLS):10–16Nov89–1236

Merritt, W.E. Where the Rivers Ran Backward.
D. Murray, 441:24Sep89–49
Merryman, J.H. & A.E. Elsen. Law, Ethics, and the Visual Arts.* (2nd ed)
B. Hoffman, 55:Mar88–93
Mersmann, W. Der Faltstuhl vom Nonnberg in Salzburg.
H. Appuhn, 683:Band51Heft2–280
Mertens, P. Les Eblouissements.
J. Decock, 207(FR):May89–1095
Mertens, V., ed. Die Grimms, die Germanistik und die Gegenwart.
C. van Kerckvoorde, 350:Sep89–669
Merton, T. The Road to Joy. (R.E. Daggy, ed)
D. Leimbach, 441:17Sep89–25
Merwin, W.S., ed & trans. Four French Plays.
R.S. Gwynn, 569(SR):Spring88–297
Merwin, W.S., ed & trans. From the Spanish Morning.*
R.S. Gwynn, 569(SR):Spring88–297
Merwin, W.S. The Rain in the Trees.*
A. Corn, 491:Jan89–237
M. Jarman, 249(HudR):Winter89–729
Merwin, W.S. Selected Poems.*
M. Jarman, 249(HudR):Winter89–729
639(VQR):Autumn88–133
van Mesdag, M. Think Marketing.
P.S. Guptara, 324:Apr89–320
Meserve, W.J. Heralds of Promise.*
R.K. Bank, 615(TJ):Dec87–535
E.M. Hayes, 432(NEQ):Sep88–461
Messenger, A. His and Hers.*
Kendall, 615(TJ):Mar88–126
P. Sabor, 178:Mar88–100
P.M. Spacks, 401(MLQ):Dec86–441
J.F. Thaddeus, 301(JEGP):Jul88–444
Messeri, M. Causa e spiegazione.*
L.S. Joy, 319:Jul89–476
Messerli, D., ed. "Language" Poetries.*
H. Lazer, 659(ConL):Spring89–142
Messick, H. Desert Sanctuary.
J. Harris, 649(WAL):Nov88–239
Mészáros, I. Philosophy, Ideology and Social Science.
J.J.W., 185:Oct88–194
Met, M. Moving Ahead in Spanish.
S.P. Walker, 399(MLJ):Summer88–247
Met, M. Welcome to Spanish.
D. Barnwell, 238:Sep88–564
S.P. Walker, 399(MLJ):Summer88–247
"Métapsychologie et philosophie."
M. Bertrand, 542:Jan–Mar88–81
Metcalf, J. Adult Entertainment.*
D. Barbour, 102(CanL):Spring88–145
K. Fraser, 168(ECW):Spring88–57
Metcalf, J., ed. The Bumper Book.
A.R. Kizuk, 627(UTQ):Fall87–150
S. Scobie, 529(QQ):Spring88–190
Metcalf, P. U.S. Dept. of the Interior.
S. Birkerts, 472:Vol15No1–163
Metcalfe, A. Canada Learns to Play.
A. Varpalotai, 529(QQ):Winter88–952
Metcalfe, P. 1933.
O. Fuerbringer, 441:5Feb89–23
Meter, H. Figur und Erzählauffassung im veristischen Roman.
M. Ainley, 402(MLR):Jul89–751
Y. Chevrel, 52:Band23Heft3–325
F-R. Hausmann, 602:Band19Heft2–192
R. Schwaderer, 547(RF):Band100Heft4–456

Mettam, R. Power and Faction in Louis XIV's France.
J. Rogister, 617(TLS):20-26Jan89-65
Metzger, L. One Foot in Eden.*
R.L. Brett, 541(RES):Feb88-120
B.E. Graver, 661(WC):Autumn88-207
W. Walling, 340(KSJ):Vol37-170
Metzidakis, S. Repetition and Semiotics.
M. Antle, 207(FR):Dec88-320
van den Meulen, J. & J. Hohmeyer. Chartres.*
W. Haas, 43:Band18Heft1-116
Meunier, J. Le Monocle de Joseph Conrad.
J. Taylor, 532(RCF):Spring88-205
Meurant, G. Shoowa Design.
M. Adams, 2(AfrA):Nov87-14
Mews, S. Bertolt Brecht: Herr Puntila und sein Knecht Matti.
D.H. Haenicke, 221(GQ):Spring87-307
Mey, J. Whose Language?
D.H., 355(LSoc):Mar88-149
M. Huspek, 567:Vol72No3/4-341
Meyer, A. "Sestra moja - žizn'" von Boris Pasternak.
A. Livingstone, 575(SEER):Oct88-649
Meyer, H. & R. Suntrup. Lexikon der mittelalterlichen Zahlenbedeutungen.
D.A. Wells, 402(MLR):Oct88-1015
Meyer, H.L. Einführung in die englische Kasusgrammatik.
H.U. Boas, 38:Band106Heft1/2-157
Meyer, M., ed. De la métaphysique à la rhétorique.*
C. Ronveaux, 209(FM):Apr88-101
Meyer, M. De la problématologie?*
W.F. Motte, Jr., 494:Vol8No3/4-729
Meyer, M. From Logic to Rhetoric.*
A. Brinton, 480(P&R):Vol21No4-312
Meyer, M. Not Prince Hamlet.
K. Worth, 617(TLS):25-31Aug89-929
Meyer, M. Science et métaphysique chez Kant.
R. Theis, 540(RIPh):Vol42fasc3-386
Meyer, M. Strindberg.
F. Rosslyn, 97(CQ):Vol17No2-196
Meyer, R., ed. Die Hamburger Oper 1678-1730.*
P.M. Mitchell, 301(JEGP):Apr88-294
M.R. Wade, 221(GQ):Winter87-151
Meyer, R., with others, eds. Bibliographia Dramatica et Dramaticorum.
D.G. John, 564:Feb88-71
Meyer-Bahlburg, H. & E. Wolff. Afrikanische Sprachen in Forschung und Lehre.
S. Brauner, 682(ZPSK):Band41Heft2-256
Meyer-Kalkus, R. Wollust und Grausamkeit.
T. Borgstedt, 224(GRM):Band38Heft1/2-210
Meyering, S.L., ed. Charlotte Perkins Gilman.
E. Hedges, 357:Fall89-63
Meyers, A. The Big Killing.
M. Stasio, 441:9Jul89-24
Meyers, D.T. & K. Kipnis, eds. Philosophical Dimensions of the Constitution.
A.S. Rosenbaum, 103:Apr89-161
Meyers, H.B. Geronimo's Ponies.
B. Hochberg, 441:22Oct89-22
Meyers, J. Hemingway.*
J.M. Cox, 569(SR):Summer88-511
E. Margolies, 179(ES):Jun88-267
Meyers, J. L'art de l'emprunt dans la poésie de Sedulius Scottus.
J. Martin, 589:Oct88-959

Meyers, J., ed. The Legacy of D.H. Lawrence.
L. Blanchard, 177(ELT):Vol31No3-355
D.R. Schwarz, 395(MFS):Summer88-279
Meyers, J. Manic Power.
R. von Hallberg, 432(NEQ):Dec88-633
M. Hofmann, 617(TLS):26May-1Jun89-578
Meyers, R.G. The Likelihood of Knowledge.
F. Dretske, 543:Mar89-632
J. Peterson, 103:Nov88-459
Meyerson, I. Ecrits 1920-1983.
J-M. Gabaude, 542:Jan-Mar88-82
Meynell, H. The Art of Handel's Operas.*
W. Dean, 410(M&L):Oct88-518
Mezey, R. Evening Wind.
G. Kuzma, 219(GaR):Fall88-624
C. Muske, 441:8Jan89-14
639(VQR):Summer88-99
Mian, M.S. - see under Shahjahan Mian, M.
Micha, A. Essais sur le Cycle du Lancelot-Graal.
G. Roques, 553(RLiR):Jul-Dec88-543
Michael, C.V. The Marquis de Sade.
L.W. Lynch, 207(FR):Mar89-684
Michael, I. & R.A. Cardwell, eds. Medieval and Renaissance Studies in Honour of Robert Brian Tate.*
B. Taylor, 86(BHS):Jul88-294
Michael, J. Emerson and Skepticism.
C. Dove, 400(MLN):Dec88-1189
Michael, S. Refuge.
M. Roshwald, 268(IFR):Winter89-85
Michaels, W.B. The Gold Standard and the Logic of Naturalism.*
A. Boyer, 395(MFS):Summer88-227
W.E. Cain, 536(Rev):Vol10-73
E. Carton, 533:Winter89-99
J. Ditsky, 26(ALR):Fall88-92
A. Habegger, 432(NEQ):Jun88-284
D. Pizer, 445(NCF):Jun88-113
B. Thomas, 27(AL):May88-301
Michaelsen, A.G. En undersøkelse av Henrik Wergelands farsediktning.
E. Beyer, 172(Edda):1988/4-372
Michailovsky, B. La langue hayu.
S. De Lancey, 350:Dec89-828
Michalski, K., ed. Der Mensch in den modernen Wissenschaften.*
K. Prätor, 687:Apr-Jun88-333
Michaud, S. & J. Sessa, eds. Pluridisciplinarité et Innovation pédagogique.
Y. Chevrel, 549(RLC):Jul-Sep88-405
Michaud, Y. La violence.
J-M. Gabaude, 542:Jan-Mar88-106
Michaux, B. & others. Philosophie.
M. Adam, 542:Jan-Mar88-121
Michaux, H. Ailleurs (Voyage en Grande Garabagne, Au pays de la Magie, Ici, Poddema). (new ed)
P. Broome, 208(FS):Jan88-110
Micheels, L.J. Doctor No. 117641.
I. Deak, 453(NYRB):28Sep89-63
442(NY):24Apr89-112
Micheels, P.A. Braving the Flames.
J.E. Butler, 441:30Apr89-39
Michel, B. Le Mémoire de Prague.
H.G. Skilling, 575(SEER):Apr88-303
Michel, G. & others. Sprachliche Kommunikation.
J.E. Schmidt, 685(ZDL):2/1988-259
Michel, J. Une mise en récit du silence.*
G. Cesbron, 535(RHL):Mar-Apr88-343

Michel, J.M. – see "Mitteilungen der Karg-Elert-Gesellschaft"
Michel, M.R. Le dessin français au XVIIIe siècle.
  A. Laing, 39:Nov88–374
Michel-Thiriet, P. The Book of Proust.
  E. Hughes, 617(TLS):13–19Oct89–1112
Michelangelo. The Sonnets of Michelangelo. (E. Jennings, trans)
  G. Maxwell, 617(TLS):5–11May89–495
Michelet, J. Les femmes de la Révolution. (F. Giroud, ed)
  M. & P. Higonnet, 617(TLS):19–25May89–541
Michelet, J. Oeuvres complètes. (P. Viallaneix, ed) [together with] L'Oiseau, L'Insecte. (E. Kaplan, ed)
  J.R. Williams, 207(FR):Mar89–687
Micheli, G. & G. Santinello, eds. Kant a due secoli dalla "Critica."
  S. Carboncini, 53(AGP):Band70Heft3–335
Michelson, A. & others, eds. October.
  42(AR):Spring88–274
  639(VQR):Spring88–68
Michelutti, D. Loyalty to the Hunt.
  D. Manganiello, 102(CanL):Spring88–220
Michener, J.A. Caribbean.
  R. Houston, 441:5Nov89–22
Michener, J.A. Journey.
  T. Fleming, 441:9Jul89–15
Michie, H. The Flesh Made Word.
  M. Hite, 395(MFS):Winter88–680
  H.M. Schor, 141:Spring88–259
  L.M. Shires, 637(VS):Winter89–247
  H. Sussman, 191(ELN):Jun88–91
  R.R. Warhol, 454:Winter89–213
Michinaga, F. Notes journalières de Fujiwara no Michinaga, ministre à la cour de Heian (995–1018).
  A. Gatten, 407(MN):Winter88–471
Michio, N. & M. Urrutia – see under Nagai Michio & M. Urrutia
Michler, C., ed. Le Somme abregiet de theologie.
  J.L. Grigsby, 545(RPh):May89–491
Michnik, A. Letters from Prison and Other Essays.
  J.K.M. Hanson, 575(SEER):Jan88–154
  E. Hoffman, 497(PolR):Vol33No3–355
Michon, J.A. & J.L. Jackson, eds. Time, Mind, and Behavior.
  J-M. Gabaude, 542:Jan–Mar88–83
Michon, P. Vie de Joseph Roulin.
  G. Macé, 450(NRF):Jul–Aug88–217
Michot, J. La destinée de l'homme selon Avicenne.
  J.W. Morris, 318(JAOS):Oct–Dec87–815
Mickelson, S. From Whistle Stop to Sound Bite.
  M. Goodman, 441:10Dec89–11
Mickle, S.F. The Queen of October.
  J. Shepard, 441:12Nov89–9
Micou, P. The Music Programme.
  C. Hawtree, 617(TLS):19–25May89–536
Micros, M., ed. The Creative Circus Book.*
  P. Denham, 168(ECW):Spring88–130
Middlebrook, M. The Fight for the "Malvinas."
  M. Carver, 617(TLS):21–27Apr89–416
Middleton, C. Selected Writings.
  M. Ford, 617(TLS):7–13Jul89–737
Middleton, C. – see von Goethe, J.W.
Middleton, H. The Earth Is Enough.
  J. Kennedy, 441:30Jul89–17

Middleton, M. Man Made the Town.
  P. Goodman, 47:Dec88–59
Middleton, R. & P. Duboy. Lequeu, une énigme.
  J. Guillerme, 98:Oct88–805
Middleton, S. Entry into Jerusalem.
  P. Vigderman, 441:12Mar89–26
Middleton, S. Vacant Places.
  M. Casserley, 617(TLS):7–13Jul89–738
Midgley, G. – see Bunyan, J.
Midgley, M. Evolution as a Religion.*
  H.B., 185:Apr89–672
Midgley, M. Wisdom, Information and Wonder.
  D.E. Cooper, 617(TLS):11–17Aug89–865
Midiohouan, G.O. L'idéologie dans la littérature négro-africaine d'expression française.
  M. Steins, 538(RAL):Fall88–398
Midwinter, E. Red Roses Crest the Caps.
  T.D. Smith, 617(TLS):23–29Jun89–696
Mieder, W. Disenchantments.
  J. Zipes, 292(JAF):Jul–Sep88–382
Mieder, W. "Findet, so werdet ihr suchen!"*
  M.E. Barrick, 292(JAF):Jan–Mar88–103
Mieder, W., ed. Grimmige Märchen.
  W. Pape, 196:Band29Heft1/2–216
Mieder, W., ed. The Prentice-Hall Encyclopedia of World Proverbs.*
  L. Bluhm, 133:Band21Heft2/3–266
Mieder, W. Tradition and Innovation in Folk Literature.
  S.S. Jones, 292(JAF):Jul–Sep88–363
  S.S. Jones, 650(WF):Oct88–310
  J. Wood, 402(MLR):Oct89–909
Mieder, W. – see "Proverbium"
Mieder, W. – see Taylor, A.
Mielke, H., with M. Angerer & W. Pfeiffer. Albrecht Altdorfer.
  B. Butts, 380:Autumn88–277
Mielsch, H. Die römische Villa.
  A. Frazer, 576:Dec88–411
  R.J.A. Wilson, 313:Vol78–244
Mielsch, H., H. von Hesberg & K. Gaertner. Die heidnische Nekropole unter St. Peter in Rom. (Vol 1)
  G. Davies, 313:Vol78–252
Mierau, F., ed. Die Erweckung des Wortes.
  A. Trebess, 654(WB):8/1988–1402
Miers, S. & R. Roberts, eds. The End of Slavery in Africa.
  R. Oliver, 617(TLS):28Jul–3Aug89–829
Miethe, T.L. – see Habermas, G.R. & A.G.N. Flew
Mighetto, D. & P. Rosengren. Diccionario reverso.
  R. Wright, 86(BHS):Apr88–177
Migliorini, B. The Italian Language. (T.G. Griffith, ed)
  M.D. Maiden, 545(RPh):Feb89–292
Mignot-Ogliastri, C. – see Cocteau, J. & A. de Noailles
Migoyo, G.D. – see under Díaz Migoyo, G.
Miguélez, A. & M. Sandoval. Jauja.
  E. Chávez, 238:Mar88–101
Mihailovich, V.D. Say It in Serbo-Croatian.
  T.F. Magner, 574(SEEJ):Winter88–684
Mihm, A., ed. Sprache an Rhein und Ruhr.
  G. Cornelissen, 680(ZDP):Band107Heft1–151
  E. Neuss, 685(ZDL):1/1988–109
Mihm, M.T. The "Songe d'Enfer" of Raoul de Houdenc.
  U. Mölk, 547(RF):Band99Heft4–460

Mihura, M. The Independent Act.
M.T. Halsey, 238:Mar88-103
Mijuskovic, B. Contingent Immaterialism.
N.O. Bernsen, 449:Jun87-280
Mijuskovic, B.L. Loneliness.
M. Adam, 542:Apr-Jun88-217
Mikhail, E.H., ed. The Abbey Theatre.
J. O'Riordan, 511:Jun88-44
Mikhail, E.H. Sean O'Casey and His Critics.
J. Coakley, 130:Spring88-84
Mikkelson, G. & M. Winchell - see Rasputin,
V.
Mikosch, I. Die Präpositionen in gesprochener
Sprache.
A.R. Wedel, 350:Mar89-188
Milbauer, A.Z. & D.G. Watson, eds. Reading
Philip Roth.
L. Field, 395(MFS):Winter88-645
Milburn, R. Early Christian Art and Archi-
tecture.*
B. Allsopp, 324:Jul89-522
Mildenberg, L. The Coinage of the Bar Kok-
hba War.* (P.E. Mottahedeh, ed & trans)
S.J.D. Cohen, 318(JAOS):Jul-Sep87-549
Miles, B. Ginsberg.
P. Berman, 441:1Oct89-3
Miles, D., comp. Something in Common.
D.C. Wixson, 534(RALS):Vol16No1&2-29
Miles, R. The Female Form.
C. Hoyser, 637(VS):Summer89-580
Miles, R. Ben Jonson.*
R.C. Evans, 250(HLQ):Autumn88-329
J. Ferns, 541(RES):Aug88-440
D. McPherson, 401(MLQ):Jun87-188
M.R.G. Spiller, 571(ScLJ):Spring88-5
Milián-Silveira, M.C. El primer Onetti y sus
contextos.
J. Walker, 238:May88-310
Miliaras, B. Pillar of Flame.
J. Meyers, 395(MFS):Winter88-695
Mill, C. Norman Collie.
D. Robertson, 637(VS):Winter89-260
Mill, J.S. Newspaper Writings. (A.P. & J.M.
Robson, eds)
A.J. Arscott, 529(QQ):Summer88-478
L. James, 635(VPR):Fall88-120
Millán-Puelles, A. Léxico Filosófico.
C. Melches, 489(PJGG):Band95Heft2-429
Millar, D. & others, eds. Chambers Concise
Dictionary of Scientists.
S. Rose, 617(TLS):4-10Aug89-845
Millar, F. & E. Segal - see "Caesar Augustus:
Seven Aspects"
Millard, P. - see North, R.
Millen, R.F. & R.E. Wolf. Heroic Deeds and
Mystic Figures.
J. Russell, 441:3Dec89-9
Miller, A. Timebends.
E. Brater, 385(MQR):Spring89-298
M. Gussow, 18:Apr88-60
R.A. Martin, 115:Summer88-321
C.P. Ryan, 157:No167-50
Miller, A. - see Haasse, H.S.
Miller, A.M. From Delos to Delphi.
A.C. Brumfield, 124:Mar-Apr89-315
N.J. Richardson, 123:Vol38No1-5
Miller, C. Emily Dickinson.*
J.L. Capps, 27(AL):Oct88-473
S.M. Gilbert, 26(ALR):Fall88-69
L. Kelly, 402(MLR):Oct89-967
L.T. Oggel, 599:Spring89-135
D. Porter, 445(NCF):Sep88-244
639(VQR):Winter88-29

Miller, C.L. Blank Darkness.*
M. Diawara, 153:Spring88-66
A. Gérard, 107(CRCL):Mar88-168
M. Schipper, 538(RAL):Winter88-567
C. Wake, 208(FS):Jan88-116
Miller, C.R. Virginia Woolf.
S. Roe, 617(TLS):3-9Feb89-100
Miller, D. Material Culture and Mass Con-
sumption.
E.S. Clemens, 185:Apr89-658
Miller, D., M. Bracher & D. Ault. Critical
Paths.
639(VQR):Spring88-52
Miller, D.A. The Novel and the Police.
S. Cohan, 454:Spring89-350
W.P. Day, 637(VS):Summer89-577
M. Edmundson, 385(MQR):Summer89-437
G.A. Hudson, 268(IFR):Winter89-80
Miller, D.L. Lewis Mumford.
P. Goldberger, 61:Jul89-9
A.L. Huxtable, 441:26Nov89-3
442(NY):18Sep89-140
Miller, E.F. - see Hume, D.
Miller, H. Henry VIII and the English Nobil-
ity.*
A.J. Slavin, 551(RenQ):Summer88-332
Miller, J. American Odalisque.
R. Katrovas, 434:Spring89-340
L. Rector, 249(HudR):Summer88-398
L. Upton, 152(UDQ):Spring88-106
Miller, J., ed. The Art of Alice Munro.*
P. Köster, 102(CanL):Summer88-166
Miller, J. Measures of Wisdom.*
M.J.B. Allen, 551(RenQ):Summer88-310
J. Nohrnberg, 589:Apr88-438
J.M. Rist, 627(UTQ):Fall87-98
Miller, J. Religion in the Popular Prints
1600-1832.
J.E. Hill, 173(ECS):Summer88-530
Miller, J. The Vision of Cosmic Order in the
Vedas.*
A.T. de Nicolás, 485(PE&W):Jan88-89
Miller, J.C. Way of Death.
S.B. Schwartz, 441:12Mar89-27
Miller, J.H. The Ethics of Reading.*
G. Joseph, 290(JAAC):Winter87-312
G. Prince, 478(P&L):Oct88-310
R. Scholes, 454:Winter89-223
Miller, J.H. The Linguistic Moment.*
J. Hill, 115:Winter88-80
I. Massey, 591(SIR):Summer88-336
Miller, J.M. & J.H. Hayes. A History of
Ancient Israel and Judah.
R.T. Anderson, 115:Winter88-90
Miller, J.P. Numbers in Presence and
Absence.*
R. Tragesser, 316:Jun88-646
Miller, J.T. Poetic License.
E.D. Hirsch, 604:Spring/Summer88-33
M. Murrin, 551(RenQ):Autumn88-523
Miller, K.A. Emigrants and Exiles.*
D. Dowling, 102(CanL):Winter87-216
M. Heale, 617(TLS):10-16Mar89-261
Miller, K.E. Denmark.
P.M. Mitchell, 562(Scan):Nov88-204
Miller, L. & A. Cohen. Music in the Royal
Society of London 1660-1806.
P. Gouk, 413:Fall88-113
Miller, M. Boogie, Pete & The Senator.
D. Rollins, 627(UTQ):Fall88-213
Miller, M. Bliss Carman.
R. Hatch, 102(CanL):Winter87-223

255

Miller, M. A Thousand and One Coffee Mornings.
    A. Soueif, 617(TLS):13–19Oct89–1132
Miller, M.A. The Russian Revolutionary Emigrés, 1825–1870.*
    J. Slatter, 575(SEER):Apr88–295
Miller, M.C. Boxed In.*
    D. Frankel, 62:Dec88–111
    M. Sidone, 590:Dec88–159
Miller, M.H., Jr. Plato's "Parmenides."*
    E. Halper, 124:Nov–Dec88–132
    M. Schofield, 303(JoHS):Vol108–229
    J.A. Towey, 24:Winter88–600
Miller, M.J. The Poetics of "Nikki Bungaku."*
    I. Schuster, 107(CRCL):Mar88–116
Miller, N. Helmut Jahn.
    A.O. Dean, 47:Feb88–37
    S. Gutterman, 45:Mar88–77
Miller, N. Spying for America.
    J.A. Adam, 441:23Jul89–15
Miller, N. Tacitus, "Annals 14."
    M. Hammond, 124:Jul–Aug89–468
    A.J. Woodman, 123:Vol38No2–417
Miller, N.K., ed. The Poetics of Gender.*
    R.D. Cottrell, 207(FR):Dec88–321
Miller, N.K. Subject to Change.
    T. Castle, 617(TLS):2–8Jun89–607
Miller, O.V., I.A. Kolobova & S.J. Bovina, comps. Biblioteka A.A. Bloka.
    D.A. Sloane, 574(SEEJ):Spring88–137
Miller, P.L. Dragonflies.
    M. Ridley, 617(TLS):3–9Feb89–118
Miller, R., ed. Region and Class in Modern Peruvian History.
    N.P. Jacobsen, 263(RIB)Vol38No2–218
Miller, R.A. Nihongo.
    J.M. Unger, 293(JASt):Nov88–891
Miller, R.F., ed. Critical Essays on Dostoevsky.
    G. Woodcock, 569(SR):Spring88–306
Miller, R.K. Carlyle's "Life of John Sterling."*
    I.B. Nadel, 637(VS):Winter89–248
Miller, R.W. Analyzing Marx.*
    A. Buchanan, 519(PhS):Jan88–157
Miller, S.S. Studies in the History and Traditions of Sepphoris.
    M. Smith, 318(JAOS):Jul–Sep87–543
Miller, S.S., with J.A. & D.E. Miller. Conquest of Aging.
    J. Viorst, 441:9Apr89–30
Miller, T. The Panama Hat Trail.*
    S. Pickering, 569(SR):Fall88–673
Millgate, J. Scott's Last Edition.
    P.T. Srebrnik, 637(VS):Winter89–253
Millgate, M. – see Hardy, T.
Millikan, R.G. Language, Thought, and Other Biological Categories.*
    P. Godfrey-Smith, 63:Dec88–556
Millington, M. Reading Onetti.*
    J. Promis, 552(REH):Oct88–137
Millman, L., comp. A Kayak Full of Ghosts.
    V.L. Smith, 650(WF):Jul88–226
Millon, H.A. & others. Emilian Painting of the Sixteenth and Seventeenth Centuries.
    A.H., 90:Jan88–46
Millon-Delsol, C. La politique dénaturée.
    M. Adam, 542:Oct–Dec88–520
Mills, A.E. The Acquisition of Gender.
    S. Strömqvist & A–B. Andersson, 452(NJL):Vol11No1/2–211
Mills, J.A. Hamlet on Stage.*
    D. Daphinoff, 156(ShJW):Jahrbuch1988–281

Mills, N. The Crowd in American Literature.*
    P.R.J., 295(JML):Fall87/Winter88–263
Mills, R.J., Jr. Each Branch.
    B. Pryor, 389(MQ):Summer89–534
Millward, E. Appropriate Noises.*
    S. O'Brien, 617(TLS):25–31Aug89–916
Milne, A.J.M. Human Rights and Human Diversity.*
    D.E. Cooper, 161(DUJ):Dec87–165
    M. Lessnoff, 518:Jul88–173
Milne, D.A. Tug of War.
    H. Thorburn, 529(QQ):Autumn88–741
    D.C. Wallace, 298:Fall88–150
Milne, J. Daddy's Girl.
    M. Stasio, 441:4Jun89–24
Milne-Tyte, R. Bloody Jeffreys.
    J. Miller, 617(TLS):8–14Dec89–1354
Milner, J. The Studios of Paris.*
    K. Cieszkowski, 324:May89–385
    T. Hilton, 617(TLS):24–30Mar89–305
    M.S. Kinsey, 446(NCFS):Spring–Summer89–432
Milo, R.D. Immorality.*
    R.K. Fullinwider, 482(PhR):Oct88–592
Milolo, K. L'Image de la femme chez les romancières de l'Afrique noire francophone.
    D. Deltel, 535(RHL):Mar–Apr88–346
Milosz, C. The Collected Poems 1931–1987.*
    S. Barańczak, 497(PolR):Vol33No4–463
    D. O'Driscoll, 493:Winter88/89–42
    B. Wormser, 472:Vol15No2–67
Milosz, C. Témoignage de la poésie.
    J. Voisine, 549(RLC):Jan–Mar88–105
Milot, L.B. Jean Papineau-Couture.
    R. Falck, 627(UTQ):Fall88–214
Milroy, J. & L. Authority in Language.
    D. Cameron, 307:Aug88–149
    P. Poussa, 439(NM):1988/2–234
    S. Romaine, 355(LSoc):Jun88–266
Milroy, L. Language and Social Networks. (2nd ed)
    E. Finegan, 350:Sep89–670
Milsted, D. Market Forces.
    T. Fitton, 617(TLS):1–7Sep89–953
Milton, C. Lawrence and Nietzsche.*
    J. Meyers, 395(MFS):Winter88–695
Milton, J. Selected Prose.* (2nd ed) (C.A. Patrides, ed)
    E. Skerpan, 568(SCN):Spring–Summer88–8
Milton, J. The Yellow Kids.
    442(NY):21Aug89–94
Milward, P. Biblical Influences in Shakespeare's Great Tragedies.
    L.S. Champion, 179(ES):Feb88–86
Minault, G. & C.W. Troll – see Douglas, I.H.
Minco, M. The Glass Bridge.
    B. Finkelstein, 441:20Aug89–20
    M. Halahmy, 617(TLS):10–16Feb89–148
Mine, D. Champions of the World.
    A. Brumer, 441:12Feb89–18
Miner, E. – see Konishi, J.
Miner, S.M. Between Churchill and Stalin.
    G.A. Craig, 453(NYRB):30Mar89–15
Miner, V. Trespassing and Other Stories.
    J. Clute, 617(TLS):21–27Jul89–803
Minervini, V. & M.L. Indini – see de San Pedro, D.
Mineur, W.H. Callimachus, "Hymn to Delos."
    A. Griffiths, 303(JoHS):Vol108–230
    D.M. Schenkeveld, 394:Vol41fasc1/2–171
Minford, J. & S–K. Wong – see Hawkes, D.
Minier, S. Madame de Charrière.
    M. Moser-Verrey, 166:Apr89–256

Mittenzwei, W. Das Leben des Bertolt Brecht.*
  K. Schuhmann, 654(WB):2/1988-333
Mitterand, H. Le regard et le signe.
  G. Toffin, 98:Nov88-895
Mitterand, H. Zola et le naturalisme.
  Y. Chevrel, 535(RHL):Mar-Apr88-322
Mitterer, E. All Our Games.
  Z. Smardz, 441:29Jan89-30
Miwa Kimitada. Nihon.
  I. Soranaka, 293(JASt):Feb88-151
Mix, Y-G. Die deutschen Musenalmanache des
  18. Jahrhunderts.
  K.F. Hilliard, 402(MLR):Jan89-234
Mjačina, E.N., ed. Suaxili-russkij slovar' -
  Kamusi ya Kiswahili-Kirusi.
  I. Herms, 682(ZPSK):Band41Heft2-265
Mo Li-feng. Chiang-hsi shih-p'ai yen-chiu.
  S. Sargent, 116:Jul87-151
Moamin. Libro de los animales que cazan
  (Kitāb al-Yawāriḥ). (J.M. Fradejas Rueda,
  ed)
  A.J. Cárdenas, 304(JHP):Winter88-153
Moatti, C. Le Prédicateur et ses masques.
  R.D. Reck, 207(FR):Dec88-342
Mocquais, P-Y. Hubert Aquin ou la quête
  interrompue.
  J.M. Paterson, 627(UTQ):Fall87-182
Modarressi, T. The Pilgrim's Rules of Eti-
  quette.
  P. Fitzgerald, 441:13Aug89-7
  442(NY):16Oct89-131
Mode, D. Syntax des Vorfeldes. (H. Henne, H.
  Sitta & H.E. Wiegand, eds)
  B. Haftka, 682(ZPSK):Band41Heft4-532
  B.J. Koekkoek, 221(GQ):Summer88-456
Modéer, K.Å. Strindberg och advokaterna.
  B. Steene, 562(Scan):Nov88-188
"Modern Greek Studies Yearbook." (Vol 2)
  (T.G. Stavrou, ed)
  M.P.L., 295(JML):Fall87/Winter88-220
Modersohn-Becker, P. Paula Modersohn-
  Becker: The Letters and Journals. (German
  title: Paula Modersohn-Becker in Briefen
  und Tagebüchern.) (G. Busch & L. von
  Reinken, eds)
  E.C. Oppler, 54:Dec88-709
Modiano, M. Domestic Disharmony and Indus-
  trialization in D.H. Lawrence's Early Fic-
  tion.
  J. Meyers, 395(MFS):Winter88-695
Modiano, P. Remise de peine.
  P. Nathaniel, 450(NRF):May88-99
Modiano, P. Vestiaire de l'enfance.
  D. Coward, 617(TLS):5-11May89-482
Modiano, R. Coleridge and the Concept of
  Nature.*
  E.W. Nye, 405(MP):Aug88-97
Modrak, D.K.W. Aristotle.
  D.H. Frank, 319:Oct89-608
  D.S. Hutchinson, 487:Spring88-76
  J.G.L., 185:Oct88-206
  S. Lovibond, 123:Vol38No2-280
  C. Shields, 124:Sep-Oct88-61
  A.M. Wiles, 543:Sep88-153
Moeglin, J-M. Les Ancêtres du prince.
  G.M. Spiegel, 589:Jan88-195
Moeller, H-B., ed. Latin America and the
  Literature of Exile.
  J. Walker, 107(CRCL):Jun88-316
Moerman, M. Talking Culture.
  J. Bilmes, 293(JASt):Nov88-942

Moffat, D., ed. The Soul's Address to the
  Body.
  A.S.G. Edwards, 402(MLR):Apr89-429
  J. Johansen, 178:Sep88-343
Moffatt, M. Coming of Age in New Jersey.
  R.R. Cooper, 441:30Apr89-27
Moggach, D. Smile.
  D. Durrant, 364:Feb/Mar89-133
Mohan, B.A. Language and Content.
  W. Perry, 608:Mar87-137
Mohanan, K.P. The Theory of Lexical Phonol-
  ogy.
  E. Gussmann, 297(JL):Mar88-232
  S. Hargus, 350:Mar89-164
Mohanty, G. Paraja.*
  J. Mellors, 364:Dec88/Jan89-132
Moi, T. Sexual/Textual Politics.*
  C.P. Havely, 447(N&Q):Sep88-416
  E.A. Hirsh, 367(L&P):Vol34No3-59
  S. Neuman, 49:Jul88-99
  V. Raoul, 107(CRCL):Jun88-254
  C.H. Smith, 128(CE):Mar88-318
Moi, T. - see Kristeva, J.
Moisan, A. Répertoire des noms propres de
  personnes et de lieux cités dans les chan-
  sons de geste françaises et les oeuvres
  étrangères dérivées.
  L.S. Crist, 589:Oct88-961
Mojsisch, B., ed. Sprachphilosophie in Antike
  und Mittelalter.
  D. Perler, 687:Apr-Jun88-324
Mojtabai, A.G. Ordinary Time.
  M. Malone, 441:24Sep89-9
Molander, M. - see le comte de Creutz
Moldea, D.E. Interference.
  G. Eskenazi, 441:3Sep89-8
Molden, F. Die Feuer in der Nacht.
  R. Knight, 617(TLS):21-27Jul89-797
Mole, J. Passing Judgements.
  T. Eagleton, 617(TLS):24-30Nov89-1291
Moleta, V. Guittone cortese.
  F. Bruni, 379(MedR):Aug88-305
Moleta, V., ed. Patronage and Public in the
  Trecento.
  J. Usher, 382(MAE):1988/2-329
Molière. Tartuffe. (H. Stenzel, ed)
  W. Henning, 72:Band224Heft2-451
de Molina, T. - see under Tirso de Molina
Molinaro, M., C. McLuhan & W. Toye - see
  McLuhan, M.
Molinsky, S.J. & B. Bliss. ExpressWays 2.
  P.F. Whittaker, 399(MLJ):Winter88-468
Molitor, J.A.L. Portraits in Sechs Fursten-
  staaten Rajasthans vom 17. bis zum 20.
  Jahrhundert.
  M.C. Beach, 318(JAOS):Jul-Sep87-522
Mollat, M. The Poor in the Middle Ages.
  S.F. Roberts, 589:Oct88-966
  N. Saul, 382(MAE):1988/1-90
Mollica, A. Mots croisés pour les débutants.
  A.J. Salvas, 207(FR):Mar89-709
Mollier, J-Y. Lettres inédites d'Ernest Renan
  à ses éditeurs Michel et Calmann Lévy.
  L. Rétat, 535(RHL):Mar-Apr88-312
Mollo, A. Army Uniforms of World War I.
  A. Powell, 364:Feb87-87
Molloy-Olund, B. In Favor of Lightning.
  639(VQR):Spring88-64
von Molnár, G. Romantic Vision, Ethical Con-
  text.*
  G. Newman, 221(GQ):Fall88-580
Molnar, M. Body of Words.
  M. Carlson, 402(MLR):Apr89-536

Molnár, N. The Calques of Greek Origin in the Most Ancient Old Slavic Gospel Texts.
W. Fiedler, 682(ZPSK):Band41Heft1-125
von Moltke, H.J. Briefe an Freya 1939-1945. (B.R. von Oppen, ed)
G. Craig, 453(NYRB):2Feb89-10
K. von Klemperer, 617(TLS):10-16Feb89-143
Momaday, N.S. The Ancient Child.
E. Marston, 441:31Dec89-14
Momberger, M. Sonne und Punsch.
A. Hartmann, 680(ZDP):Band107Heft4-609
Momen, M. An Introduction to Shi'i Islam.
M. Bayat, 293(JASt):Aug88-574
Monaghan, D. The Novels of John le Carré.* Smiley's Circus.*
J.R. Cohn, 594:Fall88-323
Monahan, A.P. Consent, Coercion, and Limit.*
B.M.D., 185:Oct88-189
J.G. Rowe, 529(QQ):Autumn88-742
Monahan, P. Politics and the Constitution.
M. Hartney, 103:Feb89-61
Monbiot, G. Poisoned Arrows.
M. Woollacott, 617(TLS):30Jun-6Jul89-716
Mondrian, P. The New Art - The New Life.* (H. Holtzman & M.S. James, eds & trans)
R. Alley, 39:Sep88-211
P. Overy, 592:Vol201No1020-61
Monducci, E. & others. Lelio Orsi.
D. Ekserdjian, 90:Jul88-539
Monego, J.P. Maghrebian Literature in French.*
E. Sellin, 538(RAL):Fall88-389
de Mones, U.K. - see under Kühl de Mones, U.
Moneti, A. Conversazioni in italiano.
A.M. Jeannet, 276:Spring88-41
Monette, P. Borrowed Time.* Love Alone.
G. Kolovakos, 472:Vol15No1-331
Mongrédien, J. La Musique en France des Lumières au Romantisme (1789-1830).*
J. Gribenski, 537:Vol74No1-114
Mongrédien, J. & Y. Ferraton, eds. Actes du colloque international de musicologie sur Le Grand Motet français (1663-1792).
M. Seares, 410(M&L):Apr88-251
Monkman, K. - see Sterne, L.
Monod, S. "Martin Chuzzlewit."*
P. Preston, 447(N&Q):Dec88-545
Monod, S. - see Conrad, J.
Monod, S., with H. Bordenave & F. du Sorbier - see Dickens, C.
Monreal, D. Cellmates [together with] Dávila Flores, O. Qué, Cómo y Quándo.
A.C. Flores, 352(LATR):Spring89-125
Monro, J. 11 Montpelier Street.
B. Scott, 324:May89-386
Montadi, C.M. - see under Morell i Montadi, C.
Montag, A.V. Syntaktische Funktionen und Wortstellungsveränderung.
A. Lutz, 38:Band106Heft3/4-466
Montagu, J. Alessandro Algardi.*
O. Raggio, 90:Mar88-233
M.S. Weil, 54:Jun88-351
Montague, J. Selected Poems.
B. Howard, 271:Winter88-182
Montale, E. The Occasions.
639(VQR):Winter88-28
Montalenti, G. & P. Rossi, eds. Lazzaro Spallanzani e la biologia del Settecento.
G. Bremner, 83:Autumn88-236

Montanari, E. La sezione linguistica del "peri hermeneias" di Aristotele. (Vol 1)
D.M. Schenkeveld, 394:Vol41fasc1/2-165
Montanari, G.B. - see under Bermond Montanari, G.
Montandon, A. La Réception de Laurence Sterne en Allemagne.*
I.C. Ross, 83:Autumn88-231
Montaner, C.A. Trama.
S. Menton, 238:Dec88-845
Montaner, M.E. Guía para la lectura de "Cien años de soledad."
V. Soto, 711(RHM):Jun88-83
Monteath, P. & E. Nicolai. Zur Spanienkriegsliteratur.
M. Lentzen, 72:Band225Heft2-459
Montefiore, J. Feminism and Poetry.
D. Chisholm, 494:Vol8No3/4-737
T. Cosslett, 447(N&Q):Jun88-281
L. Sail, 565:Spring88-73
Montefusco, L.C. - see under Calboli Montefusco, L.
Monteith, M., ed. Women's Writing.*
M. Del Sapio, 402(MLR):Oct89-959
Montell, W.L. Killings.*
H. Willett, 292(JAF):Jan-Mar88-96
Montenegro Duque, A., J.M. Blázquez Martinez & J.M. Solan Sáinz. España Romana.
J. Clack, 124:May-Jun89-397
Montero, M.C.M. - see under Martín Montero, M.C.
Montes Huidobro, M. Persona.
F. Dauster, 36:Fall-Winter88-235
de Montfleury, A.J. Le Mary sans femme.* (E. Forman, ed)
M. Farrell, 475:Vol15No28-288
Montgomerie, W. From Time to Time.
R. Watson, 588(SSL):Vol23-254
Montgomery, K.C. Target: Prime Time.
M. Winn, 441:26Mar89-5
Montgomery, L.M. Anne...La Maison aux pignons verts.
E-M.K., 102(CanL):Winter87-290
Montgomery, M. Imperialist Japan.*
639(VQR):Summer88-95
Montgomery, M. An Introduction to Language and Society.
G. Philipsen, 355(LSoc):Dec88-612
Montgomery, M. Possum, and Other Receits for the Recovery of "Southern" Being.*
J.N. Gretlund, 392:Winter87/88-113
L.A. Lawson, 396(ModA):Summer88-255
Montgomery, M.B. & G. Bailey, eds. Language Variety in the South.*
J. Baugh, 35(AS):Fall88-265
Montgomery, M.E. Gilded Prostitution.
A.S. Grossman, 617(TLS):15-21Dec89-1395
Montgomery, M.R. Saying Goodbye.
C. McFadden, 441:4Jun89-7
Montgrédien, J. La Musique en France des lumières au romantism, 1789-1830.
J. Barzun, 309:Vol8No3/4-375
Montias, J.M. Vermeer and His Milieu.
J. Russell, 441:11Jun89-13
"The Montpellier Codex." (Vol 4) (S. Stakel & J.C. Relihan, trans)
H. van der Werf, 589:Oct88-1000
Montoya Martínez, J. - see de Berceo, G.
Montredon, J. Imparfait et compagnie.*
D.A. Kibbee, 399(MLJ):Winter88-471
Montserrat, C.D. - see under Duarte i Montserrat, C.

259

Montupet, J. The Lacemaker.
L. Belfer, 441:16Apr89-20
Moody, K. An Injury to All.
R. Cornuelle, 617(TLS):9-15Jun89-632
Moog, H. Die Wasserfrau.
J. Bauer, 196:Band29Heft1/2-218
Mooij, J.J.A. De Wereld der Waarden.
H. van Gorp, 204(FdL):Jun88-151
Moon, J.D., ed. Responsibility, Rights, and
Welfare.
R.K. Fullinwider, 103:Aug89-323
Moon, M. The Children's Book of Mary
(Belson) Elliott. John Harris's Books for
Youth 1801-1803.
C. Hurst, 78(BC):Summer88-281
Moon, P. The British Conquest and Dominion
of India.
P.J. Marshall, 617(TLS):8-14Sep89-978
Mooney, C.F. Public Virtue.
R. Harries, 185:Jan89-437
Mooney, M. Vico in the Tradition of Rhet-
oric.*
H. White, 173(ECS):Winter88/89-219
K. Zimmermann, 53(AGP):Band70Heft3-
332
Moonsammy, R.Z., D.S. Cohen & L.E. Williams,
eds. Pinelands Folklife.
A.K. Gillespie, 292(JAF):Jan-Mar88-111
R.B. St. George, 658:Winter88-265
Moor, M. Studien zum lesgische Verb.
H-J. Sasse, 361:Nov88-255
Moore, A. Opia.*
S. Rae, 364:Mar87-87
Moore, B. The Color of Blood.*
P. Saari, 42(AR):Spring88-271
Moore, E.W. The Fairs of Medieval England.
R.H. Bowers, 589:Apr88-443
Moore, F. Concepts and Practice of Architec-
tural Daylighting.*
H. Bryan, 505:Jan88-151
Moore, G. In Minor Keys.* (D.B. Eakin & H.E.
Gerber, eds)
R.H., 305(JIL):Jan88-60
Moore, G. George Moore on Parnassus. (H.E.
Gerber, with O.M. Brack, Jr., eds)
J. Kelly, 617(TLS):28Apr-4May89-451
Moore, G.E. The Early Essays.* (T. Regan,
ed)
T. Baldwin, 393(Mind):Jan88-129
Moore, J. The Left Coast of Paradise.*
C. Hitchens, 617(TLS):17-23Feb89-157
Moore, J. A Zeal for Responsibility.
D.C. Hine, 637(VS):Summer89-588
Moore, J., J. Tener & A. Steele, eds. The
Alice Munro Papers: First Accession.
H. Hoy, 102(CanL):Spring88-203
S.C. Spragge, 470:Vol26-192
Moore, J., J. Tener & A. Steele, eds. The
Joanna M. Glass Papers.
H. Hoy, 102(CanL):Spring88-203
S.C. Spragge, 470:Vol26-192
Moore, J.H. The Emergence of the Cotton
Kingdom in the Old Southwest.
639(VQR):Summer88-84
Moore, J.N. - see Elgar, E.
Moore, J.R., ed. Religion in Victorian Britain.
(Vol 3)
P. Butler, 617(TLS):4-10Aug89-852
Moore, K.D. Pardons.
A.M. Dershowitz, 441:16Jul89-7

Moore, M. The Complete Prose of Marianne
Moore.* (P.C. Willis, ed)
L. Bar-Yaacov, 577(SHR):Spring88-196
J. Barker, 4:Autumn88-63
S. Burris, 536(Rev):Vol10-113
R.B.D., 295(JML):Fall87/Winter88-356
Moore, M.B. & M.Z. Pease-Philippides. The
Athenian Agora. (Vol 23)
J. Boardman, 123:Vol38No1-177
Moore, S. The Whiteness of Bones.
J. Anderson, 441:26Mar89-5
R. Towers, 453(NYRB):27Apr89-50
Moore, T. The Style of Connectedness.*
J.M. Davis, 594:Winter88-436
D. Eddins, 536(Rev):Vol10-155
R. Merrill, 27(AL):Mar88-136
S. Moore, 532(RCF):Summer88-321
J.W. Slade, 395(MFS):Winter88-665
M. Winston, 268(IFR):Winter89-77
42(AR):Winter88-121
Moore, T.J. Heart Failure.
H.H. Hiatt, 441:24Sep89-15
Moore, W. Schrödinger.
C. Kilmister, 617(TLS):29Sep-5Oct89-
1059
Moore-Blunt, J. - see Plato
Moore-Gilbert, B.J. Kipling and "Oriental-
ism."*
Z.T. Sullivan, 402(MLR):Jan89-140
Moorehead, C. - see Stark, F.
Moorhead, F. Remember the Tarantella.
S. Hampton, 581:Mar88-55
Moorhouse, F. Forty-Seventeen.
A. Carter, 441:13Aug89-3
J. Mellors, 364:Feb/Mar89-136
Moorjani, A. Abysmal Games in the Novels of
Samuel Beckett.
L. Ben-Zvi, 299:No11&12-193
von Moos, S. L'Esprit Nouveau.
M. Spens, 592:Vol201No1019-62
Moosa, M. The Origins of Modern Arabic Fic-
tion.
M.M. Badawi, 294:Mar88-79
Mora, G. Walker Evans: Havana 1933.
A. Grundberg, 441:3Dec89-20
Mora, G. En torno al cuento.*
M.A. Salgado, 552(REH):May88-136
Morales, H.L. - see under López Morales, H.
Morales, J.L.O. - see under Onieva Morales,
J.L.
Morán, J.M.M. - see under Martín Morán, J.M.
Morani, G. & M. Tragedie e frammenti di Es-
chilo.
E. Flintoff, 123:Vol38No2-205
Moraux, P. Galien de Pergame.
J. Longrigg, 123:Vol38No1-149
Moravec, H. Mind Children.
B. Leithauser, 442(NY):9Jan89-84
M.M. Waldrop, 441:1Jan89-10
Morazzoni, M. Girl in a Turban.
S. Salisbury, 441:7May89-24
I. Thomson, 364:Jul88-109
Mordden, E. A Guide to Opera Recordings.
E. Forbes, 415:Sep88-462
Mordden, E. The Hollywood Studios.*
J.G. Dunne, 453(NYRB):18May89-28
Mordek, H., ed. Überlieferung und Geltung
normativer Texte des frühen und hohen
Mittelalters.
D.H. Miller, 589:Apr88-445
More, T. In Defense of Humanism. (D. Kin-
ney, ed)
A.L. Prescott, 551(RenQ):Autumn88-515

Morpurgo Davies, A. & Y. Duhoux, eds. Linear
B: A 1984 Survey.
　R. Schmitt, 260(IF):Band93-305
Morreall, J., ed. The Philosophy of Laughter
and Humor.*
　N. McAdoo, 89(BJA):Winter88-83
　G. Morin, 616:Vol10No1-57
Morrell, R.E. Early Kamakura Buddhism.
　M.H. Childs, 407(NM):Autumn88-368
　T.P. Kasulis, 293(JASt):Nov88-893
Morrice, K. When Truth is Known.
　B. Franks, 571(ScLJ):Spring88-34
　R. Watson, 588(SSL):Vol23-254
Morris, C. The Papal Monarchy.
　A. Murray, 617(TLS):15-21Sep89-1007
Morris, C.R. Iron Destinies, Lost Opportun-
ities.*
　639(VQR):Autumn88-131
Morris, G.H. Grandmother, Grandmother, Come
and See.
　J-A. Goodwin, 617(TLS):14-20Apr89-404
Morris, H. Last Things in Shakespeare.*
　K. Muir, 402(MLR):Oct89-924
Morris, I. Burial and Ancient Society.
　G. Cadogan, 617(TLS):13-19Jan89-45
Morris, I. Mr. Collins Considered.
　D. Birch, 175:Summer88-165
　P. Honan, 447(N&Q):Sep88-381
Morris, J. Hong Kong.*
　F. Ching, 441:29Jan89-35
　J. Haylock, 364:Oct/Nov88-133
Morris, J. Jane Morris to Wilfrid Scawen
Blunt.* (P. Faulkner, ed)
　G.A. Cevasco, 402(MLR):Apr89-449
　K. Flint, 447(N&Q):Sep88-392
　R.K.R. Thornton, 161(DUJ):Dec87-153
Morris, J. Pleasures of a Tangled Life.
　P. Levy, 441:12Nov89-16
　F. Partridge, 617(TLS):8-14Dec89-1370
Morris, M. The Waiting Room.
　B. Lott, 441:2Jul89-9
Morris, M.M. Vanished.*
　M. Brandham, 617(TLS):12-18May89-518
Morris, R. Richard Milhous Nixon.
　K. Starr, 441:12Nov89-1
Morris, R.J., ed. Class, Power, and Social
Structure in British Nineteenth-Century
Towns.
　J.H. Wiener, 635(VPR):Summer88-76
Morris, T.V., ed. The Concept of God.*
　M. Adam, 542:Oct-Dec88-504
Morris, T.V., ed. Philosophy and the Chris-
tian Faith.
　S. Grover, 617(TLS):19-25May89-534
Morris, W. The Collected Letters of William
Morris.* (Vol 2, Pts 1 & 2) (N. Kelvin, ed)
　G.B. Tennyson, 445(NCF):Sep88-276
Morris, W. Contre l'art d'élite.
　P. Somville, 542:Jan-Mar88-93
Morris, W. & M. Harper Dictionary of Contem-
porary Usage. (2nd ed)
　T. Du Bose, 35(AS):Winter88-364
Morris, W.F., Jr. Living Maya.*
　P. Malarcher, 139:Feb/Mar88-41
Morris-Suzuki, T. Beyond Computopia.
　J.A.A. Stockwin, 617(TLS):28Apr-
4May89-459
Morrison, B. Dark Glasses.
　B. O'Donoghue, 617(TLS):1-7Dec89-1336
Morrison, J. & R.K. From Camelot to Kent
State.*
　42(AR):Spring88-277
Morrison, J.J. & others - see Wing, D.

Morrison, J.S. & J.F. Coates. The Athenian
Trireme.*
　J.F. Lazenby, 303(JoHS):Vol108-250
　H. Williams, 124:Jan-Feb89-215
Morrison, K. Canters and Chronicles.
　K. Cushman, 299:No11&12-176
Morrison, K.F. "I Am You."
　B. Stock, 617(TLS):21-27Apr89-434
Morrison, M. White Rabbit.
　M. Massing, 453(NYRB):30Mar89-22
Morrison, T. Beloved.*
　D. Flower, 249(HudR):Spring88-211
Morrison, T. - see Mee, M.
Morrissette, B. Novel and Film.*
　B. Stoltzfus, 149(CLS):Vol25No1-91
Morrisson, C. & others. L'Or monnayé. (Vol
1)
　R. Bland, 313:Vol78-256
Morrow, A. Inside the Sanctuary.
　42(AR):Winter88-124
Morrow, B. - see Rexroth, K.
Morse, D. American Romanticism.
　C. Gerrard, 541(RES):Nov88-594
Morse, D.D. Women in Trollope's Palliser
Novels.
　N. Dean, 115:Summer88-330
　R. apRoberts, 637(VS):Spring89-440
Morse, D.E., ed. The Fantastic in World Lit-
erature and the Arts.
　D.M. Hassler, 561(SFS):Nov88-381
Morse, F. The Shakers and the World's
People.
　M. Heale, 617(TLS):10-16Mar89-261
Morse, P. Hokusai One Hundred Poets.
　P-L. Adams, 61:Oct89-116
Morse, R.E. Evocation of Virgil in Tolkien's
Art.
　K.J. Reckford, 121(CJ):Dec88-Jan89-174
Morse, R.M., ed. Haiti's Future.
　A.P. Maingot, 263(RIB):Vol38No4-536
Morson, G.S., ed. Bakhtin.*
　V.K. Beards, 295(JML):Fall87/Winter88-
252
Morson, G.S. Hidden in Plain View.*
　C. Lock, 627(UTQ):Summer88-542
　R. Silbajoris, 574(SEEJ):Winter88-651
Morson, G.S., ed. Literature and History.*
　T.D. Cohen, 141:Winter88-149
　D. Shepherd, 575(SEER):Apr88-270
von Morstein, P. On Understanding Works of
Art.
　S. Davies, 478(P&L):Apr88-142
Mort, G. A Halifax Cider Jar.
　J. May, 493:Summer88-54
"Morte Arthure."* (M. Hamel, ed)
　J. Finlayson, 589:Oct88-936
Mortensen, F.H. & P. Schmidt, eds. Profiler.
　S.C. Brantly, 563(SS):Summer88-421
Mortensen, K.P. Thomasines opprør.
　A.G. Michaelsen, 172(Edda):1988/2-188
Mortier, R. & H. Hasquin, eds. Etudes sur le
XVIIIe siècle. (Vol 13)
　D. Gembicki, 549(RLC):Jan-Mar88-97
Mortimer, A.K. La Clôture narrative.*
　C. Dickson, 207(FR):Oct88-155
Mortimer, G.L. Faulkner's Rhetoric of Loss.
　R.D. Parker, 402(MLR):Jan89-148
Mortimer, J. The Narrowing Stream.
　A. Arensberg, 441:15Oct89-37
Mortman, D. Rightfully Mine.
　L.S. Cohen, 441:13Aug89-16

Moylan, T. Demand the Impossible.*
   B. Garvey, 561(SFS):Jul88–244
   T.A. Shippey, 447(N&Q):Jun88–269
Moyle, N.K., M.B. Kelly & L.K. Wolynetz. God-
desses and their Offspring.
   L. Robinson, 662:Spring/Summer88–44
Moynahan, B. Claws of the Bear.
   D. Holloway, 441:6Aug89–20
   442(NY):4Sep89–107
Moynihan, M. – see Lewis, C.S. & G. Calabria
Moynihan, R. A Recent Imagining.
   A. Fairweather, 295(JML):Fall87/
   Winter88–253
Moyo, S.P.C., T.W.C. Sumaili & J.A. Moody, eds.
Oral Traditions in Southern Africa.
   M. Kasonde, 538(RAL):Fall88–431
Mozart, W.A. Correspondance. (G. Geffray, ed)
   J. Gribenski, 537:Vol74No1–110
Możejko, E., with B. Briker & P. Dalgård, eds.
Vasiliy Pavlovich Aksenov.*
   S. McLaughlin, 550(RusR):Oct88–466
   R. Porter, 575(SEER):Jul88–478
   G.N. Slobin, 574(SEEJ):Spring88–145
Mozet, N. La ville de province dans l'oeuvre
de Balzac.
   G. Jacques, 356(LR):Feb–May88–133
Mozingo, H.N. Shrubs of the Great Basin.
   T.J. Lyon, 649(WAL):Aug88–183
Mphahlele, E. Poetry and Humanism.
   N. Masilela, 538(RAL):Spring88–117
Mphahlele, E. Renewal Time.
   H.W. French, 441:30Apr89–38
   M. Hope, 617(TLS):16–22Jun89–670
Mphahlele, E. & M. Lotter. Effective English.
   S. Kroma, 538(RAL):Fall88–418
Mral, B. Poetiska bidrag i arbetarpress 1882–
1900.
   R. McKnight, 563(SS):Summer88–412
"Mūasir azerbajdžan dili, II džild: mor-
fologija."
   G.F. Meier, 682(ZPSK):Band41Heft5–674
Mück, H–D. Untersuchungen zur Überliefe-
rung und Rezeption spätmittelalterlicher
Lieder und Spruchgedichte im 15. und 16.
Jahrhundert.
   F. Delbono, 684(ZDA):Band117Heft2–87
Mück, H–D. – see Oswald von Wolkenstein
Mückenhausen, G. Wissenschaftstheorie und
Kulturprogressismus.
   A. Stanguennec, 542:Jul–Sep88–367
Mudge, B.K. Sara Coleridge, a Victorian
Daughter.
   B. Fields, 441:8Oct89–42
   S. Raitt, 617(TLS):1–7Dec89–1341
Mudimbe, V.Y. Before the Birth of the Moon.
   R. McKnight, 441:30Apr89–43
Muecke, F. Plautus "Menaechmi."
   P. Jeffreys-Powell, 123:Vol38No1–151
Mueller, I.J. – see Wyclif, J.
Mueller, J. Retreat From Doomsday.
   M. Howard, 441:30Apr89–14
Mueller, J.M. The Native Tongue and the
Word.*
   B. Vickers, 191(ELN):Dec88–65
Mueller, W.H. Eros und Sexus im Urteil der
Philosophen.
   P. Trotignon, 542:Apr–Jun88–221
Mueller-Goldingen, C. Untersuchungen zu
den "Phönissen" des Euripides.
   E. Craik, 123:Vol38No1–11

Mueller-Vollmer, K., ed. The Hermeneutics
Reader.*
   J.M. Peck, 221(GQ):Spring87–271
   R. Zimmermann, 133:Band21Heft2/3–185
Muendel, R. George Meredith.
   A. St. George, 447(N&Q):Jun88–256
Muenzer, C.S. Figures of Identity.*
   C.E. Schweitzer, 400(MLN):Apr88–681
Mugdan, J. Jan Baudouin de Courtenay
(1845–1929).*
   G. Rössler, 685(ZDL):2/1987–239
Mugdan, J. – see Baudouin de Courtenay, J.
Mugerauer, R. Heidegger's Language and
Thinking.
   M. Pomedli, 103:May89–188
Mugnier, A. Journal de l'Abbé Mugnier
(1879–1939). (M. Billot, G. de Diesbach &
J. d'Hendecourt, eds)
   P. McDonald, 207(FR):Feb89–577
Mühlenberg, H.M. Die Korrespondenz Heinrich
Melchior Mühlenbergs. (Vols 1 & 2) (K.
Aland, ed)
   A.G. Roeber, 656(WMQ):Jan88–191
Mühlhäusler, P. Pidgin & Creole Linguistics.
   J. Aitchison, 353:Vol26No2–303
   D.K. Nylander, 297(JL):Sep88–564
   P.A.M. Seuren, 603:Vol12No2–504
Mui, H–C. & L.H. Shops and Shopkeeping in
Eighteenth-Century England.
   P. Earle, 617(TLS):4–10Aug89–853
Muir, E. Edwin Muir: Selected Prose. (G.M.
Brown, ed)
   H. Hewitt, 571(ScLJ):Winter88–13
   P. Lewis, 565:Spring88–35
Muir, E. The Truth of Imagination. (P.H.
Butter, ed)
   M. Baron, 175:Autumn88–266
   A. Noble, 617(TLS):3–9Mar89–218
Muir, K., ed. Interpretations of Shakespeare.*
   E.A.J. Honigmann, 677(YES):Vol19–314
Muir, W. Imagined Corners.
   A. Smith, 571(ScLJ):Spring88–52
Mujanto, G. The Concept of Power in Javan-
ese Culture.
   M.R. Woodward, 293(JASt):Nov88–943
Mujica, B. Iberian Pastoral Characters.*
   A.J. Cárdenas, 238:Sep88–543
   F.P. Casa, 552(REH):May88–124
   W. Ferguson, 240(HR):Winter88–104
Mukand, J., ed. Sutured Words.
   27(AL):Dec88–698
Mukařovský, J. Schriften zur Ästhetik,
Kunsttheorie und Poetik. (H. Siegel, ed &
trans)
   W.F. Schwarz, 52:Band23Heft1–94
Mukherjee, A. The Gospel of Wealth in the
American Novel.
   R.W. Dowell, 27(AL):May88–303
   P. Lapp, 150(DR):Fall88–369
   S. de Paul, 106:Summer88–253
Mukherjee, B. Jasmine.
   M. Gorra, 441:10Sep89–9
   442(NY):2Oct89–119
Mukherjee, B. The Middleman and Other
Stories.*
   S. Chew, 617(TLS):21–27Jul89–804
Mukherjee, M. Realism and Reality.*
   S. Suleri, 402(MLR):Jul89–728
Mukherjee, R. Awadh in Revolt 1857–1858.
   R.J. Young, 318(JAOS):Jan–Mar87–202
Mulch, R. & R., comps. Südhessisches Wörter-
buch. (Vol 4, Pts 13–16)
   E. Wagner, 685(ZDL):2/1988–239

Muldoon, P., ed. The Faber Book of Contemporary Irish Poetry.*
    T. Eagleton, 565:Winter87/88–65
Muldoon, P. Meeting the British.*
    N. MacMonagle, 272(IUR):Autumn88–343
Muldoon, P. Selected Poems, 1968–1986.*
    S. Birkerts, 473(PR):Vol55No3–484
Mulford, C. – see Leacock, J.
Mulisch, H. Last Call.*
    P–L. Adams, 61:Apr89–100
    L. Bamber, 441:18Jun89–24
    J. Mellors, 364:Dec87/Jan88–136
    J. Updike, 442(NY):24Jul89–87
Mulkerns, V. A Friend of Don Juan.
    D. Durrant, 364:Dec88/Jan89–136
Mullaly, E. Desperate Stages.
    M.E. Smith, 627(UTQ):Fall88–150
Mullaney, S. The Place of the Stage.
    K. Newman, 570(SQ):Winter88–501
Mullen, R. & J. Munson. Victoria.
    R. Tobias, 637(VS):Winter89–292
Müller, C.W. Erysichthon.
    N. Hopkinson, 123:Vol38No2–401
Müller, D.K., F. Ringer & B. Simon, eds. The Rise of the Modern Educational System.
    G. Hogg, 637(VS):Summer89–592
Müller, E. Der Nationalreichtum.
    P. Träger, 654(WB):11/1988–1929
Müller, E. – see Zhang Xinxin & Sang Ye
Müller, H. Friedrich Wolf – Weltbürger aus Neuwied.
    K. Kändler, 654(WB):12/1988–2092
Müller, H–H. Der Krieg und die Schriftsteller.
    H.M. Klein, 301(JEGP):Oct88–609
    R.C. Reimer, 406:Winter88–522
    A. Solbach, 680(ZDP):Band107Heft4–628
Muller, J.M. Rubens.
    J. Russell, 441:3Dec89–9
Muller, J.W., ed. The Revival of Constitutionalism.
    W. Brock, 617(TLS):8–14Sep89–979
Müller, K. Schlossgeschichten.*
    W.L. Zwiebel, 221(GQ):Spring88–315
Müller, K–D., ed. Bertolt Brecht.
    K–H. Schoeps, 462(OL):Vol43No1–78
Müller, K.E. – see Benya, R.
Müller, M. Die "Deutsche Dichter–Gedächtnis–Stiftung."
    T. Salumets, 406:Summer88–232
Muller, M. The Shape of Dread.
    M. Stasio, 441:24Dec89–23
Muller, M. There's Something in a Sunday.
    M. Stasio, 441:12Mar89–24
Müller, P. Transzendentale Kritik und moralische Teleologie.
    W. Steinbeck, 342:Band79Heft1–107
Müller, P.E. Goya's Black Paintings.
    I. Mateo Gómez, 48:Apr–Jun88–191
Müller, P.I. & C. Pfaff. Thesaurus Fabariensis.*
    G. Kornbluth, 589:Apr88–446
Müller, U., ed. "Minne is ein swaerez spiel."*
    A. Gier, 72:Band224Heft2–368
Müller, U. & others, eds. Richard Wagner 1883–1983.
    H.R. Vaget, 400(MLN):Apr88–689
Müller, U. & P. Wapnewski, ed. Richard Wagner Handbuch.
    T.R. Nadar, 406:Fall88–386
Müller–Jahncke, W–D. Astrologisch–magische Theorie und Praxis in der Heilkunde der frühen Neuzeit.
    P.R. Blum, 687:Oct–Dec88–725

Müller–Schmid, P.P. Emanzipatorische Sozialphilosophie und pluralistisches Ordnungsdenken.
    C. Schefold, 489(PJGG):Band95Heft2–376
Müller–Schmid, P.P. Der rationale Weg zur politischen Ethik.
    C. Schefold, 489(PJGG):Band95Heft2–376
Müller–Schwefe, G. Corpus Hamleticum.
    D. Daphinoff, 156(ShJW):Jahrbuch1988–281
    F. Stock, 52:Band23Heft1–102
Müller–Seidel, W. Die Deportation des Menschen.*
    R.V. Gross, 406:Winter88–488
    E. Schlant, 221(GQ):Summer88–472
Mullin, D., comp. Victorian Plays.
    D. Barrett, 610:Autumn88–286
Mullins, E. The Master Painter.
    S.S. Wells, 441:23Jul89–18
Munanga, K. Negritude.
    W.F. Feuser, 538(RAL):Winter88–583
Munch, M–M., ed. Recherches sur l'histoire de la poétique.
    D. Millet–Gérard, 549(RLC):Jul–Sep88–407
Munenori, Y. The Sword and the Mind.
    J. Kirkup, 617(TLS):25–31Aug89–925
Mungello, D.E. Curious Land.*
    R.P. Kramers, 318(JAOS):Apr–Jun87–348
Mungoshi, C. The Setting Sun and the Rolling World.*
    S.G. Freedman, 441:24Sep89–23
Munich, A.A. – see "Browning Institute Studies"
Munich, A.A. & J. Maynard – see "Browning Institute Studies"
Munif, A. Cities of Salt.*
    I. Hill, 617(TLS):3–9Mar89–226
Munitiz, J.A. – see Nicephorus Blemmydes
Muñoz Delgado, V. – see de Oria, J.
Munro, A. The Progress of Love.*
    D. Durrant, 364:Apr–May87–158
    R. Thacker, 102(CanL):Winter87–239
Munro, A., ed. Spectacular Helmets of Japan, 16th–19th Century.
    S. Markbreiter, 60:Sep–Oct87–140
Munro, J. The Trees Just Moved Into a Season of Other Shapes.
    S.R. Dorscht, 102(CanL):Winter87–257
Munro, J.S. Mademoiselle de Scudéry and the Carte de Tendre.
    J–D. Biard, 402(MLR):Oct89–976
Munsch, R. Le Dodo.
    A. Kertzer, 102(CanL):Winter87–165
Munson, G. The Awakening Twenties.*
    E.R. Hagemann, 534(RALS):Vol16No1&2–157
    D. Kleine, 396(ModA):Summer89–263
Münster, A. Pariser philosophisches Journal.
    P. Trotignon, 542:Jul–Sep88–368
Munter, R. A Dictionary of the Print Trade in Ireland 1550–1775.
    M. Pollard, 617(TLS):31Mar–6Apr89–346
Munz, P. Our Knowledge of the Growth of Knowledge.
    H.T. Wilson, 488:Dec88–577
Münz, W. – see Tieck, L.
Murakami, H. A Wild Sheep Chase.
    P–L. Adams, 61:Dec89–127
    A. Arensberg, 441:3Dec89–82
    B. Leithauser, 442(NY):4Dec89–182
Murari, T.N. The Imperial Agent.
    M. Buck, 441:6Aug89–18

Muraro, M.T. & F. Rossi, eds. Galuppiana 1985.
    M. Hunter, 410(M&L):Apr88-257
Murdoch, D. Niels Bohr's Philosophy of Physics.
    R.H. Schlagel, 543:Sep88-140
Murdoch, I. Acastos.
    R.K., 185:Jan89-457
Murdoch, I. The Book and the Brotherhood.*
    A. Bloom, 249(HudR):Autumn88-543
    J. Mellors, 364:Dec87/Jan88-136
    42(AR):Spring88-272
    639(VQR):Summer88-91
Murdoch, I. The Message to the Planet.
    C. Sinclair, 617(TLS):20-26Oct89-1149
Murdoch, I. Sartre.
    J. Parini, 249(HudR):Summer88-363
    42(AR):Winter88-119
de Muret, M-A. Commentaires au premier livre des "Amours" de Ronsard.* (J. Chomarat, M-M. Fragonard & G. Mathieu-Castellani, eds)
    F.C. Cornfield, 207(FR):Mar89-680
Murfin, R.C. "Sons and Lovers."*
    D.R. Schwarz, 395(MFS):Summer88-279
Murken-Altrogge, C. Paula Modersohn-Becker.
    E.C. Oppler, 54:Dec88-709
Murnaghan, S. Disguise and Recognition in the "Odyssey."*
    R.D. Griffith, 529(QQ):Winter88-899
    V. Pedrick, 124:May-Jun89-397
    R.B. Rutherford, 123:Vol38No2-392
Murnane, G. Inland.
    H. Harris, 617(TLS):9-15Jun89-634
    J. Tittensor, 381:Summer88-751
Muro, A. The Collected Stories of Amado Muro.
    J. Byrne, 532(RCF):Summer88-328
Murphy, B. American Realism and American Drama, 1880-1940.*
    D.L. Cook, 27(AL):Mar88-124
    J.W. Crowley, 432(NEQ):Dec88-624
    L. Kerjan, 189(EA):Oct-Dec88-496
    J.D. Mason, 615(TJ):Dec88-571
    L.T. Oggel, 26(ALR):Spring88-89
Murphy, D. Cameroon with Egbert.
    C. Moorehead, 617(TLS):29Sep-5Oct89-1073
Murphy, D. Imagination and Religion in Anglo-Irish Literature 1930-1980.
    J. Devitt, 235:Summer88-149
Murphy, H. Murder Keeps a Secret.
    R. Herbert, 441:27Aug89-16
Murphy, J.W. Postmodern Social Analysis and Criticism.
    A. Miles, 103:Dec89-490
Murphy, M. Blanco White.
    J. Lynch, 617(TLS):13-19Oct89-1120
Murphy, P. The City, Not Long After.
    G. Jonas, 441:21May89-26
Murphy, R. New Selected Poems. The Mirror Wall.
    S. O'Brien, 617(TLS):4-10Aug89-850
Murphy, R. Realism and Tinsel.
    J.K.L. Walker, 617(TLS):1-7Sep89-939
Murray, C. & C.B. Cox. Apollo.
    M. Collins, 441:16Jul89-26
    D. King-Hele, 617(TLS):29Sep-5Oct89-1071
Murray, D., ed. Literary Theory and Poetry.
    T. Eagleton, 617(TLS):24-30Nov89-1291

Murray, D.H. Pirates of the South China Coast, 1790-1810.
    E.S. Rawski, 293(JASt):Aug88-611
Murray, D.M. Write to Learn. (2nd ed)
    J. Clifford, 126(CCC):Feb88-99
Murray, I. - see Mitchison, N.
Murray, J. Pleasure.
    D. Durrant, 364:Mar88-109
    P. Lewis, 565:Spring88-35
Murray, J. Samarkand. Kin.
    P. Lewis, 565:Spring88-35
Murray, L.A. The Daylight Moon.
    S. Birkerts, 472:Vol15No2-31
    W. Scammell, 364:Aug/Sep88-108
    P. Scupham, 493:Spring88-8
    H. Vendler, 453(NYRB):17Aug89-26
Murray, N.D. - see Flanner, J.
Murray, P. Marx's Theory of Scientific Knowledge.
    F.R. Cristi, 103:Feb89-63
Murray, R. Adam and Eve in Middle Age.
    J. Donlan, 102(CanL):Spring88-153
Murray, R. The Indigo Dress.
    M. Jenkins, 526:Summer88-84
    D. McGifford, 102(CanL):Spring88-170
Murray, S. Beauvais Cathedral.
    P. Crossley, 617(TLS):8-14Sep89-982
Murray, S. Building Troyes Cathedral.*
    N. Coldstream, 90:May88-374
Murray, T. Theatrical Legitimation.*
    J. Goldberg, 141:Winter88-124
    A.K. Pask, 400(MLN):Dec88-1191
Murray, W. The King of the Nightcap.
    M. Stasio, 441:13Aug89-14
    442(NY):25Sep89-122
Musacchio, E. & G. Pellegrini - see Mazzoni, J.
Musaeus. Hero et Leander. (E. Livrea, ed)
    J.M. Bremer, 394:Vol41fasc1/2-187
Muşat, M. & I. Ardeleanu. România după Marea Unire. (Pt 1)
    D. Deletant, 575(SEER):Apr88-301
Muscatine, C. The Old French Fabliaux.*
    G.S. Burgess, 382(MAE):1988/2-325
    W. Calin, 131(CL):Spring88-179
    P. Nykrog, 545(RPh):Feb89-285
    R. Pensom, 208(FS):Jan88-70
    M.J. Schenck, 141:Fall88-519
    J. Simons, 366:Spring88-116
    E.B. Vitz, 589:Jan88-199
    H.F. Williams, 345(KRQ):May88-232
Muscettola, S.A., A. Balasco & D. Gianpaola - see under Adamo Muscettola, S., A. Balasco & D. Gianpaola
Musgrave, M., ed. Brahms 2.*
    J. Dunsby, 410(M&L):Apr88-284
    J.H., 412:Feb88-78
Musgrave, P.W. From Brown to Bunter.*
    T. Wright, 161(DUJ):Dec87-156
Musgrave, S. Cocktails at the Mausoleum.*
    R. Bevis, 102(CanL):Winter87-186
Muske, C. Applause.
    W. Koestenbaum, 441:24Sep89-50
Muske-Dukes, C. Dear Digby.
    S. McCauley, 441:16Apr89-13
    442(NY):19Jun89-99
Musseleck, K-H. Untersuchungen zur Sprache katholischer Bibelübersetzungen der Reformationszeit.
    F. Simmler, 685(ZDL):1/1988-89
Musselwhite, D.E. Partings Welded Together.*
    G.A. Hudson, 594:Winter88-437

de Musset, A. Correspondance d'Alfred de
Musset.* (Vol 1) (M. Cordroc'h, R. Pierrot &
L. Chotard, eds)
S. Jeune, 535(RHL):Jan–Feb88–132
de Musset, A. On ne badine pas avec l'amour.
A. Vasak, 450(NRF):Jun88–91
Mustacchi, M.M. & P.J. Archambault – see
Helisenne de Crenne
Musto, D.F. The American Disease.
M. Massing, 453(NYRB):30Mar89–22
Musto, M. Manhattan on the Rocks.
W.J. Harding, 441:8Oct89–24
Musto, R.G. The Catholic Peace Tradition.
C.A.J. Coady, 185:Jan89–446
Musto, R.G. – see Gilles, P.
Musto, R.G. – see Petrarch
Muthmann, G. Rückläufiges deutsches Wör-
terbuch.
R. Raffelsiefen, 350:Dec89–905
"Al–Muwajaha." (Bk 3)
N. Rejwan, 390:Feb/Mar88–52
Muysken, P. & H. van Riemsdijk. Features
and Projections.*
R.D. Borsley, 297(JL):Mar88–259
Muysken, P. & N. Smith, eds. Substrata
Versus Universals in Creole Genesis.
J. Aitchison, 353:Vol26No5–895
Muzerelle, D. Des Termes français relatifs
aux manuscrits.
R. McKitterick, 78(BC):Summer88–278
Muzerelle, D. Vocabulaire codicologique.*
L. Light, 589:Oct88–969
Muzzolini, A. L'art Rupestre Prehistorique
des Massifs Centraux Sahariens.
R.J. McIntosh, 2(AfrA):May88–80
Mycoff, D.A., ed. A Critical Edition of the
Legend of Mary Magdalena from Caxton's
"Golden Legende" of 1483.*
R. Hamer, 382(MAE):1988/1–123
Myer, V.G., ed. Samuel Richardson.*
L. Fletcher, 594:Spring88–111
I. Haywood, 447(N&Q):Mar88–96
Myers, A., ed & trans. An Age Ago.
H. Gifford, 617(TLS):14–20Apr89–390
Myers, G.E. William James.*
M. Lebowitz, 344:Spring89–154
M. Migotti, 518:Apr88–65
J.J. Stuhr, 478(P&L):Oct88–305
L. Willson, 569(SR):Summer88–482
Myers, J. & M. Sims, eds. The Longman Dic-
tionary of Poetic Terms.
G. Ewart, 617(TLS):21–27Jul89–807
Myers, L.T. Stories From Latin America.
C. Baker, 399(MLJ):Summer88–224
Myers, R. & M. Harris, eds. Economics of the
British Booktrade 1605–1939.* Bibliophily.
D. Pearson, 83:Autumn88–212
Myers, R. & M. Harris, eds. Pioneers in Bibli-
ography.
R.C. Alston, 617(TLS):31Mar–6Apr89–346
Myers, R.J., ed. International Ethics in the
Nuclear Age.
S.G., 185:Apr89–684
Myers, T., K. Brown & B. McGonigle, eds. Rea-
soning & Discourse Processes.*
F. Nuessel, 307:Nov88–232
Myers, W. Milton and Free Will.*
S. Archer, 568(SCN):Spring–Summer88–8
P. Barry, 175:Spring88–74
T.N. Corns, 447(N&Q):Dec88–535
G.R. Evans, 541(RES):Nov88–604
T. Healy, 402(MLR):Jul89–717

Myers, W., ed. Restoration and Revolution.*
N.C. Jaffe, 677(YES):Vol19–325
Myerscough, J. Facts about the Arts 2.
A. Cameron, 610:Spring88–70
Myerson, J. Emily Dickinson.
W.J. Buckingham, 534(RALS):Vol16
No1&2–127
de Mylius, J. & others, eds. Nordica. (Vol 3)
B.D. Eddy, 563(SS):Summer88–427
Mylius, K., ed & trans. Gautama Buddha.
L. Hurvitz, 293(JASt):Aug88–684
Mylius, K. Geschichte der Literatur im alten
Indien.
A. Bharati, 293(JASt):May88–405
Myrivilis, S. Life in the Tomb.
J. Taylor, 268(IFR):Winter89–75

Nabb, M. The Marshal and the Madwoman.*
M. Stasio, 441:22Jan89–30
Nabe, M–E. L'Ame noire de Billie Holiday.
A.J.M.P., 91:Spring88–114
Nabholtz, J.R. "My Reader My Fellow–
Labourer."*
P. Marshall, 677(YES):Vol19–330
J. North, 447(N&Q):Mar88–126
Nabokov, P. Architecture of Acoma Pueblo.
J.B. Wolford, 292(JAF):Jan–Mar88–85
Nabokov, V. The Enchanter.*
P.J. Thibault, 529(QQ):Winter88–902
Nabokov, V. Vladimir Nabokov: Selected Let-
ters, 1940–1977. (D. Nabokov & M.J. Bruc-
coli, eds)
V. Erofeyev, 441:1Oct89–16
442(NY):13Nov89–147
Nachtwey, J. Deeds of War.
M.W. Browne, 441:5Nov89–24
Nadel, A. Invisible Criticism.
K. Byerman, 395(MFS):Winter88–634
J.D. Kalb, 115:Fall88–430
Nadler, S.M. Arnauld and the Cartesian Phil-
osophy of Ideas.
S. James, 617(TLS):29Sep–5Oct89–1069
Naeve, M.M. John Lewis Krimmel.
W.T. Oedel, 658:Winter88–273
Nagai Michio & M. Urrutia, eds. Meiji Ishin.
S.D. Brown, 293(JASt):Feb88–153
Nagarajan, S. & S. Viswanathan. Shakespeare
in India.*
K. Tetzeli von Rosador, 156(ShJW):
Jahrbuch1988–306
Nagasawa, K. Das Ich im Deutschen Idealis-
mus und das Selbst im Zen–Buddhismus.
A.K. Soller, 489(PJGG):Band95Heft2–423
Nagel, B. Das Reimproblem in der deutschen
Dichtung.*
N. Gabriel, 680(ZDP):Band106Heft4–637
E.R. Haymes, 406:Spring88–120
U. Rainer, 400(MLN):Apr88–672
Nagel, J., ed. Ernest Hemingway.*
E. Pifer, 677(YES):Vol19–351
Nagel, J.H. Participation.
P.A. Weiss, 185:Jan89–441
Nagel, P.C. The Adams Women.
M.B. Norton, 432(NEQ):Dec88–620
Nagel, T. The View from Nowhere.*
M. Adam, 542:Apr–Jun88–221
J. Dancy, 518:Jan88–1
E.F. Mooney, 262:Jun88–223
J.A. Schuler, 258:Jun88–207
Nagel, T. What Does It All Mean?
E. Craig, 617(TLS):22–28Sep89–1034
483:Jul88–414

Nägele, R. Reading After Freud.
 S.L. Gilman, 400(MLN):Dec88-1193
 R.C. Holub, 406:Fall88-364
Nägele, R. Text, Geschichte und Subjektivi-
 tät in Hölderlins Dichtung.*
 P-A. Alt, 224(GRM):Band38Heft1/2-217
 E.E. George, 406:Fall88-394
 A.A. Kuzniar, 221(GQ):Winter87-121
Nagle, J. The Nagle Journal.* (J.C. Dann, ed)
 F. McLynn, 617(TLS):1-7Sep89-949
 R.B. Smith, 441:26Feb89-35
Nagle, R.J. American Conservatism.
 R.E. Tyrrell, Jr., 441:3Dec89-45
Naharro, B.D. - see under de Torres Naharro,
 B.
Naifeh, S. & G.W. Smith. The Mormon Mur-
 ders.*
 M. Ruthven, 617(TLS):9-15Jun89-629
Naipaul, V.S. The Enigma of Arrival.
 C. Hope, 364:Mar87-91
Naipaul, V.S. A Turn in the South.
 G.M. Fredrickson, 617(TLS):5-11May89-
 477
 N. Lemann, 61:Mar89-89
 R. Shattuck, 453(NYRB):30Mar89-3
 C.V. Woodward, 441:5Feb89-7
Naïr, S. Machiavel et Marx.
 J-F. Duvernoy, 192(EP):Oct-Dec88-563
Nairn, T. The Enchanted Glass.*
 R. Chesshyre, 441:7May89-31
 P. Jenkins, 453(NYRB):12Oct89-46
Nairne, S. State of the Art.
 H. James, 89(BJA):Winter88-93
Najita, T. Visions of Virtue in Tokugawa
 Japan.*
 R. Rubinger, 407(MN):Winter88-483
Nakaji, Y. Combat spirituel ou immense déri-
 sion?
 K. Dillman, 446(NCFS):Spring-Summer89-
 420
Nakamura, H. A Comparative History of
 Ideas. (2nd ed)
 F.E. Reynolds, 293(JASt):May88-329
Nakhimovsky, A.D. & R.L. Leed. Advanced
 Russian. (2nd ed)
 M.I. Levin, 558(RLJ):Winter-Spring-
 Fall88-344
 N. Loseff, 574(SEEJ):Fall88-495
Nam, J-H. America's Commitment to South
 Korea.
 B.C. Koh, 293(JASt):Feb88-158
Namjoshi, S. & G. Hanscombe. Flesh and
 Paper.
 L. York, 102(CanL):Spring88-185
Nancy, J-L. L'oubli de la philosophie.
 A.M. Hjort, 154:Summer88-367
Nannestad, E. Jump.
 D. McDuff, 565:Spring88-64
Nantell, J. Rafael Alberti's Poetry of the
 Thirties.
 S.J. Fajardo, 238:May88-299
 P. McDermott, 345(KRQ):Nov88-498
Napier, D. Masks, Transformation and Para-
 dox.
 J.R. Rayfield, 488:Dec88-569
Napier, E.R. The Failure of Gothic.*
 B. Roth, 447(N&Q):Jun88-244
 J. Wilt, 402(MLR):Jul89-720
Naquin, S. & E.S. Rawski. Chinese Society in
 the Eighteenth Century.
 W.S. Atwell, 293(JASt):Nov88-867

Narboni, J. & N. Simsolo. Il était une fois ...
 Samuel Fuller.
 T. Milne, 707:Summer88-215
Nardin, J. He Knew She Was Right.
 J. Bayley, 453(NYRB):17Aug89-6
Nardocchio, E.F. Theatre and Politics in
 Modern Québec.*
 L.E. Doucette, 627(UTQ):Fall87-186
 J. Moss, 102(CanL):Winter87-175
Narens, L. Abstract Measurement Theory.
 H.E. Kyburg, Jr., 606:Jul88-179
Nash, M. Skulls Are Forever.
 G. Gessert, 448:Vol26No2-124
Nash, P. Outline.
 R. Cardinal, 617(TLS):31Mar-6Apr89-336
Nash, R. Psalms from the Suburbs.
 B. Pell, 102(CanL):Autumn88-171
Nash, R.F. The Rights of Nature.
 E.C. Hargrove, 103:Nov89-455
 P. Shabecoff, 441:9Apr89-26
Nasio, J-D. Les yeux de Laure.
 A. Reix, 542:Jan-Mar88-83
Nasrallah, E. Flight Against Time.*
 A.C. Morrell, 198:Spring88-103
 C. Somerville, 102(CanL):Summer88-144
Natanson, M. Anonymity.*
 B. Baran, 543:Sep88-154
 D.K., 185:Oct88-200
Naterop, B.J. & R. Revell. Telephoning in
 English.
 J.M. Fayer, 399(MLJ):Summer88-229
Nath, P., ed. Fresh Reflections on Samuel
 Johnson.
 J.F. Woodruff, 627(UTQ):Spring89-419
Nathan, A.J. Chinese Democracy.
 W. Wei, 318(JAOS):Oct-Dec87-834
Nathan, M. Anthologie du roman populaire,
 1836-1918.*
 P. Maurus, 535(RHL):Jan-Feb88-142
Nathanson, R.M. A Dirty Distant War.
 639(VQR):Winter88-20
Nathanson, S. The Ideal of Rationality.*
 G. Weiler, 488:Sep88-415
Natoli, J., ed. Tracing Literary Theory.
 W.E. Cain, 478(P&L):Oct88-319
 S. Scobie, 376:Mar88-101
Natsuki, S. Innocent Journey.
 M. Stasio, 441:14May89-30
Nattiez, J-J. Musicologie générale et sémi-
 ologie.
 A. Whittall, 410(M&L):Apr88-294
Naudé, G. Lettres de Naudé à Grémonville.
 (K.W. & P.J. Wolfe, eds)
 J.L. Pallister, 568(SCN):Spring-
 Summer88-21
Naughton, J. Colloquial Czech.
 L.A. Janda, 399(MLJ):Spring88-81
 D. Short, 575(SEER):Oct88-631
Naumann, B. Grammatik der deutschen
 Sprache zwischen 1781 und 1856. (W.
 Binder & others, eds)
 K-Å. Forsgren, 597(SN):Vol60No2-273
 G. Schmidt, 682(ZPSK):Band41Heft4-534
Naumann, H. Familiennamenbuch.
 W.F.H. Nicolaisen, 424:Sep-Dec88-239
Naumoff, L. The Night of the Weeping
 Women.*
 R. Kaveney, 617(TLS):24Feb-2Mar89-191
Nava, M., ed. Finale.
 M. Stasio, 441:10Dec89-41
Navajas, G. Mímesis y cultura en la ficción.*
 C. Alborg, 552(REH):Jan88-148
 B.J. McGuirk, 402(MLR):Apr89-414

Navarre, Y. The Little Rogue in Our Flesh.
  A. Mars-Jones, 617(TLS):22-28Dec89-
  1422
Navarre, Y. Romans, un roman.
  T. Spear, 207(FR):Apr89-904
Navarri, R. André Breton: "Nadja."
  R. Cardinal, 208(FS):Jan88-108
  P. Powrie, 208(FS):Apr88-232
Naveh, J. & S. Shaked. Amulets and Magic
  Bowls.
  C.H. Gordon, 318(JAOS):Jan-Mar87-133
Naversen, K. West Coast Victorians.
  M.J. Crosbie, 47:Jul88-45
Naves, M.D.B. - see under Bobes Naves, M.D.
Nay, C. Les Sept Mitterand ou les métamor-
  phoses d'un septennat.
  H.B. Sutton, 207(FR):Apr89-934
Nayer, A. & S. Capiau. Le droit social et fis-
  cal des artistes.
  P. Chesnais, 537:Vol74No2-246
Naylor, C.D. Private Practice, Public Pay-
  ment.
  B. Burk, 529(QQ):Winter88-958
Naylor, G. Mama Day.*
  42(AR):Summer88-401
Naylor, T.H. The Gorbachev Strategy.
  L. Gruliow, 42(AR):Summer88-383
Naylor, T.H. & C.W. Polzer, eds. The Presidio
  and Militia on the Northern Frontier of New
  Spain.
  M.A. Burkholder, 377:Nov88-208
Ndiaye, A.R. La place de la femme dans les
  rites au Sénégal.
  B.J. Soko, 538(RAL):Summer88-250
Neal, F. Sectarian Violence.
  W.L. Arnstein, 637(VS):Spring89-426
Neale, W.S. Scenes of the Crime.
  529(QQ):Summer88-507
Nebehay, C.M. Egon Schiele: Sketchbooks.
  J. Russell, 441:3Dec89-77
Needell, J.D. A Tropical Belle Époque.
  M.L. Conniff, 263(RIB):Vol38No4-537
  A. Hennessy, 617(TLS):14-20Jul89-763
Needham, J. - see under Tsien Tsuen-hsun
Needham, J. & others. The Hall of Heavenly
  Records.
  D.L. Baker, 293(JASt):Aug88-664
Needham, J. & Lu Gwei Djen. Science and
  Civilization in China. (Vol 6, Pt 1)
  D.A. Griffiths, 302:Vol24No1-94
Neeld, J. Sea Fire.
  D. Hopes, 236:Spring-Winter88-74
Neëlov, E.M. Volšebno-skazočnye korni
  naučnoj fantastiki.
  A. Liberman, 574(SEEJ):Spring88-143
Neely, C.T. Broken Nuptials in Shakespeare's
  Plays.*
  C. McEachern, 702:Vol20-306
Neely, M.E., Jr., H. Holzer & G.S. Boritt, eds.
  The Confederate Image.*
  F. Allen, 577(SHR):Summer88-286
  D. Tatham, 658:Winter88-287
Neff, J. Mobbed Up.
  A.H. Raskin, 441:10Dec89-22
Neff, W., Jr., comp. Wallace Neff. (text by A.
  Clark)
  D. Gantenbein, 45:Jan88-53
Nehamas, A. Nietzsche.*
  T.E. Heeney, 480(P&R):Vol21No3-240
  F.R. Love, 221(GQ):Summer87-513
  R. Schacht, 482(PhR):Apr88-266
Neher, A. Faust et le Maharal de Prague.
  A. Reix, 542:Apr-Jun88-254

Neider, C. - see Twain, M.
Neidle, A. Fables for the Nuclear Age.
  D.A. Hofmann, 441:8Jan89-23
Neidle, C. The Role of Case in Russian Syn-
  tax.
  L.H. Babby, 350:Dec89-832
Neidle, C. & R.A. Nuñez Cedeño, eds. Studies
  in Romance Languages.
  F. Nuessel, 361:May88-85
  R. Posner, 353:Vol26No3-501
Neil, B. Someone Wonderful.
  N. Sonenberg, 441:6Aug89-18
Neill, S. A History of Christianity in India
  1707-1858.*
  M. Laird, 83:Spring88-118
Neill, W. Wild Places.
  R. Watson, 588(SSL):Vol23-254
Neilson, M. Even Mississippi.
  J. Berry, 441:24Sep89-49
Nelde, P.H., P.S. Ureland & I. Clarkson, eds.
  Language Contact in Europe.
  B.J. Koekkoek, 221(GQ):Fall87-653
Nelson, B. Workers on the Waterfront.
  N. Lichtenstein, 441:4Jun89-23
Nelson, B. - see Giono, J.
Nelson, C., ed. Theory in the Classroom.*
  H. Davidson, 301(JEGP):Jul88-425
  W. Slinn, 478(P&L):Oct88-322
Nelson, C. & E. Folsom, eds. W.S. Merwin.*
  M. Christhilf, 301(JEGP):Jul88-467
Nelson, C. & L. Grossberg, eds. Marxism and
  the Interpretation of Culture.*
  W.E. Cain, 580(SCR):Fall88-71
  639(VQR):Summer88-97
Nelson, C. & M. Seccombe, comps. British
  Newspapers & Periodicals, 1641-1700.
  J.J. McCusker, 517(PBSA):Vol82No3-373
  D. McKitterick, 78(BC):Winter88-461
Nelson, D. Tar and Feathers.
  A. Higgins, 070(IUR):Spring88-104
Nelson, D.H. & H. van der Werf - see Adam de
  la Halle
Nelson, E. The British Counter-Culture,
  1966-73.
  E. Svarny, 617(TLS):29Dec89/4Jan90-
  1436
Nelson, E. Predicative Arithmetic.
  P. Pudlák, 316:Sep88-987
Nelson, J.A., ed. "Le Chevalier au Cygne" and
  "La fin d'Elias."
  P.F. Dembowski, 589:Jul88-702
Nelson, J.A., ed. The Old French Crusade
  Cycle. (Vol 2)
  G. Roques, 553(RLiR):Jan-Jun88-318
Nelson, J.R., Jr. Liberty and Property.*
  S.R. Boyd, 656(WMQ):Apr88-383
  R.E. Ellis, 106:Fall88-386
Nelson, K. The Art of Reciting Qur'an.
  J. Pacholczyk, 355(LSoc):Jun88-294
Nelson, K. Making Sense.
  C. Feldman, 567:Vol68No1/2-159
Nelson, L., Jr. - see Cavalcanti, G.
Nelson, M.C. & M. Eigen, eds. Evil.
  J.O. Wisdom, 488:Sep88-426
Nelson, P. The Hard Shape of Paradise.
  639(VQR):Autumn88-135
Nelson, R.J. Willa Cather and France.
  L. Wagner-Martin, 659(ConL):Fall89-444
  42(AR):Summer88-398
Nelson, W., with B. Shrake. I Didn't Come
  Here and I Ain't Leaving.
  D. Hill, 617(TLS):29Dec89/4Jan90-1438

"New Vico Studies."* (Vols 1 & 2) (G. Tagliacozzo & D.P. Verene, eds)
  K. Zimmermann, 53(AGP):Band70Heft3–332
"New Vico Studies." (Vol 3) (G. Tagliacozzo & D.P. Verene, eds)
  R. Holub, 141:Summer88–403
Newberry, F. Hawthorne's Divided Loyalties.
  J. Dolis, 27(AL):Oct88–470
Newbrook, M. Sociolinguistic Reflexes of Dialect Interference in West Wirral.
  C. Feagin, 35(AS):Spring88–76
Newbury, A.H. Julien Green.*
  M. Autrand, 535(RHL):Mar–Apr88–338
  A. Grewe, 72:Band225Heft2–446
Newcomb, D. & K. The Complete Vegetable Gardener's Sourcebook.
  L. Yang, 441:3Dec89–75
Newfield, J. & W. Barrett. City for Sale.
  J. Alter, 441:15Jan89–7
Newhouse, J. War and Peace in the Nuclear Age.
  M.S. Sherry, 441:22Jan89–7
Newhouse, V. Wallace K. Harrison, Architect.
  T. Hines, 617(TLS):8–14Dec89–1358
  J.H. Kay, 441:10Sep89–38
Newland, G. Compassion.
  U. Bernis, 485(PE&W):Oct88–421
Newlove, J. The Night the Dog Smiled.*
  D. Barbour, 168(ECW):Spring88–90
  R. Berry, 102(CanL):Autumn88–147
  S. Glickman, 168(ECW):Spring88–95
  A.R. Kizuk, 102(CanL):Autumn88–152
Newlyn, L. Coleridge, Wordsworth, and the Language of Allusion.*
  J. Hodgson, 88:Spring89–122
  S.M. Kearns, 591(SIR):Winter88–611
  J. Sturrock, 402(MLR):Oct89–934
Newman, B. Searching for the Figure in the Carpet in the Tales of Henry James.
  J.R. Frakes, 573(SSF):Spring88–172
  R. Hewitt, 395(MFS):Winter88–617
Newman, B., with B. Rogan. The Covenant.
  L. Wenzel, 441:16Jul89–25
Newman, F.X., ed. Social Unrest in the Late Middle Ages.
  J.O. Fichte, 38:Band106Heft3/4–516
  J. Scattergood, 677(YES):Vol19–301
  F.C. de Vries, 541(RES):Aug88–425
Newman, G. The Rise of English Nationalism.
  L.E. Klein, 173(ECS):Summer88–539
Newman, H. An Illustrated Dictionary of Silverware.
  M. Snodin, 90:Oct88–782
Newman, J. Saul Bellow and History.*
  E. Hollahan, 594:Spring88–104
Newman, J. The Mental Philosophy of John Henry Newman.*
  M. Vertin, 627(UTQ):Fall87–119
Newman, J.K. The Classical Epic Tradition.*
  D. Kremers, 547(RF):Band99Heft4–443
  D. Quint, 405(MP):May89–417
Newman, K. Shakespeare's Rhetoric of Comic Character.*
  R. Vince, 610:Autumn88–276
Newman, M. John Strachey.
  M. Pugh, 617(TLS):3–9Nov89–1207
Newman, P.C. Caesars of the Wilderness.
  G.W., 102(CanL):Autumn88–193
Newman, R.D. Understanding Thomas Pynchon.*
  S. Moore, 532(RCF):Summer88–321

Newman, R.D. & W. Thornton, eds. Joyce's "Ulysses."
  B.W. Shaffer, 481(PQ):Summer88–396
  R. Spoo, 329(JJQ):Fall88–148
Newman, R.P. The Cold War Romance of Lillian Hellman and John Melby.
  N. Robins, 441:9Jul89–19
Newmeyer, F.J. Linguistic Theory in America. (2nd ed)
  E.L. Barton, 660(Word):Apr88–71
Newmeyer, F.J., ed. Linguistics.
  R. Hudson, 350:Dec89–812
Newmeyer, F.J. The Politics of Linguistics.
  J. Leiber, 543:Mar89–633
  T. Pateman, 297(JL):Mar88–263
Newsham, B. All the Right Places.
  J. Krich, 441:11Jun89–12
Newton, J. & D. Rosenfelt, eds. Feminist Criticism and Social Change.*
  J. Simons, 541(RES):Feb88–156
Newton, K.M. In Defence of Literary Interpretation.
  F. Berry, 541(RES):Feb88–155
Newton, W., with D. Maurice. Once Before I Go.
  J. Kaufman, 441:26Nov89–31
Nexo, M.A. Pelle the Conqueror. (Vol 1)
  C.D. Kennedy, 441:3Sep89–14
Ngugi wa Thiong'o. Matigari.
  R. Gibson, 617(TLS):16–22Jun89–670
"Nicaraguan Peasant Poetry from Solentiname." (D. Gullette, trans)
  A. Josephs, 441:1Jan89–5
Nicephorus Blemmydes. Autobiographia sive curriculum vitae necnon epistula universalior. (J.A. Munitiz, ed)
  A. Angelou, 303(JoHS):Vol108–272
Nicephorus Blemmydes. Nikephoros Blemmydes, "Gegen die Vorherbestimmung der Todesstunde." (W. Lackner, ed & trans)
  M. Philippides, 589:Oct88–903
Nichol, BP. The Martyrology. (Bk 6)
  E. Quigley, 102(CanL):Autumn88–175
Nicholas, D. The Metamorphosis of a Medieval City.
  639(VQR):Spring88–44
Nicholl, C. Borderlines.
  E. Beattie, 441:3Sep89–15
  V. Fitzpatrick, 364:Dec88/Jan89–140
Nicholls, B. Bluejackets and Boxers.
  D.P. Crook, 635(VPR):Fall88–128
Nicholls, J.W. The Matter of Courtesy.*
  R.F. Green, 589:Jan88–202
Nichols, A. Yves Congar.
  P. Hebblethwaite, 617(TLS):29Dec89/4Jan90–1450
Nichols, A. The Poetics of Epiphany.
  M. Bidney, 661(WC):Autumn88–205
  P.A. Dale, 637(VS):Winter89–289
Nichols, D. – see Pyle, E.
Nichols, M. Socrates and the Political Community.
  T.V. Kaufman-Osborn, 478(P&L):Apr88–145
Nichols, M. & G.B. Schaller. Gorilla.
  M. Nichols, 441:9Apr89–32
Nichols, R., ed. Ravel Remembered.*
  R. Crichton, 415:Mar88–133
Nichols, R. & R.L. Smith. Claude Debussy: "Pelléas et Mélisande."
  W. Mellers, 617(TLS):8–14Sep89–985
Nichols, S.G., Jr. Romanesque Signs.*
  E. Sears, 54:Jun88–347

Nicholson, M. The New Environmental Age.
G.E.V., 185:Jan89-468
Nickel, G. & J.C. Stalker, eds. Problems of
Standardization and Linguistic Variation in
Present-Day English.
W. Viereck, 257(IRAL):May88-167
Nicol, E. & D. More. The U.S. or Us?
529(QQ):Spring88-223
Nicol, M. The Powers that Be.
W. Finnegan, 441:26Nov89-9
Nicoloff, A. The Bulgarian Resurgence.
R.J. Crampton, 575(SEER):Apr88-293
Nicolova, P. Pragmatičen aspekt na izrečen-
ieto v b"lgarskija knižoven ezik.
W. Fiedler, 682(ZPSK):Band41Heft2-260
Nic Pháidín, C. Cnuasach Focal ó Uíbh Ráth-
ach.
B. Ó Cuív, 112:Vol20-212
Niderst, A., ed. Pierre Corneille.
M-O. Sweetser, 475:Vol15No28-312
Niderst, A. - see Corneille, P.
Niebaum, H. Naar een taalgeschiedenis van
Oostnederland.
H. Tiefenbach, 685(ZDL):2/1988-249
Niebaum, H. & H. Taubken, comps. Westfäl-
isches Wörterbuch. (Pt 7)
G.H. Kocks, 685(ZDL):2/1988-243
Niedecker, L. "Between Your House and
Mine." (L.P. Faranda, ed)
A. Askenase, 295(JML):Fall87/Winter88-
227
R. Caddell, 161(DUJ):Dec87-160
Niederehe, H-J. & B. Schlieben-Lange, eds.
Die Frühgeschichte der romanischen Phil-
ologie: von Dante bis Diez.
H. Kalverkämper, 72:Band225Heft2-423
Nieh, H. Mulberry and Peach.
M. Buck, 441:22Jan89-22
Niehüser, W. Redecharakterisierende Ad-
verbiale.
W.V. Davies, 402(MLR):Oct89-1015
Niel, J-B. Vous qui passez dans l'ombre.
J. Kirkup, 617(TLS):13-19Oct89-1130
Nielsen, A.M. Corpus of Cypriote Antiquities:
8.
Y. Calvet, 555:Vol61fasc1-108
Nielsen, H.J. Kaetterier og dialoger.
I. Laerkesen, 172(Edda):1988/1-79
Nienhauser, W.H., Jr., ed. The Indiana Com-
panion to Traditional Chinese Literature.*
D.R. Knechtges & T. Chang, 318(JAOS):
Apr-Jun87-293
Nies, F. & K. Stierle, eds. Französische
Klassik.*
E.M. Zimmermann, 475:Vol15No28-316
Nietzsche, F. Dithyrambs of Dionysus. (R.J.
Hollingdale, ed & trans)
A. Del Caro, 221(GQ):Winter87-156
Niezabitowsky, M. & T. Tomaszewski. Rem-
nants.*
J. Riemer, 287:Sep/Oct87-27
Niggemann, G. Untersuchungen zur Nominal-
komposition im Tschechischen.*
D. Short, 575(SEER):Oct88-667
Nightingale, F. Ever Yours, Florence Night-
ingale. (M. Vicinus & B. Nergaard, eds)
A. Summers, 617(TLS):29Dec89/4Jan90-
1433
Nightingale, F. "I have done my duty." (S.M.
Goldie, ed)
A. Summers, 637(VS):Spring89-454
Nightingale, P. Journey through Darkness.
H.S. Mann, 395(MFS):Summer88-255

Nightingale, P., ed. A Sense of Place in the
New Literatures in English.
M.P.L., 295(JML):Fall87/Winter88-215
R. Ross, 538(RAL):Spring88-130
Niiniluoto, I. Is Science Progressive?*
R.J. Gomez, 449:Jun88-316
Nikolaev, G.A., ed. Russkoe sravnitel'noe i
sopostavitel'noe slovoobrazovanie.
R.D. Schupbach, 574(SEEJ):Fall88-492
Nikolitseas, D. Ban Hemlock Laws.
P. Levi, 617(TLS):31Mar-6Apr89-345
Ní Laoire, S. Bás Cearbhaill Agus Farb-
hlaidhe.
S. Ua Súilleabháin, 112:Vol20-204
Nill, M. Morality and Self-Interest in Pro-
tagoras, Antiphon and Democritus.
R. Ferwerda, 394:Vol41fasc1/2-160
M.R. Wright, 41:Spring88-117
Nilsson, N.A., ed. The Slavic Literatures and
Modernism.
M. Pursglove, 575(SEER):Oct88-643
Nimier, M. La Girafe.
D. Brautman, 207(FR):Feb89-551
Nin, A. The Early Diary of Anaïs Nin.* (Vol
4)
D. Schneider, 534(RALS):Vol16No1&2-197
Nin, A. & H. Miller. A Literate Passion.* (G.
Stuhlmann, ed)
639(VQR):Spring88-48
"1990 Chevrolet S-10 Owner's Manual." "The
1990 Buick LeSabre Owner's Manual."
N. Perrin, 441:24Dec89-18
"Nineteenth Century Short Title Catalogue."
(Ser II, Phase 1)
R. Landon, 470:Vol26-200
Nir, Y. The Lost Childhood.
T. Swick, 441:31Dec89-6
Nisbet, H.B., ed. German Aesthetic and Liter-
ary Criticism.
R. Rundell, 221(GQ):Winter87-118
Nisbet, R. History of the Idea of Progress.
G. Trompf, 488:Jun88-274
Nischik, R.M. Short Short Stories.
G. Düsterhaus, 72:Band224Heft2-467
Nischik, T-M. Das volkssprachliche Natur-
buch im späten Mittelalter.
F. Tobin, 221(GQ):Summer88-461
Nish, I. The Origins of the Russo-Japanese
War.*
P. Berton, 293(JASt):May88-379
Nishi, K. & K. Hozumi. What is Japanese
Architecture? (H.M. Horton, ed & trans)
N.S. Steinhardt, 576:Mar88-95
Nishida Kitarō. Last Writings.
V.H. Viglielmo, 407(MN):Autumn88-353
Nishikawa, N. Le Roman japonais depuis
1945.
J. Ducruet, 605(SC):15Apr89-242
Nitze, P.H., with A.M. Smith & S.L. Rearden.
From Hiroshima to Glasnost.
S. Hoffmann, 453(NYRB):23Nov89-13
W. Isaacson, 441:15Oct89-15
Niven, A., ed. Under Another Sky.
M. Hulse, 364:Feb88-110
J. Welch, 493:Spring88-31
Niven, J. John C. Calhoun and the Price of
Union.
J.M. McPherson, 453(NYRB):19Jan89-16
Nixon, C. Lawrence's Leadership Politics and
the Turn Against Women.*
K. Cushman, 177(ELT):Vol31No1-114
K.M. Hewitt, 541(RES):Feb88-143
[continued]

[continuing]
    D.T.O., 295(JML):Fall87/Winter88-345
    M. Storch, 402(MLR):Oct89-954
Nixon, C.E.V. - see Pacatus
Nixon, R. 1999.*
    A. Roberts, 617(TLS):27Jan-2Feb89-80
Noakes, S. Timely Reading.
    M.G. Rose, 446(NCFS):Spring-Summer89-
    401
Noakes, V. - see Lear, E.
Noble, C.D. - see under Donatelli Noble, C.
Noble, I. Language and Narration in Céline's
    Writings.*
    B. Stoltzfus, 395(MFS):Summer88-298
Noble, T.A. - see Eliot, G.
Nochlin, L. Women, Art, and Power.
    M.D. Carroll, 441:15Jan89-23
Nockels, A. - see Wallraff, G.
Noël, B. Onze romans d'oeil. Journal du re-
    gard.
    H. Carn, 450(NRF):Jun88-79
    J. Taylor, 532(RCF):Summer88-319
Noel, R. - see "Joufroi de Poitiers"
Noiray, J. - see Zola, É.
Nojgaard, M. En kvaelerslange som kaeledyr.
    N. Sjursen, 535(RHL):Mar-Apr88-342
Nokes, D. Jonathan Swift, a Hypocrite Re-
    versed.*
    J. Mezciems, 541(RES):Aug88-447
Nolan, J.E. Guardians of the Arsenal.
    M.S. Sherry, 441:24Dec89-11
Noll, R. Die griechischen und lateinischen
    Inschriften der Wiener Antikensammlung.
    (2nd ed)
    A. Donati, 229:Band60Heft6-550
Noller, J. Engagement und Form.
    E. Reimer, 416:Band3Heft3-270
Nomberg-Przytyk, S. Auschwitz. (E. Pfeffer-
    korn & D.H. Hirsch, eds)
    H.A. Schmitt, 569(SR):Winter88-158
Nonnos. Nonnos de Panopolis, "Les Dionys-
    iaques." (Vol 4) (G. Chrétien, ed & trans)
    J. Schiavi, 555:Vol61fasc1-127
Noomen, W. & N. van den Boogaard, eds. Nou-
    veau Recueil des fabliaux.* (Vol 3)
    A.J. Holden, 402(MLR):Jan89-155
Noonan, H.W. Personal Identity.
    S. Shoemaker, 617(TLS):29Sep-5Oct89-
    1069
Noonan, P. What I Saw at the Revolution.
    J. Didion, 453(NYRB):21Dec89-3
Nooteboom, C. Philip and the Others.
    P. Glossop, 441:8Jan89-22
van Noppen, J-P. & others, eds. Metaphor.
    U. Albrecht, 685(ZDL):3/1988-394
Nora, P., ed. Essais d'ego-histoire.
    M. Jarrety, 450(NRF):Mar88-90
Norbeck, E. & M. Lock, eds. Health, Illness,
    and Medical Care in Japan.
    E. Ohnuki-Tierney, 293(JASt):Nov88-894
    S.R. Smith, 407(MN):Winter88-512
Norberg-Schulz, C. New World Architecture.
    T. Fisher, 505:Dec88-103
Nordberg, B. Der mångskiftande språket.
    P. Linell, 355(LSoc):Mar88-118
Nordhjem, B. What Fiction Means.
    M. McGuire, 38:Band106Heft3/4-559
Nordland, G. Richard Diebenkorn.*
    L. Malen, 55:Oct88-94
Nordquist, G.C. A Middle Helladic Village.
    S. Dietz, 303(JoHS):Vol108-256
Noreng, H. Fra Tullin til Sandemose.
    R. Eide, 172(Edda):1988/4-371

Norge. Le Stupéfait.
    R. Jacquelin, 450(NRF):Jul-Aug88-207
Norman, D. Terrible Beauty.
    L.R. Pratt, 637(VS):Winter89-265
Norman, E. The Victorian Christian Social-
    ists.
    J. Cox, 637(VS):Winter89-288
Norman, H. Kiss in the Hotel Joseph Conrad.
    S. Dobyns, 441:8Oct89-16
Norman, P. Words of Love.
    M. Illis, 617(TLS):22-28Dec89-1421
Norman, R. Free and Equal.*
    B. Almond, 483:Apr88-276
    A. Brown, 518:Jul88-171
Norr, D. Causa Mortis.
    B.W. Frier, 24:Winter88-618
Nørretranders, T. Det udelelige.
    R. Fossum, 563(SS):Winter88-79
Norrick, N. How Proverbs Mean.
    D. Tannen, 355(LSoc):Sep88-455
Norrington, A.L.P. - see Clough, A.H.
Norris, C. The Contest of Faculties.*
    K.Z. Moore, 295(JML):Fall87/Winter88-
    254
    É. Morot-Sir, 535(RHL):Jul-Aug88-801
Norris, C. Deconstruction.
    M. Folch-Serra, 529(QQ):Autumn88-618
Norris, C. Deconstruction and the Interests
    of Theory.
    M. Walters, 617(TLS):22-28Dec89-1419
Norris, C. The Deconstructive Turn.*
    D.A. Foster, 107(CRCL):Jun88-250
Norris, C. Derrida.*
    A. Segal, 89(BJA):Autumn88-387
Norris, C. Paul de Man.
    S. Corngold, 144:Winter89-117
    T. Eagleton, 617(TLS):26May-1Jun89-
    573
Norris, C., ed. Music and the Politics of Cul-
    ture.
    J. Deathridge, 617(TLS):1-7Dec89-1328
Norris, F. Frank Norris: Collected Letters.
    (J.S. Crisler, ed)
    V. Albertini, 649(WAL):Aug88-153
    H.J. Dawson, 26(ALR):Fall88-90
Norris, G., ed. New American Short Stories.
    G. Davenport, 569(SR):Spring88-323
Norris, H. Walk with the Sickle Moon.
    D. Stead, 441:24Dec89-16
Norris, K., ed. Canadian Poetry Now.
    D. Precosky, 168(ECW):Spring88-123
Norris, K. In the Spirit of the Times.
    S.R. Dorscht, 102(CanL):Winter87-257
    529(QQ):Spring88-226
Norris, L. The Girl from Cardigan.*
    E. McGraw, 455:Sep88-64
Norse, H. Memoirs of a Bastard Angel.
    D. Kaufman, 441:31Dec89-13
North, J.S., ed. The Waterloo Directory of
    Irish Newspapers and Periodicals, 1800-
    1900. (Phase II)
    R. Morton, 178:Mar88-94
    P.V. O'Dea, 635(VPR):Summer88-84
North, R. General Preface & Life of Dr. John
    North. (P. Millard, ed)
    R.A. Beddard, 447(N&Q):Mar88-92
North, S.B., ed. Studies in Medieval French
    Language and Literature Presented to Brian
    Woledge in Honour of his 80th Birthday.
    H.R. Runte, 207(FR):Apr89-887

Northcutt, W. The French Socialist and Communist Party under the Fifth Republic, 1958–1981.
  T. Scanlan, 207(FR):Apr89–932
Northey, A. Kafkas Mischpoche.
  R. Robertson, 402(MLR):Oct89–1043
Norti Gualdani, E. – see de Padilla, J.
Norton, C. & D. Park, eds. Cistercian Art and Architecture in the British Isles.*
  D. Hibberd, 161(DUJ):Dec87–129
  J.P. McAleer, 576:Sep88–302
Norton, C., D. Park & P. Binski. Dominican Painting in East Anglia.
  M. Michael, 90:Oct88–774
Norton, R. Tonality in Western Culture.*
  C. Dahlhaus, 416:Band3Heft3–264
Norwich, J.J. Byzantium.
  M. Angold, 617(TLS):27Jan–2Feb89–83
  G.W. Bowersock, 441:16Apr89–9
Norwood, V. & J. Monk, eds. The Desert Is No Lady.
  P.R. Howell, 649(WAL):May88–78
  S. Rosowski, 357:Spring89–74
de Nostredame, C. – see under César de Nostredame
Nostwich, T.D. – see Dreiser, T.
"Le notion de liberté au moyen âge: Islam, Byzance, Occident."
  A.L. Ivry, 589:Jan88–203
Notker der Deutsche. Notker latinus zum Martianus Capella. (J.C. King, ed) Boethius, "De consolatione Philosophiae." (Bks 1 & 2) (P.W. Tax, ed)
  H.D. Schlosser, 133:Band21Heft4–326
Noto, S. – see London, J.
Nova, C. Tornado Alley.
  A. Codrescu, 441:23Jul89–7
Novak, B. Alice's Neck.
  42(AR):Winter88–121
Novak, B., with others. The Thyssen-Bornemisza Collection: Nineteenth-Century American Painting.*
  H. Adams, 90:Jan88–42
Novak, M.E., G.R. Guffey & A. Roper – see Dryden, J.
Nováková, M. & Z. Lešková. Bibliografie české lingvistiky 1983, 1984, 1985.
  C. Müller-Roewer, 682(ZPSK):Band41 Heft6–830
Novarr, D. The Lines of Life.*
  H.P. Abbott, 402(MLR):Jul89–696
Nove, A. Glasnost' in Action.
  H. Robinson, 441:10Sep89–13
Novelli, B. A Grammar of the Karimojong Language.
  K.H. Schmidt, 685(ZDL):2/1987–276
Novick, P. That Noble Dream.
  A. Brinkley, 617(TLS):10–16Nov89–1246
Novick, S.M. Honorable Justice.
  E. Morris, 441:20Aug89–3
  442(NY):2Oct89–120
Novitski, J. Wind Star.*
  639(VQR):Summer88–103
Novitz, D. Knowledge, Fiction & Imagination.
  G. Hermerén, 103:Apr89–164
Novy, M.L. Love's Argument.*
  R.L. Widmann, 191(ELN):Jun88–82
Nowak, K. Schleiermacher und die Frühromantik.
  G. Heinrich, 654(WB):5/1988–854
  N. Saul, 83:Autumn88–241

Nowak, S., ed. Społeczeństwo polskie czasu kryzysu.
  P. Swistak, 497(PolR):Vol33No1–107
Nowicki, S. Pół wieku czyśćca.
  J.T. Baer, 497(PolR):Vol33No2–242
Nowra, L. Palu.
  K. Kalfus, 441:9Jul89–18
Noxon, G. Teresina Maria.
  C. Ackerley, 102(CanL):Autumn88–138
Noyes, S. Backing Into Heaven.*
  A. Brown, 526:Winter88–102
  R. Donovan, 198:Autumn88–102
  S.R. Dorscht, 102(CanL):Winter87–257
Nozick, R. The Examined Life.
  W. Gaylin, 441:29Oct89–15
"La nozione di 'Romano' tra cittadinanza e universalità."
  J–C. Richard, 555:Vol61fasc2–335
Nugel, B. The Just Design.
  R. Borgmeier, 38:Band106Heft1/2–243
Nugent, S.G. Allegory and Poetics.
  R. Hexter, 589:Apr88–448
Núñez Cabeza de Vaca, A. La "Relación" o "Naufragios" de Alvar Núñez Cabeza de Vaca. (M.A. Favata & J.B. Fernández, eds)
  F.J. Cevallos, 238:Mar88–78
  J.S. Cummins, 402(MLR):Apr89–498
  N.W. Rokas, 552(REH):Oct88–130
Núñez Cedeño, R., I. Páez Urdaneta & J.M. Guitart, eds. Estudios sobre la fonología del español de Caribe.
  J.R. Gutiérrez, 238:Dec88–847
Nunley, J.W. Moving with the Face of the Devil.
  D. Cosentino, 2(AfrA):Aug88–26
Nunn, K. Unassigned Territory.
  C.L. Crow, 649(WAL):Aug88–167
Nunn, P.G., ed. Canvassing.
  H.E. Roberts, 635(VPR):Spring88–41
  662:Spring/Summer88–51
Nunn, P.G. Victorian Women Artists.
  B.C. Rezelman, 637(VS):Spring89–429
Nürnberger, H. – see Fontane, T.
Nussbaum, F. & L. Brown, eds. The New Eighteenth Century.
  W.A. Speck, 366:Autumn88–246
Nussbaum, G.B. Homer's Metre.
  J. Williams, 124:Mar–Apr89–314
Nussbaum, G.B. Vergil's Metre.
  H.V. Bender, 124:Jan–Feb89–207
Nussbaum, M. – see Owen, G.E.L.
Nussbaum, M.C. The Fragility of Goodness.*
  H.E. Barnes, 131(CL):Winter88–76
  J.M. Cooper, 482(PhR):Oct88–543
  C.L. Griswold, Jr., 31(ASch):Spring88–314
  S. Halliwell, 41:Fall88–313
  T.H. Irwin, 311(JP):Jul88–376
  A.A. Long, 122:Oct88–361
  D.L. Roochnik, 41:Fall88–285
  N.P. White, 185:Oct88–136
Nusser, K–H. Kausale Prozesse und sinnerfassende Vernunft.
  F.W. Graf, 489(PJGG):Band95Heft1–210
Nusser, R. Walking After Midnight.
  M. Stasio, 441:4Jun89–24
Nuttall, A.D. Pope's "Essay on Man."*
  M.G.H. Pittock, 83:Autumn88–223
Nuttall, A.D. "Timon of Athens."
  R. Hapgood, 617(TLS):25–31Aug89–927
Nuttgens, P., ed. Mackintosh & his Contemporaries in Europe and America.
  D. Farr, 324:Jan89–124

Nuttgens, P. The Story of Architecture.
   D.P. Crouch, 576:Mar88–76
Nuttgens, P. Understanding Modern Archi-
   tecture.
   J. Frew, 324:May89–383
Nuttin, J. Théorie de la motivation humaine.
   P. Livet, 192(EP):Jan–Mar88–130
Nye, A. Feminist Theory and the Philoso-
   phies of Man.
   J. Butler, 103:Aug89–326
   N.T., 185:Jul89–968
Nye, D.E. Image Worlds.*
   R. Cuff, 106:Spring88–126
Nye, R. The Memoirs of Lord Byron. A Col-
   lection of Poems, 1955–1988.
   N. Berry, 617(TLS):17–23Nov89–1271
Nygren, E.J. & B. Robertson, with others.
   Views and Visions.
   D.M. Sokol, 658:Summer/Autumn88–187
Nyholm, K., ed. Grammatik im Unterricht.
   H–W. Eroms, 685(ZDL):2/1987–283
Nyiri, J. Battlefields and Playgrounds.
   P. Sherwood, 617(TLS):8–14Dec89–1369
Nyíri, J.C. Am Rande Europas.
   V. Nemoianu, 543:Jun89–847
Nyiri, J.C. – see Lukács, G.
Nyiri, J.C. & B. Smith, eds. Practical Know-
   ledge.
   F. Adams, 103:Jul89–283
Nykrog, P. L'Amour et la rose.
   L.C. Brook, 208(FS):Apr88–196
   D.F. Hult, 545(RPh):May89–485
   S. Huot, 589:Apr88–449
Nykrog, P. La Recherche du don perdu.
   E. Hughes, 208(FS):Apr88–226
   M. Slater, 402(MLR):Jan89–184
Nyquist, M. & M.W. Ferguson, eds. Re-mem-
   bering Milton.
   M. Stocker, 617(TLS):27Jan–2Feb89–90
Nysenholc, A. Charles Chaplin ou la légende
   des images.
   P. Aron, 193:Autumn88–142
Nystrand, M., with M. Himley & A. Doyle. The
   Structure of Written Communication.
   C.I. Schuster, 126(CCC):Feb88–89
   S.P. Witte & D. Elias, 599:Winter88–670

Oakeshott, M. The Voice of Liberal Learning.
   (T. Fuller, ed)
   J. Passmore, 617(TLS):26May–1Jun89–
   567
Oakley, A. The Men's Room.
   E. Feldman, 441:9Apr89–19
Oates, J.C. American Appetites.
   P. Craig, 617(TLS):15–21Sep89–997
   R. Towers, 441:1Jan89–5
   442(NY):3Apr89–116
Oates, J.C. The Assignation.*
   G. Johnson, 219(GaR):Winter88–840
Oates, J.C. Marya.
   J. Mellors, 364:Mar87–98
Oates, J.C. On Boxing.*
   G. Early, 271:Fall88–173
   R. Roberts, 598(SoR):Summer89–771
Oates, J.C. (Woman) Writer.*
   J. Saari, 42(AR):Fall88–522
Oates, J.C. You Must Remember This.*
   D. Flower, 249(HudR):Spring88–210
Oates, S.B., ed. Biography as High Adven-
   ture.*
   I.B.N., 295(JML):Fall87/Winter88–254

Oates, S.B. William Faulkner.
   A.F. Kinney, 395(MFS):Winter88–622
   D. Trouard, 392:Summer88–463
Ó Baoill, D.P. Lárchanúint don Ghaeilge.
   Foclóir Póca.
   B. Ó Cuív, 112:Vol20–218
Obenaus, S. Literarische und politische Zeit-
   schriften 1830–1848.
   R. Godwin–Jones, 221(GQ):Summer88–468
Ober, J. Fortress Attica.*
   P. Harding, 487:Spring88–61
Ober, J. Mass and Elite in Democratic
   Athens.
   P. Millett, 617(TLS):29Dec89/4Jan90–
   1449
Oberg, J.E. Uncovering Soviet Disasters.*
   639(VQR):Summer88–95
Oberleitner, W. Geschnittene Steine. (G.
   Langthaler, ed)
   E. Zwierlein–Diehl, 229:Band60Heft5–469
Obermayer, A., ed. Die Ehre als literarisches
   Motiv.
   C.N. Genno, 564:Feb88–94
Obidinski, E.E. & H.S. Zand. Polish Folkways
   in America.
   I. Nagurski, 497(PolR):Vol33No2–231
O'Brian, J. – see Greenberg, C.
O'Brian, P. Joseph Banks.
   J. Wilson, 364:Apr–May87–150
O'Brien, C.C. The Siege.
   D.V. Segre, 473(PR):Vol55No2–341
O'Brien, D. Eminent Domain.*
   P. Glasser, 455:Jun88–61
O'Brien, D. Murder in Little Egypt.
   W. Kaminer, 441:12Mar89–23
O'Brien, D. The Rites of Autumn.
   H. Middleton, 441:29Jan89–31
   J. Ure, 617(TLS):10–16Nov89–1248
O'Brien, D. Spirit of the Hills.*
   J. Clute, 617(TLS):1–7Sep89–952
O'Brien, E. The Beckett Country.
   M.B., 295(JML):Fall87/Winter88–293
   J.C.C. Mays, 541(RES):May88–324
O'Brien, E. The High Road.*
   T. Rafferty, 442(NY):30Jan89–92
O'Brien, G. The Village of Longing [and]
   Dancehall Days.
   R. Kearney, 617(TLS):25–31Aug89–929
O'Brien, G. with S. Wasserstein & H. Morris,
   eds. The Reader's Catalog.
   M. Richler, 441:8Oct89–7
O'Brien, G.W. The Legal Fraternity and the
   Making of a New South Community, 1848–
   1882.*
   J.T. O'Brien, 106:Fall88–339
O'Brien, M. A Character of Hugh Legaré.
   J.D. O'Donnell, Jr., 392:Winter87/88–102
O'Brien, M. Reproducing the World.
   C. Overall, 103:Oct89–420
O'Brien, S. Willa Cather.*
   P.J. Casagrande, 594:Summer88–206
   G.F. Day, 649(WAL):May88–69
   S.P., 295(JML):Fall87/Winter88–304
   J. Simons, 541(RES):Nov88–587
   L. Wagner–Martin, 659(ConL):Fall89–444
   J. Woodress, 447(N&Q):Sep88–424
O'Brien, S. The Frighteners.*
   H. Lomas, 364:Mar88–81
Obuchowski, C.W. The Franco–File.
   R. Cormier, 399(MLJ):Autumn88–355
Occleshaw, M. Armour against Fate.
   K. Jeffery, 617(TLS):10–16Nov89–1232

Oceja Gonzalo, I., ed. Documentación del monasterio de San Salvador de Oña (1032–1284; 1285–1310; 1311–1318; 1319–1350).*
    P. Freedman, 589:Apr88–452
Ochs, M. The African Press.
    D. Lamb, 639(VQR):Spring88–352
William of Ockham. Guillelmi de Ockham: Quaestiones in Librum Quartum Sententiarum (Reportatio). (Opera Theologica VII). (R. Wood & G. Gál, with R. Green, eds)
    M.M. Adams, 482(PhR):Jul88–417
Ó Coigligh, C. Raiftearaí.
    S. Ua Súilleabháin, 112:Vol20–208
O'Connell, D.C. Critical Essays on Language Use and Psychology.
    W.E. Cooper, 348(L&S):Oct–Dec88–379
O'Connell, J. & C.B. Kelly. The Blame Game.
    E. Couric, 639(VQR):Winter88–170
O'Connell, M. Robert Burton.
    J.B. Bamborough, 447(N&Q):Jun88–230
    M. Elsky, 551(RenQ):Winter88–757
    E. Heale, 677(YES):Vol19–309
O'Connell, N. At the Field's End.
    D.A. Hecker, 649(WAL):Aug88–176
    S. Weisenburger, 395(MFS):Winter88–660
O'Connell, R.L. Of Arms and Men.
    G.A. Craig, 453(NYRB):17Aug89–31
O'Connor, A. Raymond Williams.
    C. Baldick, 617(TLS):3–9Nov89–1205
O'Connor, D. The Metaphysics of G.E. Moore.
    J.G. Hanink, 438:Winter88–112
O'Connor, F. & B. Cheney. The Correspondence of Flannery O'Connor and the Brainard Cheneys.* (C.R. Stephens, ed)
    S.G. Driggers, 577(SHR):Summer88–291
    J.L. Idol, Jr., 534(RALS):Vol16No1&2–250
    L. Willson, 569(SR):Spring88–283
O'Connor, G. Sean O'Casey.*
    D. Mills, 157:No169–50
O'Connor, J. & E.I. Koch. His Eminence and Hizzoner.
    A. Hacker, 441:26Mar89–3
O'Connor, M. John Davidson.*
    M. Pittock, 571(ScLJ):Spring88–8
O'Connor, R.A. A Theory of Indigenous Southeast Asian Urbanism.
    R. Provencher, 293(JASt):Nov88–944
O'Connor, S. Rescue.
    C. Verderese, 441:10Sep89–26
O'Connor, S. Tomorrow Was Another Day.
    G. West, 174(Éire):Winter88–156
O'Connor, T.F. Jean Rhys: The West Indian Novels.*
    C.A. Howells, 541(RES):Aug88–464
O'Connor–Visser, E.A.M.E. Aspects of Human Sacrifice in the Tragedies of Euripides.
    J. Wilkins, 123Vol38No1–12
O'Crohan, T. Island Cross-Talk.
    S. Pickering, 569(SR):Fall88–673
O'Dea, A.C. Bibliography of Newfoundland. (A. Alexander, ed)
    D.G. Lochhead, 470:Vol26–181
Odegard, D., ed. Ethics and Justification.
    J.U. Lewis, 103:Jun89–240
Odelman, E. Corpus troporum VI.
    J. Caldwell, 410(M&L):Jul88–365
    M–N. Colette, 537:Vol74No1–102
Odelman, E., ed. Glossarium mediae Latinitatis Sueciae. (Vol 2, fasc 1 & 2)
    P. Dinter, 229:Band60Heft6–539

Oderman, K. Ezra Pound and the Erotic Medium.*
    R.B.D., 295(JML):Fall87/Winter88–370
    D.P. Tryphonopoulos, 468:Fall&Winter88–255
Ó Dochartaigh, C. Dialects of Ulster Irish.
    D.P. Ó Baoill, 112:Vol20–192
O'Donnell, W.H. The Poetry of William Butler Yeats.*
    R.J. Finneran, 177(ELT):Vol31No3–320
O'Driscoll, D. Hidden Extras.*
    N. MacMonagle, 272(IUR):Autumn88–343
O'Driscoll, G.P., Jr. & M.J. Rizzo. The Economics of Time and Ignorance.
    P. Davidson, 144:Summer/Fall89–467
Odwarka, K., ed. Methods II.
    P. Markham, 399(MLJ):Autumn88–334
Ōe, K. The Silent Cry.
    L. Allen, 617(TLS):28Apr–4May89–466
Oesterreicher, W. Sprachtheorie und Theorie der Sprachwissenschaft.
    L. Saltveit, 685(ZDL):3/1987–349
O'Faolain, S. And Again?
    C. Gaiser, 441:17Sep89–18
Offe, C. Contradictions of the Welfare State.* (J. Keane, ed)
    J. Cohen, 482(PhR):Jul88–435
Offner, R. A Critical and Historical Corpus of Florentine Painting. (The Fourteenth Century, Section 3, Vol 1)
    J.C., 90:Jan88–46
Offord, D. The Russian Revolutionary Movement in the 1880s.
    R.G. Suny, 550(RusR):Apr88–191
    W.G. Wagner, 575(SEER):Jul88–489
O'Flaherty, W.D. Other Peoples' Myths.
    J. Boon, 441:29Jan89–18
O'Flaherty, W.D. Tales of Sex and Violence.*
    F. Staal, 293(JASt):Aug88–686
O'Gara, M. Triumph in Defeat.
    P. Hebblethwaite, 617(TLS):27Oct–2Nov89–1188
Ogden, D.H. Performance Dynamics and the Amsterdam Werkteater.
    L. Champagne, 615(TJ):Dec88–570
Oggel, L.T. – see Booth, M.D.
Ogilvie–Thomson, S.J., ed. Walter Hilton's "Mixed Life" edited from Lambeth Palace MS 472.
    Toshiyuki Takamiya, 382(MAE):1988/1–113
O'Gorman, H.J. – see Klassen, A.D., C.J. Williams & E.E. Levitt
O'Gorman, J.F. H.H. Richardson.*
    P.R. Baker, 432(NEQ):Jun88–306
    K.A. Breisch, 658:Spring88–94
    J. Coolidge, 576:Jun88–214
    L.K. Eaton, 505:Dec88–103
O'Grady, T. Motherland.
    G. Mangan, 617(TLS):24–30Mar89–300
Oguibénine, B. Essais sur la culture védique et indoeuropéenne.
    F. Crevatin, 259(IIJ):Apr88–142
Ohala, J.J. & J.J. Jaeger, eds. Experimental Phonology.*
    P.M. Bertinetto, 297(JL):Sep88–571
O'Halpin, E. The Decline of the Union.*
    M. Banotti, 272(IUR):Autumn88–349
O'Halpin, E. Head of the Civil Service.
    G. Peden, 617(TLS):20–26Oct89–1158
O'Hanlon, R. In Trouble Again.*
    J. Krich, 441:11Jun89–12

Ó hAnnracháin, S. An Comchaidreamh.
  R. Ó Glaisne, 272(IUR):Spring88-154
O'Hara, D.T. The Romance of Interpretation.
  R.L., 295(JML):Fall87/Winter88-254
  D.E. Pease, 290(JAAC):Fall87-91
O'Hara, J. Collected Stories of John O'Hara.*
  (F. MacShane, ed)
  P.B. Eppard, 534(RALS):Vol16No1&2-254
O'Hear, A. What Philosophy Is.*
  R. Crisp, 291:Vol5No2-233
Ohlgren, T.H., ed. Insular and Anglo-Saxon
  Illuminated Manuscripts.*
  L. Nees, 589:Jan88-207
Ohlin, B., ed. Correspondance littéraire
  secrète, 29 juin-28 décembre 1776.
  A. Grafström, 553(RLiR):Jul-Dec88-560
  J. Lough, 208(FS):Jan88-92
Ohmann, R. Politics of Letters.
  H. Fromm, 219(GaR):Spring88-183
Ohnuki-Tierney, E. The Monkey as Mirror.
  C.W. Kiefer, 293(JASt):Aug88-645
  D.W. Plath, 407(MN):Summer88-256
Oickle, D. Edgar Potato.
  A. Kertzer, 102(CanL):Winter87-165
Oikonomides, N. A Collection of Dated Byz-
  antine Lead Seals.
  A. Dunn, 303(JoHS):Vol108-274
Oinas, F.J. Essays on Russian Folklore and
  Mythology.*
  J.L. Perkowski, 574(SEEJ):Winter88-680
  E.V. Žygas, 292(JAF):Jan-Mar88-102
Ojtozi, E. Slavyanskiye i rumynskiye knigi
  kirillovskoy pechati Biblioteki Grekokato-
  licheskoy Dukhovnoy Akademii/g. Nired'-
  khaza, Vengriya/.
  C.L. Drage, 575(SEER):Jul88-473
Okada, T. Sō-Min tetsugaku no honshitsu.
  B.D. Steben, 485(PE&W):Oct88-459
Okken, L. Das goldene Haus und die goldene
  Laube.
  K. Pratt, 382(MAE):1988/2-293
Okrent, D. & S. Wulf. Baseball Anecdotes.
  M. Gallagher, 441:23Apr89-36
Okri, B. Stars of the New Curfew.*
  N. Bissoondath, 441:13Aug89-12
  A. Maja-Pearce, 364:Jul88-114
  442(NY):25Sep89-121
Oksaar, E. Spracherwerb im Vorschulalter.
  (2nd ed)
  H. Ramge, 685(ZDL):3/1988-393
Olbrich, J.M. Architecture.
  I.B. Whyte, 617(TLS):12-18May89-523
Oldenburg, H. The Correspondence of Henry
  Oldenburg. (Vols 12 & 13) (A.R. & M.B.
  Hall, eds & trans)
  R. Burch, 568(SCN):Spring-Summer88-13
Oldenburg, R. The Great Good Place.
  R.B. Gratz, 441:24Dec89-2
Oldenburg, V.T. The Making of Colonial
  Lucknow, 1856-1877.
  R.J. Young, 318(JAOS):Jan-Mar87-201
Oldenquist, A. The Non-suicidal Society.
  N.S. Care, 185:Jul89-946
Oldfield, D. German Paintings in the National
  Gallery of Ireland.
  J.O. Hand, 90:Jan88-41
Oldham, J. The Poems of John Oldham. (H.F.
  Brooks, with R. Selden, eds)
  D.L.F. Hills, 541(RES):Aug88-445
Olds, S. The Gold Cell.*
  R. Flint, 496:Spring88-39
  P. Harris, 639(VQR):Spring88-265
  455:Mar88-72

Oldsey, B. & J. Browne, eds. Critical Essays
  on George Orwell.
  R.D.B., 295(JML):Fall87/Winter88-365
O'Leary, P. My Story.
  B. Ó Cuív, 112:Vol20-224
Olesch, R. & H. Rothe, eds. Festschrift für
  Herbert Bräuer zum 65. Geburtstag am 14.
  April 1986.
  W. Busch, 688(ZSP):Band48Heft2-436
  H. Leeming, 575(SEER):Apr88-258
Olinger, P. Images of Transformation in Tra-
  ditional Hispanic Poetry.*
  M. Frenk, 86(BHS):Jul88-290
  E.H. Friedman, 552(REH):Oct88-139
  A. Sánchez Romeralo, 240(HR):Summer88-
  366
Olivares, J., ed. International Studies in
  Honor of Tomás Rivera.
  J. Bruce-Novoa, 238:May88-309
Olivares, J. La novela decadente en Venezu-
  ela.*
  A.A. Fernández-Vázquez, 345(KRQ):
  Feb88-122
Oliver, D. Return to Tahiti.
  G. Milner, 617(TLS):1-7Sep89-955
Olivier, J-M. & M-A. Monégier du Sorbier.
  Catalogue des manuscrits grecs de Tchéco-
  slovaquie.*
  B. Mondrain, 555:Vol61fasc1-131
Ollard, R. Clarendon and His Friends.*
  639(VQR):Summer88-88
Ollerenshaw, P. Banking in Nineteenth-
  Century Ireland.
  A.J. Marrison, 637(VS):Winter89-267
Ollier, C. The Mise-en-scène.
  I. Hill, 617(TLS):11-17Aug89-879
Olmedo, A.S. - see under Soria Olmedo, A.
Olmstead, A. Conversations with Roger Ses-
  sions.*
  C. Shaw, 607:Sep88-63
Olney, J., ed. T.S. Eliot.
  J. Olney, 598(SoR):Spring89-503
Olney, J., ed. Studies in Autobiography.
  E.A.J. Honigmann, 453(NYRB):7Dec89-16
Olschner, L.M. Der feste Buchstab.*
  N.J. Meyerhofer, 406:Fall88-399
Olschowsky, H., ed. Der Mensch in den
  Dingen.
  K. Hirdina, 601(SuF):Nov-Dec88-1323
Olsen, A.L. & N.P. Stilling, eds. Et nyt liv.
  P. Houe, 562(Scan):May88-45
Olsen, B.M. L'étude des auteurs classiques
  latins aux XIe et XIIe siècles.* (Vols 1 &
  2)
  P. Flobert, 555:Vol61fasc2-355
Olsen, B.M. L'Étude des auteurs classiques
  latins aux XIe et XIIe siècles. (Vol 3, Pt 1)
  B.C. Barker-Benfield, 123:Vol38No2-371
Olsen, D.J. The City as a Work of Art.*
  J.S. Ackerman, 576:Mar88-90
  S.M. Gaskell, 366:Autumn88-252
Olsen, J. "Doc."
  A. Jones, 441:18Jun89-12
Olsen, L. Ellipse of Uncertainty.
  E.A. Kaplan, 395(MFS):Winter88-733
  D.W. Madden, 594:Fall88-354
Olsen, M. Amore, virtù e potere nella novel-
  listica rinascimentale.
  R. Morabito, 462(OL):Vol43No4-382
  H.H. Wetzel, 72:Band225Heft1-236
Olsen, M.A., ed. Libro del cavallero Çifar.
  M. Vaquero, 345(KRQ):Feb88-108

Olsen, S.H. The End of Literary Theory.*
    P. Barry, 175:Spring88-74
    L. Stern, 290(JAAC):Summer88-522
Olsen, W. The Hand of God and a Few Bright
    Flowers.
    A. Hudgins, 249(HudR):Winter89-737
Olshan, J. The Waterline.
    C. Geeslin, 441:5Nov89-9
Olson, C. The Collected Poems of Charles
    Olson.* (G.F. Butterick, ed)
    639(VQR):Spring88-63
Olson, J.S. Saving Capitalism.
    A. Schlesinger, Jr., 453(NYRB):16Feb89-
    20
Olson, P.A. "The Canterbury Tales" and the
    Good Society.
    P.R. Cross, 366:Autumn88-229
    G. Olson, 589:Oct88-972
Olson, S. John Singer Sargent.*
    W.A. Coles, 432(NEQ):Mar88-122
Olson, T. Millennialism, Utopianism and Pro-
    gress.
    G. Trompf, 488:Jun88-274
Olsson, H. La Concurrence entre "il," "ce" et
    "cela (ça)" comme sujet d'expressions im-
    personnelles en français contemporain.
    G. Price, 208(FS):Oct88-497
Oltra Tomás, J.M. La parodia como referente
    en "La pícara Justina."
    G. Díaz-Migoyo, 240(HR):Autumn88-499
    J.A. Jones, 86(BHS):Oct88-407
Omaggio, A.C. Teaching Language in Con-
    text.*
    T.D. Terrell, 238:Mar88-98
O'Marie, C.A. The Missing Madonna.
    M. Stasio, 441:22Jan89-30
O'Meally, R., ed. New Essays on Invisible
    Man.
    K. Byerman, 395(MFS):Winter88-634
O'Meara, J.J. Eriugena.
    G. Leff, 617(TLS):7-13Jul89-756
Omesco, I. Hamlet ou la tentation du pos-
    sible.
    A. Reix, 542:Oct-Dec88-516
Ondaatje, M. The Collected Works of Billy the
    Kid.
    J. Loose, 617(TLS):3-9Nov89-1217
Ondaatje, M. In the Skin of a Lion.*
    L. Hutcheon, 102(CanL):Summer88-132
    N. Schmitz, 529(QQ):Summer88-452
"One Half of the Sky."* (R.A. Roberts & A.
    Knox, trans)
    L. Dawson-Evans, 565:Summer88-54
O'Neal, J.C.C. Seeing and Observing.*
    F. Juranville, 535(RHL):Mar-Apr88-281
O'Neal, W.B. & C. Weeks. The Work of William
    Lawrence Bottomley in Richmond.
    R.C. Cote, 576:Jun88-216
O'Neill, E. As Ever, Gene. (N.L. & A.W.
    Roberts, eds)
    T.P. Adler, 130:Fall88-283
    D.B. Wilmeth, 610:Autumn88-291
O'Neill, E. Eugene O'Neill: Comments on the
    Drama and the Theater. (U. Halfmann, ed)
    E. Törnqvist, 610:Autumn88-292
O'Neill, E. The Unknown O'Neill. (T. Bogard,
    ed)
    27(AL):Dec88-698
O'Neill, E. & S. Commins. "Love and Admira-
    tion and Respect."* (D. Commins, ed)
    S.A. Black, 397(MD):Mar88-117
    R.A. Martin, 115:Winter88-97

O'Neill, J. Disturbance.
    A-M. Conway, 617(TLS):31Mar-6Apr89-
    344
O'Neill, J. Five Bodies.
    M. Roche, 488:Jun88-259
O'Neill, J.H. George Villiers, Second Duke of
    Buckingham.
    R.D. Hume, 173(ECS):Summer88-511
O'Neill, J.M. Canon Bang Bang.
    G. Gardiner, 617(TLS):1-7Dec89-1337
O'Neill, J.M. Duffy is Dead.
    J. Bowen, 364:Mar87-102
O'Neill, O. Faces of Hunger.*
    S. Dodds, 63:Mar88-118
O'Neill, P., ed. Critical Essays on Günter
    Grass.
    M. Minden, 402(MLR):Jan89-265
O'Neill, R.H. & N.M. Boretz. The Director as
    Artist.
    P.A. Davis, 615(TJ):Dec87-544
O'Neill, R.K. English-Language Dictionaries,
    1604-1900.
    R. Rulon-Miller, Jr., 517(PBSA):
    Vol82No3-376
Onetti, J.C. La Vie brève.
    M. Alhau, 450(NRF):Mar88-95
Ong, A. Spirits of Resistance and Capitalist
    Discipline.
    L. Lim, 293(JASt):Nov88-945
Ong, W.J. Hopkins, the Self, and God.*
    N. Belins, 577(SHR):Winter88-82
    B. Bergonzi, 402(MLR):Oct89-953
    A.M. Garab, 599:Spring89-168
    C. Lock, 627(UTQ):Fall87-126
    R.K.R. Thornton, 541(RES):Aug88-459
    N. White, 447(N&Q):Jun88-255
Onians, J. Bearers of Meaning.
    J. Summerson, 617(TLS):2-8Jun89-615
Onieva Morales, J.L. Fundamentos de gramá-
    tica estructural del español.
    A. Roca, 238:May88-317
Onions, C.T. A Shakespeare Glossary.* (rev
    by R.D. Eagleson)
    B. Cottle, 541(RES):May88-291
    E. Standop, 38:Band106Heft3/4-454
Ono, M. Morphologische Untersuchungen zur
    deutschen Sprache in einem Stadtbuch der
    Prager Neustadt vom 16.-18. Jahrhundert.
    M. Bürgisser, 685(ZDL):1/1988-93
    R. Peilicke, 682(ZPSK):Band41Heft3-400
Ōoka Makoto & T. Fitzsimmons, eds. A Play
    of Mirrors.
    L. Allen, 565:Summer88-26
    R. Epp, 407(MN):Spring88-107
    T. Rimer, 293(JASt):Aug88-648
    Takachi Jun'ichirō, 285(JapQ):Jan-
    Mar88-95
Oomen, U. Die englische Sprache in den USA.*
    (Pt 1)
    W. Sauer, 38:Band106Heft1/2-188
Oon, K.C. - see under Khong Cho Oon
Oosterhoff, F.G. Leicester and the Nether-
    lands 1586-1587.
    A. Hamilton, 617(TLS):24Feb-2Mar89-
    205
Mrs. Opie. Adeline Mowbray, or, The Mother
    and Daughter.
    J. Wheare, 447(N&Q):Jun88-248
Opie, I. & P. The Singing Game.
    G. Boyes, 203:Vol99No1-135
Opitz, M. - see Heine, H.
Oppel, F.N. Mask and Tragedy.
    L.R. Pratt, 637(VS):Winter89-265

Ortiz Ibarz, J.M. El origin radical de las cosas.
 B. Orio de Miguel, 706:Band20Heft2-217
Ortmann, W.D. Wortbildung und Morphem-struktur hochfrequenter deutscher Wort-formen.
 I. Barz, 682(ZPSK):Band41Heft2-261
Ortner, H. Die Ellipse.
 F. Hundsnurscher, 685(ZDL):3/1988-389
"Ortnît and Wolfdietrich."* (J.W. Thomas, trans)
 A. Classen, 597(SN):Vol60No2-282
 F. Tobin, 221(GQ):Winter87-105
Orton, J. Joe Orton's Diaries.* (J. Lahr, ed)
 A. Cameron, 610:Spring88-69
Orwell, G. The War Commentaries.* (W.J. West, ed)
 R.D.B., 295(JML):Fall87/Winter88-365
Ory, P. & others. Nouvelle histoire des idées politiques.
 J-M. Le Lannou, 98:Jan/Feb88-156
Ory, P. & J-P. Sirinelli. Les Intellectuels en France, de l'affaire Dreyfus à nos jours.
 K.A. Reader, 208(FS):Oct88-499
Osa, O. Nigerian Youth Literature.
 N.J. Schmidt, 538(RAL):Fall88-413
Osborne, C. The Complete Operas of Richard Strauss.
 B. Nelson, 465:Summer89-92
Osborne, C. Rethinking Early Greek Philoso-phy.*
 J. Barnes, 520:Vol33No3-327
 A.C.J.H., 185:Jan89-455
Osborne, C. Verdi.*
 D.W. Wakeling, 465:Spring89-108
Osborne, J. The Meiningen Court Theatre.
 H. Rorrison, 402(MLR):Jul89-795
Osborne, R. Classical Landscape with Fig-ures.
 R.A. Knox, 123:Vol38No2-312
 J.E. Ziolkowski, 124:Nov-Dec88-120
Osborne, R. Demos.
 G.J.D. Aalders H. Wzn., 394:Vol41 fasc1/2-224
 J. Ober, 122:Jan88-70
 R.K. Sinclair, 303(JoHS):Vol108-251
O'Shea, M.J. James Joyce and Heraldry.*
 P. Parrinder, 402(MLR):Jan89-141
Oshima, H.T. Economic Growth in Monsoon Asia.
 M.T. Skully, 293(JASt):Aug88-575
Osinski, Z. Grotowski and His Laboratory. (L. Vallee & R. Findlay, eds & trans)
 R.N.C., 295(JML):Fall87/Winter88-277
'Osmān Aġa. Die Autobiographie des Dol-metschers 'Osmān Aġa aus Temeschwar. (R.F. Kreutel, ed)
 S. Soucek, 318(JAOS):Jul-Sep87-532
Ossner, J. Konvention und Strategie.
 D. Müller & M. Roloff, 682(ZPSK):Band41 Heft6-818
Ostenfeld, E. Ancient Greek Psychology and the Modern Mind-Body Debate.
 H. Du Lac, 543:Mar89-635
 C. Gill, 123:Vol38No2-427
Oster, P. The Mexicans.
 J.M. Hamilton, 441:2Jul89-13
Ostergard, D.E., ed. Bent Wood and Metal Furniture 1850-1946.*
 S. Jervis, 39:Aug88-144
 P. Kirkham, 90:Jan88-43
Osterle, H.D., ed. Bilder von Amerika.
 S. Mews, 222(GR):Spring88-103

Ostler, G., ed. The Little Oxford Dictionary of Current English. (6th ed rev by J. Swannell)
 E. Standop, 38:Band106Heft3/4-455
Östling Andersson, A. L'Identification automatique des lexèmes du français contemporain.*
 S.F. Noreiko, 208(FS):Apr88-248
Östör, A. Culture and Power.
 W.S. Sax, 293(JASt):Aug88-687
Ostriker, A.S. Stealing the Language.*
 S.A.S., 295(JML):Fall87/Winter88-271
"The Ostroh Bible."
 U. Schweier, 559:Vol12No2-215
Ostrovsky, E. Under the Sign of Ambiguity.*
 S. Winspur, 546(RR):Nov88-686
Ostwald, M. From Popular Sovereignty to the Sovereignty of Law.*
 J.V. Dolan, 185:Jan89-436
 S.D. Olson, 124:Mar-Apr89-323
O'Sullivan, A., with P. Ó Riain, eds. Poems on Marcher Lords.
 B. Ó Cuív, 112:Vol20-215
O'Sullivan, J.C. Joyce's Use of Colors.*
 J. Voelker, 177(ELT):Vol31No4-505
O'Sullivan, V. The Pilate Tapes.
 L. Mackinnon, 617(TLS):26May-1Jun89-593
O'Sullivan, V. & M. Scott – see Mansfield, K.
Osuna, R. Las revistas españolas entre dos dictaduras: 1931-1939.
 P. Ilie, 238:Sep88-549
Oswald, S. Italienbilder.
 M. Beller, 52:Band23Heft2-182
Oswald von Wolkenstein. Die Lieder Oswalds von Wolkenstein. (K.K. Klein & others, eds) (new ed rev by H. Moser, N.R. Wolf & N. Wolf)
 A. Classen, 201:Vol14-220
 A. Robertshaw, 402(MLR):Oct89-1020
Oswald von Wolkenstein. Streuüberliefe-rung.* (H-D. Mück, ed)
 F. Delbono, 684(ZDA):Band117Heft2-87
Otaka, Y. – see Marie de France
O'Toole, F. The Politics of Magic.
 C. Murray, 272(IUR):Spring88-161
Otsuka, K., G. Ranis & G. Saxonhouse. Com-parative Technology Choice in Develop-ment.
 R. Evans, Jr., 293(JASt):Nov88-841
Ott, A. Hegel et la philosophie allemande ou exposé et examen critique des principaux systèmes de la philosophie allemand depuis Kant, et specialement de celui de Hegel.
 R.M., 342:Band79Heft2-252
Ott, H. Martin Heidegger.
 M. Zimmerman, 617(TLS):5-11May89-481
Otten, C.F. Environ'd With Eternity.*
 E. Mackenzie, 447(N&Q):Jun88-216
Otten, C.F. A Lycanthropy Reader.
 R.M. Davis, 577(SHR):Fall88-400
 C. Oates, 203:Vol99No2-266
 J. Wood, 402(MLR):Jul89-693
 J.M. Ziolkowski, 589:Apr88-451
Otten, F. Der Reisebericht eines anonymen Russen über seine Reise nach Westeuropa im Zeitraum 1697/1699.
 E. Donnert, 688(ZSP):Band48Heft2-393
Otten, F. Untersuchungen zu den Fremd- und Lehnwörtern bei Peter dem Grossen.
 W.F. Ryan, 575(SEER):Jan88-137

Pacheco, C.C. Breaking Patterns.
J. Viorst, 441:9Apr89-30
Pacheco, F. Libro de descripción de verda-
deros retratos de ilustres y memorables
varones (Sevilla, 1599). (P.M. Piñero Ram-
írez & R. Reyes Cano, eds)
M. Chevalier, 92(BH):Jan-Dec87-380
Pachet, P. Autobiographie de mon père.*
F. Trémolières, 450(NRF):Feb88-96
Pachoński, J. Generał Franciszek Paszkowski,
1778-1856.
A.A. Hetnal, 497(PolR):Vol33No4-475
Pachoński, J. & R.K. Wilson. Poland's Carib-
bean Tragedy.
J.W. Wieczerzak, 497(PolR):Vol33No1-101
Pächt, O. Book Illumination in the Middle
Ages.*
M. Camille, 377:Mar88-50
L.F. Sandler, 54:Sep88-521
78(BC):Autumn88-313
Pack, R. Clayfield Rejoices, Clayfield La-
ments.
S.J. Rosowski, 502(PrS):Summer88-127
Pack, R., S. Lea & J. Parini, eds. The Bread
Loaf Anthology of Contemporary American
Poetry.
C. Clausen, 569(SR):Winter88-131
Pack, R. & J. Parini, eds. The Bread Loaf
Anthology of Contemporary American Short
Stories.*
639(VQR):Winter88-21
Packalén, S. Zum Hölderlinbild in der
Bundesrepublik und der DDR.
H. Gaskill, 133:Band21Heft2/3-221
E.E. George, 301(JEGP):Apr88-300
A.A. Kuzniar, 564:May88-196
O. van Weerdenburg, 224(GRM):
Band38Heft1/2-220
Packard, V. The Ultra Rich.
M. Gallagher, 441:19Feb89-21
Packer, N.H. The Women Who Walk.
S. Ferguson, 441:23Jul89-18
de Paco, M. - see Medina, V.
Padden, C. & T. Humphries. Deaf in America.
K. Ray, 441:26Mar89-17
Paden, W.D., T. Sankovitch & P.H. Stäblein -
see Bertran de Born
Padfield, P. Armada.*
J.R. Hale, 453(NYRB):16Feb89-30
Padilla, G. - see Chavez, A.
de Padilla, J. Los doce triunfos de los doce
apóstoles. (Vol 3)(E. Norti Gualdani, ed)
T. O'Reilly, 86(BHS):Apr88-181
Padley, G.A. Grammatical Theory in Western
Europe, 1500-1700.*
A. Scaglione, 276:Spring88-44
Paduano, G. & M. Fusillo - see Apollonius
Paech, J., ed. Methodenprobleme der Analyse
verfilmter Literatur. Literatur und Film:
Mephisto.
B. Murray, 221(GQ):Spring87-267
Paehlke, R.C. Environmentalism and the
Future of Progressive Politics.
T. Burke, 324:Nov89-816
J. Porritt, 617(TLS):30Jun-6Jul89-708
J.I. Weinberg, 441:9Apr89-33
Pagani, I. La teoria linguistica di Dante.
Z.G. Barański, 545(RPh):Aug88-51
Pagano, R. Scarlatti.
F. Hammond, 410(M&L):Oct88-519
Pagden, A., ed. The Languages of Political
Theory in Early-Modern Europe.
F. Gilbert, 551(RenQ):Autumn88-482

Pagden, A. - see Cortés, H.
Page, C. Voices and Instruments of the Mid-
dle Ages.*
J. Caldwell, 382(MAE):1988/2-333
M. Everist, 410(M&L):Apr88-246
Page, K. Island Paradise.
C. Greenland, 617(TLS):7-13Jul89-738
Page, M. & R. Ingpen, eds. Encyclopedia of
Things That Never Were.
W.N., 102(CanL):Winter87-284
Page, N. A Conrad Companion.
J.H. Stape, 177(ELT):Vol31No2-237
Page, N. A Dickens Chronology.
G. Storey, 617(TLS):17-23Feb89-173
Page, N. - see "Thomas Hardy Annual"
Page, P.K. Brazilian Journal.*
C. Messenger, 102(CanL):Autumn88-161
Page, R.I. Runes.
E.A. Ebbinghaus, 215(GL):Vol28No2-149
Page, T. - see Gould, G.
Pagels, E. Adam, Eve, and the Serpent.*
639(VQR):Autumn88-138
Pagetti, C. I Marziani alla Corte della Regina
Vittoria.
I.F. Clarke, 561(SFS):Jul88-240
Pagis, D. Variable Directions.
C. Kizer, 441:12Nov89-63
Pagliai, F., G. Folena & M. Scotti - see Fos-
colo, U.
Pagnini, M., ed. Il Romanticismo.
R. Ceserani, 494:Vol8No1-202
Pagnol, M. Jean de Florette [and] Manon of
the Springs.*
639(VQR):Autumn88-138
Pagnotta, L. Bugiardini.
E. Fahy, 90:Sep88-704
F. Russell, 39:Sep88-210
Pagnoulle, C. David Jones.
W. Cookson, 4:Winter88-81
Paikeday, T.M. The Native Speaker Is Dead!
Z.P. Thundy, 35(AS):Fall88-271
Paillard, D. Enonciation et détermination en
russe contemporain.
T.M. Nikolaeva, 559:Vol12No3-351
Paine, F. & N.E. Magazines.
B. Katz, 87(BB):Mar88-63
Painter, D.S. Oil and the American Century.
J.N. McDougall, 106:Spring88-121
Painter, G.D. Marcel Proust. (rev)
E. Hughes, 617(TLS):13-19Oct89-1112
Painter, N.I. Standing at Armageddon.
639(VQR):Summer88-82
Painting, D. Amy Dillwyn.
S. Mitchell, 637(VS):Autumn88-138
Pakenham, T. & V., eds. Dublin.
A. Haverty, 617(TLS):6-12Jan89-7
Pal, P., ed. American Collectors of Asian Art.
J. Leoshko, 60:Jul-Aug88-127
Pal, P. Indian Sculpture. (Vol 1)
90:Jan88-45
Palau, B. Historia de la gloriosa santa Oro-
sia.* (O. Mazur, ed)
L.L. Cofresí, 552(REH):Jan88-137
A.A. Heathcote, 402(MLR):Jan89-204
Paley, M.D. The Apocalyptic Sublime.*
J.A. Dando, 637(VS):Winter89-250
C. Powell, 59:Mar88-135
J. Wittreich, 88:Summer88-21
Palisca, C.V. The Florentine Camerata.
D. Fallows, 617(TLS):1-7Sep89-943
Palisca, C.V. Humanism in Italian Renais-
sance Musical Thought.*
J. Haar, 551(RenQ):Spring88-138

Palissy, B. Recepte veritable. (K. Cameron, ed)
  G. Roques, 553(RLiR):Jul-Dec88-557
Palliser, C. The Quincunx.
  R.B. Martin, 617(TLS):15-21Sep89-1006
Pallot, G.B. L'art du siege au XVIIIe siècle.
  H. Roberts, 39:Jul88-68
Palma Caetano, J.A. & others. Grammatik Portugiesisch.
  J. Schmidt-Radefeldt, 547(RF):Band100 Heft4-380
Palmer, A. The Banner of Battle.*
  J.W. Kipp, 550(RusR):Apr88-192
Palmer, B.D., ed. The Character of Class Struggle.
  J. Mouat, 102(CanL):Spring88-109
Palmer, B.D. Solidarity.
  D. Swartz, 529(QQ):Winter88-962
Palmer, C. - see Machen, A.
Palmer, F.R. The English Verb. (2nd ed)
  W.N. Francis, 350:Jun89-435
Palmer, F.R. Mood and Modality.
  E.E. Davies, 361:Jul88-268
  R. Salkie, 297(JL):Mar88-240
Palmer, H. & T., eds. Peoples of Alberta.
  B. Ferguson, 298:Spring/Summer88-219
Palmer, J. The Logic of the Absurd.
  P.D. Murphy, 590:Jun89-47
Palmer, M. Sun.
  W. Logan, 441:28May89-24
Palmer, R. The Sound of History.
  T. Hoppen, 617(TLS):7-13Apr89-358
Palmer, R.D. & T.J. Reckford. Building ASEAN.
  S.A. Douglas, 293(JASt):Aug88-712
Palomino, A. Lives of the Eminent Spanish Painters and Sculptors. (Spanish title: Antonio Palomino: Vidas.) (N. Ayala Mallory, ed & trans)
  E.H., 90:Mar88-242
  V. Lleó Cañal, 617(TLS):20-26Jan89-66
Pálsson, H. & P. Edwards - see "Knytlinga saga"
Pálsson, H. & P. Edwards - see "Magnus' Saga"
Paludan, P.S. "A People's Contest."
  R. Snow, 441:29Jan89-7
Palumbo, D., ed. Spectrum of the Fantastic.
  D.M. Hassler, 561(SFS):Nov88-381
Panati, C. Panati's Extraordinary Endings of Practically Everything and Everybody.
  E. Zotti, 441:24Sep89-22
Pančenko, A.M., ed. Russkaja literatura XVIII veka v ee svjazjax s iskusstvom i naukoj.
  T. Barran, 574(SEEJ):Summer88-312
Panetta, V.J., Jr. - see Denis, J.
Pangle, T.L., ed. The Roots of Political Philosophy.
  S.R. Hemmenway, 543:Dec88-398
Pangle, T.L. The Spirit of Modern Republicanism.
  W. Brock, 617(TLS):8-14Sep89-979
Pangle, T.L. - see Strauss, L.
Panichas, G.A. The Burden of Vision.*
  G. Woodcock, 569(SR):Spring88-306
Pāṇini. Aṣṭādhyāyī of Pāṇini. (S.M. Katre, trans)
  M.M. Deshpande, 350:Sep89-646
  W.G. Regier & R. Wallace, 400(MLN): Dec88-1195
Panisse, M.D.R. - see under Rios Panisse, M.D.
Panizzolo, P. Die schweizerische Variante des Hochdeutschen.
  R. Hinderling, 685(ZDL):3/1987-400

Pankowski, M. Le Gars de Lvov.
  L. Kovacs, 450(NRF):May88-111
Pannenberg, W. Christianity in a Secularized World.
  A. Webster, 617(TLS):27Oct-2Nov89-1188
Panter-Downes, M. & others. The New Yorker Book of War Pieces.
  P. French, 617(TLS):12-18May89-506
Paolini, C.J. Valle-Inclán's Modernism.*
  A. Sinclair, 86(BHS):Oct88-413
Papadiamantis, A. The Murderess.
  K.M., 295(JML):Fall87/Winter88-216
Papadiamantis, A. Tales From a Greek Island.*
  W.C. Hamlin, 573(SSF):Winter88-84
Papanghelis, T.D. Propertius.*
  K. Gries, 124:Nov-Dec88-134
Papàsogli, B. La Lettera e lo Spirito, Temi e figure del Seicento francese.
  H. Bordes, 535(RHL):Nov-Dec88-1136
Paperno, L. & R.D. Sylvester. Getting Around Town in Russian Situational Dialogs.
  J.E. Bernhardt, 399(MLJ):Summer88-245
  K.L. Nalibow, 574(SEEJ):Winter88-681
"The Papers of Dorothy Livesay."*
  L.B. Thompson, 102(CanL):Spring88-179
Papineau, D. Reality and Representation.*
  J. Heil, 518:Jul88-151
  P.F. Snowdon, 393(Mind):Oct88-629
  P. Trotignon, 542:Jul-Sep88-392
Paquet, M., with R. Ralston & D. Cardinal. A Handbook for Cultural Trustees.
  B.J. Wry, 476:Spring88-81
Paquin, W. Arthur de Bussières, poète, et l'Ecole littéraire de Montréal.
  D.M. Hayne, 627(UTQ):Fall87-178
Paradis, M., H. Hagiwara & N. Hildebrandt. Neurolinguistic Aspects of the Japanese Writing System.*
  C. Futter, 320(CJL):Mar88-95
Paral, V. Catapult.
  D.J. Enright, 453(NYRB):18May89-37
  O. Wickerhauser, 441:18Jun89-20
Paras, J. The Music for Viola Bastarda.* (G. & G. Houle, eds)
  R. Boenig, 568(SCN):Spring-Summer88-21
  J.A. Sadie, 415:May88-246
Paratore, E. - see Bernard of Clairvaux
Pardo Bazán, E. Los Pazos de Ulloa. (M. Mayoral, ed)
  G. Gullón, 240(HR):Autumn88-505
Pardo de Andrade, M. La Conversione de Sant'Agostino, tragicommedia. (M.R. Saurín de la Iglesia, ed)
  I.L. McClelland, 86(BHS):Apr88-188
Parekh, B. Gandhi's Political Philosophy.
  S. Khilnani, 617(TLS):6-12Oct89-1080
Paret, P. Art as History.
  S.S. Prawer, 617(TLS):27Oct-2Nov89-1193
Parfit, M. Chasing the Glory.
  J.B. Cooke, 441:1Jan89-10
Parfitt, G. Fiction of the First World War.*
  P. Parker, 364:Jul88-101
Parfitt, T. The Thirteenth Gate.
  R. Fainlight, 364:Nov87-109
Pargetter, W. Observations on Maniacal Disorders.
  R. Brown, 617(TLS):7-13Jul89-749
Pariente, A., ed. En torno a Góngora.
  W.J. Weaver 3d, 240(HR):Spring88-262

Parini, J. Town Life.
  B. Bennett, 441:12Mar89-38
  639(VQR):Summer88-97
Paris, B. Louise Brooks.
  N. Gabler, 441:22Oct89-11
Paris, R-M. Camille.*
  A. Adams, 39:Dec88-447
"Paris, 1979-1989."
  D. Waterman, 55:Oct88-94
Parish, P.J. Slavery.
  442(NY):30Oct89-118
Parish, R. Pascal's "Lettres Provinciales."
  G. Strickland, 617(TLS):14-20Jul89-769
Parizeau, A. L'amour de Jeanne.
  E. Potvin, 102(CanL):Summer88-156
Park, C. The Househusband.
  M. Stimpson, 617(TLS):10-16Mar89-256
Park, P. Sugar Rain.
  G. Jonas, 441:20Aug89-24
Parke, H.W. The Oracles of Apollo in Asia
  Minor.*
  J. Pouilloux, 555:Vol61fasc2-304
Parker, D., ed. Essays on Modern American
  Drama.
  B. Murphy, 130:Fall88-274
  B.N. Olshen, 397(MD):Mar88-127
Parker, F. Linguistics for Non-Linguists.*
  C.F. Meyer, 35(AS):Summer88-167
Parker, G.F. Johnson's Shakespeare.
  R. Hapgood, 617(TLS):25-31Aug89-927
Parker, K.L. The English Sabbath.
  P. Collinson, 617(TLS):17-23Feb89-155
Parker, P. Ackerley.
  H. Carpenter, 617(TLS):15-21Sep89-993
  A. Lurie, 441:12Nov89-12
Parker, P. The Old Lie.
  P. Dickinson, 364:Mar87-104
Parker, P. & G. Hartman, eds. Shakespeare
  and the Question of Theory.*
  J. Drakakis, 447(N&Q):Sep88-369
  M.H. Keefer, 627(UTQ):Fall87-109
  B.M., 494:Vol8No2-468
  M. Pfister, 156(ShJW):Jahrbuch1988-235
  R. Strier, 405(MP):Aug88-56
  P. Wenzel, 38:Band106Heft3/4-529
Parker, P. & D. Quint, eds. Literary Theory/
  Renaissance Texts.*
  J.P. Bednarz, 250(HLQ):Autumn88-319
  M. Evans, 551(RenQ):Spring88-158
  R. Flores, 478(P&L):Oct88-311
  B.M., 494:Vol8No2-460
  A. Patterson, 627(UTQ):Fall87-106
  N.W. Rodman, 188(ECr):Summer88-98
  J. Tylus, 276:Autumn88-285
Parker, R. The Subversive Stitch.
  B.M. Ward, 658:Summer/Autumn88-193
Parker, R.A.C. Struggle for Survival.
  M. Carver, 617(TLS):1-7Sep89-935
Parker, R.B. Playmates.
  R.W.B. Lewis, 441:23Apr89-13
  442(NY):3Jul89-96
Parker, R.D. Faulkner and the Novelistic
  Imagination.
  C.S. Brown, 569(SR):Spring88-271
  J.T. Matthews, 301(JEGP):Jan88-146
Parker, R.D. The Unbeliever.
  B.C. Millier, 617(TLS):12-18May89-516
Parker, S.T., ed. The Roman Frontier in Cen-
  tral Jordan.
  B. Isaac, 313:Vol78-240
Parker, S.T. Romans and Saracens.
  B. Isaac, 313:Vol78-240
  M. Sartre, 122:Apr88-173

Parker, T. A Place Called Bird.
  C. Hitchens, 617(TLS):17-23Feb89-157
Parkes, G., ed. Heidegger and Asian Thought.
  Y. Saito, 293(JASt):Aug88-576
Parkes, K.S. Writers and Politics in West
  Germany.*
  V.K., 295(JML):Fall87/Winter88-217
  J.M. Ritchie, 366:Spring88-137
Parkin, A. - see Boucicault, D.
Parkin, F. The Mind and Body Shop.
  639(VQR):Winter88-20
Parkin, S. Green Parties.
  J. Buchan, 617(TLS):20-26Oct89-1159
Parkinson, D.B. Constructing the Social Con-
  text of Communication.
  A.S. Kaye, 320(CJL):Sep88-265
Parkinson, M.H. The Rural Novel.
  J. Warwick, 107(CRCL):Mar88-142
  P. Zimmermann, 52:Band23Heft3-321
Parks, M. - see De Mille, J.
Parks, T. Family Planning.
  P. Reading, 617(TLS):26May-1Jun89-592
Parks, T. Loving Roger.*
  D. Teagle, 42(AR):Summer88-390
Parnell, T. Collected Poems of Thomas Par-
  nell. (C. Rawson & F.P. Lock, eds)
  D. Davie, 617(TLS):8-14Dec89-1365
Paroissien, D. "Oliver Twist."
  J.J. Fenstermaker, 158:Mar88-33
Paroussis, M. Les Listes de champs de Pylos
  et Hattuša et le régime foncier mycénien et
  hittite.
  J.T. Hooker, 123:Vol38No2-451
Parović-Pešikan, M. Corpus Vasorum Anti-
  quorum. (Yugoslavia, Vol 4)
  B.A. Sparkes, 303(JoHS):Vol108-268
Parra, R. El álbum secreto del Sagrado Cora-
  zón.
  D.L. Heyck, 238:Mar88-94
Parret, H. Les passions.
  C.P. Morinet, 567:Vol68No1/2-185
Parret, H. & H-G. Ruprecht, eds. Exigences et
  perspectives de la sémiotique.
  D.H., 355(LSoc):Jun88-310
Parrinder, G., ed. A Dictionary of Religious
  and Spiritual Quotations.
  B. Brindley, 617(TLS):22-28Dec89-1404
Parrinder, P. The Failure of Theory.
  W. van Peer, 204(FdL):Spring88-233
  R. Selden, 677(YES):Vol19-363
  P. Stevick, 395(MFS):Summer88-313
Parrish, S.M. - see Coleridge, S.T.
Parrish, T.M. & R.M. Willingham, Jr. Confed-
  erate Imprints.
  87(BB):Sep88-217
Parroni, P. - see Pomponius Mela
Parrott, B. The Soviet Union and Ballistic
  Missle Defense.
  J. Snyder, 550(RusR):Apr88-221
Parry, G.J.R. A Protestant Vision.
  A.J. Slavin, 551(RenQ):Winter88-727
Parsons, C. Mathematics in Philosophy.*
  S. Shapiro, 316:Mar88-321
Parsons, C. & M. Ward. A Bibliography of
  Salon Criticism in Second Empire Paris.*
  R. Lethbridge, 208(FS):Jan88-103
Parsons, G., ed. Religion in Victorian Britain.
  (Vols 1, 2 & 4)
  P. Butler, 617(TLS):4-10Aug89-852
Parsons, M.J. How We Understand Art.*
  M.K. Di Blasio, 289:Winter88-103
  D.H. Feldman, 289:Winter88-85
                              [continued]

Paul, E.F. & others, eds. Nuclear Rights/Nuclear Wrongs.
  J.S. Hellman, 575(SEER):Jan88-157
Paul, J-M., ed. Situation de l'homme et histoire de la philosophie dans l'oeuvre de Karl Jaspers.
  J-J. Wunenburger, 192(EP):Jan-Mar88-118
Paul, J.M. The Victorian Heritage of Virginia Woolf.*
  H. Richter, 594:Winter88-417
Paul, S. In Search of the Primitive.*
  P. Christensen, 472:Vol15No1-125
Prince Paul of Hohenzollern-Roumania. King Carol II.
  N. Malcolm, 617(TLS):10-16Feb89-137
Paulhan, C. - see Pozzi, C.
Paulhan, J. Choix de lettres. (Vol 1) (D. Aury & J-C. Zylberstein, eds; rev by B. Leuilliot)
  J-J. Didier, 356(LR):Feb-May88-146
Paulhan, J. Fautrier l'enragé.
  J-Y. Pouilloux, 98:Mar88-187
Paulhan, J. & A. Suarès. Correspondance 1925-1940.
  R. Jacquelin, 450(NRF):Jan88-105
Paulin, R. Ludwig Tieck.*
  T.C. Fox, 591(SIR):Winter88-616
  W.J. Lillyman, 221(GQ):Fall87-672
Paulin, T., ed. The Faber Anthology of Political Verse.
  S. Burris, 639(VQR):Summer88-546
Paulin, T. Fivemiletown.*
  S. O'Brien, 364:Apr/May88-118
Paulos, J.A. Innumeracy.
  M. Kline, 441:15Jan89-9
Paulsen, W. Deutsche Literatur des Expressionismus.
  R. Cardinal, 133:Band21Heft4-355
  E. Krispyn, 301(JEGP):Jan88-93
Paulson, R. Representations of Revolution (1789-1820).*
  G.G. Brittan, Jr., 207(FR):May89-1107
Paulson, W.R. Enlightenment, Romanticism, and the Blind in France.*
  W. Greenberg, 207(FR):Oct88-174
  E.J. MacArthur, 188(ECr):Winter88-120
Paulston, C.B., ed. International Handbook of Bilingualism and Bilingual Education.
  B. Spolsky, 350:Sep89-632
Pauly, P.J. Controlling Life.
  R.C. Lewontin, 453(NYRB):27Apr89-18
Pavel, T. Le Mirage linguistique.
  A.M. Hjort, 400(MLN):Sep88-905
Pavel, T.G. Fictional Worlds.*
  M. Cornis-Pop, 141:Winter88-134
  S.L. Feagin, 290(JAAC):Spring88-428
  B.K. Horvath, 532(RCF):Spring88-197
  A. Leighton, 617(TLS):1-7Sep89-950
  U. Niklas, 567:Vol71No1/2-165
  L. Rodríguez-Carranza, 494:Vol9No4-853
  A.S., 295(JML):Fall87/Winter88-264
Pavić, M. Dictionary of the Khazars.* (French title: Le Dictionnaire Khazar.)
  E. Korn, 617(TLS):3-9Mar89-225
  L. Kovacs, 450(NRF):Jul-Aug88-226
Pavković, A., ed. Contemporary Yugoslav Philosophy.
  M. Detlefsen, 103:Dec89-492
Pavlova, K. A Double Life.
  D. Greene, 574(SEEJ):Winter88-654
Pavlowitch, S.K. The Improbable Survivor.
  M. Wheeler, 617(TLS):16-22Jun89-659

Pawel, E. The Labyrinth of Exile.
  P. Loewenberg, 441:31Dec89-9
Pawling, C., ed. Popular Fiction and Social Change.*
  M. Jensen, 102(CanL):Winter87-176
Paxton, J. Companion to the French Revolution.
  C. Lucas, 617(TLS):19-25May89-554
Payer, L. Medicine and Culture.*
  D. Gould, 617(TLS):7-13Jul89-748
Payer, P.J. Sex and the Penitentials.
  B.E. Ferme, 382(MAE):1988/1-83
Payerle, G. Unknown Soldier.
  C. Hunter, 376:Dec88-135
Payette, L. La Bonne Aventure.
  S.A. Bergersen, 102(CanL):Spring88-189
Payne, A.J. Politics in Jamaica.
  G.K. Lewis, 617(TLS):3-9Feb89-104
Payne, D. Early from the Dance.
  B. Cole, 441:26Nov89-30
Payne, J. Colloquial Hungarian.
  P. Sherwood, 575(SEER):Oct88-633
Payne, R.O. Geoffrey Chaucer. (2nd ed)
  E. Brown, Jr., 589:Jan88-210
Payot, R. L'intuition ontologique et l'introduction à la métaphysique.
  P. Trotignon, 542:Apr-Jun88-222
"Au pays d'Eros."
  G. Ferroni, 539:Summer88-245
de Paysac, H. - see Gide, A.
Payzant, G. - see Hanslick, E.
Paz, O. The Collected Poems of Octavio Paz, 1957-1987.* (E. Weinberger & others, eds & trans)
  D. Lyon, 37:Nov/Dec88-60
  A. Terry, 617(TLS):14-20Apr89-402
  639(VQR):Spring88-64
Paz, O. Convergencies.*
  639(VQR):Spring88-53
Pazzi, R. Searching for the Emperor.
  P. Bailey, 617(TLS):11-17Aug89-878
  J. Roux, 441:12Feb89-18
Pazzi, R. Vangelo di Giuda.
  P. Bailey, 617(TLS):11-17Aug89-878
Peacock, D.P.S. Pottery in the Roman World.
  J.J. Paterson, 313:Vol78-241
Peacock, D.P.S. & D.F. Williams. Amphorae and the Roman Economy.
  J.J. Paterson, 313:Vol78-241
Peacock, M. Take Heart.
  J. Parini, 441:22Oct89-16
Peacock, S.J. Jane Ellen Harrison.
  M. Beard, 617(TLS):27Jan-2Feb89-82
Peacocke, C. Thoughts.*
  G. Forbes, 484(PPR):Sep88-178
  J-L. Gardies, 542:Jul-Sep88-393
Peacocke, M.R. Marginal Land.
  S. Knight, 364:Dec88/Jan89-118
  G. Mort, 493:Winter88/89-57
  S. O'Brien, 617(TLS):25-31Aug89-916
Pearce, D. & J. Wolenski, eds. Logischer Rationalismus.
  P. Engel, 542:Jul-Sep88-393
Pearce, M. The Mamur Zapt and the Night of the Dog.
  T.J. Binyon, 617(TLS):21-27Jul89-810
Pearce, R.H. Gesta Humanorum.*
  J. Longenbach, 705:Fall88-185
Pearcy, L.T. The Mediated Muse.*
  S. Chaudhuri, 447(N&Q):Mar88-74
  A.K. Hieatt, 539:Summer88-242
Pears, D. The False Prison. (Vol 2)
  M. Budd, 617(TLS):3-9Feb89-115

Pears, I. The Discovery of Painting.
  D. Solkin, 617(TLS):10–16Feb89–149
Pearsall, D. "The Canterbury Tales."*
  J.O. Fichte, 72:Band224Heft2–396
  J.B. Friedman, 677(YES):Vol19–305
Pearsall, D.A., ed. Manuscripts and Texts.
  N.F. Blake, 402(MLR):Oct89–914
  B. Cottle, 179(ES):Aug88–360
  E.G. Stanley, 447(N&Q):Jun88–212
Pearsall, D.A. – see Chaucer, G.
Pearson, B.L. Sounds So Good to Me.
  D.G. Such, 292(JAF):Jan–Mar88–99
Pearson, N.W., Jr. Goin' to Kansas City.*
  G.L. Starks, Jr., 91:Fall88–254
Pearson, R. Stendhal's Violin.*
  D. Place, 402(MLR):Jul89–743
Pearson, R. Undercurrents.
  T.J. Binyon, 617(TLS):6–12Oct89–1104
Pearson, T.R. Call and Response.
  442(NY):4Sep89–106
Pearson, T.S. Russian Officialdom in Crisis.
  J. Keep, 617(TLS):11–17Aug89–868
Peart–Binns, J.S. Maurice B. Reckitt.
  G. Irvine, 617(TLS):27Jan–2Feb89–82
Pease, D.E. Visionary Compacts.*
  E. Carton, 533:Winter89–99
  W.G. Heath, 106:Summer88–263
  M.W. Thomas, 646(WWR):Fall88–97
  K.P. Van Anglen, 445(NCF):Jun88–116
Peattie, M.R. Nan'yō.
  H. Frei, 407(MN):Autumn88–379
Peck, J. & M. Coyle. How to Study a Shake-
  speare Play.
  L. Potter, 402(MLR):Jul89–710
Peck, R.A. Chaucer's "Romaunt of the Rose"
  and "Boece," "Treatise on the Astrolabe,"
  "Equatorie of the Planetis," Lost Works,
  and Chaucerian Apocrypha.
  R. Beadle, 617(TLS):16–22Jun89–676
Peckham, M. The Birth of Romanticism 1790–
  1815.
  R. Nicholls, 131(CL):Winter88–87
Pédech, P. Historiens, Compagnons d'Alex-
  andre.*
  S. Hornblower, 123:Vol38No1–144
Pedersen, J.S. The Reform of Girls' Secondary
  and Higher Education in Victorian England.
  C. Dyhouse, 637(VS):Summer89–589
Pedersen, R. & F.G. Andersen, eds. The Con-
  cept of Tradition in Ballad Research.*
  J. Harris, 563(SS):Spring88–315
Pedroni, P.N. Existence as Theme in Carlo
  Cassola's Fiction.*
  H. Moss, 402(MLR):Apr89–495
Peel, E. The Painter Joaquín Sorolla y Bas-
  tida.
  R. Thomson, 617(TLS):23–29Jun89–697
van Peer, W. Stylistics and Foregrounding.
  R. Carter, 506(PSt):Sep88–108
Peeters, L. Une prose du monde.*
  M. Watthee-Delmotte, 356(LR):Nov88–522
Péguy, C. Oeuvres en prose complètes. (Vol
  1) (R. Burac, ed)
  N. Wilson, 208(FS):Oct88–488
"Peindre dans la lumière de la Méditerranée."
  F. de Mèredieu, 450(NRF):Mar88–93
Peirce, C.S. Writings of Charles S. Peirce.*
  (Vol 3) (C.J.W. Kloesel, ed)
  C. Hookway, 567:Vol69No3/4–331
Peirone, L. Tra Dante e "Il Fiore." Il "Detto
  d'Amore" tra "Il Fiore" e Dante.
  Z.G. Barański, 545(RPh):Aug88–51

Pekar, H. More American Splendor.* Ameri-
  can Splendor.
  S. Gutterman, 62:Dec88–112
Pelayo, M.M. – see under Menéndez Pelayo, M.
Pelckmans, P. Le Rêve apprivoisé.
  G.J. Mallinson, 208(FS):Jan88–82
  P. Ronzeaud, 535(RHL):Mar–Apr88–347
Pelen, M.M. Latin Poetic Irony in the "Roman
  de la Rose."
  L.C. Brook, 402(MLR):Apr89–466
Peli, P. Torah Today.
  J. Riemer, 390:Feb/Mar88–63
Pelikan, J. The Christian Tradition. (Vol 5)
  The Melody of Theology.
  J. Drury, 617(TLS):29Dec89/4Jan90–1450
Pellegrin, H. – see Shadwell, T.
Pellegrin, P. Aristotle's Classification of
  Animals.
  S.R.L. Clark, 319:Apr89–300
Pelletier, C. Once Upon a Time on the Banks.
  F. Flagg, 441:22Oct89–21
Pelletier, J. Lecture politique du roman qué-
  bécois contemporain.
  A.L. Amprimoz, 345(KRQ):May88–223
Pelletier, J., ed. Le Social et le Littéraire.*
  G. Cesbron, 535(RHL):Jan–Feb88–167
Pellón, G. & J. Rodríguez-Luis, eds. Upstarts,
  Wanderers or Swindlers.*
  F. Baasner, 72:Band225Heft2–477
  F.P. Casa, 447(N&Q):Jun88–267
Peltason, T. Reading "In Memoriam."*
  J. Kolb, 481(PQ):Fall88–532
  S. Shatto, 301(JEGP):Jan88–125
Peltenburg, E.J. Lemba Archaeological Proj-
  ect. (Vol 1)
  H. Matthäus, 229:Band60Heft6–553
Pelton, W.J., S. Sackmann & R. Boguslaw.
  Tough Choices.
  K. Konolige, 441:29Oct89–41
Pelzer, J. "Kritik durch Spott."
  M. Wedel, 654(WB):10/1988–1756
Pemble, J. The Mediterranean Passion.
  A. Ryall, 637(VS):Summer89–597
Peña, L. El ente y su ser.
  A. Reix, 542:Oct–Dec88–506
Peña Pérez, F.J., ed. Documentación del mon-
  asterio de San Juan de Burgos (1091–
  1400).
  P. Freedman, 589:Apr88–452
Penelhum, T. Butler.*
  J.B. Schneewind, 482(PhR):Jul88–425
Penfield, J. The Media.
  S. Stempleski, 608:Mar89–142
Penfield, J., ed. Women and Language in
  Transition.
  B.S. McElhinny, 350:Dec89–906
Penfield, J. & J.L. Ornstein-Galicia. Chicano
  English.
  J. Amastae, 355(LSoc):Sep88–436
Penfold, J. Craft, Design and Technology.
  P. Green, 324:Jun89–441
Penhaligon, A. Penhaligon.
  J. Campbell, 617(TLS):29Sep–5Oct89–
  1054
Penn, J. Outrageous Exposures.
  T.J. Binyon, 617(TLS):10–16Mar89–262
Penna, S. Croix et délice. [together with]
  Ginsburg, N. Sandro Penna.
  F. Mary, 450(NRF):Feb88–103
Penner, P. Robert Needham Cust, 1821–1909.
  R.E. Frykenberg, 637(VS):Winter89–258
Penner, T. Ascent from Nominalism.
  F.C. White, 63:Sep88–429

Pennington, S. & B. Westover. A Hidden Workforce.
 D. Atkinson, 617(TLS):15–21Sep89–1014
Pennock, J.R. & J.W. Chapman, eds. NOMOS XXIX.
 J.T. Kloppenberg, 185:Oct88–163
Penrose, A. The Lives of Lee Miller.*
 A. Winand, 441:30Jul89–17
Penrose, B. & S. Freeman. Conspiracy of Silence.
 A. MacAdam, 55:Feb88–51
 639(VQR):Spring88–61
Penrose, J. Letters from Bath 1766–67 by the Rev. John Penrose. (B. Mitchell & H. Penrose, eds)
 P. Rogers, 83:Spring88–90
Penrose, R. The Emperor's New Mind.
 D.C. Dennett, 617(TLS):29Sep–5Oct89–1055
 T. Ferris, 441:19Nov89–3
Pensado, J.L. & C. Pensado Ruiz. "Gueada" y "geada" gallegas.
 D. Woll, 547(RF):Band99Heft4–434
Pensado Ruiz, C. Cronología relativa del castellano.
 Y. Malkiel, 545(RPh):May89–408
 H. Meier, 72:Band224Heft2–435
Pensado Ruiz, C. El orden histórico de los processos fonológicos.
 H. Meier, 72:Band224Heft2–435
Penuel, A.M. Psychology, Religion, and Ethics in Galdós's Novels.
 G. Gullón, 238:Dec88–828
 T.A. Sackett, 395(MFS):Winter88–726
Penzias, A. Ideas and Information.
 T. Bay, 441:9Apr89–33
Penzl, H. Althochdeutsch.
 B.J. Koekkoek, 221(GQ):Summer87–465
Peperzak, A.T. Philosophy and Politics.*
 J–F. Kervegan, 192(EP):Jan–Mar88–123
Pepió, V.B. – see under Beltrán Pepió, V.
Peppe, L. Posizione giuridica a e ruolo sociale della donna romana in età repubblicana.
 J.F. Gardner, 313:Vol78–205
Pepper, C.D., with H. Gorey. Pepper.
 639(VQR):Spring88–50
Pepper, M., ed. A Dictionary of Religious Quotations.
 B. Brindley, 617(TLS):22–28Dec89–1404
Pepper, S. & N. Adams. Firearms and Fortifications.*
 J. Coolidge, 576:Jun88–196
Pepper–Smith, R. Six Stories.
 J. Taylor, 532(RCF):Summer88–323
Perani, J. & M. Fleming. Yoruba Art of West Africa.
 2(AfrA):Feb88–93
Percas de Ponseti, H. Cervantes the Writer and Painter of "Don Quijote."
 E. Urbina, 304(JHP):Autumn88–80
Percival, A. Galdós and His Critics.*
 A. Risco, 627(UTQ):Fall87–211
Percy, H.R. A Model Lover.*
 B. Leckie, 102(CanL):Winter87–278
Percy, H.R. Tranter's Tree.
 M. Ware, 198:Summer88–112
Percy, W. The Thanatos Syndrome.*
 E. Current–Garcia, 577(SHR):Summer88–294
 J. Mellors, 364:Dec87/Jan88–136
Perdue, P.C. Exhausting the Earth.
 Y–C. Wang, 293(JASt):Aug88–612

Perec, G. La clôture et autres poèmes. Alphabets.
 A. Chevrier, 98:May88–416
Perec, G. Life: A User's Manual.*
 D. Flower, 364:Dec87/Jan88–140
 T. McGonigle, 532(RCF):Summer88–314
Perec, G. Voeux. L'Infraordinaire. 53 jours.
 J. Sturrock, 358:Dec89–6
Perec, G. W or the Memory of Childhood.
 G. Craig, 617(TLS):10–16Feb89–148
 L. Simon, 441:8Jan89–16
Pereda Llarena, F.J., ed. Documentación de la catedral de Burgos (1254–1293; 1294–1316).*
 P. Freedman, 589:Apr88–452
Pereira, B. Texteis.
 2(AfrA):Nov87–84
Perelman, C. Le raisonnable et le déraisonnable en droit.
 J–L. Gardies, 542:Jan–Mar88–106
Perelman, M. Marx's Crises Theory.
 F. Vorhies, 144:Summer/Fall89–531
Perelman, S.J. Don't Tread on Me.* (P. Crowther, ed)
 42(AR):Winter88–123
Peres, C. Die Struktur der Kunst in Hegels Aesthetik.
 P. Somville, 542:Jan–Mar88–94
Pérez, A.J. Poética de la prosa de J.L. Borges.
 G.H. Bell–Villada, 240(HR):Autumn88–528
 H.M. Cavallari, 238:Dec88–837
Pérez, F.J.P. – see under Peña Pérez, F.J.
Pérez, J. Contemporary Women Writers of Spain.
 K. Burke, 532(RCF):Fall88–161
 N.M. Valis, 238:Dec88–832
Pérez, L.A., Jr., comp. Cuba: An Annotated Bibliography.
 M. Goslinga, 263(RIB):Vol38No3–409
Pérez, L.A., Jr. Cuba: Between Reform and Revolution.
 A. Hennessy, 617(TLS):19–25May89–531
Pérez, O.B. – see under Barrero Pérez, O.
Pérez Firmat, G. The Cuban Condition.
 J. Labanyi, 617(TLS):20–26Oct89–1165
Pérez Firmat, G. Literature and Liminality.*
 H.R.M., 295(JML):Fall87/Winter88–217
 J. Tittler, 345(KRQ):May88–252
Pérez Galdós, B. Our Friend Manso.* (R. Russell, trans)
 K.O. Austin, 240(HR):Winter88–114
 I. Malin, 532(RCF):Fall88–175
 S. Miller, 238:Dec88–850
Pérez–López, J.F. Measuring Cuban Economic Performance.
 R. Moncarz, 263(RIB):Vol38No1–78
Pérez Rojas, F.J. Cartagena 1874–1936.
 W. Rincón García, 48:Apr–Jun88–188
Pérez Sánchez, A.E. & E.A. Sayre. Goya and the Spirit of Enlightenment.
 P–L. Adams, 61:Apr89–100
 R. Hughes, 453(NYRB):29Jun89–26
Pérez Villanueva, J. & B. Escandell Bonet, eds. Historia de la Inquisición en España y América.
 A. Márquez, 240(HR):Summer88–368
Pergnier, M. Le mot.
 A. Lecomte–Hilmy, 207(FR):Apr89–924
 S. Levin, 215(GL):Vol28No2–131
Perissa Torrini, A. Disegni del Figino.
 J.B. Shaw, 90:Nov88–862

Perkin, H. The Rise of Professional Society.
G. Hawthorn, 617(TLS):14–20Jul89–766
Perkin, J. Women and Marriage in Nineteenth-Century England.
A. Summers, 617(TLS):7–13Apr89–357
Perkins, D. A History of Modern Poetry: From the 1890s the High Modernist Mode.
B. McHale, 494:Vol8No3/4–743
Perkins, D. A History of Modern Poetry: Modernism and After.*
D.L. Eder, 639(VQR):Autumn88–729
G. Gunn, 494:Vol8No3/4–740
B. McHale, 494:Vol8No3/4–743
M.K. Spears, 569(SR):Winter88–95
Perl, J. Paris without End.
L. Nesbitt, 62:Oct88–16
R. Siegel, 441:23Apr89–21
Perl, M. & others. Studien zur Herausbildung der kubanischen Variante der spanischen Sprache.
N. Weinhold, 685(ZDL):1/1988–125
Perl, M. & J. García González, eds. Estudios sobre la formación y características del español de Cuba.
P. Stein, 72:Band225Heft1–199
J. Thiele, 682(ZPSK):Band41Heft2–263
Perlemuter, V. & H. Jourdan-Morhange. Ravel According to Ravel.
P. Hill, 607:Dec88–47
Perlina, N. Varieties of Poetic Utterance.*
E. Chances, 558(RLJ):Winter–Spring–Fall88–357
Perlmann, M.L. Arthur Schnitzler.
W.E. Yates, 402(MLR):Jan89–252
Perloff, M. The Dance of the Intellect.*
R. Berry, 102(CanL):Autumn88–147
M.L. Rosenthal, 405(MP):Aug88–112
Perloff, M. The Futurist Moment.*
B.C., 295(JML):Fall87/Winter88–200
S. Connor, 402(MLR):Oct89–904
J. Korg, 477(PLL):Spring88–212
T. Materer, 301(JEGP):Jan88–153
G.L. Ulmer, 141:Spring88–263
Permut, J.B. Embracing the Wolf.
E. Rosenthal, 441:19Nov89–43
Pernstich, K. Der italienische Einfluss auf die deutsche Schriftsprache in Südtirol, dargestellt an der Südtiroler Presse.
E. Kühebacher, 686(ZDL):3/1987–393
Perosa, S., ed. Henry James e Venezia.
P. Buitenhuis, 106:Fall88–325
Pérouse, G–A. & M. Simonin – see Poissenot, B.
Perreault, G. Curved Like an Eye.
W.H. Green, 649(WAL):Nov88–266
Perret, G. A Country Made by War.
G.A. Craig, 453(NYRB):17Aug89–31
H.G. Summers, Jr., 441:28May89–11
Perrett, R.W. Death and Immortality.
J. Donnelly, 543:Dec88–401
Perrie, M. The Image of Ivan the Terrible in Russian Folklore.
E.A. Warner, 575(SEER):Oct88–653
F. Wigzell, 402(MLR):Apr89–542
Perrier, F. Les corps malades du signifiant.
A. Reix, 542:Jan–Mar88–78
Perrin, N. A Reader's Delight.*
639(VQR):Autumn88–138
Perrin, U. The Looking-Glass Lover.
G. Krist, 441:20Aug89–11
Perrone, C.A. Masters of Contemporary Brazilian Song.
J. Ryle, 617(TLS):14–20Jul89–778

Perry, D.M. The Politics of Terror.
639(VQR):Autumn88–117
Perry, G. The Complete "Phantom of the Opera."
M.O. Lee, 465:Autumn88–147
Perry, M. Four Stars.
R.F. Weigley, 441:12Mar89–9
Perry, N. & L. Echeverría. Under the Heel of Mary.
T. Kselman, 617(TLS):11–17Aug89–867
Perry, R. The Celebrated Mary Astell.*
I. Grundy, 83:Spring88–89
M.G. Mason, 77:Spring88–181
F.A. Nussbaum, 173(ECS):Summer88–499
Perry, T.A. – see Santob de Carrión
Persico, J.E. Edward R. Murrow.
J. Konner, 441:15Jan89–11
Persin, M.H. Recent Spanish Poetry and the Role of the Reader.
A.P. Debicki, 238:Sep88–552
D. Harris, 86(BHS):Jul88–312
Persius. The Satires of Persius. (G. Lee, trans; W. Barr, ed)
W. Kissel, 229:Band60Heft6–505
Person, L.S., Jr. Aesthetic Headaches.
J.L. Idol, Jr., 580(SCR):Spring89–81
Pertschuk, M. & W. Schaetzel. The People Rising.
S. Labaton, 441:19Nov89–15
Perucho, J. Natural History.
N. Shrady, 441:5Feb89–24
Perusino, F. Dalla commedia antica alla commedia di mezzo.
R.L. Hunter, 303(JoHS):Vol108–228
Perutz, L. Leonardo's Judas.
C.G. Segrè, 441:10Sep89–37
Perutz, L. The Marquis of Bolibar.
P–L. Adams, 61:Oct89–116
Perutz, L. La Nuit sous le pont de pierre.
L. Kovacs, 450(NRF):Apr88–101
Perutz, M.F. Is Science Necessary?
R. Kanigel, 441:9Apr89–29
S. Rose, 617(TLS):4–10Aug89–845
Peruzzi, E. Money in Early Rome.
J. Champeaux, 555:Vol61fasc1–158
Pesetsky, B. Confessions of a Bad Girl.
C. Dickinson, 441:28May89–17
Pessoa, F. O manuscrito de "O guardador de rebanhos" de Alberto Caeiro. (I. Castro, ed)
J. Parker, 86(BHS):Jul88–315
Pessoa, F. The Surprise of Being.
R.A. Preto-Rodas, 238:Dec88–851
Pestalozzi, K., A. von Bormann & T. Koebner, eds. Kontroversen, alte und neue. (Vol 10)
J.G. Pankau, 564:May88–188
A.A. Wallas, 602:Band19Heft1–208
Peter, J. Vladimir's Carrot.
M. Patterson, 610:Autumn88–300
Peter, K.A. The Dynamics of Hutterite Society.*
G.W., 102(CanL):Summer88–179
Peter the Venerable. Adversus Iudeorum inveteratam duritiem. (Y. Friedman, ed)
J. Cohen, 589:Jan88–212
Peterman, M. Robertson Davies.*
S. Buswell, 102(CanL):Spring88–149
J. Hart, 298:Winter88/89–145
Peters, A.K. Jean Cocteau and His World.*
W. Fowlie, 569(SR):Fall88–lxxxv

Peters, C. Thackeray's Universe.*
  R.A. Colby, 405(MP):May89-441
  A. St. George, 184(EIC):Jan88-80
  D.J. Taylor, 364:Mar87-106
Peters, E. The Confession of Brother Haluin.*
  M. Stasio, 441:22Jan89-30
Peters, E. The Heretic's Apprentice.
  T.J.B., 617(TLS):14-20Jul89-783
Peters, E. Naked Once More.
  F. King, 441:15Oct89-46
Peters, E. A Rare Benedictine.
  M. Stasio, 441:24Dec89-23
Peters, J-U. Russische Satire im 20. Jahr-
  hundert.
  W. Busch, 688(ZSP):Band48Heft2-400
Peters, R. Red Army.
  D. Murray, 441:18Jun89-20
Peters, S. Ludvig Holbergs Menippeische
  Satire.
  L.V.R., 568(SCN):Spring-Summer88-36
Petersen, D. – see Guthrie, A.B., Jr.
Petersen, K.H. & A. Rutherford, eds. A Double
  Colonization.
  C.O. Ogunyemi, 538(RAL):Summer88-234
Peterson, A. Death in Wessex.
  M. Stasio, 441:30Apr89-45
Peterson, B.L., Jr. Contemporary Black Amer-
  ican Playwrights and Their Plays.
  27(AL):Dec88-707
Peterson, C.L. The Determined Reader.
  N.A. Haxell, 345(KRQ):Nov88-485
  A. Lebowitz, 102(CanL):Winter87-152
Peterson, D. The Deluge and the Ark.
  P. Schullery, 441:24Sep89-14
Peterson, I.J. William of Nassington.
  R. Bradley, 589:Oct88-974
Peterson, L.H. Victorian Autobiography.*
  H.P. Abbott, 494:Vol8No3/4-720
Peterson, M.D. The Great Triumvirate.
  I.H. Bartlett, 432(NEQ):Sep88-455
  E.M. Yoder, Jr., 639(VQR):Autumn88-723
Peterson, M.J. Family, Love and Work in the
  Lives of Victorian Gentlewomen.
  A. Summers, 617(TLS):29Sep-5Oct89-
  1050
Peterson, R.F., A.M. Cohn & E.L. Epstein, eds.
  Work in Progress.
  P. Parrinder, 402(MLR):Jan89-141
Peterson, R.S. Imitation and Praise in the
  Poems of Ben Jonson.
  E. Platz-Waury, 38:Band106Heft3/4-537
Petherbridge, D., ed. Art for Architecture.*
  C.S. Smith, 46:Jul88-64
Petievich, G. Earth Angels.
  M. Stasio, 441:5Nov89-28
Petievich, G. Shakedown.*
  T.J. Binyon, 617(TLS):18-24Aug89-902
Petit, J. Acquisition linguistique et inter-
  férences.
  D.A. Kibbee, 399(MLJ):Autumn88-335
Petit, R. Rainer Maria Rilke in und nach
  Worpswede.
  S.R. Cerf, 221(GQ):Spring88-336
Petitfils, P. Rimbaud.*
  W. Fowlie, 569(SR):Fall88-lxxxv
Petitot-Cocorda, J. Les catastrophes de la
  parole, de Roman Jakobson à René Thom.
  R. Marty, 567:Vol68No1/2-121
Petke, W. Kanzlei, Kapelle und königliche
  Kurie unter Lothar III. (1125-1137).
  P.W. Strait, 589:Jan88-214

Petrarch. The Revolution of Cola di Rienzo.
  (M.E. Cosenza, trans; 2nd ed rev by R.G.
  Musto)
  R.E. Proctor, 589:Oct88-975
Petrioli Tofani, A., ed. Uffizi, Gabinetto Dis-
  egni e Stampe.
  J.B. Shaw, 90:Nov88-862
Petrocchi, G. Vita di Dante.
  Z.G. Barański, 545(RPh):Aug88-51
Petroff, E.A., ed. Medieval Women's Visionary
  Literature.*
  J. Yunck, 115:Spring88-195
Pettersen, E., ed. Hamarkrøniken.
  J.M. Jochens, 563(SS):Winter88-91
  H. Schottmann, 172(Edda):1988/1-88
Pettersson, T. Att söka sanningen.
  G. Orton, 562(Scan):May88-83
Pettigrew, J. & J. Portman. Stratford: The
  First Thirty Years.*
  A. Dawson, 102(CanL):Spring88-200
Pettit, P. & J. McDowell, eds. Subject,
  Thought and Context.*
  R. Kirk, 518:Jan88-44
Pétursson, M. – see Orešnik, J.
Petyt, K.M. Dialect and Accent in Industrial
  West Yorkshire.
  W. Elmer, 38:Band106Heft3/4-452
Peylet, G. Les Evasions manquées, ou les
  illusions de l'artifice dans la littérature
  "fin de siècle."
  I. Finel-Honigman, 207(FR):Dec88-336
Peyser, J. Leonard Bernstein.*
  M.J. Anderson, 607:Jun88-51
  A. Jacobs, 415:Jan88-21
Peyton, J. Zion's Cause.*
  639(VQR):Spring88-57
Pfaff, W. Barbarian Sentiments.
  A. Tonelson, 441:28May89-9
Pfanner, H.F., ed. Kulturelle Wechselbezie-
  hungen im Exil – Exil across Cultures.*
  J. Riesz, 549(RLC):Jul-Sep88-413
  A. Stephan, 406:Winter88-530
Pfanz, H.W. Gettysburg.*
  639(VQR):Summer88-85
Pfau, T. – see Hölderlin, F.
Pfeffer, J.A. Deutsches Sprachgut im Wort-
  schatz der Amerikaner und Engländer.*
  G. Cannon, 350:Mar89-189
  S. Clausing, 133:Band21Heft4-376
  B.J. Koekkoek, 221(GQ):Fall88-567
Pfeffer, W. The Change of Philomel.
  F. Goldin, 589:Apr88-455
Pfefferkorn, E. & D.H. Hirsch – see Nomberg-
  Przytyk, S.
Pfeiffer, B.B. Frank Lloyd Wrights ungebaute
  Architektur.
  I. Boyken, 43:Band18Heft2-202
Pfeiffer, B.B. – see Wright, F.L.
Pfeiffer, H. Phantasiemorde.
  K. Kändler, 654(WB):12/1988-2095
Pfister, G.G. & Y. Poser. Culture, Proficiency,
  and Control in FL Teaching.
  L.M. Crawford-Lange, 399(MLJ):
  Autumn88-337
Pfister, M. Einführung in die romanische
  Etymologie.
  P. Swiggers, 260(IF):Band93-316
Pfrimmer, T. Freud, lecteur de la Bible.
  A. Juranville, 192(EP):Oct-Dec88-552
Pharies, D.A. Charles S. Peirce and the Lin-
  guistic Sign.
  C. Hookway, 567:Vol69No3/4-331
  D. Justice, 545(RPh):Aug88-77

Pharies, D.A. Structure and Analogy in the Playful Lexicon of Spanish.*
F. Hodcroft, 304(JHP):Autumn88-67
J. Lengert, 547(RF):Band99Heft4-426
R. Penny, 545(RPh):May89-472
R. Wright, 86(BHS):Jul88-283
Pheby, J. – see "The Oxford-Duden Pictorial English Dictionary"
Phelan, N. Home is the Sailor and the Best of Intentions.
D. Adelaide, 581:Sep88-339
Phelan, N. Charles Mackerras.*
D.R.P., 412:May88-155
Phelps, A. Orchidée nègre.
A.L. Amprimoz, 102(CanL):Autumn88-140
Philbrick, T. & M. Geracht – see Cooper, J.F.
Philip, G. – see under le comte de Creutz
Philip, L. The Road Through Miyama.
P-L. Adams, 61:May89-100
M. Porges, 441:20Aug89-29
Philip, N., ed. The Cinderella Story.
M. Warner, 617(TLS):24-30Nov89-1309
Philipp, H. Mira et magica.
M. Henig, 123:Vol38No2-450
Philippa, M-L.I. Noord-Zee-Germaanse Ontwikkelingen.
J. Goossens, 685(ZDL):3/1987-361
Philippides, D., ed. Greek Traditional Architecture.
G. Fowden, 617(TLS):22-28Dec89-1424
Philipson, G. Aycliffe and Peterlee New Towns 1946-1988.
A. Saint, 46:Sep88-12
Phillips, A. Winnicott.
P.L. Rudnytsky, 617(TLS):7-13Jul89-750
Phillips, C. Higher Ground.
A. Lively, 617(TLS):2-8Jun89-619
B. Smith, 441:24Sep89-27
Phillips, C. – see Hopkins, G.M.
Phillips, C.R. Six Galleons for the King of Spain.*
T.J. Oertling, 568(SCN):Fall88-52
Phillips, D.Z. Belief, Change, and Forms of Life.
V.M. Cooke, 258:Jun88-227
J.H. Whittaker, 521:Apr88-166
Phillips, D.Z. R.S. Thomas.
R. Williams, 521:Oct88-336
Phillips, J.A. Fast Lanes.
B.K. Horvath, 152(UDQ):Spring88-97
Phillips, K.C. Language and Class in Victorian England.
J.C. Beal, 355(LSoc):Mar88-133
Phillips, M. Blood Rights.
M. Stasio, 441:13Aug89-14
Phillips, M. – see Blake, W.
Phillips, R. Personal Accounts.*
J. Mazzaro, 569(SR):Winter88-149
Phillips, R. Putting Asunder.
P. Laslett, 617(TLS):4-10Aug89-843
L. Stone, 453(NYRB):2Mar89-12
Phillips, R. – see Schwartz, D.
Phillips, S.H. Aurobindo's Philosophy of Brahman.
R.N. Minor, 485(PE&W):Oct88-455
Phillips, T. A Humument.
A.J. MacAdam, 55:Summer88-90
Phillipson, J.S., ed. Critical Essays on Thomas Wolfe.
C. Johnston, 580(SCR):Spring89-84
Phillipson, N. Hume.
J. Cannon, 617(TLS):25-31Aug89-926

Philodemus. Über die Musik IV. (A.J. Neubecker, ed & trans)
E.K. Borthwick, 123:Vol38No1-145
D.A. Campbell, 24:Fall88-450
M.L. West, 303(JoHS):Vol108-236
Philoponus. Against Aristotle on the Eternity of the World. (C. Wildberg, trans)
H.S. Lang, 543:Dec88-403
M. Schofield, 520:Vol33No1-116
"Philosophie und Begründung."
P. Trotignon, 542:Oct-Dec88-508
Philp, M. Godwin's Political Justice.*
P. Marshall, 677(YES):Vol19-328
K.E. Smith, 83:Autumn88-222
Phimister, I. An Economic and Social History of Zimbabwe, 1890-1948.
T. Ranger, 617(TLS):10-16Feb89-146
Phinney, E., P.E. Bell & B. Romaine, eds. Cambridge Latin Course Unit 1.
J.H. Hall, 399(MLJ):Winter88-483
Phipps, C. – see Lord Buckingham
Phipps, F. Let Me Be Los.
J. Bishop, 329(JJQ):Spring89-456
Phocas, P. Gide et Guéhenno polémiquent.
J.S.T. Garfitt, 208(FS):Oct88-489
Pholien, G. Les deux "Vie de Jésus" de Renan.*
J. Gaulmier, 535(RHL):Jul-Aug88-786
Photius. Epistulae et Amphilochia. (Vols 2 & 3) (B. Laourdas & L.G. Westerink, eds)
R. Browning, 303(JoHS):Vol108-271
Piacentino, E.J. T.S. Stribling.
V.A. Kramer, 395(MFS):Winter88-631
M.E. Summerlin, 392:Fall88-573
Piaget, J. & R. Garcia. Psychogenèse et histoire des sciences.*
R.F. Kitchener, 679:Band19Heft1-157
Picard, H.R. Der Geist der Erzählung.
U. Schulz-Buschhaus, 547(RF):Band100 Heft4-395
"Picasso Linoleum Cuts."
T. Foster, 324:Jun89-446
Piccione, A. Seeing It Was So.
D. Revell, 460(OhR):No43-116
Pichl, R. & others, eds. Grillparzer und die europäische Tradition.
B. Mullan, 402(MLR):Jul89-792
Pichois, C. Baudelaire.
R. Sennett, 617(TLS):6-12Oct89-1089
Pichois, C., with others – see Colette
Pichois, C. & J. Ziegler. Baudelaire.*
A. Kies, 356(LR):Feb-May88-137
R. Sennett, 617(TLS):6-12Oct89-1089
Pick, J.B. – see Gunn, N.M.
Pickering, O.S., ed. The South English Ministry and Passion Edited from St. John's College, Cambridge, MS B.6.*
N.F. Blake, 72:Band225Heft1-234
A.S.G. Edwards, 677(YES):Vol19-300
Pickering, P. The Blue Gate of Babylon.
N. Callendar, 441:17Dec89-17
M. Illis, 617(TLS):19-25May89-536
Pickering, S.F., Jr. May Days. The Right Distance.
P.C. Hoy 2d, 569(SR):Fall88-688
Pickett, T.H. The Unseasonable Democrat.*
H.T. Tewarson, 222(GR):Summer88-156
Pickles, J.D. & J.L. Dawson, eds. A Concordance to John Gower's "Confessio Amantis."
L.D. Benson, 589:Oct88-977
E.G. Stanley, 447(N&Q):Dec88-517
Pickles, S., ed. A Victorian Posy.
42(AR):Spring88-275

Pickvance, R. Van Gogh in Arles.
J. Hulsker, 600:Vol18No3-177
Pickvance, R. Van Gogh in Saint-Rémy and Auvers.
J. Hulsker, 600:Vol18No3-177
E. Van Uitert, 39:Jun88-454
Pico della Mirandola, G. Commentary on a Canzone of Benivieni. (S. Jayne, trans)
C.V. Kaske, 301(JEGP):Jul88-442
Picoche, J. Structures sémantiques du lexique français.*
C. Blanche-Benveniste, 209(FM):Apr88-131
D. Gaatone, 545(RPh):May89-463
G. Kleiber, 553(RLiR):Jan-Jun88-298
Picoche, J-L. - see Zorrilla, J.
Picone, M., ed. Il racconto.
M. Lecco, 379(MedR):Aug86-273
Pidal, R.M. - see under Menéndez Pidal, R.
Pienkos, A.T. The Imperfect Autocrat.
P. Wozniak, 497(PolR):Vol33No4-477
Pieper, M. Daniel Sudermann (1550-ca. 1631) als Vertreter des mystischen Spirtualismus.
M.K. Kremer, 406:Winter88-507
Pierce, C. When Things Get Back to Normal.
G.L. Morris, 455:Sep88-68
Pierce, C. & D. Van De Veer. AIDS.*
E.D.P., 185:Apr89-690
Pierce, D. The False Prison.
P. Trotignon, 542:Jul-Sep88-369
Pierce, F. Alonso de Ercilla y Zúñiga.
R. Perelmuter-Pérez, 345(KRQ):Feb88-119
Pierce, P. & R. Hunter, with others, eds. The Oxford Literary Guide to Australia.*
B. Elliott, 71(ALS):May88-381
Pierce, R. & R. Fuszek. The P-F Guide. (rev)
510:Fall88-8
Piercy, M. Summer People.
P. Craig, 617(TLS):15-21Sep89-997
S. Schiff, 441:11Jun89-26
Pierson, C. Marxist Theory and Democratic Politics.
G.P., 185:Oct88-189
Pierson, R. The Queen of Mean.
S. Shapiro, 441:5Nov89-25
Pierson, R.R. "They're Still Women After All."*
J. Sangster, 298:Spring/Summer88-234
Pierson, R.R., ed. Women and Peace.
S.H., 185:Jan89-464
Piesman, M. Unorthodox Practices.
M. Stasio, 441:8Oct89-20
Pietrkiewicz, J. Literatura polska w perspektywie europejskiej.
D.P.A. Pirie, 575(SEER):Jul88-479
Piette, I. Littérature et musique.
F. Claudon, 549(RLC):Jan-Mar88-89
Pietzcher, C., ed. Kontroversen, alte und neue. (Forum 10)
S.K. Johnson, 221(GQ):Fall87-647
Pietzcker, C. Trauma, Wunsch und Abwehr.
J.T. Adams, 221(GQ):Fall88-540
Pifer, E. Critical Essays on John Fowles.
I.V., 295(JML):Fall87/Winter88-319
Pigeaud, J. Folie et cures de la folie chez les médecins de l'antiquité gréco-romaine.
V. Nutton, 123:Vol38No2-375
Pigeaud, T.G.T. & P. Voorhoeve. Handschriften aus Indonesien.
M. Nihom, 318(JAOS):Oct-Dec87-843
Piggott, S., ed. William Stukeley.
C.S. Briggs, 83:Autumn88-210

Pignatti, T. Disegni antichi del Museo Correr in Venezia.* (Vol 4)
J.B. Shaw, 90:Nov88-862
Piguet, J-C. Le Dieu de Spinoza.
J. Brun, 192(EP):Jul-Sep88-434
Piguet, J-C. - see Ansermet, E.
Piirainen, I.T. Das Stadt- und Bergrecht von Banská Štiavnica/Schemnitz.
L. Sattler, 682(ZPSK):Band41Heft1-139
Pike, A. Prose Sketches and Poems Written in the Western Country. (D.J. Weber, ed)
R.D. Harper, 649(WAL):Aug88-172
Pike, D. Lukács and Brecht.*
K-H. Schoeps, 406:Winter88-525
Pike, D. Vietnam and the Soviet Union.
W.S. Turley, 293(JASt):Nov88-947
Piker, S. A Peasant Community in Changing Thailand.
D.K. Swearer, 318(JAOS):Apr-Jun87-373
Pikulik, L. E.T.A. Hoffmann als Erzähler.
A. Robertshaw, 402(MLR):Jul89-784
Pikulik, L., H. Kurzenberger & G. Guntermann, eds. Deutsche Gegenwartsdramatik.
W.G. Sebald, 402(MLR):Jan89-266
Pilisuk, M. & S.H. Parks. The Healing Web.
M.E. Benjamin, 529(QQ):Autumn88-749
Pilkington, M. - see Tosi, P.F.
Pillsbury, K.H., R.D. Hale & J. Post, eds. The Duxbury Book, 1637-1987.
P.H. Tedesco, 432(NEQ):Jun88-282
Pilnyak, B. Chinese Story and Other Tales.
S. Laird, 617(TLS):21-27Jul89-808
Z. Smardz, 441:16Apr89-20
Pilzer, P.Z., with R. Deitz. Other People's Money.
A.M. Solomon, 441:29Oct89-27
Pimlott, J.L., ed. The World at Arms.
M. Carver, 617(TLS):1-7Sep89-935
Pinar, S. & others, eds. A History of Turkish Painting.
J.M. Rogers, 617(TLS):6-12Oct89-1100
Pinches, M. & S. Lakha, eds. Wage Labour and Social Change.
D.L. Wolf, 293(JASt):Nov88-948
Pincoffs, E.L. Quandaries and Virtues.
J-C. Wolf, 489(PJGG):Band95Heft2-420
Pinder, L.H. Under the House.*
H.W. Connor, 102(CanL):Autumn88-144
Pine, M.L. Pietro Pomponazzi.
A. Poppi, 319:Jul89-471
C. Trinkaus, 589:Oct88-978
Piñera, V. Cold Tales.
S. Salisbury, 441:15Jan89-22
Piñero, M. Outrageous.
E.C. Ramírez, 615(TJ):Dec88-572
Piñero Ramírez, P.M. & R. Reyes Cano - see Pacheco, F.
Pinget, R. L'Ennemi.*
O. Beetschen, 450(NRF):Apr88-92
Pinkard, T. Democratic Liberalism and Social Union.*
R.M. Lemos, 484(PPR):Jun89-755
Pinkard, T. Hegel's Dialectic.
H.S. Harris, 103:Nov89-460
Pinkney, T. - see Williams, R.
Pinkwater, D. Fish Whistle.
B. Franzen, 441:12Nov89-55
Pinney, T. - see Kipling, R.
Piñon, N. The Republic of Dreams.
J. Polk, 441:30Jul89-22
Pinsker, H. & W. Ziegler, eds. & trans. Die altenglischen Rätsel des Exeterbuchs.
J.E. Anderson, 589:Oct88-981

Polizzi, G. Forme de sapere e ipotezi di traduzione.
P. Engel, 542:Jul–Sep88–394
Polkinghorne, D.E. Narrative Knowing and the Human Sciences.
L.C., 185:Jul89–971
Pollak, E. The Poetics of Sexual Myth.*
K. Flint, 447(N&Q):Dec88–538
V. Kelly, 49:Apr88–98
Pollak, V.R. Dickinson.
L.Y. Gossett, 569(SR):Summer88–469
Pollard, A.J. The Wars of the Roses.
C.T. Allmand, 617(TLS):28Apr–4May89–468
Pollard, P., ed. André Gide et l'Angleterre.*
R. Gibson, 208(FS):Jul88–360
A. Goulet, 535(RHL):Jul–Aug88–792
F. Mouret, 549(RLC):Jul–Sep88–435
Pollin, B.R. – see Poe, E.A.
Pollitt, J.J. Art in the Hellenistic Age.*
A.M. Berlin, 124:Jan–Feb89–199
Pollmann, L. Geschichte des lateinamerikanischen Romans. (Vol 2)
W. Theile, 72:Band225Heft1–225
Pollock, D. Lair of the Fox.
N. Callendar, 441:17Dec89–17
Pollock, G. & R. Parker, eds. Framing Feminism.
N.B. Kampen, 662:Fall88/Winter89–45
Pollock, J. Contemporary Theories of Knowledge.
H. Kornblith, 484(PPR):Sep88–167
P.K. Moser, 84:Mar88–131
Pollock, S. Doc.*
J.T. Goodwin, 102(CanL):Spring88–157
Polo, M. Il Milione. (R.M. Ruggieri, ed)
A. Dardi, 708:Vol14fasc1–140
Poloma, M.M. The Assemblies of God at the Crossroads.
P.W. Wood, 441:24Sep89–49
Polonsky, A. – see Lewin, A.
Polovchak, W., with K. Klose. Freedom's Child.
639(VQR):Summer88–96
Póltawska, W. And I Am Afraid of My Dreams.*
I. Deak, 453(NYRB):28Sep89–63
P. Lewis, 565:Spring88–34
Polvinen, T. Between East and West. (D.G. Kirby & P. Herring, eds & trans)
S. Oakley, 562(Scan):May88–82
A.F. Upton, 575(SEER):Jan88–150
Poma, G. Tra legislatori e tiranni.*
J–C. Richard, 555:Vol61fasc1–168
Pombo, A. The Hero of the Big House.*
J. Mellors, 364:Feb/Mar89–136
Pombo, A. The Resemblance.
A.L. Six, 617(TLS):22–28Dec89–1422
Pomeau, R. Beaumarchais ou la bizarre destinée.
T.M. Pratt, 208(FS):Apr88–209
Pomeau, R. D'Arouet à Voltaire (1694–1734).*
J. Sareil, 546(RR):Nov88–683
Pomeroy, E. The Huntington Library: Art Collections; Botanical Gardens. (rev)
G. Ashton, 39:Jan88–68
Pomeroy, S.B. Women in Hellenistic Egypt.*
H.W. Pleket, 394:Vol41fasc1/2–227
Pomian, K. Collectionneurs, amateurs et curieux.
J. Tribby, 400(MLN):Dec88–1198

Pommer, R., D. Spaeth & K. Harrington. In the Shadow of Mies.
M.A. Branch, 505:Oct88–113
Pommier, R. Roland Barthes ras le bol!*
A.K. Mortimer, 210(FrF):Jan88–123
J. Voisine, 549(RLC):Jan–Mar88–107
Pommier, R. Un marchand de salades qui se prend pour un prince.*
M. Autrand, 535(RHL):Jul–Aug88–803
J. Voisine, 549(RLC):Jan–Mar88–107
Pomorska, K. & others, eds. Language, Poetry and Poetics.*
Y. Tobin, 361:Aug88–373
Pomorska, K. & S. Rudy – see Jakobson, R.
Pomper, P. – see Trotsky, L.
Pomponius Mela. Pomponii Melae "De Chorographia libri tres."* (P. Parroni, ed)
E.C.L. van der Vliet, 394:Vol41fasc3/4–438
Ponce, J.G. Encounters.
G.H. Bell-Villada, 441:25Jun89–17
Ponce, M.H. Taking Control.
S. Magnarelli, 238:Dec88–844
Pong, D. & E.S.K. Fung, eds. Ideal and Reality.
A.Y.C. Lui, 302:Vol24No1–119
Ponnau, G. La Folie dans la littérature fantastique.*
R. Pearson, 208(FS):Jul88–374
L. Vax, 189(EA):Oct–Dec88–491
Ponomareff, C.V. On the Dark Side of Russian Literature, 1709–1910.
R. Freeborn, 575(SEER):Oct88–639
E. Thompson, 574(SEEJ):Winter88–647
A.C. Wright, 627(UTQ):Fall88–197
Pons, A., ed. Encyclopédie ou Dictionnaire raisonné des sciences, des arts et des métiers.*
A.M. Chouillet, 530:Apr88–169
de Ponseti, H.P. – see under Percas de Ponseti, H.
Pontiero, G. Eleonora Duse.
F.H. Londré, 615(TJ):Mar88–141
Pontiggia, G. The Invisible Player.
J. Baumel, 441:26Feb89–16
Ponting, C. Breach of Promise.
J. Turner, 617(TLS):3–9Mar89–215
Ponting, C. Whitehall.
W. Plowden, 617(TLS):29Dec89/4Jan90–1432
Pontormo, J.C. Il libro mio. (S.S. Nigro, ed)
A. Di Benedetto, 228(GSLI):Vol165fasc529–124
Poole, A. Tragedy.*
D.S. Carne-Ross, 184(EIC):Jul88–237
L.S. Champion, 179(ES):Feb88–86
M. Lomax, 366:Autumn88–231
A.D. Nuttall, 541(RES):May88–329
Poovey, M. The Proper Lady and the Woman Writer.*
A. Leighton, 617(TLS):1–7Sep89–950
Poovey, M. Uneven Developments.
A. Summers, 617(TLS):7–13Apr89–357
Pope, A. The Prose Works of Alexander Pope.* (Vol 2) (R. Cowler, ed)
P. Dixon, 447(N&Q):Jun88–237
V. Newey, 506(PSt):Sep88–99
Pope, A. Selected Prose of Alexander Pope.* (P. Hammond, ed)
J.A. Downie, 506(PSt):Sep88–100
D. Hopkins, 447(N&Q):Sep88–375
639(VQR):Winter88–10

Pope-Hennessy, J. Cellini.*
   A. Radcliffe, 90:Dec88-929
Pope-Hennessy, J., with L.B. Kanter. The
Robert Lehman Collection.* (Vol 1)
   C.B. Strehlke, 90:Nov88-859
Popelar, I. - see Baldinger, K.
Popkin, R.H., ed. Millenarianism and Messi-
anism in English Literature and Thought
1650-1800.
   G.F. Nuttall, 617(TLS):11-17Aug89-880
Popper, K.R. Logik der Forschung. (8th ed)
   J. Dölling, 682(ZPSK):Band41Heft4-536
Popper, K.R. Quantum Theory and the Schism
in Physics. (W.W. Bartley 3d, ed)
   J.D. Barrow, 617(TLS):29Sep-5Oct89-
1072
"Popular Music Perspectives, 2."
   R.S. Denisoff, 498:Spring88-89
"The Population Atlas of China."*
   W. Lavely, 293(JASt):Nov88-871
Por, P. Das Bild in der Lyrik des Jugendstils.
   F. Claudon, 549(RLC):Jan-Mar88-104
Poratti, A. & others, eds & trans. Los filóso-
fos presocráticos. (Vol 3)
   R. Torretti, 160:Jan88-221
Portch, S.R. Literature's Silent Language.
   D. Lateiner, 599:Winter88-664
Porter, A. Musical Events.*
   G. Martin, 465:Autumn88-76
Porter, A. Victorian Shipping, Business and
Imperial Policy.
   W. Minchinton, 637(VS):Autumn88-148
Porter, B. Plots and Paranoia.
   N. Hiley, 617(TLS):22-28Dec89-1408
Porter, D.H. Horace's Poetic Journey.
   V. Pöschl, 229:Band60Heft8-699
Porter, D.H. Only Connect.
   M. Comber, 123:Vol38No2-420
Porter, E. & E. Auerbach, with D. Pierce.
Mexican Churches.
   J.B. Esser, 263(RIB):Vol38No4-539
Porter, F.W. 3d, comp. Native American Bas-
ketry.
   658:Winter88-296
Porter, G. The Politics of Counterinsurgency
in the Philippines.
   R. Marlay, 293(JASt):May88-439
Porter, J. Dover and the Claret Tappers.
   M. Stasio, 441:5Nov89-28
Porter, J.C. Paper Medicine Man.*
   A.M. Gibson, 77:Spring88-184
Porter, L.M., ed. Critical Essays on Gustave
Flaubert.
   R.A. Hartzell, 207(FR):Apr89-894
Porter, M.C. Through Parisian Eyes.
   M.P.L., 295(JML):Fall87/Winter88-218
   L.A. MacKenzie, Jr., 207(FR):Dec88-344
Porter, P. The Automatic Oracle.*
   S. O'Brien, 364:Apr/May88-118
   A. Wallace, 581:Sep88-350
   J. Whitworth, 493:Spring88-60
Porter, P. Possible Worlds. A Porter Selected.
   S. O'Brien, 617(TLS):15-21Dec89-1392
Porter, P.A. Metaphors and Monsters.
   E. Yamauchi, 318(JAOS):Jul-Sep87-552
Porter, R. Gibbon.
   J. Kenyon, 617(TLS):15-21Dec89-1379
Porter, R. Health for Sale.
   P. Rogers, 617(TLS):20-26Oct89-1146
Porter, R. & M. Teich, eds. Romanticism in
National Context.
   R. Ashton, 617(TLS):24-30Mar89-302

Pörtl, K., ed. Reflexiones sobre el nuevo
teatro español.*
   D. Gagen, 86(BHS):Oct88-417
Pörtl, K., ed. Das spanische Theater.*
   M. Lentzen, 72:Band225Heft1-218
Portmann, P.F., ed. Di letschti Chue tuet's
Törli zue.
   A. Lötscher, 685(ZDL):3/1987-410
Portz, R. Sprachliche Variation und Sprache-
instellungen bei Schulkindern und -jug-
endlichen.
   C. Pollner, 38:Band106Heft1/2-182
Porush, D. The Soft Machine.*
   J.R. Wytenbroek, 102(CanL):Spring88-140
Pöschl, V., ed. 2000 Jahre Vergil.*
   J. den Boeft, 394:Vol41fasc1/2-198
"Posidonius." (Vol 1: The Fragments) (2nd
ed) (L. Edelstein & I.G. Kidd, eds)
   R.W. Sharples, 617(TLS):25-31Aug89-923
Posner, R. Rational Discourse and Poetic
Communication.*
   E. Noronha, 567:Vol69No3/4-355
Posner, R. & J.N. Green, eds. Trends in Ro-
mance Linguistics and Philology.
   H. Meier, 72:Band224Heft2-423
Pososhkov, I. The Book of Poverty and
Wealth. (A.P. Vlasto & L.R. Lewitter, eds &
trans)
   P. Dukes, 575(SEER):Oct88-655
Post, J.F. The Faces of Existence.
   K. Campbell, 484(PPR):Dec88-358
   D. Weissman, 543:Sep88-163
Post, R. Romanische Entlehnungen in den
westmitteldeutschen Mundarten.
   H. von Gadow, 685(ZDL):2/1988-223
Postal, P.M.H. Studies of Passive Clauses.
   G. Legendre, 209(FM):Apr88-113
Postel, G. De Etruriae regionis, originibus
institutis religione et moribus. (G. Cipri-
ani, ed)
   P.P. Bober, 551(RenQ):Summer88-313
Postema, G.J. Bentham and the Common Law
Tradition.
   C. Silver, 185:Oct88-164
Poster, J. - see Crabbe, G.
Postgate, O. & N. Linnell. Becket.
   J.R. Maddicott, 617(TLS):7-13Apr89-381
Postgate, R. 1848: The Story of a Year.
   J.F. McMillan, 617(TLS):21-27Jul89-792
Postman, N. Conscientious Objections.*
   L. Menand, 617(TLS):21-27Jul89-796
Poteet, M., ed. Textes de l'exode.
   A. Chartier, 207(FR):Oct88-159
Pothen, S. Divorce.
   G. Minault, 293(JASt):Nov88-814
Potocki, J. Manuscrit trouvé à Saragosse. (R.
Radrizzani, ed)
   D. Coward, 617(TLS):13-19Oct89-1111
Potrebenko, H. Sometimes They Sang.
   C. Somerville, 102(CanL):Summer88-144
Pott, H.G., ed. Literatur und Provinz.
   P. Zimmermann, 52:Band23Heft3-321
Potter, B. The Journal of Beatrix Potter
1881-1897. (L. Linder, ed) Beatrix Pot-
ter's Letters. (J. Taylor, ed)
   P. Keating, 617(TLS):22-28Dec89-1423
Potter, D. Ticket to Ride.
   P. McGrath, 441:15Oct89-37
Potter, D.C. India's Political Administrators,
1919-83.
   C.H. Kennedy, 293(JASt):Aug88-688

Potter, J. Independent Television in Britain.
(Vol 3)
L. Taylor, 617(TLS):24Feb-2Mar89-192
Potter, J. The Long Lost Journey.
S. Altinel, 617(TLS):24-30Nov89-1312
Potter, J. & M. Wetherell. Discourse and
Social Psychology.
G. Myers, 126(CCC):Dec88-465
Potter, N. Legacies.*
C. Hardesty, 455:Mar88-67
Potter, T.W. Roman Italy.
H.V. Bender, 124:Jul-Aug89-450
T.J. Cornell, 313:Vol78-202
J.J. Wilkes, 617(TLS):7-13Apr89-374
Poucet, J. Les Origines de Rome.*
J.M. Alonso-Núñez, 123:Vol38No1-169
Poulat, É. Liberté, laïcité.
M. Larkin, 617(TLS):3-9Feb89-117
Poulet, G. La Pensée indéterminée.* (Vol 1)
J. Roudaut, 450(NRF):Feb88-98
Poulin, A., Jr. A Momentary Order.
455:Mar88-72
Poulin, J. Spring Tides.*
D. Homel, 168(ECW):Spring88-87
J. Urquhart, 102(CanL):Spring88-129
Poulin, J. Volkswagen Blues.
M.A. Jarman, 376:Jun88-187
Poulton, A., ed. Alan Rawsthorne.
L. East, 415:Feb88-88
Pound, E. The Dying Sorcerer. (R. Spoo, ed)
M.T. Davis, 468:Fall&Winter88-269
Pound, E. Hugh Selwyn Mauberley. (M. Baci-
galupo, ed) Omaggio a Sesto Properzio. (M.
Bacigalupo, ed & trans)
S.M. Casella, 468:Fall&Winter88-265
Pound, E. Mauberley en Andere Gedichten.
(P. Claes & M. Nys, trans)
M. Buning, 468:Spring88-147
Pound, E. Ezra Pound and Japan. (S. Ko-
dama, ed)
C.D.K. Yee, 27(AL):Oct88-501
Pound, E. Pound/The Little Review. (T.L.
Scott & M.J. Friedman, with J.R. Bryer, eds)
H. Levin, 453(NYRB):9Nov89-45
Pound, E. & L. Zukofsky. Pound/Zukofsky.*
(B. Ahearn, ed)
K. Cox, 4:Spring88-60
Pound, O. & R. Spoo, eds. Ezra Pound and
Margaret Cravens.
H. Levin, 453(NYRB):9Nov89-45
Poundstone, W. Labyrinths of Reason.*
M. Gardner, 453(NYRB):16Mar89-26
Poupard, D. Twentieth-Century Literary
Criticism. (Vols 20 & 21)
L. Austin, 365:Winter87-52
Poupard, D., ed. Twentieth-Century Literary
Criticism. (Vol 22)
E. Pilon, 470:Vol26-205
Pourbaix, J. Dans les plis de l'écriture.
A.L. Amprimoz, 102(CanL):Autumn88-140
Pourjavady, N. & P.L. Wilson. Kings of Love.
V.R. Holbrook, 318(JAOS):Apr-Jun87-374
Pourquery, D. Parlez-vous business?
S.I. Spencer, 207(FR):Feb89-568
Poverman, C.E. My Father in Dreams.
D.A. Hofmann, 441:23Jul89-18
Pow, T. Rough Seas.
T. Nairn, 571(ScLJ):Spring88-49
Powe, B.W. The Solitary Outlaw.*
B. Testa, 627(UTQ):Fall88-145
Powell, A. Athens and Sparta.
P. Cartledge, 617(TLS):6-12Jan89-19

Powell, C. Turner in the South.*
A. Tennant, 59:Mar88-140
Powell, D. Tom Paine.
M. Fitzpatrick, 83(Spring88-73
617(TLS):22-28Dec89-1426
Powell, H. Trammels of Tradition.
P. Skrine, 402(MLR):Oct89-1023
Powell, L.C. An Orange Grove Boyhood.
G. Haslam, 649(WAL):Nov88-240
Powell, P. A Woman Named Drown.
R. Kaveney, 617(TLS):15-21Sep89-998
639(VQR):Winter88-20
Powell, V. The Life of a Provincial Lady.
H. Mantel, 364:Dec88/Jan89-130
Powell, W., with P. Powell & A. Bannister.
The Wisden Guide to Cricket Grounds.
T.D. Smith, 617(TLS):23-29Jun89-696
Powers, D.S. Studies in Qur'an and Ḥadīth.
L. Librande, 589:Oct88-982
Powers, J.F. How the Fish Live.
D. Durrant, 364:Feb/Mar89-133
Powers, J.F. A Society Organized for War.
639(VQR):Autumn88-116
Powers, L.H., ed. Leon Edel and Literary Art.
P. Buitenhuis, 106:Fall88-325
W.H. Epstein, 395(MFS):Winter88-646
I.B. Nadel, 177(ELT):Vol31No4-465
Powers, M.N. Oglala Women.*
J. Rice, 128(CE):Feb88-206
Powers, R. Prisoner's Dilemma.*
J. Sutherland, 617(TLS):21-27Apr89-436
Powers, R.G. Secrecy and Power.
A. Theoharis, 77:Winter88-76
Powers, W.K. Sacred Language.*
S. Niles, 292(JAF):Jan-Mar88-80
Pownall, D. The White Cutter.
P-L. Adams, 61:Apr89-100
P. Hampl, 441.20Feb89-20
Pozzi, C. Journal 1913-1934. (C. Paulhan,
ed)
V. Kaufmann, 98:Nov88-883
M.C. Weitz, 207(FR):Feb89-552
van Praag, M.C.V. The Status of Tibet.
C.I. Beckwith, 293(JASt):Aug88-626
Pradier, J. Correspondance.* (Vols 1 & 2) (D.
Siler, ed)
J. Vercruysse,547(RF):Band99Heft4-468
Prado, C.G. The Limits of Pragmatism.
H.I. Brown, 543:Sep88-166
R. Eldridge, 103:Aug89-328
Prado, C.G. Making Believe.*
C. Korsmeyer, 290(JAAC):Fall87-90
Pradon, J. Phèdre et Hippolyte. (O. Classe,
ed)
C. Smith, 208(FS):Oct88-472
Praeger, M. Les Romans de Robert Pinget.
S. Hand, 208(FS):Apr88-236
W.F. Motte, Jr., 210(FrF):Sep88-378
Prag, A.J.N.W. The "Oresteia."*
S. Fineberg, 124:Mar-Apr89-312
B.A. Sparkes, 123:Vol38No1-111
Prager, E. Clea and Zeus Divorce.
M. Gorra, 249(HudR):Summer88-404
Prandi, J.D. Spirited Women Heroes.
E.D. Bernhardt, 221(GQ):Winter87-116
Prange, G.W., with D.M. Goldstein & K.V.
Dillon. Dec 7 1941.
W.F. Kimball, 617(TLS):12-18May89-505
Prantera, A. Conversations with Lord Byron
on Perversion.*
J. Mellors, 364:Mar87-98
639(VQR):Winter88-20

Proclus. Commentaire sur le Parménide de Platon: traduction de Guillaume de Moerbeke.* (Vol 2) (C. Steel, ed)
 K. Bormann, 53(AGP):Band70Heft1-111
Proclus. Proclus' Commentary on Plato's "Parmenides." (J.M. Dillon, ed; G.R. Morrow & J.M. Dillon, trans)
 H.J. Blumenthal, 123:Vol38No2-407
 A.C. Lloyd, 319:Apr89-299
 A. Smith, 235:Summer88-113
Proclus. Proclus, "Elementatio Theologica," translata a Guillielmo de Moerbecca. (H. Boese, ed)
 J. Dillon, 123:Vol38No2-455
Proclus. Sur le premier "Alcibiade" de Platon. (Vol 1) (A.P. Segonds, ed & trans)
 M. Lassègue, 542:Apr-Jun88-245
 É. des Places, 555:Vol61fasc1-125
Proclus. Sur le premier "Alcibiade" de Platon. (Vol 2) (A.P. Segonds, ed & trans)
 M. Lassègue, 542:Apr-Jun88-245
 A. Sheppard, 123:Vol38No1-150
Proctor, R.N. Racial Hygiene.
 D. Kevles, 617(TLS):3-9Mar89-214
Proffer, C.R. The Widows of Russia and Other Writings.*
 K. Bushnell, 550(RusR):Oct88-465
Proffer, C.R. & others, eds. Russian Literature of the Twenties.
 G.L. Browning, 574(SEEJ):Summer88-330
Profitlich, U. Volker Braun.
 F.R. Love, 564:Feb88-92
Profumo, D. In Praise of Trout.
 G. Melly, 617(TLS):10-16Nov89-1248
Prokhovnik, S.J. Light in Einstein's Universe.
 R. Jones, 486:Mar88-153
Prontera, F., ed. Strabone. (Vol 1)
 J.M. Alonso-Núñez, 303(JoHS):Vol108-235
Pronzini, B., ed. Wild Westerns.
 E.C. Lynskey, 649(WAL):May88-55
Pronzini, B. & M.H. Greenberg — see Patten, L.B.
Propertius. Sexti Properti "Elegiarum" libri IV.* (P. Fedeli, ed)
 A. La Penna, 229:Band60Heft1-25
Prosch, H. Michael Polanyi.*
 G.D. Martin, 89(BJA):Autumn88-388
von Proschwitz, G., ed. Gustave III par ses lettres.*
 R. Boyer, 549(RLC):Apr-Jun88-301
 Y. Coirault, 535(RHL):Mar-Apr88-272
 J. Heidner, 597(SN):Vol60No1-141
 H-J. Lope, 547(RF):Band100Heft4-433
 J. Lough, 208(FS):Apr88-214
Prose, F. Bigfoot Dreams.
 I. Malin, 532(RCF):Fall88-176
"Prose et prosateurs de la Renaissance."
 K. Christodoulou, 539:Summer89-245
Pross, A.P. & S. McCorquodale. Economic Resurgence and the Constitutional Agenda.
 D.C. Wallace, 298:Fall88-150
Prosterman, R.L. & J.M. Riedinger. Land Reform and Democratic Development.
 R.J. Herring, 293(JASt):Aug88-578
Prou, S. Le Temps des innocents.
 C.F. Demaray, 207(FR):May89-1098
Proudfoot, W. Religious Experience.
 K.P. Pedersen, 485(PE&W):Apr88-209
 N. Smart, 311(JP):Mar88-151
Proulx, E.A. Heart Songs.
 K. Rosen, 441:29Jan89-30

Proust, J. Questions de forme.*
 A. Reix, 542:Jul-Sep88-394
Proust, M. Albertine Gone.
 E. Hughes, 617(TLS):13-19Oct89-1112
Proust, M. Un amour de Swann.* (M. Raimond, ed) Du côté de chez Swann. (A. Compagnon, ed)
 J. Murray, 207(FR):Mar89-690
Proust, M. Correspondance. (Vols 16 & 17) (P. Kolb, ed)
 F. Steegmuller, 617(TLS):24-30Nov89-1304
Proust, M. On Reading Ruskin.* (J. Autret, W. Burford & P.J. Wolfe, eds & trans)
 M. Bright, 445(NCF):Sep88-259
 B.J. Bucknall, 529(QQ):Winter88-933
 D. Gervais, 97(CQ):Vol17No3-256
Proust, M. Marcel Proust, Selected Letters. (Vol 2) (P. Kolb, ed)
 O. Conant, 441:17Dec89-19
Proust, M. A la recherche du temps perdu. (Vol 1) La Prisonnière. La Fugitive (Albertine disparue).
 M. Pierssens, 98:Apr88-320
Proust, M. & G. Gallimard. Correspondance: 1912-1922. (P. Fouché, ed)
 J. Sturrock, 617(TLS):24-30Nov89-1304
Prout, C. Market Socialism in Yugoslavia.
 S. Popov, 575(SEER):Apr88-327
"Proverbium, 1." "Proverbium, 2." "Proverbium, 3." (W. Mieder, ed)
 M.E. Barrick, 292(JAF):Jan-Mar88-104
"Les provinces hellénophones de l'empire romain."
 P. Guyot, 229:Band60Heft4-369
Prucha, F.P. The Indians in American Society.
 M. Heale, 617(TLS):10-16Mar89-261
Pruñonosa, M. & others. Teoría: Lenguajes.
 J.N. Green, 86(BHS):Apr88-177
Pryce-Jones, A. The Bonus of Laughter.
 R. Fuller, 364:Feb87-89
Pryce-Jones, D. The Closed Circle.
 D. Morgan, 617(TLS):16-22Jun89-658
 D.K. Shipler, 441:12Feb89-13
Pryor, E.B. Clara Barton, Professional Angel.
 639(VQR):Spring88-48
Przyboś, J. L'Entreprise mélodramatique.
 B.T. Cooper, 446(NCFS):Spring-Summer89-436
 M-P. Le Hir, 207(FR):May89-1069
Przybylowicz, D. Desire and Repression.*
 J.W. Gargano, 587(SAF):Spring88-124
Przybylski, R. An Essay on the Poetry of Osip Mandelstam.
 P. France, 617(TLS):10-16Mar89-245
Psellus, M. Michael Psellus: The Essays on Euripides and George of Pisidia and on Heliodorus and Achilles Tatius. (A.R. Dyck, ed & trans)
 B. Baldwin, 589:Apr88-460
Pseudo-Phocylides. Pseudo-Phocylide: "Sentences." (P. Derron, ed)
 J.R. March, 123:Vol38No1-142
Pucci, P. Odysseus Polutropos.*
 A.T. Edwards, 124:May-Jun89-398
Pucci, S.L. Diderot and a Poetics of Science.
 J. Chouillet, 530:Apr88-162
 P. Saint-Amand, 188(ECr):Winter88-123
Pucciani, O.F. & J. Hamel. Langue et Langage.* (5th ed)
 M. Donaldson-Evans, 399(MLJ):Spring88-90

Pucciarelli, E. I Cristiani e il servizio militare.
E.D. Hunt, 123:Vol38No2-440
Puel, G. Au feu (Le dé bleu); L'Incessant, l'incertain.
D. Leuwers, 450(NRF):May88-96
Pugel, T.A., with R.G. Hawkins, eds. Fragile Interdependence.
S.D. Cohen, 293(JASt):Feb88-154
Pugh, A.R. The Composition of Pascal's "Apologia."*
D. Wetsel, 475:Vol15No28-322
Pughe, T. - see Shakespeare, W.
Pugliese, O.Z. - see Valla, L.
Puhvel, J. Comparative Mythology.*
K.J. Gutzwiller, 124:Jul-Aug89-476
M.S. Jensen, 196:Band29Heft1/2-221
C.S. Littleton, 292(JAF):Jul-Sep88-360
Puig, M. Blood of Requited Love.
S. Dobyns, 617(TLS):11-17Aug89-877
Puig, M. The Buenos Aires Affair.
S. Dobyns, 617(TLS):11-17Aug89-877
Pulbrook, M. - see Ovid
Pulleyblank, D. Tone in Lexical Phonology.
D. Odden, 297(JL):Mar88-218
Pullinger, K. When the Monster Dies.
M. Ford, 617(TLS):2-8Jun89-619
Pullum, G.K. & W.A. Ladusaw. Phonetic Symbol Guide.*
R. Coates, 297(JL):Sep88-570
A.S. Kaye, 608:Mar89-143
Pulzer, P. The Rise of Political Anti-Semitism in Germany and Austria. (rev)
M. Ignatieff, 453(NYRB):29Jun89-21
Punter, D. - see Blake, W.
Puppo, M.M. - see under Moreno Puppo, M.
Purdy, A. The Collected Poems of Al Purdy.* (R. Brown, ed)
R. Donovan, 198:Autumn88-102
D. Gutteridge, 102(CanL):Spring88-159
Purdy, A. & G. Woodcock. The Purdy-Woodcock Letters. (G. Galt, ed)
D.M.R. Bentley, 105:Fall/Winter88-90
Purdy, J. Garments the Living Wear.
B. Harris, 441:29Oct89-13
Purdy, R.L. & M. Millgate - see Hardy, T.
Pursglove, M. D.V. Grigorovich.
P. Henry, 402(MLR):Oct89-1052
Purvis, T.L. Proprietors, Patronage, and Paper Money.
L.R. Gerlach, 656(WMQ):Apr88-373
Puschman, A. Adam Puschman, "Gründlicher Bericht des deutschen Meistergesangs." (B. Taylor, ed)
H-J. Schlütter, 564:Nov88-386
Putnam, H. Representation and Reality.*
J. Foss, 103:Dec88-491
Putnam, M.C.J. Artifices of Eternity.*
W.R. Nethercut, 24:Winter88-615
E.A. Schmidt, 229:Band60Heft6-501
Puttfarken, T. Roger de Piles' Theory of Art.*
P.R. Radisich, 173(ECS):Winter88/89-228
Pütz, P. Die Leistung der Form.*
E. Glass, 221(GQ):Fall87-665
L. Löb, 83:Autumn88-237
Py, A. Imitation et Renaissance dans la poésie de Ronsard.
J.A. Della Neva, 207(FR):Feb89-516
Pybus, R. Cicadas in Their Summers.*
K. Turner, 493:Winter88/89-53
Pye, L.W. Asian Power and Politics.
A.W. Burks, 293(JASt):Nov88-842

Pyle, E. Ernie's America. (D. Nichols, ed)
D.B. Johnson, 441:12Nov89-55
Pyle, J. Greengold.
G. Gessert, 448:Vol26No2-123
Pylyshyn, Z.W. Computation and Cognition.*
A. Clark, 479(PhQ):Oct88-526
Pyne, S.J. Fire on the Rim.
A.H. Malcolm, 441:14May89-7
Pynson, P. La France à table.
A.J.M. Prévos, 207(FR):Dec88-350
Pyritz, H. & I. Bibliographie zur deutschen Literaturgeschichte des Barockzeitalters.* (Pt 1, fasc 1) (R. Bölhoff, comp)
J. Alexander, 406:Summer88-221
Pyrse, M. - see Austin, M.

Qian Zhongshu. Cinq essais de poétique. (N. Chapuis, ed & trans)
M. Détrie, 549(RLC):Jan-Mar88-67
Qian Zhongshu. Guanzhuibian. (2nd ed)
M. Motsch, 52:Band23Heft2-208
Quackenbush, H.L. Teatro del absurdo hispanoamericano.
D. Zalacaín, 352(LATR):Fall88-137
Quarantotto, C. Dizionario del nuovo italiano.
L. Serianni, 708:Vol14fasc1-130
Quartermain, P., ed. American Poets, 1880-1945. (2nd Ser)
A. Glover, 534(RALS):Vol16No1&2-144
Queffélec, Y. The Wedding.*
42(AR):Winter88-119
Quella-Villéger, A. Pierre Loti l'incompris.
H.H. Poggenburg, 446(NCFS):Fall-Winter 88/89-244
R. Stanley, 207(FR):Mar89-691
Queller, D.E. The Venetian Patriciate.
J. Anderson, 59:Dec88-565
B.G. Kohl, 589:Jul88-707
E. Muir, 551(RenQ):Summer88-288
Quemada, B., ed. Datations et documents lexicographiques. (2nd Ser, fasc 30) (rev by P. Enckell)
R. Arveiller, 553(RLiR):Jul-Dec88-512
Quennell, P. The Pursuit of Happiness.*
J.D. Bloom, 441:22Jan89-23
H. Mantel, 364:Feb/Mar89-132
Quenneville, J-G. René Richard.
P.G. Socken, 627(UTQ):Fall88-206
Quenot, Y. Les Lectures de La Ceppède.*
A. Baïche, 539:Summer88-237
Querry, R. I See by My Get-Up.
R.M. Davis, 649(WAL):May88-77
Quesada, L. La novela española y el cine.
E.D. Myers, 238:May89-301
"Qu'est-ce que Dieu?"
J. Colette, 192(EP):Apr-Jun88-271
Questa, C. Parerga Plautina.
J. Soubiran, 555:Vol61fasc2-327
Questa, C. & R. Raffaelli, eds. Atti del Convegno Internazionale Il Libro e il Testo.
G.J.M. Bartelink, 394:Vol41fasc3/4-389
Questa, C. & R. Raffaelli, eds. Il libro e il testo.
P.F., 555:Vol61fasc2-354
Quigley, A.E. The Modern Stage and Other Worlds.*
M. Göring, 402(MLR):Apr89-428
Quigley, P. Armed and Female.
L. Williams, 441:2Jul89-13
Quigly, I. - see Kipling, R.

Quignard, P. Les Escaliers de Chambord.
   R. Buss, 617(TLS):22–28Dec89–1422
Quignard, P. La leçon de musique.*
   J. Taylor, 532(RCF):Summer88–313
Quilis, A. & H–J. Niederehe, eds. The History
  of Linguistics in Spain.*
   C.J. Pountain, 402(MLR):Jan89–198
Quill, M. The Veil of Ignorance.
   M. Stasio, 441:22Jan89–30
Quinan, J. Frank Lloyd Wright's Larkin
  Building.
   W.J.R. Curtis, 617(TLS):24–30Mar89–315
   A. Gorlin, 47:Jun88–47
   D. Jenkins, 46:Jun88–10
   J. Lipman, 576:Dec88–431
   E. Weiss, 505:Sep88–133
Quinault, P. Stratonice. (E. Dubois, ed)
   H.T. Barnwell, 208(FS):Oct88–471
Quine, J.B. The Bridesmaids.
   S. Chassler, 441:11Jun89–46
   C. Seebohm, 617(TLS):22–28Sep89–1040
Quine, W.V. Philosophy of Logic. (2nd ed)
   M. Jubien, 316:Mar88–303
Quine, W.V. Quiddities.
   A. Orenstein, 103:Jun89–249
   42(AR):Winter88–121
Quine, W.V. The Time of My Life.
   D. Davidson, 316:Mar88–301
Quinn, E. The Private Picasso.
   M. Esterow, 55:Summer88–89
Quinn, E.V. & J.M. Prest, eds. Dear Miss
  Nightingale.
   639(VQR):Spring88–46
Quinn, S. A Mind of her Own.*
   639(VQR):Spring88–51
Quinn, V. & J. Prest – see Jowett, B.
Quinones, R. Mapping Literary Modernism.
   L. Wesseling, 107(CRCL):Mar88–158
Quintas, D.R. see under Rivas Quintas, F.
Quirk, R. & others. A Comprehensive Gram-
  mar of the English Language.*
   F.G.A.M. Aarts, 179(ES):Apr88–163
Quirk, R. & H.G. Widdowson, eds. English in
  the World.*
   A. Ellegard, 355(LSoc):Mar88–151

Raab, L. Other Children.
   P. Stitt, 491:Jun88–163
Raaflaub, K. Die Entdeckung der Freiheit.
   M. Ostwald, 123:Vol38No1–82
   R. Sealey, 229:Band60Heft2–163
Raaflaub, K.A., ed. Social Struggles in Ar-
  chaic Rome.
   G.P. Verbrugghe, 124:Mar–Apr89–318
van Raalte, M. Rhythm and Metre.
   M.L. West, 123:Vol38No1–78
Raaz, F. Ost–West–Kulturaustausch.
   W. Barthel, 654(WB):11/1988–1926
Raban, J. For Love & Money.
   J.T. Hospital, 441:1Oct89–20
   W. Scammell, 364:Feb88–101
   442(NY):4Dec89–188
Rábanos Faci, C. Vanguardia frente a tradic-
  ión en la arquitectura aragonesa (1925–
  1939).
   W. Rincón García, 48:Jan–Mar88–86
Rabaté, J–M. Language, Sexuality and Ideol-
  ogy in Ezra Pound's "Cantos."*
   R.B.D., 295(JML):Fall87/Winter88–370
   J. Kronick, 598(SoR):Autumn89–859
Rabbi, S.G. – see under Gargantini Rabbi, S.

Rabel, R.G. Between East and West.
   639(VQR):Autumn88–131
Rabey, D.I. British and Irish Political Drama
  in the Twentieth Century.
   R.N.C., 295(JML):Fall87/Winter88–277
Rabinbach, A. & J. Zipes, eds. Germans and
  Jews since the Holocaust.
   C. Poore, 221(GQ):Spring88–339
Rabine, L.W. Reading the Romantic Heroine.*
   M. Donaldson–Evans, 207(FR):Oct88–153
Rabinovitch, A. Jerusalem on Earth.
   442(NY):6Feb89–108
Rabinovitch, I. Le psychisme. (Vol 1)
   J–M. Gabaude, 542:Jan–Mar88–86
Rabinovitch, J.N., ed & trans. Shōmonki.*
   H. Shirane, 318(JAOS):Apr–Jun87–343
Rabinowitz, P.J. Before Reading.
   B.K. Horvath, 395(MFS):Winter88–649
   27(AL):May88–322
Rabinowitz, S., ed & trans. The Noise of
  Change.
   J. Graffy, 575(SEER):Jul88–475
Rabotti, G., ed. Breviarium ecclesiae Raven-
  natis (Codice Bavaro), secoli VII–X.
   A.O. Citarella, 589:Apr88–462
Rabushka, A. The New China.
   T.R. Gottschang, 293(JASt):Nov88–857
Racault, J–M., ed. Etudes sur "Paul et Vir-
  ginie" et l'oeuvre de Bernardin de Saint-
  Pierre.
   M–T. Veyrenc, 535(RHL):Mar–Apr88–285
Race, W.H. Pindar.*
   C. Carey, 123:Vol38No1–6
   A. Köhnken, 303(JoHS):Vol108–223
de Rachewiltz, S. De Sirenibus.
   C.S. Brown, 569(SR):Fall88–lxxx
Racine, D., ed. Saint–John Perse. (Vol 1)
   R. Little, 208(FS):Oct88–490
Racine, J. Britannicus, Phaedra, Athaliah.
  (C.H. Sisson, ed & trans)
   W.D. Howarth, 208(FS):Oct88–471
   H. Phillips, 402(MLR):Oct89–976
Racine, J. Phaedra.* (R. Wilbur, trans)
   R.S. Gwynn, 569(SR):Spring88–297
Rackham, B. Catalogue of the Glaisher Col-
  lection of Pottery and Porcelain in the
  Fitzwilliam Museum Cambridge.
   J.E. Poole, 39:Jan88–70
Rackham, O. The Last Forest.
   T. Hinde, 617(TLS):31Mar–6Apr89–348
Radcliff–Umstead, D. Carnival Comedy and
  Sacred Play.*
   L.G. Clubb, 551(RenQ):Spring88–151
   K. Eisenbichler, 539:Summer88–238
Radcliff–Umstead, D. The Exile into Eternity.
   H. Davis, 402(MLR):Apr89–496
Radcliffe, S. Fontane: "Effi Briest."
   P. Howe, 402(MLR):Jan89–246
Raddatz, F.J. The Survivor.
   O. Conant, 441:25Jun89–24
Radding, C.M. A World Made by Man.
   J.J. Contreni, 589:Jul88–709
Radest, H.B. Can We Teach Them?
   S. Morrison, 103:Nov89–462
Radford, J., ed. The Progress of Romance.*
   S. Smith, 366:Autumn88–266
Radl, H., ed. 200 Australian Women.
   D. Adelaide, 581:Dec88–487
Radice, G. Labour's Path to Power.
   M. Pugh, 617(TLS):3–9Nov89–1207
Radice, W. – see Tagore, R.

Radice, W. & B. Reynolds, eds. The Translator's Art.
　R. Stoneman, 123:Vol38No2-386
Radiguet, R. Count d'Orgel's Ball.
　G. Annan, 453(NYRB):12Oct89-8
de Radkowski, G-H. Métamorphoses de la valeur.
　M. Deguy, 98:May88-365
Radley, S. This Way Out.
　M. Stasio, 441:10Dec89-41
Radner, G. It's Always Something.
　J. Kennedy, 441:25Jun89-25
Radnitzky, G. & P. Bernholz, eds. Economic Imperialism.
　R. Sassower, 488:Dec88-551
Radrizzani, R. - see Potocki, J.
Radway, J.A. Reading the Romance.
　R.R. Hellenga, 223:Fall88-359
Rae, N.C. The Decline and Fall of the Liberal Republicans.
　H. Goodman, 441:19Mar89-23
Rae, S., ed. The Orange Dove of Fiji.
　S. Carnell, 617(TLS):15-21Dec89-1392
Raedts, P. Richard Rufus of Cornwall and the Tradition of Oxford Theology.
　J. Goering, 589:Oct88-984
Raeper, W. George MacDonald.
　P.R. Nancarrow, 637(VS):Autumn88-144
Raevsky-Hughes, O. - see Remizov, A.
Rafal'skij, S. Ix pamjati.
　V. Terras, 574(SEEJ):Winter88-658
Raffel, B. Politicians, Poets, and Con Men.*
　G.J. Harp, 106:Summer88-267
Rafferty, K. City on the Rocks.
　B. Winterton, 617(TLS):22-28Dec89-1406
Ragen, N. Jephte's Daughter.
　K. Blickle, 441:2Apr89-28
Ragland-Sullivan, E. Jacques Lacan and the Philosophy of Psychoanalysis.*
　K. Racevskis, 577(SHR):Spring88-174
Ragussis, M. Acts of Naming.*
　M. Couturier, 189(EA):Oct-Dec88-467
　M. Rosenblum, 637(VS):Winter89-274
　S. Scobie, 376:Mar88-101
　L. Yelin, 158:Jun88-90
Rahming, M.B. The Evolution of the West Indian's Image in the Afro-American Novel.
　C. Werner, 395(MFS):Spring88-125
Rai, A. A House Divided.
　R.S. McGregor, 318(JAOS):Jan-Mar87-198
Rai, A. Orwell and the Politics of Despair.
　M. Shelden, 617(TLS):26May-1Jun89-570
Raikes, P. Modernising Hunger.
　M. Douglas, 617(TLS):7-13Apr89-355
Raimes, A. Exploring Through Writing.*
　J. Costello, 399(MLJ):Winter88-470
Raimond, M. - see Proust, M.
Raina, B. Dickens and the Dialectic of Growth.*
　J. Hill, 115:Spring88-210
　R. Mason, 447(N&Q):Jun88-254
　A. Sanders, 402(MLR):Oct89-943
Rainbow, B., ed. Classic Texts in Music Education. (Nos 12, 15, 16 & 18)
　N. Temperley, 415:Feb88-83
Raine, K. The Presence.
　J. MacVean, 4:Spring88-54
　W.S. Milne, 4:Spring88-58
Rainini, I. Il santuario di Mefite in valle d'Ansanto.*
　D. Briquel, 555:Vol61fasc2-341

Rainold, J. John Rainold's Oxford Lectures on Aristotle's "Rhetoric."* (L.D. Green, ed & trans)
　K. Eden, 551(RenQ):Spring88-169
Raitt, A., P.G. Castex & J.M. Bellefroid - see de Villiers de l'Isle-Adam, P.A.M.
Raitt, A.W. - see Lowe, M.
Raitt, J., with B. McGinn & J. Meyendorff. Christian Spirituality.
　A.E. McGrath, 589:Oct88-988
Raj, M.K., ed. Women's Studies in India.
　G. Minault, 293(JASt):Nov88-814
Rajan, B. The Dark Dancer.
　K.D. Verma, 314:Summer-Fall87-60
Rajan, B. The Form of the Unfinished.*
　L.M. Findlay, 591(SIR):Summer88-323
Rajchman, J. Michel Foucault.*
　G. Crichfield, 345(KRQ):May88-236
　P. Trotignon, 542:Jul-Sep88-369
Rajchman, J. & C. West, eds. Post-Analytic Philosophy.
　H.B. Veatch, 449:Sep88-471
Rajemisa-Raolison, R. Rakibolana malagasy.
　B. Schmidt, 682(ZPSK):Band41Heft3-401
Rajendra, C. Dove on Fire.
　B. Raffel, 363(LitR):Winter89-263
Rajš, F. Stawizny Domowiny we słowje a wobrazu.
　G. Stone, 575(SEER):Oct88-667
Raju, P.T. Structural Depths of Indian Thought.*
　R. Martin, 293(JASt):Feb88-186
　K.G. Zysk, 318(JAOS):Jul-Sep87-521
Räkel, H-H.S. Der deutsche Minnesang.
　S. Hägeli & M. Schiendorfer, 680(ZDP):Band107Heft3-462
　H. Heinen, 406:Summer88-215
　H. Heinen, 564:Nov88-384
　I. Kasten, 684(ZDA):Band117Heft2-74
Ralph, R. The Life and Works of John Weaver.
　C.H. de Robilant, 611(TN):Vol42No2-83
Ramage, E.S. The Nature and Purpose of Augustus' "Res Gestae."
　J. Carter, 123:Vol38No2-436
Ramage, J.A. Rebel Raider.
　R.G. Haycock, 106:Spring88-105
Ramalho, A.D. - see under da Costa Ramalho, A.
Ramamoorthy, P. Rangoli.
　J.O. Perry, 314:Winter-Spring88-238
Ramanujan, A.K., ed & trans. Poems of Love and War.*
　W.S. Merwin, 473(PR):Vol55No3-514
　I.V. Peterson, 318(JAOS):Apr-Jun87-351
　S.B. Steever, 318(JAOS):Oct-Dec87-786
Ramanujan, A.K. Second Sight.
　J. John, 314:Winter-Spring88-236
　D. McDuff, 565:Spring88-64
　J. Welch, 493:Spring88-31
Ramat, A.G., O. Carruba & G. Bernini, eds. Papers from the 7th International Conference on Historical Linguistics.
　R. Lass, 159:Vol5-239
Ramat, P. Linguistic Typology.
　F. Müller-Gotama, 350:Jun89-437
Ramaya, S. Flute.
　S. Curtis, 617(TLS):10-16Mar89-256
Rameau, J-P. Jean-Philippe Rameau letzter Musiktraktat.* (H. Schneider, ed)
　T. Christensen, 416:Band3Heft1-81
Ramírez, P.M.P. & R. Reyes Cano - see under Piñero Ramírez, P.M. & R. Reyes Cano

Ramírez, S.F. – see under Fernández Ramírez, S.

Ramírez Trejo, A. Heródoto, padre y creador de la historia científica.
  D. Arnould, 555:Vol61fasc1–115

Ramón, F.R. – see under Ruiz Ramón, F.

Ramos–Kuethe, L. Valle–Inclán: Las "Comedias bárbaras."*
  A. Sinclair, 86(BHS):Oct88–414

Rampersad, A. The Life of Langston Hughes.* (Vol 1)
  R.D.B., 295(JML):Fall87/Winter88–333
  R.K. Barksdale, 534(RALS):Vol16No1&2–215
  H. Eley, 617(TLS):16–22Jun89–671
  D. Pinckney, 453(NYRB):16Feb89–38
  R. Willett, 447(N&Q):Sep88–425

Rampersad, A. The Life of Langston Hughes.* (Vol 2)
  H. Eley, 617(TLS):16–22Jun89–671
  D. Pinckney, 453(NYRB):16Feb89–38

Ramsay, J. Raw Spiritual.
  H. Buckingham, 565:Winter87/88–71

Ramsey, B. & M. Waldvogel. The Quilts of Tennessee.
  L. Horton, 292(JAF):Jan–Mar88–89
  S. James, 662:Spring/Summer88–51

Ramsey, D. Jazz Matters.
  B. Morton, 617(TLS):29Dec89/4Jan90–1438

Ramsey, P., ed. Contemporary Religious Poetry.
  639(VQR):Spring88–64

Ramsey, S.R. The Languages of China.
  J.L. Packard, 293(JASt):Aug88–613

Ramus, P. Arguments in Rhetoric against Quintilian.* (C. Newlands, trans)
  P.J. Smith, 402(MLR):Jul89–690

Ramusi, M.C. & R.S. Turner. Soweto, My Love.
  L. May, 441:19Mar89–23

Rancour–Laferriere, D. Signs of the Flesh.
  U. Kutter, 196:Band29Heft1/2–222

Randall, B. Webster's New World Guide to Current American Usage.
  W.N. Francis, 350:Dec89–907

Randall, D. The Sin Eater.
  M. Wormald, 617(TLS):9–15Jun89–641

Randall, D.B.J. "Theatres of Greatness."
  N.G. Brooks, 447(N&Q):Jun88–228

Randall, F.B. Vissarion Belinskii.
  V. Terras, 550(RusR):Jul88–352

Randall, J. Moving in Memory.
  639(VQR):Winter88–29

Randall, J.G., with J.C.B. Foster & D.F. Kennedy. Learning Latin.
  V.J. Cleary, 121(CJ):Dec88–Jan89–176

Randall, R.H., Jr. Masterpieces of Ivory from the Walters Art Gallery.
  M. Estella, 48:Jul–Sep88–327

Randel, D.M., ed. The New Harvard Dictionary of Music.*
  C. Dahlhaus, 416:Band3Heft3–265
  D.E. McGinty, 91:Spring88–106

Randolph, R.S. The United States and Thailand.
  C.D. Neher, 293(JASt):Feb88–195

Randolph, V. Ozark Folklore. (Vol 1)
  R. Cochran, 292(JAF):Jul–Sep88–371

Randolph, V. & G. McCann. Ozark Folklore. (Vol 2)
  R. Cochran, 292(JAF):Jul–Sep88–371

"The Random House Dictionary of the English Language, Unabridged."* (2nd ed) (S.B. Flexner, ed–in–chief)
  H. Homa, 35(AS):Winter88–371
  L. Mackinnon, 617(TLS):21–27Apr89–431

Randriamasimanana, C. The Causatives of Malagasy.
  B. Schmidt, 682(ZPSK):Band41Heft3–403

Ranger, P., ed. "The School for Scandal" by Richard Sheridan.
  C. Price, 402(MLR):Oct89–932

Ranke, K., ed. Enzyklopädie des Märchens. (Vol 5, Pt 1)
  E. Ettlinger, 203:Vol99No2–256
  A. Gier, 72:Band224Heft2–362

Ranke, K., ed. Enzyklopädie des Märchens. (Vol 5, Pts 2 & 3)
  E. Ettlinger, 203:Vol99No2–256

Ranke, K. & others, eds. Enzyklopädie des Märchens.* (Vol 4, Pts 4 & 5)
  A. Gier, 72:Band224Heft2–362

Ránki, G., ed. Bartók and Kodály Revisited.
  A. Pople, 410(M&L):Apr88–287

Rankin, N. Dead Man's Chest.*
  R.A. Boyle, 637(VS):Spring89–450
  T.M. Robinson, 364:Nov87–107

Ransel, D.L. Mothers of Misery.
  L. Pollock, 617(TLS):17–23Mar89–281

Ransford, T. Shadows from the Greater Hill.
  C. Gow, 571(ScLJ):Winter88–51

Ransmayr, C. Die letzte Welt.
  M. Hofmann, 617(TLS):21–27Apr89–435

Ransom, D.J. Poets at Play.*
  I. Bishop, 677(YES):Vol19–304

Ransom, E.N. Complementation.*
  R. Hudson, 297(JL):Mar88–258

Rao, S.B. A Still, Small Voice.
  J.O. Perry, 314:Winter–Spring88–238

Rapaport, H. Milton and the Postmodern.*
  G. Teskey, 153:Spring88–42

Raper, J.R. – see Glasgow, E.

Raper, P.E. Dictionary of Southern African Place Names.
  A. Room, 424:Mar–Jun88–111

Raphael, D. The Alhambra Decree.
  B. Finkelstein, 441:23Apr89–20

Raphael, F. After the War.
  J. Roux, 441:4Jun89–22

Raphael, R. The Men From the Boys.
  B. Lovenheim, 441:12Mar89–23

Rapoport, J.L. The Boy Who Couldn't Stop Washing.
  G. Hochman, 441:26Feb89–35

Rapp, F. & R. Wiehl, eds. Whiteheads Metaphysik der Kreativität.
  L.S. Ford, 619:Spring88–302

Rappaport, G.C. Grammatical Function and Syntactic Structure.
  C.V. Chvany, 574(SEEJ):Summer88–346

Rappaport, S. Worlds within Worlds.
  P. Clark, 617(TLS):20–26Oct89–1162

Rasch, J.J. Das Maxentius–Mausoleum an der Via Appia in Rom.
  K. de Fine Licht, 229:Band60Heft6–569

Rasch, R. – see Huygens, C.

Rasch, R. – see Sauveur, J.

Rasch, R. – see Werckmeister, A.

Rasch, W. Die literarische Décadence um 1900.*
  M. Anderson, 400(MLN):Apr88–692
  N.H. Donahue, 222(GR):Spring88–111
  J. Hardin, 406:Summer88–242
  [continued]

Rasch, W. Die literarische Décadence um
1900. [continuing]
   W. Paulsen, 564:Feb88-84
   J. Rieckmann, 221(GQ):Winter88-146
Raskin, V. & I. Weiser. Language and Writing.
   R. Evans, 350:Mar89-190
Rasky, H. Tennessee Williams.
   R.C., 295(JML):Fall87/Winter88-400
Rasmussen, D. & J. Sterba. The Catholic
Bishops and the Economy.
   P.H., 185:Oct88-209
Rasnake, R.N. Domination and Cultural Re-
sistance.
   B.Y. Butler, 263(RIB):Vol38No4-539
Raspa, A. - see Donne, J.
Raspail, J. Who Will Remember the People...*
(French title: Qui se souvient des
hommes...)
   E.M. Thomas, 441:15Jan89-18
Rasputin, V. Siberia on Fire. (G. Mikkelson &
M. Winchell, eds & trans)
   J.B. Dunlop, 441:17Dec89-1
Rastier, F. Sémantique Interprétative.
   R. Posner, 402(MLR):Apr89-460
Ratherius. Ratherii Veronensis Praeloquiorum
Libri VI. (P.L.D. Reid & others, eds)
   B.R. Reece, 377:Mar88-58
Rathmayr, R. Die russischen Partikeln als
Pragmalexeme.
   G. Hüttl-Folter, 559:Vol12No3-337
Rathofer, C. Ciceros "Brutus" als literar-
isches Paradigma eines Auctoritas-Ver-
hältnisses.
   A. Douglas, 123:Vol38No2-414
   J.G.F. Powell, 313:Vol78-216
Ratkowitsch, C. Maximianus amat.
   D. Shanzer, 229:Band60Heft3-259
Rattay, B. Entstehung und Rezeption politis-
cher Lyrik im 15. und 16. Jahrhundert.
   A. Classen, 201:Vol14-232
Ratushinskaya, I. Beyond the Limit.
   P. Debreczeny, 473(PR):Vol55No3-497
Ratushinskaya, I. Grey is the Colour of
Hope.*
   J.M. Cameron, 453(NYRB):1Jun89-33
   J. Lucas, 493:Winter88/89-18
Ratushinskaya, I. Pencil Letter.*
   J. Lucas, 493:Winter88/89-18
Ratušinskaja, I. Skazka o trex golovax. (D.N.
Ignashev, ed & trans)
   T. Pogacar, 574(SEEJ):Summer88-337
Ratz, N. Der Identitätsroman.
   E. Boa, 402(MLR):Oct89-1025
Rault-Leyrat, L. La cithare chinoise zheng.
   C. Despeux, 537:Vol74No2-237
Raupp, H-J. Bauernsatiren.
   P. Vandenbroeck, 600:Vol18No1/2-69
Raval, S. The Art of Failure.*
   B. Stampfl, 401(MLQ):Dec86-447
   I.V., 295(JML):Fall87/Winter88-306
Ravel, M. Lettres, écrits, entretiens. (A.
Orenstein, ed)
   R. Nichols, 617(TLS):1-7Dec89-1330
Raven, S. Blood of My Bone.
   T. Fitton, 617(TLS):10-16Mar89-256
Ravenel, S., ed. New Stories from the South:
The Year's Best, 1987.
   S.M. Jones, 577(SHR):Fall88-406
   G.L. Morris, 455:Mar88-70
   P. Samway, 392:Winter87/88-105
Ravenel, S., ed. New Stories from the South:
The Year's Best, 1988.
   P. Lyons, 110:Winter89-65

Rawles, S. & M.A. Screech. A New Rabelais
Bibliography.
   I.D. McFarlane, 617(TLS):16-22Jun89-
   676
Rawlinson, J. Cargo.
   C. Verderese, 441:7May89-24
Rawls, J. Théorie de la justice.*
   A. Reix, 542:Jan-Mar88-107
Raworth, T. Tottering State.
   R. Sheppard, 617(TLS):10-16Mar89-257
Rawson, B., ed. The Family in Ancient Rome.*
   R.P. Saller, 122:Jul88-263
Rawson, C. & F.P. Lock - see Parnell, T.
Rawson, C., with J. Mezciems, eds. English
Satire and the Satiric Tradition.
   G. Midgley, 541(RES):May88-331
   F. Price, 83:Autumn88-230
Rawson, C.J. Order from Confusion Sprung.*
   M. Price, 173(ECS):Summer88-514
   J. Richetti, 141:Spring88-256
Rawson, C.J., with J. Mezciems - see "The
Yearbook of English Studies"
Rawson, E. Intellectual Life in the Late Ro-
man Republic.*
   G.W. Bowersock, 487:Autumn88-272
   R. Saller, 41:Vol7-251
   A. Wallace-Hadrill, 122:Jul88-224
Ray, D. Sam's Book.*
   C. Inez, 152(UDQ):Summer88-115
Ray, L. Approches du lieu.
   M-N. Little, 207(FR):Apr89-906
Ray, L. Le Nom perdu.
   G. Goffette, 450(NRF):Feb88-95
Ray, M. Self Portrait.
   R. Cardinal, 617(TLS):31Mar-6Apr89-336
Ray, R.H., ed. Approaches to Teaching
Shakespeare's "King Lear."*
   D.A. Carroll, 702:Vol20-311
Ray, V. Advertising the Contradictions.
   G. Gessert, 448:Vol26No2-121
Ray, W. Literary Meaning.*
   E.F. Kaelin, 289:Fall88-120
Rayl, A.J.S. & C. Gunther. Beatles '64.
   D. Kelly, 441:31Dec89-12
Raymond, J.G. A Passion for Friends.
   M.S., 185:Oct88-190
   P. Summerfield, 637(VS):Summer89-595
Raymond, M. Le travail d'écriture.
   D. Devoto, 92(BH):Jan-Dec87-331
Raynaud de Lage, G., ed. Choix de fabliaux.*
   B.J. Levy, 382(MAE):1988/1-131
   A.V., 379(MedR):Dec88-462
Rayner, R. Los Angeles Without a Map.*
   D. Stillman, 441:22Jan89-18
Raz, J. The Morality of Freedom.*
   P. Engel, 542:Jan-Mar88-108
   S. Guest, 518:Oct88-196
   R.A. Shiner, 483:Jan88-119
Rāzī, N.A. The Path of God's Bondsmen from
Origin to Return. (H. Algar, ed & trans)
   H. Landolt, 318(JAOS):Oct-Dec87-803
Read, A. & D. Fisher. The Deadly Embrace.*
   G.A. Craig, 453(NYRB):30Mar89-15
Read, C. Children's Creative Spelling.
   P. Freyd, 355(LSoc):Mar88-153
Read, D. Peel and the Victorians.
   P. Dunkley, 637(VS):Winter89-273
Read, P.P. A Season in the West.*
   J. De Lynn, 441:13Aug89-21
   J. Mellors, 364:Dec88/Jan89-132
Reade, C. Plays by Charles Reade.* (M. Ham-
met, ed)
   M.R. Booth, 677(YES):Vol19-344

Reading, P. Final Demands.*
  H. Lomas, 364:Jul88-92
  B. O'Donoghue, 493:Summer88-62
Reading, P. Perduta Gente.
  M. Imlah, 617(TLS):25-31Aug89-916
Reagan, M. First Father, First Daughter.
  D. Ephron, 441:26Mar89-8
Reagan, M., with J. Hyams. On the Outside
  Looking In.*
  C. Hitchens, 617(TLS):21-27Apr89-418
Reagan, N., with W. Novak. My Turn.
  F. Barnes, 441:19Nov89-9
  J. Didion, 453(NYRB):21Dec89-3
Reagan, R. Speaking My Mind.
  J. Didion, 453(NYRB):21Dec89-3
Real, H.J. & H.J. Vienken, eds. Proceedings of
  the First Münster Symposium on Jonathan
  Swift.*
  D.C. Mell, Jr., 173(ECS):Fall88-95
Reale, G. A History of Ancient Philosophy.*
  (Vols 1 & 3) (J.R. Catan, ed & trans)
  R. Torretti, 160:Jan88-226
"Reallexikon für Antike und Christentum."
  (Pts 97-101)
  J. André, 555:Vol61fasc2-348
"Reallexikon für Antike und Christentum."
  (Supp, Pts 1/2 & 3)
  J. André, 555:Vol61fasc2-349
Reames, S.L. The "Legenda aurea."
  M.L. Day, 589:Apr88-463
Reaves, D. Secrets of the Giants.
  G. Gessert, 448:Vol26No1-70
Reay, B., ed. Popular Culture in Seven-
  teenth-Century England.
  D. Smith, 568(SCN):Fall88-50
Recanati, F. Meaning and Force.
  C. Bernstein, 350:Sep89-672
  N. Brown, 643:Dec88-405
  355(LSoc):Sep88-465
"Les récits de voyage."
  S. Moussa, 547(RF):Band99Heft4-453
Recker, J.A.M. Appelle-moi "Pierrot."
  H.J. Barnwell, 208(FS):Apr88-203
  P.A. Wadsworth, 207(FR):Oct88-168
Reckford, K.J. Aristophanes' Old-and-New
  Comedy. (Vol 1)
  T.J. Moore, 568(SCN):Fall88-39
  S.D. Olson, 124:Nov-Dec88-140
Reddé, M. Mare Nostrum.*
  B. Campbell, 313:Vol78-239
Rédei, K. Zu den indogermanisch-uralischen
  Sprachkontakten.
  P. Sherwood, 575(SEER):Apr88-262
Redfern, H.B. Questions in Aesthetic Educa-
  tion.*
  T. Anderson, 290(JAAC):Winter87-318
  E.L. Lankford, 289:Summer88-114
Redfern, W.D. Georges Darien.*
  M. Autrand, 535(RHL):Jan-Feb88-149
Redfield, J. La tragédie d'Hector.
  A. Bonnafé, 555:Vol61fasc2-301
Redford, B. The Converse of the Pen.*
  H. Anderson, 401(MLQ):Mar87-93
  M. Myers, 173(ECS):Fall88-84
  V. Newey, 506(PSt):Sep88-101
  P. Rogers, 191(ELN):Jun88-96
  P. Sabor, 629(QQ):Winter88-926
Redgrove, P. The First Earthquake. Poems
  1954-87.
  S. Medcalf, 617(TLS):22-28Dec89-1417
Redgrove, P. The Mudlark Poems and Grand
  Buveur.*
  H. Buckingham, 565:Winter87/88-71

Redhead, M. Incompleteness, Non-Locality
  and Realism.*
  P. Gibbins, 518:Apr88-117
  A. Heathcote, 63:Dec88-560
Redmond, J., ed. Farce.
  S. Wall, 617(TLS):24-30Mar89-301
Redner, H. The Ends of Science.
  M. Neumann, 103:Nov89-465
Redon, J. Bloodstream.
  M. Mifflin, 441:20Aug89-20
Redondi, P. Galileo Heretic.* (French title:
  Galilée hérétique.)
  R. Flannagan, 391:Mar88-21
Redondo, A., ed. Amours légitimes, amours
  illégitimes en Espagne.
  M.S. Sánchez, 551(RenQ):Winter88-731
Redonnet, M. Forever Valley.
  D. Pierson, 207(FR):Apr89-907
Redpath, P. William Golding.*
  S. Vice, 447(N&Q):Jun88-263
Redslob, E. Schicksal und Dichtung.
  S. Samples, 221(GQ):Summer88-443
Rée, J. Philosophical Tales.*
  J. Mason, 478(P&L):Oct88-318
  T.M.R., 185:Jul89-971
Reece, R.D. & H. Siegal. Studying People.
  E.M.M., 185:Oct88-212
Reed, A., ed. Romanticism and Language.*
  J.E. Grant, 88:Spring89-124
Reed, C. Henry Chapman Mercer and the
  Moravian Pottery and Tile Works.*
  C.A. Robertson, 658:Winter88-289
Reed, E.S. James J. Gibson and the Psychol-
  ogy of Perception.
  E.H. Gombrich, 453(NYRB):19Jan89-13
Reed, H.H. The Reader in the Picaresque
  Novel.
  J.V. Ricapito, 346(KRQ):Feb88-113
Reed, H.M. Decorated Furniture of the
  Mahantongo Valley.
  S.T. Swank, 658:Winter88-285
Reed, I. The Terrible Threes.
  G. Early, 441:7May89-34
  D. Pinckney, 453(NYRB):12Oct89-20
Reed, I. The Terrible Twos. The Free-Lance
  Pallbearers. Yellow Back Radio Broke-
  Down. Mumbo Jumbo. The Last Days of
  Louisiana Red. New and Collected Poems.
  Writin' Is Fightin'.
  D. Pinckney, 453(NYRB):12Oct89-20
Reed, J. Engaging Form.*
  S. O'Brien, 493:Autumn88-56
Reed, J. Red Eclipse.
  T.D. Smith, 617(TLS):1-7Sep89-953
Reed, J. Schubert.*
  E.N. McKay, 410(M&L):Apr88-267
Reed, J. The Schubert Song Companion.
  E. West, 410(M&L):Apr88-265
Reed, J. Selected Poems.*
  T. Eagleton, 565:Summer88-67
Reed, J.R. Victorian Conventions.
  M. Moseley, 569(SR):Spring88-243
  P.T. Srebrnik, 635(VPR):Fall88-130
Reed, J.S. Southern Folk, Plain and Fancy.*
  J.G. Flanagan, 585(SoQ):Winter89-103
Reed, P. Longing.
  G. Kolata, 441:19Feb89-20
Rees, B. A Musical Peacemaker.*
  V. Crowther, 637(VS):Winter89-287
Rees, E. Libri Walliae.
  J. Roberts, 354:Dec88-351
Rees, I.B., comp. The Mountains of Wales.
  A. Adams, 39:Jul88-67

305

Rees, J. Shelley's Jane Williams.
N. Brown, 340(KSJ):Vol37-200
Rees, J.C. John Stuart Mill's "On Liberty."*
(G.L. Williams, ed)
L. Kreimendahl, 687:Oct-Dec88-704
Rees-Davies, J. - see "Fétis on Clarinettists
and Clarinet Repertoire"
Reese, T.J. Archbishop.
P.F. Drucker, 441:28May89-10
Reeve, A., ed. Modern Theories of Exploita-
tion.
C.B., 185:Jan89-453
Reeve, A. Property.
J.C., 185:Apr89-666
Reeve, C.D.C. Philosopher-Kings.
J. Annas, 617(TLS):2-8Jun89-600
Reeve, W.C. In Pursuit of Power.
A. Bohm, 529(QQ):Summer88-463
H.M. Brown, 402(MLR):Jan89-236
Reeves, H. & others. Chaos et Cosmos.
M. Espinoza, 542:Jul-Sep88-396
Reeves, M. & W. Gould. Joachim of Fiore and
the Myth of the Eternal Evangel in the
Nineteenth Century.
R. Ashton, 541(RES):Nov88-577
Regan, D.T. For the Record.*
R.S. Leiken, 617(TLS):10-16Feb89-127
Regan, J.J. Your Legal Rights in Later Life.
J. Viorst, 441:9Apr89-30
Regan, T. Bloomsbury's Prophet.*
T. Baldwin, 393(Mind):Jan88-129
B. Faulk, 637(VS):Summer89-608
Regan, T. - see Moore, G.E.
"Regensburger Buchmalerei."
V.R. Kaufmann, 90:Feb88-145
Regn, G. Torquato Tassos zyklische Liebes-
lyrik und die petrarkistische Tradition.
G. Güntert, 547(RF):Band100Heft4-452
Regnard, J-F. Le Joueur. (J. Dunkley, ed)
B. Griffiths, 208(FS):Jul88-343
Regneri, C. Demonstratio logicae verae juri-
dica. (G. Kalinowski, ed)
A. Reix, 542:Apr-Jun88-256
van Regteren Altena, J.Q. Jacques de Gheyn.
M. Roethlisberger, 380:Spring88-52
M. Schapelhouman, 600:Vol18No4-264
Reh, A.M. Literatur und Psychologie.
J.T. Adams, 221(GQ):Fall88-540
Rehder, P., ed. Slavistische Linguistik 1983.
F.E. Knowles, 575(SEER):Apr88-254
Rehder, R. The Poetry of Wallace Stevens.
J.S. Leonard, 27(AL):Dec88-693
J.N. Serio, 705:Fall88-183
Reibetanz, J. Ashbourn.*
B.N.S. Gooch, 102(CanL):Summer88-154
Reich, R.B., ed. The Power of Public Ideas.
L.B.G., 185:Jan89-464
Reich, W. Passion of Youth.* (M.B. Higgins &
C.M. Raphael, eds)
R.M. Young, 617(TLS):5-11May89-480
Reich-Ranicki, M., with D. von Briel & H-U.
Treichel - see Koeppen, W.
Reichardt, L. Ortsnamenbuch des Kreises
Reutlingen.
T. Steiner, 685(ZDL):3/1987-416
Reichardt, R. & E. Schmitt, with others, eds.
Handbuch politisch-sozialer Grundbegriffe
in Frankreich 1680-1820.* (Pts 1-7)
A. Gier, 72:Band225Heft2-432
Reichart, E. February Shadows.
M. Halahmy, 617(TLS):10-16Feb89-148

Reichel, J. Der Spruchdichter Hans Rosen-
plüt.*
E. Schumann, 684(ZDA):Band117Heft1-24
Reichel, S. What Did You Do in the War,
Daddy?
I. Buruma, 453(NYRB):26Oct89-31
A. Owings, 441:25Jun89-28
Reichelt, K., ed. Historisch-politische
Schauspiele.
P. Skrine, 402(MLR):Oct89-1024
Reichenbach, B.A. Handbook of German
Grammar.
W. Keel, 399(MLJ):Autumn88-361
Reichler, C. L'Age libertin.
J.G. Turner, 536(Rev):Vol10-1
Reichley, A.J. Religion in American Public
Life.
L.A.K., 185:Jan89-471
Reichmann, O. - see Anderson, R.R., U. Goebel
& O. Reichmann
Reid, A. Southeast Asia in the Age of Com-
merce, 1450-1680. (Vol 1)
C. Geertz, 453(NYRB):16Feb89-28
Reid, C.J., ed. Peace in a Nuclear Age.
C.A.J. Coady, 185:Jan89-446
Reid, C.W. Open Secret.
C. Bedient, 569(SR):Winter88-137
Reid, J. Emperors of the Turf.
A. Ross, 617(TLS):17-23Nov89-1285
Reid, J.H. Heinrich Böll.
K. Bullivant, 402(MLR):Oct89-1045
Reid, J.M. Basic Writing.
A. Bollati, 399(MLJ):Autumn88-349
Reid, J.P. The Concept of Liberty in the Age
of the American Revolution.
R.L., 185:Jul89-978
Reid, J.P. Constitutional History of the
American Revolution: The Authority of
Rights. Constitutional History of the
American Revolution: The Authority to
Tax.
S.A. Conrad, 656(WMQ):Oct88-775
P.S. Onuf, 173(ECS):Summer88-551
Reid, M. All-Change in the City.
C. Johnson, 617(TLS):10-16Mar89-243
Reid, M. Ask Sir James.
W.B. Ober, 441:9Apr89-33
Reid, P.L.D. & others - see Ratherius
Reid, R., ed. Problems of Russian Romanti-
cism.*
L.G. Leighton, 574(SEEJ):Spring88-132
Reid, R.L., ed. A Treasury of the Sierra
Nevada.
O. Burmaster, 649(WAL):May88-81
Reid, T. The Philosophical Orations of
Thomas Reid. (D.D. Todd, ed)
C. Stewart-Robertson, 103:Aug89-338
Reif, M. Film und Text.
E. Wright, 494:Vol8No2-461
Reiff, D.D. Small Georgian Houses in England
and Virginia.*
D. Leatherbarrow, 173(ECS):Winter88/89-
274
M. Whiffen, 576:Jun88-210
Reilly, B.F. The Kingdom of León-Castilla
under King Alfonso VI 1065-1109.
F.C. Cesareo, 377:Nov88-210
Reilly, E., M. McManus & W. Chadwick. The
Monkees - a Manufactured Image.
B.L. Cooper, 498:Spring88-85
Reilly, E.J., ed. Approaches to Teaching
Swift's "Gulliver's Travels."
A.H. de Quehen, 166:Jul89-338

Reilly, J.M. Care and Identification of 19th-Century Photographic Prints.
P.S. Koda, 87(BB):Sep88-215
Reiman, D.H. - see Shelley, M.W. & P.B.
Reiman, D.H., with D.D. Fischer, eds. Shelley and his Circle: 1773-1822. (Vols 7 & 8)
L.A. Marchand, 591(SIR):Summer88-330
R. Woodman, 340(KSJ):Vol37-188
Reimarus, H.S. Die vornehmsten Wahrheiten der natürlichen Religion.* (G. Gawlick, ed)
R. Finster, 706:Band20Heft1-119
Rein, K. Einführung in die Kontrastive Linguistik.
G. Ineichen, 260(IF):Band93-271
Reiner, E. Les Doublets étymologiques.
D. Justice, 545(RPh):Nov88-197
Reiner, E. Études de linguistique dualiste.*
W. Ayres-Bennett, 208(FS):Oct88-495
J. Erfurt, 682(ZPSK):Band41Heft6-831
C. Schmitt, 72:Band224Heft2-358
Reiner, E., with D. Pingree. Babylonian Planetary Omens. (Pts 1 & 2)
W.G. Lambert, 318(JAOS):Jan-Mar87-93
Reinhard, J. Burning the Prairie.
E. Butscher, 496:Fall88-44
Reischauer, E.O. The Japanese Today.
J. Parry, 617(TLS):13-19Jan89-31
Reising, R.J. The Unusable Past.*
N. Baym, 301(JEGP):Jan88-136
J.W. Crowley, 26(ALR):Fall88-63
E. Emerson, 125:Fall87-100
R.L., 295(JML):Fall87/Winter88-255
T.M. Leitch, 536(Rev):Vol10-35
D.S. Reynolds, 27(AL):Mar88-109
Reiss, K.P. - see von Hassell, U.
Reiss, T.J. The Discourse of Modernism.*
D.R. Lachterman, 480(P&R):Vol21No1-69
Reith, H.R. René Descartes.*
R.A. Watson, 319:Apr89-299
von Reitzenstein, W-A. Lexikon bayerischer Ortsnamen.
E. Meineke, 685(ZDL):2/1988-251
W.F.H. Nicolaisen, 424:Sep-Dec88-239
H. Rosenfeld, 72:Band224Heft2-372
Rejhon, A.C., ed & trans. Cân Rolant.
J.F. Nagy, 589:Apr88-464
Remak, H.H.H. Novellistische Struktur.
G. Gillespie, 107(CRCL):Mar88-136
"Remembering the Future."
H. Rubin, 441:8Oct89-24
Remi-Giraud, S. & M. Le Guern, with others, eds. Sur le verbe.*
L. Melis, 209(FM):Apr88-107
Remizov, A. Iveren'.* (O. Raevsky-Hughes, ed)
G.N. Slobin, 550(RusR):Apr88-229
Remnant, M. English Bowed Instruments from Anglo-Saxon to Tudor Times.*
I. Woodfield, 410(M&L):Oct88-505
Rempel, R.A., A. Brink & M. Moran - see Russell, B.
Remy, M. L'Évolution administrative de l'Anatolie aux trois premiers siècles de notre ère.
S. Mitchell, 123:Vol38No2-437
"Renaissance Drama." (Vol 16 ed by L. Barkan; Vol 17 ed by M.B. Rose)
R. Soellner, 130:Fall88-269
Renard, M. & P. Laurens, eds. Hommages à Henri Bardon.
P.F., 555:Vol61fasc2-349

Renart, J. Jean Renart: "Le Lai de l'Ombre."* (M.E. Winters, ed)
G.S. Burgess, 208(FS):Jul88-332
Renaud, B. Bach et Bottine.
R. Viau, 102(CanL):Spring88-240
Renaud, P. Ramuz ou l'intensité d'en bas.*
R. Mathé, 535(RHL):Nov-Dec88-1169
Renaut, A. L'Ere de l'individu.
M. Lilla, 617(TLS):17-23Nov89-1255
Rendell, R. The Bridesmaid.
M. Stasio, 441:10Sep89-28
Renfrew, C. Archaeology and Language.*
K.R. Norman, 361:Sep88-91
Rengakos, A. Form und Wandel des Machtdenkens der Athener bei Thukydides.*
H.D. Westlake, 123:Vol38No2-307
Renkema, J. Tekst en uitleg.
M. Schasfoort, 204(FdL):Sep88-237
Renner, R.G. Peter Handke.*
T.F. Barry, 221(GQ):Winter87-88
T.R. Nadar, 406:Fall88-405
Renner, R.G. Lebens-Werk.
S.R. Cerf, 221(GQ):Summer87-497
Rennert, H.H. Eduard Mörike's Reading and the Reconstruction of his Extant Library.
M.C. Crichton, 221(GQ):Winter87-126
Rennison, J. Bidialektale Phonologie.
H. Scheutz, 685(ZDL):3/1987-378
Renov, M. Hollywood's Wartime Woman.
P.D. Murphy, 590:Jun89-47
Rensch, R. Harps and Harpists.
C. Ehrlich, 617(TLS):16-22Jun89-667
Rentoul, J., with J. Ratford. Me and Mine.
B. Barnes, 617(TLS):17-23Mar89-270
Rentschler, E., ed. German Film and Literature.*
F.A. Birgel, 221(GQ):Fall87-697
P.C. Lutze, 406:Fall88-384
Renwick, J. Chamfort devant la postérité 1794-1984.
G.E. Rodmell, 402(MLR):Jan89-176
D. Wood, 208(FS):Jul88-348
Renzi, L., with G. Salvi. Nuova introduzione alla filologia romanza.
J. Albrecht, 547(RF):Band99Heft4-401
"Répertoire des écrivains franco-ontariens."
L.E. Doucette, 627(UTQ):Fall88-191
"Report of the National Economic Commission, March 1, 1989."
B.M. Friedman, 453(NYRB):1Jun89-23
Rescher, N. Ethical Idealism.*
H.J. Johnson, 103:Mar89-112
T. McConnell, 484(PPR):Jun89-748
Rescher, N. Die Grenzen der Wissenschaft.
J. Seibt, 679:Band19Heft1-165
Resnick, P. Parliament vs. People.
F. Cunningham, 529(QQ):Spring88-209
Resnick, P. & R. Walkey. The Centaur's Mountain.
D.M.A. Relke, 102(CanL):Spring88-118
Restagno, E., ed. Nono.
R. Fearn, 410(M&L):Oct88-554
Restak, R.M. The Mind.
T. Bay, 441:1Jan89-15
Reston, J., Jr. The Lone Star.
N. Lemann, 61:Oct89-109
K. Northcott, 441:26Nov89-9
Resweber, J-P. Qu'est-ce qu'interpréter?
A. Reix, 542:Oct-Dec88-507
Rétat, P. Les Journaux de 1789.
A. Forrest, 617(TLS):6-12Oct89-1097
"Retskrivningsordbogen."
R. Baudusch, 682(ZPSK):Band41Heft4-537

Reuchlein, G. Bürgerliche Gesellschaft, Psychiatrie und Literatur.*
S.L. Gilman, 301(JEGP):Oct88-603
R.C. Holub, 406:Fall88-364
G. Lehnert-Rodiek, 52:Band23Heft2-189
C. Poore, 221(GQ):Fall88-582
Reula, J.F.G. - see under Galván Reula, J.F.
Reuland, E.J. & A.G.B. ter Meulen, eds. The Representation of (In)definiteness.
J. Hoeksema, 350:Mar89-115
Reulos, M. Comment transcrire et interpréter les références juridiques.
J. Pineaux, 535(RHL):Mar-Apr88-255
Reuter, O.R. Proverbs, Proverbial Sentences and Phrases in Thomas Deloney's Works.
W. Mieder, 292(JAF):Apr-Jun88-250
J.E. Van Domelen, 568(SCN):Spring-Summer88-12
Reuter, P., G. Crawford & J. Cave. Sealing the Borders.
M. Massing, 453(NYRB):30Mar89-22
Reutter, M. Sparrows Point.
C.F. Sabel, 441:5Feb89-3
Reuzeau, J.V., ed. French Poets of Today.
M. Bishop, 150(DR):Winter87/88-528
"Le Rêve et la vie: 'Aurélia,' 'Sylvie,' 'Les Chimères' de Gérard de Nerval."
S. Dunn, 535(RHL):Nov-Dec88-1150
de Revenga, F.J.D. - see under Díez de Revenga, F.J.
Reverby, S.M. Ordered to Care.*
N.N., 185:Jan89-467
"The Revised English Bible with the Apocrypha."
G. Hill, 617(TLS):17-23Nov89-1273
Revon, M., ed. Anthologie de la littérature japonaise.
M. Détrie, 549(RLC):Jan-Mar88-67
Revuelta Sañudo, M. - see Menéndez Pelayo, M.
Rewald, J. Cézanne and America.
R. Kendall, 441:16Apr89-13
Rex, J. The Ghetto and the Underclass.
N.D. Deakin, 617(TLS):3-9Mar89-216
Rex, W.E. The Attraction of the Contrary.*
M. Cardy, 166:Apr89-244
Rexach, R. Estudios sobre Martí.*
J. Marbán, 552(REH):May88-131
Rexroth, K. World Outside the Window.* (B. Morrow, ed)
B. Almon, 649(WAL):Nov88-274
Rey Rosa, R. The Beggar's Knife.*
I. Malin, 532(RCF):Spring88-200
Rey Rosa, R. Dust on Her Tongue.
G. Martin, 617(TLS):14-20Jul89-782
Reydellet, M. - see Isidore of Seville
Reyerson, K.L. Business, Banking, and Finance in Medieval Montpellier.
S.F. Roberts, 589:Jan88-217
Reyle, U. & C. Rohrer, eds. Natural Language Parsing and Linguistic Theories.
J. Hoeksema, 350:Jun89-437
Reynolds, D., with D.P. Columbia. Debbie.
B. Shulgasser, 441:29Jan89-31
Reynolds, D.S. Beneath the American Renaissance.*
N. Baym, 183(ESQ):Vol33No3-180
J.E. Becker, 363(LitR):Winter89-278
J. Myerson, 432(NEQ):Dec88-595
D. Van Leer, 357:Fall89-61
Reynolds, G. English Portrait Miniatures. (rev)
M. Rogers, 617(TLS):7-13Apr89-375

Reynolds, J. & R. Tannenbaum. Jews and Godfearers at Aphrodisias.
M. Goodman, 313:Vol78-261
J. Pouilloux, 555:Vol61fasc2-314
Reynolds, L. Kate O'Brien.*
M. Koenig, 272(IUR):Spring88-146
P. O'Leary, 395(MFS):Summer88-286
Reynolds, L.D., ed. Texts and Transmission.
A. Grafton, 354:Mar88-53
Reynolds, M. The Young Hemingway.*
E. Margolies, 179(ES):Jun88-267
E. Pifer, 677(YES):Vol19-351
Reynolds, M.S. "The Sun Also Rises."
234:Fall88-66
Reynolds, O. The Player Queen's Wife.*
W. Scammell, 364:Aug/Sep88-108
Reynolds, P. & T. Shachtman. The Gilded Leaf.
A. Cooper, 441:20Aug89-21
Reynolds, V., V. Falger & I. Vine, eds. The Sociobiology of Ethnocentrism.
F. Gifford, 185:Oct88-183
Reynolds-Cornell, R. Witnessing an Era.
A.R. Larsen, 207(FR):Feb89-517
D. Russell, 188(ECr):Summer88-101
Rézeau, P. Les "Prières" aux saints en français à la fin du Moyen Age.*
U. Mölk, 547(RF):Band99Heft4-461
Rézeau, P. Répertoire d'incipit des prières françaises à la fin du moyen âge.*
B.J. Levy, 208(FS):Jan88-73
Reznek, L. The Nature of Disease.
T.S. Champlin, 291:Vol5No2-240
A. Flew, 518:Oct88-228
von Rezzori, G. The Snows of Yesteryear.
A. Bernays, 441:26Nov89-10
Rheinheimer, H.P. Topo.
J. Ure, 617(TLS):24-30Nov89-1294
Rheinwald, R. Der Formalismus und seine Grenzen.*
S.J. Wagner, 316:Jun88-645
Rhenisch, H. Eleusis.
A. Munton, 102(CanL):Spring88-227
Rhoads, S.E. The Economist's View of the World.
M. Schabas, 488:Dec88-559
J.O. Wisdom, 488:Sep88-424
Rhodes, P.J. The Greek City States.*
D.G. Kyle, 124:Jan-Feb89-209
M. Stahl, 229:Band60Heft6-543
Rhodes, R. Farm.
M. Kumin, 441:24Sep89-1
Rials, S. La Déclaration des droits de l'homme et du citoyen.
W. Scott, 617(TLS):19-25May89-554
Ribaillier, J. - see William of Auxerre
Ribeiro, A. Dress and Morality.
J. Arnold, 39:Sep88-209
Ribeiro, J.U. An Invincible Memory.
J. Gledson, 617(TLS):6-12Oct89-1088
M. Morris, 441:16Apr89-18
Riberette, P. - see de Chateaubriand, F.R.
Ribeyro, J.R. Silvio in the Rose Garden.
A. Whitehouse, 441:26Nov89-30
Ribhegge, W. Frieden für Europa.
J. Joll, 453(NYRB):27Apr89-53
Ribowsky, M. He's a Rebel.
A. Peck, 441:14May89-23
Ricapito, J.V., ed. Tri-linear Edition of "Lazarillo de Tormes" of 1554.
B.M. Damiani, 240(HR):Autumn88-498

Ricard, S. Theodore Roosevelt et la justification de l'impérialisme.
A. Desbiens, 106:Fall88-398
Ricard, S. & J. Bolner, eds. La République Impérialiste.
J-P. Brunet, 106:Fall88-396
Ricardou, J. Révolutions minuscules, précédé de "Révélations minuscules, en guise de préface à Jean Paulhan." La Cathédrale de Sens.
T.H. Jones, 207(FR):Mar89-720
Riccards, M.P. A Republic, If You Can Keep It.
T. Guinsburg, 106:Summer88-276
Ricci, L.B. Dante e la tradizione letteraria medievale.
Z.G. Barański, 545(RPh):Aug88-51
Riccio, F. Genealogia dell'esperienza sociale.
P. Trotignon, 542:Oct-Dec88-521
Ricco, R. & F. Maresca. American Primitive.
M. Nixon, 441:5Feb89-24
Riccòmini, E. & others. "La più bella di tutte."
C. Smyth, 54:Mar88-150
Rice, A. The Mummy.
F.J. Prial, 441:11Jun89-9
Rice, C. Night Freight.
D.L. Walker, 649(WAL):Aug88-173
Rice, T.J. "Barnaby Rudge."
I. Crawford, 155:Autumn88-182
B.F. Fisher 4th, 365:Winter88-53
"Ricerche di pittura ellenistica."
B. Gossel-Raeck, 229:Band60Heft5-467
Rich, A. Time's Power.
L. Norfolk, 617(TLS):15-21Sep89-1000
J. Parini, 441:22Oct89-16
Rich, A. Your Native Land, Your Life.*
H. Buckingham, 565:Winter87/88-71
Rich, D.L. Amelia Earhart.
D.M. Kennedy, 441:26Nov89-1
Rich, D.Z. The Dynamics of Knowledge.
C. Ripley, 103:Apr89-167
Rich, P.V., T.H. Rich & M.A. Fenton - see Fenton, C.L. & M.A.
Rich, W.C. Coleman Young and Detroit Politics.
J. Thomas, 441:24Sep89-49
Richard, J-P. Pages Paysages.*
C. Scott, 208(FS):Apr88-242
Richard, M. The Ice at the Bottom of the World.
S. MacNeille, 441:28May89-18
Richards, A., with P. Knobler. Straight From the Heart.
E.W. Sunstein, 441:10Dec89-14
Richards, D.A. Nights Below Station Street.
C. Rooke, 376:Jun88-188
Richards, E.J. Modernism, Medievalism and Humanism.*
W. Weiss, 38:Band106Heft3/4-523
Richards, J. Happiest Days.*
G.B. Tennyson, 445(NCF):Mar89-552
Richards, J. & D. Sheridan, eds. Mass-Observation at the Movies.*
J. Petley, 707:Spring88-142
Richards, J.C. & T.S. Rodgers. Approaches and Methods in Language Teaching.*
S.K. Gill, 355(LSoc):Jun88-309
Richards, R.J. Darwin and the Emergence of Evolutionary Theories of Mind and Behavior.*
W. Montgomery, 637(VS):Spring89-444

Richardson, D., ed. Bristol, Africa and the Eighteenth-Century Slave Trade to America. (Vol 1)
G.M. Ditchfield, 83:Autumn88-206
Richardson, D. Journey to Paradise. (T. Tate, ed)
B. Hardy, 617(TLS):1-7Dec89-1341
Richardson, H.E. A Corpus of Early Tibetan Inscriptions.
J.W. de Jong, 259(IIJ):Apr88-163
Richardson, J. Existential Epistemology.*
L. Stevenson, 479(PhQ):Jul88-383
Richardson, J. Wallace Stevens: The Early Years, 1879-1923.*
J. Applewhite, 569(SR):Winter88-121
R. Asselineau, 189(EA):Oct-Dec88-498
S.S. Baskett, 115:Summer88-324
J. Bayley, 432(NEQ):Jun88-252
F.J. Lepkowski, 77:Fall88-326
P. Mariani, 534(RALS):Vol16No1&2-207
D.T.O., 295(JML):Fall87/Winter88-387
J. Thorpe 3d, 363(LitR):Winter89-267
Richardson, J. Wallace Stevens: The Later Years, 1923-1955.
M.J. Bates, 441:5Feb89-27
Richardson, J. Vanishing Lives.
A. St. George, 617(TLS):21-27Jul89-807
Richardson, J.S. Hispaniae.
A.A. Barrett, 124:Jan-Feb89-208
R. Collins, 86(BHS):Jul88-288
C.F. Konrad, 121(CJ):Oct-Nov88-61
N. Mackie, 123:Vol38No2-318
J.W. Rich, 313:Vol78-212
Richardson, P., with D. Granskou, eds. Anti-Judaism in Early Christianity. (Vol 1)
S. Westerholm, 627(UTQ):Fall87-240
Richardson, R. Death, Dissection and the Destitute.*
T.M.R., 185:Jul89-989
442(NY):4Dec89-188
Richardson, R.C. & G.M. Ridden, eds. Freedom and the English Revolution.*
J. Sawday, 506(PSt):May88-103
Richardson, R.D., Jr. Henry Thoreau.*
R. Lebeaux, 432(NEQ):Mar88-144
S. Paul, 301(JEGP):Jan88-144
"Richelieu et le monde de l'esprit."*
D. Clarke, 208(FS):Jan88-82
Richert, D. Beste Gelegenheit zum Sterben. (A. Tramitz & B. Ulrich, eds)
R. Woods, 617(TLS):1-7Dec89-1342
Richeson, D. - see Cameron, A.D.
Richetti, J.J. Daniel Defoe.*
I.A. Bell, 566:Autumn88-77
Richie, D. Different People.*
Takahashi Osamu, 285(JapQ):Jul-Sep88-324
42(AR):Summer88-399
Richter, D. Das fremde Kind.
D. Simonides, 196:Band29Heft1/2-223
Richter, D.K. & J.H. Merrell, eds. Beyond the Covenant Chain.
R. Aquila, 656(WMQ):Oct88-789
Richter, G. - see Krauss, F.
Richter, H. Verwandeltes Dasein.
H. Haase, 654(WB):12/1988-2088
Richter, L. & others, eds. Literatur im Wandel.
W. Beitz, 654(WB):12/1988-2105
Richter, W. Transliteration and Transkription.
W. Weinberg, 318(JAOS):Jul-Sep87-547

Richter–Schröder, K. Frauenliteratur und
weibliche Identität.*
R.C. Holub, 406:Fall88–364
Rickards, M. Collecting Printed Ephemera.
T. Russell–Cobb, 324:Aug89–594
Rickert, H. The Limits of Concept Formation
in Natural Science.
G.R. Weaver, 543:Sep88–167
Ricketson, S. The Berne Convention for the
Protection of Literary and Artistic Works:
1886–1986.
J.J. Fishman, 476:Fall88–82
Rickett, W.A. – see "Guanzi"
Rickford, J.R. Dimensions of a Creole Contin-
uum.*
L.D. Carrington, 350:Jun89–389
Ricks, C. T.S. Eliot and Prejudice.
H. Haughton, 617(TLS):17–23Mar89–285
Ricks, C., ed. The New Oxford Book of Victo-
rian Verse.
B. Richards, 447(N&Q):Sep88–406
G.R. Stange, 636(VP):Winter88–487
Ricks, C. – see Tennyson, A.
Rico, F., ed. Lazarillo de Tormes.
P.J. Smith, 86(BHS):Jul88–296
Ricoeur, P. Lectures on Ideology and Utopia.*
(G.H. Taylor, ed)
A. Collier, 506(PSt):Sep88–106
J. McGowan, 473(PR):Vol55No4–690
Ricoeur, P. Time and Narrative.* (French
title: Temps et Récit.) (Vol 1)
L. Lerner, 128(CE):Sep88–572
C. Malabou, 542:Jul–Sep88–317
M.J. Valdés, 107(CRCL):Mar88–90
Ricoeur, P. Time and Narrative.* (French
title: Temps et Récit.) (Vol 2)
L. Lerner, 128(CE):Sep88–572
Riconda, G. Invito al pensiero di Kant.
A. Stanguennec, 542:Jul–Sep88–334
Ricou, L. Everyday Magic.
D.J. Napoli, 350:Mar89–191
M.H. Rubio, 599:Summer89–322
J–A. Wallace, 178:Dec88–477
Riden, P. Rebuilding a Valley.
A. Saint, 46:Sep88–12
Ridley, H. Thomas Mann: "Buddenbrooks."
K. Fickert, 395(MFS):Winter88–714
K.M. Hewitt, 447(N&Q):Dec88–552
H. Siefken, 402(MLR):Oct89–1041
Riecke–Niklewski, R. Die Metaphorik des
Schönen.
T. Kontje, 221(GQ):Winter88–130
W. Wittkowski, 133:Band21Heft4–340
Rieckmann, J. Aufbruch in die Moderne.*
E. Middell, 654(WB):5/1988–875
D.G. Richards, 221(GQ):Winter87–137
Riede, B. Luigi Nonos Kompositionen mit
Tonband.
K. Ebbeke, 416:Band3Heft3–261
Riede, D.G. Matthew Arnold and the Betrayal
of Language.
S. Coulling, 445(NCF):Dec88–414
S.D. Edwards, 636(VP):Winter88–479
639(VQR):Spring88–54
Riedel, N. Internationale Günter–Kunert-
Bibliographie. (Vol 1)
M. Humble, 402(MLR):Jan89–265
Riedel, N. Untersuchungen zur Geschichte der
internationalen Rezeption Uwe Johnsons.
W.G. Cunliffe, 406:Fall88–403
M. Durzak, 52:Band23Heft2–203
H.D. Osterle, 221(GQ):Spring88–327

Riedel, W. Die Anthropologie des jungen
Schiller.*
J. Golz, 406:Summer88–227
Riedhauser, H. Essen und Trinken bei Jere-
mias Gotthelf.
E. Gallati, 564:Sep88–276
Riedl, P.A. & M. Seidel, eds. Die Kirchen von
Siena.
H. van Os & K. van der Ploeg, 600:Vol18
No3–157
Riedweg, C. Mysterienterminologie bei Platon,
Philon, und Klemens von Alexandrien.*
H. Chadwick, 123:Vol38No1–164
Rieff, D. Going to Miami.*
R.J. Cortina, 36:Fall–Winter88–237
Riegel, M. L'adjectif attribut.
J–M. Léard, 320(CJL):Mar88–109
Rieger, D., ed. Die französische Erzählkunst
des 17. Jahrhunderts.
G. Berger, 475:Vol15No28–326
Rieger, P.E. The Upper Ohio Valley.
G.A. Hunt, 87(BB):Jun88–158
Riel, L. The Collected Writings of Louis Riel/
Les Ecrits complets de Louis Riel. (G.F.G.
Stanley, general ed)
N. Voisine, 627(UTQ):Fall87–174
van Riemsdijk, H. & E. Williams. Introduction
to the Theory of Grammar.
J. Goldsmith, 350:Mar89–150
A. Radford, 297(JL):Mar88–207
A. von Stechow, 353:Vol26No2–325
Riera Melis, A. La corona de Aragón y el
reino de Mallorca en el primer cuarto del
siglo XIV. (Vol 1)
M. Aurell, 589:Apr88–465
Ries, G. Prolog und Epilog in Gesetzen des
Altertums.
M. Ducos, 555:Vol61fasc1–166
Ries, W. Franz Kafka.
R.V. Gross, 406:Winter88–488
Riese, T.A., ed. Die weiten Horizonte – The
Vast Horizons.*
A.P. Frank, 38:Band106Heft1/2–262
Riesz, J., ed. Frankophone Literaturen aus-
serhalb Europas.
W.F. Feuser, 538(RAL):Fall88–394
R. Pageard, 549(RLC):Jan–Mar88–108
Rifelj, C.D. Word and Figure.
J.C. Kessler, 546(RR):Mar88–396
C. Scott, 402(MLR):Apr89–477
D. Scott, 208(FS):Oct88–486
M.L. Shaw, 446(NCFS):Fall–Winter88/89–
220
Rifkin, J. Time Wars.*
639(VQR):Winter88–23
Rifkin, N. Robert Moskowitz.
C. Ratcliff, 617(TLS):29Sep–5Oct89–1064
Rigamonti, G. Teoria e Osservazione.
F. Orilia, 449:Dec88–641
Rigau Canardo, M. Lugar y espacio.
A. Reix, 542:Apr–Jun88–248
Rigaud, N.J. La veuve dans la comédie ang-
laise au temps de Shakespeare, 1600–1625.
J.L. Lepage, 599:Winter88–681
Rigby, P. Original Sin in Augustine's "Con-
fessions."
M. Adam, 542:Apr–Jun88–249
Rigg, A.G., ed & trans. Gawain on Marriage.
K. Busby, 589:Apr88–467
Riggio, T.P. – see Dreiser, T. & H.L. Mencken

Rizk, B.J. El Nuevo Teatro latinoamericano.*
C. Lucía Garavito, 352(LATR):Spring89-
128
Rizkalla, J. The Jericho Garden.*
J. Mellors, 364:Jul88-105
Rizza, C. - see Gautier, T.
Roa Bastos, A. I the Supreme.
I. Malin, 532(RCF):Fall88-173
Roach, J. A History of Secondary Education
in England, 1800-1870.
W.B. Stephens, 637(VS):Autumn88-135
Roach, J.R. The Player's Passion.
C.M. Mazer, 610:Summer88-175
Robbe-Grillet, A. Angélique.*
T. Spear, 207(FR):Oct88-202
Robbe-Grillet, A. Ghosts in the Mirror.
A. Ross, 364:Feb/Mar89-140
Robbins, B. The Servant's Hand.*
K. Quinlan, 219(GaR):Fall88-643
G.C. Sorensen, 594:Spring88-114
Robbins, C.D., ed. Mottoes.
R.B. Harder, 424:Mar-Jun88-124
Robbins, C.L. Daylighting.*
H. Bryan, 505:Jan88-151
Robbins, K. Buttermilk Bottoms.
N. German, 152(UDQ):Summer88-111
Robbins, R.G., Jr. The Tsar's Viceroys.
639(VQR):Summer88-85
Robello, F. - see de Claireville, O.S.
Robert, J-N. Les plaisirs à Rome.
H. Schneider, 229:Band60Heft2-172
Robert, M. As Lonely as Franz Kafka.
W. Phillips, 473(PR):Vol55No4-675
Robert, P-E. - see Dabit, E.
Roberts, C. Schemes & Undertakings.*
J.M. Rosenheim, 568(SCN):Fall88-48
Roberts, C.H. & T.C. Skeat. The Birth of the
Codex.*
K.W. Humphreys, 447(N&Q):Dec88-505
Roberts, G., ed. Gerard Manley Hopkins: The
Critical Heritage.
P.E. Mitchell, 177(ELT):Vol31No3-361
R.K.R. Thornton, 541(RES):Aug88-459
Roberts, G. Unamuno.
N.R. Orringer, 238:May88-297
R.H. Webber, 240(HR):Spring88-270
Roberts, G. - see under "Beowulf"
Roberts, J-M. Mon Père américain.
R.J. Hartwig, 207(FR):Mar89-721
Roberts, K. Picking the Morning Colour.
P. Kokotailo, 102(CanL):Spring88-213
Roberts, M. British Poets and Secret Socie-
ties.*
H. Ormsby-Lennon, 661(WC):Autumn88-
219
P. Partner, 447(N&Q):Mar88-132
Roberts, M. The Mirror of the Mother.*
H. Buckingham, 565:Winter87/88-71
Roberts, M.S. & D. Gallagher - see Dufrenne,
M.
Roberts, N.L. & A.W. - see O'Neill, E.
Roberts, P. The Royal Court Theatre, 1965-
1972.*
G. Doty, 615(TJ):Mar88-129
J. Fisher, 397(MD):Sep88-468
H. Hunt, 611(TN):Vol42No2-81
K. Worth, 447(N&Q):Sep88-426
Roberts, P.A. West Indians and Their Lan-
guage.
L. Hart-González, 350:Sep89-673
Roberts, R.A. & A. Knox - see "One Half of
the Sky"

Roberts, W., J.T. Boulton & E. Mansfield - see
Lawrence, D.H.
Robertson, A. Atkinson Grimshaw.
F. Spalding, 617(TLS):9-15Jun89-640
Robertson, C.L. The International Herald
Tribune.*
P. Desbarats, 106:Fall88-387
Robertson, H. Lily.
L. Lamont-Stewart, 102(CanL):Winter87-
275
Robertson, H.W. To the Fierce Guard in the
Assyrian Saloon.
S.S. Moorty, 649(WAL):Aug88-184
Robertson, J., ed. Mélanges de littérature
française offerts à M. Shackleton et C.J.
Greshoff par leurs collègues et amis.
A. Tooke, 208(FS):Jan88-114
Robertson, J.C. The Hidden Cinema.
C. Gearty, 617(TLS):21-27Jul89-796
Robertson, J.I., Jr. General A.P. Hill.
639(VQR):Spring88-46
Robertson, M.E. What I Have to Tell You.
R. Weinreich, 441:31Dec89-13
Robertson, M.G. The Sculpture of Palenque.
B. Riese, 54:Jun88-359
Robertson, R. Heine.
H. Zohn, 402(MLR):Jul89-790
Robertson, R. Kafka.*
P.F. Dvorak, 221(GQ):Spring88-321
M.H. Gelber, 395(MFS):Summer88-303
T. Kuhn, 447(N&Q):Dec88-554
A. Udoff, 400(MLN):Apr88-694
Robertson, W.B. Standing On Our Own Two
Feet.
A. Brooks, 102(CanL):Summer88-160
Robez-Ferraris, J. Les Richesses du lexique
d'Henri Vincenot, auteur bourguignon.
J-P. Chambon, 553(RLiR):Jan-Jun88-303
Robidoux, R. La Création de Gérard Bessette.
N.B. Bishop, 627(UTQ):Fall88-188
Robin, R. Le Réalisme socialiste.*
J. Brooks, 550(RusR):Jul88-327
Robinet, A. Architectonique disjonctive, au-
tomates systémiques et idéalité transcen-
dentale dans l'oeuvre de G.W. Leibniz.*
J-L. Gardies, 542:Apr-Jun88-257
Robinson, A. Instabilities in Contemporary
British Poetry.
T. Eagleton, 617(TLS):24-30Nov89-1291
Robinson, A. Maharaja.
I. Buruma, 453(NYRB):18May89-9
Robinson, B. Focus.
K.M. Wilson, 608:Dec89-690
Robinson, C. & J. Herschman. Architecture
Transformed.*
M. Branch, 505:Jan88-151
D. Gantenbein, 45:Mar88-75
J. Stallabrass, 90:Aug88-642
Robinson, D. American Apocalypses.*
J.E. Becker, 363(LitR):Winter89-278
L. Olsen, 70:Oct88-157
Robinson, E. The Language of Mystery.*
M. Austin, 89(BJA):Autumn88-389
Robinson, E. & D. Powell - see Clare, J.
Robinson, F. Atlas of the Islamic World Since
1500.
M.R. Waldman, 318(JAOS):Oct-Dec87-802
Robinson, F.C. "Beowulf" and the Appositive
Style.*
W.G. Busse, 38:Band106Heft1/2-203
Robinson, F.G. In Bad Faith.*
E.L. Galligan, 569(SR):Spring88-265
J. Hurt, 402(MLR):Jul89-730

Robinson, H. Sergei Prokofiev.*
  C. Emerson, 550(RusR):Jul88-323
  G.D. McQuere, 574(SEEJ):Fall88-487
Robinson, J.C. Radical Literary Education.
  S. Simpkins, 128(CE):Nov88-812
Robinson, J.M., with S. Emmel. The Facsimile
  Edition of Nag Hammadi Codices.
  D.W. Young, 318(JAOS):Oct-Dec87-836
Robinson, K.M. Stepchildren of Progress.
  A.L. Stoler, 293(JASt):Feb88-199
Robinson, K.S. The Gold Coast.*
  C. Greenland, 617(TLS):8-14Dec89-1368
Robinson, M. Mother Country.
  L. Ackland, 441:16Jul89-7
  M.F. Perutz, 453(NYRB):23Nov89-51
  442(NY):14Aug89-92
Robinson, P. More about the Weather.
  G. Foden, 617(TLS):29Sep-5Oct89-1065
Robinson, P. Necessary End.
  T.J. Binyon, 617(TLS):29Dec89/4Jan90-
  1448
Robinson, P. Opera and Ideas.*
  A.W. Hayward, 290(JAAC):Winter87-316
Robinson, R. Bad Dreams.
  C. Hawtree, 617(TLS):27Oct-2Nov89-
  1180
Robinson, R. Georgia O'Keeffe.
  H. Herrera, 441:5Nov89-3
Robinson, T. Stones of Aran.
  A. Broyard, 441:3Dec89-22
  B. O hEithir, 617(TLS):9-15Jun89-633
Robinson, T.A. Greek Verb Endings: a Re-
  verse Index.
  M.H.B. Marshall, 123:Vol38No2-431
Robinson, T.M. Heraclitus, Fragments.
  W. Graham, 627(UTQ):Fall88-100
  E. Hussey, 123:Vol38No2-219
  M. Ring, 518:Jul88-129
  S.D. Sullivan, 487:Spring88-72
Robinson, W.S., ed. Early American Indian
  Documents, Treaties and Laws. (Vols 4-6)
  H.C. Rountree, 656(WMQ):Jul88-596
Robinson-Hammerstein, H., ed. The Trans-
  mission of Ideas in the Lutheran Reforma-
  tion.
  A. Hamilton, 617(TLS):23-29Jun89-683
Robison, A. Piranesi: Early Architectural
  Fantasies.*
  J. Wilton-Ely, 90:Jul88-542
  J. Wilton-Ely, 576:Dec88-412
Robison, J. The Illustrator.*
  J. Clute, 617(TLS):17-23Feb89-170
de Roblès, J-M.B. - see under Blas de Roblès,
  J-M.
Robson, A.P. & J.M. - see Mill, J.S.
Robson, B. The Road to Kabul.
  E. Ingram, 637(VS):Autumn88-131
Robson, R. The Rise and Fall of the English
  Highland Clans.
  R.W. Hoyle, 617(TLS):20-26Oct89-1163
Robson, W.W. - see Kipling, R.
Roby, K.E. Joyce Cary.
  C. Cook, 447(N&Q):Sep88-398
Roch, H.J. Santiago Rusiñol (1861-1931).
  J-L. Marfany, 86(BHS):Oct88-420
Roche, J.F. The Colonial Colleges in the War
  for American Independence.
  L.L. Tucker, 656(WMQ):Jul88-612
Roche, M. Je ne vais pas bien, mais il faut
  que j'y aille.
  L. Enjolras, 207(FR):May89-1099
Rochefort, C. La Porte du fond.
  B. Wright, 617(TLS):27Jan-2Feb89-88

Rochemont, M.S. Focus in Generative Gram-
  mar.*
  R.W. Ostler, 307:Nov88-234
Rocher, L., ed. Ezourvedam.
  R. Salomon, 293(JASt):Nov88-924
Rocher, L. The Purāṇas.
  J.W. de Jong, 259(IIJ):Apr88-149
Rochester, M. & others. Bonjour, ça va? (2nd
  ed)
  M. Donaldson-Evans, 399(MLJ):
  Autumn88-356
Rochfort, D. The Murals of Diego Rivera.
  O. Baddeley, 59:Jun88-271
Rochon, E. Coquillage.
  T. Vuong-Riddick, 102(CanL):Spring88-
  133
Rock, W.R. Chamberlain and Roosevelt.
  G.A. Craig, 453(NYRB):12Oct89-11
  W.F. Kimball, 617(TLS):12-18May89-505
"Rock 'N' Roll: 100 of the Best."
  B.L. Cooper, 498:Summer88-87
Röcke, W. Die Freude am Bösen.
  P. Strohschneider, 72:Band225Heft2-352
Rockett, K., L. Gibbons & J. Hill. Cinema and
  Ireland.*
  D. Fitzsimons, 272(IUR):Spring88-159
Rockett, W.H. Devouring Whirlwind.
  P.B. McElwain, 590:Jun89-44
Rockland, M.A. A Bliss Case.
  C. McWilliam, 441:15Oct89-14
Rockmore, T. Hegel's Circular Epistemology.*
  D. Janicaud, 192(EP):Jul-Sep88-442
Röd, W. Dialektische Philosophie der Neuzeit.
  P. Trotignon, 542:Apr-Jun88-224
Roddaz, J-M. Marcus Agrippa.*
  P. Jal, 555:Vol61fasc1-162
Rodden, J. The Politics of Literary Reputa-
  tion.
  J. Symons, 441:4Jun89-25
Roddewig, M. Dante Alighieri, "Die göttliche
  Komödie."*
  G.C. Alessio, 379(MedR):Aug86-315
Rodenbeck, J. - see Mahfouz, N.
Rodger, N.A.M. Wooden World.*
  D. Schurman, 529(QQ):Autumn88-716
Rodgers, A.T. Virgin and Whore.
  M. Dickie, 27(AL):Mar88-137
Rodgers, D.D. Bookseller as Rogue.
  T.R. Adams, 78(BC):Summer88-276
Rodgers, E. From Enlightenment to Realism.
  S. Miller, 345(KRQ):Aug88-373
Rodgers, M.E. - see Mencken, H.L. & S. Haardt
Rodimzeva, I., N. Rachmanov & A. Raimann.
  The Kremlin and Its Treasures.
  J. Cracraft, 617(TLS):15-21Dec89-1397
Rodley, L. Cave Monasteries of Byzantine
  Cappadocia.*
  A. Grishin, 576:Jun88-194
  P. Mackridge, 575(SEER):Jan88-132
  A.J. Wharton, 589:Jan88-219
Rodman, H., B. Sarvis & J.W. Bonar. The
  Abortion Question.
  N.A.D., 185:Oct88-213
Rodowick, D.N. The Crisis of Political Mod-
  ernism.
  P.D. Murphy, 590:Jun89-47
Rodrígues Suro, J. Erico Veríssimo.
  H.J. Dennis, 238:Mar88-89
Rodriguez, F.I. & J. Weisman. Shadow Warrior.
  J.M. Hamilton, 441:5Nov89-25
Rodríguez, J.R.S. - see under Sampayo Rodrí-
  guez, J.R.

Rodríguez, L.A. The Search for Public Policy.
  D.J. Cubitt, 86(BHS):Apr88-205
Rodríguez Cuadros, E., ed. Novelas amorosas
  de diversos ingenios del siglo XVII.
  P.N. Dunn, 86(BHS):Oct88-410
Rodríguez de Laguna, A., ed. Images and
  Identities.
  B. Torres Caballero, 240(HR):Winter88-
  128
Rodríguez López-Vázquez, A. Andrés de
  Claramonte y "El Burlador de Sevilla."
  B. Wittmann, 547(RF):Band100Heft4-473
Rodríguez López-Vázquez, A. – see de Clara-
  monte, A.
Rodríguez Marín, R. – see Alas, L.
Rodríguez Matos, C.A. El narrador pícaro.*
  P. López-Adorno, 345(KRQ):Feb88-115
  D.P. Testa, 593:Spring88-78
Rodríguez-Salgado, M.J. The Changing Face
  of Empire.
  H. Kamen, 617(TLS):12-18May89-522
Rodríguez-Salgado, M.J. & others, eds.
  Armada: 1588-1988.*
  J.R. Hale, 453(NYRB):16Feb89-30
Rodríguez Stone, E. & C. Navarro Berkeley.
  Por Hispanoamérica.
  R.M. Carter, 399(MLJ):Spring88-114
  H.H. Ryan, 238:Mar88-102
Roe, N. Wordsworth and Coleridge.
  M. O'Neill, 184(EIC):Oct88-334
Roe, S., ed. Women Reading Women's Writing.*
  B.L. Harman, 637(VS):Summer89-601
  E.B. Thompson, 395(MFS):Winter88-747
Roegiest, E. & L. Tasmowski, eds. Verbe et
  phrase dans les langues romanes.
  L. Löfstedt, 439(NM):1988/1-104
Roemer, J., with B. Austin. Two to Four From
  9 to 5.
  A.P. Murphy, 441:13Aug89-15
Roemer, J.E. Free to Lose.
  J. Gray, 617(TLS):24Feb-2Mar89-183
Roemer, W.F., Jr. Roemer.
  D. Dawson, 441:15Oct89-51
Roeper, T. & E. Williams, eds. Parameter Set-
  ting.
  J. Aitchison, 297(JL):Sep88-527
  Y. Roberge, 320(CJL):Sep88-291
Roessler, H.R. Deutsche Geschäftskorres-
  pondenz.
  A. Galt, 399(MLJ):Autumn88-360
Roff, W.R., ed. Islam and the Political Econ-
  omy of Meaning.
  C. Dobbin, 293(JASt):Nov88-844
Rogan, B. Cafe Nevo.
  Y. Luria, 390:Feb/Mar88-62
Rogers, D.D. Bookseller as Rogue.
  J. Black, 83:Spring88-75
  J.D.C. Buck, 365:Winter87-42
  J. Feather, 447(N&Q):Sep88-380
  R.R. Rea, 577(SHR):Winter88-77
  J.E. Tierney, 40(AEB):Vol2No2-82
Rogers, E.R. & T.J., eds. In Retrospect.
  A. Rosman-Askot, 711(RHM):Jun88-85
Rogers, J.M., ed. Topkapi Carpets.
  R. Chenciner, 39:Jul88-67
Rogers, J.N. The Country Music Message:
  Revisited.
  D. Hill, 617(TLS):29Dec89/4Jan90-1438
Rogers, P. Eighteenth-Century Encounters.*
  J. Richetti, 141:Spring88-256
Rogers, P. Legendary Performance.
  D. Sampson, 249(HudR):Summer88-392
  P. Stitt, 491:Jun88-166

Rogers, P. Literature and Popular Culture in
  Eighteenth-Century England.*
  J. Richetti, 141:Spring88-256
Rogers, W.E. Upon the Ways.
  H. Cooper, 541(RES):May88-337
  J.M. Dean, 589:Apr88-469
Rogin, M. "Ronald Reagan," the Movie.
  R. Combs, 707:Winter87/88-70
  W.B. Hixson, Jr., 115:Spring88-204
  G.S. Smith, 529(QQ):Winter88-797
Rohlfs, G. Dizionario storico dei cognomi sal-
  entini (Terra d'Otranto). Dizionario storico
  dei soprannomi salentini (Terra d'Otranto).
  G. Holtus, 72:Band224Heft2-471
Rohlfs, G. Panorama delle lingue neolatine.*
  J-M. Klinkenberg, 209(FM):Apr88-149
Rohlfs, G. Von Rom zur Romania.
  C. Schmitt, 72:Band225Heft1-190
Rohls, H.W. & T. Böhm, comps. Berlin um
  1900.
  F. Bugenhagen & E. Schüttauf, 654(WB):
  6/1988-1047
Rohmer, R. Rommel & Patton.
  E. Thompson, 102(CanL):Spring88-177
Rohmer, R. Starmageddon.
  J.R. Wytenbroek, 102(CanL):Spring88-140
Rohrbach, G. Studien zur Erforschung des
  mittelhochdeutschen Tageliedes.
  A. Classen, 201:Vol14-235
  H. Heinen, 589:Oct88-990
Röhrich, L. Wage es, den Frosch zu küssen.
  W. Pape, 196:Band29Heft1/2-225
Roiphe, A. Lovingkindness.*
  E.M. Avery, 390:Feb/Mar88-61
Rojahn-Deyk, B. – see Shakespeare, W.
de Rojas, F. Celestina. (M. Marciales, ed)
  V.A. Burrus, 345(KRQ):May88-244
Rojas, F.J.P. – see under Pérez Rojas, F.J.
Rojas, J.N. & R.A. Curry. Gramática para la
  comunicación.
  J.M. Chaston, 399(MLJ):Autumn88-375
Rojas Aravena, F. & L.G. Solis Rivera. ¿Súb-
  ditos o aliados?
  S.S. Volk, 263(RIB):Vol38No2-220
Rolán, T.G. – see under González Rolán, T.
Rolán, T.G. & P. Saquero Suárez-Somonte –
  see under González Rolán, T. & P. Saquero
  Suárez-Somonte
Roland, C.G. Secondary Sources in the His-
  tory of Canadian Medicine.
  M.J. Giacomelli, 470:Vol26-184
Rolf, R. & N. Ayuzawa – see Yamamoto, H.
Rolin, D. Trente ans d'amour fou.
  L. Enjolras, 207(FR):May89-1100
Röll, W. & H-P. Bayerdörfer, eds. Kontrover-
  sen, alte und neue. (Vol 5)
  S.L. Gilman, 564:May88-182
Roll-Hansen, N. Ønsketenkning som viten-
  skap.
  J.A. Dellenbrant, 575(SEER):Apr88-306
Rölleke, H. "Wo das Wünschen noch geholfen
  hat."*
  R.B. Bottigheimer, 221(GQ):Spring87-321
Rölleke, H. – see Gorgias, J.
Rölleke, H. – see Grimm, J. & W.
Rolleston, J. Narratives of Ecstasy.
  R. Salter, 221(GQ):Fall88-561
Rollfinke, D. & J. The Call of Human Nature.
  W.G. Cunliffe, 406:Fall88-381
  S. Mews, 400(MLN):Apr88-702
Rollyson, C. Lillian Hellman.*
  P.M. Spacks, 534(RALS):Vol16No1&2-37

314

Rollyson, C.E., Jr. Uses of the Past in the Novels of William Faulkner.
C.S. Brown, 569(SR):Spring88-271
Roloff, V. & H. Wentzlaff-Eggebert, eds. Der spanische Roman vom Mittelalter bis zur Gegenwart.*
G. Sobejano, 547(RF):Band99Heft4-476
Romaine, S. Bilingualism.
K. Hakuta, 617(TLS):17-23Nov89-1263
Romaine, S. Pidgin and Creole Languages.*
P.L. Patrick, 350:Sep89-674
"Romanesque and Gothic: Essays for George Zarnecki."
P.W., 90:Dec88-937
Romano, E. La capanna e il tempio.
E. Rawson, 123:Vol38No2-416
Romano, G. & others. I modi. (L. Lawner, ed & trans)
R.M. Adams, 453(NYRB):18May89-40
de Romans, F. - see under Falquet de Romans
Romer, J. Testament.
B.J. Brooten, 441:25Jun89-33
Römer, R. Sprachwissenschaft und Rassenideologie in Deutschland.*
K.H. Schmidt, 685(ZDL):1/1988-82
Romer, S. Idols.*
S. Rae, 364:Mar87-87
J. Saunders, 565:Autumn88-72
Romera Castillo, J. El comentario semiótico de textos. (2nd ed) La literatura como signo.
M. Rector, 567:Vol69No3/4-369
Romero, F. Gli Stati Uniti e il sindacalismo europeo 1944-1951.
C. Maier, 358:Dec89-16
Romero, P.W. E. Sylvia Pankhurst.*
E. Sypher, 77:Fall88-336
Rømhild, L.P. Slags.
L. Longum, 172(Edda):1988/1-100
de Romilly, J. La modernité d'Euripide.
D. Arnould, 555:Vol61fasc2-307
de Romilly, J. Perspectives actuelles sur l'épopée homérique. Homère.
S.R. Slings, 394:Vol41fasc1/2-125
de Romilly, J. Problèmes de la démocratie grecque.
D. Arnould, 555:Vol61fasc1-102
Ronald, A., ed. Words for the Wild.
S.E. Marovitz, 649(WAL):Nov88-237
Ronan, F. The Men Who Loved Evelyn Cotton.
A. Clyde, 441:8Oct89-24
G. Gardiner, 617(TLS):19-25May89-536
442(NY):2Oct89-120
Ronat, M. & D. Couquaux, eds. La grammaire modulaire.
A. Zribi-Hertz, 209(FM):Apr88-103
von Roncador, M. Zwischen direkter und indirekter Rede.
J.R.P. King, 350:Dec89-914
Rondeau, M-J. Les commentaires patristiques du Psautier (IIIe-Ve siècles). (Vol 2)
J. Irigoin, 555:Vol61fasc2-332
Ronell, A. Dictations.*
S.L. Gilman, 221(GQ):Winter88-118
Ronner, A.D. W.H. Hudson.
D. Shrubsall, 177(ELT):Vol31No1-100
Ronning, C.N. & A.P. Vannucci, eds. Ambassadors in Foreign Policy.
J.D. Cochrane, 263(RIB):Vol38No1-79
Ronsac, C. Trois noms pour une vie.
F. George, 98:Oct88-858

Röntgen, K-H. Einführung in die katalanische Sprache.
A. Quintana, 547(RF):Band99Heft4-433
P. Swiggers, 553(RLiR):Jul-Dec88-506
Ronzeaud, P., ed. Racine: La Romaine, la Turque et la Juive.
R.W. Tobin, 475:Vol15No28-336
Roob, J-D. Alain Resnais.
R.J. Nelson, 207(FR):Dec88-354
Rood, K.L., ed. American Literary Almanac.
T. Wortham, 445(NCF):Dec88-420
Rooke, P.T. & R.L. Schnell. No Bleeding Heart.
L. Good, 529(QQ):Autumn88-722
Roome, A. A Real Shot in the Arm.
T.J. Binyon, 617(TLS):6-12Oct89-1104
Rooney, A.A. Not That You Asked...
A. Rome, 441:23Apr89-21
Rooney, D.F. Folk Pottery in South-East Asia.*
E.H. Moore, 293(JASt):Nov88-949
Roos, L., ed. Church and Economy in Dialogue.
P.H., 185:Oct88-209
Roos, P. Sentenza e proverbio nell'antichità e i "Distici di Catone."
W. Bühler, 229:Band60Heft2-116
Roos, P. Survey of Ruck-Cut Chamber-Tombs in Caria. (Pt 1)
W. Radt, 229:Band60Heft2-184
Roose-Evans, J. - see Grenfell, J.
Roosen, W. Daniel Defoe and Diplomacy.
D. De Luna, 173(ECS):Fall88-87
Roosevelt, E. Murder in the Oval Office.
M. Stasio, 441:16Apr89-31
Roosevelt, P.R. Apostle of Russian Liberalism.
G.M. Hamburg, 550(RusR):Apr88-190
Roper, J.H. C. Vann Woodward, Southerner.*
42(AR):Spring88-276
639(VQR):Summer88-86
Roper, R. Mexico Days.
R. Ward, 441:10Sep89-15
Rorem, N. The Nantucket Diary, 1973-1985.
42(AR):Winter88-119
Rorty, A.O. Mind in Action.
A. Kenny, 441:27Aug89-21
Rorty, R. Contingency, Irony, and Solidarity.
J. Bell, 617(TLS):24-30Nov89-1296
J. Teichman, 441:23Apr89-30
Rorty, R. Philosophy and the Mirror of Nature.
J.P. Cadello, 321:Jan88-71
Rosa, A. Citoyennes, les femmes et la Révolution française.
M. & P. Higonnet, 617(TLS):19-25May89-541
Rosa, A.A. - see under Asor Rosa, A.
Rosa, G. - see Hugo, V.
Rosa, R.R. - see under Rey Rosa, R.
Rosand, D., ed. Interpretazioni veneziane.
L. Armstrong, 551(RenQ):Spring88-144
Rose, D. Our Lady of the Pickpockets.
T. Glyde, 617(TLS):1-7Dec89-1337
Rose, F. West of Eden.
S. Kinsley, 441:7May89-14
Rose, G.J. Trauma and Mastery in Life and Art.
E.H. Spitz, 289:Fall88-124
Rose, J. The Edwardian Temperament: 1895-1919.*
A. Bowie, 447(N&Q):Sep88-409
M.P.L., 295(JML):Fall87/Winter88-193
D. Rutenberg, 635(VPR):Fall88-124

Rose, J. Kill the Poor.
W. Smith, 441:5Mar89-22
Rose, J. & C. Texier, eds. Between C & D.
T. McGonigle, 532(RCF):Summer88-327
Rose, M. Indonesia Free.
D. Hindley, 293(JASt):Aug88-718
Rose, M. Lives on the Boundary.
G. Kolata, 441:23Apr89-21
Rose, M.B., ed. Women in the Middle Ages and
the Renaissance.*
J.M. Ferrante, 545(RPh):Aug88-117
E.H. Hageman, 570(SQ):Summer88-247
J.W. Nicholls, 402(MLR):Jan89-114
Rose, M.B. - see "Renaissance Drama"
Rose, M.G., ed. Translation Excellence.
J.L. Malone, 215(GL):Vol28No2-151
W.M. Park, 399(MLJ):Spring88-115
Rose, M.G., ed. Translation Perspectives:
Selected Papers 1982-83.
A. Lefevere, 107(CRCL):Mar88-108
Rose, P. Jazz Cleopatra.
J.R. Mellow, 441:5Nov89-12
Rose, P. & R. Kahn. Pete Rose.
T. Whitaker, 441:10Dec89-16
Rose, R. & Rei Shiratori, eds. The Welfare
State.*
P.M. Lewis, 293(JASt):May88-382
Rose, T. Freeing the Whales.
J.A. Hennessee, 441:26Nov89-6
Rosemont, H., Jr., ed. Explorations in Early
Chinese Cosmology.
R.T. Ames, 485(PE&W):Jan88-68
A.H. Black, 293(JASt):Aug88-590
Rosen, D. & A. Porter, eds. Verdi's
"Macbeth."*
G. Duval-Wirth, 537:Vol74No1-119
Rosén, H. Studies in the Syntax of the Verbal
Noun in Early Latin.
A.M. Bolkestein, 394:Vol41fasc1/2-193
Rosén, H.B. East and West. (Pt 2)
A.S. Kaye, 318(JAOS):Jan-Mar87-141
Rosen, M. Did I Hear You Write?
C.A. Duffy, 617(TLS):7-13Apr89-381
Rosen, M.J. - see Thurber, J.
Rosen, R. Fadeaway.
D. Lehman, 473(PR):Vol55No1-149
Rosen, S. Hermeneutics as Politics.
P. Gottfried, 543:Sep88-168
Rosen, S. The Quarrel Between Philosophy
and Poetry.
K. Dorter, 543:Jun89-848
L.P. Gerson, 103:Dec88-495
Rosenbaum, A.S., ed. Constitutionalism.
E.R. Gill, 103:May89-194
Rosenbaum, S.P. Victorian Bloomsbury.*
P.R. Broughton, 177(ELT):Vol31No1-81
639(VQR):Winter88-9
Rosenbaum, W. Naturrecht und positives
Recht.
C. Schefold, 489(PJGG):Band95Heft2-376
Rosenberg, A. Philosophy of Social Science.
V. di Norcia, 103:May89-197
D. Papineau, 617(TLS):30Jun-6Jul89-724
Rosenberg, A. The Structure of Biological
Science.*
R.N. Brandon, 311(JP):Apr87-224
Rosenberg, D., ed. Congregation.*
S. Pinsker, 219(GaR):Spring88-194
B.V. Qualls, 533:Spring89-134
Rosenberg, J. King and Kin.
R.T. Anderson, 115:Winter88-99

Rosenberg, J.D. Carlyle and the Burden of
History.*
W. Myers, 402(MLR):Jan89-132
Rosenberg, J.F. The Thinking Self.*
R. Foley, 543:Dec88-407
Rosenberg, K-P. Der Berliner Dialekt - und
seine Folgen für die Schüler.
B.J. Koekkoek, 221(GQ):Winter88-120
Rosenberg, P. Fragonard.
M. Sheriff, 127:Winter88-368
Rosenberg, S. A Soviet Odyssey.
A. Austin, 441:15Jan89-23
Rosenberg, S.N. & S. Danon - see Gace Brulé
Rosenblatt, A. Virginia Woolf for Beginners.
J.E. Fisher, 395(MFS):Winter88-692
Rosenblum, M. Back Home.
L. Green, 441:22Oct89-23
Rosenblum, R. The Dog in Art from Rococo to
Post-Modernism.*
C.V. Miller, 62:Dec88-109
R. Snell, 617(TLS):24-30Mar89-314
Rosenblum, R. Paintings in the Musée
d'Orsay.
M. Kimmelman, 441:12Nov89-20
Rosenblum, R. The Romantic Child.
R. Snell, 617(TLS):24-30Mar89-314
Rosenfeld, A.H. Imagining Hitler.
J. Santore, 222(GR):Winter88-46
H.A. Schmitt, 569(SR):Winter88-158
Rosenfeld, I. Preserving the Hunger. (M.
Shechner, ed) Passage from Home.
J. Atlas, 453(NYRB):29Jun89-42
Rosenman, E.B. The Invisible Presence.*
T.C. Caramagno, 405(MP):Feb89-324
E.C.R., 295(JML):Fall87/Winter88-403
Rosenmeyer, T.G. Deina ta polla.
S.D. Goldhill, 123:Vol38No2-423
Rosenstone, R.A. Mirror in the Shrine.
I. Nish, 617(TLS):28Apr-4May89-460
Rosenthal, B.G., ed. Nietzsche in Russia.*
P. Davidson, 402(MLR):Apr89-535
A.P. Fell, 529(QQ):Summer88-472
J.P. Scanlan, 550(RusR):Apr88-206
R.C. Williams, 574(SEEJ):Fall88-473
Rosenthal, D.A. La Grande Manière.
D. Rice, 127:Spring88-46
Rosenthal, M. Jasper Johns.
W. Gass, 453(NYRB):2Feb89-22
Rosenthal, M.L. The Poet's Art.*
R. Asselineau, 189(EA):Oct-Dec88-500
Rosenthal, M.M. Health Care in the People's
Republic of China.
G. Henderson, 293(JASt):Aug88-616
Rosenwald, L. Emerson and the Art of the
Diary.
H. Marten, 441:12Feb89-22
Roses, L.E. Voices of the Storyteller.*
G. Ibieta, 295(JML):Fall87/Winter88-360
Rosidor [C-F. Guillemay du Chesnay]. Les
Valets de chambre nouvellistes. (M.S.
Djelassi, ed)
G. Roques, 553(RLiR):Jul-Dec88-559
Rosinski, N.M. Feminist Futures.
N. Easterbrook, 295(JML):Fall87/
Winter88-264
Rosmarin, A. The Power of Genre.
H. Dubrow, 131(CL):Summer88-283
J.N. Schmidt, 38:Band106Heft3/4-557
Rosner, D. & G. Markowitz, eds. Dying for
Work.
S.P. Schneider, 106:Fall88-373

Rosowski, S.J. The Voyage Perilous.*
J.E. Miller, Jr., 502(PrS):Fall88-126
A.H. Petry, 577(SHR):Summer88-300
P. Reilly, 447(N&Q):Sep88-423
Ross, A. No Respect.
D. Papineau, 617(TLS):8-14Dec89-1364
Ross, A. - see Vaughan, K.
Ross, A. & D. Woolley - see Swift, J.
Ross, A.M. The Imprint of the Picturesque on
Nineteenth-Century British Fiction.*
J.B. Bullen, 541(RES):May88-303
R. Gilmour, 571(ScLJ):Spring88-11
I. Goody, 627(UTQ):Fall87-121
I.S. MacLaren, 178:Mar88-108
Ross, C. & K.M.W. Brown, eds. Women Who
Dared.
G. London, 563(SS):Autumn88-512
Ross, D.O., Jr. Virgil's Elements.*
P.R. Hardie, 123:Vol38No2-241
F. Muecke, 313:Vol78-233
Ross, J.F. Portraying Analogy.
W.G. Lycan, 359:Feb88-107
Ross, L. & M.A. Silk. Environmental Law and
Policy in the People's Republic of China.
W.C. Jones, 293(JASt):Aug88-617
Ross, M. The Impossible Sum of Our Tradi-
tions.*
W.J. Keith, 627(UTQ):Fall87-145
Ross, R. Museology.
R. Ranck, 441:19Nov89-24
Ross, T.W. - see Chaucer, G.
Ross, V. Homecoming.
W. Connor, 198:Spring88-109
Rossen, J. The World of Barbara Pym.
L.L. Doan, 395(MFS):Summer88-290
Rosser, G. Medieval Westminster 1200-1540.
P. Basing, 617(TLS):8-14Dec89-1373
Rossi, L.D. The Politics of Fantasy.
N. Easterbrook, 295(JML):Fall87/
Winter88-230
Rossi, Z. Spravočnik po GULagu.
H.E. Marquess, 574(SEEJ):Winter88-682
Rossiter, S. Beyond This Bitter Air.
M. Hallissy, 573(SSF):Winter88-85
C. Hardesty, 455:Mar88-67
Rossi, J. & H. Konrad. Tacuinum Sanitatis.
78(BC):Autumn88-313
Rössler, F.G. Paul Hindemith, Messe (1963).
G. Metz, 416:Band3Heft2-189
Rosslyn, W. The Prince, the Fool and the
Nunnery.
S.I. Ketchian, 574(SEEJ):Fall88-477
Rosso, C. Procès à la Rochefoucauld et à la
maxime.
L.K. Horowitz, 207(FR):Oct88-167
J. Lafond, 475:Vol15No28-338
L. Thirouin, 547(RF):Band99Heft4-461
Rosso, C. Les Tambours de Santerre.*
M. Delon, 535(RHL):Mar-Apr88-282
D. Gembicki, 549(RLC):Jan-Mar88-95
P. Jimack, 208(FS):Oct88-477
R. Waller, 83:Autumn88-234
Rosso, C. Transhumances culturelles.
M.J. Muratore, 546(RR):Nov88-689
R. Waller, 83:Spring88-88
Rosso, J. & S. Lukins. The New Basics Cook-
book.
R. Flaste, 441:3Dec89-40
Rost, M. & J. Lance. PAIRallels.
G. Kimzin, 608:Mar87-143
Rosten, L. The Joys of Yinglish.
R. Shepard, 441:8Oct89-11

Roston, M. Renaissance Perspectives in Lit-
erature and the Visual Arts.*
D. Evett, 149(CLS):Vol25No2-184
R. Studing, 568(SCN):Winter88-76
Rotberg, R.I. & T.K. Rabb, eds. Art and His-
tory.
D. Carrier, 617(TLS):6-12Jan89-17
Rotberg, R.I., with M.F. Shore. The Founder.*
A. Porter, 617(TLS):5-11May89-494
G. Wheatcroft, 441:1Jan89-4
Roteta de la Maza, A.M. La Ilustración del
Libro en la España de la Contrarreforma.*
D.W. Cruickshank, 86(BHS):Apr88-185
W. Rincón García, 48:Jan-Mar88-86
Roth, H. Shifting Landscape.* (M. Materassi,
ed)
L. Schneiderman, 390:Feb/Mar88-58
Roth, J. The Spider's Web [and] Zipper and
His Father.
M. Hofmann, 617(TLS):3-9Feb89-114
J. Mellors, 364:Feb/Mar89-136
Roth, J. & A. Devil's Advocates.
P-L. Adams, 61:Sep89-111
Roth, J.K. & R.L. Rubenstein. Approaches to
Auschwitz.
D. Kirby, 150(DR):Spring/Summer88-184
Roth, L., ed. Musical Life in Sweden.
J.H., 412:May88-158
Roth, M. & J. Kroll. The Reality of Mental
Illness.
T.S. Champlin, 483:Jan88-122
Roth, N. Maimonides.*
D. Hook, 86(BHS):Apr88-180
Roth, P. The Facts.*
B. Cheyette, 617(TLS):17-23Feb89-159
Roth, P.A. Meaning and Method in the Social
Sciences.
R. Paden, 543:Dec88-409
A.L. Stinchcombe, 185:Jan89-434
Roth, R.A. The Democratic Dilemma.
J. Daniell, 432(NEQ):Dec88-629
Rothenberg, J. New Selected Poems: 1970-
1985.
P. Christensen, 472:Vol15No1-125
Rothenberg, J., ed. Shaking the Pumpkin.
Technicians of the Sacred. (2nd ed)
P. Christensen, 472:Vol15No1-125
Rothenberg, J., with H. Lenowitz & C. Doria,
eds. A Big Jewish Book.
P. Christensen, 472:Vol15No1-125
Rothenberg, J. & D., eds. Symposium of the
Whole.
P. Christensen, 472:Vol15No1-125
Rothgeb, J. - see Schenker, H.
Rothman, B.K. Recreating Motherhood.
L. Gordon, 441:16Apr89-29
Rothman, T. Censored Tales.
C. Rumens, 617(TLS):13-19Oct89-1132
Rothstein, A., ed. How Does Treatment Help?
P.L. Wachtel, 441:6Aug89-14
Rothstein, A. Peter the Great and Marlbor-
ough.
J. Cracraft, 550(RusR):Apr88-183
Rotman, B. Signifying Nothing.
P. MacHamer, 148:Summer88-106
Rotrou, J. La Soeur. (R.G. Le Page, ed)
P. Gethner, 475:Vol15No28-302
Q.M. Hope, 207(FR):Oct88-167
Rotter, A.J. The Path to Vietnam.*
639(VQR):Summer88-95
Rouart, D. Degas.
P-L. Adams, 61:Jan89-120
Rouart, D. - see Morisot, B.

Rozental, S. NB: Erindringer om Niels Bohr.
R. Fossum, 563(SS):Winter88-79
Rozett, M.T. The Doctrine of Election and the
Emergence of Elizabethan Tragedy.*
D.J. Gless, 570(SQ):Spring88-129
Rozman, G. The Chinese Debate About Soviet
Socialism, 1978-1985.
J.T. Paltiel, 293(JASt):May88-359
Rozman, G. A Mirror for Socialism.*
Shum Kui-Kwong, 302:Vol24No1-87
Ruben, D-H. The Metaphysics of the Social
World.*
M. Hollis, 393(Mind):Jan88-141
Rubenberg, C.A. Israel and the American Na-
tional Interest.
E.S. Shapiro, 390:Jan88-57
Rubenstein, C. The Honey Tree Song.
J. Knappert, 203:Vol99No2-260
Rubenstein, R. Boundaries of the Self.
M. Alcorn, 599:Summer89-312
B. Draine, 395(MFS):Summer88-327
C.D. Edelberg, 27(AL):May88-318
J.D. Kalb, 115:Summer88-331
Rubenstein, R.A., C.D. Laughlin, Jr. & J.
McManus. Science as a Cognitive Process.
R. Almeder, 606:Sep88-447
Rubin, B. Istanbul Intrigues.
M.W. Browne, 441:22Oct89-23
Rubin, D. After the Raj.*
E.W.C., 295(JML):Fall87/Winter88-218
M. Green, 293(JASt):Feb88-187
S. Suleri, 402(MLR):Jul89-728
Rubin, D.L., ed. La poésie française du prem-
ier XVIIe siècle.*
J. Grimm, 547(RF):Band100Heft4-430
I. Piette, 356(LR):Feb-May88-132
Rubin, D.L. & W.M. Dodd. Talking into Writ-
ing.
V.H. Wilson, 126(CCC):Dec88-481
Rubin, E.R. Abortion, Politics and the Courts.
N.A.D., 185:Oct88-213
Rubin, L. Frank Stella: Paintings 1958 to
1965.
S. Wilson, 39:Feb88-144
Rubin, L.D., Jr., with others, eds. The History
of Southern Literature.*
J.N. Gretlund, 534(RALS):Vol16No1&2-52
Rubin, L.D., Jr. & J.L. Idol, Jr. - see Wolfe, T.
Rubin-Dorsky, J. Adrift in the Old World.
R.D. Rust, 165(EAL):Vol24No2-155
Rubinsohn, W.Z. Der Spartakus-Aufstand und
die sowjetische Geschichtsschreibung.
H. Heinen, 229:Band60Heft7-657
Rubinstein, A.Z. Soviet Foreign Policy Since
World War II, Imperial and Global. (3rd ed)
A.G. Meyer, 385(MQR):Fall89-772
Rubio Cremades, E. - see Valera, J.
Rubio de Lértora, P. & R.A. Young. Carpentier
ante la crítica.*
V. Smith, 86(BHS):Apr88-206
Rubió i Balaguer, J. Obres. (Vols 1-5)
J-L. Marfany, 86(BHS):Apr88-198
Rubio Tovar, J., ed. Libros españoles de vi-
ajes medievales (Selección).
P.E. Grieve, 240(HR):Winter88-95
D.P. Seniff, 86(BHS):Jul88-289
Ruck, C.A.P. Latin.
P. Jeffreys-Powell, 123:Vol38No2-432
J.S. Ruebel, 399(MLJ):Winter88-484
J. Sarkissian, 124:Mar-Apr89-316
Rucker, R. Mind Tools.*
R.M. Smullyan, 316:Dec88-1254

Rucker, R. & L., comps. MUSI*KEY.
B.L. Cooper, 498:Fall88-106
Rudall, B.H. & T.N. Corns. Computers and
Literature.
R. Alston, 354:Jun88-173
Rudd, N. Themes in Roman Satire.*
J. Adamietz, 229:Band60Heft3-257
E.S. Ramage, 487:Summer88-183
Rudd, N. & E. Courtney - see Juvenal
de Rudder, O. Le Français qui se cause.*
J.T. Chamberlain, 207(FR):Oct88-185
Ruddick, S. Maternal Thinking.
M. Quilligan, 441:21May89-15
Rudé, G. The French Revolution.
P.L. Adams, 61:Feb89-83
H. Goodman, 441:9Jul89-13
N. Hampson, 453(NYRB):13Apr89-11
C. Lucas, 617(TLS):19-25May89-554
Ruderman, J. William Styron.*
M.J. Bolsterli, 395(MFS):Winter88-642
S. Felton, 392:Spring88-194
D.J. Greiner, 27(AL):Oct88-500
Rudes, B.A. Tuscarora Roots, Stems, and Par-
ticles.
M. Mithun, 350:Mar89-159
Rudes, B.A. & D. Crouse. The Tuscarora Leg-
acy of J.N.B. Hewitt.
M. Mithun, 350:Mar89-159
Rudlin, J. Jacques Copeau.*
J. Norwood, 615(TJ):May88-285
Rudnick, P. I'll Take It.
S. Isaacs, 441:11Jun89-14
Rueda, J.M.F. - see under Fradejas Rueda,
J.M.
Rueda, L.F., ed. Robert A.M. Stern.
S. Gutterman, 45:Mar88-77
Ruelle, P. Les "Apologues" de Guillaume Tar-
dif et les "Facetiae morales" de Laurent
Valla.
D. Evans, 208(FS):Apr88-201
Ruelle, P. Chartes en langue française an-
térieures à 1271 conservées dans la pro-
vince de Hainaut.*
C. Marchello-Nizia, 554:Vol107No4-554
C. Rebuffi, 379(MedR):Aug86-297
Ruelle, P., ed. Le "Dialogue des créatures."*
(C. Mansion, trans)
W.R. Laird, 589:Jul88-717
Ruether, R.R. & H.J. The Wrath of Jonah.
B.M. Weir, 441:9Apr89-22
Ruetz, M. Goethes Italienische Reise.
G. Hoffmeister, 221(GQ):Spring87-286
Ruffinatto, A. Semiotica ispanica.*
J. Weiss, 86(BHS):Apr88-180
Rugaleva, A. Elementary Russian. Interme-
diate Russian. Advanced Russian.
J. Lake, 574(SEEJ):Spring88-170
Rugaleva, A. Reading Russian. (Vols 1 & 3)
F. Ingram, 574(SEEJ):Spring88-172
Rugaleva, A., K. McKenna & A. Nakhimovsky.
Reading Russian. (Vol 2)
F. Ingram, 574(SEEJ):Spring88-172
Rugg, D.S. Eastern Europe.
A.H. Dawson, 575(SEER):Jan88-161
Ruggieri, R.M. - see Polo, M.
Rugoff, M. America's Gilded Age.
R.C. Skidmore, 441:9Jul89-19
Ruh, K., ed. Abendländische Mystik im Mit-
telalter.
F.L. Borchardt, 221(GQ):Fall88-571
Ruhlen, M. A Guide to the World's Lan-
guages.* (Vol 1)
B. Blake, 297(JL):Mar88-261

Ruiz, C.P. – see under Pensado Ruiz, C.
Ruiz, U.E. – see under Espinosa Ruiz, U.
Ruiz–Domenec, J.E. La caballeria o la imagen cortesana del mundo.
  R. Ayerbe–Chaux, 589:Jan88–221
Ruiz Ramón, F. Calderón y la tragedia.*
  F.A. de Armas, 238:Mar88–81
  E. Oostendorp, 547(RF):Band100Heft4–477
Ruiz Veintemilla, J.M., ed. Estudios dedicados a James Leslie Brooks.
  G. Ribbans, 86(BHS):Apr88–179
Rule, J. After the Fire.
  R. Kaveney, 617(TLS):1–7Dec89–1338
Rule, J. The Labouring Classes in Early Industrial England 1750–1850.
  R. Glen, 637(VS):Winter89–237
Rule, J. Memory Board.*
  S. Havener, 647:Fall88–80
Rull, E. – see Tirso de Molina
Rumens, C. The Greening of the Snow Beach.
  S. Laird, 617(TLS):31Mar–6Apr89–345
Rumens, C. Plato Park.*
  J. Mellors, 364:Apr–May87–153
Rumi. Mystical Poems of Rumi: Second Selection. (A.J. Arberry, trans)
  V.R. Holbrook, 318(JAOS):Jul–Sep87–530
Rummel, E. Erasmus as a Translator of the Classics.
  J. Kraye, 447(N&Q):Mar88–72
  M. Lowry, 123:Vol38No1–134
Rumney, A., ed. New Directions in Vocational Education.
  F.D. Flower, 324:Oct89–752
Rumrich, J.P. Matter of Glory.
  639(VQR):Spring88–54
Runciman, L. & S. Sher, eds. Northwest Variety.
  C.S. Long, 649(WAL):May88–80
Runia, D.T., ed. Plotinus Amid Gnostics and Christians.
  S. Gersh, 41:Vol7–253
Ruoff, A. Alltagstexte I. Alltagstexte II.
  K. Rein, 685(ZDL):3/1988–353
Ruotolo, L.P. The Interrupted Moment.
  M. De Koven, 395(MFS):Summer88–275
  H. Richter, 594:Winter88–417
Rupe, C.J. La dialéctica del amor en la narrativa de Juan Valera.
  C. De Coster, 238:Dec88–827
Rüping, K. – see Hacker, P.
Rupnik, J. The Other Europe.
  W. Brus, 617(TLS):10–16Mar89–244
Rupp, G. Religion in England, 1688–1791.
  W.R. Ward, 83:Spring88–119
Ruppert, P. Reader in a Strange Land.*
  R.R. Hellenga, 223:Fall88–359
  K.M. Roemer, 561(SFS):Mar88–88
Ruse, M. The Darwinian Paradigm.
  P.J. Bowler, 617(TLS):1–7Dec89–1345
Ruse, M. Homosexuality.
  J. McCarthy, 103:Oct89–423
Ruse, M. Taking Darwin Seriously.*
  D. Gordon, 258:Mar88–105
  A. Holland, 518:Apr88–116
  P. Simpson, 63:Jun88–256
Rushdie, S. The Jaguar Smile.*
  M.A. Rygiel, 577(SHR):Winter88–63
Rushdie, S. The Satanic Verses.*
  D.J. Enright, 453(NYRB):2Mar89–25
  B. Leithauser, 442(NY):15May89–124
  A.G. Mojtabai, 441:29Jan89–3

Rushton, J. Classical Music.
  P. Robinson, 83:Autumn88–247
  J. Smaczny, 410(M&L):Oct88–526
Rushton, W.F. The Cajuns.
  M. Lacombe, 102(CanL):Spring88–168
Rusinko, S. Tom Stoppard.*
  D.S. Morettini, 447(N&Q):Mar88–123
Ruskin, C., M. Herron & D. Zemke. The Quilt.*
  A. Korner, 62:Dec88–109
Ruskin, J. Modern Painters.* (D. Barrie, ed)
  T. Harrod, 39:Aug88–145
Ruskin, J. & C.E. Norton. The Correspondence of John Ruskin and Charles Eliot Norton.* (J.L. Bradley & I. Ousby, eds)
  J.B. Bullen, 541(RES):Nov88–574
  K.O. Garrigan, 445(NCF):Sep88–261
  M. Hardman, 402(MLR):Apr89–446
Russ, C.V.J. Studies in Historical German Phonology.
  P. Wiesinger, 685(ZDL):3/1987–367
Russ, J. The Hidden Side of the Moon.*
  C. Greenland, 617(TLS):12–18May89–518
Russell, B. The Collected Papers of Bertrand Russell.* (Vol 7) (E.R. Eames, with K. Blackwell, eds)
  R.E. Tully, 154:Summer88–299
Russell, B. The Collected Papers of Bertrand Russell.* (Vol 12) (R.A. Rempel, A. Brink & M. Moran, eds)
  R.E. Tully, 154:Winter88–701
Russell, D. Popular Music in England, 1840–1914.
  C. Ehrlich, 415:Apr88–192
  M. Pickering, 637(VS):Winter89–246
Russell, D.E.H. Lives of Courage.
  A. McClintock, 441:17Dec89–11
Russell, D.S. The Emblem and Device in France.*
  B.C. Bowen, 535(RHL):Mar–Apr88–254
  G.J. Brault, 188(ECr):Summer88–102
  D. Graham, 475:Vol15No28–341
Russell, F. Portraits of Sir Walter Scott.
  R. Walker, 90:Jul88–543
Russell, F. Sacco & Vanzetti.
  R.J. Tosiello, 432(NEQ):Jun88–313
Russell, I., ed. Singer, Song and Scholar.
  S. Roud, 203:Vol99No1–129
Russell, J. The Mosaic Inscriptions of Anemurium.
  J. Nollé, 229:Band60Heft7–662
Russell, J. Reading Russell.
  F. Kermode, 441:22Oct89–13
Russell, J.B. The Prince of Darkness.
  J.N.D. Kelly, 617(TLS):5–11May89–496
Russell, J.G. Peacemaking in the Renaissance.
  J.H.M. Salmon, 551(RenQ):Winter88–715
Russell, N. The Novelist and Mammon.*
  R.D. Altick, 405(MP):Aug88–109
  E.M. Sigsworth, 366:Spring88–132
Russell, R. Hot Wire.
  M. Stasio, 441:30Apr89–45
Russett, C.E. Sexual Science.
  J.H. Murray, 441:9Apr89–34
  E. Showalter, 617(TLS):27Oct–2Nov89–1177
"Russia – The Land, The People: Russian Painting 1850–1910."
  J. Kennedy, 550(RusR):Apr88–202
Russo, C.F. – see Seneca
Russo, J. Omero, "Odissea, V": libri XVII–XX.
  M.M. Willcock, 123:Vol38No1–1

Russo, J.P. I.A. Richards.
 H. Vendler, 453(NYRB):27Apr89–44
Russo, R. The Risk Pool.*
 J. Clute, 617(TLS):9–15Jun89–634
 442(NY):6Feb89–106
Russolo, L. The Art of Noises.
 J.C.G. Waterhouse, 410(M&L):Jul88–413
Russom, G. Old English Meter and Linguistic Theory.
 C.B. McCully, 361:Aug88–379
Rust, A. Die organismische Kosmologie von Alfred N. Whitehead.
 P. Trotignon, 542:Jul–Sep88–370
Rust, A., Jr., with M. Marley. Legends.
 M. Lichtenstein, 441:17Sep89–25
Ruta, S. Stalin in the Bronx.
 42(AR):Winter88–122
Rutherford, A. – see Kipling, R.
Rutherford, M. This Day Dawning.
 S. O'Brien, 617(TLS):25–31Aug89–916
Ruthven, K.K. Feminist Literary Studies.*
 T. McCormack, 102(CanL):Winter87–142
Ruthven, M. The Divine Supermarket.
 R.J. Neuhaus, 617(TLS):6–12Oct89–1086
Rutledge, J. & D. Allen. Rust to Riches.
 S.J. Govoni, 441:29Oct89–40
Rutter, P. Sex in the Forbidden Zone.
 G. Hochman, 441:10Dec89–33
Ruurs, R. Saenredam.* (Vol 1)
 W. Liedtke, 90:Jan88–39
Ryals, C.D. & K.J. Fielding – see Carlyle, T. & J.W.
Ryan, A., ed. The Idea of Freedom.
 R.L. Holmes, 449:Jun88–330
Ryan, A. Property.
 L.C.B., 185:Apr89–666
Ryan, A. Bertrand Russell.*
 S. Hampshire, 453(NYRB):2Feb89–7
Ryan, B.A. Gertrude Stein's Theatre of the Absolute.
 V.K., 295(JML):Fall87/Winter88–385
Ryan, C. House of Cards.
 H. Goodman, 441:2Jul89–12
Ryan, J. Remembering How We Stood.
 P. Craig, 617(TLS):7–13Apr89–362
Ryan, J. The Uncompleted Past.
 J. Zipes, 222(GR):Fall88–209
Ryan, M. God Hunger.
 C. Muske, 441:5Nov89–32
Ryan, M. Innocence and Estrangement in the Fiction of Jean Stafford.
 W.R. Allen, 27(AL):Oct88–495
 J.J. Firebaugh, 395(MFS):Winter88–644
 W. Leary, 569(SR):Summer88–lv
Ryan, W.F. & C.B. Schmitt, eds. Pseudo–Aristotle, "The Secret of Secrets."
 E.K. Rowson, 318(JAOS):Jan–Mar87–188
Rybakov, A. Children of the Arbat.*
 R. Garis, 249(HudR):Winter89–752
Rybczynski, W. Home.*
 N.Z. Tausky, 627(UTQ):Fall88–198
Rybczynski, W. The Most Beautiful House in the World.
 P–L. Adams, 61:Jun89–97
 E.V. Walter, 441:21May89–1
Rychard, A. & A. Sulek, eds. Legitymacja.
 Z. Bauman, 617(TLS):24–30Nov89–1295
Rychner, J. Du Saint Alexis à François Villon.*
 A. Hindley, 208(FS):Jan88–72
Rychner, J. & M. Schlup, eds. Aspects du livre neuchâtelois.*
 J. Renwick, 402(MLR):Oct89–970

Ryckmans, P. – see Confucius
Ryden, H. Lily Pond.
 K. Ray, 441:17Dec89–19
Rydén, M. & S. Brorström. The BE/HAVE Variation with Intransitives in English.
 T.F. Shannon, 350:Sep89–676
Rylance, R., ed. Debating Texts.
 M. Baron, 175:Summer88–173
 S. Scobie, 376:Mar88–101
Rymkiewicz, J. Umschlagplatz.
 J.R. Clark, 497(PolR):Vol33No3–359
Rymkiewicz, J.M. Żmut.
 R. Koropeckyj, 497(PolR):Vol33No1–88
Rzepka, C.J. The Self as Mind.*
 J.O. Allsup, 591(SIR):Winter88–622
 L. Newlyn, 541(RES):Aug88–460
 S. Simpkins, 128(CE):Nov88–812
Rževskij, L. Za Okolicej, Rasskazy Raznyx Let.
 J.T. Baer, 558(RLJ):Winter–Spring–Fall88–365

Saakyants, A. Marina Tsvetayeva.
 A. Smith, 575(SEER):Apr88–274
von Saar, F. Kritische Texte und Deutungen. (Vol 3 ed by D. Haberland; Vol 4 ed by J. Stüben)
 J. Strelka, 133:Band21Heft4–350
de Saavedra, A., Duque de Rivas. Don Alvaro o la fuerza del sino. (E. Caldera, ed)
 M.A. Rees, 86(BHS):Jul88–307
Saavedra, M.D. – see under de Cervantes Saavedra, M.
Saba, G – see de Viau, T.
Saba, R.P. Political Development and Democracy in Peru.
 S.C. Bourque, 263(RIB):Vol38No1–80
Saba, U. Atroce paese che amo. (G. Lavezzi & R. Saccani, eds)
 E. Favretti, 228(GSLI):Vol165fasc532–580
Sabar, Y. Midrashim ba–Aramit Yehudey Kurdista'n la–Parashiyot Va–Yehi, Be–Shallah ve–Yitro.
 R.D. Hoberman, 318(JAOS):Jul–Sep87–551
Sabato, L.J. The Party's Just Begun.
 J. Latimer, 639(VQR):Summer88–554
Sabbah, G., ed. Centre Jean Palerne: Mémoires V.
 P. Flobert, 555:Vol61fasc2–346
Sabean, D.W. Power in the Blood.
 P. Milbouer, 221(GQ):Spring87–314
"Saber ver el Gótico."
 J. Huidobro Pérez–Villamil, 48:Jul–Sep88–329
Sabiston, E.J. The Prison of Womanhood.
 C. Hoyser, 637(VS):Summer89–580
 S. Oldfield, 89(BJA):Autumn88–397
Sablich, S. Busoni.
 J.C.G. Waterhouse, 410(M&L):Jan88–99
Sabloff, J.A. The Cities of Ancient Mexico.
 W. Bray, 617(TLS):15–21Sep89–1011
Sablosky, I., ed. What They Heard.*
 G. Martin, 465:Autumn88–83
Sabor, P. Horace Walpole: A Reference Guide.*
 P. Rogers, 83:Spring88–91
Sacco, G. Iscrizioni greche d'Italia, Porto.
 J.P., 555:Vol61fasc1–112
Saccone, M.S. – see under Squillante Saccone, M.
Sacerio Cari, E. & E. Rodríguez Monegal – see Borges, J.L.

Sacher, R. & Nguon Phan. Lehrbuch des Khmer.
 G.F. Meier, 682(ZPSK):Band41Heft4-547
Sachs, H. Music in Fascist Italy.
 J.C.G. Waterhouse, 415:Jun88-298
Sachslehner, J. Führerwort und Führerblick.*
 S.K. Johnson, 221(GQ):Summer87-502
Sacks, O. Seeing Voices.
 P. West, 441:8Oct89-17
Sacks, P.M. The English Elegy.*
 P.H. Fry, 539:Summer88-227
 S.A.S., 295(JML):Fall87/Winter88-272
Sacristán, C.H. - see under Hernández Sacristán, C.
Saddlemyer, A. & C. Smythe, eds. Lady Gregory, Fifty Years After.
 L.R. Pratt, 637(VS):Winter89-265
Sadek, M.M. The Arabic "Materia Medica" of Dioscorides.*
 G. Saliba, 318(JAOS):Apr-Jun87-374
Sadie, S., ed. The New Grove Dictionary of Musical Instruments.
 A.P. Larson, 317:Summer88-375
 T. Mace, 143:No43-76
Sadie, S., with A. Latham, eds. The Norton/Grove Concise Encyclopedia of Music.
 H.C. Schonberg, 441:8Oct89-10
Sadler, F. The Unified Ring.
 K.L. Spencer, 561(SFS):Nov88-374
Sadler, L. Welsh Syntax.
 D.L. Everett, 350:Dec89-907
Sadrin, P. Nicolas-Antoine Boulanger (1722-1759) ou avant nous le déluge.*
 J-L. Lecercle, 535(RHL):Mar-Apr88-274
Saeed, J.I. The Syntax of Focus and Topic in Somali. Somali Reference Grammar.
 D. Biber, 350:Sep89-628
Sáenz, M.S.D. - see under de Cruz Sáenz, M.S.
Saerheim, I. Namn som fortel om oss.
 C.S. Hale, 563(SS):Winter88-107
Sáez Vidal, J. La ciudad de Alicante y las formas artísticas de la cultura barroca, 1671-1770.
 M. Estella, 48:Apr-Jun88-187
Safa Isfehani, N. Rivāvat-i Namīt-i Ašawahištān.
 J.R. Russell, 318(JAOS):Oct-Dec87-835
Safarik, A., ed. Vancouver Poetry.*
 M. Doyle, 102(CanL):Winter87-188
Safir, K.J. Syntactic Chains.*
 A. Giorgi, 297(JL):Sep88-536
Safrian, H. & H. Witek, eds. Und Keiner war dabei.
 R. Knight, 617(TLS):21-27Jul89-797
Sagan, F. Freud, Women, and Morality.*
 C.C., 185:Jul89-969
Sagaris, L. Exile Home/Exilio en la patria.*
 J. MacDonald, 137:Fall88-56
Sage, H. Incorporating Literature in ESL Instruction.
 J. Costello, 399(MLJ):Summer88-230
Sage, V. Horror Fiction in the Protestant Tradition.
 J. Blumberg, 617(TLS):24-30Mar89-302
Sage, W.W. & J.A.N. Henchy. Laos.
 J.M. Halpern, 293(JASt):Aug88-714
Sagers, M. & M. Green. The Transportation of Soviet Energy Resources.
 G. Hausladen, 550(RusR):Apr88-217
Sagiv, D. Hebrew-Arabic Dictionary of the Contemporary Hebrew Language.
 J.M. Landau, 318(JAOS):Jan-Mar87-194

Sagoff, M. The Economy of the Earth.
 J.S. Dryzek, 185:Jul89-962
Sagredo, D. Medidas del Romano.
 A. Rodríguez G. de Ceballos, 48:Apr-Jun88-190
Sahgal, N. Mistaken Identity.*
 J. Mellors, 364:Apr/May88-133
 M. Simon, 441:9Jul89-18
Sahuquillo, A. Federico García Lorca y la cultura de la homosexualidad.
 D. Eisenberg, 86(BHS):Oct88-415
Said, E. & J. Mohr. After the Last Sky.*
 C.A. Easton, 577(SHR):Winter88-67
Said, E.W. The World, the Text, and the Critic.*
 C. Bode, 224(GRM):Band38Heft4-471
Saïd, L. A Bridge through Time.
 E. Accad, 538(RAL):Summer88-248
Saïd, S. Sophiste et tyran ou le problème du "Promethée enchaîné."*
 M. Lloyd, 123:Vol38No1-8
 A.J. Podlecki, 303(JoHS):Vol108-224
Sail, L. Aquamarine.
 N. Powell, 493:Autumn88-66
Sail, L., ed. First and Always.
 T. Dooley, 617(TLS):5-11May89-495
Saine, T.P. - see "Goethe Yearbook"
Saine, T.P. & J.L. Sammons - see von Goethe, J.W.
Sainsbury, J. Disaffected Patriots.
 J.L. Bullion, 656(WMQ):Jul88-608
 N. Mackinnon, 529(QQ):Winter88-916
 D.O. Thomas, 83:Spring88-77
Saint-Amand, P. Séduire, ou la passion des Lumières.*
 J. Creech, 188(ECr):Fall88-92
St. Andrews, B.A. Forbidden Fruit.*
 R. Rubenstein, 538(RAL):Summer88-268
St. Armand, B.L. Emily Dickinson and Her Culture.*
 L.Y. Gossett, 569(SR):Summer88-469
St. Clair, W. The Godwins and the Shelleys.
 R. Lansdown, 617(TLS):25-31Aug89-912
 L.A. Marchand, 441:5Nov89-38
 A. Ryan, 453(NYRB):23Nov89-21
de Saint-Exupéry, A. Wartime Writings, 1939-1944.
 C.S. Brosman, 295(JML):Fall87/Winter88-379
St. Onge, S.S., D.W. King & R.R. St. Onge. Interaction. (2nd ed)
 L.K. Martin, 399(MLJ):Summer88-234
St. Onge, S.S., D.W. King & R.R. St. Onge. Interculture. (2nd ed)
 L.K. Martin, 399(MLJ):Summer88-234
St. Onge, S.S., R.R. St. Onge & R.M. Terry. Intersections.
 L.K. Martin, 399(MLJ):Summer88-234
de Saint-Victor, R. Trois opuscules spirituels de Richard de Saint-Victor. (J. Châtillon, ed)
 H. Feiss, 589:Oct88-989
Saith, A., ed. The Re-Emergence of the Chinese Peasantry.
 P. Howard, 293(JASt):Aug88-619
Sajavaara, K., ed. Discourse Analysis.
 A.S. Kaye, 350:Dec89-908
Sakai, C. Histoire de la littérature populaire japonaise.
 J. Bésineau, 407(NM):Autumn88-367
Sakaki, N. Break the Mirror.
 T.J. Lyon, 649(WAL):Feb89-392

Sakayan, D. Formen der Textkohärenz.
  K-E. Sommerfeldt, 682(ZPSK):Band41
  Heft1-127
Salaman, N. Forces of Nature.
  M. Imlah, 617(TLS):30Jun-6Jul89-714
Salaman, R. The History and Social Influence
  of the Potato. (rev) (J.G. Hawkes, ed)
  S.L. Hoch, 550(RusR):Apr88-180
Salamun, K., ed. Karl Popper und die Philos-
  ophie des Kritischen Rationalisus.
  J. Agassi, 103:Sep89-378
Salamun, T. The Selected Poems of Tomaz
  Salamun. (R. Haas, ed)
  R. Jackson, 219(GaR):Winter88-856
Salanitro, G. Theodorus Gaza.
  J.G.F. Powell, 123:Vol38No2-455
Salazar Rincón, J. El mundo social del "Qui-
  jote."
  F. Pierce, 86(BHS):Jul88-302
Salel, H. Oeuvres poétiques complètes.*
  (H.H. Kalwies, ed)
  V. Worth, 208(FS):Oct88-463
Salih, T. Season of Migration to the North.
  D. Pryce-Jones, 441:23Jul89-15
Salimbene de Adam. The Chronicle of Salim-
  bene de Adam. (J.L. Baird, G. Baglivi & J.R.
  Kane, trans)
  L. Martines, 589:Jan88-222
de Salinas, J. Poesías humanas. (H. Bonne-
  ville, ed)
  C. Maurer, 304(JHP):Autumn88-77
Salinas, L.O. The Sadness of Days.
  C.M. Wright, 649(WAL):May88-91
Salingar, L. Dramatic Form in Shakespeare
  and the Jacobeans.*
  M. Charney, 570(SQ):Spring88-126
  T.W. Craik, 161(DUJ):Dec87-145
  E.A.J. Honigmann, 677(YES):Vol19-314
  M. Lomax, 366:Spring88-117
  R.W.F. Martin, 541(RES):May88-289
  D. Mehl, 156(ShJW):Jahrbuch1988-296
  R. Simard, 615(TJ):May88-290
Salinger, S.V. "To serve well and faithfully."
  J.K. Alexander, 656(WMQ):Oct88-801
Salins, P.D., ed. New York Unbound.
  D. Harvey, 617(TLS):7-13Apr89-356
Salisbury, H.E. The Great Black Dragon Fire.
  H. Bruno, 441:14May89-7
Salisbury, H.E. Tiananmen Diary.
  J. Mirsky, 617(TLS):20-26Oct89-1156
  S. Shapiro, 441:10Sep89-13
Salisbury, R. Birds of the Air.
  442(NY):3Apr89-115
Sallenave, D. Adieu.
  F. Mary, 450(NRF):May88-100
  M. Naudin, 207(FR):Apr89-907
  J. Taylor, 532(RCF):Summer88-319
Sallenave, D. Phantom Life.
  P. Erens, 441:24Dec89-17
Sallés, A. Quan Catalunya era d'Esquerra.
  A. Shubert, 86(BHS):Oct88-422
Salling, A. Laer at tale dansk. (3rd ed)
  J.E. Granger, 399(MLJ):Autumn88-346
Sallis, J. Die Krisis der Vernunft.
  C-A. Scheier, 489(PJGG):Band95Heft2-
  413
  W. Steinbeck, 342:Band79Heft2-236
Sallis, J.C., G. Moneta & J. Taminiaux. The
  Colleguim Phaenomenologicum, The First
  Ten Years.
  R. Bruzina, 103:Nov89-468

Sallmann, N., ed. Acta omnium gentium ac
  nationum conuentus quinti Latinis litteris
  linguaeque fouendis.
  H. Zehnacker, 555:Vol61fasc2-354
Salloum, S. Malcolm Lowry: Vancouver Days.*
  C. Lillard, 102(CanL):Autumn88-154
Salm, P. Pinpoint of Eternity.
  R.C. Holub, 406:Fall88-364
Salmon, E. - see Granville-Barker, H.
Salmon, J.B. Wealthy Corinth.
  H.W. Singor, 394:Vol41fasc1/2-223
  É. Will, 555:Vol61fasc1-105
Salmon, J.H.M. Renaissance and Revolt.
  J.H. Franklin, 551(RenQ):Autumn88-488
Salmon, N. Frege's Puzzle.*
  A.D. Smith, 393(Mind):Jan88-136
Salmon, T.C. Unneutral Ireland.
  C. Townshend, 617(TLS):27Oct-2Nov89-
  1175
Salmon, V. & E. Burness, eds. A Reader in the
  Language of Shakespearean Drama.*
  M. Lehnert, 72:Band225Heft1-161
Salmon, W.C. Scientific Explanation and the
  Causal Structure of the World.*
  R.N. Giere, 482(PhR):Jul88-444
  J. Woodward, 449:Jun88-322
Salomé, L. Ibsen's Heroines.
  H.S. Naess, 563(SS):Winter88-108
Salska, A. Walt Whitman and Emily Dickin-
  son.*
  L.Y. Gossett, 569(SR):Summer88-469
Salter, D., ed. New Canadian Drama 3.
  P. Brask, 108:Fall88-88
Salter, E. Fourteenth-Century English Poet-
  ry.
  G.C. Britton, 447(N&Q):Mar88-70
Salter, J. Dusk and Other Stories.*
  M.A. Jarman, 376:Jun88-189
  J. Saari, 42(AR):Spring88-270
  P. Wild, 649(WAL):Feb89-375
  639(VQR):Summer88-92
Saltykov-Shchedrin, M.E. The Golovlevs.
  R. Freeborn, 575(SEER):Jan88-160
Salusinsky, I. Criticism in Society.
  C. Bode, 224(GRM):Band38Heft4-471
  D. Cottom, 141:Spring88-272
  S. Scobie, 376:Dec88-144
  639(VQR):Winter88-9
Salzberg, J. Bernard Malamud.*
  L. Field, 534(RALS):Vol16No1&2-258
Salzman, J., ed. The Cambridge Handbook of
  American Literature.
  R. King, 541(RES):Feb88-157
  M.P.L., 295(JML):Fall87/Winter88-188
  T. Wortham, 445(NCF):Dec88-419
Salzman, P. English Prose Fiction, 1558-
  1700.*
  M.E. Novak, 536(Rev):Vol10-59
Samaltanos, K. Apollinaire.*
  A-M. Christin, 535(RHL):Jul-Aug88-788
Samarakis, A. Wanted: Hope.
  K.M., 295(JML):Fall87/Winter88-216
Samaraweera, V., comp. Sri Lanka.
  P. Peebles, 293(JASt):Nov88-914
Sambrook, J. The Eighteenth Century.*
  A. Varney, 447(N&Q):Mar88-93
  T. Woodman, 83:Spring88-91
Sambrook, J. - see Thomson, J.
Sammons, J.L. Wilhelm Raabe.
  L.A. Lensing, 221(GQ):Fall88-585
  G. Opie, 402(MLR):Jan89-244
Sammons, M.C. "A Better Country."
  R. Reilly, 561(SFS):Nov88-380

Sampaoli, L. Guillaume Dufay.
  D. Fallows, 309:Vol8No1/2-194
Sampayo Rodríguez, J.R. Rasgos erasmistas
  de la locura del "Licenciado Vidriera" de
  Miguel de Cervantes.
  F. Márquez Villanueva, 304(JHP):
    Autumn88-82
  T. O'Reilly, 402(MLR):Apr89-502
  H.R. Picard, 547(RF):Band100Heft4-472
  J.V. Ricapito, 552(REH):May88-122
Sampford, C.J.G. & D.J. Galligan, eds. Law,
  Rights and the Welfare State.
  R.E.G., 185:Jan89-454
Sams, E. - see Shakespeare, W.
Samuel, A.E. From Athens to Alexandria.*
  J.D. Thomas, 123:Vol38No1-91
Samuel, A.E. The Promise of the West.
  M. Goodman, 617(TLS):27Jan-2Feb89-93
Samuel, R., ed. Patriotism.
  D. Cannadine, 617(TLS):22-28Dec89-
    1407
Samuels, E. Henry Adams.
  H. Brogan, 441:19Nov89-22
Samuels, E., with J.N. Samuels. Bernard Ber-
  enson: The Making of a Legend.*
  W.L. Vance, 432(NEQ):Dec88-575
Samuels, R.J. The Business of the Japanese
  State.
  L.E. Hein, 293(JASt):Nov88-895
Sánchez, A.E.P. & E.A. Sayre - see under
  Pérez Sánchez, A.E. & E.A. Sayre
Sanchez, T. Mile Zero.
  E. Abeel, 441:1Oct89-7
  R. Towers, 453(NYRB):7Dec89-46
Sánchez Beltrán, M.J. La porcelana del Buen
  Retiro de Madrid en el Museo Arqueológico
  Nacional.
  I. Mateo Gómez, 48:Oct-Dec88-454
Sanchez de La Torre, A. Le droit dans
  l'aventure européenne de la liberté.
  M. Adam, 542:Jan-Mar88-109
  S. Goyard-Fabre, 154:Winter88-728
Sánchez-Eppler, B. Habits of Poetry; Habits
  of Resurrection.
  J.P. Devlin, 402(MLR):Apr89-508
Sánchez Vidal, A. - see Hernández, M.
Sancisi-Weerdenburg, H., ed. Achaemenid
  History. (Vol 1)
  M.C. Root, 617(TLS):13-19Oct89-1126
Sancisi-Weerdenburg, H. & A. Kuhrt, eds.
  Achaemenid History. (Vol 2)
  M.C. Root, 617(TLS):13-19Oct89-1126
Sandbach, F.H. Aristotle and the Stoics.*
  A.P. Bos, 394:Vol41fasc1/2-170
  R.B. Todd, 41:Fall88-304
Sandberg, B. Untersuchungen zur Graphemik
  und Phonemik eines Tiroler Autographs aus
  dem Ende des 15. Jahrhunderts.
  E. Neuss, 260(IF):Band93-365
Sandberg, B. Zur Repräsentation, Besetzung
  und Funktion einiger zentraler Leerstellen
  bei Substantiven.
  A. Lötscher, 685(ZDL):3/1987-366
Sandburg, C. Carl Sandberg at the Movies.
  (D. & D. Fetherling, eds)
  G.C. Wood, 534(RALS):Vol16No1&2-185
Sandburg, H. "...Where Love Begins."
  J. Baumel, 441:1Oct89-27
Sander, V. - see Benn, G.
Sanders, A. The Companion to "A Tale of Two
  Cities."
  G. Storey, 617(TLS):17-23Feb89-173

Sanders, A.F. Michael Polanyi's Post-Critical
  Epistemology.
  W. Gulick, 103:Aug89-330
Sanders, C.R. - see Carlyle, T. & J.W.
Sanders, D. John Dos Passos.
  L. Wagner-Martin, 365:Fall87-221
Sanders, E.P. & M. Davies. Studying the Syn-
  optic Gospels.
  M. Goulder, 617(TLS):20-26Oct89-1166
Sanders, J. E.E. Smith.
  R. Letson, 561(SFS):Mar88-97
Sanders, J.B. La Correspondance d'André
  Antoine.
  B.L. Knapp, 446(NCFS):Spring-Summer89-
    435
Sanders, L. Capital Crimes.
  W.H. Banks, Jr., 441:13Aug89-16
Sanders, M. & M. Rock. Waiting for Prime
  Time.
  S.B. Levine, 441:22Jan89-18
Sanders, R. Shores of Refuge.*
  J. Fischel, 390:Nov88-54
Sanders, S.R. The Paradise of Bombs.
  J. Eis, 219(GaR):Summer88-435
Sanders, W. "The Winter's Tale."*
  M. Baron, 175:Spring88-84
Sanderson, J. "But the People's Creatures."
  R. Lockyer, 617(TLS):29Dec89/4Jan90-
    1434
Sandford, J. Rules of Prey.
  M. Stasio, 441:30Jul89-18
Sandison, A. - see Kipling, R.
Sandler, I. & A. Newman - see Barr, A.H., Jr.
Sandler, L.F. Gothic Manuscripts, 1285-
  1385.*
  78(BC):Autumn88-313
Sandler, R. - see Frye, N.
Sandqvist, S., ed. La mort du roi Souvain.*
  T. Hobbs, 382(MAE):1988/1-154
di Sandro, N. Le anfore archaiche dallo Sca-
  rico Gosetti, Pithecusa.
  A. Johnston, 123:Vol38No2-447
Sands, H. Wall Systems Analysis by Detail.
  D.E. Gordon, 47:Mar88-49
Sandulescu, C.G. & C. Hart, eds. Assessing
  the 1984 "Ulysses."*
  T.P. Martin, 295(JML):Fall87/Winter88-
    339
Sandved, A.O. Introduction to Chaucerian
  English.*
  382(MAE):1988/1-151
Sandy, S. Man in the Open Air.
  H. Hart, 385(MQR):Summer89-417
Sanford, A. Lasting Attachments.
  E. Lotozo, 441:14May89-22
Sanford, G. Military Rule in Poland.
  G. Davies, 575(SEER):Apr88-319
Sangren, P.S. History and Magical Power in a
  Chinese Community.
  H. Gates, 293(JASt):Aug88-620
Sangsue, D. Le Récit excentrique.
  M-F. Étienne, 446(NCFS):Spring-Sum-
    mer89-404
  J-J. Hamm, 529(QQ):Winter88-921
  R. Pearson, 208(FS):Oct88-482
Sani, B. Rosalba Carriera.*
  F. Haskell, 617(TLS):24-30Mar89-312
Sankaranarayanan, S. Śrīmadbhagavadgītā
  with Gītārthasaṅgraha of Abhinavagupta.
  A. Sharma, 485(PE&W):Apr88-200

de San Pedro, D. "Càrcer d'Amor," "Carcer d'Amore."* (V. Minervini & M.L. Indini, eds)
    R. Rohland de Langbehn, 240(HR): Spring88-253
    P. Taravacci, 379(MedR):Aug88-310
de San Pedro, D. Diego de San Pedro's "Tractado de amores de Arnalte y Lucenda."* Diego de San Pedro's "Cárcel de amor."* (I.A. Corfis, ed of both)
    D. Hook, 402(MLR):Jan89-201
Sansom, W. Proust.
    M.P.L., 295(JML):Fall87/Winter88-372
Santayana, G. Persons and Places.* (W.G. Holzberger & H.J. Saatkamp, Jr., eds)
    T.N. Munson, 432(NEQ):Mar88-154
    I.K. Skrupskelis, 619:Winter88-155
Santiago Baca, J. Martin & Meditations on the South Valley.
    L. Rector, 249(HudR):Summer88-393
Santiago Kastner, M. The Interpretation of 16th- and 17th-Century Iberian Keyboard Music.*
    A. Howell, 410(M&L):Jul88-372
Sāntideva. La Marche à la Lumière (Bodhicaryâvatâra). (L. Finot, trans)
    L. Chouteau, 450(NRF):Sep88-101
Santirocco, M.S. Unity and Design in Horace's "Odes."
    W.S. Anderson, 122:Apr88-165
    R.A. Hornsby, 481(PQ):Spring88-265
    W. Kissel, 229:Band60Heft4-314
Santner, E.L. Friedrich Hölderlin.
    P. Hayden-Roy, 221(GQ):Winter88-137
Santob de Carrión. Proverbios morales.* (T.A. Perry, ed)
    L.P. Harvey, 86(BHS):Jul88-292
    J. Joset, 304(JHP):Spring88-258
Santoli, A. New Americans.
    A. Codrescu, 441:2Apr89-32
Santore, C. The Windsor Style in America. (Vol 2) (T.M. Voss, ed)
    658:Winter88-295
dos Santos, M.H.C. – see under Carvalho dos Santos, M.H.
Santschi, M. Portrait d'Antonio Pizzuto.*
    J. Roudaut, 450(NRF):Oct88-99
Sañudo, M.R. – see under Revuelta Sañudo, M.
San Vicente, A. – see Andrés de Uztarroz, J.F.
Saperstein, A. How Old Was Lolita?*
    J. Saari, 42(AR):Spring88-268
Sarah, R. Becoming Light.
    K. McGuirk, 137:Fall88-50
Saramago, J. Baltasar and Blimunda.*
    J. Mellors, 364:Mar88-102
Saramago, J. Das Kloster zu Mafra.
    H-J. Ille, 654(WB):3/1988-471
Sargent, M. & J. Hogg, eds. The "Chartae" of the Carthusian General Chapter, Paris, Bibliothèque Nationale Ms. Latin 10888. (Pt 1)
    R.B. Marks, 589:Jan88-224
Sargent, P. Venus of Shadows.
    G. Jonas, 441:26Feb89-32
Sarkissian, A., ed. Contemporary Authors: Autobiography Series. (Vol 2)
    P. Stitt, 534(RALS):Vol16No1&2-271
Sarkonak, R., ed. The Language of Difference.
    E-M. Kröller, 107(CRCL):Jun88-304
Sarkonak, R. Claude Simon.
    R. Bim, 295(JML):Fall87/Winter88-381
    [continued]

[continuing]
    R. Gay-Crosier, 207(FR):Feb89-537
    R. Gay-Crosier, 207(FR):Mar89-692
    S. Petit, 345(KRQ):Nov88-400
    R. Runyon, 188(ECr):Spring88-110
Sarlo, B. Una modernidad periférica.
    N. Lindstrom, 263(RIB):Vol38No4-540
Sarna, J., ed. The American Jewish Experience.
    B. Levine, 287:Sep/Oct87-25
Saroyan, W. Madness in the Family. (L. Hamalian, ed)
    P. Wild, 649(WAL):Nov88-283
    42(AR):Summer88-401
Sarraute, C. Allô Lolette, c'est Coco.
    L. Lazar, 207(FR):Dec88-368
Sarraute, N. Tu ne t'aimes pas.
    G. Josipovici, 617(TLS):13-19Oct89-1130
Sarton, M. The Education of Harriet Hatfield.
    A. Corn, 441:2Jul89-5
Sartori, G. The Theory of Democracy Revisited.
    D. Zolo, 185:Jan89-431
Sartre, J-P. The Family Idiot.* (Vol 2)
    J. Parini, 249(HudR):Summer88-363
Sartre, J-P. Mallarmé, or The Poet of Nothingness.
    C.S. Brosman, 207(FR):Apr89-899
Sarup, M. An Introductory Guide to Post-Structuralism and Postmodernism.
    M. Walters, 617(TLS):22-28Dec89-1419
Šašel, A. & J. Inscriptiones Latinae quae in Iugoslavia inter annos MCMII et MCMXL repertae et editae sunt.
    M. Clauss, 229:Band60Heft7-661
Sass, G. Redcoat.
    J. Gellert, 102(CanL):Winter87-220
Sasson, J.M., ed. Studies in the Literature of the Ancient Near East Dedicated to Samuel Noah Kramer.
    B. Groneberg, 318(JAOS):Apr-Jun87-321
Sassoon, A. & G. Wilson. Decorative Arts.
    G. Ashton, 39:Jan88-68
Sassoon, S. Siegfried Sassoon: Letters to Max Beerbohm, with a Few Answers. (R. Hart-Davis, ed)
    M. Thorpe, 179(ES):Feb88-91
Sather, L.B., comp. Norway.
    H.S. Naess, 563(SS):Winter88-107
Sato, E.M.T. & M. Sakihara. Japanese Now. (Vol 3)
    T.J. Vance, 399(MLJ):Autumn88-366
Sattelmeyer, R. & J.D. Crowley, eds. One Hundred Years of "Huckleberry Finn."
    E.L. Galligan, 569(SR):Spring88-265
Satterthwait, W. Miss Lizzie.
    T. Nolan, 441:15Oct89-50
Sattin, A. – see Tytler, H.
Satty, H.J. & C.C. Smith. Olaf Stapledon.
    R.M.P., 561(SFS):Nov87-410
Satyamurti, C. Broken Moon.*
    S. O'Brien, 364:Apr/May88-118
Sauder, G. & J. Schlobach, eds. Aufklärungen.* (Vol 1)
    J. Mondot, 547(RF):Band99Heft4-465
    H.B. Nisbet, 402(MLR):Jan89-232
Sauerberg, L.O. Secret Agents in Fiction.
    J.R. Cohn, 594:Fall88-323
Sauermann, E. Zur Datierung und Interpretation von Texten Georg Trakls.
    G.M. Sakrawa, 222(GR):Winter88-49
    E. Williams, 221(GQ):Winter87-139

Saugnieux, J., ed. Foi et Lumières dans l'Espagne du XVIIIe siècle.
  P. Deacon, 86(BHS):Apr88-186
Saul, J.R. The Paradise Eater.*
  E. Toynton, 441:1Jan89-6
Saulniers, A.H. Public Enterprises in Peru.
  M.S. Grindle, 263(RIB):Vol38No4-541
Saunders, A. Fortress Britain.
  S. Pepper, 617(TLS):22-28Dec89-1424
Saunders, A. The Sixteenth-Century French Emblem Book.
  J.M. Massing, 617(TLS):21-27Jul89-806
Saunders, E.D. - see Hisatoyo Ishida
Saunders, J. Prescriptives.
  G. Gessert, 448:Vol26No1-78
Saunders, R.H. & E.G. Miles. American Colonial Portraits, 1700-1776.
  K. Calvert, 656(WMQ):Oct88-803
Saurín de la Iglesia, M.R. - see Pardo de Andrade, M.
Sauter, H. & E. Loos - see d'Holbach, P.H.D.
Sauveur, J. Collected Writings on Musical Acoustics (Paris 1700-1713). (R. Rasch, ed)
  A. Cohen, 410(M&L):Jan88-68
Savage, M. The Dynamics of Working-Class Politics.
  P. Stead, 637(VS):Spring89-448
Savard, M. Le Sourire des chefs.
  A. Moorhead, 207(FR):Mar89-722
Savary, R. Ordre langagier, champ spatial et emplois figurés.*
  B. Lamiroy, 545(RPh):Feb89-311
Savater, F. - see de Unamuno, M.
Savile, A. Aesthetic Reconstructions.
  M.L. Morgan, 543:Mar89-636
Savinio, A. Childhood of Nivasio Dolcemare.*
  B.K. Horvath, 532(RCF):Fall88-162
Savinio, A. Speaking to Clio.
  M. Rainbow-Vigourt, 593:Spring88-72
Savoie, J. Le récif du prince.
  N.B. Bishop, 102(CanL):Winter87-169
Savran, D. The Wooster Group, 1975-1985.*
  P. Epstein, 295(JML):Fall87/Winter88-278
  B. King, 130:Summer88-183
Sawyer, P. Christopher Rich of Drury Lane.
  G. Barlow, 610:Spring88-58
  J. Milhous, 611(TN):Vol42No2-89
Sawyer-Lauçanno, C. An Invisible Spectator.
  A. Broyard, 441:6Aug89-3
  R. Craft, 453(NYRB):23Nov89-6
  J. Ryle, 617(TLS):15-21Sep89-995
Saxon, A.H. P.T. Barnum.
  H. Brogan, 617(TLS):17-23Nov89-1262
Saxonhouse, G.R. & K. Yamamura, eds. Law and Trade Issues of the Japanese Economy.
  G.S. Fukushima, 293(JASt):Nov88-897
Sayer, G. Jack.
  C. Rawson, 617(TLS):11-17Aug89-863
Sayer, P. The Comforts of Madness.*
  J. Vandenburgh, 441:24Dec89-7
Sayers, J., M. Evans & N. Redclift, eds. Engels Revisited.
  L.J.N., 185:Oct88-201
Sayers, J.E. Papal Government and England during the Pontificate of Honorius III (1216-1227).
  J.C. Moore, 589:Apr88-471
Sayers, R., with R. Rinzler. The Korean "Onggi" Potter.
  L.A. Cort, 293(JASt):Aug88-666

Sayers, V. How I Got Him Back.
  A. Corn, 441:29Jan89-7
Sayles, G.O. The Functions of the Medieval Parliament of England.
  G.L. Harriss, 617(TLS):28Apr-4May89-468
Saylors, R., ed. Liquid City.
  T.W. Ford, 649(WAL):Aug88-177
Sayre-McCord, G., ed. Essays on Moral Realism.
  R. Bett, 103:Jun89-252
Scaglia, G., F.D. Prager & U. Montag - see Taccola, M.
Scaglione, A., ed. The Emergence of National Languages.*
  G. Holtus, 72:Band224Heft2-469
Scalapino, R.A. & S-J. Han, eds. United States-Korea Relations.
  B.C. Koh, 293(JASt):Feb88-158
Scalapino, R.A. & Chen Qimao, eds. Pacific-Asian Issues.
  E.K. Lawson, 293(JASt):Feb88-100
Scalapino, R.A. & H. Lee, eds. North Korea in a Regional and Global Context.
  R. Kim, 293(JASt):May88-391
Scambray, K. A Varied Harvest.
  A. Boyer, 395(MFS):Summer88-227
  R.B. Salomon, 27(AL):Dec88-676
Scammell, W. Keith Douglas.*
  E. Garrett, 493:Winter88/89-60
  P. Parker, 364:Jul88-101
Scammell, W. Eldorado.*
  H. Lomas, 364:Mar88-82
Scanlan, J.P. Marxism in the USSR.
  A. Brown, 575(SEER):Apr88-315
Scarfe, N. Suffolk in the Middle Ages.
  R. Abels, 589:Oct88-992
Scarpa Bonazza Buora, A. Libertà e tirannide in un discorso "Siracusano" di Diodoro Siculo.
  W. Orth, 229:Band60Heft3-263
Scarpat, G. - see Tertullian
Scarron, P. Les Nouvelles tragi-comiques.* (R. Guichemerre, ed) Le Jodelet ou le Maistre Valet.* (W.J. Dickson, ed)
  I. Landy-Houillon, 535(RHL):Jul-Aug88-763
Scarry, E. The Body in Pain.*
  A. Stoekl, 577(SHR):Winter88-49
Scatozza Höricht, L.A. I vetri romani di Ercolano.
  K. Goethert-Polaschek, 229:Band60 Heft8-745
Scatozza Höricht, L.A. Il volto dei filosofi antichi.
  R.R.R. Smith, 123:Vol38No2-449
Scattergood, J., ed. Literature and Learning in Medieval and Renaissance England.
  A. Samson, 677(YES):Vol19-307
Scatton, E.A. A Reference Grammar of Modern Bulgarian.*
  J.E. Augerot, 399(MLJ):Spring88-80
Schabus, S. Die Präfixverben in den südbairischen Dialekten Kärntens.
  A. Rowley, 685(ZDL):3/1987-385
Schacher, T. Idee und Erscheinungsformen des Dramatischen bei Hector Berlioz.
  F. Andrieux, 537:Vol74No2-238
Schachermeyr, F. Mykene und das Hethiterreich.
  D.F. Easton, 123:Vol38No2-303
  D.F. Easton, 303(JoHS):Vol108-259
  H.G. Güterbock, 229:Band60Heft4-360

Schacht, R. Nietzsche.
  A. Del Caro, 221(GQ):Spring87–317
Schadel, E., ed. Bibliotheca Trinitariorum.
  (Vol 1)
  H. Kraft, 229:Band60Heft2–159
Schaedler, K-F. Weaving in Africa South of
  the Sahara.
  F.T. Smith, 2(AfrA):Aug88–23
Schaefer, F. The Scapeweed Goat.
  J. Clute, 617(TLS):1–7Sep89–952
  G.M. Henry, 441:3Sep89–14
Schaefer, S. & P. Fusco, with P-T. Wiens.
  European Painting and Sculpture in the Los
  Angeles County Museum of Art.
  G. Ashton, 39:Jan88–68
Schaeffer, S.F. Buffalo Afternoon.
  F. Baveystock, 617(TLS):24–30Nov89–
  1313
  N. Proffitt, 441:21May89–7
Schaeken, J. Die Kiever Blätter. (A.A. Bar-
  entsen, B.M. Groen & R. Sprenger, eds)
  H.G. Lunt, 574(SEEJ):Winter88–595
  C.M. MacRoberts, 402(MLR):Jan89–268
  W.R. Veder, 575(SEER):Apr88–252
Schäfer, A. Aufklärung und Verdinglichung.
  P. Trotignon, 542:Oct–Dec88–509
Schafer, E.H. Mirages on the Sea of Time.
  Wong Shiu Hon, 302:Vol24No1–117
Schafer, E.N. Our Remarkable Memory.
  J. Viorst, 441:9Apr89–30
Schäfer, J. Geschichte des amerikanischen
  Dramas im 20. Jahrhundert.
  W. Binder, 38:Band106Heft3/4–550
Schafer, R.M. Dicamus et Labyrinthos.
  B. Whiteman, 102(CanL):Winter87–148
Schäfer, W. Komik in den Romanen George
  Eliots.
  M. Verch, 72:Band225Heft2–406
Schaidenreisser, S. "Odyssea," Augsburg
  1537.* (T. Sodmann & G. Weydt, eds)
  J.P. Clark, 400(MLN):Apr88–676
Schall, J.V. Reason, Revelation, and the
  Foundations of Political Philosophy.
  J.A.G., 185:Apr89–664
Schaller, M. Douglas MacArthur.
  R. Dallek, 441:14May89–12
Schama, S. Citizens.
  N. Hampson, 453(NYRB):13Apr89–11
  C. Jones, 617(TLS):21–27Jul89–791
  G. Steiner, 442(NY):17Apr89–131
  E. Weber, 441:19Mar89–1
Schama, S. The Embarrassment of Riches.*
  I. Gaskell, 90:Aug88–636
  639(VQR):Winter88–14
Schanze, H., ed. Friedrich Schlegel und die
  Kunsttheorie seiner Zeit.
  K. Peter, 221(GQ):Winter87–120
Schanzer, G.O. The Persistence of Human
  Passions.
  J.M. Flint, 402(MLR):Jan89–219
Schaper, E. & W. Vossenkuhl, eds. Reading
  Kant.
  J. Roberts, 617(TLS):27Oct–2Nov89–1189
Schapiro, L. Russian Studies.* (E. Dahren-
  dorf, ed)
  D.W. Treadgold, 396(ModA):Winter88–66
Scharfmann, R.L. "Engagement" and the Lan-
  guage of the Subject in the Poetry of Aimé
  Césaire.
  A.J. Arnold, 538(RAL):Winter88–586
  A. Chambers, 402(MLR):Jan89–185

Scharnhorst, G., with J. Bales. The Lost Life
  of Horatio Alger, Jr.*
  C. Brucker, 534(RALS):Vol16No1&2–138
Schastok, S.L. The Śāmalājī Sculptures and
  6th Century Art in Western India.
  M.W. Meister, 318(JAOS):Apr–Jun87–367
Schatt, P.W. Exotik in der Musik des 20.
  Jahrhunderts.
  W. Rathert, 416:Band3Heft3–273
Shatz, M.S. Jan Waclaw Machajski.
  J. Keep, 617(TLS):22–28Sep89–1039
Schatz, T. The Genius of the System.
  E. Kendall, 441:6Aug89–7
  R. Schickel, 61:Apr89–96
Schatzberg, W., R.A. Waite & J.K. Johnson,
  eds. The Relations of Literature and
  Science.
  J.L. Greenway, 70:Oct88–158
  S.J. Linden, 111:Fall89–13
  T.L. Warren, 365:Spring/Summer87–157
Schauber, E. & E. Spolsky. The Bounds of
  Interpretation.*
  J. John, 257(IRAL):Feb88–69
  K. Kuiper, 478(P&L):Apr88–147
Schaum, M. Wallace Stevens and the Critical
  Schools.
  D.T. O'Hara, 705:Spring88–69
Schaus, G.P. Cyrene.* (Vol 2)
  H.P. Isler, 229:Band60Heft1–54
Schechter, B. The Path of No Resistance.
  B. Sharp, 441:9Apr89–32
Schechter, H. The Bosom Serpent.
  S.C., 219(GaR):Fall88–657
Schechter, J. Durov's Pig.*
  J. Fisher, 397(MD):Jun88–310
Scheckner, P. Class, Politics, and the Indi-
  vidual.*
  J. Blackmon, 389(MQ):Spring89–387
Schecter, J. & others. Back in the U.S.S.R.
  H. Robinson, 441:12Feb89–14
Scheer, R. Thinking Tuna Fish, Talking
  Death.
  J.G. Dunne, 453(NYRB):18May89–28
Scheetz, G.H. Names' Names.
  T.J. Gasque, 424:Sep–Dec88–245
Scheffler, L. Evgenij Zamjatin.
  W. Busch, 688(ZSP):Band48Heft2–405
Schehr, L.R. Flaubert and Sons.*
  L.M. Porter, 599:Winter88–691
Scheibert, B. Jean-Henry D'Angelbert and
  the Seventeenth-Century Clavecin School.*
  R. Cormier, 568(SCN):Winter88–81
Scheichl, S.P. & E. Timms, eds. Karl Kraus in
  neuer Sicht: Londoner Kraus-Symposium/
  Karl Kraus in a New Perspective: London
  Kraus Symposium.
  L.A. Lensing, 221(GQ):Spring88–287
Scheier, L. Second Nature.*
  J. Donlan, 102(CanL):Spring88–153
Scheina, R.L. Latin America.
  J. Child, 263(RIB):Vol38No2–221
Scheitz, E. Dictionary of Russian Abbrevia-
  tions.
  S. Aslanoff, 559:Vol12No3–331
Schele, L. & M.E. Miller. The Blood of Kings.*
  D. Ades, 59:Jun88–268
  C.F. Klein, 127:Spring88–42
Schell, J. Observing the Nixon Years.
  D.M. Oshinsky, 441:9Apr89–7
Schell, O. Discos and Democracy.*
  J.K. Fairbank, 453(NYRB):16Mar89–17
  M.B. Yahuda, 617(TLS):11–17Aug89–869

Schlobach, J., ed. Correspondances littéraires inédites – Etudes et extraits – Suivies de Voltairiana.
   M. Moog-Grünewald, 52:Band23Heft3-317
Schlobinski, P. Stadtsprache Berlin.
   D. Stellmacher, 685(ZDL):3/1987-373
de Schloezer, B., with M. Scriabine. Scriabin.
   D. Murray, 415:May88-248
Schloss, E., with E.J. Kent. Eva's Story.
   I. Deak, 453(NYRB):28Sep89-63
   R. Wisse, 441:2Jul89-2
von Schlosser, J. Die Kunstliteratur.
   (French title: La littérature artistique.)
   M. Marmor, 90:Oct88-783
Schlossman, B. Joyce's Catholic Comedy of Language.*
   P. Parrinder, 402(MLR):Jan89-141
Schlueter, J. & J.K. Flanagan. Arthur Miller.
   B. Murphy, 130:Fall88-274
Schlunk, H. Las cruces de Oviedo.
   D.L. Simon, 589:Oct88-993
Schlüter, M.V. – see Benn, G.
Schmalenbach, W., ed. African Art from the Barbier-Mueller Collection, Geneva.
   K. Barber, 617(TLS):7-13Apr89-375
Schmalstieg, W.R. A Lithuanian Historical Syntax.
   V. Zeps, 350:Dec89-909
Schmeling, M. Der labyrinthische Diskurs – Vom Mythos zum Erzählmodell.*
   E. Koppen, 52:Band23Heft3-312
   W. Pabst, 547(RF):Band100Heft4-398
   P.V. Zima, 602:Band19Heft2-188
Schmetzer, H. Traditional Architecture in Zambia.
   J. Chanda, 2(AfrA):May88-83
Schmid, H-U. Althochdeutsche und frühmittelhochdeutsche Bearbeitungen lateinischer Predigten des "Dahlschen Homiliars."*
   K.O. Seidel, 684(ZDA):Band117Heft3-117
Schmid, U., ed. Codex Vindobonensis 2885.*
   T. Kerth, 221(GQ):Spring87-279
   D.F. Tinsley, 301(JEGP):Apr88-293
Schmid, W. Ausgewählte philologische Schriften. (H. Erbse & J. Kueppers, eds)
   A. Novara, 555:Vol61fasc2-325
Schmid-Cadalbert, C. Der "Ortnit AW" als Brautwerbungsdichtung.*
   F.H. Bäuml, 589:Apr88-472
   E.R. Haymes, 133:Band21Heft2/3-200
   S.M. Johnson, 221(GQ):Spring87-277
   M.E. Kalinke, 301(JEGP):Jan88-77
Schmidhuber, G. Por las tierras de Colón.
   A.G. Labinger, 352(LATR):Spring89-127
Schmidt, A. Young People's Dyirbal.
   E.L. Bavin, 355(LSoc):Sep88-440
Schmidt, A.V.C. The Clerkly Maker.
   M.T. Tavormina, 447(N&Q):Sep88-355
   M. Wakelin, 175:Summer88-151
Schmidt, D.J. The Ubiquity of the Finite.
   F. Schalow, 103:Mar89-114
Schmidt, H. Die lebendige Sprache.
   L. Seppänen, 439(NM):1988/2-219
Schmidt, H. Quellenlexikon der Interpretationen und Textanalysen.* (2nd ed)
   R. Grimm, 406:Winter88-498
Schmidt, H. Wörterbuchprobleme.
   A. Classen, 221(GQ):Winter88-122
   G. Drosdowski, 685(ZDL):3/1987-356
Schmidt, H-J. Bettelorden in Trier.
   J.B. Freed, 589:Jan88-227

Schmidt, J. Die Geschichte des Genie-Gedankens in der deutschen Literatur, Philosophie und Politik 1750-1945.*
   W. Goetschel, 221(GQ):Summer87-455
Schmidt, J. & T. Simon. Frontiers.
   O. Zarzour, 608:Dec89-689
Schmidt, J.E. Die mittelfränkischen Tonakzente (Rheinische Akzentuierung).*
   G. Lerchner, 682(ZPSK):Band41Heft4-539
Schmidt, J-U. Adressat und Paraineseform.
   L. Lenz, 229:Band60Heft4-292
Schmidt, M. The Love of Strangers.
   M. O'Neill, 617(TLS):20-26Oct89-1148
Schmidt, M. Reading Modern Poetry.
   T. Eagleton, 617(TLS):24-30Nov89-1291
Schmidt, M. – see von Biberach, R.
Schmidt, P. Gebrauchstheorie der Bedeutung und Valenztheorie.
   G. Van der Elst, 133:Band21Heft2/3-270
Schmidt, P. William Carlos Williams, the Arts, and Literary Tradition.
   C. Rapp, 219(GaR):Winter88-879
Schmidt-Dengler, W. – see von Doderer, H.
Schmidt-Dounas, B. Der lykische Sarkophag aus Sidon.*
   G. Davies, 303(JoHS):Vol108-270
Schmidt-Wiegand, R., ed. Text-Bild-Interpretation.
   J. Bumke, 684(ZDA):Band117Heft2-55
Schmiegelow, M., ed. Japan's Response to Crisis and Change in the World Economy.
   R. Napier, 293(JASt):Nov88-899
Schmit, R. Husserls Philosophie der Mathematik.
   R. Tragesser, 316:Jun88-646
Schmitt, M.C. Peter Weiss, "Die Ästhetik des Widerstands."
   C. Poore, 221(GQ):Fall88-605
Schmitt, R. Introduction to Marx and Engels.
   R. Hudelson, 484(PPR):Jun89-745
Schmitz, D. Singing.
   C. Bedient, 569(SR):Winter88-137
Schmitz, D.F. The United States and Fascist Italy, 1922-1940.
   J. Gooch, 617(TLS):1-7Sep89-936
Schmitz, H. Die Ideenlehre des Aristoteles. (Vol 1, Pts 1 & 2)
   A. Schmitt, 229:Band60Heft2-107
Schmitz-Emans, M. Schnupftuchsknoten oder Sternbild.
   W. Koepke, 133:Band21Heft2/3-214
Schmolke-Hasselmann, B. – see "Chanson de Guillaume"
Schnädelbach, H. Vernunft und Geschichte.
   P. Trotignon, 542:Oct-Dec88-509
Schnapp, J.T. The Transformation of History at the Center of Dante's "Paradise."
   P.S. Hawkins, 478(P&L):Apr88-132
Schneble, H. Krankheit der ungezählten Namen.
   K. Dieckhöfer, 229:Band60Heft4-361
Schneider, A. Brecht-Dramen auf Russisch.
   W.F. Schwarz, 688(ZSP):Band48Heft2-412
Schneider, A. Entrances.
   M. Yacowar, 106:Summer88-257
Schneider, H. – see Rameau, J-P.
Schneider, J. & M. Leger-Orine, eds. Frontiers and Space Conquest.
   C. Mitcham, 103:Aug89-333
Schneider, J-C. Là, respirant, sur le chemin qui nous reste. Lamento.
   P. Chappuis, 450(NRF):Apr88-88

Schneider, J.C. Should America Go to War?
  W.F. Kimball, 617(TLS):12–18May89–505
Schneider, K. Gotische Schriften in deutscher
  Sprache. (Vol 1)
  W. Schröder, 684(ZDA):Band117Heft3–101
Schneider, M. Vengeance of the Victim.*
  M.B. Cloud, 532(RCF):Spring88–205
  M.P.L., 295(JML):Fall87/Winter88–292
Schneider, P. Matisse.
  J.D. Herbert, 59:Jun88–297
Schneider, P–P. Die "Denkbücher" Friedrich
  Heinrich Jacobis.
  X. Tilliette, 192(EP):Apr–Jun88–269
Schneider, S.H. Global Warming.
  D.J. Kevles, 453(NYRB):21Dec89–32
Schneider, U. Die Londoner Music Hall und
  ihre Songs 1850–1920.*
  H.G. Klaus, 224(GRM):Band38Heft3–358
Schnell, R. Causa amoris.*
  I. Glier, 133:Band21Heft2/3–192
  S. Westphal–Wihl, 221(GQ):Fall87–657
Schnell, R. Die Literatur der Bundesrepublik.
  U. Rainer, 406:Fall88–401
  M.W. Rectanus, 221(GQ):Fall88–604
Schnitzler, A. Illusion and Reality.
  M.W. Roche, 221(GQ):Spring88–317
Schnitzler, A. Tagebuch 1879–1892.* (W.
  Welzig & others, eds)
  W.E. Yates, 402(MLR):Jan89–250
Schnyder, A. Die Ursulabruderschaften des
  Spätmittelalters.
  S. Jefferis, 133:Band21Heft4–331
  F. Tobin, 221(GQ):Spring88–300
Schodek, D.L. Landmarks in American Civil
  Engineering.
  42(AR):Winter88–124
Schoedel, W.R. Ignatius of Antioch.
  D.W.H. Arnold, 161(DUJ):Dec87–168
Schoeman, F., ed. Responsibility, Character,
  and the Emotions.*
  L. Thomas, 185:Jul89–950
Schoeman, K. Promised Land.
  S. Gordon, 441:30Apr89–36
Schoemperlen, D. Frogs & Other Stories.*
  R.J. Merrett, 102(CanL):Autumn88–158
Schoenbaum, S. Shakespeare and Others.*
  A.J. Cook, 702:Vol20–314
Schoenbrun, D. On and Off the Air.
  M. Sanders, 441:9Jul89–19
Schofer, P. & D. Rice. Autour de la littéra-
  ture.
  R. Reynolds–Cornell, 207(FR):Feb89–557
Schofield, M. & G. Striker, eds. The Norms of
  Nature.*
  R.J. Hankinson, 41:Vol7–343
  P. Mitsis, 319:Jul89–465
Schofield, M.A. & C. Macheski, eds. Fetter'd
  or Free?*
  E.L. Steeves, 403(MLS):Winter88–199
Schofield, P. – see Bentham, J.
Scholz, H. Brouwer invenit.*
  H–J. Raupp, 683:Band51Heft4–584
Schomperlen, D. Frogs and Other Stories.
  Hockey Night in Canada.
  C. Rooke, 376:Mar88–94
Schön, F. Der Beginn der römischen Herr-
  schaft in Rätien.
  J.F. Drinkwater, 313:Vol78–228
  R. Frei–Stolba, 229:Band60Heft2–137
Schon, I. Basic Collection of Children's Books
  in Spanish.*
  R.D. Woods, 238:Sep88–567

Schönbein, M. Das Kibyōshi 'Happyakuman ryō
  kogane no kamibana' von Santō Kyōden
  (1791).
  P.F. Kornicki, 407(MN):Summer88–235
Schönberger, R. Die Transformation des
  klassischen Seinsverständnisses.*
  R. Imbach, 687:Jul–Sep88–476
  J. Owens, 319:Jul89–470
Schönborn, C. L'icône du Christ. (3rd ed)
  D.J. Sahas, 589:Oct88–994
Schönbuber, F. Ich war dabei. Freunde in
  der Not. Macht. Trotz allem Deutschland.
  G.A. Craig, 453(NYRB):15Jun89–22
Schöne, A., ed. Kontroversen, alte und neue.*
  (Vol 1)
  S.L. Gilman, 564:May88–182
Schönzeler, H–H. Dvořák.
  J. Smaczny, 410(M&L):Jul88–399
Schönzeler, H–H. Zu Bruckners IX. Sym-
  phonie.
  P. Banks, 410(M&L):Apr88–283
Schoor, G. 100 Years of Army–Navy Football.
  M. Lichtenstein, 441:10Dec89–32
Schopen, B. The Big Silence.
  M. Stasio, 441:5Feb89–26
Schopenhauer, A. Textes sur la vue et sur
  les couleurs. (M. Elie, ed & trans)
  A. Reix, 542:Jul–Sep88–351
Schopf, A., ed. Essays on Tensing in English.
  (Vol 1)
  R.D. Botne, 350:Jun89–439
Schopf, A. Das Verzeitungssystem des En-
  glischen und seine Textfunktion.*
  B. Brömser, 260(IF):Band93–337
Schopp, C. Alexandre Dumas.*
  O. Conant, 441:8Jan89–23
Schoppa, R.K. Xiang Lake.
  J. Shapiro, 441:2Apr89–29
Schor, N. Breaking the Chain.*
  J. Bem, 535(RHL):Mar–Apr88–298
  J. Humphries, 153:Spring88–18
  J.M. Todd, 131(CL):Winter88–73
Schor, N. Reading in Detail.*
  F.L. Restuccia, 454:Winter89–228
  C. Rigolot, 207(FR):Feb89–512
  P. Suchin, 89(BJA):Autumn88–380
Schorr, J.L. – see van Effen, J.
Schøsler, J. La Bibliothèque Raisonnée,
  1728–1753.* Bibliographie des éditions et
  des traductions d'ouvrages philosophiques
  français, et particulièrement des écrivains
  obscurs, 1680–1800.*
  J. Caron, 462(OL):Vol43No1–93
Schouls, P.A. Descartes and the Enlighten-
  ment.
  S. James, 617(TLS):29Sep–5Oct89–1069
Schourup, L.C. Common Discourse Particles in
  English Conversation.
  D.H., 355(LSoc):Jun88–310
Schrader, G. Expressive Sachlichkeit.
  R.C. Holub, 406:Fall88–364
  T. Steinfeld, 564:May88–202
Schrag, C.O. Communicative Praxis and the
  Space of Subjectivity.
  R. Donovan, 258:Jun88–215
  J.C. Flay, 480(P&R):Vol21No4–294
  J–M. Gabaude, 542:Apr–Jun88–224
Schram, M. The Great American Video Game.
  639(VQR):Winter88–24
Schramke, J. Wilhelm Heinse und die Franzö-
  sische Revolution.
  F.J. Lamport, 402(MLR):Jul89–782
  A.E. Ratz, 133:Band21Heft4–343

Schreiner, O. Olive Schreiner Letters.* (Vol
1) (R. Rive, ed)
R.G. Hampson, 175:Autumn88-233
Schreiner, O. An Olive Schreiner Reader. (C.
Barash, ed)
M. May, 177(ELT):Vol31No4-484
Schrenck, G. – see d'Aubigné, A.
Schriber, M.S. Gender and the Writer's Imagi-
nation.
G. Scharnhorst, 395(MFS):Winter88-611
Schrickx, W. Foreign Envoys and Travelling
Players in the Age of Shakespeare and
Jonson.*
D.B. Hamilton, 570(SQ):Winter88-512
Schröder, G. Logos und List.*
P. Hess, 406:Fall88-379
R. Reschke, 654(WB):4/1988-696
Schröder, J. Deutsche Präpositionen im
Sprachvergleich.
G. Kleiber, 553(RLiR):Jul-Dec88-487
Schröder, J. Lexikon deutscher Präposition-
en.
G. Kleiber, 553(RLiR):Jul-Dec88-486
Schröder, P. Beratungsgespräche.
M. Lissek, 682(ZPSK):Band41Heft3-405
Schroder, T. The National Trust Book of En-
glish Domestic Silver 1500-1900.*
J.K.D. Cooper, 39:Oct88-296
Schröder, W. Vom "Rheinauer Paulus" zur
"Millstätter Sündenklage."
R.H. Lawson, 133:Band21Heft2/3-187
Schröder, W., ed. Wolfram-Studien VIII.
L.B. Parshall, 301(JEGP):Jan88-73
Schroeder, A. Dustship Glory.*
A. Shucard, 102(CanL):Winter87-196
Schrömbges, P. Tiberius und die res publica
Romana.
M. Pani, 229:Band60Heft4-343
Schubert, B. Der Künstler als Handwerker.
H. Nabbe, 564:May88-198
J.L. Sammons, 406:Summer88-214
Schubert Kalsi, M-L. Meinong's Theory of
Knowledge.
A. Mickunas, 543:Jun89-850
Schubnell, M. N. Scott Momaday.
J. Rice, 128(CE):Feb88-206
Schulkind, J. – see Woolf, V.
Schuller, G. Early Jazz.*
E.J. Hobsbawm, 453(NYRB):13Apr89-32
Schuller, G. Musings.*
P. Dickinson, 410(M&L):Jan88-113
Schuller, G. The Swing Era.
W. Balliett, 442(NY):10Apr89-121
S. Crouch, 441:2Apr89-7
C. Fox, 617(TLS):21-27Jul89-794
E.J. Hobsbawm, 453(NYRB):13Apr89-32
Schüller, W. Frauen in der römischen
Geschichte.
G. Clark, 123:Vol38No1-173
S.B. Pomeroy, 229:Band60Heft3-265
N. Smits, 124:Nov-Dec88-124
Schullery, P. The Bear Hunter's Century.
M. Nichols, 441:19Feb89-14
Schulman, G. Marianne Moore.*
S. Burris, 536(Rev):Vol10-113
Schulman, H. Not a Free Show.*
L. Mintz, 390:Jun/Jul88-64
Schulman, I.A., ed. Nuevos asedios al mod-
ernismo.
A. González, 240(HR):Summer88-395
Schulman, I.A. & E.P. Garfield, eds. Poesía
modernista hispanoamericana y española.
G. Hambrook, 86(BHS):Jul88-321

Schulte, B. Die Goldprägung der gallischen
Kaiser von Postumus bis Tetricus.
R. Bland, 313:Vol78-258
Schultz, B. & R. It Did Happen Here.
S. MacNeille, 441:6Aug89-19
Schulz, B. The Fictions of Bruno Schulz.
J. Mellors, 364:Feb/Mar89-136
Schulz, B. Letters and Drawings of Bruno
Schulz with Selected Prose.* (J. Ficowski,
ed)
J. Bayley, 453(NYRB):13Apr89-3
Schulz, G., ed. Lessing und der Kreis seiner
Freunde.
E. Moore, 221(GQ):Summer87-472
Schulz, M.F. Paradise Preserved.*
F. Garber, 301(JEGP):Jan88-120
P. Rogers, 173(ECS):Summer88-502
W. Walling, 340(KSJ):Vol37-170
M.D. Yeager, 366:Spring88-124
Schulz, R. Puškin i Knidskij mif/Puschkin und
die Knidos-Sage.
R-D. Keil, 52:Band23Heft3-304
Schulz, R.A., R.C. Helt & D.J. Woloshin. Aktu-
elle Themen.
K.O. Anderson, 399(MLJ):Spring88-94
Schulz, W. Metaphysik des Schwebens.
S. Majetschak, 489(PJGG):Band95Heft2-
406
C. Schacke-Bauer, 687:Apr-Jun88-330
Schulze, H-J. & C. Wolff. Bach Compendium.*
(Vol 1)
C.M.B., 412:Aug88-227
S. Daw, 410(M&L):Apr88-254
Schulze, R. Höflichkeit im Englischen.
K. Kohn, 38:Band106Heft1/2-177
Schunnesson, T. Framtidsstaden.
E. Trousdell, 563(SS):Winter88-99
Schur, E.M. The Americanization of Sex.
P.S.R., 185:Apr89-686
Schürer, E. The History of the Jewish People
in the Age of Jesus Christ. (Italian title:
Storia del popolo giudaico al tempo di Gesù
Cristo (175 a.C. – 135 d.C.).) (Vol 1) (G.
Vermes & others, eds)
E.P., 555:Vol61fasc1-129
Schürer, E. The History of the Jewish People
in the Age of Jesus Christ (175 B.C. – A.D.
35). (Vol 3)(2nd ed)(G. Vermes, F. Millar &
M. Goodman, eds)
A.H.J. Gunneweg, 229:Band60Heft2-167
Schürer, E. & P. Jenkins, eds. B. Traven.
D.O. Chankin, 395(MFS):Summer88-233
Schuster, G. – see Benn, G.
Schuster, I. Theodor Storm.
M.T. Peischl, 221(GQ):Summer87-486
Schuster, T.E. & R. Engen. Printed Kate
Greenaway.
B. Alderson, 78(BC):Winter88-581
Schüttauf, K. Die Kunst und die bildenden
Künste.
G. Scholtz, 53(AGP):Band70Heft3-340
Schutte, J. Einführung in die Literaturinter-
pretation.*
S.D. Martinson, 406:Spring88-116
Schutte, J. & P. Sprengel, eds. Die Berliner
Moderne 1885-1914.
R. Furness, 402(MLR):Jan89-247
Schütz, A. & A. Gurwitsch. Briefwechsel
1939-1959. (R. Grathoff, ed)
R. Crispin, 706:Band20Heft1-121
Schütz, E. Romane der Weimarer Republik.
H.F. Pfanner, 221(GQ):Winter88-147
R.C. Reimer, 406:Winter88-522

Schütz, H. In Annas Namen.
E. Kaufmann, 601(SuF):Nov–Dec88–1316
G. Krieger, 654(WB):8/1988–1318
Schuyler, J. Selected Poems.*
A. Hudgins, 249(HudR):Winter89–742
639(VQR):Autumn88–136
Schwab, A.T. – see Huneker, J.G.
Schwabe, K. Woodrow Wilson, Revolutionary
Germany, and Peacemaking, 1918–1919.
F.M. Carroll, 106:Summer88–211
Schwaller, J.F. The Church and Clergy in
Sixteenth-Century Mexico.
P. Ganster, 263(RIB):Vol38No3–410
Schwandner, E-L., with others. Der ältere
Porostempel der Aphaia auf Aegina.*
R.A. Tomlinson, 303(JoHS):Vol108–264
Schwartz, B.I. The World of Thought in An-
cient China.*
R.E. Hegel, 116:Jul87–161
D.S. Nivison, 485(PE&W):Oct88–411
H. Rosemont, Jr., 293(JASt):Aug88–621
Schwartz, B.M. A World of Villages.
S. Pickering, 569(SR):Fall88–673
Schwartz, D. The Ego is Always at the Wheel.
(R. Phillips, ed)
R. Raider, 97(CQ):Vol17No3–284
Schwartz, J.B. Bicycle Days.
P. Payne, 441:9Jul89–11
Schwartz, J.I. Encouraging Early Literacy.
D.J. Napoli, 350:Sep89–678
Schwartz, L.S. Leaving Brooklyn.
S. Birkerts, 441:30Apr89–16
Schwartz, R.B. Daily Life in Johnson's Lon-
don.
N.C. Jaffe, 677(YES):Vol19–325
Schwartz, R.M. Remembering and Repeating.
N. Forsyth, 617(TLS):22–28Sep89–1036
Schwartz Lerner, L. Quevedo: Discurso y rep-
resentación.
J. Olivares, 304(JHP):Winter88–165
Schwarz, B. French Instrumental Music
Between the Revolutions (1789–1830).
J. Gribenski, 537:Vol74No1–114
Schwarz, D.R. The Humanistic Heritage.*
T. Morgan, 177(ELT):Vol31No1–117
S.P., 295(JML):Fall87/Winter88–265
P. Rae, 49:Apr88–90
Schwarz, D.R. Reading Joyce's "Ulysses."
M. Fludernik, 395(MFS):Winter88–687
M.J. Friedman, 329(JJQ):Fall88–152
S. Pinsker, 177(ELT):Vol31No3–324
Schwarz, E. – see Rilke, R.M.
Schwarz, H-G. Dasein und Realität.
J. Guthrie, 83:Autumn88–239
Schwarz, J.A. Liberal.*
A. Schlesinger, Jr., 453(NYRB):16Feb89–
20
Schwarz, W. The New Dissenters.
B. Godlee, 617(TLS):11–17Aug89–867
Schwarze, C. & D. Wunderlich, eds. Handbuch
der Lexikologie.*
R.B. Howell, 406:Winter88–500
D. Nehls, 257(IRAL):Nov88–334
G. Rössler, 685(ZDL):3/1988–372
L. Zgusta, 361:Nov88–254
Schwauss, M. Wörterbuch der regionalen
Umgangssprache in Lateinamerika: Ameri-
kaspanisch-Deutsch.
H. Kubarth, 72:Band225Heft2–454
Schweda-Nicholson, N., ed. Languages in the
International Perspective.*
J. John, 257(IRAL):Aug88–251
Schweik, R.C. – see Hardy, T.

Schweikart, L. Banking in the American
South from the Age of Jackson to Recon-
struction.
639(VQR):Summer88–82
Schweikert, U. – see Tieck, L.
Schweitzer, C.E. – see Albertinus, A.
"Schweizer Jahrbuch für Musikwissenschaft/
Annales Suisses de Musicologie." (Vol 3,
1983)
W. Dömling, 416:Band3Heft3–266
Schwenk, R.L. Onward Christians!
V.L. Rafael, 293(JASt):May88–411
Schwering, M. Epochenwandel im spätroman-
tischen Roman.
L. Tatlock, 221(GQ):Spring87–287
Schwerner, A. Sounds of the River Naranjana
& The Tablets I–XXIV.
P. Christensen, 472:Vol15No1–125
Schwertfeger, R., ed. Women of Theresien-
stadt.
K. Ray, 441:4Jun89–23
Schwinge, E-R. Künstlichkeit von Kunst.
J.J. Clauss, 24:Fall88–447
N. Hopkinson, 123:Vol38No1–158
Schwob, M. The King in the Golden Mask.
I. Malin, 532(RCF):Summer88–324
Sciascia, L. Il cavaliere e la morte.
J. Sturrock, 617(TLS):3–9Mar89–225
Sciascia, L. The Moro Affair [and] The Mys-
tery of Majorana.
D. Day, 577(SHR):Spring88–171
U. Eisenzweig, 153:Fall88–32
Sciascia, L. To Each His Own. 1912 + 1.
J. Rosselli, 617(TLS):21–27Jul89–802
Scigaj, L.M. The Poetry of Ted Hughes.*
V.S., 295(JML):Fall87/Winter88–333
Ščiraliev, M. Dialekty gorovy azerbajžan-
skogo jazyka.
G.F. Meier, 682(ZPSK):Band41Heft6–822
Scliar, M. The Enigmatic Eye.
I. Stavans, 441:25Jun89–24
Scliar, M. The Strange Nation of Rafael
Mendes.*
G. Kidder, 37:Sep/Oct88–61
Sclippa, N. Texte et idéologie.
A.D. Hytier, 166:Apr89–254
Scobie, S. The Ballad of Isobel Gunn.
M. Estok, 198:Winter88–106
Scodel, H.R. Diaeresis and Myth in Plato's
"Statesman."
C. Gill, 123:Vol38No2–225
Scofield, S. Gringa.
M. Wolf, 441:23Apr89–20
Scolnicov, H. & P. Holland, eds. The Play Out
of Context.
J. Willett, 617(TLS):30Jun–6Jul89–728
Scolnikov, S. Plato's Metaphysics of Educa-
tion.
A. Preus, 103:Dec89–496
Scott, A., ed. Voices of our Kind.
C. Whyte, 571(ScLJ):Spring88–47
Scott, A. – see Soutar, W.
Scott, A.M. Bonnie Dundee.
D. Stevenson, 617(TLS):18–24Aug89–891
Scott, B.K. James Joyce.*
C. Herr, 395(MFS):Winter88–684
Scott, C. A Question of Syllables.*
A.L. Amprimoz, 345(KRQ):Nov88–484
J. Birkett, 402(MLR):Oct89–986
W.L. McLendon, 210(FrF):May88–249
Scott, D.C. Powassan's Drum.
R. Hatch, 102(CanL):Winter87–223

Scott, D.D. & R.A. Fox, Jr. Archaeological Insights into the Custer Battle.
  D.E. Gribble, 649(WAL):Nov88-277
Scott, F.J.D. - see James, W.
Scott, F.R. A New Endeavour.
  G.W., 102(CanL):Spring88-242
Scott, G. Heroine.*
  L. Robinson, 618:Fall88-31
Scott, J. Behind the Urals. (S. Kotkin, ed)
  B. Keller, 441:24Sep89-37
Scott, J. The Closest Possible Union.*
  P. Reading, 617(TLS):17-23Mar89-268
Scott, J. Fading, My Parmacheene Belle.*
  (British title: My Parmacheene Belle.)
  J. Mellors, 364:Mar88-102
Scott, J. Algernon Sidney and the English Republic 1623-1677.
  J. Miller, 617(TLS):4-10Aug89-853
Scott, J. The Widow of Desire.
  J. Cohen, 441:4Jun89-22
Scott, J.W. Gender and the Politics of History.*
  M. Pugh, 617(TLS):27Jan-2Feb89-83
Scott, K.W. Zane Grey, Born to the West.
  G. Topping, 649(WAL):Aug88-154
Scott, M. The Great Caruso.*
  J.K. Law, 465:Spring89-102
  R. Osborne, 617(TLS):6-12Jan89-9
Scott, M., ed. Harold Pinter.
  D.S. Morettini, 447(N&Q):Mar88-123
Scott, R. Glory Days.
  M. Stasio, 441:25Jun89-24
Scott, T. The Dirty Business.*
  R. Watson, 588(SSL):Vol23-254
Scott, T.L. & M.J. Friedman, with J.R. Bryer - see Pound, E.
"Scottish Short Stories 1987."
  J. Hendry, 571(ScLJ):Winter88-58
Scotus, J.D. Duns Scotus on the Will and Morality.* (A.B. Wolter, ed & trans)
  B. Kent, 319:Apr89-303
Scovell, E.J. Collected Poems.*
  H. Buck, 4:Autumn88-73
  R. Garfitt, 364:Aug/Sep88-112
  L. Sail, 493:Spring88-75
Scovell, E.J. Listening to Collared Doves.*
  D. McDuff, 565:Spring88-64
Scribner, C. 3d. Rubens.
  J. Russell, 441:11Jun89-56
Scriven, M. Paul Nizan.
  P. McCarthy, 617(TLS):17-23Mar89-284
Scruton, R. Spinoza.
  M-H. Belin, 192(EP):Oct-Dec88-559
Scruton, R. Thinkers of the New Left.
  D. O'Keeffe, 396(ModA):Winter88-75
Scull, A. Social Order/Mental Disorder.
  J.K. Wing, 617(TLS):7-13Jul89-747
Scupham, P. The Air Show.
  B. O'Donoghue, 617(TLS):31Mar-6Apr89-345
  C. Rumens, 493:Winter88/89-68
Scupham, P. Out Late.
  R. John, 4:Autumn88-69
  J. Saunders, 565:Autumn88-72
Seabury, P. & A. Codevilla. War.
  G.A. Craig, 453(NYRB):17Aug89-31
  M. Howard, 441:30Apr89-14
Seaford, R. Euripides, "Cyclops."*
  A. Harder, 394:Vol41fasc1/2-148
Seager, R. Ammianus Marcellinus.
  J.M. Alonso-Núñez, 123:Vol38No1-157
  T.G. Elliott, 487:Spring88-89
  E.T. Salmon, 124:Nov-Dec88-144

Seagrave, S. The Marcos Dynasty.*
  M. Leifer, 617(TLS):28Apr-4May89-465
Seale, P., with M. McConville. Asad of Syria.
  J. Kifner, 441:30Apr89-15
Sealey, R. The Athenian Republic.*
  D. Lateiner, 124:Mar-Apr89-311
  P.J. Rhodes, 123:Vol38No1-85
Sealts, M.M., Jr. Melville's Reading.* (rev)
  W. Kelley, 534(RALS):Vol16No1&2-19
Sealy, I.A. The Trotter-Nama.*
  J. Mellors, 364:Oct/Nov88-111
Seanor, D. & N. Fotion, eds. Hare and Critics.
  B. Hooker, 617(TLS):14-20Jul89-784
Searcy, M.C. The Georgia-Florida Contest in the American Revolution, 1776-1778.
  C.R. Ferguson, 656(WMQ):Jan88-198
Searle, G.R. Corruption in British Politics, 1895-1930.*
  A. Doig, 637(VS):Summer89-609
Searle, J. Minds, Brains and Science.*
  W.J. Rapaport, 449:Dec88-585
Searles, G.J. The Fiction of Philip Roth and John Updike.
  S. Pinsker, 587(SAF):Spring88-120
Sears, E. The Ages of Man.
  M.L. Colish, 589:Apr88-474
Sears, S.W. - see McClellan, B.G.
Seaton, J.P & J. Cruyer - see "Li Po and Tu Fu Bright Moon, Perching Bird"
Seaver, T., with H. Resnicow. Beanball.
  M. Stasio, 441:19Feb89-23
Seavey, O. Becoming Benjamin Franklin.
  B. Granger, 165(EAL):Vol24No3-262
Seaward, P. The Cavalier Parliament and the Reconstruction of the Old Regime, 1661-1667.
  J. Miller, 617(TLS):23-29Jun89-686
Sebald, W.G. Die Beschreibung des Unglücks.
  W. Nehring, 221(GQ):Winter87-135
Sebbar, L. J.H. cherche âme soeur.
  M. Mortimer, 207(FR):Dec88-369
Sebbar, L. & N. Huston. Lettres parisiennes.
  F. Lionnet, 207(FR):Feb89-553
Sebeok, T.A. I Think I Am A Verb.
  T. Ingold, 567:Vol69No1/2-179
Sebeok, T.A. & J. Umiker-Sebeok, eds. The Semiotic Sphere.
  G. Withalm, 567:Vol69No1/2-149
Sebold, R.P., ed. Gustavo Adolfo Bécquer.*
  J.R. Arboleda, 345(KRQ):Feb88-116
Sebold, R.P. Descubrimiento y fronteras del neoclasicismo español.*
  I.L. McClelland, 86(BHS):Jul88-306
Sebold, R.P. - see de Torres Villarroel, D.
Secor, R. & D. Moddelmog, comps. Joseph Conrad and American Writers.*
  R. Davis, 534(RALS):Vol16No1&2-173
Sedgwick, E.K. Between Men.*
  M. Lynch, 637(VS):Autumn88-129
Sedgwick, E.K. The Coherence of Gothic Conventions.
  P. Clemit, 447(N&Q):Jun88-247
Sedgwick, P. Psychopolitics.
  N. Laor, 488:Mar88-142
See, C. Golden Days.
  C.L. Crow, 649(WAL):May88-59
See, F.G. Desire and the Sign.
  A. Boyer, 395(MFS):Summer88-227
  E. Cheyfitz, 445(NCF):Sep88-264
  E. Prioleau, 26(ALR):Fall88-66
  R.B. Salomon, 27(AL):Dec88-676
von See, K., ed. Die Strindberg-Fehde.
  H. Uecker, 52:Band23Heft2-198

von See, K. & others. Neues Handbuch der Literaturwissenschaft.* (Vol 6: Europäisches Frühmittelalter.)
    W.H. Jackson, 402(MLR):Apr89-424
See, K.O. First World Nationalisms.
    R. Cook, 529(QQ):Summer88-489
Seebass, G. & R. Tuomela, eds. Social Action.
    J.A. López Cerezo, 488:Jun88-276
Seebass, T., with T. Russell - see "Imago Musicae"
Seeber, H.U. & P.G. Klussman, eds. Idylle und Modernisierung in der europäischen Literatur des 19. Jahrhunderts.
    G. Gillespie, 564:Sep88-279
    E.H. Rockwell, 133:Band21Heft2/3-223
Seebohm, A., ed. The Vienna Opera.
    B. Brisk, 465:Autumn88-92
Seebohm, C. The Country House.
    F. Partridge, 617(TLS):1-7Sep89-938
Seebohm, T.M. Philosophie der Logik.
    W. Marx, 687:Apr-Jun88-340
Seebold, E. Das System der Personalpronomina in den frühgermanischen Sprachen.
    R. Lühr, 684(ZDA):Band117Heft1-18
Seeck, G.A. Dramatische Strukturen der griechischen Tragödie.
    J.C. Kamerbeek, 394:Vol41fasc1/2-141
Seed, D. The Fictional Labyrinths of Thomas Pynchon.*
    D. Eddins, 536(Rev):Vol10-155
    S. Moore, 532(RCF):Fall88-174
    S. Weisenburger, 395(MFS):Winter88-660
Seel, L. Studien zu Klangraum und Klangordnung in der Motette der späten Ars antiqua.
    A. Traub, 416:Band3Heft3-277
Seel, M. Die Kunst der Entzweiung.*
    R. Rochlitz, 98:Jan/Feb88-95
Seelbach, U. Kommentar zum "Helmbrecht" von Wernher dem Gartenaere.
    D.H. Green, 402(MLR):Apr89-516
Seemann, K-D., ed. Beiträge zur russischen Volkskunde.
    P. Grzybek, 196:Band29Heft1/2-232
Seeskin, K. Dialogue and Discovery.*
    D. Browne, 478(P&L):Oct88-302
    J. Creed, 123:Vol38No2-277
    M.L. Gillespie, 103:Jul89-285
    N.D. Smith, 41:Vol7-215
Segal, C. Interpreting Greek Tragedy.*
    R. Buxton, 123:Vol38No1-54
Segal, C. Pindar's Mythmaking.*
    A. Köhnken, 303(JoHS):Vol108-223
    D. Kovacs, 124:Sep-Oct88-67
    J.B. Lidov, 24:Summer88-256
    I. Rutherford, 161(DUJ):Dec87-132
Segal, C. - see Conte, G.B.
Segal, E., ed. Oxford Readings in Greek Tragedy.
    A.E. Hinds, 235:Summer88-104
Segal, H.H. Corporate Makeover.
    J.D. Donahue, 441:29Oct89-32
Segal, N. Narcissus and Echo.
    K. Gore, 617(TLS):17-23Mar89-284
Segal, N. The Unintended Reader.*
    J.C. Hayes, 188(ECr):Winter88-121
    V. Mylne, 83:Spring88-113
    R.C. Rosbottom, 207(FR):Oct88-172
Segalman, R. & D. Marsland. Cradle to Grave.
    R. Cullen, 617(TLS):15-21Dec89-1383
Segel, H.B. Turn-of-the-Century Cabaret.*
    A.B. Harris, 615(TJ):Oct88-434

Segert, S. A Basic Grammar of the Ugaritic Language.
    D. Marcus, 318(JAOS):Jul-Sep87-487
Segev, S. The Iranian Triangle.*
    T. Draper, 453(NYRB):19Jan89-38
Segev, T. Soldiers of Evil.
    I. Deak, 453(NYRB):28Sep89-63
Segger, M. The Buildings of Samuel Maclure.
    L.K. Eaton, 576:Sep88-313
    J. McKendry, 627(UTQ):Fall88-201
Segonds, A.P. - see Proclus
Segre, C. Avviamento all'analisi del testo letterario.
    M. Ferraresi, 567:Vol68No1/2-175
Sei-wha, C. - see under Chung Sei-wha
Seidel, K.L. The Southern Belle in the American Novel.*
    V. Kling, 577(SHR):Winter88-80
    A.H. Petry, 587(SAF):Autumn88-248
Seidel, K.O. Mittelniederdeutsche Handschriften aus Bielefelder Bibliotheken.
    A. Classen, 201:Vol14-241
Seidel, M. Exile and the Narrative Imagination.*
    J. Meyers, 131(CL):Winter88-93
    J. Richetti, 405(MP):Feb89-335
    F. Robertson, 447(N&Q):Mar88-129
    M.A. Salgado, 149(CLS):Vol25No3-275
    R.C. Wood, 569(SR):Summer88-lix
Seidel, W. & B. Cooper. Entstehung nationaler Traditionen.
    B.V. Rivera, 410(M&L):Jul88-379
Seidel Menchi, S. Erasmo in Italia, 1520-1580.* [shown in prev under Menchi, S.S.]
    A.J. Schutte, 551(RenQ):Winter88-723
    A. Sottili, 72:Band225Heft2-465
Seideman, D. The New Republic.
    F. Matthews, 106:Spring88-69
Seidler, V.J. Kant, Respect and Injustice.*
    E. Schaper, 323:May88-203
Seielstad, G.A. At the Heart of the Web.
    R. Kanigel, 441:16Jul89-31
Seifert, J. Back to "Things in Themselves."*
    P. Lee, 543:Jun89-852
    P. Trotignon, 542:Jul-Sep88-370
    D. Willard, 103:Feb89-66
Seifert, J. The Selected Poetry of Jaroslav Seifert.* (G. Gibian, ed)
    W.W. Werner, 577(SHR):Winter88-90
Seiler, F. Die griechische Tholos.
    R.A. Tomlinson, 123:Vol38No2-350
Seiler, H. Possession as an Operational Dimension of Language.
    A. Orlandini, 260(IF):Band93-260
Seiler, H. & G. Brettschneider, eds. Language Invariants and Mental Operations.
    P. Sgall, 603:Vol12No1-252
Seiler, R.M., ed. Walter Pater.*
    B.A. Inman, 177(ELT):Vol31No3-312
Seiler, T.B. & W. Wannenmacher, eds. Begriffs- und Wortbedeutungsentwicklungen.
    K. Goede, 682(ZPSK):Band41Heft3-392
Sekine, M., ed. Irish Writers and Society at Large.*
    C. Barrow, 174(Éire):Spring88-153
Sekine, M., ed. Irish Writers and the Theatre.*
    J.W. Flannery, 235:Summer88-132
    H. Pyle, 541(RES):May88-318
Selbmann, R. Der deutsche Bildungsroman.
    T. Kontje, 222(GR):Winter88-48

Selbourne, H. A Doctor's Life. (D. Selbourne, ed)
    J.F. Watkins, 617(TLS):18–24Aug89–893
Selby, H., Jr. Song of the Silent Snow.
    J. Byrne, 532(RCF):Summer88–316
Selden, R. A Reader's Guide to Contemporary Literary Theory.*
    R.J. Dingley, 447(N&Q):Jun88–279
    W. van Peer, 204(FdL):Mar88–77
    478(P&L):Oct88–325
Selden, R., ed. The Theory of Criticism.
    M. Ellmann, 617(TLS):17–23Feb89–172
"Selected Paintings at The Norton Simon Museum, Pasadena, California."
    G. Ashton, 39:Jan88–68
Self, G. In Town Tonight.
    S. Banfield, 415:Jul88–348
Selgin, G. The Theory of Free Banking.
    S. Horwitz, 144:Summer/Fall89–411
Selkirk, E.O. Phonology and Syntax.*
    D.H., 355(LSoc):Jun88–308
Sell, R.D. The Reluctant Naturalism of Amelia.
    566:Autumn88–73
Selleri, F. Le grand débat de la théorie quantique.
    A. Reix, 542:Jul–Sep88–397
Sellers, S. Delighting the Heart.
    P. Raine, 617(TLS):7–13Jul89–740
Sellick, R., ed. Gwen Harwood.
    M. MacLeod, 71(ALS):May88–393
Sellstrom, A.D. Corneille, Tasso and Modern Poetics.
    W.O. Goode, 207(FR):Oct88–164
    A. Niderst, 475:Vol15No28–351
van Selm, B. Een menighte treffelijcke Boecken.
    J. Gerritsen, 354:Sep88–270
Selous, T. The Other Woman.
    D. Quinn, 617(TLS):0–8Jun89–608
Seltzer, M. Henry James and the Art of Power.*
    M. Banta, 284:Spring88–142
    M. Steele, 454:Winter89–237
Al-Selwi, I. Jemenitischer Wörter in den Werken von al-Hamdānī und Naśwän und ihre Parallelen in den semitischen Sprachen.
    A.S. Kaye, 350:Jun89–440
Selz, G. Die Bankettszene.
    D.L. Stein, 318(JAOS):Oct–Dec87–797
Sembach, K–J. Henry van de Velde.
    I.B. Whyte, 617(TLS):8–14Dec89–1358
Semsel, G.S., ed. Chinese Film.
    P. Clark, 293(JASt):Aug88–623
Sen, A. On Ethics and Economics.*
    J.L. Gorman, 518:Jul88–183
Sen, A. The Standard of Living. (G. Haworth, ed)
    R.E.G., 185:Apr89–665
    P. Weirich, 518:Jul88–180
Sen, S. The Working Women and Popular Movements in Bengal.
    R. Ghose, 302:Vol24No1–112
de Sena, J. By the Rivers of Babylon. (D. Patai, ed)
    A. Boaz, 441:24Sep89–48
Sena, J.F. The Best-Natured Man.
    C. Fox, 566:Autumn88–79
    M. Kelsall, 541(RES):Aug88–446
Sénac de Meilhan, G. Des Principes et des causes de la Révolution en France.
    J–P. Guinle, 450(NRF):Feb88–102

Sendak, M. Caldecott & Co.
    E. Blishen, 617(TLS):7–13Apr89–381
    M. Cart, 441:29Jan89–31
Sender Barayón, R. A Death in Zamora.
    W. Herrick, 441.18Jun89–29
Sendich, M. An Undergraduate Course in Transcriptional Phonetics of Russian.
    V.I. Kozyrev, 558(RLJ):Winter–Spring–Fall88–348
Seneca. Medea. Phaedra. Trojan Women. (F. Ahl, trans of all)
    J. Clack, 124:Sep–Oct88–66
    A.L. Motto & J.R. Clark, 121(CJ):Apr–May89–365
Seneca. L. Annaei Senecae, "Divi Claudii Apokolokyntōsis." (6th ed) (C.F. Russo, ed)
    P. Flobert, 555:Vol61fasc2–324
Seneca. Seneca's "Hercules Furens." (J.G. Fitch, ed)
    M. Colakis, 124:Nov–Dec88–145
    O. Zwierlein, 229:Band60Heft4–333
Seneca. Seneca's "Phaedra." (A.J. Boyle, ed & trans)
    R. Mayer, 123:Vol38No2–250
Seneca. Tragoediae. (O. Zwierlein, ed)
    R. Mayer, 313:Vol78–245
"Senefiance No. 19."
    E. Suomela–Härmä, 439(NM):1988/2–229
Senelick, L. The Age and Stage of George L. Fox, 1825–1877.
    M. Steyn, 511:Sep88–47
Senelier, J. Au pays des chimères.
    J. Bony, 535(RHL):Mar–Apr88–303
Senft, G. Kilivila.
    N. Besnier, 353:Vol26No2–305
    D.H., 355(LSoc):Dec88–619
Senn, A.E., J.C. Bowlt & D. Staskevicious. Mikalojus Konstantinas Ciurlionis.
    C.L., 90:Jun88–478
Sennett, T. Hollywood's Golden Year, 1939.
    D. Finkle, 441:10Dec89–7
Sephiha, H.V. Le judéo-espagnol.
    M. Sala, 553(RLiR):Jan–Jun88–287
Seppänen, L. Meister Eckeharts Konzeption der Sprachbedeutung.*
    F.L. Borchardt, 221(GQ):Spring88–301
Sepper, D.L. Goethe contra Newton.
    J.J. Kockelmans, 543:Jun89–853
    R. Smook, 103:Dec89–498
Šeptunov, I.M., ed. Slavjanskij i balkanskij fol'klor.
    D.E. Bynum, 574(SEEJ):Spring88–150
Serbat, G. Linguistique latine et linguistique générale.
    P. Baldi, 350:Mar89–192
Sereni, V. Tutte le poesie.
    P. Robinson, 364:Apr–May87–124
Sermain, J–P. Rhétorique et roman au dix-huitième siècle.
    P. France, 544:Autumn88–419
Sernin, A. Alain, Un sage dans la cité (1868–1951).
    J–L. Dumas, 192(EP):Jan–Mar88–133
Seroka, J. & R. Smiljković. Political Organizations in Socialist Yugoslavia.
    R. Kindersley, 575(SEER):Jan88–152
Serote, M. To Every Birth Its Blood.
    W. Finnegan, 441:7May89–38
Serpa, F. Il punto su: Virgilio.
    N. Horsfall, 123:Vol38No2–411
"Serra."
    L.E. Nesbitt, 55:Nov88–105
Serrano, C.F. – see under Foresti Serrano, C.

Service, J.S., ed. Golden Inches.
   T.B. Strong, 441:5Nov89-37
Service, R. Lenin. (Vol 1)
   H-D. Lowe, 550(RusR):Oct88-460
Sessions, W. Henry Howard, Earl of Surrey.
   W.D. McGaw, 447(N&Q):Sep88-361
Seth, V. The Golden Gate.*
   R.T. Smith, 577(SHR):Winter88-96
Settle, M.L. Charley Bland.
   D. Leavitt, 441:22Oct89-12
Severo, R. & L. Milford. The Wages of War.
   G.A. Craig, 453(NYRB):17Aug89-31
   M.S. Sherry, 441:9Apr89-12
Sewell, D.R. Mark Twain's Languages.*
   E.L. Galligan, 569(SR):Spring88-265
   S. Gillman, 26(ALR):Fall88-73
   J.D. Wilson, 27(AL):May88-298
Seyfert, M. Im Niemandsland.
   W. Riedel, 107(CRCL):Mar88-155
Seymour, J.D. China's Satellite Parties.
   B.L. McCormick, 293(JASt):May88-360
Seymour, M. A Ring of Conspirators.*
   P-L. Adams, 61:Jul89-94
   J. Bayley, 453(NYRB):7Dec89-21
   H. Bevington, 441:16Jul89-11
   442(NY):7Aug89-96
Seymour-Smith, M. Rudyard Kipling.
   D. Trotter, 617(TLS):3-9Feb89-99
Sezgin, F. Geschichte des arabischen
   Schrifttums. (Vol 8)
   E.L. Ormsby, 318(JAOS):Jan-Mar87-171
Sgard, J. L'Abbé Prévost.*
   A. Rosenberg, 627(UTQ):Winter87/88-348
Sgard, J. Les trente récits de la Journée des
   Tuiles.
   V.D.L., 605(SC):15Jul89-338
Sgard, J. - see Prévost, M.
Shabtai, Y. Past Perfect.
   L. Rapoport, 390:May88-62
Shackelford, R. - see Dallapiccola, L.
Shackleton Bailey, D.R., ed. Anthologia
   Latina. (Vol 1, fasc 1)
   J.M. Hunt, 122:Oct88-328
Shackleton Bailey, D.R. - see Cicero
Shackleton Bailey, D.R. - see Horace
Shacochis, B. The Next New World.
   R. Bausch, 441:19Feb89-10
Shadbolt, D. Bill Reid.*
   G. Moray, 627(UTQ):Fall88-208
Shadwell, T. The Libertine. (H. Pellegrin, ed)
   566:Autumn88-83
Shafer, D.M. Deadly Paradigms.
   639(VQR):Autumn88-132
Shaffer, E. Erewhons of the Eye.*
   G. Cavaliero, 324:Mar89-260
Lord Shaftesbury - see under Cooper, A.A.
Shagan, S. Pillars of Fire.
   N. Callendar, 441:22Oct89-37
Shah, R.C. Yeats and Eliot.
   P. Bonila, 295(JML):Fall87/Winter88-230
Shahar, D. Summer in the Street of the
   Prophets [and] A Voyage to Ur of the Chal-
   dees.
   J. Kaplan, 441:21May89-27
Shahîd, I. Rome and the Arabs. Byzantium
   and the Arabs in the Fourth Century.
   W.E. Kaegi, Jr., 318(JAOS):Jan-Mar87-
   177
Shahjahan Mian, M. Bangla Pandulipi Patha-
   samiksha.
   C. Salomon, 318(JAOS):Oct-Dec87-785
Shain, Y. The Frontier of Loyalty.
   K.J. Uva, 441:13Aug89-17

Shainberg, L. Memories of Amnesia.*
   442(NY):23Jan89-118
Shaked, G. The Shadows Within.
   L. Field, 395(MFS):Winter88-645
Shakespeare, L.M. Utmost Good Faith.
   N. Callendar, 441:12Feb89-20
Shakespeare, N. The Vision of Elena Silves.
   A. Feinstein, 617(TLS):27Oct-2Nov89-
   1180
Shakespeare, W. All's Well That Ends Well.*
   (R. Fraser, ed) The Merchant of Venice.
   (M.M. Mahood, ed)
   D. Mehl, 156(ShJW):Jahrbuch1988-261
Shakespeare, W. The Complete Works: Mod-
   ern-Spelling Edition.* (S. Wells & G.
   Taylor, general eds)
   B. Engler, 179(ES):Jun88-277
   R.A. Foakes, 402(MLR):Apr89-436
   E.A.J. Honigmann, 447(N&Q):Jun88-218
Shakespeare, W. The Complete Works, Origi-
   nal-Spelling Edition.* (S. Wells & G.
   Taylor, general eds)
   P. Davison, 354:Sep88-255
   E.S. Donno, 702:Vol20-317
   B. Engler, 179(ES):Jun88-277
   R.A. Foakes, 402(MLR):Apr89-436
   B. Gibbons, 541(RES):Nov88-544
   E.A.J. Honigmann, 447(N&Q):Jun88-218
Shakespeare, W. Hamlet. (G.R. Hibbard, ed)
   T.H. Howard-Hill, 541(RES):Aug88-432
   H.M. Klein, 447(N&Q):Sep88-365
   D. Mehl, 156(ShJW):Jahrbuch1988-261
Shakespeare, W. Henry IV, Part I. (D. Bev-
   ington, ed)
   M.G. Brennan, 447(N&Q):Jun88-221
   D. Mehl, 156(ShJW):Jahrbuch1988-261
   J. Rees, 541(RES):Aug88-431
Shakespeare, W. Julius Caesar/Julius Cäsar.
   (T. Pughe, ed)
   H.R. Mickisch, 72:Band225Heft1-163
Shakespeare, W. King Lear.* (J.S. Bratton,
   ed)
   J. Yettram, 157:No166-49
Shakespeare, W. Romeo and Juliet. (W.T.
   Betken, ed)
   K. Bartenschlager, 156(ShJW):
   Jahrbuch1988-305
Shakespeare, W. Shakespeare's Lost Play
   "Edmund Ironside." (E. Sams, ed)
   D.W. Foster, 570(SQ):Spring88-118
   K. Tetzeli von Rosador, 156(ShJW):
   Jahrbuch1988-305
Shakespeare, W. The Tempest. (S. Orgel, ed)
   M. Butler, 447(N&Q):Jun88-222
   D. Mehl, 156(ShJW):Jahrbuch1988-261
Shakespeare, W. Troilus and Cressida/Troilus
   und Cressida. (W. Brönnimann-Egger, ed)
   The Taming of the Shrew/Der Widerspens-
   tigen Zähmung. (B. Rojahn-Deyk, ed)
   Hamlet. (H.M. Klein, ed)
   W.G. Müller, 156(ShJW):Jahrbuch1988-
   273
Shakespeare, W. Twelfth Night, or What You
   Will.* (E.S. Donno, ed)
   R.G. Barlow, 615(TJ):Mar88-143
   D. Mehl, 156(ShJW):Jahrbuch1988-261
Shakespeare, W. The Winter's Tale/Das Win-
   termärchen. (I. Boltz, ed)
   W.G. Müller, 156(ShJW):Jahrbuch1988-
   273
   M. Steppat, 72:Band225Heft1-168

Shakespeare, W. The Winter's Tale/Das Win-
termärchen. (H. Geisen, ed & trans)
   M. Steppat, 72:Band225Heft1–168
"Shakespeare Survey." (Vol 36) (S. Wells, ed)
   R. von Ledebur, 72:Band225Heft1–174
"Shakespeare Survey." (Vol 39) (S. Wells, ed)
   G. Giesekam, 610:Summer88–173
   M. Grivelet, 189(EA):Oct–Dec88–483
   R.S. White, 541(RES):Nov88–549
"Shakespeare Survey." (Vol 41) (S. Wells, ed)
   R. Hapgood, 617(TLS):25–31Aug89–927
Shalev, C. Birth Power.
   M.E. Gale, 441:17Dec89–12
Shalom, A. The Body/Mind Conceptual
Framework and the Problem of Personal
Identity.*
   B. Morito, 543:Jun89–797
Shames, L. The Hunger for More.
   D. Cole, 441:25Jun89–25
Shanin, T. The Roots of Otherness.
   J. Bushnell, 550(RusR):Jan88–75
Shanker, S.G., ed. Gödel's Theorem in Focus.
   J.F. Post, 103:Jul89–287
Shanker, S.G., ed. Philosophy in Britain
Today.*
   I.G., 185:Oct88–196
Shanker, S.G. Wittgenstein and the Turning-
Point in the Philosophy of Mathematics.
   S. Mulhall, 518:Jan88–32
Shann, P. Untersuchungen zur strukturellen
Semantik.*
   H. Geckeler, 547(RF):Band99Heft4–409
Shannon, E. Desperadoes.*
   M. Massing, 453(NYRB):30Mar89–22
Shannon, P. Broken Promises.
   J.W. Tollefson, 608:Dec89–679
Shannon, T.F. Aspects of Complementation
and Control in Modern German.
   R.G. Hoeing, 350:Dec89–841
Shanor, R.R. The City That Never Was.
   R. Campbell, 441:8Jan89–11
Shanzer, D. A Philosophical and Literary
Commentary on Martianus Capella's "De
nuptiis Philologiae et Mercurii," Book 1.
   J.A. Willis, 229:Band60Heft5–451
Shapcott, J. Electroplating the Baby.
   M. Wormald, 617(TLS):9–15Jun89–641
Shapcott, T. Limestone and Lemon Wine.*
   D. Durrant, 364:Mar88–109
Shapere, D. Reason and the Search for Know-
ledge.
   M.A. Finocchiaro, 488:Mar88–135
Shapin, S. & S. Schaffer. Leviathan and the
Air-Pump.*
   R.C. Jennings, 84:Sep88–403
   A.P. Martinich, 319:Apr89–308
Shapiro, A.R. Unlikely Heroines.
   B. Draine, 395(MFS):Summer88–327
   J.W. Warren, 357:Fall88–66
Shapiro, K. New and Selected Poems.
   D. Sampson, 249(HudR):Summer88–384
Shapiro, L. A Book of Days in American His-
tory.
   639(VQR):Winter88–14
Shapiro, M. Japan.
   B. Slavin, 441:27Aug89–17
Shapiro, M.E. & P.H. Hassrick, eds. Frederic
Remington.
   E. Johns, 127:Fall88–241
Sharansky, N. Fear No Evil.*
   J.M. Cameron, 453(NYRB):1Jun89–33
Sharlitt, J.H. Fatal Error.
   L. Greenhouse, 441:6Aug89–20

Sharma, A., ed. Women in World Religions.
   L. Harlan, 293(JASt):May88–330
   W.A. Tomm, 485(PE&W):Oct88–452
Sharma, L.R. In Defence of J. Middleton
Murry.
   S. Cassavant, 177(ELT):Vol31No1–103
Sharma, P. Days of the Turban.
   J. Mellors, 364:Feb87–103
Sharon, A., with D. Chanoff. Warrior.
   L. Anderson, 441:3Sep89–3
Sharp, C. The Crystal Spring.* (M. Karpeles,
ed)
   G. Boyes, 203:Vol99No1–129
Sharp, P. The Woman Who Was Not All There.*
   D. Blackwell, 441:15Jan89–22
Sharpe, D. Rochdale.
   P. Colgan, 529(QQ):Autumn88–715
Sharpe, J.A. Crime and Law in English Satir-
ical Prints 1600–1832.
   J.E. Hill, 173(ECS):Summer88–530
Sharpe, K. Criticism and Compliment.*
   R.A. Anselment, 481(PQ):Fall88–524
   T. Healy, 175:Summer88–155
   W.H. Herendeen, 568(SCN):Winter88–70
   A.G.R. Smith, 366:Autumn88–238
Sharpe, K. Politics and Ideas in Early Stuart
England.
   R. Lockyer, 617(TLS):29Dec89/4Jan90–
1434
Sharpe, K. & S.N. Zwicker, eds. Politics of
Discourse.*
   A.C. Labriola, 568(SCN):Winter88–69
Sharpe, T. Porterhouse Blue.
   442(NY):27Mar89–115
Sharples, R.W. Alexander of Aphrodisias on
Fate.
   J. Mansfeld, 394:Vol41fasc3/4–416
Sharples, R.W. – see Plato
Sharrow, G. – see Borie, B. 4th
Shatto, S. – see Tennyson, A.
Shattock, J., ed. Dickens and Other Victo-
rians.
   P. Rogers, 617(TLS):7–13Apr89–360
Shattock, J. Politics and Reviewers.
   J.D. McClure, 617(TLS):29Dec89/4Jan90–
1436
Shavit, Z. Poetics of Children's Literature.*
   494:Vol8No2–461
Shaw, B.A. & N. Vera-Godwin, eds. Critical
Perspectives on Gabriel García Márquez.*
   J. Tittler, 140(CH):Vol10–139
Shaw, C.B. – see under Byam Shaw, C.
Shaw, D. Molière: "Les Précieuses ridicules."
   P. Tomlinson, 402(MLR):Jan89–164
Shaw, G.B. Agitations.* (D.H. Laurence & J.
Rambeau, eds)
   J–C. Almaric, 189(EA):Oct–Dec88–490
Shaw, G.B. Dear Mr. Shaw.* (V. Elliot, ed)
   P. Craig, 617(TLS):7–13Apr89–362
Shaw, G.B. The Diaries 1885–1897.* (S.
Weintraub, ed)
   F.D. Crawford, 572:Vol8–139
   B.F. Dukore, 615(TJ):Dec87–539
   A.E.W. Maurer, 536(Rev):Vol10–219
   M. Meisel, 177(ELT):Vol31No2–215
   B. Richardson, 477(PLL):Winter88–98
Shaw, G.B. Bernard Shaw: Collected Letters.*
(Vol 4) (D.H. Laurence, ed)
   J. Updike, 442(NY):2Jan89–65
Shaw, G.B. Shaw on Dickens.* (D.H. Laurence
& M. Quinn, eds)
   B.B. Watson, 572:Vol8–143

Shaw, G.B. Bernard Shaw's Letters to Sieg-
fried Trebitsch.* (S.A. Weiss, ed)
   B.F. Dukore, 615(TJ):Dec87-540
   J.L. Wisenthal, 572:Vol8-149
Shaw, G.B. & A. Douglas. Bernard Shaw and
Alfred Douglas: A Correspondence. (M.
Hyde, ed)
   617(TLS):1-7Dec89-1344
Shaw, J.C. Introducing Thai Ceramics, Also
Burmese and Khmer.
   N.V. Robinson, 60:Nov-Dec88-144
Shaw, L.R., N.R. Cirillo & M.S. Miller, eds.
Wagner in Retrospect.
   R. Furness, 402(MLR):Oct89-1034
   B. Millington, 415:Feb88-87
Shaw, R. The Arts and the People.
   R. Fuller, 364:Feb87-111
Shaw, R.B. The Wonder of Seeing Double.
   A. Corn, 491:Jan89-235
Shaw, W.D. The Lucid Veil.*
   C.T. Christ, 445(NCF):Jun88-111
   D.S. Hair, 627(UTQ):Winter87/88-350
   D.G. Riede, 301(JEGP):Jul88-452
Shaw, Y-M., ed. Chinese Modernization.
   K.L. Macpherson, 302:Vol24No1-114
"Shaw: The Annual of Bernard Shaw
Studies."* (Vol 6) (S. Weintraub, ed)
   J.J. Conlon, 177(ELT):Vol31No1-120
Shawcross, W. Kowtow!
   B. Winterton, 617(TLS):22-28Dec89-1406
Shawcross, W. The Shah's Last Ride.*
   M. Ruthven, 617(TLS):20-26Jan89-53
Shcheglov, Y. & A. Zholkovsky. Poetics of
Expressiveness.
   C. Lyas, 307:Nov88-239
Shcherbak, I. Chernobyl.
   S. Thomas, 617(TLS):20-26Oct89-1159
Shead, R. Constant Lambert. (2nd ed)
   S. Banfield, 415:Mar88-135
Sheaf, C. & R. Kilburn. The Hatcher Porcelain
Cargoes.
   M. Butler, 463:Autumn88-220
Shechner, M. After the Revolution.
   A. Gordon, 536(Rev):Vol10-251
   M. Greenstein, 106:Fall88-333
   E.M. Kauvar, 659(ConL):Fall89-452
   S. Pinsker, 560:Fall88-239
   A. Wald, 385(MQR):Winter89-130
Shechner, M. - see Rosenfeld, I.
Sheed, W. The Boys of Winter.
   G. Garrett, 569(SR):Summer88-516
   639(VQR):Winter88-19
Sheehan, E.R.F. Agony in the Garden.
   J. Chace, 453(NYRB):17Aug89-46
Sheehan, H. Irish Television Drama.
   C. Murray, 272(IUR):Spring88-161
Sheehan, N. A Bright Shining Lie.*
   M. Woollacott, 617(TLS):28Apr-4May89-
   446
Sheeran, J.G. & J.P. McCarthy. Exploring
French.
   R.A. Hartzell, 207(FR):Feb89-559
Sheeran, J.G. & J.P. McCarthy. Exploring
German.
   J.S. Biemel, 399(MLJ):Winter88-478
Sheeran, J.G. & J.P. McCarthy. Exploring
Spanish.
   V.E. Sherer, 399(MLJ):Winter88-492
Sheingorn, P. The Easter Sepulchre in En-
gland.
   V. Sekules, 90:Oct88-774

Shelden, M. Friends of Promise.
   I. Hamilton, 617(TLS):10-16Feb89-131
   L. Klepp, 441:10Sep89-27
   442(NY):20Nov89-155
Sheldon, S. The Sands of Time.
   D. Murray, 441:8Jan89-22
Shelley, M. The Journals of Mary Shelley
1814-1844. (P.R. Feldman & D. Scott-Kil-
vert, eds)
   B.T. Bennett, 340(KSJ):Vol37-197
   N. Crook, 339:Autumn88-77
   A. Leighton, 541(RES):Nov88-566
   A.K. Mellor, 445(NCF):Mar89-535
   A. Morvan, 189(EA):Oct-Dec88-433
   D. Womersley, 447(N&Q):Sep88-385
Shelley, M.W. The Letters of Mary Wollstone-
craft Shelley.* (Vol 3) (B.T. Bennett, ed)
   A.K. Mellor, 445(NCF):Mar89-535
Shelley, M.W. & P.B. Peter Bell the Third
[and] The Triumph of Life. (D.H. Reiman,
ed)
   J.A. Butler, 340(KSJ):Vol37-196
Shelnutt, E. The Musician.
   M. Greene, 271:Spring-Summer88-174
Shelton, C.J. The Mills of Manayunk.
   S. Rosswurm, 656(WMQ):Jul88-621
Shelton, J. The Coming Soviet Crash.
   N. Eberstadt, 441:5Feb89-9
   O. Figes, 617(TLS):4-10Aug89-841
Shelton, R. The Other Side of the Story.
   T. Hansen, 271:Winter88-177
Shen Fu, G.D. Lowry & A. Yonemura. From
Concept to Context.
   R. Hillenbrand, 463:Summer87-190
Shenfield, S. The Nuclear Predicament.
   J.S. Hellman, 575(SEER):Oct88-665
Shengold, L. Soul Murder.
   F.R. Rodman, 441:17Dec89-14
Shennan, J.H. Liberty and Order in Early
Modern Europe.
   W. Doyle, 83:Spring88-80
Shennan, S.J., ed. Archaeological Approaches
to Cultural Identity.
   P.G. Bahn, 617(TLS):11-17Aug89-881
Shepard, C.E. Forgiven.
   P. Sims, 441:24Sep89-7
   G. Wills, 453(NYRB):21Dec89-20
Shepard, L. The Jaguar Hunter.
   C. Greenland, 617(TLS):31Mar-6Apr89-
   343
Shepherd, N. The Quarry Wood.
   A. Smith, 571(ScLJ):Spring88-52
Shepherd, S. Marlowe and the Politics of
Elizabethan Theatre.*
   D. Feldmann, 156(ShJW):Jahrbuch1988-
   287
   R. Wilson, 366:Autumn88-210
Sheppard, A. Aesthetics.*
   S.L. Feagin, 103:Nov88-444
   G. Graham, 518:Jul88-186
Sher, A. Middlepost.*
   L. Freed, 441:21May89-20
Sher, G. Desert.
   B. Gert, 185:Jan89-426
Sherbo, A. The Birth of Shakespeare
Studies.*
   A.W. Bellringer, 179(ES):Aug88-363
   J.D. Fleeman, 405(MP):Aug88-90
   K. Walker, 173(ECS):Winter88/89-286
Shergold, N.D. & J.E. Varey, with C. Davis.
Teatros y comedias en Madrid: 1699-1719.
   J.M. Ruano de la Haza, 402(MLR):Jan89-
   210

Sheridan, F. Memoirs of Miss Sidney Bidulf.
42(AR):Spring88-276
Sheringham, M. Beckett: "Molloy."*
E. Jacquart, 535(RHL):Jan-Feb88-166
Sherk, R.K. Rome and the Greek East to the
Death of Augustus.
M.H. Crawford, 123:Vol38No2-435
A.J.L. van Hooff, 394:Vol41fasc3/4-452
Sherlock, J. State of Emergency.
R.C. Skidmore, 441:12Mar89-22
Sherry, M.S. The Rise of American Air
Power.*
E.J. Sundquist, 639(VQR):Summer88-541
Sherry, N. The Life of Graham Greene. (Vol
1)
R. Coles, 441:18Jun89-1
S. Hynes, 617(TLS):26May-1Jun89-575
Sherry, V. The Uncommon Tongue.*
N. Smith, 184(EIC):Apr88-167
Sherwin-White, A.N. Roman Foreign Policy in
the East, 168 B.C. to A.D. 1.*
S. Podes, 229:Band60Heft1-36
Sherwood, J. A Bouquet of Thorns.
T.J. Binyon, 617(TLS):18-24Aug89-902
Sherwood, J. Menacing Groves.*
M. Stasio, 441:5Feb89-26
Sherwood, J.E. Nebraska Football.
R.B. Heilman, 31(ASch):Spring88-308
Sherzer, D. Representation in Contemporary
French Fiction.*
M. Praeger, 494:Vol8No3/4-704
E. Smyth, 535(RHL):Nov-Dec88-1174
Sherzer, J. & G. Urban, eds. Native South
American Discourse.
N. Besnier, 353:Vol26No3-510
S. Niles, 292(JAF):Jan-Mar88-80
Sherzer, J. & A.C. Woodbury. Native American
Discourse.
E.B. Basso, 350:Jun89-381
E. Désveaux, 98:Dec88-989
K. Kroeber, 292(JAF):Jul-Sep88-375
Shevoroshkin, V.V. & T.L. Markey, eds &
trans. Typology, Relationships, and Time.*
R. Anttila & S. Embleton, 320(CJL):
Mar88-79
Shibamoto, J.S. Japanese Women's Language.
P. Downing, 355(LSoc):Jun88-278
B. Saint-Jacques, 320(CJL):Jun88-201
Shields, C. Swann.*
P-L. Adams, 61:Aug89-92
M. Helwig, 99:Feb/Mar88-48
R.E. Jones, 198:Autumn88-114
J. Rubins, 441:6Aug89-11
Shields, C. Various Miracles.
J. Rubins, 441:6Aug89-11
Shields, D. Dead Languages.
R. Towers, 453(NYRB):20Jul89-30
E. Toynton, 441:18Jun89-22
442(NY):3Jul89-95
Shields, J.C. - see Wheatley, P.
Shigemastu, S., ed & trans. A Zen Harvest.
J. Kirkup, 617(TLS):1-7Dec89-1340
Shillingsburg, P.L. Scholarly Editing in the
Computer Age.
T.H. Howard-Hill, 40(AEB):Vol2No2-73
T.L. Warren, 365:Spring/Summer87-155
Shimazaki, T. - see under Tôson Shimazaki
Shinn, T.J. Radiant Daughters.*
E.C.R., 295(JML):Fall87/Winter88-266
Shinn, T.J. Worlds Within Women.*
M. Barr, 561(SFS):Nov87-405
N. Easterbrook, 295(JML):Fall87/
Winter88-266

Shinran. The True Teaching, Practice and
Realization of the Pure Land Way. (Vol 3)
(Y. Ueda, general ed)
M.L. Rogers, 407(MN):Spring88-120
Shipman, H.L. Humans in Space.
W.G. Kolata, 441:9Apr89-32
Shipman, N. The Silent Screen and My Talk-
ing Heart.
S. Kahin, 649(WAL):May88-66
Shîrâzî, M.S. Le Livre des pénétrations méta-
physiques. (H. Corbin, ed & trans)
J. Brun, 192(EP):Jul-Sep88-433
Shirley, J. The Lady of Pleasure.* (R. Hue-
bert, ed) The Cardinal.* (E.M. Yearling,
ed)
B. Gibbons, 541(RES):Nov88-550
H. Love, 402(MLR):Oct89-925
Shirley, R.W. Printed Maps of the British
Isles 1650-1750.
S. Bendall, 617(TLS):21-27Apr89-426
Shive, D.M. Naming Achilles.
G. Nagy, 487:Winter88-364
Shively, C., ed. Drum Beats.
E. Folsom, 646(WWR):Spring89-200
Shklar, J. Montesquieu.*
C. Brown, 518:Jul88-131
Shloss, C. In Visible Light.*
E-M.K., 102(CanL):Winter87-290
Shmidt, S.O. & S.E. Kniaz'kov. Dokumenty
deloproizvodstva pravitel'stvennykh uchr-
ezhdenii Rossii XVI-XVII vv. Uchebnoe
posobie.
P.B. Brown, 550(RusR):Jul88-328
Shnayerson, M. Irwin Shaw.
D. Cole, 441:20Aug89-21
Shoemaker, S. Identity, Cause, and Mind.
J.J. Altham, 393(Mind):Apr88-285
C. McGinn, 311(JP):Apr87-227
"Shona Sculpture of Zimbabwe."
2(AfrA):Nov87-83
Shonfield, Z. The Precariously Privileged.*
G.K. Behlmer, 637(VS):Spring89-421
Shopen, T., ed. Language Typology and Syn-
tactic Description.
D.H., 355(LSoc):Mar88-154
A.S. Kaye & F. Muller-Gotama, 320(CJL):
Sep88-267
C. Lehmann, 297(JL):Mar88-175
Shor, I., ed. Freire for the Classroom.
A.E. Berthoff, 126(CCC):Oct88-359
Shore, D.R. Spenser and the Poetics of Pasto-
ral.*
S. Chaudhuri, 447(N&Q):Dec88-525
J. Dundas, 402(MLR):Jan89-119
Shore, E. Talkin' Socialism.
G. De Gruson, 389(MQ):Winter89-259
Shore, H. Arts Administration and Manage-
ment.
K. Neely, 615(TJ):Dec88-579
Shore, J. The Minute Hand.*
P. Filkins, 363(LitR):Winter89-241
Shore, L. Southern Capitalists.*
J.P. Kaetz, 577(SHR):Spring88-180
Shore, M. Music Video.
R.S. Denisoff, 498:Winter88-91
Shore, M. The Science of Social Redemption.
N.J. Christie, 529(QQ):Winter88-954
Shore, M.M.J. The Tempest.
G. Noonan, 102(CanL):Summer88-135
529(QQ):Spring88-224
Shore, P. Acts of Faith.
G. Gessert, 448:Vol26No1-74

339

Shorley, C. Queneau's Fiction.*
 E. Smyth, 535(RHL):Mar—Apr88—341
Short, A. The Origins of the Vietnam War.
 R. Smith, 617(TLS):15—21Dec89—1381
Short, E. Whip to Wilson.
 J. Turner, 617(TLS):3—9Mar89—215
Short, I. — see de Thaon, P.
Short, M. Inside the Brotherhood.
 A. Rusbridger, 617(TLS):21—27Apr89—421
"A Short—Title Catalogue of Books Printed in
 England, Scotland, and Ireland and of En-
 glish Books Printed Abroad 1475—1640."*
 (2nd ed) (Vol 1) (W.A. Jackson, F.S. Fer-
 guson & K.F. Pantzer, comps)
 D. Pearson, 402(MLR):Oct89—919
 G. Williams, 541(RES):Feb88—148
"Short—Title Catalogue of Books Printed in
 Italy and of Italian Books Printed in Other
 Countries from 1465 to 1600 Now in the
 British Library." (Supplement)
 L. Baldacchini, 354:Mar88—61
Shoumatoff, A. African Madness.
 L. Green, 441:22Jan89—23
Showalter, E. Exiles and Strangers.
 J. Sarocchi, 535(RHL):Mar—Apr88—336
Showalter, E., ed. The New Feminist Criti-
 cism.*
 J.O. Newman, 221(GQ):Winter87—160
Showalter, E. — see Alcott, L.M.
Shrake, E. Blessed McGill.
 J.T. Flanagan, 649(WAL):Nov88—254
Shreve, A. Eden Close.
 C. Banks, 441:3Sep89—6
Shreve, A. Women Together, Women Alone.
 A.K. Shulman, 441:13Aug89—10
Shreve, S.R. A Country of Strangers.
 J. Parini, 617(TLS):24—30Nov89—1313
 M. Watkins, 441:5Mar89—24
Shroff, H.J. The Eighteenth—Century Novel.*
 C. Lamont, 83:Spring88—99
Shtromas, A. & M.A. Kaplan, eds. The Soviet
 Union and the Challenge of the Future.
 (Vol 1)
 O. Figes, 617(TLS):4—10Aug89—841
Shubin, S. Never Quite Dead.
 J.F. Clarity, 441:20Aug89—21
Shue, V. The Reach of the State.
 J. Mirsky, 617(TLS):17—23Mar89—270
Shuichi, K. — see under Katō Shuichi
Shūji Takashina & J.T. Rimer, with G.D. Bolas.
 Paris in Japan.
 F. Baekeland, 407(MN):Autumn88—386
Shukla, H.L. Language, Ethnicity and His-
 tory.
 M. Gatzlaff, 682(ZPSK):Band41Heft6—832
Shukman, H., ed. The Blackwell Encyclopedia
 of the Russian Revolution.
 R. Pipes, 617(TLS):21—27Apr89—428
Shull, M.S. & D.E. Wilt. Doing Their Bit.
 P. Kemp, 707:Summer88—217
Shulman, D.D. The King and the Clown in
 South Indian Myth and Poetry.
 S.S. Bean, 318(JAOS):Jul—Sep87—516
 W.J. Jackson, 314:Winter—Spring88—230
Shulman, F.J. Burma.
 J. Badgley, 293(JASt):Feb88—201
Shulman, R. Social Criticism and Nineteenth-
 Century American Fictions.
 R.E. Burkholder, 587(SAF):Autumn88—246
 S. Pinsker, 27(AL):Oct88—475
 M.W. Thomas, 646(WWR):Fall88—97
Shumaker, P. Esperanza's Hair.
 R. Pybus, 565:Summer88—72

Shumway, N. & D. Forbes. Español en Españ-
 ol. (2nd ed)
 R.H. Gilmore, 399(MLJ):Winter88—492
Shusterman, R., ed. Analytic Aesthetics.
 S. Gardner, 617(TLS):23—29Jun89—698
Shusterman, R. T.S. Eliot and the Philosophy
 of Criticism.*
 R. Eldridge, 290(JAAC):Summer88—529
 R. Seamon, 103:Feb89—70
 639(VQR):Autumn88—122
Shuttle, P. Adventures with My Horse.
 C. Wills, 617(TLS):17—23Feb89—169
Shuttle, P. The Lion from Rio.*
 J. Saunders, 565:Autumn88—72
Siatkowski, J., ed. Gesta Romanorum Linguae
 polonicae (1543), cum fontibus latinis et
 bohemicis.
 R.B. Pynsent, 575(SEER):Jan88—160
Sibley, C. Turned Funny.
 K. Ferguson, 441:22Jan89—23
Sicca, C.M., with C. Harpum & E. Powell.
 Committed to Classicism.*
 R.W. Liscombe, 576:Sep88—309
 R. O'Donnell, 90:Aug88—638
Sichel, B.A. Moral Education.
 R.K. Fullinwider, 185:Jul89—954
Sicher, E. Style and Structure in the Prose of
 Isaac Babel.*
 P.R. Hart, 395(MFS):Summer88—307
Sichtermann, B. Femininity.
 C. Poore, 221(GQ):Summer88—489
Sicker, M. The Judaic State.
 M.D. Yaffe, 103:Feb89—72
Sid—Ahmad, R. Ikhtiraq al—Aql al—Misri.
 N. Rejwan, 390:Feb/Mar88—52
Siddons, A.R. Peachtree Road.
 S. Ferguson, 441:1Jan89—14
Sidebotham, S.E. Roman Economic Policy in
 the Erythra Thalassa 30 B.C.—A.D. 217.
 G.W. Bowersock, 123:Vol38No1—101
 T.W. Gallant, 124:Mar—Apr89—325
Sidenbladh, C. Ty så roar mig at måla.
 N. Kent, 562(Scan):Nov88—184
 H. Lund, 172(Edda):1988/2—183
 A. Melberg, 172(Edda):1988/2—180
Sidhwa, B. Ice—Candy—Man.*
 J. Mellors, 364:Mar88—102
Sidney, P. Selected Writings. (R. Dutton, ed)
 M.G. Brennan, 447(N&Q):Sep88—363
Sidwell, K. — see "Lucian"
Siebenmann, G. & J.M. López, eds. Spanische
 Lyrik des 20. Jahrhunderts.*
 H. Merkl, 72:Band225Heft1—223
Sieber, R., D. Newton & M.D. Coe. African,
 Pacific, and Pre—Columbian Art in the
 Indiana University Art Museum.
 D. Jenkins, 2(AfrA):Nov87—74
Sieber, R. & R.A. Walker. African Art in the
 Cycle of Life.
 S.P. Blier, 2(AfrA):May88—21
Siebers, T. The Ethics of Criticism.*
 42(AR):Summer88—397
Siebers, T. The Romantic Fantastic.
 D.V. Traas, 188(ECr):Fall88—89
Siebert, W. Max Rychner.
 J. Ricker—Aberhalden, 133:Band21
 Heft4—370
Siegel, H. — see Mukařovský, J.
Siegel, H. — see Schenker, H.
Siegel, P.N. Shakespeare's English and Roman
 History Plays.
 S.K. Fischer, 570(SQ):Autumn88—368

Simmons, J.C. Passionate Pilgrims.
  M. Brose, 177(ELT):Vol31No3-339
Simmons, R.C. & P.D.G. Thomas, eds. Proceedings and Debates of the British Parliaments Respecting North America, 1754-1783. (Vols 3 & 4)
  B.S. Schlenther, 83:Autumn88-206
Simmons, W.S. Spirit of the New England Tribes.*
  C.F. Feest, 196:Band29Heft1/2-234
Simms, C. Eyes Own Ideas.
  L. Sail, 565:Spring88-73
Simms, K. From Kings to Warlords.
  B. Ó Cuív, 112:Vol20-221
Simo, M.L. Loudon and the Landscape.
  J. Summerson, 617(TLS):3-9Feb89-106
Simocatta, T. - see under Theophylactus Simocatta
Simon, B. Bending the Rules.
  S.J. Prais, 617(TLS):17-23Feb89-175
Simon, C. The Georgics.
  J. Sturrock, 441:1Oct89-37
  A. Tahourdin, 617(TLS):17-23Nov89-1272
Simon, C. L'Invitation.*
  R. Jacquelin, 450(NRF):May88-98
Simon, D., ed. Fontes Minores VII.
  W. Selb, 229:Band60Heft2-175
Simon, E. Augustus.
  J. Carter, 313:Vol78-226
  P. Gros, 229:Band60Heft1-76
Simon, J. Sheep from the Goats.
  A. Barnet, 441:19Mar89-23
Simon, J.F. The Antagonists.
  B. Schwartz, 441:15Oct89-18
Simon, K. A Renaissance Tapestry.*
  639(VQR):Summer88-102
Simon, P. Winners and Losers.
  H. Goodman, 441:5Mar89-23
Simon, R.K. The Labyrinth of the Comic.*
  P.M. Briggs, 594:Spring88-116
  M. Sokolyansky, 402(MLR):Jul89-687
  R.M. Torrance, 223:Summer88-240
Simon, Y. The Road to Vichy: 1918-1938.
  E. Papa, 543:Dec88-410
Simon, Y.R. The Definition of Moral Virtue.* (V. Kuic, ed)
  P. Redpath, 438:Autumn88-483
Simon of Faversham. Quaestiones super Libro Elenchorum. (S. Ebbesen, ed)
  W. Wehrle, 606:Dec88-403
Simonis, W. Ursprung und Geschichte der Kunst.
  H-J. Werner, 489(PJGG):Band95Heft1-203
Simons, J. Fanny Burney.*
  C.A. Howells, 83:Spring88-97
Simons, J. Women Writers.
  L. Speirs, 179(ES):Oct88-454
Simons, P. Parts.
  H.W. Noonan, 393(Mind):Oct88-638
Simonson, H.P. Prairies Within.
  P.A. Greasley, 395(MFS):Summer88-237
  A.C. Huseboe, 649(WAL):Aug88-155
  S. Øksenholt, 563(SS):Autumn88-521
Simonson, R. & S. Walker, eds. The Graywolf Annual Five.
  D. Lazere, 441:17Dec89-22
Simonton, D.K. Scientific Genius.
  B. Kevles, 617(TLS):16-22Jun89-662
"Simpliciana." (Vol 8)
  H. Wagener, 133:Band21Heft2/3-205

"Simposio Virgiliano Commemorativo del Bimilenario de la muerte de Virgilio."
  J. den Boeft, 394:Vol41fasc1/2-198
Simpson, B.J. City Centre Planning and Public Transport.
  P. Hall, 324:May89-380
Simpson, C. Artful Partners.* (British title: The Partnership.)
  W.L. Vance, 432(NEQ):Dec88-575
Simpson, D. Dead By Morning.
  T.J. Binyon, 617(TLS):22-28Sep89-1022
  N. Wartik, 441:15Oct89-50
Simpson, D. The Politics of American English, 1776-1850.*
  B. Cottle, 541(RES):Feb88-93
  V. McDavid, 405(MP):Nov88-212
Simpson, D. Suspicious Death.*
  M. Stasio, 441:1Jan89-23
Simpson, D. Wordsworth's Historical Imagination.*
  A. Liu, 661(WC):Autumn88-172
Simpson, E., ed. Anti-Foundationalism and Practical Reasoning.*
  K.B., 185:Jul89-970
Simpson, E. Orphans.
  T.M. Robinson, 364:Jun88-108
Simpson, J.A. & E.S.C. Weiner - see "The Oxford English Dictionary"
Simpson, K. The Protean Scot.
  J.D. McClure, 617(TLS):26May-1Jun89-579
Simpson, L. Collected Poems.*
  W. Scammell, 617(TLS):5-11May89-495
Simpson, L. Selected Prose.
  A. Stevenson, 441:7May89-28
Simpson, L.P., J. Olney & J. Gulledge, eds. "The Southern Review" and Modern Literature, 1935-1985.
  639(VQR):Autumn88-120
Simpson, M.A. Dying, Death and Grief.
  87(BB):Dec88-280
Simpson, M.S. L'art islamique, Asie.
  R. Hillenbrand, 463:Summer87-190
Simpson, M.S. The Russian Gothic Novel and its British Antecedents.*
  R.F. Miller, 550(RusR):Apr88-223
Simpson, P. Goodness and Nature.*
  M. Slote, 543:Mar89-640
Simpson, R.A. Words for a Journey.*
  J. Forth, 364:Apr-May87-128
Simpson-Cooke, J. Future Rivers.
  L.M. York, 628(UWR):Vol21No2-90
Sin, A.S. - see under Szaszkóné Sin, A.
Sinari, R.A. The Structure of Indian Thought.
  E. Harzer, 318(JAOS):Oct-Dec87-787
Sinclair, A. John Ford.
  J.G. Dunne, 453(NYRB):18May89-28
Sinclair, A. King Ludd.*
  J. Mellors, 364:Oct/Nov88-110
Sinclair, A. The Red and the Blue.
  639(VQR):Spring88-60
Sinclair, A., ed. The War Decade.
  H. Carpenter, 617(TLS):10-16Nov89-1231
Sinclair, A. War Like a Wasp.
  H. Carpenter, 617(TLS):10-16Nov89-1231
Sinclair, C. Cosmetic Effects.
  B. Cheyette, 617(TLS):22-28Sep89-1022
Sinclair, I. Flesh Eggs & Scalp Metal.
  G. Maxwell, 617(TLS):4-10Aug89-850
Sinclair, J. - see "Collins COBUILD English Language Dictionary"

Sinclair, K.V. Prières en ancien français.
    A.J. Holden, 402(MLR):Oct89-974
Sinclair, R.K. Democracy and Participation in
    Athens.
    P. Cartledge, 617(TLS):6-12Jan89-19
Sinclair-Stevenson, C. When in France.
    639(VQR):Spring88-66
Sinfield, A. Alfred Tennyson.*
    S. Shatto, 447(N&Q):Mar88-108
Singer, B.D. Advertising and Society.
    T. McCormack, 529(QQ):Summer88-504
Singer, D. Is Socialism Doomed?
    P. McCarthy, 617(TLS):24Feb-2Mar89-
    184
Singer, I. The Nature of Love. (Vol 1)
    C.C. Park, 249(HudR):Winter89-716
Singer, I. The Nature of Love.* (Vol 2)
    C.C. Park, 249(HudR):Winter89-716
    R.C. Solomon, 449:Sep88-467
Singer, I. The Nature of Love.* (Vol 3)
    C.C. Park, 249(HudR):Winter89-715
    C.W., 185:Jan89-470
Singer, I.B. The King of the Fields.*
    S.S. Prawer, 617(TLS):1-7Sep89-952
Singer, I.B. Love and Exile.
    S.P., 295(JML):Fall87/Winter88-382
Singer, M.G., ed. American Philosophy.*
    P. Engel, 542:Apr-Jun88-226
    J.J. Stuhr, 619:Spring88-279
Singerman, A.J. L'Abbé Prévost.
    R. Ellrich, 210(FrF):Jan88-115
    J.A. Fleming, 166:Jan89-153
    J.P. Gilroy, 207(FR):Apr89-890
Singh, A.K.J. Himalayan Triangle.
    J. Snelling, 617(TLS):12-18May89-522
Singh, G. Language, Race and Education.
    G. James, 324:Apr89-316
Singh, G. - see Leavis, F.R.
Singh, G. - see Leavis, Q.D.
Singh, K., ed. The Writer's Sense of the Past.
    D. Haskell, 581:Sep88-347
Singh, R. Jaishankar Prasad.
    K. Hansen, 314:Winter-Spring88-246
Singleton, F. The Economy of Finland in the
    Twentieth Century.
    D. Kirby, 575(SEER):Jan88-163
Sinos, S. Die Klosterkirche der Kosmosoteira
    in Bera (Vira).
    R. Ousterhout, 589:Jan88-229
Sinyard, N. Filming Literature.
    J.M., 295(JML):Fall87/Winter88-283
Sinyavsky, A. - see under Tertz, A.
Sircello, G. Love and Beauty.
    J.E. Bachrach, 103:Apr89-169
Siriwardena, R., ed. Equality and the Reli-
    gious Traditions of Asia.
    J.I. Cabezon, 293(JASt):May88-331
Sirois, A. & Y. Francoli - see Grignon, C-H.
Siskin, C. The Historicity of Romantic Dis-
    course.
    D.H. Bialostosky, 661(WC):Autumn88-194
Sisson, C.H. God Bless Karl Marx!*
    J.F. Cotter, 249(HudR):Spring88-231
    H. Lomas, 364:Mar88-82
    J. Whitworth, 493:Spring88-60
Sisson, C.H. On the Look-Out.
    A. Ross, 617(TLS):6-12Oct89-1091
Sisson, C.H. - see Racine, J.
Siu, P.C.P. The Chinese Laundryman.* (J.K.W.
    Tchen, ed)
    A.B. Chan, 106:Summer88-275

Sivan, D. Grammatical Analysis and Glossary
    of the Northwest Semitic Vocables in Akka-
    dian Texts of the 15th-13th C. B.C. from
    Canaan and Syria.
    J. Huehnergard, 318(JAOS):Oct-Dec87-
    713
de Sivry, L.P. - see under Poinsinet de Sivry,
    L.
Sizemore, C.C. A Mind of My Own.
    J. Kennedy, 441:12Nov89-55
Sjöberg, Å.W. & others, eds. The Sumerian
    Dictionary. (Vol 2)
    J. Bauer, 318(JAOS):Apr-Jun87-324
Skaff, W. The Philosophy of T.S. Eliot.*
    R. Crawford, 447(N&Q):Mar88-120
    H. Davidson, 301(JEGP):Jul88-425
    W. Harmon, 569(SR):Winter88-105
    T.H.J., 295(JML):Fall87/Winter88-313
    P. Lamarque, 677(YES):Vol19-355
Skårdal, D.B. & I.R. Kongslien, eds. Essays on
    Norwegian-American Literature and His-
    tory.
    S. Øksenholt, 563(SS):Autumn88-521
Skei, H.H. William Faulkner.*
    C.S. Brown, 569(SR):Spring88-271
Skelton, R. Memoirs of a Literary Blockhead.
    P.J. Clark, 376:Jun88-197
Skelton, R. The Parrot Who Could.
    W. Connor, 198:Spring88-109
Skelton, R. - see Faludy, G.
Skenazi, C. - see Gevers, M.
"Sketches, Projects and Executed Buildings by
    Otto Wagner."
    P.D., 46:May88-14
Skidelsky, R., ed. Thatcherism.
    L. Kolakowski, 617(TLS):24-30Mar89-319
Skidmore, T.E. The Politics of Military Rule
    in Brazil, 1964-85.
    D. Lehmann, 617(TLS):10-16Mar89-244
Skilton, B. - see Carter, B.
Skinner, M., ed. Rescuing Creusa.
    J.F. Gardner, 123:Vol38No2-337
    F. Van Keuren, 124:Jul-Aug89-479
Skinner, Q. & E. Kessler, with J. Kraye, eds.
    The Cambridge History of Renaissance Phi-
    losophy.
    L.V.R., 568(SCN):Winter88-91
Skinner, Q. & R. Price - see Machiavelli, N.
Skipp, F.E. - see Wolfe, T.
Sklute, L. Virtue of Necessity.^
    E.H.C., 382(MAE):1988/1-151
Skom, E. The Mark Twain Murders.
    M. Stasio, 441:4Jun89-24
Skomal, S.N. & E.C. Polomé, eds. Proto-Indo-
    European.*
    J.C. Kerns, 159:Vol5-181
Skram, A. Hellemyrsfolket I-IV.
    A. Aarseth, 172(Edda):1988/3-281
Skrebnev, J.M. Vvedenie kollokvialistiku.
    M. Neumann, 682(ZPSK):Band41Heft1-128
Skutsch, O. - see Ennius
Škvorecký, J. Dvořák in Love.*
    S. Solecki, 102(CanL):Spring88-175
Škvorecký, J. Sins for Father Knox.
    D.J. Enright, 453(NYRB):18May89-37
    M. Stasio, 441:12Mar89-24
van Skyhawk, H., ed. "Minorities" on Them-
    selves.
    R.H. Davis, 293(JASt):Aug88-689
Skyrms, B. Pragmatics and Empiricism.
    E. Eells, 482(PhR):Jan88-118
Slack, R. English Pressed Glass 1830-1900.
    T. Hughes, 324:Feb89-186

Slade, L.A., Jr. Another Black Voice.
R.K. Barksdale, 95(CLAJ):Mar89-379
Sladek, J. Bugs.
C. Greenland, 617(TLS):28Jul-3Aug89-830
Slate, R. & E. Slawson. Dear Girl. (T. Thompson, ed)
P. Summerfield, 637(VS):Summer89-595
Slater, J.A. The Colonial Burying Grounds of Eastern Connecticut and the Men Who Made Them.
K.M. Sweeney, 432(NEQ):Jun88-279
Slater, W.J. - see Aristophanes of Byzantium
Slatin, J.M. The Savage's Romance.*
L. Bar-Yaacov, 577(SHR):Spring88-196
S. Burris, 536(Rev):Vol10-113
Slatoff, W.J. The Look of Distance.*
T. Docherty, 541(RES):Feb88-146
Slatta, R.W., ed. Bandidos.
G.M. Joseph, 263(RIB):Vol38No2-223
Slaughter, C. Dreams of the Kalahari.
639(VQR):Autumn88-129
Slavin, M. The Making of an Insurrection.*
N. Hampson, 83:Autumn88-217
Slavitt, D. Salazar Blinks.
D.A. Hofmann, 441:26Feb89-34
Slavov, A. With the Precision of Bats.
R.J. Crampton, 575(SEER):Apr88-318
Sławek, T. The Outlined Shadow.
N. Hilton, 88:Spring89-121
Slawson, W. Sound Color.
J. Dubiel, 413:Spring89-329
Slee, P.R.H. Learning and a Liberal Education.*
T.W. Heyck, 637(VS):Winter89-257
Sleeper, R.W. The Necessity of Pragmatism.*
R. Donovan, 258:Jun88-215
M. Migotti, 518:Apr88-65
Slesin, S. & S. Cliff, with others. Caribbean Style.
H. Muschamp, 139:Jun/Jul88-21
Sless, D. In Search of Semiotics.*
G. Sampson, 144:Winter89-93
Slezak, F. Beethovens Wiener Originalverleger.
O. Neighbour, 410(M&L):Apr88-264
Slide, A. - see Blaché, A.G.
Śliwowski, R. Antoni Czechow.
J.T. Baer, 574(SEEJ):Fall88-470
Sljivic-Simsic, B., with R. Price. Serbo-Croatian Just for You.
T.F. Magner, 574(SEEJ):Spring88-178
Sljivic-Simsic, B. & K. Vidakovic. Elementary Serbo-Croatian. (Vols 1 & 2) Intermediate Serbo-Croatian. (Vol 1)
T.F. Magner, 574(SEEJ):Spring88-178
Sloane, T.O. Donne, Milton and the End of Humanist Rhetoric.*
A. King, 480(P&R):Vol21No1-73
B. Vickers, 551(RenQ):Autumn88-525
Slobin, D.I. & K. Zimmer, eds. Studies in Turkish Linguistics.
J. Kornfilt, 350:Jun89-441
Sloboda, J.A., ed. Generative Processes in Music.
A. Storr, 415:Aug88-403
Slonim, R. To Kill a Rabbi.
G. Tulchinsky, 529(QQ):Autumn88-725
Slonimsky, N. Lectionary of Music.
A. Jacobs, 617(TLS):29Sep-5Oct89-1068
Slonimsky, N. Perfect Pitch.*
P. Rapoport, 607:Dec88-46

Slusser, G., C. Greenland & E.S. Rabkin, eds. Storm Warnings.
D.M. Hassler, 395(MFS):Summer88-325
P.J. Snyder, 561(SFS):Nov88-378
Slusser, G.E. & E.S. Rabkin, eds. Aliens.
A.B. Sandback, 62:Dec88-108
Slusser, R.M. Stalin in October.
639(VQR):Spring88-45
Small, C. Music of the Common Tongue.
W. Mellers, 415:Jan88-19
R. Middleton, 410(M&L):Jul88-423
Smallwood, I. A Childhood at Green Hedges.
R. Dinnage, 617(TLS):7-13Apr89-377
Smarczyk, B. Bündnerautonomie und athenische Seebundspolitik im Dekeleischen Krieg.
D.W. Rathbone, 123:Vol38No1-169
Smarr, J.L. Boccaccio and Fiammetta.
J.H. McGregor, 589:Jul88-721
G. Mazzotta, 551(RenQ):Summer88-295
J. Usher, 402(MLR):Jan89-190
Smart, A. Villages of Glasgow. (Vol 1)
I. Gow, 617(TLS):10-16Mar89-259
Smart, E. Necessary Secrets. (A. Van Wart, ed)
P. Morley, 102(CanL):Spring88-225
Smart, I. Central American Writers of West Indian Origin.*
L. King, 86(BHS):Jul88-325
Smart, J.J.C. Essays Metaphysical and Moral.
I. Hinckfuss, 393(Mind):Apr88-306
P. Trotignon, 542:Apr-Jun88-227
Smart, N. & others, eds. Nineteenth Century Religious Thought in the West.
W. Schwarz, 617(TLS):24Feb-2Mar89-203
Smart, N. & Swami Purnananda. Prophet of a New Hindu Age.
K.N. Upadhyaya, 485(PE&W):Oct88-436
Smedts, W. De beheersing van de woordvorming.
H. Hulshof, 204(FdL):Sep88-229
Smeed, J.W. German Song and its Poetry.
K.G. Knight, 447(N&Q):Dec88-555
J. Warrack, 415:Apr88-187
Smeets, J.R., ed. La Bible de Macé la Charité V: Cantique des Cantiques, Maccabées.
J.L. Grigsby, 545(RPh):Nov88-174
Smelser, R. Robert Ley.
G. Craig, 453(NYRB):2Feb89-10
Smetana, J. & M-R. Myron. Plein vol.*
E.W. Munley, 399(MLJ):Autumn88-357
Smethurst, M.J. The Artistry of Aeschylus and Zeami.
O. Taplin, 617(TLS):27Oct-2Nov89-1187
Smethurst, R.J. Agricultural Development and Tenancy Disputes in Japan, 1870-1940.*
R. Bowen, 293(JASt):Nov88-821
Smil, V. Energy in China's Modernization.
B.J. Esposito, 293(JASt):Nov88-872
Smiley, J. Ordinary Love & Good Will.
J. Humphreys, 441:5Nov89-1
Smit, D.W. The Language of a Master.
J.A. Rowe, 27(AL):Dec88-675
Smith, A.B. The Anonymous Parts of the Old English Hexateuch.*
J.E. Cross, 589:Jan88-232
Smith, B. & A. Wheeler, eds. The Art of the First Fleet and Other Early Australian Drawings.
R.J. Varney, 324:Dec88-66

Smith, R.C. The Global Bankers.
  H. Lampert, 441:29Oct89-28
Smith, R.J. The Gothic Bequest.
  C. Haydon, 366:Autumn88-247
Smith, R.J. Japanese Society.
  A.H. Ion, 529(QQ):Summer88-498
Smith, R.P. In the Forest at Midnight.
  R. Bromley, 441:30Jul89-16
Smith, S. W.H. Auden.
  I. Smith, 447(N&Q):Mar88-121
Smith, S. Blind Zone.
  E. Tihanyi, 102(CanL):Winter87-200
Smith, S. Edward Thomas.
  M.G.H. Pittock, 677(YES):Vol19-346
  M. Scofield, 175:Spring88-65
Smith, T.C. Native Sources of Japanese In-
  dustrialization, 1750-1920.
  W.B. Hauser, 407(MN):Winter88-491
Smith, T.G. Classical Architecture.
  M.A. Branch, 505:Sep88-133
Smith, T.R. Keeping the Star.
  E. Butscher, 496:Fall88-44
Smith, V., ed. Australian Poetry 1986.
  T. Eagleton, 565:Summer88-67
Smith, W. & D. Carley, eds. New Works I.
  L. van Luven, 108:Winter87-81
Smith, W.F., ed. Modern Media in Foreign
  Language Education.
  K.E. Kintz, 207(FR):Feb89-558
  D.R. Long, 399(MLJ):Autumn88-336
Smith, W.J. & F.D. Reeve – see Voznesensky,
  A.
Smith Brindle, R. The New Music. (2nd ed)
  P. Owens, 410(M&L):Jul88-425
Smith-Soto, M.I. El arte de Alfonsina Storni.
  C. Davies, 402(MLR):Apr89-507
Smither, E. Professor Musgrove's Canary.
  B. O'Donoghue, 493:Spring88-34
Smither, H.E. The Oratorio in the Classical
  Era.
  W. Drabkin, 415:Mar88-131
  J. Rushton, 410(M&L):Oct88-522
Smither, H.E., ed. Oratorios of the Italian
  Baroque. (Vol 1)
  R.R. Holzer, 317:Fall88-533
Smither, W.J. El mundo gallego de Valle-In-
  clán.
  S.M. Greenfield, 238:May88-295
Smithers, G.V., ed. Havelok.*
  F. Chevillet, 189(EA):Oct-Dec88-469
  N. Jacobs, 382(MAE):1988/2-303
  E. Wilson, 447(N&Q):Sep88-351
Smithyman, K. Stories About Wooden Key-
  boards.
  R. Pybus, 565:Summer88-72
Smock, A. Double Dealing.
  M.H. Gelber, 395(MFS):Summer88-303
Smoke, T. A Writer's Workbook.*
  J. Costello, 399(MLJ):Winter88-471
Smolla, R.A. Jerry Falwell v. Larry Flynt.
  E.R. Shipp, 441:5Mar89-26
Smollett, T. The Adventures of Ferdinand
  Count Fathom. (J.C. Beasley, ed)
  P. Rogers, 166:Jul89-343
Smoryński, C. Self-Reference and Modal
  Logic.
  G. Boolos, 316:Mar88-306
Smuts, R.M. Court Culture and the Origins of
  a Royalist Tradition in Early Stuart En-
  gland.
  A.G.R. Smith, 366:Autumn88-238

Smyth, E. The Memoirs of Ethel Smyth.* (R.
  Crichton, ed)
  M. Hurd, 410(M&L):Jul88-416
Smyth, W. & N. Cohen, comps. Country Music
  Recorded Prior to 1943.
  B. Ellis, 650(WF):Jan88-58
Snead, J.A. Figures of Division.
  R. Blann, 594:Winter88-440
  I. Jackson, 447(N&Q):Mar88-139
  J.T. Matthews, 27(AL):Mar88-144
  W.R., 295(JML):Fall87/Winter88-315
Snellgrove, D. Indo-Tibetan Buddhism.
  J.I. Cabezón, 293(JASt):Nov88-925
Sneyd, L. The Concrete Giraffe.
  A. & S. Munton, 102(CanL):Spring88-231
Snodgrass, A.M. An Archaeology of Greece.
  G. Cadogan, 617(TLS):13-19Jan89-45
Snodgrass, W.D. Selected Poems, 1957-1987.*
  D. Hall, 473(PR):Vol55No3-505
  D. McDuff, 565:Autumn88-61
  639(VQR):Summer88-98
Snoke, A.W. Hospitals, Health, and People.
  B.J., 185:Oct88-212
Snorri Sturluson. Edda. (A. Faulkes, ed &
  trans)
  D. Whaley, 562(Scan):May88-86
Snow, B. & D. Birds and Berries.
  M. Brooke, 617(TLS):3-9Feb89-118
Snow, J.T. "Celestina" by Fernando de Rojas.*
  K. Kish, 545(RPh):Nov88-239
  P.E. Russell, 86(BHS):Oct88-404
Snyder, J. Medieval Art.
  J. Russell, 441:11Jun89-56
Snyder, S.H. Brainstorming.
  D.X. Freedman, 441:22Oct89-39
Sŏ Chŏngju. Unforgettable Things.
  J-H.K. Haboush, 293(JASt):Aug88-667
Sobchack, V. Screening Space.
  A. Gordon, 561(SFS):Nov87-386
Sobel, M.I. Light.*
  J.D. Barrow, 617(TLS):29Sep-5Oct89-
  1072
Sober, E. The Nature of Selection.*
  A. Heathcote, 63:Jun88-260
Soboul, A. Understanding the French Revolu-
  tion.
  A. Forrest, 617(TLS):6-12Oct89-1097
Sobrino, H.E. – see under Escolar Sobrino, H.
Sochor, A. Soziologie und Musikkultur. (J.
  Hahn & D. Lehmann, eds)
  E. Binas, 654(WB):1/1988-167
"Sociolinguistique des langues romanes."*
  T.M. Stephens, 545(RPh):Aug88-79
Söding, U. Das Grabbild des Peter Paul
  Rubens in der Jakobskirche zu Antwerpen.
  C. Lawrence, 600:Vol18No1/2-73
Sodmann, T. & G. Weydt – see Schaidenreis-
  ser, S.
Soffer, W. From Science to Subjectivity.
  T.L. Prendergast, 103:Feb89-78
"Soho Square II." (I. Hamilton, ed)
  L. Menand, 617(TLS):22-28Dec89-1411
Sohravardî, S.Y. Le livre de la sagesse ori-
  entale. (H. Corbin, ed & trans)
  A. Reix, 542:Apr-Jun88-250
  Y. Richard, 192(EP):Apr-Jun88-272
de Soissons, M. Welwyn Garden City.
  C. Ward, 46:Dec88-10
Sōjun, I. – see under Ikkyū Sōjun
Sokolov, S. Astrophobia.
  R. Lourie, 441:17Dec89-27
Sokolowski, R. Moral Action.*
  V. Cobb-Stevens, 258:Jun88-236

Solanki, M. Shadows of my Making.
  J. Welch, 493:Spring88-31
Söldner, M. Untersuchungen zu liegenden
Eroten in der hellenistischen und römis-
chen Kunst.
  B. Schmaltz, 229:Band60Heft4-346
Solé, C.A. & Y.R. Español. (2nd ed)
  J.E. McKinney, 399(MLJ):Autumn88-376
Solecki, S., ed. Spider Blues.*
  R.F.G. Harding-Russell, 627(UTQ):Fall87-
  166
  J. Hart, 298:Winter88/89-145
Solèr, C. & T. Ebneter. Romanisch und
Deutsch am Hinterrhein/GR. (Pt 1)
  G.A. Plangg, 547(RF):Band99Heft4-423
Sollers, P. Les Folies françaises.
  C. Michael, 207(FR):Apr89-908
Sollors, W. Beyond Ethnicity.*
  R.J. Maiman, 366:Spring88-114
Solnon, J-F. La Cour de France.
  J. Rogister, 617(TLS):20-26Jan89-65
  J-C. Vuillemin, 207(FR):Mar89-728
Solomita, S. Force of Nature.
  M. Stasio, 441:8Oct89-20
Solomon, B.P. Horse-Trading and Ecstasy.
  K. Weber, 441:2Apr89-29
Solomon, C. Enchanted Drawings.
  L. Anderson, 441:3Dec89-11
Solomon, D. Jackson Pollock.
  B.B. Stretch, 55:Feb88-52
Solomon, E. & S. Arkin - see Weiss, D.
Solomon, J.L. Die Kriegsdramen Reinhard
Goerings.*
  G.P. Knapp, 221(GQ):Fall87-683
  W.J. Lillyman, 564:Feb88-90
Solomon, M. Beethoven Essays.*
  T. Ziolkowski, 617(TLS):17-23Feb89-161
Solomon, R.C. Continental Philosophy Since
1750.*
  R. Stern, 483:Jul88-410
Solomon, R.C. From Hegel to Existentialism.*
  S. Houlgate, 518:Oct88-205
  R. Stern, 483:Jul88-410
  P. Trotignon, 542:Jul-Sep88-371
Solomos, J. Black Youth, Racism and the
State.
  N.D. Deakin, 617(TLS):3-9Mar89-216
Solotaroff, T. A Few Good Voices in My Head.
  G. Garrett, 569(SR):Summer88-516
  42(AR):Spring88-273
Solotaroff, T., ed. Many Windows.
  G. Davenport, 569(SR):Spring88-323
Solov'eva, I.I. & V.V. Šitova. K.S. Stanislav-
skij.
  L. Hecht, 574(SEEJ):Winter88-672
Soloviev, S.M. History of Russia. (Vol 45)
(W.H. Hill, ed & trans)
  I. de Madariaga, 575(SEER):Jan88-140
Sołtan, K.E. The Causal Theory of Justice.
  W.A. Galston, 185:Apr89-637
Solzhenitsyn, A. August 1914.
  J. Bayley, 453(NYRB):21Dec89-11
  I. Howe, 441:2Jul89-1
Somerville, E.O. & M. Ross. The Real Char-
lotte. (V. Beards, ed)
  G. O'Brien, 402(MLR):Apr89-457
Somerville, E.O. & M. Ross. The Selected Let-
ters of Somerville and Ross. (G. Lewis, ed)
  R. Foster, 617(TLS):27Oct-2Nov89-1191
Sommella, P.P. La moda nell'opera di Marcel
Proust.
  M. Tilby, 208(FS):Jan88-106

Sommer, P., ed. Antologia nowej poezji bry-
tyjskiej.
  J. Jarniewicz, 97(CQ):Vol17No1-92
Sommer, P. Zapisy rozmów.
  J. Jarniewicz, 97(CQ):Vol17No1-92
Sommer, S. Still Lives.
  G. Johnson, 441:30Jul89-16
Sommerfeldt, K-E. & W. Spiewok, eds. Beit-
räge zu einer funktionalsemantischen
Sprachbetrachtung.
  J. Herrgen, 685(ZDL):3/1988-383
Sommerstein, A.H. - see Aristophanes
Sommerville, J.P. Politics and Ideology in
England 1603-1640.
  K. Sharpe, 250(HLQ):Spring88-99
Somville, P. Art et symbole dans la peinture
moderne.
  M. Adam, 542:Oct-Dec88-516
Soncini, A., ed. Cheminements dans la littér-
ature francophone de Belgique au XXe
siècle.
  P. Halen, 356(LR):Aug88-252
Sondrup, S.P. & D. Chisholm, comps. Verskon-
kordanz zu Goethes "Faust, Erster Teil."
  J.K. Brown, 221(GQ):Summer88-437
Sonenberg, M. Cartographies.
  M. Buck, 441:22Oct89-23
Sonenscher, M. The Hatters of Eighteenth-
Century France.*
  J. Barry, 83:Autumn88-216
Soniat, K. Notes of Departure.
  R. Gibbs, 198:Winter86-99
Sonn, R.D. Anarchism and Cultural Politics in
Fin de Siècle France.
  J. Joll, 453(NYRB):23Nov89-38
Sonoda, K. - see under Kyōichi Sonoda
Sontag, S. AIDS and Its Metaphors.
  P. Robinson, 441:22Jan89-11
  A. Scull, 617(TLS):10-16Mar89-239
Soong, S.C., ed. A Brotherhood in Song.
  P.W. Kroll, 318(JAOS):Oct-Dec87-833
  L.Y-X., 295(JML):Fall87/Winter88-218
Sophocleous, S. Atlas des Représentations
Chypro-Archaïques des Divinités.*
  R. Senff, 229:Band60Heft4-372
Sophocles. Antigone. (A. Brown, ed & trans)
  G.M. Kirkwood, 124:Jan-Feb89-213
  P. Mason, 123:Vol38No1-9
Sophocles. Oedipus Rex. (R.D. Dawe, ed)
  A.E. Hinds, 235:Summer88-100
Sophocles. The Oedipus Trilogy of Sophocles.
  (S. Spender, trans)
  J. Saunders, 565:Winter87/88-26
Sophocles. The Three Theban Plays. (R.
Fagles, trans)
  A.E. Hinds, 235:Summer88-104
Sophocles. Three Theban Plays. (C.A. Tryp-
anis, ed & trans)
  S. Ireland, 123:Vol38No2-396
Sophocles. Trachiniae. (P.E. Easterling, ed)
  S. Esposito, 24:Spring88-135
  A.E. Hinds, 235:Summer88-100
  W.E.M. Klostermann, 394:Vol41fasc1/2-
  143
Soprani, A. La Révolution et les femmes.
  M. & P. Higonnet, 617(TLS):19-25May89-
  541
Sorabji, R. Matter, Space, and Motion.
  D.J. Furley, 617(TLS):21-27Jul89-793
Sorabji, R. Time, Creation, and the Con-
tinuum.*
  D. Bostock, 466:Vol6-255
  R. Bunn, 486:Jun88-304

Sordi, M. The Christians and the Roman Empire.
 R.L. Bates, 124:Jan–Feb89–217
 J. Molthagen, 229:Band60Heft3–245
Sorell, T. Hobbes.*
 A.P. Martinich, 319:Jan89–152
Sorell, T. Moral Theory and Capital Punishment.
 M. Powers, 518:Jul88–162
Soren, D., ed. Excavations at Kourion, Cyprus: The Sanctuary of Apollo Hylates at Kourion, Cyprus.
 E.J. Peltenburg, 123:Vol38No2–445
Soren, D. The Sanctuary of Apollo Hytates at Kourion, Cyprus.
 A.O. Koloski-Ostrow, 124:Jan–Feb89–214
Sörensen, D. Theory Formation and the Study of Literature.
 R. Fowler, 402(MLR):Oct89–897
Sørensen, F., ed. Aspects of Aspect.*
 C.F. Meyer, 179(ES):Oct88–462
Sorensen, V. The Downfall of the Gods.
 E. Hower, 441:9Jul89–19
Sorensen, V. Tutelary Tales.
 A. Boaz, 441:29Jan89–30
Sorescu, M. The Youth of Don Quixote.
 N. MacMonagle, 272(IUR):Autumn88–343
Sorfleet, R. – see Leprohon, J.L.
Sorge, P. D'Annunzio, vita di un superuomo.
 F. Donini, 617(TLS):10–16Mar89–254
Soria Olmedo, A., ed. Lecciones sobre Federico García Lorca.
 S.M. Hart, 402(MLR):Jan89–214
 L.H. Klibbe, 240(HR):Winter88–119
 A. Vargas Churchill, 552(REH):Oct89–127
Sorley, C.H. Collected Poems. (J.M. Wilson, ed)
 J. Saunders, 565:Spring88–22
Sornig, K. Soziosemantik auf der Wortebene.
 W. Wolski, 685(ZDL):2/1987–257
Sorrell, T. Descartes.
 E. Matthews, 518:Apr88–84
Sorrell, T. Hobbes.*
 R. Burch, 568(SCN):Spring–Summer88–13
Sorrell, T. Moral Theory and Capital Punishment.
 S. Nathanson, 185:Jul89–964
Sorrentino, F. Sanitary Centennial & Selected Short Stories.
 P–L. Adams, 61:Jan89–120
Sorrentino, G. The Sky Changes. Mulligan Stew.
 S. Moore, 532(RCF):Summer88–313
Sōseki, N. The Miner.* (J. Rubin, trans)
 L. Allen, 617(TLS):28Apr–4May89–466
 A. Turney, 407(NM):Autumn88–365
Soskice, J.M. Metaphor and Religious Language.*
 W.P. Alston, 482(PhR):Oct88–595
 J.F. Ross, 355(LSoc):Dec88–609
Sosnowski, S., comp. Represión, exilio y democracia.
 N.R. Olivera-Williams, 238:Dec88–836
Sosower, M.L. Palatinus Graecus 88 and the Manuscript Tradition of Lysias.
 D.M. MacDowell, 123:Vol38No2–403
Soto, G., ed. California Childhood.
 M. Kowalewski, 649(WAL):Feb89–380
Soto, G. Small Faces.
 G.W. Haslam, 649(WAL):Aug88–162
Souhami, D. Gluck.
 B. O'Donoghue, 617(TLS):10–16Mar89–252

Souiller, D. La littérature baroque en Europe.
 J–C. Vuillemin, 207(FR):May89–1072
Soulez, P. & G. Vigarello, eds. Cahiers de l'éducation.
 P. Trotignon, 542:Jan–Mar88–86
Soulié, H. La Brasse coulée.
 M. Alhau, 450(NRF):Jun88–81
de Sousa, R. The Rationality of Emotion.*
 J.D., 185:Apr89–673
 J.M. Robinson, 103:Jun89–224
Souster, R. It Takes All Kinds.
 L. Boone, 102(CanL):Winter87–209
 S. Noyes, 198:Spring88–106
Soutar, W. Poems of William Soutar.* (W.R. Aitken, ed) Diaries of a Dying Man.* (A. Scott, ed)
 C. Whyte, 571(ScLJ):Winter88–54
South, M., ed. Mythical and Fabulous Creatures.
 J. Ziolkowski, 149(CLS):Vol25No2–182
Southam, B., ed. Jane Austen: The Critical Heritage. (Vol 2)
 P. Honan, 447(N&Q):Dec88–543
 G. Koppel, 50(ArQ):Summer88–107
Southern, R.W. Robert Grosseteste.
 B. Eastwood, 589:Jan88–233
Southerne, T. The Works of Thomas Southerne.* (R. Jordan & H. Love, eds)
 M. Baron, 175:Summer88–178
Southwold, M. Buddhism in Life.
 K.G. Zysk, 318(JAOS):Jan–Mar87–206
Southworth, E.D.E.N. The Hidden Hand or, Capitola the Madcap. (J. Dobson, ed)
 S. Coultrap-McQuin, 357:Fall88–70
Souza, G.B. The Survival of Empire.
 J. Cushman, 293(JASt):Aug88–624
de Souza, T.R., ed. Indo-Portuguese History.
 P.E.H. Hair, 86(BHS):Jan88–102
 G. Parker, 318(JAOS):Jul–Sep87–524
Sowa, C.A. Traditional Themes and the Homeric Hymns.
 I.M. Cohen, 487:Autumn88–264
Sowards, J.K. – see Erasmus
Sowell, M. The Pitch That Killed.
 S. Jacoby, 441:17Sep89–11
Sowell, T. Choosing a College.
 A. Hacker, 453(NYRB):12Oct89–63
Soyinka, W. Isara.
 R. Dove, 441:12Nov89–11
Spade, P.V. & G.A. Wilson – see Wyclif, J.
Spaemann, R. Etica.
 A. Reix, 542:Apr–Jun88–228
Spaeth, D. – see Dearstyne, H.
Spaethling, R. Music and Mozart in the Life of Goethe.
 G. Birrell, 221(GQ):Fall88–576
 H.M.K. Riley, 133:Band21Heft2/3–210
 F.W. Sternfeld, 410(M&L):Oct88–528
Spahn, P. Gesellschaft – Komponisten – Medien.
 G. Olias, 654(WB):7/1988–1217
Spalding, F. Stevie Smith.*
 G. Ewart, 364:Feb/Mar89–123
 R. Hill, 493:Winter88/89–14
 C. Kino, 441:13Aug89–17
Spalding, L. Daughters of Captain Cook.
 B. Finkelstein, 441:22Oct89–22
 B. Wallace, 376:Jun88–189
Spalinger, A.J. Aspects of the Military Documents of the Ancient Egyptians.
 A.F. Rainey, 318(JAOS):Jan–Mar87–89

Spaltenstein, F. Commentaire des "Punica" de Silius Italicus (livres 1 à 8).
D.W.T. Vessey, 123:Vol38No2-254

Spang, M.G. The Spy Who Longed for Home.
N. Callendar, 441:16Jul89-23

Spangenberg, K., comp. Thüringisches Wörterbuch. (Vol 5, Pt 2 thru Vol 6, Pt 5)
H. Schönfeld, 682(ZPSK):Band41Heft2-267

Spanier, E. – see Herzog, I.

Spanier, S.W. Kay Boyle.*
J.M.M., 295(JML):Fall87/Winter88-299
E.S. Watts, 115:Winter88-96

Spann, E.K. Brotherly Tomorrows.
M. Kazin, 617(TLS):3-9Nov89-1209

Spann, P.O. Quintus Sertorius and the Legacy of Sulla.
A. Keaveney, 123:Vol38No2-321

Spark, M. A Far Cry from Kensington.*
A. Lumsden, 571(ScLJ):Winter88-56
J. Mellors, 364:Jun88-100

Spark, M. The Stories of Muriel Spark.
W. Scammell, 364:Apr-May87-157

Sparke, P. Design in Context.*
90:Aug88-641

Sparks, E. Univeral Limited Art Editions.
J. Russell, 441:3Dec89-9

Sparks, K. & V.H. Vail. German in Review. (2nd ed)
W.E. Petig, 399(MLJ):Spring88-94

Sparshott, F. Off the Ground.
M. Sirridge, 103:May89-206

Sparshott, F. Storms and Screens.
I. Sowton, 102(CanL):Summer88-163

Spate, O.H.K. Paradise Found and Lost.
G. Milner, 617(TLS):28Apr-4May89-462

Spaulding, J. The Heroic Age in Sinnār.
M.W. Daly, 318(JAOS):Apr-Jun87-376

Spearing, A.C. Medieval to Renaissance in English Poetry.*
G.C. Britton, 447(N&Q):Dec88-509
G. Schmitz, 38:Band106Heft3/4-520

Spearing, A.C. Readings in Medieval Poetry.*
G.C. Britton, 447(N&Q):Dec88-509
P. Brown, 175:Summer88-145

Spears, H. How to Read Faces.*
C. Smart, 529(QQ):Spring88-185

Spears, M.K. American Ambitions.*
42(AR):Winter88-123

Spears, R. & J. Cassidy, with R. Coles, eds. Agee, His Life Remembered.
V.A. Kramer, 534(RALS):Vol16No1&2-242

Speck, C. Boccherinis Streichquartette.
H. Unverricht, 416:Band3Heft3-257

Specker, K. Weber im Wettbewerb.
W. Hauser, 293(JASt):Feb88-188

Spector, S., ed. Essays in Paper Analysis.
S. Boorman, 410(M&L):Oct88-495

"Speculum." (Index Vols 1-49, 1926-1974)
A.V., 379(MedR):Dec88-469

Speirs, R. Bertolt Brecht.
O. Durrani, 402(MLR):Jan89-260

Spellerberg, G. – see Hallmann, J.C.

Spelman, E.V. Inessential Woman.
M. Frye, 441:30Apr89-18

Spence, G. With Justice For None.
P-L. Adams, 61:Jun89-97
S. Wishman, 441:7May89-35

Spence, J.D. The Question of Hu.*
C. Jones, 617(TLS):24-30Nov89-1294
J. Updike, 442(NY):3Apr89-109

Spence, N.C.W. Ups and Downs in Semantics.
H. Geckeler, 547(RF):Band99Heft4-407

Spencer, J. The Rise of the Woman Novelist.*
A.K. Mellor, 173(ECS):Summer88-495
M. Scheuermann, 594:Summer88-234
A.J. Smallwood, 447(N&Q):Jun88-238
H. Wilcox, 83:Spring88-101

Spencer, M. Site, citation et collaboration chez Michel Butor.*
J.A. Fleming, 627(UTQ):Fall88-135

Spencer, P. The Maasai of Matapato.
J. Mack, 617(TLS):6-12Jan89-18

Spencer, S. & B. Millington – see Wagner, R.

Spencer, S.I., ed. French Women and the Age of Enlightenment.
M.E. Birkett, 345(KRQ):Feb88-102

Spender, D. Mothers of the Novel.*
J. Barron, 566:Autumn88-76
A.K. Mellor, 173(ECS):Summer88-495
A. Messenger, 102(CanL):Winter87-234
H. Wilcox, 83:Spring88-101

Spender, D. & J. Todd, eds. Anthology of British Women Writers.
A. Leighton, 617(TLS):22-28Sep89-1024

Spender, S. Collected Poems, 1928-1985.*
W.H. Pritchard, 31(ASch):Winter88-148
J. Saunders, 565:Winter87/88-26

Spender, S. Journals, 1939-1983. (J. Goldsmith, ed)
W.H. Pritchard, 31(ASch):Winter88-148
J. Saunders, 565:Winter87/88-26

Spender, S. The Temple.*
M. Baron, 175:Spring88-84

Sperber, D. & D. Wilson. Relevance.*
P. Meara, 402(MLR):Oct89-894
J.L. Mey & M. Talbot, 567:Vol72No3/4-291
R.E. Sanders, 355(LSoc):Dec88-604

Sperling, S. Animal Liberators.
M.S. Dawkins, 617(TLS):3-9Mar89-214
P. Singer, 453(NYRB):2Feb89-36

Spevack, M. & J.W. Binns, eds. Renaissance Latin Drama in England. (Vols 5-7, 10, 11, 13)
H. Kelliher, 354:Mar88-66

Spicker, S.F., W.B. Bondeson & H.T. Engelhardt, Jr., eds. The Contraceptive Ethos.
H.K., 185:Jul89-987

Spicker, S.F., S.R. Ingman & I.R. Lawson, eds. Ethical Dimensions of Geriatric Care.
M.H.W., 185:Jul89-989

Špidlík, T. The Spirituality of the Christian East.
D.J. Constantelos, 589:Apr88-476

Spiegel, H. – see "Marie de France: Fables"

Spiegelman, A. Maus.*
P. Lewis, 565:Spring88-34

Spiegelman, A. & F. Mouly, eds. Raw.
442(NY):21Aug89-94

Spiers, E.M. Chemical Weaponry.
M.I. Chevrier, 441:27Aug89-19

Spillane, M. The Killing Man.
M. Friedman, 441:15Oct89-43

Spilling, H. Die Handschriften der Staats- und Stadtbibliothek Augsburg 2° Cod 101-250.
B. Schnell, 684(ZDA):Band117Heft1-1

Spina, L. Il cittadino alla tribuna.
T.R. Martin, 124:Jul-Aug89-478

Spindel, C. In the Shadow of the Sacred Grove.
J. North, 441:17Sep89-44

Spinelli, E. & M. Rosso-O'Laughlin. Encuentros.
M.E. Beeson, 399(MLJ):Autumn88-376

Spinner, H. Ist der Kritischer Rationalismus am Ende?
F. Eidlin, 488:Mar88-138
Spire, A. Plaisir poétique et plaisir musculaire.* (new ed)
A. Sonnenfeld, 207(FR):Mar89-675
Spires, E. Annonciade.
C. Muske, 441:5Nov89-32
Spires, R.C. Beyond the Metafictional Mode.*
H.R.M., 295(JML):Fall87/Winter88-219
Spisak, J.W. & W. Matthews − see Malory, T.
Spittel, O.R., ed. Science-Fiction.
D. Wuckel, 654(WB):12/1988-2098
Spitz, B. Bob Dylan.
A. Day, 617(TLS):18-24Aug89-904
Spivak, G.C. In Other Worlds.*
U. Fitzgerald, 49:Oct88-101
R. Fowler, 402(MLR):Oct89-897
P.D. Murphy, 590:Dec88-163
S. Suleri, 400(MLN):Dec88-1201
Spivey, T.R. The Writer as Shaman.*
E.T. Carroll, 395(MFS):Summer88-251
N.S. Grabo, 27(AL):Dec88-668
A.L.T., 295(JML):Fall87/Winter88-231
Spleth, J.S. Léopold Sédar Senghor.
C.L. Dehon, 207(FR):Oct88-177
Spock, B. & M. Morgan. Spock on Spock.
E. Crow, 441:5Nov89-11
Spofford, H.P. "The Amber Gods" and Other Stories. (A. Bendixen, ed)
A. Tucker, 357:Fall89-68
Spohr, M. Mas Schöpferische widerspiegelt sich selbst.
J. Chouillet, 530:Apr88-166
Spolsky, B., ed. Language and Education in Multilingual Settings.*
I.B. Casey, 399(MLJ):Autumn88-343
Sponheuer, B. Musik als Kunst und Nicht-Kunst.
C. Dahlhaus, 410(M&L):Jul88-384
Spoo, R. − see Pound, E.
Spore, P. & others, eds. Actes du VIIIe Congrès des Romanistes Scandinaves, Odense, 17-21 août 1981.
C. Schmitt, 72:Band224Heft2-425
Spoto, D. Lenya.
P. Brady, 617(TLS):1-7Dec89-1335
H. Dudar, 441:30Apr89-12
Spotts, F. − see Woolf, L.
Sprague, C. Rereading Doris Lessing.*
M.M. Rowe, 395(MFS):Winter88-708
Sprague, L.F., ed. Agreeable Situations.
E.A. Churchill, 432(NEQ):Sep88-471
Spratt, G.K. The Music of Arthur Honegger.
M. Anderson, 607:Dec88-48
R. Nichols, 415:Sep88-463
Spreda, K.W. Tonologie des Metta (Western Grassfields).
B. Sietsema, 350:Mar89-193
Sprengel, P. − see Brahm, O. & G. Hauptmann
Sprigg, J. & D. Larkin, with M. Freeman. Shaker Life, Work and Art.
R.L. Emerson, 106:Fall88-369
Sprigge, T.L.S. The Rational Foundations of Ethics.
D. Collinson, 89(BJA):Autumn88-391
J.P. Griffin, 617(TLS):17-23Mar89-287
C. Megone, 291:Vol5No2-237
Sprinchorn, E. − see Strindberg, A.
Spring, R. Salisbury Cathedral.
N.C., 90:Oct88-784
Springer, M. & H. − see Farnsworth, M.

Sprinker, M. Imaginary Relations.*
G. O'Sullivan, 141:Summer88-399
Sprotte, S. Farbige Kalligraphie/Coloured Calligraphy/Caligrafia Colorida.
S.S. Prawer, 617(TLS):20-26Jan89-66
Sproxton, B., ed. Trace.
R. Thacker, 649(WAL):Nov88-268
Spruit, J.E. & K.E.M. Bongenaar. Ulpianus, Papinianus en kleinere Fragmenten.
G. Crifò, 229:Band60Heft4-364
Sprung, M. The Magic of Unknowing.
A.R. Kelkar, 529(QQ):Autumn88-737
Spufford, P., with W. Wilkinson & S. Tolley. Handbook of Medieval Exchange.*
J.H. Munro, 589:Oct88-998
Spuhler, F. Oriental Carpets in the Museum of Islamic Art, Berlin.
R. Chenciner, 39:Jul88-67
Spurling, J. The Ragged End.
R. Kaveney, 617(TLS):2-8Jun89-619
Spurr, M.S. Arable Cultivation in Roman Italy c. 200 B.C.-c. A.D. 100.
K.D. White, 123:Vol38No1-94
Squarotti, G.B. − see under Bàrberi Squarotti, G.
Squier, S.M. Virginia Woolf and London.*
C. Williams, 177(ELT):Vol31No2-232
Squillante Saccone, M. Le "Interpretationes Vergilianae" di Tiberio Claudio Donato.*
J. Soubiran, 555:Vol61fasc1-154
Squire, J.R., ed. The Dynamics of Language Learning.
S. Stotsky, 126(CCC):Feb88-91
Squires, M. & D. Jackson, eds. D.H. Lawrence's "Lady."*
M. Bell, 402(MLR):Jan89-146
Srebrnik, P.T. Alexander Strahan.*
J.W. Stedman, 635(VPR):Spring88-37
Sri, P.S. T.S. Eliot.*
J.M. Reibetanz, 627(UTQ):Fall87-128
Srzednicki, J.T.J. Stepan Körner − Philosophical Analysis and Reconstruction.
P. Butchvarov, 103:Sep89-381
Stacey, P.F. Boulez and the Modern Concept.
P. Griffiths, 415:Mar88-136
N. Le Fanu, 607:Jun88-47
Stacey, S. Knife at the Opera.
P-L. Adams, 61:Sep89-112
M. Stasio, 441:13Aug89-14
Stacey, T. Deadline.
J.F. Clarity, 441:24Dec89-16
Stache, U.J., W. Maaz & F. Wagner, eds. Kontinuität und Wandel.
K.A. Neuhausen, 52:Band23Heft2-173
Stachowiak, H., ed. Pragmatik. (Vol 1)
A. Pieper, 489(PJGG):Band95Heft1-218
Stack, E. The West.
C.D. Kennedy, 441:30Apr89-38
Stack, F. Pope and Horace.*
W. Frost, 131(CL):Summer88-293
Stack, T.W. & C. Stainback − see Charlesworth, B. & C. Hagen
Madame de Staël. Delphine.* (Vol 1) (S. Balayé & L. Omacini, eds)
J. Kitchin, 208(FS):Oct88-478
M. Lehtonen, 439(NM):1988/3-429
Madame de Staël. An Extraordinary Woman. (V. Folkenflik, ed & trans)
K.J. Crecelius, 446(NCFS):Fall-Winter 88/89-216
Stafford, D. Camp X.*
639(VQR):Winter88-32

Stafford, F. The Sublime Savage.
  R. Ashton, 617(TLS):24-30Mar89-302
Stafford, K.R. Having Everything Right.*
  G.A. Love, 448:Vol26No2-133
  L.R., 102(CanL):Spring88-259
Stafford, W. An Oregon Message.*
  J. Kitchen, 219(GaR):Summer88-407
  V. Shetley, 491:May88-108
  K. Wilson, 649(WAL):Nov88-265
  639(VQR):Spring88-63
Stafford, W. Socialism, Radicalism, and Nos-
  talgia.
  K.D.M. Snell, 366:Autumn88-249
Stafford, W. You Must Revise Your Life.
  T.O., 295(JML):Fall87/Winter88-384
  K. Wilson, 649(WAL):Nov88-265
Stafford-Clark, M. Letters to George.
  D. Nokes, 617(TLS):20-26Oct89-1151
Stahl, A. - see Storm, T., H. Brinkmann & L.
  Brinkmann
Stahl, H-P. Propertius: "Love" and "War."
  W.R. Johnson, 122:Jan88-85
Stahl, P-H. Histoire de la décapitation.
  A. Reix, 542:Jan-Mar88-110
Stainer, P. The Honeycomb.
  M. Wormald, 617(TLS):9-15Jun89-641
Staines, D., ed. The Forty-Ninth and Other
  Parallels.
  S.E. Grace, 295(JML):Fall87/Winter88-
  219
  S. Scobie, 529(QQ):Spring88-190
  G.W., 102(CanL):Winter87-294
Staines, D., ed. Stephen Leacock.*
  J. Hart, 298:Winter88/89-145
  A.F. Moritz, 627(UTQ):Fall88-161
Stainton, L. & C. White. Drawing in England
  from Hilliard to Hogarth.
  D.B. Brown, 380:Autumn88-274
Štajner, K. Seven Thousand Days in Siberia.*
  639(VQR):Autumn88-125
Stakel, S. & J.C. Relihan - see "The Montpel-
  lier Codex"
Stalley, R. The Cistercian Monasteries of
  Ireland.*
  P. Fergusson, 90:Feb88-144
  J.P. McAleer, 576:Sep88-302
Stallman, R. The Orphan.
  C. Greenland, 617(TLS):29Dec89/4Jan90-
  1448
Stallybrass, P. & A. White. The Politics and
  Poetics of Transgression.*
  L. Lerner, 128(CE):Sep88-572
  W. Ruddick, 366:Autumn88-227
  C. Wills, 529(QQ):Spring88-201
Stambaugh, J. The Real Is Not the Rational.
  V.M. Fóti, 485(PE&W):Apr88-187
Stambler, I. The Encyclopedia of Pop, Rock
  and Soul.
  P. Oldfield, 617(TLS):18-24Aug89-904
Stamelman, R. & M.A. Caws, eds. Écrire le
  livre.
  M. Edwards, 617(TLS):29Dec89/4Jan90-
  1443
Stamp, T. Double Feature.
  C. Bray, 617(TLS):22-28Sep89-1040
Standen, E.A. European Post-Medieval Tap-
  estries and Related Hangings in the Metro-
  politan Museum of Art, New York.*
  C. Adelson, 90:Jan88-37
Standish, P. - see Fuentes, C.
Standop, E. Englishe Wörterbücher unter der
  Lupe.*
  W. Viereck, 257(IRAL):Feb88-73

"Stanford Slavic Studies." (Vol 1) (L. Fleish-
  man & others, eds)
  A. McMillin, 575(SEER):Oct88-668
Stangerup, H. In the Courts of Power.
  W.G. Jones, 562(Scan):Nov88-201
Stanguennec, A. Etudes post-kantiennes.
  A. Reix, 542:Jul-Sep88-351
Stanguennec, A. Hegel critique de Kant.
  R. Theis, 342:Band79Heft1-101
Stanguennec, A., ed. L'homme et ses normes.
  (Pt 2)
  P. Somville, 542:Jan-Mar88-95
Stankiewicz, E. The Slavic Languages.
  M. Bayuk, 399(MLJ):Winter88-487
  H. Birnbaum, 574(SEEJ):Summer88-342
Stankiewicz, M.A. & E. Zimmerman, eds.
  Women Art Educators II.
  R. Sandell, 662:Fall88/Winter89-49
Stanley, E.G. Unideal Principles of Editing
  Old English Verse.*
  N. Jacobs, 382(MAE):1988/1-94
Stanley, E.G. & T.F. Hoad, eds. Words.*
  M. Lehnert, 72:Band225Heft2-369
Stanley, G.F.G. - see Riel, L.
Stannard, M. Evelyn Waugh: The Early Years,
  1903-1939.*
  J. Meyers, 659(ConL):Winter89-589
Stanton, G.N. The Gospels and Jesus.
  M. Goulder, 617(TLS):20-26Oct89-1166
Stanton, M. The Country I Come From.
  M. Chernoff, 441:26Feb89-30
Stanton, M. Tales of the Supernatural.
  H. Hart, 385(MQR):Summer89-417
Stanwood, P.G. & H.R. Asals, eds. John Donne
  and the Theology of Language.*
  A. Pritchard, 627(UTQ):Fall87-111
  W. Schleiner, 405(MP):Feb89-296
Stanzel, F.K. & W. Zacharasiewicz, eds. En-
  counters and Explorations.*
  H. Dahlie, 627(UTQ):Fall87-156
  S. Slemon, 102(CanL):Spring88-122
Stap, D. Letters at the End of Winter.
  G. Kuzma, 219(GaR):Fall88-624
Stapanian, J.R. Mayakovski's Cubo-Futurist
  Vision.
  H.R.M., 295(JML):Fall87/Winter88-353
  D.E. Peterson, 550(RusR):Jan88-93
  J. Woll, 574(SEEJ):Spring88-139
Stapledon, O. & A. Miller. Talking Across the
  World. (R. Crossley, ed)
  P.A. McCarthy, 561(SFS):Jul88-237
  639(VQR):Spring88-48
Starck, T. & J.C. Wells, eds. Althoch-
  deutsches Glossenwörterbuch, mit Stellen-
  nachweis zu sämtlichen gedruckten
  althochdeutschen und verwandten Glossen.
  H. von Gadow, 72:Band224Heft2-366
Stärk, E. Hermann Nitschs "Orgien Mysterien
  Theater" und die "Hysterie der Griechen."
  M. Winkler, 221(GQ):Fall88-590
Stark, F. Over the Rim of the World. (C.
  Moorehead, ed)
  S. Guppy, 617(TLS):5-11May89-493
  A. Higgins, 364:Feb/Mar89-126
Starkell, D. Paddle to the Amazon. (C. Wil-
  kins, ed)
  T. Cahill, 441:24Sep89-13
  J. Donlon, 37:Nov/Dec88-61
Starobinski, J. Montaigne in Motion.*
  M.K. Spears, 249(HudR):Summer88-302
Starobinski, J. Le Remède dans le mal.
  P. France, 617(TLS):14-20Jul89-769

Starobinski, J. Jean-Jacques Rousseau.*
P.W., 185:Jul89-977
Starobinski, J. - see Jouve, P-J.
Starosta, S. The Case for Lexicase.
B.J. Blake, 350:Sep89-614
Starr, B. Clearing the Bases.
C. Sommers, 441:6Aug89-19
Starr, K. Inventing the Dream.
J.G. Dunne, 453(NYRB):18May89-28
Starr, S.F. & R.S. Brantley. Southern Comfort.
A. Rice, 441:31Dec89-7
Stashower, D. Elephants in the Distance.
M. Stasio, 441:14May89-30
Stassen, L. Comparison and Universal Grammar.*
A.S. Kaye & F. Müller-Gotama, 603:
Vol12No1-186
Stassinopoulos-Huffington, A. Picasso.
A. Adams, 39:Dec88-447
States, B.O. Great Reckonings in Little Rooms.
P. Hernadi, 494:Vol8No2-439
I. Smith, 223:Spring88-123
States, B.O. The Rhetoric of Dreams.
P.N. Johnson-Laird, 617(TLS):27Oct-2Nov89-1178
States, B.O. The Shape of Paradox.
D. McMillan, 299:No11&12-166
Stattkus, M.H. Claudio Monteverdi.*
N.C.F., 410(M&L):Jan88-64
Stauffenberg, H.J., ed. The Southern Version of "Cursor Mundi." (Vol 3)
J.L. Ball, 589:Oct88-1001
D. Pearsall, 541(RES):Feb88-99
O.S. Pickering, 38:Band106Heft1/2-215
J.J. Thompson, 382(MAE):1988/1-118
Stauffer, G. & E. May, eds. J.S. Bach as Organist.*
J. Dalton, 410(M&L):Oct88-515
R. Stinson, 143:No43-71
Stauth, G. & B.S. Turner. Nietzsche's Dance.
M. Tanner, 617(TLS):12-18May89-509
Stavely, K.W.F. Puritan Legacies.*
J. Holstun, 656(WMQ):Oct88-791
L.L. Knoppers, 568(SCN):Winter88-73
M. Stocker, 617(TLS):27Jan-2Feb89-90
K.P. Van Anglen, 27(AL):Dec88-660
639(VQR):Summer88-81
Stavrou, T.G. - see "Modern Greek Studies Yearbook"
Stavrou, T.G. & P.R. Weisensel. Russian Travelers to the Christian East from the Twelfth to the Twentieth Century.
D.C. Waugh, 550(RusR):Apr88-182
Stead, C. I'm Dying Laughing.
A. Blake, 381:Autumn88-135
Stead, C.K. Between.
L. Mackinnon, 617(TLS):26May-1Jun89-593
Stead, C.K. Pound, Yeats, Eliot and the Modernist Movement.
J. Williams, 366:Spring88-135
Stead, C.K. Sister Hollywood.
T. Moore, 617(TLS):11-17Aug89-877
Steadman, J.M. Milton and the Paradoxes of Renaissance Heroism.*
T.N. Corns, 447(N&Q):Dec88-535
D. Loewenstein, 551(RenQ):Winter88-758
Steadman, J.M. The Wall of Paradise.*
D. Loewenstein, 551(RenQ):Winter88-758
Steadman, R. The Big I Am.
M. Cart, 441:14May89-22

Stearns, C. The Transparency of Skin.
E. Butscher, 496:Fall88-44
Stedman, J.G. Narrative of a Five Years Expedition against the Revolted Negroes of Surinam. (R. & S. Price, eds)
D.B. Davis, 453(NYRB):30Mar89-29
Steed, N. Chipped.
M. Stasio, 441:12Mar89-24
Steegmuller, F. Apollinaire.
M. Davies, 208(FS):Apr88-228
Steel, C. - see Proclus
Steel, D. Against Goliath.
J. Campbell, 617(TLS):29Sep-5Oct89-1054
Steel, D. Daddy.
E. Stumpf, 441:10Dec89-43
Steel, D. Star.
S. Kellerman, 441:26Mar89-16
Steel, J. Paul Nizan.
P. McCarthy, 617(TLS):17-23Mar89-284
Steele, B. - see Lawrence, D.H.
Steele, H. Chasing the Gilded Shadow.
C. McCullough, 571(ScLJ):Winter88-62
Steele, H. Lord Hamlet's Castle.
S. Watts, 571(ScLJ):Spring88-55
Steele, J. Hassan Fathy.
C. Ward, 46:Sep88-12
Steele, J. The Representation of the Self in the American Renaissance.
E. Carton, 445(NCF):Dec88-403
L.J. Reynolds, 27(AL):Dec88-664
639(VQR):Summer88-79
Steele, M. The Hat of My Mother.*
639(VQR):Autumn88-126
Steele, R. & T. Threadgold, eds. Language Topics.
M. Gregory, 660(Word):Dec88-229
A.S. Kaye, 350:Dec89-910
Steever, S.B. The Serial Verb Formation in the Dravidian Languages.
H.H. Hock, 350:Jun89-398
Stéfan, J. Faux Journal.*
J. Taylor, 532(RCF):Summer88-331
Stefenelli, A. Die lexikalischen Archaismen in den Fabeln von La Fontaine.
L. Bray, 547(RF):Band100Heft4-369
Steffens, H.J. & M.J. Dickerson. Writer's Guide: History.
T. Haring-Smith, 126(CCC):Dec88-485
Steffensen, E. Oprør fra oven.
E. Egeberg, 172(Edda):1988/4-376
Steffler, J. The Wreckage of Play.
S. Scobie, 376:Sep88-163
Stegmüller, W. Kripkes Deutung der Spätphilosophie Wittgensteins.
J. Riha, 167:May88-431
Stegner, W. Crossing to Safety.
R. Burrows, 649(WAL):Aug88-145
G. Oldham, 42(AR):Winter88-113
639(VQR):Spring88-55
Stegner, W.E. The American West as Living Space.
C.L. Rawlins, 649(WAL):Aug88-180
Steiger, K.P. Die Geschichte der Shakespeare-Rezeption.
H. Priessnitz, 72:Band225Heft2-394
Steigerwald, J. Exploring French, German, and Spanish.
C.W. Nickisch, 399(MLJ):Autumn88-333
Stein, A. The House of Death.*
G.R. Evans, 541(RES):Aug88-467
[continued]

[continuing]

O.B. Hardison, Jr., 551(RenQ):Winter88-742

D.L. Miller, 401(MLQ):Jun87-190

Stein, D. Ada.*

L.A. Marchand, 340(KSJ):Vol37-186

Stein, D.J. Hugo Wolf's Lieder and Extensions of Tonality.

T. Howell, 411:Mar88-93

Stein, G. Operas and Plays. Mrs. Reynolds.

G. Voros, 472:Vol15No1-45

Stein, G. & C. Van Vechten. The Letters of Gertrude Stein and Carl Van Vechten, 1913-1946.* (E. Burns, ed)

G. Voros, 472:Vol15No1-45

R.L. White, 534(RALS):Vol16No1&2-190

Stein, H. Governing the $5 Trillion Economy.

G. Harmon, 441:26Mar89-17

Stein, H. Die romanischen Wandmalereien in der Klosterkirche Prüfening.

W. Sanderson, 589:Oct88-1003

Stein, J. & S.B. Flexner, eds. The Random House Thesaurus. (College ed)

L. Mackinnon, 617(TLS):21-27Apr89-431

Stein, P. Connaissance et emploi des langues à l'Ile Maurice.

I. Werlen, 685(ZDL):2/1987-266

Stein, R.L. Léger Félicité Sonthonax.*

G. Lewis, 83:Spring88-84

Stein, R.L. Victoria's Year.

C. Dawson, 445(NCF):Dec88-392

J. Sutherland, 617(TLS):13-19Jan89-43

R. Tobias, 637(VS):Winter89-292

Stein, S. A Deniable Man.

N. Callendar, 441:25Jun89-31

Stein, S. A Feast for Lawyers.

J. Taylor, 441:10Dec89-11

Stein, S.A., ed. Van Gogh.

E. Van Uitert, 39:Jun88-454

Stein, S.R., ed. The Architecture of Richard Morris Hunt.*

M.G. Broderick, 576:Jun88-215

Steinbeck, J. The Grapes of Wrath.

W. Kennedy, 441:9Apr89-1

Steinbeck, J. Working Days. (R. De Mott, ed)

W. Kennedy, 441:9Apr89-1

B. Leithauser, 442(NY):21Aug89-90

Steinberg, L. La Sexualité du Christ dans l'art de la Renaissance et son refoulement moderne.

F. Trémolières, 450(NRF):Apr88-96

Steinberger, P.J. Logic and Politics.

H.P. Kainz, 543:Mar89-641

Steinbrecher, M. Der delisch-attische Seebund und die athenischspartanischen Beziehungen in der kimonischen Ära (ca. 478/7-462/1).

D.W. Rathbone, 123:Vol38No1-168

Steinbrügge, L. Das moralische Geschlecht.

I. Selle, 654(WB):11/1988-1932

Steinecke, H. Romanpoetik von Goethe bis Thomas Mann.

J.H. Petersen, 680(ZDP):Band107Heft4-603

Steiner, A. Corpus Vasorum Antiquorum. (U.S.A., fasc 21)

J. Boardman, 123:Vol38No1-177

Steiner, D. The Crown of Song.*

T.K. Hubbard, 24:Summer88-254

Steiner, G. Freimaurer und Rosenkreuzer.

T.P. Saine, 462(OL):Vol43No1-76

Steiner, G. Real Presences.

R. Kimball, 441:30Jul89-11

R. Scruton, 617(TLS):19-25May89-533

Steiner, R. The Essential Steiner. (R.A. McDermott, ed)

S.H. Phillips, 485(PE&W):Oct88-457

Steiner, R. In Spite of Everything, Yes.

B.B. Stretch, 55:Apr88-53

Steiner, R. La philosophie de la liberté.

M. Adam, 542:Jul-Sep88-372

Steiner, S. The Vanishing White Man.

J.L. Davis, 649(WAL):May88-83

Steinhagen, H., ed. Zwischen Gegenreformation und Frühaufklärung.

R.E. Schade, 221(GQ):Winter87-107

Steinhoff, H-H., ed. Ein schöne Historia von Engelhart auss Burgunt.

W. Wunderlich, 196:Band29Heft1/2-238

Steinhoff, M. Zeitbewusstsein und Selbsterfahrung.

K.B. Beils, 342:Band79Heft3-358

Steinke, D. Up Through the Water.

R. Olmstead, 441:2Jul89-14

Steinke, K.B. Die mittelalterlichen Vatikanpaläste und ihre Kapellen, Baugeschichtliche Untersuchung anhand der schriftlichen Quellen.

G.M. Radke, 576:Jun88-192

Steinlein, R. Die domestizierte Phantasie.

W. Paulsen, 406:Fall88-392

Steinman, L.M. Made in America.*

D. Minter, 432(NEQ):Jun88-294

J.M. Reibetanz, 106:Fall88-365

G. Rotella, 27(AL):Mar88-139

Steinman, M. Yeats's Heroic Figures.*

D.T.O., 295(JML):Fall87/Winter88-408

Steinmetz, J-L. Pétrus Borel.*

V. Brombert, 535(RHL):Nov-Dec88-1149

Steinmetz, S. Yiddish and English.

D.L. Gold, 35(AS):Fall88-276

Steinsaltz, A. The Talmud: A Reference Guide.

L. Wieseltier, 441:17Dec89-3

Stella, F. Working Space.*

J. Mundy, 39:Feb88-143

Stellmacher, D. - see Dock, A.

Stellmacher, W., ed. Auseinandersetzung mit Shakespeare.*

F. Amrine, 133:Band21Heft2/3-216

Stendhal. Chroniques italiennes. (R. André, ed)

P. Berthier, 535(RHL):Mar-Apr88-296

Stendhal. Vie de Henry Brulard. (V. Del Litto, ed)

P. Neaud, 605(SC):15Apr89-243

Stendhal. Vie de Rossini.

A. Suied, 98:Dec88-1049

Stenger, K.L. Die Erzählstruktur von Friedrich Theodor Vischers "Auch Einer."

J.T. Adams, 221(GQ):Spring88-312

A.T. Alt, 406:Winter88-516

Stenner-Pagenstecher, A.M. Das Wunderbare bei Jung-Stilling.

D. Dowdey, 221(GQ):Spring87-284

Stennik, J.V. Russkaja satira XVIII veka.

I.R. Titunik, 550(RusR):Apr88-222

Stenson, F., ed. Alberta Bound.

N. Besner, 647:Spring88-111

C. Wiseman, 526:Summer88-82

Stenzel, H. - see Molière

Stenzel, H. & H. Thoma, eds. Die französische Lyrik des 19. Jahrhunderts.

M.H. Parkinson, 402(MLR):Oct89-987

Stepanowa, M.D. & W. Fleischer. Grundzüge der deutschen Wortbildung.
J. Eichhoff, 301(JEGP):Apr88-283
W. Motsch, 682(ZPSK):Band41Heft3-406
Stepansky, P.E. – see Mahler, M.S.
Stephan, A. & H. Wagener, eds. Schreiben im Exil.
R. Kieser, 406:Winter88-527
Stephan, I., ed. Kontroversen, alte und neue. (Forum 9)
S.K. Johnson, 221(GQ):Fall87-647
Stephanson, A. Kennan and the Art of Foreign Policy.
W.F. Kimball, 617(TLS):6-12Oct89-1081
R. Steel, 453(NYRB):17Aug89-3
Stephen, M., ed. Never Such Innocence.
D. Hibberd, 617(TLS):10-16Feb89-134
Stephens, C.R. – see O'Connor, F. & B. Cheney
Stephens, H.G. & E.M. Shoemaker. In the Footsteps of John Wesley Powell.
J. Aton, 649(WAL):Nov88-347
Stephens, M., ed. A Book of Wales.*
G. Davies, 447(N&Q):Sep88-401
Stephens, W.B. Education, Literacy and Society, 1830-70.
P. Gosden, 637(VS):Autumn88-150
Stephenson, E.A. What Sprung Rhythm Really Is.
C. Lock, 627(UTQ):Fall88-116
Steptoe, A. The Mozart-Da Ponte Operas.
R. Osborne, 617(TLS):16-22Jun89-667
L.L. Tyler, 465:Summer89-88
Stern, D. Twice Told Tales.
A. Arensberg, 441:18Jun89-13
Stern, F. Dreams and Delusions.*
639(VQR):Spring88-43
Stern, G. Lovesick.*
S. Pinsker, 363(LitR):Winter89-256
D. Walker, 199:Spring88-87
Stern, I., ed-in-chief. Dictionary of Brazilian Literature.
K. Müller-Bergh, 263(RIB):Vol38No3-412
Stern, J.P. & J.J. White, eds. Paths and Labyrinths.*
P.F. Dvorak, 221(GQ):Summer87-492
Stern, M.B. – see Alcott, L.M.
Stern, R. The Position of the Body.
G. Garrett, 569(SR):Summer88-516
Stern, R.A.M. Modern Classicism.
M. Filler, 617(TLS):24-30Mar89-295
Stern, R.A.M., G. Gilmartin & T. Mellins. New York 1930.
H. Muschamp, 139:Jun/Jul88-20
R.G. Wilson, 47:Apr88-49
Stern, S. No Tricks in My Pocket.
M. Bloom, 441:3Sep89-17
Stern, S. Marcel Proust: "Swann's Way."
E. Hughes, 617(TLS):13-19Oct89-1112
Stern, S.J., ed. Resistance, Rebellion, and Consciousness in the Andean Peasant World, 18th to 20th Centuries.
J.L. Klaiber, 263(RIB):Vol38No2-225
Stern, S.M. Studies in Early Ismā'ilism.
A.A. Nanji, 318(JAOS):Oct-Dec87-741
Sternberg, M. The Poetics of Biblical Narrative.*
G.A. Rendsburg, 318(JAOS):Jul-Sep87-554
Sternberg, R.D.L. The Unquiet Self.
J. Courteau, 238:May88-304
J. Gledson, 86(BHS):Jan88-109

Sternberg, R.J. & M.L. Barnes, eds. The Psychology of Love.*
S. Sutherland, 617(TLS):1-7Dec89-1344
Sternberg, W. & M.C. Harrison, Jr. Feeding Frenzy.
J. Beatty, 61:Dec89-124
Sterne, L. Sterne's Memoirs.* (K. Monkman, ed)
W.G. Day, 536(Rev):Vol10-193
Sternlicht, S. John Galsworthy.
L. Strahan, 177(ELT):Vol31No2-235
Stetson, D.M. Women's Rights In France.
M. Sarde, 207(FR):Mar89-724
Stevens, D. Musicology in Practice. (Vol 1) (T.P. Lewis, ed)
D. Fallows, 415:Aug88-403
Stevens, J. Words and Music in the Middle Ages.*
J. Caldwell, 382(MAE):1988/2-333
T.G. Duncan, 541(RES):Nov88-531
D. Pearsall, 402(MLR):Oct89-916
H. van der Werf, 309:Vol8No3/4-378
Stevens, J.E. Hoover Dam.
S.C. Florman, 441:12Feb89-23
Stevens, M. Four Middle English Mystery Cycles.
P. Happé, 130:Spring88-86
Stevens, M. Sudden Death.
J.E. Garten, 441:29Oct89-42
Stevens, P. Imagination and the Presence of Shakespeare in "Paradise Lost."*
G. Teskey, 627(UTQ):Fall87-114
Stevens, P. Out of the Willow Trees.
A. Munton, 102(CanL):Spring88-227
Stevens, R. In Sickness and in Wealth.
U.E. Reinhardt, 441:20Aug89-14
Stevens, S. Malaria Dreams.
442(NY):23Oct89-147
Stevens, S. Rosalía de Castro and the Galician Revival.
C. Davies, 402(MLR):Jan89-211
R. Havard, 86(BHS):Jul88-308
Stevens, W. & J. Rodríguez Feo. Secretaries of the Moon.* (B. Coyle & A. Filreis, eds)
R.W.B., 295(JML):Fall87/Winter88-227
M. Perloff, 405(MP):Nov88-217
Stevenson, A. Selected Poems, 1956-1986.*
J. Forth, 364:Nov87-85
R.B. Shaw, 491:Apr88-41
Stevenson, A., with others. Bitter Fame.
A. Alvarez, 453(NYRB):28Sep89-34
D. Middlebrook, 617(TLS):27Oct-2Nov89-1179
R. Pinsky, 441:27Aug89-11
Stevenson, D. The First World War and International Politics.
G. Best, 617(TLS):10-16Mar89-241
Stevenson, D. The Origins of Freemasonry. The First Freemasons.
G. Donaldson, 617(TLS):3-9Feb89-116
Stevenson, K.C. & H.W. Jandl. Houses by Mail.*
D.D. Reiff, 576:Jun88-212
Stevenson, L.C. Praise and Paradox.*
R. Strickland, 570(SQ):Spring88-125
Stevenson, R. The British Novel since the Thirties.*
M.P.L., 295(JML):Fall87/Winter88-266
B.M., 494:Vol8No2-462
Stevenson, R.L. Island Landfalls. (J. Calder, ed)
K. Gelder, 571(ScLJ):Spring88-6

Storey, C. An Annotated Bibliography and
Guide to Alexis Studies (La Vie de Saint
Alexis).
  A.J. Holden, 402(MLR):Apr89-462
Storey, G. Charles Dickens: "Bleak House."*
  L. Hartveit, 179(ES):Apr88-183
  A. Sanders, 402(MLR):Apr89-447
Storey, G., K. Tillotson & N. Burgis – see
Dickens, C.
Storey, M. Byron and the Eye of Appetite.
  W.H. Galperin, 340(KSJ):Vol37-178
  A. Nicholson, 402(MLR):Jan89-131
  W.W. Robson, 541(RES):Feb88-128
Storey, R. Pierrots on the Stage of Desire.*
  P. Baggio, 704(SFR):Fall-Winter88-411
  J. Bem, 535(RHL):Jan-Feb88-138
Storm, T., H. Brinkmann & L. Brinkmann.
Theodor Storm – Hartmuth und Laura
Brinkmann, Briefwechsel.* (A. Stahl, ed)
  A.T. Alt, 400(MLN):Apr88-684
Storm, T. & W. Petersen. Theodor Storm-Wil-
helm Petersen Briefwechsel.* (B. Coghlan,
ed)
  M.T. Peischl, 221(GQ):Spring87-290
Storni, A. Selected Poems.
  D. Meyer, 238:Sep88-569
Storoni Mazzolani, L. Tibère ou la spirale du
pouvoir.
  P. Schrömbges, 229:Band60Heft2-173
Storr, A. Churchill's Black Dog, Kafka's Mice.
(British title: Churchill's Black Dog and
Other Phenomena of the Human Mind.)
  P.L. Adams, 61:Feb89-83
  L.E. Beattie, 441:5Mar89-23
  R. Davenport-Hines, 617(TLS):1-7Sep89-
  942
Storr, A. Freud.
  R. Davenport-Hines, 617(TLS):1-7Sep89-
  942
Story, G. Black Swan.*
  D. McGifford, 102(CanL):Spring88-170
Stott, M. Forgetting's No Excuse.
  617(TLS):29Sep-5Oct89-1072
Stotz, P. Sonderformen der sapphischen
Dichtung.
  F. Rädle, 229:Band60Heft1-69
Stouck, D. – see Wilson, E.
Stourac, R. & K. McCreery. Theatre as a
Weapon.*
  C.H., 615(TJ):Mar88-133
Stout, H.S. The New England Soul.*
  J.M. Bumsted, 656(WMQ):Apr88-360
  E. Emerson, 115:Summer88-312
  D.A. Ringe, 70:Jul88-117
  K.E. Rowe, 27(AL):May88-288
  D. Weber, 405(MP):May89-443
Stout, J. Ethics after Babel.
  J.B. Schneewind, 103:Dec88-498
Stove, D. Popper and After.
  D. Dutton, 478(P&L):Apr88-155
Stove, D.C. The Rationality of Induction.*
  D. Baird, 543:Dec88-411
  N. Griffin, 154:Spring88-178
  D. Miller, 483:Apr88-286
Stover, L. Robert A. Heinlein.
  D.N. Samuelson, 561(SFS):Nov88-361
Stover, L. The Prophetic Soul.
  H.M. Geduld, 561(SFS):Nov88-376
Stowe, H.B. Oldtown Folks.* (D. Berkson, ed)
  S.K. Harris, 26(ALR):Fall88-68

Stowe, S.M. Intimacy and Power in the Old
South.*
  C. Simpson, 106:Fall88-347
  C.S. Watson, 392:Fall88-575
Stowe, W.W. Balzac, James, and the Realistic
Novel.*
  C.B. Cox, 569(SR):Summer88-497
  P.A. Walker, 284:Fall88-221
Stowers, S.K. Letter Writing in Greco-Roman
Antiquity.
  M. Morford, 124:May-Jun89-394
Stradling, R.A. Philip IV and the Government
of Spain, 1621-1665.
  I.A.A. Thompson, 617(TLS):13-19Jan89-
  44
Strasberg, L. A Dream of Passion.
  M. Wolf, 511:Jul88-46
Strasser, S. Satisfaction Guaranteed.
  L.J. Davis, 441:19Nov89-34
Strassner, E. Ideologie – SPRACHE – Politik.
  J. Erfurt, 682(ZPSK):Band41Heft3-408
Stratford, P. All the Polarities.*
  A.E. Davidson, 395(MFS):Winter88-655
Strathern, M. The Gender of the Gift.
  A. Gell, 617(TLS):16-22Jun89-663
Strattis. Estratis, "Fragmentos." (A. Ropero
Gutierrez, ed)
  W.G. Arnott, 123:Vol38No1-141
Stratton, C. & M.M. Scott. The Art of Sukho-
thai.
  J. Ayers, 324:Jun89-447
Stratton, J. The Virgin Text.
  P. McGee, 454:Winter89-244
Straub, K. Divided Fictions.
  K.M. Rogers, 166:Jan89-160
Straughan, R. & J. Wilson, eds. Philosophers
on Education.
  O. Hanfling, 483:Apr88-279
Straumanis, A., ed. Baltic Drama. Fire and
Night.
  S. Rubene, 610:Summer88-181
Strauss, B. Niemand anderes.
  K. Pankow, 601(SuF):Jul-Aug88-876
Strauss, B.S. Athens after the Peloponnesian
War.*
  P. Cartledge, 235:Summer88-105
  R.A. Knox, 123:Vol38No2-308
  R.R. Simms, 124:Jul-Aug89-457
Strauss, D. & H.W. Drescher, eds. Scottish
Language and Literature, Medieval and
Renaissance 1984: Fourth International Confer-
ence 1984, Proceedings.*
  D.A. Low, 541(RES):Nov88-539
Strauss, F.J. Die Erinnerungen.
  H. James, 617(TLS):15-21Dec89-1382
Strauss, L. La cité et l'homme.
  A. Reix, 542:Jan-Mar88-111
Strauss, L. Philosophy and Law.
  M.J. Plax, 390:Jun/Jul88-62
Strauss, L. The Rebirth of Classical Political
Rationalism. (T.L. Pangle, ed)
  S. Holmes, 617(TLS):1-7Dec89-1319
Strauss, W. Allgemeine Pädagogik als trans-
zendentale Logik der Erziehungswissen-
schaft.
  E. Hufnagel, 342:Band79Heft4-485
Strawson, G. Freedom and Belief.
  C.J. Hookway, 479(PhQ):Oct88-533
  N.M.L. Nathan, 518:Jan88-48
Strawson, G. The Secret Connexion.
  D.M. Armstrong, 617(TLS):22-28Dec89-
  1425

Sunstein, E.W. Mary Shelley.
  C. Heibrun, 441:12Feb89-14
  R.B. Martin, 453(NYRB):29Jun89-13
Sunter, R.M. Patronage and Politics in Scotland 1707-1832.
  R. Scott, 83:Autumn88-213
Suny, R.G. The Making of the Georgian Nation.
  J. Keep, 617(TLS):21-27Apr89-415
Suojanen, P. Finnish Folk Hymn Singing.
  M. Ramsten, 64(Arv):Vol42-203
Suomela-Härmä, E. Les Structures narratives dans le "Roman de Renart."
  M.T. Bruckner, 545(RPh):Nov88-231
Super, R.H. The Chronicler of Barsetshire.
  J. Bayley, 453(NYRB):17Aug89-6
  S. Collini, 617(TLS):30Jun-6Jul89-712
Supičić, I. Music in Society.
  W. Weber, 415:Sep88-465
Suppan, W. Musica Humana.
  V. Karbusicky, 416:Band3Heft2-187
Suppes, P. Probabilistic Metaphysics.*
  I. Levi, 486:Dec88-646
Supple, J.J. Racine: "Bérénice."
  J.P. Short, 402(MLR):Jan89-166
Suro, J.R. - see under Rodrígues Suro, J.
Surtz, E. & V. Murphy, eds. The Divorce Tracts of Henry VIII.
  L.V.R., 568(SCN):Winter88-92
Surya, M. Georges Bataille.
  R.W. Schoolcraft 3d, 400(MLN):Sep88-920
Susskind, L. & J. Cruikshank. Breaking the Impasse.
  S.K., 185:Apr89-683
Sussman, S. The Dieter.
  C. Fein, 441:2Apr89-29
Suter, A. Das portugiesische Pretérito perfeito composto.
  J. Schmidt-Radefeldt, 547(RF):Band99 Heft4-430
Sutherland, C.H.V. Roman History and Coinage: 44 B.C. - A.D. 69.
  C. Cheal, 124:Mar-Apr89-319
Sutherland, F. Whitefaces.
  J. Donlan, 102(CanL):Spring88-153
Sutherland, J. The Longman Companion to Victorian Fiction.
  R. Jenkyns, 617(TLS):28Jul-3Aug89-817
Sutherland, J. The Restoration Newspaper and its Development.*
  J. Black, 366:Spring88-122
  N.H. Keeble, 506(PSt):May88-105
  J. Morrill, 541(RES):Feb88-111
  H.L. Snyder, 354:Jun88-170
Sutherland, J.D. Fairbairn's Journey into the Interior.
  P. Lomas, 617(TLS):1-7Sep89-942
Sutherland, L.S. & L.G. Mitchell, eds. The History of the University of Oxford.* (Vol 5)
  P. Kelly, 235:Summer88-123
  W.R. Ward, 83:Spring88-78
Sutherland, S. Macmillan Dictionary of Psychology.
  S. Wilson, 617(TLS):3-9Mar89-214
Sutton, D. Edgar Degas.
  R. Thomson, 90:Mar88-239
Sutton, D. Flints.*
  S. Rae, 364:Mar87-87
Sutton, D.F. Seneca on the Stage.
  C.D.N. Costa, 123:Vol38No1-153
Sutton, D.F. Two Lost Plays of Euripides.
  E.M. Craik, 123:Vol38No2-399

Sutton, P.C. & others. Masters of 17th-Century Dutch Landscape Painting.*
  C. Brown, 600:Vol18No1/2-76
  M. Russell, 39:Jun88-452
Sutton, W.A. - see Anderson, S.
Suttoni, C. - see Liszt, F.
Suvin, D.R. The Long March.
  B.N.S. Gooch, 102(CanL):Summer88-154
Suworow, V. Der Eisbrecher.
  G.A. Craig, 453(NYRB):12Oct89-11
Suyin, H., M. Langford & G. Mason - see under Han Suyin, M. Langford & G. Mason
Suzuki, D. Metamorphosis.
  G.W., 102(CanL):Summer88-179
  529(QQ):Autumn88-753
Suzuki, D. & B. Hehner. Looking at Insects.
  J. Gellert, 102(CanL):Winter87-220
Suzuki, D. & P. Knudtson. Genethics.
  S. Rose, 617(TLS):15-21Dec89-1384
Svane, B. Le Monde d'Eugène Sue.
  M. Tilby, 208(FS):Jul88-352
Svarny, E. "The Men of 1914."
  H. Haughton, 617(TLS):17-23Mar89-285
Svedjedal, J. Almqvist - berättaren på bokmarknaden.
  K. Petherick, 562(Scan):May88-84
Švejcer, A.D. Contemporary Sociolinguistics.*
  J. Harris, 402(MLR):Jul89-681
  Xu Daming, 320(CJL):Sep88-310
Švejcer, A.D. & L.B. Nikol'skij. Introduction to Sociolinguistics.*
  J. Harris, 402(MLR):Jul89-681
  Xu Daming, 320(CJL):Sep88-310
Svenbro, J. Phrasikleia.
  O. Murray, 617(TLS):16-22Jun89-655
Svendsen, H.M. The Gold Ball.
  P-L. Adams, 61:Sep89-111
  V. Moberg, 441:24Dec89-16
"Den svenska Polenbilden och Polsk prosa i Sverige 1939-1960."
  O.M. Selberg, 172(Edda):1988/2-177
Svensson, Ö. Saxon Place-Names in East Cornwall.
  M. Gelling, 447(N&Q):Jun88-201
  M. Wakelin, 382(MAE):1988/1-101
Svevo, I.V. Memoir of Italo Svevo.
  G. Josipovici, 617(TLS):16-22Jun89-668
Svoboda, F.J. Hemingway and "The Sun Also Rises."
  C.L. Ross, 517(PBSA):Vol82No2-235
Swados, E. Listening Out Loud.
  M. Kimmelman, 441:22Jan89-10
Swaim, K.M. Before and After the Fall.*
  F.M. Keener, 677(YES):Vol19-321
  I. Simon, 541(RES):May88-295
Swain, E. David Edgar.
  A.E. Kalson, 397(MD):Jun88-313
Swain, N. Collective Farms Which Work?
  A. Brown, 575(SEER):Apr88-307
Swain, R.B. The Practical Gardener.
  A. Lacy, 441:11Jun89-30
Swales, M., ed. German Poetry.*
  P. Hayden-Roy, 221(GQ):Fall88-563
  639(VQR):Spring88-64
Swales, M. The Sorrows of Young Werther.
  L. Sharpe, 402(MLR):Oct89-1027
Swan, M. & B. Smith, eds. Learner English.
  S.R. Schecter, 399(MLJ):Winter88-461
Swan, C. Intermediate Polish.*
  M.J. Mikoś, 574(SEEJ):Spring88-167
Swann, B., ed. Smoothing the Ground.
  J. Rice, 128(CE):Feb88-206

Swann, B. Song of the Sky.*
    J. Rice, 128(CE):Feb88-206
Swann, P. The Hollywood Feature Film in Postwar Britain.
    R. Murphy, 161(DUJ):Dec87-166
Swannell, J. - see Ostler, G.
Swanson, H. Medieval Artisans.
    P. Basing, 617(TLS):8-14Dec89-1373
Swanson, R.N. Church and Society in Late Medieval England.
    P. Heath, 617(TLS):8-14Dec89-1373
Swartz, N. The Concept of Physical Law.*
    M. Ruse, 154:Autumn88-523
Sway, M. Familiar Strangers.*
    T. Martin, 42(AR):Fall88-526
Swearingen, R., ed. Siberia and the Soviet Far East.
    R.U.T. Kim, 293(JASt):Nov88-845
Sweeney, A. A Full Hearing.
    L.J. Sears, 293(JASt):Nov88-950
Sweeney, J.G. 3d. Jonson and the Psychology of Public Theater.*
    M. Shapiro, 570(SQ):Summer88-258
Sweeney, M. Blue Shoes.
    L. Norfolk, 617(TLS):7-13Apr89-365
Sweeny, M.K. Walker Percy and the Postmodern World.
    G.M. Ciuba, 27(AL):Mar88-148
Sweet, W.E. Sport and Recreation in Ancient Greece.
    H.M. Lee, 124:Jul-Aug89-474
Sweetman, J. The Oriental Obsession.*
    J.S. Curl, 324:Jan89-126
Sweetser, M-O. La Fontaine.*
    J-P. Collinet, 475:Vol15No28-353
Swennen, R. Les Trois Frères.
    J.A. Reiter, 207(FR):Mar89-723
Swenson, M. In Other Words.*
    D. Sampson, 249(HudR):Summer88-387
Swietlicki, C. Spanish Christian Cabala.*
    E.T. Howe, 589:Jul88-722
    S.N. McCrary, 552(REH):May88-121
    T. O'Reilly, 402(MLR):Apr89-499
    J.H. Silverman, 240(HR):Spring88-259
    A. Vermeylen, 356(LR):Feb-May88-126
Swift, E. The Christopher Park Regulars.
    E. Pall, 441:20Aug89-7
Swift, E. A Place With Promise.
    639(VQR):Summer88-94
Swift, G. Out of this World.*
    H. Mantel, 364:Mar88-101
    C. Rooke, 376:Jun88-191
    442(NY):6Feb89-105
Swift, J. The Oxford Authors: Jonathan Swift.* (A. Ross & D. Woolley, eds)
    J. Mezciems, 541(RES):May88-297
Swift, R. & S. Gilley, eds. The Irish in Britain, 1815-1939.
    F. McLynn, 617(TLS):27Oct-2Nov89-1192
Swiggers, P. & W. Van Hoecke, with others. Mot et parties du discours/Word and Word Classes/Wort und Wortarten.*
    C. Römer, 682(ZPSK):Band41Heft4-541
Swinburne, R. The Evolution of the Soul.*
    M. Adam, 542:Oct-Dec88-508
    A. Flew, 518:Apr88-97
    D. Gordon, 258:Jun88-233
    J. Knox, Jr., 484(PPR):Jun89-738
    P. Sherry, 483:Apr88-281
Swindells, J. Victorian Writing and Working Women.
    C.A. Martin, 635(VPR):Summer88-77

Swiny, S. & others. The Kent State University Expedition to Episkopi Phaneromeni. (Vol 2)
    E.J. Peltenburg, 303(JoHS):Vol108-261
Sykes, C.J. ProfScam.
    M. Birnbaum, 396(ModA):Summer89-245
    R. Kimball, 441:19Feb89-16
Sylvest, O. Det litteraere karneval.
    E. Rasmussen, 172(Edda):1988/4-379
Sylvie, A. Gobineau et la féminité.
    A. Smith, 446(NCFS):Spring-Summer89-412
"Symbolae Lvdovico Mitxelena septuagenario oblatae."
    P. Flobert, 555:Vol61fasc2-350
Syme, R. The Augustan Aristocracy.
    R. Seager, 123:Vol38No2-327
Syme, R. Roman Papers. (Vol 3) (A. Birley, ed)
    J. Beaujeu, 555:Vol61fasc2-335
Symeonoglou, S. The Topography of Thebes: From the Bronze Age to Modern Times.*
    M. Bernal, 318(JAOS):Jul-Sep87-557
Symington, R. - see Böschenstein, H.
Symmons, S. Goya.
    J. Bareau, 617(TLS):14-20Apr89-398
Symonds, R. Alternative Saints.
    A. Webster, 617(TLS):21-27Jul89-812
Symons, A. Selected Letters, 1880-1935. (K. Beckson & J.M. Munro, eds)
    J. Stokes, 617(TLS):16-22Jun89-668
Symons, J. Dashiell Hammett.
    W. Marling, 534(RALS):Vol16No1&2-220
Symons, J. Makers of the New.*
    H. Haughton, 617(TLS):17-23Mar89-285
    42(AR):Spring88-274
Symons, J. A.J.A. Symons.
    D. Flower, 364:Mar87-93
    J.A. Stein, 31(ASch):Summer88-462
Symons, J. - see Lewis, W.
Symons, S. Helmet of Flesh.
    E. Jewinski, 168(ECW):Spring88-71
    S. Solecki, 102(CanL):Winter87-146
"Symposium in honorem prof. M. de Riquer."
    C. de Nigris, 379(MedR):Aug88-295
Syndikus, H.P. Catull. (Vols 1 & 3)
    R.G.M. Nisbet, 313:Vol78-218
Syréhn, G. Makten och ensamheten.
    C.S. McKnight, 563(SS):Winter88-113
Syrokomla-Stefanowska, A.D. - see Kaneko Mitsuharu
Sysyn, F.E. Between Poland and the Ukraine.*
    D. Van Horn, 497(PolR):Vol33No3-353
Syverson-Stork, J. Theatrical Aspects of the Novel.
    J.A. Parr, 238:Sep88-545
Szacka, B., ed. Polska Dziecięca.
    Z. Bauman, 617(TLS):24-30Nov89-1295
Szarkowski, J. Winogrand.
    H. Martin, 507:Sep/Oct88-162
Szarmach, P.E., ed. Studies in Earlier Old English Prose.*
    E.G. Stanley, 402(MLR):Oct89-911
Szarmach, P.E., with V.D. Oggins, eds. Sources of Anglo-Saxon Culture.
    J.D. Pheifer, 541(RES):May88-278
    E.G. Stanley, 402(MLR):Oct89-913
Szaszkóné Sin, A., ed. Magyarország történeti helynévtára.
    M. Rady, 575(SEER):Apr88-291
Szávai, J. André Malraux.
    T. Gorilovics, 535(RHL):Jan-Feb88-153

Talese, G., ed. The Best American Essays 1987.
 639(VQR):Spring88-53
Tallack, D., ed. Literary Theory at Work.
 P. Stevick, 395(MFS):Summer88-313
Tallent, E. Time with Children.*
 M. Gorra, 249(HudR):Summer88-404
 42(AR):Winter88-118
 639(VQR):Spring88-56
Talley, R. The Cubs of '69.
 R.L. Bray, 441:23Apr89-36
Tallis, R. Not Saussure.*
 A. Berman, 144:Winter89-40
Talmadge, H.E., with M.R. Winchell. Talmadge.
 J.E. Brown, 580(SCR):Fall88-69
"The Talmud." (Vol 1) (A. Steinsaltz, commentary) (I.V. Berman, ed & trans)
 L. Wieseltier, 441:17Dec89-3
Tálos, E., E. Hanisch & W. Neugebauer, eds. NS-Herrschaft in Österreich 1939-1945.
 R. Knight, 617(TLS):21-27Jul89-797
Tamari, M. "With All Your Possessions."
 E.N.D., 185:Apr89-678
Tambiah, S.J. Sri Lanka.
 A. Shastri, 293(JASt):Feb88-170
Tames, R. Servant of the Shogun.
 K.W. Berger, 293(JASt):Nov88-900
Tammi, P. Problems of Nabokov's Poetics.*
 J. Grayson, 575(SEER):Jan88-128
 494:Vol8No2-463
Tam'si, T.U. Das Geheimnis der Medusen.
 C. Kunze, 654(WB):8/1988-1336
Tan, A. The Joy Luck Club.
 C. Ong, 617(TLS):29Dec89/4Jan90-1447
 O. Schell, 441:19Mar89-3
 442(NY):26Jun89-91
Tanabe Hajime. Philosophy as Metanoetics.
 D.A. Dilworth, 407(MN):Winter88-497
Tanabe, K. Sculptures of Palmyra, I.
 M.A.R. Colledge, 123:Vol38No1-184
Tanabe, W.J. Paintings of the Lotus Sutra.
 C. Guth, 407(MN):Winter88-502
Tanaka, M. Platon. (Vols 1-4)
 S. Kawada, 303(JoHS):Vol108-212
Tanaka, Y., ed. To Live and to Write.*
 C.I. Mulhern, 407(MN):Summer88-239
 V.V. Vernon, 293(JASt):Aug88-652
 L. Wagner-Martin, 573(SSF):Winter88-93
Tancke, G. Die italienischen Wörterbücher von den Anfängen bis zum Erscheinen des "Vocabolario degli Accademici della Crusca" (1612).*
 R. Coluccia, 279(GSLI):Vol165fasc529-112
 E. Radtke, 260(IF):Band93-325
Tandon, D. Birds and Other Relations.
 P. Sherwood, 402(MLR):Apr89-543
Tanenbaum, R.K. Depraved Indifference.
 N. Callendar, 441:26Nov89-33
Tångeberg, P. Mittelalterliche Holzskulpturen und Altarschreine in Schweden.
 P. Williamson, 90:Feb88-148
Tanitch, R. Gielgud.
 J.C. Trewin, 511:Sep88-46
Tanizaki, J. Childhood Years.*
 P. Anderer, 407(MN):Winter88-473
Tankard, J.B. & M.R. Van Valkenburgh. Gertrude Jekyll.
 A. Urquhart, 617(TLS):19-25May89-558
 442(NY):24Apr89-112

Tannenbaum, M. Conversations with Stockhausen.
 N. Le Fanu, 607:Jun88-47
 C. Wintle, 617(TLS):20-26Jan89-67
Tanner, M. - see Furtwängler, W.
Tanner, R.L. The Humor of Irony and Satire in the "Tradiciones peruanas."*
 M-G. Jackson, 345(KRQ):May88-251
Tanner, S.L. Paul Elmer More.
 W. Randel, 27(AL):Mar88-126
Tanner, T. Jane Austen.*
 D. Birch, 175:Summer88-165
 W.A. Craik, 447(N&Q):Jun88-245
 F.M. Keener, 677(YES):Vol19-333
 L.R. Leavis, 179(ES):Apr88-177
 D. Le Faye, 541(RES):May88-308
 A.W. Neumann, 599:Spring89-129
 S. Tave, 454:Winter89-231
Tanner, T., ed. Aldo Leopold.
 S.E. Campbell, 649(WAL):Nov88-239
 S. Paul, 271:Fall88-163
Tanner, T. Scenes of Nature, Signs of Men.*
 R.S. Peckham, 364:Dec88/Jan89-125
 G. Scharnhorst, 395(MFS):Winter88-611
Tanner, T. The Writer and His Work: Henry James.*
 P.B. Armstrong, 131(CL):Spring88-187
 J.A. Ward, 284:Fall88-218
Tannery, C. Malraux, l'agnostique absolu ou la métamorphose comme loi du monde.
 G. Cesbron, 356(LR):Feb-May88-149
Tanselle, G.T. Textual Criticism since Greg.
 J.B. Gabel, 40(AEB):Vol2No4-168
 27(AL):Oct88-520
Tao, X. - see under Xue Tao
Tao-ching, H. - see under Hsu Tao-ching
Taplin, O. - see Macleod, C.
Tappan, D.W. & W.A. Mould, eds. French Studies in Honor of Philip A. Wadsworth.
 H.G. Hall, 208(FS):Jan88-85
Tapply, W.G. Dead Winter.
 M. Stasio, 441:18June9-28
Tapscott, S. American Beauty.
 G.S. Lensing, 569(SR):Winter88-113
Taraborrelli, J.R. Call Her Miss Ross.
 V. Kaufman, 441:17Dec89-21
Tarcov, N. Locke's Education for Liberty.
 R. Burch, 568(SCN):Spring-Summer88-13
Tardat, C. Sweet Death.*
 S. Roe, 617(TLS):17-23Feb89-170
Tardieu, J. Margeries.
 A.V. Williams, 207(FR):Feb89-554
Tardieu, J. & J-P. Vallotton. Causeries devant la fenêtre.
 J. Roudaut, 450(NRF):Oct88-93
Tarkanian, J. & T. Pluto. Tark.
 C. Salzberg, 441:5Mar89-23
Tarrow, S. Democracy and Disorder.
 A. Kelikian, 617(TLS):10-16Nov89-1234
Tarrow, S. Exile from the Kingdom.
 J. Guérin, 535(RHL):Jul-Aug88-790
Tarugi, G., ed. Validità perenne dell'Umanesimo.
 D. Marsh, 276:Autumn88-289
Tasso, T. Jerusalem Delivered. (R. Nash, trans)
 R. Flannagan, 391:Mar88-22
Tatár, B. Russkaja Leksikografija.
 F. Häusler, 682(ZPSK):Band41Heft1-132
Tatar, M. The Hard Facts of the Grimms' Fairy Tales.
 J.M. McGlathery, 406:Winter88-512

Terlecka, A.M. Stanisław Wyspiański and Symbolism.
G.T. Kapolka, 497(PolR):Vol33No2-237
Terman, D. Enemy Territory.
N. Callendar, 441:17Dec89-17
"Terminologijaja aid ädäbijjatyn vä termin-oloži luģetlärin bibliografijasy."
G.F. Meier, 682(ZPSK):Band41Heft6-831
Terpening, R.H. Charon and the Crossing.
G. Costa, 131(CL):Spring88-174
Terrasse, A. Pierre Bonnard.
B. Thomson, 617(TLS):28Apr-4May89-449
Terrasse, J. Le Sens et les Signes.
D. Trott, 627(UTQ):Fall87-134
Terrasse, M. Bonnard et Le Cannet.
B. Thomson, 617(TLS):28Apr-4May89-449
Terrell, C.F. A Companion to the "Cantos" of Ezra Pound.* (Vol 2)
R. Casillo, 534(RALS):Vol16No1&2-199
Terry, A., ed. Homage to Joan Gili on his Eightieth Birthday.
G. Ribbans, 86(BHS):Jul88-317
Terry, G.M. East European Languages and Literature III.
A.G. Cross, 575(SEER):Apr88-332
Terry, J. Miss Abigail's Part or Version & Diversion.*
A. Lebowitz, 102(CanL):Winter87-152
Terry, M. Dallas Stories.
J.W. Byrd, 649(WAL):Feb89-387
Terry, M., ed. Prize Stories.
D.A. Carpenter, 649(WAL):Aug88-163
Terry, M. Ringer.
J.W. Lee, 649(WAL):Aug88-168
Terry, R.C., ed. Trollope.
M. Laine, 627(UTQ):Fall88-113
C. Lansbury, 637(VS):Winter89-263
639(VQR):Spring88-48
Tertullian. De Idololatria. (J.H. Waszink & J.C.M. Van Winden, eds & trans)
R.P.C. Hanson, 123:Vol38No2-419
Tertullian. Q.S.F. Tertulliano, "Contro Prassea." (G. Scarpat, ed & trans)
G.J.M. Bartelink, 394:Vol41fasc1/2-213
Tertullian. Tertullien, "Exhortation à la chasteté." (C. Moreschini, ed; J-C. Fredouille, trans)
M. Reydellet, 555:Vol61fasc1-148
Tertullian. Tertullien, "Les spectacles" (De spectaculis). (M. Turcan, ed & trans)
I. Opelt, 229:Band60Heft2-158
Tertz, A. (A. Sinyavsky). Goodnight.
J. Bayley, 441:17Dec89-1
Testard, M. – see "Saint Ambroise, 'Les devoirs'"
Tester, S.J. A History of Western Astrology.*
J.D. North, 447(N&Q):Dec88-502
"I testi di medicina latini antichi."
J. André, 555:Vol61fasc2-347
Testori, G. In Exitu.
J. Burckhardt, 62:Dec88-110
Tete, P. A Missionary Social Worker in India.
R.F. Young, 318(JAOS):Oct-Dec87-840
Tetel, M., R.G. Witt & R. Goffen, eds. Life and Death in Fifteenth-Century Florence.
L. Martines, 617(TLS):1-7Sep89-956
Tétreau, J. Hertel: l'homme et l'oeuvre.*
E-M.K., 102(CanL):Summer88-180
R. Major, 627(UTQ):Fall87-185
Tetreault, R. The Poetry of Life.
R.C. Casto, 178:Jun88-231
G. Durrant, 627(UTQ):Fall88-111
[continued]

[continuing]
D. Hughes, 301(JEGP):Jul88-449
A.D. Knerr, 340(KSJ):Vol37-193
D.H. Reiman, 191(ELN):Sep88-71
Teulon-Nouailles, S. & B. Michel Butor.
F.C. St. Aubyn, 207(FR):Apr89-897
"Texte."* (Vol 2)
C. Jordens, 356(LR):Aug88-235
"Texte." (Vol 4) (B.T. Fitch & A. Oliver, eds)
E. Apter, 494:Vol8No3/4-717
"Le Texte et ses représentations."
R.W., 555:Vol61fasc2-321
Teymur, N., T.A. Markus & T. Woolley, eds. Rehumanising Housing.
C. Ward, 46:Jun88-8
Thackara, J., ed. Design After Modernism.
N. Whiteley, 324:Feb89-184
Thaden, E.C., with M.F. Thaden. Russia's Western Borderlands, 1710-1870.
D. Kirby, 575(SEER):Jan88-138
Thaker, R. & C.A. Thayer, eds. The Soviet Union as an Asian Power.
R.U.T. Kim, 293(JASt):Nov88-845
Thalmann, W.G. Conventions of Form and Thought in Early Greek Epic Poetry.*
I.J.F. de Jong, 394:Vol41fasc1/2-127
de Thaon, P. Comput.* (I. Short, ed)
G. Hesketh, 382(MAE):1988/1-126
A.J. Holden, 208(FS):Jan88-69
Thapar, R. From Lineage to State.*
R.W. Lariviere, 318(JAOS):Jul-Sep87-517
Tharoor, S. The Great Indian Novel.
T. Raychaudhuri, 617(TLS):8-14Sep89-969
Thayer, E.L. Casey at the Bat.
J. Gindin, 385(MQR):Spring89-283
Theau, J. Certitudes et questions de la raison philosophique.*
M. Adam, 542:Apr-Jun88-232
G. Nicholson, 627(UTQ):Fall87-220
Theau, J. Le crépuscule de l'homme.
M. Adam, 542:Apr-Jun88-232
Thelen, D. Paths of Resistance.*
G.G. Suggs, Jr., 389(MQ):Autumn88-124
Thelle, N.R. Buddhism and Christianity in Japan.*
J.E. Ketelaar, 293(JASt):May88-383
Themba, D.C. The World of Can Themba. (E. Patel, ed)
H. Willemse, 538(RAL):Spring88-101
Themerson, S. Hobson's Island.
P. Reading, 617(TLS):6-12Jan89-21
Theocritus. The Idylls. (R. Wells, trans)
J. Heath-Stubbs, 4:Autumn88-24
C. Martindale, 617(TLS):31Mar-6Apr89-341
Theophylactus Simocatta. The "History" of Theophylact Simocatta.* (M. & M. Whitby, trans)
W.E. Kaegi, 589:Apr88-478
Theotocas, G. To Daimonio.
K.M., 295(JML):Fall87/Winter88-216
Theroux, A. An Adultery.*
D. Flower, 249(HudR):Spring88-216
R.A. Scaramelli, 532(RCF):Spring88-190
639(VQR):Summer88-91
Theroux, P. My Secret History.
W. Lesser, 441:4Jun89-1
W. Steiner, 617(TLS):7-13Jul89-739
Theroux, P. Riding the Iron Rooster.*
J. Haylock, 364:Oct/Nov88-133
"These and Other Lands."
H.W. Stauffer, 649(WAL):Nov88-283

Thesing, W.B. – see "Dictionary of Literary Biography"

Thevet, A. André Thevet's North America. (R. Schlesinger & A.P. Stabler, eds)
S. Greenblatt, 551(RenQ):Spring88–164
C.J. Jaenen, 529(QQ):Spring88–198

Theweleit, K. Male Fantasies. (Vol 1) Männer Phantasien. (Vol 2)
B. Bettelheim, 617(TLS):14–20Apr89–392

Thibault, P.R. Pope Gregory XI.
J.E. Weakland, 589:Jul88–724

Thickstun, M.O. Fictions of the Feminine.
L.L. Knoppers, 568(SCN):Winter88–74
639(VQR):Autumn88–120

Thieberger, R. Georg Büchner: "Lenz." (2nd ed)
D. Horton, 402(MLR):Jan89–241

Thiel, C. – see Frege, G.

Thiel-Horstmann, M., ed. Bhakti in Current Research, 1979–1982.*
M.C. Shapiro, 318(JAOS):Jan–Mar87–200

Thieme, J. The Web of Tradition.
H.S. Mann, 395(MFS):Winter88–656

Thiériot, G. Franz Xaver Kroetz et le nouveau théâtre populaire.
M. McGowan, 402(MLR):Jul89–809

wa Thiong'o, N. – see under Ngugi wa Thiong'o

Thistle, P.C. Indian–European Trade Relations in the Lower Saskatchewan River Region to 1840.
C.J. Jaenen, 298:Spring/Summer88–243

Thomaneck, J.K.A. & J. Mellis, eds. Politics, Society and Government in the German Democratic Republic.
R. Morgan, 617(TLS):13–19Oct89–1115

Thomas, A. Goodbye Harold, Good Luck.*
M. Fee, 102(CanL):Winter87–218

Thomas, A. La Variation Phonetique.
G. Lessard, 529(QQ):Summer88–458

Thomas, B. Cross–Examinations of Law and Literature.
R. Asselineau, 189(EA):Oct–Dec88–495
A.J. von Frank, 445(NCF):Mar89–548
D.A. Ringe, 27(AL):Mar88–117

Thomas, C. Caitlin.
A. Suied, 98:Jan/Feb88–157

Thomas, C. Casanova.*
D. Coward, 208(FS):Apr88–211

Thomas, C.Y. The Poor and the Powerless.
G.K. Lewis, 617(TLS):3–9Feb89–104

Thomas, D. Robert Browning.
617(TLS):1–7Dec89–1344

Thomas, D. & D.K. Jackson. The Poe Log.*
B.F. Fisher 4th, 27(AL):Mar88–115
J.M. Hutchisson, 536(Rev):Vol10–177
K. Ljungquist, 392:Winter87/88–99
639(VQR):Winter88–8

Thomas, D.K., comp. A Checklist of Editions of Major French Authors in Oxford Libraries 1526–1800.
H.G. Hall, 208(FS):Apr88–243

Thomas, D.M. Memories and Hallucinations.*
G. Ewart, 364:Jul88–113
W. Magee, 493:Winter88/89–24

Thomas, E. Sir John Johnson.
S.C. Spragge, 529(QQ):Summer88–454
C. Wilton-Siegel, 298:Winter88/89–135

Thomas, F. The Fall of Man.
S. Herbert, 617(TLS):10–16Mar89–256

Thomas, G. Selected Short Stories.
R. Burgin, 441:6Aug89–18

Thomas, G.S. The Rock Garden and Its Plants.
L. Yang, 441:3Dec89–74

Thomas, H. Un détour par la vie.
J. Roudaut, 450(NRF):Jul–Aug88–209

Thomas, J. Coventry Cathedral.
N.C., 90:Oct88–784

Thomas, J. Le Dépassement du quotidien dans l'"Énéide," les "Métamorphoses" d'Apulée et le "Satiricon."
K. Dowden, 123:Vol38No1–59

Thomas, J. Reading "Middlemarch."
C. Crosby, 637(VS):Autumn88–119

Thomas, J.W. – see "Ortnît and Wolfdietrich"

Thomas, L. The Adventures of Goodnight & Loving.
J. Rascoe, 441:1Oct89–9

Thomas, M. Antonia Saw the Oryx First.*
R. Gibson, 617(TLS):27Jan–2Feb89–88

Thomas, M.W. The Lunar Light of Whitman's Poetry.*
E. Folsom, 481(PQ):Summer88–393
R.W. French, 30:Winter89–88
S. Hutchinson, 447(N&Q):Sep88–419
D. Kuebrich, 405(MP):May89–445
R. Rehder, 541(RES):Nov88–570
A. Salska, 445(NCF):Sep88–253

Thomas, P. Strangers from a Secret Land.
G.W., 102(CanL):Summer88–179

Thomas, P. The Welsher.
D. Glover, 198:Summer88–108

Thomas, P.D.G. The American Revolution.
J.E. Hill, 173(ECS):Summer88–531

Thomas, R. Bad Girls, Good Women.
G. Courter, 441:7May89–16

Thomas, R. The Fourth Durango.
M. Stasio, 441:24Sep89–29

Thomas, R. Oral Tradition and Written Record in Classical Athens.
O. Murray, 617(TLS):8–14Dec89–1353

Thomas, R. The Ruby Slippers of Oz.
K. Olson, 441:24Dec89–18

Thomas, R.G. Edward Thomas.*
P.E. Mitchell, 177(ELT):Vol31No4–458
M.G.H. Pittock, 677(YES):Vol19–346
M. Scofield, 175:Spring88–65

Thomas, R.G.C. Indian Security Policy.
T.P. Thornton, 293(JAST):May88–407

Thomas, R.S. The Echoes Return Slow.
T. Curtis, 493:Summer88–48
S. O'Brien, 364:Oct/Nov88–99
B. O'Donoghue, 617(TLS):14–20Apr89–402

Thomas, R.S. Experimenting With An Amen.*
H. Buckingham, 565:Winter87/88–71

Thomas, V. The Moral Universe of Shakespeare's Problem Plays.*
A.W. Bellringer, 179(ES):Aug88–363
J.G. Saunders, 541(RES):Nov88–547
157:No168–49

Thomas, W. Die Erforschung des Tocharischen (1960–1984).
D.Q. Adams, 318(JAOS):Apr–Jun87–370

Thomas, Y. Mommsen et "l'Isolierung" du droit (Rome, l'Allemagne et l'Etat).
J–C. Richard, 555:Vol61fasc2–343

Thomas Aquinas – see under Aquinas, T.

Thomas of Britain. Tristan. (G. Bonath, ed & trans)
G. Pinkernell, 72:Band224Heft2–448

Thomas of Hales. The Lyfe of Oure Lady.* (S.M. Horrall, ed)
A.S.G. Edwards, 677(YES):Vol19–300
M. Wakelin, 382(MAE):1988/1–121

Thomason, S.G. & T. Kaufman. Language Contact, Creolization, and Genetic Linguistics.*
  J.H. Jasanoff, 350:Sep89-623
Thomasseau, J-M., ed. Commerce et commerçants dans la littérature.
  V.D.L., 605(SC):15Jul89-340
Thompson, A. & J.O. Shakespeare, Meaning and Metaphor.
  O.M. Meidner, 89(BJA):Spring88-193
Thompson, B. The Art of Graphic Design.
  R. McLean, 441:22Jan89-28
Thompson, B., with B.L. Reitman. Boxcar Bertha.
  L. Sante, 453(NYRB):27Apr89-15
Thompson, D., ed. The Leavises.*
  G. Singh, 396(ModA):Spring89-179
Thompson, D. - see Finch, A.
Thompson, D.J. Memphis under the Ptolemies.
  T.G.H. James, 617(TLS):6-12Oct89-1096
Thompson, E.M. Understanding Russia.
  D.M. Fiene, 574(SEEJ):Spring88-151
Thompson, F.M.L. The Rise of Respectable Society.*
  H. Ritvo, 441:26Feb89-38
Thompson, J. Between Self and World.
  D.D. Rogers, 166:Jul89-347
Thompson, J.B. Studies in the Theory of Ideology.
  H.T. Wilson, 488:Mar88-134
Thompson, J.B. - see Lefort, C.
Thompson, J.J. Robert Thornton and the London Thornton Mauscript.
  R. Beadle, 617(TLS):13-19Jan89-46
Thompson, J.M. Leaders of the French Revolution.
  J.F. McMillan, 617(TLS):21-27Jul89-792
Thompson, J.M. Robespierre. (new ed)
  C. Lucas, 617(TLS):19-25May89-554
Thompson, K. Leaping Up Sliding Away.
  C. Creede, 628(UWR):Vol21No1-94
  J. Doyle, 102(CanL):Spring88-183
  D. Glover, 198:Spring88-101
  D. Schoemperlen, 526:Summer88-78
  P. Stevens, 529(QQ):Autumn88-568
Thompson, K.W., ed. The Nixon Presidency.
  R.A. Strong, 639(VQR):Summer88-525
Thompson, L. The Political Mythology of Apartheid.
  S.G.M. Ridge, 538(RAL):Spring88-94
Thompson, M. & R. Shakespeare and the Sense of Performance.
  R. Hapgood, 617(TLS):25-31Aug89-927
Thompson, N. On Their Return.
  L. Dawson-Evans, 565:Summer88-54
Thompson, N. Wellington after Waterloo.
  W.L. Arnstein, 637(VS):Winter89-244
  A.G. Jones, 83:Autumn88-207
Thompson, P. Accidental Chords.
  M. Hardie, 581:Dec88-475
Thompson, R. Sex in Middlesex.
  R.P. Gildrie, 656(WMQ):Jan88-175
Thompson, T. - see Slate, R. & E. Slawson
Thomsen, C.W. & I. Schneider, eds. Grundzüge der Geschichte des europäischen Hörspiels.
  R. Usmiani, 107(CRCL):Jun88-313
Thomson, A. The Life and Times of Charles-Marie Widor, 1844-1937.*
  C. Shuster, 537:Vol74No2-242
Thomson, A.W. The Poetry of Tennyson.*
  D. Birch, 541(RES):Feb88-135
Thomson, B. Vuillard.
  E. Cowling, 617(TLS):24-30Mar89-306
Thomson, F.C. - see Eliot, G.

Thomson, G. Needs.*
  S. Sayers, 518:Oct88-229
  A.R. White, 521:Jul88-268
Thomson, J. "Liberty," "The Castle of Indolence" and Other Poems.* (J. Sambrook, ed)
  R. Inglesfield, 354:Dec88-366
  J.R. Watson, 161(DUJ):Dec87-147
  T. Woodman, 83:Spring88-91
Thomson, R. Degas: The Nudes.*
  T. Hilton, 617(TLS):24-30Mar89-305
Thomson, R. Seurat.
  J-C. Lebensztejn, 98:Mar88-236
Thomson, V. Music with Words.
  N. Rorem, 617(TLS):22-28Dec89-1409
Thoolen, H., ed. Indonesia and the Rule of Law.
  D.S. Lev, 293(JASt):Aug88-708
Thorau, H. Augusto Boals Theater der Unterdrückten in Theorie und Praxis.
  D. Woll, 72:Band224Heft2-462
Thordarson, A. A Medal of Distinction.
  I. Hill, 617(TLS):14-20Jul89-783
Thoreau, H.D. Translations. (K.P. Van Anglen, ed)
  W.G. Heath, 106:Summer88-262
Thorlby, A. Leo Tolstoy: "Anna Karenina."
  A.D.P. Briggs, 402(MLR):Apr89-533
  K.M. Hewitt, 447(N&Q):Dec88-552
Thorman, C. Fifty Years of Eternal Vigilance.
  K. Ray, 441:5Mar89-22
Thorn, J. & P. Palmer, with D. Reuther, eds. Total Baseball.
  A. Clymer, 441:8Oct89-10
Thornbury, C. - see Berryman, J.
Thorndike, J. The Potato Baron.
  D. Jersild, 441:9Jul89-18
Thornton, J.E. & E.R. Winkler, eds. Ethics and Aging.
  M.H. Waymack, 103:Aug89-336
Thornton, L. Women as Portrayed in Orientalist Painting.
  F.N. Bohrer, 127:Spring89-49
Thorpe, A. Mornings in the Baltic.*
  M. Crucefix, 493:Winter88/89-51
  S. Knight, 364:Dec88/Jan89-118
Thorpe, D.R. Selwyn Lloyd.
  G. Peele, 617(TLS):17-23Mar89-271
Thorpe, N. The Glory of the Page.
  M. Michael, 90:Oct88-774
Thoursie, S.A.O. Die Verbalflexion eines sudbairischen Autographs aus dem Jahre 1464.
  E. Neuss, 260(IF):Band93-366
Threadgold, T. & others, eds. Semiotics Ideology Language.
  494:Vol8No2-464
Threlfall, R. Frederick Delius: a Supplementary Catalogue.*
  S. Banfield, 410(M&L):Apr88-286
Thubron, C. Behind the Wall.*
  J.K. Fairbank, 453(NYRB):16Mar89-17
Thubron, C. Falling.
  P. Reading, 617(TLS):8-14Sep89-968
Thulstrup, N. Kierkegaard og kirken i Danmark.*
  J.S. Veisland, 563(SS):Summer88-403
Thunberg, L. Man and the Cosmos.
  J.E. Rexine, 589:Jan88-237
Thunecke, J., ed. Leid der Worte.
  J.M. Ritchie, 402(MLR):Jan89-256

Thurber, J. Collecting Himself. (M.J. Rosen, ed)
  F. Raphael, 617(TLS):29Dec89/4Jan90–1437
  E. Sorel, 441:5Nov89–36
Thürlemann, F. Kandinsky über Kandinsky.
  M. Rummens, 90:Oct88–781
Thurley, J. The Enigma Variations.
  N. Callendar, 441:23Apr89–33
Thurley, J. Household Gods.
  J. Mellors, 364:Nov87–102
Thurston, A.F. Enemies of the People.
  L.W. Pye, 293(JASt):Feb88–130
Thurston, C. The Romance Revolution.*
  M. Honey, 115:Summer88–314
  J.M. Roller, 27(AL):May88–317
Thwaite, A. Letter from Tokyo.*
  H. Lomas, 364:Dec87/Jan88–122
Thwaite, A. Poems 1953–1988.
  S. Rae, 617(TLS):10–16Nov89–1245
Thwaite, A. – see Larkin, P.
Tibaut. Le Roman de la Poire.* (C. Marchello-Nizia, ed)
  J.H. Marshall, 208(FS):Apr88–196
Tibbetts, J. The American Theatrical Film.
  R.N.C., 295(JML):Fall87/Winter88–284
Tibi, B. The Crisis of Modern Islam.
  F. Halliday, 617(TLS):14–20Apr89–387
Tichane, R. Ash Glazes.
  N.V. Robinson, 60:Mar–Apr88–127
Tichi, C. Shifting Gears.*
  J.I. McClintock, 115:Winter88–89
  D. Minter, 432(NEQ):Jun88–294
  M. Schleier, 658:Spring88–106
Tichy, E. Onomatopoetische Verbalbildungen des Griechischen.
  O. Wenkus, 260(IF):Band93–308
Tidrick, G. & C. Jiyuan, eds. China's Industrial Reform.
  W.A. Fischer, 293(JASt):Nov88–874
Tieck, L. William Lovell. (W. Münz, ed)
  W.J. Lillyman, 221(GQ):Fall87–672
Tieck, L. Ludwig Tieck: Schriften. (Vol 6 ed by M. Frank; Vol 12 ed by U. Schweikert)
  W.J. Lillyman, 221(GQ):Fall87–672
  R. Paulin, 402(MLR):Jul89–785
Tiedemann, R. – see Arorno, T.W.
Tiee, H.H–Y. A Reference Grammar of Chinese Sentences.
  J.H.Y. Tai, 399(MLJ):Winter88–465
"Domenico Tiepolo: The Punchinello Drawings."*
  J. Anderson, 59:Dec88–565
Tierney, B. Foundations of the Conciliar Theory. Church Law and Constitutional Thought in the Middle Ages. Religion, Law and the Growth of Constitutional Thought 1150–1650.
  J–F. Spitz, 98:Jan/Feb88–114
Tierney, J.E. – see Dodsley, R.
Tiersma, P.M. A Frisian Reference Grammar.
  W.M. Sijtsma, 353:Vol26No1–177
Tiessen, P., with N. Strobel – see Lowry, M. & G. Noxon
Tigay, J.H., ed. Empirical Models for Biblical Criticism.
  A. Berlin, 318(JAOS):Jan–Mar87–145
Tikkanen, H. The 30 Years' War.
  W.G. Jones, 562(Scan):Nov88–197
Tiktin, H. Rumänisch–Deutsches Wörterbuch. (2nd ed) (Pts 1–6) (P. Miron, ed)
  D. Deletant, 575(SEER):Apr88–264

Tiles, J.E. Dewey.
  M. Grossman, 103:Jul89–296
Tilliette, X. L'Absolu et la philosophie.
  P. David, 192(EP):Jul–Sep88–440
Tilliette, X. La mythologie comprise.
  L. Procesi, 192(EP):Jan–Mar88–124
Tillinghast, D. Women Hoping for Rain.
  G. Kuzma, 219(GaR):Fall88–624
  639(VQR):Winter88–27
Tillman, L. Haunted Houses.
  B.K. Horvath, 532(RCF):Spring88–201
Tillotson, G.H.R. The Rajput Palaces.
  R. Head, 324:Dec88–63
Tilly, C. The Contentious French.*
  R.M. Davis, 577(SHR):Winter88–71
Tilman, R.O. Southeast Asia and the Enemy Beyond.
  D.E. Weatherbee, 293(JASt):May88–440
Timaios of Locri. On the Nature of the World and the Soul.* (T.H. Tobin, ed & trans)
  J. Whittaker, 487:Autumn88–285
"The Times Atlas of the Second World War." (J. Keegan, general ed)
  M. Carver, 617(TLS):1–7Sep89–935
  P. Kennedy, 441:31Dec89–10
Timko, M., F. Kaplan & E. Guiliano – see "Dickens Studies Annual"
Timm, E. W.B. Yeats.
  J. Duytschaever, 272(IUR):Autumn88–342
Timmerman, J.H. John Steinbeck's Fiction.*
  P.R.J., 295(JML):Fall87/Winter88–385
Timms, E. Karl Krauss, Apocalyptic Satirist.*
  L.J. King, 406:Winter88–521
  L.A. Lensing, 221(GQ):Spring88–287
Timms, E. & P. Collier, eds. Visions and Blueprints.*
  M. James, 364:Aug/Sep88–126
  J.M. Ritchie, 402(MLR):Jan89–254
Timms, E. & D. Kelley, eds. Unreal City.
  P.A. Miller, 577(SHR):Spring88–176
Timms, E. & N. Segal, eds. Freud in Exile.*
  S.B. Girgus, 30:Spring89–64
Timofeev, L. Posledniaia nadezhda vyzhit'.
  K. Brooks, 550(RusR):Jul88–346
Timpanaro, S. Per la storia della filologia virgiliana antica.*
  H.D. Jocelyn, 229:Band60Heft3–199
von Timroth, W. Russian and Soviet Sociolinguistics and Taboo Varieties of the Russian Language (Argot, Jargon, Slang and "Mat").* (rev) (German title: Russische und sowjetische Soziolinguistik und tabuisierte Varietäten des Russischen.)
  S. Marder, 575(SEER):Jul88–472
Tindall, W. Give Them All My Love.
  A. Hollinghurst, 617(TLS):5–11May89–483
Tinkler-Villani, V. Visions of Dante in English Poetry.
  R. Wells, 617(TLS):1–7Dec89–1339
Tinnell, R.D. Federico García Lorca.
  A. Josephs, 238:Sep88–550
Tintner, A.R. The Book World of Henry James.*
  J. Auchard, 177(ELT):Vol31No3–349
  P. Buitenhuis, 106:Fall88–325
  R.L. Gale, 26(ALR):Spring89–83
Tintner, A.R. The Museum World of Henry James.*
  P. Buitenhuis, 106:Fall88–325
  C.B. Cox, 569(SR):Summer88–497
  R.L. Gale, 284:Spring88–145

Tintner, A.R. The Pop World of Henry James.
J. Bayley, 453(NYRB):7Dec89-21
Tintoré, M.J. "La Regenta" de Clarín y la
crítica de su tiempo.
N.M. Valis, 547(RF):Band100Heft4-478
Tioutchev, F. Poésies.
J. Blot, 450(NRF):Jul-Aug88-222
Tipton, F.B. & R. Aldrich. An Economic and
Social History of Europe from 1939 to the
Present.
639(VQR):Summer88-85
Tirso de Molina. Damned for Despair ("El
condenado por desconfiado"). (N.G. Round,
ed & trans)
P.W. Evans, 86(BHS):Jul88-300
M. Wilson, 402(MLR):Jan89-208
Tirso de Molina. The Trickster of Seville and
the Stone Guest.* (G. Edwards, ed & trans)
D. Rogers, 86(BHS):Jul88-299
Tirso de Molina. El vergonzoso en palacio.
(E. Rull, ed)
R. ter Horst, 240(HR):Winter88-110
Tiruchelvam, N. & R. Coomaraswamy, eds.
The Role of the Judiciary in Plural Socie-
ties.
R.M. Hayden, 293(JASt):Aug88-579
Tischler, B.L. An American Music.*
D. Harvey, 410(M&L):Jan88-111
Tisdale, S. The Sorcerer's Apprentice.
L. Kirkwood, 529(QQ):Winter88-950
Tissier, A., ed. Recueil de Farces (1450-
1550).* (Vol 1)
B. Faivre, 535(RHL):Mar-Apr88-244
F-R. Hausmann, 547(RF):Band100Heft4-
424
Tissier, A., ed. Recueil de Farces (1450-
1550).* (Vol 2)
E.E. Du Bruck, 201:Vol14-243
F-R. Hausmann, 547(RF):Band100Heft4-
424
A. Hindley, 402(MLR):Apr89-468
G.A. Runnalls, 208(FS):Oct88-463
Tissier, A., ed. Recueil de Farces (1450-
1550). (Vol 3)
G. Roques, 553(RLiR):Jul-Dec88-554
Tissoni Benvenuti, A. L'Orfeo del Poliziano.
E. Bigi, 228(GSLI):Vol165fasc531-463
Titi, F. Studio di pittura, scultura, et arch-
itettura, nelle chiese di Roma (1674-1763).
(B. Contardi & S. Romana, eds)
J. Montagu, 90:Aug88-637
Titley, E.B. A Narrow Vision.*
O.P. Dickason, 298:Fall88-170
K.P. Stich, 102(CanL):Spring88-187
Titon, J.T. Powerhouse for God.
B.M. Sietsema, 350:Dec89-911
Tivnan, E. The Lobby.
D. Stone, 390:Apr88-52
Tixonov, A.N. Slovoobrazovatel'nyj slovar'
russkogo jazyka.
M. Rammelmeyer, 559:Vol12No3-315
Tobin, F. Meister Eckhart.*
F.L. Borchardt, 221(GQ):Spring88-302
Tobin, J.J., D.Y.H. Wu & D.H. Davidson. Pre-
school in Three Cultures.
P. Leach, 441:25Jun89-26
Tobin, T.H. - see Timaios of Locri
de Tocqueville, A. Oeuvres complètes. (Vol
7)
H. Brogan, 617(TLS):6-12Jan89-4
"The Tocqueville Review-La Revue Tocque-
ville." (Vol 8) (J. Pitts & H. Mendras, eds)
L. Wylie, 207(FR):May89-1103

Todd, D.D. - see Reid, T.
Todd, J., ed. Dictionary of British Women
Writers.
A. Leighton, 617(TLS):22-28Sep89-1024
Todd, J. Feminist Literary History.*
M. Baron, 175:Summer88-174
Todd, J. Sensibility.*
C.A. Howells, 83:Spring88-93
C.L. Johnson, 173(ECS):Fall88-111
W.A. Speck, 366:Autumn88-244
Todd, J. The Sign of Angellica.
T. Castle, 617(TLS):2-8Jun89-607
Todd, J., ed. Women and Film.
P.D. Murphy, 590:Jun89-47
Todd, L. & I. Hancock. International English
Usage.*
A.D. Horgan, 447(N&Q):Dec88-521
Todd, W.B. & A. Bowden. Tauchnitz Interna-
tional Editions in English 1841-1955.
J. Sutherland, 617(TLS):9-15Jun89-644
Todd, W.M. 3d. Fiction and Society in the Age
of Pushkin.*
W.H. Truitt, 290(JAAC):Spring88-430
Toesca, M., P. Conrath & R. Kolpa-Kopoul.
Guide de tube, 1000 tubes de 1950 à 1987.
A.J.M. Prévos, 498:Summer88-78
Tofani, A.P. - see under Petrioli Tofani, A.
Toker, F. Pittsburgh.
D. Gebhard, 576:Mar88-94
Tolchin, N.L. Mourning, Gender, and Creativ-
ity in the Art of Herman Melville.
M. Fisher, 268(IFR):Winter89-65
M.R. Stern, 587(SAF):Autumn88-245
Toledano, E.R. The Ottoman Slave Trade and
its Suppression, 1840-1890.
S. Soucek, 318(JAOS):Jul-Sep87-530
Toliver, H. Lyric Provinces in the English
Renaissance.*
J. Roe, 447(N&Q):Mar88-88
A. Rudrum, 49:Apr88-87
P. Thomson, 677(YES):Vol19-311
Toliver, S.S. Exile and the Elemental in the
Poetry of Erich Arendt.
D.C.G. Lorenz, 222(GR):Winter88-47
Tölle-Kastenbein, R. Frühklassische Peplos-
figuren.*
B. Sismondo Ridgway, 229:Band60Heft6-
523
Tollerson, M.S. Mythology and Cosmology in
the Narratives of Bernard Dadié and Birago
Diop.*
J.A. Mayes, 538(RAL):Fall88-404
Tolley, A.T. The Poetry of the Forties in
Britain.*
J. Reibetanz, 627(UTQ):Fall87-132
Tolstaya, T. On the Golden Porch.
P.K. Bell, 441:30Apr89-1
H. Gifford, 453(NYRB):1Jun89-3
Tolstoy, N. The Tolstoys.
G. Woodcock, 569(SR):Spring88-306
Tom, G., comp. Ekeyi, Gyo Cho Chu, My Coun-
try, Big Salmon River.
J. Kari, 424:Mar-Jun88-121
Tomalin, C. Katherine Mansfield.*
P. Craig, 617(TLS):7-13Apr89-362
R. Fuller, 364:Nov87-93
D. Rifkind, 31(ASch):Autumn88-628
639(VQR):Autumn88-123
Toman, J., ed. Studies in German Grammar.*
L. Travis, 603:Vol12No2-513
Tomás, J.M.O. - see under Oltra Tomás, J.M.

Tomasek, T. Die Utopie im "Tristan" Gotfrids von Strassburg.*
    W. McConnell, 221(GQ):Winter87-105
    P.W. Tax, 301(JEGP):Apr88-289
Tomaselli, K. & others, eds. Myth, Race, and Power.
    D. Walder, 538(RAL):Spring88-97
Tomaselli, S. & R. Porter, eds. Rape.
    S. Kappeler, 59:Mar88-118
Tomasoni, F. Ludwig Feuerbach e la natura non umana.
    F. Bazzani, 319:Jul89-489
    P. Trotignon, 542:Jul-Sep88-352
Tomašpol'skij, V.I. Obščeromanskij glagol.
    Y. Malkiel, 215(GL):Vol28No1-63
Tomberlin, J.E., ed. Agent, Language, and the Structure of the World.
    R. Hilpinen, 449:Jun88-307
Tomin, Z. Stalin's Shoe.
    P. Lewis, 565:Spring88-35
Tomkowiak, I. Curiöse Bauer-Historien.
    W. Theiss, 196:Band29Heft1/2-240
Tomlin, F. T.S. Eliot.
    H. Lomas, 364:Feb/Mar89-118
    J. Olney, 598(SoR):Spring89-503
Tomlin, R.S. Basic Word Order.
    W.J. Ashby, 320(CJL):Jun88-167
    B.B. Blake, 297(JL):Mar88-213
    W. Croft, 353:Vol26No5-892
Tomlinson, C. Annunciations.
    M. Edwards, 617(TLS):22-28Dec89-1417
Tomlinson, C. The Return.*
    H. Lomas, 364:Mar88-82
Tomlinson, G. Monteverdi and the End of the Renaissance.*
    B.R. Hanning, 309:Vol8No1/2-195
    H.W. Hitchcock, 551(RenQ):Summer88-320
    M. Somville, 465:Autumn88-87
Tommasini, A. Virgil Thomson's Musical Portraits.*
    M. Meckna, 414(MusQ):Vol73No1-144
Tompkins, J. Sensational Designs.*
    B.M., 494:Vol8No2-463
Tompkins, J.M.S. William Morris.
    A. St. George, 617(TLS):21-27Jul89-807
Tondeur, C-L. Gustave Flaubert, critique.*
    A. Schweiger, 535(RHL):Jan-Feb88-142
Tong, X. - see under Xiao Tong
de Tonnac, J-P., ed. Qui vive?
    J. Taylor, 617(TLS):2-8Jun89-618
Toohey, T.J. Piety and the Professions.
    T.W. Heyck, 637(VS):Summer89-582
Tooley, M. Causation.*
    J.H. Fetzer, 103:Mar89-121
Toomer, J. The Collected Poems of Jean Toomer. (R.B. Jones & M.T. Latimer, eds)
    L. Rosenberg, 441:19Feb89-24
van den Toorn, P.C. Stravinsky and "The Rite of Spring."*
    P. Wilson, 607:Sep88-64
Topolski, J. An Outline History of Poland.
    P.S. Wandycz, 497(PolR):Vol33No1-94
Torańska, T. "Them."*
    M.A. Abidor, 287:Jan/Feb88-28
    639(VQR):Winter88-25
Torchiana, D.T. Backgrounds for Joyce's "Dubliners."*
    M.H. Begnal, 174(Éire):Spring88-149
    R.A. Cave, 541(RES):May88-321
    P. Miles, 447(N&Q):Sep88-396
    P. Parrinder, 402(MLR):Jan89-141
    B. Tippett, 366:Autumn88-262

Tordi, R., ed. Umberto Saba, Trieste e la cultura mitteleuropea.
    E. Favretti, 228(GSLI):Vol165fasc532-580
Torelli, M. Lavinio e Roma.
    C. Ampolo, 123:Vol38No1-117
Torgovnick, M. The Visual Arts, Pictorialism, and the Novel.*
    D. Mehl, 72:Band224Heft2-465
de Toro, A., ed. Gustave Flaubert.
    L.R. Schehr, 446(NCFS):Fall-Winter 88/89-235
de Toro, F. Semiótica del teatro.*
    M. Carlson, 610:Autumn88-302
"Toronto Modern."
    A. Payne, 627(UTQ):Fall88-204
Torrance, J.M. Public Violence in Canada, 1867-1982.*
    J. Mouat, 102(CanL):Spring88-109
Torrell, J-P. & D. Bouthillier. Pierre le Vénérable et sa vision du monde.
    B.H. Rosenwein, 589:Oct88-1004
Torres, A. Blues for a Lost Childhood.
    J. Gledson, 617(TLS):15-21Dec89-1386
Torres, D. Studies on Clarín.
    M. Junquera, 552(REH):Jan88-141
    J. Rutherford, 402(MLR):Oct89-1012
    N.M. Valis, 238:Dec88-828
Torres, J. Fire & Fear.
    R. Strauss, 441:30Jul89-17
Torres, O. Al partir.
    J.J. Rodríguez-Florido, 238:Mar88-93
Torres, V.B. - see Calderón de la Barca, P.
de Torres Naharro, B. Comedias. (H. López Morales, ed)
    J. Lihani, 240(HR):Spring88-255
de Torres Villarroel, D. Vida. (R.P. Sebold, ed)
    I.L. McClelland, 86(BHS):Apr88-186
Torrijos, R.L. - see under López Torrijos, R.
Torrini, A.P. - see under Perissa Torrini, A.
Tosches, N. Country.
    D. Hill, 617(TLS):29Dec89/4Jan90-1438
Toselli, F. Nicola De Maria: Trionfo della carità.
    L.L. Ponti, 62:Dec88-109
Tosi, P.F. Observations on the Florid Song. (M. Pilkington, ed)
    H.M. Brown, 415:Feb88-86
Tōson Shimazaki. Before the Dawn.*
    M.C. Brownstein, 293(JASt):Aug88-650
Toulet, P-J. Oeuvres diverses.
    P.W.M. Cogman, 208(FS):Jan88-104
Touloumakos, J. Die theoretische Begründung der Demokratie in der klassischen Zeit Griechenlands.
    C.J. Rowe, 123:Vol38No2-282
Toulouse, T. The Art of Prophesying.*
    M.A. Bellesiles, 106:Summer88-233
    L. Henigman, 27(AL):Mar88-112
    E.B. Holifield, 656(WMQ):Jan88-177
    N.W. Shankle, 568(SCN):Spring-Summer88-17
Touratier, C., ed. Syntaxe et Latin.
    P. Flobert, 555:Vol61fasc1-135
Tourlakis, G.J. Computability.
    A. Yasuhara, 316:Dec88-1255
Tournier, M. The Golden Droplet.
    J. Updike, 442(NY):10Jul89-95
    639(VQR):Spring88-56
Tournier, M. Petites proses.
    J. Taylor, 532(RCF):Spring88-203

Tournier, M. Le Tabor et le Sinaï. Le Média-
noche amoureux.
 M. Sheringham, 617(TLS):11–17Aug89–
 879
Tournier, M. The Wind Spirit.*
 M. Sheringham, 617(TLS):11–17Aug89–
 879
 J. Updike, 442(NY):10Jul89–92
Tousignant, C. La Variation sociolinguis-
tique.
 L.B. Mignault, 627(UTQ):Fall88–182
Toussaint, J–P. L'Appareil–photo. The
Bathroom.
 D. Gunn, 617(TLS):28Apr–4May89–452
Toussaint–Dekker, A. Boek en school.
 H. Bekkering, 204(FdL):Jun88–152
Touzot, J. – see Cocteau, J.
Tovar, A. Relatos y diálogos de los Matacos,
seguidos de una gramática de su lengua.
 K.H. Schmidt, 685(ZDL):2/1987–250
Tovar, J.J.D. & J.H. Silverman – see under de
Bustos Tovar, J.J. & J.H. Silverman
Tovar, J.R. – see under Rubio Tovar, J.
Townsend, C. & E. War Wives.
 P. Willmott, 617(TLS):19–25May89–539
Townsend, C.E. & T. McAuley. Advanced
Czech.
 H. Arie–Gaifman, 574(SEEJ):Spring88–
 179
Townsend, C.E., T. McAuley & P. Kussi. In-
termediate Czech. (Vol 2)
 H. Arie–Gaifman, 574(SEEJ):Spring88–
 179
Townsend, C.E. & E. McKee. Elementary
Czech. (Vols 1 & 2) Intermediate Czech.
(Vol 1)
 H. Arie–Gaifman, 574(SEEJ):Spring88–
 179
Townsend, K. Sherwood Anderson.*
 W.B. Rideout, 569(SR):Summer88–lii
 J. Schevill, 536(Rev):Vol10–285
 D. Stouck, 395(MFS):Winter88–619
Townshend, C., ed. Consensus in Ireland.
 T. Hadden, 617(TLS):6–12Jan89–7
Toye, F. Rossini.
 M.S. Cole, 465:Autumn88–100
Toynbee, P. End of a Journey.*
 A. Ross, 364:Apr/May88–137
Trace, A. Furnace of Doubt.
 V. Terras, 268(IFR):Winter89–81
Trachtenberg, A. Reading American Photo-
graphs.
 W.S. McFeely, 441:20Aug89–15
Trachtenberg, M. & I. Hyman. Architecture.*
 J.J. Poesch, 576:Mar88–77
 R. Pommer, 505:May88–107
Trachtenberg, S., ed. The Postmodern
Moment.
 M.P.L., 295(JML):Fall87/Winter88–257
Tracy, C. English Gothic Choir–stalls 1200–
1400.*
 N. Coldstream, 90:Jun88–468
Tracy, C. A Portrait of Richard Graves.
 H. Cochrane, 566:Autumn88–87
 J. Gray, 166:Oct88–71
 L.G. Mitchell, 447(N&Q):Jun88–242
Tracy, W. Letters of Credit.*
 W. Rueter, 470:Vol26–206
Tracy, W. The Typographic Scene.
 S. Carter, 617(TLS):21–27Apr89–437
 B. Crutchley, 324:Nov89–824

"Traditions polémiques."
 M–M. de La Garanderie, 535(RHL):Nov–
 Dec88–1133
"Le traducteur cleptomane."
 P. Chardin, 549(RLC):Jan–Mar88–115
Traeger, J. Der Tod des Marat.
 M. Bleyl, 683:Band51Heft2–292
Träger, C., ed. Wörterbuch der Literatur-
wissenschaft.
 W. Thierse, 654(WB):3/1988–508
Traill, C.P. Canadian Crusoes. (R. Schieder,
ed)
 M. Peterman, 627(UTQ):Fall87–160
Train, J. The New Money Masters.
 R. Krulwich, 441:29Oct89–25
Traina, A. & M. Bini, eds. Supplementum
Morelianum.*
 P. Flobert, 555:Vol61fasc1–136
Tramitz, A. & B. Ulrich – see Richert, D.
Tramontano Magno, C. & D.V. Erdman – see
Blake, W.
Tranel, B. The Sounds of French.
 S.R. Anderson, 350:Dec89–912
 B. Ebling 2d, 399(MLJ):Winter88–474
"Transpositions."*
 J–M. Bailbé, 535(RHL):Nov–Dec88–1184
Tranströmer, T. Collected Poems.
 A. Brownjohn, 493:Spring88–22
Tranströmer, T. Tomas Tranströmer: Selected
Poems, 1954–1986. (R. Hass, ed)
 S. Friebert, 199:Spring88–54
 N. Van Winckel, 271:Spring–Summer88–
 178
Transue, P.J. Virginia Woolf and the Politics
of Style.*
 N. Bradbury, 541(RES):May88–317
 R.B.D., 295(JML):Fall87/Winter88–403
 J. Gindin, 401(MLQ):Dec86–422
Trapnell, W.H. Eavesdropping in Marivaux.
 F. Deloffre, 166:Jan89–149
 D.C. Spinelli, 207(FR):Mar89–685
Trapp, A.D. & others – see Gregory of Rimini
Trasancos, A.V. – see under Vigo Trasancos,
A.
Trasko, M. Heavenly Soles.
 E. Jong, 441:3Dec89–45
Trassard, J–L. L'érosion intérieure. Paroles
de laine. L'Ancolie. Des cours d'eau peu
considérables. Tardifs instantanés.
 J–P. Richard, 98:Nov88–867
Traube, E.G. Cosmology and Social Life.
 J.C. Kuipers, 293(JASt):Feb88–202
 S. McKinnon, 292(JAF):Jan–Mar88–108
Traversagni, L.G. The "Epitoma Margarite
Castigate Eloquentie" of Laurentius Guliel-
mus Traversagni de Saona.* (R.H. Martin,
ed & trans)
 R.P.H. Green, 123:Vol38No1–188
Traversi, D. Chaucer: The Earlier Poetry.
 E. Brown, Jr., 191(ELN):Sep88–77
Travisano, T.J. Elizabeth Bishop.
 M. Holley, 27(AL):Dec88–692
 B.C. Millier, 617(TLS):12–18May89–516
Treffert, D.A. Extraordinary People.
 S. Sutherland, 617(TLS):2–8Jun89–601
Trefousse, H.L. Andrew Johnson.
 J.M. McPherson, 61:Aug89–84
Trefusis, V. Violet to Vita. (M.A. Leaska &
J. Phillips, eds)
 C. Harman, 617(TLS):29Sep–5Oct89–1053
Tregebov, R. No One We Know.*
 L. York, 102(CanL):Summer88–142
Treglown, J. – see Stevenson, R.L.

Truman, H.S. Where the Buck Stops. (M. Truman, ed)
  H. Thomas, 441:31Dec89-15
Truman, M. Murder at the Kennedy Center.
  B. Kent, 441:17Sep89-24
Truman, M. Murder in the CIA.
  639(VQR):Spring88-57
Trump, D.J., with T. Schwartz. Trump.*
  639(VQR):Spring88-51
Trump, M., ed. Armed Vision.
  M. Hope, 617(TLS):16-22Jun89-670
Truscott, L.K. 4th. Army Blue.
  D. Murray, 441:17Sep89-14
Trusted, J. Free Will and Responsibility.
  T. Horgan, 449:Jun88-332
Trusted, J. Moral Principles and Social Values.*
  P. Benn, 518:Jul88-165
Tryon, T. The Night of the Moonbow.
  C. Salzberg, 441:6Aug89-18
Trypanis, C.A. - see Sophocles
Tsai Wen-hui. Patterns of Political Elite Mobility in Modern China, 1912-1949.
  J.L. Saari, 302:Vol24No1-84
Tsao, J.T.H. China's Development Strategies and Foreign Trade.
  C-Y. Cheng, 293(JASt):May88-362
Tsatsos, C. Dialogues in a Monastery.
  E. Current-Garcia, 577(SHR):Summer88-282
Tscherpel, R. Mörikes lemurische Possen.
  M.C. Crichton, 221(GQ):Winter87-126
Tsien Tsuen-hsun. Science and Civilization in China.* (Vol 5, Pt 1) [shown in prev under Needham, J.]
  Ho Peng Yoke, 302:Vol24No1-92
Tsuda, A. Sales Talk in Japan and in the United States.
  P. Schlobinski, 355(LSoc):Mar88-147
Tsuen-hsun, T. - see under Tsien Tsuen-hsun
Tsuji, N. Playfulness in Japanese Art.
  M. Takeuchi, 293(JASt):May88-367
Tsung-hsi, H. - see under Huang Tsung-hsi
Tsurumi, S. A Cultural History of Postwar Japan, 1945-1980.* An Intellectual History of Wartime Japan, 1931-1945.
  M. Silverberg, 293(JASt):Aug88-654
Tsushima, Y. The Shooting Gallery and Other Stories.* (G. Harcourt, comp & trans)
  L. Allen, 617(TLS):28Apr-4May89-466
  L. Dunlop, 363(LitR):Winter89-288
Tsvetayeva, M. Selected Poems.
  C. Rumens, 493:Spring88-23
Tuan, N.A. South Vietnam Trial and Experience.
  G.C. Larsen, 293(JASt):May88-438
Tuan, Y-F. Morality and Imagination.
  M. Midgley, 441:25Jun89-29
Tuchman, G., with N.E. Fortin. Edging Women Out.
  A. Snitow, 441:3Sep89-15
Tucker, H.F. Tennyson and the Doom of Romanticism.
  M. Bailin, 344:Summer89-159
  G. Joseph, 637(VS):Winter89-280
  W.H. Pritchard, 249(HudR):Autumn88-560
  J. Sendry, 445(NCF):Mar89-537
  M. Stone, 150(DR):Fall88-366
  639(VQR):Summer88-80
Tucker, J.B. The Man Who Looked Like Howard Cosell.
  N. Callendar, 441:12Feb89-20

Tucker, J.G. Innokentij Annenskij and the Acmeist Doctrine.
  C. Kelly, 575(SEER):Apr88-272
  E. Rusinko, 574(SEEJ):Summer88-322
Tucker, M.M., comp. Harvest Time Stories.
  R. Finnegan, 538(RAL):Fall88-424
Tucker, R.C. Political Culture and Leadership in Soviet Russia.
  S. Welch, 575(SEER):Apr88-314
  639(VQR):Summer88-96
Tucker, S. Telling Memories Among Southern Women.
  442(NY):23Jan89-119
Tufts, E. Luis Meléndez, Eighteenth-Century Master of the Spanish Still Life, With a Catalogue Raisonné.
  A. Ubeda de los Cobos, 48:Apr-Jun88-189
Tugendhat, E. Selbstbewusstsein und Selbstbestimmung.
  R. Rochlitz, 98:May88-370
Tulard, J. Napoleon.
  C. Jones, 83:Autumn88-218
Tuleja, T. The Catalog of Lost Books.
  F. Gannon, 441:23Jul89-12
Tulloch, H. Acton.
  J.P. Kenyon, 617(TLS):5-11May89-494
Tulloch, L. Fabulous Nobodies.
  C. Heimel, 441:11Jun89-14
Tung, C. & C. MacKerras, eds. Drama in the People's Republic of China.
  H-Y.L. Mowry, 293(JASt):Aug88-625
Tuohy, J. & R. Warden. Greylord.
  M.E. O'Connell, 441:12Feb89-19
Tuomela, R. A Theory of Social Action.*
  M. Brand, 449:Dec88-624
Tuomi, R. Omma Sofokleen draamassa Oidipus Tyrannos 81.
  F. Vian, 555:Vol61fasc1-116
Tuomi, R. & Kai Nyn. Solons Gedicht an Mimnermos im Lichte der Tradition.
  F. Vian, 555:Vol61fasc1-116
Tuppen, J. France under Recession, 1981-1986.
  T.H. Jones, 207(FR):Apr89-933
Tur, R. & W. Twining, eds. Essays on Kelsen.*
  J.H.B., 185:Oct88-198
Turcan, M. - see Tertullian
Turchetti, M. Concordia o Toleranza, François Bauduin (1520-1573) e i "Moyenneurs."*
  M. Adam, 542:Apr-Jun88-258
Turco, L. The New Book of Forms.*
  S. Cushman, 569(SR):Winter88-ii
Turgenev, I. A Sportsman's Notebook.
  G. Woodcock, 569(SR):Spring88-306
Turienzo, F.F. - see under Fernández Turienzo, F.
Turk, E.B. Child of Paradise.
  P. Biskind, 441:16Apr89-28
  D. Coward, 617(TLS):10-16Nov89-1242
von dem Türlin, H. The Crown.
  E. Hower, 441:24Sep89-48
Turnbull, R., ed. The Opera Gazetteer.
  E. Forbes, 415:Sep88-462
Turner, A. Early Scientific Instruments: Europe 1400-1800.
  D. Howse, 324:Apr89-317
Turner, B., ed. Building Community.
  D. Lewis, 47:Dec88-55
Turner, B.S. The Body and Society.*
  L. Brodkey, 128(CE):Jan88-89

Turner, E. The Spirit and the Drum.
42(AR):Spring88-278
Turner, E.G. Greek Manuscripts of the Ancient World. (2nd ed rev by P.J. Parsons)
J.N. Birdsall, 354:Jun88-158
S.G. Daitz, 124:Jul-Aug89-477
N.G. Wilson, 123:Vol38No2-452
Turner, G.W., ed. The Australian Pocket Oxford Dictionary. (2nd ed)
H. Ulherr, 38:Band106Heft1/2-197
Turner, H.A., Jr. The Two Germanies since 1945.
639(VQR):Winter88-25
Turner, H.A., Jr. - see Wagener, O.
Turner, J.G. One Flesh.
R. Flannagan, 391:Dec88-129
T. Healy, 175:Summer88-155
J. Holstun, 568(SCN):Winter88-72
Turner, P. English Literature 1832-1890, Excluding the Novel.
R. Altick, 617(TLS):14-20Apr89-390
Turner, S. The Search for a Methodology of Social Science.
D. Ginev, 679:Band19Heft2-391
Turner, T. English Garden Design, History and Style since 1650.
P.D., 46:Apr88-12
Turnley, D., P. Turnley & M. Liu. Beijing Spring.
M. Gottschalk, 441:10Dec89-13
Turnley, D.C. Why Are They Weeping?
A. Barnet, 441:1Jan89-15
Turow, J. Playing Doctor.
M. Oppenheim, 441:9Apr89-33
Tuten, F. Tallien.*
S. Moore, 532(RCF):Fall88-161
Tutuola, A. Yoruba Folktales.
O. Owomoyela, 538(RAL):Fall88-426
Tveterås, H.L. Den norske bokhandels historie. (Vol 3)
R. Eide, 172(Edda):1988/1-94
Tvorogov, O.V. - see Lixačev, D.S.
Twain, M. Adventures of Huckleberry Finn.* (W. Blair & V. Fischer, eds)
H. Beaver, 677(YES):Vol19-350
Twain, M. Plymouth Rock and the Pilgrims, and Other Salutary Platform Opinions. (C. Neider ed) Mark Twain at His Best. (C. Neider ed) Mark Twain Laughing. (P.M. Zall, ed)
E.L. Galligan, 569(SR):Spring88-265
Twain, M. Roughing It.
E.L. Galligan, 569(SR):Spring88-265
Twain, M. Mark Twain's Letters. (Vol 1) (E.M. Branch, M.B. Frank & K.M. Sanderson, eds)
W. Baker, 42(AR):Summer88-391
M. Millgate, 627(UTQ):Winter88/89-327
Twain, M. The Wit & Wisdom of Mark Twain. (A. Ayres, ed)
E.L. Galligan, 569(SR):Spring88-265
42(AR):Winter88-123
Tweyman, S. Scepticism and Belief in Hume's Dialogues Concerning Natural Religion.*
J. Noxon, 154:Autumn88-551
M.A. Stewart, 319:Jul89-481
Twining, W., ed. Legal Theory and Common Law.
C.M. Gray, 185:Apr89-650
Twining, W. Theories of Evidence.*
A. Welsh, 125:Fall87-91

Twitchett, D. & M. Loewe, eds. The Cambridge History of China. (Vol 1)
J.L. Dull, 293(JASt):Feb88-131
C-Y. Hsu, 244(HJAS):Dec88-535
Tydeman, W. "Doctor Faustus."*
R. Dutton, 402(MLR):Oct89-922
Tydeman, W. English Medieval Theatre 1400-1500.*
C. Gauvin, 189(EA):Oct-Dec88-475
C.W. Marx, 382(MAE):1988/1-123
P. Meredith, 402(MLR):Oct89-918
Tye, M. The Metaphysics of Mind.
H.M. Robinson, 617(TLS):27Oct-2Nov89-1189
Tyler, A. Breathing Lessons.*
M. Wood, 617(TLS):20-26Jan89-57
Tyler, J. & P. Sparks. The Early Mandolin.
I. Woodfield, 617(TLS):4-10Aug89-854
Tyler, S.A. The Unspeakable.
P.J. Hopper, 350:Mar89-194
Tyler, W.T. The Lion and the Jackal.*
639(VQR):Summer88-92
Tymieniecka, A-T. Logos and Life.
D. Laskey, 543:Jun89-855
Tymowski, M., J. Kieniewicz & J. Holzer. Historia Polski.
N. Pease, 497(PolR):Vol33No1-99
Tynan, K. The Life of Kenneth Tynan.*
M. Coveney, 157:No167-47
M. Gussow, 18:Apr88-60
C. Osborne, 364:Feb88-97
W.H. Pritchard, 31(ASch):Autumn88-620
de Tyr, G. - see under Guillaume de Tyr
Tyrrell, J. Czech Opera.
G. Martin, 465:Summer89-80
G. Melville-Mason, 324:Apr89-321
M. Zemanová, 617(TLS):20-26Jan89-67
Tyson, A. Mozart.*
C. Hatch, 465:Summer89-96
A.H. King, 309:Vol8No3/4-386
S. Sadie, 415:Mar88-128
Tyson, G.P. & S.S. Wagonheim, eds. Print and Culture in the Renaissance.
M. Lowry, 551(RenQ):Winter88-717
Tyson, N.J. Eugene Aram.
M. Cotsell, 158:Dec88-201
Tytell, J. Ezra Pound.*
J.T. Barbarese, 219(GaR):Fall88-656
B. Duffey, 579(SAQ):Fall88-821
H. Levin, 453(NYRB):9Nov89-45
C.D.K. Yee, 27(AL):Oct88-501
Tytler, H. An Englishwoman in India. (A. Sattin, ed)
J.E. Early, 635(VPR):Summer88-75
Tzavella-Evjen, H. Lithares.
J.M. Fossey, 121(CJ):Feb-Mar89-260
Tzonis, A. & L. Lefaivre. Classical Architecture.*
C. Tadgell, 576:Dec88-413

Ua Laoghaire, P. Séadna.
S. Ua Súilleabháin, 112:Vol20-209
Uchida, F.Y. L'Enigme onomastique et la création romanesque dans "Armance."
S.C. Witkin, 446(NCFS):Spring-Summer89-405
Udall, M.K. Too Funny To Be President.*
639(VQR):Summer88-102
al-Udhari, A. - see Darwish, M., S. al-Qasim & Adonis

374

Udoff, A., ed. Kafka and the Contemporary Critical Performance.*
P.F. Dvorak, 221(GQ):Fall88-591
R.V. Gross, 406:Winter88-488
Ueckermann, G. Renaissancismus und Fin de siècle.
M.P. Alter, 221(GQ):Spring87-294
Ueda, M., ed. The Mother of Dreams and Other Short Stories.
P.I. Lyons, 407(MN):Spring88-104
Ueda, Y. - see Shinran
Ueding, G., ed. Karl-May-Handbuch.
C.F. Lorenz, 602:Band19Heft1-186
Uggla, A.N. Den svenska Polenbilden och polsk prosa i Sverige 1939-1960.
B. Steene, 563(SS):Winter88-112
Uglione, R., ed. Atti del Convegno Nazionale di Studi su La Città Ideale nella Tradizione Classica e Biblico-Cristiana, Torino 2-4 Maggio 1985.
J. Ferguson, 123:Vol38No1-73
Uglow, J. George Eliot.
C. Crosby, 637(VS):Autumn88-119
Ugrinsky, A., ed. Lessing and the Enlightenment.
H.H.F. Henning, 406:Fall88-390
A.C. Leidner, 221(GQ):Summer88-462
Uhlenbruch, E. - see Kvetnickij, F.
Uhlig, C. Theorie der Literarhistorie.
E. Możejko, 107(CRCL):Mar88-79
Ulbert, T. Die Basilika des Heiligen Kreuzes in Resafa-Sergiupolis.
J. Kramer, 229:Band60Heft3-281
Ule, L. A Concordance to the Shakespeare Apocrypha. (J. Jofen, ed)
E. Sams, 447(N&Q):Sep88-372
Ulivi, F. D'Annunzio.
F. Donini, 617(TLS):10-16Mar89-254
Ullman, L. Dreams by No One's Daughter.
B. Howard, 491:Nov88-111
C. Muske, 441:8Jan89-14
Ullmann-Margalit, E. The Emergence of Norms.
A.M.S. Piper, 482(PhR):Jan88-99
Ulloa, J.C. Sobre José Lezama Lima y sus lectores.
R.D. Woods, 238:Dec88-840
Ulmer, G.L. Applied Grammatology.
C. Koelb, 149(CLS):Vol25No1-95
Umehara Kaoru. Sōdai kanryō seido kenkyū.
P. Ebrey, 244(HJAS):Dec88-493
Umiker-Sebeok, J., ed. Marketing and Semiotics.
R.B. Wilbur, 350:Sep89-679
Umpierre-Herrera, L.M. The Margarita Poems.
R.S. Platizky, 36:Fall-Winter88-232
de Unamuno, M. San Manuel Bueno, mártir. (F. Fernández Turienzo, ed)
M. Gordon, 240(HR):Winter88-116
de Unamuno, M. Del sentimiento trágico de la vida en los hombres y en los puebllos. (F. Savater, ed) Niebla. (A. Suárez Miramón, ed) La agonía del cristianismo. (A. García Calvo, ed)
H.C. Raley, 240(HR):Summer88-378
de Unamuno, M. Vida de Don Quijote y Sancho. La tía Tula.
T.R. Franz, 240(HR):Autumn88-510
Unbescheid, G., ed & trans. Märchen aus Nepal.
U. Kölver, 196:Band29Heft1/2-242
Underdown, D. Revel, Riot and Rebellion.*
K. Sharpe, 250(HLQ):Spring88-112

Underhill, N. Testing Spoken Language.
J.D. Brown, 608:Mar89-144
R. Caminero, 399(MLJ):Autumn88-337
A.G. Lo Re, 238:Dec88-846
Underwood, L. On Dangerous Ground.
B. Hochberg, 441:3Sep89-14
Unger, D. El Yanqui.
G.L. Morris, 502(PrS):Spring88-121
Unger, J.M. The Fifth Generation Fallacy.
M.M. Strauss & M. Tomita, 293(JASt): Nov88-901
Unger, R.M. Social Theory. False Necessity. Plasticity into Power.
P. Anderson, 617(TLS):13-19Jan89-37
G. Poggi, 676(YR):Autumn88-134
Ungerer, M. Summertime Food.
R. Flaste, 441:11Jun89-18
Unschuld, P.U. Medicine in China: A History of Pharmaceutics.
S. Kuriyama, 293(JASt):May88-364
Unschuld, P.U., ed & trans. Medicine in China: Nan-ching - the Classic of Difficult Issues.
S. Kuriyama, 293(JASt):May88-364
Unsworth, C. The Politics of Mental Health Legislation.
J. Neu, 185:Oct88-174
Unterreitmeier, H. Tristan als Retter.*
D. Mieth, 224(GRM):Band38Heft1/2-203
Unwin, T. Constant: "Adolphe."
C.P. Courtney, 208(FS):Oct88-479
M.A. Wégimont, 446(NCFS):Spring-Summer89-406
D. Wood, 402(MLR):Jan89-178
Updike, D. Out on the Marsh.*
J. Clute, 617(TLS):21-27Jul89-803
Updike, J. La Condition naturelle.
G. Goffette, 450(NRF):Jun88-87
Updike, J. Just Looking.
A.C. Danto, 441:15Oct89-12
Updike, J. S.*
T. Wilhelmus, 249(HudR):Autumn88-550
Updike, J. Self-Consciousness.
P-L. Adams, 61:Apr89-100
D. Donoghue, 441:5Mar89-7
E. Hardwick, 453(NYRB):18May89-3
A. MacCurtain, 617(TLS):5-11May89-479
Upham, F.K. Law and Social Change in Postwar Japan.
Fujiwara Jun'ichirō, 285(JapQ):Jan-Mar88-91
W. Kelly, 293(JASt):Aug88-656
Upton, D., ed. America's Architectural Roots.
B.F. Le Beau, 576:Sep88-316
Upton, D. Holy Things and Profane.*
P.D. Zimmerman, 658:Spring88-81
Upton, D. & J.M. Vlach, eds. Common Places.*
M.C. Perdue, 292(JAF):Apr-Jun88-248
D.F. Ward, 440:Winter-Spring88-149
Upward, E. The Night Walk and Other Stories.*
S. Spender, 364:Mar87-29
Ur, P. Grammar Practice Activities.
I. Leki, 608:Dec89-688
Urban, G.R., ed. Can the Soviet System Survive Reform?
O. Figes, 617(TLS):4-10Aug89-841
Urban, M. Emil Nolde.* (Vol 1)
J. Lloyd, 90:Apr88-300
Urban, S., ed. Z Husowa po berła rektorskie.
T.N. Cieplak, 497(PolR):Vol33No2-215

Urbanas, A. La notion d'accident chez Aristote.
  L.J. Elders, 543:Dec88–413
Urdang, L. Dictionary of Differences.
  D.J. Enright, 617(TLS):24Feb–2Mar89–202
Urdang, L. & F.R. Abate. Loanwords Dictionary.*
  G. Cannon, 660(Word):Apr88–67
Urdang, L. & F.G. Ruffner, Jr., eds. Allusions – Cultural, Literary, Biblical and Historical. (2nd ed)
  K.B. Harder, 424:Mar–Jun88–124
Ureland, P.S. & I. Clarkson, eds. Scandinavian Language Contacts.*
  W. Lehmann, 320(CJL):Jun88–194
Uris, L. Mitla Pass.
  D. Fitzpatrick, 441:1Jan89–14
Urmson, J.O. Aristotle's Ethics.*
  483:Jul88–413
Urrutia, J. Imago Litterae.
  P.W. Evans, 86(BHS):Oct88–418
Ursua Lezaun, N. & others. Filosofía de la Ciencia y Metodología Crítica.
  R. Torretti, 449:Jun88–327
Urzidil, J. Le Triptyque de Prague.
  L. Kovacs, 450(NRF):Nov88–121
"Use of Laboratory Animals in Biomedical and Behavioral Research."
  P. Singer, 453(NYRB):2Feb89–36
Ustinov, P. The Disinformer.
  L.E. Nesbitt, 441:17Sep89–30
Uszkoreit, H. Word Order and Constituent Structure in German.
  E.W. Hinrichs & T. Nakazawa, 350:Mar89–141
Utas, B. A Persian Sufi Poem.
  V.R. Holbrook, 318(JAOS):Jul–Sep87–529
Utermöhlen, G. & S. Sellschopp – see Leibniz, G.W.
Uther, H–J. Katalog zur Volkserzählung.
  C. Daxelmüller, 196:Band29Heft1/2–245
  R.M.J., 203:Vol99No2–265
  H. Rölleke, 52:Band23Heft1–97
Uyemoto, H. Rebel Without a Clue.
  P. Cytrynbaum, 441:10Dec89–32
de Uztarroz, J.F.A. – see under Andrés de Uztarroz, J.F.

Väänänen, V. Le Journal–Épître d'Égérie.*
  M. Winterbottom, 123:Vol38No2–419
de Vaca, A.N.C. – see under Núñez Cabeza de Vaca, A.
Vachek, J. Written Language Revisited. (P.A. Luelsdorff, ed)
  Z. Salzmann, 350:Dec89–914
Vajda, G.M. & J. Riesz, eds. The Future of Literary Scholarship/Die Zukunft der Literaturwissenschaft/L'Avenir des sciences littéraires.*
  Y. Chevrel, 549(RLC):Jul–Sep88–405
  H.H.H. Remak, 107(CRCL):Jun88–236
Vakalopoulos, K.A. Neoterē istoria tēs Makedonias (1830–1912) apo tē genesē toy neoellēnikoy kratoys ōs tēn apeleytherōsē [and] E Makedonia stis paramones toy Makedonikoy agōna (1894–1904).
  G.P. Henderson, 303(JoHS):Vol108–277
Vaksman, F. Ideological Struggle.
  R. Walker, 575(SEER):Oct88–663
Valais, G. Les deux soeurs.
  M. Andersen, 102(CanL):Winter87–182

de Valdés, A. Dialogue of Mercury and Charon.
  M.T. Ward, 238:Sep88–569
Valdes, J.M., ed. Culture Bound.
  L.M. Crawford-Lange, 399(MLJ):Autumn88–337
  H.L. Nostrand, 399(MLJ):Spring88–77
Valdés, M.J. Phenomenological Hermeneutics and the Study of Literature.
  D. Dowling, 102(CanL):Summer88–149
  J. Weinsheimer, 177(ELT):Vol31No4–512
Valdivieso, E. Historia de la pintura sevillana, siglos XIII al XX.
  E. Bermejo, 48:Jan–Mar88–89
Valencia, P., F. Merlonghi & M. Weissenrieder. En contacto. (3rd ed)
  A.L. Prince, 399(MLJ):Winter88–494
Valency, M. Julie.
  P–L. Adams, 61:Mar89–98
  L. Rosenberg, 441:2Apr89–25
Valensi, L. Venise et la sublime porte.
  M. Schaub, 98:Oct88–860
Valentin, J–M., ed. "Monarchus Poeta."*
  K.F. Otto, Jr., 406:Fall88–389
Valentiner, T. – see Kant, I.
Valera, J. Juanita la Larga.* (E. Rubio Cremades, ed)
  M. Hemingway, 86(BHS):Apr88–190
Valéry, P. Cahiers 1894–1914. (N. Celeyrette-Pietri & J. Robinson-Valéry, eds)
  R. Sieburth, 617(TLS):22–28Sep89–1019
"Valéry, pour quoi?"
  H. Merkl, 72:Band225Heft2–443
Valet, P. Études, témoignages, inédits. Vertiges.
  F. Mary, 450(NRF):Jan88–102
Valette, J–P., G.S. Kupferschmid & R.M. Valette. Con Mucho Gusto. (3rd ed)
  R.J. Griffin, 399(MLJ):Winter88–495
Valgardson, W.D. The Carpenter of Dreams.
  I. Sowton, 102(CanL):Summer88–163
Valin, J. Extenuating Circumstances.
  M. Stasio, 441:16Apr89–31
Valin, R., W. Hirtle & A. Joly – see Guillaume, G.
Valis, N.M. Leopoldo Alas (Clarín).
  H.C. Woodbridge, 345(KRQ):Aug88–378
Valis, N.M. The Novels of Jacinto Octavio Picón.*
  A.H. Clarke, 345(KRQ):Aug88–372
  J. Dial, 552(REH):Jan88–140
Valla, L. The Profession of the Religious and the Principal Arguments from The Falsely-Believed and Forged Donation of Constantine.* (O.Z. Pugliese, ed & trans)
  L.V.R., 568(SCN):Spring–Summer88–33
Valla, L. De professione religiosorum. (M. Cortesi, ed)
  D. Marsh, 551(RenQ):Summer88–297
Vallance, A. William Morris.
  D. McKitterick, 78(BC):Spring88–134
Valle-Inclán, R. The Lamp of Marvels (Aesthetic Meditations).*
  W.J. Smither, 238:May88–318
Vallee, L. & R. Findlay – see Osinski, Z.
Vallejo, C. Poemas humanos. (F. Martínez García, ed)
  D. Harris, 402(MLR):Apr89–507
  J.C. Marset, 711(RHM):Jun88–79
Vallejo, C. Tungsten.
  N. Shakespeare, 617(TLS):14–20Jul89–781
  A. Whitehouse, 441:26Feb89–34

Varley, H.P. Japanese Culture. (3rd ed)
L.A. Serafim, 399(MLJ):Spring88-99
Varloot, J. - see Diderot, D.
Varnado, S.L. Haunted Presence.
E.F. Bleiler, 445(NCF):Dec88-394
D.A. Ringe, 395(MFS):Summer88-317
J. Wilt, 637(VS):Autumn88-137
Varnedoe, K. Northern Light.*
J. Abdy, 39:Sep88-218
Varnedoe, K. Vienna 1900.*
P.D., 46:May88-14
Varnedoe, K.T. Gustave Caillebotte.*
K. Adler, 90:Jun88-472
R.D. Reck, 446(NCFS):Spring-Summer89-
430
Varriano, J. Italian Baroque and Rococo Ar-
chitecture.*
S.F. Ostrow, 54:Sep88-528
Varro. M. Terentius Varro, "Saturarum Men-
ippearum Fragmenta." (R. Astbury, ed)
J-P. Cèbe, 229:Band60Heft3-196
H.D. Jocelyn, 123:Vol38No1-33
Varro. Varron, La langue latine. (Bk 6) (P.
Flobert, ed & trans)
D. Briquel, 555:Vol61fasc2-323
Varro. Varron, "Satires Ménippées." (Fasc 8)
(J-P. Cèbe, ed & trans)
H. Dahlmann, 229:Band60Heft8-691
Vàrvaro, A. Letterature romanze del Medio-
evo.*
A. Scaglione, 545(RPh):Nov88-220
Vàrvaro, A. La parola nel tempo.
F. Bruni, 545(RPh):Feb89-306
G. Holtus, 72:Band225Heft1-203
Vàrvaro, A., with R. Sornicola. Vocabolario
Etimologico Siciliano. (Vol 1)
H. Meier, 72:Band225Heft1-207
Vasa, A. Logica, scienze della natura e
mondo della vita, Lezioni 1978-1980. (L.
Handjaras & A. Marinotti, eds)
P. Trotignon, 542:Jul-Sep88-399
Vasina, A. & others. Ricerche e studi sul
Breviarium ecclesiae Ravennatis (Codice
Bavaro).
A.O. Citarella, 589:Apr88-483
Vasquez, E.P.M., with A.L. Sanarabia & others
- see under Martinez Vasquez, E.P., with
A.L. Sanarabia & others
Vassalli, S. The Night of the Comet.
A.H.C. Danti, 617(TLS):1-7Sep89-954
Vassallo, P. Byron.*
M. Storey, 339:Autumn88-101
Vattimo, G. The End of Modernity.* (Italian
title: La fine della modernità.)
B. Rotman, 617(TLS):7-13Apr89-373
Vaughan, K. Journals 1939-1977. (A. Ross,
ed)
F. MacCarthy, 617(TLS):29Sep-5Oct89-
1053
Vax, L. La séduction de l'étrange. (2nd ed)
M. Potet, 549(RLC):Jul-Sep88-411
Vaz Ferreira, M.E. Poesías Completas. (H.J.
Verani, ed)
A.H. Martínez, 238:Mar88-88
Vázquez Estévez, M. Comedias sueltas del
"Institut del Teatre" en Barcelona.
D.W. Cruickshank, 402(MLR):Apr89-502
Veatch, R.M. The Foundations of Justice.
M. Lappé, 185:Oct88-172
Vecce, C. Gli umanisti e la musica.
W.R. Bowen, 551(RenQ):Spring88-143
Vecsey, G. A Year in the Sun.
K. Stabiner, 441:26Mar89-7

Veeder, W. Mary Shelley and Frankenstein.*
A.F. Janowitz, 402(MLR):Oct89-938
M. Smith, 577(SHR):Winter88-78
Veeder, W. & G. Hirsch, eds. Dr. Jekyll and
Mr. Hyde after One Hundred Years.
H-P. Breuer, 395(MFS):Winter88-677
B. Kalikoff, 637(VS):Spring89-452
Veen, H-J., ed. From Brezhnev to Gorbachev.
M. McCauley, 575(SEER):Oct88-661
de Veer, E. & R.J. Boyle. Sunlight and Shad-
ow.*
F. Murphy, 432(NEQ):Dec88-612
Vega, E. Mendoza's Dreams.
A. Ramírez, 238:Mar88-97
de la Vega, G.L.L. - see under Lasso de la
Vega, G.L.
de Vega Carpio, L. La bella malmaridada. (D.
McGrady & S. Freeman, eds)
M.C. Quintero, 238:Dec88-823
de Vega Carpio, L. La fábula de Perseo o la
bella Andrómeda.* (M.D. McGaha, ed)
S.N. McCrary, 345(KRQ):Feb88-111
de Vega Carpio L. Lo fingido verdadero/
Acting is Believing.* (M.D. McGaha, trans)
A.J. Cruz, 552(REH):Jan88-136
J.M. Ruano de la Haza, 86(BHS):Jul88-
298
de Vega Carpio, L. Las hazañas del segundo
David. (J.B. Avalle-Arce & G. Cervantes
Martín, eds)
W.F. Hunter, 86(BHS):Jul88-299
de Vegvar, C.L.N. The Northumbrian Renais-
sance.
I. Henderson, 90:Dec88-934
Veintemilla, J.M.R. - see under Ruiz Veinte-
milla, J.M.
Veisland, J.S. Kierkegaard and the Dialectics
of Modernism.*
Ø. Rottem, 172(Edda):1988/4-365
Veit, W. Siegel und Siegelschrift der Chou-,
Ch'in- und Han-Dynastie.
W.G. Boltz, 318(JAOS):Oct-Dec87-833
Veith, W.H. & W. Putschke, eds. Kleiner
Deutscher Sprachatlas.* (Vol 1, Pt 1)
W. Kleiber, 260(IF):Band93-357
Veltruský, J.F., ed. A Sacred Farce from
Medieval Bohemia: Mastičkář.*
A. Měšťan, 688(ZSP):Band48Heft2-431
A. Thomas, 549(RLC):Jan-Mar88-110
H. Voisine-Jechova, 107(CRCL):Mar88-
120
Velz, J.W. & F.N. Teague - see Crosby, J.
van de Ven, C. Space in Architecture. (3rd
ed)
90:Aug88-641
van der Ven, J.J.M. Ius humanum.
C. Schefold, 489(PJGG):Band95Heft2-376
Vena, G. O'Neill's "The Iceman Cometh."
M. Matlaw, 610:Autumn88-294
Venclova, T. Neustojčivoe ravnovesie.
B.P. Scherr, 574(SEEJ):Summer88-315
Vendler, H., ed. The Harvard Book of Con-
temporary American Poetry.* (British title:
The Faber Book of Contemporary American
Poetry.)
C. Clausen, 569(SR):Winter88-131
R. Pybus, 565:Summer88-72
Vendler, H. The Music of What Happens.*
B. Bawer, 249(HudR):Winter89-617
N. Miller, 42(AR):Spring88-269
Vendler, H., ed. Voices & Visions.
639(VQR):Summer88-100

Vetter, T. Der Buddha und seine Lehre in Dharmakīrtis Pramāṇavārittika.
  J.P. McDermott, 318(JAOS):Oct-Dec87-776
van der Veur, P.W., ed. Toward a Glorious Indonesia.
  D. Hindley, 293(JASt):Aug88-718
Veyne, P. Did the Greeks Believe in Their Myths?
  R.K., 185:Apr89-681
Veyne, P., ed. A History of Private Life. (Vol 1)
  C. Edwards, 313:Vol78-224
  W. Goffart, 627(UTQ):Spring89-409
  S.C. Humphreys, 123:Vol38No2-339
Vial, C. Délos indépendante (314-167 avant J-C.).
  D. Hennig, 229:Band60Heft6-516
Vial, G. Le Conte du Graal.*
  L. Stephens, 382(MAE):1988/2-323
Viala, A. Naissance de l'écrivain.*
  C. Spenser, 475:Vol15No28-362
Viale, O. Teatro I.
  J.A. Dubatti, 352(LATR):Spring89-136
Viallaneix, P. - see Michelet, J.
Vian, B. Round About Close to Midnight.* (M. Zwerin, ed & trans)
  D. Flower, 364:Oct/Nov88-118
de Viau, T. Oeuvres complètes. (Vol 4) G. Saba, ed)
  C. Abraham, 475:Vol15No28-345
Viazzo, P.P. Upland Communities.
  D. Siddle, 617(TLS):1-7Sep89-956
Vicent, M. Balada de Caín.
  K.M. Glenn, 238:Dec88-831
Vicinus, M. & B. Nergaard - see Nightingale, F.
Vickerman, A. The Fate of the Peasantry.
  G. Porter, 293(JASt):May88-443
Vickers, B., ed. Arbeit, Musse, Meditation.*
  F.C. De Vries, 541(RES):May88-325
  C. Trinkaus, 551(RenQ):Autumn88-474
Vickers, B., ed. English Science, Bacon to Newton.
  P.C. Dust, 599:Spring89-127
Vickers, B. In Defence of Rhetoric.*
  J. Fuchs, 175:Autumn88-251
Vickers, B., ed. Public and Private Life in the Seventeenth Century.
  D. Low, 447(N&Q):Sep88-373
Vickers, B. - see Mackenzie, G.
Vickers, H. Vivien Leigh.*
  A. Aronson, 441:9Jul89-20
Vickers, M. Pots and Pans.*
  J.F. Healy, 123:Vol38No1-179
Vico, G. De la très ancienne philosophie des peuples italiques.
  G. Navet, 98:Apr88-280
Vico, R.M. - see Gentile da Cingoli
Victoroff, J.I. The Wild Type.
  N. Callendar, 441:7May89-18
Vidal, A.S. - see under Sánchez Vidal, A.
Vidal, F.C. - see under Canals Vidal, F.
Vidal, G. Hollywood.
  M. Wood, 617(TLS):10-16Nov89-1243
Vidal, J.S. - see under Sáez Vidal, J.
Vidal-Naquet, P., ed. Atlas historique.
  J. Piel, 98:Jan/Feb88-152
Vidal-Naquet, P. The Black Hunter.
  N. Robertson, 24:Summer88-282
  D. Sinos, 124:Jan-Feb89-211

Vidén, G. The Roman Chancery Tradition.
  S.J.B. Barnish, 313:Vol78-271
  D. Conso, 555:Vol61fasc1-156
Vidler, A. The Writing of the Walls.
  T. Matthews, 45:Jan88-49
Vieillefond, J-R. - see Longus
Vieilliard, F. & J. Monfrin. Manuel bibliographique de la littérature française du Moyen Age de Robert Bossuat.* (3rd Supp, Vol 1)
  B. Guidot, 547(RF):Band100Heft4-418
  C.S., 379(MedR):Dec88-457
Vieilliard, F., ed. Le Roman de Troie en prose (Version du Cod. Bodmer 147).
  J.L. Grigsby, 545(RPh):Nov88-174
Viera, D.J. Medieval Catalan Literature.
  P.J. Boehne, 304(JHP):Autumn88-71
Viereck, P. Archer in the Marrow.*
  M. Edmundson, 560:Fall88-216
  P. Filkins, 271:Spring-Summer88-184
Viereck, W. & W-D. Bald, eds. English in Contact with Other Languages.*
  M. Görlach, 685(ZDL):1/1988-76
  J.M. Lipski, 35(AS):Winter88-360
  D. Nehls, 257(IRAL):May88-171
Viereck, W., E.W. Schneider & M. Gorlach, comps. A Bibliography of Writings on Varieties of English, 1965-1983.
  E. Callary, 40(AEB):Vol2No2-71
Vierne, S. Jules Verne.
  W. Butcher, 561(SFS):Mar88-94
  D. Compère, 535(RHL):Mar-Apr88-324
Vierneisel, K., W. Haftmann & O. Kokoschka. Oskar Kokoschka: Zeichnungen zur Antike.
  J.P.H., 90:Jun88-478
Vieth, D.M., ed. Essential Articles for the Study of Jonathan Swift's Poetry.
  J. Mezciems, 447(N&Q):Dec88-539
Vieth, H. Pamberi nechiShona.
  S. Brauner, 682(ZPSK):Band41Heft3-409
Vietor, J.L. & J. Redinger. Format-Büchlein [together with] Rist, J. Depositio Cornuti Typographici.
  J.L. Flood, 354:Dec88-358
"Viga-Glums Saga with the Tales of Ögmund Bash and Thorvald Chatterbox." (J. McKinnell, trans)
  H. Martin, 563(SS):Spring88-322
Vigarello, G. Concepts of Cleanliness.
  E. Weber, 617(TLS):24Feb-2Mar89-185
Vigée-Le Brun, E. The Memoirs of Elisabeth Vigée-Le Brun.
  M. Jordan, 617(TLS):18-24Aug89-890
Vigevani, A. - see Orioli, G.
de Vigny, A. Oeuvres complètes. (Vol 1) (F. Germain & A. Jarry, eds)
  J-P. Saint-Gerand, 535(RHL):Mar-Apr88-291
Vigo Trasancos, A. Arquitectura y Urbanismo en el Ferrol del siglo XVIII.
  A. Úbeda de los Cobos, 48:Oct-Dec88-451
Vila, M.O. - see under Ordóñez Vila, M.
Vilallonga, M. - see Pau, J.
Vilenkin, V. V sto perkale.
  S.I. Ketchian, 574(SEEJ):Winter88-664
Viljamaa, T. Infinitive of Narration in Livy.
  G. Calboli, 229:Band60Heft7-583
  H. Pinkster, 394:Vol41fasc3/4-428
Villacañas Berlanga, J.L. Racionalidad crítica.
  M. Caimi, 342:Band79Heft3-354
de Villanova, A. - see under Arnaldus de Villanova
Villanueva, D. - see Bécquer, G.A.

Vogel, D. Fluctuating Fortunes.
  T.B. Edsall, 453(NYRB):20Jul89-20
  D. Henriques, 441:9Apr89-21
Vogel, D. Married Life.*
  A. Whitehouse, 441:13Aug89-16
Vogel, E.F. One Step Ahead in China.
  A.S. Cohen, 441:29Oct89-41
Vogel, S. Life's Devices.
  P. Harvey, 617(TLS):3-9Mar89-214
Vogel, S. Reasonable Doubt.
  J.E. Butler, 441:15Oct89-51
Vogel, S.M. Aesthetics of African Art.
  2(AfrA):Nov87-83
Vogelaar, C. Netherlandish Fifteenth and
  Sixteenth Century Paintings in the Nation-
  al Gallery of Ireland.
  L. Campbell, 600:Vol18No1/2-68
  M. Russell, 39:Sep88-219
Vogeler, M.S. Frederic Harrison.*
  M.M. Garland, 637(VS):Winter89-233
Voges, M. Aufklärung und Geheimnis.
  R. Baasner, 224(GRM):Band38Heft4-461
Vogt, D. Ritterbild und Ritterlehre in der
  lehrhaften Kleindichtung des Stricker und
  im sog. Siegfried Helbling.
  O. Ehrismann, 224(GRM):Band38Heft3-
  351
Vogt, H. Johann Sebastian Bach's Chamber
  Music.
  P. Williams, 617(TLS):19-25May89-557
Vogt, H. Flagstad.*
  W.R. Moran, 465:Winter88/89-93
Voight, E.B. The Lotus Flowers.*
  M. Collier, 473(PR):Vol55No3-490
  J.F. Cotter, 249(HudR):Spring88-228
  P. Harris, 639(VQR):Spring88-262
  S. Pinsker, 363(LitR):Winter89-256
  P. Stitt, 491:Jun88-168
Voigts, L.E. A Handlist of Middle English in
  Harvard Manuscripts.*
  J.R. Goodman, 589:Jul88-730
Voinovich, V. The Fur Hat.
  P-L. Adams, 61:Nov89-135
  M. Carlson, 441:5Nov89-12
Volbach, W.F. Monumenti Musei e Gallerie
  Pontificie. (Vol 2)
  C.B. Strehlke, 90:Nov88-859
Volek, E. Metaestructuralismo.
  H.M. Cavallari, 238:Sep88-556
Volk, S. Grenzpfähle der Wirklichkeit.
  G. Schmitz, 72:Band225Heft2-415
Volkov, G.N. & others, eds. Antologiia peda-
  gogicheskoi mysli Rossii XVIII v.
  M.J. Okenfuss, 550(RusR):Oct88-445
Volland, B. Französische Entlehnungen im
  Deutschen.
  B.J. Koekkoek, 221(GQ):Fall87-653
Vollmann, W.T. The Rainbow Stories.
  C. James, 441:13Aug89-9
Vollmann-Profe, G. Geschichte der deutschen
  Literatur von den Anfängen bis zum Beginn
  der Neuzeit.* (Vol 1, Pt 2)
  H. Freytag, 684(ZDA):Band117Heft3-132
  S.N. Werbow, 406:Spring88-121
Volodarskii, M.I. Sovety i ikh iuzhnye so-
  sedy.
  E. Naby, 550(RusR):Oct88-463
Vološinov, V.N. Marxism and the Philosophy
  of Language.
  S. Prince, 144:Summer/Fall89-568
Volpi, F. Heidegger e Aristotele.
  D. Webb, 323:Jan88-105

Volpilhac-Auger, C. Tacite et Montesquieu.*
  J.F. Jones, Jr., 207(FR):Apr89-888
Volponi, P. Le mosche del capitale.
  I. Thomson, 617(TLS):13-19Oct89-1131
Volta, O., ed. Satie.
  J. Sams, 617(TLS):1-7Dec89-1330
  442(NY):4Dec89-188
de Voltaire, F.M.A. The Complete Works of
  Voltaire/Oeuvres complètes de Voltaire.
  (Vol 33) (J. Vercruysse & others, eds)
  G. Gargett, 402(MLR):Oct89-979
  F. Moureau, 530:Apr88-170
de Voltaire, F.M.A. The Complete Works of
  Voltaire.* (Vol 50) (W.D. Howarth, C.
  Duckworth & J. Balcou, eds)
  E.D. James, 208(FS):Apr88-208
de Voltaire, F.M.A. The Complete Works of
  Voltaire/Oeuvres complètes de Voltaire.
  (Vol 62) (J. Marchand, R. Mortier & J. Ren-
  wick, eds)
  G. Gargett, 402(MLR):Oct89-979
de Voltaire, F.M.A. Correspondance. (Vol 11)
  (T. Besterman, ed)
  J.H. Brumfitt, 208(FS):Jul88-344
Vomperskij, V.P. Slovari XVIII veka.
  H. Keipert, 559:Vol12No2-222
Von Eckhardt, W. Please Write.
  639(VQR):Autumn88-137
Von Eckardt, W., S.L. Gilman & J.E. Chamber-
  lin. Oscar Wilde's London.*
  K. Beckson, 177(ELT):Vol31No3-329
Von Gunden, H. The Music of Ben Johnston.
  P. Dickinson, 410(M&L):Jan88-114
  K. Potter, 415:Feb88-85
  P. Rapoport, 607:Mar88-44
Vonnegut, K. Bluebeard.*
  L. Rackstraw, 455:Mar88-65
Voous, K.H. Owls of the Northern Hemisphere.
  R.O. Paxton, 453(NYRB):21Dec89-39
Vorländer, K. Kant - Schiller - Goethe.
  R.M., 342:Band79Heft2-253
Vörös, I., ed. Lettre à Mr. de Voltaire ou
  Plainte d'un Hongrois (1764).
  G.F. Cushing, 575(SEER):Oct88-657
Voss, L. Literarische Präfiguration darges-
  tellter Wirklichkeit bei Fontane.*
  V.G. Doerksen, 564:Nov88-393
  W.L. Zwiebel, 221(GQ):Winter88-145
Voss, T.M. - see Santore, C.
Vosskamp, W., ed. Utopieforschung. (Vols 1-
  3)
  M. Harbsmeier, 462(OL):Vol43No2-187
Vosskamp, W. - see Harbsmeier, M.
Vosskamp, W. & E. Lämmert, eds. Kontrover-
  sen, alte und neue. (Vol 11)
  J.M. Ellis, 564:May88-190
  A.A. Wallas, 602:Band19Heft1-210
Vozgrin, V.E. Rossiia i evropeiskie strany v
  gody Severnoi voiny.
  J. Cracraft, 550(RusR):Apr88-183
Voznesensky, A. An Arrow in the Wall.*
  (W.J. Smith & F.D. Reeve, eds)
  K. Fitzlyon, 364:Dec87/Jan88-127
  G. Szirtes, 493:Spring88-24
Vranich, S.B. - see de Arguijo, J.
Vray, N. Des Femmes dans la tourmente.
  M. & P. Higonnet, 617(TLS):19-25May89-
  541
Vuillemin, J. Nécessité ou contingence.
  E. Karger-Jannin, 192(EP):Oct-Dec88-
  539

Vysotskii, V.S. Sobranie Stikhov I Pesen n
Trekh Tomakh. (A. Lvov & A. Sumerkin,
eds)
  G.S. Smith, 617(TLS):21-27Jul89-808

de Waal, F. Peacemaking Among Primates.
  S.B. Hrdy, 441:9Apr89-24
Waanders, F.M.J. The History of "telos" and
"teleő" in Ancient Greek.
  D. Gourevitch, 555:Vol61fasc1-95
  J-L. Perpillou, 555:Vol61fasc1-101
Wabnegger, E. Literaturskandal.
  J.L. Sammons, 680(ZDP):Band107Heft4-
  611
Wacher, J., ed. The Roman World.
  M. Grant, 123:Vol38No1-92
  N.B. Kampen, 124:Jul-Aug89-470
  G. Woolf, 313:Vol78-225
Wachill, H. Jour après jour.
  G. Goffette, 450(NRF):Mar88-85
Wachsmann, S. Aegeans in the Theban Tombs.
  V. Hankey, 303(JoHS):Vol108-260
Wacker, M., ed. Sturm und Drang.
  A.C. Leidner, 221(GQ):Spring88-305
  H.B. Nisbet, 402(MLR):Apr89-524
Wade, E.L., ed. The Arts of the North Amer-
ican Indian.*
  Z. Pearlstone, 54:Mar88-144
Wadlington, W. Reading Faulknerian Tragedy.
  A.F. Kinney, 395(MFS):Winter88-622
  S.M. Ross, 392:Summer88-471
Waelkens, M. Die kleinasiatischen Türsteine.
  R.R.R. Smith, 123:Vol38No2-349
Waelti-Walters, J., ed. Jeanne Hyvrard.
  F.C. St. Aubyn, 207(FR):Apr89-882
Wagener, O. Hitler - Memoirs of a Confidant.
(H.A. Turner, Jr., ed)
  H.A. Schmitt, 569(SR):Winter88-158
Wagenknecht, C. - see Kraus, K.
Waggoner, N. Macedonia I.
  W.J. Cherf, 124:Jul-Aug89-458
Wagner, A. A Herald's World.
  A. Payne, 617(TLS):14-20Apr89-400
Wagner, B. Gärten und Utopien.
  G. Grün, 647(RF):Band100Heft4-439
Wagner, H. Aesthetik der Tragödie.
  M.S. Silk, 123:Vol38No2-422
  W. Wittkowski, 133:Band21Heft4-339
Wagner, J. La Ballade du nègre blanc.
  A.D. Ranwez, 207(FR):Oct88-204
Wagner, P. Eros Revived.
  P. Lewis, 54:Mar88-94
Wagner, R. Sämtliche Briefe. (Vol 6) (H-J.
Bauer & J. Forner, eds)
  B. Millington & R. Anderson, 415:May88-
  240
Wagner, R. Selected Letters of Richard Wag-
ner.* (S. Spencer & B. Millington, eds &
trans)
  R. Anderson, 415:May88-241
  A. Gray, 465:Winter88/89-87
  C. Hatch, 465:Winter88/89-85
Wagner-Martin, L. Sylvia Plath.*
  R. von Hallberg, 432(NEQ):Dec88-633
  D. Holbrook, 364:Oct/Nov88-124
  J.T. Newcomb, 27(AL):Oct88-511
Wahba, M., ed. Samuel Johnson.
  A.F.T. Lurcock, 447(N&Q):Sep88-379
Wahlgren, E. The Vikings and America.
  E.H. Antonsen, 562(Scan):May88-73
  N.L. Hatch, 563(SS):Autumn88-511

Waldhas, D. Kants System der Natur.
  V. Mudroch, 342:Band79Heft3-363
Wain, J. Where the Rivers Meet.*
  J. Mellors, 364:Oct/Nov88-112
Waisman, C.H. Reversal of Development in
Argentina.
  A. Ciria, 263(RIB):Vol38No2-226
Waite, D.B. Artefacts from the Solomon Is-
lands in the Julius L. Brenchley Collection.
  J. Feldman, 2(AfrA):Feb88-91
Waite, P. Lord of Point Grey.
  D.C. Savage, 150(DR):Winter87/88-529
Waith, E.M. Patterns and Perspectives in
English Renaissance Drama.
  C.W. Cary, 130:Winter88/89-381
Waithe, M.E., ed. A History of Women Philos-
ophers. (Vol 1)
  P. Allen, 103:Nov88-464
  C.C., 185:Jan89-456
  G. Clark, 123:Vol38No2-429
Waitzkin, F. Searching for Bobby Fischer.
  M. Amis, 617(TLS):30Jun-6Jul89-709
Wajda, A. Double Vision.
  D. Jacobs, 441:7May89-25
Wajemann, H. Die Chorkompositionen von
Richard Strauss.
  K. Birkin, 410(M&L):Jan88-96
Wakabayashi, B.T. Anti-Foreignism and
Western Learning in Early-Modern Japan.*
  J.V. Koschmann, 244(HJAS):Dec88-538
  R.H. Minear, 318(JAOS):Jul-Sep87-504
Wakefield, T. Lot's Wife.
  J. Melmoth, 617(TLS):27Oct-2Nov89-
  1180
van der Wal, M.J. Passiefproblemen in oudere
taalfasen.
  F. Weerman, 204(FdL):Jun88-166
van der Wal, N. & J.H.A. Lokin. Historiae
iuris Graeco-Romani delineatio.*
  J. Konidaris, 229:Band60Heft3-275
Walbruck, H. & R.H. Specht. Deutsch gestern
und heute.
  C.J. James, 399(MLJ):Spring88-95
Walcott, D. The Arkansas Testament.
  F. D'Aguiar, 493:Spring88-16
  J. Figueroa, 364:Aug/Sep88-116
  P. Filkins, 271:Spring-Summer88-184
  V. Shetley, 491:May88-106
  639(VQR):Spring88-63
Walcott D. Collected Poems, 1948-1984.*
  T. Eagleton, 565:Winter87/88-65
Wald, A.M. The New York Intellectuals.*
  D. Felix, 396(ModA):Winter88-79
  F. Matthews, 106:Spring88-69
  W.B. Rideout, 27(AL):Oct88-489
Walden, G. The Shoeblack and the Sovereign.
  P. Grose, 441:26Feb89-27
Walder, A.G. Communist Neo-Traditionalism.
  D. Chirot, 293(JAfst):Feb88-134
Waldinger, R., ed. Approaches to Teaching
Voltaire's "Candide."
  A. Mason, 402(MLR):Jan89-173
  L.K. Penrod, 399(MLJ):Autumn88-358
Waldman, A. The Romance Thing.
  D. Kolokithas, 703:Fall88-213
Waldman, D. Willem de Kooning.
  R. Bass, 55:Summer88-90
Waldoff, L. Keats and the Silent Work of
Imagination.*
  D. Perkins, 591(SIR):Spring88-146

383

Waldron, A. Close Connections.*
    J.L. Idol, Jr., 392:Fall88–579
    M. Jones, 577(SHR):Summer88–287
    D. Middlebrook, 249(HudR):Autumn88–
    581
    D.R. Noble, 585(SoQ):Winter89–95
    M.K. Spears, 453(NYRB):2Mar89–35
    639(VQR):Summer88–89
Waldron, J., ed. Nonsense upon Stilts.*
    J.C., 185:Jan89–460
    B.A. Haddock, 521:Oct88–340
Waldron, J. The Right to Private Property.
    J. Dunn, 617(TLS):5–11May89–489
Waldrop, R. The Reproduction of Profiles.*
Streets Enough to Welcome Snow.
    R. Hadas, 472:Vol15No1–217
Waldstein, W. Operae libertorum.
    T.E.J. Wiedemann, 123:Vol38No2–331
"Waldungen – Die Deutschen und ihr Wald."
    I. Rogoff, 90:Jun88–474
Wales, K. A Dictionary of Stylistics.
    L. Milic, 617(TLS):17–23Nov89–1266
H.R.H. the Prince of Wales. A Vision of Brit-
ain.
    A. Saint, 617(TLS):8–14Dec89–1351
Walesa, L. A Way of Hope.
    I.G. Gross, 497(PolR):Vol33No4–487
Walker, A. Franz Liszt. (Vol 2)
    L. Botstein, 441:20Aug89–9
    P. Griffiths, 358:Dec89–8
Walker, A. Living by the Word.*
    A. Solanke, 617(TLS):13–19Jan89–30
Walker, A. Revolutionary Petunias.
    A. Solanke, 617(TLS):13–19Jan89–30
Walker, A. The Temple of My Familiar.
    J.M. Coetzee, 441:30Apr89–7
    A. Gurnah, 617(TLS):22–28Sep89–1023
Walker, A.R. The Toda of South India.
    P. Hocking, 293(JASt):Aug88–691
Walker, D. Fool's Paradise.*
    J.A.C. Greppin, 617(TLS):20–26Jan89–54
Walker, D. The Transparent Lyric.
    J. Applewhite, 569(SR):Winter88–121
Walker, D.D. The Aventures of Barney Tullus.
    T. Barnous, 649(WAL):Feb89–390
Walker, G.D. The Rule of Law.
    G. Marshall, 617(TLS):30Jun–6Jul89–707
Walker, I.M., ed. Edgar Allan Poe: The Criti-
cal Heritage.*
    C. Gerrard, 541(RES):Nov88–594
    J.M. Hutchisson, 536(Rev):Vol10–177
    B.R. Pollin, 495(PoeS):Jun88–23
Walker, J.M., ed. Milton and the Idea of
Woman.
    M. Stocker, 617(TLS):27Jan–2Feb89–90
Walker, K. – see Dryden, J.
Walker, L.E. Terrifying Love.
    T. Carpenter, 441:31Dec89–17
Walker, N.A. A Very Serious Thing.
    M.R. Higonnet, 617(TLS):29Dec89/
    4Jan90–1437
Walker, P. Zola.*
    D. Baguley, 535(RHL):Mar–Apr88–318
    F.S. Heck, 345(KRQ):Feb88–103
Walker, R.C.S. The Coherence Theory of
Truth.
    B. Stroud, 617(TLS):7–13Jul89–741
Walker, S. – see "The Graywolf Annual Four"
Walker, T. In Spain.
    P. Lewis, 565:Spring88–35
    D. Mitchell, 364:Dec87/Jan88–132

Walker, W. The Immediate Prospect of Being
Hanged.
    M. Stasio, 441:28May89–27
Walker, W. The Southern Harmony & Musical
Companion. (G.C. Wilcox, ed)
    D.W. Patterson, 578:Fall88–95
Walkiewicz, E.P. John Barth.
    S. Moore, 532(RCF):Spring88–199
Wall, R. An Anglo-Irish Dialect Glossary for
Joyce's Works.*
    T.P. Dolan, 272(IUR):Spring88–156
Wall, R. & J. Winter, eds. The Upheaval of
War.
    A.J.A. Morris, 617(TLS):1–7Dec89–1342
Wall, S. Trollope.
    J. Bayley, 453(NYRB):17Aug89–6
Wallace, D. Chaucer and the Early Writings of
Boccaccio.*
    J.O. Fichte, 38:Band106Heft1/2–224
Wallace, D.F. Girl with Curious Hair.
    J. Levin, 441:5Nov89–31
Wallace, D.R. Bulow Hammock.
    J. Rudloe, 441:16Apr89–28
Wallace, I. The Guest of Honor.
    M. Dowd, 441:16Jul89–24
Wallace, J.D. Early Cooper and His Audi-
ence.*
    M. Lopez, 115:Spring88–200
Wallace, M., ed. Sisters in Crime.
    M. Stasio, 441:30Apr89–45
Wallace, R. Beethoven's Critics.*
    T.S. Grey, 451:Spring89–257
Wallace, R., ed. Quebec Voices.
    V. Comensoli, 102(CanL):Autumn88–136
    J.C. Godin, 108:Fall88–86
Wallace, R.K. Emily Brontë and Beethoven.*
    P. Barford, 410(M&L):Jan88–85
Wallace, S. War and the Image of Germany.
    G. Best, 617(TLS):10–16Mar89–241
Wallace-Crabbe, C. I'm Deadly Serious.
    S. O'Brien, 493:Autumn88–56
Wallace-Hadrill, J.M. Bede's Ecclesiastical
History of the English People.
    H.R. Loyn, 617(TLS):5–11May89–492
Wallach, J. & J. Still Small Voices.
    L.E. Beattie, 441:9Jul89–19
Wallenstein, P. From Slave South to New
South.
    D.L. Carlton, 106:Summer88–268
    639(VQR):Winter88–14
Waller, B. Marie–Fée Marie–Sol.
    R. Henkels, 207(FR):Apr89–909
Waller, C. Expressionist Poetry and its Crit-
ics.
    G. Benda, 406:Winter88–524
Waller, G. English Poetry of the Sixteenth
Century.
    M.G. Brennan, 447(N&Q):Mar88–77
    R.R. Hellenga, 223:Fall88–359
Waller, J.O. A Circle of Friends.*
    D.M. MacDowell, 123:Vol38No1–190
Wallerstein, J.S. & S. Blakeslee. Second
Chances.
    C. Tavris, 441:26Feb89–13
Wallingford, K. Robert Lowell's Language of
the Self.
    M. Hofmann, 617(TLS):26May–1Jun89–
    578
Wallis, B., ed. Blasted Allegories.*
    639(VQR):Summer88–102
Wallis, R.V. & P.J. Biobibliography of British
Mathematics and its Applications.* (Pt 2)
    R. Gaskell, 354:Dec88–368

Wallmann, K. Minnebedingtes Schweigen in Minnesang, Lied und Minnerede des 12. bis 16. Jahrhunderts.
D. Joschko, 680(ZDP):Band107Heft1-132

Wallock, L., ed. New York.
H. Rubin, 441:18Jun89-21

Wallraff, G. Ganz unten. (A. Nockels, ed)
A. Williams, 402(MLR):Jul89-807

Walpole, R.N., ed. Le Turpin français, dit le Turpin I.*
K.H. Rogers, 403(MLS):Winter88-204

Walravens, H. - see Laufer, B.

Walser, M. Breakers.
D. Flower, 249(HudR):Spring88-215

Walser, M. No Man's Land.
A. Hyde, 441:22Jan89-8
J. Updike, 442(NY):9Oct89-135

Walsh, J.E. Into My Own.
P-L. Adams, 61:Jan89-120

Walsh, J.P. A School for Lovers.
J. O'Grady, 617(TLS):7-13Jul89-738

Walsh, M. The Secret World of Opus Dei.
D. Martin, 617(TLS):22-28Sep89-1035

Walsh, M. Andrew Lloyd Webber.
P. Holland, 617(TLS):8-14Dec89-1364

Walsh, P.G. - see Livy

Walsh, S. The Music of Stravinsky.*
P. Driver, 607:Dec88-45

Walter, B. The Jury Summation as Speech Genre.
A.G. Walker, 350:Dec89-915

Walter, E.V. Placeways.*
J.S.D., 185:Jul89-981

Walter, H. Le Français dans tous les sens.
A. Valdman, 207(FR):Feb89-566

Walter of Châtillon. "The Alexandreis." (R.T. Pritchard, ed & trans)
A.B.E. Hood, 123:Vol38No1-127

Walter-Karydi, E. Die äginetische Bildhauerschule.
P.E. Arias, 229:Band60Heft5-435

Walters, D.G. The Poetry of Francisco de Aldana.
E.L. Rivers, 304(JHP):Spring88-267

Walters, D.G. Francisco de Quevedo, Love Poet.*
J. Fernández Jiménez, 552(REH):Oct88-133

Walters, G.J. Karl Jaspers and the Role of "Conversion" in the Nuclear Age.
W.C. Gay, 103:Feb89-81

Walters, H. Y Wasg Gyfnodol Gymreig/The Welsh Periodical Press 1735-1900.
A. Jones, 635(VPR):Summer88-77

Walthall, A. Social Protest and Popular Culture in Eighteenth-Century Japan.*
R. Bowen, 293(JASt):Nov88-821

Walther, J. Logik der Fragen.
R. Schmit, 687:Oct-Dec88-706

Walther, J.G. Johann Gottfried Walther: Briefe. (K. Beckmann & H-J. Schulze, eds)
M. Boyd, 415:Oct88-533

Walton, D.N. Courage.*
L. Thomas, 154:Winter88-687

Walton, D.N. Physician-Patient Decision-Making.
G. Hélal, 154:Spring88-163

Walton, J., P.B. Beeson & R.B. Scott, eds. Oxford Companion to Medicine.
V. Ludwin, 529(QQ):Spring88-218

Walton, S. William Walton.*
M. Kennedy, 415:May88-245

Walton, S.P. Mode in Javanese Music.*
R.A. Sutton, 293(JASt):Aug88-720

Walworth, A. Wilson and His Peacemakers.
N.A. Graebner, 639(VQR):Winter88-157

Walz, G., ed. Flashback.
D. Clandfield, 627(UTQ):Fall87-231

Walzer, M. The Company of Critics.
D. Donoghue, 617(TLS):3-9Mar89-217
J.P. Euben, 441:8Jan89-18

Walzer, M. Interpretation and Social Criticism.*
E.P. Nassar, 396(ModA):Summer89-269

Wambaugh, J. The Blooding.
P-L. Adams, 61:May89-99
W. Walker, 441:19Feb89-11

Wamlek-Junk, E. Hans Pfitzner und Wien.
J. Williamson, 410(M&L):Jan88-107

Wandor, M. Carry On, Understudies.
E. Diamond, 615(TJ):Dec87-531
R.C. Lamont, 397(MD):Mar88-135

Wandor, M. Look Back in Gender.*
H. Keyssar, 615(TJ):May88-280

Wandruszka, A. & P. Urbanitsch, eds. Die Habsburger Monarchie 1848-1918. (Vol 4)
T.V. Thomas, 575(SEER):Jul88-491

Wang Anyi. Lapse of Time. Baotown.
J. Mirsky, 453(NYRB):26Oct89-27

Wang, H. Beyond Analytic Philosophy.*
B. Humphries, 482(PhR):Apr88-270
G. Landini, 543:Mar89-642

Wang, H. Reflections on Kurt Gödel.
M. Giaquinto, 393(Mind):Oct88-634
T.C. Holyoke, 42(AR):Spring88-268

Wangerin, W., Jr. Miz Lil & the Chronicles of Grace.
P. Payne, 441:8Jan89-9

Wanless, P.T. Taxation in Centrally Planned Economies.
Z. Popov, 575(SEER):Apr88-326

Wanley, H. Letters of Humfrey Wanley. (P.L. Heyworth, ed)
P. Rogers, 617(TLS):1-7Sep89-949

Wanner, D. The Development of Romance Clitic Pronouns.
A.G. Ramat, 350:Sep89-606

Wanner, I. Sailing to Corinth.*
J. Purdy, 649(WAL):Feb89-383

Wapnewski, P., ed. Mittelalter-Rezeption.
O. Ehrismann, 680(ZDP):Band107Heft3-460
J. Haustein, 684(ZDA):Band117Heft2-93

Warburg, T.L. A Voice at Twilight.
R. Dinnage, 617(TLS):13-19Jan89-33

Ward, A. The New York Intellectuals.
J. Seaton, 115:Spring88-207

Ward, A.J., ed. Northern Ireland.
J.B. Davenport, 174(Éire):Spring88-150

Ward, B.K. Dostoevsky's Critique of the West.
C.R. Pigden, 478(P&L):Apr88-133

Ward, D.F., ed. Personal Places.
J. Benincasa, 440:Winter-Spring88-147

Ward, E. & A. Silver. Raymond Chandler's Los Angeles.
M. Anderson, 441:15Oct89-51

Ward, G. Wandering Girl.
H. Dakin, 581:Dec88-473

Ward, G.C. A First-Class Temperament.
S.R. Graubard, 441:20Aug89-13
G. Wills, 453(NYRB):23Nov89-3
442(NY):11Sep89-123

Ward, J.R. British West Indian Slavery, 1750-1834.
R. Blackburn, 617(TLS):14-20Apr89-388

Ward, J.W. Andrew Jackson.
G.S. Smith, 529(QQ):Winter88-797
Ward, R. Baccio Bandinelli 1493-1560.
J.D. Draper, 380:Summer88-137
Ward, R.E. & Sakamoto Yoshikazu, eds. Demo-
cratizing Japan.
G.K. Goodman, 407(MN):Summer88-247
M. Schaller, 293(JASt):Feb88-156
Warden, P.G. The Metal Finds from Poggio
Civitate (Murlo) 1966-1978.
M.J. Chavane, 555:Vol61fasc1-121
Wardhaugh, R. An Introduction to Sociolin-
guistics.*
Y. Lastra, 269(IJAL):Oct88-470
P. Mühlhäusler, 353:Vol26No2-310
P. Sgall, 603:Vol12No2-499
Wardhaugh, R. Language in Competition.
J.M. Fayer, 399(MLJ):Autumn88-340
Ware, S. Partner and I.*
J.T. Patterson, 432(NEQ):Jun88-316
Warhol, A. The Andy Warhol Diaries. (P.
Hackett, ed)
M. Amis, 441:25Jun89-9
Waring, M. If Women Counted.
M.H. Stevenson, 441:29Oct89-36
Warland, B. serpent (w)rite.
S. Scobie, 376:Mar88-95
Warnant, L. Dictionnaire de la prononciation
française dans sa norme actuelle.
G. Straka, 553(RLiR):Jul-Dec88-524
Warner, E. "The Waves."
G. Cunningham, 541(RES):Nov88-591
M. Di Battista, 177(ELT):Vol31No4-494
Warner, J.A. Blake and the Language of Art.
B.O. Lindberg, 591(SIR):Spring88-159
Warner, M. The Lost Father.*
A. Cornelisen, 441:7May89-26
Warner, M., ed. Management Reforms in
China.
W.A. Fischer, 293(JASt):Nov88-874
Warner, R. Freedom, Enjoyment, and Happi-
ness.*
D. Braybrooke, 185:Apr89-625
W.A. Davis, 484(PPR):Jun89-758
Warner, S.T. T.H. White.
P. Craig, 617(TLS):7-13Apr89-362
Warner, W.B. Chance and the Text of Experi-
ence.
A. Calder, 478(P&L):Apr88-136
D. Hunter, 615(TJ):Oct88-438
R.P. Wheeler, 570(SQ):Autumn88-364
Warnicke, R.M. The Rise and Fall of Anne
Boleyn.
M.W. Ferguson, 441:26Nov89-31
Warnke, G. Gadamer.
M.K., 185:Jul89-974
Warnock, J.W. The Politics of Hunger.
O.O., 185:Apr89-685
Warnock, M. A Common Policy for Education.
E.F. Candlin, 324:Jun89-442
S.J. Prais, 617(TLS):17-23Feb89-175
Warnock, M. Universities.
J. Campbell, 617(TLS):29Dec89/4Jan90-
1432
Warren, C. T.S. Eliot on Shakespeare.*
W. Harmon, 569(SR):Winter88-105
K. Smidt, 179(ES):Dec88-534
Warren, D.B., K.S. Howe & M.K. Brown. Marks
of Achievement.
I.M.G. Quimby, 658:Spring88-79
Warren, L. Madeleine de janvier à septembre.
T. Vuong-Riddick, 102(CanL):Spring88-
132

Warren, M. Nietzsche and Political Thought.
M. Tanner, 617(TLS):12-18May89-509
Warren, R.P. New and Selected Essays.
R. Siegel, 441:28May89-19
Warren, R.P. Portrait of a Father.
M. Walters, 617(TLS):17-23Feb89-158
639(VQR):Autumn88-122
Warrick, P.S. Mind in Motion.
E.B. Thompson, 395(MFS):Summer88-257
G.K. Wolfe, 561(SFS):Jul88-234
Warshofsky, F. The Chip War.
J. Markoff, 441:14May89-23
von Wartburg, W. & J-P. Chambon. Franzö-
sisches Etymologisches Wörterbuch. (fasc
148)
A. Stefenelli, 553(RLiR):Jan-Jun88-289
Washington, M.H., ed. Invented Lives.*
C. Werner, 395(MFS):Spring88-125
Wasiolek, E., ed. Critical Essays on Tolstoy.*
G.N. Slobin, 149(CLS):Vol25No1-98
Wasserman, G. Samuel Butler and the Earl of
Rochester.*
K. Combe, 447(N&Q):Jun88-236
Wasserman, J.N. & R.J. Blanch, eds. Chaucer
in the Eighties.*
H. Cooper, 382(MAE):1988/1-107
Wasson, J.M., ed. Records of Early English
Drama: Devon.*
T. Pettitt, 539:Fall88-318
C.C. Rutter, 611(TN):Vol42No3-136
Waswo, R. Language and Meaning in the Ren-
aissance.
M.L. Colish, 589:Oct88-1008
E. Eldridge, 568(SCN):Fall88-42
Waswo, R., ed. On Poetry and Poetics.
494:Vol8No2-465
Waszek, N. Man's Social Nature.
D. Winch, 83:Autumn88-214
Waszink, J.H. & J.C.M. Van Winden - see Ter-
tullian
Waterhouse, E. The Dictionary of Sixteenth
and Seventeenth-Century British Painters.
M. Rogers, 617(TLS):24-30Nov89-1299
Waterhouse, H. The British School at Athens:
the First Hundred Years.
D. Hunt, 123:Vol38No1-138
Waterhouse, K. On Newspaper Style.
W. Redfern, 617(TLS):29Dec89/4Jan90-
1436
Waterman, A. Selected Poems.*
S. Rae, 364:Mar87-87
Waters, F. The Woman at Otowi Crossing.
(rev)
C.L. Adams, 649(WAL):May88-45
Waters, G.R. Three Elegies of Ch'u.*
J. Pease, 318(JAOS):Jul-Sep87-493
Waters, K.H. Herodotos the Historian.*
G. Nagy, 124:May-Jun89-400
Waters, L. - see de Man, P.
Waters, L. & W. Godzich, eds. Reading de Man
Reading.
D. Donoghue, 453(NYRB):29Jun89-32
T. Eagleton, 617(TLS):26May-1Jun89-
573
Waters, M.A. The Exact Place.
H. Humes, 649(WAL):Nov88-268
P. Stitt, 491:Jun88-161
Wates, N. & C. Knevitt. Community Architec-
ture.
D. Lewis, 47:Dec88-55

Watkin, D. A History of Western Architecture.*
P. Goodman, 47:Feb88-37
P.L. Goss, 576:Mar88-79
R. Pommer, 505:May88-107
Watkin, D. & T. Mellinghoff. German Architecture and the Classical Ideal, 1740-1840.
B. Bergdoll, 90:Jan88-42
J.C. Garcias, 46:Mar88-10
T. Matthews, 45:Jan88-49
Watkins, C., ed. Studies in Memory of Warren Cowgill (1929-1985).
M. Mayrhofer, 350:Mar89-135
Watkins, D.P. Social Relations in Byron's Eastern Tales.
T.A. Hoagwood, 661(WC):Autumn88-188
P. Story, 340(KSJ):Vol37-176
Watkins, P. Calm at Sunset, Calm at Dawn.
M. Wormald, 617(TLS):10-16Nov89-1244
Watmough, D. The Unlikely Pioneer.
R. Elliott, 529(QQ):Spring88-176
Watmough, D. Vibrations in Time.*
J.A. Wainwright, 102(CanL):Spring88-134
529(QQ):Spring88-225
Watney, S. Policing Desire.
R.D.M., 185:Jul89-990
Watson, A. Roman Slave Law.*
K.R. Bradley, 487:Autumn88-274
Watson, A.G. - see Ker, N.R.
Watson, D. Liszt.
P. Griffiths, 358:Dec89-8
Watson, J. - see Wooden, W.W.
Watson, J.G. William Faulkner: Letters and Fictions.*
M.M. Dunn, 27(AL):May88-307
A.F. Kinney, 395(MFS):Winter88-622
Watson, J.N.P. Millais.
O. Beckett, 324:Jun89-450
Watson, J.R. English Poetry of the Romantic Period 1789-1830.*
N. Roe, 661(WC):Autumn88-202
Watson, J.R., ed. Everyman's Book of Victorian Verse.
B. Richards, 447(N&Q):Sep88-406
Watson, O. Persian Lustre Ware.
R. Hillenbrand, 463:Winter88/89-282
Watson, P. Wisdom and Strength.
S. Coates, 441:26Nov89-31
Watson, R.N. Ben Jonson's Parodic Strategy.
A.D. Hammond, 599:Winter88-685
E.J. Jensen, 130:Winter88/89-373
K.E. Maus, 551(RenQ):Autumn88-530
Watson, R.N. Shakespeare and the Hazards of Ambition.*
A.W. Bellringer, 447(N&Q):Mar88-82
Watson, S. Winning Women.
M. Beard, 617(TLS):24Feb-2Mar89-192
Watson, W. The Architectonics of Meaning.*
E. Garver, 480(P&R):Vol21No1-60
G.B. Pepper, 485(PE&W):Apr88-193
Watt, D.C. How War Came.
M. Carver, 617(TLS):1-7Sep89-935
G.A. Craig, 453(NYRB):12Oct89-11
G. Smith, 441:3Sep89-1
442(NY):23Oct89-147
Watt, F.W. It's Over It's Beginning.
D.M.A. Relke, 102(CanL):Spring88-118
Wattenberg, B.J. The Birth Dearth.
W. Petersen, 31(ASch):Spring88-312
Watts, S. The Republic Reborn.
M. Meranze, 656(WMQ):Oct88-814

Waugh, E. A Tourist in Africa.
S. Pickering, 569(SR):Fall88-673
Waugh, E. Evelyn Waugh, Apprentice.* (R.M. Davis, ed)
B. Stovel, 223:Fall88-371
Waugh, H. A Death in a Town.
M. Stasio, 441:5Nov89-28
Waugh, T. Song at Twilight.
P. Craig, 617(TLS):17-23Nov89-1271
Wawn, A. - see Holland, H.
Waxman, M. The Promised Land.
H.W. Connor, 102(CanL):Autumn88-144
C. Mavrow, 376:Jun88-192
Wayman, T. The Face of Jack Munro.*
G. Boire, 102(CanL):Spring88-194
Waywell, G.B. The Lever and Hope Sculptures.
C. Picón, 90:Dec88-933
M. Robertson, 123:Vol38No1-183
Waźbiński, Z. L'Accademia Medicea del Disegno a Firenze nel Cinquecento.
K-E. Barzman, 90:Nov88-856
Wearing, J.P., ed. Bernard Shaw. (Vol 1)
A. Silver, 365:Winter87-48
S. Weintraub, 572:Vol8-147
Wearne, A. Out Here.
R. McDowell, 249(HudR):Autumn88-566
Weart, S.R. Nuclear Fear.*
A.Y. Kaplan, 62:Apr89-19
Weatherby, W.J. James Baldwin.
J. Berry, 441:25Jun89-25
Weatherilt, M. - see Champfleury
Weaver, G. The Eight Corners of the World.
J. Baumbach, 441:8Jan89-15
E. Campbell, 344:Spring89-146
Weaver, M., ed. British Photography in the Nineteenth Century.
A. Hollinghurst, 617(TLS):20-26Oct89-1155
Weaver, S.A. John Fielden and the Politics of Popular Radicalism 1832-1847.
W.L. Arnstein, 637(VS):Winter89-244
Weaver, W. A Gravestone Made of Wheat.
A. Solomon, 441:12Mar89-22
Weaver, W. - see Eco, U.
Webb, P. Portrait of David Hockney.
V. Raynor, 441:24Dec89-9
Webb, S. & B. Indian Diary. (N.G. Jayal, ed)
J. Motion, 617(TLS):27Jan-2Feb89-81
Webb, W.H. & others. Sources of Information in the Social Sciences. (3rd ed)
J.W. Geary, 87(BB):Mar88-65
Webber, P.E. Pella Dutch.
W.J. de Reuse, 350:Dec89-917
Weber, B. O Rio de Janeiro.
I. Jeffrey, 364:Mar87-79
Weber, D. Heimito von Doderer.
M. McInnes, 133:Band21Heft4-367
Weber, D. Rhetoric and History in Revolutionary New England.
P.F. Gura, 432(NEQ):Sep88-439
H.S. Stout, 165(EAL):Vol24No2-152
639(VQR):Autumn88-115
Weber, D.J. Relativization and Nominalized Clauses in Huallaga (Huanuco) Quechua.
R.H. Crapo, 269(IJAL):Oct88-475
Weber, D.J. - see Pike, A.
Weber, E. France: Fin de Siècle.*
C.L. Lloyd, 345(KRQ):Nov88-491
G.A.O., 295(JML):Fall87/Winter88-201
D.H. Pinkney, 31(ASch):Winter88-155

Weber, H. A travers le seizième siècle.* (Vol 2)
B.C. Bowen, 207(FR):Oct88-164
Weber, H.B., ed. The Modern Encyclopedia of Russian and Soviet Literatures. (Vol 8)
R. Cockrell, 402(MLR):Jan89-269
V. Terras, 574(SEEJ):Summer88-312
Weber, H.M. The Restoration Rake-Hero.*
J. Conaghan, 541(RES):Aug88-442
C. Hill, 366:Spring88-120
D. Hughes, 401(MLQ):Jun87-192
M. Jones, 447(N&Q):Jun88-235
S. Staves, 405(MP):Feb89-306
J.G. Turner, 536(Rev):Vol10-1
L. Woods, 615(TJ):Mar88-127
Weber, M.J. Perspectives.
R.A. Silverman, 2(AfrA):Nov87-19
Weber, N.F. The Art of Babar.
M. Cart, 441:17Dec89-18
Weber, S. Institution and Interpretation.
W.E. Cain, 580(SCR):Fall88-71
C.S. Schreiner, 478(P&L):Apr88-138
Weber, T. Bronzekannen.
G. Zahlhaas, 229:Band60Heft6-555
Weber-Caflisch, A. La Scène et l'Image.
J-N. Segrestaa, 535(RHL):Mar-Apr88-332
Webster, P. Schwarz-Rot-Gold.
W. Keel, 399(MLJ):Winter88-479
Webster, S. Small Tales of a Town.*
D. Stead, 441:2Apr89-28
442(NY):13Feb89-93
Wechsler, H.J. Offerings of Jade and Silk.
J. Lee, 318(JAOS):Jan-Mar87-157
Wedde, I. Driving into the Storm.
L. Mackinnon, 617(TLS):26May-1Jun89-593
Wedde, I. Symmes Hole.
J. Mellors, 364:Feb87-103
Wedekind, A. "Die Verlobung in St. Domingo."
B. Fischer, 221(GQ):Summer87-481
Wedekind, F. Die Tagebücher.* (G. Hay, ed)
R. Stäblein, 680(ZDP):Band107Heft4-621
Wedgwood, C.V. History and Hope.*
A.S. Byatt, 441:8Oct89-25
Weedon, C. Feminist Practice and Poststructuralist Theory.*
J.B., 185:Apr89-668
E. Jordan, 366:Autumn88-223
Weegee. The Village.
A. Grundberg, 441:3Dec89-73
Weeramantry, C.G. Nuclear Weapons and Scientific Responsibility.
S.I., 185:Apr89-684
Weevers, T. Vision and Form in the Poetry of Albert Verwey.
T.D., 295(JML):Fall87/Winter88-393
Wegeler, F. & F. Ries. Remembering Beethoven.*
V. Beahrs, 415:Nov88-602
Wegener, L.E. A Concordance to Herman Melville's "Pierre; or, The Ambiguities."
H. Parker, 534(RALS):Vol16No1&2-109
Wegener, L.E. A Concordance to Herman Melville's "The Confidence Man: His Masquerade."
S. Garner, 534(RALS):Vol16No1&2-105
Wegera, K-P., ed. Zur Entstehung der neuhochdeutschen Schriftsprache.
W. Neumann, 682(ZPSK):Band41Heft6-826
H. Penzl, 221(GQ):Fall87-655
Wegman, W. $19.84.
G. Gessert, 448:Vol26No1-81

Wegmann, B. Ocho Mundos. (3rd ed)
D.P. Hill, 399(MLJ):Spring88-114
Wegner, D.M. White Bears and Other Unwanted Thoughts.
G. Kolata, 441:1Oct89-27
Wegner, I. Frame-Theorie in der Lexikographie.
A. Blumenthal, 260(IF):Band93-267
Wegstein, W., ed. Studien zum "Summarium Heinrici."*
K. Ridder, 685(ZDL):2/1988-245
J. Splett, 680(ZDP):Band107Heft1-117
Wehr, B. Diskurs-Strategien im Romanischen.
E. Mayr, 260(IF):Band93-314
Wehr, D.S. Jung and Feminism.
H. Goldgar, 249(HudR):Autumn88-580
42(AR):Winter88-121
Wehr, G. Jung.*
H. Goldgar, 249(HudR):Autumn88-575
M. Lebowitz, 344:Spring89-154
Wehrli, R. Environmental Design Research.
C.C. Marcus, 47:Aug88-39
Wehrmann, R.F. L'Art de Roger Martin du Gard dans "Les Thibault."
R. Gibson, 208(FS):Jul88-364
C. Toloudis, 207(FR):Dec88-341
Weidenfeld, W. & H. Zimmermann, eds. Deutschland-Handbuch.
R. Morgan, 617(TLS):13-19Oct89-1115
Weidner, M., E.J. Laing & I.Y. Lo. Views from Jade Terrace.
J. Rawson, 617(TLS):6-12Oct89-1099
Weier, W. Phänomene und Bilder des Menschseins.
P. Trotignon, 542:Apr-Jun88-236
Weiger, J.G. The Substance of Cervantes.*
E. Williamson, 86(BHS):Jul88-301
Weigl, B. & T.R. Hummer, eds. The Imagination as Glory.
L. Goldstein, 289:Summer88-118
Weil, F. L'Interdiction du roman et la librairie, 1728-1750.
C.P. Courtney, 208(FS):Oct88-474
Weil, J. Life With a Star.
L. Chamberlain, 617(TLS):8-14Dec89-1369
I. Deak, 453(NYRB):28Sep89-63
T. Rafferty, 442(NY):2Oct89-115
A. Tyler, 441:18Jun89-3
Weil, S. Formative Writings 1929-1941.* (D.T. McFarland & W. van Ness, eds)
P. Winch, 521:Jul88-255
Weil, S. Oeuvres complètes. (Vol 1) (G. Kahn & R. Kühn, eds)
L. Chouteau, 450(NRF):Dec88-86
J. Hayward, 617(TLS):28Jul-3Aug89-821
Weil, S. Oeuvres complètes. (Vol 2) (G. Leroy, ed)
J. Hayward, 617(TLS):28Jul-3Aug89-821
Weimer, J.M. - see Woolson, C.F.
Weinberg, F.M. Gargantua in a Convex Mirror.*
F-R. Hausmann, 52:Band23Heft2-177
Weinberg, S. Armand Hammer.
A. Sampson, 441:29Oct89-36
Weinberger, E. & others - see Paz, O.
Weinbrot, H.D. Alexander Pope and the Traditions of Formal Verse Satire.*
M. Schuchard, 38:Band106Heft1/2-248
Weiner, A.B. & J. Schneider, eds. Cloth and Human Experience.
I. Poliski, 441:17Dec89-15

Weiner, M.A. Arthur Schnitzler and the Crisis of Musical Culture.
   P. Franklin, 410(M&L):Jan88-97
Weinfeld, M. Justice and Righteousness in Israel and the Nations.
   N.M. Sarna, 318(JAOS):Jan-Mar87-144
Weingarden, L.S. Louis H. Sullivan: The Banks.
   R.B. Elstein, 576:Dec88-432
   D. Jenkins, 46:Apr88-10
Weinhold, N. Sprachgeographische Distribution und chronologische Schichtung.
   K. Heger, 685(ZDL):3/1988-344
   O. Lurati, 553(RLiR):Jul-Dec88-484
Weinreb, B. & C. Hibbert, eds. The London Encyclopaedia.
   D.P., 46:Jun88-10
Weinreb, L.L. Natural Law and Justice.
   R.P. George, 518:Oct88-248
   J.G. Hanink, 185:Jan89-435
Weinrebe, H.M.A. Märchen - Bilder - Wirkungen.
   H-J. Uther, 196:Band29Heft1/2-249
Weinreich, B.S., ed. Yiddish Folktales.
   J. Hadda, 441:5Mar89-30
Weinreich, R. The Spontaneous Poetics of Jack Kerouac.*
   M. Green, 363(LitR):Fall88-123
   H. Isernhagen, 224(GRM):Band38Heft3-363
Weinrich, H. Wege der Sprachkultur.
   H-M. Gauger, 547(RF):Band99Heft4-405
Weinsheimer, J.C. Gadamer's Hermeneutics.*
   D. Dutton, 478(P&L):Apr88-155
   D. Marshall, 494:Vol8No1-199
   H. Rapaport, 481(PQ):Spring88-272
Weinstein, P.M. The Semantics of Desire.*
   B. Wilshire, 449:Jun87-277
Weinstein, S. Buddhism Under the T'ang.
   V.H. Mair, 244(HJAS):Dec88-551
Weintraub, E.R. General Equilibrium Analysis.
   R. Sassower, 488:Dec88-551
Weintraub, S. - see Shaw, G.B.
Weintraub, S. - see "Shaw: The Annual of Bernard Shaw Studies"
Weisberg, G.P. Art Nouveau Bing, Paris Style 1900.*
   S. Braybrooke, 507:Mar/Apr88-153
Weisbrot, R. Freedom Bound.
   D.J. Garrow, 441:17Dec89-28
Weisbuch, R. Atlantic Double-Cross.*
   N. Baym, 301(JEGP):Jan88-136
   E. Carton, 533:Winter89-99
   C. Gerrard, 541(RES):Nov88-594
   H. Levin, 131(CL):Spring88-183
   E.F. Shields, 529(QQ):Spring88-203
   L. Willson, 401(MLQ):Mar87-95
Weisenburger, S. A "Gravity's Rainbow" Companion.
   S. Moore, 532(RCF):Fall88-174
Weisheipl, J.A. Nature and Motion in the Middle Ages.* (W.E. Carroll, ed)
   S. Baldner, 438:Autumn88-479
"Weismanns Petersburger Lexikon von 1731." (Vols 1-3)
   J. Biedermann, 559:Vol12No2-228
Weiss, B. The Hell of the English.*
   A.L. Harris, 268(IFR):Winter89-74
Weiss, D. The Critic Agonistes.* (E. Solomon & S. Arkin, eds)
   M. Sokolyansky, 402(MLR):Jul89-687

Weiss, E. City in the Woods.
   R.M. Candee, 576:Sep88-317
Weiss, H.F., ed. Unbekannte Briefe von und an Achim von Arnim aus der Sammlung Varnhagen und anderen Beständen.
   R. Burwick, 221(GQ):Fall87-677
Weiss, J.M. French-Canadian Theater.
   L.E. Doucette, 627(UTQ):Fall87-186
Weiss, M.A. The Rise of the Community Builders.
   R. Harris, 529(QQ):Winter88-956
Weiss, M.J. The Clustering of America.
   R. Blount, Jr., 441:22Jan89-24
Weiss, P. Philosophy in Progress. (Vol 10)
   P. Young, 543:Sep88-172
Weiss, S.A. - see Shaw, G.B.
Weiss, T. From Princeton One Autumn Afternoon.
   R.B. Shaw, 491:Apr88-43
   639(VQR):Summer88-99
Weissbort, D. Leaseholder.*
   T. Eagleton, 565:Winter87/88-65
   J. Saunders, 565:Autumn88-72
Weissenberger, K., ed. Prosakunst ohne Erzählen.*
   J.M. Van Der Laan, 301(JEGP):Jan88-96
Weisskopf, V.F. The Privilege of Being a Physicist.
   M.M. Waldrop, 441:14May89-28
Weissman, D. Intuition and Ideality.
   J.F. Post, 543:Dec88-415
Weissman, J. Half Savage and Hardy and Free.
   J. Eis, 219(GaR):Winter88-867
   V.J. Emmett, Jr., 389(MQ):Autumn88-125
   K.E. Welsh, 637(VS):Winter89-234
Weitzmann, K. & H.L. Kessler. The Cotton Genesis.
   S.E. Gerstel, 589:Jul88-731
   J. Lowden, 54:Jun88-346
   M. Wenzel, 90:Aug88-631
Wekker, H. & L. Haegeman. A Modern Course in English Syntax.*
   R. Declerck, 361:Jan88-67
Welbourne, M. The Community of Knowledge.
   N. Everitt, 518:Jan88-34
Welburn, A.J. Power and Self-Consciousness in the Poetry of Shelley.
   S.C. Behrendt, 340(KSJ):Vol37-193
Welch, B.L. Ronsard's Mercury.*
   H. Fournier, 539:Summer88-232
Welch, C. Linguistic Responsibility.
   R. Ginsberg, 103:Dec89-501
Welch, D. Fragments of a Life Story. (M. Dela-Noy, ed)
   J. Lewis, 364:Mar88-111
Welch, L. Word-House of a Grandchild.
   M. Estok, 198:Winter88-106
Welch, T.L., comp. The Indians of South America.
   263(RIB):Vol38No4-547
Welcomme, G. & C. Willerval. Juniorscopie.
   A.J.M. Prévos, 207(FR):Oct88-188
Weldon, F. The Cloning of Joanna May.
   P. Craig, 617(TLS):12-18May89-518
Weldon, F. The Hearts and Lives of Men.*
   A. Bloom, 249(HudR):Autumn88-540
Weldon, F. Leader of the Band.*
   R. Ward, 441:4Jun89-1
   442(NY):7Aug89-96
Weldon, F. Polaris and Other Stories.
   R. Ward, 441:4Jun89-1

389

Weldon, F. The Shrapnel Academy.*
   P. Stevens, 529(QQ):Autumn88-568
Welfeld, I. Where We Live.
   G. Winslow, 441:19Mar89-23
Welke, K., ed. Sprache, Bewusstsein, Tätig-
keit.
   L. Seppänen, 439(NM):1988/2-215
Wellbery, D.E., ed. Positionen der Literatur-
wissenschaft.*
   B. Fischer, 221(GQ):Spring87-262
Wellek, R. A History of Modern Criticism
1750-1950.* (Vols 5 & 6)
   C.S. Brown, 131(CL):Winter88-67
   J. Culler, 322(JHI):Apr-Jun88-347
   G. Gunn, 494:Vol8No1-205
   C. Uhlig, 52:Band23Heft2-166
Wellens, B., K. de Bot & T. van Els, eds. Lan-
guage Attrition in Progress.
   J.W. de Vries, 204(FdL):Sep88-240
Weller, R.P. Unities and Diversities in Chi-
nese Religion.
   D.R. De Glopper, 293(JASt):Aug88-629
Wellershoff, D. Der Sieger nimmt alles.
   U. Reinhold, 654(WB):2/1988-283
Wellershoff, D. Winner Takes All.
   M. Hulse, 364:Jul88-115
Welles, M.L. Arachne's Tapestry.*
   F.A. de Armas, 86(BHS):Jul88-304
   N.C. Davis, 345(KRQ):Nov88-496
Welles, O. & others. Isak Dinesen/Karen
Blixen.
   D.W. Hannah, 538(RAL):Summer88-271
Welles, O., with O. Kodar. The Big Brass Ring.
   S. French, 707:Winter87/88-70
   G. Vidal, 453(NYRB):1Jun89-12
Wellesley, K. - see Tacitus
Wellm, A. Morisco.
   K. Hirdina, 601(SuF):Jul-Aug88-858
Wellmer, A. Zur Dialektik von Moderne und
Postmoderne.*
   V. Kaiser, 221(GQ):Summer87-463
Wells, C., ed. Perspectives in Vernacular
Architecture, II.
   G.L. Pocius, 292(JAF):Jan-Mar88-87
Wells, C.J. German.
   M. Bürgisser, 72:Band225Heft2-350
Wells, H.G. The Definitive Time Machine.
(H.M. Geduld, ed)
   D. Lake, 561(SFS):Nov88-369
Wells, N. Just Bounce/Wilderness.
   M. Wormald, 617(TLS):9-15Jun89-641
Wells, R. Selected Poems.*
   S. Rae, 364:Mar87-87
Wells, R.G. A Woman of Her Time and Ours.
   D.C. Hine, 637(VS):Summer89-588
Wells, R.H. Shakespeare, Politics and the
State.
   M. Butler, 447(N&Q):Jun88-223
   J. Clare, 541(RES):Aug88-436
   A. Thompson, 402(MLR):Jul89-713
   P. Yachnin, 539:Fall88-324
Wells, S. The Cambridge Companion to
Shakespeare Studies.*
   I. Boitz, 72:Band225Heft1-159
   B. Gaines, 702:Vol20-332
   B. Gibbons, 611(TN):Vol42No2-92
   M. Jones, 541(RES):Aug88-438
   L. Potter, 402(MLR):Jul89-710
Wells, S. The Dialectics of Representation.*
   L. Bliss, 131(CL):Summer88-281
   E. White, 494:Vol8No1-210

Wells, S. Re-Editing Shakespeare for the
Modern Reader.*
   M. Warren, 301(JEGP):Jan88-111
Wells, S., ed. "Twelfth Night."
   R.G. Barlow, 615(TJ):Mar88-143
Wells, S. - see "Shakespeare Survey"
Wells, S. & G. Taylor. William Shakespeare, A
Textual Companion.*
   P. Davison, 354:Sep88-255
   B. Engler, 179(ES):Jun88-277
Wells, S. & G. Taylor - see Shakespeare, W.
Wells, S.M., ed. Coral Reefs of the World.
   K. Brower, 61:Jun89-87
Wellwarth, G.E. Modern Drama and the Death
of God.
   L.S. Butler, 447(N&Q):Sep88-410
   B. Crow, 610:Spring88-66
Welsch, R.L. & L.K. Cather's Kitchens.
   G.F. Day, 649(WAL):May88-69
Welsh, A. George Eliot and Blackmail.*
   M. Moseley, 569(SR):Spring88-243
Welsh, A. From Copyright to Copperfield.*
   N. Auerbach, 637(VS):Autumn88-116
   M. Baumgarten, 599:Spring89-165
   R.J. Dunn, 445(NCF):Sep88-268
   D.F. Sadoff, 158:Dec88-192
Welsh-Ovcharov, B. Van Gogh à Paris.
   J. Hulsker, 600:Vol18No3-177
Weltner, L. No Place Like Home.
   F.W. Burck, 441:26Mar89-13
Welz, D. Writing against Apartheid.
   R.N. Choonoo, 538(RAL):Fall88-416
Welzig, W., ed. Katalog gedruckter deutsch-
sprachiger katholischer Predigtsammlung-
en.
   D.L. Paisey, 354:Dec88-355
Welzig, W. & others - see Schnitzler, A.
Wemyss, C.T. & A. Ugrinsky, eds. George
Orwell.
   R.J. Voorhees, 395(MFS):Winter88-702
Wen-hui, T. - see under Tsai Wen-hui
Wendelius, L. Fredrika Bremers Amerikabild.*
   A. Swanson, 563(SS):Winter88-111
Wendland, P. La cultura ellenistico-romana
nei suoi rapporti con giudaismo et cris-
tianesimo.
   E. des Places, 555:Vol61fasc1-130
Wendt, I. Singing the Mozart Requiem.
   L. Baker, 448:Vol26No3-106
   P. Varner, 649(WAL):Nov88-258
Wenfu, L. - see under Lu Wenfu
Wengert, T.J. Philip Melanchthon's "Annota-
tiones in Johannem" in Relation to its Pre-
decessors and Contemporaries.
   K. Meerhoff, 544:Autumn88-414
   L.V.R., 568(SCN):Fall88-67
Wengst, K. Pax Romana and the Peace of
Jesus Christ.
   R.P.C. Hanson, 123:Vol38No2-441
Wenhua, C. - see under Cui Wenhua
Wenke, J. Mailer's America.*
   J.A. Halprin, 27(AL):Dec88-685
Wenkums, S., ed. Mein Gespräch, meine Lied-
er.
   R. Minert, 399(MLJ):Summer88-242
Wente-Lukas, R., with A. Jones. Handbook of
Ethnic Units in Nigeria.
   S. Brauner, 682(ZPSK):Band41Heft3-411
Wentzlaff-Eggebert, H., ed. Die Legitimation
der Alltagssprache in der modernen Lyrik.*
   H. Merkl, 72:Band225Heft1-147

Wenzel, H-E. Antrag auf Verlängerung des Monats August.
M. Gratz, 601(SuF):Sep-Oct88-1096
Wenzel, H.V., ed. Simone de Beauvoir.*
T. Moi, 208(FS):Apr88-235
Wenzel, S. Preachers, Poets, and the Early English Lyric.*
M.G. Briscoe, 401(MLQ):Sep87-279
G. Cigman, 589:Apr88-484
T.G. Duncan, 402(MLR):Apr89-433
V. Gillespie, 382(MAE):1988/2-300
S.J. Ogilvie-Thomson, 541(RES):Aug88-423
M.W. Twomey, 301(JEGP):Jul88-439
Wenzler, L. Die Freiheit und das Böse nach Vladimir Soloviev.*
P. Trotignon, 542:Jul-Sep88-353
Weöres, S. Eternal Moment.
G. Gömöri, 617(TLS):24Feb-2Mar89-200
Werckmeister, A. Musicalische Temperatur (Quedlinburg 1691). (R. Rasch, ed)
A. Cohen, 410(M&L):Jan88-68
Werkner, P. Physis und Psyche.
I. Sármány-Parsons, 90:Jul88-543
Werlen, E. Studien zur Datenerhebung in der Dialektologie.
W. Viereck, 685(ZDL):2/1988-203
Werner, B.C. Blake's Vision of the Poetry of Milton.
J. Warner, 88:Summer88-25
Werner, F. Gesprächsverhalten von Frauen und Männern.
K.J. Mattheier, 680(ZDP):Band107Heft3-474
Werner, H-J. Eins mit der Natur.
P. Trotignon, 542:Apr-Jun88-236
Werner, S. Socratic Satire.
N. Sclippa, 207(FR):Feb89-521
Wernham, J.C.S. James's Will-to-Believe Doctrine.
G. Cotkin, 26(ALR):Spring89-79
J.R. Horne, 154:Autumn88-568
S. Nathanson, 619:Summer88-423
P. Rae, 529(QQ):Summer88-474
I.K. Skrupskelis, 319:Apr89-320
Wertheim, S. & P. Sorrentino - see Crane, S.
Wertheimer, A. Coercion.
S.D. Warner, 185:Apr89-642
Wertsch, J.V., ed. Culture, Communication, and Cognition.*
B. Sutton-Smith, 355(LSoc):Jun88-298
Wertsch, J.V. Vygotsky and the Social Formation of Mind.
E. Gellner, 575(SEER):Apr88-309
Wesley, J. The Journal of John Wesley. (E. Jay, ed)
W.R. Ward, 83:Autumn88-244
Wesley, M. Second Fiddle.*
E. Kraft, 441:30Jul89-8
Wesley, S. The Wesley Bach Letters.
N. Temperley, 415:Oct88-535
Wesselink, A. - see Poliziano, A.
Wessels, W. Hörspiele im Dritten Reich.
G.R. Cuomo, 221(GQ):Summer87-500
Wessely, G. Nebensätze im spontanen Gespräch.
A. Lötscher, 685(ZDL):3/1987-383
West, C. Routine Complications.
J.F. Kess, 567:Vol68No1/2-165
West, F. Gilbert Murray.
E.C. Kopff, 396(ModA):Spring89-160

West, J.L.W. 3d, ed. Conversations with William Styron.
J.F. Desmond, 392:Fall88-553
S. Felton, 392:Spring88-194
E.B. Mills, 534(RALS):Vol16No1&2-261
West, J.L.W. 3d. A "Sister Carrie" Portfolio.
J.K. Davis, 569(SR):Summer88-507
West, L.L. Welding.
S. Rippert-Davila, 399(MLJ):Spring88-85
West, M.L. Greek Metre.
B. Gentili, 229:Band60Heft6-481
West, M.L. The Hesiodic Catalogue of Women.
S.C. Shelmerdine, 124:Sep-Oct88-54
West, M.L. - see Euripides
West, M.L. - see Hesiod
West, N. Molehunt.
R.W. Winks, 441:16Apr89-1
West, P. Lord Byron's Doctor.
A. Goreau, 441:3Sep89-2
West, P. The Place in Flowers Where Pollen Rests.*
S. Moore, 532(RCF):Fall88-156
West, P. Sheer Fiction.* The Universe, and Other Fictions.*
S. Moore, 532(RCF):Spring88-188
West, R. The Diamonds and the Necklace.
S. Watson, 617(TLS):12-18May89-524
West, R. Family Memories.* (F. Evans, ed)
639(VQR):Autumn88-123
West, R.S. Satire on Stone.*
639(VQR):Autumn88-140
West, W.J. - see Orwell, G.
Westall, R. Antique Dust.
G. Wilson, 441:15Oct89-11
Westarp, K-H. & J.N. Gretlund, eds. Realist of Distances.*
S. Felton, 392:Winter87/88-119
Westenholz, A. The Power of Aries.*
D. Kennedy, 538(RAL):Summer88-270
Westergaard, M.R. Definite NP Anaphora.*
R. Chen, 350:Jun89-444
C. Lyons, 297(JL):Sep88-561
Westerink, L.G. - see Damascius
Westfall, P.T. Real Farm.
S. MacNeille, 441:8Oct89-25
Westin, A.F. & J.D. Aram. Managerial Dilemmas.
L.E.L., 185:Jul89-984
Westlake, D.E. Sacred Monster.
D. Ryan, 441:30Jul89-12
Westlake, D.E. Tomorrow's Crimes.
R. Short, 441:15Oct89-50
Westlake, M. The Utopian.
J. Melmoth, 617(TLS):26May-1Jun89-592
Westney, D.E. Imitation and Innovation.
A. Fraser, 407(MN):Summer88-244
Westphal, J. Colour.
E.W. Averill, 518:Oct88-210
Westphal, M. God, Guilt and Death.
J.H. Thomas, 323:May88-212
Westphal, M. Kierkegaard's Critique of Reason and Society.
P.J.W. Miller, 319:Jul89-488
Westphalen, T. & others. Erich Maria Remarque Bibliographie.
C.R. Owen, 150(DR):Winter87/88-523
Westra, H.J., ed. The Commentary on Martianus Capella's "De nuptiis Philologiae et Mercurii" Attributed to Bernardus Silvestris.
C. Baswell, 589:Jul88-733

[continuing]
R.L. Emerson, 106:Summer88-227
J. Ryder, 619:Spring88-287
White, M. & L. Journeys to the Japanese, 1952-1979.
I. Nish, 302:Vol24No1-105
White, M.J. Agency and Integrality.*
P.M. Huby, 123:Vol38No2-286
B. Leftow, 258:Dec88-467
A. Reix, 542:Apr-Jun88-237
White, N. New York.*
R.G. Wilson, 47:Apr88-49
White, R.S. Innocent Victims.* (2nd ed)
R. Hillman, 539:Fall88-315
White, S. The Recent Work of Jürgen Habermas.
R.H.N., 185:Jan89-455
White, S. John Thomson.
J. Sturman, 55:Apr88-54
White, S.D. Custom, Kinship, and Gifts to Saints.
J. Muldoon, 377:Nov88-218
White, S.F., ed & trans. Poets of Nicaragua. Culture and Politics in Nicaragua.
G. Simon, 448:Vol26No3-58
Whited, C. Knight.
J.V. Turk, 441:5Mar89-23
Whitehead, D. The Demes of Attica 508/7 - ca. 250 B.C.*
J. Ober, 122:Jan88-70
R.K. Sinclair, 303(JoHS):Vol108-251
Whitehead, K. The Third Programme.
A. Thwaite, 617(TLS):10-16Feb89-130
Whitehead, M.B., with L. Schwartz-Nobel. A Mother's Story.
J. Greenfeld, 441:12Mar89-14
Whitelaw, M. - see Lord Dalhousie
Whitelaw, W. The Whitelaw Memoirs.
J. Turner, 617(TLS):19-25May89-540
Whiteley, P.J. Knowledge and Experimental Realism in Conrad, Lawrence, and Woolf.
J. Gindin, 395(MFS):Summer88-270
Whiteman, B. The Invisible World Is in Decline.
E. Tihanyi, 102(CanL):Winter87-200
Whiteman, B., C. Stewart & C. Funnell. A Bibliography of Macmillan of Canada Imprints 1906-1980.
G.L. Parker, 102(CanL):Spring88-115
Whitenack, J.A. The Impenitent Confession of Guzmán de Alfarache.*
D.P. Testa, 593:Spring88-77
Whiteside, A. & M. Issacharoff, eds. On Referring in Literature.*
T. Kowzan, 567:Vol72No1/2-159
Whitfield, A. Le jeu illocutoire.
P. Perron, 627(UTQ):Fall88-193
Whitfield, S.J. A Critical American.
F. Matthews, 106:Spring88-69
Whitford, D. A Payroll to Meet.
G.S. White, Jr., 441:22Oct89-29
Whiting, R. The Blind Devotion of the People.
F. Heal, 617(TLS):1-7Dec89-1343
Whiting, R. The Enterprise of England.*
J.R. Hale, 453(NYRB):16Feb89-30
Whiting, R. You Gotta Have Wa.
R.J. Collins, 441:11Jun89-45
Whitman, J. Allegory.
G.L. Bruns, 131(CL):Fall88-384
J.G. Lidaka, 599:Spring89-124
G. Teskey, 405(MP):May89-418
Whitman, R. The Testing of Hannah Senesh.
E. Pennant, 287:May/Jun87-28

Whitmore, J.K. Vietnam, Ho Quy Ly, and the Ming (1371-1421).
C.M. Wilson, 293(JASt):May88-444
Whitney, C. Francis Bacon and Modernity.*
A. Guibbory, 301(JEGP):Oct88-579
A.G.R. Smith, 366:Autumn88-237
Whitney, M.L. & D. Hussey. Bob Marley.
D.E.M., 91:Fall88-252
Whitrow, G.J. Time in History.
D. King-Hele, 617(TLS):21-27Jul89-793
Whittaker, H. Whittaker's Theatre. (R. Bryden & B. Neil, eds)
R. Plant, 108:Winter87-79
Whittall, A. Romantic Music.*
N. Temperley, 410(M&L):Apr88-270
Whittemore, R. Poets and Anthologists.
C. Clausen, 569(SR):Winter88-131
Whittemore, R. Pure Lives.*
M. Seymour-Smith, 617(TLS):27Jan-2Feb89-92
C. Winton, 396(ModA):Spring89-142
Whittemore, R.C. The Transformation of the New England Theology.
J. Hoopes, 619:Summer88-432
Whitton, D. Stage Directors in Modern France.
N.H. Paul, 610:Spring88-71
L.C. Pronko, 615(TJ):Dec88-567
J. Rudlin, 402(MLR):Oct89-995
Whitworth, J. Tennis and Sex and Death.
G. Maxwell, 617(TLS):3-9Nov89-1216
Whyte, A-J. Economic Sex.
L. Surette, 102(CanL):Winter87-245
Whyte, W.H. City.
E.A. Schwartz, 441:26Feb89-15
Wickens, D.C. The Instruments of Samuel Green.
N. Thistlethwaite, 415:Apr88-215
Wickert-Micknat, G. Die Frau.
J.M. Hemelrijk, 394:Vol41fasc1/2-131
Wickham, C.J. Diendorf Kr. Nabburg (Oberpfalz) [together with] Hinderling, R. Zinzenzell Kr. Bogen (Niederbayern).
L. Zehetner, 685(ZDL):2/1988-218
Wickham, C.J. The Mountains and the City.
D. Abulafia, 617(TLS):20-26Jan89-64
Wickremeratne, L.A. The Genesis of an Orientalist.
C. Hallisey, 318(JAOS):Jul-Sep87-514
Widdowson, P. Hardy in History.
K. Millard, 617(TLS):29Dec89/4Jan90-1445
Wideman, J.E. Fever.
S.F. Schaeffer, 441:10Dec89-1
Wideman, J.E. Reuben.*
M.S. Bell, 455:Jun88-60
M. Gorra, 249(HudR):Summer88-407
Widmer, E. The Margins of Utopia.
R.E. Hegel, 293(JASt):Feb88-136
R.K. McMahon, 244(HJAS):Dec88-545
Wiebe, M.G. & others - see Disraeli, B.
Wiebe, M.G., J.B. Conacher & J. Matthews - see Disraeli, B.
"The Rudy Wiebe Papers, First Accession."
S.C. Spragge, 470:Vol26-192
Wiegels, R. Die Tribusinschriften des römischen Hispanien.*
N. Mackie, 313:Vol78-269
Wieland, W. Strukturwandel der Medizin und der ärztlichen Ethik.
J-C. Wolf, 687:Apr-Jun88-345
Wiener, J.H., ed. Innovators and Preachers.*
W. Ruddick, 366:Autumn88-255

Wier, D. The Book of Knowledge.
  G. Conoley, 152(UDQ):Winter/Spring89-
  129
  R. Katrovas, 434:Spring89-340
Wierzbicka, A. Lexicography and Conceptual
  Analysis.*
  D. Geeraerts, 355(LSoc):Sep88-449
  A. Lehrer, 603:Vol12No1-235
Wiese, J. Berliner Wörter & Wendungen.
  H. Kuntz, 685(ZDL):3/1988-365
Wiesel, E. Le Crépuscule, au loin.
  R. Bleizman, 207(FR):Apr89-911
Wiesel, E. Twilight.*
  I. Halperin, 390:Aug/Sep88-61
Wiesel, E. & A.H. Friedlander. The Six Days
  of Destruction.
  B. Southworth, 441:30Apr89-39
Wiesinger, P., ed. Beiträge zur bairischen und
  ostfränkischen Dialektologie.
  J.E. Schmidt, 685(ZDL):2/1988-214
Wiggins, D. Needs, Values, Truth.*
  W. Charlton, 483:Oct88-550
Wiggins, G. Fiddlin' Georgia Crazy.
  G.T. Meade, 292(JAF):Jan-Mar88-97
Wiggins, M. John Dollar.
  G. Annan, 453(NYRB):15Jun89-12
  M. Gorra, 441:19Feb89-3
  P. Reading, 617(TLS):3-9Mar89-226
Wiggins, P.D. Figures in Ariosto's Tapestry.*
  M. Davie, 402(MLR):Oct89-1005
  C. Jordan, 604:Winter88-10
  M. Sherberg, 405(MP):Aug88-79
Wightman, E.M. Gallia Belgica.*
  H.C. Boren, 124:Sep-Oct88-69
Wihl, G. Ruskin and the Rhetoric of Infalli-
  bility.*
  P. Mallett, 677(YES):Vol19-345
Wiingaard, J. Teatersemiotik.
  A. Jørgensen, 172(Edda):1988/2-189
Wijeyewardene, G. Place and Emotion in
  Northern Thai Ritual Behavior.
  M.R. Rhum, 293(JASt):Feb88-191
Wikander, M.H. The Play of Truth and State.*
  R. Ingram, 366:Autumn88-226
  R. Nicholls, 131(CL):Summer88-276
  A. Thompson, 402(MLR):Jul89-713
  S. Watt, 130:Summer88-180
Wikander, Ö. Acquarossa. (Vol 6, Pt 1)
  D. Ridgway, 123:Vol38No1-180
von Wilamowitz-Moellendorff, U. The Pre-
  served Letters of Ulrich von Wilamowitz-
  Moellendorff to Eduard Schwartz. (W.M.
  Calder 3d & R.L. Fowler, eds & trans)
  N. Horsfall, 123:Vol38No1-191
Wilberforce, O. The Autobiography of a Pio-
  neer Woman Doctor. (P. Jalland, ed)
  A. Summers, 617(TLS):2-8Jun89-606
Wilbert, J. & K. Simoneau, eds. Folk Litera-
  ture of the Chamococo Indians.
  H-J. Uther, 196:Band29Heft1/2-252
Wilbur, C.M. The Nationalist Revolution in
  China, 1923-1928.
  D. Lary, 302:Vol24No1-86
Wilbur, R. New and Collected Poems.*
  I. Hamilton, 617(TLS):15-21Sep89-999
  A. Hudgins, 249(HudR):Winter89-743
Wilbur-Cruce, E.A. A Beautiful, Cruel Coun-
  try.
  J.N. Lensink, 649(WAL):Aug88-166
Wilcox, D.J. The Measure of Times Past.
  M.L. Colish, 589:Oct88-1011
Wilcox, G.C. - see Walker, W.

Wilcox, J. Miss Undine's Living Room.
  L. Dawson-Evans, 565:Summer88-54
  42(AR):Spring88-277
Wilcox, J. Sort of Rich.
  J. McCorkle, 441:28May89-25
Wilcox, J.C. Self and Image in Juan Ramón
  Jiménez.
  M.A. Salgado, 140(CH):Vol10-136
Wilczek, F. & B. Devine. Longing for the Har-
  monies.*
  J. Polkinghorne, 617(TLS):17-23Mar89-
  273
Wild, N. Décors et costumes du XIXe siècle.
  (Vol 1)
  J-M. Nectoux, 537:Vol74No2-241
Wild, R. Literatur im Prozess der Zivilisation.
  J. Neubauer, 107(CRCL):Mar88-76
Wilde, A. Middle Grounds.
  J. Klinkowitz, 587(SAF):Autumn88-249
  S. Weisenburger, 395(MFS):Winter88-660
Wilde, O. Oscar Wilde's Oxford Notebooks.
  (P.E. Smith 2d & M.S. Helfand, eds)
  J. Stokes, 617(TLS):16-22Jun89-668
Wilde, W.H., J. Hooton & B. Andrews. The
  Oxford Companion to Australian Litera-
  ture.*
  B. Cottle, 541(RES):May88-334
  J. Scheckter, 481(PQ):Spring88-275
  E.J. Zinkhan, 49:Jan88-91
Wilden, A. Man and Woman, War and Peace.*
  J.B.E., 185:Apr89-684
Wilden, A. The Rules Are No Game.
  R. Ginsberg, 103:Jan89-39
Wilder, T. The Journals of Thornton Wilder,
  1939-1961.* (D. Gallup, ed)
  H-J. Lang, 38:Band106Heft3/4-555
Wildhaber, R. Der Altersvers des Wechsel-
  balges und die übrigen Altersverse.
  J. Erickson, 203:Vol99No2-259
  G. Petschel, 196:Band29Heft1/2-254
Wilding, M. Dragons Teeth.*
  T. Healy, 175:Summer88-155
Wilentz, A. The Rainy Season.
  K.M. Brown, 617(TLS):17-23Nov89-1257
  H.W. French, 441:25Jun89-18
Wilentz, S., ed. Rites of Power.
  A.R. Smith, 382(MAE):1988/1-155
Wiles, D. Shakespeare's Clown.
  M. Archer, 157:No166-50
  S. Billington, 610:Summer88-155
  M. Coyle, 447(N&Q):Dec88-527
  T.J. King, 570(SQ):Winter88-518
  M. Willems, 189(EA):Oct-Dec88-480
Wiles, P., ed. The Soviet Economy on the
  Brink of Reform.
  R.W. Davies, 617(TLS):17-23Mar89-282
Wiles, R.C. & A.K. Zimmermann, eds. The Liv-
  ingston Legacy.
  J. Judd, 656(WMQ):Jul88-601
Wiley, R. Fools' Gold.*
  J. Melmoth, 617(TLS):27Jan-2Feb89-89
Wiley, R. Serenity.
  B. Kirsch, 441:3Sep89-15
Wiley, R.J. Tchaikovsky's Ballets.*
  H.Z., 412:May88-150
Wiley, T. & H.S. Wrigley. Communicating in
  the Real World.
  R.M. Ramsey, 399(MLJ):Summer88-226
Wilgus, D.K. & B. Toelken. The Ballad and the
  Scholars.*
  T. Cheesman, 196:Band29Heft1/2-255

Wilson, J. What Philosophy Can Do.*
  D. Carr, 518:Jul88-136
  T.M.R., 185:Oct88-192
Wilson, J.D. A Reader's Guide to the Short
  Stories of Mark Twain.
  S.I. Bellman, 573(SSF):Winter88-96
  L.T. Oggel, 26(ALR):Fall88-75
Wilson, J.F. Tearing Down the Color Bar.
  R. Cornuelle, 617(TLS):22-28Sep89-1026
Wilson, J.M. Charles Hamilton Sorley.
  J. Saunders, 565:Spring88-22
Wilson, J.M. - see Sorley, C.H.
Wilson, J.V.K. - see under Kinnier Wilson,
  J.V.
Wilson, K. Lion's Gate.
  J. Harris, 649(WAL):Nov88-260
Wilson, K. - see Gwynne, H.A.
Wilson, K.M., ed. British Foreign Secretaries
  and Foreign Policy.
  J.A. Thompson, 637(VS):Winter89-271
Wilson, K.M. Empire and Continent.
  N. Etherington, 637(VS):Summer89-573
Wilson, K.M., ed. Women Writers of the Ren-
  aissance and Reformation.
  L. Woodbridge, 551(RenQ):Autumn88-510
Wilson, L.A. Wind.
  J. Krauss, 441:2Apr89-28
Wilson, M.N. The Marginal World of Ōe Kenz-
  aburō.*
  P. McCarthy, 407(MN):Winter88-478
Wilson, N.G. Scholars of Byzantium.
  K. Alpers, 122:Oct88-342
Wilson, R. Conrad's Mythology.*
  J. Gindin, 395(MFS):Summer88-270
  B. Teets, 177(ELT):Vol31No2-240
Wilson, R., Jr. Kingdoms of the Ordinary.*
  P. Stitt, 491:Jun88-164
Wilson, R., Jr. Terrible Kisses.
  D. Jersild, 441:16Jul89-15
Wilson, R. & D.J. Carter, eds. Minorities in
  Higher Education.
  A. Hacker, 453(NYRB):12Oct89-63
Wilson, R.B. Near the Magician.
  P.K. Bell, 441:10Dec89-26
Wilson, R.C. Gypsies.
  S.O. Warner, 441:28May89-18
Wilson, R.M. Ripley Bogle.
  P. Reading, 617(TLS):21-27Jul89-804
Wilson, S. Feuding, Conflict and Banditry in
  Nineteenth-century Corsica.
  J.F. McMillan, 617(TLS):26May-1Jun89-
  572
Wilson, S.G., ed. Anti-Judaism in Early
  Christianity. (Vol 2)
  S. Westerholm, 627(UTQ):Fall87-240
Wilson, T. Utah's Wasatch Front.
  S. Cheney, 649(WAL):Nov88-256
Wilson, T., with P. Collins & H. Blake. British
  Museum, Ceramic Art of the Italian Renais-
  sance.*
  W.M. Watson, 551(RenQ):Winter88-735
Wilson, W.D. Humanität und Kreuzzugside-
  ologie um 1780.*
  J.W. Van Cleve, 221(GQ):Winter88-128
Wilt, J. Secret Leaves.*
  M. Moseley, 569(SR):Spring88-243
Wilton, A. Turner in his Time.
  C. Powell, 59:Mar88-135
Wiltshire, S. Cities.
  S. Sutherland, 617(TLS):2-8Jun89-601
Wimmer, D. Irish Wine.
  C.D.B. Bryan, 441:9Apr89-16

Winch, P. Trying to Make Sense.
  H.O. Mounce, 521:Jul88-236
Winch, P. Simone Weil.
  J.M. Cameron, 617(TLS):17-23Nov89-
  1256
Winchester, S. Their Noble Lordships.
  S. Pickering, 569(SR):Spring88-259
Windeatt, B.A., ed & trans. Chaucer's Dream
  Poetry.
  N. Jacobs, 382(MAE):1988/1-104
van Windekins, A.J. Dictionnaire étymolo-
  gique complémentaire de la langue grecque.
  M.E. Huld, 24:Fall88-463
  J-L. Perpillou, 555:Vol61fasc2-298
Winder, R. No Admission.
  N. Callendar, 441:7May89-18
Windrow, M. Uniforms of the French Foreign
  Legion 1831-1981.
  A. Powell, 364:Feb87-87
Wines, J. De-Architecture.
  D. Kessler, 505:Nov88-139
  E. Posner, 45:Jun88-77
Wing, D., comp. Short-Title Catalogue of
  Books Printed in England, Scotland, Ire-
  land, Wales, British America & of English
  Books Printed in Other Countries, 1641-
  1700. (Vol 3) (2nd ed) (J.J. Morrison &
  others, eds)
  D. McKitterick, 78(BC):Winter88-461
Wing, N. The Limits of Narrative.*
  C.D. Rifelj, 446(NCFS):Fall-Winter88/89-
  233
Wingrove, D. Run, Madrina, Run!
  P. Stenberg, 102(CanL):Summer88-147
Winkler, H.A. Von der Revolution zur Stabili-
  sierung. Der Schein der Normalität. Der
  Weg in die Katastrophe.
  A.J. Nicholls, 617(TLS):17-23Mar89-283
Winkler, M. "Décadence Actuelle."
  N. Addinall & H. Peitsch, 402(MLR):
  Oct89-990
  D. Wood, 208(FS):Apr88-215
Winks, R.W. Cloak and Gown.*
  R.T. Arndt, 639(VQR):Autumn88-736
Winn, J.A. John Dryden and his World.*
  T.A.B., 179(ES):Oct88-465
  P. Bruckmann, 627(UTQ):Summer89-517
  P. Harth, 405(MP):May89-425
  C. Hill, 366:Autumn88-239
  S. Staves, 385(MQR):Winter89-143
  L. Zionkowski, 391:Dec88-133
Winner, A. Culture and Irony.*
  D.L. Higdon, 395(MFS):Winter88-679
  D.R. Schwarz, 445(NCF):Mar89-545
Winner, E. The Point of Words.
  V. Washington, 42(AR):Summer88-393
Winnicott, D.W. Conversations ordinaires.
  H. Cronel, 450(NRF):Dec88-91
Winnicott, D.W. Human Nature.
  R. Dinnage, 453(NYRB):21Dec89-60
Winnifrith, T.J. The Vlachs.
  C.F. Natunewicz, 124:Mar-Apr89-324
Winslow, K. Henry Miller.*
  P.R.J., 295(JML):Fall87/Winter88-355
Winston, G.C. & R.F. Teichgraeber 3d. The
  Boundaries of Economics.
  A.N., 185:Apr89-675
Winter, H-G. J.M.R. Lenz.
  J. Guthrie, 402(MLR):Oct89-1028
  U. Kaufmann, 654(WB):7/1988-1224
  T. Menke, 221(GQ):Fall88-573

de Winter, P.M. La bibliothèque de Philippe le Hardi, duc de Bourgogne (1364-1404).*
A. Châtelet, 683:Band51Heft1-147
C. Reynolds, 90:Mar88-231
A.H. Van Buren, 54:Dec88-699
Winter, W. Studia Tocharica.
W. Thomas, 260(IF):Band93-298
Winterbourne, A.T. The Ideal and the Real.
R.R. Wojtowicz, 103:Jul89-300
Winters, A. The Key to the City.
C. Bedient, 569(SR):Winter88-137
Winters, M.E. - see Renart, J.
Winters, S. Shelley II.
K. Olson, 441:10Sep89-30
Winterson, J. Sexing the Cherry.
S. Mackay, 617(TLS):15-21Sep89-1006
Winton, T. In the Winter Dark.
H. Harris, 617(TLS):9-15Jun89-634
Wintour, C. The Rise and Fall of Fleet Street.
O.R. McGregor, 617(TLS):8-14Sep89-971
Wippel, J.F. Metaphysical Themes in Thomas Aquinas.
D.B. Burrell, 438:Spring88-228
Wisdom, J.O. Challengeability in Modern Science.
M. Baghramian, 235:Summer88-135
C. Wright, 518:Apr88-114
Wise, D. The Spy Who Got Away.*
639(VQR):Autumn88-132
Wise, S. & L. Stanley. Georgie Porgie.
S.H., 185:Jan89-463
Wiseman, C. Postcards Home.
N. Ruddick, 647:Spring88-99
Wiseman, T.P. Catullus and his World.*
J.H. Dee, 124:Jul-Aug89-465
J.E.G. Zetzel, 122:Jan88-80
Wiseman, T.P. Roman Studies.*
R.G.M. Nisbet, 123:Vol38No2-380
Wisniewski, R. Mittelalterliche Dietrich-dichtung.
J. Heinzle, 684(ZDA):Band117Heft2-82
W. McConnell, 221(GQ):Summer88-457
K.J. Meyer, 406:Fall88-387
Wisse, R.R. A Little Love in Big Manhattan.*
S.S. Prawer, 617(TLS):24Feb-2Mar89-197
Wisskirchen, H. Zeitgeschichte im Roman.*
K. Hasselbach, 221(GQ):Spring88-323
Wister, O. Owen Wister's West. (R.M. Davis, ed)
C. Beyers, 649(WAL):Nov88-278
Wister, S. The Journal and Occasional Writings of Sarah Wister. (K.Z. Derounian, ed)
L. Chambers-Schiller, 165(EAL): Vol24No2-160
Wistrich, E. After 1992.
P. Jenkins, 617(TLS):8-14Dec89-1356
Wistrich, R. Hitler's Apocalypse.
V. Caron, 287:Nov/Dec88-29
P. Milbouer, 221(GQ):Winter88-162
Wistrich, R.S. The Jews of Vienna in the Age of Franz Joseph.
M. Ignatieff, 453(NYRB):29Jun89-21
Witcover, J. Sabotage at Black Tom.
R.H. Ferrell, 441:6Aug89-21
Witherup, W. Black Ash, Orange Fire, Collected Poems 1959-1985.
C.H. Daughaday, 649(WAL):Feb89-391
Withrow, J. Effective Writing.
A. Bollati, 399(MLJ):Autumn88-349
Witkam, A.P.M. DLT - Distributed Language Translation.
G.F. Meier, 682(ZPSK):Band41Heft6-827

Witke, J. William Blake's Epic.*
D. Fuller, 161(DUJ):Dec87-148
Witt, R.G. Hercules at the Crossroads.
A. Mazzocco, 276:Autumn88-251
Witte, B. Walter Benjamin.
R. Rochlitz, 98:Oct88-786
Witte, E. & H.B. Beardsmore, eds. The Interdisciplinary Study of Urban Bilingualism in Brussels.
C.A. Klee, 399(MLJ):Winter88-464
Wittich, J. Catholic London.
A. Symondson, 617(TLS):5-11May89-496
Wittkowski, W., ed. Verlorene Klassik?*
T. Kontje, 221(GQ):Winter88-131
Wittreich, J. Interpreting "Samson Agonistes."*
G. Campbell, 447(N&Q):Dec88-536
J.M. Evans, 541(RES):Feb88-109
W. Furman, 481(PQ):Summer88-389
T. Healy, 402(MLR):Jan89-128
J. Mueller, 405(MP):Feb89-300
Witz, C. Religionspolitik in Britisch-Indien 1793-1813.
R.F. Young, 318(JAOS):Oct-Dec87-790
Wixted, J.T. Poems on Poetry.*
M.A. Fuller, 293(JASt):Feb88-137
Wode, H. Papers on Language Acquisition, Language Learning and Language Teaching.
C. El-Solami-Mewis, 682(ZPSK):Band41 Heft1-142
Wodehouse, P.G. The World of Jeeves.
T. Rafferty, 442(NY):22May89-94
Wodsak, M. Die Complainte.
R.R. Grimm, 547(RF):Band100Heft4-419
E. Weber, 535(RHL):Jan-Feb88-159
Woesler, W. - see Heine, H.
Woiwode, L. The Neumiller Stories.
E. Tallent, 441:17Dec89-7
Wojahn, D. Glassworks.*
G. Looney, 502(PrS):Fall88-128
C. Muske, 441:8Jan89-14
Wolandt, G., ed. Die Aesthetik, das tägliche Leben und die Künste.
P. Somville, 542:Jan-Mar88-96
Wolchik, S.L. & A. Meyer, eds. Women, State, and Party in Eastern Europe.
A. Feltham, 575(SEER):Apr88-321
Wolf, A.J. New York Society of Women Artists, 1925.
J. Loughery, 662:Spring/Summer88-54
Wolf, B. Cowboy.
S. Cheney, 649(WAL):May88-90
Wolf, C. Accident/A Day's News.
M. Gordon, 441:23Apr89-3
Wolf, C. Ansprachen. Sommerstück.
P. Graves, 617(TLS):21-27Apr89-435
Wolf, C. Die Dimension des Autors.
B. Leistner, 601(SuF):Jan-Feb88-229
Wolf, F.A. Prolegomena to Homer (1795).* (A. Grafton, G.W. Most & J.E.G. Zetzel, eds & trans)
C. Martindale, 402(MLR):Apr89-422
M.D. Reeve, 303(JoHS):Vol108-219
Wolf, L. & W. Hupka. Altfranzösisch.
G.A. Plangg, 685(ZDL):1/1988-119
Wolf, M.E. Eros under Glass.*
P. Dayan, 402(MLR):Apr89-479
Wolf, S. Die Augustusrede in Senecas Apocolocyntosis.
R. Jakobi, 229:Band60Heft3-202

Wong, J.Y., ed. Sun Yatsen.
   L.H.D. Gordon, 293(JASt):Nov88-875
Wong, R. Teaching Pronunciation.
   R.T. Williams, 399(MLJ):Summer88-231
Wood, A.G. Literary Satire and Theory.*
   P. Gethner, 577(SHR):Winter88-75
Wood, B. Green City in the Sun.*
   639(VQR):Autumn88-128
Wood, D. Constant: "Adolphe."
   C.P. Courtney, 208(FS):Oct88-479
   B. Fink, 207(FR):Mar89-687
   R. Le Huenen, 166:Apr89-258
   T. Unwin, 446(NCFS):Spring-Summer89-
   408
Wood, E.M. Peasant-Citizen and Slave.
   P. Cartledge, 617(TLS):6-12Jan89-19
Wood, F. A Companion to China.
   D. Davin, 617(TLS):28Apr-4May89-464
Wood, J.R. The Train to Estelline.
   A. Putnam, 649(WAL):Nov88-248
Wood, N. John Locke and Agrarian Capital-
ism.*
   J.C., 185:Oct88-205
Wood, N. Swift.*
   C. Fabricant, 83:Autumn88-228
   D.C. Mell, Jr., 173(ECS):Fall88-95
Wood, R. Hollywood from Vietnam to Reagan.
   B. Testa, 627(UTQ):Fall87-238
Wood, R. & G. Gál, with R. Green - see William
of Ockham
Wood, S. Roman Portrait Sculpture 217-260
A.D.*
   B. Burrell, 124:Jul-Aug89-452
   M.A.R. Colledge, 123:Vol38No1-181
   R.R.R. Smith, 313:Vol78-257
Wood, T. When the Killing Starts.
   T.J. Binyon, 617(TLS):17-23Nov89-1288
Woodcock, G. Northern Spring.
   C.G. Holland, 529(QQ):Autumn88-734
   B. Trehearne, 105:Spring/Summer88-78
Woodcock, G. A Social History of Canada.
   G. Martin, 617(TLS):10-16Nov89-1246
Woodcock, G. Strange Bedfellows.
   J.E. Chamberlin, 627(UTQ):Fall87-148
Woodcock, S. & P. Dyer. The Theatre Museum
Unpacks.
   J. Arnold, 611(TN):Vol42No2-90
Woodcock, T. & J.M. Robinson. The Oxford
Guide to Heraldry.
   A. Payne, 617(TLS):14-20Apr89-400
Wooden, W.W. Children's Literature of the
English Renaissance.* (J. Watson, ed)
   P. Hollindale, 541(RES):Aug88-428
Woodfield, M. R.H. Hutton.*
   E. Block, 637(VS):Autumn88-127
   S. Gilley, 402(MLR):Oct89-947
   D. Mehl, 72:Band224Heft2-408
   G. Rowell, 447(N&Q):Mar88-112
Woodford, S. An Introduction to Greek Art.
   B. Cohen, 124:Jan-Feb89-212
   E. Moignard, 303(JoHS):Vol108-265
Woodhouse, C.M. George Gemistos Plethon.*
   M. Angold, 123:Vol38No1-129
   J. Monfasani, 551(RenQ):Spring88-116
Woodman, A.J. Rhetoric in Classical Histori-
ography.*
   T.P. Wiseman, 123:Vol38No2-262
Woodress, J. Willa Cather.*
   M.A. O'Connor, 115:Fall88-431
   C. Petty-Schmitt, 649(WAL):Aug88-150
   M.M. Skaggs, 27(AL):Oct88-493
   L. Wagner-Martin, 659(ConL):Fall89-444

Woodruff, J. China in Search of Its Future.
   B.D. Sanders, 441:4Jun89-17
Woods, A., P. Fletcher & A. Hughes. Statistics
in Language Studies.
   L.K. Edwards, 355(LSoc):Dec88-614
   L. Hamp-Lyons, 608:Mar89-127
   E. Schils & R. van Hout, 353:Vol26No2-
   321
Woods, J.M. Rebellion and Realignment.
   C. Simpson, 106:Fall88-347
Woods, L. Garrick Claims the Stage.
   P. Rogers, 83:Spring88-96
Woods, M.C., ed. An Early Commentary on the
"Poetria nova" of Geoffrey of Vinsauf.
   M. Camargo, 589:Jul88-736
   H.A. Kelly, 377:Mar88-54
Woods-Marsden, J. The Gonzaga of Mantua
and Pisanello's Arthurian Frescoes.
   D.S. Chambers, 617(TLS):3-9Nov89-1220
Woodson, T. & others - see Hawthorne, N.
Woodson, T., L.N. Smith & N.H. Pearson - see
Hawthorne, N.
Woodward, A. Living in the Eternal.
   P.G. Kuntz, 543:Mar89-644
Woodward, C.V. The Future of the Past.
   W. Leuchtenburg, 61:Nov89-129
Woodward, D., ed. Art and Cartography.
   N. Adams, 551(RenQ):Autumn88-498
Woodwell, R.H. John Greenleaf Whittier.*
   J.E. Rocks, 534(RALS):Vol16No1&2-122
Woolf, L. Letters of Leonard Woolf. (F.
Spotts, ed)
   L. Edel, 441:29Oct89-7
Woolf, S. The Poor in Western Europe in the
Eighteenth and Nineteenth Centuries.
   M. Hughes, 83:Autumn88-215
Woolf, V. The Essays of Virginia Woolf.* (Vol
1) (A. McNeillie, ed)
   C. Camper, 219(GaR):Fall88-653
Woolf, V. The Essays of Virginia Woolf.* (Vol
2) (A. MacNeillie, ed)
   D. Seed, 161(DUJ):Dec87-153
Woolf, V. The Essays of Virginia Woolf. (Vol
3) (A. McNeillie, ed)
   A. Barnet, 441:23Apr89-21
   L. Menand, 617(TLS):24-30Mar89-298
Woolf, V. Moments of Being. (J. Schulkind,
ed)
   P.R. Broughton, 536(Rev):Vol10-125
Woolgar, S., ed. Knowledge and Reflexivity.
   G. Myers, 126(CCC):Dec88-465
Woolgar, S. Science.
   G. Myers, 126(CCC):Dec88-465
Woolmer, J.H. The Poetry Bookshop 1912-
1935.
   J. Byrne, 617(TLS):10-16Mar89-247
Woolsey, G. One Way to Love.
   J. Mellors, 364:Apr-May87-153
Woolson, C.F. Woman Artists, Women Exiles.
(J.M. Weimer, ed)
   E. Gillooly, 441:5Feb89-24
Wooten, C.W. Cicero's "Philippics" and Their
Demosthenic Model.*
   H.C. Gotoff, 121(CJ):Dec88-Jan89-170
Wooten, C.W. - see Hermogenes
Wordsworth, J., M.C. Jaye & R. Woof. Words-
worth and the Age of English Romanticism.
   42(AR):Spring88-273
Wordsworth, W. "The Tuft of Primroses," with
Other Late Poems for "The Recluse."* (J.F.
Kishel, ed) The Fourteen-Book "Prelude."*
(W.J.B. Owen, ed) Peter Bell. (J.E. Jordan,
   [continued]

Wu, Y-L. & others. Human Rights in the People's Republic of China.
J.D. Seymour, 293(JASt):Nov88-876
Wuilleumier, P., H. Le Bonniec & J. Hellegouarc'h - see Tacitus
Wulff, H.J. Die Erzählung der Gewalt.
W. Höfig, 196:Band29Heft1/2-256
Wulff, H.J. Konzeptionen der psychischen Krankheit im Film.
W. Höfig, 196:Band29Heft1/2-259
Wunderli, P., ed. Der kranke Mensch in Mittelalter und Renaissance.
R. Schieffer, 72:Band225Heft1-145
Wunderli, P. L'intonation des séquences extraposées en français.
F. Carton, 553(RLiR):Jan-Jun88-294
Wundt, M. Kant als Metaphysiker.
R.M., 342:Band79Heft1-113
Würffel, S.B. Ophelia.*
M. Prinz, 406:Summer88-245
D.G. Richards, 221(GQ):Summer87-459
Würffel, S.B. Der produktive Widerspruch.
R.C. Holub, 301(JEGP):Jul88-410
G.F. Peters, 221(GQ):Summer88-469
J.L. Sammons, 133:Band21Heft2/3-227
Wurmbach, H. Christopher Marlowes "Tamburlaine"-Dramen.
R. Böhm, 72:Band225Heft2-391
R. Noll-Wiemann, 38:Band106Heft1/2-238
Wuss, P. Die Tiefenstruktur des Filmkunstwerks.
E.M. Scherf, 654(WB):5/1988-870
Wuthnow, R. The Restructuring of American Religion.
M. Ruthven, 617(TLS):9-15Jun89-629
Wyatt, D. The Fall into Eden.*
C.L. Crow, 649(WAL):Nov88-233
S. Fender, 250(HLQ):Spring88-139
J. Hurt, 402(MLR):Oct89-963
D. Miller, 569(SR):Summer88-xlviii
Wyatt, R. Time in the Air.*
C.A. Howells, 102(CanL):Winter87-150
"Sir Thomas Wyatt, A Literary Portrait."*
(H.A. Mason, ed)
R.A. Rebholz, 97(CQ):Vol17No2-187
P. Thomson, 541(RES):Feb88-103
Wyatt, W., ed. The Way We Lived Then.
P. Craig, 617(TLS):1-7Sep89-953
Wyclif, J. On Universals (Tractatus de Universalibus).* (I.J. Mueller, ed)
L.A. Kennedy, 438:Autumn88-472
Wyclif, J. Johannis Wyclif "Summa Insolubilium." (P.V. Spade & G.A. Wilson, eds)
I. Boh, 589:Jan88-244
A. Hudson, 541(RES):Feb88-160
Wyczynski, P. - see Laberge, A.
Wyczynski, P., F. Gallays & S. Simard, eds. L'Essai et la prose d'idées au Québec.
E-M.K., 102(CanL):Spring88-259
Wyden, P. Wall.
D. Spanier, 441:5Nov89-7
Wylie, H. The Gould Collection of Netsuke.
R. Bushell, 407(MN):Autumn88-388
Wylie, J. The Faroe Islands.
J.O. Haehn, 650(WF):Jan88-64
S.A. Mitchell, 292(JAF):Jan-Mar88-118
Wylleman, A., ed. Hegel on the Ethical Life, Religion, and Philosophy (1793-1807).
G. di Giovanni, 103:Dec89-503
Wymer, R. Suicide and Despair in the Jacobean Drama.*
R.J. Stilling, 570(SQ):Spring88-123

Wynand, D. Heat Waves.
S. McCartney, 376:Dec88-139
Wyndham, F. The Other Garden.*
J. Mellors, 364:Nov87-110
Wynn, M. Wolfram's "Parzival."*
B. Schirok, 680(ZDP):Band107Heft1-133
Wynne, M. Later Italian Paintings in the National Gallery of Ireland.*
H. Brigstocke, 90:Jan88-40
Wynne-Davies, M., ed. The Bloomsbury Guide to English Literature.
D. Hibberd, 617(TLS):29Dec89/4Jan90-1445
Wyrick, D.B. Jonathan Swift and the Vested Word.
W.B. Carnochan, 173(ECS):Winter88/89-222
Wyschogrod, E. Spirit in Ashes.
H.A. Schmitt, 569(SR):Winter88-158
Wysling, H., with W. Pfister - see Mann, T. & J. Ponten

Xenakis, I. Arts/Sciences: Alloys.
E.R. Flint, 513:Summer88-312
Xian-liang, Z. - see under Zhang Xian-liang
Xiao Hong. Market Street.
R.E. Hegel, 116:Jul87-163
Xiao Tong. Wen xuan or Selections of Refined Literature. (Vol 2)(D.R. Knechtges, ed & trans)
C.S. Goodrich, 116:Jul87-145
Xinxin, Z. & Sang Ye - see under Zhang Xinxin & Sang Ye
Xitu, U. The World of "Mestre" Tamoda.*
A. Maja-Pearce, 364:Dec88/Jan89-142
Xrakovskij, B.S. & A.P. Volodin. Semantika i tipologija imperativa.
W. Lehfeldt, 559:Vol12No3-307
Xue, C. - see under Can Xue
Xue Tao. Brocade River Poems. (J. Larsen, ed & trans)
C.L. Chennault, 116:Jul87-148
Xueqin, L. - see under Li Xueqin
"Xunzi: A Translation and Study of the Complete Works." (Vol 1) (J. Knoblock, ed & trans)
A.C. Graham, 617(TLS):7-13Apr89-370
Xuto, S., ed. Government and Politics of Thailand.
C.J. Reynolds, 293(JASt):Nov88-940

Yack, B. The Longing for Total Revolution.*
A.J. Arscott, 529(QQ):Summer88-476
Yaeger, P. Honey-Mad Women.
E.E. Berry, 454:Winter89-219
P.D. Murphy, 590:Dec88-163
Yakovlev, A., ed. Perestroika Annual.
O. Figes, 617(TLS):4-10Aug89-841
Yalden, J. Principles of Course Design for Language Teaching.
J.M. Hendrickson, 238:Sep88-564
R.B. Kaplan, 350:Mar89-194
Yalland, Z. Traders and Nabobs.*
R. Head, 324:May89-383
Yalof, I. Life and Death.
F. Mullan, 441:12Feb89-22
Yalom, I.D. Love's Executioner.
E. Simpson, 441:3Sep89-5
Yalom, M. Maternity, Mortality, and the Literature of Madness.
N. Auerbach, 402(MLR):Apr89-419

Zapf, H. Hermann Zapf & His Design Philos-
ophy.*
J. Dreyfus, 78(BC):Summer88-274
A. Hoyem, 441:23Apr89-28
Zardoya, C. Altamor. Los perplejos hallaz-
gos.
C.G. Bellver, 238:May88-300
Zebouni, S.A., ed. Actes de Baton Rouge.*
C. Smith, 208(FS):Jan88-85
Zecchini, G. Il Carmen de Bello Actiaco.
J. Carter, 313:Vol78-236
Zecha, G. & P. Weingartner, eds. Conscience.
D.M.F., 185:Oct88-191
Zedong, M. - see under Mao Zedong
Zee, A. An Old Man's Toy.
M. Bartusiak, 441:30Jul89-3
Zeeman, P. The Later Poetry of Osip Mandel-
stam.
P. France, 617(TLS):10-16Mar89-245
Zeidner, L. Limited Partnerships.
R.R. Cooper, 441:24Sep89-15
Zelaya Kolker, M. Testimonios americanos de
los escritores españoles transterrados de
1939.*
G. Ibieta, 240(HR):Winter88-123
Zelazny, R. Frost and Fire.
G. Jonas, 441:20Aug89-24
Zeldin, T. Happiness.*
P. Vansittart, 364:Oct/Nov88-136
Zeller, L. The Marble Head and Other Poems.
M.T. Lane, 198:Summer88-100
D. Precosky, 102(CanL):Spring88-172
Zelnik, R.E. - see Kanatchikov, S.I.
Zelzer, K., ed. Basili regula a Rufino Latine
versa.
S. Lundström, 229:Band60Heft7-587
Zeman, Z.A.B. Pursued by a Bear.
C.M. Woodhouse, 617(TLS):10-16Feb89-
142
Zemanová, M. - see Janáček, L.
Zenck, M. Die Bach-Rezeption des späten
Beethoven.
B. Cooper, 410(M&L):Apr88-263
Zenkovsky, S.A., ed. The Nikonian Chronicle.
W.K. Hanak, 589:Jan88-246
Zenowich, C. The Cost of Living.
E. Allen, 441:6Aug89-8
Zeri, F., with E.B. Gardner. Italian Paintings.
C.B. Strehlke, 90:Nov88-860
Zeri, F. & M. Natale, eds. La Pittura in Italia:
Il Quattrocento.
J. Anderson, 59:Dec88-565
Zerlang, P. Dansk litterær opslagsbog.
A. Jørgensen, 172(Edda):1988/1-95
Zeruneith, K. Soldigteren, en biografi om
Johannes Ewald.
S.H. Rossel, 563(SS):Winter88-94
von Zesen, P. Philipp von Zesen: Sämtliche
Werke. (Vols 2; 12; 13; 15, Pts 1 & 2) (F.
van Ingen, with U. Maché & V. Meid, eds)
P. Skrine, 402(MLR):Apr89-522
von Zesen, P. Philipp von Zesen: Sämtliche
Werke. (Vol 4, Pt 1) (V. Meid, ed)
E.A. Philippson, 301(JEGP):Oct88-600
P. Skrine, 402(MLR):Apr89-522
Zgusta, L. The Old Ossetic Inscription from
the River Zelenčuk.
D.D. Testen, 350:Mar89-195
Zgusta, L., ed. Probleme des Wörterbuchs.
D. Herberg, 682(ZPSK):Band41Heft1-126
Zhadova, L.A., ed. Tatlin.
N. Lynton, 617(TLS):28Jul-3Aug89-827
S.F. Starr, 441:26Mar89-9

Zhang Jie. Leaden Wings.
J. Mellors, 364:Apr-May87-153
Zhang Jie. Love Must Not Be Forgotten.*
R.E. Hegel, 116:Jul87-162
Zhang Jie. Schwere Flügel.
E. Müller, 654(WB):6/1988-1002
Zhang Xian-liang. Half of Man is Woman.*
J. Mellors, 364:Mar88-102
J. Updike, 442(NY):3Apr89-112
Zhang Xinxin & Sang Ye. Eine Welt voller
Farben. (E. Müller, ed)
F. Gruner, 654(WB):6/1988-1009
Zholkovskii, A.K. & I.K. Shcheglov. Mir av-
tora i struktura teksta.
C. Isenberg, 550(RusR):Apr88-231
"Zhongguo bijiao wenxue." (Vol 4)
M. Motsch, 52:Band23Heft2-220
"Zhongguo bijiao wenxue nianjian." [1986]
(Yang Zhouhan & others, eds)
M. Motsch, 52:Band23Heft2-220
Zhongshu, Q. - see under Qian Zhongshu
Zhouhan, Y. & others - see under Yang
Zhouhan & others
Zickenheiner, O. Untersuchungen zur Credo-
Fuge der Missa Solemnis von Ludwig van
Beethoven.
R.S. Winter, 317:Spring88-186
Ziechmann, J. & others - see Frederick the
Great
Ziegeler, H-J. Erzählen im Spätmittelalter.*
J. Heinzle, 224(GRM):Band38Heft1/2-207
Ziegler, C.E. Environmental Policy in the
Soviet Union.
D. Weiner, 550(RusR):Apr88-212
Ziegler, G., ed. Shakespeare Study Today.*
L. Potter, 402(MLR):Jul89-710
Ziegler, H., ed. Facing Texts.
B.K. Horvath, 395(MFS):Winter88-649
S. Moore, 532(RCF):Fall88-177
Ziegler, P. - see Earl Mountbatten of Burma
Ziegler, R. Der Schatzfund von Brauweiler.
R. Bland, 313:Vol78-258
Ziegler, R. Städtisches Prestige und kaiser-
liche Politik.
H. Halfmann, 229:Band60Heft6-520
Zielonka, A. Alphonse Esquiros (1812-76).*
P. Whyte, 402(MLR):Oct89-993
Ziembinski, Z., ed. Polish Contributions to
the Theory and Philosophy of Law.
J-L. Gardies, 542:Oct-Dec88-523
Zieroth, D. When the Stones fly up.
A. Taylor, 102(CanL):Winter87-197
Ziff, P. Epistemic Analysis.
G. Harman, 482(PhR):Jan88-122
Zigerell, J. John Oldham.
M. Pittock, 447(N&Q):Mar88-99
Zim, R. English Metrical Psalms.
L. Adey, 184(EIC):Jul88-245
Zima, P.V. Manuel de sociocritique.
S. Sarkany, 107(CRCL):Jun88-247
Zima, P.V. Roman und Ideologie.
M. Rössner, 602:Band19Heft2-199
Zimbardo, R.A. A Mirror to Nature.*
H. Love, 402(MLR):Apr89-439
M.E. Novak, 173(ECS):Summer88-506
Zimic, S. Las Églogas de Garcilaso de la Vega.
W.H. Clamurro, 304(JHP):Autumn88-75
Zimic, S. - see del Encina, J.
Zimmer, H. Maya ou le rêve cosmique dans la
mythologie hindoue.
G. Bugault, 192(EP):Jul-Sep88-415
Zimmer, P. Family Reunion.
S. Pinsker, 363(LitR):Winter89-256

de Zulueta, C. Misioneras, feministas, educa-
doras.
  K.O. Austin, 345(KRQ):Aug88-371
Zumthor, P. La lettre et la voix de la "littér-
ature" médiévale.
  J. Kittay, 589:Oct88-1017
Zuntz, G. Drei Kapitel zur griechischen Met-
rik.
  J-L. Perpillou, 555:Vol61fasc2-297
  A.H. Sommerstein, 123:Vol38No1-166
  M.L. West, 303(JoHS):Vol108-240
Žuravlëv, V.K. Diaxroničeskaja fonologija.
  W.R. Schmalstieg, 215(GL):Vol28No2-142
Zürn, U. Anagrammes.
  A. Chevrier, 98:May88-416
Zvelebil, K.V., ed & trans. The Lord of the
Meeting Rivers.*
  D.A. Chekki, 293(JASt):May88-409
Zviadadze, G. Dictionary of Contemporary
American English Contrasted with British
English.
  D. Küster, 38:Band106Heft3/4-457
Zwerdling, A. Virginia Woolf and the Real
World.*
  T.C. Caramagno, 405(MP):Feb89-324
  R.B.D., 295(JML):Fall87/Winter88-403
  J. Gindin, 401(MLQ):Dec86-422
  E. Jay, 447(N&Q):Jun88-261
  K.L. Levenback, 396(ModA):Spring89-169
Zwerin, M. - see Vian, B.
Zwicky, F., ed. Procession.
  C. Clutterbuck, 581:Sep88-356
Zwicky, J. Wittgenstein Elegies.
  529(QQ):Summer88-508
Zwiebach, B. The Common Life.
  R. Eldridge, 185:Apr89-641
Zwierlein, O. Kritischer Kommentar zu den
Tragödien Senecas.
  R. Mayer, 313:Vol78-245
Zwierlein, O. Der prägende Einfluss des an-
tiken Epos auf die "Alexandreis" des Walter
von Châtillon.
  A.B.E. Hood, 123:Vol38No1-127
Zwierlein, O. Prolegomena zu einer kritischen
Ausgabe der Tragödien Senecas.
  R. Mayer, 313:Vol78-245
Zwierlein, O. Senecas Hercules im Lichte
kaiserzeitlicher und spätantiker Deutung.*
  H.J. Tschiedel, 229:Band60Heft6-532
Zwierlein, O. Senecas "Phaedra" und ihre
Vorbilder.
  R. Mayer, 123:Vol38No2-250
Zwierlein, O. - see Seneca
Zwierlein-Diehl, E. Glaspasten im Martin-
von-Wagner-Museum der Universität Würz-
burg. (Vol 1)
  C. Maderna-Lauter, 229:Band60Heft4-
  373